# ACCOUNTS RENDERED BY PAPAL COLLECTORS
## IN ENGLAND 1317-1378

Memoirs of the

AMERICAN PHILOSOPHICAL SOCIETY

*Held at Philadelphia*

*For Promoting Useful Knowledge*

Volume 70

# ACCOUNTS RENDERED BY

# PAPAL COLLECTORS IN ENGLAND

## 1317–1378

Transcribed with Annotations and Introduction by

## WILLIAM E. LUNT

*Late Scull Professor of English Constitutional History,*
*Haverford College*

Edited with Additions and Revisions by

## EDGAR B. GRAVES

*Professor of History, Hamilton College*

THE AMERICAN PHILOSOPHICAL SOCIETY
INDEPENDENCE SQUARE. PHILADELPHIA
1968

Library of Congress Catalog
Card Number 67-19647

PRINTED IN THE UNITED STATES OF AMERICA
BY J. H. FURST COMPANY, BALTIMORE, MARYLAND

# PREFACE

At the time of his death on 10 November 1956, William Edward Lunt left two completed manuscripts concerning the financial relations of the Papacy with England in the Middle Ages. These manuscripts as well as the notes and photostats associated with them were committed to me by Professor Lunt's widow with the authorization to promote and edit the printing of the manuscripts. One of them was published as *Financial Relations of the Papacy with England 1327-1534* by the Mediaeval Academy of America in 1962. The second of Lunt's manuscripts was a typewritten transcription of the reports of papal collectors in England from 1317 to 1378-1379, preceded by an introduction. It is this manuscript which is printed herewith.

The typescript of the collectors' reports was for some years in the custody of the Mediaeval Academy of America, whose search for a subsidy to supplement a contribution from its own publication fund was not fruitful. At the 1962 meeting of the Council of the Academy, I once again urged the publication of the Lunt manuscript and suggested that the American Philosophical Society might be approached. Through the good offices of Professor Albert C. Baugh and Professor Kenneth Setton, the Committee on Publications of the American Philosophical Society accepted the manuscript for publication in October 1962, on the condition that I assume full responsibility for the proofreading and completion of the edition.

The commission to publish the work of a teacher and friend who can no longer be consulted entails decisions which may diverge from the author's intentions. In this case I hope that the divergence has been reduced by my possession of Lunt's handwriten notes and annotations. His notes indicate that he had corrected his transcriptions afresh in the early 1940's. Yet numerous doubtful readings seem still to meet the eye; on re-examining scores, perhaps hundreds, of these with the photostats, it becomes obvious, as one would expect that the doubtful readings are almost always inherent in the scribe's spelling or carelessness. I have felt warranted, however, in making a few emendations. To save space on the printed page, Lunt typed on consecutively where gaps occur in the documents; to diminish the confusion which may thus arise, I have sought to describe towards the end of the Introduction the procedures which Lunt presumably used. Furthermore the photographs of four folios (figs. 1-4) which illustrate the formats of the collectors' reports may help to elucidate the methods of transcription.

Some portions of the Introduction which Lunt had written have now been recast; these including particularly the descriptions of the changes of scribal hands and the postscript are my responsibility. The dates assigned to each collector are the dates of his tenure, not necessarily the period of his reports; accordingly Arnald Garnerii's collectorate is carried on into 1379. The Table of Contents, the List of Books cited, and the Index have been compiled by me. The lengthy Table of Contents seemed to me to justify the restriction of the Index to persons and places.

Finally I am happy to report that the Board of Managers of Haverford College and former students of Professor Lunt provided a sum which was used for stenographic and editorial assistance. All scholars in this field of study will applaud, I feel certain, the American Philosophical Society for having undertaken the publication of such a long and detailed book.

EDGAR B. GRAVES

Hamilton College
Clinton, New York

# CONTENTS

## ILLUSTRATIONS

# ACCOUNTS RENDERED BY PAPAL COLLECTORS
## IN ENGLAND 1317-1378

# INTRODUCTION

## 1. THE ACCOUNTS

The general accounts rendered to the papal camera by papal general collectors in England, which are known to be extant, extend from 1304 [1] to 1378, with some gaps in the series. The first account printed below is that of Rigaud d'Assier, who was commissioned as general collector in May, 1317.[2] The reports of Gerard of Pecorara, who was collector in 1304, and of William Testa, who was collector from 1306 to 1313, have been published.[3] No accounts of William de Balaeto, who held office from 1313 to 1317, of Hugh of Angoulême, who was appointed on 29 July 1323, and allowed to retire on 22 May 1328,[4] or of Raymond Pelegrini, who became collector on 26 June 1343,[5] and was superseded by his brother Hugh on 8 July 1350,[6] have been discovered, though all three probably rendered accounts. William de Balaeto was ordered to report to the camera when he was dismissed from office,[7] and in 1323 William's executor, his brother Raymond, paid " the balance of the account rendered of money received in England for the papal *camera*." [8] In 1335 Hugh of Angoulême, who meanwhile had become bishop of Carpentras, assigned to the camera £16 6 s. 8 d. of the money which he had received while he was collector in England.[9] Though not conclusive, this would seem to indicate that a balance had been struck with the camera. Raymond Pelegrini's render of accounts is attested both by references in his brother's accounts [10] and by a letter of the camerarius dated 3 February 1369,[11] but when he died in 1365 he had not closed his account, because he had received money and made payments since the date of his last account.[12] After 1378 general collectors continued to perform the functions of their office in England until the separation under Henry VIII, but an extensive search in the Vatican Archives, in the Archivio di Stato in Rome, which contains many reports rendered by collectors in other countries after 1378, and in English repositories of manuscripts has yielded none of their accounts to the papal camera.[13]

The account of Rigaud d'Assier apparently carries the record of his receipts through the year 1321. The last recorded date on which a payment was received is 14 January 1321,[14] but several payments of census and one of Peter's pence due in 1321 are entered.[15] The former was customarily paid to the collector at Michaelmas.[16] The latter was received by the bishops and archdeacons at Michaelmas,[17] but usually was not delivered by them to the collector until the next spring,[18] though occasionally a delivery was made to the collector before the end of the year in which the bishop or archdeacon received the pence.[19] Since Rigaud left England in January 1322 to go to the papal court as the ambassador of Edward II and remained there until his death on 12 April 1323,[20] it seems reasonable to assume that this account was delivered to the camera in that period and included the receipts only to the beginning of 1322. The subsequent receipts were probably accounted for by Rigaud's successor, Hugh of Angoulême,[21] or by his brother, Gerard d'Assier, who acted as one of his executors.[22] Rigaud's account contains no statement of expenses, though the deduction of them was authorized.[23] It also omits the assignments of money which were made to the camera.[24]

---

[1] There are a few surviving accounts drawn up between 1283 and 1299 by Geoffrey of Vezzano, who was a general collector, but they relate only to tenths and other receipts for the crusades: Lunt in *Eng. Hist. Rev.*, xxxi (1916) 110-112; xxxii (1917) 55-58.

[2] Below, p. xxi.

[3] That of Gerard in Lunt in *Eng. Hist. Rev.*, xxviii (1913) 318-321; those of William Testa in *ibid.*, xli (1926) 352-357 and in Lunt's *Financial Relations . . . to 1327*, pp. 682-685.

[4] Lunt, *Financial Relations . . . to 1327*, pp. 623-624.

[5] *Clement VI, Lettres Closes*, ed. Déprez, i, no. 243.

[6] *Cal. Pap. Regs. Letters*, iii, 46.

[7] *Ibid.*, ii, 436.

[8] *Ibid.*, ii, 453. See also E. Göller, *Die Einnahmen der apostolischen Kammer unter Johann XXII*, pp. 310-311.

[9] Vatican Archives, Introitus et Exitus 146, fol. 23.

[10] Below, pp. 116, 130.

[11] Vatican Archives, Collectorie 353, fol. 107.

[12] *Cal. Pap. Regs. Letters*, iv, 18, 19. This summary seems to imply that he had made no accounting to the camera, but this clearly was not the case.

[13] Some other Collectorie in the Vatican Archives contain documents relating to England. Number 287, for example, contains a list of English benefices collated by Clement VI in 1351 and 1352 and by Innocent VI in 1352 and 1353 which was sent to the English collector: fols. 160-164. It is simliar in form to the list given in Arnald Garnerii's report, below, pp. 418-452. Peter Griphus, who was collector in England from 1508 to 1513, wrote a treatise tracing the history and describing the functions of the office: Vatican Library MS. Ottoboniano Latino 2948.

[14] Below, p. 28. Rigaud's account is found in Vat. Arch. Introitus et Exitus 15, fols. 1-46ᵛ.

[15] Below, pp. 26-28.

[16] Below, p. 417.

[17] Below, p. 418; Lunt *Financial Relations . . . to 1327*, p. 76.

[18] Below, p. 418.

[19] E. g., below, p. 518.

[20] Below, p. xxii.

[21] His assignments to the camera included arrears left by Rigaud: Göller, *Die Einnahmen unter Johann XXII*, pp. 632-633.

[22] He accounted to the royal exchequer for the arrears of annates: *Regs. of Sandale and Asserio*, ed. F. J. Baigent, pp. 584,586; P. R. O., Pipe Roll 173, m. 13ᵛ; 175, mems. 10, 13ᵛ, 14ᵛ, 17, 30ᵛ, 39, 41.

[23] Below, p. xxiii.

[24] The acquittances issued to him by the camera were for

The hand of the text and of the marginal comments is uniform throughout. Ordinarily this would indicate that the report was written at the camera because the cameral clerks who inspected a report generally wrote comments in the margins. It is possible, however, that Rigaud made the marginal comments in his report. They are of two types. Against several items appears the comment: *vacans per constitutionem,* and against several others *non est in certificatione.* The former designates a benefice which had become vacant by the bull *Execrabilis* issued on 19 November 1317. The bishop of each diocese was ordered to send to the pope a list of the benefices so vacated, but Rigaud requested copies of the lists.[25] The second refers to lists of all benefices which became vacant during the years when annates were being levied. After the expiration of the period each bishop was required to supply the collector with such a list for his diocese.[26] Since the camera may have received copies of these lists, it seems impossible to determine with certainty whether the account is an original rendered by Rigaud, a copy of his account made at the camera, or a compilation made by officials of the camera from more than one account rendered by him. The frequent use of the first person throughout the document makes the last supposition appear improbable.

The only report of Itier de Concoreto known to be extant records receipts for only a portion of the period during which he held the office of collector. He was commissioned on 22 August 1328,[27] and was superseded by Bernard de Sistre on 13 September 1335.[28] The earliest payment noted in the report was received on 18 February 1329 and the latest on 16 February 1333.[29] The payments of annual census listed as received became due in the years from 1329 to 1332 inclusive.[30] References in the account of his successor indicate that Itier later rendered an account which included receipts from census and other revenues due in 1333 and 1334.[31]

The account under consideration is incomplete. The first part of it appears to have been lost.[32] The extant portion contains receipts only from census and bequests for the Holy Land. It omits receipts from Peter's Pence, from a quadrennial tenth imposed on the English clergy by John XXII on 3 January 1330 and from the general levy of annates ordered on 31 August 1329.[33] Yet Itier probably accounted to the camera for the last two revenues in 1333, since, at his request, the pope on 7 February granted him permission to come to the papal court at Easter for that purpose,[34] and on 13 March a royal license for him to cross the sea was issued.[35]

The account printed below appears to be a portion of the original delivered by Itier. The marginal comments, such as *approbatum,* are in a different hand from that of the text and were made presumably by the auditors in the camera.

The account of Bernard de Sistre includes the whole period from 13 September 1335[36] to 18 June 1343 during which he was collector. He died on the latter date[37] while still in office,[38] and the account was rendered by the executors of his will.[39] The hands indicate that Bernard may have had the account nearly finished before his death. The main account[40] and the assignments[41] seem to have been written by one hand. The *Conclusio compoti*[42] were written by another hand, the same hand that wrote folio 133r. The *compotus brevis*[43] was written by a third hand. The list of arrears from England and Ireland still due at the time of Bernard's death[44] was composed by a fourth hand. Finally a fifth scribe drew up the receipts of arrears charged to Itier[45] on elongated and narrow folios. The marginal comments are in hands different from those of the text and were made by the cameral clerks who audited the account.

Hugh Pelegrini rendered two accounts to the papal camera. The first covers his transactions as collector from 1 August 1349 to 1 June 1358.[46] He probably took it with him to the camera soon after its conclusion, though it apparently did not receive its final audit at the camera until 1360,[47] when Hugh was again at the

---

receipts from annates only, and they may not be complete for that revenue. The last was dated 9 March 1322: Göller, *Die Einnahmen unter Johann XXII,* pp. 631-632; *Cal. Pap. Regs. Letters,* ii, 449.

[25] Lunt, *Financial Relations . . . to 1327,* pp. 495-496.

[26] Wells Diocesan Registry, Reg. of Drokensford, fols. 132-133; W. Brown, *Yorkshire Arch. Soc., Record Ser.,* lxi *Miscellanea,* i (1920), 138-148.

[27] Below, pp. 32-33. Itier's account is found in Vat. Arch. Collectorie 227, fols. 34-45v.

[28] Below, pp. xxvii-xxviii.

[29] Below. pp. 31, 34.

[30] Below, pp. 29-31.

[31] Below, pp. 35-37; 43-44; 68; 77.

[32] Below, p. 29.

[33] Below, p. xxiv.

[34] *Cal. Pap. Regs. Letters,* ii, 510. It is also significant in this connection that a view of Itier's account for these taxes, of which the king was entitled to a share, was made at the royal exchequer on 21 February 1333: P. R. O.; K. R. Memo. Roll 109, m. 125.

[35] *Cal. Pat. Rolls 1330-34,* p. 414.

[36] Bernard's account is found in Vat. Arch. Collectorie 227, fols. 103-55. Technically it did not begin until 10 October when he left Avignon for England: below, p. xxix.

[37] Below, p. 69.

[38] His successor, Raymond Pelegrini, was appointed on 26 June after Bernard's death was known at the curia: *Cal. Pap. Regs. Letters,* iii, 2. One payment was received by Bernard on 2 May 1343: below, p. 42.

[39] Below, pp. 68-69.

[40] Fols. 105-130; below, pp. 35-63.

[41] Fols. 131-134r, except for fol. 133r; below, pp. 64-67.

[42] Fols. 130v, 135r, 135v; below, pp. 63-64, 67-68.

[43] Fols. 138-141; below, pp. 68-69. This is a typical *compotus brevis,* whose format is described below p. li.

[44] Fols. 146-153r; below, pp. 69-76.

[45] Fols. 154-155; below, pp. 76-77.

[46] Below, p. xxxii, 78, 164. Hugh's first account is found in Vat. Arch. Collectorie 14, fols. 23-89v.

[47] *Cal. Pap. Regs. Letters,* iii, 633.

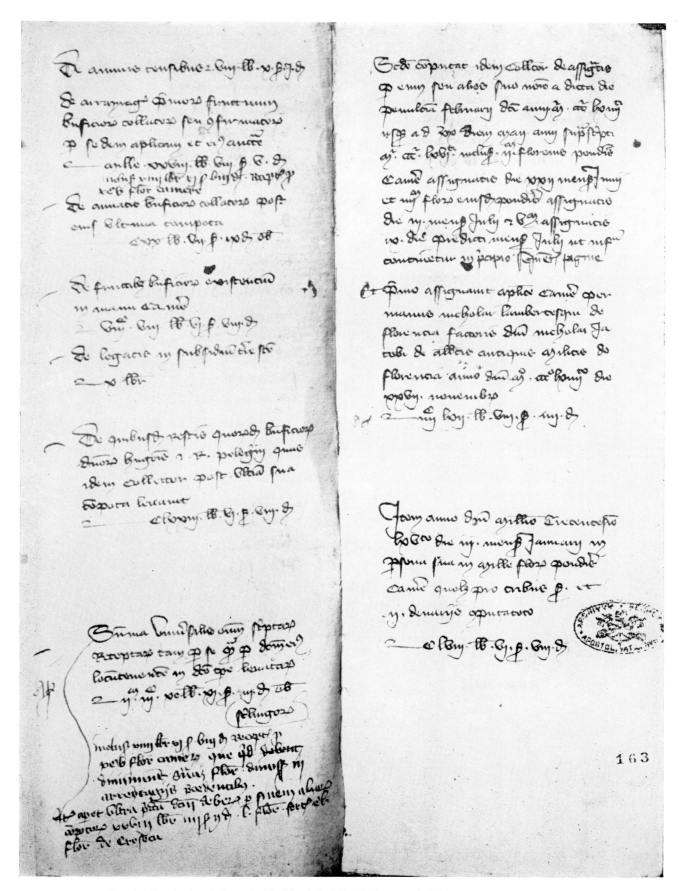

FIG. 1. Vat. Arch., Collectorie 11, fols. 162ᵛ-163ʳ (29.8 cm. × 10.7-11.2 cm.). Printed on p. 226.

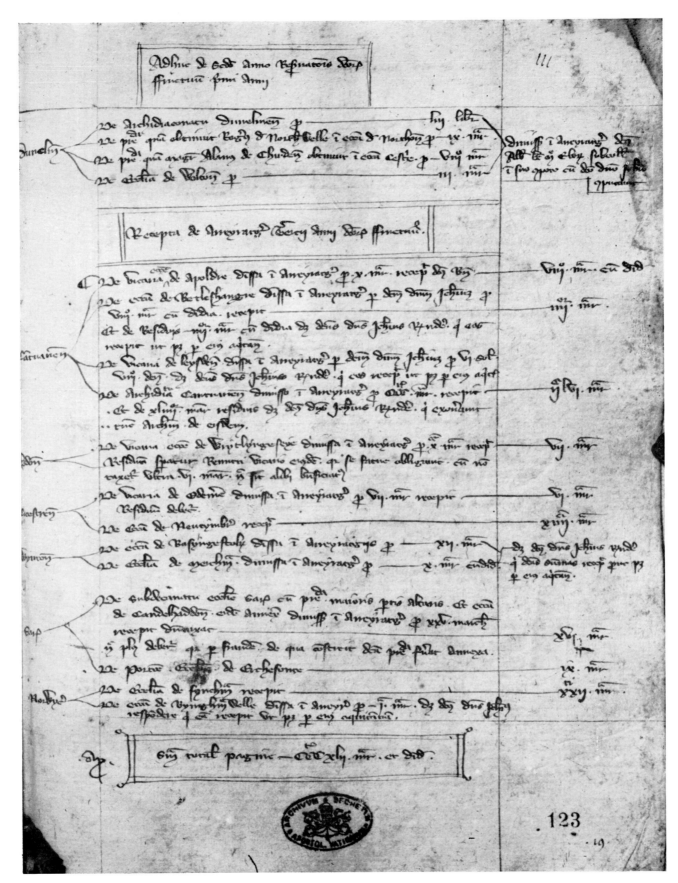

Fig. 2. Vat. Arch., Collectorie 227, fol. 123 (31.1 cm. × 23 cm.). Printed on p. 56.

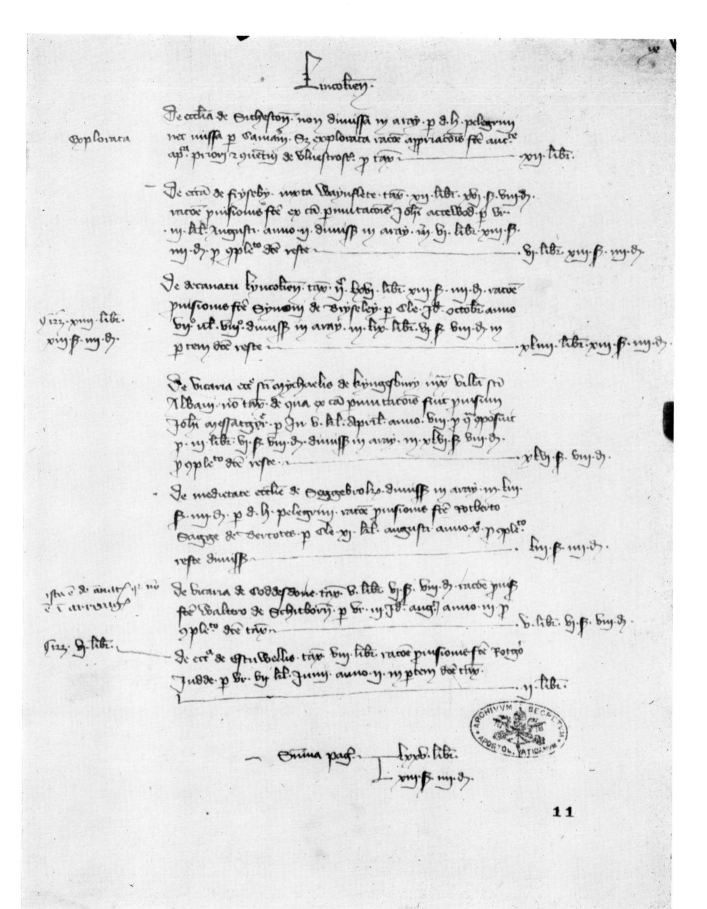

Fig. 3. Vat. Arch., Collectorie 12, fol. 11 (30.4 cm. × 22.2 cm.). Printed on pp. 261-262.

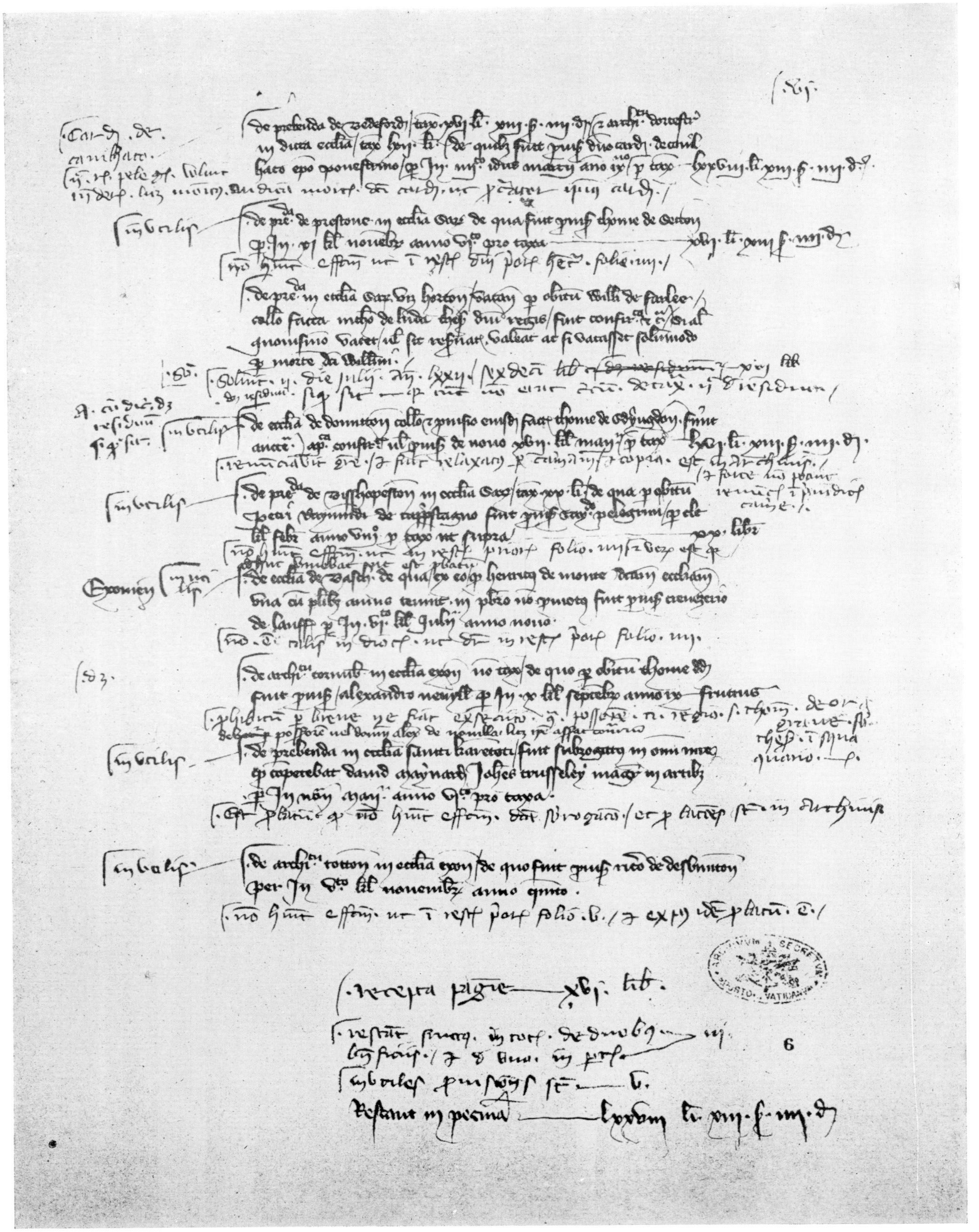

FIG. 4. Vat. Arch., Collectorie 13, fol. 6 (30.4 cm. × 22.6 cm.). Printed on pp. 366-367.

papal court.[48] The document was written by two main hands,[49] which presumably are those of scribes employed by the collector. The summary of the account is in a different hand [50] and its form suggests that it was compiled at the camera.[51] The marginal comments were also made at the camera in hands different from the two main hands. The second account extends from the date when the first was ended to 1 September 1363,[52] when Hugh terminated his career as collector.[53] The account was written by one hand with a few corrections by another. Many of the marginalia are in the same hand as the text, but others in a different hand were written at the camera.[54]

John de Cabrespino submitted four reports. The first deals with the period from 1 September 1363 to 31 March 1364.[55] It includes receipts from arrears left uncollected by Hugh Pelegrini, of which John was informed by a copy of Hugh's account left in London with Hugh's brother Raymond,[56] and from payments which fell due in 1363. There are two copies of this account in Collectorie 11. The first (folios 1-71ᵛ) is here designated as **a**, and the second (folios 74-137ᵛ) as **b**. The text of **a**[57] was written by four scribes. The first hand, which runs to folio 21, (below, p. 186) enters the receipts obtained by Cabrespino from Raymond Pelegrini. The second hand wrote folios 27 to 62ᵛ (below, pp. 186-210) which concern the arrears of annates reported to John de Caroloco. The third hand, covering folios 64-66 (below, pp. 210-213), listed the ineffective provisions reported to Cabrespino. A fourth scribe composed the *compotus brevis* of folios 70-71ᵛ (below, pp. 213-214).[58] The text of **b** seems to have been written by at least three hands. As in **a**, the section on the receipts from Raymond Pelegrini, which in **b** comprises folios 76 to 87ᵛ and 92 to 95, was the work of one scribe. The rest of the text of **b** which runs from folio 97 to folio 137ᵛ was the work of another scribe. The hand of the *compotus brevis* of **b** on folios 88-89ᵛ differs from that of the *compotus brevis* of **a**. The use of the third person to designate the collector suggests that the *compotus brevis* was compiled in the camera.

The main text of **b** was copied either from **a** or from a common original. It is a careless copy. In several instances faulty copying or the omission of words or phrases destroys the meaning or the grammar.[59] The items cancelled in **a** are omitted in **b**.[60] The omissions which are inserted in the margin of **a** find their regular places in **b**.[61] Summary statements and sums at the bottom of the page [62] which are written in **b** do not appear in **a**. The *compotus brevis* of **b** includes computations and annotations which are absent from that of **a**.[63] The word *approbatum* appears only in **b**. It seems clear, therefore, that the copy of the account audited by the cameral clerks was **b**.

Cabrespino's second report carries the account forward to 20 May 1366. It is fundamentally the account of John de Caroloco, prior of Lewes, whom John de Cabrespino had appointed his deputy collector and *locumtenens* before Cabrespino left England on 6 March 1364. Caroloco now dispatched his account to Cabrespino who was then at Avignon.[64] There are two copies of this report in Collectorie 11. The first, here called **a**, occupies folios 138 to 196ᵛ (below, pp. 214-56), and the second, here called **b**, folios 202 to 262ᵛ (which are not printed below). Omitting the *compotus brevis* for each account, four scribes seem to have compiled these reports. Scribe 1 wrote folios 140 to 178ᵛ (below, pp. 214-237) in **a** and folios 239 to 244 in **b**; conversely Scribe 2 wrote folios 179 to 184 (below, pp. 237-241) in **a** and 202 to 238ᵛ in **b**. The changes in penmanship occur at exactly the same places in **a** and **b**. Where changes of penmanship occur, there are unique markings. Thus folios 179 and 239 bear the number i; and folios 185 and 248, where the reports of arrears on benefices begin, bear the number ii. On folio 179, a scribe has written *hic*.[65] The sections of each copy which report the arrears of benefices (folios 185-96ᵛ in **a** and folios

---

[48] Below, p. xxxiii.

[49] The first fols. 24-55, 59-66ᵛ (below, pp. 78-95, 96-103) and the second fols. 69-89ᵛ (below, pp. 103-118).

[50] Fols. 56-58 (below, pp. 95-96). This *compotus brevis* is composed in the common form; see below, p. li.

[51] Many items begin *dicit se recepisse*.

[52] Below, p. 118.

[53] Below, p. 164. John de Cabrespino was commissioned as his successor on 15 June 1363: *Cal. Pap. Regs. Letters*, iv, 28.

[54] E. g., fol. 121 (below, p. 141).

[55] Below, p. 172. These dates are given also in the summary of the account in **b**, but in **a** the dates are 1 August 1363 and 12 April 1364; below, p. 213. The latter are the dates on which John left the papal court and returned to it: below, p. 183. See also below, p. 226.

[56] Below, pp. 172, 182.

[57] Below, pp. 172-214.

[58] For the format and characteristics of a *compotus brevis*, see below, p. li and figure 1.

[59] Note the many mistakes or variants given as **b** in the footnotes of page after page.

[60] Below, pp. 177-210, footnotes 83, 120, 229, 424, 462, 699, 809.

[61] The following entries are inserted in the margin of **a**, but in the text of **b**: p. 179, right column lines 1-5; p. 180, left column lines 15-19; p. 180, right column lines 10-15.

[62] Summary statements in footnotes 195, 651, 799; the *summa pagine* at the foot of most pages: e. g., footnotes 236, 239, 249, 253, 270, 729, 738, 764.

[63] Footnotes 863, 864, 865, 867.

[64] Below, pp. xxxvi, 186, 214. John de Caroloco had probably been appointed before 11 October 1363; below, p. xxxvi.

[65] It may plausibly be suggested that the confusion of hands arises from the transposition of two sheafs of folios; but this conjecture cannot be affirmed from the photostats alone, where the gatherings of folios are not clearly indicated. If folios 179 to 184, now in **a**, were transferred to follow immediately after folio 238ᵛ, now in **b**, and if folios 239 to 244, now in **b**, were shifted to follow folio 178ᵛ, now in **a**, then the hand of each of the two scribes would run on continuously. In any case, the transposition, if there were one, occurred before the auditing at the camera. The markings and notations made in the camera appear on folios 179 to 184 as they appear elsewhere in copy **a**; they do not appear on folios 239 to 244 as they do not appear elsewhere in copy **b**.

248-59ᵛ in **b**; below, pp. 241-256) were written by different hands, neither of them the hand of Scribe 1 or Scribe 2.

In copy **a**, assessment of a few benefices and the words *fructus* or *taxa*, which were omitted in **b**, were added in a different hand by another scribe.[66] Two entries which are canceled in **b** are not copied in **a**;[67] and several items which are not canceled in **b** are canceled in **a** with the reason for the cancelation given.[68] Two items of Peter's pence given separately in **b** are combined correctly in one item in **a**.[69] Many marginal notes which do not appear in **b** are written in **a** in a hand different from that of the text.[70] Sums and comments thereon which are not entered in **b** are given in **a**.[71] The word *approbatum* appears only in **a**.[72] The *compotus brevis*[73] of **a** includes several items[74] which are not entered in **b**; these items seem to be in the same hand which wrote the marginal notes referred to in footnote 70. The additions by hands different from the text are presumably the work of cameral clerks. The copy of the account which they audited was obviously **a**.

John de Cabrespino's third account covers his transactions as collector from 20 May 1366 to 18 February 1368, though it was not delivered to the camera until July and was not audited until August of the latter year.[75] It was written by one hand with the following exceptions. An occasional page was written by a second hand[76] and numerous notations in the margins and at the feet of pages were made by two other hands,[77] one of which is the same hand that made similar notations on the second report. This hand is also one of the several hands which appear in the summary of the account.[78]

John de Cabrespino closed his fourth and final report with business done on 1 November 1370,[79] and accounted to the camera in April 1371.[80] It was written by two hands, folios 59ᵛ to 62ᵛ [81] and 95 to 139 [82] by the first and folios 63 to 82ᵛ [83] and 83ᵛ to 86ᵛ [84] by the second. A page of sums [85] and two added explanations of sums [86] were written by a third hand which was probably that of a cameral official. The summary of the account [87] and several marginal comments [88] were written by still other hands.

On or before 12 July 1371, John de Cabrespino was appointed papal collector in Germany, Hungary, Bohemia, and Poland.[89] At the order of the camera he designated John de Caroloco, who had been his deputy collector and *locumtenens* throughout the period of his English collectorship,[90] to continue in that capacity and to act as collector without the title.[91] Arnald Garnerii was appointed English collector on 8 October 1371, but he did not arrive in London until 8 February 1372,[92] and did not begin to exercise the functions of his office until 22 February.[93] His first report contains a copy of the account of John de Caroloco from 1 November 1370 to 22 February 1372, which was rendered to him on the latter date, and his own account from that date to 27 July 1374,[94] when he left London to go to the papal court for the purpose of accounting. He finally delivered his report to the camera on 9 November. A cameral clerk audited the account and pronounced it correct; and the treasurer issued an acquittance on 12 February 1375.[95]

The manuscript of Caroloco's report, folios 2-37,[96] of his receipts of sums, folios 38-42,[97] and of Garnerii account for 1372-74, folios 47ᵛ-121ᵛ,[98] was first prepared

---

[66] Below, pp. 231-250; for assessment, footnote 379; for *fructus* or *taxa*, footnotes 307, 309, 314, 317, 365, 376, 379, 400, 412, 414, 416, 577, 583, 593, 636.

[67] Below, p. 235, n. 420.

[68] Below, pp. 225-237, footnotes 198, 200, 264, 278, 473.

[69] Below, p. 227, n. 228.

[70] Below, pp. 218-241, footnotes 64, 254, 311, 354, 367, 377, 397, 400, 414, 473, 525, 530.

[71] Below, pp. 222-241, footnotes 145, 150, 172, 188, 190, 192, 196, 204, 531.

[72] Fols. 159, 160, 161, 183.

[73] The *compotus brevis* of **a** occupies folios 162-165 (below, pp. 225-227; the *compotus brevis* of **b** fills folios 260-262 and is not printed here. In each case, the abbreviated account exemplifies the format described below, p. li.

[74] Below, pp. 226-227, footnotes 207, 209, 210, 211, 213, 214, 218, 219, 220, 221, 222.

[75] Below, pp. 256, 308. John de Cabrespino's third account is found in Vat. Arch. Collectorie 12, fols. 1-57 (below, pp. 256-307).

[76] E. g., the list of payers of Peter's pence, fol. 2ᵛ (p. 256); the expense account, fol. 16ᵛ (pp. 265-266); the cameral summary, fol. 21 (pp. 267-268); and the six provisions fol. 34ᵛ (p. 280).

[77] For marginal annotations, see footnotes 55, 114, 117 and 160. For sums at the foot of the folio, see fols. 3ᵛ, 4, 7ᵛ, 14, 16ᵛ, 23, 32, 49.

[78] The *compotus brevis* is on fols. 17-21; but fol. 19ᵛ is in a different hand (below, pp. 266-268).

[79] Below, p. 307. John de Cabrespino's fourth account is found in Vat. Arch. Collectorie 12, fols. 58-139 (below, pp. 307-362).

[80] Below, p. 322.

[81] Below, pp. 307-309.

[82] Below, pp. 324-363.

[83] Below, pp. 309-320.

[84] Below, pp. 321-322.

[85] Fol. 83, below, pp. 320-321.

[86] Fols. 107, 108, below, pp. 333, 334.

[87] Fols. 87-94, below, pp. 322-324.

[88] E. g., pp. 307-362: wherever the word "Approbatum" appears, it is abbreviated.

[89] The date of his safe-conduct: *Cal. Pap. Regs. Letters*, iv, 148.

[90] Above p. xix.

[91] Collectorie 358, fol. 129.

[92] Below, pp. xxxix, 411.

[93] Below, p. 363. The date is given as 27 February in Collectorie 358, fol. 129.

[94] Arnald's first report is found in Vat. Arch. Collectorie 13, in which fols. 2-37 (below, pp. 363-415) form John de Caroloco's report, fols. 43-44 present John de Cabrespino's excuses for arrears, and fols. 47-198 (pp. 417-484) contain Arnald's own account to 27 July 1374.

[95] Below, pp. 474-475; Obligationes Reg. 42, fols. 3-4.

[96] Below, pp. 363-411.

[97] Below, pp. 411-415.

[98] Below, pp. 417-474.

in a neat chancery hand. To this prepared document were added under each entry notations in cursive writing reporting the action on the preceding item. Thus on folio 6 [99] we find in the chancery hand: *De archidiaconatu Cornubie . . . fructus* followed in a cursive hand by *Prohibitum per breve . . . contrarium*. This is the procedure for nearly every entry on folios 2 to 37 and 47ᵛ to 49 and for every item for which a report of a receipt is made on folios 54 to 121ᵛ. For these folios the additions reporting payments are in a cursive hand. Another hand wrote folios 123-124 [100] on assignments and expenses and folios 125ᵛ-132.[101] This same hand wrote folio 155, which is misplaced and belongs between 157 and 157ᵛ, and folios 161-185,[102] which, called *brevetus*, duplicates those items and only those items for which receipts are recorded in the earlier portions of the document. Finally this third hand seems to have drawn up the *compotus brevis*, which covers folios 188 to 198.[103] In the margins and on several therefore blank pages are entered many comments in hands not found elsewhere in the manuscript. These comments appear to be cameral notations.[104]

Arnald's last known report takes the business of his office forward from the date when his previous report closed to 6 March 1378, when the collector, after a long illness, left London for Avignon to render his account.[105] Arnald gives the year as 1377, but he is reckoning from the Incarnation. Elsewhere in the report he designates its final date as 6 March 1378.[106] Since he calculated the year indiscriminately from the Nativity [107] or from the Incarnation and does not always specify which system he is using,[108] his dates are sometimes confusing.[109] Many payments recorded in the report were received in 1377 after 6 March.[110] When Arnald left for the papal court, he appointed Laurence de Nigris, who had previously served as his deputy collector,[111] as his *locumtenens*.[112] He does not appear to have returned to England, though he retained the office of collector until

he was superseded by Cosmatus Gentilis in 1379.[113]

The second report was written by two principal hands. The first goes from folio 145ᵛ to folio 210 (below pp. 484-519) and the second from folio 225 to 255ᵛ (below, pp. 520-538). There are several headings, marginal comments, entries, and additions to items in the collector's hand, though they are not as extensive as in the first report. Most of the remaining marginal notations, which are not in one of the two main hands, and many of the sum totals are in a fourth hand.[114] Since this hand notes that Cardinal Gibanensis (Robert of Geneva) had become Pope Clement VII,[115] its notations were probably made after 20 September 1378, when his election took place. Presumably they were made at Avignon, where the arrears in this report were collated with those in another copy and corrections made in October, 1378.[116] The short summary of the account was written in still another hand.[117]

## 2. THE COLLECTORS

### RIGAUD D'ASSIER

John XXII, on 8 December 1316, named Rigaud d'Assier collector in the British Isles of the annates [118] which, on the same day, he imposed on his clerical subjects for the next three years.[119] At that time Rigaud was a professor of civil law, cantor and master of schools at Orléans, a papal chaplain, and an auditor of causes in the papal palace.[120] He was appointed collector of Peter's pence and the arrears of tenths on 1 May 1317 and on 29 May he superseded William de Balaeto as general collector and nuncio in the British Isles.[121] In this capacity he was given exemption from ordinary jurisdiction and from the commands of papal delegates and was granted the procurations of seven shillings a day. The procurations consisted, however, of sums of seven shillings or less owed annually by many chapters and religious communities whose liability had been estab-

---

[99] Below, p. 367 and figure 4.

[100] Below, pp. 475-476.

[101] Below, pp. 477-480.

[102] Below, pp. 480-481.

[103] Below, pp. 481-484.

[104] E. g., fols. 37 (p. 411), 43-44 (pp. 415-417), 49 (p. 418), 122 (pp. 474-475), 125 (p. 476).

[105] Below, p. 484. Arnald's second report is found in Vat. Arch. Collectorie 12, fols. 143-266.

[106] Below, p. 538.

[107] The date of the beginning of his first report is given as 22 February 1372 from the nativity of the Lord: below, p. 363.

[108] Examples in his second report, *passim*.

[109] The year from the Nativity began on 25 December and the year from the Incarnation on 25 March. At the papal court the former was the common usage. E. g., on 1 October 1355 Hugh Pelegrini assigned to the camera 1500 florins which were received on 29 December 1356: Below, p. 91. Hoberg, *Die Einnahmen unter Innocenz VI*, p. 102.

[110] Below, pp. 488, 492, 504-507, 510, 513-516, 518-519, 532, 535.

[111] Below, p. 479.

[112] Below, p. 484.

[113] Cosmatus took an oath of fidelity to the king in his capacity of papal collector on 3 June: *Cal. Close Rolls, 1377-81*, p. 257. His papal commission was dated 27 August: *Cal. Pap. Regs. Letters*, iv, 257.

[114] E. g., fols. 148ᵛ (p. 486), 160 (p. 492), 164ᵛ (p. 494), 167 (p. 496), 205ᵛ-206 (p. 517), 252ᵛ (pp. 536-537).

[115] Fol. 158 (below, p. 491, n. 98).

[116] Below, p. 519. Other corrections were made in London on 25 February and in Avignon on 25 July.

[117] Fols. 261-266ᵛ (below, pp. 538-541) form a typical *compotus brevis*.

[118] *Cal. Pap. Regs. Letters*, ii, 127.

[119] *Si gratanter advertitis: Reg. of John de Halton, Bishop of Carlisle*, ed. W. N. Thompson and T. F. Tout, ii, 157-161. It is translated from another copy in Lunt, *Papal Revenues*, ii, 324-328.

[120] *Cal. Pat. Rolls, 1317-21*, p. 26; *Cal. Pap. Regs. Letters*, ii, 126, 421; O. Jensen, " The 'Denarius Sancti Petri' in England," *T. R. H. S.*, new ser., xix (1905), 271.

[121] *Cal. Pap. Regs. Letters*, ii, 126, 127, 436; Collectorie 350, fol. 57.

lished by custom.[122] On 18 June 1317, Rigaud was still at the papal court, whence he dispatched to English prelates and to the king copies of his commissions and of papal bulls imposing annates and ordering the bishops to pay the full amount of Peter's pence received from the payers of the due.[123] The papal letter recommending the new collector to the king demanded that he and his deputies should not be tried in lay courts or by a jury.[124] It was dated 20 June, but Rigaud does not appear to have reached England until September. His royal safe conduct bore the date 24 September [125] and on the next day he issued an official letter at York.[126] After his arrival he was further commissioned to collect the annual tribute of one thousand marks owed by the king.[127]

By the middle of October, Rigaud had established his office and residence in the house of the dean of St. Paul's in London,[128] which his two immediate predecessors had occupied before him.[129] There he probably received the letters and documents pertaining to the work of the office which William de Balaeto was directed to deliver to him,[130] though he may have received a copy of William's account either there or at Avignon.[131] When Rigaud later became bishop of Winchester, he moved his residence,[132] but he continued to maintain the collector's office staffed with clerks in London,[133] where the general collectors had conducted their business for a long time.[134]

In the performance of some of his duties the new collector met with difficulties. The full amount of Peter's pence, which he was ordered to collect, was a much larger sum than that which the papacy customarily received from this revenue. Since the reign of Henry II, and probably before that time, the annual income of the pope from this source had been a few shillings less than £200. The collector received from the bishop or the archdeacons in each diocese where Peter's pence was levied fixed portions of this sum. The large remainder of the pennies paid by those who owed them was retained by these local collectors and the many others who participated in their local exaction and transmission to the bishops and the archdeacons. Several popes had claimed this remainder before John XXII made a determined effort to obtain possession of it. Because the claim ran counter to time-honored English custom, Rigaud placed it before the convocation of Canterbury in February 1318. On the order of the king, he received the reply that parliament would have to be consulted. On 1 March the king forbade both the papal collector and the local English collectors to levy Peter's pence in any other than the accustomed manner until parliament should have considered the question. Parliament in its Michaelmas session at York ordained the arrest of Rigaud and his agents if they should disobey the prohibition.[135] John XXII protested the action of convocation and the royal prohibition in vain and finally instructed Rigaud to collect Peter's pence in the traditional manner. The king also interfered with the levy of other revenues. He, for example, prohibited the collection of annates from priories or from prebends in royal chapels.[136] At last the pope became so exasperated that he demanded of Edward II a clear statement of the rights of his chapels and other liberties in order that the collector might know what was allowed and what was not and be free from " obscure and captious prohibitions " in the exercise of his commission.[137]

The royal prohibitions, though addressed to the collector, were directed against the papal demands, and the relations between the king and the collector appear to have been friendly. On one occasion Rigaud accommodated the king with a temporary loan of £200.[138] The king conferred upon him the prebend of Bedwin in the church of Salisbury,[139] and later expressed his pleasure when the pope provided Rigaud with the rich bishopric of Winchester.[140] After Rigaud became bishop, the king employed him on diplomatic missions. On 19 January 1321, he was one of several envoys sent to Scotland to treat with Robert Bruce for peace.[141] A year later he was sent as one of two ambassadors to the papal court at Avignon,[142] where he remained until he died on 12 April 1323.[143]

[122] 20 May 1317: *Cal. Pap. Regs. Letters*, ii, 127. Lunt, *Financial Relations . . . to 1327*, pp. 548-549.

[123] *Cal. Pap. Regs. Letters*, ii, 126; Collectorie 350, fol. 57.

[124] *Cal. Pap. Regs. Letters*, ii, 434.

[125] *Cal. Pat. Rolls, 1317-21*, p. 26; Rymer, *Foedera*, ii, 343.

[126] *Reg. of Halton*, ii, 156-161.

[127] 29 October 1317: Rymer, *Foedera*, ii, 345.

[128] Salisbury Diocesan Registry, Reg. of Mortivall, ii, fol. 75ᵛ; *Reg. Ade de Orleton, Episcopi Herefordensis*, ed. A. T. Bannister, p. 40.

[129] Lunt, *Financial Relations . . . to 1327*, p. 581.

[130] *Cal. Pap. Regs. Letters*, ii, 436.

[131] The latest document issued by William in London, which I have discovered, was dated 17 May: Wells Diocesan Registry, Reg. of Drokensford, fol. 106ᵛ. The papal mandate to deliver documents to Rigaud and to account was dated 29 May 1317.

[132] *Regs. of Sandale and Asserio*, p. xxxvii.

[133] Reg. of Drokensford, fol. 133.

[134] Lunt, *Financial Relations . . . to 1327*, p. 580.

[135] *Documents illustrative of English History in the thirteenth and fourteenth centuries*, ed. H. Cole, p. 8.

[136] *Cal. Close Rolls, 1313-18*, p. 596.

[137] *Cal. Pap. Regs. Letters*, ii, 426. Except as noted, the paragraph is based on Lunt, *Financial Relations . . . to 1327*, pp. 39, 51-66, 78-79, 494-495.

[138] 12 April 1318: *Cal. Pat. Rolls, 1317-21*, pp. 131, 161.

[139] 18 October 1319; *ibid.*, p. 395. On 8 December 1319 the king granted it to Bertrand d'Assier: *ibid.*, p. 406.

[140] *Cal. Pap. Regs. Letters*, ii, 424; *Cal. Pat. Rolls, 1317-21*, pp. 438, 441. Rigaud was appointed on 26 November 1319 and consecrated on 16 November 1320: *Regs. of Sandale and Asserio*, pp. xxxvii, 443.

[141] *Cal. Pat. Rolls, 1317-21*, pp. 554, 560, 567.

[142] 3 January 1322: *ibid., 1321-24*, pp. 46, 53; *Cal. Close Rolls, 1318-23*, pp. 411, 510.

[143] *Cal. Pat. Rolls, 1321-24*, pp. 229, 280; *Cal. Close Rolls, 1318-23*, pp. 514, 523, 697; Public Record Office, Exchequer K. R. Accounts, 309/27, m. 3; *Regs. of Sandale and Asserio*, p. xxxvii.

The collector also transacted for the pope much business which was not financial. He was placed on commissions to see that papal provisions were executed, to issue a papal citation, to receive the resignation of a benefice and to fill the vacancy created, to revise the valuation of the church of Scarborough, and to act as papal delegate.[144] After he was provided to Winchester, the pope requested him to come to the curia on business relating to England,[145] and thereafter he was charged with affairs of state. He was instructed to use his efforts to foster peace between the kings of England and Scotland and also between Edward II and Thomas earl of Lancaster. In 1322 John XXII asked him to report on the relations between the king and his barons and to suggest any papal remedies which might be appropriate.[146]

Rigaud fared exceptionally well in the matter of remuneration. As was the custom, he received procurations,[147] and though his expenses are not recorded in his report, he was authorized to deduct them from the arrears of the tenth which he collected.[148] He was allowed to enjoy the fruits of his benefices in which he did not reside, and the pope provided him with prebends in the churches of London and Salisbury.[149] His provision to a bishopric while he was still collector was an unusually rich reward,[150] and two further financial privileges bestowed by John XXII were unique in the annals of English general collectors to that time. He was given permission to demand a subsidy from the prelates and clergy of his diocese to meet the expenses incurred by his services to the camera,[151] and the king was requested to exempt the bishopric of Winchester from a tenth on clerical income levied in 1319 and 1320, which the pope had granted to the king, on the ground that the revenues of the bishopric had gone to the royal exchequer during the vacancy of the see preceding Rigaud's appointment.[152]

## ITIER DE CONCORETO

Itier de Concoreto was given formal notification on 21 August 1328 that he was to take the place of Hugh of Angoulême, who was the successor of Rigaud and had recently been granted permission to end his term

of office on account of ill health.[152] Itier was a native of Aquitaine,[154] apparently resident at the papal court at the time of his appointment.[155] He had received the degree of bachelor of civil and canon law and of master, and he had recently been provided by the pope with a canonry and prebend in Salisbury.[156]

His general commission,[157] which was issued the next day, authorized him to collect in England, Wales, Ireland, and Scotland the arrears of tenths imposed by Gregory X, Nicholas IV, Boniface VIII, and Clement V, of other revenues owed to the Holy Land or to the Roman church, of procurations of legates or nuncios of the apostolic see which belonged to the Roman church in accordance with an ordinance of Boniface VIII,[158] and of the goods of Geoffrey of Vezzano, a former papal collector in England, whose possessions were owed to the camera because he died at the papal court in 1300.[159] It further empowered him to collect current income as well as arrears of Peter's pence, annual census, bequests and redemptions of vows in aid of the Holy Land, indistinct legacies and pecuniary penalties promised to the Holy Land for breaches of contracts. It also conferred upon him the usual powers to compel the render of accounts and payment of sums owed, and revoked all earlier commissions issued to others. The document was supplemented by several others. By a separate commission he was ordered to collect the full amount of Peter's pence and the prelates of his collectorate were commanded to pay it.[160] The prelates were also directed to assist the collector and his agents and to pay to him the customary procurations of seven shillings.[161] Letters commending the new collector were addressed to the king, the two queens, the two archbishops, three bishops, and several nobles.[162]

Later the collector's duties were altered in several particulars. In April and May 1329, Scotland was removed from his collectorate and assigned to other collectors.[163] Itier was appointed on 6 June 1329 to collect the subsidy which in 1326 John XXII had requested of English prelates and clergy to aid the

---

[144] *Cal. Pap. Regs. Letters*, ii, 151, 189, 194, 197, 200.
[145] *Ibid.*, ii, p. 424.
[146] *Ibid.*, ii, 428, 442, 447, 449.
[147] W. H. Turner and H. O. Coxe, *Calendar of Charters and Rolls preserved in the Bodleian Library*, p. 341.
[148] *Cal. Pap. Regs. Letters*, ii, 190.
[149] *Ibid.*, ii, 127, 152, 186.
[150] Pandulph became bishop-elect of Norwich while he was collector. Otherwise this reward was reserved for the conclusion of a collector's term of office and granted only rarely: Lunt, *Financial Relations . . . to 1327*, pp. 611, 619, 621; Vatican Archives, Regesta Avinionensia 101, fol. 71 (Hugh of Angoulême).
[151] *Cal. Pap. Regs. Letters*, ii, 213.
[152] *Ibid.*, ii, 424. There the letter is dated only " anno 4," but it was sent from Avignon by messenger on 17 August 1320: Collectorie 350, fol. 48.

[153] *Ibid.*, ii, 488.
[154] *Cal. Pat. Rolls, 1334-38*, p. 487.
[155] Göller, *Die Einnahmen unter Johann XXII*, pp. 211, 219 n. 4.
[156] *Cal. Pap. Regs. Letters*, ii, 269, 282, 485.
[157] *Ibid.*, ii, 486; below, pp. 32-33.
[158] He reserved part of the procurations levied by the nuncios, Cardinals Bernard of Albano and Simon of Palestrina, between 1295 and 1297: Lunt, *Financial Relations . . . to 1327*, p. 556.
[159] *Ibid.*, p. 512.
[160] This is not made clear in the summaries in *Cal. Pap. Regs. Letters*, ii, 486. Letters issued by Itier on 9 December 1328 specify that the pope was demanding the whole sum of Peter's pence which the local collectors received from the payers: *Reg. of John de Grandisson, Bishop of Exeter*, i, 457-458; York Diocesan Registry, Reg. of Melton, fol. 529; Salisbury Diocesan Registry, Reg. of Mortivall, ii, fol. 259.
[161] *Cal. Pap. Regs. Letters*, ii, 486.
[162] *Ibid.*, ii, 488.
[163] *Ibid.*, ii, 489-490; below, p. 30.

Roman church against Italian rebels and heretics.[164] Six days later he was instructed to collect the fruits of the church of Haughton in the diocese of Durham from the beginning of its voidance by the papal provision of its incumbent to another church.[165] On 31 August 1329 he was named collector of a new general levy of annates imposed by the pope for three years [166] and subsequently extended for an additional year.[167] Finally he was designated on 30 June 1330 as the receiver of the proceeds of a quadrennial tenth which John XXII commanded the clergy to pay.[168]

After Itier received his original commission, he remained at the papal court several days before beginning his journey. It was probably during this interval that he had an interview with the pope in which he was informed of the pope's desire to obtain the full amount of Peter's pence.[169] Presumably he also studied the records in the camera which related to his collectorate.[170] On 11 September he received from the camera fifty pounds of small Tours for the expenses of his journey and soon after left the papal court. He did not go directly to England, since he was ordered to assist an envoy who was being sent at the same time to the royal court of France.[171] He reached England probably not long before 15 November, when his royal safe conduct was issued.[172]

Before he began the work of collection he had to attend to several affairs in London. His predecessor, Hugh of Angoulême, had been instructed to provide him with information concerning the state of the affairs of the collectorship,[173] and this he had to have before he could begin operations.[174] Another preliminary was to have his commission published in the Court of Arches.[175] He also established his residence and place of business. For this purpose he selected a house which had not been occupied by any of his three immediate predecessors.[176] It was near St. Paul's and the conduit [177] and nearly in the center of the city. When the archbishop of Canterbury was summoned to appear before Itier in the house, his proctor described it as " a private place of no distinction " " to which the archbishop had not access or approach except by dirty, unseemly, and low places and through which it was not fitting that he, the archbishop, with any regard to his own dignity, should pass," but the proctor of the opponents of the archbishop in the case which was the cause of the summons told the pope that it was " one of the honourable and greater dwellings of the . . . city." [178] From this office, on 9 December, the collector issued his first letters to the bishops informing them of his appointment and demanding payment of Peter's pence and his procurations.[179]

Athough Itier sent to the camera large sums of money derived mainly from annates and the tenth,[180] he failed to obtain any return from several of the revenues which he was ordered to collect. Previous attempts to secure the full yield of Peter's pence had been without exception unsuccessful,[181] and Itier fared no better. To his demand of 9 December, 1328, for the full amount due for the past time during which payment had ceased, the archbishop of York replied that no Peter's pence would be due from him until after the next Easter when he would owe £11 10 s.[182] This was the sum which he customarily paid to the pope each year, though he received much more.[183] All other payments which I have noted were likewise the traditional sums,[184] and in later demands the collector apparently gave up the effort to secure more.[185] The collection of legacies indistinctly bequeathed and of fines pledged to the Holy Land for breaches of contracts had been forbidden by

[164] Below, pp. 33-34; Lunt, *Financial Relations . . . to 1327*, pp. 238-239.

[165] *Cal. Pap. Regs. Letters*, ii, 491.

[166] *Ibid.*, ii, 492; *Reg. of John de Grandisson*, i, 543-545.

[167] 13 December 1329: *Cal. Pap. Regs. Letters*, ii, 495.

[168] *Literae Cantuarienses*, ed. J. B. Sheppard, i, 322-333; Winchester Diocesan Registry, Reg. of Stratford, fols. 48ᵛ, 49; Lincoln Diocesan Registry, v, Reg. of Burghersh, fol. 436ᵛ.

[169] York Diocesan Registry, Reg. of Melton, fol. 529.

[170] C. Samaran and G. Mollat, *La Fiscalité pontificale*, p. 79.

[171] Schäfer, *Die Ausgaben der apostolischen Kammer unter Johann XXII*, p. 505.

[172] *Cal. Pat. Rolls, 1327-30*, p. 331. On 9 December he stated that he had already supported his household for two months and more: *Reg. of John de Grandisson*, i, 457. Since it was customary for a collector to bring with him some foreign clerks who formed part of his staff (Lunt, *Financial Relations . . . to 1327*, p. 581), Itier may have been supporting a household before he arrived in England.

[173] 21 August 1328: *Cal. Pap. Regs. Letters*, ii, 488.

[174] Hugh received his royal safe conduct which enabled him to leave England for Avignon on 11 September: *Cal. Pat. Rolls, 1327-30*, p. 320. Since Itier left the papal court on that date or soon after, Hugh must have met him in London, unless he met him enroute, which is not probable. The bishop of Exeter addressed a letter to Hugh as nuncio on 10 October: *Reg. of John de Grandisson*, i, 409.

[175] *Reg. of John de Grandisson*, i, 458.

[176] William Testa and Rigaud had occupied the house of the dean of St. Paul's and Hugh of Angoulême lived near Lombard Street: Lunt, *Financial Relations . . . to 1327*, p. 581.

[177] *Reg. of John de Grandisson*, i, 457; *Reg. of Ralph of Shrewsbury*, ed. T. S. Holmes, i, 16.

[178] William Thorne's *Chronicle*, ed. A. H. Davis, pp. 445-446.

[179] *Reg. of John de Grandisson*, i, 456-458; York Diocesan Registry, Reg. of Melton, fol. 529; Salisbury Diocesan Registry, Reg. of Mortivall, ii, fol. 259; Hist. MSS. Comm., *Reports*, ix, 74.

[180] Göller, *Die Einnahmen unter Johann XXII*, pp. 377-378, 544-549, 567-568; Göller, *Die Einnahmen unter Benedikt XII*, p. 198; *Cal. Pap. Regs. Letters*, ii, 501, 502, 504-508, 513-515, 560.

[181] Lunt, *Financial Relations . . . to 1327*, pp. 38-40, 56-59, 61-66.

[182] York Diocesan Registry, Reg. of Melton, fol. 529.

[183] Lunt, *Financial Relations . . . to 1327*, pp. 78-79.

[184] Salisbury Diocesan Registry, Reg. of Mortivall, i, fol. 275; York Diocesan Registry, Reg. of Melton, fols. 27ᵛ, 46ᵛ, 57ᵛ, 535ᵛ; *Cal. Reg. of Drokensford*, p. 297; *Reg. of John de Grandisson*, i, 481.

[185] Reg. of Mortivall, i, fol. 275ᵛ; Reg. of Melton, fol. 535ᵛ; Wells Diocesan Registry, Reg. of Ralph of Shrewsbury, fol. 42; Salisbury Diocesan Registry, Reg. of Wyville, i, fol. 10ᵛ.

the parliament of Carlisle in 1307.[186] In Itier's report there is no mention of receipts from these sources in the section relating to the crusades,[187] where they would normally appear. Neither are they listed in the papal acquittances issued to Itier among the revenues specified as the sources of the sums of money forwarded by him to the camera. Itier also failed to obtain anything from the subsidy which John XXII had requested of the clergy in 1326.[188]

Among the payers of some of the revenues Itier's administration caused complaint. When his successor, Bernard de Sistre was appointed in 1335, he was instructed to inquire whether his two immediate successors or their deputies had harmed the taxpayers or defrauded the camera in their work of collection.[189] Bernard asked the bishops to obtain the desired information from their archdeacons and deans and to report to him. The bishop of Bath and Wells replied that three deputy collectors in his diocese had burdened many of his subjects. They had ordered executors of deceased persons to exhibit testaments and inventories, they had drawn many of them to divers places until fines had been paid, they had received extortions and rewards, and they had often defamed the apostolic camera. The residents of the diocese had been so dissatisfied that they no longer wished to give anything to the Holy Land. The inquiry yielded no evidence whether the camera had been satisfied or defrauded.[190] If this reply was typical, the complaints were concerned only with the collection of legacies for the Holy Land, which had been a source of friction for a long time.[191] At least one of the deputy collectors whom the bishop accused of malpractices had been appointed by Itier.[192]

Despite these criticisms of his subordinates, some members of the clergy had reason to be grateful to him. He withdrew his demand for procurations from the prioress and sisters of Maiden Bradley when he learned of their poverty, which had been attested by his predecessor, William Testa.[193] It was at his representation that John XXII allowed the quadrennial tenth to be levied in the dioceses of Carlisle, Durham and part of York on the new valuation made partly in 1318, partly in 1327 and in a few instances in 1331, on account of the devastation caused by Scottish invasions.[194] Since

the pope estimated that the amount of the tenth would be £2,000 less each year than the yield by the old valuation made between 1291 and 1293, the grant was a boon to the clergy of the northern province. No doubt it was appreciated the more because some of the taxpayers by Itier's orders received back what they had paid in excess of the new valuation before the papal concession was made.[195]

In addition to his regular duties Itier was assigned many other tasks. Assessments of the incomes of prelates who had petitioned the pope for financial concessions had to be made.[196] Papal citations or warnings had to be served on several occasions.[197] He was frequently called upon to act as one of a committee of three to attend to the execution of papal provisions or expectancies.[198] In one instance he was directed to appropriate a church to a monastery[199] and in another to assist in the sequestration of the fruits of an office in a cathedral chapter.[200] Papal absolution was conveyed by him to beneficed members of Queen Isabella's household who had administered sacraments in Scotland when the country was under interdict.[201] It became his duty to procure the arrest of William of Ockham, if he could be found in England,[202] and of two friars minors accused of heresy.[203] He was ordered to have published copies of the book which John XXII wrote in refutation of the heresies of Michael de Cesena and to see that they were distributed to the universities and the bishops. A papal letter announcing the abjuration of the antipope, Peter de Corbario, had to be presented to the king and the two queens.[204] He was appointed to ascertain the facts in suits appealed to the pope,[205] and in one such case he was delegated to act as judge.[206]

The last commission caused him much trouble. The suit was brought by the abbot and convent of St. Augustine's Canterbury against Simon Meopham, archbishop of Canterbury, who had visited churches of the abbot and convent which they claimed were exempt. Itier summoned the archbishop to appear before him in his house, but the archbishop, who thought it beneath his dignity to be tried by the collector, appears to have ignored the summons.[207] On 21 March 1331 Itier sent three proctors to deliver another summons to the arch-

[186] Lunt in *Eng. Hist. Rev.*, xli (1926), 342-343.
[187] Below, p. 34.
[188] Below, p. 34.
[189] Theiner, *Vetera Monumenta Hibernorum*, pp. 267-268; *Cal. Pap. Regs. Letters*, ii, 559.
[190] *Reg. of Ralph of Shrewsbury*, i, 267, 289.
[191] Lunt, *Financial Relations . . . to 1327*, pp. 433, 443-444.
[192] William Skynard or Esquinard, dean of Crantock: below, p. 34. *Cal. Pat. Rolls, 1330-34*, p. 107.
[193] 16 January 1330, Itier to the prioress and sisters: P. R. O., Ancient Correspondence 50, no. 141.
[194] *Cal. Close Rolls, 1330-33*, pp. 65, 77-78; York Dioecesan Registry, Reg. of Melton, fols. 530, 578ᵛ; Carlisle Diocesan Registry, Reg. of Kirkby, p. 438; *Cal. Pap. Regs. Letters*, ii, 509; *Reg. Palatinum Dunelmense*, iii, 218-219; P. R. O., Ancient Correspondence 42, no. 82.

[195] Muniments of the Dean and Chapter of Durham, Misc. Charters 4319.
[196] *Cal. Pap. Regs. Letters*, ii, 288, 306, 413.
[197] *Ibid.*, ii, 320, 344, 369, 383.
[198] *Ibid.*, ii, 317, 325, 326, 335, 339, 340, 342, 346, 363, 370, 377, 510.
[199] *Ibid.*, ii, 316, 381.
[200] *Ibid.*, ii, 379, 400.
[201] *Ibid.*, ii, 296.
[202] *Ibid.*, ii, 490.
[203] *Ibid.*, ii, 492-493.
[204] *Ibid.*, ii, 497.
[205] *Ibid.*, ii, 321, 383; *Reg. of John de Grandisson*, i, 593.
[206] 27 July 1330; *Cal. Pap. Regs. Letters*, ii, 318; *Literae Cantuarienses*, i, 512-515.
[207] William Thorne's *Chronicle*, ed. A. H. Davis, pp. 440-445. The chronology of the chronicle appears to be confused.

bishop at his manor of Slyndon. They were attacked by the archbishop's retainers and some of them were severely injured. The proctor of the abbot and convent reported the incident to the pope and cardinals in consistory, and the pope commissioned Armand, archbishop of Aix (not Aquino), to investigate. Archbishop Simon attested under oath that he was ill in the manor at the time and was not responsible for those deeds which he abhorred. He also persuaded the king and several bishops to write in his behalf.[208] The king expressed his belief that the injuries had not been inflicted with the connivance or consent of the archbishop and furthermore he declared that it was a scandal to have one of such authority tried before the nuncio.[209] The archbishop of Aix, on the other hand, reported to the pope that the archbishop of Canterbury was responsible because he had heard the commotion and had done nothing to stop it.[210]

Archbishop Simon next tried to stop Itier's proceedings against him by bringing the question before the Michaelmas session of parliament.[211] He claimed that the nuncio was attempting to draw before an ecclesiastical court a case which belonged to the king's throne and asked that Itier should be prevented by royal letters from proceeding further with the suit. Some of the archbishop's supporters in parliament demanded that the collector should be banished from the realm, but it was finally decided to summon him to answer the archbishop's accusation. When he appeared, he claimed that the cause came under canon law and the ecclesiastical forum.[212] Since he was allowed to continue the case, his claim apparently was accepted by parliament. The proctors of the abbot and convent reported the archbishop's action to John XXII who apparently received the impression that Simon had tried to secure the exclusion from England of nuncios of the apostolic see who were foreigners. The king thereupon wrote to the pope that this view was erroneous.[212]

After this experience with parliament, Itier continued to issue summonses to the archbishop, who still refused to acknowledge the collector's jurisdiction by appearing before him. Eventually Itier gave final sentence declaring the acts of the archbishop against the abbot and convent void and condemning him to pay the costs of the abbot and convent which were assessed at £700. Ultimately Itier's judgment was set aside by a compromise made between the abbot and convent and John Stratford, Simon Meopham's successor.[214]

Like most collectors Itier received emoluments and privileges in addition to his procurations and customary allowance for expenses. While he was in office the pope conferred upon him the churches of Kirk Ella in Yorkshire and Adderbury in Oxfordshire, the prebends of Overhall in Ledbury, Herefordshire and Ealdland in the church of St. Paul's London, and the archdeaconry of London.[215] He also acquired the prebends of Hinton in the church of Hereford and Faringdon in Salisbury.[216] The pope authorized him to collect the fruits of all his benefices as long as he should be in the service of the apostolic see, provided he supplied vicars for those with cure of souls.[217] The king appointed Itier one of his clerks,[218] and he allowed the collector to deduct the expenses which he incurred in the collection of the royal half of the quadrennial levies of the tenth and annates.[219] The king also extended his favor to Colinus Draperii of Vermentone, a notary from the diocese of Auxerre, who was a member of the collector's staff.[220] He requested the pope to provide the notary with an English benefice on account of his extensive labors in the collection of the tenth and annates.[221] John XXII authorized Itier to dispose of his personal property by will and at the hour of death to receive plenary remission from a confessor of his choice.[222]

In 1333 the collector went to the papal court at Avignon. Papal permission to make the journey was given on 7 February and a royal safe conduct was issued on 13 March.[223] He probably left soon after the latter date, since he was expected at the papal court at Eastertide.[224] His principal purpose was to account with the papal camera.[225] He also represented the king[226] and undertook to expedite business for the clergy of the archdeaconry of Durham.[227] He returned to London

---

[208] *Ibid.*, pp. 447-450.

[209] 16 July 1331: Rymer, *Foedera*, ii, 822-823.

[210] William Thorne's *Chronicle*, pp. 450-451.

[211] Thorne makes this event appear to have happened before the attack on the proctors on 21 March 1331 (*Chronicle*, pp. 445-446), but the king, writing on 6 January 1332, states that it took place in his last parliament: Rymer, *Foedera*, ii, 830.

[212] William Thorne's *Chronicle*, pp. 445-446. The chronicler does not state the outcome of the dispute.

[213] Rymer, *Foedera*, ii, 830.

[214] William Thorne's *Chronicle*, pp. 451-458, 484-489; *Literae*

*Cantuarienses*, i, 511-519; Dugdale, *Monasticon*, i, 133-134.

[215] *Cal. Pap. Regs. Letters*, ii, 314, 327, 339, 357; *Cal. Pat. Rolls, 1334-38*, p. 487.

[216] *Cal. Pat. Rolls, 1327-30*, p. 542; *1334-38*, p. 487. After he ceased to be collector, the bishop of Winchester gave him, on 23 March 1336, a pension of 30 marks a year to last for the life of the donor or until he provided the recipient with a benefice worth 30 marks annually with cure or 50 marks without cure: Winchester Diocesan Registry, Reg. of Orlton, i, fol. 33ᵛ.

[217] *Cal. Pap. Regs. Letters*, ii, 498.

[218] *Cal. Pat. Rolls, 1327-30*, p. 542.

[219] *Ibid.*, *1330-34*, p. 454; P. R. O., K. R. Memo. Roll 109, m. 125 r and v; P. R. O., Chancery Misc., Bundle 18, File 9, no. 7; Bundle 87, File 3, general, no. 4.

[220] *Reg. of John de Grandisson*, ii, 737; *Reg. Hamonis Hethe*, pp. 538-539.

[221] P. R. O., Ancient Correspondence 38, no. 155.

[222] *Cal. Pap. Regs. Letters*, ii, 404.

[223] Above, p. xiv.

[224] *Cal. Pap. Regs. Letters*, ii, 510. He made deposits with Italian bankers in England on 11 and 12 March: *ibid.*, ii, 508. Commissioners were acting for him in the collection of the tenth on 22 June.

[225] *Cal. Pap. Regs. Letters*, ii, 510.

[226] *Cal. Pat. Rolls, 1330-34*, p. 414.

[227] Muniments of the Dean and Chapter of Durham, Misc. Charter 4278.

before 4 August.[228] During his absence the work of collection was carried on by his subordinates.[229]

Itier was superseded by Bernard de Sistre on 13 September 1335 and ordered to deliver to his successor all letters in his possession relating to the collector's office.[230] Actually he seems to have ceased to act as collector in 1334. During the period from December 1333 to March 1334 inclusive, he audited the final accounts of the deputy collectors of annates and the tenth,[231] and in July he deposited some of his funds with English factors of the Florentine firm of Azayali.[232] This was his last official act in England in 1334 of which record has come to light. Thereafter he probably availed himself of a royal license, dated 2 March 1334,[233] to cross to the continent. On 10 December 1334, while Itier was on the continent,[234] the king forbade the Bardi to pay any of the proceeds of the tenth and the annates which might be in their hands until the king had received the balance of his share which was still due. He also ordered the mayor and sheriffs of London to seize any of the money they could find in their bailiwick.[235] Had the collector been in England, the royal government would probably have dealt with him directly. Other evidence tends to substantiate this inference. Two series of documents which record the payments of Itier's procurations made by two payers in several years both terminate with his sixth year which came to a conclusion in 1334. The payments for that year were due in the spring of 1334.[236] Itier's successor had to collect all but a few items of the census and Peter's pence which fell due in 1334.[237] The former were due at Michaelmas 1334 and the latter before 25 March 1335.[238]

Itier's absence in 1335 is well attested. On 22 January the king addressed a letter concerning the tenth being levied in the diocese of Hereford to Itier or his commissioners or his deputy collector in the diocese.[239] On 19 April Bertandus Itherii, acting as Itier's *locumtenens*, demanded payment at his house from a deputy collector

of annates within fifteen days.[240] On 12 May the king summoned Bertrandus and Poncius de Sancto Egidio, Itier's proctor, to come to York to consult with the royal council concerning the collection and receipt of the tenth and annates which were still owed to the king and the pope. The problem arose because John XXII had died, Benedict XII had not yet appointed a new collector and the powers of Itier, according to the assumption of the royal government, had lapsed.[241] Under these conditions the collector would have been summoned rather than his agents if he had been available. Itier did not return until some time in 1336. On 8 April he was given a safe conduct to come to England from beyond the seas in order to forward business laid upon him by the king [242] and on 26 May he was authorized to account with the exchequer for annates and the tenth by attorney.[243] He was in England in 1337, since on 3 August he was given a royal protection explaining that because he had been born in Aquitaine, he was exempt from the royal order for the confiscation of the goods of Frenchmen subject to the king of France.[244]

Itier left the affairs of his office in some disorder. While he was away, his staff carried on the business,[245] but the large number of payments of Peter's pence and census due in 1334 which Bernard de Sistre had to collect after he took over late in 1335 [246] indicate that its work was not efficient. After John XXII died on 4 December 1334, some of the collector's work was still maintained by the staff,[247] but the view of the king that the powers of the collector appointed by the deceased pope were no longer valid probably was the prevalent view,[248] and this disrupted the work still further. Not a single debtor who owed census paid what was due on Michaelmas 1335 until after 3 February 1336,[249] when Bernard began to demand payments of census and other dues which were in arrears.[250] In normal years many payers were that much behind, but there were always some who paid before the close of the year in which payment became due.[251]

[228] *Reg. of Ralph of Shrewsbury*, i, 156. His royal letter of protection was good only until Michaelmas.

[229] Lincoln Diocesan Registry, Reg. v, Burghersh, fols. 465ᵛ, 466; Wells Diocesan Registry, Reg. of Shrewsbury, fol. 83; *Reg. of Ralph of Shrewsbury*, i, 146.

[230] Theiner, *Vetera Monumenta Hibernorum*, pp. 266-268; *Cal. Pap. Regs. Letters*, ii, 559.

[231] British Museum, Addit. MS. 41612, fols. 84ᵛ, 85; *Reg. Hamonis Hethe*, pp. 536-539; I. H. Jeayes, *Descriptive Catalogue of the Charters and Muniments belonging to the Marquis of Anglesey*, p. 130, no. 493; *Reg. of John de Grandisson*, ii, 736.

[232] Göller, *Die Einnahmen unter Benedikt XII*, p. 198; Theiner, *Vetera Monumenta Hibernorum*, p. 270.

[233] *Cal. Pat. Rolls, 1330-34*, p. 519.

[234] Lunt, *Financial Relations . . . 1327-1534*, pp. 82-83.

[235] Rymer, *Foedera*, ii, 899.

[236] Muniments of the Dean and Chapter of Lincoln, B. j. 2. 5; Muniments of the Dean and Chapter of Durham, Misc. Charters, 4193, 4338, 4765, 5020.

[237] Below, pp. 35-37; 43-44.

[238] Below, pp. 417, 418.

[239] *Reg. Thome de Charlton*, ed. W. W. Capes, pp. 68-69.

[240] Winchester Diocesan Registry, Reg. of Orlton, i, fol. 17.

[241] *Cal. Close Rolls, 1333-37*, pp. 485-486.

[242] *Cal. Pat. Rolls, 1334-38*, p. 245.

[243] P. R. O., K. R. Memo. Roll 113, m. 37.

[244] *Cal. Pat. Rolls, 1334-38*, p. 487. On 17 March the king acquitted Itier for £500 of arrears of the tenth and annates which he had paid to the Bardi: *ibid*., p. 391.

[245] *Cal. Close Rolls, 1333-37*, p. 485; Winchester Diocesan Registry, Reg. of Orlton, i, fol. 17.

[246] Above, this page.

[247] *Cal. Close Rolls, 1333-37*, p. 485; below, p. 219; York Diocesan Registry, Reg. of Melton, fols. 46ᵛ, 52.

[248] There was often doubt on this question during the fourteenth century: Samaran and Mollat, *La Fiscalité pontificale*, pp. 77-78.

[249] Below, pp. 43-44.

[250] Winchester Diocesan Registry, Reg. of Orlton, i, fol. 32; Worcester, Reg. of Montacute, ii, fol. 18; *Winchester Cathedral Chartulary*, ed. A. W. Goodman, p. 53; *Reg. of Ralph of Shrewsbury*, i, 262-263.

[251] Below, pp. 29-32.

Itier not only left an undue amount of arrears, but he also was found to have collected more than he had delivered to the camera. The account rendered by Itier, which Bernard had copied before leaving Avignon,[252] left a balance due the camera of £237 19 s. 11 d.[253] In addition Bernard discovered many items entered in the account as still owed by the debtors for which the debtors produced acquittances issued by Itier, his *locumtenens* or his deputies, items of receipt similarly established by acquittances which were not included in the account at all and one forgiveness of a debt for annates which the collector had no power to grant.[254] Part of this indebtedness was met by a deposit which Itier had made with the Peruzzi before leaving England and the remainder by distraint of the fruits of his English benefices and of some of the procurations still owed to him.[255] Itier was also in debt to the king for part of the royal share of the tenth and annates. After a view of his account had been made at the exchequer in 1339,[256] writs were issued to the bishops of London and Lincoln ordering them to levy respectively from Itier's ecclesiastical goods £537 8¼ d. and £600.[257] In 1340 Bernard delivered to the exchequer £21 raised from the issues of the archdeaconry of London, but the exchequer continued without result to send writs of *levari facias* to the two bishops for many years.[258]

Itier ultimately lost all his English benefices. He was deprived of Adderbury because he held it for a year without being ordained a priest.[259] On 13 September 1338 the king presented another clerk to the archdeaconry of London.[260] Then or sometime before 17 June 1343 Itier sacrificed his other benefices in order to take unto himself a wife.[261] Rumor had it that he also became a soldier.[262] He died long before 1364.[263]

---

[252] Below, p. 67.

[253] Below, p. 77.

[254] Below, pp. 43, 55-58, 62, 76.

[255] Below, pp. 54, 68, 77. The bishop of Exeter suspected that Bernard was collecting for himself these revenues belonging to Itier: *Reg. of John de Grandisson*, i, 303.

[256] P. R. O., K. R. Memo. Roll 115, Status et Visus Compotorum, Hilary Term, anno XIII, m. 1ᵛ; Exchequer K. R. Accounts 311/37.

[257] P. R. O., K. R. Memo. Roll 115, Brevia Retorn., Hilary Term, m. 1.

[258] *Reg. Simonis de Sudbiria*, ed. R. C. Fowler, i, 46, 59, 62, 67, 71, 82; P. R. O., K. R. Memo. Rolls, under Michaelmas Term, 117, Brevia Irretorn.; 118, Brevia Retorn.; 142, Brevia Retorn.; 156, Brevia Retorn.; in subsequent rolls under Brevia Retorn. et Irretorn., 175, 177, 178, 180, 188, 191, 199, 200, 202, 203, 211.

[259] Below, p. 54.

[260] *Cal. Pat. Rolls, 1338-40*, p. 125.

[261] *Cal. Pap. Regs. Petitions*, i, 52, 57, 288. In 1350 the king claimed that Itier resigned his benefices in 1335, while he was still papal nuncio, but the claim was a necessary part of a complicated claim that the king had the right to present to the canonry and prebend of Overhall in Ledbury: *Cal. Pat. Rolls, 1348-50*, p. 545. Itier seems to have been in possession of Hinton in 1338: Le Neve, *Fasti* (Hereford), 27. Furthermore Bernard de Sistre was levying on several of his benefices after 1335.

[262] *Cal. Pap. Regs. Petitions*, i, 288.

## BERNARD DE SISTRE

When Master Bernard de Sistre was appointed collector, he was rector of Saint-Hippolyte-Majan in Villemagne in the neighborhood of Béziers, vicar of Coursan in the diocese of Narbonne and canon of St. Hilary in Poitiers.[264] He had acted as one of the executors of Raymond, cardinal bishop of Sabina, and he had been the chamberlain of Gaillard de Mota, cardinal deacon of St. Lucy in Silice. In the latter capacity he seems to have resided at the papal court.[265] He had previously been in England. In 1318 he was acting there as proctor of Vitalis, cardinal priest of Ss. Silvestro e Martino ai Monti.[266]

His commission, dated 13 September 1335, named him collector and nuncio in England, Wales, Ireland and Scotland,[267] but his report included no receipts from Scotland. He was empowered to collect Peter's pence and census, to transact other business and to finish any business touching the pope and the camera which had been entrusted by John XXII to Hugh of Angoulême or Itier de Concoreto. Bernard's commission did not instruct him specifically to seek the full amount of Peter's pence, and he did not ask for it in his first demands for payment of the due. While he was absent from England in 1337, his *locumtenens*, relying perhaps on Hugh's commission, put forward a claim to the full amount,[268] but met with no success.[269] Whether Bernard sanctioned the act of his *locumtenens* is not apparent, but he was thereafter content with the customary sums. Bernard received the usual power to enforce payments with ecclesiastical censures, letters of commendation to the king, and various English magnates, and the right to exact procurations.[270] On 30 December 1336 the papal treasurer ordered him to collect during vacancies the fruits of benefices in his collectorate which became vacant at the apostolic see, Benedict XII having reserved them for the papal camera on 8 January 1335, the day of his consecration.[271] Bernard was further directed to obtain private information concerning the patronage and value of prebends, monasteries, priories and other regular and secular benefices and to forward it to the pope in a written report.[272] The purpose of this inquiry was

---

[263] *Reg. Simonis de Sudbiria*, i, 59.

[264] Göller, *Die Einnahmen unter Johann XXII*, p. 287, n. 4; *Benoit XII: Lettres Communes*, no. 4206.

[265] Göller, *op. cit.*, pp. 287, n. 4, 340.

[266] Hist. MSS. Comm., *Report* ix, app. 1, p. 34.

[267] Theiner, *Vetera Monumenta Hibernorum*, pp. 266-267; *Cal. Pap. Regs. Letters*, ii, 559; *Reg. of Ralph of Shrewsbury*, i, 261-262.

[268] *Reg. of John de Grandisson*, i, 297-299.

[269] Below, p. xxx, 35-43.

[270] Theiner, *Vetera Monumenta Hibernorum*, pp. 266-267; *Reg. of Ralph of Shrewsbury*, i, 261-262; *Cal. Pap. Regs. Letters*, ii, 561.

[271] Winchester Diocesan Registry, Reg. of Orlton, ii, fol. 28. From time to time the pope called the attention of Bernard to specific benefices in this category: *Cal. Pap. Regs. Letters*, ii, 558, 560, 561, 590.

[272] 12 October 1335: *Cal. Pap. Regs. Letters*, ii, 560.

not stated in the papal mandate, but it brings to mind the suspicions entertained by the English at times in the thirteenth century that papal agents in England were spotting rich benefices for papal collation. On one occasion the king addressed Bernard as collector of the sexennial tenth imposed for the crusade by John XXII on 26 July 1333, and renewed by Benedict XII on 31 January 1335.[273] Though he seems to have attended to the business committed to him in the royal letter,[274] the English bishops had been appointed collectors of the tenth [275] and Bernard had no responsibility for its levy.[276] Bernard retained the office of general collector under Clement VI,[277] who was consecrated on 19 May 1342, though no trace of the renewal of his commission has been discovered. He must also have been notified of the imposition of annates on benefices reserved to papal disposal made by Clement VI on 21 May 1342 [278] and ordered to collect them, since he accounted for them in his report.[279] On 20 May 1343 Clement VI ordered him to collect the visitation tax owed every three years by the archbishops of Canterbury, York and Armagh,[280] which previously had been payable at the camera by the debtors.[281] This commission must have arrived too late for him to execute it.

After Bernard was appointed collector by Benedict XII he remained at Avignon for a few weeks, during which he had copies made of the accounts of his predecessor and of the valuation of English benefices. He left the papal court on 10 October 1335 and arrived in London on 21 November. Before he could begin to exercise the duties of his office he had to obtain the royal *exequatur*, and for this he went to Scotland where the king was.[282] The royal approval was signified by a safe conduct for himself, his household and his commissioners, dated 18 December.[283] He arrived back in London 9 January 1336,[284] where he established himself and his household in a house, the location of which he did not specify in his correspondence. On 3 February, Bernard had his commissions published by the official of the Court of Arches, and issued his first demands for payment of Peter's pence, census and arrears of annates, and for the render of accounts for arrears by deputy

collectors of the quadrennial tenth.[285] In 1337 he was away from England for several months acting as an envoy of Edward III to the pope. His safe conduct bore the date 6 March and it was good for his return to England until Michaelmas.[286] He had his interview with the pope on or before 16 May.[287] During his absence Master Durantus acted as his *locumtenens*.[288] Bernard died on 18 June 1343, while still in office.[289] He was succeeded by Raymond Pelegrini, who, on 26 June, was directed by Clement VI to continue the work of Bernard, and on 30 January 1344 was commissioned as general collector in his own right.[290]

Bernard appears to have been an efficient collector. When he died, the affairs of his office were in such good order that his executors, a nephew of the same name and Poncius de Puteo,[291] were able to settle them within four months.[292] They recovered the goods of the camera from the exchequer, which had seized them for sums owed by the collector to the king, and from some ecclesiastics who were obliged to Bernard probably for loans which he had made to them,[293] concluded Bernard's account, provided the new collector with the information which he needed and delivered to him the property of the camera which had been in the keeping of the deceased collector.[294] Before 10 December 1344 they rendered an account to the camera for the whole period of Bernard's collectorship which left a moderate amount of arrears still to be recovered from the taxpayers and a balance due from the collector of £149 5 s. 8½ d.[295] This was met from Bernard's personal property, which the pope had ordered Raymond Pelegrini to sequestrate and forward to the camera, and enough was left to pay a bequest of fifty florins which Bernard made to the

---

[273] 10 November 1336: *Cal. Close Rolls, 1333-37*, p. 720.

[274] *Cal. Pap. Regs. Letters*, ii, 568.

[275] *Ibid.*, ii, 369, 523; P. R. O., K. R. Memo. Roll 113, m. 161, 161ᵛ.

[276] A large number of documents concerned with the levy of the tenth indicate that the archbishops, the bishops and the deputy collectors appointed by them in their respective dioceses were responsible for the collection. They contain no reference to any liability of Bernard for its administration: below, pp. xlv-xlvi.

[277] Below, pp. 42, 48, 53.

[278] Lunt, *Papal Revenues*, ii, 358-361.

[279] Below, p. 53.

[280] *Cal. Pap. Regs. Letters*, iii, 1.

[281] Below, pp. 43, 44.

[282] Below, pp. 67, 69.

[283] Rymer, *Foedera*, ii, 928; *Cal. Pat. Rolls, 1334-38*, p. 189.

[284] Below, p. 67.

[285] *Reg. of Ralph of Shrewsbury*, i, 260-263; *Chartulary of Winchester Cathedral*, p. 53; Winchester Diocescan Registry, Reg. of Orlton, i, fol. 32, 32ᵛ; Worcester, Reg. of Montacute, ii, fol. 18. He issued one letter at Carlton in Lindrick (Notts) on 5 January presumably when he was making his return journey from Scotland. It was an order for the sequestration of the revenues of the archdeacon of Winchester for debts owed to the camera. The nature of the debts was not specified: Reg. of Orlton, i, fol. 32ᵛ.

[286] *Cal. Pat. Rolls, 1334-38*, p. 427; *Cal. Close Rolls, 1337-39*, p. 118.

[287] *Cal. Pap. Regs. Letters*, ii, 563.

[288] *Reg. of John de Grandisson*, i, 297-298.

[289] Below, p. 35.

[290] *Cal. Pap. Regs. Letters*, iii, 2, 6; *Clement VI: Lettres closes*, ed. Déprez, i, no. 243; York Diocesan Registry, Reg. of la Zouche, fols. 255ᵛ, 256.

[291] Mohler, *Die Einnahmen unter Klemens VI*, p. 353.

[292] Below, p. 68. Both Bernard's successor and Androynus de Rocha, Bernard Dortali and John Bonaura, a notary and member of Bernard's household, were ordered to render an account (*Cal. Pap. Regs. Letters*, iii, 2), but the account which has survived was rendered by his executors.

[293] E. g. *Reg. Palatinum Dunelmense*, iii, 240.

[294] Below, pp. 67-68. The property of the camera was delivered to Raymond Pelegrini on 3 August 1343: Vatican Archives, Arm. xxxv, 140, fol. 24.

[295] *Cal. Pap. Regs. Letters*, iii, 13; below, pp. 64-77.

papal camera and to provide approximately 2700 florins for Bernard's heirs.[296] Bernard's account with the king for his half of the quadrennial annates and tenth imposed by John XXII was, on the face of it, in much worse shape. In 1343, after Bernard's death, £1,010 were still recorded as due the king,[297] but a goodly part of it probably consisted of hopeless debts, exemptions granted by the king and similar items which in this account were not credited to the collector.[298] Four years earlier in a view of account at the exchequer Bernard was left owing no more than a little over £100.[299]

The duties other than those associated with his office which Benedict XII asked Bernard to perform were few,[300] but Clement VI called upon him frequently to act as one of the executors of papal grants and citations.[301] The cardinals, Peter, priest of S. Prassede, and Bertrand, deacon of S. Maria in Aquiro, required him in 1340 to act as the colleague of the archbishop of Canterbury for the collection of the procurations which as papal nuncios they demanded of the English clergy.[302] Bernard received from Benedict XII collation to a canonry and prebend in Bayeux,[303] and from Clement VI provision to the archdeaconry of Canterbury to which the archbishop of Canterbury had previously collated him.[304] Benedict XII conferred upon him several privileges which it was becoming customary to grant to the papal collector in England. He was authorized to enjoy the fruits of his benefices as long as he was engaged upon his mission, to dispose of his personal property by will, to receive plenary remission from his confessor at the hour of death and to confer the office of notary public on two persons selected by him.[305]

With Edward III Bernard seems to have been *persona grata*. The king made the collector one of his clerks.[306] In 1337, when he sent Bernard to negotiate in his behalf with the pope, he provided for his transportation across the Channel, gave him 200 marks for his expenses and granted him an annual pension of fifty marks until he should provide him with a benefice.[307]

A year later Bernard was given permission to send servants to Aquitaine to purchase fifty tuns of wine.[308] On another occasion, at the request of the collector and out of reverence for Clement VI, the king restored to Guy de Calma the prebend of Gretton in the church of Lincoln which had been seized because Guy was a subject of the king of France.[309] But the best evidence of Bernard's standing with the king is a letter of 1 May 1340 attested by the king himself. It explains that an examination of Bernard in the presence of the king had established the falsity of a report that he had written letters to correspondents beyond seas defaming the king and his councillors. It concludes, according to the summary in the Calendar: " Wherefore the king as well for his watchfulness and loving bearing as for the gentle services rendered by him holds him very dear and beloved." [310] The collector reciprocated these favors to some extent between 1339 and 1342 by accomodating the king with loans which amounted to over £2,400, a sum so large that it probably came wholly or in part from the funds of the papal camera in the collector's possession. They were temporary loans which for the most part were to be repaid promptly from the proceeds of various royal taxes.[311]

Bernard's relations with the English clergy appear in some instances to have been friendly and in others quite the contrary. When the collector went to the papal court in 1337 on a mission for the king, he carried letters to the pope for the archbishop of Canterbury.[312] Two years later the archbishop collated him to the archdeaconry of Canterbury.[313] With Richard of Bury, bishop of Durham, Bernard was sufficiently friendly to make him a small loan from the papal money in his possession.[314] From John de Grandisson, bishop of Exeter, who was somewhat cantankerous, the collector received stringent criticism. He complained to Bernard that his proceedings against debtors were too hasty and that dates for payment assigned by him could not be met from such distant places.[315] This was an old grievance. In 1329 he had suggested to Itier that he ought to appoint someone in the diocese of Exeter with power to receive payments and give acquittances for his procurations on account of the difficulties of delivery in London from places so distant.[316] The bishop was much offended by a demand from Master Durantus, when he was acting as *locumtenens*, for payment of the full amount of Peter's pence. He expressed his resentment that the collector had taken the word of others to the

[296] *Cal. Pap. Regs. Letters*, iii, 13; Mohler, *Die Einnahmen unter Klemens VI*, pp. 353-354.

[297] P. R. O., L. T. R. Enrolled Accounts, Subsidies etc., no. 3, m. 17ᵛ.

[298] E. g., below, pp. 67, 71-72; *Cal. Close Rolls, 1337-39*, p. 600: Muniments of the Dean and Chapter of Durham, Reg. Secundum, fols. 133ᵛ, 134; 3, xiii. 8 Pontificalium.

[299] P. R. O., Exchequer K. R. Accounts, 311/37. The sum was probably less than £100, but a stain renders the end of the account illegible.

[300] *Cal. Pap. Regs. Letters*, ii, 549, 560.

[301] *Ibid.*, iii, 61, 71, 80, 112.

[302] *Reg. of Shrewsbury*, i, 424-425.

[303] *Benoit XII: Lettres communes*, no. 4206.

[304] *Cal. Pap. Regs. Letters*, iii, 53.

[305] *Ibid.*, ii, 530, 561, 562.

[306] *Cal. Pat. Rolls, 1334-38*, pp. 427, 436; *1338-40*, pp. 198, 260, 450, 470.

[307] *Ibid.*, *1334-38*, p. 436; *Cal. Close Rolls, 1337-39*, pp. 118, 600; P. R. O., K. R. Memo. Roll 115, Brevia directa Baronibus, Hilary Term, m. 2.

[308] *Cal. Pat. Rolls, 1334-38*, p. 568.

[309] *Cal. Close Rolls, 1341-43*, pp. 577-578.

[310] *Cal. Pat. Rolls, 1338-40*, p. 470.

[311] *Ibid.*, *1338-40*, pp. 308, 450; *1340-43*, p. 479; *Cal. Close Rolls, 1339-41*, pp. 526, 556; *1341-43*, pp. 594, 684.

[312] *Cal. Pap. Regs. Letters*, ii, 563.

[313] *Ibid.*, iii, 53; Le Neve, *Fasti* (Monastic Cathedrals, Southern Province), p. 7.

[314] *Reg. Palatinum Dunelmense*, iii, 240.

[315] *Reg. of John de Grandisson*, i, 297.

[316] *Ibid.*, i, 204-205.

effect that he had held back payments of Peter's pence, explained that he received not an obol more than he paid to the Roman church, that he had acquittances up to the past year, and that he would pay for the current year at his convenience. He also stated his disbelief that the collector's commission gave him power to depose or degrade a bishop, threatened to write to friends at the Roman court about it, and asked the *locumtenens* to bring his reply to the attention of Bernard upon his return. When Durantus answered this letter, the indignant bishop denied the collector's legal right to issue compulsory letters against him, because he had been able to find no law that Peter's pence must be received or paid at a certain time.[317] Later the bishop carried out his threat and wrote to Bertrand de Monte Faventio, cardinal deacon of Santa Maria in Aquiro. He asserted that Bernard collected from both rich and poor prelates and clergy procurations which he was entitled to receive only from colleges and cells [318] and that he acknowledged receipt of five marks more than the seven shillings a day of procurations to which he was entitled. He complained that Bernard was collecting arrears owed to Itier for the benefit of neither Itier nor the pope but of Bertrand himself, an accusation which was probably false. He stated further that the collector used excommunication and interdict against allegedly delinquent payers of procurations who actually had paid what they owed.[319] Bishop Grandisson's enmity toward the collector may have been exceptional, but apparently several English prelates were contemplating some common action in opposition to Bernard in 1341, because Benedict XII, on 17 December, forbade the archbishops, bishops, abbots and secular and regular prelates of England, Wales and Ireland " to attempt anything contrary to the letters appointing Master Bernard de Sistre and his officers charged with a certain mission in those parts." [320] This prohibition taken in conjunction with the false rumors about Bernard reported to the king in 1340 gives color to a surmise that the collector at that time was disliked by more than a few individuals. Possibly the collector's procurations were the subject of adverse comment by others than the bishop of Exeter, or possibly the antagonism to a French collector, which had been displayed against Itier de Concoreto in the parliament of 1331,[321] was becoming stronger with the progress of the war against France. Both sentiments came to a head in the parliament of 1346 when Raymond Pelegrini was collector. The commons petitioned that the procurations of seven shillings taken by him annually from each religious house should be annuled

for all time and that he should leave the country before Michaelmas or be held outside the common law. The petition was denied with the explanation that Raymond was a liege of the king born in Gascony and sworn of the council and that he took procurations for his sustenance as others had long done.[322] The petition is, nevertheless, striking testimony to the strength of popular sentiment against French collectors and the collectors' procurations.

## HUGH PELEGRINI

The brothers, Hugh and Raymond Pelegrini, were born in the English king's lordship of Aquitaine and were ' not of the power of the king of France.' [323] In 1349 Edward III designated Raymond as a denizen and not an alien.[324] Their childhood home was in Le Vigan in the diocese of Cahors,[325] and they remained closely associated with that diocese throughout their lives.[326] Both held benefices there.[327] Raymond in his will, drawn up in 1365, left property to found and endow a college named after him in the University of Cahors, and Hugh in 1378 added to the endowment by leaving to the college all his property.[328] Raymond appears to have been the first to go to England. In 1322 Gaillard de Duroforti, a nephew of Clement V and prebendary of Wetwang in York, named Raymond one of his attorneys during his absence from England.[329] In following years Raymond served Gaucelme, cardinal of Albano, and several other aliens beneficed in England as attorney or proctor.[330] He also held English benefices of his own. Through presentation by the abbot of Lire and a papal provision he became parson of Arreton in the Isle of Wight in 1323.[331] With the aid of papal provisions he exchanged that benefice for East Grinstead in Sussex and the new benefice in turn for the canonry and prebend of Henstridge in the church of Wells.[332] In 1339 he was also parson of Withington in Gloucestershire, and before he was appointed collector

---

[317] *Ibid.*, i, 297-300. The letters of the bishop are dated 15 May and 16 June 1337. The letters of the *locumtenens* are lacking.

[318] This statement was inaccurate: Lunt, *Financial Relations . . . to 1327*, pp. 548-549.

[319] Below, pp. 54, 77; 5 March 1338: *Reg. of John de Grandisson*, i. 302-304.

[320] *Cal. Pap. Regs. Letters*, ii, 590.

[321] Above, p. xxvi.

[322] *Rot. Parl.*, ii, 163.

[323] *Ibid.*, *Cal. Pat. Rolls, 1324-27*, p. 56; *1364-67*, p. 188.

[324] *Cal. Pat. Rolls, 1348-50*, p. 346.

[325] Marcel Fournier, *Les Statuts et Privilèges des Universités françaises*, iii, no. 1430.

[326] Collectorie 354, fol. 27.

[327] Raymond was beneficed in France in 1329, held a canonry with expectation of a prebend in 1344, the archdeaconry of Saint-Ceré in 1359 and the deanery of Le Vigan in 1365: *Cal. Pap. Regs. Letters*, ii, 301; iii, 166, 632; Fournier, *Les Statuts*, iii, no. 1430. Hugh was a canon of Le Vigan in 1342: *Cal. Pap. Regs. Letters*, iii, 82.

[328] Fournier, *Les Statuts*, iii, nos. 1430, 1431, 1444, 1449.

[329] *Cal. Pap. Regs. Letters*, ii, 558; *Cal. Pat. Rolls, 1321-24*, p. 111.

[330] *Cal. Pat. Rolls, 1321-24*, p. 403; *1324-27*, pp. 93, 119; *1330-34*, p. 477; *1334-38*, pp. 317, 330, 336; *1343-45*, p. 5; *Cal. Close Rolls, 1327-30*, p. 550; *1330-33*, p. 620.

[331] *Cal. Pat. Rolls, 1321-24*, p. 354; *Cal. Pap. Regs. Letters*, ii, 230.

[332] *Cal. Pap. Regs. Letters*, ii, 326, 328.

in 1343 he had acquired a canonry in London.[333] In these various capacities he came into contact with several branches of the royal government. He received the royal proctection on several occasions[334] and transacted business with the chancery, the exchequer and the royal courts.[335] In 1331 he was sent to the continent on the king's service.[336] By the time that he was appointed collector in 1343, he had become so well known to the royal government that he was made a king's clerk and a member of the king's council.[337] He was also well enough known at the papal court to have been asked several times to serve as an executor of papal provisions.[338]

Hugh's earliest association with England, of which I have found record, was on 6 March 1333, when the pope provided him with a prebendal portion in the church of Lanchester at the request of the king.[339] Ten years later he was provided with the church of Boxley in Kent which had become vacant because he had previously held it without having been ordained a subdeacon within the prescribed period. Presumably he was ordained later, since he was still in possession in 1349.[340] In 1342 Hugh had the bachelor's degree. Six years later he had received the degree of doctor of civil law and was lecturing at Oxford.[341] In the same year he was provided with the treasurership of Lichfield.[342] There is no indication that up to that time Hugh was particularly well known at either the royal or the papal court.[343]

On 26 June 1343 Raymond had merely taken over Bernard de Sistre's commissions.[344] On 30 January 1344, when he received his own commission to collect Peter's pence and census, he was also empowered to continue to use the letters addressed by Benedict XII to Bernard de Sistre.[345] He was given separate commissions by Clement VI to collect annates[346] as well as the power to levy his own procurations.[347]

When Hugh became collector, he simply took over Raymond's commissions. On 30 April 1349 Hugh was named papal nuncio and was commissioned to act for Raymond in the business of the papal camera during his brother's absence.[348] The appointment was temporary and Raymond was still regarded as collector.[349] Hugh began to keep an account of his own on 1 August 1349,[350] and Raymond apparently soon left England to go to the papal court.[351] Subsequently the pope kept Raymond occupied with other affairs for several years[352] and on 8 July 1350 Hugh was named Raymond's successor for the transaction of the business of the papal camera in England, Wales and Ireland.[353] Like other collectors, Hugh maintained a house in London where he conducted the affairs of his office, but he did not locate the house in his official letters.[354] Hugh was given commissions in addition to those which he inherited from Raymond. In 1350 the camera asked him to report on the value of the property of three prelates who owed common services and to collect these obligations.[355] In the same year, Raymond Pelegrini, writing from the papal camera, informed his brother of a priest in the diocese of London who owed the fruits of his benefices for two years to the camera as a composition for fruits which he had collected illegally.[356] When Innocent VI became pope, he notified Hugh that the commission which Clement VI had granted him was to continue in effect.[357] Hugh retained his office throughout Innocent's pontificate. In 1355 he was ordered to visit all ecclesiastical places in his collectorate once and receive procurations.[358] He does not appear to have acted on this mandate until 1357, when, instead of conducting the visitation himself, he sent a copy of the papal bull of 1355 to each bishop.[359] It ordered the recipient to visit

---

[333] Ibid., iii, 2; Cal. Close Rolls, 1339-41, pp. 271, 291.

[334] Cal. Pat. Rolls, 1321-24, p. 403; 1324-27, pp. 56, 93, 119, 342.

[335] Ibid., 1321-24, p. 534; 1324-27, p. 287; 1334-38, p. 216; Cal. Close Rolls, 1327-30, p. 201; 1330-33, pp. 325, 620, 621; 1333-37, p. 493; 1339-41, pp. 88, 135, 271, 291, 314-315.

[336] Cal. Pat. Rolls, 1330-34, p. 188.

[337] Ibid., 1343-45, p. 111.

[338] Cal. Pap. Regs. Letters, ii, 516, 553; iii, 61, 63, 80, 94, 99.

[339] Ibid., ii, 373. For Hugh, consult Emden, Register . . . Oxford, iii, 1452-1453.

[340] Ibid., iii, 82, 293.

[341] Ibid., iii, 277.

[342] Ibid., iii, 277; Reg. of Roger de Norbury, ed. Bishop Hobhouse, p. 277.

[343] On 13 January 1343 he was named one of three executors of a papal provision: Cal. Pap. Regs. Letters, iii, 55.

[344] Ibid., iii, 2; York Diocesan Registry, Reg. of la Zouche, fols. 255ᵛ, 256.

[345] Cal. Pap. Regs. Letters, iii, 6.

[346] Ibid., iii, 5, 9, 40.

[347] Ibid., iii, 6.

[348] Ibid., iii, 40; Cal. Close Rolls, 1349-54, p. 186.

[349] 21 May 1350: Lunt, Papal Revenues, ii, 273.

[350] Below, p. 78.

[351] His royal safe conduct was dated 20 June, but his letters naming attorneys to act for him during his absence were recorded under the date of 20 August: Cal. Pat. Rolls, 1348-50, pp. 346, 356.

[352] Raymond remained at the papal court until the autumn of 1350, unless for an interval he went to Rome to obtain the indulgence of the jubilee: Mohler, Die Einnahmen unter Klemens VI, pp. 35-36; Collectorie 497, fol. 44ᵛ; Cal. Pap. Regs. Letters, iii, 353. On 3 September 1350 he was accredited to Edward III as a papal envoy to arrange negotiations for peace between him and the king of France, and in 1353 and 1354 he served again in a similar capacity: Cal. Pap. Regs. Letters, iii, 47, 48, 610-614.

[353] Cal. Pap. Regs. Letters, iii, 46.

[354] Reg. Johannis de Trillek, ed. J. H. Parry, p. 148; Lincoln Diocesan Registry, Reg. viii, Gynwell, fols. 133, 185ᵛ.

[355] Lunt, Papal Revenues, ii, 273, 311-312.

[356] Collectorie 497, fol. 44ᵛ.

[357] 5 January 1353: Theiner, Vetera Monumenta Hibernorum, p. 301; Cal. Pap. Regs. Letters, iii, 610.

[358] 23 August: Cal. Pap. Regs. Letters, iii, 617; Samaran and Mollat, La Fiscalité pontificale, pp. 37-39.

[359] Diocesan Registry of Lincoln, Reg. viii, Gynwell, fols. 86, 106-108ᵛ, 136-137; of Worcester, Reg. of Brian, i, fols. 77, 80-82; of Lichfield, Reg. of Northburgh, ii, fol. 143; Muniments of the Dean and Chapter of Worcester, Liber Albus, fols. 215-217.

immediately—or in the next year if he had already visited within the year—in person or by deputy the ecclesiastical places in his diocese which he customarily visited and to receive from them the procurations due the bishop when he was making a personal visitation. The letter said nothing about any papal share of the proceeds, but a portion was reserved by the popes.[360] From the bishop of Llandaff the papal camera received one-half of them and from the bishop of Lincoln two-thirds.[361] The bishops paid the sums directly to the camera and the collector seems to have had no responsibility for the levy other than to notify the ordinaries of the papal mandate.[362] On 10 June 1356 Hugh was ordered to enforce the payment within six months by the archbishop of Canterbury of 6750 florins which he owed for the arrears of his visitation tax.[363] In the next year he was directed to collect annates on benefices reserved to the pope without regard for any indult to the contrary.[364] In 1358 he was instructed to receive the money which Archbishop Simon owed for a loan which his predecessor had contracted in order to pay his common services, but Cardinal Talleyrand de Périgueux, bishop of Albano, who was a nuncio in England, was ordered to enforce the payment.[365] The pope utilized Hugh in 1360 to explain a request for help against Barnabo Visconti, who had invaded the patrimony of the Roman church.[366] However, the subsidy of 100,000 florins granted by the clergy in 1362 for that purpose was collected by the archbishops and their suffragans without the intervention of the collector.[367] One task committed to Hugh seems to substantiate the English suspicion that some of the money collected from the English clergy for French popes by French collectors was finding its way into the hands of the king of France.[368] At least, during the period after the battle of Poitiers when King John of France was in captivity in England, Hugh and Raymond Pelegrini were ordered in 1357 by the pope to pay secretly and cautiously to the king of France 5,000 florins as a loan and in 1359 another 5,000 florins.[369] Of this amount Hugh delivered to the king or his agents 8,000 florins.[370]

During his term of office Hugh was absent from England several times. After 1 September 1352 he went to the papal court as a royal envoy, whence he returned with a verbal answer from the pope apparently before 18 December.[371] In each of the three years from 1358 to 1360 he went overseas on the king's behalf. In the first year letters naming his attorneys during his absence were dated 18 June and a royal letter of protection dated 5 October stated that he was staying overseas.[372] On this occasion he acted also as a special proctor for making the triennial visitation due from the bishop of Rochester at the tombs of the apostles.[373] From this trip he appears to have returned before 2 November 1358.[374] In 1359 letters of attorney dated 20 August referred to the collector as staying beyond seas,[375] and apparently he had been abroad for several months. On 8 February 1359 he was ordered to exact from Gerald Mercatoris, a papal commissary, sums owed to the papal camera from revenues arising in Cahors and other places in southern France.[376] In this year he left the papal court before 25 October[377] and he was in England by 26 November.[378] On 1 April 1360 new letters of attorney designated him as beyond seas.[379] This time he was at the papal court on 23 January and 25 September,[380] and he had returned to England before 13 January 1361.[381] Hugh appears to have been absent from England in 1362 and 1363.

During some of these absences Poncius de Vereriis, his kinsman and registrar, probably served as his *locum-tenens*;[382] but Raymond acted in that capacity in 1359 and 1362 when he submitted sums through other agents

[360] Reg. Avinionensia 149, fol. 68; Hoberg, *Die Einnahmen . . . unter Innocenz VI*, p. 395.

[361] The bishop of Llandaff in 1360 and of Lincoln in 1362: Introitus et Exitus 293, fol. 70; Hoberg, *op. cit.*, pp. 321, 395.

[362] Hugh delivered the procurations of the bishop of Llandaff to the camera, but only as an agent for the transport of the funds and not in his capacity as collector. The procurations do not appear in his accounts.

[363] *Cal. Pap. Regs. Letters*, iii, 620; below, p. xliv.

[364] *Cal. Pap. Regs. Letters*, iii, 624.

[365] *Ibid.*, iii, 632, 634, 635.

[366] *Ibid.*, iii, 631.

[367] Below, pp. xlvi–xlvii.

[368] *Rot. Parl.*, ii, 228, where the suspicion is recorded.

[369] *Cal. Pap. Regs. Letters*, iii, 624–625, 632.

[370] Below, pp. 92, 140.

[371] *Cal. Pap. Regs. Letters*, iii, 51, 469; *Cal. Pat. Rolls, 1350-54*, pp. 325, 378.

[372] *Cal. Pat. Rolls, 1358-61*, pp. 59, 102.

[373] His appointment as proctor was dated 1 July 1358: Rochester Diocesan Registry, Reg. of Sheppey, fol. 291ᵛ.

[374] He issued an acquittance at London on that date: *Cal. of Charters and Documents relating to Selborne and its Priory*, ed. W. D. Macray, i, 93.

[375] *Cal. Pat. Rolls, 1358-61*, p. 258.

[376] *Cal. Pap. Regs. Letters*, iii, 632; Reg. Vaticana 241, fol. 19ᵛ; Hoberg, *op. cit.*, p. 278.

[377] On that date the camera sent to him by messenger a list of benefices collated by the pope: *Cal. Pap. Regs. Petitions*, i, 313. On 14 November a delivery of 3000 florins was made to his credit at the papal camera not by him but by his *locum-tenens*, Bertrand de Aragono, papal serjeant at arms: Introitus et Exitus 271, fol. 135; Hoberg, *op. cit.*, p. 270.

[378] Below, p. 140.

[379] *Cal. Pat. Rolls, 1358-61*, p. 351.

[380] Lists of collations to English benefices were handed to him in person on 23 January and 20 September: *Cal. Pap. Regs. Petitions*, i, 314, 316. On 17 September he delivered a payment to the camera by his own hand: Introitus et Exitus 293, fol. 70; Hoberg, *op. cit.*, pp. 304, 321. On 25 September the pope wrote that he had commissioned Hugh to explain his intimate thoughts to the kings of France and England: *Cal. Pap. Regs. Letters*, iii, 631.

[381] On that date and on 20 January he wrote letters from London: Lincoln Diocesan Registry, Reg. viii, Gynwell, fol. 133; Muniments of the Dean and Chapter of Worcester, Liber Albus, fol. 223ᵛ.

[382] *Cal. Pap. Regs. Petitions*, i, 327, 329, 359. Poncius died before 23 August 1361: Le Neve, *Fasti: Bath and Wells*, p. 37.

to the camera.[383] By 11 January 1362 Hugh had been captured by the French in Berry since on that date Edward III requested his envoys in France to secure Hugh's release.[384] It was Raymond who in Hugh's name transferred the equipment and documents of the collector's office to John de Cabrespino in 1363.[385] Similarly Raymond supplied Cabrespino with the necessary information concerning arrears.[386] If Raymond was conducting the business of the collectorate in England in 1362 and 1363,[387] nonetheless Hugh was nominally collector until his tenure was technically ended by Urban V's appointment of John de Cabrespino to succeed him on 15 June 1363.[388] In reality the new collector did not arrive until 28 August and the collectorate continued in Hugh's name until 1 September 1363.[389]

When Hugh rendered his final account to the camera at the close of his term of office, he owed only a small sum which he paid immediately.[390] Nevertheless, in 1367 property which belonged to him and his brother Raymond in the diocese of Cahors was sequestrated and ordered to be held until they had satisfied the camera for the sums which they had received in their collectorate above those reported in their last accounts. Their property was released from sequestration within a few months, after Hugh had appeared before the treasurer and clerks of the camera and had undertaken to meet any debts still owed to the camera by him and his brother.[391] It seems probable that most of the debts were owed by Raymond, who died in 1365[392] and of whose will Hugh was the principal executor.[393] When Raymond ended his term as collector, he had not yet accounted for all that he owed the camera. Soon after his

death, the pope ordered the sequestration of Raymond's goods in England, until his executor and his heirs had given full satisfaction for his debts.[394] Hugh, however, was not entirely free of financial obligation to the camera, despite the balancing of his account in 1363. For one debt the brothers appear to have been jointly responsible. A cardinal who was provided by Innocent VI with a prebend in Lincoln made Raymond his proctor. Raymond leased the prebend and received the income for two years but remitted none of it to the cardinal. He also acted as proctor of a new incumbent and received the income for two more years. Hugh, who was the collector at the time, should have collected annates twice, but they were still owed to the camera. In 1369 the camerarius ordered John de Cabrespino, if he should find the statement true, to levy the annates from the goods of Raymond, Hugh and the new incumbent.[395] John de Cabrespino also found a few items received by Hugh which he had not included in his accounts.[396] John's successor, Arnald Garnerii, attempted to recover the debt from the income of Hugh's English benefices, but he failed because the king had taken possession of this revenue.[397]

The pope imposed upon Hugh a few burdensome duties in addition to those of the collector's office. He was asked to serve as one of three executors of many papal provisions, to confer some canonries with expectancies of prebends, to examine several candidates for the office of notary public and some applicants for expectancies to benefices and to perform a few other duties of a similar routine nature.[398] He was further ordered to receive two papal couriers carrying letters to Edward III and to assist them in their business.[399] Hugh acted as proctor or attorney for several foreigners, among whom were Cardinal Talleyrand de Périgueux and Cardinal Peter Roger.[400] It was probably as the administrator of their benefices rather than in his capacity as collector that a clerk and two laymen acknowledged in chancery that they owed him substantial sums.[401]

Hugh was named by the king one of his clerks,[402] a position which was now customarily conferred upon the papal collector. He was also sent to the papal court on several occasions as a royal envoy. The king ratified his estate as the holder of many of his benefices, protecting him against possible royal claims of the right

[383] Hoberg, op. cit., pp. 270, 405, 411. In the last two references for May and June 1362, Raymond is called in the papal document (Registrum Avinionense 149) "collectore apostolico in regno Anglie."
[384] Emden, Register . . . Oxford, iii, p. 1453; Chaplais, Documents . . . on Treaty of Bretigny, p. 29.
[385] Below, pp. 182, 183-184.
[386] Below, pp. 172, 173, 210.
[387] Reg. Avinionensia 149, fols. 77ᵛ, 82ᵛ; Introitus et Exitus 271, fol. 159ᵛ; 300, fol. 34; 303, fol. 43ᵛ; 305, fol. 10ᵛ; 307, fol. 32. Some of these entries of sums assigned to the camera by Raymond designate him as the collector, but he was acting for his brother. They are the assignments entered in Hugh's account: below, pp. 140-141. His report and John de Cabrespino's leave no doubt.
[388] Cal. Pap. Regs. Letters, iv, 28.
[389] Below, pp. 118, 172, 183.
[390] Below, pp. 141, 183. He left in arrears part of the annates which he and his brother owed for some of the benefices to which the pope had collated them, but this was paid to John de Cabrespino between 1364 and 1366: below, p. 224.
[391] Letters of 3 February and 11 October: Collectorie 353, fol. 107; 354, fol. 27.
[392] Reg. Simonis de Sudbiria, i, 62. In his will, drawn up on 10 August 1365, he spoke of himself as in poor health: M. Fournier, Les Statuts et Privilèges des Universités françaises, iii, no. 1430. He was dead by 4 September 1365; Fierens and Tihon, Lettres d'Urbain V, i, no. 1595.
[393] Cal. Pat. Rolls, 1364-67, pp. 188, 339; 1367-70, pp. 26, 309.

[394] Cal. Pap. Regs. Letters, iv, 18-19.
[395] 27 April: Collectorie 353, fols. 211-212.
[396] E. g., below, pp. 257, 323.
[397] Below, p. 478.
[398] Cal. Pap. Regs. Letters, iii, 55, 318, 325, 331, 338, 342, 343, 358, 365, 367, 389, 418, 420, 430, 457, 479, 480, 487, 498, 501, 546.
[399] Ibid., iii, 50.
[400] Cal. Pat. Rolls, 1348-50, p. 447; 1354-58, pp. 136, 156, 593; Cal. Close Rolls, 1349-54, p. 309.
[401] Cal. Close Rolls, 1354-60, p. 301.
[402] Cal. Pat. Rolls, 1348-50, p. 492; 1350-54, p. 187; 1364-67, p. 188.

of presentation which might conflict with his papal provisions to them.[403] Royal protection was given to John de Empyngham, Hugh's sequestrator,[404] who had to travel about the kingdom on the collector's business.[405] On the other side of the ledger, the king forbade Hugh to levy annates from benefices collated by the pope before the collation had been made effective. The king claimed that the practice by which annates were charged against benefice-holders presented by normal patrons rather than by papal provisions had not previously been followed in England.[406] He also prohibited the collection of annates from several specific benefices.[407] Hugh appears to have had little business with the exchequer,[408] but he wrote to the chancellor occasionally asking him, as previous chancellors had customarily done, to exempt from the payment of a royal tenth granted by the English clergy specified benefices which were in the hands of the pope at the time.[409]

While Hugh was collector, he had remarkable success in the accumulation of English benefices. In addition to those which he already possessed, he obtained by papal provision between 1349 and 1351 a canonry and prebend in both Lincoln and Salisbury and the rich church of Maidstone.[410] The church was exempt from the jurisdiction of the archdeacon of Canterbury and under the immediate jurisdiction of the archbishop. In 1367 the archbishop conferred his jurisdiction upon Hugh.[411] When Hugh received the church, he had to resign the churches of Boxley and Horncastle.[412] He still retained a large income. In 1366, when pluralists had to inform their diocesans of the value of their benefices, one hundred and sixty-nine reported to the bishop of London. Hugh's benefices were assessed at a total of £293 6 s. 8 d., which was exceeded only by William de Wykeham whose benefices attained the princely sum of £873 6 s. 8 d.[413] Hugh enjoyed an income from procurations for an exceptionally long period. His first year

was calculated from 8 July 1350, when he was appointed collector in his own right, and the procurations for that year were paid in 1351.[414] Thereafter he received them once a year until 1363, when the thirteenth year of his term of office was concluded.[415] In the field of papal privileges Hugh apparently did not fare as well as some of his predecessors. He was authorized to select three candidates for receipt of the office of notary public and he was indulged to choose a confessor who could give him, being penitent, plenary remission at the hour of death.[416]

After Hugh retired from the collectorship, he appears to have traveled back and forth from England to southern France frequently for several years.[417] In this period the royal government seized the fruits of his benefices on the ground that he was of the obedience of the king of France, though as late as 1365 a royal letter of protection stated that he had been born of the English king's lordship of Aquitaine.[418] In 1371 the pope requested the king to restore his benefices and their fruits.[419] The papal plea seems to have been unsuccessful, since the benefices were still in the hands of the king in 1374 [420] and in 1376 the king revoked his former ratification of Hugh's estate in his benefices on the ground that Hugh had become the adherent of the king's enemies in Aquitaine and elsewhere.[421] The pope also intervened in Hugh's behalf with the count of Savoy in order to obtain justice with regard to money owed to Hugh by some merchants.[422] In 1376 he was sent with a colleague on a papal mission to the duke of Austria and to other distant parts.[423] He probably died in 1378.[424]

## JOHN DE CABRESPINO

When John de Cabrespino was appointed papal collector in England, he had the degree of Doctor of Decrees, he was a canon of Narbonne,[425] and he appears

---

[403] *Ibid.*, 1348-50, pp. 336, 492; 1350-54, pp. 187, 227.

[404] *Reg. of Ralph of Shrewsbury*, ii, 691.

[405] *Cal. Pat. Rolls, 1350-54*, p. 378; *1354-58*, p. 76.

[406] *Cal. Close Rolls, 1349-54*, p. 457; Rymer, *Foedera*, iii, 250.

[407] *Cal. Close Rolls, 1349-54*, pp. 186, 407, 560; *Gesta Abbatum Sancti Albani*, ii, 393-394.

[408] He collected one item of the quadrennial levy of annates imposed by John XXII about which the exchequer had to be consulted (below, p. 91), but normally the arrears due the king were being collected by the exchequer by orders to the bishops to distrain the goods of the debtors: *Reg. of Ralph of Shrewsbury*, ii, 601; *Reg. Simonis de Sudbiria*, i, 46, 59, 62, 67, 82.

[409] P. R. O., Ancient Correspondence 40, nos. 99, 114, 115. His letters are dated 28 October 1349 and 27 January and 16 April 1352. For earlier examples of such exemptions see Rymer, *Foedera*, ii, 1060; *Cal. Close Rolls, 1346-49*, pp. 418-419, 592.

[410] *Cal. Pap. Regs. Letters*, iii, 293, 415, 419, 435.

[411] Churchill, *Canterbury Administration*, i, 83-91; *Reg. Simonis de Langham*, p. 150.

[412] *Cal. Pap. Regs. Letters*, iii, 419, 542. He had received Horncastle before 18 March 1350: *Cal. Pat. Rolls, 1348-50*, p. 492.

[413] *Reg. Simonis de Sudbiria*, ii, pp. xxxvii, 150.

[414] His deputy collector, the abbot of St. Mary York, designated it as the eighth year of Hugh's stay as nuncio, but it would have been the eighth year of Raymond's collectorship. The payment in 1352 was correctly stated to be for Hugh's second year: Muniments of the Dean and Chapter of Durham, Misc. Charters, 4251, 4360.

[415] *Ibid.*, nos. 4239, 4252, 4336, 4348, 4356, 4358, 4656, 4772, 4854, 5023, 5086.

[416] *Cal. Pap. Regs. Letters*, iii, 401, 583, 586.

[417] *Cal. Pat. Rolls, 1364-67*, pp. 188, 339; *1367-70*, pp. 26, 151, 309, 356; Churchill, *Canterbury Administration*, i, 91; *Reg. Simonis de Sudbiria*, ii, 150; Collectorie 354, fol. 27. The last date at which he is mentioned as present in England in these references was 2 February 1370.

[418] *Cal. Pat. Rolls, 1364-67*, p. 188.

[419] *Cal. Pap. Regs. Letters*, iv, 92.

[420] Below, p. 478.

[421] *Cal. Pat. Rolls, 1374-77*, pp. 211-212, 241, 285.

[422] 12 January 1372: *Cal. Pap. Regs. Letters*, iv, 114.

[423] 13 January: Schäfer, *Die Ausgaben unter Urban V und Gregor XI*, p. 632.

[424] Fournier, *Les Statuts*, iii, no. 1444.

[425] Rymer, *Foedera*, iii, 707.

to have been a member of the staff of the papal camera. Shortly before his appointment he was sent to Hungary, Bohemia and Poland for the transaction of cameral business.[426] His commission as collector and nuncio to England and Ireland was issued on 15 June 1363.[427] His letter of credence to the king was dated 29 June,[428] on 8 July he was granted several privileges [429] and on 30 July William Wykeham, who was then archdeacon of Lincoln, was asked to obtain from the king permission for the new collector to enter and remain in England, a safe conduct and an *exequatur*.[430] John left Avignon on 1 August and reached London four weeks later. On the day of his arrival he summoned Raymond Pelegrini to come to London to render his brother's account; that accounting took place on 1 September.[431] Before 11 October he established his combined dwelling and office in London at a location not specified in his letters, and on that and successive days he issued his first letters demanding payment of sums owed to the camera for various revenues or to him for procurations.[432] He remained in England less than a year before he returned to the camera to render his first account.[433] The terminal date of his first account is doubtful. His first account is said to have run to 31 March 1364,[434] but in his second account the first is said to have ended on 28 February 1364.[435] The statement in the first account is probably correct, since it speaks of Easter 1364 as past [436] and Easter fell in that year on 24 March. The account was terminated before 24 June 1364, since it mentions a payment due on that date as still unpaid,[437] and the payment was actually made on that date.[438] The day of his departure from England is likewise stated variously. In the second report he is said to have left on 28 February.[439] This seems improbable, though not impossible, since he wrote an executory letter to the bishop of Carlisle on that day.[440] In the first report John states that he left England on 6 March

and arrived at the papal court on 12 April.[441] Since the camera allowed traveling expenses for that length of time,[442] the dates are probably correct. Since he was going to the camera for the purpose of rendering his account, it seems probable that he took with him the data in hand at the time of his departure and reduced it to the form of an account after 31 March.

When John de Cabrespino departed from England, he left John de Caroloco, whom he had appointed his deputy collector, commissioner and *locumtenens*, to administer the collector's office.[443] John de Caroloco was then the prior of Bermondsey and soon became the prior of Lewes.[444] He maintained a residence in Southwark in which he conducted the affairs of the collectorship.[445] For the remainder of John de Cabrespino's tenure of the office, the prior did most of the actual work of collection and the collector spent the major portion of his time outside of England.

The second account was sent by John de Caroloco to John de Cabrespino, who rendered it at the papal camera on 20 May 1366, the day on which he received it.[446] During the interval of over two years the deputy collector appears to have been responsible for the conduct of the collector's business,[447] and the collector appears to have been at Avignon.[448] He probably remained there until the summer of 1367.[449] On 3 December 1366 he was given royal protection for coming to and returning from England,[450] but he was still at the papal court on 15 December.[451] A new royal protection for him was dated 24 March 1367.[452] On 9 April, however, he was present at the papal camera,[453] and he accompanied the papal court on its journey from Avignon to Viterbo

---

[426] Schäfer, *Die Ausgaben unter Klemens VI und Innocenz VI*, p. 812; *unter Urban V und Gregor XI*, p. 15.

[427] *Cal. Pap. Regs. Letters*, iv, 28.

[428] Rymer, *Foedera*, iii, 707; P. R. O., Papal Bulls 35/13.

[429] *Cal. Pap. Regs. Letters*, iv, 2, 87.

[430] P. R. O., Papal Bulls 35/10; Rymer, *Foedera*, iii, 708.

[431] Below, pp. 172, 173, 183, 185, 210.

[432] *Reg. Simonis de Sudbiria*, i, 197-198; Carlisle Diocesan Registry, Reg. of Appelby, p. 159; Library of the Dean and Chapter of Durham, Reg. of Hatfield, p. 103.

[433] His presence in England up to and including 28 February 1364 is amply attested by documents which he issued: below, pp. 183-184; Carlisle Diocesan Registry, Reg. of Appelby, pp. 158-159, 161; Muniments of the Dean and Chapter of Westminster, 8574.

[434] Below, pp. 172, 184.

[435] Below, pp. 214, 224.

[436] E. g., below, p. 176.

[437] Below, p. 174.

[438] Muniments of the Dean and Chapter of Westminister, 8575. For this reference I am indebted to Professor Alfred H. Sweet.

[439] In the third person: below, p. 214.

[440] Carlisle Diocesan Registry, Reg. of Appelby, p. 161.

[441] In the first person: below, p. 183.

[442] Below, p. 213.

[443] Below, p. 186. John de Caroloco was probably appointed as early as 11 October 1363. In letters issued by John de Cabrespino on that and two successive days debtors were cited to appear before him or his commissioner who was not named: *Reg. Simonis de Sudbiria*, i, 197-198; Carlisle Diocesan Registry, Reg. of Appelby, p. 159; Library of the Dean and Chapter of Durham, Reg. of Hatfield, p. 103.

[444] Below, pp. 186, 224; York Diocesan Registry, Reg. of Thoresby, fol. 321ᵛ.

[445] Worcester Diocesan Registry, Reg. of Whittelsey, fol. 29ᵛ; Carlisle Diocesan Registry, Reg. of Appelby, pp. 229-230; Lincoln, Reg. xii, Buckingham, fol. 72ᵛ.

[446] Below, pp. 224-225.

[447] Below, p. 225; a receipt for a payment of Peter's pence issued by him on 4 February 1365: York Diocesan Registry, Reg. of Thoresby, fol. 321ᵛ.

[448] Below, pp. 225, 256-257. On January 1365 he delivered a payment to the camera in person: Introitus et Exitus 303, fol. 54.

[449] On 22 June and 3 and 9 July 1366 he made payments to the camera in person: Introitus et Exitus 303, fol. 63ᵛ; below, p. 225. On 24 October 1366 John de Caroloco issued an acquittance for a payment of Peter's pence: York Diocesan Registry, Reg. of Thoresby, fol. 324.

[450] *Cal. Pat. Rolls, 1364-67*, p. 338; Rymer, *Foedera*, iii, 813.

[451] Introitus et Exitus 321, fol. 10.

[452] *Cal. Pat. Rolls, 1364-67*, p. 386.

[453] Introitus et Exitus 321, fol. 34.

in May and June.[454] He remained with the court at Viterbo, apparently in the service of the camera, during July.[455] On 26 July Urban V appointed him to go on a special mission to Edward III, the Black Prince and the duke of Lancaster,[456] and on 2 August 1367 he received 100 florins from the camera for his expenses.[457]

John de Cabrespino was in England during the autumn of 1367 [458] and was still there on 20 February 1368,[459] two days after he closed his third account.[460] He probably left England not long after that date, since on 11 February he was given license to cross from Dover on the way to the Roman court.[461] He did not go directly to the court, however. On 30 March the camera paid two scribes for copying the accounts of Jean Maubert, deputy collector in the province of Reims, for the information of John de Cabrespino who was going to Reims.[462] Since the collector did not render his third account until August,[463] it may be surmised that he stopped at Reims on the way from England to the papal court. John reached the papal camera at Montefiascone in time to deliver on 7 August some of the money which he had collected in England [464] and to have his account audited on 22 August 1368.[465]

Thereafter the collector seems to have returned to England for only two short periods. In November 1368 he sent to England from the papal court a list of benefices which the pope had collated.[466] On 10 March and 13 June 1369 John de Caroloco gave acquittances for sums received from debtors to the camera.[467] John de Cabrespino may have been in England in May 1369, since he sent to Bruges a member of his household who

had to cross the sea to get there.[468] On 17 June, however, a cursor was sent to him from Montefiascone with instructions that if the collector was not found in Paris he would be in Bruges.[469] In August, John sent letters to England and in January 1370 he sent to England to have the assessment of English benefices copied.[470] In the same month and in March, John de Caroloco made assignments to the agents of the cameral merchants in London,[471] but on 5 September 1370 John de Cabrespino made a similar delivery.[472] On 1 November his last account was concluded.[473] In February and March 1371 he made in person several payments to the camera at Avignon,[474] and in April he delivered his fourth account.[475] On 28 March John de Caroloco sent to him by John de Strensall, the registrar in the English collector's office, an account for the period from 1 November 1370 to 28 March 1371, but it did not arrive in time for John de Cabrespino to receive it,[476] and it was consequently included in the account which John de Caroloco rendered to Arnald Garnerii on 22 February 1372.[477] The prior acted as collector from 1 November 1370 to 22 February 1372 by mandate of the camerarius and by commission of John de Cabrespino, but did not have the title of collector.[478] On November 1371 John de Cabrespino appointed John de Wendlyngburgh, the treasurer of Chichester, his *locumtenens* and in that capacity he delivered to an Italian firm for transmission to the camera £192 13 s.,[479] but John de Caroloco's account from 1 November 1370 to 22 February 1372 leaves no doubt that he was in charge of the collectorship throughout the period.[480]

When the final account of John de Cabrespino was audited, he was found to have paid to the camera 8 s. 8 d. more than he had received from the papal revenues, but he was debited with 150 florins of the cross which

[454] J. P. Kirsch, *Die Rückkehr . . . von Avignon nach Rom*, pp. 27, 28.

[455] *Ibid.*, pp. 32, 33, 40, 43.

[456] The date of his letter of credence to the king: P. R. O., Papal Bulls, 34/16. See also below, p. 267.

[457] Kirsch, *Die Rückkehr*, p. 55.

[458] Below, p. 265; letters issued by him on 20 November and 23 December: Worcester Diocesan Registry, Reg. of Whittelsey, fol. 29ᵛ; York Diocesan Registry, Reg. of Thoresby, fol. 324.

[459] On that date he delivered money to the English factor of the Alberti Antiqui: Collectorie 357, fol. 26.

[460] Below, p. 256.

[461] *Cal. Pat. Rolls, 1367-70*, pp. 126, 129.

[462] Schäfer, *Die Ausgaben unter Urban V und Gregor XI*, p. 268.

[463] Below, pp. 256, 308.

[464] Introitus et Exitus 325, fol. 28; below, pp. 265, 266. He made another delivery on 16 August: below, p. 268.

[465] Collectorie 357, fol. 26ᵛ. The following item indicates that he stopped at Avignon, and, finding the camera gone, set out for Rome: "Item conclusio compotorum domini Johannis de Cabrespino, collectoris Anglie, non est hic incerta quia non reperitur in dictis suis compotis fuisse conclusum, sed ipsa compota apud Romam secum portavit ut concludatur in eisdem:" Reg. Avinionensia 259, fol. 40; Collectorie 114, fol. 53.

[466] Below, p. 321.

[467] York Diocesan Registry, Reg. of Thoresby, fol. 326; Lincoln Diocesan Registry, Reg. xii, Buckingham, fol. 72ᵛ. On 14 June he wrote to the bishop of Carlisle: Carlisle Diocesan Registry, Reg. of Appelby, pp. 229-230.

[468] Below, p. 321.

[469] Collectorie 354, fol. 69ᵛ.

[470] Below, p. 321.

[471] Introitus et Exitus 331, fols. 11ᵛ, 21ᵛ.

[472] *Ibid.*, fol. 58.

[473] Below, pp. 307, 309.

[474] Below, p. 322; Collectorie 464, fols. 102ᵛ, 104, 109ᵛ.

[475] Below, p. 322. According to a statement in Arnald Garnerii's account it was rendered before the end of 1370: below, p. 416. An acquittance for the sums paid to the credit of this account was dated 3 June 1371: *Cal. Pap. Regs. Letters*, iv, 98.

[476] Below, p. 414. John de Strensall received a royal license to make the journey dated 28 March: *Cal. Pat. Rolls, 1370-74*, p. 64.

[477] Below, p. 411.

[478] On 14 January 1372 John de Cabrespino was designated as collector and John de Caroloco as deputy collector (Introitus et Exitus 336, fol. 4), though John de Cabrespino had been appointed collector in Germany, Hungary, Bohemia and Poland on 12 July 1371 and Arnald Garnerii had been commissioned collector in England on 8 October 1371: *Cal. Pap. Regs. Letters*, iv, 148-149.

[479] Delivery was made to the camera by the firm on 15 February 1374: Collectorie 466, fol. 148; Introitus et Exitus 340, fol. 11ᵛ.

[480] Below, pp. 363-417.

the camera had supplied to him as a loan for the expenses of his initial journey to England in 1363.[481] There were also four items of annates left in arrears in his account for which he was said to have received payment from the debtors and for which he was consequently responsible to the camera. They amounted to £39 13 s. 4 d.[482] There was some doubt whether John still owed the loan,[483] and he explained in detail why he was not liable for the four items of annates.[484] Whatever the camera may have decided finally with regard to his indebtedness, on 22 April 1372 the camerarius wrote to Arnald ordering him to collect any procurations still owed to his predecessor and to pay them to the camera to meet the balance due from John. Although this mandate would appear to have been canceled by another order of the camerarius written the same day instructing Arnald to deliver whatever arrears of procurations he recovered to John de Cabrespino or his agents,[485] Arnald sent to the camera £14 16 s. from that source with the explanation that the money could be given to John if the camera should decide that the charge against him was in error.[486] Arnald did not assign the sum to the camera without protest. It represented part of a total sum of £63 4 s. 8 d. which had become due for procurations between 8 October 1371 and 22 February 1372 and which had been collected by John de Caroloco.[487] Arnald claimed that the whole amount belonged to him, since he had been appointed collector on the former date; John de Cabrespino opposed this claim on the ground that he had to meet the expenses of the collector's office during the period. The camerarius ruled that John was entitled to the procurations until Arnald began to exercise the functions of his office.[488] John de Caroloco therefore retained £48 8 s. 8 d. of the procurations for John de Cabrespino. After 22 February 1372 he still continued to act as commissioner of John de Cabrespino for the collection of the arrears of his procurations until 4 May 1375[489] or after.

A copy of the commission of John de Cabrespino is lacking. It may be presumed that it was similar to those of his predecessors. The commissions of collectors were by this time becoming standardized. They usually contained clauses authorizing the collector to use his immediate predecessor's commissions in addition to his own and to collect any debts owed to the papal camera in his collectorate not specifically mentioned in his commission.[490] His reports display no types of revenues which previous collectors had not received. The archbishops and bishops of his collectorate, as was customary, were ordered to assist the collector,[491] and he was given normal supplementary instructions about his work. The camera sent to him from time to time lists of benefices collated or confirmed by the pope in his collectorate[492] and notices of new reservations of benefices made by the pope.[493] It also ordered him to collect specific debts owed to the camera,[494] to render accounts,[495] or to assign his receipts to specified firms of Italian bankers.[496] Odd jobs which he performed as collector were to purchase clothing for use in the papal alms office and to pack and ship to the pope bows and arrows delivered to him by Raymond Pelegrini. They were sent to Genoa by the way of Bruges and transported thence to Arles, their ultimate destination being the armory of the papal palace at Avignon.[497]

The pope appears to have asked John to do nothing in England beyond his duties as collector except to act as his ambassador on a special mission in 1367. Joanna, queen of Naples, had heard a rumor that John of Gaunt intended to invade the county of Provence and the ambassador was sent to dissuade him.[498] Possibly the reason for the collector's freedom from additional duties in England was the extent of his responsibilities elsewhere. He spent much time at the papal court where he appears still to have been in the service of the camera. He seems also to have been in some measure responsible for the conduct of the affairs of the collectorate in the province of Reims. On his way to England in 1363 he stopped at Bruges on the business of the camera and on 13 September he sent his clerk, Berengar Ferrarii, to Bruges with a commission, directed to P. Marchewell, ordering him to make an inventory of the goods of Guiraud de Marssenacho,[499] the collector in the province of Reims who had recently died there, and to manage the collector's office until the camera should ordain otherwise.[500] In 1367 he went to Reims on the business of the collectorate,[501] and in the account for his English collectorate which he closed on 18 February 1368 he entered the receipt of an item of census paid by a monastery in the diocese of Thérouanne[502] which is in the province of Reims. On 2 October 1368 he was appointed collector and nuncio in that province when he

[481] Below, pp. 213-214, 324.
[482] Below, pp. 411, 414-415.
[483] Below, p. 267.
[484] Below, pp. 415-417.
[485] Collectorie 358, fols. 43ᵛ-44ᵛ.
[486] Below, p. 415.
[487] Below, p. 411.
[488] 30 November 1372: Collectorie 358, fols. 129-130.
[489] *Cal. of Charters and Documents relating to Selborne and its Priory*, i, 93.
[490] Below, pp. 32-34; above, pp. xxviii, xxxii.
[491] *Cal. Pap. Regs. Letters*, iv, 18.
[492] Collectorie 354, fol. 69; below, pp. 241-256, 321.
[493] Collectorie 354, fol. 69ᵛ.
[494] *Cal. Pap. Regs. Letters*, iv, 25, 26; Collectorie 353, fols. 7ᵛ, 41, 211-213.
[495] Collectorie 353, fol. 227.
[496] *Ibid.*, fol. 227ᵛ; *Cal. Pap. Regs. Letters*, iv, 18, 148.
[497] Below, p. 184; Schäfer, *Die Ausgaben unter Urban V und Gregor XI*, p. 134.
[498] P. R. O., Papal Bulls 34/16.
[499] Otherwise Geraldus Marcenaco: Samaran and Mollat, *La Fiscalité pontificale*, p. 181, n. 3.
[500] Below, p. 183.
[501] Above, p. xxxvii.
[502] Below, p. 265.

should have been recalled from the same office in England.[503] He, however, retained the English collectorship until 8 October 1371,[504] and on 29 May 1369 was designated as collector in England as well as in the province of Reims.[505] On 17 June letters were sent to him by courier concerning the affairs of both collectorates.[506]

John de Cabrespino was given authority by the pope to confer the office of notary on ten persons and power of dispensation more extensively than is known to have been granted to any previous collector. He could dispense sixty persons for irregularity, sixty persons of illegitimate birth to be ordained and to hold benefices with cure of souls, thirty sons of priests or illegitimate sons of married men or of married women to receive minor orders and to hold benefices without cure and twenty-five men and twenty-five women related in the fourth degree of kindred or affinity to remain in the marriages which they had contracted.[507] Most of these were dispensations which could be obtained ordinarily only from the pope. On the other hand, John appears to have received no pecuniary rewards in England other than his procurations. He does not appear to have received the customary appointment as king's clerk, nor is there record of his provision by the pope to any English benefice.

If John went to his new collectorate in Germany, Poland, Bohemia and Hungary after 12 July 1371, his tenure of office must have been brief, or he must have been absent frequently, as he had been from his English collectorate. In September of the three successive years from 1373 to 1375, acting as an agent of the camera together with an agent of the cardinal college, he made trips through parts of southern France to make contracts for new wines.[508] In 1375 he was sent by the pope to Sitten in Switzerland and in 1376 to the Dauphiné, to Rome and to the king of Aragon.[509] In 1375 he was rewarded by papal provision to the archdeaconry of Murviedro in the diocese of Valencia.[510]

### ARNALD GARNERII

Arnald Garnerii was appointed collector and nuncio on 8 October 1371 and given the customary powers.[511] He had been born in the French dominion of the king

of England,[512] and he was at the time a licentiate in laws and a canon of Châlons.[513] His papal safe conduct was issued on 8 October[514] and his letter of credence to the king ten days later.[515] On 29 October he was further empowered to recover, with the help of the secular arm if necessary, money or other property bequeathed to the aid of the Holy Land by members of the clergy.[516] He also received the proceeds of a subsidy of 60,000 florins paid by the English clergy in 1375 and 1376, but the collection of it was entirely in the hands of the English clergy.[517] In 1373 he became subject to a papal prohibition, placed generally on collectors under penalty of excommunication, to lend money collected for the papal camera or to sell any property reserved to the pope without special mandate from the pope, the camerarius or the treasurer.[518]

Arnald's appointment marked a new departure in the size of the collectorate. It had previously included Ireland as well as England and Wales, and the collector in Ireland had been a deputy of the collector in England.[519] In 1368 John Duncan was appointed collector in Ireland with responsibility for accounting to the camera.[520] Arnald as a consequence was accredited as collector only in England and Wales.[521]

Arnald's journey to England took a long time because he had to wait six weeks at Calais for a license to make the crossing to England.[522] He arrived in London on 8 February 1372. Before he began his work, he had to take an oath of fealty to the king. This requirement appears to have been new,[523] but thereafter it became part of the routine for every new collector upon his arrival.[524] In this oath he made the customary promise to be faithful and loyal to the king and his crown, to procure or suffer to be done nothing prejudicial to the king, his realm, his laws, his rights or his subjects, to give good and loyal counsel upon request, and to keep

---

[503] *Cal. Pap. Regs. Letters*, iv, 28.
[504] The date of Arnald Garnerii's commission: *Cal. Pap. Regs. Letters*, iv, 149. John was appointed collector in Germany and neighboring countries on 12 July 1371: *ibid.*, iv, 148; above, p. xxxvii, n. 478.
[505] Collectorie 353. fol. 227.
[506] Collectorie 354, fol. 69ᵛ.
[507] *Cal. Pap. Regs. Letters*, iv, 2, 87.
[508] Schäfer, *Die Ausgaben unter Urban V und Gregor XI*, pp. 429, 483, 545, 611.
[509] *Ibid.*, pp. 575, 650; Kirsch, *Die Rückkehr*, p. 174.
[510] Collectorie 391, fol. 90; Obligationes Reg. 42, fol. 63ᵛ.
[511] *Cal. Pap. Regs. Letters*, iv, 149; below, p. 411. The camerarius spoke of the date as 7 October: Collectorie 358, fol. 129.

[512] 'de patria tibi . . . obedienti et subiecta': copy of a papal letter of 23 November ⟨1371⟩: British Museum, Cotton MSS., Cleopatra E ii, fol. 117 (or 127).
[513] P. R. O., Papal Bulls 17/10.
[514] *Cal. Pap. Regs. Letters*, iv, 148.
[515] P. R. O., Papal Bulls 17/10; Rymer, *Foedera*, iii, 924. *Cf. Cal. Pap. Regs. Letters*, iv, 100.
[516] *Cal. Pap. Regs. Letters*, iv, 100.
[517] Below, pp. xlvii.
[518] *Cal. Pap. Regs. Letters*, iv, 151.
[519] Below, pp. 28, 29, 35, 63, 78, 172.
[520] *Cal. Pap. Regs. Letters*, iv, 28, 258. His appointment was renewed in 1372: *ibid.*, iv, 149.
[521] P. R. O., Papal Bulls 17/10.
[522] Below, p. 476.
[523] Collectors who had been appointed to the King's Council presumably took the councillor's oath of loyalty and fealty, but it contained no restrictions with regard to the relation of the collector with the pope. This is the first mention of this type of oath which I have discovered. *Cf.* Perroy, *L'Angleterre et le Grand Schisme*, p. 28, n. 4. The oath later aroused the opposition of the papacy, because it conflicted with the oath taken by the collector to the pope and the camera: *Cal. Pap. Regs. Letters*, iv, 289.
[524] *Cal. Close Rolls, 1377-81*, pp. 224, 257.

secret what he might learn. He further agreed not to execute or to allow to be executed papal letters or mandates displeasing or prejudicial to the king, his laws, his rights or his subjects, to deliver any papal letters received by him to the king's council before publication or delivery to another, to send no money out of the realm by letters of exchange or otherwise without the consent of the king or his council, and not to leave England without the king's special license.[525]

Before 20 February 1372 Arnald established his headquarters in a house in London. On that day he issued an executory letter with regard to census and annates,[526] although he dated the beginning of his exercise of the function of his office from 22 February, when John de Caroloco accounted to him for his conduct of the office since John de Cabrespino had left England.[527] He remained in England until 27 July 1374,[528] when he concluded his first account and set out for the papal camera to present it.[529] Delivery was made to the camera on 9 November [530] and on 12 February 1375, after the account had been audited by a cameral clerk, he was given an acquittance for the receipts listed therein.[531] He had already received a papal safe-conduct for his return to England,[532] but letters of credence for him addressed to several persons were not issued until late in March.[533] He had to break his journey at Paris and Bruges to conduct papal business entrusted to him,[534] and he did not reach England until late in May or early in June 1375.[535]

During this absence the collector's office was managed by Laurence de Nigris, his *locumtenens*,[536] whom he had appointed his deputy collector in 1373.[537] Laurence was a citizen of Rome,[538] a bachelor of law and a canon of Lincoln.[539] He was still in charge on 8 June 1375, but a week later Arnald was again directing affairs.[540]

Arnald remained in England the second time until 6 March 1378,[541] when he closed his second account and departed for the papal court to deliver it.[542] In April Robert de Grantham, who was the registrar in the collector's office, went to Rome on business connected with the account, returning to England in October.[543] The account, which apparently was not audited and approved before 22 March 1379, left the collector owing nothing.[544]

Arnald does not appear to have returned to England though he remained collector until he was superseded by Cosmatus Gentilis, who took the oath of fealty to the king on 3 June 1379,[545] though his papal commission was not dated until 27 August.[546] During the interval Laurence de Nigris, whom Arnald had appointed his *locumtenens* on his departure on 6 March 1378,[547] performed the functions of the collector. On 5 October 1378 the king licensed Arnald to demand and receive the money due to the church of Rome whether for annates by authority of Gregory XI or for other revenues long accustomed to be paid to that church.[548] It was, however, Laurence who acted under this license, since it was he who took an oath of fealty to the king similar to that which Arnald had taken. It omitted the clauses with regard to counsel and it contained the additional promises not to claim annates from benefices to which the king had made presentation or from benefices granted by the pope in expectancy.[549] Presumably these actions were taken by the royal government to remove any doubt with regard to the collector's powers which may have arisen from the death of Gregory XI, the subsequent schism and the failure of Urban VI to commission a collector immediately. Concerning the transaction of business by Laurence during this period there is little evidence,[550] since any report he may have rendered is lacking.

The principal task which the pope placed upon Arnald Garnerii in addition to his duties as collector was to act as papal envoy to the parties who were engaged in an

[525] 13 February 1372: Rymer, *Foedera*, iii, 933-934; *Cal. Close Rolls, 1369-74*, p. 424.

[526] Carlisle Diocesan Registry, Reg. of Appelby, pp. 248-249.

[527] Below, p. 363. The camerarius gave the date as 27 February: Collectorie 358, fol. 129.

[528] Documents which establish dates when he was in England during this period: below, pp. 475-476; 478-479; Carlisle Diocesan Registry, Reg. of Appelby, p. 251; P. R. O., Chancery Misc., bundle 16, file 7, no. 8; York Diocesan Registry, Reg. of Thoresby, fols. 326-327; *Reg. of Thomas de Brantyngham*, ed. F. C. Hingeston-Randolph, i, 179-180, 281-282, 296-298, 300, 305, 324-326; *Wykeham's Reg.*, ii, 191; Introitus et Exitus 340, fols. 22ᵛ, 61; Collectorie 465, fols. 57, 77ᵛ; 466, fol. 148. Perroy places his departure in June: *L'Angleterre et le Grand Schisme*, p. 38, n. 4.

[529] Below, pp. 475, 476.

[530] Below, p. 363.

[531] Obligationes Reg. 42, fols. 3-4.

[532] 25 January 1375: *Cal. Pap. Regs. Letters*, iv, 153.

[533] *Ibid.*, iv, 142, 146; *Wykeham's Reg.*, ii, 246.

[534] He arrived in Bruges on or shortly before 16 May: Perroy, *L'Angleterre et le Grand Schisme*, p. 38.

[535] Below, pp. 533, 537.

[536] Below, pp. 476, 533, 537; Obligationes Reg. 42, fol. 17, 17ᵛ.

[537] Below, p. 484.

[538] In cameral documents he was designated as Laurence de Alma Urbe: Obligationes Reg. 42, fol. 17; Introitus et Exitus 343, fol. 42.

[539] Below, p. 484; *Cal. Pap. Regs. Letters*, iv, 420-421.

[540] Below, p. 533.

[541] The following documents indicate Arnald's presence in England at frequent intervals: below, pp. 533-537; *Wykeham's Reg.*, ii, 243-244, 274-275; Ely Diocesan Registry, Reg. of Arundell, fols. 14, 17ᵛ, 83ᵛ, 84; Introitus et Exitus 306, fol. 27; 344, fol. 27; Obligationes Reg. 42, fols. 55ᵛ, 62; *Cal. Close Rolls, 1374-77*, pp. 419, 478; *1377-81*, p. 16; P. R. O., Ancient Correspondence 38, no. 53.

[542] Below, p. 484.

[543] Below, p. 538.

[544] Below, p. 538.

[545] *Cal. Close Rolls, 1377-81*, p. 257.

[546] *Cal. Pap. Regs. Letters*, iv, 257.

[547] Below, p. 479.

[548] *Cal. Pat. Rolls, 1377-81*, p. 276.

[549] *Cal. Close Rolls, 1377-81*, p. 224.

[550] There is record of a payment which he made at the end of March 1378 in accordance with a cameral mandate: below, p. 535.

attempt to negotiate peace between the kings of France and England in 1375. Late in March he was accredited to the king of France,[551] to papal envoys who were taking part in the peace negotiations at Bruges or were about to leave England in order to take part in them.[552] He was also recommended to William Wykeham, bishop of Winchester, whose influence the pope desired to be used in behalf of peace.[553] On this mission Arnald was further instructed to convey to the papal nuncios and to the bishop of Winchester the pope's wishes with regard to a subsidy from the English clergy,[554] for which the pope had been negotiating since 1372.[555] He was called upon further to present papal letters concerning the advisability of reforming the religion of the Hospitallers to the bishops of his collectorate and to obtain their written replies and to present to Edward III papal letters requesting that the English benefices of cardinals should be exempt from royal tenths levied on the clergy.[556]

During the period of Arnald's collectorship protests were made by the commons in several parliaments against papal fiscal practices. In 1373 they complained that the treasure of the realm was carried outside the realm by the payment of annates to the impoverishment of the realm and people and to the comfort and strength of the enemy.[557] In the first parliament of Richard's reign they even raised the question of the discontinuance of Peter's pence,[558] which was by many centuries the oldest revenue received by the papacy from England. The pope's collector did not escape his share of criticism. In the Good Parliament of 1376 the commons claimed that the collector was an alien of the obedience of the king of France. He and his agents spied vacant benefices which were reported to cardinals and others at the court of Rome who then bought the benefices from the pope. They also betrayed the secrets of the realm. The collector kept a great hostel in London for the receipt of papal money, as if it were the exchequer of a prince or a duke. From thence he sent to the pope the income derived from annates, subsidies and procurations amounting to 20,000 marks annually. The commons wanted Master John Strensall, parson of St. Botolph, who had been serving the collector as a clerk and living with him for five years, to give testimony before the lords and commons, and demanded that the papal collector should be excluded from England.[559] In the Hilary session of parliament in 1377 the commons repeated these charges with some

variations and said that the collector ought to be an English prelate or person.[560] Though the commons did not attain their purpose with regard to the collector, the general state of public opinion in England concerning papal fiscal policies, which these and earlier expressions of grievance[561] indicate, may well have had some influence in bringing about the establishment by the royal government of the collector's oath. This made it possible for the king to place many restrictions on the collector. The limitations of which Arnald complained to the king's council[562] were for the most part not new, but perhaps they were more strictly enforced. He could not, for example, export money from the realm even by bill of exchange without the royal license.[563]

There is no record that Arnald received any special privileges or any English benefices from the pope. The only suggestion of a reward in addition to his procurations was his acquisition before 12 June 1377 of a canonry in Narbonne in addition to the one which he held in Châlons.[564]

## 3. THE REVENUES

### PETER'S PENCE

Of the revenues which the papal collectors received in England, Peter's pence was by far the oldest. Like most mediaeval institutions of such venerable antiquity its administration was regulated by custom. There were local variations in the customs which prescribed the laymen who were liable for the annual payment of the pennies and in the hierarchial arrangement of the ranks of the clergy who took part in the collection of them within each diocese. The final recipients of the pennies were in most dioceses the bishops and in the others the archdeacons. They were responsible for the payment of Peter's pence to the pope, and the amount which each owed annually had been established at a definite sum as early as the twelfth century and possibly before. The papacy, therefore, received from this revenue in the fourteenth century a fixed annual sum which was a few shillings less than £200.[565]

The total of the amount paid by those who owed the due was much in excess of this sum and the surplus was retained by the series of local collectors through whose hands the money passed. The papacy began at least as early as 1115 to attempt from time to time to

[551] Below, p. 537.
[552] Cal. Pap. Regs. Letters, iv, 142, 146.
[553] Wykeham's Reg., ii, 245-246.
[554] Ibid., ii, 245-246, Cal. Pap. Regs. Letters, iv, 142.
[555] Ibid., iv, 101, 106-107, 115-118, 123-124, 127, 136. See also below, p. xlvii.
[556] Ibid., iv, 105, 121, 143.
[557] Rot. Parl., ii, 320.
[558] Ibid., iii, 21.
[559] Ibid., ii, 338-340.

[560] Ibid., ii, 373. A document in the archives of the Dean and Chapter of Durham contains headings of subjects which apparently were to be discussed at some parliament early in the reign of Richard II. Among them is the heading: "Concerning the collector of the pope": Locellus 20, no. 7.
[561] Above, pp. xxvi, xxx-xxxi.
[562] Below, pp. 477-478.
[563] Below, p. 477; Cal. Close Rolls, 1374-77, pp. 419, 478; 1377-81, p. 16; Rymer, Foedera, iv, 16.
[564] Ely Diocesan Registry, Reg. of Arundell, fol. 83ᵛ.
[565] Lunt, Financial Relations . . . to 1327, ch. i; below, pp. 256, 307.

obtain the full amount of Peter's pence paid by those who owed them. After 1282 a continuous effort to bring about this result was maintained by successive popes for many years.[566] The demands reached a climax during the pontificate of John XXII. Apparently Benedict XII repeated them early in his pontificate,[567] but thereafter nothing further was heard of them. They produced no change in the established system, and throughout the period covered by the collectors' accounts printed below the annual sum due the papacy from Peter's pence remained without alteration.

The papal collectors did not intervene in the local collection. They dealt only with the bishop or archdeacons who customarily paid the sum owed to the papacy from each diocese. In the autumn or early winter the collector would send a warning to deliver the amount of Peter's pence due at the collector's house in London at dates varying from early in January to some time in April. The warning usually gave the recipient from two to four months in which to make the delivery.[568] In the dioceses where the archdeacons were responsible for render of the money to the collector he would order the bishop to notify them of the date when delivery was to be made.[569] If a bishop who owed the payment had not yet received the money from his archdeacons, he might request a postponement of the date, which would usually be granted.[570] If a bishop or an archdeacon fell into arrears, the collector issued a more peremptory warning which might include a threat of ecclesiastical censures for failure to comply.[571] If John de Grandisson, bishop of Exeter, was threatened with deposition or degradation, as he implied,[572] the instance would appear to have been unique. It may be doubted whether in practice any of the collectors carried out a threat to apply ecclesiastical censures to a bishop for failure to pay Peter's pence on time, but the reason seems to have been the deference due from a collector to a prelate of higher rank. The contention of John de Grandisson that the collector had no right to enforce payment by compulsory process seems to have been without foundation, since the collectors sometimes did

employ sequestration. They directed bishops to sequestrate the revenues of archdeacons who were behind in their remittances of Peter's pence,[573] and one collector ordered sequestration of the goods of a bishop who died owing Peter's pence. This order failed of immediate result because the royal escheator had taken possession of the property to meet the bishop's debts to the king,[574] but it was successful ultimately.[575] More commonly the collector recovered the debt of a deceased bishop or archdeacon from his executors, if the debtor had received the money from the local collectors who owed it to him.[576] If he had not received it, his successor became responsible for the payment.[577]

Similarly a translated bishop was held responsible for any Peter's pence which he had collected in his former diocese and his successor to his former bishopric for any arrears which he had not received.[578] On 3 February 1336, for example, Bernard de Sistre ordered Simon Montacute to pay the Peter's pence owed from the diocese of Worcester for the past five years. The bishop discovered by inquiry that his predecessor, Adam Orlton, who had been translated to Winchester, had received the money. He therefore informed the collector that Adam Orlton would explain orally in London at the next parliament to be held that for the first three years he had paid Itier de Concoreto and for the last two years produce letters of acquittance. If it should appear that any had remained unpaid, he would give satisfaction at that time.[579] When a see remained vacant for a long period, whoever exercised the spiritual jurisdiction might become responsible for the payment of the due to the collector.[580]

The collection of Peter's pence seems to have given the collectors comparatively little trouble. Payments were made on time more frequently than not. It was not uncommon for a debtor to be one to three years in arrears, but longer periods were exceptional. Sometimes payments listed as in arrears for a year were nominal than real on account of the method of keeping books used by the collector.

## CENSUS

The census in its narrowest meaning was an annual payment made by a small number of English religious houses in return for papal protection or exemption.

---

[566] Lunt, *Financial Relations . . . to 1327*, ch. i.

[567] Above, pp. xxii, xxiii.

[568] *Reg. of John de Grandisson*, i, 457-458; *Reg. of Ralph of Shrewsbury*, i, 16, 20, 27, 77; *Reg. of Brantyngham*, i, 324-325; Worcester Diocesan Registry, Reg. of Orlton, fol. 17ᵛ; Salisbury Diocesan Registry, Reg. of Mortivall, i, fol. 275ᵛ, ii, fol. 84; York Diocesan Registry, Reg. of Melton, fol. 535ᵛ.

[569] Winchester Diocesan Registry, Reg. of Orlton, i, fol. 32, 32ᵛ; *Winchester Cathedral Chartulary*, p. 53; Ely Diocesan Registry, Reg. of Arundell, fol. 14, 83ᵛ, 84.

[570] *Reg. of John de Grandisson*, i. 204, 220, 344, 351, 360; Salisbury Diocesan Registry, Reg. of Wyville, i, fol. 10ᵛ; Lincoln Diocesan Registry, Reg. xii, Buckingham, fol. 72ᵛ.

[571] *Reg. of John de Grandisson*, i, 344, 360; *Reg. Johannis de Trillek, Episcopi Herefordensis*, p. 136; *Reg. Ade de Orleton, Episcopi Herefordensis*, p. 298; Winchester Diocesan Registry, Reg. of Orlton, i, fol. 32, 32ᵛ.

[572] Above, p. xxxi.

[573] Winchester Diocesan Registry, Reg. of Orlton, i, fol. 32ᵛ; *Wykeham's Reg.*, ii, 191, 243-244.

[574] *Reg. of the Diocese of Worcester during the Vacancy of the See*, ed. J. W. Willis Bund, pp. 266-267.

[575] Below, pp. 39, 40.

[576] Below, pp. 35, 37-40, 70, 172.

[577] Below, pp. 40, 186, 517-518; Salisbury Diocesan Registry, Reg. of Mortivall, ii, fols. 56ᵛ, 57.

[578] Below, pp. 37, 38, 257, 517-518.

[579] Worcester Diocesan Registry, Reg. of Montacute, ii, fol. 18, 18ᵛ; below, p. 36.

[580] Below, pp. 27, 41-43, 70, 186; Lambeth Palace Library, Reg. of Reynolds, fol. 148.

St. Augustine's Canterbury paid its census directly to the papal camera. The other twelve houses which were known by the camera to be subject to the due in 1317 made delivery to the papal collector.[581]

During the period four new payers of census were established. In 1343 the abbess and nuns of the order of minoresses, who had moved in the preceding year from Waterbeach to Denney,[582] were granted exemption from the jurisdiction of the metropolitan. In acknowledgment they were to pay to the pope annually a pound of wax.[583] On 5 August 1345 the master and all the members of the English order of Sempringham were exempted from ordinary jurisdiction and made subject immediately to the papacy. As a sign of this " liberty " they were to pay a pound of gold to the pope once every two years.[584] Queen Isabella, who had supported the petition for this grant, regarding the census as too heavy, joined with the king to request its reduction to a mark of gold every two years.[585] The change was conceded on 8 October 1345.[586] The gold mark was valued by the camera at sixty-four florins,[587] which were computed by John de Cabrespino as equal to £9 12 s.[588] and by Arnald Garnerii at £9 15 s. The abbot and convent of St. Werburgh Chester, on 3 January 1345, sought to be given exemption and to be made immediately subject to the apostolic see, offering in return to pay a yearly census.[589] The petition was approved on 2 January 1346 and the census was set at ten marks a year, with the understanding that a mark was to be computed as worth five florins.[590] The monks of the abbey protested the exemption on the ground that the convent had not been consulted with regard to the petition for it and appealed to the apostolic see. The appeal was ultimately successful, and on 23 May 1363 the exemption was revoked.[591] Clement VI, on 19 November 1349, conferred upon the dean of the chapel of St. Stephen, which Edward III had established as a college in his palace of Westminster, ecclesiastical jurisdiction over the clergy attached to the chapel and exempted them from the jurisdiction of the bishop, excepting the dean's cure of souls. In recognition of

the exemption a mark was to be paid annually to the papal camera.[592]

None of these recipients of exemptions appears to have paid census during the period under review except the order of Sempringham.[593] Receipts from the others do not appear in the collector's accounts, or in the Introitus et Exitus registers where payments made directly to the camera were usually entered and where the payments from the order of Sempringham were noted regularly.[594] In 1367 and again in 1377 the order paid the census to the papal collector in England,[595] but ordinarily the collector had no responsibility for collecting the census from the order.

The collector dealt with the religious houses which customarily paid census to him through the bishop. He ordered the bishop to cite the debtor to render payment at the collectors' house in London before a certain day. If a payment was delayed too long, the bishop would be directed to excommunicate the delinquent, to sequestrate his income and to cite him to come before the collector on a stated day. When the payment had been rendered, the bishop would be called upon to relax the sentence.[596]

## TRIBUTE

The annual tribute of one thousand marks which King John pledged himself and his successors to pay to the papacy was regarded by the officials of the papal camera as census.[597] Nevertheless, a collector's general commission to levy census was not interpreted as including tribute.[598] Rigaud d'Assier received a special commission to collect the tribute [599] and he reported the receipt of two thousand marks.[600] Itier de Concoreto noted in his report an arrangement made between Edward III and John XXII for the payment of the arrears of thirty-three years by instalments extending over many years and for the current render of future payments as they fell due each year. He concluded the entry with the statement that he did not yet have any special mandate to receive the money.[601] During Itier's tenure

[581] Lunt, *Financial Relations . . . to 1327*, ch. ii; *Financial Relations . . . 1327-1534*, pp. 55-66.

[582] Knowles and Hadcock, *Medieval Religious Houses: England and Wales*, p. 232.

[583] 18 January: *Cal. Pap. Regs. Letter*, iii, 68.

[584] Collectorie 282, fol. 143.

[585] *Cal. Pap. Regs. Petitions*, i, 86. The king in giving his approval to the petition apparently did not realize the nature of the exemption, for in 1366 he ordered the master of the order to acknowledge the jurisdiction of the bishop under pain of the king's displeasure: *Cal. Close Rolls, 1364-68*, p. 227.

[586] *Cal. Pap. Regs. Letters*, iii, 189; *Le Liber Censuum de l'Église romaine*, ed. P. Fabre and L. Duchesne, i, 225.

[587] Introitus et Exitus 238, fol. 37.

[588] Below, p. 265.

[589] *Cal. Pap. Regs. Petitions*, i, 91.

[590] *Reg. of Robert de Stretton*, William Salt Archaeol. Soc., *Collections*, new series, x, pt. 2, 156.

[591] *Cal. Pap. Regs. Petitions*, i, 274, 423.

[592] *Cal. Pap. Regs. Letters*, iii, 330; *Petitions*, i, 186-187; *Liber Censuum*, ii, 121.

[593] Denney and Chester do not appear in the Liber Censuum.

[594] Introitus et Exitus 238, fol. 37; 270, fol. 37ᵛ; 277, fol. 6ᵛ; 283, fol. 27; 295, fol. 3ᵛ; 300, fol. 4; 325, fol. 28; 333, fol. 36ᵛ; Collectorie 231, fol. 140. Hoberg, *Die Einnahmen unter Innocenz VI*, pp. 6, 86, 167, 258, 354.

[595] Below, pp. 264-265.

[596] Bodleian Library, MS. Kent Roll 6, entries r, pp, and qq; Worcester Diocesan Registry, Reg. of Montacute, ii, fol. 18, 18ᵛ; Winchester Diocesan Registry, Reg. of Orlton, i, fol. 32, 32ᵛ; Carlisle Diocesan Registry, Reg. of Appelby, pp. 248-249; *Reg. of Brantyngham*, i, 324-325.

[597] Lunt, *Financial Relations . . . to 1327*, pp. 130-131.

[598] *Ibid.*, p. 173.

[599] Above, p. xxii.

[600] Below, p. 27.

[601] Below, p. 29; for a summary on Royal Tribute in Edward III's reign, consult Lunt, *Financial Relations . . . 1327-1534*, pp. 66-73.

of office the king made three payments of the tribute, sending them to the papal camera by the agency of his envoys or of Italian merchants.[602] Bernard de Sistre explained that he had received no money from this source because the king was bound to make payment directly to the Roman court.[603] He and his successors to 1378 received no special commissions with regard to the tribute and his successors did not mention it in their reports. After 1333 the king made no further payments of the tribute and in 1366 the obligation was repudiated by Edward III with the advice and consent of parliament.[604] A pope occasionally reminded the king of his indebtedness for the tribute, but the reminder was presented to the king through agents other than the collectors.[605]

### VISITATION TAX

Associated with the census by some of the collectors [606] and confused with it by cameral officials [607] was a revenue known more properly as the visitation tax. It arose in connection with the duty incumbent upon all English archbishops and bishops and upon some abbots of exempt monasteries to visit the tombs of the apostles once every three years. On the occasion of each visitation the archbishops of Canterbury and York and the abbot of St. Augustine's Canterbury were required to pay a sum of money to the papal camera. Each of the two archibishops owed three hundred marks and the abbot of St. Augustine's ten marks.[608]

Ordinarily the debtors sent the money to their proctors who made the visitation for them and the proctors assigned it to the camera.[609] When one of the payers was badly in arrears, the pope might direct the collector to recover them. In 1343 Bernard de Sistre was ordered to exact 600 marks from the archbishop of Canterbury for payments due in 1317 and 1341 and the like from the archbishop of York for the same two terms.[610] Both

archbishops paid the sum due in 1341 at the papal court,[611] but the archbishop of York paid the amount due on 1317 to Bernard's successor, Raymond Pelegrini, on 6 June 1349.[612] On 10 July 1356 Hugh Pelegrini was ordered to enforce payment of 6750 florins owed by the archbishop of Canterbury for four and one-half triennial periods.[613] The archbishop, however, did not make delivery to the collector. On 7 January 1359 he made an arrangement with the pope for the payment of the arrears. Fifteen hundred florins which would become due on the next 3 February were to be added to them, making the total 8250 florins. On 3 February 1362 he was to pay the additional 1500 florins which would become due on that date and 500 florins on the arrears. Thereafter at the conclusion of each triennial period he was to pay the current amount due and 2000 florins toward the arrears.[614] In 1360 this agreement was superseded. On 8 July the pope and cardinals in consistory pardoned him 3750 florins which he owed for his predecessors to the cameras of the pope and the college of cardinals, and on 22 July he paid 2250 florins through his proctor to the papal camera for the three triennial periods which had accumulated during his own time.[615] The remaining 2250 florins were owed to the camera of the college of cardinals. Presumably they were paid, since it was customary to make payments to both cameras at the same time, but I have discovered no record of the transaction. The archbishop of York was also in arrears in 1356, but the aid of the collector was not invoked. On 8 July the proctors of the archbishop pledged him to the officials of both cameras to pay 3600 florins for three triennial visitations left unpaid by his predecessor at the rate of 600 florins every three years,[616] and the contract was fulfilled.[617]

### TENTHS

The papal imposition of mandatory tenths upon the incomes of the English clergy became much less common in this period than it had been in preceding years. While Rigaud d'Assier was collector, John XXII, at the petitions of Edward II, ordered the whole English clergy to pay two annual tenths [618] and one biennial

[602] In 1329, Obligationes Reg., 11, fol. 61ᵛ; in 1330, Theiner, *Vetera Monumenta Hibernorum*, p. 250; *Cal. Pat. Rolls, 1327-30*, p. 513; Rymer, *Foedera*, ii, 789; in 1333, Rymer, *Foedera*, ii, 864; *Cal. Pat. Rolls, 1330-34*, p. 407.

[603] Below, p. 43.

[604] *Rot. Parl.*, ii, 289-290; *Chronica Johannis de Reading*, p. 171; *Eulogium Historiarum*, ed. F. S. Hayden, iii, 239.

[605] *Chronicon Henrici Knighton*, ii, 98; Lambeth Palace Library, Reg. of Islip, fol. 141ᵛ; Theiner, *Vetera Monumenta Hibernorum*, p. 329.

[606] Below, pp. 29, 43, 44.

[607] Lunt, *Financial Relations . . . to 1327*, pp. 121-122; Collectorie 464, fol. 150; 465, fol. 69; Introitus et Exitus 300, fol. 3ᵛ.

[608] Lunt, *Financial Relations . . . to 1327*, pp. 482-486.

[609] Obligationes Reg. 8, fol. 85ᵛ; 10, fols. 85, 88ᵛ, 89, 90ᵛ, 91; 11, fols. 60, 60ᵛ; 12, fols. 35, 36ᵛ, 71ᵛ; 17, fols. 55ᵛ, 78ᵛ; 18, fols. 24, 31ᵛ, 46ᵛ; 19, fol. 136ᵛ; Collectorie 353, fol. 7; 375, fols. 27, 28, 29ᵛ; 464, fol. 150; 465, fol. 69; Introitus et Exitus 272, fol. 5; 278, fol. 3ᵛ; 300, fol. 3; 303, fols. 3ᵛ, 5ᵛ, 7ᵛ; 321, fol. 24; 325, fols. 1, 1ᵛ; York Diocesan Registry, Reg. of Melton, fols. 26ᵛ, 27, 36ᵛ, 38, 55ᵛ, 56ᵛ, 62ᵛ-63ᵛ; Reg. of Thoresby, fols. 303, 308, 308ᵛ, 319ᵛ-320ᵛ, 323, 325; Lambeth Palace Library, Reg. of Islip, fols. 64ᵛ, 207.

[610] *Cal. Pap. Regs., Letters*, iii, 1; above, p. xxix.

[611] Introitus et Exitus 238, fols. 6ᵛ, 11ᵛ; 278, fol. 3ᵛ; Obligationes Reg. 19, fol. 136ᵛ.

[612] York Diocesan Registry, Reg. of la Zouche, fol. 269.

[613] 6650 florins in the text: *Cal. Pap. Regs. Letters*, iii, 620.

[614] Collectorie 385, fol. 170ᵛ.

[615] 8 July: Obligationes Reg. 10, fols. 91, 91ᵛ; Introitus et Exitus 238, fol. 7; 293, fols. 4ᵛ, 5. Hoberg, *op. cit.*, p. 290. In Obligationes Reg. 23A he is said to have paid in 1360 the share of the papal camera for one period, which would be 750 florins, and Innocent VI is said to have remitted the remainder to him in consistory: fol. 62ᵛ.

[616] York Diocesan Registry, Reg. of Thoresby, fols. 30ᵛ, 303, 308ᵛ, 309, 319-320ᵛ, 323, 325.

[617] Obligationes Reg. 23A, fol. 113; Introitus et Exitus 300, fol. 3; 303, fol. 5ᵛ; 304, fol. 4; 325, fol. 1ᵛ; Hoberg, *op. cit.*, pp. 124-125, 126, 257-258.

[618] The first of these was imposed before Rigaud's appointment, but it was levied while he was collector.

tenth, and the clergy of the province of Canterbury to pay an additional tenth for one year. These taxes were collected by English prelates and delivered by them or their deputy collectors to the royal exchequer without the intervention of the papal collector. The pope reserved a quarter of the proceeds of the biennial tenth for himself, but the king, to whom all the proceeds were delivered, transmitted only a small part of the quarter to the pope.[619] The only income taxes which Rigaud collected were the arrears of tenths which had been imposed by Nicholas IV and Clement V.[620]

The next tenth which the English clergy were compelled to pay by papal mandate was imposed at the request of Edward III. In 1329 he sent to the papal court envoys who pledged the king to pay in instalments 33,000 marks of arrears owed for the royal tribute and obtained from John XXII the grant of half the yield of a tenth to be paid by the English clergy for four years and of half the proceeds of a levy of annates begun in 1329 for a period of three years.[621] On 3 January 1330 the pope appointed the archbishops of Canterbury and York and their suffragans collectors of the tenth in their respective dioceses. The methods of administration prescribed in the bull were the same as those which had been used in the levy of previous tenths. The collectors or their deputies were to deliver the proceeds of each semi-annual payment to a receiver to be named by the pope.[622] On 30 June 1330 John XXII appointed Itier de Concoreto to that post.[623] He had no part in the collection of the tenth from the payers. After each instalment became due, he ordered the diocesan collectors to appear before him at his house in London to account for and to deliver their receipts.[624] Early in 1334, after the last payment had become due from the payers, Itier received from the collectors accounts for the whole four years of the tenth. He then issued to each a notarial instrument recording the amount due from the collector, the amount delivered by him and the balance still owed.[625] It was his responsibility to render to the pope and to the king their

shares of the yield, but his accounts with the papal camera in which the deliveries of the papal share were recorded are not known to be extant.

Bernard de Sistre, who followed Itier de Concoreto in 1335, took up the business, which his predecessor left unfinished, of obtaining the arrears of the tenth. He dealt with the diocesan collectors as Itier had done.[626] The amounts which he recovered and the deliveries which he made to the papal camera are set forth in his report.

Before the final instalment of this tenth had become due, John XXII ordered the English clergy to pay another tenth for the purpose of financing a crusade to the Holy Land. On 26 July 1333 Philip VI of France took an oath to go on a crusade.[627] On the same day John XXII ordered a general passage to begin on 1 August 1336, appointed Philip captain-general of the expedition and issued a series of decrees arranging for the crusade to be preached, establishing indulgences, seeking gifts and legacies for the cause and imposing a tenth on the clergy universally. Copies of all these bulls were addressed to the archbishops of Canterbury and York and their suffragans.[628]

The tenth was to run for six years. If it would be concurrent with another papal tenth, it was to be postponed until the current tenth had ceased, and it was to be levied only for enough years in addition to those of the current tenth to make a total of six years. Since the period of the quadrennial tenth would not expire until 5 January 1334 and the last instalment of that tenth would not be due until 11 November 1333, the English clergy owed the crusading tenth for only two years and were entitled to a delay in the levy of the tax.

Actually the machinery for the collection of the tenth was not put into operation until 1335. On 31 January Benedict XII renewed the crusading bulls of John XXII and commanded that they be executed. On 7 May the archbishop of Canterbury sent copies of the letters of John XXII and Benedict XII with a mandate to put them into effect. The first semi-annual instalment became due on 2 February 1336.[629] After two further instalments had been levied,[630] the archbishop of Canterbury, between 17 and 21 March 1337, announced that

[619] Lunt, Financial Relations . . . to 1327, pp. 404-416.

[620] Below, p. 28.

[621] Rymer, Foedera, ii, 786; Annales Paulini in Chronicles of the Reigns of Edward I and Edward II, ed. W. Stubbs, i, 348; Vatican Library, Fondo Barberiniano Latino 2166, fol. 132ᵛ; for the Tenths during Edward III's reign, see Lunt, Financial Relations . . . 1327-1534, pp. 75-94.

[622] Literae Cantuarienses, ed. Sheppard, i, 322-333; Cal. Pap. Regs. Letters, ii, 494.

[623] Cal. Pap. Regs. Letters, ii, 496; P. R. O., K. R. Memo Roll 109, m. 122ᵛ

[624] E. g., Lincoln Episcopal Archives, Reg. v, Burghersh, fols. 436ᵛ-437ᵛ, 440, 440ᵛ, 448ᵛ, 452ᵛ, 462, 465ᵛ-466; York Diocesan Registry, Reg. of Melton, fols. 532, 532ᵛ, 535, 535ᵛ, 578ᵛ-579; Reg. of Ralph of Shrewsbury, i, 58. 60, 99; Reg. of John de Grandisson, i, 582.

[625] Reg. Hamonis Hethe, pp. 536-538; Jeayes, Descriptive Catalogue of the Charters ond Muniments belonging to the Marquis of Anglesey, p. 130; British Museum, Addit. MS. 41612, fol. 84ᵛ-85.

[626] Reg. of Ralph of Shrewsbury, i, 263; Worcester Diocesan Registry, Reg. of Montacute, ii, fol. 18; Winchester Diocesan Registry, Reg. of Orlton, i, fol. 32, 32ᵛ.

[627] Samaran and Mollat, La Fiscalité pontificale, p. 15.

[628] Salisbury Diocesan Registry, Reg. of Wyville, i, fols. 23-27; Winchester Diocesan Registry, Reg. of Orlton, ii, fols. 12-14; Worcester Diocesan Registry, Reg. of Montacute, ii, fols. 11-16; Lincoln Episcopal Archives, Rsg. v, Burghersh, fols. 509-514ᵛ; York Diocesan Registry, Reg. of Melton, fols. 543ᵛ-544; Cal. Pap. Regs. Letters, ii, 369.

[629] York Diocesan Registry, Reg. of Melton, fol. 57; Muniments of the Dean and Chapter of Salisbury, Press iv, Box A i; of Durham, Misc. Charters 3383, 4653, 5048.

[630] Bodleian Library, MS. Charter Oxon, A 1, no. 60; Muniments of Dean and Chapter of Salisbury, Press iv, Box A i; of Durham, Misc. Charters 4158, 4979; Worcester Diocesan Registry, Reg. of Montacute, fol. 34.

Benedict XII had ordered the collection of the tenth to cease, because the crusade had been given up.[631] The pope directed that what had been collected was to be restored to the payers,[632] but this provision was disregarded in England on account of actions previously taken by the convocations of Canterbury and York. In response to royal requests the clergy of both provinces in 1336 had granted the king two tenths, with the restriction that the concession would become operative only if the sexennial tenth imposed by John XXII in 1333 should be revoked. If the revocation should be made, whatever had been collected or had become due of the papal tenth previously would be paid to the king and enough more would be collected to make up the balance of a biennial tenth.[633] Thus the tenth ceased to be a papal tax.

For the collection of the sexennial tenth the general papal collectors had no responsibility. Neither Itier de Concoreto, who held office when John XXII decreed the tenth, nor Bernard de Sistre, who was collector when the tenth was levied, received any commission from the pope as collector or receiver of the tenth. The English archbishops and bishops collected the tenth without papal supervision. According to the papal instructions in the bull which imposed the tax, each bishop was to keep the proceeds or to deposit them with the dean and chapter. Each bishop was to disburse the funds among the crusaders who went from his diocese. Since no crusade took place, the money was on deposit in each diocese when the king took over the tenth.[634]

This was the last mandatory tenth imposed upon the English clergy by the papacy previous to 1378. Both Innocent VI and Gregory XI threatened to require the payment of tenths, if the clergy did not grant requested subsidies, but on both occasions the clergy accepted payment of the subsidies.

## SUBSIDIES

During the period under review a few popes asked the English clergy to grant subsidies. They differed from mandatory taxes in that the clergy were either free to grant or deny the request, or to have some voice in the nature or amount of the subsidy to be levied.[635] John XXII, in 1326, asked for a voluntary subsidy from the English clergy. The clergy of the whole country, meeting in council on 17 January 1327, declined to make

a grant.[636] The pope, apparently believing that a subsidy had been promised, commissioned Itier de Concoreto in 1329 to collect it, but the collector found it could not be levied because it had not been granted.[637]

Innocent VI was the next pope to seek a subsidy from the English clergy. During his pontificate Barnabo Visconti of Milan occupied portions of the States of the Church for several years and the attempted defense exhausted the resources of the papal camera. As long as the war between France and England continued, the pope refrained from asking the English clergy for a subsidy,[638] but after peace had been made at Calais, he sent individual requests to the two archbishops and their suffragans to assist his nuncios, Androin abbot of Cluny and Hugh Pelegrini, his collector in England, whom he was sending to seek a subsidy for the defense of the Patrimony of the Church.[639] Apparently in response to this letter, Simon Islip, archbishop of Canterbury, on 31 March 1361, summoned a convocation of the province, in which the lower clergy were represented, to meet at Southwark on 31 May to deliberate on the questions raised in the papal letter.[640] Convocation seems to have postponed giving a definite answer.[641] Later the archbishop learned from friends at the papal court that Innocent VI was planning to place an unbearable tax on the English clergy.[642] In the light of this information the two archbishops and their bishops took the occasion, when they met at Westminster to consider the affairs of the kingdom, to discuss further the papal request for a subsidy. They decided to offer a sum of florins as a gracious aid, if the pope would forego his intention to levy a larger amount. They sent a messenger to put the proposal before the pope, who then agreed to accept the gracious aid.[643]

The amount of the subsidy was 100,000 florins,[644] which the council of archbishops and bishops estimated to be the equivalent of a tenth, though it was actually

---

[631] Reg. of Montacute, fol. 34; Winchester Diocesan Registry, Reg. of Orlton, i, fol. 52ᵛ; Reg. of Ralph of Shrewsbury, i, 301.

[632] 18 December 1336: Cal. Pap. Regs. Letters, ii, 534; York Diocesan Registry, Reg. of Melton, fol. 545; Vatican Library, Fondo Barberiniano Latino, 2126, fol. 154, 154ᵛ.

[633] P. R. O., L. T. R. Enrolled Accounts, Subsidies 3, mems. 20, 22; K. R. Memo. Roll 113, m. 176.

[634] Actually the king had seized a large part of the money on deposit before it became a royal tenth: Lunt, " Collectors of Clerical Subsidies," English Government at Work, 1327-1336, ii: 260-261.

[635] Lunt, Financial Relations . . . to 1327, p. 175.

[636] Ibid., pp. 238-239.

[637] Below, pp. 33-34.

[638] Rymer, Foedera, iii, 623.

[639] 25 September 1360: Cal. Pap. Regs. Letters, iii, 631; for the subsidies of 1362 and 1372, see Lunt, Financial Relations . . . 1327-1534, pp. 95-114.

[640] The archbishop in his summons did not explain the contents of the papal letter, but he said that each of the bishops would receive a copy addressed to him individually: Reg. of John de Grandisson, iii, 1223.

[641] In a letter of 14 April 1362 the archbishop of Canterbury said that consent had been delayed: Reg. Simonis de Sudbiria, i, 183.

[642] On 25 April 1361 he repeated his request for a subsidy. On the same date he imposed a tenth for two years on the English clergy by one bull and a tenth for one year by another bull: Reg. Litterarum Innocentii Sexti, in Martène et Durand, Thesaurus Novus, ii, 938-942, 965-969. Probably it was the threat of a biennial tenth of which the archbishop heard.

[643] Letter of the archbishop of Canterbury, 14 April 1362: Reg. Simonis de Sudbiria, i, 182-184.

[644] Ibid., i, 184-185.

less than a tenth.[645] On 14 April 1362 the archbishop of Canterbury ordered the bishops of his province to levy a tenth.[646] Later a mandate of the pope, dated 1 April 1362, was received. It ordered the archbishop of Canterbury and the bishop of Ely to collect the " gracious subsidy." On 21 May 1362 the two collectors issued a new mandate to collect the tenth, quoting the papal letter of 1 April.[647] By an arrangement made by the pope with the kings of England and France, the latter was to pay 100,000 florins to the pope. The former was to deduct that sum from the ransom owed to him by King John and receive the 100,000 florins which the English clergy owed to the pope for the subsidy.[648] The local receiver of the tenth, who had been appointed by the two collectors, delivered to the royal exchequer in instalments between 9 December 1362 and 12 October 1365 £15,000, which was accepted as the equivalent of 100,000 florins.[649] Thus the general collectors of papal revenues in England intervened neither in the collection of the subsidy nor in the disposal of the proceeds.

The next request for a subsidy was made by Gregory XI. On 10 March 1372 he asked the king and several prelates to use their influence to persuade the English clergy to grant a subsidy for purposes with which his nuncio, William bishop of Carpentras, would acquaint them.[650] This request was followed on 1 July by two mandates. One ordered the archbishops and their suffragans each to collect a tenth in his own diocese and to deliver the money to the banking firm of Benedict Nerotii. The other commanded the clergy to pay, if they preferred, a subsidy of 100,000 florins in accordance with the precedent set in the time of Innocent VI. If they chose the subsidy, the order to pay a tenth would become void.[651] These letters were not allowed to enter the realm. Gregory XI expostulated and issued several further mandates, but they likewise failed to reach those to whom they were addressed.[652] The pope attributed the failure of his letters to be delivered to the influence of English ecclesiastics. Their influence may have been responsible for it, but only the royal government could have seized the papal letters at the ports of entry.

The king's opposition to the subsidy became apparent in 1373. In July he sent ambassadors to the pope.[653]

Their principal business was to obtain a moderation of the papal policy with regard to provisions and reservations, but they also petitioned to have the subsidy postponed until after the war with France ended.[654] The most which the pope conceded with regard to the subsidy was to defer its levy until 1374.[655] With regard to the other questions he proposed that further negotiations should take place between papal and royal ambassadors. Edward III agreed in a letter of 11 March 1374 to send envoys to Bruges or Calais.[656] The pope replied on 4 May naming nuncios whom he would send to Bruges.[657] The subsidy, which was not being collected, finally became a subject of negotiation at Bruges. The outcome was announced in a papal mandate of 15 July 1375. The negotiators agreed that the English clergy in 1375 and 1376 should pay a subsidy of 60,000 florins. If the negotiations between England and France taking place at Bruges should result in peace, the clergy would pay an additional 40,000 florins. The mandate ordered the archbishops to collect the subsidy of 60,000 florins.[658] The archbishops ordered their suffragans to collect in two equal portions one-half a tenth to meet that sum.[659]

Though the collection of this subsidy was left to the English bishops and the deputies whom they appointed, this time papal agents had some oversight of the administration. On 22 September 1375 the pope notified the bishop of Ely that he was sending back to England William, formerly bishop of Carpentras and then archbishop-elect of Rouen, to explain the pope's wishes with regard to the subsidy.[660] On 31 December the pope notified William that he was instructing the archbishops of Canterbury and York to assign the proceeds of the subsidy to him, and exhorted him to be solicitous in exacting the subsidy. He was also given power to compel payment of the subsidy by ecclesiastical censures and to issue acquittances to the archbishops.[661] There is no indication that he intervened with the bishops, their deputies or the taxpayers. His authority was apparently limited to the exaction of the collected funds from the archbishops. In practice the two archbishops made nearly all of their deliveries to Arnald Garnerii, the papal collector.[662] The only exception noted by him was a payment made by the archbishop of York to the archbishop of Rouen.[663] The collector delivered some of his receipts from the subsidy to the archbishop of Rouen or at his orders, but he assigned the bulk of them to papal bankers for payment to the camera.[664] When

---

[645] The sum of florins was calculated at 3 s. to a florin, making £15,000: Rymer, *Foedera*, iii, 776. The yield of a tenth was over £18,000: P. R. O., K. R. Memo. Roll 109, mm. 125v-126.

[646] *Reg. Simonis de Sudbiria*, i, 182-184.

[647] *Ibid.*, i, 184-185.

[648] Rymer, *Foedera*, iii, 643.

[649] *Ibid.*, iii, 776; Broome, *The Ransom of John II*, Camden Third Series, xxxvii, 18-22.

[650] *Cal. Pap. Regs. Letters*, iv, 115-116.

[651] *Ibid.*, iv, 101.

[652] *Ibid.*, iv, 106-107, 116-118, 123-124. The later mandates were dated 17 December 1372 and 2 February and 13 May 1373.

[653] Perroy, *L'Angleterre et le Grand Schisme*, pp. 31-32.

[654] *Ibid.*, pp. 32-33; *Cal. Pap. Regs. Letters*, iv, 127.

[655] *Cal. Pap. Regs. Letters*, iv, 127, 136.

[656] *Cal. Close Rolls, 1374-77*, pp. 69-70.

[657] Rymer, *Foedera*, iii, 1002.

[658] *Cal. Pap. Regs. Letters*, iv, 111, 218.

[659] Lambeth Palace Library, Reg. of Sudbury, fols. 21, 23-24v.

[660] Lambeth Palace Library, Reg. of Arundell, fol. 11v.

[661] *Cal. Pap. Regs. Letters*, iv, 112.

[662] Below, pp. 531-532.

[663] Below, p. 532.

[664] Below, pp. 535-536; Obligationes Reg., 42, fol. 62; Introitus et Exitus 344, fol. 27.

Arnald closed his account on 6 March 1378 £6246 11 s. had been received from the archbishop of Canterbury and £1780 from the archbishop of York.[665] The amount in arrear was £973 9 s.[666] The collector, therefore, calculated the total subsidy of 60,000 florins equal to £9,000.

## ANNATES

The revenue which occupies more space in the accounts of the collectors than any other was that derived from annates. During the pontificate of John XXII there were two general levies of annates similar to that which had first been made by Clement V in 1306.[667] The first was imposed on 8 December 1316 for a period of three years. All benefices which became vacant within that period were to pay the fruits of the first year except archiepiscopal, episcopal and abbatial churches, benefices worth six marks or less annually, benefices vacant by exchange or for a second time within a year and daily distributions made to those who attended the hours. The amount of the first fruits was normally the value of the benefice as assessed in the current valuation for the tenth. This was a nominal value which was expected to leave the incumbent enough income to provide for the services and to pay the charges on the benefice. If it would not, the collector might require less than the assessed value for annates. The collector at his option could take the remainder for the first fruits and leave the assessed value for the incumbent. If a benefice was not assessed in the valuation, one-half the average annual income was taken for annates.

Rigaud d'Assier who was appointed collector of the annates, required each bishop to notify him at intervals of the benefices which became vacant in his diocese. He or one of his deputies then made a contract with the new incumbent of the vacant benefice for the payment of annates by instalments, of which there were usually two. Failure to pay on time would result in excommunication of the debtor and sequestration of the fruits of the benefice. Rigaud obtained most of the annates which were owed, but he left some arrears for his two immediate successors, Hugh of Angoulême and Itier de Concoreto, to recover. Of this levy of annates the king received half the proceeds of the first year and the remainder went to the papal camera.[668]

The second general levy of this type and the last during the period was decreed on 31 August 1329 for the next three years,[669] and on 13 December 1329 the period of the imposition was extended for another year.[670] Soon after this extension of the time, John XXII granted to the king half the proceeds for the whole four years.[671]

Itier de Concoreto was appointed collector and given the same instructions and powers that Rigaud had received for the earlier levy. In the administration of the tax he followed the precedents set by Rigaud.[672] Itier's account printed below does not include his receipts from annates, but other sources indicate that he left large sums due both to the pope and the king. Bernard de Sistre recovered from the taxpayers who were still in debt and from the ecclesiastical revenues of Itier the bulk of the annates due the pope and part of those due the king.[673]

Meanwhile John XXII began a practice which ultimately came to govern the benefices which should pay annates and made the revenue a permanent instead of an occasional source of income. On 20 February 1326 he decreed that benefices vacant at the apostolic see then and during the next year should pay to the papal camera the fruits accumulating during the period of the vacancy and annates for the year following the vacancy. Excepted from the decree were cathedral churches, regular abbeys and benefices vacant by exchange. Thereafter the decree was renewed each year to the end of his pontificate.[674] His successor claimed from such benefices only the fruits during their vacancies,[675] but Clement VI and his successors to 1378 exacted annates from these benefices.[676]

The number of benefices subject to annates by this arrangement increased steadily. In the time of John XXII benefices vacant at the apostolic see were interpreted to be all those to which the pope for any reason

---

[665] Below, pp. 531-532.

[666] Below, p. 484.

[667] On this levy see Lunt, *Financial Relations . . . to 1327*, pp. 486-494; and *Financial Relations . . . 1327-1534*, pp. 307-319. Rigaud collected some arrears of this levy: below, p. 28.

[668] For fuller details see Lunt, *Financial Relations . . . to 1327*, pp. 494-501.

[669] The bull, *Duras persecutiones et*, is published *in extenso* in *Reg. of John de Grandisson*, i, 543-545.

[670] *Dudum videlicet: Cal. Pap. Regs. Letters*, ii, 495; P. R. O., K. R. Memo. Roll 109, m. 123; Winchester Diocesan Registry, Reg. of Stratford, fol. 72; York Diocesan Registry, Reg. of Melton, fol. 533ᵛ.

[671] *Dudum dilecti filii*: Fondo Barberiniano Latino 2166, fol. 132ᵛ (dated 5 January 1330); P. R. O., K. R. Memo. Roll 109, m. 22 (dated 30 June 1330). Edward III acknowledged the grant on 12 April 1330: Rymer, *Foedera*, ii, 786.

[672] *Reg. of John de Grandisson*, i, 543-549; ii, 614, 687-688, 694, 723, 736: *Reg. of Ralph of Shrewsbury*, i, 16, 23, 40, 45, 57-58, 60-62, 102, 107-108, 116, 126, 156; *Reg. of Roger of Norbury*, p. 260: Diocesan Registries, Lichfield, Reg. of Norbury, ii, fol. 44; Salisbury, Reg. of Mortivall, ii, fols. 276-278; of Wyville, fols. 3-4, 8-9; Lincoln, Reg. v, Burghersh, fols. 425ᵛ-427; Winchester, Reg. of Stratford, fols. 44ᵛ, 45; of Orlton, i, fols. 17, 17ᵛ; York, Reg. of Melton, fols. 530-531, 533-534, 536-537; Carlisle, Reg. of Kirkby, p. 278.

[673] Below, pp. 54-60, 70.

[674] Lunt, *Papal Revenues*, i, 95; ii, 374-375; Göller, *Die Einnahmen unter Johann XXII*, pp. 91*, 92*, 113*; Samaran and Mollat, *La Fiscalité pontificale*, pp. 24, 25; Vatican Archives, Instrumenta Misc. 1008, 1208.

[675] Lunt, *Papal Revenues*, ii, 375-376; Samaran and Mollat, *La Fiscalité pontificale*, p. 25; Göller, *Die Einnahmen unter Benedikt XII*, pp. 20*, 22*.

[676] Lunt, *Papal Revenues*, i, 95; ii, 358-361; Samaran and Mollat, *La Fiscalité pontificale*, pp. 25-26.

had the right of collation.[677] They included benefices which were filled by the pope by the law of devolution, benefices vacant by the death of the incumbents at the papal court or within two days' journey of the court, benefices vacant anywhere by the death of cardinals or of many other papal officials, and benefices vacant by papal deposition, privation, promotion [678] or translation of their incumbents, by papal quashing of an election or by resignation into the hands of the pope.[679] Clement VI, soon after his accession in 1342, designated the benefices subject to annates in the more general terms of those at his disposal by the reservations of himself or his predecessors vacant at the apostolic see or anywhere else. It may be doubted that they included more classes of benefices than the reservation of John XXII, and Clement VI exempted more classes of benefices from annates than were specified in the bull of 1326, making the exemptions about the same as they were in the general levy imposed in 1316.[680] Yet the number of English benefices to which he made provision increased so greatly that complaints began to be made early in his pontificate.[681] In 1344 he subjected to annates benefices united or appropriated to monasteries or other churches by the apostolic see or with papal confirmation,[682] and at some time in his pontificate he began to demand annates from benefices of which the pope had confirmed the collation.[683] Innocent VI added benefices to which the contested right of possession was settled by the pope and benefices vacant by exchange effected at the papal court.[684] Gregory XI, on 17 April 1371, required payment of annates to the papal camera from any benefice acquired as the result of a papal expectative grace, whoever the local collator had been.[685]

Itier de Concoreto, in 1329, had to discover by inquiries addressed to the bishops the benefices to which John XXII had made collation since 1326.[686] In 1330 the papal camera began to keep registers of benefices filled by papal provision and to forward from time to time lists of those coming under the jurisdiction of the respective collectors.[687] Occasionally the recipient of a papal provision was required to notify the collector of it.[688] After the collector learned of a papal provision, he had to ascertain whether it had been effective.[689] This he often did by an inquiry addressed to the bishop of the diocese in which the benefice was located.[690] Discoveries of provisions which had not been put into effect were frequent. The next step was to establish the amount of annates. In the large majority of instances this was the value of the benefice as it was listed in the assessment for the tenths, of which the collector had a copy.[691] If any doubt arose concerning the assessed value, the bishop would be consulted.[692] If the benefice was not assessed for the tenth, the true value in common years was established by the oath of the holder of the benefice [693] or by the certification of the bishop.[694] From these benefices a half of the true value was claimed. Arrangements would then be made with the debtor for the payment of the whole sum before a fixed date or for payment by instalments at certain times.[695] If the payment was not rendered on time, the collector would order the bishop to excommunicate the debtor, to cite him to appear before the collector and to sequestrate the fruits of the benefice.[696] If the debtor obeyed the citation, the collector might grant new dates for payment which the debtor was required to take oath to observe under penalty of excommunication.[697] In carrying out these details of administration the collectors in many instances met with difficulties such as royal prohibitions and inability to locate benefices on their lists. These are amply illustrated in their accounts.

## INTERCALARY FRUITS

On 20 February 1326, when John XXII reserved the annates of certain benefices, he also reserved the fruits of the same benefices during their actual vacancies.[698] The fruits owed during the period of vacancy are known as intercalary fruits. Their reservation was renewed

---

[677] Constitutions *Ex debito* and *Multarum necessitatum*; Lunt, *Papal Revenues*, ii, 222-225, 375.

[678] If, for example, the pope appointed a bishop, the benefices which he held at the time became subject to papal collation: below, p. 49. It included also benefices which the constitution *Execrabilis* forced those who received provision to incompatible benefices to resign: Lunt, *Financial Relations . . . 1327*, pp. 495-496; *Papal Revenues*, ii, 225-228.

[679] Lunt, *Papal Revenues*, i, 84-85; ii, 217, 220-225.

[680] Muniments of the Dean and Chapter of York, Chapter Act Bk., pt. 3, fol. 100ᵛ; pt. 4, fol. 1, 1ᵛ; Lunt, *Papal Revenues*, ii, 358-361; *Cal. Pap. Regs. Letters*, iii, 5, 9, 40; Lunt, *Financial Relations . . . 1327-1534*, pp. 320-380.

[681] *Reg. of John de Grandisson*, i, 111-112; *Rot. Parl.*, ii, 144-145, 153-154; *Chronicon domini Walteri de Hemingburgh*, ii, 401-111; *Adae Murimuth, Cont.*, pp. 138-154, 230, 233-241; Rymer, *Foedera*, ii, 1233-34; *Cal. Close Rolls, 1343-46*, pp. 247, 356-357; *Cal. Pap. Regs. Letters*, iii, 2, 5, 9, 11; *Cal. Pat. Rolls, 1343-45*, pp. 277, 279.

[682] Samaran and Mollat, *La Fiscalité pontificale*, p. 25. E. g., below, pp. 93, 99, 102.

[683] E. g., below, pp. 93-99; 173, 175-176. Samaran and Mollat attribute this reservation to Innocent VI: p. 26.

[684] Samaran and Mollat, p. 26. They date the reservation in 1357, but Innocent VI was exercising it as early as 1353: below, pp. 93, 97, 100, 101, 102.

[685] Samaran and Mollat, p. 26; *Wykeham's Reg.*, ii, 167-169.

[686] York Diocesan Registry, Reg. of Melton, fol. 529ᵛ.

[687] Collectorie 280, fols. 7, 22. For an example of such a list see below, pp. 241-256.

[688] *Cal. Pap. Regs. Petitions*, i, 235.

[689] E. g., below, pp. 103-118; 210-213.

[690] E. g., below, pp. 190-192, 195-196.

[691] Below, pp. 183, 234.

[692] Below, pp. 182, 192.

[693] Below, pp. 174, 179, 181, 187, 222, 223.

[694] Below, pp. 177, 192.

[695] Below, pp. 527-531.

[696] *Reg. of Ralph of Shrewsbury*, ii, 691; *Reg. of Brantyng-ham*, i, 281-284, 296-299, 305; *Wykeham's Reg.*, ii, 191; below, pp. 186-187, 189, 191-198.

[697] Below, pp. 174-195 *passim*.

[698] Lunt, *Papal Revenues*, ii, 374-375.

every year to the end of his pontificate, and both Itier de Concoreto [699] and Bernard de Sistre [700] appear to have collected the fruits of some benefices falling under this reservation. Benedict XII did not retain annates, but he continued to reserve the intercalary fruits of benefices vacant at the apostolic see.[701] They were collected by Bernard de Sistre by means of local custodians or farmers of the benefices.[702]

Clement VI did not renew the general reservation of intercalary fruits made by his predecessor, but it was revived by Innocent VI and maintained by his successors to 1378.[703] Gregory XI extended it to include consistorial benefices.[704] None of these reservations was put into force in England, since they were not mentioned in the commissions or accounts of the collectors. The successors of Benedict XII sometimes reserved the intercalary fruits of specific benefices, but Urban V seems to have been the only pope who made such reservations in England previous to 1378. His reservations were few, and with one exception they were confined to the benefices of deceased cardinals.[705]

### FRUITS WRONGFULLY RECEIVED

Fruits wrongfully received were revenues collected from a benefice by a clerk who was in actual occupation of the benefice but had no legal right to it. The occupier might be too young, or of illegitimate birth without a dispensation, or otherwise disqualified by the canon law. When he sought to legalize his position by obtaining dispensation for the future and absolution for the past, he was required to pay part of the fruits which he had received illegally from the benefice to the camera for the war against the Turks, for the use of the camera, or for some other purpose. The amount of the payment would be fixed by the camera, but the money might be received by the collector.[706] A few instances of such payments are entered in some accounts.[707]

### LEGACIES AND COMMUTATION OF VOWS

In their wills the faithful sometimes left legacies for the crusade, the war against the Turks or the Roman church.[708] In the time of Rigaud d'Assier they yielded a substantial sum, and they were still sufficiently numerous in the time of Itier de Concoreto to justify the maintenance of local deputies to collect them.[709] Bernard de Sistre received the proceeds of several legacies which for the most part had been made during the collectorship of Itier. After Benedict XII postponed the crusade which had been projected by his predecessor, he instructed Bernard not to seek such legacies any longer.[710] Nevertheless, legacies continued to be made to the above causes throughout the period and small sums from them appear in the reports of all the subsequent collectors to 1378.[711]

Generally entered along with the legacies were sums received for the commutation of vows. They were vows to make pilgrimages to the Holy Land, Rome or some other shrine which could not be fulfilled on account of illness or some other good reason. The confessor who gave the release from the vow required in its place the payment of a sum which was usually calculated at the estimated cost of the journey to and from the shrine.[712] The money went to the papal camera and in a few instances was received by the collector.[713]

### SERVICE TAXES

The service taxes in England were payments made by archbishops, bishops and some abbots when they were appointed or confirmed by the pope in consistory. The principal payment was a sum equal to one-third of the annual income of the payer. Ordinarily the debtor delivered the money due directly to the camera and the collector had no concern with the tax. If the camera did not have a record of the value of the income of a prelate who had received a papal provision, it might send the bull of provision to the collector with instructions to assess the income and before delivery of the bull to receive from the prelate a letter binding him to pay to the camera the amount thus established. Occasionally a collector might also be required to collect a service tax which was in arrears.[714] Hugh Pelegrini was asked to perform each of these functions once,[715] though no receipts from this revenue are noted in his report.

[699] Lunt, *Financial Relations . . . to 1327*, pp. 502, 504-505; above, p. xxiv.

[700] Below, pp. 49-50. The heading does not indicate whether the payments are for annates or for fruits during vacancies. When the sum is the same as the assessed value of the benefice, presumably only annates were taken, but when the sum is larger than the assessed value probably both taxes were taken. E. g., Habbesthorp and Wenlock's Barn.

[701] 8 January 1335; Lunt, *Papal Revenues*, ii, 375-376.

[702] Below, pp. 50-53.

[703] Samaran and Mollat, *La Fiscalité pontificale*, pp. 64-65.

[704] *Cal. Pap. Regs. Letters*, iv, 152, 157.

[705] Below, pp. 182-183, 224, 264, 321. On 6 July 1366 Urban V ordered the collector to exact the fruits of the archiepiscopal *mensa* of Canterbury during a vacancy (*Cal. Pap. Regs. Letters*, iv, 25-26), but receipts from that source do not appear in the collector's account.

[706] Lunt, *Papal Revenues*, i, 101-102; *Financial Relations . . . to 1327*, pp. 528-529; above, p. xxxii.

[707] E. g., below, pp. 149-150, 154, 509.

[708] Lunt, *Financial Relations . . . to 1327*, ch. viii.

[709] Below, pp. 28, 34; above, p. xxv.

[710] Below, pp. 48-49.

[711] Below, pp. 83-84, 120, 224, 321, 453-454, 528; See also above, p. xxxix.

[712] Lunt, *Financial Relations . . . to 1327*, pp. 424-426, 527-528.

[713] Below, pp. 49, 84, 120, 321, 453, 528, 530.

[714] Lunt, *Papal Revenues*, i, 81-91; for Service Taxes, see Lunt, *Financial Relations . . . 1327-1534*, chaps. v and vi.

[715] Above, pp. xxxii.

Arnald Garnerii mentioned in his report two payments for the service tax made by English prelates, but he had no part in exacting or receiving them.[716]

## 4. CONVENTIONS FOR TRANSCRIPTION [717]

The accounts printed herein have been drawn from Introitus et Exitus Register 15 and from Collectorie 11, 12, 13, 14, and 227 which are deposited in the Vatican Archives.

The collector was expected to submit at least two copies of each report, one of which was to be returned to him.[718] Among the accounts, duplicate copies survive.[719]

In addition to the collector's reports themselves, these documents contain annotations made on them in the papal camera and in each of the fuller surviving reports a summary account, called *compotus brevis*.[720] The *compotus brevis*, giving only the totals of receipts, arrears, assignments and expenses, was normally drawn up under the direction of a cameral clerk to whom the camera had entrusted the examination of the account.[721] It is composed in the third person and committed to a special format. The folios of the *compotus brevis* are about the height of those of the collector's accounts, but are only half as wide; they are therefore narrow and elongated.[722] They are written with careful legibility.

The transfer of the entries in the manuscripts to the printed page presented several problems. To conserve space, Professor Lunt apparently adopted for the typescript the following conventions. (1) No matter where the caption for the diocese is written on the folio, it is invariably centered in the typescript. In the manuscripts, the caption is sometimes written at the top of the folio, sometimes it is centered immediately above the entry, and sometimes it is written in the left-hand margin opposite the entry. (2) In the manuscripts the abbreviation for *approbatum* is invariably in the left-hand margin; in the typescript the word *approbatum* is placed at the end of the item which has been approved. (3) The marginal notes made by the collector or by a cameral clerk are transferred to footnotes in the typescript. (4) No indication of a change in handwriting is given in the typescript. (5) The sums, normally

separated from the main entry and placed in the right-hand margin of the folio, are in the typescript annexed immediately to the end of the entry. This procedure may give rise to confusion if it is not remembered that the terminal sum of an entry is normally in the right-hand margin of the folio. (6) Another convention is the printing of monetary symbols in type indistinguishable from the adjacent type. Thus *libre* is printed as li. not as *l.* or *li.*; *solidi* as s., not as *s.*; *denarii* as d., not as *d.* Similarly other monetary symbols are not italicized. A peculiar sequence of letters occurs when the sum is fifty-one pounds, printed as li li. The usage of these conventions may be illustrated by the comparison of the four figures on pages xv to xviii, with the transcriptions of them printed in the text. Convention 1 is illustrated by figures 1, 2, and 3; convention 2 by figures 1 and 2; conventions 3 and 4 by figure 4; convention 5 by figures 2, 3, and 4; convention 6 by figures 1, 2, 3, 4. Figure 1 shows two folios of a typical *compotus brevis*.

Some obvious mistakes in syntax have been corrected, but faulty grammar which seemed to be inherent in the documents has not been emended. When the superscribed line or symbol of abbreviation is lacking, the omitted letters are not added in the transcription; thus the letters *m* and *n* are often left out. The original spelling has been retained; hence orthographic variations are numerous. The Latin word for " arrears " appears in diverse forms. Conjecture, supported by numerous tests, indicates that Lunt extended the abbreviated names of dioceses to conform with the spelling used by the current scribe when at some point the latter extended the abbreviation. Considerable diversity occurs in the spelling of repeated surnames and in the reproduction of place names; the transcribed text follows the scribe's spelling, but the index attempts to establish a broader uniformity.

The sections concerning Peter's pence in the collectors' accounts for the Avignonese period have been previously printed by Jensen.[723] They are transcribed afresh below with a few corrections of Jensen's readings.

## 5. COMMENTARY ON CHRONOLOGY

The longest sections of the collectors' accounts report on papal provisions, confirmations of benefices, and expectancies.[724] The dates assigned to these papal graces should be treated with circumspection. Discrepancies between the dates given in collectors' accounts and those given in papal chancery records are not infrequent. By and large it seems that chronological conformity between these two sources is greater with the papal provisions

---

[716] Below, pp. 453, 536.

[717] The final sections of the introduction have been supplied by E. B. Graves.

[718] Samaran and Mollat, *La Fiscalité pontificale*, p. 124.

[719] Below, p. 214, note 880; p. 256, note 711.

[720] Below, pp. 68, 95, 213, 225, 266, 538. *Cf.* fig. 1.

[721] Gasnault, " Notes et documents," *MAH*, XX (1958), 368-370, contravenes the opinion of Samaran and Mollat, *La Fiscalité pontificale*, p. 128 that the collector himself had condensed his account into the *compotus brevis*.

[722] Gasnault, *loc. cit.*, p. 369, where the *compotus brevis* is said to be about 29-30 cm. high and 11-12 cm. wide. The folios of the *compotus brevis*, which are printed here as figure 1, measure 29.8 cm. by 10.7-11.2 cm. The measurements of the folios printed here as figures 1, 2, 3, and 4 were supplied through the kindness of Msgr. Hermann Hoberg, Vice-Prefect of the Vatican Archives.

[723] O. Jensen, " The ' Denarius Sancti Petri ' in England," *T. R. H. S.* n. s. xv (1901) 204-241. The matching pages below are pp. 256, 35-43, 78, 95, 81-82, 172-173, 186, 214-215, 227, 256, 257, 268, 308, 309-310, 324-325, 411-412, 417, 474-475, 363-364, 517-518, 525-526, 538, 539.

[724] See Lunt, *Financial Relations . . . 1327-1534*, pp. 356 ff.

for 1363-1378 than for those for the period 1349-1363. Although many of the dates in Pelegrini's accounts agree with those found elsewhere, a considerable number diverge. In his first account, for example, there are for pages 96 to 100 below, sixty-nine footnotes assigning modern dates analogous to those in the Latin text. Of these sixty-nine, fifty-two can also be found for the appropriate entries in the Bliss-Twemlow calendars of papal chancery letters and petitions. Twenty-six of the fifty-two, so traced, bear identical dates in both chancery documents and collector's accounts; but twenty-six others carry different dates in the two sources. Twenty of the latter vary by a year or more [725] and six differ by only a few days.[726] Other random illustrations of inaccurate copying occur in the repetitions of items on the prebend of Sutton [727] and on the deanery of Chichester.[728]

In John de Cabrespino's accounts, a date once recorded is quite regularly repeated without variation each time that the item occurs.[729] The dates for provisions made between 6 March 1363 and 1366 as given in Cabrespino's second account normally agree with those in papal chancery petitions.[730]

For the numerous provisions and expectancies made between 1367 and 1378 and reported in the third and fourth accounts of John de Cabrespino and in the two accounts of Arnald Garnerii, only a few counterparts can be found in print. For the Avignonese period, the *Calendar of Papal Registers, Petitions,* ends with the year 1366, and the Vatican Registers, which are calendared in the Bliss-Twemlow series, contain relatively few provisions and expectancies for this decade. It is well known that most of the letters of Innocent VI, Urban V, and Gregory XI which were entered in the paper *Registra Avinionensia* were not recopied into the parchment *Registra Vaticana.* The beneficial graces, provisions and expectancies were only rarely transferred to the Vatican series of registers. Papal letters granting the favors requested in petitions were enrolled in the *Registra Avinionensia.*[731] Since the latter series of

registers were not calendared by Bliss and Twemlow, the collectors' accounts which are printed below open a fresh and fertile source on provisions and expectancies during the final decade of the Avignonese period. Since the outstanding ineffective graces were withdrawn upon the accession of a new pope, the first year of a pontificate regularly produced an inordinately large number of new or renewed graces. For the first year of Gregory XI, about 600 grants of English benefices which might entail the payment of annates are recorded in Garnerii's account, while for the second year only 260 or so are reported. A substantial majority were expectancies, many of which presumably never became effective; certainly some faced difficulties.[732] On the other hand, for a considerable number the payment of annates is noted and for these and others the papal grace presumably became effective.[733] The accuracy of the entries in the collectors' accounts can be attested by reference to their counterparts in the *Registra Avinionensia.* Since a comparison between the two sources indicates an almost invariable conformity in names and dates,[734] the lists in the collector's accounts for this last decade of the Avignonese period may be accepted as having been copied with care.

## 6. PRINTED WORKS CITED

*Adae Murimuth Continuatio chronicarum,* ed. Edward M. Thompson. (Rolls Series) London, 1889.
*Benoît XII (1334-1342). Lettres communes analysées d'après les registres dits d'Avignon et du Vatican,* ed. J-M. Vidal. 3 vols. (Biblio. Écoles franç. d'Athènes et de Rome) Paris, 1903-1911.
BROOME, DOROTHY M. "The Ransom of John II, King of France 1360-1370" (*Camden Miscellany* XIV) [Camden Soc., Third Ser. XXXVII]. London, 1926.
BROWN, W. "A List of Benefices in the Diocese of York Vacant Between 1316 and 1319." *Yorkshire Archaeological Society: Record Series* LXI. *Miscellanea* vol. i (1920) 138-148.
*Calendar of charters and documents relating to Selborne and its priory preserved in the Muniment Room of Magdalen College, Oxford.* Ed. W. D. Macray. 2 vols. (Hampshire Rec. Soc.). London 1891-1894.
*Calendar of the Close Rolls preserved in the Public Record Office,* [(1313-1381) 18 vols. London, 1893-1914].

[725] The footnotes on pages 96 to 100 below, numbered 113, 114, 122, 123, 126, 127, 131, 142, 151, 152, 154, 168, 170, 171, 172, 174, 184, 185, 189.

[726] Footnotes 102, 140, 158, 160, 162, 166.

[727] The dates for the prebend of Sutton are given as anno 8 (below, p. 99), anno 6 (below, p. 126) and anno 7 (*Cal. Pap. Regs. Petitions,* i, 157).

[728] The date for the deanery of Chichester is given as 14 Kal. Junii anno 7 (below, p. 93), 4 Kal. Junii anno 8 (below, p. 122) and 14 Kal. Julii anno 8 (*Cal. Pap. Regs. Petitions,* i, 166).

[729] For the many examples that might be cited, two will serve, namely the date 8 Ides Augusti anno xi for the church of Stockbury on pages 186, 228, 269, 325, 364; and the date for the archdeaconry of Lewes on pages 188, 228, 269, 326, 365.

[730] Below, pp. 222-224 and 242-256, and *Cal. Pat. Regs. Petitions,* i, 417-504, *passim.*

[731] The petitions for 1362-1363 which are abstracted in *Cal. Pap. Regs. Petitions,* i, resulted in papal graces which were copied in the *Registra Avinionensia* and are printed in abridgment in

*Urban V (1362-70), Lettres Communes,* ed. M-H. Laurent, i (Paris, 1954-58). *Cf.* footnote no. 733 below.

[732] Below, pp. 484 ff.

[733] For the payment of annates, for example, below pp. 410, 421-447, 453-458 *passim.* As another sample, at least 14 candidates for prebends and dignities listed on pages 419-426 below turn up in appropriate places in the new edition of Le Neve's *Fasti Ecclesiae Anglicanae.* Many of the graces were, of course, for benefices which would not properly be listed in Le Neve.

[734] This statement is based on notes, made some thirty-five years ago, from several volumes numbered between 156 and 200 of the *Registra Avinionensia.* From some of these registers I collected about 370 references regarding provisions and expectancies for English benefices for the period 1366 to 1376. Two hundred and twenty-one of these references for the period 1367 to 1372 are reproduced in part in the collectors' accounts, wherein the dates and names coincide almost uniformaly with my notes. No attempt was made to calendar all the references to English benefices in the *Registra Avinionensia.*

*Calendar of Entries in the Papal Registers relating to England and Ireland: Papal Letters.* ed. W. H. Bliss and J. A. Twemlow. vol. ii, 1305-1342, London, 1895; vol. iii, 1342-1362, London, 1897; vol. iv, 1362-1404. London, 1902.

*Calendar of entries in the Papal Registers relating to Great Britain and Ireland: Petitions to the Pope.* ed. W. H. Bliss. vol. 1 (1342-1419). London, 1896.

*Calendar of the Patent Rolls preserved in the Public Record Office,* (1317-1377, 19 vols. London, 1903-1916).

*Calendar of the Register of John de Drokensford, Bishop of Bath and Wells, A.D. 1309-1329.* ed. Bishop Hobhouse. (Somerset Rec. Soc.). London, 1887.

CHAPLAIS, PIERRE, ed. "Some Documents Regarding the Fulfillment and Interpretation of the Treaty of Brétigny (1361-1369)," *Camden Miscellany* XIX 1-84 (Camden Soc., Third Series LXXX). London, 1952.

*Chartulary of Winchester Cathedral,* ed. in English by A. W. Goodman. Winchester, 1927.

*Chronica Johannis de Reading et anonymi Cantuariensis, 1346-1367,* ed. James Tait. Manchester, 1914.

*Chronicles of the Reigns of Edward I and Edward II,* ed. William Stubbs. 2 vols. (Rolls Series). London, 1882-1883.

*Chronicon domini Walteri de Hemingburgh, vulgo Hemingford nuncupati . . . de gestis regum Angliae.* ed. H. C. Hamilton. 2 vols. (Eng. Hist. Soc. Pubns.). London, 1848-1849.

*Chronicon Henrici Knighton,* ed. J. R. Lumby. 2 vols. (Rolls Series) London, 1889-1895.

CHURCHILL, IRENE J. *Canterbury Administration.* 2 vols. London, 1933.

*Clement VI, Lettres closes, patentes et curiales se rapportant à la France,* ed. Eugène Déprez et G. Mollat. (Biblio. Écoles franç. d'Athènes et de Rome). Paris, 1901-1961.

*Documents illustrative of English History in the thirteenth and fourteenth centuries,* ed. H. Cole. (Record Commission). London, 1844.

DUGDALE, WILLIAM. *Monasticon Anglicanum.* New edition by John Caley, Henry Ellis and B. Bandinel. 6 vols. in 8 parts. London, 1846.

EMDEN, A. B. *A Biographical Register of the University of Oxford to A.D. 1500.* 3 vols. Oxford, 1957-1959.

EUBEL, CONRAD, ed. *Hierarchia catholica medii aevi (1198-1605).* 3 vols. Münster, 1898-1910.

*Eulogium historiarum sive temporis . . . a monacho quodam Malmesburiensi exaratum,* ed. F. S. Haydon. 3 vols. (Rolls Series). London, 1858-1863.

FIERENS, ALPHONSE, and CAMILLE TIHON. *Lettres d'Urbain V (1362-1370).* 2 vols. (Analecta Vaticano-Belgica). Rome, Brussels, Paris, 1928-1932.

FOURNIER, MARCEL. *Les statuts et les privilèges des universités françaises depuis leur fondation jusqu'en 1789.* 3 vols. Paris, 1890-1894.

GASNAULT, PIERRE. "Notes et documents sur la Chambre Apostolique à l'époque d'Urbain V," *Mélanges d'archéologie et d'histoire.* (Paris) LXX (1958) 369-394.

*Gesta Abbatum Monasterii Sancti Albani a Thoma Walsingham, regnante Ricardo Secundo, ejusdem ecclesiae praecentore, computata,* ed. H. T. Riley. 3 vols. (Rolls Series). London, 1867-69.

GÖLLER, EMIL. *Die Einnahmen der apostolischen Kammer unter Benedikt XII.* Paderborn, 1920.

—— *Die Einnahmen der apostolischen Kammer unter Johann XXII.* Paderborn, 1910.

GUILLEMAIN, BERNARD. *La Cour pontificale d'Avignon (1309-1376)* : étude d'une société. Paris, 1962.

Historical Manuscripts Commission, *Reports,* IX, part 1, London, 1883.

HOBERG, HERMANN. *Die Einnahmen der apostlischen Kammer unter Innocenz VI.* Erster Teil: die einnahmeregister des päpstlichen thesaurars. Paderborn, 1955.

JEAYES, I. H., ed. *Descriptive Catalogue of the charters and muniments belonging to the Marquis of Anglesey* (Staffordshire Rec. Soc.). 1937.

JENSEN, O. "The 'Denarius Sancti Petri' in England." *Trans. Royal Hist. Soc.,* new ser. XV (1901) 171-261; XIX (1905) 209-277.

KIRSCH, JOHANN P. *Die Rückkehr der Päpste Urban V und Gregor XI von Avignon nach Rom: Auszüge aus den Kameralregistern der vatikanischen Archivs.* Paderborn, 1898.

KNOWLES, DAVID, and R. NEVILLE HADCOCK. *Medieval Religious Houses: England and Wales,* London, 1953.

LE NEVE, JOHN. *Fasti Ecclesiae Anglicanae 1300-1541,* (compiled by various authors). Institute of Historical Research, University of London. 11 vols. 1962-1965.

*Le Liber Censuum de l'Eglise romaine,* ed. P. Fabre and L. Duchesne. (Biblio. Écoles franç. d'Athènes et de Rome) Paris, 1889-1905. (1910).—Table des matières by G. Mollat (1952).

*Literae Cantuarienses: the Letter Books of the Monastery of Christ Church, Canterbury,* ed. J. B. Sheppard. 3 vols. (Rolls Series). London, 1887-1889.

LUNT, WILLIAM E. "The Account of a papal collector in England in 1304," *Eng. Hist. Rev.* XXVIII (1913) 313-321.

—— "Collectors' Accounts for the Clerical Tenth levied in England by order of Nicholas IV," *Eng. Hist. Rev.* XXXI (1916) 102-119.

—— "Collectors of Clerical Subsidies," in *English Government at Work 1327-1336,* ed. W. A. Morris and J. R. Strayer. Cambridge, Mass. 1947. Vol. ii, pp. 227-280.

—— *Financial Relations of the Papacy with England to 1327.* Cambridge, Mass., 1939.

—— *Financial Relations of the Papacy with England 1327-1534.* Cambridge, Mass., 1962.

—— *Papal Revenues in the Middle Ages.* 2 vols. New York, 1934.

—— "A Papal Tenth Levied in the British Isles from 1274 to 1280," *Eng. Hist. Rev.* XXXII (1917) 49-89.

—— "William Testa and the Parliament of Carlisle," *Eng. Hist. Rev.* xli (1926) 332-357.

MARTÈNE, EDMOND ET URSIN DURAND. *Thesaurus novus anecdotorum.* 5 vols. Paris, 1717.

MOHLER, LUDWIG. *Die Einnahmen der apostolischen Kammer unter Klemens VI.* Paderborn, 1931.

PERROY, ÉDOUARD. *L'Angleterre et le grand Schisme d'Occident: Étude sur la politique religieuse de l'Angleterre sous Richard II (1378-1399).* Paris, 1933.

*Register of the Diocese of Worcester during the vacancy of the See (1301-1435),* ed. J. W. Willis-Bund. (Worcestershire Hist. Soc.). Oxford, 1897.

*Register of John de Grandisson, Bishop of Exeter (A.D. 1327-1369),* ed. F. C. Hingeston-Randolph. 3 vols. London, 1894-1899.

*Register of John de Halton, Bishop of Carlisle, A.D. 1292-1324,* ed. W. N. Thompson and T. F. Tout. 2 vols. (Canterbury and York Soc.). London, 1913.

*Registers of John de Sandale and Rigaud de Asserio, Bishops of Winchester (A.D. 1316-1323),* ed. F. J. Baigent. (Hampshire Rec. Soc.). London, 1897.

*Register of Ralph of Shrewsbury, Bishop of Bath and Wells, 1329-1363,* ed. T. S. Holmes. 2 vols. (Somerset Rec. Soc.). London, 1896.

*Register of Robert de Stretton:* The registers and act books of the bishops of Coventry and Lichfield. Books 4 and 5, ed. R. A. Wilson. (William Salt. Arch. Soc.). 1907, 1905.

*Register of Roger de Norbury, Bishop of Lichfield and Coventry from A.D. 1322 to A.D. 1358:* an abstract of contents and remarks by Bishop Hobhouse. (*Collections for a history of Staffordshire*) (Wm. Salt Arch. Soc. I, 241-288). Birmingham, 1880.

*Register of Thomas de Brantyngham, Bishop of Exeter (A.D. 1370-1394)*, ed. F. C. Hingeston-Randolph. 2 vols. London, 1901-1906.

*Registrum Ade de Orleton, episcopi Herefordensis, A.D. MCCCXVIII-MCCCXXVII*, ed. A. T. Bannister. (Canterbury and York Soc.). London, 1908.

*Registrum Hamonis Hethe, diocesis Roffensis, A.D. 1319-1352*, ed. Charles Johnson, 2 vols. (Canterbury and York Soc.). London, 1948.

*Registrum Simonis de Sudbiria, diocesis Londoniensis, A.D. MCCCXLIV-MCCCLXI*, ed. J. H. Parry. (Canterbury and York Soc.). London, 1912.

*Registrum Palatinum Dunelmense: The Register of Richard de Kellawe, Lord Palatine and Bishop of Durham 1311-1316*, ed. T. D. Hardy. 4 vols. (Rolls Series). London, 1873-1878.

*Registrum Simonis de Gandavo, diocesis Saresbiriensis, A.D. 1297-1315*, ed. C. T. Flower and M. C. B. Dawes. 2 vols. (Canterbury and York Soc.). London, 1934.

*Registrum Simonis de Langham, Cantuariensis archiepiscopi (1366-68)*, ed. A. C. Wood. (Canterbury and York Soc.). London, 1956.

*Registrum Simonis de Sudbiria diocesis Londoniensis, A.D. 1362-1375*, ed. R. C. Fowler. 2 vols. (Canterbury and York Soc.). London, 1927, 1938.

*Registrum Thome de Charlton Episcopi Herefordensis, A.D. MCCCXXVII-MCCCXLIV*, ed. W. W. Capes. (Canterbury and York Soc.). London, 1913.

*Richard d'Aungerville of Bury, Fragments of his Register, and other documents*. (Surtees Soc. Pubns.). Durham, etc., 1910.

*Rotuli Parliamentorum, ut et Petitiones et Placita in Parliamento*. 6 vols. (Record Comm.). [1783-1832].

RYMER, T., and R. SANDERSON. *Foedera, conventiones, litterae et cuiuscumque generis acta publica inter reges Angliae et alios quovis imperatores, reges, pontifices, principes, vel communitates*, ed. A. Clarke and F. Holbrooke. 4 vols. (Record Comm.). London, 1816-1869.

SAMARAN, C., and G. MOLLAT. *La fiscalité pontificale en France au XIVᵉ siècle*. (Biblio. Écoles franç. d'Athènes et de Rome). Paris, 1905.

SCHÄFER, KARL H. *Die Ausgaben der apostolischen Kammer unter Johann XXII. Nebst den Jahresbilanzen von 1316-1375*. Paderborn, 1911.

—— *Die Ausgaben der apostolischen Kammer unter Benedikt XII, Klemens VI und Innocenz VI (1335-1362)*. Paderborn, 1914.

—— *Die Ausgaben der apostolischen Kammer unter den Päpsten Urban V und Gregor XI (1362-1378)*. Paderborn, 1937.

*Taxatio ecclesiastica Angliae et Walliae auctoritate P. Nicholai IV. circa A.D. 1291*. (Record Comm.). London, 1802.

THEINER, AUGUSTIN. *Vetera Monumenta Hibernorum et Scotorum Historiam illustrantia*, Rome, 1864.

TURNER, WILLIAM H., and HENRY O. COXE. *Calendar of Charters and rolls preserved in the Bodleian Library*. Oxford, 1878.

*Urbain V (1362-1370), Lettres communes analysées d'après les registres dits d'Avignon et du Vatican*, par les membres de l'école française de Rome et M-H. Laurent. vol. 1. Paris, 1954-1958.

*William Thorne's Chronicle of Saint Augustine's Abbey Canterbury*, now rendered into English by A. H. Davis. Oxford, 1934.

*Wykeham's Register*, ed. T. F. Kirby. 2 vols. (Hampshire Rec. Soc.). London, 1886-1889.

# ACCOUNT OF RIGAUD D'ASSIER COLLECTOR FROM 1317 TO 1323

Vatican Archives, Introitus et Exitus 15 [1]

(fol. 1) Hec sunt beneficia vacantia in provinciis Cantuariensi et Eboracensi in primo anno reservationis omnium beneficiorum ecclesiasticorum in ipsis provinciis vacantium per dominum nostrum Dominum Johannem divina providentia papam XXII ad triennium facte, videlicet a vi$^{to}$ idus Decembris anno domini millesimo CCC$^{mo}$ sextodecimo usque ad vi$^{to}$ idus Decembris anno domini millesimo CCC$^{mo}$ decimo nono, ad quorum collectionem fructuum venerabilis vir Dominus Rigaudus de Asser'; tunc canonicus Aurelianensis nunc autem episcopus Wyntoniensis, commissarius principalis fuerat per supradictum dominum papam deputatus.

Nomina beneficiorum vacantium in dyocesi Cantuariensi primo anno reservationis predicte, videlicet a vi$^{to}$ idus Decembris anno domini millesimo CCC$^{mo}$ sextodecimo usque ad idem tempus anno revoluto.

## Cantuariensis

Ecclesia de Demecherch' (Dymchurch) dimissa ad firmam pro taxatione xvii m.; solvit nobis Rigaudo totum.

Prepositura ecclesie prebendalis de Wengham (Wingham) dimissa pro taxatione lx m.; solvit nobis totum.

Ecclesia de Frithendene (Frittenden) dimissa pro taxatione x li.; solvit nobis totum.

Ecclesia de Hope dimissa pro taxatione xx m.; solvit nobis totum.

Vicaria de Apuldre (Appledore) dimissa pro taxatione x m.; inde solvit nobis v m. et commissario v m., et sic solvit totum.

Ecclesia de Wytrichesham (Wittersham) dimissa pro taxatione xxx m; inde solvit nobis xv m. et commissario xv m., et sic solvit totum.

Ecclesia de Boklond (Buckland) dimissa pro taxatione xii m.; inde solvit nobis viii m. et dimidiam.

(fol. 1$^v$) Ecclesia de Stouutyng' (Stowting) dimissa pro taxatione xx m.; solvit nobis totum.

Summa recepta per nos Cantuariensis c iiii$^{xx}$ m. et dimidia.

## Roffensis

Primus annus in dyocesi Roffensi

Vicaria de Lesnes dimissa ad firmam pro taxatione viii m.; solvit nobis totum.

Ecclesia de Northcreye (North Cray) dimissa pro taxatione x m.; solvit nobis totum.

Ecclesia de Dytton' (Ditton) taxata xii m.; dimissa propter exilitatem pro v m.; solvit nobis totum.

Ecclesia de Netlestede (Nettlestead) dimissa pro taxatione viii m.; solvit nobis totum.

[1] Brief extracts from this account have been published in translation: Lunt, *Papal Revenues*, ii, 41-43, 68-70, 330-335.

Ecclesia de Chelesfeld (Chelsfield) dimissa pro taxatione xxx m.; inde solvit nobis xv m.

Summa recepta Roffensis per nos xlvi m.

## (fol. 2) Cycestrensis

Primus annus in dyocesi Cycestrensi

Ecclesia de Berecomp' (Barcombe) dimissa ad firmam pro taxatione xx m.; solvit nobis totum.

Ecclesia de Compton' dimissa pro taxatione xv m.; solvit nobis totum.

Ecclesia de Watlyngton' (Whatlington) taxata vii m., dimissa propter exilitatem pro xx s.; solvit nobis totum.

Ecclesia de Fokynton' (Folkington) dimissa pro taxatione x li.; solvit nobis totum.

Portio prebendalis de Wertlyng' (Wartling) in capella Castri Hasting' taxata xxv m., et quia residuum non sufficit pro oneribus supportandis dimissa pro xvii m. viii s.; solvit nobis totum.

Vicaria de Wysebergh' (Wisborough Green) dimissa pro taxatione x m.; solvit nobis totum.

Prebenda de Selseye (Selsey) in ecclesia Cycestrensi taxata xxx m., dimissa ad firmam pro xxxii m.; solvit nobis totum.

Vicaria de Brighthalmeston' (Brighton) dimissa pro taxatione c s.; solvit nobis totum.

Ecclesia de Fletchyng' (Fletching) dimissa pro taxatione xxv m.; solvit nobis totum.

Ecclesia de Litlington' dimissa pro taxatione x li.; solvit nobis totum.

Ecclesia de Pycombe (Pyecombe) dimissa pro taxatione xxvi m.; solvit nobis totum.

Ecclesia de Rya (Rye) dimissa pro taxatione vii m. dimidia; solvit nobis totum.

(fol. 2$^v$) Ecclesia de Retherefeld (Rotherfield) taxata iiii$^{xx}$ m., dimissa propter exilitatem pro lx m.; inde solvit nobis l m.

Capella de Bello (Battle) dimissa pro taxatione xx m.; solvit nobis totum.

Ecclesia de Alfricheston' (Alfriston) dimissa pro taxatione xxvi m.; solvit nobis totum.

Ecclesia de Erdinglegh' (Ardingley) dimissa pro taxatione xxx m.; solvit nobis totum.

Vicaria de Bolneye (Bolney) taxata c s., dimissa propter exilitatem pro xl s.; solvit nobis totum.

Ecclesia de Torring' (West Tarring) dimissa pro taxatione x m.; solvit nobis totum.

Vicaria de Wylingdon' (Willingdon) dimissa pro taxatione viii m.; solvit nobis totum.

Ecclesia de Nuthurst dimissa pro taxatione x m.; solvit nobis totum.

Ecclesia de Lutegershale (Lurgashall) dimissa pro taxatione x m.; solvit nobis totum.

Ecclesia de Fordes (Ford) dimissa pro taxatione viii m.; solvit nobis totum.

Vicaria de Bernham (Barnham) dimissa pro taxatione viii m.; solvit nobis totum.

Vicaria de Launcyng' (Lancing) dimissa pro taxatione viii m.; solvit nobis totum.

Vicaria de Westfeld (Westfield) taxata x m., dimissa pro v m.; solvit nobis totum.[2]

Summa recepta per nos Cicestrensis ccc iiii^xx viii m. xvi d.

### (fol. 3) Londoniensis

Primus annus in dyocesi Londoniensi [3]

Vicaria de Hilyngdon' (Hillingdon) taxata c s., dimissa ad firmam pro viii m.; solvit nobis totum.

Ecclesia de Reyndon' (Roydon) taxata xx m.; dimissa propter exilitatem pro x m.; solvit nobis totum.

Prebenda de Iseldon' (Islington) dimissa pro taxatione viii m.; solvit nobis totum.

Ecclesia de Berneston' (Barnston) dimissa pro taxatione viii m.; solvit nobis totum.

Ecclesia de Stanewell' (Stanwell) dimissa pro taxatione lx m.; solvit nobis totum.

Ecclesia de Bedefonte (Bedfont) dimissa pro taxatione viii m.; solvit nobis totum.

Ecclesia de Borle (Borley) dimissa pro taxatione xii m.; solvit nobis totum.

Ecclesia de Wokyndon' Episcopi (Cranham or Ockendon Episcopi) dimissa pro taxatione xii m.; solvit nobis totum.

Ecclesia de Upmynstr' (Upminster) dimissa pro taxatione xviii m.; solvit nobis totum.

Ecclesia de Chigewell' (Chigwell) taxata xxv m., dimissa propter exilitatem pro xxii m.; solvit nobis totum.

Ecclesia de Magna Teye (Great Tey) dimissa pro taxatione xxv m.; solvit nobis totum.

Ecclesia de Bergholt' dimissa pro taxatione xi m.; solvit nobis totum.

Ecclesia de Farnham taxata viii m., dimissa pro ix m.; solvit nobis totum.

Ecclesia de Beumont (Beaumont) dimissa pro taxatione vii m.; solvit nobis totum.

Ecclesia de Hakeneye iuxta Londoniam (Hackney) dimissa pro taxatione l m.; solvit nobis totum.

Ecclesia de Pentelowe (Pentlow) dimissa pro taxatione xvii m.; solvit nobis totum.

Prebenda de Kentishton' (Kentish Town) dimissa pro x m.; solvit nobis totum.[4]

Summa recepta Londoniensis cc iiii^xx xv m.

### (fol. 3^v) Wyntoniensis

Primus annus in dyocesi Wyntoniensi

Ecclesia de Ewell' dimissa ad firmam pro taxatione l m.; solvit nobis totum

Ecclesia de Tyches' (Titsey) taxata xviii m. cum portione, dimissa propter exilitatem pro xv m.; solvit nobis totum.

Ecclesia de Ritherhith' (Rotherhithe) taxata x m., dimissa propter exilitatem pro v m.; solvit nobis totum.

Ecclesia Sancti Georgii in Suwerk' (Southwark) dimissa pro taxatione x m.; solvit nobis totum.

Ecclesia de Wynchefeld (Winchfield) dimissa pro taxatione xx m.; solvit nobis totum.

Ecclesia de Wolferton' (Woolverton) dimissa pro taxatione xi m.; solvit nobis totum.

Ecclesia de Alresford dimissa pro taxatione xl m.; solvit nobis totum.

Ecclesia de Gratele (Grately) taxata x m., dimissa pro xiii m.; solvit nobis totum.

Ecclesia de Anna Bek' (Anne Beck) taxata x m, dimissa pro xi m.; solvit nobis totum.

Ecclesia de Eston' Crok' (Easton in Longparish) dimissa pro taxatione viii m.; solvit nobis totum.

Ecclesia de Compton' dimissa pro taxatione xx m.; solvit nobis totum.

Ecclesia Beate Marie de Vall' (St. Mary in the Valley, Winchester) cum capella de Wyk' (Weeke) dimissa pro taxatione xv m.; solvit nobis totum.

Ecclesia de Bynteworth' (Bentworth) dimissa pro taxatione xxvi m.; solvit nobis totum.

Ecclesia de Wymbeldon' (Wimbledon) dimissa pro taxatione lx m.; solvit nobis totum.

Ecclesia de Cheyham (Cheam) dimissa pro taxatione xxv m.; solvit nobis totum.[5]

Summa recepta Wintoniensis per nos cccxxix m.

### (fol. 4) Sarisberiensis

Primus annus in dyocesi Sarisberiensi

Vicaria de Portesham (Portisham) taxata c s., dimissa pro viii m.; solvit nobis totum.

Vicaria de Abbodesbur' (Abbotsbury) taxata x m., dimissa pro xii m.; solvit nobis totum.

Ecclesia de Swyntolre (Toller Porcorum) taxata ix m., dimissa pro xii m.; solvit nobis totum.

Ecclesia de Wyk' (Wyke Regis) dimissa pro taxatione xx m.; solvit nobis totum.

Ecclesia de Betescombe (Bettiscombe) taxata vi m. dimidia, dimissa pro ix m.; solvit nobis totum.

Ecclesia de Stupel (Steeple) dimissa pro taxatione vii m.; solvit nobis totum.

Ecclesia seu prebenda de Gyllingham (Gillingham) taxata xxx li., dimissa pro l m., solvit nobis totum.

Ecclesia de Fifhyde (Fifehead) dimissa pro taxatione vi m. dimidia; solvit nobis totum.

---

[2] Entered in the margin at the papal camera: *non est in certificatione*. It probably refers to the list of all benefices vacant during the three years which each bishop was required to compile for his diocese and send to the camera at the end of the period.

[3] *Londoniensi* repeated MS.

[4] In the margin: *Non est in certificatione*.

---

[5] In the margin: *Non est in certificatione*.

Ecclesia de Holewale (Holwell) taxata c s., dimissa pro xi m.; solvit nobis totum.

Ecclesia de Caneford (Canford) dimissa pro taxatione x m.; solvit nobis totum.

Ecclesia de Lytchet Mautravers (Lytchet Matravers) dimissa pro taxatione x m.; solvit nobis totum.

Ecclesia de Wynterborn' Hughtton' (Winterborne Houghton) dimissa pro taxatione c s.; solvit nobis totum.

(fol. 4v) Ecclesia de Boklond (Buckland Ripers) dimissa pro taxatione xv m.; solvit nobis totum.

Ecclesia de Mapudre (Mappowder) taxata c s., dimissa pro viii m.; solvit nobis totum.

Ecclesia de Tarente Hyneton' (Tarrant Hinton) dimissa pro taxatione x m.; solvit nobis totum.

Ecclesia de Tarente Keygnes (Tarrant Keynston) taxata vi m., dimissa pro vii m.; solvit nobis totum.

Prebenda de Writelyngton' (Writhlington) et Fordington' taxata xxv m., dimissa pro xl m.; solvit nobis totum.

Prebenda de Cherdestok (Chardstock) dimissa pro taxatione xxiiii m.; solvit nobis totum.

Ecclesia Sancti Nicholai Abbendon' (Abingdon) dimissa pro taxatione xiii m.; solvit nobis totum.

Ecclesia de Chelreye (Childrey) dimissa pro taxatione xxx m.; solvit nobis totum.

Ecclesia de Clyfware (Clewer) dimissa pro taxatione xv m.; solvit nobis totum.

Ecclesia de Fynchamstede (Finchhampstead) dimissa pro taxatione vi m. dimidia; solvit nobis totum.

Vicaria de Okham[6] (Cookham) dimissa pro taxatione vi m. dimidia; solvit nobis totum.

Ecclesia de Estgarston' (East Garston) taxata xviii m., dimissa pro xx m.; solvit nobis totum.

Ecclesia de Westhildesle (West Ilsley) dimissa pro taxatione xv m.; solvit nobis totum.

Ecclesia de Brightewell' (Brightwell) taxata xxv m., dimissa pro xxx m.; solvit nobis totum.

Prebenda de Blebur' (Blewbury) taxata lx m., et quia residuum non sufficit pro oneribus dimissa pro l m.; solvit nobis totum.

Ecclesia de Compton' Chamberlayn (Compton Chamberlain) taxata xx m., dimissa pro xxv m.; solvit nobis totum.

Ecclesia de Tidols fide (Tilshead) taxata xxv m., et quia residuum non sufficit pro oneribus dimissa pro xv m.; solvit nobis totum.

Prebenda de Archesfonte (Urchfont) taxata xviii m., dimissa pro xx m.; solvit nobis totum.

Vicaria de Edyndon' (Edington) dimissa pro taxatione x m.; solvit nobis totum.

Ecclesia de Kyvele (Keevil) dimissa pro taxatione xl m.; solvit nobis totum.

Ecclesia de Wyntereslewe (Winterslow) dimissa pro taxatione xviii m.; solvit nobis totum.

Ecclesia de Boscombe dimissa pro taxatione vi m. dimidia; solvit nobis totum.

Thesauraria in ecclesia Sarisberiensi cum prebenda de Calne dimissa pro taxatione cxxx m.; solvit nobis totum.

Ecclesia de Yatesbur' (Yatesbury) dimissa pro taxatione xv m.; solvit nobis totum.

Ecclesia de Colynburn' (Collingbourne) Comitis taxata x m., dimissa pro xv m; solvit nobis totum.

Archidiaconatus Wyltes' (Wilts) dimissus pro taxatione l m.; solvit nobis totum.

Prebenda de Rothefen' (Rotefen) dimissa pro taxatione x m.; solvit nobis totum.[7]

Prebenda de Rosecamp' (Ruscombe) dimissa pro xv m.; solvit nobis totum.

Vicaria de Canyng' (Cannings) dimissa pro xvi m.; solvit nobis totum.

Summa recepta per nos Sarisberiensis viii[c] xxxviii m. et dimidia.

## (fol 5) Exoniensis

Primus annus in dyocesi Exoniensi.

Ecclesia de Merewode (Marwood) dimissa pro taxatione viii li.; solvit nobis totum.

Ecclesia de Suthmeton' (South Molton) dimissa pro taxatione xx m.; solvit commissario[8] totum.

Ecclesia de Biri Nerberd (Berry Narbor) taxata viii li.; dimissa pro xiii m. dimidia; solvit commissario totum.

Precentoria in ecclesia Exoniensi cum ecclesia de Peyngton' (Paignton) dimissa pro taxatione xlv m.; solvit commissario totum.

Ecclesia de Mouseby (Musbury) dimissa pro taxatione viii li. xiii s. iiii d.; solvit commissario totum.

(fol. 5v) Ecclesia de Newenton' (Newton St. Cyres) dimissa pro taxatione viii li.; solvit commissario totum.

Ecclesia de Kentelesber' (Kentisbeare) dimissa pro taxatione ix m. dimidia; solvit commissario totum.

Ecclesia de Torre Brian (Tor Bryan) dimissa pro taxatione vii m.; solvit commisario totum.

Ecclesia de Inwardelegh' (Inwardleigh) taxata vi li. vi s. viii d., dimissa pro c s.; solvit commissario totum.

Ecclesia de Thurleston' (Thurlestone) dimissa pro taxatione vii m.; solvit commissario totum.

Ecclesia de Lodeswell' (Loddiswell) dimissa pro taxatione xii m.; solvit commissario totum.

Ecclesia de Manaton' dimissa pro taxatione vii m.; solvit commissario totum.

Ecclesia de Nortbur' (Norbury) dimissa pro xii m.; solvit commissario totum.

Ecclesia de Northull' (North Hill) dimissa pro taxatione ix m.; solvit commissario totum.

---

[6] The vicarage which the bishop of Salisbury certified to Rigaud as vacant was *Coxham* in the deanery of Reading: Salisbury Diocesan Registry, Reg. of Mortivali, ii, fol. 82(90).

[7] In the margin bracketed against this and the next two items: *Non sunt in certificatione.*

[8] The commissioner in the diocese of Exeter was the abbot of Tavistock: Lunt, *Papal Revenues*, ii, 330.

Ecclesia de Mahynieth' (Menheniot or Menhynnet) dimissa pro taxatione xii m.; solvit commissario totum.

Ecclesia de Quedyk (Quethlock or Quithick) dimissa pro taxatione c s.; solvit commissario totum.

Ecclesia de Bonelegh (Bondleigh) dimissa pro taxatione iiii li. v s.; solvit commissario totum.

Ecclesia de Northtauton' (North Tawton) dimissa pro taxatione viii li. xiii s. iiii d.; solvit commissario totum.

Ecclesia de Lappeford (Lapford) dimissa pro taxatione vi li.; solvit commissario totum.

Ecclesia de Esse (Ash) dimissa pro xiiii m.; solvit commissario totum.

Ecclesia de Wytherigg' (Witheridge) dimissa pro taxatione xx li.; inde solvit commissario xviii m.

Summa recepta per nos Exoniensis xii m. Item per commissarium ccliiii m. v s.

### (fol. 6) Bathoniensis et Wellensis

Primus annus in dyocesi Bathoniensi et Wellensi.

Ecclesia de Corston' dimissa ad firmam pro taxatione xx m.; solvit nobis totum.

Ecclesia de Compton' Pauncefot taxata x m.; dimissa pro xi m.; solvit nobis totum.

Ecclesia de Hemyngton' (Hemington) dimissa pro taxatione xix m.; solvit nobis totum.

Ecclesia de Pulton' (Paulton) pro precentore dimissa pro taxatione xxx m.; solvit nobis totum.

Ecclesia de Exeford (Exford) dimissa pro taxatione x m.; solvit nobis totum.

Ecclesia de Compton' Martyn (Compton Martin) dimissa pro taxatione xiiii m.; solvit nobis totum.

Prebenda de Wondestr' (Wanstrow) dimissa pro taxatione viii m.; solvit nobis totum.

Ecclesia de Blakedon' (Blagdon) taxata xii m., dimissa pro xiii m.; solvit nobis totum.

Summa recepta per nos Bathoniensis cxxv m.

### (fol. 6ᵛ) Coventrensis

Primus annus in dyocesi Coventrensi et Lychfeldensi.

Ecclesia de Solihull' taxata xxx m., dimissa pro xxxv m.; solvit nobis totum.

Ecclesia de Stokton' (Stockton) dimissa pro taxatione ix m.; solvit nobis totum.

Ecclesia de Berkeswell' (Berkswell) dimissa pro taxatione xx m.; solvit nobis totum.

Portio quondam Rolandi in ecclesia de Wroxcestr' (Wroxeter) dimissa pro taxatione xx m.; solvit nobis totum.

Ecclesia de Mudle (Middle) dimissa pro taxatione xxx m.; solvit nobis totum.

Ecclesia de Wityngton' (Whittington) taxata x m.; dimissa propter exilitatem pro lxxiiii s. viii d. obolo quadrante; solvit nobis totum.

Vicaria de Cesterfeld (Chesterfield) dimissa pro taxatione x m.; solvit nobis totum.

Ecclesia de Kersington' (Carsington) dimissa pro taxatione c s.; solvit nobis totum.

Ecclesia de Sudbur' (Sudbury) dimissa pro taxatione xx m.; solvit nobis totum.

Ecclesia de Eyum (Eyam) taxata xx m., et quia residuum non sufficit pro oneribus dimissa pro xvi m.; solvit nobis totum.

Ecclesia de Cloune (Clown) dimissa pro taxatione x m.; solvit nobis totum.

Ecclesia de Aldeford (Aldford) dimissa pro taxatione x li.; solvit nobis totum.

Ecclesia de Haywarthyn (Hawardon) dimissa pro taxatione xx m.; solvit nobis totum.

Ecclesia de Mottrum (Mottram) taxata x li., dimissa pro xvi m.; solvit nobis totum.

Ecclesia de Elleford (Elford) dimissa pro taxatione viii m.; solvit nobis totum.

Prebenda quondam Willelmi de Eston' in Gnoushale (Gnosall) taxata x m., dimissa ad firmam pro xi m.; solvit nobis totum.

(fol. 7) Ecclesia de Stok' (Stoke-on Trent) dimissa pro taxatione lx m.; solvit nobis totum.

Decanatus de Tameworth' (Tamworth) dimissus pro taxatione x m.; solvit nobis totum.

Ecclesia de Worfeld (Worfield) dimissa pro taxatione l m.; inde solvit nobis xlv m.

Ecclesia Lullyngton' (Lullington) dimissa pro xii m.; solvit nobis totum.[9]

Ecclesia de Acton' Blundel (Acton Burnell) non taxata, dimissa pro vi m.; solvit nobis totum.

Prebenda de Salwe (Sawley) dimissa pro taxatione c m.; solvit nobis totum.

Summa recepta Coventrensis per nos iiiiᶜ iiiiˣˣ v m. iiii s. viii d. obolus quadrans.

### Wygorniensis

Primus annus in dyocesi Wygorniensi.

Portio decanatus ecclesie collegiate de Westbur' (Westbury) dimissa pro xv m. dimidia; solvit nobis totum.

Ecclesia de Chaddeseye (Chaddesley Corbett) dimissa pro xlv m.; solvit commissario[10] totum.

Ecclesia de la Holte (Holt) dimissa pro xx m.; solvit commissario totum.

Ecclesia de Solautr' Superiori (Upper Slaughter) taxata x m., dimissa pro xiii m.; solvit commissario totum.

Ecclesia de Herforton' (Harvington) dimissa pro taxatione x m.; solvit commissario totum.

Ecclesia de Wytton Beate Marie (Witton St. Mary) taxata vii m., dimissa pro x m.; solvit commissario totum.

---

[9] In the margin bracketed against this and the next two items: *Non sunt in certificatione.*

[10] The commissioner in the diocese of Worcester was the abbot of Evesham.

Ecclesia de Overbur' (Overbury) taxata xxiii m., dimissa pro xxxvi m.; solvit commissario totum.

Ecclesia de Kemeseye (Kempsey) taxata xl m., dimissa pro l m;. solvit commissario totum.

(fol. 7ᵛ) Ecclesia de Wotton' (Wooton Leek) taxata liii m., dimissa pro lxi m. dimidia; solvit commissario totum.

Vicaria de Berkeleye (Berkeley) taxata xix m., dimissa pro xxv m.; inde solvit nobis vi m. xii s. iiii d. et commissario xviii m. xii d. et sic solvit [11] totum.

Ecclesia de Wodechestr' (Woodchester) dimissa pro taxatione x m.; solvit commissario totum.

Ecclesia de Maderefeld (Madresfield) taxata vi m., dimissa pro c s.; solvit commissario totum.

Ecclesia de Crombe (Croome) dimissa pro taxatione vii m.; solvit commissario totum.

Ecclesia de Weston' bret (Weston Birt) dimissa pro taxatione c s.; solvit commissario totum.

Ecclesia de Baggeleye (Beoley) dimmissa pro taxatione xii m. dimidia; solvit commissario totum.

Ecclesia de Estouwe (Stow on the Wold) dimissa pro taxatione xii m.; solvit commissario totum.

Ecclesia de Hullecombe (Croome Hill) dimissa pro taxatione vii m. iiii s.; solvit commissario totum.

Vicaria Beate Marie ante Portam Albam (Gloucester) dimissa pro taxatione xxiii m.; solvit commissario totum.

Ecclesia de Frompton' Cotel (Frampton Cotterell) dimissa pro taxatione xi m.; solvit commissario totum.

Ecclesia de Elkeston' (Elkstone) taxata xv m., dimissa pro v m.; solvit commissario totum.

De archidiaconatu Gloucestrie recepimus xxi m.[12]

Summa recepta per nos Wygoriensis xliii m. v s. viii d. Item per commissarium ccclxvi m. v s.

### (fol. 8) Herefordensis

Primus annus in dyocesi Herefordensi.

Prebenda de Cherchewythynton' (Church Withington) taxata vii li. xvi d., dimissa pro vii li.; solvit nobis totum.

Ecclesia de Staunton' (Staunton on Arrow) dimissa pro taxatione x m.; solvit nobis totum.

Ecclesia de Munstreworth' (Minsterworth) dimissa pro taxatione x li.; solvit nobis totum.

Ecclesia de Aure (Awre) dimissa pro taxatione lx m.; solvit nobis totum.

Ecclesia de Chircham (Churcham) dimissa pro taxatione viii m.; solvit nobis totum.

Prebenda de Berton' (Barton) cum thesauraria Herfordensi dimissa pro taxatione xxix li. x s.; solvit commissario [13] totum.

Vicaria ecclesie Omnium Sanctorum (Hereford) dimissa pro taxatione c s.; solvit commissario totum.

Vicaria de Norton' (Norton Canon) dimissa pro taxatione vii m.; solvit commissario totum.

Vicaria de Eya (Eye) dimissa pro taxatione vi m. dimidia; solvit commissario totum.

Ecclesia de Sapy (Sapey) dimissa pro taxatione vii m.; solvit commissario totum.

Ecclesia de Thaddesterne de la Mare (Tedstone Delamere) dimissa pro taxatione vii m.; solvit commissario totum.

Ecclesia de Westbur' (Westbury) dimissa pro taxatione l m.; solvit commissario totum.

Ecclesia de Culmynton' (Culmington) dimissa pro taxatione x li.; solvit commissario totum.

Portio in ecclesia de Holgate (Holdgate) dimissa pro taxatione vi li.; solvit commissario totum.

Portio in ecclesia de Burford dimissa pro taxatione ix li.; solvit commissario totum.

Ecclesia de Hopesay dimissa pro taxatione x m.; solvit commissario totum.

Summa recepta per nos Herfordensis ciii m. et dimedia. Item per commissarium clxxvi m. x s.

### (fol. 8ᵛ) Menevensis

Primus annus in dyocesi Menevensi.

Ecclesia de Burton' dimissa pro taxatione xii m.; solvit commissario [14] totum.

Ecclesia de Laurenny (Lawrenny) dimissa pro taxatione xii m.; solvit commissario totum.

Ecclesia de Talagharn (Talycharn or Laugharne) dimissa pro taxatione xl m.; solvit commissario totum.

Ecclesia de Lamethly (Llanelly) dimissa pro taxatione x li.; solvit commissario totum.

Ecclesia de Swynese (Swansea) dimissa pro taxatione x li.; solvit commissario totum.

Ecclesia de Lansanfred (Llansantfraed) dimissa pro taxatione viii m.; solvit commissario totum.

Ecclesia de Trachlan (Talachddu) dimissa pro taxatione viii m.; solvit commissario totum.

Ecclesia de Lancadok (Llangattock) iuxta Crughowel (Crickhowel) taxata xxiiii m., dimissa ad firmam pro lv s. quia nichil plus haberi potuit, ut asseruit commissarius; solvit nobis totum.

Ecclesia de Castro Walwayn (Walwyn's Castle) dimissa pro taxatione xiiii m.; inde solvit nobis vii m. dimidiam et commissario vi m. dimidiam; et sic solvit totum.

Summa recepta per nos Menevensis vii m. et dimidia. Item per commissarium cxx m. viii s. iiii d.

### (fol. 9) Landavensis

Primus annus in dyocesi Landavensi.

---

[11] Followed by *commissario* deleted by a line in manuscript.

[12] In the margin: *Non est in certificatione. Dies non annus vacatur.*

[13] The commissioner in the diocese of Hereford was the bishop of Hereford.

[14] The bishop of Hereford was the commissioner in the diocese of St. Davids.

Ecclesia de Troya (Troy) dimissa pro taxatione xx li.; solvit commissario [15] totum.

Summa patet.

### Bangorensis

Primus annus in dyocesi Bangorensi.

Portio David in ecclesia de Landynan (Llandinam) taxata vii m., dimissa pro vi m.; solvit commissario [16] totum.

Portio alterius decani in ecclesia de Twyn (Towyn) taxata viii m. dimidia, dimissa pro c s.; solvit commissario totum.

Portio Jevan Velyn in ecclesia de Aberdaron dimissa pro taxatione vi m. dimidia; solvit commissario totum.

Summa recepta Bangorensis per commissarium xx m.

### (fol. 9ᵛ) Assavensis

Primus annus in dyocesi Assavensi.

Decanatus Assavensis dimissus pro xxxv m.; solvit commissario totum.

Ecclesia de Lavoryn (Llanwrin) taxata ix, dimissa pro xii m.; solvit commissario totum.

Ecclesia de Landervael (Llandderfel) dimissa pro taxatione vii m. dimidia; solvit commissario totum.

Ecclesia de Machynlleyth (Machynlleth) taxata ix m., dimissa pro iiii m. dimidia; solvit commissario totum.

Summa recepta Assavensis per commissarium lix m.

### Norwycensis

Primus annus in dyocesi Norwycensi.

Ecclesia de Causton' (Cawston) dimissa pro taxatione l m.; solvit nobis totum.

Ecclesia de Acle dimissa pro taxatione xlv m.; solvit nobis totum.

Ecclesia de Fornsete (Forncett) dimissa pro taxatione xxx m.; solvit nobis totum.

Ecclesia de Brisingham (Bressingham) dimissa pro taxatione xxiiii m.; solvit nobis totum.

Ecclesia de Fyncham (Fincham) Sancti Michaelis dimissa pro taxatione xvi m.; solvit nobis totum.

Ecclesia de Thurgarton' dimissa pro taxatione xiiii m.; solvit nobis totum.

Ecclesia de Kertlyng' (Kirtling) dimissa pro taxatione xx li.; solvit nobis totum.

Ecclesia de Kenet (Kennett) dimissa pro taxatione xviii m.; solvit nobis totum.

Ecclesia de Rysangle (Rishangles) dimissa pro taxatione viii li.; solvit nobis totum.

Ecclesia de Thorndon' dimissa pro taxatione xl m.; solvit nobis totum.

(fol. 10) Ecclesia de Brandenesene (Barnardiston) dimissa pro taxatione xx li.; solvit nobis totum.

Ecclesia de Welles (Wells-next-the-Sea) dimissa pro taxatione xxxii m.; solvit commissario [17] totum.

Ecclesia de Wytton' (Wighton) dimissa pro taxatione xii m.; solvit commissario totum.

Ecclesia de Saham taxata xvii m., dimissa pro xl m.; solvit commissario totum.

Ecclesia de Puddyng Northon' (Pudding Norton) dimissa pro taxatione x li.; solvit commissario totum.

Ecclesia de Refham (Reepham) Omnium Sanctorum dimissa pro taxatione x li.; solvit commissario totum.

Ecclesia de Estbarsham (East Barsham) taxata x li., dimissa pro xx m.; solvit commissario totum.

Ecclesia de Wetacr' (West Acre) Omnium Sanctorum dimissa pro taxatione c s.; solvit commissario totum.

Ecclesia de Wetacre Sancti Petri dimissa pro taxatione xi m.; solvit commissario totum.

Ecclesia de Morlee (Morley) taxata xxxiiii m., dimissa pro xxx m.; solvit commissario totum.

Ecclesia de Colton' dimissa pro taxatione x li.; solvit commissario totum.

Ecclesia de Kirkestede (Kirstead) taxata x m., dimissa pro xii m.; solvit commissario totum.

Medietas ecclesie de Northtodenham (North Tuddenham) taxata xii m., dimissa pro xiii m.; solvit commissario totum.

Ecclesia de Haleholm (Holme Hale) Sancti Andree dimissa pro taxatione x m.; solvit commissario totum.

Ecclesia de Cranewyg (Cranwich) dimissa pro taxatione x li.; solvit commissario totum.

Ecclesia de Wynbodesham (Wimbotsham) dimissa pro taxatione x m.; solvit commissario totum.

Ecclesia de Lesingham (Lessingham) dimissa pro taxatione xi m.; solvit commissario totum.

Ecclesia de Cressingham dimissa pro taxatione xxi m.; solvit commissario totum.

Ecclesia de Eston' (Easton) taxata x m., dimissa pro xii m.; solvit commissario totum.

Ecclesia de Brandon' dimissa pro taxatione x m. dimidia; solvit commissario totum.

Ecclesia de Fakenhamdam (Hempton) dimissa pro taxatione iiiiˣˣ m.; solvit commissario totum.

Ecclesia de Estbradenham (East Bradenham) taxata xxii m. et propter sterilitatem dimissa pro ix m.; solvit commissario totum.

Ecclesia seu vicaria de Hecham (Heacham) dimissa pro taxatione viii m.; solvit commissario totum.

Ecclesia de Palegrave (Palgrave) dimissa pro taxatione xx li.; solvit commissario totum.

Ecclesia de Wrottyng' parva (Little Wratting) dimissa pro taxatione viii m.; solvit commissario totum.

Ecclesia de Neweton' (Newton) dimissa pro taxatione x m.; solvit commissario totum.

Ecclesia de Briseword (Braiseworth) dimissa pro taxatione c s.; solvit commissario totum.

---

[15] The commissioner in the diocese of Llandaff was the bishop of Hereford.

[16] The commissioner in the dioceses of Bangor and St. Asaph was the bishop of Hereford.

[17] The commissioner in the diocese of Norwich was Master Thomas de Hales (or Helles).

Ecclesia de Stanstede (Stanstead) dimissa pro taxatione x li.; solvit commissario totum.

Ecclesia de Brom (Brome) dimissa pro taxatione c s.; solvit commissario totum.

Ecclesia de Hornyngesherth' (Horningsheath) dimissa pro taxatione vii m.; solvit commissario totum.

(fol. 10ᵛ) Ecclesia de Henstede (Henstead) dimissa pro taxatione xviii m.; solvit commissario totum.

Ecclesia de Coulyng' (Cowlinge) dimissa pro taxatione xx li.; inde solvit nobis x m. et commissario xx m., et sic solvit totum.

Medietas ecclesie de Westwalton' (West Walton) dimissa pro taxatione xviii m.; inde solvit nobis x m.

Ecclesia de Byskele (Bixley) taxata x li., dimissa pro xviii m.; inde solvit nobis viii m.

Portio de Shetford in ecclesia de Mendham dimissa pro taxatione vi m. dimidia; inde solvit commissario xl s.

Vicaria de Acton' dimissa pro taxatione xiiii m.; solvit commissario totum.[18]

Summa recepta Norwycensis per nos cccxxxvii m. Item per commissarium vᶜ xlix m.

## (fol. 11) Elyensis

Primus annus in dyocesi Elyensi.

Ecclesia de Pappeworth' (Papworth St. Agnes) dimissa pro taxatione x li.; solvit commissario [19] totum.

Ecclesia de Teveresham (Teversham) dimissa pro taxatione xxii m.; solvit commissario totum.

Ecclesia de Shelford parva taxata xvi m., dimissa pro xix m.; solvit commissario totum.

Ecclesia de Gritton' (Girton) dimissa pro taxatione lv m.; solvit nobis totum.

Ecclesia de Staunton (Long Stanton) Sancti Michaelis dimissa pro taxatione xx m.; inde solvit nobis v m. et commissario xv m., et sic solvit totum.

Summa recepta per nos Eliensis lx m. Item per commissarium lxxi m.

## (fol. 11ᵛ) Lincolniensis

Primus annus in dyocesi Lincolniensi

Ecclesia de Horsington' dimissa pro taxatione xii m. dimidia; solvit nobis totum.

Ecclessia de Enderby Malbys (Mavis Enderby) dimissa pro taxatione xvii m.; solvit nobis totum.

Medietas ecclesie de Carleby (Carlby) dimissa pro taxatione xv m.; solvit nobis totum.

Ecclesia de Walseby (Walesby) dimissa pro taxatione xlii m.; solvit nobis totum.

Ecclesia de Swalowe (Swallow) dimissa pro taxatione xxiiii m.; solvit nobis totum.

Vicaria Sancti Jacobi de Grimesby (Great Grimsby) dimissa pro taxatione xiiii m.; solvit nobis totum.

Ecclesia de Irby dimissa pro taxatione xxii m.; solvit nobis totum.

Ecclesia de Wassingburn' (Washingborough) dimissa pro taxatione iiiixx xii m.; solvit nobis totum.

Ecclesia de Gedeneye (Gedney) dimissa pro taxatione xxii m.; solvit nobis totum.

Ecclesia de Suthichame (South Hykeham) taxata xxx m. xl d., et quia residuum non sufficit pro oneribus quia terre fuerunt inculte dimissa pro xx m.; solvit nobis totum.

Vicaria partis borealis de Graham (Grantham) dimissa pro taxatione xvi m. dimidia; solvit nobis totum.

Vicaria de Haxay (Haxey) dimissa pro taxatione xx m.; solvit nobis totum.

Ecclesia de Halton' (Halton) dimissa pro taxatione xl m.; solvit nobis totum.

Ecclesia de Bringhurst taxata xxxix m. x s. iiii d., dimissa pro xl m.; solvit nobis totum.

Ecclesia de Saxeby (Saxby) dimissa pro taxatione vii m. dimidia; solvit nobis totum.

Ecclesia de Wymondesham (Wymondham) dimissa pro taxatione xvi m.; solvit nobis totum.

Ecclesia de Scaldeford (Scalford) taxata xvi m., dimissa propter exilitatem pro viii m.; solvit nobis totum.

Ecclesia de Peghtelton' (Peckleton) dimissa pro taxatione ix m. vi s. viii d.; solvit nobis totum.

Ecclesia de Blyseworth' (Blisworth) dimissa pro taxatione x m.; solvit nobis totum.

Ecclesia de Hargrave dimissa pro taxatione xiii m.; solvit nobis totum.

Ecclesia de Barthon' Henred (Barton Seagrave) dimissa pro taxatione xvi m.; solvit nobis totum.

Ecclesia de Deen' (Deene) dimissa pro taxatione xx m.; solvit nobis totum.

Ecclesia de Corby dimissa pro taxatione x m.; solvit nobis totum.

Ecclesia de Cotherstok' (Cotterstock) dimissa pro taxatione xx m.; solvit nobis totum.

Ecclesia de Barthon' (Barton) dimissa pro taxatione xxiiii m.; solvit nobis totum.

Ecclesia de Everdon' dimissa pro xviii m.; solvit nobis totum.

Vicaria de Kymeton' (Kimpton) taxata vii m. dimidia, dimissa pro xi m.; solvit nobis totum.

(fol. 12) Ecclesia de Aldenham dimissa pro taxatione xix m.; solvit nobis totum.

Ecclesia de Baudak' (Baldock) dimissa pro taxatione ix m.; solvit nobis totum.

Vicaria de Lutton' taxata xxiiii m., et quia residuum non sufficit pro oneribus dimissa pro xv m.; solvit nobis totum.

Medietas ecclesia de Elnestouwe (Elstow) dimissa pro taxatione vii m.; solvit nobis totum.

Ecclesia de Craunfeld (Cranfield) dimissa pro taxatione xxx m.; solvit nobis totum.

Ecclesia de Bledelawe (Bledlow) taxata xxx m., dimissa pro l m.; solvit nobis totum.

Ecclesia de Magna Hampden' dimissa pro taxatione x m.; solvit nobis totum.

---

[18] In the margin: *Non est in certificatione.*
[19] The commissioner was Master Thomas de Hales.

Ecclesia de Drayton' Beauchamp (Drayton Beauchamp) taxata xiii m.; dimissa pro xiiii m.; solvit nobis totum.

Ecclesia de Swerford dimissa pro taxatione x m.; solvit nobis totum.

Ecclesia de Crowell' dimissa pro taxatione x m.; solvit nobis totum.

Ecclesia de Torresmere (Tusmore) dimissa pro taxatione ix m.; solvit nobis totum.

Ecclesia de Hanewell' (Hanwell) taxata xi m.; dimissa pro xiiii m.; solvit nobis totum.

Ecclesia de Broghton' (Broughton) taxata xx m., dimissa pro xxv m.; solvit nobis totum.

Tertia pars ecclesie de Repinghale (Rippingale) dimissa pro taxatione xviii m.; solvit nobis totum.

Medietas ecclesie de Westburgh' (Westborough) dimissa pro taxatione xxx m.; solvit nobis totum.

Vicaria ecclesie de Multon' (Moulton) dimissa pro taxatione l m.; solvit nobis totum.

Ecclesia de Houghton' dimissa pro taxatione l m.; solvit nobis totum.

Ecclesia de Magna Lynford (Great Linford) dimissa pro taxatione xv m.; solvit nobis totum.

Thesauraria ecclesie Lincolniensis taxata xxx m., dimissa pro xxxvi m.; solvit nobis totum.

Ecclesia de Emynton' (Emmington) dimissa pro taxatione vi m. dimidia; solvit nobis totum.

Ecclesia de Staynton' iuxta Langwath' (Stainton by Langworth) cum pensione dimissa pro taxatione xxx m.; solvit commissario [20] totum.

Medietas ecclesie de Claypol (Claypole) dimissa pro taxatione xxv m.; solvit commissario totum.

Ecclesia de Salmanby (Salmonby) dimissa pro taxatione viii m. dimidia; solvit commissario totum.

Medietas ecclesie de Saltfleteby (Saltfleetby) Sancti Clementis dimissa pro xii m.; solvit commissario totum.

Ecclesia de Graynesby (Grainsby) dimissa pro taxatione xx m.; solvit commissario totum.

Ecclesia de Magna Cotes (Great Coates) dimissa pro taxatione l m.; solvit commissario totum.

Ecclesia de Gretham (Greetham) dimissa pro taxatione xx m. dimidia; inde solvit commissario xvii m. dimidiam et nobis iii m., et sic solvit totum.

Ecclesia de Ouston' (Owston) dimissa pro taxatione lx m.; inde solvit abbati Beate Marie Eboracensis [21] lx m., solvit totum abbati Eboracensi.

(fol. 12ᵛ) Ecclesia de Retherefeld Grey (Rotherfield Greys) dimissa pro taxatione xii m.; inde solvit nobis vi m.

Item recepta de prebenda de Cropery (Cropredy), taxata ad c m., xxiii m. xl d.

Ecclesia de Hamerton' dimissa pro taxatione vii m.

Vicaria in ecclesia de Bampton' dimissa pro taxatione xx m.

Summa recepta Lincolniensis per nos mˡ xxxix m. x s. Item per commissarium ccxxiii m.

## (fol. 13) Eboracensis

Primus annus in dyocesi Eboracensi

Ecclesia de Spoford (Spofforth) dimissa pro taxatione cxx m.; solvit nobis totum.

Ecclesia de Ewesleye (Yearsley) dimissa pro taxatione xxxviii m.; solvit nobis totum.

Archidiaconatus Richem' (Richmond) taxatus cc li., dimissus propter exilitatem pro c li.; solvit nobis totum.

Prebenda de Fenton' dimissa pro lx m.; solvit nobis totum.

Prebenda Sancti Michaelis in ecclesia Sancti Johannis Beverlaci (Beverley) dimissa pro taxatione xvii li., solvit nobis totum.

Prebenda de Northwell' (Norwell) in ecclesia Suwell' (Southwell) dimissa pro taxatione xl m.; solvit nobis totum.

Ecclesia Sancti Michaelis ad pontem Use (St. Michael at Ouse Bridge, York) dimissa pro taxatione c s.; solvit commissario [22] totum.

Ecclesia Sancte Crucis Eboracensis dimissa pro taxatione c s.; solvit commissario totum.

Ecclesia Omnium Sanctorum in Havergate (York) dimissa pro taxatione vii m.; solvit commissario totum.

(fol. 13ᵛ) Ecclesia de Hoton Wandesley (Hutton Wandesley) dimissa pro taxatione xxii m.; solvit commissario totum.

Ecclesia de Munketon' super Moram (Moor Monkton) dimissa pro taxatione xxv m.; solvit commissario totum.

Ecclesia de Akastr' Malebys (Acaster Malbis) dimissa pro taxatione xl m.; inde solvit nobis xx m. et commissario xx m., et sic solvit totum.

Ecclesia de Adel dimissa pro taxatione xvi m.; solvit nobis totum.

Ecclesia de Gergrave (Gargrave) dimissa pro taxatione l m.; solvit commissario totum.

Ecclesia de Arneclyf (Arncliffe) taxata l m., dimissa pro xxii li.; solvit commissario totum.

Ecclesia de Slayteburn' (Slaidburn) taxata xx li., dimissa pro xl m.; solvit commissario totum.

Ecclesia de Broghton' in Cravene (Broughton) dimissa pro taxatione xx li., solvit commissario totum.

Ecclesia de Bradeforth' (Bradford) dimissa pro taxatione iiiiˣˣ m.; solvit commissario totum.

Ecclesia de Almanbyr' (Almondbury) dimissa pro taxatione xl li.; solvit commissario totum.

Ecclesia de Barneburgh (Barmborough) dimissa pro taxatione xviii m.; solvit commissario totum.

Ecclesia de Styvelyngflete (Stillingfleet) dimissa pro taxatione xl li., solvit commissario totum.

Ecclesia de Dalby dimissa pro taxatione x li.; solvit commissario totum.

---

[20] The prior of St. Katherine without Lincoln and the abbot of Osney were commissioners in the diocese of Lincoln.

[21] Commissioner in the province of York.

[22] The commissioner was the abbot of St. Mary, York.

Ecclesia de Bossale (Bossall) taxata lx m., dimissa pro xlvi li.; solvit commissario totum.

Ecclesia de Tyverington' (Terrington) dimissa pro taxatione xxx li.; solvit commissario totum.

Vicaria de Sutton' in Galtres (Sutton on the Forest) dimissa pro taxatione xviii m.; solvit commissario totum.

Ecclesia de Foston' prope Kirkham dimissa pro taxatione xx m., solvit commissario totum.

Ecclesia de Esington' (Easington) taxata xx li., et quia destructa et inculta dimissa pro xii m.; solvit commissario totum.

Ecclesia de Halnby (Hawnby) taxata xx m., ad instantiam comitis Lancastrie dimissa pro x m.; solvit commissario totum.

Medietas ecclesie de Bubwyth' (Bubwith) dimissa pro taxatione xl m.; solvit commissario totum.

Ecclesia de Foule Sutton' (Full Sutton) dimissa pro taxatione x m.; solvit commissario totum.

Ecclesia de Baynton' (Bainton) dimissa pro taxatione c m.; solvit commissario totum.

Ecclesia de Rouleye (Rowley) dimissa pro taxatione lxx m.; solvit commissario totum.

Ecclesia de Haselarton' (Heslerton) dimissa pro taxatione xx m.; solvit commissario totum.

Ecclesia de Beforth' (Beeford) dimissa pro taxatione xx li.; solvit commissario totum.

Ecclesia de Hornse (Hornsea) dimissa pro taxatione l m.; solvit commissario totum.

Ecclesia de Ruddestan (Rudston) dimissa pro taxatione lx m.; solvit commissario totum.

Ecclesia de Folketon' (Folkton) dimissa pro taxatione xl m.; solvit commissario totum.

Ecclesia de Misne (Misson) dimissa pro taxatione xii li.; solvit commissario totum.

(fol. 14) Vicaria de Edenestouwe (Edwinstow) dimissa pro taxatione x li.; solvit commissario totum.

Medietas ecclesie de Eykering' (Eakring) dimissa pro taxatione c s.; solvit commissario totum.

Ecclesia de Nitteshale (Nuthall) dimissa pro taxatione c s.; solvit commissario totum.

Vicaria ecclesie de Baseforth' (Basford) dimissa pro taxatione viii m.; solvit commissario totum.

Ecclesia de Gresleye (Greasley) dimissa pro taxatione xxxv m.; solvit commissario totum.

Medietas ecclesie de Cotegrave (Cotgrave) dimissa pro taxatione x m.; solvit commissario totum.

Ecclesia de Radeclyve super Sore (Ratcliffe on Soar) dimissa pro taxatione lxx m.; solvit commissario totum.

Ecclesia de Wilughby super Waldham (Willoughby on the Wolds) dimissa pro taxatione xx li.; solvit commissario totum.

Ecclesia Sancti Nicholai in Beverlaco (Beverley) dimissa pro taxatione x m.; solvit commissario totum.

Ecclesia de Scorresburgh' (Scorbrough) dimissa pro taxatione viii m.; solvit commissario totum.

Ecclesia de Patrington' taxata x li., dimissa pro xx m.; solvit commissario totum.

Prebenda de Drifeld (Driffield) dimissa pro taxatione c li.; solvit commissario totum.

Prebenda de Skelton' in ecclesia Hoveden' (Howden) dimissa pro taxatione l m.; solvit commissario totum.

Vicaria de Brymston' (Burneston) taxata xl m., dimissa pro combustione Scotorum pro xv m.; solvit commissario totum.

Ecclesia de Brigham taxata iiii<sup>xx</sup> m., dimissa pro l m.; inde solvit nobis xxx m. et commissario xx m., et sic solvit totum.

Prebenda de Brichull' cum Knaresburgh (Bichhill cum Knaresborough) dimissa pro taxatione lxx m.; inde solvit nobis xxx m.

Ecclesia de Lounesburgh' (Londesborough) dimissa pro taxatione xxxv m.; inde solvit commissario xv m.

Prebenda de Buggethorp (Bugthorpe) dimissa pro taxatione lx m.; inde solvit nobis l m.

Ecclesia de Hemmyngburgh' (Hemingborough) dimissa pro taxatione clx m.; inde solvit commissario clvi m.

Ecclesia de Welleton' (Welton) taxata xl m., dimissa pro xxxix m.; inde solvit nobis xxxvi m. dimidiam.

(fol. 14ᵛ) Precentoria ecclesie Eboracensis taxata xvi li.; dimissa pro xx m.

Ecclesia de Haukeswell' (Hauxwell) taxata xxxv m.; dimissa pro xviii m.

Ecclesia de Deen' (Dean) dimissa pro xviii m.; solvit nobis totum.[23]

Ecclesia de Wirkyngton' (Workington) dimissa pro xxv m.; solvit nobis totum.

Summa recepta per nos Eboracensis vi<sup>c</sup>xliii m. Item per commissarium m<sup>l</sup>vii<sup>c</sup>xxx m.

## (fol. 15) Dunolmensis

Primus annus in dyocesi Dunolmensi

Prebenda quondam Magistri Stephani de Malolacu in ecclesia de Aukelond (Auckland) dimissa pro xxiiii m.; solvit nobis totum.

Ecclesia de Hucheword (Hurworth) dimissa pro xlvi li. xiii s. iiii d.; solvit commissario [24] totum.

Prebenda quondam Domini Ade de Middelton' in ecclesia de Derlyngton' (Darlington) dimissa pro xxv m.; solvit commissario totum.

Prebenda quondam Magistri Johannis de Snaynton' in eadem ecclesia dimissa pro xxv m.; solvit commissario totum.

Vicaria de Gayneford (Gainford) dimissa pro c s.; solvit commissario totum.

Ecclesia de Halghton' (Haughton le Skerne) dimissa pro iiii<sup>x</sup>x m.; solvit nobis totum.

Ecclesia de Elton' dimissa pro iiii li. vi s. viii d.; inde solvit commissario xliii s. iiii d.

Ecclesia de Hoghton' (Houghton le Spring) dimissa

---

[23] In the margin bracketed against this item and the next: *Non sunt in certificatione.*

[24] The commissioner in the diocese of Durham was the abbot of St. Mary, York.

pro iiii[xx] vi li. xiii s. iiii d.; inde solvit commissario lxv m. et nobis xxxv li. vi s. viii d.

Prebenda quondam Domini Lodowyci in ecclesia de Aukelond (Auckland) dimissa pro xlvi li. xiii s. iiii d.

Prebenda quondam Domini Lodowyci in ecclesia de Northon' (Norton) dimissa pro lx m.

Ecclesia de Gatesheved (Gateshead) dimissa pro xiii li. vi s. viii d.

Summa recepta Dunelmensis per nos clxvii m. Item per commissarium c iiii[xx]xv m. x s.

### (fol 15[v]) Karleolensis

Primus annus in dyocesi Karleolensi

Ecclesia de Wyggeton' (Wigton) dimissa pro xv m.; solvit nobis totum.

Ecclesia de Clyfton' (Clifton) dimissa pro cvi s. viii d.; solvit commissario [25] totum.

Ecclesia de Clybburn' (Cliburn) dimissa pro viii li.; solvit commissario totum.

Ecclesia de Dacre dimissa pro xl li.; solvit commissario totum.

Ecclesia de Croglyn (Croglin) dimissa pro ii m.; solvit commissario totum.

Ecclesia de Musgrave dimissa pro xl s.; solvit commissario totum.

Summa recepta per nos Carleolensis xv m. Item per commissarium iiii[xx] v m.[26]

### (fol. 16[v]) Cantuariensis

Secundus annus et tertius in dyocesi Cantuariensi

Ecclesia de Chertham (Chartham) dimissa ad firmam pro taxatione xl m.; solvit nobis totum.

Ecclesia de Smerdon' (Smarden) dimissa pro taxatione xxx m.; solvit nobis totum.

Vicaria de Tenderden' (Tenterden) taxata xv m., dimissa propter exilitatem pro vi m.; solvit nobis totum.

Ecclesia de Milstede (Milstead) taxata xx m., et quia residuum non sufficit pro oneribus dimissa pro xv m.; solvit nobis totum.

Ecclesia de Fordwyco (Fordwich) taxata x m., dimissa pro viii m.; solvit nobis totum.

Ecclesia de Boxle (Boxley) taxata xl m., dimissa pro l m.; solvit nobis totum.

Ecclesia de Holyngburn' (Hollingbourn) dimissa pro taxatione lx m.; solvit nobis totum.

Ecclesia de Sandehurst (Sandhurst) dimissa pro xxxv m.; solvit nobis totum.

Ecclesia de Dale (Deal) dimissa pro xxx m.; solvit nobis totum.

Ecclesia de Hathewoldenn' (Hathwolding) dimissa pro taxatione x li.; solvit nobis totum.

Ecclesia de Langele (Langley) dimissa pro taxatione x m.; solvit nobis totum.

Ecclesia de Berfreyston' (Barfreston) dimissa pro vi m.; solvit nobis totum.

Ecclesia de Herietesham (Harrietsham) dimissa pro taxatione xxiiii m.; solvit nobis totum.

Archidiaconatus Cantuariensis dimissus pro taxatione ccc m.; solvit nobis totum.

Ecclesia de Esshetesford (Ashford) dimissa pro taxatione xxiiii m.; solvit nobis totum.

Ecclesia de Northon' (Norton) taxata xxviii m., et quia terre fuerunt inculte dimissa pro xii m.; solvit nobis totum.

Ecclesia de Cherleton' (Charlton) taxata xv m., et quia de residuo non potuit deserviri dimissa pro vi m.; solvit nobis totum.[27]

Ecclesia de Quelton (Walton) dimissa pro xx m.; solvit nobis totum.

Ecclesia de Ocham (Ockham) dimissa pro taxatione x m.

Summa recepta Cantuariensis per nos vi[c] iiii[xx] xi m.

### (fol. 17) Roffensis

Secundus annus et tertius in dyocesi Roffensi.

Ecclesia de Coulyng' (Cooling) dimissa pro taxatione xx m.; solvit nobis totum.

Ecclesia de Lodesdon' (Luddesdon) dimissa pro taxatione xv m.; solvit nobis totum.

Vicaria de Plumstede (Plumstead) dimissa pro taxatione x m.; solvit nobis totum.

Ecclesia de Clyve (Cliffe) dimissa pro taxatione cx m.; solvit nobis totum.

Vicaria de Cobeham (Cobham) dimissa pro taxatione vii m.; solvit nobis totum.

Vicaria de Estpecham (East Peckham) dimissa pro taxatione xii m.; solvit nobis totum.

Ecclesia de Coudenn' (Cowden) dimissa pro taxatione xv m.; solvit nobis totum.[28]

Archidiaconatus Roffensis non taxatus, dimissus pro xx m.; solvit nobis totum.

Ecclesia de Shorham (Shoreham) dimissa pro taxatione iiii[xx] m.; solvit nobis totum.

Ecclesia de Erde (Hardres) dimissa pro taxatione xl m.; solvit nobis totum.

Ecclesia de Huntyndon' (Hunton) dimissa pro taxatione xv m.; inde solvit nobis xiiii m.

Summa recepta per nos cccxliii m.

### (fol. 17[v]) Cicestrensis

Secundus annus et tertius in dyocesi Cicestrensi

Ecclesia Sancti Egidii de Wynchels' (Winchelsea) taxata x m., dimissa pro vii m. dimidia; solvit nobis totum.

---

[25] The commissioner in the diocese of Carlisle was the abbot of St. Mary, York.

[26] Folio 16 is blank.

[27] In the margin bracketed against this item and the next: *Vacant per constitutionem.* The constitution *Exsecrabilis*, 21 November, 1317: Extravag. Ioann. XXII, Tit. iii, Cap. un.

[28] In the margin bracketed against this item and the next four: *Vacant per constitutionem.*

Ecclesia de Worth' taxata xii m., dimissa pro xiii m.; solvit nobis totum.

Ecclesia de Idenn' (Iden) taxata vi m., dimissa pro vii m.; solvit nobis totum.

Vicaria de Coufeld (Cowfold) dimissa pro taxatione x m.; solvit nobis totum.

Ecclesia de Gestlyng' (Guestling) dimissa pro taxatione xx m.; solvit nobis totum.

Vicaria [29] de Hanefeld (Henfield) taxata c s., dimissa pro v m.; solvit nobis totum.

Capella de Echinghame (Etchingham) dimissa pro taxatione xii m.; solvit nobis totum.

Vicaria de Iklesham (Icklesham) dimissa pro taxatione xx m.; solvit nobis totum.

Vicaria de Stoghton' (Stoughton) dimissa pro taxatione xii m.; solvit nobis totum.

Ecclesia de Clopham (Clapham) dimissa pro taxatione x m.; solvit nobis totum.

Ecclesia de Sullyngton' (Sullington) taxata xv m., dimissa pro xvii m.; solvit nobis totum.

(fol. 18) Ecclesia de Northstok' (North Stoke) dimissa pro taxatione x m.; solvit nobis totum.

Ecclesia de Coumbes (Coombes) dimissa pro taxatione xii m.; solvit nobis totum.

Ecclesia de Pagham dimissa pro taxatione clx m.; solvit nobis totum.

Ecclesia seu capella de Estwistering' (East Wittering) dimissa pro taxatione c s.; solvit nobis totum.

Vicaria de Wandhurst (Wadhurst) exempte iurisdictionis Cantauriensis taxata ix m., dimissa propter exilitatem pro vii m.; solvit nobis totum.

Prebenda de Ertham (Eartham) in ecclesia Cycestrensi dimissa pro taxatione xv m.; solvit nobis totum.

Prebenda de Somerle (Somerley) in dicta ecclesia dimissa pro taxatione xii m.; solvit nobis totum.

Prebenda de Waltham in eadem ecclesia dimissa pro taxatione x li.; solvit nobis totum.

Prebenda de Wysburgh' (Wisborough Green) in eadem ecclesia dimissa pro xx m.; solvit nobis totum.

Ecclesia de Bery (Bury) dimissa pro xxx m.; solvit nobis totum.

Ecclesia de Westfeld (Westfield) taxata x m., dimissa pro v m.; solvit nobis totum.

Ecclesia de Plumpton' dimissa pro taxatione xx m.; solvit nobis totum.

Ecclesia de Hangelton' (Hangleton) dimissa pro taxatione x li.; solvit nobis totum.

Ecclesia de Kyngeston' (Kingston) dimissa pro taxatione xxv m.; solvit nobis totum.

Ecclesia de Pette (Pett) dimissa pro taxatione c s.; solvit nobis totum.

Prebenda de Huvavilla (Hove) in ecclesia Cycestrensi dimissa pro taxatione xl m.; solvit nobis totum.

Ecclesia de Northihame (Northiam) dimissa pro xx m.; solvit nobis totum.[30]

Ecclesia de Blachynton' (Blatchington) dimissa pro taxatione xx m.; solvit nobis totum.

Ecclesia de Stedeham (Stedham) cum capella de Eishete (Heyshott) dimissa pro taxatione xxv m.; inde solvit nobis xii m. dimidiam.

Ecclesia de Horstede Kaynot (Horsted Keynes) dimissa pro xx m.; inde solvit nobis iiii m.

Ecclesia de Fletchyng' (Fletching) dimissa pro taxatione xxv m.

Summa recepta per nos Cicentrensis v^c iiii^xx xi m.

### (fol. 18^v) Londoniensis

Secundus annus et tertius in dyocesi Londoniensi

Ecclesia de Bradewell' (Bradwell) dimissa pro taxatione lx m.; solvit nobis totum.

Ecclesia de Thurrok parva (Little Thurrock) dimissa pro taxatione viii m.; solvit nobis totum.

Ecclesia de Estwode (Eastwood) dimissa pro taxatione xii m.; solvit nobis totum.

Ecclesia de Fifhide (Fyfield) dimissa pro taxatione xviii m.; solvit nobis totum.

Ecclesia de Bolefanne (Bulphan) dimissa pro taxatione xx m.; solvit nobis totum.

Ecclesia de Hadham (Much Hadham) dimissa pro taxatione lx m.; solvit nobis totum.

Ecclesia de Heydon' taxata c s.; dimissa pro viii m.; solvit nobis totum.

Ecclesia de Reed dimissa pro taxatione x m.; solvit nobis totum.

Ecclesia de Chesthunt' (Cheshunt) dimissa pro taxatione xl m.; solvit nobis totum.

Ecclesia de Gilham parva (Little Yeldham) dimissa pro taxatione c s.; solvit nobis totum.

Ecclesia de Wodyton' (Widdington) non taxata, dimissa pro x m.; solvit nobis totum.

Ecclesia de Bassingeshagh' (St. Michael, Bassishaw) dimissa pro taxatione x m.; solvit nobis totum.

Ecclesia Sancti Swithuni (London) dimissa pro taxatione vi m.; solvit nobis totum.

Ecclesia de Ronewell' (Runwell) dimissa pro taxatione viii m.; solvit nobis totum.

Ecclesia de Lamburn' (Lambourne) dimissa pro taxatione x m.; solvit nobis totum.

Ecclesia de Berneston' (Barnston) dimissa pro taxatione viii m.; solvit nobis totum.

Archidiaconatus Londoniensis non taxatus, dimissus pro xlviii li.; solvit nobis totum.

Ecclesia de Shordych' (Shoreditch) annexa dicto archidiaconatui dimissa pro taxatione xiiii li.; solvit nobis totum.

---

[29] Substituted for *Ecclesia* erased.

[30] In the margin bracketed against this and the next item: *Vacant per constitutionem.*

Ecclesia de Shenefeld (Shenfield) dimissa pro taxatione xv m.; solvit nobis totum.

Ecclesia de Chelchith' (Chelsea) dimissa pro taxatione xiii m.; solvit nobis totum.

Ecclesia de Sheperton' (Shepperton) taxata xx m., dimissa pro xxii m.; solvit nobis totum.

Ecclesia de Cestreford (Chesterford) taxata xxv m., dimissa pro xxxv m.; solvit nobis totum.

Ecclesia de Sampford parva dimissa pro taxatione xv m.; solvit nobis totum.

Ecclesia de Tholesbur' (Tollesbury) dimissa pro taxatione xxx m.; solvit nobis totum.

Ecclesia de Berden' dimissa pro taxatione xv m.; solvit nobis totum.

Vicaria de Staundon' (Standon) dimissa pro vi m. iii s.; solvit nobis totum.

Ecclesia Sancti Vedasti (Vedast) Londonie dimissa pro taxatione x m.; solvit nobis totum.

Ecclesia de Alvithele (Aveley) taxata xlv m., et quia residuum non sufficit pro oneribus dimissa pro xxxv m.; inde solvit nobis xxx m. dimidiam.

(fol. 19) Ecclesia de Langham dimissa pro taxatione xvi m.; inde solvit nobis viii m.

Ecclesia de Fairstede (Fairsted) dimissa pro taxatione xi m.; inde solvit nobis iiii m. dimidiam.

Ecclesia Omnium Sanctorum ad Fenum (All Hallows the Great, London) taxata x m., dimissa pro xii m.; inde solvit nobis iiii m. xiii s. ii d.

Ecclesia de Stebbenhith' iuxta Londoniam (Stepney) taxata lx m., dimissa pro lxxv m.; inde solvit nobis xxxvii m. dimidiam.

Ecclesia de Craunford (Cranford) taxata viii m.; dimissa pro x m.; inde solvit nobis vi m.

Ecclesia de Sabrichesworth' (Sawbridgeworth) dimissa pro taxatione lxx m.

Prebenda de Wallokesbern' (Wenlock's Barn, St. Giles) dimissa pro taxatione c s.

Ecclesia Sancti Petri Colecestrie dimissa pro iiii m.; solvit nobis totum.[32]

Summa recepta Londoniensis vi[c] xlv m. ii s. x d.

### (fol. 20)[33] Wyntoniensis

Secundus annus et tertius in dyocesi Wyntoniensi.

Ecclesia de Kyngesclere (Kingsclere) taxata c li., dimissa propter exilitatem pro c m.; solvit nobis totum.

Ecclesia de Bedhampton' dimissa pro taxatione xvi m. xl d.; solvit nobis totum.

Ecclesia de Abbodeston' (Abbotstone) dimissa pro taxatione x m.; solvit nobis totum.

Ecclesia de Alta Clera (Highclere) dimissa pro taxatione xii m.; solvit nobis totum.

Ecclesia de Mikelham (Mickleham) dimissa pro taxatione xxviii m.; solvit nobis tutum.

Ecclesia de Crauele (Crawley) dimissa pro taxatione xxxii m.; solvit nobis totum.

Ecclesia de Croundale (Crondall) dimissa pro taxatione iiii[xx] li.; solvit nobis totum.

Medietas ecclesie de la Waye (Weyhill) dimissa pro taxatione v m. dimidia; solvit nobis totum.

Ecclesia de Westhorsle (West Horsley) dimissa pro taxatione xxxv m.; solvit nobis totum.

Ecclesia de Wordy Comitis (Worthy Martyr) dimissa pro taxatione xv m.; solvit nobis totum.

Vicaria de Godalmyng' (Godalming) dimissa pro taxatione xx m.; solvit nobis totum.

Ecclesia de Minnestok' (Meon Stoke) dimissa pro taxatione l m.; solvit nobis totum.

Ecclesia de Candevere (Brown Candover) dimissa pro taxatione xviii m.; solvit nobis totum.

Ecclesia de Byflete (Byfleet) dimissa pro taxatione c s.; solvit nobis totum.[34]

Ecclesia de Wodyton' (Wootton) dimissa pro taxatione xii m.; solvit nobis totum.

Ecclesia de Westuderlegh' (West Tytherly) dimissa pro taxatione xvi m.; solvit nobis totum.

Ecclesia de Farlegh' (Farleigh Wallop) dimissa pro taxatione viii m.; solvit nobis totum.

Ecclesia de Warneford (Warnford) dimissa pro taxatione xxxii m.; solvit nobis totum.

Ecclesia de Freshwater taxata lx m.; dimissa pro l m.; solvit nobis totum.

Ecclesia de Atherton' (Arreton) dimissa pro taxatione l m.; solvit nobis totum.

Ecclesia de Ichenestok' (Itchen Stoke) dimissa pro taxatione xv m.; solvit nobis totum.

Ecclesia de Muchelmersh' (Michelmersh) dimissa pro taxatione xxxv m.; solvit nobis totum.

Ecclesia de Bedyngton' (Beddington) dimissa pro taxatione xl m.; inde solvit nobis xxxii m.

Ecclesia de Werplesdon' (Worplesdon) dimissa pro taxatione xxxv m.

Ecclesia de Cherchocle (Church Oakley) dimissa pro taxatione xii m.

(fol. 20[v]) Ecclesia de Brittesdon' (Brixton) dimissa pro taxatione xxx m.[34a]

Vicaria de Mulford (Milford) dimissa pro taxatione xxx m.; inde solvit nobis xxvi m. dimidiam.

Ecclesia de Everslegh' (Eversley) dimissa pro taxatione xii m.; inde solvit nobis vi m.

Ecclesia de Ashtede (Ashtead) dimissa pro taxatione xx m.; inde solvit nobis x m.

Vicaria de Farnham dimissa pro taxatione xxi m.; inde solvit nobis x m. dimidiam.

---

[31] In the margin bracketed against this and the next eight items: *Vacant per constitutionem.*

[32] In the margin: *Non est in certificatione.*

[33] The verso of folio 19 is blank.

[34] In the margin bracketed against this and the next eleven items: *Vacant per constitutionem.*

[34a] In the margin: *Vacat per constitutionem.*

Ecclesia de Warneburn' (Warnborough) dimissa pro xv m.; solvit nobis totum.[35]

Ecclesia de Hedeley (Headley) dimissa pro vii m. dimidia; solvit nobis totum.

Ecclesia de Suthwaltham (Bishops Waltham) dimissa pro xxx m.; solvit nobis totum.

Ecclesia de Suthtudeworth' (South Tidworth) dimissa pro xv m.; solvit nobis totum.

Summa totius recepte per nos Wintoniensis viii^c xlvii m. x s.

### (fol. 21) Sarisberiensis

Secundus annus et tertius in dyocesi Sarisberiensi

Ecclesia de Brudeport (Bridport) taxata x m., dimissa pro xi m.; solvit nobis totum.

Vicaria de Cherdestok' (Chardstock) dimissa pro taxatione c s.; solvit nobis totum.

Vicaria de Porstok (Poorstock) non taxata, dimissa pro vi m.; solvit nobis totum.

Ecclesia de Wynterborn' Wast (Winterborne Monkton) dimissa pro taxatione vi m.; solvit nobis totum.

Ecclesia de Acford Alfredi (Okeford Fitzpaine) dimissa pro taxatione xv m.; solvit nobis totum.

Ecclesia de Spetebur' (Spettisbury) dimissa pro taxatione xv m.; solvit nobis totum.

Ecclesia de Blaneford Langeton' (Long Blandford) dimissa pro taxatione ix m.; solvit nobis totum.

Ecclesia de Westhildesle (West Ilsley) dimissa pro taxatione xv m.; solvit nobis totum.

Vicaria de Ebbelesburn' Episcopi (Ebbesborne Wake) dimissa pro taxatione vi m. dimidia; solvit nobis totum.

Ecclesia de Wyli (Wylye) dimissa pro taxatione xv m.; solvit nobis totum.

Ecclesia de Stourton' dimissa pro taxatione xv m.; solvit nobis totum.

Ecclesia de Coueleston' (Coulston) dimissa pro taxatione c s.; solvit nobis totum.

Ecclesia de Cristemaleford (Christian Malford) dimissa pro taxatione lx m.; solvit nobis totum.

Ecclesia de Sopworth' dimissa pro taxatione vi m. dimidia; solvit nobis totum.

Ecclesia de Pole (Poole Keynes) dimissa pro taxatione x m.; solvit nobis totum.

Vicaria de Hanyndon' (Hannington) taxata vi m. dimidia, dimissa pro vii m.; solvit nobis totum.

Ecclesia de Tytecombe (Tidcombe) dimissa pro taxatione viii m.; solvit nobis totum.

Ecclesia de Sottesbrok (Shottesbrook) dimissa pro taxatione xiii m.; solvit nobis totum.

(fol. 21^v) Ecclesia seu vicaria de Lavynton' Episcopi (West Lavington) dimissa pro taxatione c s.; solvit nobis totum.

Vicaria de Uphavene (Uphaven) non taxata, dimissa pro c s.; solvit nobis totum.

Ecclesia de Dounton' (Downton) dimissa pro taxatione c m.; solvit nobis totum.

Vicaria de Lacok (Lacock) dimissa pro taxatione c s.; solvit nobis totum.

Ecclesia de Crudewell' (Crudwell) dimissa pro taxatione x m.; solvit nobis totum.

Capella de Wrockeshale (North Wraxhall) dimissa pro taxatione x m.; solvit nobis totum.

Ecclesia de Yatton' Kaynel (Yatton Keynell) dimissa pro taxatione xii m.; solvit nobis totum.

Ecclesia de Aulton' Berners (Alton Barnes) taxata c s., dimissa pro x m.; solvit nobis totum.

Ecclesia de Swyndon' (Swindon) dimissa pro taxatione xx m.; solvit nobis totum.

Prebenda de Stratford Sancti Laurentii dimissa pro taxatione c s.; solvit nobis totum.

Ecclesia de Brideton' (Burton) taxata xx m., et quia residuum non sufficit pro oneribus dimissa pro xv m.; solvit nobis totum.

Ecclesia de Fysherton' (Fisherton) iuxta Sarum dimissa pro taxatione x m.; solvit nobis totum.

Ecclesia de Alnyng' (All Cannings) dimissa pro taxatione xx m.; solvit nobis totum.

Ecclesia seu capella de Compton' Hawey (Nether Compton) dimissa pro x m.; solvit nobis totum.[36]

Ecclesia de Compton' Pontelarg' (Valence Compton) dimissa pro taxatione x m.; solvit nobis totum.

Ecclesia de Henton' (Hinton) dimissa pro xxvi m.; solvit nobis totum.[37]

Ecclesia Sancti Sampsonis Crikelad (Cricklade) dimissa pro taxatione xx m.; solvit nobis totum.

Ecclesia de Wotton' Basset (Wootton Bassett) dimissa pro taxatione xxiiii m.; solvit nobis totum.

Ecclesia seu prebenda de Gilyngham (Gillingham) dimissa pro taxatione xxx li.; inde solvit nobis xiiii li.

Ecclesia de Wollanynton' (Woolhampton) dimissa pro taxatione vii m.

Ecclesia de Swere (Swyre) dimissa pro taxatione c s.

Prebenda de Axeford (Axford) dimissa pro taxatione c. s.

(fol. 22) Ecclesia de Silhamstede Abbatis (Sulhampstead Bannister) dimissa pro taxatione c s.; solvit nobis totum.[38]

Ecclesia de Sonnyngwell' (Sunningwell) dimissa pro viii m.; solvit nobis totum.

Prebenda de Hulle deverel (Hill Deverill) dimissa pro xii m.; solvit nobis totum.

Ecclesia de Langeworth' (Longworth) dimissa pro xv m.; solvit nobis totum.

Vicaria de Fighelden' (Figheldean) dimissa pro vi m. dimidia; solvit nobis totum.

---

[35] In the margin bracketed against this and the next three items: *Non sunt in certificatione.*

[36] In the margin bracketed against this and the next item: *Non sunt in certificatione.*

[37] In the margin bracketed against this and the next two items: *Vacant per constitutionem.*

[38] In the margin bracketed against this and the next five items: *Non sunt in certificatione.*

Ecclesia de Corf castel (Corfe Castle) dimissa pro xxii m.; solvit nobis totum.

Summa totalis recepta Sarisberiensis per nos vi^c lii m.

### Exoniensis

Secundus annus et tertius in dyocesi Exoniensi

Archidiaconatus Exoniensis non taxatus, dimissus pro x m.; solvit nobis totum.

Ecclesia de Bradenech' (Bradninch) dimissa pro taxatione xiii m.; solvit nobis totum.

Ecclesia de Ludwon (Ludgvan) dimissa pro taxatione x li.; solvit nobis totum.

Ecclesia Sancti Maugani (St. Mawgan in Kerrier) dimissa pro taxatione x li.; solvit nobis totum.

Archidiaconatus Barnastapol' (Barnstaple) non taxatus, set sunt due ecclesie eidem annexe, dimissus pro x m.; solvit nobis totum.

Ecclesia de Byr (Beer) dimissa pro taxatione viii li.; solvit commissario totum.

Ecclesia de Tattecote (Tetcott) dimissa pro taxatione vi m. dimidia; solvit commissario totum.

Ecclesia de Dertyngton' (Dartington) dimissa pro taxatione vi li.; solvit commissario totum.

(fol 22^v) Ecclesia de Rupe (Roche) dimissa pro taxatione ix m. dimidia; solvit commissario totum.

Ecclesia de Cardynan (Cardinham) taxata vi li. xiii s. iv d., dimissa pro cxii s. iiii d.; solvit commissario totum.

Ecclesia de Eglosheyl (Egloshayle) dimissa pro taxatione c s.; solvit commissario totum.

Ecclesia de Duelton' (Dowlton) dimissa pro taxatione c s.; solvit commissario totum.

Ecclesia de Bidiford (Bideford) dimissa pro taxatione xii li. vi s. viii d. solvit commissario totum.

Ecclesia de Alfyngton' (Alphington) dimissa pro taxatione viii li.; solvit nobis totum.[89]

Ecclesia de Stok' in Tynhide (Stoke in Teignhead) dimissa pro taxatione xi m.; solvit commissario totum.

Portio Magistri Thome de Teffonte quondam in ecclesia de Tyverton' (Tiverton) taxata vii li. xii d., dimissa pro vii m.; solvit commissario totum.

Ecclesia Sancte Ladoce (St. Ladock) dimissa pro taxatione vi li.; solvit commissario totum.

Ecclesia de Atherington dimissa pro taxatione vii li. iiii s.; solvit commissario totum.

Ecclesia de Brideford (Bridford) dimissa pro taxatione iiii li. xiii s. iiii d.

Ecclesia de Lomene (Uplowman) dimissa pro taxatione iiii li. ix s. iiii d.

Ecclesia de Honyton' (Honiton) dimissa pro taxatione xv li.

Ecclesia de Exemynstr' (Axminster) dimissa pro taxatione xvii li. vi s. viii d.

Ecclesia de Lusteslegh' (Lustleigh) dimissa pro taxatione iiii li. xiii s. iiii d.

Ecclesia de Neweton' Ferers (Newton Ferrers) dimissa pro taxatione vi li. xiii s. iiii d.

(fol. 23) Ecclesia Sancte Ermete (St. Erme) dimissa pro taxatione vi li.

Ecclesia de Bukynton' (Bickington) dimissa pro taxatione c s.

Ecclesia de Morcestr' Episcopi (Morchard Bishop) dimissa pro taxatione vi li. xiii s. iiii d.

Summa recepta per nos Exoniensis lxiii m. Item per commissarium cxxviii m. ix s. viii d. Vera.

### (fol. 23^v) Bathoniensis et Wellensis

Secundus annus et tertius in dyocesi Bathoniensi et Wellensi

Ecclesia de Ak' (Oak) taxata c s., dimissa pro x m.; solvit nobis totum.

Ecclesia de Camelarton' (Camerton) dimissa pro taxatione x li. xviii s. viii d.; solvit nobis totum.

Ecclesia de Brokton' (Broughton) dimissa pro taxatione c s.; solvit nobis totum.

Ecclesia de Pristh' ton' (Priston) dimissa pro taxatione vi m. v s. iiii d.; solvit nobis totum

Ecclesia de Porlok (Porlock) dimissa pro taxatione xii m.; solvit nobis totum.

Ecclesia de Sok' (Sock) dimissa pro taxatione xi m. iiii s. iiii d.; solvit nobis totum.

Ecclesia de Stratton' Sancti Victoris dimissa pro taxatione ix m.; solvit nobis totum.

Ecclesia de Chyw (Chew Magna) dimissa pro taxatione l m.; solvit nobis totum.

Ecclesia de Stok' super Mare (Kewstoke) dimissa pro taxatione c s.; solvit nobis totum.

Ecclesia de Cherdelynch' (Charlinch) dimissa pro taxatione x li.; solvit nobis totum.

Ecclesia de Donyate (Donyatt) dimissa pro taxatione viii m.; solvit nobis totum.

Vicaria de Frome dimissa pro taxatione xi m. dimidia; solvit nobis totum.

Ecclesia de Chisebrigg' (Chiselborough) taxata xx m., dimissa pro xxvii m.; solvit nobis totum.

Ecclesia de Estludeford (East Lydford) dimissa pro taxatione x m.; solvit nobis totum.

Prebenda de Ilton' dimissa pro taxatione xviii m.; solvit nobis totum.

Ecclesia de Kyngeston' (Kingston or Kingstone) dimissa pro taxatione xx m.; solvit nobis totum.

Prebenda de Lutton' (Litton) dimissa pro taxatione x m.; solvit nobis totum.

Prebenda de Estharpetr' (East Harptree) dimissa pro taxatione xii m.; solvit nobis totum.

Ecclesia de Lympesham (Lympsham) dimissa pro taxatione xx m.; solvit nobis totum.[40]

---

[89] In the margin bracketed against this and the next four items: *Vacant per constitutionem.*

[40] In the margin bracketed against this and the next six items: *Vacant per constitutionem.*

Ecclesia de Cory malet (Curry Malet) dimissa pro xv m.; solvit nobis totum.

Ecclesia de Uphull' (Uphill) dimissa pro taxatione x m.; solvit nobis totum.

Ecclesia de Chedesy (Chedzoy) dimissa pro taxatione xxx m.; solvit nobis totum.

Ecclesia de Baudryp (Bawdrip) dimissa pro taxatione xii m.; solvit nobis totum.

Ecclesia de Babbecary (Babcary) dimissa pro taxatione xx m.; solvit nobis totum.

Ecclesia de Wrockeshale (Wraxall) dimissa pro taxatione xxxii m.; solvit nobis totum.

Ecclesia de Lollyngton' (Lullington) dimissa pro taxatione ix m.; inde solvit nobis iiii m. dimidiam.

(fol. 24) Ecclesia de Westcanttokesheved (West Quantockshead) dimissa pro taxatione vi m. dimidia; inde solvit nobis xliii s. iiii d.

Prebenda de Compton' dimissa pro taxatione xx li.; inde solvit nobis x li.

Ecclesia de Henton' (Hinton) Sancti Georgii non taxata; dimissa pro x m.

Ecclesia de Magna Weston (Weston super Mare) taxata viii m.; dimissa pro c s.

Summa recepta per nos Bathoniensis iiii$^c$ xxiii m. v s.

### (fol. 24$^v$) Coventrensis et Lychfeldensis

Secundus annus et tertius in dyocesi Coventrensi et Lychfeldensi.

Prebenda de Bobenhill' (Bubbenhall) in ecclesia Lychfeldensi dimissa pro taxatione x m.; solvit nobis totum.

Prebenda de Ruyton' (Ryton upon Dunsmoor) in ecclesia Lychfeldensi dimissa pro taxatione xv m.; solvit nobis totum.

Ecclesia de Sheldon' taxata viii m., dimissa pro xiiii m.; solvit nobis totum.

Ecclesia de Chetewynde (Chetwynd) taxata vii m., dimissa pro x m.; solvit nobis totum.

Medietas ecclesia de Megynton (Mugginton) taxata xiii m., dimissa pro ix m.; solvit nobis totum.

Tertia portio ecclesie de Derleye (Darley) dimissa pro taxatione ix m.; solvit nobis totum.

Ecclesia de Swerkeston' (Swarkeston) dimissa pro taxatione vii m. dimidia; solvit nobis totum.

Ecclesia de Mackeworth' (Mackworth) dimissa pro taxatione xlv m.; solvit nobis totum.

Ecclesia de Tibbeshulf (Tibshelf) dimissa pro taxatione xii m.; solvit nobis totum.

Medietas ecclesie de Malo passu (Malpas) taxata xx m., dimissa pro lx m.; solvit nobis totum.

Prebenda que fuit Roberti de Hemmyngton' in ecclesia Sancti Johannis Cestr' (Chester) dimissa pro x m.; solvit nobis totum.

Vicaria de Acton' (Acton) iuxta vicum Malbanum (Middlewich) dimissa pro taxatione vii m.; solvit nobis totum.

Ecclesia de Croston' dimissa pro taxatione l m.; solvit nobis totum.

Ecclesia de Rolleston' dimissa pro taxatione xx m.; solvit nobis totum.

Prebenda Gaye Maiora (Gaia Major [41]) dimissa pro taxatione x m.; solvit nobis totum.

Ecclesia de Ledebrok' (Ladbrooke) taxata xv m., dimissa pro xvii m.; solvit nobis totum.

Ecclesia de Adderdeleye (Adderley) dimissa pro taxatione vii m. dimidia; solvit nobis totum.

Ecclesia de Biriton' (Berrington) taxata viii m., dimissa pro viii m. ii s.; solvit nobis totum.

Ecclesia de Egmenden' (Edgmond) taxata xviii m., dimissa pro xxx m.; solvit nobis totum.

Ecclesia de Routheshorn' (Rostherne) taxata xx m., dimissa pro xl m.; solvit nobis totum.

Ecclesia de Caleston' (Castleton) taxata xviii m., dimissa pro xx m.; solvit nobis totum.

Ecclesia de Draycote dimissa pro taxatione xx m.; solvit nobis totum.

Ecclesia de Tatenhull' (Tatenhill) dimissa pro taxatione xxv m., solvit nobis totum.

Ecclesia de Aston' super Trentham (Aston on Trent) dimissa pro taxatione l m.; solvit nobis totum.

Medietas ecclesie de Malo passu (Malpas) dimissa pro taxatione xx m.; solvit nobis totum.

Ecclesia de Torperlegh' (Tarporley) dimissa pro taxatione vii m. dimidia; solvit nobis totum.

Ecclesia de Nesse (Ness) dimissa pro taxatione xv m.; solvit nobis totum.

(fol. 25) [42] Ecclesia de Sutton' dimissa pro taxatione xx m.; solvit nobis totum. [43]

Ecclesia de Conede (Cound) dimissa pro traxatione xxx m.; solvit nobis totum.

Ecclesia de Albrichton' (Albrighton) taxata viii m., dimissa pro xx m.; solvit nobis totum.

Ecclesia we Davenham taxata xxx m., dimissa pro xl m.; solvit nobis totum.

Ecclesia de Wermyngham (Warmingham) taxata x m., dimissa pro xv m.; solvit nobis totum.

Ecclesia de Cristelton' (Christleton) dimissa pro taxatione xviii m.; solvit nobis totum.

Ecclesia Beate Marie Cestr' (Chester) taxata xvi m., dimissa pro xxx m.; solvit nobis totum.

Decanatus ecclesie Sancti Johannis Cestr' taxatus vi m., dimissus pro xx m.; solvit nobis totum.

Ecclesia de Bradelegh' (Bradley) dimissa pro taxatione xl m.; solvit nobis totum.

Ecclesia de Mecleston' (Mucklestone) dimissa pro taxatione xx m.; solvit nobis totum.

---

[41] In St. Chads, Lichfield.

[42] At the top of the folio occurs the heading: *Adhuc coventrensis.*

[43] In the margin bracketed against this and the next ten items: *Vacant per constitutionem.*

Prebenda de Preez (Prees) in ecclesia Lychfeldensi dimissa pro taxatione xl m.; solvit nobis totum.

Ecclesia de Haversegg' (Hathersage) dimissa pro taxatione xxiii m.; inde solvit nobis xi m. dimidiam.

Decanatus Lychfeldensis non taxatus, dimissus pro cxx m.; inde solvit nobis lxxii m.

Ecclesia de Walton, taxata lx m., dimissa pro iiiixx x m.; inde solvit nobis xlv m.

Ecclesia seu capella de Brayton' (Drayton Bassett) dimissa pro viii m.

Summa recepta Coventrensis per nos ixᶜ lxx m. ii s.

### (fol. 25ᵛ) Wygorniensis

Secundus annus et tertius in dyocesi Wygorniensi

Ecclesia de Iweby (Uley) dimissa pro xi m.; solvit nobis totum.

Ecclesia de Bredon' dimissa pro xl m.; solvit nobis totum.

Ecclesia de Shenyndon' (Shenington) dimissa pro xviii m. dimidia; solvit nobis totum.

Ecclesia de Otyndon' (Oddington) dimissa pro xvi m.; solvit nobis totum.

Ecclesia de Slymbrugg' (Slimbridge) dimissa pro xliii m.; solvit nobis totum.

Ecclesia de Toneworth' (Tanworth) dimissa pro l m.; solvit nobis totum.

(fol. 26) Ecclesia de Wyk' Risingdon' (Rissington Wick) dimissa pro vi m. dimidia; solvit nobis totum.

Ecclesia de Synesbur' (Saintbury) dimissa pro x m.; solvit nobis totum.

Ecclesia de Duntesburn' (Duntisborne) dimissa pro taxatione x m.; solvit nobis totum.

Ecclesia de Compton' Magna (Great Compton) dimissa pro taxatione xxiii m.; solvit nobis totum.

Ecclesia de Hertlebur' (Hartlebury) dimissa pro xxx m.; solvit commissario totum.

Ecclesia de Dumbleton' dimissa pro vii m.; solvit commissario totum.

Ecclesia de Wolvardynton (Wolverton) dimissa pro x m.; solvit commissario totum.

Ecclesia de Clyfford (Clifford Chambers) dimissa pro ix m.; solvit commissario totum.

Ecclesia de Dadelyngworth' (Daglingworth) dimissa pro vii m.; solvit commissario totum.

Secunda portio de Bisleya (Bisley) dimissa pro xxi m. dimidia; solvit commissario totum.

Ecclesia de Totteworth' (Tortworth) dimissa pro xi m. dimidia; solvit commissario totum.

Ecclesia de Lench' Randulf (Rouse Lench) dimissa pro vi m. dimidia; solvit commissario totum.

Vicaria de Sobbery (Sodbury) dimissa pro vii m.; solvit commissario totum.

Ecclesia de Bagendon' (Badgington) dimmissa pro viii m.; solvit commissario totum.

Ecclesia de Withyndon' (Withington) dimissa pro xxx m.; solvit commissario totum.

Ecclesia de Cumbertone magna (Great Comberton) dimissa pro vii m. iiii s.; solvit commissario totum.

Ecclesia de Strengesham (Strensham) dimissa pro xiii m. dimidia; solvit commissario totum.

Ecclesia de Rokant' (Rockhampton) dimissa pro ix m.; solvit commissario totum.

Ecclesia de Bourghton' (Bourton on the Water) dimissa pro xx m.; solvit commissario totum.

Ecclesia de Aston' Canerteltu (Aston Cantlow) dimissa pro xxxiii m.; solvit commissario totum.

Ecclesia de Musardr' (La Miserden) taxata x m., dimissa pro v m.; solvit commissario totum.

Vicaria de Hayle (Hayles) alias Tydebrok' (Didbrook) dimissa pro v m.; solvit commissario totum.

Ecclesia de Northpydele (North Piddle) taxata vi m. dimidia, dimissa pro xl s.; solvit commissario totum.

Ecclesia de Cuberleye (Coberly) taxata x m., dimissa pro xl s.; solvit commissario totum.

Prebenda Magistri Thome de Orleton' in ecclesia de Westbur' (Westbury) dimissa pro taxatione xv m.; solvit commissario totum.

Ecclesia de Beverston' (Beverstone) taxata xv m.; dimissa pro xx m.; inde solvit nobis x m. et commissario x m., et sic solvit totum.[44]

Ecclesia de Burton' dimissa pro taxatione vi m.; solvit nobis totum.

Ecclesia de Cropthorn' (Cropthorne) taxata xi m., dimissa pro xii m.; solvit commissario totum.

(fol. 26ᵛ) Ecclesia de Alvechirch' (Alvechurch) dimissa pro xxx m.; inde solvit nobis xxiii m.[45]

Ecclesia de Swyndon' (Swindon) dimissa pro vi m. dimidia; inde solvit nobis iii m. dimidiam.

Ecclesia de Salwarp' (Salwarpe) dimissa pro xii m.; inde solvit commissario x m. dimidiam.

Ecclesia de Ullebregg' (Oldberrow) dimissa pro taxatione vi m. dimidia; inde solvit nobis xx s.

Prebenda de Inceberg' (Inkberrow) in ecclesia Herfordensi et in dyocesi Wygorniensi taxata xv m., dimissa pro xii m.; inde solvit nobis vi m.

Ecclesia de Ekleshale (Exhall) dimissa pro x m.

Vicaria de Clardon' (Claverdon) dimissa pro vi m. dimidia.

Summa recepta per nos Wygorniensis cclxxviii m. Item per commissarium cc iiiixx iii m.[46] s.

### (fol. 27) Herfordensis

Secundus annus et tertius in dyocesi Herfordensi

Portio in ecclesia de Ledebur' (Ledbury) dimissa pro taxatione xl m.; solvit nobis totum.

Ecclesia de Castro Ricardi (Richard's Castle) dimissa pro taxatione xxiii li. vi s. viii d.; solvit nobis totum.

Prebenda de Morton' (Moreton Magna) dimissa pro taxatione xx li.; solvit nobis totum.

---

[44] In the margin bracketed against this and the next two items: *Vacant per constitutionem.*

[45] In the margin: *Vacat per constitutionem.*

[46] The number of shillings is cut off.

Archidiaconatus Salopie dimissus pro taxatione x li.; solvit commissario totum.

Ecclesia de Zedefenne (Edvin Ralph) dimissa pro taxatione c s.; solvit commissario totum.

Ecclesia de Tylton' (Tillington?) dimissa pro taxatione xii m.; solvit commissario totum.

Ecclesia de Kynardesleye (Kinnersley) dimissa pro taxatione xx m.; solvit commissario totum.

Ecclesia de Chetynton' (Chetton) dimissa pro taxatione xxiiii m.; solvit commissario totum.

Ecclesia de Maddeleye (Madley) dimissa pro taxatione viii li.; solvit commissario totum.

Ecclesia de Mora (More) dimissa pro taxatione vi m. dimidia; solvit commissario totum.

(fol. 27ᵛ) Portio in ecclesia de Pontesbur' (Pontesbury) dimissa pro taxatione viii m.; solvit commissario totum.

Vicaria de Welynton' (Wellington) dimissa pro taxatione vi m. dimidia; solvit commissario totum.

Ecclesia de Monynton' (Monnington) dimissa pro taxatione x m.; solvit commissario totum.

Ecclesia de Mordeford (Mordiford) dimissa pro taxatione xii m.; solvit commissario totum.

Ecclesia de Wytteburn' (Whitbourne) dimissa pro taxatione ix m.; solvit commissario totum.

Ecclesia Sancti Dubricii (St. Devereux) dimissa pro taxatione viii li.; solvit commissario totum.

Ecclesia de Mockres (Moccas) dimissa pro taxatione ix m.; solvit commissario totum.

Ecclesia de Dorsyndon' (Dorstone) dimissa pro taxatione xx li.; solvit commissario totum.

Ecclesia de Humbr' (Humber) dimissa pro taxatione c s.; solvit commissario totum.

Ecclesia de Wistanstouwe (Wistanstow) dimissa pro taxatione xx m.; solvit commissario totum.

Ecclesia de Nentsolers (Neen Sollars) dimissa pro taxatione viii li.; solvit commissario totum.

Ecclesia de Acle Pychard (Ocle Pychard) dimissa pro taxatione vii m.; solvit nobis totum.

Archidiaconatus Herfordensis dimissus pro taxatione xx li.; solvit commissario totum.[47]

Ecclesia de Aka (Rock) dimissa pro taxatione xx m.; solvit commissario totum.

Ecclesia de Kynton' (Kington) dimissa pro taxatione xx li.; inde solvit nobis x li.

Ecclesia de Radenor' veteri (Radnor) dimissa pro taxatione xl m.; inde solvit nobis xx m.

Ecclesia de Clonegunford (Clungunford) dimissa pro taxatione vi li.; inde solvit commissario c s.

Prebenda de Hyneton' (Hinton) dimissa pro taxatione viii m.

Ecclesia de Thurleston (Thruxton) dimissa pro taxatione iiii li.

[47] In the margin bracketed against this item and the next: *Vacant per constitutionem.*

(fol. 28) Portio in ecclesia de Pontesbur' (Pontesbury) dimissa pro taxatione viii m.

Summa recepta per nos Herfordensis cxl m. Item per commissarium cc iiiixx xvii m. et dimidia.

### Menevensis

Secundus annus et tertius in dyocesi Menevensi

Ecclesia de Florent' (St. Florence) taxata xx m., dimissa pro xv m.; solvit nobis totum.

Ecclesia de Lannenyth' (Lawrenny) taxata xii m., dimissa pro x m.; solvit nobis totum.

Ecclesia de Landenaylok (Llandefeilog) dimissa pro taxatione xx m.; solvit commissario totum.

Ecclesia de Lanpet' in Wilfrey (Lampeter-Velvrey) dimissa pro taxatione viii m.; solvit commissario totum.

Ecclesia de Morvill' (Morvil) dimissa pro taxatione vi m. dimidia; solvit commissario totum.

(fol. 28ᵛ) Ecclesia de Landestnian (Llanstinan?) non taxata, dimissa pro v m. dimidia; solvit commissario totum.

Ecclesia de Villa Lamberti (Lambston) dimissa pro taxatione vii m.; inde solvit commissario iii m. dimidiam.

Ecclesia Sancti Bernachi (Llanfyrnach) dimissa pro taxatione vi m. dimidia; inde solvit commissario iii m. xl d.

Ecclesia de Kilredyn (Kilrhedyn) dimissa pro taxatione c s.; inde solvit commissario l s.

Ecclesia de Langathen (Llangathen) taxata viii m.; dimissa pro vi m. dimidia.

Archidiaconatus de Kermerdyn (Carmarthen) dimissus pro taxatione xxiii m.

Ecclesia de Lanwenok (Llanwenog) dimissa pro taxatione c s.

Ecclesia de Treflegh' (Llanbadarn-Treveglwys) dimissa pro taxatione xii m.

Ecclesia de Langenchlan (Llancynvelyn) dimissa pro taxatione viii m.

Ecclesia de Lannothul (Llanwrthwl) dimissa pro taxatione viii m.

Summa recepta per nos xxv m. Item per commissarium l m. et dimidia.

### (fol. 29) Landavensis

Secundus annus et tertius in dyocesi Landavensi

Ecclesia de Coyccherch' (Coychurch) dimissa pro taxatione x li.; solvit nobis totum.

Ecclesia de Porscuet (Portskewett) taxata xii m., dimissa pro vii m.; solvit nobis totum.

Prebenda quondam Walteri de Ludeford in ecclesia Landavensi dimissa pro taxatione viii m. v s.; solvit nobis totum.

Ecclesia de Shirrevesneuton' (Shire-Newton) dimissa pro taxatione xii m.; solvit nobis totum.

Thesauraria in ecclesia Landavensi dimissa pro taxatione vii li. v s.; solvit nobis totum.

Ecclesia de Dinaspoys (Dinas Powys) dimissa pro

taxatione xx m.; inde solvit nobis x m. et commissario x m., et sic solvit totum.

Ecclesia de Rogeiate (Roggiett) dimissa pro taxatione ix m.; solvit commissario totum.

Archidiaconatus Landavensis dimissus pro taxatione xx li. xiii s. iiii d.

Summa recepta per nos Landavensis lxiii m. xl d. Item per commissarium xix m.

### (fol. 29ᵛ) Bangorensis

Secundus annus et tertius in dyocesi Bangorensi

Ecclesia de Lanbebblyk (Llanbeblig) dimissa pro taxatione viii m. dimidia; solvit nobis totum.

Prepositura ecclesie Castr' Kiby (Holyhead) dimissa pro taxatione xxxix m.; solvit nobis totum.

Ecclesia de Aberfraw (Aberffraw) dimissa pro taxatione xi m.; solvit nobis totum.

Archidiaconatus Engles' (Anglesey) dimissus pro taxatione xxx m.; solvit nobis totum.

Ecclesia de Rosfeyr (Rhosfair or Newborough) dimissa pro taxatione x m.; inde solvit nobis v m. dimidiam.

Ecclesia de Penmynye (Penmynydd) dimissa pro taxatione vi m. dimidia.

Ecclesia Sancti Petri dimissa pro taxatione viii m.

Summa recepta Bangorensis per nos iiiiˣˣ xiiii m.

### (fol. 30) Assavensis

Secundus annus et tertius in dyocesi Assavensi

Ecclesia de Monte Alto (Mold) dimissa pro taxatione l m.; inde solvit nobis xxxviii m.

Ecclesia de Machinlleith' (Machynlleth) cum ecclesia de Langyweir (Llangower or Llangywair) dimissa pro x m. dimidia; inde solvit nobis ix m. dimidiam.

Vicaria de Monte Alto (Mold) dimissa pro taxatione xv m.; inde solvit nobis x m.

Decanatus Assavensis dimissus pro xxx m.; solvit nobis totum.

Portio Lewelyn ap Ithel in ecclesia de Lannengayn (Llaneurgain or Northop) dimissa pro taxatione xviii m.; solvit nobis totum.

Portio David ap Lewath in ecclesia de Lansannan (Llansannan) dimissa pro taxatione xv m.; solvit nobis totum.

Vicaria ecclesie de Skenyok (Ysceifiog) dimissa pro taxatione ix m.; solvit nobis totum.

Vicaria de Caerwe (Caerwys) dimissa pro taxatione vi m. xx d.; solvit nobis totum.

Summa recepta per nos Assavensis cxxxv m. viii s. iiii d.

### (fol. 30ᵛ) Norwycensis

Secundus annus et tertius in dyocesi Norwycensi

Ecclesia de Stivekeye (Stiffkey) Beate Marie dimissa pro taxatione x m.; solvit nobis totum.

Ecclesia de Hadesco (Haddiscoe) dimissa pro taxatione xv m.; solvit nobis totum.

Ecclesia de Beston' (Beeston All Saints) taxata xxxiii m., dimissa pro xxiiii m.; solvit nobis totum.

Ecclesia de Hasketon' dimissa pro taxatione xx m.; solvit nobis totum.

Ecclesia de Hyntlesham (Hintlesham) dimissa pro taxatione xxxiiii m.; solvit nobis totum.

Ecclesia de Akenham dimissa pro taxatione x m.; solvit nobis totum.

Ecclesia de Stok' iuxta Gypp' (Stoke near Ipswich) dimissa pro taxatione xv m.; solvit nobis totum.

Ecclesia de Thorpmorieus (Thorpe Morieux) taxata xxviii m., dimissa pro xxv m.; solvit nobis totum.

Ecclesia de Baketon' (Baton) dimissa pro taxatione xxx m., solvit nobis totum.

Ecclesia sive capella de Tweyt (Thwaite) dimissa pro taxatione viii m.; solvit nobis totum.

Ecclesia de Whelwetham parva (Little Whelnetham) taxata vii m., dimissa pro c s.; solvit nobis totum.

Ecclesia de Leyham (Layham) dimissa pro taxatione xxii m.; solvit nobis totum.

### (fol. 31) Ecclesia de Wridelington' (Worlington) dimissa pro taxatione xxx m.; solvit nobis totum.

Ecclesia de Blyclyng' (Blickling) dimissa pro taxatione xvi m.; solvit nobis totum.

Ecclesia de Haddelegh' (Hadleigh) dimissa pro taxatione lx m.; solvit nobis totum.

Ecclesia de Waldyngfeld magna (Great Waldingfield) dimissa pro taxatione xxx m.; solvit nobis totum.

Ecclesia de Oxewyk (Oxwick) taxata x m., dimissa pro xii m.; solvit nobis totum.

Ecclesia de Lirlyng' (Larling) dimissa pro taxatione xiiii m.; solvit nobis totum.

Medietas ecclesie de Northtodenham (North Tuddenham) dimissa pro taxatione xii m.; solvit nobis totum.

Ecclesia de Fakenhamdam aspes (Fakenham Magna) taxata xviii m., dimissa pro xii m.; solvit nobis totum.

Ecclesia de Soham Monachorum (Monk Soham) dimissa pro taxatione xxv m.; solvit nobis totum.

Ecclesia de Castelrising' (Castle Rising) dimissa pro taxatione x m. dimidia; solvit nobis totum.

Ecclesia de Hevyngham (Hevingham) dimissa pro taxatione x m.; solvit nobis totum.

Ecclesia de Neweton' Floteman (Newton Flotman) dimissa pro taxatione ix m.; solvit nobis totum.

Ecclesia de Eyk (Eyke) dimissa pro taxatione xv m.; solvit nobis totum.

Ecclesia de Burgo in Carleford (Burgh, St. Andrew) dimissa pro taxatione xii m.; solvit nobis totum.

Ecclesia de Salthus (Salthouse) dimissa pro taxatione xl m.; solvit nobis totum.

Ecclesia de Bokenhamferie (Buckenham Blofield) dimissa pro taxatione vii m. dimidia; solvit nobis totum.

Ecclesia de Sandcroft (South Elmham, St. Cross) dimissa pro taxatione xv m.; solvit nobis totum.

Ecclesia de Palegrave (Palgrave) taxata xxv m., dimissa pro xxvii m.; solvit nobis totum.

Ecclesia de Refham Marie (Reepham, St. Mary) dimissa pro taxatione xvii m. dimidia; solvit nobis totum.

Medietas ecclesie de Brom (Broome) dimissa pro taxatione vii m. dimidia; solvit nobis totum.

Ecclesia de Foston' dimissa pro taxatione viii m.; solvit nobis totum.

Ecclesia de Stepelcretyng' (Creeting All Saints) dimissa pro taxatione xv m.; solvit nobis totum.

Ecclesia de Thebertone (Theberton) taxata xl m.; dimissa propter exilitatem pro xxii m.; solvit nobis totum.

Ecclesia de Naringes (Little Snoring) taxata xvii m., dimissa pro xx m.; solvit nobis totum.

Ecclesia de Byskele (Bixley) dimissa pro taxatione xvi m.; solvit nobis totum.

Ecclesia de Morlee (Morley) dimissa pro taxatione xxiiii m.; solvit nobis totum.

Ecclesia de Burgo Margarete in Flegg' (Burgh, St. Margaret) dimissa pro taxatione xiii m.; solvit nobis totum.

Ecclesia de Marleford (Marlingford) dimissa pro taxatione xiiii m.; solvit nobis totum.

Ecclesia de Falsham (Felsham) dimissa pro taxatione xiii m. dimidia; solvit nobis totum.

Ecclesia de Beston' (Beeston Regis) dimissa pro taxatione xxvii m.; solvit nobis totum.[48]

(fol. 31ᵛ) Medietas ecclesie de Leringsete (Letheringsett) dimissa pro taxatione xv m.; solvit nobis totum.[49]

Ecclesia de Aysle (Ashill) dimissa pro taxatione xx m.; solvit nobis totum.

Ecclesia de Suthreppes (Southrepps) taxata xxii m., dimissa pro xxiiii m.; solvit nobis totum.

Ecclesia de Geldeston' dimissa pro taxatione x m.; solvit nobis totum.

Ecclesia de Shadenefeld (Shadingfield) dimissa pro taxatione xviii m.; solvit nobis totum.

Ecclesia de Bradeleye magna (Great Bradley) dimissa pro taxatione xxx m.; solvit nobis totum.

Ecclesia de Elmesete (Elmsett) taxata xxii m.; dimissa pro xxiiii m.; solvit nobis totum.

Ecclesia de Lacford (Lackford) dimissa pro taxatione xxx m.; solvit nobis totum.

Ecclesia de Erpingham taxata xxv m., dimissa pro xxx m.; solvit nobis totum.

Ecclesia de Alfleton' (Alpheton) dimissa pro taxatione xv m.; solvit nobis totum.

Ecclesia de Bergh (Burgh) dimissa pro taxatione xxiiii m.; solvit nobis totum.

Ecclesia de Walepol (Walpole) taxata cx m.; dimissa pro cxv m.; solvit nobis totum.

Ecclesia de Gymyngham (Gimingham) dimissa pro taxatione xv m.; solvit nobis totum.

Ecclesia de Elyngham parva (Little Ellingham) tax-

ata x m., dimissa pro xi m.; inde solvit nobis v m. et commissario vi m., solvit totum.

Ecclesia de Refham Marie (Reepham, St. Mary) taxata xvii m.; dimissa pro xviii m. dimidia; solvit commissario totum.

Ecclesia de Byntr' (Bintree) dimissa pro taxatione xx m.; solvit commissario totum.

Ecclesia de Thomeston' (Thompson) taxata xx m., dimissa pro xxiiii m.; solvit commissario totum.

Ecclesia de Thirnyng' (Thurning) taxata xiii m., dimissa pro xiiii m.; solvit commissario totum.

Ecclesia de Wremyngham (Wreningham) dimissa pro taxatione vi m.; solvit commissario totum.

Ecclesia de Snyterton' Omnium Sanctorum (Snetterton, All Saints) taxata xviii m., dimissa pro xx m.; solvit commissario totum.

Ecclesia de Aysshwellethorp' (Ashwellthorpe) dimissa pro taxatione ix m.; solvit commissario totum.

Ecclesia de Carleton' taxata xxvi m., dimissa pro xxvii m. dimidia; solvit commissario totum.

Medietas ecclesie de Neweton' Floteman (Newton Flotman) dimissa pro taxatione ix m.; solvit commissario totum.

Ecclesia de Kirketon' in Saunford (Kirton in Shotley) dimissa pro taxatione xiii m.; solvit commissario totum.

Ecclesia de Elton' (Elveden?) taxata xx m., dimissa pro xxii m.; solvit commissario totum.

Ecclesia de Throston (Troston) taxata xvi m., dimissa pro xxii m.; inde solvit nobis v m. et commissario xvii m.; solvit totum.

Ecclesia de Irstede (Irstead) taxata xii m., dimissa pro xvi m.; solvit commissario totum.

Ecclesia de Meleford (Long Melford) dimissa pro taxatione xxx m.; solvit commissario totum.

(fol. 32 Ecclesia de Redgrave dimissa pro taxatione xl m.; solvit commissario totum.

Ecclesia de Ryston' taxata lv m., dimissa pro lx m.; solvit commissario totum.

Ecclesia de Thurston' taxata xxx m., dimissa pro xxxiiii m.; solvit commissario totum.

Ecclesia de Saxham magna taxata xx m., dimissa propter sterilitatem pro xv m.; solvit commissario totum.

Ecclesia de Suthburn' (Sudbourne) cum capella de Oreford (Orford) dimissa pro taxatione l m.; solvit commissario totum.

Ecclesia de Aldebergh (Aldeburgh) dimissa pro taxatione xvii m.; inde solvit commissario xv m. et nobis ii m., solvit totum.

Ecclesia Sancti Gregorii Subyr' (Sudbury) taxata xxv m., dimissa pro xxvii m.; solvit commissario totum.

Ecclesia de Laxefeld (Laxfield) taxata lvii m. et quia terre fuerunt inculte dimissa pro xxx m.; solvit commissario totum.

Medietas ecclesie de West Walton' dimissa pro taxatione xxi m.

---

[48] In the margin: *Vacat per constitutionem.*
[49] In the margin bracketed against this and the next thirty-six items: *Vacant per constitutionem.*

Ecclesia de Anemer' (Anmer) taxata xii m., dimissa pro xiii m.; solvit commissario totum.

Ecclesia de Lyng' taxata xx m., dimissa pro xxi m.; solvit commissario totum.

Ecclesia de Drayton' taxata x m., dimissa pro xii m.; solvit commissario totum.

Ecclesia de Antynham (Antingham) dimissa pro taxatione vi m.; solvit commissario totum.

Ecclesia de Northrungeton' (North Runcton) dimissa pro taxatione xv m.; solvit commissario totum.

Ecclesia de Burgo parva (Burgh Parva) dimissa pro taxatione vi m.; solvit commissario totum.

Ecclesia de Northbarsham taxata xii m., dimissa pro xiii m.; solvit commissario totum.

Ecclesia de Sislonde (Sisland) dimissa pro taxatione vii m.; solvit commissario totum.

Ecclesia de Stratton' Sancti Petri dimissa pro taxatione vi m.; solvit commissario totum.

Ecclesia de Denton' taxata xxxvi m., dimissa pro xxxvii m.; solvit commissario totum.

Ecclesia de Sotherton' dimissa pro taxatione viii m.; solvit commissario totum.

Ecclesia de Kirketon' in Colnese (Kirton in the deanery of Colneys) dimissa pro taxatione xvi m.; solvit commissario totum.

Ecclesia de Dalyngho (Dallinghoo) dimissa pro taxatione xx m.; solvit commissario totum.

Ecclesia de Somerleton' (Somerleyton) taxata xvi m., dimissa pro xx m.; solvit commissario totum.

Ecclesia de Heggesete (Hessett) taxata xv m., dimissa pro c s.; inde solvit nobis l s. et commissario l s., solvit totum.

(fol. 32ᵛ) Ecclesia de Ikelingham (Icklingham) Omnium Sanctorum dimissa pro taxatione xx m.; solvit commissario totum.

Ecclesia de Cretyng' (Creeting) Sancti Petri dimissa pro taxatione xv m.; solvit commissario totum.

Ecclesia de Melles (Mellis) dimissa pro taxatione xv m.; solvit commissario totum.

Ecclesia de Wychingham (Witchingham) Sancte Fidis dimissa pro taxatione c s.; solvit commissario totum.

Ecclesia de Freton' in Luthynglond (Fritton in the deanery of Lothingland) dimissa pro taxatione x m.; solvit commissario totum.

Ecclesia de Blundeston' dimissa pro taxatione xx m.; solvit commissario totum.

Ecclesia de Tremeleye (Trimley) Sancti Martini dimissa pro taxatione xv m.; inde solvit nobis vi m. et commissario ix m., solvit totum.

Ecclesia de Toft Monachorum (Toft Monks) taxata viii m., dimissa pro x m. dimida; solvit commissario totum.

Ecclesia de Castr' Trinitatis (Caister next Yarmouth) taxata xxx m., dimissa pro xxv m.; inde solvit nobis viii m. dimidiam et commissario xvi m. dimidiam, solvit totum.

Medietas ecclesie de Howe dimissa pro taxatione vi m. dimidia; inde solvit nobis xliii s. iiii d. et commissario xliii s. iiii d., solvit totum.

Ecclesia de Warham Marie dimissa pro taxatione c s.; solvit commissario totum.

Ecclesia de Longa Stratton' Marie (Stratton, St. Mary) taxata xviii m., dimissa pro xx m.; inde solvit nobis ix m. dimidiam et commissario x m. dimidiam, solvit totum.

Ecclesia de Cleye iuxta mare (Cleye next the Sea) dimissa pro taxatione xxxiiii m.; inde solvit nobis xvi m. dimidiam et commissario xvii m. dimidiam, solvit totum.

Ecclesia de Ufford taxata x m., dimissa pro xii m.; solvit commissario totum.

Ecclesia de Hoo dimissa pro taxatione xi m.; inde solvit nobis v m. et commissario vi m., solvit totum.

Ecclesia de Huneworth' (Hunworth) non taxata, dimissa pro xl s.; solvit commissario totum.

Vicaria de Gaysle (Gazeley) taxata x m., dimissa pro x m. dimidia.; solvit commissario totum.

Vicaria de Ludham (Loudham) dimissa pro taxatione viii m.; inde solvit nobis vii m. xl d. et commissario x s., solvit totum.

Medietas ecclesie de Sidestronde (Sidestrand) dimissa pro taxatione x m.; inde solvit nobis v m. et commissario v m., solvit totum.

Ecclesia de Suthbirlingham (South Burlingham) dimissa pro taxatione xx m.; solvit commissario totum.

Ecclesia de Santon' taxata lx s., dimissa pro iiii m.; solvit commissario totum.

Vicaria de Eye dimissa pro taxatione viii m.; solvit commissario totum.[50]

(fol. 33) Decanatus de Holt' non taxatus, dimmissus pro ii m.; solvit commissario totum.[51]

Vicaria de Elvergate (Halvergate?) dimissa pro taxatione vi m. ix s.; solvit commissario totum.

Vicaria de Codenham (Coddenham) dimissa pro taxatione xvi m.; inde solvit nobis vii m. dimidiam et commissario viii m. dimidiam; solvit totum.

Ecclesia de Molton' (Moulton) dimissa pro xxxv m.; solvit nobis totum.

Ecclesia de Wetherefeld (Withersfield) dimissa pro taxatione xvii m.; inde solvit nobis viii m. dimidiam.

Ecclēsia de Brecham (Bircham) dimissa pro xv m.; solvit nobis totum.

Ecclesia de Tatyngton' (Tannington) cum capella de Burnedysh' (Brundish) dimissa pro taxatione xl m.; inde solvit nobis xxx m.

Ecclesia de Suthelmham (South Elmham) Omnium Sanctorum taxata xii m.; dimissa pro xiii m.

Summa recepta Norwicensis per nos mˡ cccvii m. x s. Item recepta ⟨per⟩ commissarium ixᶜ lxxv m. v s. viii d.

---

[50] In the margin: *Non est in certificatione.*

[51] In the margin bracketed against this and the next five items: *Non sunt in ceritificatione.*

(fol. 33ᵛ) Elyensis

Secundus annus et tertius in dyocesi Elyensi

Ecclesia de Abyndon' magna (Great Abington) dimissa pro taxatione xvi m.; solvit nobis totum.

Ecclesia de Leveryngton' (Leverington) dimissa pro taxatione cxxvii m. dimidia; solvit nobis totum.

Ecclesia de Elm cum capella de Elmeth' (Emneth) dimissa pro taxatione l m.; solvit nobis totum.

Ecclesia de Stepelmordon' (Steeple Morden) taxata c m., dimissa pro lxx m.; solvit nobis totum.

Ecclesia de Pappeworth' Agneys (Papworth, St. Agnes) dimissa pro taxatione xv m.; solvit nobis totum.

Ecclesia de Wyvelyngham (Willingham) dimissa pro taxatione xl m.; solvit nobis totum.[52]

Ecclesia de Barnton' (Barrington) dimissa pro taxatione xl li.; solvit commissario totum.

Ecclesia de Hildresham (Hildersham) dimissa pro xx m.; solvit commissario totum.

Ecclesia de parva Eversdon' (Little Eversden) taxata x m., dimissa propter exilitatem pro v m.; solvit commissario totum.

Ecclesia Sancte Marie Cantebr' (Cambridge) dimissa pro taxatione vi m. dimidia; inde solvit nobis iii m. xl d. et commissario iii m. xl d., solvit totum.

Ecclesia Omnium Sanctorum de Longa Staunton' (Long Stanton) dimissa pro taxatione l m.; inde solvit nobis xxv m.

Ecclesia de Pappeworth' Everard (Papworth Everard) taxata xv m., dimissa propter exilitatem pro x m.; solvit commissario totum.

(fol. 34) Ecclesia de Litlyngton' (Litlington) dimissa pro taxatione xxxi m.; solvit nobis totum.

Ecclesia de Trumpeton' (Trumpington) dimissa pro taxatione xxx m.; solvit nobis totum.

Ecclesia de Erdwyk (Hardwick) taxata xvi m., dimissa pro xv m.; solvit nobis totum.

Summa recepta per nos Eliensis iiiiᶜ xxii m. x s. Item per commissarium iiiiˣˣ xviii m. xl ⟨d.⟩

Lyncolniensis

Secundus annus et tertius in dyocesi Lyncolniensi

Ecclesia de Candelesby (Candlesby) dimissa pro taxatione xiii m. dimidia; solvit nobis totum.

Ecclesia de Friseby (Firsby) dimissa pro taxatione xix m. dimidia; solvit nobis totum.

Ecclesia de Bokenhale (Bucknall) dimissa pro taxatione xv m. dimidia; solvit nobis totum.

Prebenda de Luda (Louth) in ecclesia Lincolniensi dimissa pro taxatione lxx m.; solvit nobis totum.

Prebenda de Northon' (Bishop Norton) dimissa pro taxatione l m.; solvit nobis totum.

Ecclesia de Whytewek (Whitwick) dimissa pro taxatione xx m.; solvit nobis totum.

Ecclesia de Outheby (Oadby) dimissa pro taxatione xix m.; solvit nobis totum.

Ecclesia de Ridelyngton' (Ridlington) dimissa pro xii m.; solvit nobis totum.

Vicaria de Okham (Oakham) dimissa pro xxx m.; solvit nobis totum.

Due partes ecclesie de Clypston' (Clipston) taxata tota ecclesia xxii m., dimissa pro xiiii m.; solvit nobis totum.

Ecclesia de Pyghtesle (Pytchley) dimissa pro taxatione xxx m.; solvit nobis totum.

(fol 34ᵛ) Ecclesia de Therfeld (Therfield) dimissa pro taxatione l m.; solvit nobis totum.

Ecclesia de Aldebur' (Aldbury) dimissa pro taxatione ix m.; solvit nobis totum.

Ecclesia de Glatton' dimissa pro taxatione xxxi m. x s.; solvit nobis totum.

Ecclesia de Stilton' dimissa pro taxatione x m.; solvit nobis totum.

Prebenda de Bykeleswade (Biggleswade) in ecclesia Lyncolniensi dimissa pro lxx m.; solvit nobis totum.

Ecclesia de Felmeresham (Felmersham) dimissa pro taxatione xl m.; solvit nobis totum.

Ecclesia de Sulthorp' (Souldrop) taxata c s., dimissa pro x m.; solvit nobis totum.

Ecclesia de Brughton' (Broughton) dimissa pro taxatione ix m.; solvit nobis totum.

Ecclesia de Stok' Hamund (Stoke Hammond) dimissa pro taxatione xii m.; solvit nobis totum.

Ecclesia de Ivyngho (Ivinghoe) dimissa pro taxatione lv m.; solvit nobis totum.

Ecclesia de Newenton' (South Newington) taxata xvi m., dimissa pro xxv m.; solvit nobis totum.

Ecclesia de Wytteneye (Witney) taxata vi m., dimissa propter exilitatem pro iii m.; solvit nobis totum.

Ecclesia de Weston' non taxata, dimissa pro vii m.; solvit nobis totum.

Ecclesia de Blechesdon' (Bletchingdon) dimissa pro taxatione xv m.; solvit nobis totum.

Prebenda de Langeford (Langford) Manerium in ecclesia Lincolniensi dimissa pro lx m.; solvit nobis totum.

Ecclesia de Denton' dimissa pro taxatione xxx m.; solvit nobis totum.

Ecclesia de Ingoldeby (Ingoldsby) taxata xxxix m. dimidia, dimissa pro xxx m.; solvit nobis totum.

Ecclesia de Askeby iuxta Partenay (Ashby by Partney) dimissa pro taxatione xviii m.; solvit nobis totum.

Ecclesia de Bernolby (Barnoldby le Beck) dimissa pro taxatione xxii m. dimidia; solvit nobis totum.

Ecclesia de Donyngton' super Blayn (Donington on Bain) dimissa pro taxatione c s.; solvit nobis totum.

Ecclesia de Cotesbergh' (Cotesbach) dimissa pro taxatione xiiii m.; solvit nobis totum.

Ecclesia de Aylmeresthorp' (Elmesthorpe) dimissa pro taxatione x m.; solvit nobis totum.

---

[52] In the margin bracketed against this and the next two items: *Vacant per constitutionem.*

Ecclesia de Louseby (Lowesby) dimissa pro taxatione vii m.; solvit nobis totum.

Ecclesia de Houby (Hoby) dimissa pro taxatione xx m.; solvit nobis totum.

Ecclesia de Shathewell' (Shawell) dimissa pro taxatione xii m.; solvit nobis totum.

Ecclesia de Stanegrunde (Standground) dimissa pro taxatione xxx m.; solvit nobis totum.

Ecclesia de Thernyng' (Thurning) dimissa pro taxatione xii m.; solvit nobis totum.

Ecclesia de Abbotesle (Abbotsley) dimissa pro taxatione xxxvi m.; solvit nobis totum.

Ecclesia de Savecamp' (Sacombe) taxata x m., dimissa propter exilitatem pro v m.; solvit nobis totum.

Ecclesia de Hattele (Cokayne Hatley) dimissa pro taxatione xi m.; solvit nobis totum.

Ecclesia de Islep (Islip) dimissa pro taxatione xvi m.; solvit nobis totum.

(fol. 35) Ecclesia de Saundeye (Sandy) dimissa pro taxatione xx m.; solvit nobis totum.

Ecclesia de Lega (North Leigh) dimissa pro taxatione xv m.; solvit nobis totum.

Prebenda de Leghton' Busard (Leighton Buzzard) in ecclesia Lyncolniensi taxata cxliii m., dimissa pro c m.; solvit nobis totum.

Ecclesia de Asshele (Ashley) taxata x m., dimissa pro xii m.; solvit nobis totum.

Ecclesia de Normanton' iuxta Empyngham (Empingham) dimissa pro taxatione c s.; solvit nobis totum.

Ecclesia de Weston' dimissa pro taxatione c s.; solvit nobis totum.

Ecclesia de Farnedon' (Farndon) dimissa pro taxatione xii m.; solvit nobis totum.

Ecclesia de Lodyngton' (Loddington) dimissa pro taxatione xi m.; solvit nobis totum.

Ecclesia de Spillebur' (Spelsbury) dimissa pro taxatione xx m.; solvit nobis totum.

Ecclesia de Heyford Warin (Heyford Warren or Upper) dimissa pro taxatione viii m. dimidia; solvit nobis totum.

Ecclesia de Staunton Harecourt (Stanton Harcourt) dimissa pro taxatione xxx m.; solvit nobis totum.

Ecclesia de Swynecombe dimissa pro taxatione vii m.; solvit nobis totum.

Ecclesia de Ewelme dimissa pro taxatione viii m.; solvit nobis totum.

Ecclesia de Tyngewyk (Tingewick) dimissa pro taxatione xi m.; solvit nobis totum.

Ecclesia de Bekenesfeld (Beaconsfield) dimissa pro taxatione xxiii m.; solvit nobis totum.

Ecclesia de Magna Brichull' (Great Brickhill) dimissa pro taxatione xi m.; solvit nobis totum.

Prebenda de Castr' (Caistor) in ecclesia Lincolnensi dimissa pro taxatione lxxviii m.; solvit nobis totum.

Ecclesia de Rypton' Abbatis (Abbots Ripton) taxata xxxv m., dimissa pro xlvii m.; solvit nobis totum.

Ecclesia de Savecamp' (Sacombe) dimissa pro taxatione x m. dimidia; solvit nobis totum.

Ecclesia de Derford (Desford) dimissa pro taxatione x m.; solvit nobis totum.

Ecclesia de Carleton' Curly (Carlton Curlieu) dimissa pro taxatione xxvi m.; solvit nobis totum.

Ecclesia de Wychamstede (Wheathamstead) dimissa pro xx m.; solvit nobis totum.

Ecclesia de Wottesdon' (Waddesdon) dimissa pro taxatione xii m.; solvit nobis totum.

Prebenda de Leghton' manerium super Bromeswold (Leighton Bromswold manor) dimissa pro taxatione lxx m.; solvit nobis totum.

Ecclesia de Byfeld (Byfield) dimissa pro taxatione xxx m.; solvit nobis totum.

Ecclesia de magna Billyng' (Great Billing) dimissa pro taxation xii m.; solvit nobis totum.

Ecclesia de Kenilingworth' (South Kilworth), taxata xvi m., dimissa pro x m.; solvit nobis totum.

Ecclesia de Kirketon (Kirton) dimissa pro taxatione iiiixx m.; solvit nobis totum.[53]

Ecclesia de Tydde (Tydd, St. Mary) dimissa pro taxatione lxxiii m.; solvit nobis totum.

Ecclesia de Holbech' (Holbeach) dimissa pro taxatione c iiiixx m.; solvit nobis totum.

Ecclesia de Northorp' (Northorpe) taxata xxiiii m., dimissa pro xxvii m.; solvit nobis totum.

(fol. 35v) Ecclesia de Brampton' dimissa pro taxatione xxiii m.; solvit nobis totum.[54]

Ecclesia de Braundeston' (Braunston) dimissa pro taxatione xxx m.; solvit nobis totum.

Ecclesia de Ibestok' (Ibstock) dimissa pro taxatione xxxv m.; solvit nobis totum.

Ecclesia de Navesby (Naseby) dimissa pro taxatione xxiiii m.; solvit nobis totum.

Ecclesia de Raundes (Rauds) dimissa pro taxatione lx m.; solvit nobis totum.

Ecclesia de Clyve (King's Cliffe) dimissa pro taxatione xxx m.; solvit nobis totum.

Ecclesia de Esenden' (Essendon) dimissa pro taxatione xxvi m.; solvit nobis totum.

Ecclesia de Catworth' taxata xxv d., dimissa pro xxvii m.; solvit nobis totum.

Ecclesia de Waulyngton' (Wallington) dimissa pro taxatione xii m.; solvit nobis totum.

Ecclesia de Badelesdon' (Battlesden) dimissa pro taxatione viii m.; solvit nobis totum.

Ecclesia de Estcleydon' (East Claydon) dimissa pro taxatione x m.; solvit nobis totum.

Ecclesia de Hamelton' (Hambleton) dimissa pro taxatione xxxv m.; solvit nobis totum.

Ecclesia de Cherchull' (Churchill) dimissa pro taxatione xx m.; solvit nobis totum.

---

[53] In the margin bracketed against this and the next three items: *Vacant per constitutionem.*

[54] In the margin bracketed against this and all the items on folio 35v: *Vacant per constitutionem.*

Ecclesia de Ardele (Ardley) taxata vi m., dimissa pro viii m. dimidia; solvit nobis totum.

Ecclesia Beate Marie Oxonie taxata xxiii m., dimissa pro xl m.; solvit nobis totum.

Ecclesia de Lyndwode (Linwood) dimissa pro taxatione xx m.; inde solvit nobis x m. et commissario x m., solvit totum.

Ecclesia de Stouwe (Stowe) taxata xv m., dimissa pro xviii m.; solvit nobis totum.

Ecclesia de Ilvertoft (Yelvertoft) dimissa pro taxatione xiii m.; solvit nobis totum.

Ecclesia de Iakesle (Yaxley) dimissa pro taxatione liii m.; solvit nobis totum.

Ecclesia de Thyngden' (Finedon) dimissa pro taxatione lx m.; solvit nobis totum.

Ecclesia de Woford (Woodford Halse) dimissa pro taxatione xx m.; solvit nobis totum.

Tertia portio ecclesie de Wadeston' (Waddesdon) dimissa pro taxatione xv m.; solvit nobis totum.

Ecclesia de Hahwell' (Holywell) dimissa pro taxatione xx m.; solvit nobis totum.

Ecclesia de Hellowe (Belleau) taxata xxiii m.; dimissa propter exilitatem pro c s.; solvit commissario totum.

Ecclesia de parva Stepyng (Little Steeping) dimissa pro taxatione xxii m.; solvit commissario totum.

Ecclesia de Helmeswell' (Helmswell) dimissa pro taxatione xxx m.; solvit commissario totum.

Ecclesia de Springthorp' (Springthorpe) dimissa pro taxatione xii m.; solvit commissario totum.

Ecclesia de Malmeton' (Manton) dimissa pro taxatione xviii m.; solvit commissario totum.

Ecclesia de Marham (Marholm) dimissa pro taxatione xii m.; solvit commissario totum.

(fol. 36) Ecclesia de Rotheby (Ratby) dimissa pro taxatione xxxiii m.; solvit commissario totum.[55]

Ecclesia de Welton' dimissa pro taxatione xxiiii m.; solvit commissario totum.

Ecclesia de Langeton' iuxta Horn' (Langton by Horncastle) dimissa pro taxatione x m.; solvit commissario totum.

Due partes ecclesie de Floteby (Saltfleetby) Sancti Petri, taxata tota ecclesia xix m., dimissa pro xi m.; solvit commissario totum.

Ecclesia de Wragby (Wrawby) dimissa pro taxatione xvi m.; solvit commissario totum.

Ecclesia de Claxby dimissa pro taxatione x m.; solvit commissario totum.

Vicaria ecclesie de Cameryngham (Cammeringham) dimissa pro taxatione vii m.; solvit nobis totum.

Ecclesia de Scampton' non taxata, dimissa pro x m.; solvit commissario totum.

Prebenda de Lidyngton' (Liddington) in ecclesia Lyncolniensi dimissa pro taxatione xlviii m.; solvit commissario totum.

Subdecanatus Lyncolniensis dimissus pro taxatione lx m.; solvit commissario totum.

Medietas ecclesie de Suthwyme (South Witham) taxata xviii m., dimissa pro x m.; solvit commissario totum.

Ecclesia de Swynthorp' (Swinhope) taxata xviii m., et quia non sufficit residuum pro oneribus dimissa pro x m.; solvit commissario totum.

Ecclesia de Douseby (Dowsby) dimissa pro taxatione xx m. dimidia; solvit commissario totum.

Ecclesia de Stikeford (Stickford) dimissa pro taxatione xvii m.; solvit commissario totum.

Ecclesia de Morton' taxata xv m., dimissa pro x m. x s.; solvit commissario totum.

Prebenda de Haydor cum Walton' dimissa pro taxatione lx m.; solvit commissario totum.

Medietas ecclesiarum de Colyntr' (Collingtree) et Midelton' (Milton) dimissa pro taxatione vi m. x s.; solvit commissario totum.

Ecclesia de Tynton' inferior' (Low Toynton) dimissa pro x m.; solvit commissario totum.

Ecclesia de Thornton' (Thornton-le-Moor) iuxta Keles' (South Kelsey) dimissa pro taxatione xx m.; solvit commissario totum.

Ecclesia de Askeby (Ashby) dimissa pro taxatione xx m.; solvit commissario totum.

Ecclesia de North Scarle dimissa pro ix m.; solvit commissario totum.

Ecclesia de Blakeneye (Blankney) dimissa pro taxatione xxxii m. dimidia; solvit commissario totum.

Ecclesia de Cateby (Cadeby) dimissa pro viii m.; inde solvit nobis vi m. et commissario ii m., solvit totum.

Ecclesia de Ardelthrop (Addlethorp) dimissa pro taxatione xv m.; solvit commissario totum.

Ecclesia de Wilye (Willian) dimissa pro taxatione xx m.; solvit commissario totum.

Ecclesia de Hannyngton' (Hannington) dimissa pro taxatione vi m. dimidia; solvit commissario totum.

Ecclesia de Colby dimissa pro xl m.; solvit commissario totum.

(fol. 36ᵛ) Due partes ecclesie de Saltfleteby (Saltfleetby) Sancti Petri dimisse pro xi m.; solvit commissario totum.

Medietas ecclesie de Lekeburn' (Legbourne) dimissa pro taxatione xi m.; solvit commissario totum.

Ecclesia de Eppeworth' (Epworth) dimissa pro taxatione xxx m.; solvit commissario totum.

Ecclesia de Shanketon' (Shangton) dimissa pro taxatione viii m.; solvit commissario totum.

Vicaria ecclesie de Friskeneye (Friskney) dimissa pro taxatione c s.; solvit commissario totum.

Vicaria de Messyngham (Messingham) dimissa pro taxatione vii m.; solvit commissario totum.

Ecclesia de Hauteberg' (Alkborough) dimissa pro taxatione viii m.; solvit commissario totum.

Ecclesia de Muston' dimissa pro taxatione xvi m. xi s. iiii d.; solvit commissario totum.

---

[55] In the margin: *Vacat per constitutionem.*

Ecclesia de Herderby (Harby) dimissa pro xl m.; inde solvit nobis xx m. et commissario xx m.; solvit totum.

Ecclesia de Botheby (Boothby) dimissa pro taxatione xxxiii m.; solvit commissario totum.

Ecclesia de Waldneuton' (Wold Newton) taxata xviii m., dimissa pro xx m.; inde solvit nobis xvi m. xx d.[56]

Ecclesia de Paykirk' (Peakirk) taxata xxv m., dimissa pro xx m.; inde solvit nobis xvi m. xl d.

Ecclesia de Hatfeld (Hatfield) dimissa pro taxatione lv m.; inde solvit nobis xlvii m. dimidiam.

Ecclesia de Fletmerston (Fleet Marston) taxata vi m,; dimissa pro v m.; inde solvit nobis i m.

Ecclesia de Dadyngton (Deddington) dimissa pro taxatione lx m.; inde solvit nobis xxii m.

Archidiaconatus Huntingdonie, Bedfordie et Stowye inde habuimus xxiiii li. vi s. viii d.

(fol. 37) Medietas ecclesie de Roxeby (Roxby) dimissa pro taxatione xii m.; inde solvit commissario viii m.

Ecclesia de Berughby (Barrowby) dimissa pro taxatione xlv m.; inde solvit commissario xl m.

Ecclesia de Swynhop' (Swinhope) dimissa pro v m.; inde solvit commissario ii m. dimidiam.

Ecclesia de Fordyngton' (Fordington) dimissa pro taxatione x m. dimidia; inde solvit commissario ix m. dimidiam.

Vicaria de Cauburn' (Cabourn) dimissa pro v m.; inde solvit commissario ii m. dimidiam.

Ecclesia de Olneye (Olney) dimissa pro taxatione l m.; inde solvit nobis xxv m.

Ecclesia de Netlesham (Nettleham) dimissa pro taxatione xii m.; inde solvit nobis vi m.

Ecclesia de Eston' (Aston le Walls or Easton on the Hill) taxata xv m., dimissa pro xiii m.

Ecclesia de Haselbech' (Haselbeech) dimissa pro taxatione x m.

Vicaria de Thame dimissa pro taxatione xii m.

Vicaria de Boterwyk' (Butterwick) dimissa pro taxatione vi m. dimidia.

(fol. 37ᵛ) Ecclesia de Walweby (Wrawby) dimissa pro taxatione xxxiiii m.

Ecclesia de Hale dimissa pro taxatione liiii m.

Ecclesia de Broughton' dimissa pro taxatione ix m.

Ecclesia de Wolyngham (South Willingham) dimissa pro taxatione xxv m.

Ecclesia de Shenle (Shenley) dimissa pro xx m.; solvit nobis totum.[57]

Ecclesia de Sileby dimissa pro xxvii m.; solvit nobis totum.

Prebenda de Nassington' dimissa pro cl m.; solvit nobis totum.

Ecclesia de Russynden' (Rushden) dimissa pro x m.; solvit nobis totum.

Ecclesia de Ravenesthorp' (Ravensthorpe) dimissa pro xxviii m.; solvit nobis totum.

Ecclesia de Gretford (Greatford) dimissa pro xl m.; solvit nobis totum.

Ecclesia de Folkyngham (Folkingham) dimissa pro xii m.; solvit nobis totum.

Ecclesia de Farnham (Farnham Royal) dimissa pro xxiiii m.; solvit nobis totum.

Ecclesia de Bynnebrok (Binbrook) dimissa pro xviii m.; solvit nobis totum.

Minor pars ecclesie de Clypston' (Clipston) dimissa pro c s.; solvit nobis totum.

Prebenda de Brampton' dimissa pro liii m.; solvit nobis totum.

Summa recepta Lincolniensis per nos mˡ cxlii m. xi s. viii d. Item recepta ⟨per⟩ commissarium viiiᶜ lxv m. iiii s. viii d.[58]

## (fol. 38) Eboracensis

Secundus annus et tertius in dyocesi Eboracensi

Ecclesia de Kyghelay (Keighley) dimissa pro taxatione xii m.; solvit nobis totum.

Ecclesia de Sprotburgh (Sprotbrough) dimissa pro taxatione xl m.; solvit nobis totum.

Ecclesia de Kilyngton' (Kilvington) dimissa pro taxatione x li.; solvit nobis totum.

Prebenda de Laghton' in Morthyng' (Laughton en le Morthen) dimissa pro taxatione cx m.; solvit nobis totum.

Prebenda de Aplesthorp' (Apesthorpe) dimissa pro taxatione x li.; solvit nobis totum.

Prebenda quondam Domini Ingelardi de Warle in ecclesia Suwell' (Southwell) dimissa pro taxatione xl m.; solvit nobis totum.

Prebenda quondam Domini Roberti de Cotyngham in ecclesia Hoveden' (Howden) dimissa pro taxatione l m.; solvit nobis totum.

Archidiaconatus Eboracensis taxatus lxvii li., dimissus pro l m.; solvit nobis totum.

Vicaria ecclesie de Otteleye (Otley) taxata x m., dimissa propter exilitatem pro v m.; solvit nobis totum.

Prebenda de Fridaythorp' (Fridaythorpe) taxata lx m., dimissa pro xxx m.; solvit nobis totum.

Due partes ecclesie de Brayton' dimisse ad firmam pro xliiii m.; solvit nobis totum.[59]

Ecclesia de Brantyngham (Brantingham) dimissa pro taxatione c m.; solvit episcopo Elyensi.

Archidiaconatus Estridyng' taxatus xlii li. vi s. viii d., dimissus pro xxv li.; solvit nobis totum.

Ecclesia de Birkyn (Birkin) dimissa pro taxatione xl m.; solvit commissario totum.

---

[56] In the margin bracketed against this and the next five items: *Vacant per constitutionem.*

[57] In the margin bracketed against this and the remaining items of this folio: *Non sunt in certificatione.*

[58] The next recto and verso are blank. They are not numbered in foliation by hand.

[59] In the margin bracketed against this and the remaining items on this folio: *Vacant per constitutionem.*

Ecclesia de Foston' (Fewston) dimissa pro xx li.; solvit commissario totum.

Ecclesia de Mirefeld (Mirfield) dimissa pro taxatione xx m.; solvit commissario totum.

Ecclesia de Treton' (Treeton) dimissa pro taxatione xx m.; solvit commissario totum.

Ecclesia de Derton' (Darton) dimissa pro taxatione xxxv m.; solvit commissario totum.

Ecclesia de Esrik (Escrick) dimissa pro taxatione xxx li.; solvit commissario totum.

Ecclesia de Lyth' (Lythe) dimissa pro taxatione l m.; solvit commissario totum.

Ecclesia de Catton' (High Catton) dimissa pro taxatione lx m.; solvit commissario totum.

Ecclesia de Eyton' (Etton) dimissa pro taxatione xxiiii m.; solvit commissario totum.

Ecclesia de Elveleye (Kirk Ella) dimissa pro taxatione lxx m.; solvit totum commissario.

Ecclesia de Aghton' (Aughton) dimissa pro taxatione lx m.; solvit commissario totum.

Ecclesia de Hugate (Huggate) taxata lx m., dimissa pro xlvii m.; solvit commissario totum.

Ecclesia de Warsop dimissa pro taxatione xxxv m.; solvit commissario totum.

Ecclesia de Tuxford dimissa pro taxatione xxx m.; solvit commissario totum.

(fol. 38ᵛ) Ecclesia de Warton taxata c m., dimissa pro l m.; solvit commissario totum.[60]

Prebenda de Thorp (Thorpe) in ecclesia de Hoveden' (Howden) dimissa pro xl m.; solvit commissario totum.

Ecclesia de Wytstan (Whiston) dimissa pro taxatione xvi m.; solvit commissario totum.

Ecclesia de Gillyng' in Ridale (Gilling in Ryedale) dimissa pro taxatione xxiiii m.; solvit commissario totum.

Ecclesia de Holm in Spaldingmor (Holm on Spalding Moor) dimissa pro taxatione xxv m.; solvit commissario totum.

Ecclesia de Hesington' in Hold (Easington in Holderness) dimissa pro taxatione lx m.; solvit commissario totum.

Ecclesia de Claworth' (Clayworth) dimissa pro taxatione xxxv m.; solvit commissario totum.

Ecclesia de Kneueton' (Caunton) dimissa pro taxatione x li.; solvit commissario totum.

Ecclesia de magna Usburn' (Great Ouseburn) taxata xviii m., dimissa pro xv m.; solvit commissario totum.

Ecclesia de Birton' super Trentham (Burton Joyce) dimissa pro taxatione xviii m.; inde solvit nobis xv m.[61]

Ecclesia Sancti Michaelis super Wyre (St. Michael on Wyre) dimissa pro taxatione c m.; inde solvit commissario l m.

Ecclesia de Goldesburgh (Goldsborough) dimissa pro taxatione xxv m.; inde solvit commissario xii m. dimidiam.

Ecclesia de Egermunde (Egremont) taxata xviii m., dimissa pro viii m.

Vicaria de Gamelton' (Ganton) dimissa pro taxatione viii m.; inde solvit commissario iiii m.

Vicaria ecclesie de Burton' Flemyng' (Burton Fleming) dimissa pro taxatione c s.; inde solvit commissario l s.

Ecclesia de Fletebur' (Fledborough) dimissa pro taxatione xx m.; inde solvit commissario x m.

(fol. 39) Ecclesia de Bramwyth' (Kirt Bramwith) dimissa pro taxatione xx m.; inde solvit commissario x m.

Ecclesia de Arkeseye (Arksey) dimissa pro taxatione lx m.; inde solvit nobis xv m.

Ecclesia de Haytefeld (Hatfield) dimissa pro taxatione lxx m.; inde solvit commissario xxxv m.

Medietas ecclesie de Derfeld (Darfield) dimissa pro taxatione lv m.; inde solvit commissario xx m.

Ecclesia de Tribergh' (Thrybergh) dimissa pro taxatione x m.; inde solvit commissario v m.

Vicaria ecclesie de Pagla' (Paull) dimissa pro taxatione x m.; inde solvit commissario v m.

Ecclesia de Hikelyng' (Hickling) dimissa pro taxatione xx li.; inde solvit commissario x li.

Ecclesia de Boneye (Bunny) dimissa pro taxatione xl m.; inde solvit nobis xx m.

Ecclesia de Thornhull' (Thornhill) dimissa pro taxatione xl li.

Vicaria ecclesie de Nyweton' Rocheford (Wold Newton) dimissa pro taxatione x m.

(fol. 39ᵛ) Ecclesia de Tatham dimissa pro taxatione x m.

Ecclesia de Leek (Leake) dimissa pro taxatione xl m.

Ecclesia de Askham Ricardi (Askham Richard) dimissa pro taxatione x m.

Vicaria de Crambu' (Crambe) dimissa pro taxatione x li.

Summa recepta per nos Eboracensis vᶜ iiiixx xviii m. et dimidia. Item per commissarium mˡ xxxv m. xl d.[62]

### (fol. 40ᵛ) Dunolmensis

Secundus annus et tertius in dyocesi Dunolmensi

Ecclesia de Quicham (Whickham) dimissa pro xx s.; solvit commissario totum.

Ecclesia de Langneuton' (Long Newton) dimissa pro xx li.; solvit commissario totum.[63]

Ecclesia de Stayndrop (Staindrop) dimissa pro lx li.; inde solvit nobis xl li.

---

[60] In the margin bracketed against this and the next item: *Vacant per constitutionem.*

[61] In the margin bracketed against this and the next three items: *Vacant per constitutionem.*

[62] Folio 40 is blank.

[63] In the margin bracketed against this item and the next: *Vacant per constitutionem.*

Ecclesia de Crayk (Crayke) dimissa pro x li.; solvit commissario totum.

Ecclesia de Redmereshill' (Redmarshall) dimissa pro xi m.; solvit commissario totum.

Vicaria de Kelhou (Kelloe) dimissa pro xxvi s. viii d., solvit commissario totum.

Ecclesia de Wessington' (Washington) dimissa pro xiii li. vi s. viii d.; solvit commissario totum.

Vicaria de Middelham (Bishop Middleham) dimissa pro xxiii s. vii d. quadrante; solvit commissario totum.

Vicaria de Stranton' dimissa pro vi li. xiii s. iiii d.; solvit commissario totum.

Vicaria de Pidyngton' (Pittington) dimissa pro li. s. viii d.; solvit commissario totum.

Ecclesia de Walsingham (Wolsingham) dimissa pro xl s.; solvit commissario totum.

(fol. 41) Prebenda que fuit Magistri Alani de Kirkham (in Auckland) dimissa pro vi li. xiii s. iiii d.

Summa recepta per nos Dunelmensis lx m. Item per commissarium iiiixx xviii m. xxiii d. et quadrans.

### Karleolensis

Secundus annus et tertius in dyocesi Karleolensi.

Archidiaconatus Karleolensis dimissus pro v m.; solvit commissario totum.

Ecclesia de Ulvesby (Ousby) dimissa pro xlviii s. x d.; solvit commissario totum.

Vicaria de Pennerith' (Penrith) dimissa pro xxxv s.; solvit commissario totum.

Vicaria de Overton' (Orton) dimissa pro xlvi s.; solvit commissario totum.

Ecclesia de Bounes (Bowness) dimissa pro x li.

Ecclesia de Askeby (Asby) dimissa pro lx s.

Vicaria de Morlund (Morland) dimissa pro vi m.

Summa recepta Carlyolensis per commissarium xiiii m. ix s. x d.[64]

(fol. 42) Et memorandum quod de summis superius contentis per manus commissariorum particulariter receptis tam de primo, secundo quam tertio annis reservationis supradicte iidem commissarii solverunt nobis per diversas acquietantias summas infrascriptas, videlicet:

Commissarius in dyocesibus Norwycensi et Elyensi ml vic m. x s.

Item commissarius Lyncolniensis viic lxvi m. x s.

Item commissarius Eboracensis mlmlml ccclxxv m. et dimidiam.

Item commissarius Wygorniensis vic xxxi m. ix s.

Item commissarius Exoniensis iiiic iiiixx v. m. viii s.

Item commissarius Herfordensis, Menevensis, Landavensis, Bangorensis et Assavensis viic vii m. iiii s. iiii d.

Summa summarum predictarum viiml iiiic lxvii m. viii s.[65]

(fol. 43) Recepta denariorum Beati Petri Cantuariensis

De archidiacono Cantuariensi de anno domini Mo CCCo XVII viii li. per manus Magistri Petri Ardi.

### Roffensis

De archidiacono Roffensi de anno domini Mo CCCmo XVII cxii s.

Item de eodem de anno domini Mo CCCmo XVIII cxii s.

Item de codem de anno domini Mo CCCmo XIX cxii s.

Item de eodem in partem solutionis de anno domini Mo CCC XX lxxii s.

### Cicestrensis

De episcopo Cycestrensi de anno domini Mo CCCmo XVII viii li.

Item de eodem episcopo de anno domini Mo CCCmo XVIII viii li.

Item de eodem de annis domini Mo CCCmo XIX, XX et XXImo xxiiii li.

### Londoniensis

De archidiacono Colcestrie de anno domini Mo CCCmo XVII cx s.

Item de eodem de anno domini Mo CCCmo XVIII cx s.

Item de eodem de anno domini Mo CCCmo XIX cx s.

### Londoniensis

De archidiacono Essexie in partem solutionis arreragiorum per ipsum debitorum xxiii m. dimidia.

### (fol. 43v) Wyntoniensis

De archidiacono Wyntoniensi de annis domini Mo CCC XIIII, XV et XVI xxxv li.

Item de eodem de anno domini Mo CCCXVII xi li. xiii s. iiii d.

Item de eodem de anno domini Mo CCCmo XVIII xi li. xiii s. iiii d.

Item de eodem de anno domini Mo CCCmo XIX xi li. xiii s. iiii d.

### Wyntoniensis

De archidiacono Surreie de annis domini Mo CCCmo XIIII, XV, XVI et XVII xxii li. xiii s. iiii d.

Item de eodem de anno domini Mo CCCmo XVIII cxiii s. iiii d.

Item de eodem de anno domini Mo CCCmo XIX iiii li.

### Sarisberiensis

De episcopo Sarisberiensi de anno[66] domini Mo CCCmo XVII xvii li.

---

[64] Folio 41v is blank.
[65] Folio 42v is blank.

[66] *de anno* is repeated in the manuscript.

Item de eodem de annis domini M° CCC<sup>mo</sup> XVIII et XIX xxxiiii li.

Item de eodem de anno domini M° CCC° XX xvii li.

### Exoniensis

De episcopo Exoniensi de anno domini M° CCC<sup>mo</sup> XVII ix li. v s.

Item de eodem de anno domini M° CCC<sup>mo</sup> XVIII ix li. v s.

Item de eodem de annis domini M° CCC<sup>mo</sup> XIX et XX xviii li. x s.

### Bathoniensis

De episcopi Bathoniensi de anno domini M° CCC<sup>mo</sup> XVII xi li. v s.

Item de eodem de anno domini M° CCC<sup>mo</sup> XVIII xi li. v s.

Item de eodem de anno domini M° CCC<sup>mo</sup> XIX xi li. v s.

### (fol. 44) Coventrensis

De espiscopo Coventrensi de arreragiis denariorum Sancti Petri supradictorum [67] xx li.

Item de arreragiis predictis de eodem episcopo xii li. x s.

Item de eodem de dictis arreragiis xiii li. vi s. viii d.

Item de eodem de anno domini M° CCC° XVIII° x li. v s.

Item de arreragiis denariorum predictis x m.

Item de eodem episcopo de anno domini M° CCCXIX in partem solutionis lxvi s. viii d.

### Wygorniensis

De episcopo Wygorniensi de anno domini M° CCC° XVII x li. v s.

Item de eodem de anno domini M° CCC° XVIII x li. v s.

Item de eodem de anno domini M° CCC° XIX x li. v s.

### Norwycensis

De episcopo Norwycensi de anno domini M° CCC<sup>mo</sup> XVII xxi li. x s.

Item de eodem de anno domini M° CCCXVIII xxi li. x s.

Item de eodem de anno domini M° CCCXIX xxi li. x s.

Item de eodem de anno domini M° CCCXX xxi li. x s.

### Elyensis

De archidiacono Elyensi de anno domini M° CCC° XVII c s.

Item de eodem de anno domini M° CCC° XVIII c s.

Item de eodem de anno domini M° CCCXIX c s.

---

[67] *supradicti*, MS.

### Lincolniensis

De episcopo Lincolniensi de anno domini millesimo CCC<sup>mo</sup> XVII xlii li.

Item de eodem de anno domini M° CCCXVIII xlii li.

Item de eodem de anno domini M° CCCXIX xlii li.

### (fol. 44ᵛ) Eboracensis

De capitulo Eboracense sede vacante de denariis predictis debitis tempore vacationis xi li. v s.

Summa recepta denariorum Beati Petri vi<sup>c</sup> lxxi li. xiiii s. viii d., videlicet m¹ vii m. viii s.

### Recepta annui census
### Cantuariensis

De .. abbate de Faversham de anno domini M° CCC<sup>mo</sup> XVII xiii s. iiii d.

Item de eodem de anno domini M° CCCXVIII xiii s. iiii d.

### Roffensis

De .. priore de Tonebrugg' (Tonbridge) de annis domini M° CCC° XVI et XVII xxvi s. viii d.

### (fol. 45) Londoniensis

De .. abbatissa Minorum ordinis Sancte Clare (London, St. Mary without Aldgate) de annis domini M° CCCXIII, XIIII, XV, XVI et XVII et XVIII vi libre cere pretium iii s.

Item de eadem abbatissa de anno domini M° CCCXIX i libra cere pretium vi d.

### Wyntoniensis

De .. abbate de Certes' (Chertsey) de annis domini M° CCC<sup>mo</sup> XIIII, XV, XVI et XVII xxxii s.

Item de eodem de anno domini M° CCC° XVIII viii s.

Item de eodem de anno domini M° CCC° XIX viii s.

Item de eodem de anno domini M° CCC° XX viii s.

Item de eodem de anno domini M° CCC XXI viii s.

### Sarisberiensis

De .. abbate Sancti Aldelmi Malmesburiensis de anno domini M° CCCXVI xiii s. iiii d.

De domino rege Anglie de arreragiis duorum annorum, videlicet annuatim m¹ m., m¹m¹ m.

### (fol. 45ᵛ) Norwycensis

De .. abbate Sancti Edmundi de anno domini M° CCCXVII xiii s. iiii d.

Item de eodem de anno domini M° CCCXVIII xiii s. iiii d.

Item de eodem de anno domini M° CCCXIX xiii s. iiii d.

Item de eodem de anno domini M° CCCXX xiii s. iiii d.

Item de eodem de anno domini Mo CCCXXI xiii s. iiii d.

### Lincolniensis

De .. priore de Chaucombe (Chacombe) de anno domini Mo CCCXVI xv d.

Item de eodem de anno domini Mo CCCXVII xv d.
Item de eodem de anno domini Mo CCCXVIII xv d.
Item de eodem de anno domini Mo CCCXIX xv d.

### Lincolniensis

De .. abbate Sancti Albani de annis domini Mo CCCXVI et XVII xxvi s. viii d.

Item de eodem de annis domini Mo CCCXVIII et XIX xxvi s. viii d.

### Eboracensis

De custode ecclesie de Scardeburgh' (Scarborough) de annis domini Mo CCCXVII et XVIII ii s. vi d.

Item de eodem de anno domini Mo CCCXIX xv d.
Item de eodem de anno domini Mo CCCXX xv d.
Item de eodem de anno domini Mo CCCXXI xv d.
Summa annui census [68] mlml xix m. xii s. i d.

(fol. 46) Recepta Hibernie nobis Rigaudo tradita

In primus Raymundus de Roserus solvit nobis ix die Junii anno domini millesimo CCCmo XVIII de pecunia domini pape per ipsum Raymundum et dominum Guillelmum Nicholai collecta in partibus Hibernie, ut dixit dictus Raymundus, lv m.

Item xii die Januarii anno predicto dictus Raymundus solvit et liberavit nobis de pecunia domini pape supradicti xvii li. iiii d. obolum.

Item eadem die liberavit nobis iiiic liii florenos, pretium cuiusque iii s. iii d. obolus, valent lxxiiii li. xi s. i d. obolus.

---

[68] Followed by *summa* deleted by a line.

Item xv die Maii anno XIX Raymundus Durandi solvit nobis pro dominis Guillelmo Nicholai et Raterio de Polverello commissariis in Hibernia de pecunia dicti domini pape c li.

Item xix die Septembris anno domini millesimo CCCXIX Dominus Raterius de Polverello supradictus venit de Hibernia et liberavit nobis pro ipso et Domino Guillelmo Nicholai predicto de pecunia domini pape per ipsos collecta in Hibernia iiiixx vi li. xi s. viii d. obolum.

Item Dominus Guillelmus Nicholai commissarius in Hibernia venit x die Decembris anno domini Mo CCCo XX apud manerium de Ivyngho ubi tunc moram trahebamus et solvit nobis de pecunia dicti domini pape iiiixx li.

Item solvit nobis idem Guillelmus xiiii die Januarii eodem anno de pecunia domini pape xix li. vii s. iiii d. quadrantem.

Summa recepta Hibernie vc xiiii li. iiii s. x d. obolus quadrans.

(fol. 46v) Item recepimus a domino rege de pecunia recepta per eundem de cistis Domini Guillelmi de Balaeto [69] post mortem Domini Clementis ml cc m.

Item de legatis Terre Sancte vc iiii m. viii s. ix d. obolum quadrantem.

Item de legato Domini Johannis de Pontoysa [70] c m.

Item de arreragiis decime Domini Nicholai IIIIti xv m. iiii s. x d. obolum quadrantem.

Item de arreragiis decime Domini Clementis ccclxv m. viii s. x d. obolum quadrantem.

Item de arreragiis fructum dicti Domini Clementis [71] iiiixx m. dimidiam.

---

[69] Rigaud's predecessor as papal collector. On this incident see Lunt, *Financial Relations . . . to 1327*, p. 584.

[70] Bishop of Winchester. On the bequest see *ibid.*, p. 515.

[71] The annates imposed in the British Isles by Clement V in 1306.

# ACCOUNT OF ITIER DE CONCORETO COLLECTOR FROM 1328 TO 1335

Vatican Archives, Collectorie *227*, fols. 34 to 45[v].[1]

(fol. 34)[2] Memorandum quod non reperitur quod isti[3] solverunt a XXX citra propter guerram continuam Scotie, nec aliquis predecessorum meorum dimisit eos michi in arreragiis, ego tamen tradidi informationem super premissis dominis Bertrando Cariti, archidiacono Vaurensis (Lavaur), et Remundo del Casse, canonico Lincolniensi,[4] qui nuper fuerunt missi in Scotiam per dominum nostrum, et ipsi debent reddere computum.

### Hibernia de diocesi de Dunde (Down)

Ecclesia Sancti Patricii de Duno (Down) dicte diocesis debet de annuo censu Romane ecclesie unciam auri iuxta provinciale.[5] Nichil.

### Lugdunensis (Louth)

Ecclesia Sancte Marie de Lugdunensi debet de annuo censu Romane ecclesie xx s. sterlingorum iuxta provinciale. Nichil.

Hospitalis Sancti Johannis Dublinensis debet ii s. sterlingorum de annuo censu Romane ecclesie iuxta provinciale. Nichil.

### (fol. 34[v]) Cancellarius ecclesie Dublinensis

Memorandum quod isti de Hibernia non fuerunt dimissi in arreragiis michi per dictum Dominum Hugonem,[6] set de hoc debent reddere computum prior Hospitalis Sancti Johannis Jerosolimitani in Hibernia et Magister Petrus de Wyleby qui fuerunt commissarii dicti Domini[7] Hugonis et mei.

Recepta census annui Romane ecclesie singulari[8] anno nuntiationis

Illustris rex Anglie obtinuit gratiam a domino nostro papa Johanne XXII, sub datum Avinione nonas Januarii pontificatus ipsius domini nostri anno xiiii,[9] quod arreragiorum tam trium annorum de tempore istius Edwardi junioris quam de xxx annis de tempore patris et avi sui solvat statim in curia mille marchas pro tempore suo et infra biennium duo millia marchas, de aliis arreragiis patris et avi quingentas marchas quolibet anno quousque plene solutum sit, et nichilominus debet fieri ordinaria solutio semper quolibet annuo. Ego tamen non habeo ad huc speciale mandatum de recipiendo.

Archiepiscopus Cantuariensis solvit in curia ccc m. singulis terminis.[10]

Abbas Sancti Augustini (Canterbury) solvit, ut dicit, in curia unam marcham de annuo censu.

Summa istius folii nichil.

(fol. 35) Anno domini M° III[c] XXIX die xx Januarii abbas de Faveresham Cantuariensis diocesis solvit de annuo censu per ipsum Romane ecclesie debito de anno domini M° III[c] XXIX° xiii s. iiii d.[11]

### Roffensis

Anno quo supra prior de Torneberg' (Tonbridge) Roffensis diocesis solvit de censu annuo per ipsum Romane ecclesie debito pro anno domini M° III[c] XXIX° unam marcham.

### Londoniensis

Anno quo supra abbatissa et sorores Sancte Clare Londonie die ultima mensis Julii solvit vi d. sterlingorum pro annuo censu unius libre cere pro anno domini M° III[c] XXIX°

### Wyntoniensis

Anno domini M° III[c] XXX die v Maii abbas de Certeseya (Chertsey) Wyntoniensis diocesis solvit viii s. sterlingorum de annuo censu per ipsum Romane ecclesie debito de anno domini M° III[c] XXIX°.

### (fol. 35[v]) Exoniensis

Anno quo supra prior de Bodemya (Bodmin) Exoniensis diocesis solvit die xx Januarii anno XXXI° ii s. pro anno XXIX.

### Norwicensis

Anno domini M° III[c] XXIX° die xii Novembris abbas Sancti Edmundi de Bury Norwicensis diocesis solvit de annuo censu per ipsum Romane ecclesie debito de anno domini M° III[c] XXIX° xiii s. iiii d.

### Lincolniensis

Anno quo supra die xxvi Januarii abbas Sancti Albani Lincolniensis diocesis solvit de annuo censu per ipsum

---

[1] Modern manuscript copies of the accounts of Itier and Bernard de Sistre are in British Museum, Addit. MS. 34273 and in Public Record Office, Roman Transcripts 110. The latter also contain copies of other reports printed below. Brief extracts from Itier's account are published in *Fragments of Registers of Richard d'Aungerville of Bury* (Surtees Soc., 119), pp. 258-259.

[2] *Collectoria Anglia* appears at the head of the folio in a modern hand.

[3] Judging by the similar statement on fol. 34[v], *isti* refers to the Scots. Taken together with the reference to *dictum dominum Hugonem* on fol. 34[v], the opening statement seems to indicate that some portion of the account is missing.

[4] A mistake for Lingonensis (Langres).

[5] The Liber Censuum.

[6] Hugh of Angoulême, Itier's immediate predecessor.

[7] Followed by *prioris* deleted by a line.

[8] Extension doubtful.

[9] 5 January 1330. For this letter see *Cal. Pap. Regs. Letters*, ii, 495. The terms are more fully explained in a royal letter of 12 April: Rymer, *Foedera*, ii, 786. *Cf.* Lunt, *Financial Relations . . .1327-1534*, pp. 66-67.

[10] The visitation tax due every three years.

[11] The amount in this and in the similar following entries is repeated in the margin.

Romane ecclesie debito de anno domini M° III^c XXIX°
xiii s. iiii d.

Anno quo supra die xxvi Januarii prior de Chaucumbe (Chacombe) Lincolniensis diocesis solvit de
annuo censu per ipsum Romane ecclesie debito de anno
domini M° III^c XXIX° xv d. sterlingorum.

Summa istius folii lxv s. i d. Approbatum.[12]

### (fol. 36) Coventrensis

Monasterium de Bredeya[13] debet secundum provinciale duos besantios.

### Elyensis

Hospitale de Angleseya (Anglesey) solvit ii s. pro
anno XXIX° die xxi Januarii anno XXXI°.

Archiepiscopus Eboracensis debet singulis terminis
iii^c marchas sterlingorum; solvit in curia ut dicit.[14]

Anno domini M° III^c XXIX° die secunda Maii custos
domus de Scaldesburgh' (Scarborough) Eboracensis
diocesis solvit de annuo censu per ipsum Romane
ecclesie debito pro anno domini M° III^c XXIX° xv d.
sterlingorum.

### (fol. 36^v) Carleolensis

Prior cathedralis ecclesie Karleolensis.

Census in Scotia anno domini M° III^c XXIX°

Memorandum quod anno predicto non intromisi me
de censu Romane ecclesie in Scotia ex eo quia dominus
noster miserat ibidem nuntios Dominos Bertrandum
Cariti, archidiaconum Vaurensem (Lavaur), et Remun-
dum del Casse, canonicum Lingoniensem (Langres),
quos ego informavi de premisso censu et in reragiis, et
ipsi debent reddere computum quia habent commissionem ad huc ut dicunt.

Census in Hibernia anno domini M° III^c XXIX°

Memorandum quod anno predicto ego feci commissarios meos in Hibernia priorem hospitalis Sancti
Johannis Jerosolomitani in Hibernia et Magistrum
Petrum de Wyleby, cancellarium ecclesie Dublinensis,
qui ceperunt commissionem et debent reddere computum tam de censu annuo quam de aliis et cetera.

Summa istius folii iii s. iii d. Approbatum.

### (fol. 37) Census Romane ecclesie anno domini M° III^c XXX^mo

### Cantuariensis[15]

Illustris rex Anglie, archiepiscopus Cantuariensis et
abbas Sancti Augustini Cantuariensis nichil, quia solvunt in curia ut dicunt.

Anno domini M° III^c XXX die prima Februarii
abbas et conventus de Faveresham solvit unam marcham

sterlingorum de annuo censu per ipsum Romane ecclesie
debito de anno domini M° III^c XXX.

### Roffensis

Prior et conventus de Torneburgh' solverunt de censu
annuo Romane ecclesie debito de anno domini M° III^c
XXX i m.

### Londoniensis

Anno quo supra die xxix Februarii abbatissa Sancte
Clare Londonie solvit vi d. pro una libra cere debita de
annuo censu pro anno domini M° III^c XXXI°.

### (fol. 37^v) Wyntoniensis

Anno quo supra die xxv Februarii abbas de Chertesey
solvit de annuo censu per ipsum Romane ecclesie debito
de anno domini M° III^c XXX viii s. sterlingorum.

### Sarisberiensis

Item anno domini M° III^c XXXI° die vii Octobris
abbas de Malmesbury solvit unam marcham de censu
annuo pro anno domini M° III^c XXX.[16]

### Exoniensis

Prior de Bodemyria solvit de censu annuo ii s. pro
anno XXX Januarii anno XXXI°.

### Norwycensis

Anno domini M° III^c XXX° die xviii Januarii abbas
et conventus monasterii Sancti Edmundi solverunt unam
marcham de annuo censu per ipsos Romane ecclesie
debito de anno domini M° III^c XXX.

Summa istius folii lxiii s. x d. Approbatum.

### (fol. 38) Lincolniensis

Item anno quo supra die i^a Februarii prior et conventus de Chaucumbe solverunt de annuo censu xv d.
per ipsos[17] Romane ecclesie debito de anno domini
M° III^c XXX.

Item anno quo supra abbas de Sancto Albano solvit
die i^a Februarii anno XXXI° unam marcham de annuo
censu de anno domini M° III^c XXX^mo.

### Elyensis

Hospitale de Angleseya solvit ii s. die xxi Februarii
anno domini M° III^c XXXI° pro anno XXX de annuo
censu.

### Eboracensis

Anno domini M° III^c XXX die secunda Septembris
custos domus de Schamburgh' Eboracensis diocesis solvit xv d. de annuo censu Romane ecclesie debito pro
anno domini M° III^c XXX.

---

[12] In the margin. Presumably the note of the cameral clerk
who audited the account.

[13] Probably a mistake for Laund in the diocese of Lincoln:
Lunt, *Financial Relations . . . to 1327*, pp. 103, 104.

[14] The visitation tax due once every three years.

[15] Followed by the entry *Anno domini M° III^c XXX die i
Februarii* deleted by a line.

[16] *XXXI^a* in the text with the *I* deleted by a line.

[17] Apparently *pro ipsum* in the text.

### Carleolensis

Prior Carleolensis nichil.

(fol. 38ᵛ) Census Romane ecclesie de anno XXXIᵒ

### Cantuariensis

Anno domini Mᵒ IIIᶜ XXXIᵒ illustris rex Anglie, archiepiscopus Cantuariensis et abbas Sancti Augustini Cantuariensis nichil quia in curia.

Anno quo supra abbas de Faveresham die vii Februarii [18] solvit unam marcham de annuo censu pro anno domini Mᵒ IIIᶜ XXX.

### Roffensis

Anno quo supra die ultima Januarii prior de Thornebreg' solvit unam marcham de annuo censu pro anno domini Mᵒ IIIᶜ XXXIᵒ.

### Londoniensis

Anno quo supra die xxix Martii abbatissa Sancte Clare Londonie solvit vi d. pro una libra cere per ipsam debita de annuo censu pro anno domini Mᵒ IIIᶜ XXXIᵒ.

Summa istius folii xlv s. Approbatum.

### (fol. 39) Wyntoniensis

Item anno quo supra abbas de Chertesey solvit viii s. de annuo censu pro anno domini Mᵒ IIIᶜ XXXIᵒ.

### Sarisberiensis

Anno quo supra abbas de Malmesburi solvit unam marcham pro anno domini Mᵒ IIIᶜ XXXIᵒ.

### Exoniensis

Anno quo supra prior de Bodimeyn solvit ii s. [19] per ipsum debito s de annuo censu de anno domini Mᵒ IIIᶜ XXXIᵒ.

### Norwycensis

Anno domini millesimo IIIᶜ XXXI die v Novembris abbas et conventus Sancti Edmundi solverunt unam marcham de annuo censu de anno XXXIᵒ.

### (fol. 39ᵛ) Lincolniensis

Anno quo supra die xxviii Januarii prior de Chacube solvit xv d. annuo censu pro anno domini Mᵒ IIIᶜ XXXIᵒ.

Item anno quo supra abbas de Sancto Albano solvit die i Februarii unam marcham de annuo censu pro anno domini Mᵒ IIIᶜ XXXIᵒ.

### Elyensis

Anno quo supra die xxi Januarii hospitale de Anglesey solvit ii s. de annuo censu pro anno domini Mᵒ IIIᶜ XXXIᵒ.

### Eboracensis

Anno domini Mᵒ IIIᶜ XXXI custos domus de Schaldeburgh' Eboracensis solvit xv d. annuo censu per ipsum Romane ecclesie debito de anno domini Mᵒ IIIᶜ XXXIᵒ.

### Carleolensis

Prior Carleolensis nichil.

Summa istius folii liiii s. vi d. Approbatum.

(fol. 40) Census Romane ecclesie anno XXXIIᵈᵒ

### Cantuariensis

Illustris rex Anglie, archiepiscopus Cantuariensis et abbas Sancti Augustini Cantuariensis nichil quia in curia.

Anno domini Mᵒ IIIᶜ XXXIIᵒ abbas de Faveresham solvit die xv Januarii i m. de censu annuo de anno domini Mᵒ IIIᶜ XXXIIᵒ.

### Roffensis

Anno quo supra prior de Tonnbrigg' solvit unam marcham de censu annuo de anno domini Mᵒ IIIᶜ XXXIIᵒ; solvit die viii Januarii.

### Londoniensis

Anno quo supra abbatissa Sancte Clare Londonie.

### Wyntoniensis

Anno quo supra die viii Januarii abbas de Chertesey solvit viii s. de annuo censu de anno domini Mᵒ IIIᶜ XXXIIᵒ.

### Sarisberiensis

Item anno quo supra abbas de Malmesbury.

### Exoniensis

Item anno quo supra die xvi Februarii prior de Bodimer solvit ii s. de annuo censu de anno domini Mᵒ IIIᶜ XXXIIᵒ.

### (fol. 40ᵛ) Norwycensis

Anno domini Mᵒ IIIᶜ XXXIIᵒ die vi Novembris abbas Sancti Edmundi Norwycensis diocesis solvit i m. de censu annuo pro anno XXXIIᵒ.

### Lincolniensis

Anno quo supra prior de Chaucumbe.

Item anno quo supra abbas de Sancto Albano solvit i m. de annuo censu de anno domini Mᵒ IIIᶜ XXXIIᵒ.

### Elyensis

Item anno quo supra die xii Januarii hospitale de Angleseya solvit ii s. de anno domini Mᵒ CCC XXXIIᵒ.

---

[18] *abbas de Faveresham* repeated in the text.
[19] The amount is omitted in the text but given in the margin.

Coventrensis [20]
Eboracensis [20]

Summa istius folii lxv s. iiii d. Approbatum.
Summa totius recepte de censu annuo xx li. viii s.
v d. Approbatum.

### (fol. 42ᵛ) [21] Commissio generalis [22]

J⟨ohannes episcopus⟩ [23] servus servorum dei dilecto
filio Itherio de Concoreto, canonico Saresburiensi, apostolice sedis nuntio, salutem et apostolicam benedictionem.

Olim felicis recordationis Gregorius X, Nicholaus
IIII, Bonifatius VIII et Clemens V, Romani pontifices,
predecessores nostri, decimas omnium proventuum et
reddituum ecclesiasticorum pro Terre Sancte subsidio
et aliis certis causis duxerunt in nonnullis provinciis
secundum certas distinctiones locorum per certa tem-
porum spatia imponendas, et ⟨circa⟩ easdem decimas
et alia que in ipsius Terre Sancte seu alias ecclesie
Romane ⟨subsidio⟩ in partibus Anglie, Scotie, Wallie
et Hibernie debebantur, per prefatos et nonnullos alios
predecessores nostros, Romanos pontifices, diversis deputatis, collectoribus et aliis nuntiis destinatis, set quia
tam circa decimas quam alia supradicta facta dudum
minus plene ⟨fuisse⟩ reperiebatur collectio [24] que multa [25] de decimis et aliis predictis adhuc tam ecclesie
quam terre predictis etiam [26] preterito tempore debebantur, nos, primo bone memorie Rigaldus, episcopum
Wyntoniensem, tunc canonicum Aurilianensem, (Orléans) et postmodum, eo sicut domino placuit sublato
de medio, dilectum filium Hugonem de Engolism
(Angoulême) archidiaconum Cantuariensem, tunc sac-
ristam ecclesie Narbonensis (Narbonne), apostolice
sedis nuntium super predictis infrascriptis omnibus
auctoritate apostolica per nostras duximus litteras
deputandos.

Sane cum eidem archidiacono propter infirmitatem
et debilitatem proprii corporis ad premissa commode
intendere non valenti se ad nos licentiam concesserimus
conferendi, nos, volentes nostris et eiusdem ecclesie
Romane in hac parte in depravitatibus precavere, discretioni tue, de qua fiduciam in domino gerimus pecu-
liarem, per apostolica scripta committimus et mandamus
quatenus in illis partibus circa collectionem et exac-
tionem huius decimarum et denarii Beati Petri et
aliorum censuum qui in illis partibus ecclesie predicte

debentur, necnon et residuarum procurationum legatorum et nuntiorum apostolice sedis que ad huc restant
solvende, queve iuxta quandam [27] ordinationem dicti
Bonefatii ad dictam ecclesiam pertinent, ac bonorum
bone memorie Giffridi, episcopi Parmensis (Parma),
nuntii dicte sedis in illis partibus, qui apud sedem
eandem intestatus decessit, et distincte [28] legatorum,
necnon et pecuniarium penarum que frequenter, sicut
accepimus, in eisdem partibus promittuntur [29] in diversis
contractibus pro eiusdem Terre subsidio et etiam con-
vertuntur, et generaliter omnia que ex testamento ac
votis [30] seu votorum redemptionibus tam crucesigna-
torum quam aliorum quorumcumque dicte Terre subsidio
aut alie ipsi ecclesie in eisdem partibus quacumque
ratione vel causa quomodolibet debentur, diligentia sic
exacta procedas quod ex derecto missis ac subtractis
pro tempore iam [31] transacto satisfactio condigna pro-
venerit et ⟨in⟩ antea cum integritate hec et alia omnia
persolventur, et nichilominus in huius negotiis et ea
tangentibus generaliter et specialiter, prout facti qualitas
suasserit et tibi videbitur [32] ex officio diligenter inquiras,
super quibus tibi tenore presentium plenam et liberam
concedimus facultatem.

⟨Eos⟩ autem [33] quibus hactenus super aliquo quevis [34]
commissio facta fuerit, quam ex nunc auctoritate apostolica revocamus, et quoscumque alios de quibus expedire videris, quod tibi quaslibet litteras apostolicas
omnes et scripturas per eos de mandato seu commissione
ipsorum ⟨factas⟩ vel quas quomodolibet [35] detinent predicta negotia vel eorum aliquid contingentes, exhibeant,
et quantum ipsi per se vel alium seu alios receperint
de predictis, et penes quos et ubi, et quomodo et qualiter
(fol. 43) et coram quibus ⟨et sub quibus⟩ securitatibus
seu cautelis pecuniam ab eis in hac parte receptam [36]
depos⟨uerunt, quantum⟩ [37] etiam adhuc de hiis de
tempore preterito et in quibus resistat locis seu partibus
colligendum, et quantum, quanto et qualiter et ubi
expenderint in prosequendis eisdem negotiis, et si de
receptis restat adhuc aliquid assignandum, et de omnibus
huius negotia tangentibus prout tibi videbitur reddant
tibi plenam rationem.

Venerabiles etiam fratres nostros, archiepiscopos et
episcopos, et dilectos filios, electos, abbates, priores,
rectores, ceterosque prelatos ecclesiasticos, et personas
ecclesiasticas, conventus et capitula dictarum partium,
cuiuscumque ordinis et conditionis existant, quos tibi
constitit de premissis aliqua preterio tempore retinuisse

---

[20] No entry under the caption.
[21] Fols. 41, 41ᵛ and 42 are blank.
[22] The caption is at the head of fol. 43. There are many
copyist's errors. Another copy of the commission exists in the
Vatican series of the chancery registers, but it was not available
on account of the war. The corrections have been made in the
light of the formulae in other commissions of the same type. *Cf.*
*Cal. Pap. Reg. Letters*, ii, 486.
[23] Obscured by a stain.
[24] *collectis*, MS.
[25] *multaque* in other commissions.
[26] *quod*, MS.

[27] *quemdam*, MS.
[28] Probably an error for *indistincte*.
[29] *promittitur* in text.
[30] *voti*, MS.
[31] Followed by *exacto* deleted by a line.
[32] *videbantur*, MS.
[33] Lacking in MS., but a blank space leaves room for it.
[34] *quivis*, MS.
[35] *quemlibet*, MS.
[36] *recepta*, MS.
[37] Obscured by a stain.

seu subtraxisse, necnon et quoscumque alios depositarios et alios penes quos aliqua ex eis existunt, quod illa omnia cessante [38] difficultate qualibet tibi exhibere procurent infra competentes terminos, a te super hiis pro qualitate facti iuxta tue discretionis ⟨arbitrium⟩ eis omnibus vel eorum cuilibet statuendos, monere et efficaciter inducere ex parte nostra procures; et nichilominus illos ex personis eisdem, qui monitis tuis paruerint in hac parte, ab excommunicationis sententiis, si quas pretextu premissorum incurri denoscuntur, auctoritate nostra iuxta ecclesie formam absolvas, et dispenses cum eis super irregularitate, si quam predictis ligati [39] sententiis divina officia celebrando vel inmiscendo se illis forsitan contraxissent. Quod si tales infra premissos terminos tuis monitis parere contempserint, eos auctoritate nostra nominatim ecclesiastica censura percellas, et si per unum mensem censuram huius animis sustinuerint induratis,[40] eos extunc peremptorie citare procures, ut infra competentis termini [41] spatium a te prefigendum eisdem post citationem tuam per se vel procuratores ydoneos, aut personaliter illi de quibus personalem citationem merito videris faciendam, episcopis et eorum superioribus dumtaxat exceptis, compareant coram nobis, nostris super hoc mandatis et beneplacitis parituri et facituri et recepturi quod iustitia suadebit. Diem vero citationis et prefixionis huius et quicquid inveneris et feceris in predictis nobis per litteras tuas et nichilominus per scripturam autenticam, harum seriem continentes, fideliter intimare procures.

Ceterum ut officium tibi in hac parte commissum utilius et efficacius exequi valeas, compellendi, si opus fuerit, prelatos aliasque personas ecclesiasticas supradictos ad providendum tibi et nuntiis tuis ac illis [42] quos ad aliqua premissorum duxeris deputandos de securo conductu, cum a te vel eis super hoc fuerint requisiti, quitationem quoque de hiis que recipere te continget illis a quibus ea receperis, et quecumque circa premissa fuerint oportuna, prout utiliter expedire videbitur, faciendi et procedendi hiis omnibus et singulis, et ea exequendi per te vel alium seu alios prout et quando expedire putaveris, plenam concedimus auctoritate presentium facultatem.

Volumus autem et apostolica auctoritate decernimus quod a dato presentium in premissis omnibus et singulis sit tibi plena et perpetua potestas et iurisdictio attributa ut eo vigore (fol. 43ᵛ) ⟨fir⟩mitate [43] possis apostolice sedis auctoritate in predictis omnibus et pro predictis, etiam apostolica sede vacante, procedere ac si tua iurisdictio in predictis omnibus et singulis per citationem vel alium modum perpetua huius extitisset; non obstantibus quibuscumque constitutionibus seu quibusvis contrariis consuetudinibus, privilegiis et litteris apostolicis, per

que potestatis et iurisdictionis tibi super hiis concessarum ⟨explicatio⟩ valeat quomodolibet impediri, et de quibus quorumque totis tenoribus de verbo ad verbum in nostris litteris habenda sit mentio specialis, aut si aliquibus ab eadem fuerit sede indultum quod interdici vel excommunicari nequeant [44] aut suspendi per litteras dicte sedis non facientes plenam et expressam ac de verbo ad verbum de indulto huius mentionem.

Considerans itaque quod in premissis negotium ecclesie predicte persequeris, et in conspectu agis eius qui cuncta decernit, sibi que necnon et nobis, qui circa ⟨hec⟩ omnem diligentiam adhibere intendimus, tenebris reddere rationem, ab utroque pro meritis recepturus, sic prudenter in illis habere te studeas, sic consulte, quod in utriusque iudicio non solum vites pene que confusionis discrimina, set laudis titulos retributionis [45] premia exinde consequi merearis.

Datum Avinione, xi kalendas Septembris, pontificatus nostri anno xiiº.[46]

Johannes episcopus servus servorum dei dilecto filio Iterrio de Concoreto canonico Saresburiensi in partibus Anglie apostolice sedis nuntio salutem et apostolicam benedictionem.

Licet verisimiliter ⟨extimemus⟩ quod prelati et persone ecclesiastice necnon [47] capitula, collegia et conventus partium Anglie subsidium pro repressione hereticorum et rebellium partium Italie contra deum et ecclesiam fidemque catholicam crudeliter sevientium ab ipsis liberaliter ecclesie Romane promissum exhibere prompte ac solvere [48] procurabunt, quia tamen eisdem hereticis et rebellibus crudelibus solito sevientibus predicto subcidio noscimus presentialiter indigere, discretioni tue per apostolica scripta committimus et mandamus quatenus prefatos prelatos et alias personas ecclesiasticas necnon capitula, collegia et conventus efficaciter requiras ut de prefato subsidio promptam satisfactionem inpendant.

Nos enim tibi dictum subsidium ab ipsis et eorum singulis nostro et ecclesie memorate nomine recipiendi, sibique de hiis que inde receperis ab eisdem quitationis cautelas faciendi et instrumenta, si qua super promissione et obligatione predicti subsidii confecta fuerint, eis restituendi seu ea cancellandi post plenam de contentis in illis tibi satisfactionem inpensam, necnon contradictores, si qui forsan fuerint, etiam si pontificali vel quavis alia premineant dignitate, auctoritate nostra, appelatione postposita, compellendi, non obstantibus exemptionibus [49] aut quibusvis privilegiis aliis quibuscumque personis aut locis sub quacumque forma vel expressione verborum concessis, etiam si de illis esset in presentibus de verbo ad verbum specialis et expressa mentio facienda, aut si eis vel eorum aliquibus com-

---

[38] *cessare* in manuscript.
[39] *legatis*, MS.
[40] *indurate*, MS.
[41] *competentem terminum*, MS.
[42] Followed by *ad* deleted by a line, MS.
[43] A stain renders several letters illegible.

[44] *nequeat*, MS.
[45] *distributionis*, MS.
[46] 22 August 1328.
[47] *necnon* repeated in manuscript.
[48] *solile*, MS.
[49] *exemtionis*, MS.

muniter vel divisim a sede apostolica sit indultum quod interdici, suspendi vel excommunicari non possint per litteras apostolicas non facientes plenam et expressam ac de verbo ad verbum de indulto huius mentionem, plenam et liberam concedimus tenore presentium facultatem.

Datum Avinione viii idus Junii pontificatus nostri anno xiii°.[50]

Ista littera non potuit excequitioni mandari quia nunquam promiserunt subcidium quod ego possim reperire, et interrogetur super hoc dominus H. episcopus Carpentortrensis.[51]

(fol. 44) Recepta legatorum Terre Sancte per me Itherium.

Cantuariensis

Anno domini M° III^c XVIII° die sabbati post festum Sancti Dionisii[52] Magister Hugo de Forsham, rector ecclesie de Sandresthe (Sandhurst?) executor testamenti Nicholai de Bonovil, rectoris ecclesie de Maidestan' (Maidstone), Cantuariensis, solvit x li. sterlingorum quas dictus rector legaverat in subcidium Terre Sancte.[53]

Londoniensis

Anno domini M° III^c XXIX° die xi Octobris recepimus xx d. quos Walterus de Depenalasa, mortuarius Londonie, legaverat in subsidium Terre Sancte.

Item anno quo supra die xxvii Octobris executores testamenti, filii quondam Radulphi le Longe, solverunt unam marcham quam dictus defunctus legaverat in subsidium Terre Sancte.

(fol. 44^v) Wyntoniensis

Anno domini M° III^c XXIX die ix Maii constitui commissarium in diocesi Wyntoniensi et Sarisberiensi super exactione legatorum Terre Sancte Magistrum Hugonem Prani, rectorem ecclesie de Ychene (Itchen) dicti diocesis, qui iuravit fideliter suum officium exercere.

Solvit die xiiii Novembris x m. sterlingorum de receptis per eum in officio predicto anno domini M° III^c XXX.

Anno domini M° III^c XXX° executores testamenti quondam Philipi de Barton', archidiaconi Surreie in ecclesia Wyntoniensi, solverunt x li. in partem solutionis xx li. quas dictus archidiaconus legavit in subsidium Terre Sancte; actum die xiiii Decembris.

Item anno quo supra dictus Magister H. Prani assignavit x li. sterlingorum de receptis per eum ut supra; actum die ultima Octobris.

Item anno domini M° III^c XXXII^do dictus Magister H. assignavit iiii li. de receptis per eum de legatis predictis; actum die xxii Novembris.

Item anno domini M° III^c XXXII° die xxii Novembris dictus Magister Hugo assignavit iiii li. de eisdam legatis.

Sarisberiensis

Anno domini M° III^c XXX die ix Maii ego constitui commissarium super legatis Terre Sancte Magistrum H. Prani, rectorem ecclesie de Ychene Wyntoniensis diocesis in diocesi Sarisberiensi qui iuravit fideliter officium suum execere.

Anno domini M° III^c XXXII° die xxi Januarii executores quondam Magistri Johannis de Tarenta, canonici Sarisberiensis, assignaverunt x m. quas dictus defunctus legaverat in testamento suo.

Summa istius folii lii m. xx d. Approbatum.

(fol. 45) Cicestrensis

Anno domini M° III^c XXX die ix Maii ego constitui commissarium in diocesi Cicestrensi pro legatis Terre Sancte Magistrum Hugonem Prani, rectorem ecclesie de Ychene Wyntoniensis diocesis, qui iuravit fideliter summ officium exercere.

Bathonensis

Anno domini M° III^c XXX die iiii Februarii ego constitui commissarium in diocesi Bathoniensi et Wellensi super legatis Terre Sancte Magistrum G. Esquinard.

Anno domini M° III^c XXX die xxvi Julii executores testamenti Roberti de la More, quondam rectoris ecclesie de Ievele (Yeovil) Bathoniensis et Wellensis diocesis, solverunt xx m. sterlingorum quas dictus[54] rector legaverat in subsidium Terre Sancte.

Item anno domini M° III^c XXXI° executores Domini Roberti de Barton', militis defuncti, assignaverunt l s. in partem solutionis c s. legatorum per dominum militem.

Item solverunt dicti ii Novembris l s. in complementum.

(fol. 45^v) Exoniensis

Anno domini M° III^c XXX ego constitui commissarium in diocesi Exoniensi super legatis Terre Sancte Magistrum Guillelmum Ecquinard, decanum Sancti Karentoci (Crantock) Exoniensis diocesis.

Anno domini M° III^c XXXI° Ricardus de Venodix, commissarius dicti Magistri Guillelmi, assignavit die xxv Januarii xxxi s. iiii d.; iuravit se nichil amplius recepisse.

Item anno domini M° III^c XXXII° die vi^a Februarii Magister Johannes de Overton', commissarius postmodum constitutus in diocesi Exoniensi, assignavit de receptis per eum vii li.

Elyensis et Norwycensis[55]

Summa istius folii xxvi li. xviii s. Approbatum.

---

[50] 6 June 1329.

[51] Hugh of Angoulême, Itier's immediate predecessor and subsequently bishop of Carpentras.

[52] 18 February 1329. It is assumed that Pope Dionisius is meant, because the other saints of that name would give dates before 15 November 1328, when Itier received his royal safe conduct.

[53] The sum of this and of the following similar items is repeated in the margin.

[54] Followed by *rectore* deleted by a line.

[55] There are no entries under the caption.

# ACCOUNT OF BERNARD DE SISTRE COLLECTOR FROM 1335 TO 1343

Vatican Archives, Collectorie 227, fols. 103 to 155

(fol. 103)[1] Compotus camere apostolice redditus per dominum Bernardum de Sistre, collectorem dicte camere in Anglia de peccuniis et aliis causis per ipsum nomine dicte camere receptis ac etiam solutis, assignatis et expensis per ipsum et etiam de resta dicte camere debita, videlicet a die x mensis Octobris anno domini M° CCC° XXXV° usque ad diem xviii° mensis Junii anno domini M° CCC° XLIII° prout in presenti[2] compoto continetur.[3]

(fol. 105)[4] In dei nomine amen.

Hic est compotus Bernardi de Sistre, felicis recordationis Domini Benedicti pape XII et successive sanctissimi in Christo patris et domini, Domini Clementis divina providentia pape VI[ti], ac sedis apostolice, in partibus Anglie, Scotie, Wallie et Ibernie nuntii deputati, de omnibus et singulis per eum, alium seu alios nomine dicte sedis receptis et liberatis, assignatis et expensis de quibuscumque obventionibus ad ecclesiam Romanam in illis partibus qualitercumque spectantibus a x[a] die mensis Octobris anno domini M° CCC° XXXV°, qua die de civitate Avinionie suum iter arripuit in Angliam accedendi, usque ad xviii[am] diem mensis Junii anno domini M° CCC° XLIII°, qua die migravit ad dominum in civitate Londonie.

Secuntur recepta per nuntium supradictum

Recepit primo dictus nuntius anno domini M° CCC° XXXV° et die vii Octobris Avinionie per manus reverendi patris, Domini Johannis dei gratia episcopi Avinionensis, dicti Domini Benedicti pape tunc thesaurarii, pro expensis suis faciendo usque in Angliam et ad dominum regem Anglie, qui tunc erat in Scotia, veniendo cl florenos auri.

Recepta de denariis Beati Petri

## Cantuariensis

Archidiaconus Cantuariensis, qui fuerat dimissus per Dominum Itherium de Concoreto, predecessorem eiusdem Bernardi, in arreyratgiis in viii° li. sterlingorum pro dictis denariis de anno domini M° CCC° XXXIIII°, solvit dicto Bernardo xxiiii die Junii anno XXXVI° pro dicto anno XXXIIII° viii° li. Item ii die Augusti anno XXXVI° predicto pro anno XXXV° viii° li. Summa xvi li. sterlingorum.

---

[1] This folio was the outside cover of the original document before it was bound in the present codex.

[2] The extension is doubtful.

[3] Below, in another hand, the following is written: *Compotus Domini Bernardi de Sistre de Receptis per eum in Anglia.* This is followed by several words written with flourishes as one would scratch words idly. *Pourquey* is repeated twice, *Johannes* once, and another word is indecipherable.

[4] Folios 103[v] to 104[v] inclusive are blank.

## Roffensis

Archidiaconus Roffensis, qui fuerat dimissus in arreyratgiis per dictum Dominum Itherium in xi li. iiii[or] s. pro annis domini M° CCC° XXX III° et XXX IIII°, videlicet pro quolibet in cxii s., solvit die xxvii Februarii anno XXXV° pro dicto anno XXXIII° cxii s. Item vii die Aprilis anno XXXVI° pro dicto anno XXXIIII° et pro anno XXXV° xi li. iiii[or] s. Summa xvi li. xvi s.

## Londoniensis

Archidiaconus Colocestrie in ecclesia Londoniensi, qui per dictum Dominum Itherium fuit dimissus in arreyratgiis in cx s. pro anno domini M° CCC° XXXIIII°, solvit v die Aprilis anno XXXVI° pro dicto anno XXX° IIII° et pro anno XXXV xi li.

Summa totalis pagine xliii li. xvi s. sterlingorum cl fl. Approbatum.

(fol. 105[v]) Adhuc recepta de denariis Beati Petri

## Londoniensis adhuc

Archidiaconus Essexie in eadem ecclesia Londoniensi dimissus fuit per eundem Dominum Itherium in arreyratgiis in xl s. de anno domini M° CCC° XXIX°, et pro annis domini M° CCC° XXX°, XXXI°, XXXII°, XXXIII° et XXXIIII° pro quolibet in cx s. que omnia assendunt ad summam xxix li. x s., de quibus Magister Hugo de Staterne, olim archidiaconus dicti archidiaconatus solvit iiii[a] die Aprilis anno XXXV xi li. Item executores testamenti Domini Stephani, quondam Londoniensis episcopi, pro duobus annis quibus idem dominus episcopus proventus eiusdem archidiaconatus receperat solverunt die iiii Julii anno XXXIX xi li. Item . . executor testamenti Magistri Roberti de Cantuaria pro uno anno quando dictum archidiaconatum idem Magister Robertus tenuerat solvit die ii Madii anno domini M° CCC° XL° cx s. Item Magister Johannes le Boussher, tunc archidiaconus Essexie, solvit ultima die Decembris anno domini M° CCC° XL° in complementum dictorum arreyratgiorum xl s. Summa xx[ti] ix li. x s.

Item idem Magister Johannes de Boussher solvit die xix Novembris anno XXXVIII° pro anno domini M° CCC° XXXV° cx s.

Archidiaconus Middelsexie in dicta ecclesia Londoniensi fuit dimissus in arreyratgiis per eundem Dominum Itherium de anno domini M° CCC° XVIII° in x s. Et pro annis domini M° CCC° XIX°, XX°, XXI° XXII°, XXIII°, XXIIII°, XXV°, XXVI°, XXVII°, XXVIII°, XXIX°, XXX°, XXXI°, XXXII,° XXXIII°, et XXXIIII°, pro quolibet in cx s., que omnia assendunt ad summam lxxx[a] viii° li. x s., de quibus dictus Dominus Itherius repperitur per compota sua recepisse subsequenter a Magistro Thoma de Asteleye c s., et sic vero restabant solvendum nisi lxxxᵃ iii li. x s., et additis cx s. pro anno XXXVᵒ erant in universo lxxxᵃ ix li., de quibus Magister Robertus de Radeswell', tunc archidiaconus Middelsexie solvit anno XXXV et xxiiiᵃ die Martii xi li. Item dictus Magister Thomas de Asteleye in complementum solutionis duorum annorum, quibus dictum archidiaconatum retinuerat et pro quibus dicto Domino Itherio dictus ⟨Thomas⟩ c s. solverat, solvit ultima die Junii anno XXXVIᵒ vi li. Item Magister Richardus de Bursted pro denariis per ipsum levatis de dicto archidiaconatu anno XXXVIᵒ de mandato domini episcopi Londoniensis solvit viii die Octobris anno XXXVIᵒ xxxᵗᵃii s. viiiᵒ d. obolum. Item post mortem dicti Magistri Roberti de Radeswell', . . executor testamenti sui, facta compositione cum eo de dictis arrerratgiis pro tempore quo dictum archidiaconatum tenuerat, solvit anno domini Mᵒ CCCᵒ XXXVIIIᵒ et xxviii die Madii xxv li. x s. Item Magister Edmundus Trocelli, qui medio tempore predicto per vi annos dictum archidiaconatum tenuerat, solvit, tam per se, quam per manus diversorum quibus in vita sua et post mortem suum custodia sequestri in beneficiis suis pro premissis appositi fuerat commissa, xxxᵃiii li. Summa lxxᵃvii li. ii s. viiiᵒ d. obolus.[5]

Summa totalis pagine cxiiᶜⁱᵐ li. ii s. viiiᵒ d. obolus. Approbatum.

(fol. 106) De denariis Beati Petri

### Cicestrensis

Dominus . . episcopus Cicestrensis, qui fuerat dimissus in arreyratgiis per dictum Dominum Itherium pro anno domini Mᵒ CCCᵒ XXXIIIIᵒ in viiiᵒ li., solvit viiᵃ die Martii anno XXXV pro dictis annis XXXIIIIᵒ et XXXVᵒ xvi li. sterlingorum.

### Wyntoniensis

Archidiaconus Wyntoniensis, qui fuerat dimissus in arreyratgiis per dictum Dominum Itherium de anno domini Mᵒ CCCᵒ XXXIIIᵒ in x li. xvi s. viiiᵒ d. et pro anno XXXIIIIᵒ in xi li. xiii s. iiiiᵒʳ d., solvit tam pro dictis arreyratgiis quam pro anno XXXVᵒ xxxᵗᵃ iiiiᵒʳ li. iii s. iiiiᵒʳ d.

Item archidiaconus Surreye in ecclesia Wyntoniensi qui per dictum Dominum Itherium dimissus fuerat in arreyratgiis pro anno domini Mᵒ CCCᵒ XXXIIIIᵒ in cxiii s. iiiiᵒ d. solvit die xviᵃ Februarii anno XXXVᵒ pro dictis annis XXXIIIIᵒ et XXXVᵒ xi li. vi s. viiiᵒ d.

### Sarisbiriensis

Dominus . . episcopus Sarisbiriensis, qui dimissus fuerat in arreyratgiis per dictum Dominum Itherium pro annis domini Mᵒ CCCᵒ XXXIIᵈᵒ, XXXIIIᵒ et

XXXIIIIᵒ, pro quolibet in xvii li. que assendunt ad summam li li., solvit die ix Martii anno XXXVIᵒ li li. Item die xxi Decembris anno domini Mᵒ CCCᵒ XXXIXᵒ pro anno XXXVᵒ xvii li. Summa lxviiiᵒ li.

### Bathoniensis et Wellensis

Dominus episcopus Bathoniensis et Wellensis, qui per dictum Dominum Itherium dimissus fuerat in arreyratgiis pro anno domini Mᵒ CCCᵒ XXXIIIIᵒ in xi li. v s., solvit pro dicto anno et pro anno XXXVᵒ, videlicet die xᵃ Martii anno XXXVᵒ, xxᵗⁱii li. x s.

### Exoniensis

Dominus episcopus Exoniensis, qui dimissus fuerat in arreyratgiis per dictum Dominum Itherium pro annis domini Mᵒ CCCᵒ XXXIIIᵒ et XXXIIIIᵒ in xviiiᵒ li. x s., videlicet in ix li. v s. pro quolibet dictorum annorum, solvit die xᵃ Martii anno XXXVᵒ pro dictis annis XXXIIIᵒ, XXXIIIIᵒ et XXXVᵒ xxvii li. xv s.

### Wygorniensis

Dominus . . episcopus Wygorniensis fuit dimissus per dictum Dominum Itherium in arreyratgiis pro annis domini Mᵒ CCCᵒ XXXIᵒ, XXXIIᵒ, XXXIIIᵒ et XXXIIIIᵒ in xli li., videlicet in x li. v s. pro quolibet annorum predictorum, de quibus Dominus Adam, olim Wygorniensis subsequenter vero Wyntoniensis episcopus, solvit die xx Decembris anno XXXIXᵒ pro dictis XXXIᵒ, XXXIIᵒ et XXXIIIᵒ annis quibus tenuit dictum episcopatum Wygorniensem xxx li. xv s.

Item Dominus Symon, olim ecclesie Wygorniensis subsequenter vero Elyensis episcopus, solvit die viiiᵃ Julii anno xliᵒ pro dicto anno XXXᵒ IIIIᵒ et pro anno XXXVᵒ quibus tenuerat dictum episcopatum Wygorniensem xxᵒ li. x s.

Summa li li. v s.

Summa totalis pagine ccxxxᵃi li. Approbatum.

(fol. 106ᵛ) Adhuc de denariis Beati Petri

### Norwycensis

Dominus . . episcopus Norwycensis, qui dimissus fuerat in arreyratgiis per dictum Dominum Itherium in lxiiiiᵒʳ li. x s. pro annis domini Mᵒ CCCᵒ XXXIIᵈᵒ, XXXIIIᵒ et XXXIIIIᵒ, videlicet in xxi li. x s. pro quolibet annorum predictorum, solvit die ix Martii anno XXXVᵒ pro dictis arreyratgiis et pro dicto anno XXXVᵒ lxxxᵃvi li. sterlingorum.

### Lincolniensis

Dominus . . episcopus Lincolniensis, qui dimissus fuerat in arreyratgiis per dictum Dominum Itherium de anno domini Mᵒ CCCᵒ XXXᵒ in xl li. et pro annis domini Mᵒ CCCᵒ XXXIᵒ, XXXIIᵒ, XXXIIIᵒ et XXXIIIIᵒ in clxviiiᵒ li., videlicet in xlii li. pro quolibet

---

[5] In the margin opposite the last item is written in a different hand: ⟨st⟩at xi li. ⟨vi⟩i s, iii d. obolus. The first word and the number of shillings are obscured by a stain.

annorum predictorum, solvit pro dictis arreyratgiis et pro anno XXXV° per diversas solutiones tam per manus Magistri Johannis de Ragenhull' tunc cancellarii sui quam per manus Magistri Symonis de Yslep' vicarii sui generalis cc<sup>tum</sup> l<sup>a</sup> li.

### Conventrensis et Lichfeldensis

Dominus . . episcopus Conventrensis et Lichfeldensis, qui dimissus fuerat in arreyratgiis per dictum Dominum Itherium in x li. v s. pro anno domini M° CCC° XXX° IIII°, solvit pro dicto anno et pro anno XXXV°, videlicet vii<sup>a</sup> die Martii anno XXXV°, xx<sup>ti</sup> li. x s.

### Elyensis

Archidiaconus Elyensis solvit die x<sup>a</sup> Februarii anno XXXVII° pro anno domini M° CCC° XXXV° c s.

### Herefordensis

Dominus . . episcopus Herefordensis solvit die xii Martii anno domini M° CCC° XXXV° pro eodem anno vi li.

### Eboracensis

Dominus . . archiepiscopus Eboracensis solvit xviii<sup>a</sup> die Martii anno XXXV° pro dictis denariis de eodem anno xi li. x s.

Summa totalis pagine iii<sup>c</sup> lxx<sup>a</sup>ix li. Approbatum.

Summa totalis omnium prescriptorum vii<sup>c</sup> lxv li. xviii° s. viii° d. obolus sterlingorum, cl floreni.

(fol. 107) Recepta de dictis denariis Beati Petri de anno domini M° CCC° XXVI°

### Cantuariensis

Archidiaconus Cantuariensis solvit anno XXXVIII° et vii<sup>a</sup> die Aprilis pro dicto anno domini M° CCC° XXXVI° viii li. sterlingorum.

### Roffensis

Archidiaconus Roffensis solvit anno XXXVIII° et xviii<sup>a</sup> die Novembris pro dicto anno XXXVI° cxii<sup>cim</sup> s.

### Londoniensis

Magister Willelmus de Stanfeld, executor testamenti Magistri Willelmi de Meleford quondam archidiaconi Colocestrie in ecclesia Londoniensi, solvit die xix<sup>a</sup> Martii anno XXXVI° pro dictis denariis per dictum quondam archidiaconum debitis de archidiaconatu predicto pro dicto anno XXXVI° cx s.

Magister Hugo de Staterne, archidiaconus Essexie in dicta ecclesia Londoniensi, solvit anno XXXVI° die x Decembris pro dictis denariis de anno predicto cx s.

Magister Robertus de Radeswell', archidiaconus Middelsexie in dicta ecclesia Londoniensi, solvit die xx Madii anno XXXVII° pro dictis denariis debitis de tempore preterito de archidiaconatu predicto cx s.

### Cicestrensis

Dominus episcopus Cicestrensis solvit anno XXXVI° xxv die Novembris pro dicto anno XXXVI° viii° li.

### Wyntoniensis

Archidiaconus Wyntoniensis solvit anno XXXVI° et xix<sup>a</sup> die Decembris pro dicto anno XXXVI° xi li. xiii s. iiii<sup>or</sup> d.

Item . . archidiaconus Surreye in ecclesia Wyntoniensi solvit anno XXXVI° et die xxi<sup>a</sup> Decembris pro dicto anno XXXVI° cxiii s. iiii<sup>or</sup> d.

### Sarisbiriensis

Dominus episcopus Sarisbiriensis solvit anno XXXIX° et die xxi<sup>a</sup> Decembris pro dicto anno XXXVI° xvii li.

### Exoniensis

Dominus . . episcopus Exoniensis solvit anno XXXVII° et ix die Januarii pro dicto anno XXXVI° ix li. v s.

### Bathoniensis et Wellensis

Dominus . . episcopus Bathoniensis et Wellensis solvit anno XXXVII° et die xix Julii pro dicto anno XXXVI° xi li. v. s.

### Herefordensis

Dominus . . episcopus Herefordensis solvit anno XXXVII° et die xxiii Madii pro dicto anno XXXVI° vi li.

Summa totalis pagine lxxxx<sup>a</sup> viii° li. xviii° s. viii° d. Approbatum.

(fol. 107<sup>v</sup>) Adhuc recepta de denariis Beati Petri de anno domini M° CCC° XXXVI°

### Wygorniensis

Dominus Symon, olim Wygorniensis nunc vero Elyensis episcopus, solvit die viii Julii anno XLI° pro dicto anno XXXVI° quando fuit Wygorniensis episcopus x li. v s.

### Conventrensis et Lichefeldensis

Dominus . . episcopus Conventrensis et Lichefeldensis solvit anno XXXVII° et die xxiii<sup>a</sup> Junii pro dicto anno XXXVI° x li. v s.

### Elyensis

Achidiaconus Elyensis solvit xxvi<sup>a</sup> die Decembris anno XXXVI° pro eodem anno c s.

### Norwycensis

Dominus . . episcopus Norwycensis nichil.

### Lincolniensis

Dominus . . episcopus Lincolniensis solvit per manus

Magistri Symonis de Yslep', vicarii sui generalis, pro dicto anno XXXVI° xlii li.

### Eboracensis

Dominus . . archiepiscopus Eboracensis solvit xv die Januarii anno XXXVI° per manus sociorum societatis de Perusiis de Florentia pro dicto anno XXX° VI° xi li. x s.

Summa usque hic [6] istius pagine lxxix li. Approbatum.

Summa receptorum de dicto anno XXXVI° clxxvii li. xviii s. viii d.

Recepta de dictis denariis Beati Petri de anno domini M° CCC° XXXVII°

### Cantuariensis

Archidiaconus Cantuariensis solvit anno XXXVIII° et die vii Aprilis pro dictis denariis de archidiaconatu suo per eum debitis de anno domini M° CCC° XXXVII° viii° li.

### Roffensis

Archidiaconus Roffensis solvit anno XXXIX° et die xix^a Julii pro dicto anno domini M° CCC° XXXVII° cxii s.

### Londoniensis

Archidiaconus Colocestrie in ecclesia Londoniensi solvit anno XXXVIII° et die xi^a Junii pro dicto anno XXXVII° cx s.

Item archidiaconus Essexie in dicta ecclesia Londoniensi solvit anno XXXVIII° et xxii die Decembris pro dicto anno XXXVII° cx s.

Item Magister Thomas Duranti archidiaconus Middelsexie in dicta ecclesia Londoniensi solvit anno XXXVII° et xxi^a die Decembris pro dictis denariis de tempore preterito pro dicto archidiaconatu debitis cx s.

### Cicestrensis

Executores testamenti Domini J. quondam Cicestrensis episcopi solverunt anno XXXVII° et die xvii^a Februarii pro dicto anno XXXVII° viii° li.

Summa totalis pagine ab alia summa citra xxxviii li. ii s.[7] Approbatum.

(fol. 108) Adhuc recepta de denariis Beati Petri de anno domini M° CCC° XXXVII°

### Wyntoniensis

Archidiaconus Wyntoniensis solvit anno XXXVII° et die xi^a Novembris pro dicto anno XXXVII° xi li. xiii s. iiii^or d.

Item archidiaconus Surreye in ecclesia Wyntoniensi

solvit anno XXXVII° et xxviii die Februarii pro dicto anno XXXVII° cxiii s. iiii^or d.

### Sarisbiriensis

Dominus . . episcopus Sarisbiriensis solvit anno XXXIX° et xxi^a die Decembris pro dicto anno XXXVII° xvii li.

### Exoniensis

Dominus . . episcopus Exoniensis solvit anno XXXVIIII° et xxii^a die Aprilis pro dicto anno XXXVII° ix li. v s.

### Bathoniensis et Wellensis

Dominus . . episcopus Bathoniensis et Wellensis solvit tam per manus officialis . . archidiaconi Wellensis quam per manus . . officialis sui inter duas solutiones, quarum prima facta fuit anno XXXVII° et xiiii^a die Decembris, altera vero anno XXXVIII° et secunda die Octobris, pro dicto anno XXXVII° xi li. v s.

### Herefordensis

Dominus . . episcopus Herefordensis solvit anno XXXIX° et vii^a die Aprilis pro dicto anno domini M° CCC° XXXVII° vi li.

### Wygorniensis

Dominus Symon, olim Wygorniensis nunc vero Elyensis episcopus, solvit die viii^a Julii anno XLI° pro dictis denariis debitis de dicto episcopatu Wygorniensi de dicto anno XXXVII° quo fuit Wygorniensis episcopus x li. v s.

### Conventrensis et Lichefeldensis

Dominus . . episcopus Conventrensis et Lichefeldensis solvit anno XXXVIII° et die xxviii^a Octobris pro dicto anno XXXVII° x li. v s.

### Elyensis

Archidiaconus Elyensis solvit anno XXXVIII° et iii die Februarii pro dicto anno domini M° CCC° XXXVII° c s.

### Norwycensis

Dominus . . episcopus Norwycensis solvit anno XXXIX° et prima die Madii pro dicto anno XXXVII°, episcopatu suo remanente pro dictis denariis debitis de anno XXXVI° nichilominus obligato, xx^tii li.[8]

### Lincolniensis

Dominus episcopus Lincolniensis solvit per manus Magistri Symonis de Yslep', vicarii sui generalis, pro dicto anno XXXVII° xlii li.

---

[6] *hic* is followed by *de an* and the first loop of another *n* deleted by a line.

[7] The original entry read *Summa totalis pagine cxvii li. ii s.* The sum has been deleted by a line and the remainder of the above sentence inserted above the line.

[8] In the margin there is an abbreviation which probably stands for *resta*.

## Eboracensis

Dominus . . archiepiscopus Eboracensis solvit anno XXXVIII° et die ix Septembris per manus . . sociorum societatis Perusiorum de Florentia pro dicto anno domini M° CCC° XXXVII° xi li. x s.

Summa totalis pagine clxi li. xvi s. viii° d. Approbatum.

Summa totalis receptorum de dicto anno XXXVII° clxxxxix li. xviii s. viii d. Approbatum.

(fol. 108ᵛ) Recepta de dictis denariis Beati Petri de anno domini M° CCC° XXX° VIII°

## Cantuariensis

Archidiaconus Cantuariensis solvit pro dicto anno domini M° CCC° XXXVIII° viii° li. sterlingorum.

## Roffensis

Archidiaconus Roffensis solvit anno xxxix° et die xiiiiᵃ Augusti pro dicto anno domini M° CCC° XXXVIII° cxiiᶜⁱᵐ s.

## Londoniensis

Archidiaconus Colocestrie in ecclesia Londoniensi solvit anno XXXIX° et die xiᵃ Novembris pro dicto anno XXXVIII° cx s.

Item archidiaconus Essexie in dicta ecclesia Londoniensi solvit anno XXXVIII° et die xvii Februarii pro dicto anno XXXVIII° cx s.

Item Magister Thomas Duranti, archidiaconus Middelsexie in dicta ecclesia Londoniensi, solvit die xvii Februarii anno XXXVIII° pro dictis denariis de dicto archidiaconatu pro tempore preterito debitis cx s.

## Cicestrensis

Dominus . . episcopus Cicestrensis solvit anno domini M° CCC° XL° et de iiii Novembris pro dicto anno XXXVIII° viii° li.

## Wyntoniensis

Archidiaconus Wyntoniensis solvit anno XXXVIII° et xxviiiᵃ die Octobris pro dicto anno XXXVIII° xi li. xiii s. iiiiᵒʳ d.

Item . . archidiaconus Surreye in ecclesia Wyntoniensi solvit anno XXXIX° et die xix Junii pro dicto anno XXXVIII° cxiiiᶜⁱᵐ s. iiii d.

## Sarisbiriensis

Dominus . . episcopus Sarisbiriensis solvit anno XXXIX° et xxiᵃ die Decembris pro dicto anno domini M° CCC° XXXVIII° xvii li.

## Exoniensis

Dominus . . episcopus Exoniensis solvit anno XXXVIII° et xxiᵃ die Januarii pro dicto anno XXXVIII° ix li. v s.

## Bathoniensis et Wellensis

Dominus . . episcopus Bathoniensis et Wellensis solvit anno XXXVIII° et die iiiᵃ Februarii pro dicto anno XXXVIII° xi li. v s.

## Herefordensis

Dominus . . episcopus Herefordensis solvit anno XXXIX° et vii die Aprilis pro dicto anno domini M° CCC° XXXVIII° vi li.

## Wygorniensis

Recipit idem Bernardus de bonis que fuerant quondam Domini Thome Wygorniensis episcopi repertis in maynerio suo de Hylyndon' (Hillingdon) pro dictis denariis de episcopatu suo debitis de dicto anno XXXVIII° x li. v s.

## Conventrensis et Lichefeldensis

Dominus . . episcopus Conventrensis et Lichefeldensis solvit anno XXXIX° xxviiiᵃ die Januarii pro dicto anno XXXVIII° x li. v s.

## Elyensis

Archidiaconus Elyensis solvit anno XXXIX° et xxviii die Januarii pro dicto anno domini M° CCC° XXXVIII° c s.

Summa totalis pagine cxxᵗⁱ iiiiᵒʳ li. viii° s. viii° d. Approbatum.

(fol. 109) Adhuc recepta de dictis denariis Beati Petri de anno domini M° CCC° XXXVIII°

## Norwycensis

Dominus . . episcopus Norwycensis solvit anno XXXIX° et prima die Madii pro dicto anno XXXVIII°, episcopatu suo remanente pro dictis denariis de anno XXXVI° debitis nichilominus obligato, xxᵗⁱ ii li.

## Lincolniensis

Dominus . . episcopus Lincolniensis solvit per manus Magistri Symonis de Yslep', vicarii sui generalis, pro dicto anno XXXVIII° xlii li.

## Eboracensis

Executores testamenti Domini W. quondam Eboracensis archiepiscopi solverunt anno xl° et die ix Decembris per manus sociorum de Bardis de Florentia pro dicto anno XXVIII° xi li. x s.

Summa ⁹ pagine usque hic lxxiiiiᵒʳ li. x s. Approbatum.

Summa receptorum pro dicto anno XXXVIII° clxxxxviii li. xviii s. viii d. Approbatum.

Recepta de dictis denariis Beati Petri pro anno domini M° CCC° XXX° IX°.

---

⁹ *to* is deleted by a line in the manuscript.

### Cantuariensis

Archidiaconus Cantuariensis solvit pro dicto anno domini M° CCC° XXX° IX° viii° li.

### Roffensis

Archidiaconus Roffensis solvit die xv Februarii anno XL° pro dicto anno XXX° IX° cxii^cim s.

### Londoniensis

Archidiaconus Colocestrie in ecclesia Londoniensi solvit anno XXXIX° et ii die Novembris pro dicto anno XXXIX° cx s.

Item archidiaconus Essexie in dicta ecclesia Londoniensi solvit anno XL° et die ultima Martii pro dicto anno XXXIX° cx s.

Item Magister Henricus de Idesworth', archidiaconus Middelsexie in dicta ecclesia Londoniensi, solvit die xxx Januarii anno XL° pro dictis denariis de tempore preterito de archidiaconatu suo predicto debitis cx s.

### Cicestrensis

Dominus . . episcopus Cicestrensis solvit anno XL° et iiii die Novembris pro dicto anno domini M° CCC° XXXIX° viii° li.

### Wyntoniensis

Archidiaconus Wyntoniensis solvit pro dicto anno XXXIX° xi li. xiii s. iiii d.

Item archidiaconus Surreye in ecclesia Wyntoniensi solvit anno XL° et die vii Julii pro dicto anno domini M° CCC° XXXIX° cxiii^cim s. iiii^or d.

### Sarisbiriensis

Dominus . . episcopus Sarisbiriensis solvit anno XXXIX° et die xxi Decembris pro eodem anno XXXIX° xvii li.

### Exoniensis

Dominus . . episcopus Exoniensis solvit anno XXXIX° et prima die Februarii pro dicto anno domini M° CCC° XXXIX° ix li. v s.

Summa totalis pagine ab alia summa citra lxxxi li. xiii s. viii d.[10] Approbatum.

(fol. 109^v) Adhuc recepta de denariis Beati Petri de anno domini M° CCC° XXXIX°

### Bathoniensis et Wellensis

Dominus . . episcopus Bathoniensis et Wellensis solvit anno XL° et die iii^a Novembris pro dicto anno domini M° CCC° XXXIX° xi li. v s.

### Herefordensis

Dominus . . episcopus Herefordensis solvit ix^a die

---

[10] The original entry was *Summa totalis pagine clvii li. iii s. viii° d.* The sum has been deleted and the above inserted above the line.

Madii anno XLIII° pro dicto anno domini M° CCC° XXXIX° vi li.

### Wygorniensis

Recipit idem nuntius tam de bonis reppertis in maynerio de Hylyndon' que quondam fuerat Domini Thome Wygorniensis episcopi quam a Domino Wlstano nunc Wygorniensi episcopo pro dictis denariis de anno predicto XXXIX° debitis x li. v s.

### Conventrensis et Lichefeldensis

Dominus . . episcopus Conventrensis et Lichefeldensis solvit anno XXXIX° et die xxviii^a Januarii pro dicto anno XXXIX° x li. v s.

### Elyensis

Archidiaconus Elyensis solvit quinta die Februarii anno XL° pro dicto anno XXXIX° c s.

### Norwycensis

Dominus . . episcopus Norwycensis solvit die ultima Octobris anno XL° pro dicto anno XXXIX°, dicto tamen episcopatu suo pro dictis denariis de anno XXXVI° debitis obligato remanente, xx^ti ii li.

### Lincolniensis

Dominus . . Lincolniensis episcopus solvit per manus Magistri Symonis de Yslep', vicarii sui generalis, pro dicto anno domini M° CCC° XXXIX° xlii li.

### Eboracensis

Executores testamenti Domini Willelmi quondam Eboracensis archiepiscopi solverunt die ix Decembris anno XL° per manus . . sociorum de Bardis de Florentia pro dicto anno domini M° CCC° XXXIX° xi li. x s.

Summa pagine usque hic cxviii li. v s. Approbatum.

Summa totalis receptorum de dicto anno XXXIX° clxxxxix li. xviii s. viii d. Approbatum.

Recepta de dictis denariis Beati Petri de anno domini M° CCC° quadragesimo

### Cantuariensis

Archidiaconus Cantuariensis solvit pro dicto anno domini M° CCC° XL° viii° li.

### Roffensis

Archidiacous Roffensis solvit xv die Februarii anno XL° pro eodem anno XL° cxii s.

### Londoniensis

Archidiaconus Colocestrie in ecclesia Londoniensi solvit prima die Octobris anno domini M° CCC° XL° pro eodem anno XL° cx s.

Item . . archidiaconus Essexie in eadem ecclesia

Londoniensi solvit iii die Julii anno XLI° pro dictis denariis debitis de anno XL° cx s.

Summa totalis pagine ab alia summa citra xxiiii li. xii s.[11] Approbatum.

(fol. 110) Adhuc recepta de denariis Beati Petri de anno domini M° CCC° XL°

### Londoniensis adhuc

Magister Henricus de Idesworth' archidiaconus Middelsexie in dicta ecclesia Londoniensi solvit die xxxª Januarii anno XL° pro dictis denariis de tempore preterito pro dicto archidiaconatu sui debitis cx s.

### Cicestrensis

Dominus . . episcopus Cicestrensis solvit die xxvii Octobris anno XLI° pro dicto anno domini M° CCC° XL° viii° li.

### Wyntoniensis

Archidiaconus Wyntoniensis solvit pro dicto anno domini M° CCC° XL° xi li. xiii s. iiii d.

Item . . archidiaconus Surreye in ecclesia Wyntoniensi solvit die xxiii Julii anno XLI° pro dicto anno XL° cxiii s. iiiiᵒʳ d.

### Sarisbiriensis

Dominus . . episcopus Sarisbiriensis nichil.[12]

### Exoniensis

Dominus . . episcopus Exoniensis solvit die xxiiiiª Octobris anno XLI° pro dicto anno domini M° CCC° XL° ix li. v s.

### Bathoniensis et Wellensis

Dominus . . episcopus Bathoniensis et Wellensis solvit iiiiª die Martii anno XLIIᵈᵒ pro dictis denariis debitis de anno XL° xi li. v s.

### Herefordensis

Dominus . . episcopus Herefordensis solvit ix die Madii anno XLIII° pro dicto anno domini M° CCC° XL° vi li.

### Wygorniensis

Dominus Wlstanus Wygorniensis episcopus solvit die prima Februarii anno XL° pro dicto anno XL° x li. v s.

### Conventrensis et Lichefeldensis

Dominus . . episcopus Conventrensis et Lichefeldensis solvit xxii die Januarii anno XLIIᵈᵒ pro dicto anno XL° x li. v s.

### Elyensis

Archidiaconus Elyensis solvit die prima Februarii anno XLI° pro dicto anno XL° c s.

### Norwycensis

Dominus . . episcopus Norwycensis solvit die xv Januarii anno XLI° pro dicto anno xl°, dicto tamen episcopatu suo pro anno XXXVI° pro dictis denariis ut supra remanente obligato, xxii li.

### Lincolniensis

Dominus Henricus episcopus Lincolniensis solvit per manus Magistri Symonis de Yslep', vicarii sui generalis, in partem dictorum denariorum pro anno XL° debitorum xv li. vi s. viii d.[13]

### Eboracensis

Capitulum Eboracense sede vacante solverunt anno XLI° et die xxiiª Junii per manus sociorum societatis Bardorum de Florentia pro dicto anno XL° xi li. x s.

Summa totalis pagine cxxxªi li. xiii s. iiiiᵒʳ d. Approbatum.

Summa totalis receptorum de dicto anno XL° clvi li. xiii s. iiii d. Approbatum

(fol. 110ᵛ) Recepta de dictis denariis Beati Petri de anno domini M° CCC° XLI°

### Cantuariensis

Archidiaconus Cantuariensis solvit pro dictis denariis debitis pro dicto anno domini M° CCC° XLI° viii° li. sterlingorum.

### Roffensis

Archidiaconus Roffensis solvit die iiiiª Januarii anno XLI° pro eodem anno XLI° cxii s.

### Londoniensis

Archidiaconus Colocestrie in ecclesia Londoniensi solvit vi die Octobris anno XLI° pro eodem anno domini M° CCC° XLI° cx s.

Item . . archidiaconus Essexie in eadem ecclesia Londoniensi solvit anno XLIIᵈᵒ et die xxiii Decembris pro dictis denariis debitis de anno XLI° cx s.

Item Magister Henricus de Idesworth', archidiaconus Middelsexie in dicta ecclesia Londoniensi, solvit die xi Novembris anno XLIIᵈᵒ pro dictis denariis de dicto archidiaconatu suo pro tempore preterito debitis cx s.

### Cicestrensis

Dominus . . episcopus Cicestrensis nichil.[14]

### Wyntoniensis

Archidiaconus Wyntoniensis solvit pro dicto anno domini M° CCC° XLI° xi li. xiii s. iiii d.

Item . . archidiaconus Surreye in ecclesia Wyntoniensi solvit die ultima Julii anno XLIIᵈᵒ pro dicto anno XLI° cxiii s. iiiiᵒʳ d.

---

[11] In the original entry, which gave the sum of the page as *cxlii li. xviii s.*, the sum has been deleted by a line.
[12] In the margin: *Resta.*

[13] In the margin: *Resta.*
[14] In the margin: *Resta.*

### Sarisbiriensis

Dominus . . episcopus Sarisbiriensis nichil.

### Exoniensis

Dominus . . episcopus Exoniensis solvit ii die Madii anno XLIII° pro dictis denariis debitis de anno predicto XLI° ix li. v s.

### Bathoniensis et Wellensis

Dominus . . episcopus Bathoniensis et Wellensis solvit iiii^a die Martii anno XLII° pro dictis denariis de dicto anno XLI° xi li. v s.

### Herefordensis

Dominus . . episcopus Herefordensis solvit die ix Madii anno XLIII° pro dicto anno XLI° vi li.

### Wygorniensis

Dominus Wlstanus episcopus Wygorniensis solvit pro dicto anno XLI° x li. v s.

### Conventrensis et Lichefeldensis

Dominus . . episcopus Conventrensis et Lichefeldensis solvit die xxii^a Januarii anno XLII^do pro dicto anno XLI° x li. v s.

### Elyensis

Archidiaconus Elyensis solvit xvii die Februarii anno XLII^do pro dicto anno XLI° c s.[15]

### Norwycensis

Dominus . . episcopus Norwycensis nichil.

### Lincolniensis

Capitulum Lincolniense sede vacante solverunt per manus . . officialis Lincolniensis die xxvi^a Februarii anno XLI° pro eodem anno XLI° xlii li.

### Eboracensis

Capitulum Eboracense sede vacante solverunt anno XLII^do et die xxii^a Julii per manus . . sociorum de Bardis de Florentia pro dicto anno XLI° xi li. x s.

Summa totalis pagine et pro toto anno XLI° clii li. xviii° s. viii° d. Approbatum.

(fol. 111) Recepta de dictis denariis Beati Petri de anno domini M° CCC° XLII^do qui fuit ultimus receptus dicti Bernardi.

### Cantuariensis

Archidiaconus Cantuariensis solvit pro dicto anno domini M° CCC° XLII^do viii° li.

### Roffensis

Archidiaconus Roffensis nichil.[16]

### Londoniensis

Archidiaconus Colocestrie in ecclesia Londoniensi solvit die ix^a Octobris anno XLII^do pro eodem anno XLII^do cx s.

Item archidiaconus Essexie in eadem ecclesia Londoniensi nichil.[16]

Magister Henricus de Idesworth', archidiaconus Middelsexie in eadem ecclesia, solvit anno XLII^do die xi Novembris pro dictis denariis de archidiaconatu predicto pro tempore preterito debitis cx s.

### Cicestrensis

Dominus . . episcopus Cicestrensis nichil.[16]

### Wyntoniensis

Archidiaconus Wyntoniensis solvit in partem dictorum denariorum pro dicto anno XLII^do debitorum ciii s. iiii^or d.[17]

Archidiaconus Surreye in ecclesia Wyntoniensi nichil.[17]

### Sarisbiriensis

Dominus . . episcopus Sarisbiriensis nichil.[17]

### Exoniensis

Dominus . . episcopus Exoniensis solvit ii^a die Madii anno XLIII° pro dictis denariis per eum debitis de dicto anno XLII^do ix li. v s.

### Bathoniensis et Wellensis

Dominus . . episcopus Bathoniensis et Wellensis solvit xx die Madii anno XLIII° pro dictis denariis de anno XLII^do xi li. v s.

### Herefordensis

Dominus . . episcopus Herefordensis nichil.[17]

### Wygorniensis

Dominus . . episcopus Wygorniensis solvit pro dicto anno XLII^do x li. v s.

### Conventrensis et Lichefeldensis

Dominus . . episcopus Conventrensis et Lichefeldensis solvit xxii^a die Januarii anno XLII^do pro eodem anno x li. v s.

### Elyensis

Archidiaconus Elyensis nichil.[18]

---

[15] In the margin: *Resta*. The note is probably placed here by mistake, and should be opposite the next item.

[16] In the margin: *Resta*.

[17] In the margin: *Resta*.

[18] In the margin: *Resta*. Placed between this item and the next.

## Norwycensis

Dominus . . episcopus Norwycensis nichil.

## Lincolniensis

Magister Walterus de Stammen', olim tempore vacationis episcopatus Lincolniensis officialis Lincolniensis, solvit prima die Februarii anno XLII^do in partem dictorum denariorum de episcopatu predicto debitorum pro dicto anno XLII^do xx^ti i li.[19]

## Eboracensis

Dominus . . archiepiscopus Eboracensis nichil.[19]

Summa totalis pagine lxxx^a vi li. iii s. iiii^or d. Approbatum.

Summa totalis receptorum per dictum Bernardum de Sistre de dictis denariis Beati Petri m^l ix^c xxx^a viii li. viii s. viii^o d. obolus. Approbatum.

(fol. 111^v) Recepta per dictum Bernardum de Sistre de censu annuo Romane ecclesie in partibus Anglie debito pro tempore quo stetit in nuntiationis officio supradicto.

Illustris dominus rex Anglie debet annis singulis m^l marchas argenti ecclesie supradicte, videlicet vii^c pro regno Anglie et iii^c pro regno Ibernie, sed de toto tempore quo dictus Bernardus de Sistre fuit in Anglia nuntius nichil eidem solvit, cum dictum censum in Romana curia solvere teneatur. Nichil.

## Cantuariensis

Dominus archiepiscopus Cantuariensis debet dicte ecclesie singulis trienniis iii^c m. argenti de quibus, quia debet eas in Romana curia solvere, dicto Bernardo de toto tempore predicto nichil solvit. Nichil.

Abbas de Farversham Cantuariensis diocesis qui dat annuatim unam marcham argenti et pro anno domini M^o CCC^o XXX^o IIII^o dimissus fuerat in arreyratgiis per Dominum Itherium de Concoreto, predecessorem dicti Bernardi in officio predicto, in xiii s. iiii^or d. sterlingorum solvit eidem Bernardo pro dicto anno XXXIIII^o et pro XXXV^o xxvi s. viii^o d. sterlingorum.

## Roffensis

Prior de Tonebbrigg' Roffensis diocesis qui dat annuatim unam marcham argenti et dimissus fuerat in arreyratgiis per dictum dominum Itherium in xxvi s. viii^o d. pro annis domini M^o CCC^o XXXIII^o et XXXIIII^o solvit die xiii Martii anno XXXV^o pro dictis annis XXXIII^o, XXXIIII^o et XXXV^o xl^a s.

## Londoniensis

Abbatissa Sancte Clare Londonie, que fuerat dimissa in arreyratgiis per dictum Dominum Itherium pro annis XXXII^o, XXXIII^o et XXXIIII^o, pro quolibet in vi d.

pro i^a libra cere quam dat singulis annis dicte ecclesie, solvit dicto Domino Itherio pro dicto anno XXXII^do vi d. et dicto Bernardo pro aliis duobus annis sequentibus et pro anno XXXV^o xviii^o d.

Ecclesia que dicitur Florescia (Floreffe) que debet censum unius monete auri secundum Provinciale Romane ecclesie in Londoniensi diocesi nimine repperitur et sic nichil potuit idem Bernardus exhigere vel levare.[20] Nichil.

## Wyntoniensis

Abbas de Cherteseye Wyntoniensis diocesis, qui secundum Provinciale dat annuatim Romane ecclesie predicte iiii^or aureos quorum quilibet valet ii s. sterlingorum, solvit dicto Bernardo pro anno domini M^o CCC^o XXXV^o viii^o s.

Et de viii^o solidis, pro quibus pro anno domini M^o CCC^o XXX^o IIII^o fuerat dimissus in arreyratgiis per dictum Dominum Itherium, debet idem Dominus Itherius respondere qui eos recepit, prout patet per eius aquietantiam. Sit ad computum Domini Itherii.[21]

Summa totalis pagine iii li. xvi s. ii d. sterlingorum. Approbatum.

(fol. 112) Adhuc recepta de censu annuo

## Sarisbiriensis

Abbas de Malmesbury Sarisbiriensis diocesis, qui secundum Provinciale dat annuatim unam unciam auri valentem i^am marcham argenti et fuerat dimissus in arreyratgiis pro anno domini M^o CCC^o XXXIII^o in xiii s. iiii^or d. per dictum Dominum Itherium, solvit die xii Martii anno XXXV^o pro dictis annis XXXIIII^o et XXXV^o xxvi s. viii^o d.

## Exoniensis

Prior Bodmye Exoniensis diocesis, qui secundum Provinciale predictum dat annuatim unum malachinum valentem ii s. sterlingorum, et per dictum Dominum Itherium fuerat dimissus in arreyratgiis pro anno domini M^o CCC^o XXXIIII^o in ii s. sterlingorum, solvit xi^a die Septembris anno XXXVI^o pro annis XXXIIII^o et XXXV^o iiii^or s.

## Norwycensis

Abbas Sancti Edmundi Norwycensis diocesis, qui dat annuatim i^am marcham argenti et fuerat dimissus in arreyratgiis in xiii s. iiii^or d. per dictum Dominum Itherium pro anno domini M^o CCC^o XXXIIII^o, de quibus idem Dominus Itherius debet respondere quia eos recepit prout patet per eius aquietantiam, solvit dicto

---

[19] In the margin: *Resta*.

[20] The monastery of Floreffe was entered under the diocese of London in the *Liber Censuum* by mistake. It was also entered correctly under the diocese of Liège: Lunt, *Financial Relations . . . to 1327*, p. 104.

[21] The last sentence is entered in the margin by the cameral hand which wrote the other marginal comments.

Bernardo pro anno XXXV° xiii s. iiii°ʳ d. Sit ad Dominum Itherium.[22]

## Lincolniensis

Abbas Sancti Albani Lincolniensis diocesis, qui secundum dictum Provinciale dat annuatim unam unciam auri valentem iᵃᵐ marcham argenti, fuit dimissus in arreyratgiis per dictum Dominum Itherium in xiii s. iiii°ʳ d. pro anno domnii M° CCC° XXXIIII°, de quibus idem Dominus Itherius qui eos recepit tenetur respondere. Item solvit idem abbas dicto Bernardo pro anno domini M° CCC° XXXV° xiii s. iiii°ʳ d. Sit ut supra.[22]

Prior de Cheucombe dicte diocesis, qui secundum dictum Provinciale dat annuatim unum obolum masabnutonum [23] valentem xv d. sterlingorum, et per dictum Dominum Itherium fuerat dimissus in arreyratgiis pro anno domini M° CCC° XXXIIII° in xv d., solvit pro dicto anno et pro anno XXXV° ii s. vi d.

Monasterium quod dicitur Malvembiense [24] quod dat annuatim secundum dictum Provinciale unam unciam auri non invenitur in dicta diocesi nec in aliis partibus Anglie, quare dictus Bernardus nichil potuit exhigere vel levare. Nichil.

## Elyensis

Prior de Angleseye Elyensis diocesis, qui secundum dictum Provinciale dat annuatum unum malechinum valentem ii s. sterlingorum, solvit pro anno domini M° CCC° XXXV° ii s.

## Conventrensis et Lichefeldensis

Monasterium quod dicitur de Bredeya et secundum dictum Provinciale tenetur singulis annis dicte Romane ecclesie in ii bisantiis non potuit in Conventrensi et Lichefeldensi diocesi nec alibi in Anglia repperiri, quare dictus Bernardus de toto tempore predicto nichil potuit exhigere vel levare. Nichil.[25]

Summa totalis pagine iii li. i s. x d. sterlingorum. Approbatum.

(fol. 112ᵛ) Adhuc recepta de censu annuo Romane ecclesie

## Eboracensis

Dominus . . archiepiscopus Eboracensis, qui singulis trienniis debet iii° marchas argenti, nichil solvit de toto tempore predicto dicto Bernardo quia ipsas debet solvere in Romana curia suis sumptibus et expensis. Nichil.

Custos ecclesie de Scardeburgh' Eboracensis diocesis, qui secundum Provinciale predictum dat annuatim unum obolum masabuntinum valentem xv d. sterlingorum, solvit pro anno domini M° CCC° XXXV° xv d.

## Karliolensis

Prior cathedralis ecclesie Karliolensis, qui dat annuatim unam marcham argenti et per dictum Dominum Itherium fuerat dimissus in arreyratgiis pro anno domini millesimo CCC° XXXIIII° in xiii s. iiii°ʳ d., solvit xviᵃ die Octobris anno XXXVI° pro dictis annis XXXIIII° et XXXV xxvi s. viii° d.

Summa istius pagine usque hic xxvii s. xi d. Approbatum.

Summa totalis solutorum de arreyratgiis dicti census et de anno XXXV° viii li. v s. xi d. Approbatum.

## De Scotia

De censu annuo dicte Romane ecclesie in Scotia debito nichil est receptum per dictum Bernardum propter gueram continuam que fuit ibidem toto tempore ipsius Bernardi, nec fuit sibi aliquid in arreyratgiis dimissum in partibus Scotie.

## De Ibernia

Magister Hugo de Calce, cancellarius Dublinensis, qui fuit commissarius dicti Bernardi toto tempore suo in partibus Ibernie, non computavit cum eo.

Recepta de dicto censu pro anno domini M° CCC° XXXVI°

## Cantuariensis

Abbas de Farversham solvit prima die Februarii anno XL° pro dicto anno domini M° CCC° XXXVI° xiii s. iiii°ʳ d.

## Roffensis

Prior de Tonnebrigg' solvit ultima die Septembris anno XXXVIII° pro dicto anno domini M° CCC° XXXVI° xiii s. iiii°ʳ d.

## Londoniensis

Abbatissa Sancte Clare Londonie solvit die xiiii Martii anno XL° pro dicto anno XXXVI° vi d.

## Wyntoniensis

Abbas de Cherteseye solvit die xx Novembris anno XXXVI° pro eodem anno XXXVI° viii° s.

Summa totalis pagine ab alia summa citra xxxv s. ii d.[26] Approbatum.

(fol. 113) Adhuc recepta de censu annuo de anno domini M° CCC° XXXVI°

---

[22] The last sentence is a marginal note by the hand of the cameral writer.

[23] In the *Liber Censuum* it is given as "obolum massemutinum": i, 225. It was a coin of the Almohades.

[24] The monastery of Malmesbury entered in the Liber Censuum under the above name in the diocese of Lincoln and also entered correctly in the diocese of Salisbury: Lunt, *Financial Relations . . . to 1327*, p. 112.

[25] Probably the monastery of Laund in the diocese of Lincoln entered in the *Liber Censuum* under the above name and diocese by mistake; *ibid.*, pp. 102-104.

[26] This sum is entered over the sum of the page, *iii li. iii s. i d.*, which is deleted by a line.

### Exoniensis

Prior Bodmye solvit viiiᵃ die Novembris anno XXXᵒ VIᵒ pro eodem anno ii s.

### Sarisbiriensis

Abbas de Malmesbury solvit viᵃ die Decembris anno XXXVIIᵒ pro dicto anno XXXVIᵒ xiii s. iiiiᵒʳ d.

### Norwycensis

Abbas Sancti Edmundi solvit prima die Madii anno XXXVIIᵒ pro dicto anno XXXVIᵒ xiii s. iiiiᵒʳ d.

### Lincolniensis

Abbas Sancti Albani solvit ultima die Januarii anno XXXVIᵒ pro eodem anno xiii s. iiiiᵒʳ d.
Prior de Cheucombe solvit xxii die Februarii anno XXXVIᵒ pro eodem anno xv d.

### Elyensis

Prior de Angleseye solvit die xviiᵃ Junii anno XXXVIIᵒ pro dicto anno XXXVIᵒ ii s.

### Eboracensis

Custos ecclesie de Scardeburgh' solvit ii die Decembris anno XXXVIᵒ pro eodem anno XXXVIᵒ xv d.

### Karleolensis

Prior Karleolensis ecclesie solvit die xviᵃ Octobris anno XXXVIᵒ pro eodem anno xiii s. iiiiᵒʳ d.
Summa pagine usque hic xxxix s. x d. Approbatum.
Summa totalis receptorum de anno XXXVIᵒ predicto iiii li. xv s. Approbatum.
De Scotia et Ibernia sicut prius.

Recepta de dicto censu annuo pro anno domini Mᵒ CCCᵒ XXXVIIᵒ

### Cantuariensis

Abbas de Farversham solvit anno XLᵒ et prima die Februarii pro dicto anno domini Mᵒ CCCᵒ XXXVIIᵒ xiii s. iiiiᵒʳ d.

### Roffensis

Prior de Tonnebrigg' solvit anno XXXVIIIᵒ ultima die Septembris pro dicto anno domini Mᵒ CCCᵒ XXXVIIᵒ xiii s. iiiiᵒʳ d.

### Londoniensis

Abbatissa Sancte Clare Londonie solvit anno xlᵒ et xiiii die Martii pro dicto anno domini Mᵒ CCCᵒ XXXVIIᵒ vi d.

### Wyntoniensis

Abbas de Cherteseye solvit anno XXXVIIᵒ et die xx Decembris pro eodem anno viiiᵒ s.

### Exoniensis

Prior de Bodmye solvit anno XXXVIIᵒ et xii die Novembris pro eodem anno ii s.

### Sarisbiriensis

Abbas de Malmesbury solvit anno XXXVIIᵒ et vi die Decembris pro eodem anno xiii s. iiiiᵒʳ d.

### Norwycensis

Abbas Sancti Edmundi solvit anno XXXVIIᵒ et xxii die Januarii pro eodem anno xiii s. iiiiᵒʳ d.

### Lincolniensis

Abbas Sancti Albani solvit anno XXXVIIᵒ et ix die Februarii pro eodem anno xiii s. iiiiᵒʳ d.
Prior de Cheucombe solvit anno XXXVIIᵒ et viii die Februarii pro eodem anno xv d.

### Elyensis

Prior de Angleseye solvit anno XXXVIIᵒ et viii die Novembris pro eodem anno ii s.
Summa totalis pagine ab alia summa citra iiii li. v d.[27] Approbatum.

(fol. 113ᵛ) Adhuc recepta de censu annuo de anno domini Mᵒ CCCᵒ XXXVIIᵒ

### Eboracensis

Custos ecclesie de Scardeburgh' solvit anno XXXVIIᵒ et xiiᵃ die Februarii pro dicto anno domini Mᵒ CCCᵒ XXXVIIᵒ xv d.

### Karleolensis

Prior Karleolensis solvit anno XXXIXᵒ et die iiiiᵃ Aprilis pro dicto anno XXXVIIᵒ xiii s. iiii d.
Summa pagine usque hic xiiii s. vii d. Approbatum.
Summa totalis receptorum de dicto anno XXXVIIᵒ iiii li. xv s. Approbatum.
De Scotia et Ibernia sicut prius.

Recepta de dicto censu annuo de anno domini Mᵒ CCCᵒ XXXVIII*

### Cantuariensis

Abbas de Farversham solvit anno domini Mᵒ CCCᵒ XLᵒ et die prima Februarii pro dicto anno domini Mᵒ CCCᵒ XXXVIIIᵒ xiii s. iiiiᵒʳ d.

### Roffensis

Prior de Tonebrigg' solvit xv die Februarii anno XXXIXᵒ pro dicto anno domini Mᵒ CCCᵒ XXXVIIIᵒ xiii s. iiiiᵒʳ d.

### Londoniensis

Abbatissa Sancte Clare Londonie solvit die xiiii

---

[27] Entered over the deleted sum for the whole page of *vii li. iii d.*

Martii anno XL° pro dicto anno domini M° CCC°
XXXVIII° vi d.

### Wyntoniensis

Abbas de Cherteseye solvit anno XXXVIII° et die x
Novembris pro dicto anno XXXVIII° viii° s.

### Exoniensis

Prior de Bodmye solvit penultima die Octobris anno
XXXIX° pro dicto anno XXXVIII° ii s.

### Sarisbiriensis

Abbas de Malmesbury solvit penultima die Januarii
anno XXXIX° pro dicto anno domini M° CCC°
XXXVIII° xiii s. iiii d.

### Norwycensis

Abbas Sancti Edmundi solvit xv die Decembris anno
XXXVIII° pro eodem anno xiii s. iiii d.

### Lincolniensis

Abbas Sancti Albani solvit iii^a die Februarii anno
XXXVIII° pro eodem anno xiii s. iiii d.
Prior de Cheucombe solvit xiii die Januarii anno
XXXVIII° pro eodem anno xv d.

### Elyensis

Prior de Angleseye solvit ultima die Novembris anno
domini M° CCC° XXXVIII° pro eodem anno ii s.

### Eboracensis

Custos ecclesie de Scardeburgh' solvit xxix die
Octobris anno domini M° CCC° XXXVIII° pro eodem
anno xv d.

### Karleolensis

Prior Karleolensis solvit iiii die Aprilis anno XXXIX°
pro dicto anno domini M° CCC° XXXVIII° xiii s.
iiii d.
De Scotia et Ibernia sicut prius.
Summa totalis pagine ab alia summa citra iiii li. xv
s.[28] Approbatum.

(fol. 114) Recepta de dicto censu annuo de anno
domini M° CCC° XXXIX°

### Cantuariensis

Abbas de Farversham solvit die prima Februarii anno
domini M° CCC° XL° pro dicto anno domini millesimo
CCC° XXXIX° xiii s. iiii^or d.

### Roffensis

Prior de Tonebrigg' solvit xv die Februarii anno
XXXIX° pro eodem anno xiii s. iiii^or d.

---

[28] The sum is entered over the deleted sum for the whole page
of v^e li. ix s. vii d.

### Londoniensis

Abbatissa Sancte Clare Londonie solvit xiiii die
Martii anno XL° pro dicto anno domini M° CCC°
XXXIX° vi d.

### Wyntoniensis

Abbas de Cherteseye solvit iii^a die Aprilis anno XL°
pro dicto anno XXXIX° viii s.

### Exoniensis

Prior de Bodmye solvit penultima die Octobris anno
XXXIX° pro eodem anno ii s.

### Sarisbiriensis

Abbas de Malmesbury solvit penultima die Januarii
anno XXXIX° pro eodem anno xiii s. iiii^or d.

### Norwycensis

Abbas Sancti Edmundi solvit xvi die Octobris anno
XXX°IX° pro eodem anno xiii s. iii^or d.

### Lincolniensis

Abbas Sancti Albani solvit vii^a die Februarii anno
XXX°IX° pro eodem anno xiii s. iiii^or d.
Prior de Cheucombe solvit xi^a die Februarii anno
XXX°IX° pro eodem anno xv d.

### Elyensis

Prior de Angleseye solvit xiii^a die Octobris anno
XXX°IX° pro eodem anno ii s.

### Eboracensis

Custos ecclesie de Scardeburgh' solvit xvi^a die
Novembris anno domini M° CCC° XXX°IX° pro
eodem anno xv d.

### Karleolensis

Prior Karleolensis solvit iiii die Aprilis anno
XXXIX° pro eodem anno xiii s. iiii^or d.

### De Scotia et Ibernia sicut prius

Summa receptorum de dicto anno XXXIX iiii^or li.
xv s. Approbatum.

Recepta de dicto censu annuo pro anno domini M°
CCC° quadragesimo

### Cantuariensis

Abbas de Farversham solvit prima die Februarii anno
domini M° CCC° XL° pro eodem anno XL° xiii s.
iiii^or d.

### Roffensis

Prior de Tonebrigg' solvit iii^a die Januarii anno XLI°
pro dicto anno XL° xiii s. iiii^or d.

## Londoniensis

Abbatissa Sancte Clare Londonie solvit xiiii die Martii anno XL° pro eodem anno vi d.

## Wyntoniensis

Abbas de Cherteseye solvit ultima die Januarii anno XL° pro eodem anno viii° s.

## Exoniensis

Prior de Bodmye solvit xiii die Decembris anno XL° pro eodem anno ii s.

## Sarisbiriensis

Abbas de Malmesbury solvit xx die Martii anno XL° pro eodem anno xiii s. iiii°ʳ d.

Summa totalis pagine ab alia summa citra l s. vi d.[29] Approbatum.

(fol. 114ᵛ) Adhuc recepta de dicto censu annuo de anno domini M° CCC° XL°

## Norwycensis

Abbas Sancti Edmundi solvit iiᵃ die Octobris anno XL° pro eodem anno xiii s. iiii°ʳ d.

## Lincolniensis

Abbas Sancti Albani solvit ii die Februarii anno XL° pro eodem anno xiii s. iiii d.

Prior de Cheucombe solvit penultima die Januarii anno XL° pro eodem anno xv d.

## Elyensis

Prior de Angleseye solvit xxv die Octobris anno XL° pro eodem anno ii s.

## Eboracensis

Custos ecclesie de Scardeburgh' solvit penultima die Januarii anno XL° pro eodem anno xv d.

## Karleolensis

Prior Karleolensis solvit xxiiiiᵃ die Januarii anno XLIIᵈᵒ pro dicto anno XL° xiii s. iiii d.

De Scotia et Ibernia sicut prius

Summa pagine usque hic xliiii°ʳ s. vi d. Approbatum.

Summa totalis receptorum de dicto anno XL° iiii°ʳ li. xv s. Approbatum.

Recepta de dicto censu annuo de anno domini M° CCC° quadragesimo primo

## Cantuariensis

Abbas de Farversham solvit die iiiiᵃ Madii anno domini M° CCC° XLI° pro eodem anno XLI° xiii s. iiii d.

## Roffensis

Prior de Tonebrigg' nichil.

## Londoniensis

Abbatissa Sancte Clare Londonie solvit xv die Februarii anno XLI° pro eodem anno vi d.

## Wyntoniensis

Abbas de Cherteseye solvit xxv die Novembris anno XLIIᵈᵒ pro dicto anno domini M° CCC° XLI° viii° s.

## Sarisberiensis

Abbas de Malmesbury solvit xxiᵃ die Decembris anno XLI° pro eodem anno xiii s. iiii°ʳ d.

## Exoniensis

Prior de Bodmye solvit xviiiᵃ die Novembris anno XLI° pro eodem anno ii s.

## Norwycensis

Abbas Sancti Edmundi solvit xvi die Martii anno XLI° pro eodem anno xiii s. iiii°ʳ d.

## Lincolniensis

Abbas Sancti Albani solvit prima die Februarii anno XLI° pro eodem anno xiii s. iiii d.

Prior de Cheucombe solvit xxixᵃ die Januarii anno XLI° pro eodem anno xv d.

## Elyensis

Prior de Angleseye solvit xiᵃ die Novembris anno XLI° pro eodem anno ii s.

## Eboracensis

Custos ecclesie de Scardeburgh' solvit xv die Octobris anno XLI° pro eodem anno xv d.

## Karleolensis

Prior Karleolensis solvit xxiiiiᵃ die Januarii anno XLII° pro dicto anno XLI° xiii s. iiii d.

De Scotia et Ibernia sicut prius

Summa totalis pagine ab alia summa citra iiii li. i s. viii d.[30] Approbatum.

(fol. 115) Recepta de dicto censu annuo pro anno domini M° CCC° XLIIᵈᵒ

## Cantuariensis

Abbas de Farversham solvit xix die Martii anno domini M° CCC° XLIIᵈᵒ pro eodem anno xiii s. iiii°ʳ d.

## Roffensis

Prior de Tonebrigg' nichil.

---

[29] The sum is inserted over the original deleted sum of the whole page, *vii li. v s. vi d.*

[30] The sum for the whole page, *vi li. vi s. ii d.* is deleted by a line.

### Londoniensis

Abbatissa Sancte Clare Londonie nichil.

### Wyntoniensis

Abbas de Cherteseye solvit xxv die Novembris anno XLII<sup>do</sup> pro eodem anno viii° s.

### Sarisbiriensis

Abbas de Malmesbury solvit xvii<sup>a</sup> die Novembris anno XLII<sup>do</sup> pro eodem anno xiii s. iiii<sup>or</sup> d.

### Exoniensis

Prior de Bodmye solvit xxx<sup>a</sup> die Novembris anno XLII<sup>do</sup> pro eodem anno ii s.

### Norwycensis

Abbas Sancti Edmundi solvit xxvii die Novembris anno XLII<sup>do</sup> pro eodem anno xiii s. iiii<sup>or</sup> d.

### Lincolniensis

Abbas Sancti Albani solvit iii<sup>a</sup> die Februarii anno XLII<sup>do</sup> eodem anno xiii s. iiii<sup>or</sup> d.

Prior de Cheucombe solvit xxx<sup>a</sup> die Novembris anno XLII<sup>do</sup> pro eodem anno xv d.

### Elyensis

Prior de Angleseye solvit v<sup>a</sup> die Novembris anno XLII<sup>do</sup> pro eodem anno ii s.

### Eboracensis

Custos ecclesie de Scardeburgh' solvit xxvii die Januarii anno XLII<sup>do</sup> pro eodem anno domini M° CCC° XLII<sup>do</sup> xv d.

### Karleolensis

Prior Karleolensis solvit xxiiii<sup>a</sup> die Januarii anno XLII<sup>do</sup> pro eodem ano xiii s. iiii<sup>or</sup> d.

De Scotia et Ibernia sicut prius

Summa totalis pagine iiii<sup>or</sup> li. i s. ii d. Approbatum.

Summa totalis receptorum de dicto censu annuo per dictum Bernardum de Sistre xl<sup>a</sup> li. iii s. ix d. Approbatum.

Summa totalis receptorum tam de denariis Beati Petri quam de censu annuo m<sup>l</sup> ix<sup>c</sup> lxx<sup>a</sup>ix li. iiii<sup>or</sup> s. v d. obolus sterlingorum.

(fol. 115<sup>v</sup>) Recepta per dictum Bernardum de Sistre de pertinentibus ad Terram Sanctam in partibus supradictis.

### Lincolniensis

Recepit idem Bernardus a Magistro Richardo de Oshyngore rectore ecclesie de Suthnewenton' (South Newington) Lincolniensis diocesis, pro exoneranda anima cuiusdam nobilis defuncte, que dicebatur legasse dicte Terre Sancte lx<sup>a</sup> m., cuius quidem defuncte dictus Magister Richardus servitor fuerat et subiectus xiii<sup>cim</sup> li. vi s. viii d.

Item a Domino Johanne de Sancto Paulo et a Johanne de Teydwell', executoribus testamenti Magistri Henrici de Cliston' solventibus pro legato facto in subsidium dicte terre per Magistrum Adam Oshalby c s.

### Eboracensis

Item a .. procuratore Willelmi de Rokeby Eboracensis, executoris testamenti Magistri Thome, quondam de Warford olim commissarii legatorum factorum dicte terre in diocesi Eboracensi qui tempore mortis sue nondum computaverat, de receptis per eum c s.

Item a Domino Willelmo de Adelvingham, presbytero Eboracensis diocesis, pro debitis per eum dicte terre iii s.

### Exoniensis

Item a Magistro Johanne de Northon', olim subcollectore legatorum in subsidium dicte terre in civitate et diocesi Exoniensi, pro receptis per eum de predictis x li.

### Herefordensis

Item a Magistro Rogero de Brethon', executore testamenti Domini Richardi de Swynefeld quondam episcopi Wygoriensis,[31] pro legato per dictum dominum episcopum dicte terre facte c s.

Item ab eodem Magistro Rogero ut executore testamenti Domini Nicholay de Reygathe, quondam thesaurarii ecclesie Herefordensis, pro legato per eundem thesaurarium dicte terre facto xl s.

Item ab eodem Magistro Rogero ut executore testamenti Domini Johannis Francisci, quondam vicarii ecclesie de Breyton' (Breinton), pro legato per dictum vicarium dicte terre facto xiii s. iiii d.

### Conventrensis et Lichefeldensis

Item a Magistro Willelmo de Corbrigg', olim commissario et subcollectore dictorum legatorum in civitate et diocesi Conventrensi et Lichefeldensi, pro receptis per eum de dictis legatis x li.

### Roffensis

Item a Domino Roberto de Stanesgrave, filio et executore testamenti Domini Roberti de Stanesgrave militis quondam Roffensis diocesis, pro legato per dictum quondam patrem suum facto in subsidium dicte terre vi li. xiii s. iiii d.

### Wyntoniensis

Item a Johanne del Luys de Suthwyk' Wyntoniensis diocesis quia commisserat penam x s. in quodam contractu appositam x s.

Item a quadam paupere muliere pro promissione per ipsam dicte terre facta iiii<sup>or</sup> d.

---

[31] An error for *Herefordensis*.

## Bathoniensis et Wellensis

Item ab Henrico de Lanye, executore testamenti Willelmi Hamon Bathoniensis et Wellensis diocesis, pro legato per dictum Willelmum dicte terre facto xx s.

Summa totalis pagine lix li. vi s. viii° d. Approbatum.

(fol. 116) Adhuc de receptis legatorum et pertinentium ad Terram Sanctam

Item a quodam homine pro voto facto per eum dicte terre recepit dictus Bernardus per manus . . confessoris sui xii d.

## Cicestrensis, Sarisbiriensis, Wyntoniensis

Item a Magistro Hugone Pranii, olim per Dominum Itherium de Concoreto predecessorem dicti Bernardi commissario deputato super predictis legatis in civitatibus et diocesibus Cicestrensi, Sarisbiriensi et Wyntoniensi, duos anulos argenti deauratos.

Summa totalis omnium receptorum de pertinentibus ad dictam terram per dictum Bernardum lix li. vii s. viii° d. li anuli.

Et est sciendum quod idem Bernardus non recepit plus de predictis ad dictam Terram Sanctam pertinentibus quia sanctissimus in Christo pater felicis recordationis Dominus Benedictus papa predictus, tempore quo idem Bernardus ultimo fuit in Romana curia, dixit sibi quod quia negotium passagii ultramarini sic differebatur ipse nolebat quod aliquid dictus Bernardus amplius peteret de premissis.

Recepta per dictum Bernardum pro redemptione et dispensionibus votorum

## Eboracensis

Recepit primo ab Alicia uxore Richardi de Thorp' Eboracensis diocesis sene et antiqua pro redemptione voti quod emiserat ad Sanctum Jacobum de Gallicia quod propter antiquitatem complere non poterat viii° li.

Item a Domino Radulpho de Brok' pro redemptione voti quod emiserat ad Sanctum Jacobum predictum quod propter guerram complere non poterat xx⁽ᵗⁱ⁾ li.

Item a Domino Bartholomeo de Broaysch' milite pro redemptione dicti voti quod ad Sanctum Jacobum predictum emiserat et quod propter guerram complere non poterat xxx⁽ᵃ⁾iii li. vi s. viii° d.

Summa totalis redemptionum pro dictis dispensationibus lx⁽ᵃ⁾i li. vi s. viii° d. Approbatum.

Summa totalis receptorum de denariis Beati Petri, de censu annuo, de pertinentibus ad Terram Sanctam et de dispensationibus votorum m¹ m¹ lxxxx⁽ᵃ⁾ix li. xviii° s. ix d. obolus ii° anuli.

(fol. 116ᵛ) Recepta per dominum Bernardum de fructibus quorumdam beneficiorum apud sedem apostolicam vacantium.

Et primo de fructibus illorum beneficiorum que vacaverunt tempore creationis felicis recordationis Domini Johannis pape XXII⁽ᵈⁱ⁾

## Wellensis

De fructibus prebende de Estharpetr' (East Harptree) in ecclesie Wellensi que vacavit apud sedem predictam per consecrationem Domini Ludovici quondam Dunelmensis episcopi, qui fuit electus tempore Domini Clementis pape V et consecratus tempore dicti Domini Johannis pape XXII⁽ᵈⁱ⁾, que quidem prebenda per dictum Dominum Johannem collata fuit Magistro Henrico de Harodon', licet eius possessionem habere nequiverit, recepit dictus Bernardus in universo xxxiii li. vi s. viii d.

Recepta de fructibus quorumdam beneficiorum que apud dictam sedem annis xviii° et xix° pontificatus dicti Domini Johannis pape XXII⁽ᵈⁱ⁾ vacaverunt

## Lincolniensis

De fructibus prebende de Langestowe (Stow Longa) in ecclesia Lincolniensi olim dicto xviii° anno vacantis per consecrationem Domini Symonis Wygorniensis episcopi recepit dictus Bernardus xlii li.

De fructibus prebende Sancti Botulphi (Lincoln) in eadem ecclesia olim vacantis per renunciationem Domini Richardi nunc Dunelmensis episcopi liii s. iiii⁽ᵒʳ⁾ d.

## Sarisbiriensis

De fructibus prebende de Remesbury (Ramsbury) in ecclesia Sarisbiriensi olim vacantis per consecrationem dicti Domini Symonis Wygorniensis episcopi xxx⁽ᵃ⁾iii li. vi s. viii d.

De fructibus prebende de Beminstre (Beminster) Sarisbiriensis ecclesie in layco feodo vacantis olim per consecrationem dicti Domini Richardi Dunelmensis episcopi x li. xviii° s. viii° d.

## Herefordensis

De fructibus parochialis ecclesie de Aka (Rock) Herefordensis diocesis vacantis olim per renunciationem Ade de Alynton' xiii li. vi s. viii° d.

## Eboracensis

De fructibus prebende de Dunham in ecclesia Beate Marie Suthwell' (Southwell) Eboracensis diocesis olim vacantis per obitum Magistri Thome de Sancto Albano cuius beneficia per dictum Dominum Johannem XXII⁽ᵈᵘᵐ⁾ collationi dicte sedis fuerunt specialiter reservata xxx⁽ᵃ⁾vi li. iii s. iiii⁽ᵒʳ⁾ d.

De fructibus prebende de Apethorp' (Apesthorpe) in ecclesia Eboracensi olim vacantis per obitum Magistri Roberti de Tanton' cuius beneficia per dictum Dominum Johannem collationi dicte sedis fuerunt etiam specialiter reservata, que per regem, vacante sede Eboracensi, fuit jure regalie collata Magistro Galfrido le Scrop' xiii⁽ᶜⁱᵐ⁾ li. vi s. viii d.

Summa totalis pagine clxxx⁽ᵃ⁾v li. ii s. Approbatum.

(fol. 117) Adhuc recepta de fructibus dictorum bene-ficiorum apud dictam sedem apostolicam vacantium xviii° et xix° annis pontificatus dicti Domini Johannis pape XXII^di

### Elyensis

De fructibus ecclesie de Hadenham (Haddenham) Elyensis diocesis olim vacantis per obitum dicti Magistri Roberti de Tanton' lxxx^a li. sterlingorum.

### Londoniensis

De fructibus prebende de Wallokesbern' (Wenlock's Barn, St. Giles) in ecclesia Londoniensi, olim vacantis per consecrationem dicti Domini Richardi episcopi Dunelmensis, perceptis usque ad diem qua vacante sede Londoniensi per . . regem jure regalie collata fuit Magistro Willelmo de Cusancia xvi li. xiii s. iiii^or d.

### Cicestrensis

De fructibus prebende de Hurst' in ecclesia Cices-trensi olim vacantis per consecrationem dicti Domini Richardi Dunelmensis episcopi perceptis usque ad diem qua per dictam sedem apostolicam fuit collata Domino Manueli de Spinol' xvi li. xiii s. iiii^or d.

### Wellensis

De fructibus decanatus Wellensis olim vacantis per consecrationem dicti Domini Richardi Dunelmensi epis-copi lxvi li. xiii s. iiii^or d.

### Dunelmensis

Pro fructibus ecclesie de Egglisclif' (Egglescliffe) Dunelmensis diocesis, olim vacantis quia Magister Symon Sapiti rector eiusdem fuit assecutus archipres-biteratum Collenden' (Colle di Val d'Elsa) Wlterane (Volterra) diocesis per sedem apostolicam sibi collatum, recepit idem Bernardus tam de fructibus eiusdem ecclesie quam de fructibus ecclesie de Dale (Deal) Cantuariensis diocesis pertinentibus Ulertino de Zannetis, qui, ante collationem sibi de dicta ecclesia de Egglisclif' per Dominum Benedictum papam XII factam, ipsam eccle-siam de facto per aliquod tempus occupaverat, lv li. xvi s. viii d.

### Conventrensis et Lichefeldensis

De fructibus prebende quam Magister Thomas de Bek' obtinuit in ecclesia Omnium Sanctorum Derleye (Darley) Conventrensis et Lichefeldensis diocesis que tempore dicti Domini Johannis pape [32] vacaverat iiii^or li.

Summa pagine ii^c xxx^aix li. xvi s. viii° d. Approbatum.

Summa totalis precedentis et presentis paginarum iiii^c xxiiii^or li. xviii° s. viii° d.[33]

Summa totalis omnium suprascriptorum et per dictum

Bernardum receptorum m^l m^l v^c xx^ti iiii^or li. xvii s. v d. obolus, ii° anuli et cl floreni.

(fol. 117^v) Recepta per dictum Bernardum de fruct-ibus beneficiorum apud dictam sedem vacantium tem-pore felicis recordationis Domini Benedicti pape XII predicti qui huiusmodi fructus pro toto tempore vaca-tionis predicte pro sua camera reservavit

Et primo de fructibus beneficiorum que fuerunt bone memorie Domini Petri de Mortuo Mari tituli Sancti Stephani in Celio Monte presbyteri cardinalis

### Eboracensis

De fructibus thesaurarie Eboracensis ecclesie et pre-bende eidem annexe recepit idem Bernardus primo de mandato domini . . camerarii dicti domini pape de hiis que dicto domino cardinali dum viveret debebantur per manus sociorum societatis Bardorum de Florentia penes eos depositis lvi li. xiii s. iiii^or d.

Item per manus Nicholay Cisteronis xx li.

Item per manus Johannis de Underwolde et Willelmi Songel vii li.

Summa predictorum lxxx^aiii li. xiii s. iiii^or d. que ad dictum dominum cardinalem pertinere dicuntur. Appro-batum.

Item recepit de fructibus dictarum thesaurarie et prebende a die obitus dicti domini cardinalis usque ad diem qua fuerunt collate Domino Francisco de Filiis Ursi de Urbe perceptis l^ai li. xv s. ix d.

Item de fructibus prebende de Rikale (Riccall) quam in dicta ecclesia dictus dominus cardinalis obtinuit, videlicet de anno domini M° CCC° XXXV lx^ai li. vi s. viii° d.

Item de fructibus eiusdem prebende de alio anno sequenti usque ad diem qua per dictum dominum papam collata fuit cuidam physico domine . . regine Anglie perceptis liiii^or li. viii° s. ix d.

### Lincolniensis

De fructibus prebende de Thame quam dictus dominus cardinalis obtinuit in ecclesia Lincolniensi perceptis de tempore vacationis eiusdem usque ad diem qua per dictum dominum papam collata fuit Domino Talayrando tituli Sancti Petri ad Vincula presbytero cardinali x li. ii s.

Summa totalis prescriptorum in pagina ab alia summa citra clxxvii li. xiii s. ii d.[34] Approbatum

(fol. 118) Recepta de fructibus beneficiorum que fuerunt Domini Arnaudi bone memorie Sancti Eus-tachii diaconi cardinalis

### Sarisbiriensis

De fructibus thesaurarie ecclesie Sarisbiriensis et prebende de Calne eidem annexe perceptis a die obitus

---

[32] *papa*, MS.
[33] The *approbatum* in the margin applies to this item as well as to the preceding item.

[34] The sum is inserted over the sum of *ii° lxi li. vi s. vi d.* for the whole page which is deleted by a line.

dicti domini cardinalis usque ad diem qua per dictum dominum Benedictum papam collata fuit Magistro Radulpho de Stratford xvii li. xviii s. x d. iii quadrantes.

### Eboracensis

Item de fructibus prebende de Thorp' (Thorpe) in ecclesia collegiata de Houden' (Howden) Eboracensis diocesis perceptis a die obitus dicti domini cardinalis usque ad festum Sancti Petri ad Vincula [35] anno domini M° CCC° XXXVI° lxvi s. x d.

Item pro perceptis a dicto festo usque ad idem festum Sancti Petri ad Vincula anno domini M° CCC° XXXVII° anno revoluto xxxᵃ li. xiii s. iiiiᵒʳ d.

Item pro perceptis a dicto festo Sancti Petri usque ad idem festum anno domini M° CCC° XXXVIII° anno revoluto xxx li. xiii s. iiiiᵒʳ d.

Item pro perceptis a dicto festo Sancti Petri usque ad idem festum anno domini M° CCC° XXXIX° anno revoluto xxix li. vi s. viii° d.

Item pro perceptis a dicto festo Sancti Petri usque ad idem festum anno domini M° CCC° XL° anno etiam revoluto xxix li. vi s. viii° d.

Item pro parte fructum dicte prebende perceptorum a dicto festo Sancti Petri ad Vincula usque ad idem festum anno domini M° CCC° XLI° anno revoluto xvii li. vi s. viii° d.

Item pro fructibus eiusdem prebende perceptis a dicto festo Sancti Petri anno domini M° CCC° XLI° usque ad idem festum anno revoluto quo tempore quidam intrusus occupavit prebendam predictam xxix li. vi s. viii° d.

Summa totalis receptorum de dicta prebenda clxx li. ii d.[36]

Recepta de fructibus beneficiorum que fuerunt bone memorie Domini Johannis Gaietani,

### Dunelmensis

De fructibus ecclesie de Wermuth' (Bishop Wearmouth) Dunelmensis diocesis que fuit dicti domini cardinalis perceptis a die obitus eiusdem usque ad diem quando per dictum Dominum Benedictum papam collata fuit Magistro Johanni de Eston' xxxᵃviii° li.

### Eboracensis

De fructibus prebende de Lagthon' in Mortyng' (Laughton en le Morthen) quam dictus dominus cardinalis obtinuit in ecclesia Eboracensi perceptis a die obitus eiusdem usque ad diem qua collata fuit per dictum dominum papam Magistro Willelmo la Zouche lxxᵃiii li. vi s. viii° d.

Summa totalis pagine iiᶜ lxxxxᵃix li. iiii s. viii° d. iii quadrantes. Approbatum.

[35] 1 August.
[36] Substituted for *clxix li. xix s. ii d.* which is deleted by a line.

(fol. 118ᵛ) Adhuc recepta de fructibus beneficiorum que quondam fuerunt dicti domini Johannis Gaietani cardinalis

### Conventrensis

De fructibus et emolumentis archidiaconatus Conventrensis quem dictus dominus cardinalis obtinuit perceptis a die obitus eiusdem usque ad diem sextam mensis Septembris anno domini M° CCC° XXXVI° recepit idem Bernardus xxᵗⁱ iiiiᵒʳ li.

Item pro fructibus et emolumentis eiusdem archidiaconatus perceptis a dicta die vi Septembris anno XXXVI° usque ad xxᵃᵐ diem Octobris vel circa anno domini M° CCC° XXXVII° xxi li. vi s. viii° d.

Item pro eisdem fructibus et emolumentis perceptis a xxix die Octobris anno XXXVII° predicto usque ad mensem Martii proximam sequentem viii° li.

Item pro eisdem fructibus et emolumentis perceptis a dicta mense Martii usque ad xviᵃᵐ diem Madii anno domini M° CCC° XXX IX° xxiii li. vi s. viii° d.

Item pro eisdem fructibus et emolumentis perceptis a dicta xviᵃ die Madii anno XXXIX° usque ad annum integrum xxᵗⁱ li.

Summa totalis lxxxxᵃvi li. xiii s. iiiiᵒʳ d.

Postea vero quidem magnus ex presentatione regis et admissione . . episcopi occuppavit et adhuc occupat dictum archidiaconatum.

Recepta de fructibus beneficiorum que fuerunt bone memorie Domini Luche de Flisco Beate Marie in Via Lata diaconi cardinalis

### Norwycensis

De fructibus ecclesie de Tyrington' (Terrington) Norwycensis diocesis, cuius presentatio spectat ad episcopum Elyensem, que fuit dicti domini cardinalis, perceptis a die obitus eiusdem usque ad mensem Januarii anno domini M° CCC° XXXVI° quo tempore dominus rex, vacante sede Elyensi, presentavit ad eamdem ecclesiam unum de clericis suis c li.

### Lichefeldensis

De fructibus prebende de Langedon' (Longdon) in ecclesia Lichefeldensi que fuit dicti domini cardinalis perceptis a die obitus eiusdem usque ad diem qua per unum de domo regis ex collatione . . episcopi Lichefeldensis contra sequestrum ibi appositum fuit et adhuc est occupata xxᵗⁱ i li.

Summa totalis pagine iiᶜ xvii li. xiiiᵗⁱᵐ s. iiiiᵒʳ d. Approbatum.

(fol. 119) Recepta de fructibus quorumdam aliorum beneficiorum que tempore dicti Domini Benedicti pape ex diversis causis apud dictam sedem vacaverunt

### Lincolniensis

De fructibus decanatus ecclesie Lincolniensis et prebende de Kelleseye (North Kelsey) in eadem, qui per consecrationem Domini Antonii Norwycensis episcopi, qui fuit in Romana curia in die annunciationis Beate Marie [37] anno incarnationis domini M° CCC° XXXVII° intrante consecratus, vacaverunt usque ad iiiiᵃᵐ diem mensis Augusti anno domini M° CCC° XL° qua die decanatus predictus per dictum dominum papam collatus fuit Magistro Willelmo de Norwyco et usque ad mensem Decembris anno XL° predicto, quando, vacante sede Lincolniensi, dicta prebenda fuit collata per regem uni de clericis suis, recepit dictus Bernardus primo de primo anno vacationis eorundem qui fuit annus domini millesimus CCCᵘˢ XXXVIIᵘˢ iiiᶜ lix li. xvi s. x d. obolum.

Item de secundo anno vacationis eorundem, videlicet de anno domini M° CCC° XXXVIII°, iiiᶜ xxxᵃiii li. iii s. xi d.

Item de tercio anno vacationis eorundem qui fuit annus domini Mᵘˢ CCCᵘˢ XXXIXᵘˢ iiiᶜ xiiiiᶜⁱᵐ li.

Allocatus Magistro Willelmo Bachalerii, canonico Lincolniensi, qui per totum tempus vacationis huiusmodi habuit custodiam ipsorum xx li. pro suis laboribus et expensis et xvi li. pauperibus tenentibus dicti decanatus non valentibus solvere propter guerram.

Item de hiis que provenerunt quarto anno vacationis huiusmodi decanatus a festo annunciationis Dominice [37] anno XL° secundum custumam Anglicane ecclesie intrante usque ad tunc proximam sequentem quartam diem Augusti qua, ut predicitur, collatus fuit dicto Magistro Willelmo de Norwyco x li.

Item pro fructibus dicte prebende de quarto anno vacationis eiusdem, videlicet de anno domini M° CCC° XL°, xxxᵃ li.

De fructibus sex annorum et certe partis alterius anni cancellarie Lincolniensis ecclesie, olim vacantis pro eo quod Magister Richardus Radulphi, olim cancellarius Lincolniensis, fuit adeptus ex gratia sedie predicte decanatum Lichefeldensem, recepit tam a capitulo Lincolniensi quam a Magistro Willelmo Bachalerii, canonico Lincolniensi, xxvii li. xiiii s. viii° d.

Item de pensione trium annorum finitorum in festo Beati Micahelis anno domini M° CCC° XL° domorum dicte cancellarie vi li. xvii s. iiiiᵒʳ d.

Item pro pensione anni proximi sequentis finiti in festo Sancti Micahelis anno domini M° CCC° XLI° lvi s. viii° d.

Summa xxxᵃvii li. viii° s. viii° d.

De fructibus prebende Lafford (Sleaford) in dicta ecclesia Lincolniensi, que vacavit per consecrationem Domini Antonii Lunensis (Luna or Luni) episcopi, recepit primo de anno domini M° CCC° XXXIX° xxᵗⁱi li. x s. ii d. iii quadrantes

Item pro fructibus secundi anni vacationis eiusdem qui fuit annus domini Mᵘˢ CCCᵘˢ XL, circa cuius finem vacante sede Lincolniensi, fuit collata per regem Magistro eius (?) de Cusancia, clerico suo, xxxᵃii li. xiii s. iiiiᵒʳ d.

Summa liiiiᵒʳ li. iii s. vi d. iii quadrantes.

Summa totalis pagine mˡ cxxxᵃviii° li. xiiiᶜⁱᵐ s. i quadrans. Approbatum.

(fol. 119ᵛ) Recepta adhuc de fructibus beneficiorum apud sedem apostolicam vacantium tempore Domini Benedicti pape XII

### Lincolniensis

De fructibus ecclesie de Uffynton' (Uffington) Lincolniensis diocesis, que vacavit per resignationem Magistri Nicholay de Ros factam in manibus domini . . vicecancellarii, recepit primo dictus Bernardus de bonis reppertis in bercaria eiusdem ecclesie tam in animalibus quam in lanis et bladis que de longo tempore debebantur xv li.

Item pro fructibus eiusdem ecclesie de anno domini M° CCC° XLI° xxvi li. xiii s. iiiiᵒʳ d.

Summa totalis xlᵃi li. xiii s. iiiiᵒʳ d.

De fructibus ecclesie de Iakesle (Yaxley) dicte diocesis, que vacavit quia Magister Willelmus de la Souche olim rector eiusdem fuit assecutus ex gratia dicte sedis prebendam de Laghton' in Morthyng' (Laughton en le Morthen) in ecclesia Eboracensi, perceptis a die vacationis eiusdem usque ad diem qua collata fuit per dictum dominum papam Magistro Radulpho de Turville xxxᵃiii li. vi s. viii d.

### Conventrensis et Lichefeldensis

De fructibus prebende de Ichynton Episcopi (Long Itchington) in ecclesia Lichefeldensi, que vacavit per resignationem Domini Petri de Columpna, perceptis de anno domini M° CCC° XXXIX° lᵃ li.

Nec plus haberi potuit quia extunc unus de clericis regis ex presentatione sua ipsam occupavit.

Item de fructibus vicarie dicte prebende, que medio tempore vacavit interim, perceptis lᵃ s.

### Cantuariensis

De fructibus ecclesie de Bichopesbourn' (Bishopsbourne) Cantuariensis diocesis, que vacavit per obitum Magistri Johannis Litterel qui obiit in curia, pro tempore vacationis ipsius perceptis usque ad diem qua fuit collata per dictum dominum papam Magistro Willelmo de Skelton' x li.

De fructibus ecclesie de Ludenham (Luddenham), olim vacantis per obitum Magistri Johannis Pilrud' qui in Romana curia diem clausit extremum ix li. vi s. viii° d.

### Norwicensis

De fructibus parochialis ecclesie de Palgrave Norwycensis diocesis, que vacavit per obitum Magistri Johannis de Ulseby qui in dicta curia obiit, perceptis a festo purificationis Beate Marie [38] anno domini M° CCC° XXXVIII° usque ad xiᵃᵐ diem mensis Junii anno XL°,

[37] 25 March.

[38] 2 February.

terris dominicalibus pro anno sequenti remanentibus seminatis, xi li. xvii s. vi d.

Item pro perceptis inde a dicta xi[a] die Junii anno XL° usque ad eandem diem anno revoluto xv li. vi s. viii° d.

Summa xxvii li. iiii[or] s. ii d.

De fructibus ecclesie de Hwepsted (Whepstead) dicte diocesis, que vacavit quia Magister Johannes de Wytcherche olim rector eiusdem fuit adeptus ex gratia dicte sedis archidiaconatum Wyltsshir' in ecclesia Sarisbiriensi, perceptis a prima die vacationis huiusmodi usque ad xxi[am] diem mensis Julii anno domini M° CCC° XLI° xx[ti] li.

Item pro eisdem fructibus perceptis a dicta xxi[a] die Julii usque ad xi[am] diem mensis Junii anno domini M° CCC° XLII[do] xv li. v s. xi d. obolus.

Summa totalis xxx[a]v li. v s. xi d. obolus.

Summa totalis pagine ii[c] ix li. vi s. ix d. obolus. Approbatum.

(fol. 120) Adhuc recepta de fructibus dictorum beneficiorum apud sedem apostolicam vacantium tempore dicti Domini Benedicti pape XII

### Adhuc Norwycensis

De fructibus ecclesie de Stalham dicte Norwycensis diocesis, que vacavit pro eo quod Magister Thomas Fastolf' olim rector eiusdem fuit adeptus ex gratia dicte sedis archidiaconatum Norwycensem, recepit pro primo anno vacationis eiusdem, videlicet pro anno domini M° CCC° XLI°, xxvi li. xiii[cim] s. iiii[or] d.

### Sarisbiriensis

De fructibus ecclesie de Doneheved Marie (Donhead St. Mary) Sarisbiriensis diocesis, que vacavit per obitum Magistri Laurentii Berne qui obiit in Romana curia, perceptis a die vacationis eiusdem usque ad diem qua per dictum Dominum Benedictum papam collata fuit cuidam clerico domini Gaucelmi Episcopi Albanensis xiii[cim] li. vi s. viii d.

De fructibus prebende de Hulle Deverel (Hill Deverill) in ecclesia Sancti Petri de Hertredbury (Heytesbury) Sarisbiriensis diocesis, que vacavit per obitum Domini Johannis de Pinibus quondam familiaris et capellani Domini R. Sancte Marie Nove diaconi cardinalis qui etiam obiit in Romana curia, recepit de anno domini M° CCC° XL° qui fuit primus annus vacationis ipsius et in partem xiiii[cim] li. xiii s. iiii[or] d. pro ipsis debitorum vi li. x s.

Item in partem xiii li. vi s. viii° d. debitorum pro fructibus eiusdem de anno domini M° CCC° XLI° ix li. vi s. viii° d.

De fructibus prebende de Bichopeston' (Bishopstone) in ecclesia Sarisbiriensi, que vacavit per obitum Magistri Richardi de Haveryngg' dicte sedis capellani, perceptis de primo anno vacationis eiusdem qui fuit annus domini M[us] CCC[us] XLI[us] xx[ti] li.

### Conventrensis et Lichefeldensis

De fructibus archidiaconatus Cestrie in ecclesia Lichefeldensi et prebende de Boulton' (Bolton) sibi annexe, qui vacaverunt per obitum dicti Magistri Richardi de Haveryngg', perceptis de primo anno vacationis eorundem, videlicet de anno domini M° CCC° XLI°, cxxx[a]iii li. vi s. viii° d.

### Herefordensis

De fructibus precentorie Herefordensis ecclesie, que vacavit per obitum dicti Magistri Richardi de Haveryngg', perceptis de primo anno vacationis eiusdem, videlicet de predicto anno domini M° CCC° XLI°, xx[ti]vi li. xiii s. iiii[or] d.

Summa totalis pagine cc[tum] xxx[a]v li. xvi s. viii° d. Approbatum.

Summa totalis receptorum de fructibus beneficiorum tam tempore Domini Johannis pape XXII[di] quam Domini Benedicti pape XII apud sedem apostolicam vacantium m[l] m[l] vii[c] lxxx[a]vi li. xviii° s. viii° d. obolus.

(fol. 120[v]) Recepta per dictum Bernardum de fructibus primi anni quorundam beneficiorum apud dictam sedem vacantium tempore sanctissimi patris Domini Clementis pape VI[ti] per eundem pro sua camera reservatis

Et primo de fructibus beneficiorum que fuerunt dicti Magistri Richardi de Haveryng' que adhuc tempore creationis eiusdem Domini Clementis pape VI vacabant

### Sarisbiriensis

De fructibus prebende de Bichopeston' (Bishopstone) in ecclesia Sarisbiriensi, que vacavit ex causa suprascripta, et in partem eorum recepit dictus Bernardus de Sistre x li.

### Lichefeldensis

De fructibus archidiaconatus Cestrie et prebende de Boulton' (Bolton) sibi annexe in ecclesia Lichefeldensi qui vacaverunt ex causa prescripta et in partem eorum recepit lxxxx[a]iii li. vi s. viii° d.

### Herefordensis

De fructibus percentorie Herefordensis ecclesie que vacavit ex causa predicta et in partem eorum recepit vi li. xiii s. iiii d.

### Norwycensis

De fructibus ecclesie de Hwepstede (Whepstead) Norwycensis diocesis, que etiam vacabat adhuc tempore creationis dicti Domini Clementis pape VI[ti] ex causa suprascripta, recepit in partem ipsorum vii li. vi s. viii° d.

### Eboracensis

De fructibus ecclesie de Brampton' Eboracensis diocesis, que vacavit per consecrationem Domini Thome Lincolniensis episcopi, recepit in partem ipsorum xx[ti]iiii li. vi s. viii° d.

Summa totalis prescriptorum in pagina cxl$^a$ li. xiii$^{cim}$ s. iiii$^{or}$ d. Approbatum.

Summa totalis receptorum per dictum Bernardum de Sistre de fructibus beneficiorum apud sedem apostolicam vacantium temporibus dominorum Johannis XXII$^{di}$, Benedicti XII et successive Clementis VI$^{ti}$ summorum pontificum m$^l$ m$^l$ ix$^c$ xx$^{ti}$vii li. xii s. obolus sterlingorum.

Et additis m$^l$ m$^l$ lxxxx$^a$ix li. xviii$^o$ s. ix d. obolo cum ii anulis supra receptis tam pro denariis Beati Petri quam pro censu annuo et legatis in subsidium Terre Sancte ac pro dispensationibus super votis, est summa totalis omnium supra receptorum v$^{ml}$ xx$^{ti}$vii li. x s. x d. ii$^o$ anuli ultra cl florenos prescriptos.

(fol. 121) Recepta per dictum Bernardum de quibusdam antiquis decimis in Ibernia impositis

### De Ibernia

Facta compositione cum domino . . archiepiscopo Cassellensi pro se et pro clero suarum diocesis et provincie super arreyratgiis diversarum decimarum olim per nonnullos summos pontifices in Ibernia impositarum, attentis prolixitate temporis et beneficiorum propter guerram continuam exilitate et quasi totali destructione, recepit ab ipso cxx$^{ti}$ li.

Item facto compoto cum Magistro G. Lescapon, canonico Dublinensi olim subcollectore arreyratgiorum decimarum sexennalium et triennalium per felicis recordationis Dominum Bonefatium papam VIII in Hibernia impositarum, recepit ab ipso in partem solutionis liiii$^{or}$ li. iii s. ix d. i quad. que debebat xxx$^a$ii li. Approbatum.[39]

Recepta de pecuniis penes mercatores depositis

### De Anglia

Anno domini M$^o$ CCC$^o$ XXXVI$^o$ et die xxv Martii recepit idem Bernardus de Sistre ab Henrico Acurcii et Richardo Terii, sociis de societate Peruciorum de Florentia, pro diversis pecuniis per ipsos receptis tam de arreyratgiis quadriennalis decime per felicis recordationis Dominum Johannem papam XXII$^{dum}$ imposite quam fructuum primi anni beneficiorum vacantium per dictum dominum papam ad quadriennium reservatorum quam etiam de denariis Beati Petri et census annui Romane ecclesie debiti ac de legatis in subsidium Terre Sancte vi$^c$ xxv li. iii s. iiii$^{or}$ d. Approbatum.

Et quia dicti socii dictas pecunias receperant per manus Magistri Itherii de Concoreto predecessoris dicti Bernardi in officio predicto vel. . . commissariorum suorum, et in illis que fuerant de arreyratgiis decime et fructuum predictorum dominus rex Anglie ex concessione apostolica debebat habere medietatem, fuit primo inter ipsum Bernardum ex una parte et Dominum Henricum tunc Lincolniensem episcopum et dicti domini regis thesau-

rarium ex altera ordinatum et conventum quod idem Bernardus dictam summam a dictis sociis Peruciorum integre reciperet pro camera domini nostri pape et dictus thesaurarius pro dicto domino rege reciperet tantam summam vel maiorem quam debebant . . socii Bardorum de Florentia de pecuniis dictorum fructuum et decime per dictum Magistrum Itherium vel . . commissarios suos penes ipsos depositis.

Summa totalis pagine vii$^c$ lxxvii li. iii s. iiii$^{or}$ d.

(fol. 121$^v$) Recepta per dictum Bernardum de fructibus beneficiorum que fuerunt dicti Domini Itherii de Concoreto et de aliis ad eum spectantibus ex causis infrascriptis

Quia idem Dominus Itherius de archidiaconatu Cantuariensi exoneravit . . archidiaconum qui tunc erat de xliiii$^{or}$ m., item quia recepit de prebenda de Preston' in ecclesia Sarisbiriensi xxv m., item de ecclesia de Blokesleye (Blockley) Wygorniensis diocesis lv m., item de precentoria ecclesie Lincolniensis xx$^{ti}$ m., de quibus in suis compotis nullam fecerat mentionem, recepit dictus Bernardus inter diversas solutiones de fructibus dictorum beneficiorum suorum lxxx$^a$ix li. xv s. xi d. Approbatum.

Item recepit de fructibus ecclesie de Adburbury (Adderbury) Lincolniensis diocesis debitis pro tempore quo dictus Dominus Itherius qui rector ipsius fuerat privatus ea censebatur ipso iure cum infra annum non se fecisset ad sacros ordines promoveri lxxx$^a$i li. xiii s. iiii$^{or}$ d., quas quidem lxxx$^a$i li. et xiii s. iiii$^{or}$ d. predictus Dominus Bernardus de mandato camere dicti domini pape servare et custodire debuit quousque fuisset cognitum ad quem pertinebant. Approbatum.

Item recepit dictus Bernardus de arreyratgiis procurationum dicto Domino Itherio pro tempore more sue debitarum in diocesi et provincia Eboracensi xx$^{ti}$ii li. iii s. ii d. Approbatum.

Summa totalis prescriptorum in pagina clxxxx$^a$iii li. xii s. v d.

Summa totalis omnium et singulorum supra per dictum Bernardum de Sistre receptorum v$^{ml}$ ix$^c$ lxxxx$^a$ viii$^o$ li. vi s. vii d. ii$^o$ anuli et cl floreni.

(fol. 122) Recepta per dictum Bernardum de arreyratgiis fructuum primi anni quorundam beneficiorum ad quadriennium olim per felicis recordationis dictum Dominum Johannem papam XXII$^{dum}$ reservatorum et domino . . regi Anglie pro medietate concessorum.[39a]

De primo anno reservationis

### Londoniensis

De ecclesia de Warlee (Warley) recepit dictus Bernardus de Sistre iiii$^{or}$ li. xiii s. iiii$^{or}$ d.

De ecclesia de Hormede parva (Little Hormead) xx$^{ti}$ s.

---

[39] The *approbatum*, which is in the margin, probably applies to the preceding item as well as to this one.

[39a] On this levy of annates, see Lunt, *Financial Relations . . . 1327-1534*, pp. 309-319.

Sarisbiriensis

De prebenda de Bonemestore (Beminster) in eccesia Sarisbiriensi x m.

De vicaria de Chessebury (Chisbury) iii m. et dimidiam.

Lincolniensis

De vicaria de Asschewell' (Ashwell) xv m.
De ecclesia de Ryskyngton' (Ruskington) x m.
De ecclesia de Magnacotes (Great Coates) xv m.

Conventrensis et Lichefeldensis

De ecclesia de Moterum (Mottram), dimissa in arreyratgiis pro c s., de ecclesia de Hormesworth' (Handsworth), dimissa in arreyratgiis pro vii li, debet Dominus Itherius de Concoreto predictus respondere, qui dictas summas recepit, prout patet de prima per restam et de secunda per litteras suas.[40]

Wygorniensis

De beneficiis que in civitate et diocesi Wygorniensi toto dicto quadriennio vacaverunt inferius respondebitur.

Eboracensis

De vicaria de Naufreton' (Nafferton), dimissa in arreyratgiis pro x m., de archidiaconatu Notynghamie, dimisso in arreyratgiis pro lxxª s.; de ecclesia de Heton' (Heaton), dimissa in arreyratgiis pro xvii m. cum dimidia, de vicaria de Gikesleswyk (Giggleswick), dimissa in arreyratgiis pro v m., de prebenda de Sharnowe (Sharow) in ecclesia Ripponensi, dimissa in arreyratgiis pro l s., abbas monasterii Beate Marie Eboracensis subcollector dicti Domini Itherii in suo compoto computavit.

Herefordensis

De beneficiis que in civitate et diocesi Herefordensi dicto quadriennio vacaverunt inferius respondebitur.

Dunelmensis

De prebenda de Rivers in ecclesia de Aukeland (Auckland) nichil.[41]

Karleolensis

De ecclesia de Duston' (Dufton), dimissa in arreyratgiis pro xlª s., dictus abbas Eboracensis in suo compoto computavit.

Menevensis, Landavensis, Assavensis, Bangorensis

De beneficiis que in Menevensi, Landavensi, Assavensi et Bangorensi civitatibus et docesibus toto dicto quadriennio vacaverunt inferius respondebitur.

Summa totalis receptorum in presenti pagina lxªii m. Approbatum.

(fol. 122ᵛ) Recepta de secundo anno reservationis dictorum fructuum

Londoniensis

De ecclesia de Southam alias de Dedham nichil quia lis procedit inter quemdam priorem qui eam possidet et illum qui composuit de fructibus primi anni dicte ecclesie.

Cicestrensis

De portione tertie partis ecclesie de Wretlyng' (Wartling), de qua dictus dominus rex pro parte sua remisit xii m. et dimidiam . . portionario eiusdem, recepit pro parte dicte camere xiiᶜⁱᵐ m. et dimidiam.
De ecclesia de Astyng' (Hastings) c s.
De ecclesia de Balecombe (Balcombe) i m.
De vicaria de Ferlee (Firle) xii m.[42]

Sarisbiriensis

De prebenda australi de Graham (Grantham) in ecclesia Sarisbiriensi, dimissa in arreyratgiis in xv m., debet dictus Dominus Itherius respondere, quia Ricardus de Motu eius commissarius eas recepit, ut patet per eius aquitantiam.[43]
De ecclesia de Brenkeworth' (Brinkworth) recepit dictus Bernardus xv m.

Lincolniensis

De ecclesia de Hertheryngton' (Harrington) dimissa in arreyratgiis pro iiiiᵒʳ m. cum dimidia ii m., et de residuis ii m. cum dimidia debet dictus Dominus Itherius respondere, qui eas recepit ut patet per eius aquitantiam.[43]

Norwycensis

De ecclesia de Mateshale (Mattishall) dimissa in arreyratgiis pro iiiiᵒʳ m. cum dimidia debet dictus Dominus Itherius respondere qui eas recepit, prout patet per eius aquitantiam.[43]
De ecclesia de Kedyngton' (Kedington or Kitton) recepit dictus Bernardus xv m.

Conventrensis et Lichefeldensis

De prebenda de Sandiacre in ecclesia Lichefeldensi ix m.[44]
De ecclesia de Rodeleye (Ratley), dimissa in arreyratgiis pro vi s. viiiᵒ d., debet dictus dominus Itherius respondere, qui eas recepit prout patet per eius aquitantium.

Bathoniensis et Wellensis

De beneficiis que in civitate et diocesi Bathoniensi et Wellensi toto dicto quadriennio vacaverunt inferius respondebitur.

---

[40] In the margin: *Attende.*
[41] In the margin: *Resta.*

[42] Opposite the items under *Cicestrensis* in the margin a cross has been placed.
[43] In the margin: *Attende.*
[44] In the margin opposite this item: *attende.* It was probably intended to call attention to the next item.

### Wygorniensis, Menevensis, Landavensis, Assavensis, Bangorensis

De beneficiis que in civitatibus et diocesibus Wygorniensi, Menevensi, Landavensi, Assavensi et Bagnorensi toto dicto quadriennio vacaverunt inferius respondebitur.

### Eboracensis

De ecclesia de Fischelak' (Fishlake) recepit dictus Bernardus lxᵃm.

De libera capella regis de Tykhill' (Tickhill) dimissa in arreyratgiis pro xxiiiiᵒʳ m. recepit pro parte dicte camere xii m.

De ecclesia de Elveleye (Kirk Ella) lxxᵃ m.⁴⁵

Summa totalis receptorum in pagina iiᶜ xvi m. Approbatum.

(fol. 123) Adhuc de secundo anno reservationis dictorum fructuum primi anni

### Dunelmensis

De archidiaconatu Dunelmensi pro liii li., de prebenda quam obtinuit Rogerus de Northewelle in ecclesia de Northon' (Norton) pro ix m.; de prebenda quam Magister Alanus de Chirden' obtinuit in ecclesia Cestrie (Chester-le-Street) pro viiiᵒ m., de ecclesia de Wolton' (Whalton) pro iii m. dimissis in arreyratgiis, dictus abbas Beate Marie Eboracensis subcollector in suo compoto cum dicto Domino Itherio computavit.

Recepta de arreyratgiis tertii anni dictorum fructuum

### Cantuariensis

De vicaria ecclesie de Apoldre (Appledore) dimissa in arreyratgiis pro x m. recepit dictus Bernardus viiiᵒ m. cum dimidia.

De ecclesia de Betleshangre (Betteshanger) dimissa in arreyratgiis per dictum Dominum Itherium pro viiiᵒ m. cum dimidia recepit iiiiᵒʳ m., et de residuis iiiiᵒʳ m. cum dimidia debet dictus Dominis Itherius respondere, qui eas recepit patet per eius aquitantiam.

De vicaria de Leysden' (Leysdown) dimissa in arreyratgiis per dictum Dominum Itherium pro vi s. viiiᵒ d. debet dictus Itherius respondere, qui eas recepit ut patet per eius aquitantiam.

De archidiaconatu Cantuariensi dimisso in arreyratgiis pro cccᵗⁱˢ m. recepit iiᶜ lvi m., et de xliiiiᵒʳ m. residuis debet dictus Dominus Itherius respondere, qui exoneravit . . tunc archidiaconum de eisdem.

### Londoniensis

De vicaria ecclesie de Wrytlyngeseye (Brightlingsea) dimissa in arreyratgiis pro xᶜᵉᵐ m. recepit vii m. Residuum speratur remitti vicario eiusdem, quia se facere

obligavit cum non taxetur ultra vi m., nec sit alibi beneficiatus.

### Cicestrensis

De vicaria de Odemore (Udimore) dimissa in arreyratgiis pro vii m. recepit vi m. Residuum debetur.

De ecclesia de Neutymbr' (Newtimber) recepit xiiiiᶜⁱᵐ m.

### Wyntoniensis

De ecclesia de Basyngestok' (Basingstoke), dimissa in arreyratgiis pro xii m., de ecclesia de Mertham (Merstham), dimissa in arreyratgiis pro x m. cum dimidia, debet dictus Dominus Itherius respondere, qui dictas summas recepit prout patet per eius aquitantias.

### Sarisbiriensis

De subdecanatu ecclesie Sarisbiriensis cum prebenda maioris partis altaris et ecclesia de Candelhaddon' (Caundle Stourton) eidem annexa dimissis in arreyratgiis pro xxv m. recepit dumtaxat xvi m., nec plus debetur quia per fraudem de qua constitit dicta prebenda fuerat annexa.

De portione ecclesie de Erchefonte (Urchfont) ix m.

### Norwycensis

De ecclesia de Fyncham (Fincham) recepit xxᵗⁱ ii m.

De ecclesia de Byngham Welle (Beechamwell?) dimissa in arreyratgiis pro iᵃ m. debet dictus Dominus Itherius respondere, qui eam recepit ut patet per eius aquitantiam.

Summa totalis pagine cccᵗᵉ xlii m. et dimidia. Approbatum.

(fol. 123ᵛ) Adhuc recepta de arreyratgiis dictorum fructuum de tertio anno reservationis ipsorum

### Norwycensis adhuc

De ecclesia de Brauncestr' (Brancaster) dimissa in arreyratgiis pro xvii m. recepit iiiiᵒʳ m., et de xiii m. residuis dictus Dominus Itherius debet respondere, qui eas recepit prout patet per eius aquitatiam.

De ecclesia de Okeryng' (Hockering) dimissa in arreyratgiis pro xv m. debet idem Dominus Itherius respondere, qui eas recepit prout patet per eius aquitantiam.

De ecclesia de Brom (Broome) iuxta Dichenham (Ditchingham) recepit dictus Bernardus v m.

De ecclesia de Thelinetham (Thelnetham), dimissa in arreyratgiis pro xii m., item de ecclesia de Illegh' (Eleigh), dimissa in arreyratgiis pro xv m., debet dictus Dominus Itherius respondere, qui dictas summas recepit ut patet per eius aquitantias.

### Elyensis

De ecclesia de Overe (Over) recepit idem Bernardus xiiiᶜⁱᵐ m.

---

⁴⁵ A cross appears in the margin opposite the items under *Eboracensis.*

### Lincolniensis

De ecclesia de Etton' (Eton) iuxta Wyndesore (Windsor) dimissa in arreyratgiis pro viiiᵒ m. debet dictus Dominus Itherius respondere, qui eas recepit prout patet per eius aquitantiam.

De ecclesia de Henlee (Henley) recepit dictus Bernardus xv m.; residuum debetur.

### Conventrensis et Lichefeldensis

De ecclesia de Pleseleye (Pleasley) recepit vii m. et dimidiam.

### Bathoniensis et Wellensis

De ecclesia de Custon', quia talis in diocesi Bathoniensi et Wellensi non repperitur, nichil.

De ceteris vero beneficiis [46] que toto dicto quadriennio in civitate et diocesi Bathoniensi et Wellensi vacaverunt inferius respondebitur.

Summa usque hic xliiii m. medietas. Approbatum.

### Wygorniensis, Herefordensis, Menevensis, Landavensis, Assavensis, Bangorensis, Eboracensis, Dunelmensis, Karleolensis

De beneficiis que dicto toto quadriennio vacaverunt in Wygorniensi, Herefordensi, Menevensi, Landavensi, Assavensi, Bangorensi, Eboracensi, Dunelmensi et Karliolensi civitatibus et diocesibus inferius respondebitur.

Recepta de arreyratgiis quarti anni fructuum predictorum.

### Cantuariensis

De ecclesia de Otrindene (Otterden) recepit dictus Bernardus de Sistre v m.

### Roffensis

De ecclesia de Stone dimissa in arreyratgiis pro vi m. recepit v m., et nichil plus debetur.

### Londoniensis

De ecclesia de Litleton' (Littleton) dimissa in arreyratgiis pro ii m. debet dictus Itherius respondere.

Summa totalis pagine liiiiᵒʳ m. de dimidia. Approbatum.

(fol. 124) Adhuc recepta de arreyratgiis quarti anni fructuum predictorum

### Londoniensis

De ecclesia de Herlawe (Harlow), dimissa in arreyratgiis pro x m., de vicaria de Southmenstre (Southminster), dimissa in arreyratgiis pro v m., ⟨debet⟩ dictus Dominus Itherius respondere, qui dictas summas recepit ut patet per eius aquitantias.

---

[46] *beneficii*, MS.

De ecclesia de Alta Rothyng' (High Roding) recepit dictus Bernardus xviiiᵒ m.

De ecclesia de Sabrichesworth' (Sawbridgeworth) lxxᵃ m.

### Cicestrensis

De vicaria de Herlyngton' (Arlington), dimissa in arreyratgiis pro iiiiᵒʳ m., de vicaria de Cokyng' (Cocking), dimissa in arreyratgiis pro iii m. xl d.; de vicaria de Glynde, dimissa in arreyratgiis pro l s., debet dictus Dominus Itherius respondere, qui dictas summas recepit ut patet per eius aquitantias.

De prebenda de Hanefeld (Henfield) dimissa in arreyratgiis pro xii m. recepit iiiiᵒʳ m., et de viiiᵒ m. residuis debet dictus Dominus Itherius respondere, qui eas recepit prout patet per eius aquitantiam.

### Wyntoniensis

De ecclesia de Iwerst (Ewhurst), dimissa in arreyratgiis pro xxv m.; de ecclesia de Hemynton' (Hinton), dimissa in arreyratgiis pro viiiᵒ m., de ecclesia de Camford (Conford in Bramshott?), dimissa in arreyratgiis pro vi m., de ecclesia de Ruywode (Ringwood), dimissa in arreyratgiis pro l m., debet dictus Dominus Itherius respondere qui dictas summas recepit ut patet per eius aquitantias et locumtenentis sui.

De ecclesia de Chepstede (Chipstead) recepit dictus Bernardus xxviiiᵒ m.

### Sarisbiriensis

De ecclesia de Piperdesclyve (Clyffe Pypard), dimissa in arreyratgiis pro vii m. cum dimidia, de vicaria de Somerford, dimissa in arreyratgiis pro iii m. xl d., debet dictus Dominus Itherius respondere, qui dictas summas recepit; patet per eius aquitantias.

De ecclesia de Wyhampton' (Witchampton), dimissa in arreyratgiis pro v m., de ecclesia de Sutton' (Sutton Veney), dimissa in arreyratgiis pro xxx m. solverunt dicto Itherio; patet per compota sua.

De portione ecclesia de Herchefonte (Urchfont) supra in tertio anno computatum est nichil.

De ecclesia de Polham (Pulham) recepit dictus Bernardus v m.

### Norwycensis

De ecclesia de Sternefeld (Sternfield) vi m.

De ecclesia de Waltinton' (Watlington) c s.

### Elyensis

De ecclesia de Dodyngton' (Doddington) dimissa in arreyratgiis pro xxvii cum dimidia debet dictus Dominus Itherius respondere, qui eas recepit prout patet per eius aquitantiam.

De vicaria de Wysebech' (Wisbech) recepit dictus Bernardus x m.

## Lincolniensis

De ecclesia de Flamsted (Flamstead), dimissa in arreyratgiis pro i$^a$ m., de ecclesia de Hamerton', dimissa in arreyratgiis pro i$^a$ m., de ecclesia de Ledenham (Leadenham), dimissa in arreyratgiis pro xxv m., debet dictus Dominus Itherius respondere qui dictas summas recepit ut patet per eius aquitantie litteras.

De ecclesia de Guniby (Gunby), dimissa in arreyratgiis pro vi m. sum dimidia, dictus Itherius habuit prout patet per compota sua.

De ecclesia de Bereford (Barford), dimissa in arreyratgiis pro viii$^o$ m., dictus Itherius habuit v m.; patet per compota sua.

De ecclesia de Mixebury (Mixbury) recepit dictus Bernardus viii$^o$ m.

De ecclesia de Kyrkeby Boyn super Bayne (Kirkby on Bane) xii m.

Summa totalis pagine clxviii$^o$ m. et dimidia. Approbatum.

(fol 124$^v$) Adhuc recepta de arreyratgiis quarti anni fructuum predictorum

## Conventrensis et Lichefeldensis

De prebenda de Freford (Freeford) in ecclesia Lichefeldensi recepit dictus Bernardus xxx$^a$ m.

De ecclesia de Crouston' (Croston), dimissa in arreyratgiis pro xxv m., debet dictus Dominus Itherius respondere, qui eas recepit prout patet per restam super hec de voluntate sua receptam.

## Bathoniensis et Wellensis

De decanatu ecclesie Wellensis dimisso in arreyratgiis pro c li. recepit de parte contingente cameram domini nostri pape xxvi li. xvi s. viii$^o$ d. obolum. Restant pro complemento partis dicte camere xxix li. iii s. iii d. obolus [47] et 1 li. pro parte regis.

De archidiaconatu Bathonie recepit xvii li. vi s. viii$^o$ d.

De aliis vero beneficiis que in civitate et diocesi Bathoniensi et Wellensi dicto quadriennio vacaverunt inferius respondebitur.

## Eboracensis

De decantu Eboracensi recepit c li.

## Wygorniensis, Herefordensis, Menevensis, Landavensis, Assavensis, Bangorensis, Eboracensis, Dunelmensis, Karleolensis

De beneficiis que in Wygorniensi, Herefordensi, Menevensi, Landavensi, Assavensi, Bangorensi, Eboracensi, Dunelmensi et Karleolensi civitatibus et diocesibus dicto quadriennio vacaverunt inferius respondebitur.

Summa totalis prescriptorum in pagina clxiiii$^{or}$ li. iii s. iiii$^{or}$ d. obolus.

Summa totalis receptorum usque hic de arreyratgiis fructuum primi anni m$^l$ lxxx$^a$ix m. x s. obolus. Valet vii$^c$ xxvi li. x s. obolum sterlingorum.

Recepta per dictum Bernardum de Sistre de dictis fructibus tam a . . subcollectoribus qui eos in certis diocesibus dicto quadriennio receperunt quam a quibusdam aliis pro quibusdam beneficiis inferius nominatis.

## Eboracensis

Facto finali compoto per dictum Bernadum cum . . abbate monasterii Beate Marie Eboracensis, subcollectore dictorum fructuum in civitate, diocesi et provincia Eboracensi per dictum Dominum Itherium deputato, de receptis per eum de dictis fructibus beneficiorum vacantium dicto quadriennio in dictis civitate, diocesi et provincia Eboracensi reppertum extitit (fol. 125) [48] dictum abbatem debere per formam dicti compoti, allocatis sibi xl li. pro expensis per eum factis circa collectionem fructuum predictorum, ccclxx$^a$ i li. xv s. sterlingorum, de quibus solvit dicto Bernardo de Sistre iii$^c$ lxx$^a$ i li. iiii$^{or}$ s. vi d.

Item de prebenda de Suthnewbald (South Newbald) in ecclesia Eboracensi recepit dictus Bernardus xx$^{ti}$ li.

Item de prebenda de Northnewbald (North Newbald) in eadem ecclesia recepit xx$^{ti}$ iii li. xiii s. x d. obolum.

## Wygorniensis

Facto finali compoto cum abbate de Teukesbury et cum Magistro Willelmo de Bosco, subcollectoribus dictorum fructuum in civitate et diocesi Wygorniensi deputatis, reppertum extitit per formam dicti compoti ipsos debere lxx$^a$ viii$^o$ li. xii s. viii$^o$ d. quas et quos solverunt dicto Bernardo de Sistre.

Item de fructibus archidiaconatus Gloucestrie in ecclesia Wygorniensi quem dicti subcollectores in arreyratgiis dimisserant recepit idem Bernardus ultra xx$^{ci}$ li. solutas pro eis dicto Domino Itherio x li. xiii s. iiii$^{or}$ d.

De ecclesia de Wythenden' (Whittington) quam dicti subcollectores in arreyratgiis dimisserant xx$^{ti}$ li.

De prebenda de Hembury (Henbury) in ecclesia de Westbury quam etiam dicti subcollectores in arreyratgiis dimisserant recepit vi li. xiii s. iiii$^{or}$ d.

## Herefordensis

Item facto finali compoto cum . . procuratore domini . . Herefordensis episcopi, subcollectoris dictorum fructuum in suis civitate et diocesi deputati, reppertum extitit ipsum debere per formam dicti compoti xxx$^a$i li. iii s. v d. quas et quos idem Bernardus recepit tam ab ispo quam ab aliis pro eo solventibus xxx$^a$ i li. iii s. v d., restantibus tamen adhuc penes ipsum viii$^o$ li. xvi s. iii d. quas et quos petiit sibi pro expensis factis per eum tam circa collectionem huiusmodi fructuum quam

---

[47] A cross appears in the margin opposite this item.

[48] The folio is headed with the caption: *Adhuc recepta de dictis fructibus.* The heading *Eboracensis* is also repeated.

portationem huiusmodi pecunie ad civitatem Londoniam allocari.

Item de prebenda de Berton' (Barton) in Colewell' (Colwall) in ecclesia Herefordensi recepit pro parte camere domini nostri pape quia rex remisserat . . prebendario partem suam lxvi s. viii° d.

Item de thesauraria ecclesie Herefordensis xl s.; debetur adhuc xvii m.

Item de prebenda de Morton' et Waddon' (Moreton and Whaddon) in dicta ecclesia Herefordensi recepit dictus Bernardus xiii<sup>cim</sup> li. vi s. viii° d.

Summa totalis pagine v<sup>c</sup> lxxx<sup>a</sup> li. xiii<sup>cim</sup> s. v d. obolus. Approbatum.

(fol. 125ᵛ) Adhuc recepta de dictis fructibus a . . subcollectoribus eorundem.

### Menevensis

Item facto finali compoto cum Magistro Willelmo Petri, clerico, procuratore domini . . episcopi Menevensis, subcollectoris dictorum fructuum in suis civitate et diocesi per dictum Dominum Itherium deputati, reppertum extitit per formam dicti compoti dictum dominum episcopum de dictis fructibus debere lii li. xiii s. iiii<sup>or</sup> d., de quibus allocatis sibi xl s. pro expensis per eum circa collectionem et portationem huiusmodi pecunie factis, recepit idem Bernardus l<sup>a</sup> li. xiii s. iiii d.

### Landavensis

Item facto finali compoto cum Domino Willelmo de Brenkeworth', procuratore domini . . episcopi Landavensis, subcollectoris dictorum fructuum in suis civitate et diocesi per dictum Dominum Itherium deputati, reppertum extitit per formam dicti compoti dictum dominum episcopum debere lxxx<sup>a</sup> iii li. vii s. vii d., de quibus allocatis sibi vi li. xiii s. iiii<sup>or</sup> d. pro expensis per eum factis circa collectionem dictorum fructuum et portationem pecunie ad civitatem Londoniam, solvit dicto Bernardo lxx<sup>a</sup> vi li. xiiii<sup>cim</sup> s. ii d.

### Assavensis

Item facto finali compoto cum Magistro Ludovico, archidiacono Assavensi, procuratore domini episcopi Assavensis, subcollectoris dictorum fructuum in suis civitate et diocesi per dictum Dominum Itherium deputati, reppertum fuit per formam dicti compoti dictum dominum episcopum debere ix li. iii s. iiii<sup>or</sup> d. quas et quos solvit dicto Bernardo ix li. iii s. iiii<sup>or</sup> d.

### Bangorensis

Item facto finali compoto cum Magistro David de Brell', archidiacono Bangorensi, procuratore domini . . episcopi Bangorensis, subcollectoris dictorum fructuum in suis civitate et diocesi deputati per Dominum Itherium supradictum, reppertum extitit per formam dicti compoti dictum dominum episcopum adhuc debere lx<sup>a</sup>i

li. ii s. vi d., de quibus solvit dicto Bernardo tam per manus suas quam per manus archidiaconi de Angleseye xlix li.; restant xii li. ii s. vi d. de quibus petit sibi allocari expensas suas.

### Bathoniensis et Wellensis

Item facto finali compoto cum . . procuratore domini . . Bathoniensis et Wellensis episcopi, subcollectoris dictorum fructuum in suis civitate et diocesi per dictum Dominum Itherium deputati, reppertum extitit dictum dominum episcopum debere per formam dicti compoti lxxxx<sup>a</sup> iiii<sup>or</sup> li., de quibus solvit dicto Bernardo lxxx<sup>a</sup> li. xiiii<sup>cim</sup> s. iiii d. Restant xx<sup>ti</sup> m. quas sibi petiit allocari pro expensis suis factis tam circa collectionem dicte pecunie quam circa portationem ipsius ad civitatem Londoniam durante quadriennio supradicto.

Summa totalis pagine ii<sup>c</sup> lxvi li. iiii<sup>or</sup> s. ii d. Approbatum.

Summa totalis receptorum tam a dictis subcollectoribus quam de aliis beneficiis intermixtis viii<sup>c</sup> xlvi li. xviii° s. vii d. obolus.

(fol. 126) Recepta per dictum Bernardum de Sistre de fructibus quorundam beneficiorum prius recelatorum que infra dictum quadriennium vacaverunt, in quibus etiam dictus dominus rex habet partem suam.

### Lincolniensis

De vicaria prebendalis ecclesie de Cropp' (Cropredy) recepit dictus Bernardus viii° li. xiii s. iiii<sup>or</sup> d.

De ecclesia de Bolewyk' (Bulwick) recepit vi li. xiii s. iiii<sup>or</sup> d.

De ecclesia de Ibestok' (Ibstock) recepit xvi li.

### Cicestrensis

De ecclesia de Pecham (Patcham), que infra dictum quadriennium bis vacaverunt et non fuerat primitus responsum nisi pro uno anno, recepit xvi li. xiii s. iiii<sup>or</sup> d.

De ecclesia de Pachyng' (Patching) recepit xx<sup>ti</sup> li.

### Wellensis

De prebenda de Werminstre (Worminster) in ecclesia Wellensi, que vocatur alio nomine portio Romani Sarisbiriensis diocesis, recepit x li. vi s. viii° d.

Summa prescriptorum in pagina lxxviii° li. vi s. viii° d. Approbatum.

Summa totalis receptorum per dictum Bernardum tam de dictis beneficiis dimissis in arreyratgiis quam a . . subcollectoribus dictorum fructuum quam etiam de dictis beneficiis recelatis m<sup>l</sup> vi<sup>c</sup>l<sup>a</sup>i li. xv s.[49] iiii<sup>or</sup> d. sterlingorum, de quibus est pars camere dicti domini nostri pape viii<sup>c</sup> xlvii li. ix s. iiii d. quadrans,[50] pars vero dicti domini

---

[49] Over *ii s.* deleted by a line.
[50] Over *viii° xlix li. ii s. viii° d. quadrans* deleted by a line.

regis, qui aliquibus remisit partem suam et aliqui qui pro parte dicte camere solverunt nondum satisfecerunt pro parte sua, est viii<sup>c</sup> iiii<sup>or</sup> li. vi s.[51] xi d. iii quadrantes.

(fol. 126<sup>v</sup>) Recepta per dictum Bernardum de Sistre de arreyratgiis quadriennalis decime, olim per dictum Dominum Johannem papam XXII<sup>dum</sup> imposite, dimissis per dictum Dominum Itherium, qui fuit collector generalis eiusdem decime, in quibus dictus dominus rex Anglie ex concessione dicti domini pape habebat medietatem.[51a]

### Cantuariensis

Ab . . abbate de Farversham Cantuariensis diocesis, subcollectore dicte decime in civitate et diocesi Cantuariensi per dominum . . Cantuariensem archiepiscopum deputato, recepit dictus Bernardus cix li. xi s. i d.

### Londoniensis

A . . priore Sancti Bartholomei Londoniensis, subcollectore dicte decime in civitate et diocesi Londoniensi per dominum . . Londoniensem episcopum deputato, dimisso in arreyratgiis per dictum Dominum Itherium de Concoreto in xxxviii<sup>o</sup> li. xviii<sup>o</sup> s. i d. i quadrante, recepit idem Bernardus xxvii li. xiiii<sup>cim</sup> s. v d. obolum i quadrantem. Residuum, ut dicit, levari non potuit, quia temporalia, pro quibus solebat solvi, dicuntur alienari.

### Cicestrensis

Ab . . abbate de Bello Cicestrensis diocesis, subcollectore dicte decime in civitate et diocesi Cicestrensi per dominum . . Cicestrensem episcopum deputato, dimisso in arreyratgiis per dictum Dominum Itherium in lxii li. xvi s. vii d., recepit idem Bernardus tam ab ipso abbate quam ab aliis pro eo solventibus l<sup>a</sup>i li. x s. viii d.

Et dictus dominus rex de dicta summa totali, videlicet de parte ipsum contingente, remisit ciii s. iii d. obolum pro temporalibus abbatis de Fiscampo (Fécamp) quia tunc fuerunt in manibus suis. Residuum vero dicte summe est in manibus trium vicariorum qui licet multi processus contra ipsos facti fuerint nondum tamen solvere potuerunt pre nimia paupertate.[52]

### Wyntoniensis

A priore Wyntoniensi, subcollectore dicte decime in archidiaconatu Wyntoniensi per dominum . . Wyntoniensem episcopum deputato, recepit dictus Bernardus lxxxx<sup>a</sup> i li. vi s. xi d.

Item a . . priore de Bermundeseye Wyntoniensis diocesis, subcollectore dicte decime in archidiaconatu Surreye Wyntoniensis diocesis per dictum dominum . . Wyntoniensem episcopum deputato, dimisso in arrey-

ratgiis per dictum dominum Itherium pro ix li. xiii s. recepit dictus Bernardus vi li. xviii<sup>o</sup> s. viii<sup>o</sup> d. Residuum debebat abbas de Waltham Londoniensis diocesis pro certis bonis que habet in diocesi Wyntoniensi, sed solvit decimam pro illis . . subcollectori in diocesi Londoniensi.

### Sarisbiriensis

Ab . . abbate monasterii de Malmesbury Sarisbiriensis diocesis, subcollectore dicte decime in certa parte dicte diocesis per dominum . . Sarisbiriensem episcopum deputato, recepit dictus Bernardus xxvii li. xvii s. x d. obolum.

Item ab . . abbate monasterii de Schirebourn' dicte diocesis, subcollectore dicte decime in alia parte dicte diocesis deputato, qui per errorem ut creditur dicto Bernardo fuerat dimissus in arreyratgiis pro xvii li., recepit xvii s. Nec plus debebat secundum compotum suum.

Summa totalis pagine iii<sup>e</sup> xv li. xvi s. viii<sup>o</sup> d. obolus. Approbatum.

(fol. 127) Adhuc recepta de arreyratgiis dicte decime quadriennalis

### Norwycensis

A . . priore ecclesie Norwycensis, subcollectore dicte decime per dominum . . episcopum Norwycensem in suis civitate et diocesi deputato, dimisso in arreyratgiis per dictum Dominum Itherium in xx<sup>ti</sup> li. vii s. ix d., nichil, quia, ut dixit, levari non possunt, pro eo quod bona, pro quibus solebant solvi, devenerunt pro parte ad manus laycorum, et pro parte sunt alia beneficia ultra vi marchas ad decimam non taxata et ea obtinentes non sunt alibi beneficiati, et de talibus non consuevit hacthenus decimam solvi.

### Elyensis

A . . prior Elyensi, subcollectore dicte decime per dominum . . Elyensem episcopum in suis civitate et diocesi deputato, dimisso in arreyratgiis per dictum Dominum Itherium in lxiiii<sup>or</sup> li. xiii d., recepit dictus Bernardus liiii<sup>or</sup> li. xiii s. i d. Residuum, ut dixit, levari non potuit, pro eo quod bona de quibus petebatur partim sunt in manibus laycorum, et partim non repperuntur in dictis civitate et diocesi Elyensi, et aliqua sunt talium qui dicunt se esse privilegiatos per sedem apostolicam super decimis non solvendis.

### Lincolniensis

Ab . . abbate monasterii de Eynesham Lincolniensis diocesis, subcollectore dicte decime in certa parte dicte diocesis per dominum . . Lincolniensem episcopum deputato, dimisso in arreyratgiis per dictum Dominum Itherium in iii<sup>c</sup> lvii li. vii s. v d. obolo quadrante, recepit dictus Bernardus tam per manus ipsius abbatis quam aliorum solventium pro beneficiis et tenementis que habent infra collectam ipsius abbatis iii<sup>c</sup> liii li. iiii<sup>or</sup> s. i d. obolum.

---

[51] I am not sure of the figure. It may be v s. This would make the addition correct.

[51a] On this quadrennial tenth see Lunt, *Financial Relations* . . . *1327-1534*, pp. 75-88.

[52] There is a cross in the margin opposite this item.

Restant iiii<sup>or</sup> li. iii s. iiii<sup>or</sup> d. i quadrans, de quibus petiit sibi allocari pro ii ecclesiis et una capella ultra sex marcas non taxatis lxvi s. viii° d., presertim quia obtinentes ipsas non sunt alibi beneficiati. Item pro bonis que moniales minorisse Londonienses habent infra decanatum de Teesd' (Shefford?) xvi s., cum dicantur fore immunes a prestatione cuiuslibet decime, quibus si allocentur deductis, debet adhuc viii° d. i quadrantem.

Facto finali compoto cum . . priore Sancte Katherine extra Lincolniam, subcollectore primi et secundi annorum ac primi termini tertii anni dicte decime in certa parte Lincolniensis diocesis per dominum . . Lincolniensem episcopum deputato, deductis eis que pro beneficiis Domini Gaucelmi, Albanensis episcopi sancte Romane ecclesie cardinalis et aliorum a prestatione dicte decime exemptorum debent deduci, et aliis deducendis, ac allocatis sibi quinquaginta libris pro expensis per eum factis circa collectionem dicte decime et portationem pecunie ad civitatem Londoniensem, reppertum extitit tam in manibus dicti prioris quam debitorum tunc remanere de dicta decima usque ad summam cxx<sup>ti</sup> iiii<sup>or</sup> li. xvi s. iiii<sup>or</sup> d. Et [53] (fol. 127<sup>v</sup>) [54] additis xii li. per ipsum collectis de ultimo termino tertii anni predicte decime priusquam commissio facta foret Magistro Willelmo Bachalerii, necnon et xvi li. ii s. viii° d. i quad. quas et quos debebat pro ultimo termino tertii anni predicti et pro toto quarto anno dicte decime pro decima bonorum suorum, prout dictus Magister Willelmus ipsum onerat in compoto suo infrascripto, remanebant in summa clii li. xix s. i quad., de quibus dictus Bernardus de Sistre recepit tam per manus dicti prioris quam per manus . . abbatis de Valle Dei (Walden) quam dicti Magistri Willelmi Bachalerii et quorundam aliorum pro dicto priore solventium un universo cxx<sup>ti</sup>ii li. ii s. xi d. quadrantem.

Restant adhuc xxx<sup>a</sup> li. xvi s. obolus, de quibus dominus rex Anglie remisit pro parte sua magistro et fratribus de Kyrkeby (Monks Kirby) pro ecclesiis de Stapilford (Stapleford) et de Kyrkeby ciii s. iiii<sup>or</sup> d., et tantum solverunt pro parte dicte camere,[55] quibus deductis remanent xxv li. xii s. viii° d. obolus, que dicuntur adhuc existere in manibus debitorum, et que adhuc non potuerant levari, pro eo quod alique de bonis, pro quibus debentur, venerunt ad manus laycorum, et aliqui de dictis debitoribus non potuerunt solvere pre nimia paupertate, aliqui etiam sunt contra quos est procedendum per invocationem brachii secularis, cum sententias ecclesiasticas non formident.

Facto finali compoto cum Magistro Willelmo Bachalerii, canonico Lincolniensi, subcollectore secundi termini tertii anni et quarti anni integri dicte decime in dicta parte Lincolniensis diocesis in qua dictus prior subcollector fuerat per dictum dominum . . Lincolniensem episcopum deputato, deductis eis que pro beneficiis Domini Gaucelmi, Albanensis episcopi sancte Romane ecclesie cardinalis, et aliorum a prestatione dicte decime exemptorum deduci debent, ac aliis rationabiliter deducendis, et allocatis sibi xxx<sup>a</sup> li. pro expensis suis circa collectionem et portationem pecunie ad civitatem Londoniensem factis, reppertum extitit tam in manibus dicti Magistri Willelmi quam prioris Sancte Katherine predicti aliorum debitorum existere, computatis xii li. per dictum priorem de dicto secundo termino tertii anni de dicta decima levatis priusquam dicto Magistro Willelmo commissio facta foret, et xvi li. ii s. viii d. i quad. per eundem priorem pro decima bonorum suorum de dicto ultimo termino tertii anni et toto quarto anno dicte decime debitis, cxxx<sup>a</sup> iii li. xii s. iiii<sup>or</sup> d. iii quad., de quibus idem Bernardus recepit tam a dicto magistro Willelmo quam per manus . . abbatis de Eynesham quam quorumdam aliorum pro eo solventium in universo lxxxx<sup>a</sup> v li. ix s. ii d.

Restant xxxviii° li. iii s. ii d. iii quad., de quibus dictus prior oneratur de xxviii° li. ii s. viii° d. i quad., ut predicitur; et dominus rex Anglie pro parte sua remisit magistro et fratribus de Kyrkeby pro ecclesiis de Kyrkeby et de Stapilford lxii s.; quibus omnibus deductis, restant vi li. xviii° s. vi d. ob., que et qui sunt adhuc in manibus debitorum quorum aliqui non possunt solvere pre nimia [56] (fol. 128) [57] paupertate, alii etiam non possunt solvere quia bona, pro quibus dabant decimam, devenerunt ad manus laycorum, alii etiam non formidant sententias ecclesiasticas contra quos erit per invocationem secularis brachii procedendum.

## Wygorniensis

A . . priore Maioris Malvernie Wygorniensis diocesis, subcollectore dicte decime in certa parte dicte diocesis per dominum . . Wygorniensem episcopum deputato, dimisso in arreyratgiis per dictum Dominum Itherium in xxxviii° s. vi d. obolo, nichil, quia, ut dixit, levari non possunt propter paupertatem monialium de Recolf' (Cook Hill [58]) que ad sollicitationem illorum tenentur et per dominum regem pars sua est eis remissa.

Item ab . . abbate Gloucestrie dicte diocesis, subcollectore dicte decime in alia certa parte dicte diocesis per dictum dominum episcopum Wygorniensem deputato, dimisso in arreyratgiis per dictum Dominum Itherium in ix li. xvii s. x d., recepit idem Bernardus ix li. xvii s. x d.

---

[53] The following appears at the bottom of the folio: *Summa totalis pagine iiii<sup>e</sup> vii li. xvii s. ii d. obolus. Approbatum.*

[54] At the top of the folio is the heading: *Adhuc recepta de arreyratgiis decime quadriennalis.* In the margin is the caption: *Lincolniensis adhuc.*

[55] In the margin opposite this item is an abbreviation which probably stands for *resta.* It is followed by a cross.

[56] The following is at the bottom of the folio: Summa totalis pagine cc<sup>tum</sup> xvii li. xii s. i d. iii quad. *Approbatum.*

[57] At the top of the folio appears the heading: *Adhuc recepta de arreyratgiis decime quadriennalis.*

[58] In Rous Lench, formerly Lench Roculf.

### Landavensis

A domino . . episcopo Landavensi, collectore dicte decime in suis civitate et diocesi deputato, dimisso in arreyratgiis in vii li. viii° s. viii° d. obolo i quadrante, recepit cxiii s. iii d. Et nichil plus debebat secundum compotum suum.

### Bangorensis

Ab . . abbate de Bardeneye (Bardsey) Bangorensis diocesis, subcollectore dicte decime in civitate et diocesi Bangorensi per domimum . . Bangorensem episcopum deputato, dimisso in arreyratgiis per dictum Dominum Itherium in iiii°r li. x s. iiii°r d., nichil, quia levari non possunt pro eo quod quidam prioratus, pro quo deberent solvi, penitus est destructus.

### Assavensis

Ab . . abbate de Valle Crucis Assavensis diocesis, subcollectore dicte decime in civitate et diocesi Assavensi pro tribus primis annis eiusdem per dominum . . Assavensem episcopum deputato, dimisso in arreyratgiis per dictum Dominum Itherium in xxiiii°r li. xix s. viii° d. obolo, recepit dictus Bernardus xx$^{ti}$ li. Debet adhuc iiii°r li. xix s. viii° d. obolum pro quibus multi processus facti sunt contra eum.

Item a domino . . episcopo Assavensi, collectore dicte decime in suis civitate et diocesi predictis pro quarto anno eiusdem deputato, dimisso in arreyratgiis per dictum Dominum Itherium in xxiiii°r li. xi s. vii d., recepit dictus Bernardus xxiiii°r li. xi s. vii d.

### Herefordensis

A domino . . Herefordensi episcopo, collectore dicte decime in suis civitate et diocesi deputato, dimisso in arreyratgiis per dictum Dominum Itherium in xxiiii°r li. xviii° s. vii d., nichil, quia levari non possunt, ut dicit, prout patet per compotum per ipsum dicto Domino Itherio redditum.

Summa totalis pagine lx$^a$ li. ii s. viii° d. Approbatum.

(fol. 128$^v$) Adhuc recepta de arreyratgiis decime quadriennalis.

### Menevensis

Facto finali compoto cum . . procuratore domini . . episcopi Menevensis, collectoris dicte decime in suis civitate et diocesi deputati, reppertum extitit per formam dicti compoti dictum dominum episcopum nichil debere, allocatis sibi lxiii li. vii s. iiii°r d. quas et quos pro minutis beneficiis ultra vi m. non taxatis cum ea obtinentes non sint alibi beneficiati, et si, prout petiit, allocentur eidem lxv li. vi d. obolus pro expensis per ipsum factis tam in colligendo pecunias quam in portando ipsas de Wallia Londonias toto quadriennio supradicto. Nichil.

### Bathoniensis et Wellensis

Ab . . abbate monasterii Glastonie Bathoniensis et Wellensem episcopum deputato, dimisso in arreyratgiis parte dicte diocesis per dominum Bathoniensem et Wellensem episcopum deputato, dimisso in arreyratgiis per dictum Dominum Itherium in l li. xiiii s. ix d. obolo, recepit dictus Bernardus tam ab ipso quam ab aliis solventibus pro bonis que habent in collecta sua xlviii° li. xvii s. v d. obolum.

Residuos xxxvii s. iiii°r d. dictus abbas restituit priori Tanton' infrascripto, quia eos receperat pro decime vicarie Sancte Decum (St. Decuman's) dicte diocesis, que est de collecta dicti prioris.

Item a . . priore Tanton' dicte diocesis, subcollectore dicte decime in altera certa parte eiusdem diocesis per dictum dominum . . episcopum deputato, dimisso in arreyratgiis per dictum Dominum Itherium in xxiiii°r li. x s. v d., recepit idem Bernardus tam per manus suas quam aliorum pro beneficiis que habent infra collectam suam solverunt xx$^{ti}$ i li. xvi s. vii d. Et de residuis liii s. x d. debent sibi allocari xxvi s. viii° d. pro decima portionis quam magister et fratres hospitalis Sancti Bartholomei Londonie percipiunt in ecclesia de Henton' (Hinton) Sancti Georgii dicte diocesis, pro qua non consueverunt solvere decimam pro eo quod pro sustentatione pauperum ad dictum hospitale confluentium est assignatam, quibus, si allocentur, deductis, restant adhuc xxvii s. ii d., quos dicit adhuc existere in manibus debitorum.

### Conventrensis et Lichefeldensis

Ab . . abbate monasterii de Burton' super Trente Conventrensis et Lichefeldensis diocesis, subcollectore dicte decime in certa parte dicte diocesis deputato per dominum . . Conventresem et Lichefeldensem, dimisso in arreyratgiis per dictum Dominum Itherium in ccc$^{tis}$ xix li. xiii s. i d., recepit dictus Bernardus cl li. v s. viii° d. Et de cxxix li. vii s. vi d. de summa restanti debet dictus Dominus Itherius respondere, qui dictam summam, cxxix li. vii s. vi d., recepit, prout patet per iii aquitantias sigillo sui officii sigillatas. De xl$^a$ libris vero residuis . . socii Bardorum de Florentia respondebunt, qui eas receperunt prout patet per eorum aquitantiam. Asserunt tamen dicti socii quod dicte xl$^a$ libre continentur in illa summa quam Dominus Henricus, tunc Lincolniensis episcopus et domini regis Anglie thesaurarius, debuit ab ipsis pro dicto domino rege recipere tempore illo quo dictus Bernardus recepit pro dicta camera summam vi$^c$ xxv li. iii s. iiii°r d. sterlingorum a . . sociis de societate Perusiorum, prout supra continetur.

Summa totalis pagine ii$^c$ xx$^{ti}$ li. xix s. viii° d. obolus Approbatum.

(fol. 129) Adhuc recepta de arreyratgiis quadriennnalis decime

### Exoniensis

Ab . . archidiacono Totton' (Totnes) in ecclesia Exoniensi, subcollectore dicte decime in archidiaconatu suo per dominum . . Exoniensem episcopum deputato, dimisso in arreyratgiis per dictum Dominum Itherium in xv li. iiii<sup>or</sup> s. vi d., qui secundum compotum dicto Domino Itherio redditum non debebat nisi ix li. vi s. vii d., recepit dictus Bernardus cvi s. vii d. Residuas iiii<sup>or</sup> libre quas secundum dictum compotum debebat dumtaxat recepit dictus Dominus Itherius, prout patet per aquitantie litteras sigillo sui officii sigillatas.

Item a . . priore Sancti Nicholay Exoniensis diocesis, subcollectore dicte decime in alia certa parte dicte diocesis per dictum dominum episcopum deputato, dimisso in arreyratgiis per dictum Dominum Itherium in xxiiii<sup>or</sup> li. xii s. ii d., recepit dictus Bernardus xx<sup>ti</sup> iiii<sup>or</sup> li. xii s. ii d.

Item ab . . abbate de Hertiland (Hartland) dicte diocesis, subcollectore dicte decime in alia certa parte eiusdem diocesis per dictum dominum episcopum deputato, dimisso in arreyratgiis per dictum Dominum Itherium in xxi li. viii<sup>o</sup> s., nichil, pro eo quod levari non possunt, nam petuntur de minutis beneficiis ultra vi marchas ad decimam non taxatis que obtinentes non sunt alibi beneficiati, et pro quodam hospitali pauperum leprosorum.

### Eboracensis

Ab . . abbate de Jervall' Eboracensis diocesis, subcollectore dicte decime per dominum . . Eboracensem archiepiscopum in certa parte dicte diocesis, videlicet in archidiaconatu Richemundie, deputato, qui, secundum antiquam taxam remanente archidiaconatu predicto et non allocata ecclesia de Thormeton' (Thornton), fuerit dimissus in arreyratgiis per dictum Dominum Itherium in xlv li., nichil propter novam taxam.

Item a . . priore de Kyrkham dicte diocesis, subcollectore dicte decime in alia certa parte eiusdem diocesis, videlicet in archidiaconatu Estredyng', per dictum dominum archiepiscopum deputato, dimisso in arreyratgiis per dictum Dominum Itherium in lxx<sup>a</sup> li. vii s. iii d., recepit dictus Bernardus lx<sup>a</sup> ii li. iiii<sup>or</sup> s. vii d. obolum, tam per manus suas quam aliorum solventium pro bonis que habebant in dicto archidiaconatu, et secundum compotum suum nichil plus debebat.

Item ab . . abbate monasterii Beate Marie Eboracensis, subcollectore dicte decime in alia certa parte dicte diocesis per dictum dominum . . archiepiscopum deputato, dimisso in arreyratgiis per dictum Dominum Itherium in ccclxxxx<sup>a</sup> vi li. iiii<sup>or</sup> s. ix d. obolo quadrante, recepit dictus Bernardus lxxix li. xvi s. ix d., nec plus debet secundum compotum suum iuxta novam taxam.

Summa totalis pagine clxx<sup>a</sup> ii li. i d. obolus. Approbatum

(fol. 129<sup>v</sup>) Adhuc recepta de arreyratgiis decime quadriennalis

Eboracensis adhuc

Item a . . priore de Thorgarthon' (Thurgarton) dicte diocesis, subcollectore dicte decime in alia certa parte eiusdem diocesis per dictum dominum . . archiepis-

copum deputato, dimisso in arreyratgiis per dictum Dominum Itherium in xvii li. v s. iii quadrantibus, recepit dictus Bernardus xvii li. v s. iii quadrantes.

### Dunelmensis

A . . priore ecclesie Dunelmensis, subcollectore dicte decime in civitate et diocesi Dunelmensi per dominum . . Dunelmensem episcopum deputato dimisso in arreyratgiis per dictum Dominum Itherium in xlv li. xiii s. viii<sup>o</sup> d. obolo quadrante, recepit dictus Bernardus xii li. vii s. obolum i quadrantem. Residuum vero dominus rex Anglie levari non permittit, quia temporalia episcopatus Dunelmensis pro quibus debetur fuerunt tunc temporis in manibus suis.

### Karleolensis

A . . priore Karleolensis ecclesie, subcollectore dicte decime in civitate et diocesi Karleolensi per dominum . . Karleolensem episcopum deputato, dimisso in arreyratgiis per dictum Dominum Itherium in viii<sup>o</sup> li. iii s. ix d., recepit dictus Bernardus vi li. Residuum petiit sibi remitti pro expensis suis.

Summa prescriptorum in pagina xxx<sup>ta</sup> v li. xii s. i d. obolus. Approbatum.

Summa totalis receptorum per dictum Bernardum de Sistre de arreyratgiis dicte decime m<sup>l</sup> iiii<sup>c</sup> xxx<sup>a</sup> li. viii<sup>o</sup> d. i quadrans.

Inde pars domini regis propter remissiones predictas est vii<sup>c</sup> iiii li. xiii s. viii d. et dimidius quadrans.[59]

Pars vero camere domini nostri pape est vii<sup>c</sup> xxv li. vii s. et dimidius quadrans.[60]

### (fol. 130) Recepta de Ibernia

Recepit idem Bernardus de Sistre a Magistro Hugone de Calce, cancellario Dublinensi commissario suo et collectore arreyratgiorum dictorum fructuum primi anni et decime predicte in Ibernia, tam de arreyratgiis dictorum fructuum quam decime supradicte, nullo finito compoto cum eodem, xxv li. In quibus etiam decimis dominus rex habet partem suam.

Summa totalis omnium receptorum tam de arreragiorum dicte decime quadriennalis quam a dicto Magistro Hugone de Calce m<sup>l</sup> iiii<sup>c</sup> lv li. viii d. quadrans. Approbatum.

Pars camere vii<sup>c</sup> xxxii li. xiii s. viii d. dimidius quadrans.

Pars vero dicti domini regis vii<sup>c</sup> xvii li. iii s. viii d. et dimidius quadrans.

Summa universalis omnium receptorum predictorum quo ad cameram dicti domini nostri pape vii<sup>ml</sup> v<sup>c</sup> lxxvii li. xviii s. vii d. et dimidius quadrans et cl floreni et ii<sup>o</sup> anuli fracti.

(fol. 130<sup>v</sup>) Conclusio compoti dicti Magistri Ber-

---

[59] Over *vii<sup>c</sup> viii li. vi s. vii d. iii quadrantes et dimidius* deleted.
[60] Over *vii<sup>c</sup> xxi li. xiiii s. vii d. iii quadrantes et dimidius* deleted.

nardi de Sistre de omnibus per eum receptis tangentibus cameram predictam.

Summa totalis receptorum de denariis Beati Petri m$^l$ ix$^c$ xxxix li. viii d. obolus.

Summa totalis receptorum de censu annuo xl li. iii s. ix d.

Summa totalis receptorum de fructibus beneficiorum apud sedem apostolicam vacantium temporibus dominorum Johannis, Benedicti et Clementis VI$^{ti}$ m$^l$ m$^l$ ix$^c$ xxvii li. xii s. obolus.

Summa totalis receptorum de antiquis decimis in Ibernia et de pecuniis depositis penes socios Perusiorum vii$^c$ lxxvii li. iii s. iiii$^{or}$ d.

Summa totalis receptorum de pertinentibus ad Terram Sanctam lix li. vii s. viii$^o$ d. duo anuli.

Summa totalis receptorum pro redemptione votorum lxi li. vi s. viii d.

Summa totalis receptorum de fructibus beneficiorum que fuerunt Domini Itherii de Concoreto et de procuratoribus pro tempore suo debitis clxxxxiii li. xii s. v d.

Summa totalis receptorum de arreyragiis fructuum primi anni, videlicet partis contingentis dictam cameram viii$^c$ xlix li. ii s. viii d. i quadrans.

Summa totalis receptorum de arreyragiis decime quadriennalis, videlicet partis contingentis dictam cameram vii$^c$ xxi li. xiiii s. vii d. iii quadrantes et dimidius

Summa partis dictam cameram contingentis receptorum de arreyragiis dicte decime et fructuum predictorum in Ibernia levatorum xii li. x s.

Summa totalis omnium predictorum et per consequens totius compoti dicti Magistri Bernardi quo ad dictam cameram vii$^m$ v$^c$ lxxvii li. xviii s. vii d. medietas quadrantis ii anuli argenti et cl floreni. Approbatum.

(fol. 131) Littere super assignandis per dictum Bernardum de Sistre pecuniis cameram domini nostri pape contingentibus . . sociis Bardorum, Peruciorum et Azayalorum, societatum de Florentia

Benedictus episcopus servus servorum dei dilecto filio Magistro Bernardo Sistre, canonico ecclesie Beati Ilarii Pictavensis (St. Hilary, Poitiers) in partibus Anglie, Scotie, Wallie et Ibernie nostro et apostolice sedis nuntio salutem et apostolicam benedictionem.

Cum nos de tue circumspectionis industria plenam in domino fiduciam obtinentes te in partibus Anglie, Scotie, Wallie et Ibernie nostrum et apostolice sedis nuntium commissis ibidem tibi diversis negotiis nos et ecclesiam Romanam tangentibus duxerimus deputandum, volumus et discretioni tue per apostolica scripta mandamus quatenus omnes pecunias quas te nostro et ecclesie predicte nomine colligere et recipere in partibus contingerit supradictis dilectis filiis . . Bardorum, Peruciorum et Azayalorum societatum mercatoribus Florentinis, cuilibet videlicet societatum predictarum mercatoribus partem de qua expedire cognoveris, assignare procures per eosdem mercatores post modum infra certos terminos de quibus cum eis conveneris seu quos sibi prefixens

exsolvendas nostre camere ac etiam assignandas, faciens super singulis assignationibus huiusmodi duo confici consimilia puta instrumenta, quorum, altero penes te retento, reliquam ad eandem procures cameram destinare, ipsam certificaturus nichilominus super hiis et etiam de quibus proventibus collecte fuerint dicte pecunie clare, particulariter et distincte.[61]

Datum apud Pontem Sorgie Avinionensis diocesis idus Septembris pontificatus nostri anno primo.[62]

Littere super assignandum etiam dictis pecuniis . . sociis societatis Albertorum de Florentia

Benedictus episcopus servus servorum dei dilecto filio Bernardo Sistre canonico ecclesie Beati Ilarii Pictavensis in partibus Anglie, Scotie, Wallie et Ibernie apostolice sedis nuntio salutem et apostolicam benedictionem.

Quamvis tibi quod pecunias per te nomine nostre camere in partibus Anglie, Scotie, Wallie et Ibernie ad quas te nuper destinavimus colligendas dilectis filiis . . Bardorum, Peruciorum et Azayalorum societatum mercatoribus Florentinis assignares per eos postmodum predicte camere persolvendas per nostras certi tenoris litteras dederimus in mandatis, volumus tamen quod partem pecuniarum ipsarum de qua tibi videbitur expedire dilectis filiis . . mercatoribus Florentinis societatis Albertorum assignes et tradas sub modis et formis quibus (fol. 131$^v$) iuxta tenorem litterarum predictarum debes aliis prefatis mercatoribus assignare, utilitatem et securitatem prefate camere tam super hiis quam aliis sicut honeste et commode poteris nichilominus concurrendo.[63]

Datum Avinione iii$^e$ idus Octobris pontificatus nostri anno primo.[64]

Sequntur assignata, missa et soluta dicte camere per dictum Bernardum de Sistre a tempore quo primo fuit in officio dicte nuntiationis usque ad obitum dicti Domini Benedicti pape XII de pecuniis supradictis.

Anno domini M$^o$ CCC$^o$ XXXVI$^o$ et die xxv mensis Martii tradidit et assignavit dictus Bernardus Henrico Acursii et Richardo Serii, sociis societatis Peruciorum de Florentia in Anglia commorantibus, vii$^c$ xii$^{cim}$ li. xi s. iiii$^{or}$ d., pro quibus promiserunt assignare dicte camere infra primam diem mensis Maii tunc proximam instantem iiii$^{m l}$ vi$^c$ xxii fl. auri et ii d. sterlingorum, quolibet floreno pro iii s. i d. sterlingorum computato, prout per H. Moreti notarium fuit incartatum, quam assignationem compleverunt prout constat per bullam acquitantie datam apud Pontem Sorgie Avinionensis diocesis x kalendas Septembris pontificatus dicti Domini Benedicti anno secundo.[65]

---

[61] In the margin opposite this item is noted: *de curia A. Fabri.*
[62] 13 September 1335.
[63] In the margin opposite this item is noted: *de curia Jo. Courteys.*
[64] 13 October 1335.
[65] 23 August 1336. The following is noted in the margin

Item iiii[a] die mensis Aprilis anno domini M[o] CCC[o] XXXVI[o] assignavit dictus Bernardus Lotho Corbucii et Raynerio Griffi, sociis Azayalorum Florentie, ii[c] li. sterlingorum, pro quibus, singulis florenis ut supra pro iii s. i d. sterlingorum computatis, promiserunt solvere et assignare dicte camere infra terminum predictum m[l] ii[c] lxxxxvii fl. auri et xi d. sterlingorum, prout per dictum notarium extitit incartatum, que quidam assignatio facta fuit, prout patet per bullam aquitantie datam apud Pontem Sorgie x[o] kalendas Septembris pontificatus ⟨anno⟩ predicto.[66]

Item quinta die mensis Aprilis anno quo supra assignavit dictus Bernardus Galeatio de Uzzano et Francisco de Castillongio, sociis societatis Albertorum de Florentia, iii[c] xxvii li. viii[o] s. iiii d. sterlingorum, pro quibus, ut supra singulis florenis pro iii s. i d. sterlingorum computatis, promiserunt[67] (fol. 132)[68] solvere et assignare dicte camere termino supradicto ii[m][l] c xx[ti] iii fl. ii s. v d. sterlingorum, prout per dictum H. Moreti notarium incartatum, de qua quidem assignatione subsequenter per eos facta constat per bullam aquitantie datum loco, die et pontificatu predictis.

Item predicta quinta die Aprilis anno quo supra assignavit idem Bernardus Bartholomeo de Bardis pro se et aliis sociis societatis Bardorum de Florentia recipienti ii[c] lx[a] li. sterlingorum, pro quibus promisit solvere et assignare dicte camere infra xv dies post presentationem instrumenti per dictum Hugonem Moreti notarium super huiusmodi assignatione confecti m[l] vi[c] lxxxvi fl. auri et xviii[o] d. sterlingorum, singulis florenis pro iii s. i[o] d. sterlingorum ut supra computatis. Que quidem solutio et assignatio facte fuerunt, prout patet per bullam equitantie datam loco, die et pontificatu predictis.[69]

Item anno domini M[o] CCC[o] XXXVI[o] et viii[a] die mensis Decembris idem Bernardus assignavit Loto Corbucii de societate Azayalorum de Florentia et Galeatio de Uzzano de societate Albertorum et Johanni Baroncelli de socitate Peruciorum de Florentia cuilibet ipsorum ii[c] xx[ti] i li. xvii s. vi d. sterlingorum, et subsequenter in crastino assignavit plus Roberto de Enfangatis de societate Bardorum de Florentia ii[c] xx[ti] i li. xvii s. vi d. sterlingorum, summa totalis viii[c] lxxx[a] vii li. x s. sterlingorum. Pro qua summa totali predicti mercatores, videlicet quilibet pro quarta parte, promiserunt solvere et assignare predicte camere infra festum purificationis Beate Marie tunc proxime venturum vi[m][l] fl. auri, singulis pro xxxv d. et obolo sterlingorum computatis,

prout per dictum H. Moreti notarium tunc extitit incartatum. Quam solutionem dicti socii compleverunt, prout patet per bullam aquitantie datam Avinione xiiii[o] kalendas Aprilis pontificatus dicti Domini Benedicti anno tertio.[70]

Item anno domini M[o] CCC[o] XXX[o] VII[o] mense Aprilis dictus Bernardus assignavit dicte camere in certis aurifrisiis et sargiis factis et emptis in Anglia pro persona dicti domini pape cxxviii[o] li. xvi s. ii d. sterlingorum, prout patet per bullam aquitantie datam Avinione viii[o] kalendas Maii pontificatus dicti Domini Benedicti pape XII anno tertio.[71]

Summa totalis pagine m[l] ii[c] lxxvi li. vi s. ii d. sterlingorum.

(fol. 132[v]) Adhuc assignata per dictum Bernardum de Sistre et soluta camere supradicte.

Item anno domini millesimo CCC[o] XXX[o] VIII[o] mense Aprilis dictus Bernardus misit dicte camere per dominum fratrem Bertrandum[71a] Ostensem (Ostia) episcopum lxxxx[a] vii li. x s. sterlingorum, quas et quos idem dominus episcopus pro dicto Bernardo solvit dicte camere in vi[c] fl. auri, singulis pro iii s. iii d. sterlingorum computatis, prout patet per bullam aquitantie datam Avinione vi kalendas Augusti pontificatus dicti Domini Benedicti anno quarto.[72]

Item anno quo supra et ix[a] die Augusti dictus Bernardus assignavit . . sociis Bardorum de Florentia vi[c] li. sterlingorum, pro quibus solverunt dicte camere iii[m][l] vi[c] fl. auri, computatis singulis pro iii s. iiii[or] d. sterlingorum, prout patet per bullam aquitantie datam Avinione xvii[o] kalendas Januarii pontificatus dicti Domini Benedicti pape XII anno iiii[o].[73]

Item anno predicto et xiii[a] die mensis Augusti dictus Bernardus assignavit Galeatio de Uzzano de societate Albertorum de Florentia iiii[c] li. sterlingorum, pro quibus fecit assignari et solvi dicte camere m[l] m[l] iiii[c] fl. auri, singulis pro iii s. iiii[or] d. sterlingorum computatis, sicut patet per bullam aquitantie datam Avinione xii kalendas Februarii pontificatus dicti Domini Benedicti anno quinto.[74]

Item anno domini M[o] CCC[o] XXXIX[o] et die xix[a] Octobris idem Bernardus assignavit Philippo de Bardis socio dicte societatis Bardorum de Florentia iiii[c] li. xii d. sterlingorum, pro quibus promisit solvere et assignare

---

opposite this item: *docet per litteras apostolicas sub data Pontsorgie x kalendas Septembris anno secundo.*

[66] In the margin opposite this item: *Docet per litteras apostolicas sub data Pontissorgie x kalendas Septembris anno secundo.*

[67] In the margin opposite this item: *Docet per litteras apostolicas sub eadem data.* At the foot of the page: *Summa totalis pagine m[l] ii[c] xxx[a] ix li. xix s. viii[o] d.*

[68] At the top of the folio is the caption: *Assignata per dictum Bernardum de Sistre camere domini nostri pape.*

[69] In the margin opposite this item: *Docet per litteras apostolicas sub eadem data.*

[70] 19 March 1337. In the margin opposite this entry: *Docet per litteras apostolicas sub data Avinione xiiii kalendas Aprilis anno tertio.*

[71] 24 April 1337. In the margin opposite this entry: *Docet per litteras apostolicas sub data Avinione viii kalendas Maii anno tertio.*

[71a] *Bernardum*, MS.

[72] 27 July 1338. In the margin opposite this item: *Docet per litteras apostolicas sub data Avinione vi kalendas Augusti anno quarto.*

[73] 16 December 1338. In the margin opposite this item: *Docet per litteras apostolicas sub data Avinione xvii kalendas Januarii anno quarto.*

[74] 21 January 1339. In the margin opposite this item: *Docet per litteras apostolicas sub data Avinione xii kalendas Februarii anno quinto.*

dicte camere in festo Sancti Andree [75] tunc proximo subsequenti ii$^{m1}$ vi$^c$ lxvii fl. auri, quolibet pro iii s. sterlingorum computato, prout per Robertum de Redyng' notarium fuit tunc temporis incartatum, de qua quidem summa subsequenter fuit dicte camere satisfactum, prout patet per bullam aquitantie datam Avinione idus Aprilis pontificatus dicti Domini Benedicti anno septimo.[76]

Item anno domini M$^o$ CCC$^o$ XL$^o$ et die viii$^a$ Martii idem Bernardus assignavit Maro Baldonineri, socio Bonacursorum de Florentia m$^l$ li. sterlingorum, pro quibus idem Marus solvit et assignavit per manus sociorum suorum, sicut cum dicto Bernardo convenerit, predicte camere vi$^{m1}$ iii$^c$ xv fl. auri et duos solidos sterlingorum, computatis singulis florenis pro iii s. ii d. sterlingorum, prout patet per bullam aquitantie datam Avinione idus Aprilis pontificatus dicti Domini Benedicti pape XII anno septimo.[77]

Summa totalis pagine ii$^{m1}$ cccc$^{te}$ lxxxx$^a$ vii li. xi s. sterlingorum.

(fol. 133) Adhuc assignata per dictum Magistrum Bernardum camere domini nostri pape

Item anno domini M$^o$ CCC$^o$ XL$^o$ II$^o$ et die xviii Aprilis idem Magister Bernardus assignavit Mariodyno Gerii Rogerii, socio societatis dictorum Acchiliorum de Florentia v$^{cl}$ li. sterlingorum, pro quibus promisit nomine suo et sociorum suorum assignare et solvere dicte camere in festo nativitatis Sancte Johannis baptiste [78] tunc proximo futuro, iiii$^{or}$ florenis singulis pro xxxiii d. sterlingorum computatis, prout per Johannem Bonaura notarium fuit incartatum, nec tunc potuit dictum cambium facere cum sociis Bardorum et Peruchiorum qui non bene respondebant nec cum sociis Albertorum qui tunc non erant in Anglia. Docet per litteras apostolicas sub data Avinione v kalendas Martii anno Domini Clementis primo.[79]

Item dictus Magister Bernardus de mandato dicti domini pape fecit fieri in Anglia xiiii$^{cim}$ sargias coloris viridis pro camera sua, quas sibi misit anno domini M$^o$ CCC$^o$ XXXVIII$^o$ circa mensem Junii per Dominum Raymundum de Cornato tunc camerarium domini cardinalis de Montefavensi,[80] pro quibus et pro pannis in quibus fuerunt involute solvit in universo xvi li. viii s. sterlingorum. Constat.[81]

Summa totalis pagine v$^c$ lxvi li. viii s. sterlingorum.

(fol. 133$^v$) Littere super assignandis pecuniis dicte camere post obitum dicti Domini Benedicti pape XII Jacobo Malabayla mercatori Astensi vel procuratoribus suis usque ad summam mille librarum sterlingorum vel ampliorem

Clemens episcopus servus servorum dei dilecto filio Bernardo de Sistre, archidiacono Cantuariensi, in partibus Anglie, Scotie, Ibernie et Wallie apostolice sedis nuntio, salutem et apostolicam benedictionem.

Cum dilectus filius, Jacobus Malabayla, mercator et civis Astensis, cum camera nostra sub certis obligationibus, modis et pactis convenerit summam mille librarum sterlingorum argenti, vel ampliorem, per te de pecuniis cameram ipsam contingentibus a te collectis eidem mercatori vel procuratoribus suis assignandam in Anglia prefate camere infra certum terminum post assignationem predictum, volumus et tue discretioni per apostolica scripta mandamus quatenus summam huiusmodi mille librarum sterlingorum argenti vel maiorem, si penes te de pecuniis antedictis habeas, memorato mercatori aut eius procuratoribus studeas assignare, faciendo super eadem assignatione confici publicum instrumentum quod ad prefatam cameram mox assignatione facta huiusmodi non differas destinare, ipsam certificaturus nichilominus super hiis clare, particulariter et distincte. Nos autem prefato mercatori a te recipiendi pecuniam huiusmodi teque quitandi per se vel eosdem procuratores de hiis que inde sibi duxeris assignanda concedimus per alias litteras potestatem.

Datum Avinione idus Octobris pontificatus nostri anno primo.[82] De curia certamus.

Tenor vero aliarum litterarum predictarum talis est Clemens episcopus servus servorum dei dilecto filio Jacobo Malabayla, mercatori et civi Astensi, salutem et apostolicam benedictionem.

Cum tu cum camera nostra sub certis obligationibus, modis et pactis conveneris summam m$^l$ librarum sterlingorum argenti vel ampliorem per dilectum filium Bernardum de Sistre, archidiaconum Cantuariensem in partibus Anglie, Scotie, Ibernie et Wallie apostolice sedis nuntium, de pecuniis cameram ipsam contingentibus per ipsum collectis tibi vel procuratoribus tuis in illis partibus assignandam infra certum terminum post assignationem predictam camere solvere supradicte, nosque predicto nuntio demus per alias litteras in mandatis ut eamdem summam vel ampliorem, si penes se de pecuniis antedictis habeat, tibi vel eisdem procuratoribus studeat assignare, tibi per te vel eosdem procuratores recipiendi ab eodem nuntio dictam summam vel etiam ampliorem, ipsumque de hiis que inde tibi seu eisdem procuratoribus duxerit assignanda quitandi et absolvendi concedimus tenore presentium facultatem.

Datum Avinione idus Octobris pontificatus nostri anno primo. De curia certamus.

(fol. 134) Assignata per dictum Bernardum de Sistre . . procuratori dicti Jacobi Malabayla virtute dictarum litterarum

Anno dominice incarnationis millesimo CCC$^o$ XLII$^{do}$ secundum computationem ecclesie Anglicane et die prima Martii dictus Bernardus de Sistre pretextu dic-

---

[75] 30 November.
[76] 13 April 1341. In the margin opposite this item: *Docet per litteras apostolicas sub data Avinione idus Aprilis anno septimo.*
[77] In the margin opposite this item the same note is repeated.
[78] 24 June.
[79] The last sentence is in the margin. 25 February 1343.
[80] Bertrand de Montfavence, deacon of S. Maria in Aquiro.
[81] In the margin.

[82] 15 October 1342.

tarum litterarum assignavit Petro Provanixe, mercatori procuratori dicti Jacobi Malabayla nomine suo recipiendo, m^l iiii^c lviii^o li. vi s. viii d. sterlingorum, de quibus dictus Petrus nomine dicti Jacobi et camere predicte, auctoritate dictarum litterarum, ipsum Bernardum quitavit, promittens pro ipsis infra quindenam resurrexionis dominice tunc proximam sequentem assignare et solvere dicte camere x^{m1} fl. auri, singulis pro xxxv d. sterlingorum computatis, prout constat [83] per instrumentum publicum manu Johannis Bonaura notarium confectum. Docet per litteras apostolicas Domini Clementis de mandato et de traditione per instrumentum confectum manu Johannis Bonaura clerici Nemausensis (Nîmes) diocesis publici apostolica auctoritate notarii, confectum Londoniis anno ab incarnatione domini M^o CCC^o XLII die prima Martii.[84]

Summa pagine m^l iiii^c lviii li. vi s. viii d.

Item assignavit Dominus Raymundus Pelegrini [85] camere dicti domini nostri pape de pecuniis receptis per dictum Dominum Bernardum de Sistre ii^c lxxxxi li. xiii s. iiii^or d. in ii^{m1} fl., computatis singulis pro xxxv d. sterlingorum.

Summa totalis omnium assignatorum predicte camere per dictum Magistrum Bernardum vii^{m1} iii^c xxx li. iiii^or s. x d. sterlingorum in xlvi^{m1} iii^c x fl. et cxlv li. xi s. ii d. sterlingorum.

(fol. 135) [86] Sequitur de expensis per dictum Magistrum Bernardum factis pretextu officii sibi commisse nuntiationis

Primo cuidam scriptori transcribenti compota Domini Itherii Avinionie de mandato domini thesaurarii ii fl. et dimidium

Item in xlii diebus quibus venit de Avinionia usque Londoniam, nec propter infirmitatem equorum et maris ventis contrariis et retardatum transitum velocius venire potuit, cum vii^{tem} equis et xii personis, videlicet per diem ii fl. et dimidium, cv fl.

Item pro transitu maris xxvii fl. et dimidium.

Item expendit in septem septimanis quibus stetit eundo de Londonia in Scotiam ad dominum regem et sequendo eum et redeundo Londoniam ultra stipendia sua liii fl.

Item pro transcribendis registris taxationum beneficiorum ad decimam xvii s. v d. sterlingorum.

Item pro loqueriis hospitiorum in civitate Londoniensi per octo annos quibus fuit, excepto uno quartario anni, in officio predicto, computato etiam dicto quartario, quia pro salvandis scripturis et memorandis ad dictum officium pertinentibus executores eiusdem Magistri Bernardi habuerunt per dictum quartarium hospitia in quibus inhabitabat necessario retinere, lviii li. viii^o s. viii d.

Item pro diversis nuntiis missis pro executionibus et monitionibus tam arrayragiorum quam aliorum debitorum camere dicti domini nostri pape et litteris super eis factis portandis ad omnes prelatos et eorum officiales et aliis diversis personis tam Anglie quam Wallie per totum ipsius nuntiationis dicti Magistri Bernardi vii li.

Item die viii Aprilis anno XXXVI^o cuidam clerico familiari suo portanti primo litteras cambii dominis pape et eius camerario et thesaurario de m^l v^c li. sterlingorum pro expensis suis usque ad curiam xvii s. sterlingorum.

Item pro diversis aliis clericis vayletis et familiaribus suis portantibus litteras cambiorum factorum per dictum Bernardum camere predicte pro expensis suis viii^o li.

Item pro pergamenis, papiris, et incausto, expensis pro officio suo predicto de toto tempore nuntiationis sue, et pro regestris inde factis xl s.

Item quia incontinenti post mortem dicti Magistri Bernardi quidam servientes et alie gentes vicecomitus Londonie, virtute cuiusdam mandati domini regis Anglie, ceperunt omnia bona camere predicte que tunc erant in custodia executorum predicti Magistri Bernardi, asserentes dictum Magistrum Bernardum teneri dicto domino regi in magnis pecuniarum quantitatibus pro arreragiis decime quadriennalis, olim per felicis recordationis Dominum Johannem papam XXII^{dum} in Anglia imposite, et fructuum primi anni beneficiorum olim ad quadriennium in Anglia vacantium, per dictum Dominum Johannem reservatorum, et dicto domino regi pro medietate concessorum per eundem Magistrum Bernardum levatorum, asserentes etiam quod dictus Magister Bernardus tenebatur dicto domino regi in certa pecunie quantitate pro decima sibi debita pro decanatu Lincolnie de tempore [87] (fol. 135^v) quo fuit in manibus dicti domini nostri pape, licet ad predicta minime teneretur, executores predicti, ne bona predicta sic capta remanerent et perderentur, pro deliberatione ipsorum expenderunt tam in pecuniis datis quam aliis serviciis factis dictis servientibus et gentibus ac aliis baronibus et clericis de scacario dicti domini regis x li. et plus.

Item tam pro predicti quam pro recuperandis aliis bonis dicte camere que erant in manibus aliquorum debitorum personarum ecclesiasticarum qui dicto Magistro Bernardo erant obligati et pro ordinandis compotis reddendis predicte camere, ac etiam pro informando domino nuntio qui nunc est super hiis et aliis que debebantur eidem camere, fuerunt dicti executores post mortem dicti Magistri Bernardi in Anglia per tres menses et amplius cum uno notario et duobus famulis et expenderunt in universo xi li. v s.

Item pro expensis dictorum executorum veniendo de Anglia et stando in curia reddendis compotis dicte camere lx fl.

Summa totalis pagine xxi li. v s. et lx fl.

Summa totalis omnium expensorum per dictum

---

[83] *consta*, MS.
[84] The last sentence is in the margin.
[85] Bernard's immediate successor.
[86] Folio 134^v is blank.

[87] At the foot of folio 135: *Summa totalis pagine lxxvii li. iii s. i d. et clxxxvii fl.*

Magistrum Bernardum clxxxvii fl. et lxxxxviii li. viii s. i d. sterlingorum.

Summa summarum omnium solutorum, assignatorum et expensorum per dictum Magistrum Bernardum vii^{m1} cxxxvi li. xix s. vii d. sterlingorum et clxxxvii fl.

(fol. 138) [88] Computus de receptis, assignatis et expensis factis per quondam Dominum Bernardum Sistre, olim in partibus Anglie apostolice sedis nuntium, redditum per Dominum Pontium de Puteo Uticensis(?) (Uzès) diocesis executorem testamenti prefati Domini Bernardi a die x Martii anno XXXV usque ad xviii die Junii anno XLIII°.

Et primo computat recepisse die x mensis Octobris anno domini M° CCC° XXXV°, qua dictus Dominus Bernardus eundo in Angliam recessit de curia, a domino Johanne nunc Avinionensi episcopo, tunc felicis recordationis Domini Benedicti pape XII thesaurario, cl fl. auri.

Item computat recepisse de arreragiis denarii Beati Petri dimissis per Dominum Itherium de Concoreto predecessorem suum et de dictis denariis pro anno XXXV° vii^c lxv li. xviii s. viii d. obolum.

Item computat recepisse de dictis denariis Sancti Petri pro anno XXXVI° clxxvii li. xviii s. viii d.

Item computat recepisse de dictis denariis pro anno XXXVII° cxcix li. xviii s. viii d.

Item computat recepisse de dictis denariis pro anno XXXVIII° cxcviii° li. xviii s. viii d.

Item computat recepisse de dictis denariis pro anno XXXIX° cxcix li. xviii s. viii d.

Item computat recepisse de dictis denariis pro anno XL° clvi li. xiii s. iiii d.

Item computat recepisse de dictis denariis pro anno XLI° clii li. xviii s. viii d.

(fol. 138^v) Item computat recepisse de dictis denariis pro anno XLII° lxxxvi li. iii s. iiii d.

Summa universalis omnium receptorum per dictum Dominum Bernardum tam de arreragiis denariorum Beati Petri quam de eisdem denariis pro annis XXXV°, XXXVI°, XXXVII°, XXXVIII, XXXIX, XL°, XLI° et XLII° m ix° xxxviii li. viii s. viii d. obolus sterlingorum.

Sequitur de censibus ecclesie Romane debitis

Et primo computat recepisse de arreragiis dictorum censuum una cum solutis pro anno XXXV° viii li. v s. xi d.

Item computat recepisse de dicto censu pro anno XXXVI° iiii li. xv s.

Item computat recepisse de dictis censibus in anno XXXVII° iiii li. xv s.

Item computat recepisse de dictis censibus pro anno XXXVIII° iiii li. xv s.

Item computat recepisse de dictis censibus pro anno XXXIX° iiii li. xv s.

Item computat recepisse de dictis censibus pro anno XL° iiii li. xv s.

Item computat recepisse de dictis censibus pro anno XLI° iiii li. i s. viii d.

Item computat recepisse de dictis censibus pro anno XLII° iiii li. i s. ii d.

Summa universalis receptorum de dictis censibus ab anno XXXV° usque ad annum XLII° unacum arreragiis xl li. iii s. ix d.

(fol. 139) Item computat recepisse pro legatis factis in subsidium Terre Sancte lix li. vii s. viii d. ii anuli de argento deaurati.

Item de redemptione et dispensatione votorum lxi li. vi s. viii d.

Item computat recepisse de fructibus beneficiorum que vacaverunt tempore felicis recordationis Domini Johannis [89] pape XXII ccccxxiiii li. xviii s. viii d.

Item computat recepisse de hiis que debebantur bone memorie domino cardinali de Mortuomari de beneficiis suis que habebat in Anglia lxxxiii li. xiii s. iiii d.

Item computat recepisse de fructibus beneficiorum que vacaverunt in toto tempore felicis recordationis Domini Benedicti pape XII pro toto tempore vacationis ipsorum ii^m ii^c lxxviii li. vii s. viii d. obolum.

Item computat recepisse de fructibus primi anni quorumdam beneficiorum collatorum per dominum nostrum Clementem papam sextum cxl li. xiii s. iiii d.

Item computat recepisse ex compositione facta super antiquissimis decimis debitis in Ybernia ante creationem Domini Clementis pape V clii li.

Item computat recepisse a sociis de societate Peruciorum, quos Dominus Itherius in recessu suo de Anglia dimiserat loco, et que dicti socii receperant tam de arreragiis quadriennalis decime concesse per Dominum [90] Johannem et fructuum beneficiorum concessorum ad quadriennium per dictum Dominum Johannem et de denariis Beati Petri ac censuum (fol. 139^v) Romane ecclesie debitorum et de legatis in subsidium Terre Sancte vi^c xxv li. iii s. iiii d.

Item quia dictus Itherius in restis camere per ipsum traditis quam archidiaconus Cantuariensis debebat xliiii m.; item de prebenda de Preston' in ecclesia Sarisberiensi xxv m., item rector ecclesie de Blakesleye (Blockley) Vigorniensis diocesis lv m., item precentor ecclesie Lincolniensis xx m. debebant, de quibus summis fuerat eidem Domino Itherio satisfactum, prout clare probatum fuit, computat recepisse de fructibus beneficiorum dicti Domini Itherii summas predictas que ascendunt ad lxxxix li. xv s. xi d.

Item computat recepisse de fructibus ecclesie de Adhurbury (Adderbury) Lincolniensis diocesis qua privatus erat quia non fuerat promotus infra tempus a novo statutum [91] lxxxi li. xiii s. iiii d.

---

[88] Folios 136 to 137^v inclusive are blank.

[89] Follows *Clementis* deleted by a line.

[90] Followed by *nostrum* deleted by a line.

[91] The extension is doubtful.

Item computat recepisse de procurationibus eidem Domino Itherio debitis xxii li. iii s. ii d.

Item computat [92] recepisse pro fructibus quorumdam beneficiorum que vacaverunt infra quadriennium quo fuit facta concessio per felicis recordationis Dominum Johannem papam XXII domino regi Anglie de quibus rex remisit partem suam pro parte cameram contingente solum xliii li. iii s. iiii d.

Item cum de fructibus beneficiorum que infra dictum quadriennium vacaverunt fuissent recepte m vi^c viii li. xii s., fuit de ipsis iuxta formam concessionis apostolice facta divisio inter cameram et dictum dominum regem, videlicet quod dictus dominus rex habuit medietatem et camera aliam medietatem que est viii^c iiii li. vi s.

(fol. 140) Item cum felicis recordationis Dominus Johannes papa XXII imposuisset in regnis Anglie et Ybernie decimas ad quadriennium et concessisset domino regi Anglie medietatem dictarum decimarum, computat recepisse de arreragiis dictarum dimissis per Dominum Itherium m iiii^c lv li. viii d. quadrantem, que summa erat inter dictum dominum regem et cameram dividenda, sed quia dictus dominus rex remisit de parte ipsum contingente certis personis [93] x li. vi s. viii d., erat pars camere vii^c xxxii li. xiii s. viii d. et octava pars unius denarii.

Summa ab alia summa citra v^m v^c xcix li. vi s. i d. obolus sterlingorum. Approbatum.

Summa universalis omnium receptorum predictorum vii^m v^c lxxvii li. xviii s. vii d. et octava pars unius denarii sterlingorum. cl fl., ii anuli fracti. Approbatum.

(fol. 140^v) Secuntur expense facte per dictum Dominum Bernardum

Et primo computat solvisse pro transcribendo restis dimissis per Dominum Itherium ii fl. medietatem.

Item computat expendisse in xlii diebus quibus stetit in eundo de Avinionia usque ad Londonias cum vii equitaturis et xii personis cv fl.

Item pro transitu maris xxvii fl. cum dimidio.

Item computat expendisse in septem septimanis quibus stetit eundo et redeundo in Scotiam liii fl.

Item pro transcribendis regestris [94] taxationum beneficiorum xvii s. v d.

Item pro loquerio [95] viii annorum hospitiorum [96] in Londoniis lviii li. viii s. viii d.

Item pro diversis nuntiis missis tam ad Romanam curiam quam ad diversas partes regni pro diversis executionibus faciendis in toto tempore suo xv li. xvii s.

Item dicunt se dedisse et solvisse diversis officialibus regiis pro bonis tam camere quam suis expediendis et dearrestandis que post mortem dicti quondam Domini Bernardi fuerant arrestata xxi li. v s.

Item pro pergameno, papiro, incausto pro toto tempore suo pro libris officii et regestris faciendis xl s.

Item pro expensis dicti executoris veniendo et stando in curia lx fl.

Summa dictarum expensarum xcviii li. viii s. i d. sterlingorum, ccxlviii fl. Approbatum.

(fol. 141) Secuntur assignationes facte camere pro parte et nomine dicti Domini quondam Bernardi

Computat camere assignasse et fidem facerunt per litteras apostolicas in xv assignationibus vii^m iii^c xxx li. iiii s. x d. sterlingorum, in xlvii^m iii^c x fl. cxlv li. xi s. ii d. sterlingorum.

Summa universalis omnium assignatorum et expensorum predictorum vii^m iiii^c xxviii li. xii s. xi d., ccxlviii fl. auri, ii anuli fracti medio valore. Approbatum.

Quibus deductis de summa receptorum predictorum restat quod debent cxlix li. v s. viii d. et octava sterlingorum. Approbatum.

Dictis autem executoribus debentur xcviii fl. Approbatum.

(fol. 146) [97] Hec sunt arreragia que debebantur in Anglia camere domini nostri pape tempore obitus venerabilis viri Domini Bernardi de Sistre quondam eiusdem domini nostri pape et apostolice sedis in Anglia nuntii, qui obiit die xviii mensis Junii anno domini M^o CCC^o XLIII^o pontificatus sanctissimi patris Domini Clementis pape VI^ti anno secundo.

Et primo de denariis Beati Petri

### Roffensis

Archidiaconus Roffensis debet pro anno domini M^o CCC^o XLII^o cxii s. sterlingorum.

### Londoniensis

Archidiaconus Middessexie in ecclesia Londoniensi debet de arreragiis dictorum denariorum pro tempore quod fuit ante annum domini M CCCXXXV^tum xi li. xvii s. iii d. obolum.

Archidiaconus Essexie in dicta ecclesia debet de anno XLII^o cx s.

### Cicestrensis

Dominus episcopus Cicestrensis debet pro annis domini M^o CCC^o XLI^o et XLII^o pro singulis viii^o li. summa xvi li.

### Wyntoniensis

Archidiaconus Wyntoniensis debet pro resta de anno domini M^o CCC^o XLII^o vi li. x s.

Archidiaconus Surreye in ecclesia Wyntoniensi debet pro anno XLII^o cxiii s. iiii^or d.

### Saresbiriensis

Dominus episcopus Saresbiriensis debet pro annis

---

[92] computant, MS.

[93] remisit repeated MS.

[94] Followed by a word of four letters deleted by a line.

[95] Followed by octo deleted by a line.

[96] Followed by s deleted by a line.

[97] Folios 141^v to 145^v inclusive are blank.

domini M° CCC° XL°, XLI° et XLII° pro quolibet xvii
li. summa li li.

### Herefordensis

Dominus episcopus Herefordensis debet pro anno
domini M° CCC° XLII° vi li.

### Elyensis

Archidiaconus Elyensis debet pro anno XLII° c s.

### Norwycensis

Dominus episcopus Norwycensis debet pro anno
domini M° CCC° XXVI° quo Norwycensi sede vacante
asserit spiritualia episcopatus sui fuisse in manu domini
Cantuariensis archiepiscopi xxi li. x ⟨s.⟩ Item pro annis
domini M° CCC° XLI° et XLII° xliii li. summa lxiiii°r
li. x s.

(fol. 146ᵛ) Adhuc de denariis Beati Petri

### Lincolniensis

Executores testamenti Domini Henrici quondam Lincolniensis episcopi debent resta dictorum denariorum de
anno domini M° CCC° XL° xxvi li. xiii s. iiii°r d.

Item dominus episcopus Lincolniensis qui nunc est
debet pro resta dictorum denariorum de anno XLII°
xxi li.

Dominus archiepiscopus Eboracensis debet pro anno
domini M° CCCXLII° xi li. x s.

Summa totalis dictorum arreragiorum denariorum
Beati Petri ccxxxvi li. v s. xi d. obolus.

Secuntur arreragia census annui Romane ecclesie
debiti

### Roffensis

Prior de Tonebrugg' debet pro annis domini millesimo
CCC° XLI° et XLII° xxvi s. viii° d.

Abbatissa Sancte Clare Londonie debet pro una libra
cere de anno domini M° CCC° XLII° vi d.

Summa arreragiorum dicti census xxvii s. ii d.

Secuntur arreragia fructuum primi anni quorundam
beneficiorum per felicis recordationis Dominum Johannem papam XXIIᵈᵘᵐ ad iiii°r annos olim in Anglia
reservatorum

De primo anno dicte reservationis

### Dunelmensis

De prebenda de Rivers in ecclesia de Aukland (Auckland) debentur l s.

(fol. 147) De secundo anno dicte reservationis

### Londoniensis

De ecclesie de Stocham alias de Dedham debentur xxv
m., tamen lis pendet inter quendam priorem qui eam
sicut sibi appropriatam possidet et quendam impetrantem qui composuit pro fructibus supradictis.

### Eboracensis

De libera capella regis de Tikhille (Tickhill) debentur
pro parte regia quia camere satisfactum est xii m.

De tertio anno dicte reservationis

### Cantuariensis

De vicaria de Apoldre (Appledore) debentur xxᵗⁱ s.

De quarto anno dicte reservationis

### Wellensis

De decanatu Wellensi debentur lxxiii li. iii s. iii d.
obolus, de quibus debentur domino regi l li. et camere
xxiii li. iii s. iii d. obolus, quia residuum est solutum.

De ecclesia de Bereford (Broford in Dulverton?)
iii m.

Arreragia dimissa per . . subcollectores dictorum fructuum in diocesi Wygorniensi de quibus nondum est
satisfactum

### Wygorniensis

De archidiaconatu Wygorniensi quem habuit Magister
Johannes de Carleton' archidiaconus eiusdem.

De ecclesia de Bredon' taxata ad xxvi li. xiii s.
iiii°r d. quam habuit Magister Johannes Trillek' rector
eiusdem.

De ecclesia de Neweton' (Newton) taxata ad x m.
quam habuit Dominus Johannes Luthebourgh' rector
eiusdem, nunc vero rector ecclesie de Rodmerton'
(Rodmarton).

De prebenda de Auste iuxta Westbury (Aust) taxata
ad x m. quam habuit Magister Johannes Trillek' prebendarius eiusdem.

De decanatu de Westbury iuxta Bristoll' taxata ad
x li. vi s. viii d. quem habuit Dominus Adam de Ayleston' tunc decanus eiusdem.

De ecclesia de Doderhull' (Dodderhill) taxata ad
xxviii li. appropriata priori et capitulo ecclesie Wygorniensis.

(fol. 147ᵛ) Sequitur de quibusdam beneficiis recelatis

### Lincolniensis

De ecclesia de Bolewyk' (Bulwick) debentur xl s.

De vicaria de Cropry (Cropredy) debentur xiiii m.

Secuntur arreragia quadriennalis decime per dictum
Dominum Johannem papam in Anglia imposite

### Londoniensis

Prior Sancti Bartholomey Londoniensis, subcollector
dicte decime in civitate et diocesi Londoniensi deputatus,
fuit dimissus in arreragiis per Dominum Itherium de
Concoreto, olim sedis apostolice in Anglia nuntium, in
xxxviii li. xviii s. i d. quadrante, de quibus solvit
Domino Bernardo de Sistre, successori dicti Domini
Itherii, xxvii li. xiiii s. v d. obolum quadrantem. Restant
xi li. iii s. vii d. obolus quas et quos dicit levari non

posse quia temporalia de quibus solebant solvi alienata dicuntur. Nichil certum.

### Cicestrensis

Vicarius de Dalyngton' (Dallington) debet pro toto quadriennio xxxiiii$^{or}$ s. viii d.

Item vicarius de Stymenefeld' (Ninfield) debet pro toto quadriennio xxxiiii$^{or}$ s. viii d.

Item vicarius de Esshebourn' (Easebourne) debet pro dicto quadriennio liii s. iiii d.

Summa vi li. ii s. viii d.

Allegant quod propter paupertatem solvere non possunt, licet multi processus facti fuerint contra ipsos.

### Wyntoniensis

Prior de Bermundeseye Wyntoniensis diocesis, subcollector dicte decime in archidiaconatu Surreye dicte diocesis deputatus, fuit dimissus in arreragiis per dictum Dominum Itherium in ix li. xiii s., de quibus solvit dicto Domino Bernardo de Sistre vi li. xviii s. viii d. Restant liiii$^{or}$ s. iiii d. quos abbas de Waltham Londoniensis diocesis solvere debebat eidem priori pro certis bonis que habet in diocesi Wyntoniensi, sed tamen solvit, ut dicitur, deciman illorum subcollectoribus in diocesi Londoniensi. Nichil certum.

### Norwycensis

Prior Norwycensis, subcollector dicte decime in civitate et diocesi Norwycensi deputatus, fuit dimissus in arreragiis per dictum Dominum Itherium in xx li. vii s. ix d. sterlingorum, de quibus nichil solvit pro eo quia, ut dixit, levari non possunt, nam bona pro quibus dicta decima solvebatur pro parte devenerunt ad manus laycorum et pro parte sunt talia beneficia ultra vi m. ad decimam non taxata et ea obtinentes non sunt alibi beneficiati. Nichil certum.

### (fol. 148) Lincolniensis

Abbas monasterii de Eynesham Lincolniensis diocesis, subcollectore dicte decimo in certa parte dicte diocesis deputatus, fuit dimissus in arreragiis per dictum Dominum Itherium in ccclvii li. vii s. v d. obolo quadrante, de quibus tam dictus abbas quam alii pro beneficiis que habebant in collecta sua solverunt dicto Domino Bernardo de Sistre cccliii li. iiii s. i d. obolum, et sic restabant iiii$^{or}$ li. iii s. iiii d. quadrans, de quibus allocatis sibi lxvi s. viii d. pro tribus ecclesiis infra taxam vi m. taxatis et xvi s. pro monialibus minorissis extra Alegate Londonie (St. Mary without Aldgate); restant quos debet viii d. quad.

### Elyensis

Prior Elyensis, subcollector dicte decime in civitate et diocesi Elyensi deputatus, fuit dimissus in arreragiis per dictum Dominum Itherium in lxiiii$^{or}$ li. xiii d., de quibus solvit dicto Domino Bernardo de Sistre liiii li. xiii s. i d. Restant ix li. viii s. que et qui non possunt

levari quia, ut dicit, aliqua bona de et pro quibus certa summa solvi debebat venerant ad manus laycorum, et aliqui asserunt habere bona in dicta diocesi que non repperiuntur ibidem, licet in registro sint taxata, et aliqui habentes ibidem sunt excepti a prestatione decime. Nichil certum.

### Wygorniensis

Prior Maioris Malvernie Wygorniensis diocesis, subcollector dicte decime in certa parte dicte diocesis deputatus, fuit dimissus in arreragiis per dictum Dominum Itherium in xxxviii s. vi d. obolo, quos dixit levari non posse propter paupertatem monalium de Recolf' (Cook Hill) que ad solutionem illorum tenentur, et per regem est eis remissum. Nichil certum.

### Bangorensis

Abbas de Bardeseye (Bardsey) Bangorensis diocesis, subcollector dicte decime in civitate et diocesi Bangorensi deputatus, fuit dimissus in arreragiis per dictum Dominum Itherium in iiii$^{or}$ li. x s. iiii d., que levari non possunt, ut dixit, pro eo quia quidam prioratus pro quo debent solvi penitus est destructus. Nichil certum.

### Assavensis

Abbas de Vallecrucis Assavensis diocesis, subcollector dicte decimo in civitate et diocesi Assavensi pro primis tribus annis eiusdem deputatus, fuit dimissus in arreragiis per dictum Dominum Itherium in xxiiii$^{or}$ li. xix s. viii d. et obolo, de quibus solvit dicto domino Bernardo de Sistre xx li.; debet iiii$^{or}$ li. xix s. viii d. obolum, pro quibus multi processus facti sunt contra eum.

### (fol. 148$^v$) Herefordensis

Dominus Herefordensis episcopus, collector dicte decime in suis civitate et diocesi deputatus, fuit dimissus in arreragiis per dictum Dominum Itherium in xxiiii li. xviii s. vii d., de quibus nichil potest levari, ut dixit, quia sunt multa ibidem beneficia de quibus decimam levari non potest, et quia in registro secundum quod dicta summa exigitur est error notorius, ut dixit, in pluribus locis visis, tamen dictis erroribus adhuc repperitur debere iii s. iii d. quadrantem.

### Bathoniensis et Wellensis

Prior Tantonie (Taunton) Bathoniensis et Wellensis diocesis, subcollector dicte decime in archidiaconatu Tanton' deputatus, fuit dimissus in arreragiis per dictum Dominum Itherium in xxiiii li. x s. vi d., de quibus dictus Dominus Bernardus de Sistre recepit tam a dicto priore quam ab aliis pro bonis que habebant in sua collecta solventibus xxi li. xvi s. vii d. quibus deductis restant liii s. x d. de quibus debent defalcari pro decima portionis quam magister et fratres hospitalis Sancti Bartholomei Londonie in Smethefeld percipiunt in ecclesia de Henton' Sancti Georgii (Hinton St. George) dicte diocesis, qui alias dicuntur fuisse ymmunes per quoscunque collectores decime in Anglia reputati, cum pro sustentatione pauperum ibidem confluentium dicta portio fuerit assignata, xxvi s viii d., quibus defalcatis restant quos debet adhuc xxvii s. ii d.

### Exoniensis

Abbas de Hartiland (Hartland) Exoniensis diocesis, subcollector dicte decime in certa parte dicte diocesis deputatus, fuit dimissus in arreragiis per dictum dominum Itherium in xxi li. viii s., que, ut dixit, levari non possunt, pro eo quia de minutis beneficiis debentur ultra vi marcas non taxatis secundum decimam, nec ea obtinentes habent plura beneficia, et de quodam hospitali pauperum leprosorum. Nichil certum.

### Eboracensis

Prior de Kirkham Eboracensis diocesis, subcollector dicte decime in archidiaconatu Estredyng' deputatis, fuit dimissus in arreragiis per dictum Dominum Itherium in lxx li. vii s. iii d., de quibus dictus Dominus Bernardus de Sistre recepit tam a dicto priore quam ab aliis pro eo solventibus lxii li. iiii s. vii d. obolum. Et secundum compotum dicto Domino Bernardo per ipsum redditum nichil plus debebat, allocatis sibi x li. xv s. xi d. obolo quos et quas dixit se solvisse sociis Bardorum de Florentia. Nichil certum.

Abbas monasterii Beate Marie Eboracensis, subcollector dicte decime in alia certa parte dicte diocesis deputatus, fuit dimissus in arreragiis per dictum Dominum Itherium in ccclxxxxvi li. iiii s. ix d. obolo quadrate, de quibus solvit dicto Domino Bernardo de Sistre lxxix li. xvi s. ix d. Et secundum computum suum et novam taxam nichil plus debebat; secundum tamen antiquam taxam debet adhuc residuum. Nichil secundum novam taxam.

### (fol. 149) Dunelmensis

Prior ecclesie Dunelmensis, subcollector dicte decime in civitate et diocesi Dunelmensi deputatus, fuit dimissus in arreragiis per dictum Dominum Itherium in xlv li. xiii s. viii d. obolo quadrante, de quibus solvit dicto Domino Bernardo de Sistre xii li. vii s. obolum quadrantem. Residuum rex levari non permittit, quia temporalia episcopatus Dunelmensis pro quibus debetur fuerunt tunc temporis in manibus suis. Habetur breve regium super hoc. Nichil certum.

Secuntur arreragia debita pro fructibus quorundam beneficiorum que apud sedem apostolicam diversis temporibus vacaverunt, et primo de illis que xviii° et xix° annis felicis recordationis Domini Johannis pape XXII^di vacaverunt

### Eboracensis

De prebenda de Dunham in ecclesia Beate Marie Suthwell' Eboracensis diocesis tunc vacante per obitum Magistri Thome de Sancto Albano, cuius beneficia fuerunt per dictum Dominum Johannem reservata, debentur x s.

De ecclesia de Misterton' dicte diocesis que fuit dicti Magistri Thome de Sancto Albano et que vacavit etiam tempore Domini Benedicti pape XII, facta compositione cum Magistro Thoma Sampson qui eam occupat clxiii li. vi s. viii d.

Sequitur de beneficiis que vacaverunt apud dictam sedem tempore dicti Domini Benedicti quorum fructus ipse pro toto tempore vacationis reservaverat

### Eboracensis

De prebenda de Thorp' (Thorpe) in ecclesia Houden' (Howden) Eboracensis diocesis olim vacante per obitum Domini Arnaldi Sancti Eustachii diaconi cardinalis debet Magister Johannes Wawayn pro resta fructuum eiusdem de anno XL° xii li.

### Lincolniensis

De ecclesia de Henlee (Henley) Lincolniensis diocesis debet vicarius de Menstr' (Minster) Cantuariensis diocesis pro arreragiis dicte ecclesie prout est obligatus v m.

De ecclesia de Uffyngton' (Uffington) Lincolniensis diocesis, que vacavit per resignationem factam in Romana curia per procuratorem Magistri Nicholay de Ros, debet Magister Willelmus Bacheler, canonicus Lincolniensis, et Richardus de Pulham respondere pro fructibus eiusdem de anno XLIII°.

### (fol. 149^v) Cantuariensis

De ecclesia de Ludenham (Luddenham) Cantuariensis diocesis, olim vacante per obitum Magistri Johannis Pikardi qui obiit in Romana curia, debent pro fructibus eiusdem, olim tempore vacationis eiusdem perceptis per Dominum Johannem de Thenham quondam, Willelmus Moche et Johannes Peper, executores testamenti dicti Domini Johannis de Thenham, xi m.

### Saresbiriensis

Prebenda de Hulle Deverel (Hill Deverill) in ecclesia Sancti Petri de Herghtredebur' (Heytesbury) Saresbiriensis diocesis vacavit per obitum Domini Johannis de Pinibus, capellani Domini R. Sancte Marie Nove diaconi cardinalis, debet Magister Willelmus de Saxeby, canonicus eiusdem, pro resta fructuum dicte prebende de primo anno vacationis eiusdem qui fuit anno domini M° CCC° XL viii li. iii s. iiii d.

Item Dominus Nicolaus de Caldecote, vicarius dicte prebende, debet pro resta fructuum eiusdem de anno domini M° CCC° XLI° iiii^or li.

### Norwycensis

Ecclesia de Palagrave (Palgrave) vacavit per mortem

Domini Johannis de Ulseby, qui in Romana curia obiit, et dictus Bernardus de Sistre recepit fructus eiusdem pro annis domini Mᵒ CCCᵒ XXXIXᵒ et XLᵒ. Postea quidam intrusus in dicta ecclesia occupavit eos pro anno XLIᵒ qui de ipsis debet respondere. Nichil certum.

Sequitur de fructibus beneficiorum apud sedem apostolicam vacantium per Dominum Clementem papam VI reservatorum

Primo de beneficiis que fuerunt Domini Bertrandi de Montefavense Sancte Marie in Aquiro diaconi cardinalis

### Eboracensis

De fructibus ecclesie de Brantyngham (Brantingham) Eboracensis diocesis que fuit dicti domini cardinalis Dominus Johannes Petri, rector ecclesie de Wersill' (Worsall) dicte diocesis, debet respondere qui eos habet ad firmam.

### Wyntoniensis

De fructibus ecclesie de Wymbledon' (Wimbledon) Wyntoniensis diocesis, que fuit dicti domini cardinalis, collate Domino Ademaro titulo Sancte Anastasie presbytero cardinali, debet respondere firmarius eiusdem.

(fol. 150) De fructibus beneficiorum que fuerunt Magistri Richardi de Haveryng', sedis apostolici capellani

### Conventrensis et Lychefeldensis

De fructibus archidiaconatus Cestrie in ecclesia Lychefeldensi et prebende sibi annexe in eadem ecclesia, collati Domino P. episcopo Sabinensi, debentur adhuc xxvi li. xiii s. iiiiᵒʳ d.

Item Magister Johannes de Cravene officialis dicti archidiaconatus debet respondere de fructibus dicti archidiaconatus perceptis a fine primi anni vacationis eiusdem usque ad diem viii kalendas Junii[98] anno domini Mᵒ CCCᵒ XLIIᵒ, qua collatus fuit dicto domino cardinali.

### Herefordensis

De fructibus precentorie Herefordensis debet Magister Egidius de Stanford, canonicus Herefordensis, ultra x marchas solutas Domino Bernardo de Sistre xl m.

### Saresbiriensis

De fructibus prebende de Bisshopeston' (Bishopstone) in ecclesia Saresbiriensi debentur per Magistros Petrum de Inkepenn' et Ricardum de Pilesgate, qui eos habuerunt, x li.

De fructibus aliorum beneficiorum apud dictam sedem vacantium

### Cantuariensis

De ecclesia de Bisshopesbourn' (Bishopsbourne) que vacavit per obitum Magistri Willelmi de Shelton', qui obiit in curia, et fuit collata domini cardinali de Gardia[99]

nichil est receptum per dictum Dominum Bernardum de Sistre.

### Eboracensis

De decanatu Eboracensi, qui vacavit per consecrationem Domini Willelmi archiepiscopi Eboracensis et fuit collatus domino . . cardinali Petragoricensi,[100] nichil est receptum per dictum Dominum Bernardum de Sistre, quia per bullam fuit scriptum quod dominus noster contentabatur et quod procuratores dicti domini Petragoricensis non impedirentur[101] circa receptionem primorum fructuum dicti decanatus.

De ecclesia de Brumpton' (Brompton) Eboracensis diocesis, vacante per consecrationem Domini Thome episcopi Lincolniensis, debentur pro resta fructuum eiusdem per priorem et conventum de Maldon' (Malton) dicte diocesis obligatos xxiii li. vi s. viii d.

### Saresbiriensis

De fructibus dicte prebende de Hulle Deverel, que vacavit ex causa predicta, debet Johannes Radulphi, nunc rector ecclesie de Eastry Cantuariensis diocesis, qui pro eis composuit et solvere debuit in festo translationis Beati Thome[102] proximo preterito vi li. xiii s. iiii d.

### (fol. 150ᵛ) Exoniensis

De fructibus prebende quam Ubertus de Zannetis tenuit in ecclesia de Credynton' (Crediton) Exoniensis diocesis, que vacavit apud sedem apostolicam, debet Willelmus Clamle, nunc prebendarius eiusdem, solvere in instanti festo purificationis Beate Marie c s.

Pro fructibus ecclesie de Stalham Norwycensis diocesis, que vacavit quia Magister Thomas Fastolf', olim rector eiusdem, fuit assecutus archidiaconatum Norwycensem ex gratia dicte sedis, debet Dominus Robertus de Killingholm, qui eos recepit, xxiii li. vi s. viii d.

De fructibus ecclesie de Whepsted (Whepstead) dicte diocesis, que vacavit quia Magister Johannes de Whitcherche, olim rector eiusdem, fuit adeptus ex gratia dicte sedis archidiaconatum Wilchir' (Wilts) in ecclesia Saresbiriensi, debentur per Symonem de Burnyngham ipsius rectorem.

Arreragia que debentur per subcollectores fructuum beneficiorum per dictum Dominum Johannem papam XXII ad quadriennium reservatorum et pro quibusdam aliis beneficiis dicto quadriennio vacantibus

### Eboracensis

Abbas monasterii Beate Marie Eboracensis, subcollector dictorum fructuum in diocesi et provincia Eboracensi, debet de resta compoti sui, allocatis sibi allocandis, x s. vi d.

---

[98] 25 May.
[99] Gerard Domar, priest of S. Sabina.

[100] Elias Talleyrand de Périgueux, priest of S. Pietro in Vincoli.
[101] *impediretur*, MS.
[102] 7 July.

### Herefordensis

De thesauraria ecclesie Herefordensis, que vacavit dicto quadriennio, debentur, ultra xl s. quos Magister Richardus de Sydenhale thesaurarius dicte ecclesie solvit [103] dicto Domino Bernardo de Sistre, xvii m.

### (fol. 151) De Hibernia

Arreragia debita de quibusdam antiquis decimis in Ibernia impositis

Magister Guillelmus Lescapon, canonicus Dublinensis, debet de compoto per ipsum facto cum Domino Bernardo de Sistre de arreragiis decimarum sexennalium et biennalium per felicis recordationis Dominum Bonifacium papam VIII in Ibernia impositarum de tempore quo fuit subcollector dictarum decimarum, ultra xxxii li. quas solvit dicto Domino Bernardo, xxii li. iii s. ix d. i quadrantem.

De aliis vero que debentur et que recepta sunt in Hibernia Magister Hugo de Calce, cancellarius Dublinensis, computavit cum dicto Domino Bernardo de Sistre, prout in quodam instrumento et in duabus cedulis infrascriptis continetur, cuius instrumenti tenor talis est.

In dei nomine amen. Anno ab incarnatione eiusdem Mᵒ CCCXXXVIᵒ, die septima mensis Maii, indictione quarta, pontificatus sanctissimi patris et domini nostri, Domini Benedicti divina providentia pape XII, anno secundo, noverint universi quod in presentia venerabilis et circumspecti viri, Domini Bernardi Sistre, canonici ecclesie Beati Ilarii Pictavensis (Poitiers), domini nostri pape et apostolice sedis in Anglia, Scotia, Wallia et Hibernia nuntii, ac mei, notarii publici, et testium subscriptorum, constitutur personaliter discretus vir, Magister Hugo de Calce, canonicus Dublinensis, receptor tam decime quadriennalis per felicis recordationis Dominum Johannem papam XXII^dum in partibus Hibernie dudum imposite quam fructuum beneficiorum ecclesiasticorum primi anni per dictum quadriennium in Hibernia vacantium sub certa forma reservatorum per Dominum Itherium de Concoreto, olim apostolice sedis in predictis partibus Anglie, Scotie, Wallie et Hibernie nuntium et collectorem principalem, precessorem dicti Domini Bernardi, et ⟨per⟩ eiusdem Domini Itherii patentes litteras deputatus, rationem et computum ⟨rendet⟩ tam pro se quam Domino Adam de Lymbergh, canonico Londoniensi, ac Domino Fratre Rogero Outlawe, priore domus Sancti Johannis Jerosolimitanis in Hibernia, suis in hac parte successive collegis, de omnibus et singulis receptis, liberatis et expensis per eos, alium seu alios vice et nomine camere dicti domini nostri pape de decima, fructibus, arreragiis et legatis predictis a quarta die mensis Decembris anno domini Mᵒ CCCᵒ XXXIᵒ usque ad decimam septimam diem mensis Februarii anno ab incarnatione domini Mᵒ CCCᵒ

XXXVᵒ. ⟨Computat⟩ universaliter recepisse mille quingentas quadraginta sex libras quinque solidos octo denarios sterlingorum, de quibus, de precepto predicti Domini Itherii et per ipsius patentes litteras eis facto liberaverunt et realiter assignaverant thesaurario domini regis Anglie in Hibernia noningentas quatuorviginti (fol. 151ᵛ) decem et septem libras sex solidos duos denarios. Item assignaverunt Byndo Mathy mercatori, recipienti dicti Domini Itherii nomine et mandato, ducentas libras sterlingorum, prout per aquietantias inde factas sub manu publica, quas penes nos ex causa retinendas duximus, evidenter apparet. Et sic remanent adhuc penes dictum priorem et Magistrum Hugonem predictos de levatis et receptis per eos de decima et fructibus et aliis supradictis trescente quadraginta octo libre decem et novem solidi sex denarii sterlingorum, de quibus petit prefatus Magister Hugo eis allocari triginta sex libras sterlingorum, quas asseruit expendidisse pro expensis factis per eos in nuntiis missis et aliis necessariis ad officium pro collectione pecunie decime ac fructuum predictorum. Item petiit dictus Magister Hugo sibi allocari pro suis stipendiis de tempore supradicto in quo sunt quatuor anni et quinquaginta et quatuor dies, pro die qualibet xl denarii sterlingorum, ducentas quinquaginta duas libras sex solidos octo denarios sterlingorum, super quibus dictus dominus nuntius voluit quod supersederetur donec de ipsis per eundem de concensu dicti domini regis Anglie seu eius consilii aliud fuerit ordinatum; quas si allocari contingant restant adhuc in manibus domini prioris et Hugonis predictorum sexaginta libre duodecim solidi decem denarii sterlingorum, de quibus prefatus Magister Hugo petiit sibi et dictus dominus nuntius eidem unum vel plura publica eiusdem tenoris instrumenta per me notarium fieri infrascriptum, que dictus dominus nuntius concessit et voluit, sigillo sui officii roborari in testimonium premissorum.

Acta fuerunt hec Londonie in hospitio habitationis prefati domini nuntii anno, mense, die, indictione et pontificatu suprascriptis, presentibus discretis viris dominis Duranto Catherini, rectore ecclesie Sancti Salvatoris de Montillis (Montels) Magalonensis (Maguelonne) diocesis, Raymundo Pelegrini, canonico ecclesie Sancti Oudomarii (Saint Omer) Morinensis (Thérouanne) diocesis, et Magistro Petro Vaurelli, clerico diocesis Caturcensis (Cahors), testibus adhibitis ad premissa.

Et ego Hugo Moreti, clericus Engolismensis (Angoulême) publicus apostolica auctoritate notarius, premissis omnibus et singulis dum agerentur prout superius continetur una cum prenominatus testibus presens fui et ea de mandato dicti domini nuntii et ad requisitionem Magistri Hugonis prefati fideliter scripsi et publicavi et huic inde confecto publico instrumento subscripsi me manu propria et consuetum apposui signum meum.

---

[103] Followed by *mag* deleted by a line.

(fol. 152) Apud Kalros (Kilrush) xiiii die Februarii

anno domini M° CCC° XXXV° receptos decime quadriennalis in diversis provinciis

## Provincia Dublinensis

Dublinensis ccxxix li. vi s. quadrans.
Darensis (Kildare) xxxv li. xi s. iiii d.
Ossoriensis (Ossory) cxxxv li. xviii s. x d.
Fernensis (Ferns) lv li. xvii s.
Legh' (Leighlin) x li. xvii s. viii d.
    Summa totalis cccclxvii li. x s. x d. quadrans.

## Provincia Thuamensis (Tuam)

Clonford (Clonfert) vi li. iiii s. viii d.
Akadensis (Achonry) xxvii s. vi d.
Thuamensis xxviii li. vi s. viii d.
Duacensis (Kilmacduagh) lxx s.
Alladensis (Killala) xxvii s. i d.
    Summa totalis xl li. xv s. xi d.

## Provincia Ardmacensis (Armagh)

Ardmachensis xxxix li. ix d.
Midensis (Meath) ccxxxiii li. iiii s. ii d. obolus quadrans.
Clogherensis (Clogher) lxxvii s. iiii d.
Drumorensis (Dromore) xxxv s. obolus quadrans.
Derensis (Derry) xxxviii s. vii d.
Tirbrinensis (Kilmore) xxx s. vii d.
Conerensis (Connor) vii li. v s. vii d. obolus.
Rathbotensis (Raphoe) xii li. xvi s. viii d.
Cluanensis (Clonmacnois) xiii s. iiiior d.
Dunensis (Down) iiii li. xv s. v d. obolus.
Ardikadensis (Ardagh) xii s.
    Summa totalis cccvii li. ix s. vii d. obolus.

## Provincia Cassellensis (Cashel)

Lysmor' (Lismore) xlix li. viii s.
Cork' viii li. xviii s. viii d.
Lymerensis (Limerick) liiii li. ii s. vi d.
Cassellensis xvii li. iiii s.
Clonensis (Cloyne) lx li. xii s. xi d. obolus.
Waterfordensis (Waterford) ix s. iiii d.
    Summa totalis c iiiixx x li. xv s. v d. obolus.
    Summa omnium summarum predictarum ml vi li. xi s. x d. quad.
    Recepta de fructibus

## Provincia Dublinensis

Diocesis Dublinensis cxlviii li. xiii s. iiii d.
Darensis xxiii li. v s. viii d.
Ossoriensis xxxii li. vi s. viii d.
Legh' iiii li.
Fernensis vi d.
    Summa totalis ccxiiii li. v s. viii d.

## Provincia Ardmacensis

Diocesis Ardmacensis xviii li.

Midensis cxiiii li. viii s. viii d.
Conerensis vi li. xiii s. iiii d.
    Summa totalis cxxxix li. ii s.

## Provincia Cassellensis

Diocesis Lismorensis xl li.
Lymorensis xxxii li. vi s. v d. obolus.
Cork' xxii li. xiii s. iiii d.
    Summa totalis iiiixx xiiii li. xix s. ix d. obolus.
    Summa omnium particularium summarum fructuum predictorum ccccxlvii li. xvii s. v d. obolus.

(fol. 152v) Item computat de arreragiis antiquis et legatis Terre Sancte receptis iiiixx xi li. xvi s. iiii d. quadrans.

    Summa totalis omnium receptorum predictorum ml vc xlvi li. v s. viii d.

De quibus solutum est thesaurario domini regis Anglie in Hibernia ixc iiiixx xvii li. vi s. ii d.

Item Byndo Masthi iic li.

Item in aliis expensis circa collectionem decimarum et aliorum xxxvi li. xviii s. vi d. obolus.

    Summa summarum solutorum ml ccxxxiiii li. iiii s. viii d. ob.

Et sic remanent in manibus tam domini prioris quam Magistri Hugonis predictorum cccxii li. xi d. obolus.

De quibus consistunt in manibus domini prioris cxxvi li. ix s. v d. obolus quadrans.

Et in manibus dicti Magistri Hugonis c iiiixx v li. xi s. v d. obolus quadrans.

Et computat vadia domini prioris per tres annos, xl d. pro die, summa c iiiixx ii li.

Et sunt a retro predicta summa in manibus suis computata lv li. x s. vi d. obolus.

Et computat vadia Magistri Hugonis per quinque annos, xl d. pro die, summa ccciii li. vi s. viii d.

Et sunt a retro dicta summa in manu sua existente computata cxvii li. xv s. ii d. quadrans.

Et sic est summa in qua sunt a retro clxxiii li. v s. viii d. obolus quadrans.

De decima quadriennali

## Provincia Dublinensis

Dublinensis diocesis ascendit de claro per quadriennium ad summam cclxxvii li. xvii s. xi d. et tres partes i quadrantis., de quibus primo respondebatur de ccxxix li. vi s. quadrante, et sic remanet in arreragiis xlviii li. xi s. x d. obolus quadrans et tres partes i quadrantis.

Legh' ascendit de claro per quadriennium ad summan xxi li. viii s. viii d., de quibus fuit responsum de x li. xvii s. viii d., et sic remanet in arreragiis x li. xi s.

(fol. 153) Ossoriensis ascendit de claro per quadriennium ad summam cli li. xiiii s. ii d., de quibus fuit responsum de cxxxv li. xviii s. x d., et sic remanet in arreragiis xv li. xv s. iiii d.

Fernensis ascendit de claro per quadriennium ad

summam lvii li. xv s., de quibus respondebatur de lv li. xvii s., et sic remanebant xxxviii s.

Darensis ascendit de claro per quadriennium ad summan xliiii li. xvii s., de quibus respondebatur de xxxv li. xi s. iiii d., et sic remanebant ix li. v s. viii d.

Summa arreragiorum in provincia Dublinensi iiii$^{xx}$ vi li. xxii d. obolus quadrans et tres partes i quadrantis.

### Provincia Cassellensis

Cassellensis diocesis ascendit de claro ad summam per quadriennium xvii li. iiii s., de quibus plene fuit responsum.

Lismorensis [104] ascendit de claro ad summam per quadriennium iiii$^{xx}$ iii li. iiii d., de quibus primo fuit responsum de xlix li. viii s., et sic remanet in arreragiis xxxiii li. xii s. iiii d.

Waterfordensis ascendit ad summam cviii s., de quibus fuit responsum de ix s. iiii d., et sic remanent iiii li. xviii s. viii d.

Clonensis ascendit ad summam lx li. xii s. xi d., de quibus plene fuit responsum.

Lismorensis ascendit ad summam iiii$^{xx}$ ii li. xviii s. vi d., de quibus fuit responsum de liiii li. ii s. vi d., et sic remanebant in arreragiis xxviii li. xvi s.

Corkensis ascendit ad summam xix li. vi s., de quibus fuit responsum de viii li. xviii s. viii d., et sic remanet in arreragiis x li. viii s. iiii d.

Summa arreragiorum in provincia Cassellensi lxxvii li. xiii s. iiii d.

### Provincia Ardmacensis

Ardmacensis diocesis ascendit ad summam xxix li. ii s. ix d., de quibus fuit responsum de xxix li. ix d., et sic remanent ii s.

Midensis ascendit ad summam ccxl li. viii s. viii d. dimidius quadrantis, de quibus fuit responsum de ccxxxiii li. iiii s. ii d. obolus quadrans, et sic remanent in arreragiis vii li. iiii s. v d. quadrans dimidius quadrantis.

(fol. 153$^v$) Conerensis Durensis plene solverunt.

Cloherensis, Drummorensis, Derensis, Tirbrinensis, Rotbothensis, Cluanensis, Auchadensis non taxuntur et plene solverunt.

Summa totalis arreragiorum in provincia Ardmacensis vii li. vii s. v d. quadrans dimidius quadrantis.

### Provincia Tuamensis

Tuamensis diocesis ascendit ad summam xxxiii li. xiii s. iiii d., de quibus fuit responsum de xxviii li. vi s. viii d., et sic remanent vi li. vi s. viii d.

Alladensis ascendit ad summam xxxviii s. iii d., de quibus fuit responsum de xxvii s. i d., et sic remanent xi s. ii d.

Duassensis ascendit ad vii li. xvi s. x d., de quibus fuit responsum de lxx s., et sic remanent iiii li. vi s. x d.

---

[104] Probably should be Limorensis.

Achadensis ascendit ad xiii s., tamen fuit responsum de xxvii s. vi d.

Clonfortensis ascendit ad summam vi li. ii s., tamen fuit responsum de vi li. iiii s. viii d.

Summa totalis arreyragiorum dictarum provinciarum c iiii$^{xx}$ ii li. vii s. ii d. quadrans et quarta pars quadrantis.

(fol. 154) Recepta per Dominum Itherium de Concoreto vel suos comissarios de contentis in arreragiis per ipsum dimissis camere domini nostri pape de fructibus primi anni beneficiorum vacantium in Anglia per Dominum Johannem papam XXII$^{dum}$ ad quadriennium reservatorum.

De primo anno reservationis

Primo de ecclesia de Moteron (Mottram) c s.

Item de ecclesia de Homesworth' (Handsworth) vii li.

De secundo anno

De prebenda australi de Graham (Grantham) xv m.

De ecclesia de Hetherington' (Harrington) ii m. et dimidia.

De ecclesia de Mateshale (Mattishall) iiii$^{or}$ m. et dimidia.

De ecclesia de Roteleye (Ratley) dimidia m.

De tertio anno

De ecclesia de Bethelessangr' (Betteshanger) iiii m. et dimidia.

De vicaria de Leysseden' (Leysdown) dimidia m.

De archidiaconatu Cantuariensi xliiii$^{or}$ m.

De vicaria de Odemere (Udimore) i m.

De vicaria de Basyngestok' (Basingstoke) xii m.

De ecclesia de Merstham x m. et dimidia.

De ecclesia de Bynghamwell' (Beechamwell?) i m.

De ecclesia de Brauncestr' (Brancaster) xiii m.

De ecclesia de Okeryng' (Hockering) xv m.

De ecclesia de Themeltham (Thelnetham) xii m.

De ecclesia de Illegh' (Eleigh) xv m.

De ecclesia de Eton' iuxta Wyndesor' (Windsor) viii m.

De quarto anno

De ecclesia de Litleton' (Littleton) ii m.

De ecclesia de Herlawe (Harlow) x m.

De vicaria de Southmestr' (Southminster) v m.

De vicaria de Herlyngton' (Arlington) iiii$^{or}$ m.

De vicaria de Cokyng' (Cocking) ii m. xl d.

De vicaria de Glynde i s.

De prebenda de Hanefeld (Henfield) viii$^o$ m.

De ecclesia de Iwerk' (Ewhurst) xxv m.

De ecclesia de Henyton' (Hinton) viii m.

De ecclesia de Clanefeld (Clanfield) vi m.

De ecclesia de Wywode (Ringwood) 1 m.

De ecclesia de Piperdesclive (Clyffe Pypard) vii m. et dimidia.

(fol. 154$^v$) De vicaria de Somerford iii m. xl d.

De ecclesia de Wyhampton' (Witchampton) v m.

De ecclesia de Sutton' (Sutton Veney) xxx m.

De ecclesia de Dodyngton' (Doddington) xxvii m. et dimidia.

De ecclesia de Flamsted (Flamstead) i m.

De ecclesia de Hamerton' i m.

De ecclesia de Guniby (Gunby) vi m. et dimidia.

De ecclesia de Lodenham (Leadenham) xxv m.

De ecclesia de Bereford (Barford) v m.

De ecclesia de Crouston' (Croston) xxv m.

Summa totalis receptorum de arreragiis supradictis iiii$^c$ xxxix m.

Adhuc recepta per dictum Dominum Itherium de dimissis per eum in arreragiis.

De denariis Beati Petri

Ab archidiacono Middessexie in ecclesia Londoniensi c s.

De censu annuo

De abbatissa Sancte Clare Londoniensis pro anno XXXII° vi d.

De abbate de Cherteseye Wyntoniensis diocesis pro anno XXXIIII° viii s.

De abbate Sancti Edmundi Norwycensis diocesis pro dicto anno xiii s. iiii$^{or}$ d.

De abbate Sancti Albani Lincolniensis diocesis pro eodem anno xiii s. iiii d.

De decima quadriennali

De abbate monasterii de Burton, subcollectore dicte decime in certa parte Conventrensis et Lychfeldensis diocesis, cxxix li. vii s. vi d.

De archidiacono Totton' in ecclesia Exoniensi, subcollectore dicte decime in certa parte Exoniensis diocesis, iiii$^{or}$ li.

Recepta per dictum Dominum Itherium de quibusdam aliis beneficiis de quibus nullam in suis compotis fecerat mentionem

De prebenda de Preston' in ecclesia Saresbiriensi xxv m.

De ecclesia de Blokeleye (Blockley) Wygorniensi diocesis lv m.

De precentoria ecclesie Lincolniensis xx m.

Summa totalis ab alia summa citra iii$^c$ x m. ii s. viii d. sterlingorum.

(fol. 155) Preter predicta debet dictus Dominus Itherius per finem compotorum suorum ii$^c$ xxxvii li. xix s. xi d. sterlingorum.

Summa totalis debitorum per dictum Dominum Itherium vii$^c$ xlix m. et ii$^c$ xxxviii li. ii s. vii d., que ambe summe converse in libris valent vii$^c$ xxxvii li. ii s. vii d. sterlingorum.

De quibus recepit Dominus Bernardus de Sistre ab Henrico Acurcii et Richardi Gerii, sociis de societate Peruchiorum de Florentia, pro diversis pecuniis per ipsos receptis tam de arreyragiis quadriennalis decime quam fructuum primi anni beneficiorum vacantium ad quadriennium reservatorum quam etiam de denariis Beati Petri et census annui ecclesie Romane debiti ac de legatis factis in subsidium Terre Sancte vi$^c$xxv li. iii s. iiii$^{or}$ d.

Item recepit dictus Dominus Bernardus de fructibus et emolumentis archidiaconatus Londonie et ecclesie de Shordwych' (Shoreditch) dicto archidiaconatui annexe et prebende de Eldelond (Ealdland) in ecclesia Londoniensi et prebende de Farendon' (Faringdon) in ecclesia Saresbiriensi que fuerunt dicti Domini Itherii inter diversas solutiones lxxxix li. xv s. xi d.

Item recepit de fructibus ecclesie de Adburbury (Adderbury) Lincolniensis diocesis debitis pro tempore quo dictus Dominus Itherius, qui rector ipsius fuerat, privatus ea censebatur ipso iure cum infra annum non fecisset se ad sacros ordines promoveri lxxxi li. xiii s. iiii$^{or}$ d.

Item recepit dictus Dominus Bernardus de arreyragiis procurationum dicto Domino Itherio pro tempore more sue debitorum in diocesi et provincia Eboracensi xxii li. iii s. ii d.

Summa totalis receptorum de beneficiis et procurationibus suprascriptis clxxxxiii li. xii s. v d. sterlingorum.[105]

---

[105] Folios 154-155 are elongated and narrow, quite different from the format of the normal folio and also from that of the usual *compotus brevis*.

# ACCOUNTS OF HUGH PELEGRINI COLLECTOR FROM 1349 TO 1363

Vatican Archives, Collectorie 14, fols. 23 to 157ᵛ ¹

## FIRST ACCOUNT 1349-1358

(fol. 23) ² Rationes Domini Hugonis Pelegrini, collectoris Anglie, per ipsum camere apostolice reddite, de pecuniis et aliis quibuscumque causis per ipsum nomine dicte camere apostolice receptis, ac etiam solutis, assignatis et expensis ac etiam de restis dicte camere debitis, videlicet a die prima mensis Augusti anno domini Mᵒ CCCᵒ XLIXᵒ usque ad diem primam mensis Junii anno domini Mᵒ CCCᵒ LVIIIᵒ, prout in presenti compoto continetur.³

(fol. 24) ⁴ Hic est compotus Hugonis Pelegrini, sanctissimi in Christo patris et domini nostri, Domini Innocentii divina providentia pape VIᵗⁱ, ac sedis apostolice in partibus Anglie, Wallie et Hibernie nuntii deputati, de omnibus et singulis per eum, alium seu alios nomine dicte sedis receptis, liberatis, assignatis et expensis de quibuscumque obventionibus ad ecclesiam Romanam in dictis partibus qualitercumque spectantibus a prima die Augusti anno domini Mᵒ CCCⁿᵒ XLIXᵒ usque primum diem Junii anno eiusdem domini LVIIIᵒ

Recepte arreragiorum denarii Beati Petri dimissorum per Dominum Raymundum Pelegrini nuper nuntium sedis apostolice prefato Hugoni Pelegrini.⁵

Episcopus Herefordensis qui dimissus fuit in arreragiis de xviii l. pro denariis Beati Petri de annis domini Mᵒ CCCᵒ XLVIᵗᵒ, XLVIIᵒ et XLVIIIᵒ solvit xviii li.

Episcopus Lincolniensis qui tenebatur pro denariis predictis in iiiiˣˣ iiii li. de annis domini M CCC XLVII et XLVIII solvit iiiiˣˣ iiii li.

Archidiaconus Wyntoniensis qui tenebatur in xi li.

xiii s. iiii d. pro anno domini Mᵒ CCCᵐᵒ XLVIIIᵒ solvit xi li. xiii s. iiii d.

Episcopus Conventrensis qui tenebatur in x li. v s. pro eodem anno XLVIIIᵒ solvit x li. v s.

Episcopus Exoniensis que tenebatur in ix li. v s. pro eodem anno solvit ix li. v s.

Episcopus Bathoniensis qui tenebatur in xi li. v s. pro eodem anno solvit xi li. v s.

Summa receptorum dictorum arreragiorum denarii Beati Petri cxliiii li. viii s. iiii d. Approbatum.

(fol. 24ᵛ) Recepta arreragiorum annui census dimissorum per Dominum Raymundum Pelegrini

Prior Bodnyne Exoniensis diocesis qui tenebatur in ii s. pro anno domini Mᵒ CCCᵒ XLVIIIᵒ et dat annuatim ii s. solvit ii s.

Prior Karliolensis qui dat annuatim i m. et fuit in arreragiis pro anno predicto solvit xiii s. iiii d.

Abbas de Faveresham Cantuariensis diocesis qui dat annuatim i m. pro eodem anno solvit xiii s. iiii d.

Abbas Sancti Albani qui dat annuatim i m. et tenebatur pro dicto eodem anno solvit xiii s. iiii d.

Summa receptorum dictorum arreragiorum census ii li. ii s. Approbatum.

(fol. 25) Sequuntur recepte arreragiorum quorundam beneficiorum per dictum dominum dimissorum

### Cantuariensis

De prioratu de Folkeston' (Folkestone) confirmato Willelmo Medico in partem reste ii li.

Item de ecclesia de Saltwode (Saltwood), vacante per resignationem Magistri Ricardi de Sudbur', de qua fuit provisum Magistro Symoni de Sudbur', pro resta dimissa xxxiii li. vi s. viii d.

Item de ecclesia de Reyculvere (Reculver), unita mense archiepiscopi Cantuariensis, cvi li.

Item de ecclesia de Ryngesvode (Ringwold), de qua per resignationem Willelmi de Pekham fuit provisum Roberto de Pekham, x li. xiii s. iiii d.

### Botidonensis (London)

De ecclesia Beate Marie de Milkstrete (London), ratione subrogationis facte de Radulpho Thursteyn in iure quod competebat Roberto de Archerich', iiii li.

Item de ecclesia Onesden' (Hunsdon), de qua, vacante per obitum Johannis de M'ton', fuit provisum Johanni de Wethfold, ii li. xiii s. iiii d.

Item de prebenda de Tetenhale (Tottenhall, parish of St. Pancras) in ecclesia Londoniensi, de qua, vacante per obitum Johannis de Offord, fuit provisum Johanni de Carleton', vii li. ix s. ii d. Non plus quia per unum annum fuit in manu collectoris et plus levari non potuit.

---

¹ Brief extracts from this account have been printed by Theiner, *Vetera Monumenta Hibernorum*, pp. 145-147, 156.

² Folios 1 to 21ᵛ contain the accounts of the camera with the firms of Italian merchants which received deposits of the funds arising in England from the sexennial tenth imposed by the council of Lyons in 1274. I have edited them in *Financial Relations ... to 1327*, pp. 641-665. Folio 22 recto and verso is blank.

³ This statement is on the outside of the original cover of the account. It is the back of a papal bull, being the rough side of the parchment. A name, which seems to be Magolonensis, is scratched on the cover.

⁴ Folio 23ᵛ, the inside of the cover, is the face of the bull. A portion of the right side has been cut away in order to make the bull fit the account as a cover. Several words of each line are lost. The bull has been engrossed, but it was marked for correction in two places, and was doubtless discarded for that reason. It was addressed by Innocent VI to the archbishop of Dublin, the archdeacon of Figeac, and a third person whose name is lost. It was dated 11 December, but the pontifical year is lacking. It was an executory letter against William de Drayton who was opposing possession by William Roberti of a canonry and prebend with which he had been provided by Clement VI apparently in the church of Dublin.

⁵ *Denarii Beati Petri* is repeated in the margin.

Item de ecclesia de Hakeneye (Hackney), de qua, vacante per obitum Gaucelmi Johannis [6] cardinalis, fuit provisum Thome Dulay, xxxiii li. vi s. viii d.

Item de prebenda de Fynesbur' (Finsbury) in ecclesia Londoniensi, de qua, vacante per obitum Thome de Asteleye, fuit provisum Johanni Cook', xiii li. vi s. viii d.

Item de ecclesia de Stebenhethe (Stepney), de qua, vacante per obitum Gaucelmi Johannis cardinalis, fuit provisum Ricardo Same, xl li.

Summa pagine cclii li. xv s. x d. Approbatum.

(fol. 25ᵛ) Item de prebenda de Kentisshton' (Kentish Town) in ecclesia Londoniensi, de qua, vacante per obitum Henrici de Iddesworth', fuit provisum Rogero Holm, in partem v li.

## Cicestrensis

De prebenda de Ferring' in ecclesia Cicestrensi, de qua per resignationem Symonis Godwyn fuit provisum Johanni de Haddon', pro parte fructuum xxiii li.

Item de ecclesia [7] de Rusthyngton' (Rustington), de qua, vacante per obitum Johannis de Mideford, fuit provisum Symoni de Bredon, xv li.

## Wyntoniensis

De archidiaconatu Surreie, de quo, vacante per obitum Willelmi Inge, fuit provisum Ricardo Vaghan, iiiixx li.

Item de ecclesia de Westmues (West Meon), de qua, vacante per obitum Bernardi Cicestr', fuit Johanni de Remyngton' confirmata, xiiii li.

## Sarisbiriensis

De ecclesia de Kyvelee (Keevil), de qua, vacante per obitum Roberti de Wymble, fuit provisum Thome de Trumpessale, in partem solutionis reste dimisse x li. xiii s. iiii d.

Item de prebenda de Netherhaven' (Netheravon) in ecclesia Sarisbiriensi, de qua, vacante per consecrationem domini Willelmi Wyntoniensis episcopi, fuit provisum Stephano la Porte, pro resta dimissa iiii li. ix s. iiii d.

Item de prebenda de Swallveclyve (Swallowcliffe) in ecclesia collegiata de Hegherdeburg' (Heytesbury) per quam, vacantem per obitum Thome de Littleton', fuit provisum Roberto Bakere, in partem fructuum iii li. vi s. viii d.

Item de prebenda de Bedewynde (Bedwin) in ecclesia Sarisbiriensi, de qua per consecrationem Johannis episcopi Lincolniensis fuit provisum Johanni de Welburi', pro resta dimissa xxv li.

Item de prebenda de Stanton' Lincolniensis diocesis in ecclesia monialium de Wylton' (Wilton) Sarisbiriensis diocesis, de qua, vacante per resignationem Pauli de Montefloro, fuit provisum Willelmo Potence, xiii li. vi s. viii d.

Summa pagine c iiiixx xiii li. xvi s. Approbatum.

(fol. 26) Item de prebenda de Bere et Chermynstre (Charminster) in ecclesia Sarisbiriensi, de qua, vacante per mortem Willelmi de Warraco, fuit provisum Guidoni de Pestello, c li.

Item de ecclesia de Donton' (Downton), de qua, vacante per mortem domini cardinalis de Columpna, fuit provisum Johanni de Carleton, pro resta dimissa lx li.

Item de prebenda in ecclesia conventuali monialium Cheston' (Shaftesbury), de quia, per obitum Johannis de Littleton', fuit provisum Thome Willelmi, xiii li. vi s. viii d.

Item de ecclesia de Bisshopeston' (Bishopstone), de qua, vacante per assecutionem dignitatis in ecclesia Wellensi per Ricardum de Tormerton', fuit provisum Lamberto Paulesholte, xxi li. vi s. viii d.

Item de prebenda de Suthneton' (South Newnton), de qua, per obitum Thome de Astele, fuit provisum Thome Trellek', xx li.

## Exoniensis

De ecclesia de Wythel (Withiel), in qua fuit subrogatus Johannes Cas in iure quod competebat Gregorio Rudik, iiii li.

## Wygorniensis

De ecclesia de Suthneubold (Newbold Pacey) unita collegio aule regine Oxonie viii li. xiii s. iiii d.

Item de ecclesia de Overb' (Overbury) unita cum vacaverit priori Wigorniensi xvi li.

Item de ecclesia de Seggesberghe (Sedgeberrow), de qua, vacante per obitum Johannis de Bardwas, fuit provisum Johanni presbytero, vi li. xiii s. iiii d.

Item de ecclesia de Dolston Cantelove (Aston Cantlow) appropriata priori de Makestoke (Maxstoke) xlvi li. xiii s. iiii d.

## Bathoniensis et Wellensis

De prebenda de Tatton' alias Yatton' in ecclesia Wellensi, de qua, vacante per renuntiationem Alani de Comsburgh', fuit provisum Thome Trellek', pro resta dimissa x li.

Summa pagine cccvi li. xiii s. iiii d. Approbatum.

(fol. 26ᵛ) Item de prebenda de Withtlakerton' (White Lackington) in ecclesia Vellensi, de qua fuit de novo provisum Thome Hacluyt, pro resta dimissa xii li.

Item de prebenda de Wyvelescumbe (Wiveliscombe) in ecclesia Wellensi, de qua per resignationem Isvardi Gasky fuit provisum Johanni Derby, xxvi li. xiii s. iiii d.

Item de prebenda in ecclesia Wellensi, vacante per obitum Johannis Offord, de qua, cum vaccaret per consecrationem dicti Johannis vel alias, fuit provisum Willelmo de Bergeveny, in partem fructuum xiii li. vi s. viii d.

## Norwicensis

De archidiaconatu Sudburie, de quo, vacante per obitum Guillelmi de Zarewell', fuit provisum Henrico la

---

[6] Gaucelme, priest of Ss. Marcellino e Pietro.
[7] Follows *prebenda* deleted by a line.

Zouche, non taxatur et est modici valoris preter procurationes, ii li.

## Lincolniensis

De ecclesia de Steratton' (Sturton) iuxta Randeby (Ranby) unita per dyocesanum auctoritate apostolica, cum vacaret, xi li. xiii s. iiii d.

Item de ecclesia de Wambry (Wrawby) unita cum vacaret collegio scolarium aule de Clare Cantebrigie xxii li. xiii s. iiii d.

Item de ecclesia de Stanton' Harecourt (Stanton Harcourt), de qua⁸ fuit de novo provisum Roberto de Stonore, xx li.

Item de prebenda de Sutton' (Sutton cum Buckingham) in ecclesia Lincolniensi, de qua, quocumque modo vacaret, fuit provisum Thome de Brembre, xx li.

Item de resta prioratus de Cogges xiii s. iiii d.

Item de prebenda de Farendon' (Farndon) in ecclesia Lincolniensi, de qua, vacante per obitum Francisci de Ursinis, fuit provisum Thome de Badeby, in partem reste xl li.

Item de prebenda de Lidynton' (Liddington), quam Magister Johannes Offord obtinuit in ecclesia Lincolniensi, de qua, vacante per obitum eiusdem, fuit provisum Johanni Provane, xiiii li.; et non plus quia fuit per unum annum in manu collectoris et non potuit plus levari, deductis omnibus.

Summa pagine c iiiiˣˣ iii li. Approbatum.

(fol. 27) Item de prebenda de Luda (Louth) in ecclesia Lincolniensi, de qua per obitum Gaucelmi Johannis cardinalis fuit provisum Matheo de Urseley, xlvi li. xiii s. iiii d.

Item de ecclesia de Keteryng' (Kettering), in qua fuit subrogatus Johannes Wade in iure quod competebat Alano de Sithryngton', xxiii li. vi s. viii d.

Item de vicaria ecclesie de Kympton' (Kempston), de qua ex causa permutationis cum ecclesia de Dalyngton' (Dallington) fuit provisum Johanni Unwyn, ii li.

Item de ecclesia de Dalyngton', de qua ex causa permutationis cum vicaria de Kympston' fuit provisum Johanni Schorp', viii li. xiii s. iiii d.

Item de archidiaconatu Norhamptonie in ecclesia Lincolniensi de quo, vacante per obitum domini cardinalis Convenari,⁹ fuit provisum Rogero Newestot', liii li. vi s. viii d.; et non plus, quia licet fuisset dimissus in arreragiis in maiori summa, tamen medietas veri valoris, deductis procurationibus de quibus camera nichil percipit, non plus ascendit, ut constat per inquisitionem super hoc factam.

## Lichfeldensis

De ecclesia de Leek', de qua fuit de novo provisum Johanni de Holand, in partem reste iiii li. xiii s. iiii d.

Item de archidiaconatu Cestrensi, de quo per mortem domini cardinalis Hyspanie ¹⁰ fuit provisum Willelmo de Navesby, iiiiˣˣ xiii li. vi s. viii d.

Item de thesauraria Lichfeldensi, de qua per obitum Gaucelmi Johannis cardinalis fuit provisum Hugoni Pelegrini, xxxiii li. vi s. viii d.; et non plus quia fuit in manu collectoris in anno mortalitatis et plus levari non potuit.

Item de decanatu de quo fuit provisum Symoni de Bruseley xl li.

Item de prebenda de Langedon' (Longdon) in ecclesia Lichfeldensi, de qua de novo fuit provisum Umfredo de Hastang, in partem solutionis vi li. vi s. viii d.

Summa pagine cccxi li. xiii s. iiii d. Approbatum.

(fol. 27ᵛ) Item de ecclesia de Northworthym (Worthen) in patem solutionis reste iii li. ix s. viii d.

## Menevensis

De ecclesia de Rudbaston' (Rudbaxton), de que fuit provisum David Martini, x li. xiii s. iiii d.

## Eboracensis

De prebenda Wetewang' (Wetwang) in ecclesia Eboracensi, de qua per mortem Georgii de Salucis fuit provisum Hanibaldo cardinali,¹¹ in partem reste xxii li. ix s. Plus levari non potuit, eo quod dicta prebenda occupatur iure regio per Ricardum de Wynwik' et est prohibitum per regem, eo quod numquam dictus Hanibaldus ipsam prebendam obtinuit.

Item de ecclesia de Brayton' unita abbati monasterii Sancti Germani de Selby xxxiii li. vi s. viii d.

Item de ecclesia de Beek' (Leake), de qua per mortem cardinalis de Farges ¹² fuit provisum Hugoni de Wymondeswold xvii li. vi s. viii d.

Item de ecclesia de Hennyngburgh' (Hemingborough), de qua per obitum Gaucelmi cardinalis fuit provisum Alano de Suthendon', cvi li. xiii s. iiii d.

Item de prebenda de Driffield' in ecclesia Eboracensi, de qua per mortem Gaucelmi Johannis cardinalis fuit provisum Willelmo de Sancto Martiali, c li.

Item de prebenda quam Magister Adam de Eselbech' in ecclesia collegiata obtinuit, de qua fuit provisum Johanni Provan', xxxiii li. vi s. viii d.

Item de ecclesia de Brantingham, de qua per obitum cardinalis de Gardia ¹⁸ fuit provisum Edmundo de Hauekesgate, in partem reste xvii li.

## Dunelmensis

De ecclesia de Houghton' (Houghton-le-Spring), de qua fuit de novo provisum Willelmo de Dalton', l li.

Item de prebenda in ecclesia collegiata Langecestr' (Lanchester), de qua per obitum Maucellini Marmion' fuit provisum Johanni de Bourghton', iii li.

---

⁸ *quo*, MS.
⁹ John Raymond of Comminges, bishop of Porto.
¹⁰ Peter Gomez, bishop of Sabina.
¹¹ Anibaldus de Ceccano, bishop of Tusculum.
¹² Raymond de Farges, deacon of S. Maria Nuova.
¹⁸ Gerard Domar, priest of S. Sabina.

Summa pagine ccc iiii$^{xx}$ xvii li. v s. iiii d. Approbatum.[14]

(fol. 28) Summa totalis arreragiorem fructuum beneficiorum m vi$^c$ xlv li. iii s. x d. Approbatum.

Summa summarum omnium arreragiorem m vii$^c$ iiii$^{xx}$ xi li. xiiii s. ii d.

(fol. 29) [15] Sequuntur recepte denariorum Beati Petri [16] de anno domini millesimo CCC$^{mo}$ XLIX$^o$ de tempore suo per ipsum receptorum

Archidiaconus Cantuariensis solvit pro dicto anno XLIX$^o$ viii li.

Archidiaconus Roffensis v li. xii s.

Archidiaconus Colcestr' v li. x s.

Episcopus Cicestrensis viii li.

Archidiaconus Essexie v li. x s.

Archidiaconus Middelsexie v li. x s.

Archidiaconus Wyntoniensis xi li. xiii s. iiii d.

Archidiaconus Surreie v li. xiii s. iiii d.

Episcopus Sarisbiriensis xvii li.

Episcopus Bathoniensis et Wellensis xi li. v s.

Episcopus Exoniensis ix li. v s.

Archidiaconus Eliensis v li.

Episcopus Norwicensis xxi li. x s.

Episcopus Lincolniensis xlii li.

Episcopus Conventrensis et Lichfeldensis x li. v s.

Episcopus Herefordensis vi li.

Episcopus Wigorniensis x li. v s.

Archiepiscopus Eboracensis xi li. x s.

Summa c iiii$^{xx}$ xix li. viii s. viii d. Approbatum.

(fol. 29$^v$) Recepte denariorum Beati Petri de anno domini millesimo CCC$^{mo}$ L$^{mo}$

Archidiaconus Cantuariensi solvit viii li.

Archidiaconus Roffensis v li. xii s.

Archidiaconus Colcestr' viii li.

Episcopus Cicestrensis v li. x s.

Archidiaconus Essexie v li. x s.

Archidiaconus Middelsexie v li. x s.

Archidiaconus Wyntoniensis xi li. xiii s. iiii d.

Archidiaconus Surreie v li. xiii s. iiii d.

Episcopus Sarisbiriensis xvii li.

Episcopus Bathoniensis et Wellensis xi li. v s.

Episcopus Exoniensis ix li. v s.

Archidiaconus Eliensis v li.

Episcopus Norwicensis xxi li. x s.

Episcopus Lincolniensis xlii li.

Episcopus Conventrensis et Lichfeldensis x li. v s.

Episcopus Herefordensis vi li.

Episcopus Wygorniensis x li. v s.

Archiepiscopus Eboracensis xi li. x s.

Summa c iiii$^{xx}$ xix li. viii s. viii d. Approbatum.

(fol. 30) Recepte denariorum Beati Petri anno LI$^o$

Archidiaconus Cantuariensis solvit viii li.

Archidiaconus Roffensis v li. xii s.

Archidiaconus Cicestrensis viii li.

Archidiaconus Colcestr' v li. x s.

Archidiaconus Essexie v li. x s.

Archidiaconus Middelsexie v li. x s.

Archidiaconus Wyntoniensis xi li. xiii s. iiii d.

Archidiaconus Surreie v li. xiii s. iiii d.

Episcopus Sarisbiriensis xvii li.

Episcopus Bathoniensis xi li. v s.

Episcopus Exoniensis ix li. v s.

Archidiaconus Eliensis v li.

Episcopus Norwicensis xxi li. x s.

Episcopus Conventrensis x li. v s.

Episcopus Herefordensis vi li.

Episcopus Lincolniensis xlii li.

Episcopus Wigorniensis x li. v s.

Archiepiscopus Eboracensis xi li. x s.

Summa c iiii$^{xx}$ xix li. viii s. viii d. Approbatum.

(fol. 30$^v$) Recepte denariorum Beati Petri de anno LII$^o$

Archidiaconus Cantuariensis solvit viii li.

Archidiaconus Roffensis v li. xii s.

Archidiaconus Cicestrensis viii li.

Archidiaconus Colcestr' v li. x s.

Archidiaconus Essexie v li. x s.

Archidiaconus Middelsexie v li. x s.

Archidiaconus Wyntoniensis xi li. xiii s. iiii d.

Archidiaconus Surreie v li. xiii s. iiii d.

Episcopus Sarisbirrensi xvii li.

Episcopus Bathoniensis xi li. v s.

Episcopus Exoniensis ix li. v s.

Archidiaconus Eliensis v li.

Episcopus Norwicensis xxi li. x s.

Episcopus Lincolniensis xlii li.

Episcopus Conventrensis x li. v s.

Episcopus Herefordensis vi li.

Episcopus Wygorniensis x li. v s.

Archiepiscopus Eboracensis xi li. x s.

Summa c iiii$^{xx}$ xix li. viii s. viii d. Approbatum.

(fol. 31) Recepte denariorum Beati Petri de anno LIII$^o$

Archidiaconus Cantuariensis solvit viii li.

Archidiaconus Roffensis v li. xii s.

Archidiaconus Colcestr' v li. x s.

Archidiaconus Essexie v li. x s.

Archidiaconus Middelsexie v li. x s.

Archidiaconus Wyntoniensis xi li. xiii s. iiii d.

Archidiaconus Surreie v li. xiii s. iiii d.

Archidiaconus Eliensis v li.

Episcopus Cicestrensis viii li.

Episcopus Sarisbiriensis xvii li.

Episcopus Bathoniensis xi li. v s.

Episcopus Exoniensis ix li. v s.

Episcopus Norwicensis xxi li. x s.

Episcopus Lincolniensis xlii li.

---

[14] This is preceded by the sum total which has been erased, and it is followed by the sum total and the sum of sums which are repeated on the next folio.

[15] Folio 28$^v$ is blank except for the notation in modern hand: *Innoccenti VI anno 1349.*

[16] For an exposition on Peter's Pence in this period, see Lunt, *Financial Relations . . . 1327-1534*, Chap. 1.

Episcopus Conventrensis x li. v s.
Episcopus Herefordensis vi li.
Episcopus Wygorniensis x li. v s.
Archiepiscopus Eboracensis xi li. x s.
Summa c iiii<sup>xx</sup> xix li. viii s. viii d. Approbatum.

(fol. 31<sup>v</sup>) Recepte denariorum Beati Petri de anno LIIII°
Archidiaconus Cantuariensis viii li.
Archidiaconus Roffensis v li. xii s.
Archidiaconus Colcestr' v li. x s.
Archidiaconus Essexie v li. x s.
Archidiaconus Middelsexie v li. x s.
Archidiaconus Wyntoniensis xi li. xiii s. iiii d.
Archidiaconus Eliensis v li.
Episcopus Cicestrensis viii li.
Episcopus Sarisbiriensis xvii li.
Episcopus Bathoniensis xi li. v s.
Episcopus Exoniensis ix li. v s.
Episcopus Norwicensis xxi li. x s.
Episcopus Lincolniensis xlii li.
Episcopus Conventrensis x li. v s.
Episcopus Herefordensis vi li.
Episcopus Wigorniensis x li. v s.
Archiepiscopus Eboracensis xi li. x s.
Summa c iiii<sup>xx</sup> xiii li. xv s. iiii d. Approbatum.
Restant v li. xiii s. iiii d. sterlingorum.[17]

(fol. 32) Recepte denariorum Beati Petri de anno LV°
Archidiaconus Cantuariensis solvit viii li.
Archidiaconus Roffensis v li. xii s.
Archidiaconus Colcestr' v li. x s.
Episcopus Wigorniensi x li. v s.
Episcopus Bathoniensis xi li. v s.
Archidiaconus Middelsexie v li. x s.
Episcopus Exoniensis ix li. v s.
Episcopus Lincolniensis xl li.
Archidiaconus Wyntoniensis xi li. xiii s. iiii d.
Episcopus Sarisbiriensis xvii li.
Archiepiscopus Eboracensis xi li. x s.
Archidiaconus Eliensis v li.
Episcopus Cicestrensis viii li.
Episcopus Conventrensis x li. v s.
Episcopus Herfordensis vi li.
Summa clxiiii li. xv s. iiii d. Approbatum.
Restant xxxiiiii li. xiii li. iiii d.[18]

(fol. 32<sup>v</sup>) Recepte denariorum Beati Petri de anno LVI<sup>to</sup>
Archidiaconus Colcestrensis solvit v li. x s.
Archidiaconus Middelsexie v li. x s.
Episcopus Exoniensis ix li. v s.
Archidiaconus Cantuariensis viii li.
Episcopus Sarisbiriensis xvii li.

Archidiaconus Roffensis v li. xii s.
Archidiaconus Wyntoniensis xi li. xiii s. iiii d.
Archidiaconus Eliensis v li.
Episcopus Cicestrensis viii li.
Episcopus Coventrensis et Lichfeldensis x li. v. s.
Episcopus Herefordensis vi li.
Episcopus Wigorniensis x li. v s.
Summa cii li. iiii d. Approbatum.
Restant xcvii li. viii s. iiii d.[18]

(fol. 33) Recepte denariorum Beati Petri anno LVII<sup>mo</sup>
Archidiaconus Colcestrensis solvit v li. v s.
Archidiaconus Cantuariensis viii li.
Summa xiii li. x s. Approbatum.
Restant clxxxv li. xviii s. viii d.[18]
Summa totalis receptarum denariorum Beati Petri est m iiii<sup>c</sup> lxxi li. iiii s. iiii d.[19] Approbatum.
Summa restarum predictorum denariorum Beati Petri de tempore suo iii<sup>c</sup> xxiii li.[20] xiii s. viii d. Approbatum.

(fol. 33<sup>v</sup>) Sequuntur recepte annui census, et primo de anno domini millesimo CCC<sup>mo</sup> XLIX°
Abbas de Faversham Cantuariensis diocesis solvit xiii s. iiii d.
Prior de Tonebrigg' Roffensis diocesis xiii s. iiii d.
Abbas de Certesseye Wyntoniensis diocesis viii s.
Abbas Sancti Edmundi Norwicensis diocesis xiii s. iiii d.
Prior Bodmyne Exoniensis diocesis ii s.
Abbas Sancti Albani Lincolniensis diocesis xiii s. iiii d.
Abbas Sancti Adelmi Malmesbur' xiii s. iiii d.
Abbatissa et sorores Sancte Clare Londoniensis que dant i libram cere solverunt vi d.
Prior de Chaucoumbe qui dat obolum masaburt xv d.
Prior de Anglesseye qui dat unum malchinum ii s.
Custos ecclesie de Scardeburgh' qui dat obolum masaburt xv d.
Prior ecclesie Karkiolensis xiii s. iiii d.
Summa iiii li. xv s.

(fol. 34) Recepte annui census de anno domini M CCC L°
Abbas de Faversham solvit xiii s. iiii d.
Prior de Tonebrigg' xiii s. iiii d.
Abbas de Certesseye viii s.
Abbas Sancti Adelmi de Malmesbur' xiii s. iiii d.
Abbas Sancti Edmundi xiii s. iiii d.
Abbas Sancti Albani xiii s. iiii d.
Prior de Chaucoumbe xv d.
Abbatissa et sorores Sancte Clare vi d.
Prior de Anglesseye ii s.
Custos ecclesie de Scardeburgh' xv d.
Prior ecclesie Karkiolensis xiii s. iiii d.
Prior de Bodminie ii s.
Summa iiii li. xv s.

---

[17] An abbreviation for *resta* appears in the margin opposite this item. Archd. Surrey defaulted.
[18] An abbreviation for *resta* appears in the margin opposite this item for several defaulters.

[19] This follows the sum, erased by a line, of *m iiii<sup>c</sup> xiii li. iiii s. iiii d.*
[20] *xxiii* is over *xxvi* erased by a line.

(fol. 34ᵛ) Recepte annui census de anno LIᵒ
Abbas de Faversham solvit xiii s. iiii d.
Prior de Tonebrigg' xiii s. iiii d.
Abbas de Certesseye viii s.
Abbas Sancti Edmudi xiii s. iiii d.
Prior Bodmine ii s.
Abbas Sancti Albani xiii s. iiii d.
Prior de Chaucoumbe xv d.
Prior de Anglesseye li s.
Custos ecclesie de Scardeburgh' xv d.
Prior ecclesie Karkiolensis xiii s. iiii d.
Abbas Sancti Adelmi de Malmesbur' xiii s. iiii d.
Abbatissa et sorores Sancte Clare Londoniensis vi d.
Summa iiii li. xv s.

(fol. 35) Recepte annui census de anno LIIᵒ
Abbas de Faversham solvit xiii s. iiii d.
Prior de Tonbrigg' xiii s. iiii d.
Abbas de Certesseye viii s.
Abbas Sancti Edmundi xiii s. iiii d.
Prior Bodmine ii s.
Abbas Sancti Albani xiii s. iiii d.
Prior de Chaucoumbe xv d.
Prior de Anglesseye ii s.
Custos ecclesie de Scardeburgh' xv d.
Prior ecclesie Karkiolensis xiii s. iiii d.
Abbas Sancti Adelmi de Malmesbur' xiii s. iiii d.
Abbatissa et sorores Londonienses vi d.
Summa iiii li. xv s.

(fol. 35ᵛ) Recepte annui census de anno LIIIIᵒ
Abbas de Faversham solvit xiii s. iiii d.
Prior de Tonbrigg' xiii s. iiii d.
Abbas de Certesseye viii s.
Abbas Sancti Edmundi xiii s. iiii d.
Prior Bodmyne ii s.
Abbas Sancti Albani xiii s. iiii d.
Prior de Chaucoumbe xv d.
Prior de Anglesseye ii s.
Custos ecclesie de Scardeburgh' xv d.
Prior ecclesie Karkiolensis xiii s. iiii d.
Abbas Sancti Adelmi de Malmesbur' xiii s. iiii d.
Abbatissa et sorores Sancte Clare Londoniensis vi d.
Summa iiii li. xv s.

(fol. 36) Recepte annui census de anno domini
MCCCLIIIIᵗᵒ
Abbas de Faversham solvit xiii s.iiii d.
Prior de Tonbrigg, xiii s. iiii d.
Abbas de Certesseye viii s.
Abbas Sancti Edmundi xiii s. iiii d.
Prior Bodmyne ii s.
Abbas Sancti Albani xiii s. iiii d.
Prior de Chaucoumbe xv d.
Prior de Anglesseye ii s.
Custos ecclesie de Scardeburgh, xv d.
Prior ecclesie de Karkiolo xiii s. iiii d.
Abbas Sancti Adelmi Malmesbur' xiii s. iiii d.

Abbatissa et sorores Londonienses vi d.
Summa iiii li. xv s.

(fol. 36ᵛ) Recepte annui census de anno LVᵗᵒ
Prior de Chaucoumbe xv d.
Prior de Tonbrigg' xiii s. iiii d.
Abbas de Certesseye viii s.
Abbas Sancti Edmundi xiii s. iiii d.
Prior Bodmyne ii s.
Custos ecclesie de Scardeburgh' xv d.
Abbas Sancti Adelmi Malmesbur, xiii s. iiii d.
Abbas de Faversham xiii s. iiii d.
Abbas Sancti Albani xiii s. iiii d.
Prior de Anglesseye ii s.
Prior Karkiolensis xiii s. iiii d.
Abbatissa Sancte Clare Londoniensis vi d.
Summa iiii li. xv d.

(fol. 37) Recepte annui census de anno domini mille-
simo CCCᵐᵒ LVIᵗᵒ
Abbas Sancti Adelmi de Malmesbur' solvit xiii s. iiii d.
Custos ecclesie de Scardeburgh' xv d.
Prior de Tonbrigg' xiii s. iiii d.
Abbas de Certesseye viii s.
Abbas de Faversham xiii s. iiii d.
Prior de Chaucoumbe xv d.
Prior Karkiolensis xiii s. iiii d.
Prior de Anglesseye ii s.
Abbas de Sancto Albano xiii s. iiii d.
Abbas Sancti Edmundi xiii s. iiii d.
Abbatissa Sancte Clare Londoniensis vi d.
Summa iiii li. xiii s. Restant al solvendum ii s.[21]

(fol. 37ᵛ) Recepte annui census de anno LVIIᵐᵒ
Abbas de Malmesbur' xiii s. iiii d.
Custos de Scardeburgh' xv d.
Abbas de Certeye viii s.
Prior de Tonbrigg' xiii s. iiii d.
Abbas Sancti Edmundi de Bury xiii s. iiii d.
Abbatissa Sancte Clare Londoniensis vi d.
Prior de Anglessere ii s.
Prior de Chaucoumbe xv d.
Summa ii li. xiii s. Restant ii li. ii s.[21]
Summa totalis receptarum annui census in predicto
tempore est xl li. xi s. Approbatum.
Restant debiti ii li. iiii s. Approbatum.[21]

(fol. 38) Sequuntur recepte de legatis ad Terram
Sanctam et redemptione votorum per tempus compoti
predicti
De Thoma Abetot, rectore ecclesie de Otundon'
(Oddington) ad expugnandum contra Turcos vii li. vi
s. viii d.
De testamento Holnarstot Norwicensis diocesis x s.
De testamento Johannis Bomfeld ii s.
De testamento Johannis Greve xl s.
De testamento Holme x s.

---

[21] An abbreviation for *resta* is in the margin opposite this item.

De legatis in testamentis diversorum in diocesi Bathoniensi xxvi s. iii d.

De legatis in testamentis diversorum in diocesi Exoniensi xxxi s.

De testamento Thome, rectoris Suthfambrugg' (South Fambridge) Londoniensis diocesis l s.

De legatis in testamentis diversorum in diocesi Wintoniensi lvii s. xi d.

De Johanne de Bello Campo milite in expugnatione contra Turcos pro indulgentia sibi concessa ac si Romam accessisset clxv fl., valent xxiii li. vii s. vi d.

De legatis cuiusdam capellani per manus Domini Ricardi, prepositi hospitalis Sancte Katherine Londoniensis, vi s. viii d.

De Willelmo Broun Lichfeldensis diocesis pro redemptione voti ad Sanctum Jacobum xx s.

De Nicolao Fabro paupere pro redemptione voti ad Terram Sanctam Lincolniensis diocesis xx s.

De testamento Symonis rectoris ecclesie de Litelham (Littleham) Exoniensis diocesis xiii s. iiii d.

Summa pagine xlv li. xvi d. Approbatum.

(fol. 38ᵛ) De testamento Petri Bakestere de parochia de Houghton' Norwicensis diocesis de legatis ad Terram Sanctam xiii s. iiii d.

De legatis in testamentis diversorum in diocesi Cicestrensi, quorum nomina in quodam certificatorio per Dominum Johannem de Donton', cui commissum fuit premissa levare, misso [22] apparent, vii li.

De Symone, vicario de Westgrenewich' (West Greenwich) Roffensis diocesis, de quadam penitentia sibi iniuncta xii d.

De Domino Adam Esgor, canonico ecclesie Herefordensis, pro legatis Aymerici Pauncefot militis ad Terram Sanctam xxii li. xiii s. iiii d.

De testamento Johannis de Bordon', rectoris ecclesie Roubur, (Rothbury) Dunelmensis diocesis, legati ad Terram Sanctam x li.

De Roberto de Otto Cicestrensis diocesis pro redemptione voti ad Sanctum Jacobum xxx s.

De testamento Johannis Haward legati ad Terram Sanctam xx s.

De testamento Magistri Roberti de Cryssale legati ad Terram Sanctam in partem solutionis x li. per manus Willelmi de Farefford de Oxonia diversis vicibus vi li.[23]

De testamento Johannis de Sixdale legati ad Terram Sanctam vii d.[24]

Summa pagine xlviii li. xvii s. iii d. Approbatum.

(fol. 39) De Sibilla Vernon' Eliensis diocesis in partem solutionis v li. pro redemptione voti ad Sanctum Jacobum xx s.

Summa xx s. Approbatum.

Summa totalis receptarum legatorum iiiiˣˣ xiiii li. xix s. vii d. Approbatum.

(fol. 40) [25] Sequuntur recepte beneficiorum, de quibus est scriptum michi Hugoni de curia tempore predicto, collatorum tam per dominos Clementem papam quam Innocentium.[25a]

### Collata per Clementem
### Cantuariensis

De ecclesia de Boxeleye (Boxley), de qua per assecutionem possesionis ecclesie de Maydestan' (Maidstone) factam per Hugonem Pelegrini fuit provisum Johanni de Haddon', xl li.

Item de ecclesia de Stokebur' (Stockbury) unita prioratui de Ledes (Leeds) in partem fructuum ix li. xiii s. iiii d.

Item de prepositura de Wyngham (Wingham), ratione confirmationis collationis facte Roberto de Sulby per resignationem Johannis de Bourne, xl li.

### Collata per Innocentium

Item de ecclesia de Bilsynton' (Bilsington), de qua per resignationem Johannis de Horton' ex causa permutationis fuit provisum Johanni Stoke, x li.

Item de ecclesia de Bouclond (Buckland), de qua per resignationem ex causa permutationis fuit provisum Johanni de Horton', in partem solutionis iiii li. xiii s. iiii d.

### Roffensis

De perpetua vicaria ecclesia Beati Petri de Schorne (Shorne), de qua per resignationem Walteri de Hemmyngford fuit provisum Johanni de Tichemerssch', vi li. xiii s. iiii d.

Summa pagine cxi li. Approbatum.

(fol. 40ᵛ) Per Clementem

### Londoniensis

De canonicatu et prebenda ecclesie Londoniensis, de quibus per consecrationem Thome archiepiscopi Cantuariensis fuit provisum Ricardo Michaelis, v li. vi s. viii d.

Item de ecclesia de Wythale (Wyddial), de qua per resignationem Symonis de Hareberghe fuit provisum Johanni de Stanton', in partem vi li. xiii s. iiii d.

Item de prebenda in ecclesia Londoniensi, de qua per obitum Ricardi de Feriby fuit provisum Henrico Lymbergh', ii li.

Item de prebenda de Brandesbur' (Brondesbury, Willesden) in ecclesia Londoniensi, cuius acceptio facta per Edmundum la Zouche fuit eidem confirmata, ii li.

Item de prebenda de Wyllesden' (Willesden) in ecclesia Londoniensi, cuius collatio facta Henrico de Thaddesden' fuit eidem confirmata, iiii li.

---

[22] *missum*, MS.
[23] The letter *b* is in the margin opposite this item.
[24] The letter *a* is in the margin opposite this item.

[25] Folio 39ᵛ is blank.
[25a] For commentary on these annates, see Lunt, *Financial Relations . . . 1327-1534*, pp. 319-380.

Collata per Innocentium
Adhuc Londoniensis

Item de decanatu ecclesie Londoniensis, de quo vacante per mortem Willelmi de Briera, fuit provisum Ricardo de Kilminton', in partem solutionis taxe xxxiii li. vi s. viii d.

Item de ecclesia de Hormade parva (Little Hormead), de qua per resignationem Roberti de Thorp' ex causa permutationis fuit provisum Waltero Trenaleyn, vi li. xiii s. iiii d.

Item de prebenda de Mapesbury (in Willesden) in ecclesia Londoniensi que Michaeli de Northburgh, fuit confirmata iii li. vi s. viii d.

Per Clementem
Cicestrensis

De prebenda de Huma (Hove) in ecclesia Cicestrensi, cuius collatio facta Rogero de Dorkyng' fuit eidem confirmata, xx li.

Item de decanatu ecclesie Cicestrensis, de quo per mortem Walteri de Segrave fuit provisum Willelmo de Lenne, in partem solutionis xxiii li. vi s. viii d.

Summa pagine cvi li. xiii s. iiii d. Approbatum.

(fol. 41) Item de vicaria ecclesie de Cokefeld (Cuckfield), de qua per resignationem Roberti Longe de Shefford fuit provisum Willelmo Cletyng', vi li. xiii s. iiii d.

Item de thesauraria ecclesie Cicestrensis, de qua per obitum Edmundi de Arundell' et prebenda ecclesie vacante per obitum Bernardi del Fawe fuit provisum Waltero Gest', in partem solutionis lxiiii li. x s. vii d.

Item de prebenda de Braklesham (Bracklesham) in ecclesia Cicestrensi, cuius collatio facta Ottoni de Northwode fuerat eidem confirmata, xvi li. xiii s. iiii d.

Item de prebenda ecclesie Cicestrensis, vacante per obitum Thome Botringham, de qua fuit provisum Thome David, vi li. xiii s. iiii d.

Per Innocentium

Item de prebenda de Sidlesham in ecclesia Cicestrensi, de qua per obitum Walteri Gest' fuit provisum Johanni de Bisshopeston', in partem solutionis xv li.

Item de prebenda de Sutton' in ecclesia Cicestrensi, de qua fuit provisum Michaeli de Northburgh', xxvi li. xiii s. iiii d.

Wyntoniensis

De prebenda quam quondam Johannes de Chastebbur' in ecclesia monialium de Whorewell' (Wherwell) obtinebat, de qua fuit provisum Thome de Enham, xxv li. vi s. viii d.

Item de prebenda de Whorewell' in ecclesia monialium de Whorewell', de qua per resignationem Nicholai Calmath' acceptio facta per Willelmum Dosberston' fuit eidem confirmata, xl li.

Summa pagine iiᶜ i li. x s. vii d. Approbatum.

(fol. 41ᵛ) De ecclesia de Laverkestoke (Laverstoke), in iure quod competebat Johanni Grom fuit subrogatus Johannes de Rennebury, in partem solutionis ii li.

Item de ecclesia de Wymbeldon' (Wimbledon), de qua per obitum Ademari Roberti cardinalis fuit provisum Willelmo de Cheston', xl li.

Sarisbiriensis

De ecclesia de Wytwaltham (Waltham Abbas) unita monasterio de Certeseye xiii li. vi s. viii d.

Item de prebenda in ecclesia Sarisbiriensi de qua per obitum Johannis de Vienna fuit provisum Rogero Sibrok' v li.

Item de prebenda in ecclesia de Sarisbiria de qua per obitum Johannis Giffardi fuit provisum Johanni de Wynewyk' viii li.

Item de prebenda de Grymstan (Grimstone) et Yatemynstr' (Yetminster), de qua per mortem Johannis de Wodefford fuit provisum Rogero de Clone, xx li.

Item de prebenda de Slape in ecclesia Sarisbiriensi, de qua, per obitum Willelmi de Crouthorn', cuius acceptio facta per Ricardum de Netherlaven' fuit eidem confirmata, xiii li. vi s. viii d.

Item de prebenda Sancti Laurentii de Stratford in ecclesia Sarisbiriensi et ecclesia Sancti Thome Martir' in Sarisbiria, de quibus, per obitum Johannis de Sarisbiria alias Pittor' fuit provisum Johanni de Wilton', xv li.

Item de prebenda de Netherlaven' (Netheravon) in ecclesia Sarisbiriensi, de qua per mortem ultimi prebendarii fuit provisum Willelmo de Melburi', in partem solutionis xiii li. vi s. viii d.

Item de prebenda de Cherdestoke (Chardstock) in ecclesia Sarisbiriensi, de qua, vacante eo quod Johannes Gough', qui eam tenebat, aliam prebendam in eadem ecclesia fuit assecutus, fuit provisum Martino Molice, xvi li.

Item de ecclesia de Briton' (Burton Bradstock), cuius collatio facta Johanni Purbik' fuit eidem confirmata, x li.

Summa pagine clvi li. Approbatum.

(fol. 42) Item de prebenda in ecclesia Sarisbiriensi, de qua, per mortem Elie Pelegrini, fuit provisum Hugoni Pelegrini, lx li.

Item de prebenda de Northwenton' (North Newnton) in ecclesia monialium de Wilton', de qua per obitum Johannis de Vienna fuit provisum Ricardo de Welyngton', in partem solutionis v li.

Item de thesauraria ecclesie Sarisbiriensis et prebenda de Calne in eadem, de quibus, per obitum domini cardinalis de Mota [26] fuit provisum domino cardinali de Florentia,[27] in partem solutionis xxviii li. xvii s. ix d.

Exoniensis

De archidiaconatu Totton' (Totnes), de quo, per

[26] Gaillard de Mota, deacon of St. Lucy in Silice.
[27] Francis de Aptis, bishop of Florence, priest of S. Marco.

obitum Johannis de Northwode, fuit provisum Petro de Gildesburgh', pro medietate veri valoris x li.

Item de prebenda Exoniensi de qua, per mortem dicti Johannis de Northwode fuit provisum dicto Petro de Guldesburgh' iiii li.

Item de prebenda in ecclesia collegiata Sancti Laurentii Carentoci (Crantock), in cuius iure quod competebat Ricardo de Wytheslade et Johanni de Northwode fuit subrogatus Johannes de Holonde, iii li.

Item de prebenda in ecclesia Exoniensi, vacante per obitum Thome de Sukingham, cuius acceptio facta per Henricum Pik' fuit eidem confirmata, iiii li.

Item de prebenda in ecclesia Exoniensi vacante per mortem Ricardi de Withleslade, cuius acceptio facta per Otthonem de Northwode fuit eidem confirmata, iiii li.

Item de prebenda in ecclesia Exoniensi vacante per obitum Johannis de Nassyngton', cuius acceptio facta per Reginaldum de Bugwell' fuit eidem confirmata, iiii li.

Summa pagine cxxii li. xvii s. ix d. Approbatum.

(fol. 42ᵛ) Item de vicaria ecclesie de Sutton', de qua, per assecutionem thesaurarie ecclesie Exoniensis per Robertum de Middellond, fuit provisum Radulpho de Ryngestede, iiii li. vi s. viii d.

Item de parochiali ecclesia de Exmynstre (Axminster), de qua per obitum Magistri Henrici de Galmygton' fuit provisum Nicholao Terrer, in partem solutionis xi li. vi s. viii d.

Item de prebenda ecclesie Exoniensis de qua per obitum Walteri Retenux fuit provisum Johanni Vilot' iiii li.

Item de archidiaconatu Exoniensi, cuius collatio fuit confirmata Ottoni de Northwode, x li.

Item de prebenda ecclesie Exoniensis de qua per obitum Hugonis de Seton' fuit provisum Humfredo de Cherleton' iiii li.

Item de prebenda in ecclesia collegiata Sancti Thethe (Saint Teath), cuius collatio facta Ottoni de Northwode fuit eidem confirmata, iiii li. x s.

Item de prebenda Sancti Thome Martiris Glasneye (Glasnay) cuius collatio fuit Ottoni de Northwode confirmata ii li.

Item de prebenda Exoniensi vacante per obitum Ricardi de Brayls, cuius acceptio facta per Nicholaum Pynnok' fuit eidem confirmata, in partem solutionis iiii li.

Item de decanatu Exoniensi vacante per mortem Ricardi Brayls, de quo fuit provisum Reginaldo de Bugwell', in partem solutionis x li.

## Wigorniensis

De ecclesia de Tredyngton' (Tredington), cuius acceptio facta per Thomam de Dunclent fuit eidem confirmata, xxvi li. xiii s. iiii d.

Item de ecclesia de Poklechirch' (Pucklechurch), de

qua per obitum Radulphi de Rovedon' fuit provisum Ricardo de Tillebur', xxxiii li. vi s. viii d.

Item de ecclesia de Knyghtwych' (Knightwick), de qua per resignationem Philipi Dym fuit ex causa permutationis provisum Johanni Charneux, in partem solutionis ii li. xiii s. iiii d.

Item de prebenda Sancti Thethe (Saint Teath) de qua per obitum Johannis Cros fuit provisum Thome David iiii li. x s.

Summa pagine cxxi li. vi s. viii d. Approbatum.

## (fol. 43) Wellensis

De ecclesia de Bledon' (Bleadon), de qua per obitum Thome de Borkenhull fuit provisum Reginaldo de Bugwell', xvi li. xiii s. iiii d.

Item de prebenda de Ilton' in ecclesia Wellensi, de qua per mortem Johannis de Northwede fuit provisum Stephano de Brokesbur', xii li.

Item de cancellaria ecclesia Vellensis et prebenda de Compton' in eadem, de quibus, per assecutionem factam per Johannem de Carleton' de decanatu dicte ecclesie Wellensis,[28] in partem solutionis xxvi li. xvi d.

Item de prebenda in ecclesia Wellensi de qua per obitum Ricardi de Sudbury fuit provisum Johanni de Saucerio v li. vi s. viii d.

Item de prebenda de Cumba prima (Combe) in ecclesia Wellensi, vacante per obitum Henrici de Carleton', cuius acceptio facta per Johannem Thursteyn fuit eidem confirmata, v li. vi s. viii d.

Item de prebenda Sancti Decumani (Saint Decuman's) in ecclesia Wellensi, cuius acceptio facta per Bernardum de Brocariis fuit eidem confirmata, xxiii li. vi s. viii d.

Item de decanatu Wellensi, de quo per obitum Walteri de London' fuit provisum Johanni de Carleton', in partem solutionis xl li.

Item de prebenda de Cumba decima (Combe) in ecclesia Wellensi, cuius collatio facta Stephano Martini fuit eidem confirmata, v li. vi s. viii d.

Item de prebenda de Wednor (Wedmore) vocata quinta in ecclesia Wellensi, cuius collatio facta Willelmo Camyell' fuit eidem confirmata, iiii li.

Item de archidiaconatu Wellensi et prebenda sibi annexa, de quibus per consecrationem Thome episcopi Menevensis fuit provisum reverendo patri Domino Guillelmo Tusculanensi episcopo cardinali, in partem solutionis xxii li. iiii s. v d.

Summa pagine clx li. v s. ix d. Approbatum.

(fol. 43ᵛ) Item de precentoria Wellensi, de qua per obitum Willelmi de Littelton', fuit provisum Edmundo Gourney, in partem solutionis vi li. xii s. iiii d.

Item de archidiaconatu Bathoniensi et prebenda vocata Cumba (Combe) secunda in ecclesia Wellensi, quorum collatio facta Johanni Power fuit eidem confirmata, xv li. vi s. viii d.

Item de prepositura Wellensi, de qua per consecra-

---

[28] The entry is incomplete.

tionem Johannis Dublinensis fuit provisum Andree de Offord, xl li.

Item de prioratu Montis Acuti (Montacute), de quo per obitum Johannis la Porte, fuit provisum Johanni la Porte, in partem solutionis xxv li.

### Herefordensis

De prebenda ecclesie collegiate de Bromyerd (Bromyard) de qua per obitum Thome de Asteleye fuit provisum Rogero de Dorkyng' xx li.

Item de prebenda de Morton' (Moreton Magna) in ecclesia Herefordensi, de qua, per mortem Thome de Stanton' fuit provisum Symoni de Sudbur', in partem solutionis xix li. vi s. viii d.

Item de cancellaria Herefordensi, vacante per obitum Johannis ultimi cancellarii, cuius collatio facta Thome Hacluyt fuit eidem confirmata, xx li.

Item de prebenda ecclesie collegiate de Brumerd (Bromyard) de qua per obitum Thome de Asteleye fuit provisum Rogero Dorkyng', xx li.

Item de ecclesia de Credeleye (Cradley), cuius collatio facta Ade Trewelove fuit eidem confirmata, xxiii li. vi s. viii d.

Item de prebenda de Hyneton' (Hinton) in ecclesia Herefordensi, cuius acceptio facta pro Nicholao Carewent fuit eidem confirmata, v li. vi s. viii d.

Item de decanatu Herefordensi, cuius electio facta de Thoma Trellek' fuit eidem confirmata, xx li. xvi s.

Item de ecclesia de Montegomeri (Montgomery), de qua fuit de novo provisum Nicholao de Upton', qui pro fructibus perceptis et etiam pro prima annata debuit solvere xii li. ex conventione facta cum domino camerario pape, in partem solutionis iii li. xviii s. x d.

Summa pagine ii$^c$ xix li. xiiii s. x d. Approbatum.

(fol. 44) Item de prebenda Herefordensi, de qua per consecrationem Michaelis episcopi Londoniensis, fuit provisum Willelmo de Somerford, vii li. xvi d.

Item de prebenda de Morton' (Norton) in ecclesia Herefordensi, vacante per assecutionem alterius beneficii factam per Reginaldum de Brynton', cuius acceptio facta per Johannem Prophete <fuit> confirmata, ad plus non taxatur, ix s.

### Eliensis

De ecclesia de Hadenham (Haddenham), in iure cuius quod competebat Henrico de Harweden' fuit subrogatus Bartholomeus de Bourne, iiii$^{xx}$ li.

Item de parochiali ecclesia de Tyd (Tydd), cuius collatio facta Roberto Michaelis fuit eidem confirmata, xlii li.

Item de ecclesia de Dodyngton' (Doddington), cuius collatio facta Gervasio de Wilford fuit eidem confirmata, xxxvi li. xiiii s. iiii d.

### Norwicensis

De archidiaconatu Norwicensi, cuius collatio facta Ricardo de Lyng' fuit eidem confirmata, vii li. vi s. viii d.

Item de ecclesia de Redgrave, cuius acceptio facta per Johannem de Eye [29] fuit eidem confirmata, in partem solutionis xxii li. xiii s. iiii d.

Item de ecclesia de Ratlesden' (Rattlesden), de qua, per resignationem Thome de Felthorp', fuit provisum Rogero de Freton', xx li.

Item de ecclesia de Schipedham (Shipdham), cuius acceptio facta per Thomam de Morle fuit eidem confirmata, xxvi li. xiii s. iiii d.

Item ecclesia de Derham (East Dereham), de qua per obitum Alani de Hothum fuit provisum Symoni Theobauld de Sudbury, in partem solutionis xxxii li. x s.

Item de ecclesia de Elveden', de qua per resignationem Ricardi de Hemesby, fuit provisum Willelmo Symonis, in partem solutionis v li. xiii s. iiii d.

Item de ecclesia de Thurston', de qua fuit provisam Roberto de Thorp', in partem solutionis xiii li. vi s. viii d.

Summa ii$^c$ iiii$^{xx}$ xiiii li. vii s. Approbatum.

(fol. 44$^v$) Item de archidiaconatu [30] Suff', qui Michaeli de Northburgh' fuit confirmatus, pro medietate veri valoris quia non taxatur, xiii li. vi s. viii d.

Item de ecclesia de Pulham, de qua per mortem Johannis de Kyldesbe, fuit provisum Michaeli de Northburg', in partem solutionis xxxvi li. iiii s. iii d.

### Lincolniensis

De decanatu Lincolniensi, de quo per obitum Johannis electi Cantuariensis fuit provisum Magistro Symoni de Bruseley, in partem solutionis iiii$^{xx}$ xiii li. vi s. viii d.

Item de prebenda de Asgarby in ecclesia Lincolniensi, de qua, per obitum Henrici de Iddesworth', fuit provisum Johanni de Welburi', xx li.

Item de prebenda Sancte Margarete Leycestr' (Leicester) in ecclesia Lincolniensi, de qua per obitum domini episcopi Portuensis cardinalis fuit provisum Johanni de Edyngdon' xxxiii li. vi s. viii d.[31]

Item de prebenda de Dunham (Dunham) in ecclesia Lincolniensi, de qua per mortem Henrici de la Dale, fuit provisum Willelmo de Gynewell', xxxviii li. xiii s. iiii d.

Item de ecclesia de Estaddon' (East Haddon) unita auctoritate apostolica per episcopum Lincolniensem abbati de Sulby x li.

Item de ecclesia de Poykirk' (Peakirk), vacante per obitum Laurentii de North', de qua fuit provisum Johanni le Feete, xvi li. xiii s. iiii d.

---

[29] Follows *Rye* deleted by a line.
[30] Follows *ecclesia* deleted by a line.
[31] Followed by *Et non plus quia fuit in manu collectoris in anno mortalitatis et non potuit plus levari* deleted by a heavy line.

Item de prebenda Sancti Botulphi in ecclesia Lincolniensi, quam Thomas de Bradwardyn obtinebat, fuit provisum Stephano de Brokesburum iii li. vi s. viii d.

Item de thesauraria ecclesie Lincolniensis, de qua per obitum Walteri de Stanreth' fuit provisum Johanni de Welburi', xx li.

Item de prebenda de Langeford (Langford) in ecclesia Lincolniensi, cuius collatio facta Magistro Johanni de Lech' fuit eidem confirmata, in partem solutionis xlv li.

Item de prebenda de Stoke (East Stoke) in ecclesia Lincolniensi, de qua per obitum Johannis de Northwede, fuit provisum Hugoni Pelegrini, xxxiii li. vi s. viii d.

Summa pagine iii^c lxiii li. iiii s. iii d. Approbatum.

(fol. 45) Item de ecclesia de Oundele (Oundle), de qua per resignationem Jacobi Beauford fuit provisum Rogero Holm, in partem solutionis vi li. xiii s. iiii d. Residuum solutionis xx li. fuerunt solute in curia, ut patet per litteras camere.

Item de prebenda de Scarles (South Scarle), de qua per obitum Thome Cruse fuit provisum et confirmatum Johanni de Kyrkeby, in partem solutionis xx li.

Item de prebenda et precentoria ecclesie Lincolniensis, de quibus per obitum Petri de Dalderby, fuit provisum Antonio de Goldesburgh', xxv li. vi s. viii d. Solvit pro prebenda xii li. et pro precentoria xiii li. vi s. viii d.

Item de prebenda de Wylton' Rekhale (Welton Beckhall) in ecclesia Lincolniensi, cuius collatio facta Johanni de Haddon' fuit eidem confirmata, x li.

Item de prebenda de Wylton' Brynkale (Welton Brinkhall) in ecclesia Lincolniensi, cuius collatio facta Willelmo de Navesby fuit eidem confirmata, x li.

Item de prebenda in ecclesia Lincolniensi cuius collatio facta Ade de Lymbergh' fuit eidem confirmata iii li.

Item de prebenda de Bedeford minore in ecclesia Lincolniensi, cuius collatio facta Willelmo de Askeby fuit eidem confirmata, iiii li. vi s. viii d.

Item de ecclesia de Suthflette (Fleet), cuius collatio facta Willelmo de Gynewell' fuit eidem confirmata, xxxii li. xiii s. iiii d.

Item de prebenda de Luda (Louth) in ecclesia Lincolniensi, de qua per obitum Mathei Eruseley fuit provisum Johanni Gough', xlvi li. xiii s. iiii d.

Item de subdecanatu Lincolniensi, cuius acceptio facta per Hamonem de Belers fuit eidem confirmata, in partem solutionis xv li.

Summa pagine clxxiii li. xiii s. iiii d. Approbatum.

(fol. 45^v) Item de ecclesia de Stanford (Stanford-on-Avon), de qua per resignationem Johannis de Wynwik' fuit provisum Johanni de Melburi', xvi li. xiii s. iiii d.

Item de prebenda de Creton' (Gretton) in ecclesia Lincolniensi, de qua per uxorationem Eymerici de Cursonio, fuit provisum Johanni de Bukyngham, in partem solutionis xxx li.

Item de media portione ecclesie de Seggebrok' (Sedgebrook), de qua per obitum ultimi rectoris fuit provisum Roberto de Seggebrok', in partem solutionis ix li. xiii s. iiii d.

Item de ecclesia Folkesworth (Folksworth), de qua per obitum Henrici de Ulceby fuit provisum Symoni Spark', in partem solutionis xxxiii s. iiii d.

Item de prebenda de Carleton' Thurleby (Carlton le Moorland cum Thurlby) in ecclesia Lincolniensi, de qua per consecrationem Nicholai episcopi Urgellensis (Urgel) fuit provisum Roberto de Wyngesworth, in partem solutionis x li.

Item de prebenda de Carleton' (Carlton Kyme) cum Dalby in ecclesia Lincolniensi, de qua, vacante ex causa permutationis cum Domino Willelmo de Dalton, fuit provisum Willelmo de Hugate, xx li.

Item de ecclesia de Edenesburgh' (Edlesborough), de qua per obitum Johannis de Belvero, fuit provisum Johanni de Swynesheved, in partem solutionis x li.

Item de ecclesia de Horncastr' (Horncastle), cuius collatio facta per ordinarium Johanni de Kyrkeby fuit eidem confirmata, in partem solutionis xv li.

### Collata per Innocentium

Item de archidiaconatu Leycestrensi, cuius collatio facta [32] Willelmo de Donne fuit eidem confirmata, pro medietate veri valoris xxx li.

Summa cxliii li. Approbatum.

(fol. 46) Item de ecclesia de Hoddesdon', de qua fuit dispensatum cum Magistro Henrico Chaddesden' ut simul posset eam retinere cum archidiaconatu Leycestr', x li.

### Lychfeldensis

De ecclesia Berkeswyk' (Baswick), de qua per obitum Johannis de Amelio, fuit provisum Johanni de Bryan, xx li.

### Per Clementem

Item de prebenda ecclesie Lychfeldensis de qua per obitum Thome de Asteleye fuit provisum Matheo de Bruseley ix li. xviii s. iiii d.

Item de prebenda Lychfeldensi ⟨de qua⟩ per obitum Johannis Zouche fuit provisum Petro de Guldesburgh' xxxiii li. vi s. viii d.

Item de prebenda ecclesie Lychfeldensis de qua per obitum Thome de Clopton' fuit provisum Thome de Guldesburgh' xxx s.

Item de prebenda ecclesie Lychfeldensis de qua per consecrationem Symonis electi Cantuariensis fuit provisum Henrico de Chaddesden' xii li.

Item de prebenda de Welyngton' (Wellington) in ecclesia Lichfeldensi, vacante per obitum Johannis de Creton, fuit acceptio facta per Hugonem de Wymondeswold [33] eidem confirmata, x li.

---

[32] Followed by *per ordinarium* deleted by a line.
[33] Followed by *et*, MS.

Item de prebenda de Stotfold (Stotfold) in ecclesia Lichfeldensi, de qua per mortem Mathei de Bruseley fuit provisum Raymundo de Sancto Claro, x li.

Item de precentoria ecclesie Lichfeldensis, cuius collatio facta Thome de Baddeby fuit eidem confirmata, in partem solutionis xxvi li. xiii s. iiii d.

Summa pagine cxxxiii li. viii s. iiii d. Approbatum.

(fol. 46ᵛ) Item de ecclesia de Bolington' (Bollington), cuius acceptio facta per Johannem de Wytfeld fuit eidem confirmata, viii li. xiii s. iiii d.

Item de prebenda de Ulfton' (Ufton) in ecclesia Lichfeldensi, de qua per resignationem Johannis de Wynwyk' fuit provisum Johanni de Melborne, in partem solutionis iiii li. xiii s. iiii d.

Item de archidiaconatu Conventrensi ac prebenda de Langedon' (Longdon) in ecclesia Lichfeldensi, de quibus per obitum Willelmi de Sallewe fuit provisum Willelmo Cros, xxxiii li. vi s. viii d., videlicet pro medietate veri ⟨valoris⟩ archidiaconatus non taxati xiii li. vi s. viii d. et pro prebenda xx li.

Item de ecclesia de Walton', de qua fuit provisum Johanni de Bulkynton', in partem solutionis xxx li.

Item de parochiali ecclesia de Burton' (Burton in Winhale) ac hospitali de Neuehall' (Denwall), de quibus per resignationem Nicholai de Heth' fuit provisum Johanni de Chirneux, x li.

Item de ecclesia de Donyngton' (Donington), de qua per resignationem Johannis de Penkrth' fuit provisum Thome de Melbur', l s.

Item de archidiaconatu Derbeie, de quo collatio facta Hugoni Mareys fuit eidem confirmata, pro medietate veri valoris, quia non taxatur, iiii li.

Item de decanatu Lichfeldensi, de quo per assecutionem decanatus Lincolniensis factam per Symonem de Bruseley fuit provisum Johanni de Bukingham, in partem solutionis xx li.

## Menevensis

De ecclesia de Bisshopeston' (Bishopston), de qua, per assecutionem factam per Johannem de Farendon' de ecclesia de Hengham (High Ham) Wellensis diocesis, fuit provisum Thome Curteys, pro medietate veri valoris, quia non taxatur et etiam est exile beneficium, xxvi s. viii d.

Item de prebenda quam R.[34] electus Menevensis in ipsa ecclesia Menevensi obtinuit, de qua per consecrationem eiusdem, fuit provisum Johanni Seys, ii li.

Summa pagine cxvi li. x s. Approbatum.

(fol. 47) Item de prebenda quam dictus Reginaldus in ecclesia collegiata de Abberwyly (Abergwili) obtinuit, de qua per consecrationem eiusdem fuit provisum Johanni Seys, viii li.

Item de eclesia de Ruddebaston' (Rudbaxton), de

qua per resignationem David Martini fuit provisum Roberto Wace, alias dicto Martini, x li. xiii s. iiii d.

Item de prebenda de Langan (Llanganten) in ecclesia collegiate de Aberwyly, de qua per mortem Griffini de Canton' fuit provisum Mauricio Molich', in partem solutionis iiii li.

### Eboracensis

De archidiaconatu Richmundie in ecclesia Eboracensi, de quo per obitum Domini Johannis Portuensis episcopi cardinalis fuit provisum Henrico de Walton', in partem solutionis xxxiii li. vi s. viii d.

Item de ecclesia Sancte Crucis (St. Crux, York), de qua per obitum Johannis de Lude fuit provisum Johanni Cokyn, v li.

Item de prebenda de Hustwayt (Husthwaite) in ecclesia Eboracensi, de qua fuit provisum Johanni de Welbur', xxvi li. xiii s. iiii d.

Item de prebenda de Dunham in ecclesia collegiata de Suthwell', de qua, per obitum Henrici de Harwedon', fuit provisum Ade de Everyncham, in partem solutionis x li.

Item de prebenda de Salso Marisco (Saltmarsh) in ecclesia collegiata de Houdon' (Howden), de qua acceptio facta per Willelmum Johannis de Aula fuit confirmata, xxxiii li. vi s. viii d.

Item de prebenda de Sithneubold (South Newbald) in ecclesia Eboracensi, de qua, per assecutionem alterius prebende in eadem ecclesia factam per Andream de Offord fuit provisum Thome de Morgne, xx li.

Item de prebenda de Nunwyk (Nunwick) in ecclesia Riponensi, de qua per consecrationem Willelmi archiepiscopi Eboracensis fuit provisum Rogero de Steanby, x li.

Summa pagine clxi li. Approbatum.

(fol. 47ᵛ) Item de prebenda de Grendale (Grindale) in ecclesia Eboracensi, de qua per obitum Johannis Giffard fuit provisum Johanni de Chestfold, xxvi li. xiii s. iiii d.

Item de prebenda que vocatur Holm Archiepiscopi (Holme Archiepiscopi), de qua per obitum Thome Sampson, fuit provisum Willelmo de Sanhynniaco, xvi li. xiii s. iiii d.

Item de ecclesia de Misterton', de qua collatio facta Johanni de Holewell' fuit eidem confirmata, xxiii li. vi s. viii d.

Item de precentoria ecclesie Eboracensis, de qua, per obitum Roberti de Patrington' fuit provisum Symoni de Bekyngham, x li.

Item de prebenda de Thorp' (Thorpe) in ecclesia collegiata de Houden' (Howden), de qua per mortem Roberti Tresk' fuit provisum Ade Robelyn,[35] xviii li.

Item de prebenda de Barneby (Barnby) in ecclesia Eboracensi, de qua per obitum Reginaldi de Donyngton', fuit provisum Johanni de Holewell', xiiii li.

---

[34] Followed by *in ecclesia collegiata* deleted by a line.

[35] Followed by *in partem* deleted by a line.

Item de [36] cancellaria ecclesie Eboracensis, de qua per obitum Willelmi de Aberwyk' fuit provisum Symoni de Belyngham, xxxiii li. vi s. viii d.

Item de precentoria ecclesia Eboracensis, de qua per assecutionem cancellarie eiusdem ecclesie factam per dictum Symonem de Bekyngham fuit provisum Hugoni de Wymondeswold, x li.

Item de prebenda in ecclesia Beverlacensi, de qua acceptio facta per Alanum de Waynflete fuit sibi confirmata, in partem solutionis viii li.

Item de prebenda [37] Sancte Katherine in ecclesia Beverlacensi, de qua acceptio facta per Ricardum de Meux fuit eidem confirmata,[38] vi li. xiii s. iiii d.

Summa pagine clxvi li. xiii s. iiii d. Approbatum.

(fol. 48) Item de prebenda de Dystmelyngton' (Stillington) in ecclesia Eboracensi, de qua per obitum Johannis Berenger acceptio facta per Thomam de London' fuit eidem confirmata, xiii li. v s. viii d.

Item de ecclesia de Welton', de qua collatio facta Henrico de Gategang' fuit eidem confirmata, in partem solutionis vi li. xiii s. iiii d.

Item de ecclesia de Warumpercy (Wharram Percy) et ecclesia de Elveley (Kirk Ella) unitis prioratui de Hautemprise (Haltemprice) xxxv li.

### Per Innocentium

Item de ecclesia de Harewode (Harewood) appropriata monasterio de Bolton' xvi li.

Item de prebenda de Donyngton' (Dunnington) in ecclesia Eboracensi, de qua per consecrationem Johannis archiepiscopi Dublinensis fuit provisum Michaeli de Nortburgh', x li.

Item de prebenda Beverlacensi de qua per mortem Ricardi de Ferby fuit provisum Andree de Offord xxv li.

Item de prebenda de Masham in ecclesia Eboracensi, de qua per consecrationem R. electi Menevensis fuit provisum Andree Offord, in partem xli li. xiii s. iiii d.

### Dunolmensis

De vicaria ecclesie de Delyngton' (Bedlington), de qua per obitum Johannis Fenrother fuit provisum Willelmo Johannis, xlii li. xiii s. iiii d.

Item de prebenda in ecclesia collegiata de Aukeland (Auckland), vacante per resignationem Reginaldi electi Menevensis, de qua collatio facta Willelmo de Dalton' fuit eidem confirmata, x li.

Item de prebenda de Assh' (Esh) in ecclesia collegiata de Langecestr' (Lanchester), de qua per consecrationem electi Londoniensis fuit provisum Johanni de Burton', iiii li. vi s. viii d.

Summa pagine ii[c] iiii li. xiii s. iiii d. Approbatum.

De ecclesia de Caldebek' (Caldbeck), de qua de novo fuit provisum Nicholao Wynhytrige, iuxta novam taxam v li.

### Hybernia
### Dublinensis

De decanatu in ecclesia Dublinensi, de quo per mortem Mathei de Brusele fuit provisum Johanni Bryan, in partem solutionis xxi li.

Item de decanatu Dubliensi, de quo per resignationem Johannis Bryan ex causa permutationis fuit provisum Willelmo de Bromeleye, xli li.

Item de dicto decanatu, de quo fuit provisum Matheo de Bruseley,[39] in partem solutionis xxvi li. xiii s. iiii d.

Item de prebenda alterius portionis de Lusk' in ecclesia Dublinensi, de qua per resignationem Willelmi de Bromelye ex causa permutationis fuit provisum Johanni Bryan, xxvi li. xiii s. iiii d.

Item de cancellaria Dublinensi, de qua collatio facta Johanni de Troye fuit eidem confirmata, in partem solutionis vi. li. xiii s. iiii d.

### Mydensis

De archidiaconatu Midensi (Meath), vacante per resignationem electi Mydensis, xl li.

Summa pagine clxvii li. Approbatum

Summa totalis fructuum beneficiorum iii[m] cxxii li. xviii s. vi d. Approbatum.

Attende quod hic non ponitur resta quia non [40] potest costare de ea, eo quod in rationibus presentibus reformandis non [41] ponitur taxa nec dies collationis beneficiorum.

(fol. 49) Sequuntur recepte de quibusdam beneficiis recelatis

### Wygorniensis

De ecclesia de Blokleye (Blockley) appropriata mense episcopi Wygorniensis xxvi li. xiii s. iiii d.

### Lincolniensis

De vicaria de Billesby (Bilsby) iii li. vi s. viii d.

Item de ecclesia de Swanton' (Swaton), appropriata abbati de Barlynges (Barlings), vacante infra tempus quadriennalis reservationis per Dominum Johannem papam facte,[42] vi li. vi s. viii d.

### Exoniensis

De prebenda in ecclesia collegiata de Crydyton' (Crediton) quam quidam Humbertus de Sametis tenuit xx s.

---

[36] Followed by *prebenda* deleted by a line.
[37] Followed by *in*, MS.
[38] *Geverlacensi*, MS.

[39] Followed by *per mortem so* deleted by a line.
[40] Extension doubtful.
[41] Followed by some form of *facio* deleted by a line.
[42] *factam*, MS.

Sarisbiriensis

De ecclesia de Uffyngton' (Uffington) abbati et conventui Abindon (Abingdon) appropriata xx li.

Item de ecclesia de Bradeford (Bradford) abbatisse et conventui Sheston' (Shaftesbury) appropriata xxvi li. xiii s. iiii d.

Adhuc Lincolniensis

Item de ecclesia de Roxeby (Roxby), vacante per constitutionem *execrabilis* xvi li.

Item de prioratu de Spalding', vacante infra tempus quadriennalis reservationis facte per Johannem papam, ex compositione facta cum priore de consensu regis Anglie, qui medietatem fructuum beneficiorum huiusmodi ex concessione apostolica debuit percipere, pro parte contingente cameram c li.

Item de ecclesiis de Ekynton' (Ecton) et Hale unitis monasterio de Bardeneye (Bardney) lxvi li.

Item de ecclesia de Salby (Saleby) appropriata prioratui de Thornholm' xiii li. vi s. viii d.

Item de ecclesia de Overton' (Orton-on-the-Hill) appropriata abbati de Miravalle (Merevale) xix li. vi s. viii d.

Norwicensis

De ecclesia de Saxthorp' (Saxthorpe) appropriata aule de Valencia Cantebrigie xiii li. vi s. viii d.

Cantuariensis

De ecclesia de Saltwode (Saltwood), de qua fuit provisum Ricardo de Hemesby, xxxiii li. vi s. viii d.

Summa pagine iii$^c$ xlv li. vi s. viii d. Approbatum.

(fol. 49$^v$) Herefordensis

De ecclesia Sancti Martini Herefordensis appropriata Magistro Sancti Antonii vi li. xiii s. iiii d.

Summa pagine vi li. xiii s. iiii d. Sic per se patet.[43]

Summa totalis receptarum de beneficiis recelatis iii$^c$ lii li. Approbatum.

Summa universalis omnium receptorum a prima die Augusti anno domini M$^o$ CCC$^{mo}$ XLIX$^o$ usque ad primam diem Junii anno domini M$^o$ CCC$^{mo}$ LVIII$^o$ vi$^m$ viii$^c$ lxxiii li. vii s. vii d. Approbatum.

(fol 50) Sequuntur assignata, missa et soluta camere apostolice et eius nomine per dictum Hugonem toto tempore predicto.

Anno domini millesimo CCC$^{mo}$ L$^{mo}$ tradit et assignavit xii die Junii idem Hugo prefate camere per manus sociorum Antonii de Malebaill' iiii$^m$ fl., computato floreno pro iii s. sterlingorum, valent vi$^c$ li.

Ista assignatio fuit facta camere xxiiii Julii anno hic contento, ut per litteras Domini B. episcopi, tunc Lomberiensis (Lombez) episcopi, et thesaurarii [44] docuit.[45]

Item iiii die Novembris eodem anno pro ii orfresiis missis domino nostro pape de mandato domini tunc archiepiscopi Sesaragustani (Saragossa) nunc vero cardinalis [46] solvit xiiii li. xiii s. iiii d. Attende; doce de mandato.[45]

Item xxviii die Maii anno domini M$^o$ CCCLI assignavit prefate camere per manus dictorum sociorum de Malebaill' iii$^m$ fl., solutis pro floreno iii solidis, valent iiii$^c$ l li.

Licet ista assignatio ista die hic contenta sit facta in Anglia, tamen camere facta reperitur die iiii Augusti dicto anno LI$^o$.[45]

Item viii die Maii anno domini M$^o$ CCC$^{mo}$ LII$^o$ assignavit prefate camere per manus dictorum sociorum iiii$^m$ fl., solutis pro floreno ut supra, valent vi$^c$ li.

Ista assignatio reperitur per bullam kalendas Augusti anno primo pontificatus domini Innocentii.[47]

Item xxii die Octobris anno domini M$^o$ CCC$^{mo}$ LIII$^o$ assignavit prefate camere per manus dictorum sociorum iiii$^m$ fl., solutis pro floreno ut supra, valent vi$^c$ li.

Ista reperitur facta camere, ut per litteras thesaurarii aparet, die vii Februarii anno LIIII$^o$.[45]

Item xxvii die Septembris anno domini M$^o$ CCC$^{mo}$ LIIII$^{to}$ assignavit dicte camere per manus dictorum sociorum v$^m$ fl., solutis pro floreno iii s. obolo, valent vii$^c$ lx li. viii s. iiii d.

Ista assignatio reperitur facta camere, ut patet per litteras thesaurarii, die xxix mensis Decembris anno LV$^o$.[45]

Item v$^{ta}$ die Junii anno domini M$^o$ CCC$^{mo}$ LV$^{to}$ assignavit dicte camere per manus dictorum sociorum iii$^m$ fl., solutis pro floreno iii s. obolo, valent iiii$^c$ lvi li. v s.

Ista assignatio reperitur facta camere, ut patet per litteras thesaurarii, die v mensis Septembris anno LV$^o$.[45]

Summa pagine iii$^m$ iiii$^c$ iiii$^{xx}$ i li. vi s. viii d. Approbatum.

(fol. 50$^v$) Item prima die Octobris eodem anno assignavit prefate camere per manus dictorum sociorum m v$^c$ fl., solutis pro floreno iii s. obolo, valent ii$^c$ xxviii li. ii s. vi d.

Ista assignatio reperitur facta camere, ut patet per litteras thesaurarii, die xxix Decembris anno LVI$^o$.[45]

Item x$^{ma}$ die Januarii [48] anno LVI$^o$ assignavit prefate camere per manus dictorum sociorum m fl., solutis pro floreno iii s., valent cl li.

Ista assignatio reperitur facta camere, ut per litteras tesaurarii aparet, die xviii mensis Junii anno LVI$^o$.[45]

Item xxiiii die Maii anno domini millesimo CCC$^{mo}$ LVI$^{to}$ assignavit prefate camere per manus dictorum sociorum iii$^m$ fl., solutis pro floreno iii s., valent iiii$^c$ l li.

Item ii die Januarii eodem anno secundum computationem ecclesie Anglicane assignavit prefate camere per

---

[43] This sentence is written in a different hand.

[44] Bertrand de Cosnac. He was made bishop of Comminges in 1352.

[45] This sentence is in the margin.

[46] William d'Aigrefeuille, priest of S. Maria in Trastevere.

[47] 1 August 1353. The sentence is in the margin.

[48] Followed by *eodem* erased by dots underneath the word.

manus dictorum sociorum v^m fl., solutis pro floreno iii s. i d., valent vii^c lxx li. xvi s. viii d.

De istis duabus solutionibus docuit [49] per bullam.[45]

Item iii die Julii anno domini M CCC^mo LVII° liberavit regi Francie de mandato domini nostri pape sub bulla v^m fl., solutis pro floreno ii s. xi d., valent vii^c xxxix li. iii s. iiii d.

Docuit de mandato eidem facto et de assignatione per litteras regis et per bullam.[45]

Item prima die Junii anno domini millesimo CCC^mo LVIII° assignavit prefate camere per manus sociorum de Malebaill' iiii^m fl. et per manus Bertrandi de Aragone ii^m fl., pretio floreni iii s., valent ix^c li.

Ista assignatio iiii^m fl. reperitur facta camere die xxx Augusti anno LVIII°, ut patet per litteras thesaurarii.[45] Docuit per bullam de istis ii^m fl.[45]

Item xv die Novembris eodem anno liberavit Johanni de Colonges domicello de mandato dominorum camerarii et thesaurarii pape xx fl., solutis pro floreno iii s., valent iii li.

Docet de mandato.[45]

Item liberavit eodem anno Karolo Jori, servienti armorum domini nostri pape, de mandato dictorum dominorum c fl., solutis pro floreno ii s. xi d., valent xiiii li. xi s. viii d.

Doce.[45]

Summa pagine iii^m ix^c xcv li. xiiii s. ii d., inclusa summa posita in sequenti pagina ad singnum.[50] Approbatum.

(fol. 51) Expense sequuntur quas dictus collector dicit se fecisse

Item solutis diversis nuntiis per totum tempus predictum portantibus diversa mandata ad diversa loca Anglie et Hybernie xx li.

Item solutis diversis commissariis ad explorandum beneficia recellata de quibus camera debebat habere emolumenta prime annate per totum tempus predictum l li.

Item solutis pro conductione hospitii ix annorum, quolibet anno vi li. xiii s. iiii d., lx li.

Item pro pergameno, papiro, incausto et cera, quolibet anno xx s., assendunt per ix annos ix li.

Item in expensis collectoris veniendo ad curiam et stando in eadem ac redeundo de eadem.[51]

Item solutis pro diversis nuntiis missis cum litteris cambii ad curiam per tempus predictum v li.

Item [52] pro amissione in auro Anglie recepto dicto tempore xv li.

Item xi die Maii anno LVII° assignavit camere per socios de Malabaile v^m fl., solutis pro floreno iii s., valent vii^c l li.

De ista assignatione docuit par litteras tesaurarii.[45] Summa universalis omnium liberatorum, missorum et expensorum per dictum tempus.[51]

(fol. 52) [53] Sequuntur arreragia dimissa per dictum Hugonem debita camere apostolice in Anglia prima die Junii anno domini millesimo CCC^mo LVIII°,

### Denarii Beati Petri

Archidiaconus Surreie debet de denariis Beati Petri de annis LIIII°, LV°, LVI° et LVII°, pro anno quolibet v li. xiii s. iiii d., xxii li. xiii s. iiii d.

Item archidiaconus Essexie de annis LV^to, LVI^to, LVII^mo, anno quolibet v li. x s., xvi li. x s.

Item episcopus Bathoniensis [54] de annis LVI^to et VII^mo, pro anno quolibet xi li. v s., xxii li. x s.

Item episcopus Norwicensis de annis LV, LVI, et VII^mo, anno quolibet xxi li. x s., lxiiii li. x s.

Item episcopus Lincolniensis pro resta anni L quinti ii li. et pro annis LVI et VII^mo, pro anno quolibet xlii li., iiii^xx vi li.

Item archiepiscopus Eboracensis pro annis LVI^to et VII^mo, anno quolibet xi li. x s., xxiii li.

Item archidiaconus Middelsexie pro anno LVII^mo v li. x s.

Item episcopus Exoniensis pro anno LVII^mo ix li. v s.

Item episcopus Sarisbiriensis pro anno LVII^mo xvii li.

Item archidiaconus Roffensis pro anno LVII^mo v li.

Item archidiaconus Wyntoniensis pro anno LVII^mo viii li.

Item episcopus Conventrensis pro dicto anno LVII x li. v s.

Item episcopus Herefordensis pro dicto anno LVII° vi li.

(fol. 52^v) Item episcopus Wygorniensis pro dicto anno LVII^mo x li. v s.

### Annui census

Prior de Bodmyne debet pro annis LVI^to et LVII^mo, anno quolibet ii s., iiii s.

Item abbas de Faversham pro anno LVII^mo xiii s. iiii d.

Item abbas Sancti Albani pro anno LVII^mo xiii s. iiii d.

Item prior Karkiolensis pro dicto anno LVII^mo xiii s. iiii d.

Item abbatissa Sancte Clare pro dicto anno LVII^mo vi d.

Sequuntur arreragia dimissa per dictum Hugonem de fructibus debitis

### Cantuariensis

De prioratu de Folkeston', ordinis Sancti Benedicti, cuius collatio facta Willelmo Medici per abbatem et con-

---

[49] Followed by *istis du* which are blurred and probably intended to be erased.
[50] The item is on last three lines of this column.
[51] No amount is entered.
[52] Followed by *p a* deleted by lines.
[53] Folio 51^v is blank.
[54] Followed by *LVI* deleted by a line.

ventum fuit eidem confirmata, debet pro resta eiusdem xv li. xiii s. iiii d.[55]

Item de ecclesia de Maydestan (Maidstone), de qua per obitum Domini Hanibaldi episcopi Tusculanensis cardinalis fuit provisum Hugoni Pelegrini, debentur fructus.[56]

Item de ecclesia de Stokebur' (Stockbury) appropriata prioratui de Ledes, debentur pro resta eiusdem xvii li. xiii s. iiii d.[55]

Item de ecclesia de Boclond (Buckland), de qua per resignationem Johannis de Stoke ex causa permutationis fuit provisum Johanni de Horton', debentur pro resta eiusdem iiii li. xiii s. iiii d.[56]

Item de ecclesia de Ikham (Ickham), de qua per resignationem Roberti de Bourne fuit provisum Rogero de Wy ii kalendas Decembris pontificatus Domini Innocentii pape VI[ti] anno iiii[to] [57] debentur fructus.[58]

(fol. 53) Item de ecclesia de Wyvelesbergh' (Willesborough), appropriata per dominum Clementem papam VI[tum] abbatie Sancti Augustini, debentur fructus.[58]

Item de ecclesia de Broclondis (Brookland), appropriata per dictum Clementem dicte abbatie Sancti Augustini, debentur fructus.[58]

## Londoniensis

De prebenda de Kenteston' (Kentish Town) in ecclesia Londoniensi, de qua per obitum Henrici de Ydesworth' fuit provisum Rogero Holm, que fuit dimissa per Dominum Raymundum Pelegrini in vi li. xiii s. iiii d., debentur de resta xxxiii s. iiii d.[58a] et iii d. quos dictus Raymundus habet litteras aquietantie de dominis camerario et thesaurario.[56]

Item de archidiaconatu Middelsexie, cuius acceptio facta per Andream de Offord fuit eidem confirmata per Dominum Clementem papam VI[tum], debentur fructus.[56]

Item de prebenda de Erlesdon' (Harlesden in Willesden) in ecclesia Londoniensi, vacante per obitum Johannis de Aumbresbur', acceptio facta per Johannem Wade fuit sibi confirmata per Dominum Clementem papam VI iiii[to] idus Maii pontificatus sui anno ix°,[59] debentur fructus.[56]

Item de ecclesia de Hese (Hayes), vacante per resignationem ultimi rectoris, de qua fuit provisum Willelmo Durandi v nonas Marcii pontificatus Clementis pape VI[ti] anno ix°,[60] debentur fructus.[56]

Item de decanatu ecclesie Londoniensis, de quo per mortem Gilberti de Bruer' fuit provisum Ricardo de

Kynlinonton' v[to] idus Aprilis pontificatus Domini Innocentii VI[ti] anno secundo,[61] debentur pro resta xx li.[56]

Item de prebenda de Iseldon' (Islington) in ecclesia Londoniensi, vacante ex causa permutationis, de qua fuit provisum Willelmo de Loughteburgh' iii nonas Decembris pontificatus Domini Innocentii pape VI anno iiii°,[62] debentur fructus.[56]

Item de ecclesia de Kellevenden' (Kelvedon) appropriata abbati Westmonasterii debentur fructus.[56]

(fol. 53[v]) Item de capella de Stanford (Stanford-le-Hope), vacante per obitum Edmundi de Grimesby, de qua fuit provisum Johanni de Torkeseye viii idus Octobris pontificatus Domini Innocentii anno iii°,[63] debentur fructus.[58]

Item de ecclesia de Brayle (Rayleigh), de qua per obitum Johannis de Hynton' fuit provisum Ricardo Broun xi[mo] kalendas Februarii pontificatus Domini Innocentii anno iiii,[64] debentur fructus.[58]

## Cicestrensis

De prebenda de Ferryngges (Ferring) in ecclesia Cicestrensi, de qua per resignationem Symonis Godwyne fuit provisum Johanni de Hatton', debentur pro resta viii li. xiii s. iiii d.[56]

Item de decanatu ecclesie Cicestrensis, de quo vacante per obitum Willelmi de Segrave fuit provisum Willelmo de Lenne xiiii kalendas Junii pontificatus Domini Clementis anno vii[mo],[65] debentur pro reste xxx li.[55]

Item de thesauraria ecclesie Cicestrensis, vacante per obitum Edmundi de Aroundell', et de prebenda in ecclesia Cicestrensi per obitum Roberti del Faw, de quibus fuit provisum Waltero Gest' xii kalendas Decembris pontificatus Domini Clementis pape VI anno viii,[66] debentur pro resta earundem xii li. ii s. ix d.[58]

Item de prebenda de Walton' in ecclesia collegiata de Bosham, de qua collatio facta Ottoni de Northwode fuit eidem confirmata vi idus Aprilis pontificatus Clementis pape anno viii°,[67] debentur fructus.[56]

Item de archidiaconatu Lewensi in ecclesia Cicestrensi, de quo collatio facta Willelmo de Loughteburgh' fuit eidem confirmata secundo idus Augusti pontificatus Domini Clementis anno xi[mo],[68] debentur fructus.[58]

Item de prebenda de Suton' (Sutton) in ecclesia Cicestrensi, de qua per consecrationem Michaelis episcopi Londoniensis fuit provisum Michaeli de Northburgh' xv kalendas Junii pontificatus Domini Innocentii anno ii,[69] debentur fructus.[58]

---

[55] In the margin opposite this item: *in resta et arayragiis.*
[56] *in resta* in the margin opposite this item.
[57] 30 November 1356.
[58] *in arayragiis* in the margin opposite this item.
[58a] The sum xxxiii s. iiii d. is in the margin.
[59] 12 May 1351.
[60] 3 March 1351.

[61] 9 April 1354.
[62] 3 December 1356.
[63] 8 October 1355.
[64] 22 January 1356.
[65] 19 May 1348.
[66] 20 November 1349.
[67] 8 April 1350.
[68] 12 August 1352.
[69] 18 May 1354.

Item de archidiaconatu Cicestrensi, de quo[70] per obitum Thome de London' fuit provisum Ricardo de Drax' xi[mo] kalendas Octobris pontificatus Domini Innocentii anno ii,[71] debentur fructus.[56]

(fol. 54) Item de prebenda ecclesia Cicestrensis, de qua per obitum Thome de London' fuit provisum Ricardo de Drax' xi kalendas Octobris pontificatus Domini Innocentii anno ii°,[71] debentur fructus.[56]

Item de prebenda Cicestrensi vacante per consecrationem Thome episcopi Norwicensis fuit provisum Henrico de Walton' vi idus Februarii pontificatus Domini Innocenti anno ii°,[72] debentur fructus.[58]

Item de prebenda de Sidlesham in ecclesia Cicestrensi, de qua per obitum Walteri Gest' fuit provisum Johanni de Bisshopeston' debentur fructus.[56]

Item de precentoria ecclesie Cicestrensis, de qua per obitum cardinalis de Mota[73] fuit provisum Domino Guillelmo Farinarii cardinali[74] viii[75] kalendas Novembris pontificatus Domini Innocentii anno iiii[to][76] debentur fructus.[58]

## Wyntoniensis

De ecclesia de Westmunes (West Meon), de qua per obitum Bernardi Cistre fuit Johanni de Kenyngton' confirmata, debentur pro resta vi li.[58]

Item de hospitali Sancte Crucis extra Wyntoniam quod fuit confirmatum Johanni de Egyndon' debentur fructus.[58]

Item de rectoria sive custodia domus Sancti Nycholai de Portesmuth' (Portsmouth), confirmata Johanni de Egyndon' kalendas v° Martii pontificatus Domini Clementis anno viii°,[77] debentur fructus.[58]

De archidiaconatu Surreie, de quo collatio facta Johanni de Egyndon' fuit eidem confirmata ii idus Februarii pontificatus Domini Clementis anno x[mo],[78] debentur fructus.[58]

Item de ecclesia de Laverkestok' (Laverstoke), in cuius iure quod competebat Johanni Croun fuit subrogatus Johannes de Bannebur', debentur pro resta xii li.[55]

Item de prebenda in ecclesia monialium de Wherewell' (Wherwell), de qua per obitum Roberti de Turre fuit provisum Johanni Brankere v[to] kalendas Januarii pontificatus Domini Innocentii anno primo,[79] debentur fructus.[58]

(fol. 54ᵛ) Item de prioratu de Appelburcop' (Appuldurcombe) collatio facta Johanni Osanna fuit sibi con-

firmata v kalendas Martii anno supradicto[80] debentur fructus.[58]

## Sarisbiriensis

De ecclesia de Elyngdon' (Elingdon), de qua per resignationem Rogeri Holm fuit provisum Jacobo Beauford, debentur fructus.[56]

Item de archidiaconatu Sarisbiriensi, vacante per obitum Roberti de Ruffenham, et prebenda eiusdem ecclesie vacante per mortem Jacobi Henont', quorum acceptio facta per Rogerum de Kynton' fuit eidem confirmata, debentur fructus.[56]

Item de prebenda [80a] de Kyveleye (Keevil) in ecclesia Sarisbiriensi, de qua per mortem Roberti le Wymble fuit provisum Thome de Trompsale et fuerat per Dominum Raymundum Pelegrini dimissa in arrerargiis in xx li. xiii s. iiii d., debentur adhuc de reste eiusdem x li.[55]

Item de prebenda de Swaclyve (Swallowcliffe) in ecclesiae collegiata de Heghtredebur' (Heytesbury), de qua per obitum Thome de Litelton' fuit provisum Roberto Bakar, debentur pro resta iii li. vi s. viii d.[56]

Item de prebenda de Wermynstre (Warminster) in ecclesia Sarisbiriensi, de qua per obitum Johannis de Abbatesbur' fuit provisum Thome de Tugall', debentur pro resta v li.[58]

Item de prebenda de Dysamynstre (Yetminster) in ecclesia Sarisbiriensi, de qua per promotionem Johannis de Offord in archiepiscopatum Cantuariensem fuit provisum Henrico de Walton, debentur pro resta xvi li. xiii s. iiii d.[58]

Item de prebenda in ecclesia Sarisbiriensi de qua per obitum Thome de Astele fuit provisum Reginaldo Bryan nonas Maii pontificatus Clementis anno viii°,[81] debentur fructus.[58]

Item de prebenda de Northnuwigton' (North Newnton) in ecclesia monialium de Wylton' (Wilton), de que acceptio facta per Johannem de Vienna fuit sibi confirmata xiiii kalendas Junii pontificatus Domini Clementis anno viii°,[82] debentur pro resta viii li. vi s. viii d.[56]

Item de prebenda de Netherhaven' (Netheravon) in ecclesia Sarisbiriensi, de qua per obitum ultimi prebendarii fuit provisum Willelmo de Melburn' nonas Maii pontificatus Clementis anno ix,[83] debentur pro resta vi li. xiii s. iiii d.[56]

(fol. 55) Item de prebenda de Netherber' (Netherbury) in ecclesia Sarisbiriensi, de qua per obitum Thome de Luco acceptio facta per Reginaldum Bryan

---

[70] *qua*, MS.
[71] 21 September 1354.
[72] 8 February 1354.
[73] Gaillard de Mota, deacon of St. Lucy in Silice.
[74] Priest of SS. Marcellino e Pietro.
[75] Followed by *idus* deleted by a line.
[76] 25 October 1356.
[77] 25 February 1350.
[78] 12 February 1352.
[79] 28 December 1353.

[80] 25 February 1353.
[80a] A mistake for *ecclesia*, see p. 123.
[81] 7 May 1350.
[82] After *viii°* the text reads: *confirmata debentur sibi pro resta*. The date is 19 May 1349.
[83] 7 May 1351.

xvi kalendas Septembris pontificatus Clementis anno viiiᵒ [84] fuit sibi confirmata, debentur fructus.[85]

Item de prebenda in ecclesia Sarisbiriensi, de qua per obitum Roberti de Horton' fuit provisum Thome de Edyndon' kalendas Februarii Domini Clementis pontificatus anno viiiᵒ [86] debentur fructus.[85]

Item de prebenda de Bisshopeston' (Bishopstone) in ecclesia Sarisbiriensi, de qua per obitum Petri Raymundi fuit provisum Raymundo Pelegrini kalendas Februarii anno predicto [86] per Dominum Clementem, debentur fructus.[85]

Item de prebenda de Heyworth' (Highworth) in ecclesia Sarisbiriensi, de qua per obitum Walteri de London' fuit provisum Raymundo Pelegrini xii kalendas Junii pontificatus Domini Clementis anno ixᵒ,[87] debentur fructus.[88]

Item de ecclesia de Scorcoumbe (Corscombe), de qua acceptio facta per Johannem de Broclond fuit sibi confirmata viiiᵒ idus Junii pontificatus Clementis anno ixᵒ,[89] debentur fructus.[85]

Item de prebenda de Wermynstr' (Warminister) in ecclesia Sarisbiriensi, de qua per obitum Baldewyni de Moyn acceptio facta per Bartholomeum de Braddon' fuit eidem confirmata v idus Septembris pontificatus Clementis anno ixᵒ,[90] debentur fructus.[85]

Item de prebenda de Hull' (Hill Deverill) in ecclesia collegiata de Hertedebur' (Heytesbury), de qua per obitum Roberti Tresk' fuit provisum Bartholomeo Patricii viii idus Martii pontificatus Domini Clementis anno ixᵒ,[91] debentur fructus.[85]

Item de prebenda de Preston' in ecclesia Sarisbiriensi, de qua per obitum Rotberti Tresk' fuit provisum Johanni Goff' viii idus Martii pontificatus Clementis anno ixᵒ,[91] debentur fructus.[92]

(fol. 56) [93] Sequitur compotus brevis redditus per Dominum Hugonem Pelegrini collectorem apostolicum in partibus Anglie, Wallie et Hibernie de omnibus et singulis suis receptis et assignatis camere apostolice ac de expensis per ipsum factis a prima die mensis Augusti anno domini Mᵒ CCCᵐᵒ XLIXᵒ usque ad diem primam mensis Junii anno domini Mᵒ CCCᵒ LVIIIᵒ.

Et primo dixit se recepisse de arrayratgiis denariorum Beati Petri dimissis per Dominum Ramundum Pelegrini predecessorem suum in officio cxliiii li. viii s. iiii d.

Item dicit se recepisse de arrayratgiis annui census dimissis per dictum Dominum Ramundum ii li. ii s.

Item dicit se recepisse de arrayratgiis beneficiorum dimissis per ipsum Dominum Ramundum m viᶜ xlv li. iii s. x d.

Summa summarum dictorum arrayratgiorum dimissorum per dictum Dominum Ramundum est m viiᶜ xci li. xiiii s. ii d.

(fol. 56ᵛ) Sequitur recepta denariorum Beati Petri de tempore suo.

Et primo dicit se recepisse de denariis Beati Petri anno XLIXᵒ cxcix li. viii s. viii d.

Item dicit se recepisse de dictis [94] denariis anno Lᵒ cxcix li. viii s. viii d.

Item dicit se recepisse de dictis denariis anno LIᵒ cxcix li. viii s. viii d.

Item dicit se recepisse de dictis denariis anno LIIᵒ cxcix li. viii s. viii d.

Item dicit se recepisse de dictis denariis anno LIIIᵒ cxcix li. viii s. viii d.

Item dicit se recepisse de dictis denariis anno LIIIIᵒ cxciii li. xv s. iiii d. Restant ad solvendum de dicto anno v li. xiii s. iiii d.

Item dicit se recepisse de dictis denariis anno LVᵒ clxiiii li. xv s. iiii d. Restant ad solvendum de dicto anno xxxiiii li. xiiii s. iiii d.

Item dicit se recepisse de dictis denariis anno LVIᵒ cii li. iiii d. Restant ad solvendum de dicto anno xcvii li. viii s. iiii d.

Item dicit se recepisse de dictis denariis anno LVIIᵒ xiii li. x s. Restant ad solvendum de dicto anno clxxxv li. xviii s. viii d.

Summa summarum dictorum denariorum est m iiiiᶜ lxxi li. iiii s. iiii d. Summa restarum predictorum denariorum Beati Petri de tempore suo iiiᶜ xxvi li. x s. viii d.

(fol. 57) Sequitur recepta annui census
Et primo dicit se recepisse de annuo censu anno XLIXᵒ iiii li. xv s.

Item dicit se recepisse de dicto annuo censu anno L iiii li. xv s.

Item dicit se recepisse de dicto annuo censu anno LI iiii li. xv s.

Item dicit se recepisse de dicto annuo censu anno LIIᵒ iiii li. xv s.

Item dicit se recepisse de dicto annuo censu anno LIIIᵒ iiii li. xv s.

Item dicit se recepisse de dicto annuo censu anno LIIIIᵒ iiii li. xv s.

Item dicit se recepisse de dicto annuo censu anno LV iiii li. xv s.

Item dicit se recepisse de dicto annuo censu anno LVI iiii li. xiii s. Restant ad solvendum de dicto anno ii s.

---

[84] 17 August 1349.

[85] In the margin opposite this item is noted *in arayragiis*.

[86] 1 February 1350.

[87] 21 May 1350.

[88] In the margin opposite this item is noted *in resta et arayragiis*.

[89] 6 June 1350.

[90] 9 September 1350.

[91] 8 March 1351.

[92] In the margin opposite this item is noted *in resta*.

[93] Folio 55ᵛ is blank. Folios 55ᵛ to 58 constitute a sheaf of three leaves which are much smaller than the preceding leaves. The sheaf is probably inserted in the wrong place. With folio 59 the leaves again become of the standard size and the account of the arrears of annates is continued from folio 55.

[94] Folowed by *de* deleted by a line.

Item dicit se recepisse de dicto annuo censu anno LVII° ii li. xiii s. Restant ad solvendum de dicto anno xlii s.

Summa summarum recepta dicti annui census est xl li. xi s. Summa restarum predicti annui census ii li. iiii s.

(fol. 57ᵛ) Item dicit se recepisse de legatis ad Terram Sanctam pro redemptione votorum per tempus supradictum xciiii li. xix s. vii d.

Item dicit se recepisse de beneficiis sibi per cameram missis in predicto tempore iiiᵐ cxxii li. xviii s. vi d.

Item dicit se recepisse de beneficiis reservatis de quibus non fuit sibi scriptum per dictam cameram iiiᶜ lii li.

Summa universalis omnium receptorum a prima die mensis Augusti anno domini Mᵒ CCCᵐᵒ XLIXᵒ usque ad diem primam mensis Junii anno domini Mᵒ CCCᵐᵒ LVIIIIᵒ viᵐ viiiᶜ lxxiii li. vii s. vii d.

(fol. 58) Sequuntur assignationes et solutiones facte in Romana curia et extra de mandato camere inclusis assignationibus et solutionibus ac misiis factis de mandato camere viiᵐ iiiiᶜ lxxvii li. x d.

Item computat expendisse [95] ratione officii prout particulariter in suis rationibus continetur, inclusis l libris [96] datis revelantibus beneficia celata et salario hospitii clix li.

Summa summarum omnium assingnatorum camere [97] et extra cameram de mandato camere et expensarum est viiᵐ viᶜ xxxvi li. x d. sterlingorum.

Facta autem deductione et compensatione de receptis ad assingnata, expensas et misias, repertum est dictum Dominum Hugonem plus assingnasse, expendisse vel misisse quam recepisse viiᶜ lxii li. xiii s. iii d. sterlingorum, que summa debet deduci de receptis futuris post datam rationum predictarum.

(fol. 59) [98] Item de prebenda de Northneweton' (North Newnton) in ecclesia monialium de Wilton', de qua per obitum Johannis de Vienna fuit provisum Willelmo de Melborne nonas Maii pontificatus Clementis anno ixᵒ,[99] debentur fructus.[100]

Item de ecclesia de Wynteborn' Fakelan' (Winterborne Stickland), de qua per resignationem Willelmi de Cheston' fuit provisum Thome Henrico xiiii kalendas Julii pontificatus Domini Innocentii anno primo,[101] debentur fructus.[100]

Item de prebenda in ecclesia Sarisbiriensi de qua ex causa permutationis fuit provisum Johanni Thursteyn

idus Martii pontificatus Innocentii anno iiiᵒ [102] debentur fructus.[100]

Item de archidiaconatu Dorcestr', de quo per obitum cardinalis Sabinensis [103] fuit provisum cardinali Autissiodorensi (Auxerre) [104] iii idus Februarii pontificatus Innocentii anno iii,[105] debentur fructus.[100]

Item de prebenda de Aulton' (Alton) Sancti Pancratii in ecclesia Sarisbiriensi, de qua fuit facta confirmatio Willelmo de Nassyngton' xi kalendas Novembris pontificatus Innocentii anno iiiiᵗᵒ,[106] debentur fructus.[107]

Item de prebenda de Remeston' (Beminster) in ecclesia Sarisbiriensi, de qua fuit facta confirmatio Petro de Woton' xi kalendas Novembris pontificatus Innocentii anno iiiiᵗᵒ,[106] debentur fructus.[107]

Item de thesauraria [108] Sarisbiriensi et prebenda de Calne in eadem, de quibus per obitum cardinalis de Mota [109] fuit provisum cardinali de Florentia [110] iiiiᵗᵒ kalendas Januarii pontificatus Innocentii anno iiiiᵗᵒ,[111] debentur pro resta lvii li. xv s. vii d.[107]

Item de subdecanatu ecclesie Sarisbiriensis cum prebenda eidem annexa, de quibus collatio facta Radulpho de Querendon' fuit confirmata iiᵒ [112] kalendas Februarii pontificatus Innocentii anno iiiiᵗᵒ,[113] debentur fructus.[100]

Item de prioratu de Lodres, de quo provisio facta per abbatem Symoni de Londa fuit sibi confirmata ii kalendas Februarii anno supradicto,[113] debentur fructus.[100]

(fol. 59ᵛ) Exoniensis

De thesauraria ecclesie Exoniensis, de qua acceptio facta per Robertum de Middelond fuit sibi confirmata xv kalendas Junii pontificatus Clementis anno viiiᵒ [114] debentur fructus.[100]

Item de archidiaconatu Barnastapol', de quo per obitum Johannis de Nassyngton' collatio facta Johanni de Reynham fuit sibi confirmata vi nonas Aprilis anno Clementis viii,[115] debentur fructus.[100]

Item de prebenda ecclesie Exoniensis de qua per obitum Johannis Petri collatio facta Nicholao Terrer fuit confirmata vi nonas Aprilis [116] debentur fructus.[107]

Item de ecclesia de Exminstr' (Axminster), de qua per obitum Henrici de Galmyngton' fuit provisum

---

[95] Followed by *prout* deleted by a line.
[96] Follows *florenis* deleted by a line.
[97] Followed by *vel extra* erased by a line.
[98] Folio 58ᵛ is blank. Folio 59 continues from folio 55, above, p. 95.
[99] 7 May 1351.
[100] In the margin opposite this item is noted *in arayragiis*.
[101] 18 June 1353.

[102] 15 March 1355.
[103] Bertrand d'Eux.
[104] Peter de Croso, priest of Ss. Silvestro e Martino ai Monti.
[105] 11 February 1355. The MS. reads "anno iii;" Eubel i, 37 dates the death of the bishop of Sabina as 21 October, 1355. See below, p. 185.
[106] 22 October 1356.
[107] In the margin opposite this item is noted *in resta*.
[108] Followed by *et prebenda* deleted by a line.
[109] Gaillard de Mota, cardinal deacon of St. Lucy in Silice.
[110] Francis de Aptis, bishop of Florence, cardinal priest of S. Marco.
[111] 29 December 1356.
[112] Followed by *idus* deleted by a line.
[113] 31 January 1356.
[114] 18 May 1350.
[115] If *vi nonas* is a mistake for *vi idus*, the date is 8 April 1350.
[116] Probably the same date as the preceding item.

Nicholao Terrer iiii kalendas Aprilis Clementis anno ix [117] debentur pro resta vi li.[107]

Item de prebenda in ecclesia Exoniensi de qua per obitum Johannis Pipard fuit facta confirmatio Jacobo Milton' iiii kalendas Martii [118] debentur fructus.[107]

Item de decanatu ecclesie Exoniensis, de quo [119] per obitum Ricardi de Brayle fuit provisum Reginaldo de Bugwell' xv kalendas Octobris Clementis anno xi[mo],[120] debentur pro resta lii li. xiii s. iiii d.[121]

Item de prebenda ecclesie Exoniensis de qua per obitum Domini Henrici de Brakelee fuit provisum Henrico de Walton' debentur fructus.[100]

Item de vicaria de Holmpton' (Yealmpton), in cuius iure quod competebet Johanni de Combe fuit subrogatus Robertus Gervays ii idus Octobris pontificatus Domini Innocentii anno primo.[122]

Item de prebenda quam Thomas David in ecclesia Exoniensi obtinet, de qua per obitum Willelmi de Crouthorn' acceptio per ipsum facta fuit sibi confirmata viii idus Maii anno Clementis x,[123] debentur fructus.[100]

Item de prioratu de Oterton' (Otterton), de quo collatio facta Thome Sedile fuit sibi confirmata ii kalendas Februarii in anno iiii[to],[124] debentur fructus.[121]

### (fol. 60) Wygorniensis

De ecclesia de Estlegh' (Astley), de qua per obitum Henrici de Stowe, qui eam acceptaverat et de ea in curia litigabat, fuit provisum Henrico de Askeby, debentur pro resta viii li.[100]

Item de ecclesia Sanctorum Philipi et Jacobi Bristoll', de qua per obitum Roberti Rene fuit provisum Nicholao de Dodyngton', debentur fructus.[100]

Item de ecclesia de Knyghtwych' (Knightwick), de qua ex causa permutationis fuit provisum Johanni Charneux pontificatus Innocentii anno primo,[125] debentur fructus.[100]

### Bathoniensis

De prebenda de Harpetre (East Harptree) in ecclesia Wellensi, de qua per consecrationem Domini Lodewyci episcopi Dunolmensis fuit provisum Henrico de Harwedon' et fuerat dimissa in arreragiis per Dominum Raymundum Pelegrini, debentur pro resta iiii li.[100]

Item de ecclesia de Hyngham (High Ham), de qua per assecutionem ecclesie de Dounton' (Donnington) fuit provisum Johanni de Farendon' et fuerat dimissa in arreragiis per Dominum Raymundum Pelegrini, debentur pro resta xviii li.[107]

Item de prebenda de Weveleston' (Wiveliscombe) in ecclesia Wellensi, de qua per obitum vel consecrationem Johannis de Ufford fuit provisum Willelmo de Bergevenny, debentur pro resta xiii li. vi s. viii d.[100]

Item de decanatu Wellensi, de quo per obitum Willelmi de London' fuit proprio motu provisum Johanni de Carleton' x kalendas Junii pontificatus Clementis anno viii,[126] debentur pro resta lx li.[107]

Item de cancellaria ecclesie Wellensi et prebenda de Compton' in eadem, de quibus per assecutionem dicti decanatus fuit provisum Johanni de Horsyngton' kalendas Junii anno supradicto,[127] debentur pro resta xx li. xii s.[121]

Item de prebenda de Wyvelescoumbe (Wiveliscombe) in ecclesia Wellensi, de qua collatio facta Thome de Boughton' fuit eidem confirmata iiii° idus Maii pontificatus Clementis anno ix°,[128] debentur fructus.[107]

(fol. 60[v]) Item de thesauraria ecclesie Wellensis, de qua per obitum Ricardi de Tilteston' acceptio facta per Ricardum de Thormerton' fuit confirmata idus Novembris pontificatus Clementis anno xi[mo],[129] debentur fructus.[121]

Item de archidiaconatu Wellensi cum prebenda sibi annexa, de quibus consecrationem electi Menevensis fuit provisum Domino Guillelmo episcopo Tusculanensi iii nonas Januarii pontificatus Innocentii anno primo,[130] debentur pro resta xliiii li. viii s. xi d.[107]

Item de precentoria ecclesie Wellensis et prebenda de Cumba (Combe) quinta in eadem, de quibus per obitum Willelmi de Lutelton' fuit provisum Edmundo Gourney iii kalendas Februarii anno supradicto,[131] debentur pro resta xliiii li. vi s. viii d.[107]

Item de prebenda de Witchurche (Whitchurch) in ecclesia Wellensi, de qua per obitum Roberti Luffyn acceptio facta per Ricardum de Tormerton' fuit eidem confirmata anno ii supradicto,[132] debentur fructus.[100]

Item de prebenda in ecclesia Wellensi, de qua per obitum Gilberti de Bruera fuit provisum Transmontano Rerebaud' iiii nonas Decembris anno Domini Innocentii iii,[133] debentur fructus.[107]

Item de ecclesia de Melles (Mells), de qua acceptio facta per Andream de Weremenstr' fuit sibi confirmata xv kalendas Martii anno supradicto,[134] debentur fructus.[107]

Item de ecclesia de Preston', de qua per assecutionem alterius beneficii fuit provisum Johanni Attewelle ii nonas Maii anno supradicto,[135] debentur fructus.[107]

---

[117] 29 March 1351.
[118] 26 February 1351 : *Cal. Pap. Regs. Letters*, iii, 384.
[119] *qua*, MS.
[120] 17 September 1352.
[121] In the margin opposite this item is noted *in resta et arayragiis*.
[122] 14 October 1353. In the margin: *in arayragiis*.
[123] 8 May 1352.
[124] 31 January 1356.
[125] 22 July 1353 : *Cal. Pap. Regs. Petitions*, i, 251.

[126] 23 May 1349.
[127] 1 June 1349.
[128] 12 May 1351.
[129] 13 November 1352.
[130] 3 January 1353.
[131] 30 January 1353.
[132] 16 October 1354 : *Cal. Pap. Regs. Petitions*, i, 263.
[133] 2 December 1355.
[134] 15 February 1355.
[135] 6 May 1355.

Item de prioratu Montis Acuti (Montacute), de quo per obitum Johannis la Porte fuit provisum Johanni la Porte, fratri eiusdem, debentur pro resta dimissa per Dominum Raymundum Pelegrini cviii li. vi s. viii d.[121]

### Herefordensis

De prebenda de Morton' (Moreton Magna) in ecclesia Herefordensi, de qua per obitum Thome de Stanton' fuit provisum Symoni de Sudbur' iiii[to] nonas Julii anno Clementis viii,[136] debentur pro resta xiii s. iiii d.[100]

(fol. 61) Item de vicaria de Ledebur' (Ledbury), de qua per assecutionem archidiaconatus Menevensis factam per Ricardum de Cleangres fuit provisum Roberto Michaelis de Florentia v[to] idus Octobris anno supradicto,[137] debentur fructus.[138]

Item de portione prebendalis ecclesie de Ledebur', de qua per consecrationem J. episcopi Dublinensis fuit provisum Nicholao de Heth', debentur fructus.[139]

Item de parochiali ecclesia de Montegomeri (Montgomery), de qua fuit de novo provisum Nicholao de Upton' et convenit de fructibus perceptis cum domino camerario in xii li., xvii kalendas Februarii pontificatus Domini Innocentii anno primo,[140] debentur pro resta viii li. xiiii d.[138]

Item de prebenda de Euthyngton' (Ewithington or East Withington), de qua per obitum Edumundi de Grymesby fuit provisum Thome Gryffin viii kalendas Octobris Domini Innocenti anno ii,[141] debentur fructus.[121]

Item de prebenda ecclesie Herefordensis de qua per obitum Stephani de Ledebur' fuit provisum Willelmo de Dalton' ix kalendas Februarii anno ii[o] [142] debentur fructus.[138]

Item de ecclesia de Kingeslond (Kingsland), de qua fuit de novo provisum Willelmo de Pembrugg' iiii kalendas Martii Innocentii anno iii,[143] debentur fructus.[138]

Item de prebenda in ecclesia Herefordensi de qua collatio facta Willelmo Wroth' fuit eidem confirmata idus Octobris pontificatus Domini Innocentii anno supradicto [144] debentur fructus.[138]

Item de prebenda de Pitteston' (Putson), de qua acceptio facta per Petrum de Upton' fuit sibi confirmata xi[mo] kalendas [145] Novembris pontificatus Domini Innocentii anno iiii[to],[146] debentur fructus.[138]

### Norwicensis

De ecclesia de Bramford unita monasterio de Bello (Battle) Cicestrensis diocesis debentur fructus.[138]

Item de prioratu de Castelacre (Castle Acre), de quo fuit ex causa permutationis de novo provisum Willelmo de Warenna et fuit dimisso per Dominum Raymundum Pelegrini, debentur fructus.[139]

(fol. 61[v]) Item de ecclesia de Herdewik' (Hardwick), de qua fuit de novo provisum Radulpho de Sutholf', debentur pro resta liiii s. iiii d.[139]

Item de ecclesia de Ulmo (Holme), de qua per resignationem Willelmi de Morton' fuit provisum Thome Michel, debentur pro resta x ii.[139]

Item de ecclesia de Pulham, de qua per obitum Johannis de Hildesle fuit provisum Michaeli de Northburgh' ii nonas Septembris Clementis anno viii[o],[147] debentur pro resta xvii li. ii s. v d.[138]

Item de prioratu Sancte ⟨Fidis⟩ de Horsham, de quo per obitum Poncii de Serveria fuit provisum Bernardo Joly viii kalendas Octobris anno supradicto,[148] debentur fructus.[121]

Item de ecclesia de Redegrage (Redgrave), de qua per obitum ultimi rectoris fuit facta confirmatio Johanni de Eya v kalendas Martii anno supradicto [149] debentur pro resta iiii li.[138]

Item de ecclesia de Derham (East Dereham), de qua per obitum Alani de Hothim fuit provisum Symoni Thebaud iii kalendas Aprilis anno Clementis x,[150] debentur pro resta xl li. xvi s. viii d.[139]

Item de ecclesia de Elvedon' (Elveden), de qua per resignationem Ricardi de Hemmesby fuit provisum Willelmo Simon' xiii kalendas Januarii anno supradicto,[151] debentur pro resta vii li. xiii s. iiii d.[138]

Item de ecclesia de Thurston', de qua fuit provisum Roberto de Thorp' xviii kalendas Junii anno Domini Innocentii supradicto,[152] debentur pro resta vi li. xiii s. iiii d.[138]

### Eliensis

De prioratu de Swaveseye, de quo fuit provisum Stephano de Gurtery, debentur pro resta x li.[153]

### Lincolniensis

De prioratu de Cogges, de quo fuit facta confirmatio Guillelmo Hamonis, debentur pro resta dimissa per Dominum Raymundum Pelegrini viii li. xiii s. iiii d.[153]

(fol. 62) Item de vicaria ecclesia de Wathford (Watford), de qua per mortem Ricardi filii Ade Blakwyne

---

[136] 4 July 1349.
[137] 11 October 1349.
[138] In the margin opposite this item is noted *in resta*.
[139] In the margin opposite this item is noted *in arayragiis*.
[140] 16 January 1353.
[141] 24 September 1354.
[142] 24 January 1354.
[143] 26 February 1355.
[144] 15 October 1355.
[145] Followed by *Decembris* deleted by a line.
[146] 22 October 1356.

[147] 4 September 1349.
[148] 24 September 1349.
[149] 25 February 1350.
[150] 30 March 1352.
[151] 20 December 1351.
[152] 15 May 1354.
[153] In the margin opposite this item is noted *in resta et arayragiis*.

et Walteri de Loveday, qui de ipsa in palatio litigabant, fuit in iure ipsorum Rogerus de Thorpegate subrogatus, debentur fructus.[138]

Item de ecclesia de Humberston' (Humberstone) unita monasterio Beate Marie Leycestr', debentur fructus.[138]

Item de prebenda de Ketone (Ketton) in ecclesia Lincolniensi, de qua per resignationem Willelmi de Hogate ex causa permutationis fuit provisum Willelmo de Dalton', debentur fructus.[138]

Item de prebenda de Farendon' (Farndon) in ecclesia Lincolniensi, de qua per obitum Francisci de Urcinis, fuit provisum Thome de Baddeby, qui fuit dimissus in arreragiis per Dominum Raymundum Pelegrini in liii li. vi s. viii d., debentur pro resta dicte summe xiii li. vi s. viii d.[138]

Item de prebenda de Sutton' (Sutton cum Buck.), de qua per resignationem Baldraci de Malbaill' fuit provisum Thome de Brembre iii kalendas Maii pontificatus Domini Clementis anno viii°,[154] debentur fructus.[138]

Item de prebenda de Langesford (Langford) in ecclesia Lincolniensi, de qua fuit facta confirmatio Johanni Lech', debentur pro resta xv li.[138]

Item de decanatu Lincolniensi, de quo per obitum Johannis electi Cantuariensis fuit provisum Symoni de Bruseley vi idus Octobris anno supradicto,[155] debentur pro resta c iiiixx vi li. xiii s. iiii d.[153]

Item de ecclesia de Ketering' (Kettering), de qua fuit provisum Johanni Wade qui composuit cum camera pro subsidio contra Turcos in ii° florenis auri, debentur dicti floreni.[139]

Item de prebenda de Beddeford maiori (Bedford Maior) in ecclesia Lincolniensi, de qua collatio facta Willelmo de Wytlesseye fuit confirmata viii idus Maii pontificatus Clementis anno viii°,[156] debentur fructus.[139]

Item de archidiaconatu Bukinghamie, de qua per obitum cardinalis Tusculanensis fuit provisum Johanni de Asshebur' pontificatus Clementis anno ix°,[157] debentur fructus.[139]

(fol. 62ᵛ) Item de subdecanatu ecclesia Lincolniensis, de quo acceptio facta per Hamonem Belers fuit confirmata iii kalendas Maii anno supradicto,[158] debentur pro resta xxv li.[153]

Item de archidiaconatu Norhamptonie, de quo collatio facta Johanni de Bukingham fuit confirmata xii kalendas Maii anno supradicto,[159] debentur fructus.[138]

Item de prebenda de Greton' (Gretton) in ecclesia Lincolniensi, de qua per uxerationem Emerici de Cusornio fuit provisum Johanni de Bukingham xii kalendas Maii anno supradicto, debentur pro resta xxxvi li. xiii s. iiii d.[138]

Item de prebenda de Walton' Ryvall' (Welton Rivall), de qua per obitum Johannis de Hatton' fuit provisum Johanni de Asshebur' iiii nonas Maii anno supradicto,[160] debentur fructus.[138]

Item de prebenda de Scarles (South Scarle), de qua per obitum Thome de Cruce fuit provisum Johanni de Kyrkeby, debentur pro resta xx li.[153]

Item de media portione ecclesie de Seggebrek' (Sedgebrook), de qua per obitum ultimi rectoris fuit provisum Roberto de Seggsbrek' ximo kalendas Augusti pontificatus Clementis anno xmo,[161] debentur pro resta ii li. xiii s. iiii d.[139]

Item de ecclesia de Folkesworth' (Folksworth), de qua per obitum Henrici de Ulceby fuit provisum Symoni Spark' xvi kalendas Februarii anno supradicto,[162] debentur pro resta v li.[138]

Item de parochiali ecclesia de Greford (Greatford), de qua fuit facta unio monasterio monialium Beate Marie Wyntoniensis iii idus Julii pontificatus Clementis anno ximo,[163] debentur fructus.[139]

Item de prebenda de Clifton' in ecclesia Lincolniensi, de qua per obitum Johannis de Hull' acceptio facta per Stephanum de Ravenesore fuit eidem confirmata vii kalendas Augusti anno supradicto,[164] debentur fructus.[139]

(fol. 63) Item de ecclesia de Edesburgh' (Edlesborough), de qua per obitum Johannis de Belvero fuit provisum Johanni de Swynesheved ii nonas Octobris anno supradicto,[165] debentur pro resta xx li.[138]

Item de prebenda de Bucleden' (Buckden) in ecclesia Lincolniensi, de qua per consecrationem Thome electi Menevensis fuit provisum Edwuardo Botiller iiii nonas Novembris anno supradicto.[166] debentur fructus.[138]

Item de ecclesia de Ouston' (Owston), de qua unio facta fuit priori et monasterio de Novoburgo (Newburgh) et confirmata, reservatione non obstante, viii kalendas Junii anno supradicto,[167] debentur fructus.[138]

Item de ecclesia de Melchebur' (Melchbourne), de qua per obitum Bartholomei de Drayton' fuit provisum Radulpho de Ulnhale vito kalendas Februarii pontificatus Domini Innocentii anno primo,[168] debentur fructus.[139]

Item de prebenda de Carleton' in Thurleby (Carleton cum Thurlby) in ecclesia Lincolniensi, de qua per consecrationem Nicholai episcopi Urgellensis (Urgel) fuit provisum Roberto de Wrigesworth ix kalendas Maii anno supradicto,[169] debentur pro resta xxiii li. vi s. viii d.[139]

---

[154] 29 April 1350.
[155] 10 October 1349.
[156] 8 May 1350.
[157] 13 November 1350.
[158] 29 April 1351.
[159] 20 April 1351.

[160] 4 May 1351.
[161] 22 July 1351.
[162] 17 January 1352.
[163] 13 July 1352.
[164] 26 July 1352.
[165] 6 October 1352.
[166] 2 November 1352.
[167] 25 May 1352.
[168] 27 January 1353.
[169] 23 April 1353.

Item de prebenda Sancti Martini in ecclesia Lincolniensi, de qua per obitum Henrici de Chaddesden' fuit provisum Rogero de Burton' viii kalendas Februarii pontificatus Innocentii anno secundo,[170] debentur fructus.[138]

Item de ecclesia de Stikeneye (Stickney), de qua per assecutionem alterius beneficii fuit provisum Johanni Auncel v kalendas Februarii anno supradicto,[171] debentur fructus.[138]

Item de ecclesia de Horncastr' (Horncastle), de qua fuit facta confirmatio Johanni de Kyrkeby ix° kalendas Februarii anno supradicto,[172] debentur pro resta xviii li. vi s. viii d.[173]

Item de ecclesia de Bukenhill' (Bucknell), de qua fuit de novo provisum Laurentio de Breton' v idus Aprilis anno supradicto,[174] debentur fructus.[173]

Item de ecclesia de Pokebrog' (Polebrooke), de qua per obitum Johannis de Wirtle fuit provisum Willelmo de Esyngdon' xi kalendas Junii anno iiii^to,[175] debentur fructus.[173]

(fol. 63^v) Item de ecclesia de Kyrkeby Bayn (Kirkby on Bain), de qua per obitum Willelmi de Corbrugg' fuit provisum Thome de Plep' nonas Augusti anno supradicto,[176] debentur fructus.[173]

Item de prebenda de Scorp' (Cropredy) in ecclesia Lincolniensi, de qua ex causa permutationis fuit provisum Willelmo de Rothewell' iii nonas Decembris anno supradicto,[177] debentur fructus.[173]

## Lychfeldensis

De archidiaconatu Conventrensi et prebenda de Langodon' (Longdon), in ecclesia Lichfeldensi, de quibus fuit de novo provisum Humfredo de Hastinges, dimissis in arreragiis per Dominum Raymundum Pelegrini, debentur fructus.[153]

Item de ecclesia de Hodynet (Hodnet), de qua per consecrationem domini reverendi episcopi Bathoniensis fuit provisum Nicholao de Heth', que fuit dimissa in arreragiis per Dominum Raymundum Pelegrini, debetur[178] taxa que est xl li.[179]

Item de ecclesia de Legh' (Leigh), de qua fuit de novo provisum Magistro Johanni de Holand, que per dictum Raymundum Pelegrini fuerat dimissa in arreragiis in ix li. xiii s. iiii d., debentur pro resta v li.[179]

Item de ecclesia de Northworthy (Northenden), de qua fuit provisum Willelmo de Hyngesle et fuerat

dimissa in arreragiis per dictum Raymundum Pelegrini, debentur pro resta x s.[173]

Item de archidiaconatu Conventrensi et prebenda de Langedon' (Longdon) in ecclesia Lichfeldensi, de quibus per obitum Humfredi de Hastinges fuit provisum Willelmo Sallowe iii° nonas Septembris anno Clementis viii,[180] debentur[181] pro resta xxvi li.[182] xiii s. iiii d.[183]

Item de prebenda in ecclesia Lichfeldensi de qua per obitum Willelmi Apeltre fuit provisum Thome Attehull' debentur fructus.[179]

Item de decanatu Lichfeldensi cum prebenda sibi annexa, de quibus per assecutionem decanatus Lincolniensis fuit provisum Johanni de Bukyngham nonas Novembris anno ii°,[184] debentur pro resta xx li.[179]

(fol. 64) De prebenda in ecclesia collegiata Sancti Cedde Salopie (Shrewsbury, St. Chad), de qua per obitum Willelmi Apeltre fuit provisum Roberto Sulgrave iii Idus Decembris anno supradicto,[185] debentur fructus.[179]

Item de precentoria Lichfeldensi cum prebenda annexa, de quibus collatio facta Thome de Badeby fuit confirmata iiii idus Maii anno Clementis ix°,[186] debentur pro resta xiii li. vi s. viii d.[173]

Item de prebenda de Ulfton' (Ufton) in ecclesia Lichfeldensi, de qua per resignationem Johannis de Wynwyk' fuit provisum Johanni de Melbur' xviii kalendas Februarii anno Clementis x,[187] debentur pro resta.[188]

Item de prebenda de Eccleshale (Eccleshall) in ecclesia Lichfeldensi, de qua per resignationem Johannis de Melbur' fuit provisum Johanni de Wynwik' xviii kalendas Februarii anno supradicto, debentur fructus.[179]

Item de ecclesia de Codyngton' (Coddington), de qua per resignationem Johannis de Charneux ex causa permutationis fuit provisum Philipo Dryn xi kalendas Augusti anno ii°,[189] debentur fructus.[173]

Item de prebenda de Berkwych' (Berkswick) in ecclesia Lichfeldensi, de qua per obitum Tidonis de Valesio fuit provisum Willelmo Clavill' vii kalendas Maii pontificatus Innocentii anno primo,[190] debentur fructus.[191]

Item de prebenda de Longedon' (Longdon) in ecclesia Lichfeldensi, de qua per obitum Willelmi Cros fuit provisum Waltero Dalby xi kalendas Octobris pontifi-

---

[170] 25 January 1354.
[171] 28 January 1354.
[172] 24 January 1354.
[173] In the margin opposite this item is noted *in resta*.
[174] 9 April 1354.
[175] 22 May 1356.
[176] 5 August 1356.
[177] 3 December 1356.
[178] Changed from *debentur*; followed by *fructus* deleted by a line.
[179] In the margin opposite this item is noted *in arayragiis*.

[180] 3 September 1349.
[181] Followed by *fructus* deleted by a line.
[182] Followed by *xiii* blotted and deleted by a line.
[183] There are two notations in the margin opposite this item. One is *in resta*. The other which is followed by a hand with the forefinger pointing to the item reads: *corigatur quia nichil est solutum*.
[184] 5 November 1349; *Cal. Pap. Regs. Petitions*, i, 184.
[185] 11 December 1349; *ibid.*, i, 191.
[186] 12 May 1351.
[187] 15 January 1352.
[188] No sum is entered. In the margin opposite this item is noted *in resta et arayragiis*.
[189] 22 July 1354.
[190] 25 April 1353.
[191] In the margin opposite this item is noted *in resta et arayragiis*.

catus Domini Innocentii anno secundo,[192] debentur fructus.[179]

Item de prebenda de Wolveye (Wolvey) in ecclesia Lichfeldensi, de qua per consecrationem Michaelis electi Londoniensis fuit provisum Johanni Barnet' anno supradicto,[193] debentur fructus.[179]

Item de archidiaconatu Conventrensi, de quo per obitum Willelmi Cros fuit provisum Willelmo de Diffreld' viii° kalendas Februarii anno supradicto,[194] debentur fructus.[173]

Item de ecclesia de Wynewyk' (Winwick), de qua per obitum Johannis de Chinale fuit provisum Johanni de Creshull' viii kalendas Februarii anno Innocentii iiii,[195] debentur fructus.[179]

(fol. 64[v]) Item de decanatu ecclesie Sancti Johannis Cestr' (Chester), de quo per assecutionem alterius beneficii fuit provisum Alexandro de Dalby, debentur fructus.[173]

Item de prebenda de Termyn (Tarvin), de qua provisio facta per Dominum Clementem Petro de Guldesburgh', qui de amissione erat in dubio, fuit confirmata xiiii kalendas Martii Domini Innocentii anno iiii°,[196] debentur fructus.[173]

Item de prebenda in ecclesia collegiata Sancti Johannis Cestr', de qua ex causa permutationis fuit provisum Guidoni de Pestello iii nonas Decembris Innocentii anno iiii°,[197] debentur fructus.[173]

Item de ecclesia de Walton', de qua fuit provisum Johanni de Bulkynton', debentur pro resta xiiii li.[179]

### Assavensis

De prebenda in ecclesia [198] Assavensi, de qua per obitum Ricardi Hernag' fuit provisum Ricardo de Midelton' iiii nonas Maii pontificatus Clementis anno ix°,[199] debentur fructus.[191]

Item de ecclesia de Dynbigh' (Denbigh) cum capella, de qua, vacante de iure ut dicebatur, fuit provisum Willelmo de Sunderlond vii idus Novembris,[200] debentur fructus.[179]

### Blangorensis

De prebenda in ecclesia Bangorensi, de qua per obitum Roberti de Tresk' fuit provisum H. de Monuton' viii idus Martii pontificatus Clementis anno ix°,[201] debentur fructus.[173]

### Menevensis

De ecclesia de Lambanglorach' (Llanfihangel ar Arth), de qua per mortem Ricardi Aprovanseis fuit provisum Ludowico Canucey, debentur fructus.[179]

Item de ecclesia de Weston' (Wiston), de qua per resignationem Rogeri alias dicti Johannis fuit provisum Willelmo de Neuton' vi idus Novembris pontificatus Domini Innocentii anno iiii[to],[202] debentur fructus.[179]

Item de ecclesia Sancti Bernachi super Tafe (Llanfyrnach), de qua per obitum Johannis de Caumton' fuit provisum Willelmo de Neuhale xix kalendas Januarii anno secundo,[203] debentur fructus.[179]

### Eboracensis

De prebenda de Wetewang' (Wetwang) in ecclesia Eboracensi, de qua per obitum Georgii de Salutis fuit provisum Domino Anibaldo cardinali, que fuit dimissa in arreragiis in iiii[xx] x li.[204] per Dominum Raymundum Pelegrini, debentur pro resta dicte summe lxvii li. xi s.

Item de prebenda de Masham in ecclesia Eboracensi, de qua per obitum Magistri Johannis Offord fuit provisum Reginaldo de Bryan, que fuit dimissa per dictum Dominum Raymundum Pelegrini, debentur fructus.[205] De ista provisione nichil debet exhigi nec fieri,[206] quia scriptum in receptis episcopatus Eboracensis aparet quod eadem fuit provisum Domino Andre Offord, qui solvit partem et residuum infra folio sequenti datur in resta et quia infra annum bis fuit provisum, ideo non solvitur nisi una taxa.

(fol. 65) Item de ecclesia de Brantingham, de qua per obitum Domini Ricardi cardinalis de Gardina [207] fuit provisum Edmundo de Haukesgate, que fuit dimissa per Dominum Raymundum Pelegrini in arreragiis in xx li., debentur pro resta dicte summe iii li.[173]

Item de archidiaconatu Richemond, de quo obitum J. Portuensis cardinalis fuit provisum Henrico de Walton' iii idus Aprilis pontificatus Clementis anno viii°,[208] debentur fructus.[191]

Item de prebenda de Dunham in ecclesia collegiata Sithwell', de qua per obitum Henrici de Harwedon' fuit provisum Ade de Everingham anno supradicto,[209] debentur pro resta xxvi li. xiii s. iiii d.[173]

Item de prebenda de Masham in ecclesia Eboracensi, de qua per consecrationem electi Menevensis fuit pro-

---

[192] 21 September 1354.
[193] 1354.
[194] 25 January 1354.
[195] 25 January 1356.
[196] 17 February 1356.
[197] 3 December 1356.
[198] Folowed by *collegiate* deleted by a line.
[199] 4 May 1351.
[200] 7 November 1355.
[201] 8 March 1351.

[202] 8 November 1356.
[203] 14 December 1354.
[204] In the margin opposite this line is the note: *ac ad taxem*.
[205] The item to this point is erased by lines. Opposite it in the margin is noted *in resta*. This is followed by two blotted words erased by a line and the following: *bis fuit in anno provisum*.
[206] Reading doubtful on account of a blot.
[207] Gerard Domar, priest of S. Sabina: *Cal. Pap. Regs. Petitions*, i, 43; *Letters*, iii 96.
[208] 11 April 1350.
[209] 18 June 1349: *Cal. Pap. Regs. Petitions*, i, 166.

visum Andree Offord anno supradicto,[210] debentur pro resta xxxviii li. vi s. viii d.[179]

Item de prebenda in ecclesia collegiata Beverlacensi, de qua acceptio facta per Alanum de Waynflet' fuit sibi confirmata iii idus Maii anno supradicto,[211] debentur pro resta vii li.[173]

Item de prebenda de Sarwe (Sharrow) in ecclesia collegiata Rippon', de qua per obitum Willelmi de Aberwik' fuit provisum Johanni de Donyngton' iii idus Maii anno Clementis ix°,[212] debentur fructus.[179]

Item de prebenda de Thorp' (Thorpe) in ecclesia collegiata de Hoveden', de qua per obitum Roberti de Tresk' fuit provisum Ade Romelyn viii° idus Martii anno supradicto,[213] debentur pro resta xii li.[191]

Item de prebenda de Westward (Husthwaite) in ecclesia Eboracensi, de qua fuit de novo provisum Johanni de Welbur' qui pro fructibus perceptis debet [214] dare ex compositione cum camera facta cc fl. in subsidium Terre Sancte xii kalendas Julii anno Clementis x^mo,[215] debentur floreni.[216]

Item de ecclesia de Walton', de qua collatio facta Henrico de Gategang' fuit sibi confirmata ii kalendas Augusti anno supradicto,[217] debentur pro resta xx li.[173]

(fol. 65ᵛ) Item de prebenda in ecclesia collegiata Suthwell', de qua per consecrationem Gilberti episcopi Karkiolensis fuit provisum Thome Gryffin x kalendas Januarii anno supradicto,[218] debentur fructus.[216]

Item de prebenda in ecclesia Eboracensi, de qua per consecrationem electi Terwynensis (Treviso?) fuit provisum Henrico Salampi vi idus Maii anno supradicto,[219] debentur fructus.[216]

Item de ecclesiis Warumpercy (Wharram Percy) et Elveley (Kirk Ella), de quibus fuit unio facta monasterio de Hautemprise (Haltemprice) idus Junii anno Clementis xi^mo,[220] debentur pro resta xxxv li.[173]

Item de prebenda de Osbaldwyk' (Osbaldwick) in ecclesia Eboracensi, de qua per obitum Bernardi de Novodampno fuit provisum Symoni de Bruselcy idus Julii anno secundo,[221] debentur fructus.[216]

Item de ecclesia Sancte Trinitatis Eboracensis, de qua per obitum Roberti Sutton' fuit provisum Willelmo de Boxeby xi kalendas Aprilis pontificatus Domini Innocentii anno ii,[222] debentur fructus.[191]

Item de prebenda de Munketon' (Monkton) in ecclesia collegiata Ripon', de qua per consecrationem M.

electi Londoniensis fuit provisum Johanni de Wellewyk' xv kalendas Junii anno supradicto,[223] debentur fructus.[216]

Item de prebenda de Stanxele (Strensall) in ecclesia Eboracensi, de qua per promotionem electi Londoniensis fuit provisum episcopo Albanensi cardinali ii idus Octobris anno supradicto,[224] debentur fructus.[216]

Item de ecclesia de Rudestan (Rudston) ,de qua fuit de novo provisum Ade de Thormenton' v idus Junii anno Domini Innocentii iii,[225] debentur fructus.[226]

Item de prebenda de Bykehull' de Knaresburgh' (Bichhill cum Knaresborough), de qua per resignationem Garcie de Galharde ex causa permutationis fuit provisum Thome de Nevill' iiii idus Julii anno iiii°,[227] debentur fructus.[226]

Item de prebenda in ecclesia collegiata Ripon' de qua per resignationem Ricardi de Thoresby ex causa permutationis fuit provisum Bertrando de Cardalhaco xiii kalendas Novembris anno supradicto [228] debentur fructus.[216]

Item de ecclesia Beati Ulfridi de Kukholm (St. Wilfrid Kirkham) de qua permutatio facta inter Adam de (fol. 66) Chesterfold cum rectore ecclesie de Anywell' et Braynford (Hanwell and Brentford) fuit confirmata v kalendas Novembris anno supradicto,[229] debentur fructus.[216]

Item de prebenda in ecclesia collegiata Beverlacensi, de qua per resignationem dicti Bertrandi ex causa permutationis fuit provisum Ricardo de Thoresby die et anno supradictis, debentur fructus.[226]

Item de prebenda in ecclesia Beverlacensi de qua per obitum Willelmi de Ferughby fuit provisum Johanni de Blebur' x nonas Februarii anno supradicto,[230] debentur fructus.[216]

Item de ecclesia de Cakton' (Catton?), de qua institutio facta per patronum in personam Johannis de Cestr' fuit sibi confirmata viii kalendas Februarii anno supradicto,[231] debentur fructus.[226]

### Dunolmensis

Item de prioratu de Tinemuta (Tynemouth), de quo per assecutionem abbacie monasterii Sancti Albani factam per Thomam priorem dicti prioratus, de quo fuit sibi data potestas providendi, pontificatus Domini Clementis anno viii°,[232] debentur fructus.[216]

Item de hospitali de Gretham, de quo per obitum Johannis de Stokton' fuit provisum Thome Johannis

---

[210] 10 October 1349: *ibid.*, i, 178.
[211] 13 May 1350.
[212] 13 May 1351.
[213] 8 March 1351.
[214] *debent*, MS.
[215] 20 June 1351.
[216] In the margin opposite this item is noted *in arayragiis.*
[217] 31 July 1351.
[218] 23 December 1351.
[219] 10 May 1352.
[220] 13 June 1352.
[221] 15 July 1354.
[222] 22 March 1354.

[223] 18 May 1354.
[224] 14 October 1354.
[225] 9 June 1355.
[226] In the margin opposite this item is noted *in resta.*
[227] 12 July 1356.
[228] 20 October 1356.
[229] 28 October 1356.
[230] Error for 14 January 1357: *Cal. Pap. Regs. Petitions*, i, 291.
[231] 25 January 1356. [1357. *Ibid.*, 293]
[232] 11 August 1349; *ibid.*, 172.

de Brydekyrke ii idus Decembris anno ix,[233] debentur fructus.[234]

Item de prebenda in ecclesia collegiata de Langecestr' (Lanchester), de qua per resignationem Henrici de Exton' fuit provisum Galfredo de Cornewaill' xv kalendas Decembris anno Domini Innocentii primo,[235] debentur [236] fructus.[216]

Item de prebenda in dicta ecclesia, de qua [237] per promotionem electi Londoniensis fuit provisum Johanni de Vinton' [238] xix kalendas Januarii anno ii°,[239] debentur pro resta [240] iiii li. vi s. viii d.[226]

Item de prebenda in ecclesia collegiata de Cestr' super Sarret' (Chester-le-Street), de qua per promotionem electi Norwicensis fuit provisum Willelmo de Loughteburg' vi idus Februarii anno predicto,[241] debentur [242] fructus.[216]

Item de prebenda in eadem ecclesia, de qua per resignationem Willelmi de Rothwell' fuit provisum Guidoni de Pestello anno Clementis iiii,[243] debentur [242] fructus.[234]

### Karkiolensis

De ecclesia de Northwath' (Crosthwaite), in cuius iure quod competebat Willelmo de Sallario fuit subrogatus Johannes Henry ii idus Januarii, debentur [242] fructus.[216]

### (fol. 66ᵛ) Dublinensis

De decanatu ecclesie Dublinensis, de quo fuit provisum Matheo de Ursele, debentur pro resta [244] xiiii li. vi s. viii d.

Item de thesauraria ecclesie Sancti Patricii Dublinensis et prebenda de Dalimor' (Ballymore) in eadem, de quibus collatio facta Johanni Attegate fuit sibi confirmata viii idus Maii anno Clementis viii,[245] debentur [246] fructus.[216]

Item de decanatu ecclesie Dublinensis, de quo per obitum Mathei de Bruseley fuit provisum Johanni Bryan, debentur pro resta [247] xx li.

Item de prebenda de Hunte (Howth) in ecclesia Dublinensi, de qua per consecrationem Stephani episcopi Lymericensis fuit provisum Willelmo de Kelsey viii idus Aprilis anno Domini Innocentii ii°,[248] debentur [249] fructus.[234]

Item de cancellaria ecclesie Sancti Patricii Dublinensis, de qua collatio facta Johanni de Troye fuit eidem confirmata iiii kalendas Junii anno supradicto,[250] debentur pro resta [251] xxxiii li. vi s. viii d.[234]

### Fernensis

De prebenda de Taghmon in ecclesia Fernensi, de qua per obitum Johannis de Sutton' et ecclesia de Colstuf' (Coolstuffe) de qua per obitum Thome Michel fuit provisum Domino Johanni Stronde, in episcopatum Fernensem electum, ne in opprobrium episcopi deberet mendicare, viᵗᵒ kalendas Augusti pontificatus Clementis anno xi,[252] debentur fructus.[253]

Item de prebenda de Holon (Clone) in ecclesia Fernensi, de qua per ingressum religionis aut mortem vel aliquovis modo Hugonis de Burgh' fuit provisum Ricardo Radulphi idus Augusti anno predicto,[254] debentur [249] fructus.[216]

Item de ecclesia de Veteri Rosse (Old Ross), de qua per resignationem Nicholai Isard ex causa permutationis fuit provisum Johanni de Wellekyk' xvi kalendas Augusti anno Domini Innocentii ii°,[255] debentur [249] fructus.[216]

(fol. 71) [256] Secuntur beneficia de quibus est scriptum michi Hugoni de curia tempore predicto, collata tam per dominos Clementem papam quam Innocentium, quorum collationes effectum non habuerunt ex causis in quolibet expressis, ut sequitur

### Cantuariensis

De ecclesia de Estringhangr' (Ostenhanger), de qua per resignationem Hugonis de Staunfeld fuit provisum Henrico de Cumpton' iiiᵗᵒ idus Martii pontificatus Domini Clementis anno viiᵐᵒ.[257] Ista ecclesia pertinet ad presentationem Domini Johannis Tirel militis, qui alium presentavit, et ideo hic non habet effectum quia de patronatu laicali.

Item de ecclesia de Boxle (Boxley), de qua cum

[233] 12 December 1350.

[234] In the margin opposite this item is noted *in resta et arayragiis*.

[235] 17 November 1353.

[236] In the same entry repeated and deleted on fol. 69 *debentur* is followed by *pro taxa* in place of *fructus*.

[237] *quo*, MS.

[238] *Burton'* in the same entry on fol. 69.

[239] 14 December 1354.

[240] In the deleted duplicate of the entry on fol. 69 *resta* is followed by *taxe*.

[241] 8 February 1354. [1355, *Cal. Pap. Regs. Petitions*, i, 282]

[241a] In a deleted duplicate of this entry on fol. 69 *resta* is deleted by dots and *taxa* is substituted.

[242] In a deleted duplicate of this entry on fol. 69 *pro taxa* is substituted for *fructus*.

[243] Between 19 May 1345 and 18 May 1346.

[244] In a deleted duplicate of this item on fol. 69ᵛ *resta* is followed by *nove taxe*.

[245] 8 May 1350.

[246] In a deleted duplicate of this item on fol. 69ᵛ *pro taxis* is substituted for *fructus*.

[247] In the deleted duplicate on fol. 69ᵛ *resta* is followed by *taxe*.

[248] 6 April 1354. In the duplicate entry on fol. 69ᵛ the date is *vii idus*.

[249] The duplicate entry has *pro taxa* in place of *fructus*.

[250] 29 May 1354.

[251] The duplicate entry on fol. 69ᵛ adds *taxe* after *resta*.

[252] 27 July 1352.

[253] The duplicate entry on fol. 69ᵛ has *pro taxis* in place of *fructus*.

[254] 13 August 1352.

[255] 17 July 1354.

[256] Folios 67 to 68ᵛ are blank. Folios 69 and 69ᵛ contain duplicates of the entries under *Dunolmensis, Karkiolensis, Dublinensis* and *Fernensis* on folios 66 and 66ᵛ. They are deleted by lines. The few variants are noted above. Folios 70 and 70ᵛ are blank.

[257] 13 March 1349.

vacaret per assecutionem ecclesie de Horncastr' (Horncastle) per Hugonem Pelegrini fuit provisum Johanni de Haddon' ii[do] idus Decembris anno supradicto.[258] Predicta ecclesia de Horncastr' non fuit assecuta per dictum Hugonem, ideo non habet effectum.

Item de potestate data nuntio sedis apostolice dispensandi in partibus Anglie ut permutationem que fieri debebat inter Gilbertum de Bruera, tunc temporis decanum Sancti Pauli Londonie, de prebendis de Edyndon' (Edington) [259] in ecclesia monialium de Romeseye (Romsey) Wyntoniensis et prebenda de Haselbete (Haselbeare) in ecclesia Wellensi et Johannem de Lech' de ecclesia parochiali de Harewe (Harrow) Londoniensis diocesis et capellis liberis sine cura de Boktoneffelde (Bockingfold) et Nunstede (Newstead) Cantuariensis diocesis reciperet et quolibet [260] provideret de beneficiis resignatis causa permutationis predicte ii[do] idus Julii anno x[mo].[261] Istud nunquam venit ad effectum, quia ille Gilbertus inactivus est, nulla facta permutatione.

Item de prepositura ecclesie de Wyngham (Wingham), de qua per resignationem Johannis de Bourn' fuit provisum Bernardo Berardi ii[do] idus Augusti anno Clementis xi[mo],[262] non habet effectum quia per dictam resignationem fuit provisum Roberto de Sudbury qui tenet et possidet et solvit pro fructis [263] supra in recepta.

Item de eadem prepositura, de qua per obitum Johannis de Bourn' fuit provisum Thome de Clipston' legum doctori vii[mo] idus Martii pontificatus Domini Innocentii anno primo,[264] non habet effectum ut supra proximo dictum est.

### (fol. 71[v]) Roffensis

De ecclesia de Eynesford' (Eynsford), de qua per resignationem Wilelmi de Blakeford' fuit provisum Johanni de Creso xviii kalendas Februarii pontificatus Domini Clementis anno x,[265] non habet effectum quia neuter eorum dictam ecclesiam habuit.

### Londoniensis

De prebenda quam Magister Adam Murimouth' in ecclesia Londoniensi obtinuit, de qua fuit provisum Roberto de Berwarn', que fuit dimissa per Dominum Raymundum Pelegrini in arreragiis, non habuit effectum quia ille Robertus non fuit gratiam suam prosecutus, set quidam Johannes de Embresbury ipsam acceptaverat auctoritate apostolica quia expectans.

De archidiaconatu Middelsexie, de quo per obitum Henrici de Iddesworth' fuit provisum Rogero Holm

vii[mo] idus Aprilis pontificatus Domini Clementis anno vii[mo],[266] non habuit effectum quia Andreas de Ufford ipsum acceptaverat et habuit confirmationem; ponitur in areyragiis.

Item de prebenda in ecclesia Londoniensi, de qua per obitum Henrici de Iddesworth fuit provisum Johanni de la Mare, non habuit effectum quia prius fuerat provisum Rogere Holm de eadem,[267] qui satisfecit camere in curia.

Item de prebenda in ecclesia Londoniensi, de qua per resignationem Guillelmi Gavyny fuit provisum Hugoni Pelegrini xv kalendas Septembris anno supradicto,[268] vocata Kenteston' (Kentish Town), quam Rogerus Holm prius in data ipsam a dicto Willemo evicerat ante ipsam provisionem, ideo non habet effectum. Dictus Rogerus satisfecit ut supra in proximo.

(fol. 72) De prebenda de Wildelonde (Wildland in Tillingham) in ecclesia Londoniensi, de qua per obitum Simonis de Stranford acceptatio facta per Thomam de Romeseye fuit sibi confirmata vi[to] idus Novembris anno supradicto,[269] non habuit effectum quia quidam expectans [270] predictam prebendam a dicto Thoma evicit.

De prebenda de Iseldon' (Islington) in ecclesia Londoniensi, de qua per obitum Humfredi de Hastinges acceptatio facta per Willelmum Gavyny fuit eidem confirmata, non habuit effectum quia Dominus Willelmus de Rothewell' dictam prebendam evicit in curia regis a quo ipse obtinuerat [271] presentationem.

Item de eadem prebenda, de qua per obitum dicti Humfredi fuit provisum Ade Lamberk' viii[vo] idus Februarii anno supradicto,[272] non habuit effectum ut supra proximo.

Item de prebenda de Kenteston' (Kentish Town) in ecclesia Londoniensi, in cuius iure quod competebat Henricus de Iddesworth' fuit subrogatus Hugo Pelegrini viii[vo] idus Aprilis anno supradicto,[273] non habet effectum quia Rogerus Holm priore data ipsam obtinuit et adhuc obtinet [274] et respondit in proximo folio supra.

Item de prebenda in ecclesia Londoniensi, de qua per resignationem Geraldi de Angolisma fuit provisum Gaillardo Alkerii secundo nonas Maii anno supradicto,[275] non habuit effectum quia quidam Humfredus de Hastinges a dicto Geraldo dictam prebendam in curia regis evicerat.

De ecclesiis de Sabrichesworth' (Sawbridgeworth) et Kelveden' (Kelvedon), de quibus fuit unio facta monasterio Westmonasterii, quo ad ecclesiam de Kel-

---

[258] 12 December 1348.
[259] Followed by *Sarisbiriensis* deleted by a line.
[260] *quilibet*, MS.
[261] 14 July 1351.
[262] 12 August 1352.
[263] Followed by *ut* deleted by a line.
[264] 9 March 1353.
[265] 15 January 1352.

[266] 7 April 1349.
[267] Two words are deleted by a line and obscured by a blot.
[268] 18 August 1348. [1349. Holm's provision was dated 7 April 1349. *Cal. Pap. Regs. Petitions,* i, 151]
[269] 8 November 1348. [1349. *Ibid.,* 185]
[270] Written over four words deleted by a line.
[271] Followed by *collationem* deleted by a line.
[272] 6 February 1349.
[273] 6 April 1349. [1350. *Ibid.,* 195]
[274] Followed by *ut supra* deleted by a line.
[275] 6 May 1349.

veden' habet effectum et de ipsa respondetur in arreragiis, set quo ad ecclesiam de Sabrechesworth' non habet effectum quia adhuc rector vivit.

(fol. 72ᵛ) Item de ecclesia de Esse (Ashen) alias de Herlawe (Harlow), de qua, vacante per resignationem Magistri Ricardi Drax, fuit provisum Willelmo Durandi vᵗᵒ nonas Martii anno supradicto,²⁷⁶ fuit scriptum per dominos camerarium et thesaurarium quod dictus Ricardus rector ecclesie de Herlawe tanquam procurator resignaverat ecclesiam de Esse Willelmo Durandi predicto, et quod erronee fuerat scriptum *est alias Herlawe*, et quod fieret ²⁷⁷ executio contra ecclesiam de Esse, que executio facta est, set certifficatus est quod dictus Willelmus Durandi nunquam illam ecclesiam habuit; ideo non habet effectum.

De ecclesia Sancti Magni Londonie, de qua vacante, quia Theobaldus de Sauxeyo nulla dispensatione obtenta eam tenuit non promotus, fuit provisum Johanni de Sauxeyo iiiiᵗᵒ kalendas Septembris anno Clementis xᵐᵒ,²⁷⁸ non habet effectum quia quidam Ricardus de Bury eam tenet iure regio.²⁷⁹

Item de prebenda in ecclesia Londoniensi, de qua per obitum Alani de Hothum fuit provisum Bernardo de Brocariis iiiᵗⁱᵒ kalendas Februarii anno supradicto,²⁸⁰ non habuit effectum quia Thomas de Brembre habuit eam iure regio.

De ecclesia de Stansted Mounfichet (Stanstead Mountfitchet), de qua cum vacaret per cessum vel decessum ultimi rectoris fuit data potestas episcopo Londoniensi quod eam posset unire auctoritate apostolica prioratui de Tremensale (Thremhall) vᵗᵒ kalendas Junii anno Clementis xiᵐᵒ,²⁸¹ dictus rector adhuc non cessit nec decessit.

Item de prebenda de Mapesbury (in Willesden) in ecclesia Londoniensi, de qua fuit provisum per obitum Johannis de Clayden' Michaeli de Northburgh' xiiᵐᵒ kalendas Novembris anno supradicto,²⁸² non habuit effectum quia Dominus Ricardus de Norwico habuit ipsam iure regio, et postea habuit confirmationem ut infra pateat in proxima pagine.

(fol. 73) Item de ecclesia Sancti Magni Londonie, in cuius iure quod competebat Willelmo Hugonis dum viveret in eadem, de qua litigabat in palatio apostolico, fuit provisum Willemo de Studmere x kalendas Maii anno supradicto,²⁸³ non habuit effectum quia Ricardus de Bury habuit eam iure regio ut supradictum est.

Item de eadem ecclesia, de qua per obitum dicti Willelmi fuit provisum Ricardo de Kereswell' et in suo

iure subrogatus xᵐᵒ kalendas Maii anno supradicto, non habuit effectum ut supra proximo.

Item de archidiaconatu Londonie, de quo cum vacaret per assecutionem decanatus dicte ecclesie fuit provisum cardinali Autizodorensis (Auxerre) ²⁸⁴ vᵗᵒ kalendas Maii pontificatus Domini Innocentii anno iido,²⁸⁵ non habuit effectum quia tunc episcopatus Londoniensis vacabat et rex eum contulit Domino Jacobo de Beauford'.

Item de ecclesia de Wikham (Wickham Bishops), de qua fuit de novo provisum Thome de Clopton, quam tunc obtinebat, quibuscumque maculis et irregularitatibus non obstantibus, iido idus Augusti anno supradicto,²⁸⁶ non habet effectum quia, facta inquisitione per episcopum et officialem suum auctoritate apostolica non est inventum quod dictus Thomas ²⁸⁷ ecclesiam de Wikham obtineat.

De prebenda de Mapesbury in ecclesia Londoniensi, de qua acceptatio facta per Ricardum de Norwico fuit sibi confirmata viiᵐᵒ idus ²⁸⁸ Februarii pontificatus Domini Innocentii anno tertio.²⁸⁹ Dictus Ricardus habuit dictam prebendam, ut supradictum est, iure regio, et renuntiavit istam confirmationem, volens et expresse confitens istam confirmationem nullum sibi tenere amodo ²⁹⁰ de qua renuntiatione levatum fuit publicum instrumentum.

(fol. 73ᵛ) Cicestrensis

De prebenda de Gates in ecclesia Cicestrensi, de qua per obitum Johannis de Medeford' fuit provisum Willelmo de Navesby, que fuit dimissa in arreragiis per Dominum Raymundum Pelegrini, fuit dimissa per errorem quia ipse respondit ²⁹¹ in compotis suis.

Item de prebenda de Fitheworth' (Fittleworth), de qua per resignationem Domini Anibaldi cardinalis fuit provisum Johanni de Melbourn' que fuit dimissa per dictum Dominum Raymundum Pelegrini,²⁹² non habuit effectum quia dictus dominus cardinalis ²⁹³ nunquam fuit in possessione,²⁹⁴ ne Johannes gratiam prossequtus.

Item de prebenda de una ecclesia, de qua per obitum ²⁹⁵ Arnaldi de Ferreno, qui non habitis litteris expiravit, fuit provisum Bartholomeo Patrici xv kalendas Junii pontificatus Domini Clementis anno viiᵐᵒ,²⁹⁶ non habuit

---

²⁷⁶ 3 March 1349. [1351. *Cal. Pap. Regs. Letters,* iii, 364].
²⁷⁷ Over *fac* deleted by a line.
²⁷⁸ 29 August 1351.
²⁷⁹ Followed by *et ordinario* deleted by a line.
²⁸⁰ 30 January 1352.
²⁸¹ 28 May 1352.
²⁸² 21 October 1352.
²⁸³ 22 April 1353. The year should be the first of Innocent VI; *Cal. Pap. Regs. Petitions,* i, 241.

²⁸⁴ Peter de Croso, priest of SS. Silvestro e Martino ai Monti.
²⁸⁵ 27 April 1354.
²⁸⁶ 12 August 1354.
²⁸⁷ The extension *dictus Thomas* is doubtful. The words *dictus Thomas* are placed over *talis* deleted by a line.
²⁸⁸ Followed by *Septembris* deleted by dots and by a line.
²⁸⁹ 7 February 1355.
²⁹⁰ Followed by two words deleted by a line.
²⁹¹ *respondidit,* MS.
²⁹² Followed by *nisi* deleted by a line.
²⁹³ Followed by *ipsam tenuit usque ad mortem suam* deleted by a line.
²⁹⁴ *possetione,* MS.
²⁹⁵ Followed by *Ala* deleted by a line.
²⁹⁶ 18 May 1349.

effectum quia prius fuerat provisum Rogero de Dorkyng', ut supra in [297] recepta.

Item de prebenda in ecclesia Cicestrensi, de qua per obitum Henrici de Iddesworth fuit provisum Thome de Edyndon xviii° kalendas Junii anno supradicto,[298] non habuit effectum quia dictus Thomas noluit prosequi gratiam suam propter exilitatem prebende.

Item de eadem prebenda, de qua per obitum dicti Henrici fuit provisum Thome de Bardeby xiiii<sup>mo</sup> kalendas Junii,[299] non habuit effectum quia nec ipse prosecutus est gratiam suam.

De prebenda una ecclesia in ecclesia Cicestrensi, de qua per obitum Vitalis de Tasta fuit provisum Arnaldo de Ferrono, qui possessione non habita expiravit, fuit provisum Ade de Hilton' v<sup>to</sup> nonas Julii anno supradicto,[300] non habuit effectum quia prius fuerat provisum Rogero de Dorkyng' ut supra.

Item de prebenda in ecclesia Cicestrensi, de qua per obitum Thome de Stere,[301] qui, dum vixit, impeditus per quemdam ⟨qui⟩ possidet, eius possessionem habere non potuit, fuit provisum Roberto de Tresk', non habuit effectum quia dictus Robertus nunquam possessionem habuit.

(fol. 74) De prebenda in ecclesia collegiata de Bosham, de qua per obitum Thome atte Cross', alias de Cruce, fuit provisum Waltero Gest iii<sup>tio</sup> kalendas Februarii anno supradicto,[302] non habuit effectum quia dicta ecclesia de Bosham est libera capella regis et ipse contulit alteri.

Item de prebenda in ecclesia Cicestrensi, de qua per obitum cardinalis Tusculanensis fuit provisum Rogero Holm iiii<sup>to</sup> idus Maii pontificatus Domini Clementis anno ix<sup>no</sup>,[303] non habuit effectum quia Dominus Johannes Wynewyk' habuit ipsam iure regio.

Item de prebenda de Silesheye (Selsey) in ecclesia Cicestrensi, de qua per obitum Ferranti Sauxeye fuit provisum Johanni Lech' iiii<sup>to</sup> nonas Maii anno supradicto;[304] dictus Johannes habet eam etiam ex collatione regis, qua collatione contentus, prohibitionem regiam ne fructus pro camera exigerentur impetravit.

Item de ecclesia de Grenestede (Grinstead), de qua per obitum cardinalis Tusculanensis fuit provisum Ricardo Derby v<sup>to</sup> kalendas Maii anno supradicto.[305] Istam ecclesiam habuit Magister Simon de Bredon' iure regio, et prohibitionem regiam impetravit.

Item de prebenda in ecclesia Cicestrensi, de qua per obitum dicti cardinalis fuit provisum Johanni de

Edingdon' v<sup>to</sup> kalendas Maii anno supradicto.[305] Istam Dominus Johannes de Wynewyk' habuit iure regio, ut supra [306] dictum est.

Item de prebenda in ecclesia Cicestrensi, de qua per assecutionem prebende in ecclesia Sagobiensi (Segovia) fuit provisum Roberto de [307] Askeby viii<sup>vo</sup> idus Julii pontificatus Domini Clementis anno x<sup>mo</sup>.[308] Ista prebenda vocatur Sileseye (Selsey), que fuit Ferandi Sauxi, quam habet Magister Johannes Lech' iure regio ut supra.

Item de prebenda in ecclesia Cicestrensi, de qua per obitum Johannis de Ildesle fuit provisum Willelmo de Samynake ii<sup>do</sup> nonas Julii anno supradicto,[309] non habuit effectum quia dictus Wilelmus non fuit gratiam suam prosecutus.

(fol. 74<sup>v</sup>) Item de prebenda in ecclesia Cicestrensi, de qua per obitum Ricardi de Everingham fuit provisum Willelmo de Rothewell' secundo idus Augusti anno Clementis xi<sup>mo</sup>,[310] non habuit effectum quia dictus Willelmus nullam prebendam in dicta ecclesia obtinet nec obtinuit ut certificatum est per [311] officialem.

De prebenda in ecclesia Cicestrensi, de qua per obitum Thome de Northwode fuit provisum Johanni Stretle viii<sup>vo</sup> kalendas Novembris pontificatus Domini Innocentii anno quarto.[312] Quidam Dominus Johannes de Severle dictam prebendam obtinet per gratiam expectationis qui litigat cum dicto Johanne Stretle, tamen obligatur ad solvendum primos fructus in casu quod succumberet.

### Wyntoniensis

De prebenda de Lecford' (Leckford)[313] in ecclesia monialium Beate Marie Wyntoniensis, de qua per obitum Johannis de Deyton' fuit provisum Edwardo de Colleston', que fuit dimissa in arreragiis per Dominum Raymundum Pelegrini, non habuit effectum quia Dominus Ricardus de Norwico habuit ipsam iure regio et ille Edwardus non fuit gratiam suam prosecutus.

Item de archidiaconatu Surreie, de quo per obitum Ricardi Wancy fuit provisum Raymundo Pelegrini sexto kalendas Martii pontificatus Domini Clementis anno vii<sup>mo</sup>,[314] non habuit effectum quia prius fuerat collatus Johanni de Edingdon' qui confirmationem habuit, ut patet in arreragiis supra.

Item de dispensatione facta cum Johanne Mikkeleye, rectore parochialis ecclesie de Hareforde (Alresford), ut preposituram capelle Sancte Elizabeth', si sibi canonice conferetur, valeret recipere et insimul licite retinere, xii<sup>mo</sup> kalendas Junii anno Clementis xi<sup>mo</sup>.[315] Videtur

---

[297] Followed by *solutionibus* deleted by a line.
[298] 15 May 1349.
[299] No year is given in the manuscript; [14 Kal. July 1349. *Cal. Pap. Regs. Petitions*, i, 167].
[300] 3 July 1348.
[301] Over *Ttere* deleted by a line.
[302] 30 January 1349.
[303] 12 May 1351.
[304] 4 May 1351.
[305] 27 April 1351.

[306] Followed by *alibi* deleted by a line.
[307] Followed by *Askby* blotted and deleted by a line.
[308] 8 July 1351.
[309] 6 July 1351.
[310] 12 August 1352.
[311] Followed by *inquisitionem* deleted by a line.
[312] 25 October 1356.
[313] Followed by *d* deleted by a dot.
[314] 24 February 1349.
[315] 21 May 1352.

quod non debent solvi primi fructus quia [316] papa nihil confert set dispensat.

(fol. 75) Item de prebenda in ecclesia monialium Beate Marie Wyntoniensis, de qua per resignationem Rogeri Holm fuit provisum Bruno de Inzico xviii$^{vo}$ kalendas Februarii anno supradicto,[317] non habuit effectum quia dictus Rogerus nullam prebendam obtinuit in ecclesia predicta.

### Saresburiensis

De ecclesia de Bruton' (Burton Bradstock), de qua per assecutionem archidiaconatus Saresburiensis fuit provisum Hugoni de Marisco, que fuit dimissa in arreragiis per Dominum Raymundum Pelegrini, non habuit effectum quia Johannes Pirbyk' tenuit eam ex collatione ordinaria et collatio fuit sibi postea confirmata, et solvit pro confirmatione sua ut supra in recepta.

De ecclesia de Elingdon', de qua per obitum Ricardi de Luthull' fuit provisum Rogero Holm ix$^{no}$ kalendas Maii pontificatus Domini Clementis anno viii$^{vo}$.[318] Infra annum Dominus Rogerus resignavit dictam ecclesiam et fuit provisum Domino Jacobo de Beauford', scilicet vi$^{to}$ idus Novembris anno supradicto,[319] qui dictus Jacobus solvit primos fructus, et pro ista vacatione non debent solvi quia infra annum.

De prebenda de Farendon' (Faringdon) in ecclesia Saresburiensi, de qua per obitum Henrici de la Dale fuit provisum Nicholao Heth' iii$^{tio}$ nonas Maii anno supradicto.[320] Dictus Nicholaus obligavit se camere in curia pro primis fructibus.[321]

De prebenda de Grantham in ecclesia Saresburiensi, in cuius iure quod competebat Johanni de Luthehest' fuit subrogatus Matheus de Brisele xiiii$^{mo}$ kalendas Junii anno supradicto.[322] Dominus Willelmus de Ratford habuit illam iure regio; ideo nihil potest levari.

(fol. 75$^v$) Item de prebenda in ecclesia Saresburiensi, de qua per obitum Willelmi de Crouthorn' fuit provisum Thome David xv$^{mo}$ kalendas Decembris anno supradicto,[323] non habuit effectum quia Ricardus de Netherhaven' prius ipsam acceptaverat et postea habuit confirmationem, qui solvit [324] supra in recepta.

Item de prebenda de Netherbury,[325] per consecrationem R. electi Menevensis fuit provisum Elie Pelegrini vi$^{to}$ idus Octobris anno supradicto,[326] debent hic solvi fructus, quia dictus R. et dictus H. habuerunt dictam prebendam infra annum,[327] et respondetur supra in areyragiis.

Item de prebenda in ecclesia Saresburiensi, de qua per obitum Johannis de Whitchurch' fuit provisum Ricardo Thoresby xvi$^{mo}$ kalendas Novembris anno supradicto,[328] non habuit effectum quia tempore dicte provisionis dictus Johannes vivebat.

De prebenda in ecclesia Saresburiensi, de qua per obitum Roberti de Orton' [329] fuit provisum Rogero Holm iii$^{tio}$ die Novembris anno supradicto,[330] non habuit effectum quia non fuit gratiam suam prosecutus et alter incumbet virtute [331] expectationis.

Item de dicta prebenda, de qua per obitum dicti Roberti fuit provisum Thome de Edindon' kalendas Februarii anno supradicto,[332] non habuit effectum quia dictus Thomas prius aliam prebendam in dicta ecclesia obtinebat et adhuc obtinet iure regio, ut supradictum est.

Item de prebenda de Brambesbury (Ramsbury), de qua per obitum Simonis de Monte Acuto, quondam episcopi Wigorniensis, fuit provisum Guillelmo de Larde, qui possessione non habita obiit, fuit provisum Magistro Johanni Strik', non habuit effectum quia dictus Johannes non fuit gratiam suam prosecutus, et Dominus Edmundus de la Beche ipsam occupavit et occupat iure regio.

(fol. 76) Item de cancellaria et prebenda in ecclesia Saresburiensi, de quibus per obitum Elie de Sancto Albano acceptatio facta per Thomam Trillek' fuit eidem confirmata vii$^{mo}$ idus Maii anno supradicto,[333] non habuit effectum quia tempore dicte acceptationis et provisionis dictus Elias vivebat.

Item de prebenda de Bisshopeston' (Bishopstone) quam Raymundus Pelegrini in ecclesia Saresburiensi obtinebat, de qua per assecutionem alterius prebende in eadem ecclesia fuit provisum Arnaldo Pelegrini xii$^{mo}$ kalendas Junii anno ix$^{no}$,[334] non debent hic solvi fructus quia infra annum fuerat provisum dictis Reymundo et Arnaldo, ideo fructus non debent solvi nisi semel, qui non solvuntur adhuc, quia Willelmus de Okebourne occupat iure regio, et lis pendet in curia.

Item de prebenda de Grantham in ecclesia Saresburiensi, de qua per obitum Mathei de Brisele fuit provisum Johanni de Grey x$^{mo}$ kalendas Maii anno supradicto,[335] non habet effectum quia dictus Matheus dictam prebendam nec obtinebat set Dominus Willelmus de Ratford' iure regio, ut supradictum est.

Item de prebenda Sancti Laurentii de Stratford in ecclesia Saresburiensi, de qua per obitum Johannis de

---

[316] Followed by *in isto casu* deleted by a line.
[317] 15 January 1352.
[318] 23 April 1350.
[319] 8 November 1349.
[320] 5 May 1350.
[321] This sentence is in the margin replacing the following deleted by a line: *Istam prebendam habet Thomas de Edingdon' iure regio: ideo nichil potest levari.*
[322] 19 May 1349.
[323] 17 November 1349.
[324] Followed by *ut* deleted by a line.
[325] Followed by *de qua* deleted by dots.
[326] 10 October 1349.

[327] Followed by *et dictus R. respondebit pro prima vacatione* deleted by a line.
[328] 17 October 1349.
[329] Apparently the name should be Worthe: *Cal. Pap. Regs. Petitions*, i, 193; or possibly Horton, see p. 95 above.
[330] 1349.
[331] Over *gratia* deleted by a line.
[332] 1 February 1350.
[333] 9 May 1350.
[334] 21 May 1350.
[335] 22 April 1351.

Saresburia acceptatio facta per Ricardum de Dursham fuit sibi confirmata iiii[to] idus Maii anno supradicto,[336] non habuit effectum quia prius fuit provisum Johanni de Welton', qui solvit ut supra in recepta.

Item de prebenda in ecclesia Saresburiensi de qua per resignationem Johannis Garrich' fuit provisum Gasberto de Cusornia iiii[to] Idus Maii anno supradicto,[336] non habuit effectum quia quidam Johannes Olyver tenuit eam iure regio, nec ille Johannes Garith' nunquam habuit prebendam in illa ecclesia.

Item de prebenda de Hareforde (Axford) in ecclesia Saresburiensi, de qua per obitum Johannis de Vyenne acceptatio facta per Gervasium de Willeford' fuit sibi confirmata ii[do] kalendas Augusti pontificatus Domini Clementis anno x[mo],[337] non habuit effectum quia quidam Rogerus de Shirbrok' qui prius ipsam acceptaverat, obtinuit dictam prebendam.

(fol. 76[v]) Item de prebenda in ecclesia monialium de Wilton' quam dictus Johannes de Vyenne obtinuit, de qua fuit provisum Johanni Upwell' vii[mo] idus Junii anno supradicto,[338] non habuit effectum quia prius fuit collata Willelmo de Melbourn' qui tenet et possidet, et responditur supra in areyratgiis.

Item de prebenda in ecclesia Saresburiensi, de qua per obitum Roberti de Lutyan fuit provisum Petro de Gildesburgh' xvi[mo] kalendas Februarii anno ix[no].[339] Ad istam rex presentavit [340] Dominum Petrum de Wotton', ideo non potuerunt levari fructus.

De prebenda in ecclesia monialium de Wilton', de qua per obitum Johannis Vyenne fuit provisum et acceptatio facta per Ricardum de Wilton' fuit sibi confirmata ix[no] kalendas Junii anno xi[mo],[341] non habet effectum quia prius collata fuit Willelmo de Melbourne,[342] qui tenet et possidet ut supradictum est in principio pagine.

Item de ecclesia de Waneye (West Hanney), de qua fuit data potestas episcopo [343] Saresburiensi ad uniendum capitulo Saresburiensi viii[vo] idus Septembris anno supradicto,[344] non sunt [345] adhuc in possessione.[346]

Item de prebenda de Cumbe (Combe) et Ernham (Harnham) in ecclesia Saresburiensi, de qua cum vacaret unio facta precentorie ecclesie Saresburiensis viii[vo] idus Septembris anno supradicto,[347] non venit adhuc ad effectum.[348]

---

[336] 12 May 1351.
[337] 31 July 1351.
[338] 7 June 1351.
[339] 17 January 1351.
[340] Over *contulit* deleted by a line.
[341] 24 May 1352.
[342] Followed by *u* deleted by a line.
[343] Over *capitulo* deleted by a line.
[344] 6 September 1352.
[345] Over *fuerunt* deleted by a line.
[346] Followed by *nec erunt quia dicta gratia sit revocata* deleted by a line. The thickness of the line renders the reading of the last two words doubtful.
[347] 6 September 1352.
[348] Followed by *quia tempore vacationis gratie pape Clementis fuerunt revocate* deleted by a line.

Item de licentia data priori monasterii de Bromore (Bromere) Wyntoniensis diocesis recipiendi resignationem a Johanne de Wilton' de prebenda de Stratforde (Stratford) in ecclesia Saresburiensi et ecclesia Sancti Thome Saresburiensis ex causa permutationis, de quibus debebat providere Helye de Sancto Albano cancellario ecclesie Saresburiensis, de qua cancellaria per eius resignationem debebat providere dicto Johanni viii[vo] idus Septembris anno supradicto,[349] non habuit effectum quia nunquam permutarunt.

(fol. 77) Item de prebenda in ecclesia collegiata de Heythresbury (Heytesbury), de qua per resignationem Bartholomei Patricii fuit provisum Ade de Hilton' [350] iiii[to] idus Decembris pontificatus Domini Innocentii anno primo,[351] non habuit effectum quia dictus Bartholomeus nunquam resignavit set tenet eam.

Item de prebenda de Rummesbury (Ramsbury) in ecclesia Saresburiensi, de qua per obitum Willelmi de Larde fuit provisum Johanni Strek' iii[tio] kalendas Februarii pontificatus Domini Innocentii anno secundo.[352] Dominus Edwardus de la Beche tenet illam iure regio; ideo nichil potest levari.

### Exoniensis

De precentoria ecclesie Exoniensis, de qua fuit provisum Magistro Johanni de Shareshull', dimissa in arreragiis per Dominum Raymundum Pelegrini in xx li., non possunt levari quia collata est auctoritate regia.

Item de prebenda in ecclesia Exoniensi, de qua per obitum Magistri Ade Murymouth' fuit provisum Magistro Johanni de Holand', que fuit dimissa in arreragiis per dictum Dominum Raymundum Pelegrini in iiii[or] li., non possunt levari quia collata est auctoritate regia Magistro Johanni Lech'.

Item de prebenda quam Thomas de Astele in ecclesia Exoniensi obtinebat, que fuit dimissa in arreragiis per dictum Raymundum Pelegrini in iiii li., et de qua fuit scriptum quod fuit provisum Ricardo Cleangre nonas Maii pontificatus Domini Clementis anno vii[mo],[353] nichil potest levari quia Johannes Bran occupat eam iure regio.

(fol. 77[v]) Item de prebenda in ecclesia Exoniensi, de qua per obitum Petri de Pateshull' acceptatio facta per Henricum de Pico fuit eidem confirmata xii[mo] kalendas Junii anno supradicto,[354] non habuit effectum quia dictus Henricus non occupavit istam prebendam, set illam quam tenuit Thomas de Bokyngham pro qua solvit ut supra in recepta.

Item de thesauraria ecclesia Exoniensis, de qua per mortem Henrici de Wydeslawe fuit provisum Jacobo de

---

[349] 6 September 1352.
[350] Follows *Ilta'* deleted by a line.
[351] 10 December 1353.
[352] 30 January 1354.
[353] 7 May 1349.
[354] 21 May 1348.

Beauford' quarto kalendas Junii anno supradicto,[355] non habuit effectum quia prius fuit confirmata Roberto de Midelond' ut supra in arreragiis.

Item de prebenda in ecclesia Exoniensi quam electus Dublinensis obtinuit, de qua fuit provisum Johanni Uphull',[356] et de archidiaconatu Exoniensi, de quo per consecrationem dicti electi fuit provisum Johanni de Harewell', viimo idus Novembris anno supradicto;[357] ista duo beneficia occupat Willelmus de Cusantia iure regio quare nichil potest levari.

De prebenda in ecclesia Exoniensi, de qua per obitum Johannis de Nassington' fuit provisum Roberto Michaelis iiiito nonas Februarii anno supradicto,[358] non habet effectum quia prius fuit confirmata Reginaldo de Bugwell', qui solvit ut supra in[359] recepta.

Item de prebenda in ecclesia Exoniensi, de qua per obitum Pauli Bray collatio facta per ordinarium Johanni de Reynham fuit sibi confirmata vito nonas Aprilis anno supradicto,[360] et de qua fuit etiam provisum Johanni Noers xiiimo kalendas Novembris pontificatus Domini Clementis anno xmo [361] dictam prebendam quidam Willelmus Mugge occupat iure regio et evicit ab ipsis, quare nichil potest levari.

Item de prebenda in ecclesia Exoniensi, de qua acceptatio facta per Jacobum de Brumpton' fuit eidem confirmata iiitio idus Maii anno nono,[362] non invenitur talis incumbens, set forte fuit erratum in nomine, et debet esse Jacobus de Multon' qui prebendam in dicta ecclesia obtinet per obitum Johannis Pippard', ut patet superius in arreragiis.

Item de ecclesia de Lansaint (Lezant), de qua per obitum Ricardi de Tideworth' fuit provisum Thome de Dyworth' xiimo kalendas Julii anno supradicto,[363] rex alteri contulit, ideo non possunt levari fructus.

(fol. 78) Item de prebenda seu portione ecclesie Sancti Tete (Teath), de qua per resignationem Johannis Gros fuit provisum Rogero de Herlaston' ixno kalendas Decembris,[364] non habuit effectum quia per mortem dicti Johannis primo fuerat provisum Thome David qui solvit ut supra.

Item de prebenda[365] in ecclesia Exoniensi, de qua per mortem Ricardi de Braile fuit provisum Reginaldo de Bugwell' xvmo kalendas Octobris anno ximo,[366] non habuit effectum quia dictus Reginaldus aliam prebendam in eadem ecclesia obtinebat et adhuc obtinet, set fuit con-

firmata Nicholao Pynnok' xvmo kalendas Octobris anno supradicto, pro quo solutum est ut supra.

Item de vicaria ecclesia Sancte Salvatoris de Monte Acuto de qua per assecutionem archidiaconatus Curat' collatus Lupo Alvaro, ultimo vicario dicte ecclesie, fuit provisum Johanni Rowici xiimo kalendas Maii pontificatus Domini Innocentii anno primo,[367] non habet effectum quia non invenitur talis vicaria nec tale benficium in tota diocesi.

Item de prebenda in ecclesia Exoniensi, de qua per assecutionem vicarie de Holmpton' fuit provisum Willelmo Sampson iiitio idus Decembris anno Innocentii secundo,[368] non habet effectum quia non invenitur talis prebendarius in ecclesia illa.

Item de prebenda in ecclesia Exoniensi, de qua per obitum Johannis de Northwode fuit provisum Radulpho de Ryngestede idus Martii anno iiitio,[369] non potest levari quia Petrus de Gildesburgh' tenet illam, set litigant in curia.

### (fol. 78v) Wigorniensis

De ecclesia de Seggebergh' (Sedgeberrow), vacante per obitum Johannis de Bradwas, fuit provisum Johanni Branketre idus Junii pontificatus Domini Clementis anno viimo,[370] alias fuit scriptum quod per obitum dicti Johannis de Bradwas fuit provisum Johanni Presbytero, et eadem persona est qui solvit ut supra in compoto.

Item fuit concessum episcopi Wigorniensi ut sex beneficia ecclesiastica curata, cum[371] vacarent in sua diocesi et etiam si ad collationem episcopi exspectarent, sex personis ydoneis posset conferre. Dictus episcopus nullum contulit quia cito post factus fuit archiepiscopus Eboracensis.

Item de ecclesia de Cropthorn' (Cropthorne), de qua, cum vacaret per cessum vel decessum ultimi rectoris, fuit unita capitulo ecclesie Wigorniensis vio idus Maii anno supradicto,[372] adhuc non vacavit.

Item de prebenda in ecclesia de Westbury, de qua per obitum Walteri de London' fuit provisum Raymundo de Monte Claro nonas Junii Domini Clementis anno ixo;[373] non est talis prebendarius in ecclesia illa.

Item de prebenda Sancte Werberge in ecclesia collegiata de Westbury, de qua per resignationem Radulphi de Daventr' fuit ⟨provisum⟩ Willelmo de Savinhaco iiiio nonas Maii anno supradicto;[374] rex[375] contulit istam prebendam Domino Willelmo de Salop', ideo nichil potest levari.

Item de ecclesia de Kynewarton' (Kinwarton), de qua, quia Willelmus Peyto ipsam tenuit non promotus

---

[355] 29 May 1348.
[356] Followed by *est* deleted by a line.
[357] 7 November 1348.
[358] 2 February 1349.
[359] Followed by *supra* deleted by a line.
[360] 2 or 8 April 1349.
[361] 20 October 1351.
[362] 13 May 1351.
[363] 20 June 1350.
[364] 23 November 1351: *Cal. Pap. Regs. Petitions*, i, 223.
[365] Over *decanatu* deleted by dots and *canonicatu* deleted by a line.
[366] 17 September 1352.

[367] 20 April 1353.
[368] 11 December 1354.
[369] 15 March 1355.
[370] 13 June 1348.
[371] Reading doubtful.
[372] 10 May 1349.
[373] 5 June 1350.
[374] 4 May 1351.
[375] Follows *res* deleted by a line.

per biennium fuit absolutus, sed debet restituere fructus inde perceptos, iii kalendis Maii pontificatus Domini Innocentii anno iiii°,[376] dictus Willelmus est coniugatus a diu est ante quam reciperet istam absolutionem.[377]

### (fol. 79) Bathoniensis Wellensis

De ecclesia de Disset (Ditcheat), de qua fuit provisum Hugoni de Morton', que fuit dimissa in arreragiis per Raymundum Pelegrini, non deberet esse dimissa quia ipse respondit[378] de ea in compotis suis.

Item de prebenda in ecclesia Wellensi, de qua per consecrationem Domini Radulphi episcopi Bathoniensis fuit provisum Henrico de Asshton' que fuerat dimissa in arreragiis per dictum Dominum Raymundum Pelegrini; istam[379] occupavit et adhuc occupat Magister Johannes de Sydenhale iure ordinario, et ille Henricus[380] nunquam habuit.

De prebenda in ecclesia Wellensi, de qua per obitum Johannis Giffard' fuit provisum Thome David xv kalendas Novembris anno Clementis vii°;[381] istam prebendam occupavit Bernardus de Brocariis iure regio et postea fuit sibi confirmata, et solvit ut patet supra in compoto.

Item de eadem prebenda, de qua fuit provisum Roberto de Askeby et confirmata Reginaldo de Bugwell', non habet effectum ut supra proximo.

Item de prebenda in ecclesia Wellensi, de qua per obitum Roberti de Luffyn fuit provisum Thome de Edyndon' v° kalendas Maii anno nono,[382] non habuit effectum quia Magister Ricardus de Tormenton' eam prius acceptavit et postea habuit confirmationem, que ponitur in arreragiis.[383]

Item de thesauraria ecclesie Wellensis, de qua per obitum Ricardi de Tiseldon' fuit provisum Ricardo de Chesterfeld' decimo kalendas Maii anno supradicto,[384] non habuit effectum quia Magister Ricardus de Tormenton' eam acceptavit et postea fuit sibi confirmata ut patet in[385] arreragiis.

Item in iure et ad omne ius quod competebat Roberto de Askeby ante eius resignationem in prebenda Sancti Decumani (St. Decuman's) in ecclesia Wellensi fuit subrogatus Petrus de Veteri Villa iii° idus Februarii anno x°;[386] istam occupat Bernardus de Brocariis, ut supradictum est.

De prebenda de Cumba Prima (Combe Prima) in ecclesia Wellensi, de qua per obitum Henrici de Carleton'

### (fol. 79ᵛ) Herefordensis

De prebenda in ecclesia Herfordensi, de qua per obitum Thome de Asteleye fuit provisum Petro de Gildesburgh', que fuit dimissa in arreragiis per Dominum Raymundum Pelegrini;[388] istam occupavit Edwardus de Grymesby iure regio; ideo nichil potuit levari.

Item de prebenda in ecclesia Herfordensi que vocatur Hunderton', de qua per obitum Walteri Carles fuit provisum Nicholai Heth' v° nonas Julii pontificatus Domini Clementis anno viii°;[389] dicto Nicholao de alia prebenda in eadem ecclesia fuit provisum quam tenet, idea ista non habet effectum.

Item de prebenda in ecclesia Herfordensi vocata Norton', de qua per assecutionem alterius prebende in eadem ecclesia factam per Rogerum de Burton' fuit provisum Willelmo de Herwyitton' vii° idus Aprilis anno supradicto,[390] non habuit effectum quia quidam Johannes Prophete prius ipsam acceptaverat et fuit sibi confirmata, qui solvit ut supra in compoto.

Item de prebenda de parva Wodington' (Withington Parva), de qua per obitum Willelmi Passemer' collatio facta Magistro Willelmo de Herwutton' fuit eidem confirmata v° idus Septembris anno ix°,[391] non habet effectum quia Magister Adam de Houghton' prius[392] ipsam acceptaverat virtute gratie sub expectatione[393] sibi facte.

Item de eadem prebenda, de qua per resignationem Johannis Grose fuit provisum Rogero de Herleston' ix° kalendas Decembris anno x°,[394] non habuit effectum quia dictus Johannes Grosse nunquam habuit illam prebendam, set Magister Adam Houton', ut supradictum est.

Item de portione parochialis ecclesie de Ledbury, de qua acceptatio facta per Willelmum de Kelseye fuit sibi confirmata iiii° kalendas Junii pontificatus Domini Innocentii anno secundo,[395] non habet effectum quia in ista ecclesia non sunt nisi due portiones prebendales quarum unam tenet Nicholaus Heth', ut continetur in arreragiis, et aliam tenet Dominus Humfredus de Charleton' et tenuit per viginti annos et ultra.

(fol. 80) Item de[396] prebenda de Ledbury, de qua per promotionem Michaelis electi Londoniensis fuit provisum cardinali de Ursinis[397] ii° kalendas Aprilis

---

[376] 29 April 1356.
[377] Followed by *ideo non debet fieri executio contra beneficium sed fiat contra personam* deleted by a line.
[378] *respondidit*, MS.
[379] *isIstam*, MS.
[380] Followed by *illam* deleted by a line.
[381] 18 October 1348.
[382] 27 April 1351.
[383] Followed by *utque patet per arreragias* deleted by a line.
[384] 22 April 1351.
[385] Over *per* deleted by a line.
[386] 11 February 1352.

[387] 12 May 1351.
[388] Followed by *non* deleted by a line.
[389] 3 July 1349.
[390] 7 April 1350.
[391] 9 September 1350.
[392] Followed by *a* in MS.
[393] *expectationis*, MS.
[394] 23 November 1351.
[395] 30 May 1354.
[396] Followed by *dicta* deleted by a line.
[397] Raynald Orsini, deacon of S. Adriano.

anno Innocentii tertio [398] non habet effectum quia dictus Michaelis non obtinuit illam prebendam.[399]

### Eliensis

De ecclesia de Fennydrayton' (Fen Drayton), in cuius iure quod competebat Roberto Abbot fuit subrogatus Attecreduk', que fuit dimissa in arreragiis per Dominum Raymundum Pelegrini; istam ecclesiam rex contulit Johanni de Hilton', quare nichil potuit levari.

Item de ecclesiis de Hadenham (Haddenham) et Letherington' (Leverington), de quibus cum vicariis per cessum vel decessum rectorum earum de illa quam episcopus eligeret fuit unio facta mense sue v$^{to}$ idus Septembris pontificatus Domini Clementis anno vii$^{mo}$,[400] non dum [401] neutra ipsarum vacavit per cessum vel decessum.

Item fuit data potestas episcopo Londoniensi ut parochialem ecclesiam de Horuwell' (Orwell) unire valeret auctoritate apostolica monasterio de Sempingham (Sempringham), retento iure archidiaconale et congrua portione vicarii,[402] et liceat eam apprehendere cum vacaret, alicuius licentia non petita, xii kalendas Junii anno x$^{mo}$,[403] non dum habuit effectum quia dicta ecclesia adhuc non vacavit.

Item fuit data potestas Domino Thome [404] episcopo Eliensi ut parochialem ecclesiam de Hinton' unire valeret cum vacaret domui seu collegio scolarium Sancti Petri universitatis Cantebrigie iii$^{tio}$ idus Augusti anno Clementis xi$^{mo}$,[405] non dum est unita.

### (fol. 80$^v$) Norwicensis

De decanatu de Fyncham (Fincham), de quo per resignationem Domini Thome Michaelis fuit provisum Willelmo de Merton', qui [406] fuit dimissus in arreragiis per Dominum Raymundum Pelegrini; Dominus Matheus de Asshton' obtinuit eum iure regio, ideo nichil potest levari.

Item de ecclesia Sancti Michaelis, de qua collatio facta Johanni Godesman iure ordinario fuit sibi confirmata, que fuit dimissa in arreragiis per dictum Dominum Raymundum Pelegrini, dictus Johannes nunquam dictam ecclesiam habuit prout patet per [407] inquisitionem.

Item de prioratu conventuali de Bernewell' (Barnwell), de quo per obitum Johannis ultimi prioris fuit provisum Simoni de Sagio vi$^{to}$ idus Octobris anno

Clementis decimo,[408] non habuit effectum quia dictus Simon non fuit gratiam suam prosecutus.

Item de ecclesia de Shipdham, de qua per obitum Johannis de Bruges fuit provisum Roberto Serle xii$^{mo}$ kalendas Maii anno supradicto anno Clementis nono,[409] non habuit effectum quia prius Thome de Morle fuit confirmata, qui solvit ut supra in compotis.

Item de vicaria de Bynham (Binham), de qua per resignationem Willelmi Alani fuit provisum Radulpho Palmere iiii$^{to}$ kalendas Martii anno supradicto; [410] dicta vicaria non taxatur nec vicarius recipit aliud preterquam victum et vestitum cum priore de Bynham, ideo nichil potest levari.

Item in iure quod competebat Roberto Serle in ecclesia de Shipdham fuit subrogatus Thomas de Clipston' v$^{to}$ idus Septembris [411] pontificatus Domini Innocentii anno primo,[412] non habuit effectum quia antequam fuit provisum Roberto Serle fuerat confirmata Thome de Morle, ut supradictum est.

Item de ecclesia de Westbradenham, de qua per assecutionem factam per Johannem de Brincle [413] de archidiaconatu Notinghamie fuit provisum Stephano de Grethull' xiiii$^{mo}$ kalendas Decembris anno supradicto [414] non habuit effectum quia pertinet ad presentationem laicalem et patronus presentavit alium qui possidet.

Item de archidiaconatu Suffolchie, de quo per promotionem M. electi Londoniensis fuit provisum Francisco de Sancto Maximino iiii$^{to}$ kalendas Martii anno Innocentii quarto,[415] non habet effectum, quia antequam esset electus permutaverat dictum archidiaconatum cum alio beneficio.

### (fol. 81) Lincolniensis

De prebenda de Grantham,[416] de qua per obitum Tidonis de Baresio fuit provisum Matheo de Brusele, que fuit dimissa in arreragiis per Dominum Raymundum Pelegrini in liii li. vi s. viii d.; dicta prebenda non est in ecclesia Lincolniensi set est in ecclesia Saresburiensi, et Dominus Willelmus de Radeford' occupavit ipsam iure regio, ut supradictum est.

Item de ecclesia de Melchebourne (Melchbourne), de qua per obitum Roberti de Kilingbury fuit provisum Radulpho de Bundeby et per mortem ipsius Radulphi infra eundem annum Bartholomeo de Draxton, que fuit dimissa in arreragiis per dictum Dominum Raymundum Pelegrini, non debuerat esse dimissa quia ipse respondebat in compotis suis.

Item de vicaria Sancti Gabrielis de Brunbrok' (Binbrooke), de qua per resignationem Walteri Abrham fuit provisum alteri, que etiam fuit dimissa in arreragiis per

---

[398] 31 March 1355.
[399] Followed by *set prebenda de Schurston' de qua fuit provisum Willelmo de Somerforde et solvit ut supra* deleted by a line.
[400] 9 September 1348.
[401] Followed by *vacavit* deleted by a line.
[402] Followed by *eat* deleted by a line.
[403] 21 May 1351.
[404] Thoma, MS.
[405] 11 August 1352.
[406] que, MS.
[407] Followed by *dictam* deleted by dots.

[408] 10 October 1351.
[409] 20 April 1351.
[410] 26 February 1351.
[411] Followed by *an* deleted by a line.
[412] 9 September 1353.
[413] Followed by *s* deleted by a line.
[414] 18 November 1353.
[415] 27 February 1356.
[416] Followed by *in ecclesia Lincolniensi* deleted by a line.

dictum Dominum Raymundum Pelegrini, non habuit effectum quia dictus Walterus illam nunquam resignavit, set tenuit eam pacifice usque ad mortem suam.

Item de prebenda in ecclesia Lincolniensi, de qua per [417] consecrationem Magistri Johannis de Ufford' fuit provisum Thome Bredwardyn, que fuit dimissa in arreragiis per dictum Raymundum Pelegrini, non habuit effectum quia dictus Magister Johannes moriebatur antequam esset consecratus, et per eius obitum fuit provisum Johanni Provane, qui solvit ut supra.

Item de ecclesia de Wirardesbury (Wyrardisbury), de qua per obitum Magistri Ade Murimouth' fuit provisum Rogero Mocelowe, que fuit dimissa in arreragiis per dictum Dominum Raymundum Pelegrini, non habuit effectum quia rex ante mortem dicti Ade adquisiverat patronatum dicte ecclesie, et post eius mortem fecit ipsam appropriari collegio de Wyndesore (Windsor), et prohibitum est, ideo nichil.

Item de ecclesia de Thindon' (Finedon), de qua cedente [418] vel decedente [419] rectore, fuit unio facta monasterio de Croxton', que fuit dimissa in arreragiis per dictum Dominum Raymundum Pelegrini, non habuit effectum quia episcopus dictam unionem impedivit, et tunc prior, qui patronus est, presentavit ad eandem unum clericum, qui illam tenet.

(fol. 81ᵛ) Item de prebenda de Brampton' in ecclesia Lincolniensi, de qua per obitum Bruni de Inzico fuit provisum Rogero Holm, que fuit dimissa in arreragiis; dictus Rogerus non habuit dictam prebendam per obitum dicti Bruni set per eius resignationem, et dictam prebendam occupavit et occupat Dominus Johannes de Wynewik' iure regio, ideo nichil.

Item de archidiaconatu Northamptonie, de quo per obitum cardinalis Convenarum [420] fuit provisum Rogero Notoft, qui fuit dimissis in arreragiis per Dominum Raymundum Pelegrini in cxxxiii li. vi s. viii d., non potuit tantum levari quia de procurationibus nichil solvitur camere, et dictus Raymundus Pelegrini credebat contrarium, ideo dimisit illam summam, set solutum est pro medietate veri valoris, deductis [421] procurationibus, quia non taxatur, ut supra.

Item de prebenda Sancte Margarete Leycestr' (Leicester) in ecclesia Lincolniensi, de qua per obitum Domini Johannis, cardinalis Portuensis (Porto), fuit provisum Henrico de Walton' iiiᵗⁱᵒ idus Aprilis pontificatus Domini Clementis anno viiᵐᵒ,[422] non habuit effectum quia non fuit gratiam suam prosecutus, set fuit provisum Johanni de Edinden', qui solvit ut supra.

Item de prebenda in ecclesia Lincolniensi, de qua per obitum Ade de Oseketh' fuit provisum Johanni de Co-

lumpna secundo kalendas Julii anno supradicto,[423] non habuit effectum quia dictus Adam prebendam nunquam obtinuit in ecclesia predicta.

Item de ecclesia de Scarlindon' alias Shiltingdon' (Shillington), de qua per obitum Willelmi Bateler fuit provisum Hugoni de Wydew xiiiiᵐᵒ kalendas Septembris anno supradicto;[424] dictam ecclesiam occupat Dominus Matheus de Aston' iure regio, ideo nichil.

Item de prebenda de Nassington' in ecclesia Lincolniensi, de qua per obitum Humfredi de Hastinges collatio facta Simoni de Sudbury fuit eidem confirmata vᵗᵒ idus Septembris anno supradicto;[425] Dominus Henricus de Walton' occupat illam prebendam iure regio, et prohibitum est, ideo nichil.

Item de unione seu appropriatione olim facta de parochialibus ecclesiis de Turkelaston' (Thurcaston), Belgrave et Byfeld (Byfield) monasterio Sancti Ebrufi (Saint-Evroult) Lexoviensis diocesis (Lisieux) fuit per papam confirmata de illa quam magister eligeret, cedente [426] vel decedente rectore, iiiiᵗᵒ nonas Octobris anno supradicto,[427] nichil factum est, immo dicte ecclesie gubernantur per rectores et illum monasterium penitus in partibus ignoratur.

(fol. 82) Item de ecclesia de Keteryng' (Kettering), de qua acceptatio facta per Alanum de Crophull' fuit sibi confirmata; prius alteri fuit provisum, scilicet Johanni Wade, qui tenet et possidet, ideo nichil hic, et solvit supra in recepta.

Item de ecclesia de Horncastr' (Horncastle), de qua, cum vacaret per consecrationem electi Cantuariensis, fuit provisum Hugoni Pelegrini nonas Novembris anno supradicto,[428] non habuit effectum quia episcopus Karliolensis patronus dicte ecclesie ante dictam consecrationem alienavit ad certos annos ius patronatus cum gleba uni laico, qui dictus laicus post dictam consecrationem presentavit quendam Johannem de Kirkeby, cui postea fuit confirmata, et respondetur supra.

Item de prebenda de Bannebury (Banbury), de qua per resignationem Hugolini de Adegoris de Parma fuit provisum Johanni de Parma xixᵐᵒ kalendas Januarii anno supradicto;[429] dictam prebendam occupat Petrus de Wotton' iure regio, ideo nichil.

Item de canonicatu et prebenda in ecclesia Lincolniensi, de quibus per consecrationem electi Cantuariensis fuit provisum Willelmo de Wittlesheye secundo idus Decembris anno supradicto;[430] dominus Willelmus de Hugate occupavit eam iure regio, ideo nichil.

Item de canonicatu et prebenda eccclesie Lincolniensis, de quibus prefatus Willelmus archidiaconus Huntyng-

[417] Followed by *consecrationem* deleted by a line.
[418] *sedente*, MS.
[419] *descendente*, MS.
[420] John Raymond of Comminges, bishop of Porto.
[421] Over *de dictis* deleted by a line.
[422] 11 April 1349.

[423] 30 June 1348.
[424] 19 August 1348.
[425] 9 September 1348.
[426] *sedente*, MS.
[427] 4 October 1348.
[428] 5 November 1348.
[429] 14 December 1348.
[430] 12 December 1348.

donie fuerat dictorum canonicatus et prebende possessionem adeptus, fuit provisum Michaeli de Northburgh'
ii^{do} idus Decembris anno supradicto,[430] non habuit effectum quia dictus Willelmus non fuit possessionem dictorum canonicatus et prebende assecutus.

De prebenda in ecclesia Lincolniensi quam Henricus
de Edenestowe obtinuit, de qua fuit provisum Reymundo
de Sancto Claro primo kalendas Februarii anno supradicto;[431] dictam prebendam occupavit Willelmus Dalton'
iure regio, ideo nichil.

Item de ecclesia de Iakesle (Yaxley), de qua per
obitum Ricardi de Tanefeld' fuit provisum Willelmo
de Sallowe kalendas Januarii anno supradicto;[432] rex
istam ecclesiam contulit cuidam consanguineo archiepiscopi Cantuariensis, ideo nichil.

(fol. 82^v) Item de prebenda de Clifton' in ecclesia
Lincolniensi, de qua per obitum Johannis de Hull'
acceptatio facta per Johannem de Aston' fuit eidem
confirmata v^{to} kalendas Martii anno supradicto,[433] non
habuit effectum quia quidam Stephanus de Raveneshere,
cui fuit etiam confirmata, evicit prebendam ab ipso, et
ponitur in areyratgiis.

Item de ecclesia de Ouston' (Owston), de qua per
resignationem Radulphi de Giseburn' fuit provisum
Willelmo de Navesby, qui vigore resignationis huius
eandem auctoritate ordinaria fuerat assecutus, et pro
fructibus perceptis, quia fuerat reservata, obtulit se
daturum ccc florenos in subsidium contra Turcos idus
Aprilis anno supradicto.[434] Dictus Willelmus solvit in
curia et monstravit acquietantiam dominorum camerarii
et thesaurarii de v^c lxvii [435] fl. solutis tam pro primis
fructibus quam pro dicta obligatione contra Turcos.

Item de prebenda de Gretton', de qua per resignationem Amorici de Cusornio fuit provisum Guidoni de
Monte Pesato iii^{tio} idus Maii anno supradicto,[436] non
habuit effectum quia Dominus Johannes de Bokingham
habuit eam auctoritate apostolica per uxorationem dicti
Americi, et solvit partem ut supra.

Item de subdecanatu ecclesie Lincolniensis, de quo
per obitum Nicholai de Tarette fuit provisum Willelmo
de Kelseye et secum dispensatum ut parochialem ecclesiam de Navesby (Naseby) insimul valeret obtinere v^{to}
kalendas Maii anno Clementis ix^{no},[437] non habuit effectum quia Hamo Bellers, qui ipsam acceptaverat, confirmationem impetravit et tenet eum, pro qua quidem
confirmatione solvit partem ut supra.

Item de prebenda in ecclesia Lincolniensi, de qua per
obitum Henrici de Edenstowe fuit provisum Roberto de
Mildenhale iiii^{to} idus Maii anno supradicto;[438] dictam

prebendam Dominus Willelmus Dalton occupat iure
regio, ut supradictum est.

Item de prebenda de Scarles (South Scarle)[439] in
ecclesia Lincolniensi, de qua per obitum Thome de
Cruce fuit provisum Willelmo de Kirkeby; dictus Willelmus non fuit gratiam suam prosecutus, set fuit provisum Johanni de Kirkeby, qui solvit partem ut supra.

(fol. 83) Item de prebenda de Welton' Ryval (Welton
Rivall), de qua acceptatio facta per Johannem Lamberti
post obitum Johannis de Acton fuit eidem confirmata
iiii^{to} idus Maii anno supradicto;[440] prius fuerat collata
Johanni de Assebourn' que a ibi [441] habuit effectum et
hic non.

Item de prebenda de Southscarle (South Scarle) in
ecclesia Lincolniensi, de qua per obitum Thome de Cros
acceptatio facta per Gilbertum de Welton' fuit sibi
confirmata iiii^{to} kalendas Martii anno supradicto,[442] non
habuit effectum quia prius fuerat provisum Johanni de
Kirkeby.

Item de ecclesia de Horpol (Harpole), de qua per
resignationem Alani de Crophull' fuit provisum Roberto
de Waplom v^{to} nonas Martii ano supradicto,[443] non
habuit effectum quia est de patronatu laicali, et Dominus
Robertus non fuit gratiam suam prosecutus, et patronus
alium presentavit.

Item de prebenda de Wilingham (Willingham) in
ecclesia Lincolniensi, de qua per obitum Johannis de
Acton' fuit provisum Bernardo de Brocariis anno Clementis x^{mo},[444] non habuit effectum quia prius fuit collata
Johanni de Assebourn' ut supra.

Item de prebenda de Langeforde (Langford) in ecclesia Lincolniensi, de qua per resignationem Johannis
de Bourn' fuit provisum Roberto de Burbage xii^{mo}
kalendas Junii anno supradicto,[445] non habuit effectum
quia prius fuit collata auctoritate ordinaria Magistro
Johanni Leth' cui postea fuit confirmata, ratione cuius
confirmationis solvit partem ut supra.

Item de cantoria ecclesie Lincolniensis quam Thomas
de Baddeby debebat dimittere per assecutionem canonicatus et prebende dicte ecclesie fuit eidem provisum
xii^{mo} kalendas Junii anno supradicto; dictus Thomas
nullam cantoriam obtinet nec obtinuit in dicta ecclesia
set in ecclesia Lichefeldensi.

Item de ecclesiis de Umberston' (Humberstone) et
Umgerston (Hungarston) cum capella de Frigwardesby
(Ingarsby) de patronatu monasterii Beate Marie Leycestr', cum vacarent per cessum vel decessum ultimi
rectoris, fuerunt unite monasterio predicto, quo ad ecclesiam de Umgerston' iam habet effectum, et solutum est,

---

[431] 1 February 1349.
[432] 1 January 1349.
[433] 25 February 1349.
[434] 13 April 1349.
[435] *lxvii* takes the place of *xlv* deleted by a line.
[436] 13 May 1349.
[437] 27 April 1351.
[438] 12 May 1351.

[439] Followed by *de qua* deleted by a line.
[440] 12 May 1351.
[441] *a* repeated MS.
[442] 26 February 1351.
[443] 3 March 1351.
[444] 19 May 1351, to 18 May 1352.
[445] 21 May 1351.

de quo respondetur supra in compoto, quo ad aliam non habet effectum adhuc, ideo nichil.

(fol. 83ᵛ) Item de prebenda de Werketon' (Warkton) in ecclesia Lincolniensi, de qua per resignationem Nicholai de Merton' fuit provisum Johanni de Astynges viiiᵛᵒ idus Maii anno supradicto,[446] non habuit effectum quia quidam Henricus Piel, qui dictam ecclesiam possidebat auctoritate ordinaria, obtinuit pro se diffinitivam sententiam in curia Romana latam per Dominum Bartholomeum de Bosco, auditorem sacri palatii.

Item de medietate parochialis ecclesie de Feruby (South Ferriby), per duos solite gubernarte rectores, de qua per cessum vel decessum rectoris fuit unio facta monasterio de Turnholm (Tupholme) xᵐᵒ kalendas Maii anno supradicto,[447] non habet adhuc effectum.

Item de ecclesia de Benyngton' (Bennington), de qua fuit provisum Roberto de Driffeld' ut ipsam ecclesiam, ad quam[448] in etate viginti quatuor annorum fuerat presentatus, et quam tenuit ultra annum dispensatione non habita non promotus xiiii kalendas Junii anno xi.[449] Dictus Robertus exhibuit bullam presentis gratie, in qua bulla de aliqua provisione nullam facit mentionem, set quod dominus noster papa habilitabat eum ad recipiendum dictam ecclesiam si sibi canonice conferetur, fructus inde perceptos sibi de gratia speciali remittendo.

Item de archidiaconatu Lincolniensi ac prebenda in eadem, de quibus per resignationem Thome de Northwode, vel alias quovismodo, fuit provisum Willelmo de Askeby kalendas Junii anno supradicto,[450] non habuit effectum quia dictus Thomas nunquam resignavit; immo post eius obitum fuit provisum Domino Hugoni Alberti.

Item de prebenda de Scarle (South Scarle) in ecclesia Lincolniensi, de qua per obitum Thome de Cruce, seu per resignationem Willelmi de Kirkeby, qui[451] non habita possessione resignavit, fuit provisum Gilberto de Welton' vᵗᵒ kalendas Junii anno supradicto,[452] non habet effectum quia prius fuerat provisam Johanni de Kirkeby, ut supradictum est.

Item de duobus beneficiis, cum vacarent in diocesi Lincolniensi unitis mense J. episcopi Lincolniensis, cum preesset in episcopatu, dicit idem episcopus quod nullam habet adhuc.

(fol. 84) Item de archidiaconatu Bukinghamie, de quo per obitum cardinalis Tusculanensis collatio facta Willelmo de Gynewell' fuit eidem confirmata, seu eidem provisum de novo quocumque modo vacante, idus Julii anno supradicto,[453] non habet effectum quia prius fuit

collatus Johanni de Assebourn' qui tenet, et ponitur in arreyratgiis.

Item de cancellaria ecclesie Lincolniensis, de que fuit provisum Roberto de [454] Renevill' clerico, non obstante quod ad illud beneficium magister vel bacularius in theologia consuevit assumi. Dictus Robertus non curavit de dicto beneficio propter exilitatem, nec aliquis curat, set vacat adhuc.

Item de ecclesia Sancti Petri Northamptonie cum capellis de Kingesthorp' (Kingsthorpe) et Upton' annexis, de qua fuit unio facta capelle Sancte Katherine iuxta Turrim Londonie quarto kalendas Novembris anno supradicto;[455] dicta unio non venit ad effectum quia episcopus impedivit, ideo nichil.

Item de prebenda quam Thomas electus Menevensis in ecclesia Lincolniensi obtinuit, de qua per eius consecrationem fuit provisum Domino Willelmo episcopo Tusculanensi, non habet effectum quia prius fuerat provisum Edwardo Botiller qui possidet, et ponitur in arreragiis.

Item de prebenda de Scarle (South Scarle) in ecclesia Lincolniensi, de qua per promotionem episcopi Karliolensis fuit provisum Nicholao de Bilton' kalendas Maii anno Innocentii primo,[456] non habet effectum ⟨quia prius fuerat provisum⟩ Johanni de Kirkeby qui tenet eam et possidet ut supra.

Item de prebenda in ecclesia Lincolniensi, de qua per resignationem Johannis de Parma fuit provisum Johanni de Stretle vᵗᵒ kalendas Septembris anno iiᵈᵒ,[457] non habet effectum quia Dominus Johannes de Perma nullam prebendam obtinuit.

Item de prebenda de Eylesbury (Aylesbury), de qua per obitum Edmundi de Bereford' fuit provisum Johanni Brian tertio idus Decembris;[458] dictus Johannes non est prosecutus gratiam suam, set filius Domini Johannis de Bello Campo tenet illam per gratiam expectationis.

Item de prebenda de Farendon' (Farndon), de qua per obitum Francisci de Urcinis fuit provisum Willelmo Woderove xviᵐᵒ kalendas Martii anno supradicto,[459] non habet effectum quia prius fuerat provisum Thome de Baddeby post mortem dicti Francisci, qui solvit partem ut supra.

(fol. 84ᵛ) Item de prebenda Sancti Martini in ecclesia Lincolniensi, de qua per obitum Henrici de Chaddesden' fuit provisum Thome Madefrey viiiᵛᵒ kalendas Februarii anno supradicto,[460] non habuit effectum quia prius fuerat provisum Rogero de Burton', qui incumbit et solvit.

[446] 8 May 1352.
[447] 22 April 1352.
[448] Followed by *ad* deleted by a line.
[449] 19 May 1352.
[450] 1 June 1352.
[451] *que*, MS.
[452] 28 May 1352.
[453] 15 July 1352.

[454] Followed by *Ryneling'* deleted by a line.
[455] 29 October 1352.
[456] 1 May 1353.
[457] 28 August 1354.
[458] 11 December 1355. Though the year is omitted in this item, the next entry, which refers to the above year, was dated 14 February 1355: *Cal. Pap. Regs. Petitions*, i, 284.
[459] 14 February 1355.
[460] 25 January 1355.

Item de ecclesia de Iakesle (Yaxley), in cuius iure quod competebat Willelmo de Sallowe fuit subrogatus Simon Bate iiii$^{to}$ idus Julii anno quarto; [461] quidam vocatus Johannes de Haddon' tenuit ipsam auctoritate ordinaria et tenuit per viii annos et ultra, tamen obligatur in casu quod [462] evincatur ab eo.

Item de ecclesia de Barewell' (Barwell), de qua per obitum ultimi rectoris fuit provisum Martino de Neuton' secundo kalendas Junii anno supradicto; [463] quidam Laurentius Ibbestoke tenet eam iure ordinaria, tamen obligatur in casu quod [464] evincatur ab eo.

Item de ecclesia de Epworth', de qua per obitum Willelmi de Clyne fuit provisum Thome de Clipston' ii$^{do}$ idus Septembris supradicto,[465] etiam quoquomodo vacaret fuit sibi de predicta ecclesia provisum secundo kalendas Decembris anno supradicto; [466] dictam ecclesiam possidet Dominus Willelmus de Navesby, et tenuit diu est, et ille [467] Thomas non.

Item de parochiali ecclesia de W. fuit de novo provisum I. de M., qui eam alias simoniace tenebat, vii$^{mo}$ idus Novembris anno tertio; [468] nomina tam beneficii quam rectoris penitus ignorantur, ideo nichil.

### (fol. 85) Conventrensis, Lichfeldensis

De ecclesia de Shottesswell' (Shotteswell), de qua fuit unio facta monasterio de Lavenden' (Lavendon), que fuit dimissa in arreragiis per Dominum Raymundum Pelegrini, non habuit effectum quia episcopus nec rex permiserunt.

Item de prebenda in ecclesia Lichfeldensi, de qua per obitum Henrici de la Dale fuit provisum Petro de Gildesburgh' iiii$^{to}$ nonas Maii anno Clementis octavo,[469] non habuit effectum quia dictus Henricus nullam prebendam obtinebat in dicta ecclesia, set dicto Petro fuit provisum de prebenda in dicta ecclesia per obitum Johannis la Zouche pro qua solvit [470] supra in recepta.

Item de archidiaconatu Staffordie, de quo per obitum Willelmi de Apeltr' fuit provisum Rogero Dorkyng' ii$^{do}$ idus Decembris anno supradicto; [471] Magister Ricardus de Bermyngham tenuit dictum archidiaconatum iure ordinario et postea habuit confirmationem, ut in arreragiis supra continetur, et dictus Rogerus nunquam habuit.

Item de prebenda de Tervyn (Tarvin), de qua per obitum Johannis la Zouche acceptatio facta per Wil-

lelum de Drayton' iiii$^{tio}$ idus Maii anno nono,[472] non habuit effectum quia prius fuit provisum Petro de Gildesburgh' qui tenet et solvit [470] supra in recepta.

Item de prebenda de Colewyk' (Colwich) in ecclesia Lichfeldensi, de qua acceptatio facta per Johannem de Charneux fuit sibi confirmata; dictus Johannes satisfecit Domino Raymundo Pelegrini antequam haberet confirmationem, de qua dictus Raymundus respondit in compotis suis per mortem Roberti de Wodhous qui dictam prebendam obtinebat.

Item de archidiaconatu Staffordie, de quo [473] per obitum Rogeri Dorkyng' fuit provisum Willelmo de Grenbury secundo die Februarii pontificatus Innocentii anno secundo,[474] non habuit effectum quia Ricardus de Bermyngham tenuit eum, ut supradictum est.

(fol. 85$^v$) Item de prebenda de Wolveye (Wolvey), de qua per consecrationem M. electi Londoniensis fuit provisum Petro le Colre et Simoni de Sudbury vii$^{mo}$ idus Novembris anno tertio,[475] non habet effectum quia prius fuit provisum Johanni Barnet, ut supra in arreragiis continetur.

Item de precentoria ecclesia Lichfeldensis, de qua per obitum Anibaldi Tusculanensis episcopi cardinalis fuit provisum Willelmo Claville viii$^{vo}$ kalendas Februarii anno iiii$^{to}$,[476] non habuit effectum quia Thomas de Baddeby tenet eam, cui fuit confirmata, et solvit partem ut supra in recepta.[477]

### Menevensis

De prebenda in ecclesia Menevensi, de qua per obitum Walteri Allexandr' fuit provisum David Martini xviii$^{mo}$ kalendas Julii pontificatus Domini Clementis anno vii$^{mo}$,[478] non habuit effectum quia tempore provisionis dictus Walterus vivebat.

Item de archidiaconatu Menevensi ac prebenda in ecclesia Menevensi, de quibus acceptatio facta per Ricardum de Cleangre fuit eidem confirmata iii$^{tio}$ idus Octobris anno supradicto; [479] rex ad dicta beneficia presentavit quendam [480] Johannem Gouf', et prohibitum est.

### (fol. 86) Eboracensis

De ecclesia de Slyngesby (Slingsby), de qua, cum contigeret [481] vacare per assecutionem ecclesie de Leek' (Leake) eiusdem diocesis, fuit provisum Magistro Ricardo de Welles, que fuit dimissa in arreragiis per

---

[461] 12 July 1356.
[462] Followed by *ipse eviceret* deleted by a line. *Quod* is repeated after the deleted words.
[463] 31 May 1356.
[464] Followed by *ipse eviceret* deleted by a line.
[465] 12 September 1356.
[466] 30 November 1356. Date repeated MS.
[467] Followed by *Willelmus* deleted by a line.
[468] 7 November 1355.
[469] 4 May 1350.
[470] Followed by *ut* deleted by a line.
[471] 12 December 1349.

[472] 13 May 1351.
[473] *qua*, MS.
[474] 2 February 1354.
[475] 7 November 1355.
[476] 25 January 1356.
[477] Followed by *Item* beginning a new paragraph which is left blank.
[478] 14 June 1348.
[479] 13 October 1348.
[480] The two preceding words are written over *contulit cuidam* deleted by a line.
[481] *contigere*, MS.

Dominum Raymundum Pelegrini, non debuit esse dimissa in arreragiis quia sibi solutum fuerat et respondit in compotis suis.

Item de prebenda de South Cave in ecclesia Eboracensi, de qua fuit provisum Paulo de Monte Floro, que fuerat dimissa in arreragiis per Dominum Raymundum Pelegrini in cvi li. xiii s. iiii d.; dicta prebenda fuit collata per regem Domino Roberto de Kildesby tempore vacationis archiepiscopatus Eboracensis et obtinuit difinitivam sententiam contra dictum Paulum in curia Romana, et sic gratia eiusdem Pauli non habuit effectum.

Item de vicaria de Whitkirk iuxta Pountfrey (Pontefract), de qua per mortem Johannis Sculthorp fuit provisum Olivero de Tygrove, que fuit dimissa in arreragiis per Dominum Raymundum Pelegrini; dictus Oliverus nunquam illam vicariam habuit ut patet per [482] certificatorum officialis [483] archiepiscopi.

De thesauraria Eboracensi, de qua per obitum Francisci de Urcinis fuit provisum Domino Anibaldo cardinali, que fuit dimissa in arreragiis per Dominum Raymundum Pelegrini; dicta thesauraria fuit collata Domino Johanni de Wynewik' per regem, et prohibitum est.

Item de ecclesia de Stratton (Stirton), de qua per obitum Ade de Estlegh' fuit provisum Roberto de Askeby, que fuit dimissa in arreragiis per Dominum Raymundum Pelegrini; dictus Robertus de Askeby non fuit gratiam suam prosecutus, ideo nichil.

Item de archidiaconatu [484] Notinham [485] quem obtinebat Dominus Anibaldus cardinalis, cum vacaret per assecutionem thesaurarie dicte ecclesie, fuit provisum Johanni de Bukingham, qui [486] fuit dimissus in arreragiis per Dominum Raymundum Pelegrini, non habuit effectum quia dictus cardinalis nunquam fuit dictam thesaurariam assecutus, ut supradictum est.

(fol. 86ᵛ) Item de ecclesia de Bonaye (Bunny), de qua per assecutionem archidiaconatus Norwicensis faciendam per Dominum Hamonem Bellers, que fuit dimissa in arreragiis per Dominum Raymundum Pelegrini, non habuit effectum quia dictus Hamo nunquam fuit dictum archidiaconatum assecutus.

De prebenda de Wetewang' (Wetwang) in ecclesia Eboracensi, de qua per obitum Willelmi de Kildesby [487] acceptatio facta per Willelmum Johannis de Aula fuit sibi confirmata ixⁿᵒ kalendas Maii pontificatus Domini Clementis anno viiᵐᵒ; [488] Ricardus de Wynewyk' habet dictam prebendam iure regio, et prohibitum est.

De prebenda in ecclesia Eboracensi, de qua per obitum Radulphi de Turvill' fuit provisum Alano de Crophull';

dictus Alanus non fuit gratiam prosecutus, set hermitariam vitam accepit quam tenet.

Item de prebenda de Esketon' [489] (Skelton) in ecclesia Oueden' (Howden), vacante per obitum Ade de Aselbech' fuit provisum Johanni de Elewell,' [490] non habuit effectum quia prius fuerat provisum Johanni de Provane, qui solvit ut supra.

De ecclesia de Appelton' in Rydale (Appleton-le-Street), de qua cum vacaret per cessum vel decessum rectoris fuit unio facta monasterio Sancti Albani, adhuc non habet effectum quia adhuc non vacavit.

Item de prebenda in ecclesia Beverlacensi, de qua per obitum Ricardi de Ferughby fuit provisum Thome de Lexham, non habuit effectum quia prius fuerat provisum Andree de Ufford', qui tenet et solvit ut supra.

Item de prebenda in ecclesia Eboracensi, de qua per obitum Johannis Beringer fuit provisum Rogero Holm nonas Novembris anno supradico,[491] non habet effectum quia quidam Thomas de London' prius ipsam acceptaverat, qui pro fructibus satisfecit ut supra.

Item de archidiaconatu Notingham, de quo, cum vacaret per assecutionem possessionis thesaurarie ecclesie Eboracensis faciendam per dominum episcopum Tusculanensem cardinalem, fuit provisum Roberto de Kildesby xᵐᵒ kalendas Decembris anno supradicto,[492] non habet effectum quia dictus cardinalis nunquam fuit [493] dictam precentoriam assecutus, ut supradictum est.

(fol. 87) Item de prebenda in ecclesia Beverlacensi, de qua per obitum Thome Sampson fuit provisum Willelmo de Savinhaco iiiᵒ nonas Aprilis anno Clementis viiiᵒ; [494] dictam prebendam quidam Alanus Wynflet' virtute gratie sibi facte acceptavit, qui postea confirmationem habuit, et solvit partem ut supra.

Item de prebenda Wethewang' (Wetwang) in ecclesia Eboracensi, de qua per obitum Domini Anibaldi cardinalis fuit provisum Johanni de Insula et de qua per obitum eiusdem Anibaldi vel Willelmi de Veraco fuit provisum Johanni de Asshebourne, non habuit effectum quia neuter predictorum possessionem dicte prebende habuit, pro eo quod Ricardus de Wynwyk' habuit eam iure regio et adhuc tenet, et prohibitum est.

Item de prebenda de South Cave in ecclesia Eboracensi, de qua per obitum Roberti de Kildesby fuit provisum Nicholao de Heth' xvi kalendas Februarii pontificatus Domini Clementis anno ixᵒ; [495] dictam prebendam Dominus Henricus de Henglesby iure regio occupavit et occupat adhuc, et prohibitum est.

Item de subthesauraria Eboracensi, de qua per assecutionem precentorie ecclesie eiusdem fuit provisum

[482] Followed by *inquisitionem* deleted by a line.
[483] Followed by *q* deleted by a line.
[484] Followed by *Bukingham* deleted by dots.
[485] Followed by *d* deleted by a line.
[486] *que*, MS.
[487] Followed by *fuit provisum* deleted by dots.
[488] 23 April 1349.

[489] Followed by *v* deleted by a line.
[490] Followed by *q* deleted by a line.
[491] 5 November 1348.
[492] 22 November 1348.
[493] Followed by *assecutus* deleted by a line.
[494] 3 April 1350.
[495] 17 January 1351.

Roberto de Beverlaco iii° nonas Maii anno supradicto,[496] non habuit effectum [497] quia dictus Robertus non fuit gratiam suam prossequutus.

Item de ecclesia de Dodyngton' (Doddington), de qua collatio facta Gervasio de Wilforde fuit eidem confirmata iiii[to] idus Maii anno supradicto; [498] dicta ecclesia est in diocesi Elyensi, et ibi solutum est ut supra.

Item de prebenda in ecclesia Southwellensi, de qua per obitum Henrici de Edenestowe acceptatio facta per Henricum de Hynglesby fuit eidem confirmata iiii[to] idus Maii anno supradicto.[498] Dictus Henricus dicit quod ad eius instantiam dicta confirmatio non fuit impetrata sed coram publico notario dicte confirmationi expresse renuntiavit, et tenet eam iure regio.

Item de prebenda in ecclesia Beverlacensi, de qua acceptatio facta per dictum Henricum fuit eidem confirmata; dictus Henricus nullam prebendam habet in illa ecclesia, quare nichil.

(fol. 87[v]) Item de prebenda de Osbaldwyk' (Osbaldwick) in ecclesia Eboracensi, de qua, vacante quia Aymericus de Cursornio, priusquam esset possetionem [499] adeptus, matrimonium carnale contraxit, collatio facta Gilberto de Welton' fuit eidem confirmata iii° idus Maii anno supradicto.[500]

Item de ecclesia de Pykerinton' (Pickering), vacante per obitum Michaelis de Whait', fuit provisum Rogero Holm iiii[to] idus Maii anno supradicto; [498] dictus Rogerus non fuit gratiam suam prosecutus, set quidam filius militis tenet eam auctoritate ordinaria.

Item de prebenda de Holm archiepiscopi (Holme), de qua, vacante per resignationem Willelmi de Samynaco, fuit provisum Radulpho Daventr' iiii[to] idus Maii anno supradicto; [498] dictus Willelmus de Samynaco nunquam habebat dictam prebendam, set quidam Johannes de Ferughby, qui post obitum Thome Sampson ipsam occupavit, et quamvis per obitum ipsius Thome fuerat provisum dicto Willelmo de Samynaco, tamen ipse Johannes voluntarie satisfecit pro illa vacatione, ut supra in recepta, propter reservationem, non obstante quod ipse alio iure possideret.

De archidiaconatu Notingham, de quo per obitum Roberti de Kildesby fuit provisum Johanni de Brincle iii[tio] nonas Maii anno supradicto,[496] non habuit effectum quia dictus Robertus nunquam habuit dictum archidiaconatum, quia sibi fuerat provisum cum vacaret per assecutionem thesaurarie Eboracensis faciendum per dominum Anibaldum cardinalem Tusculanensem, quam thesaurariam nunquam fuit assecutus.

Item de prebenda in ecclesia Eboracensi, de qua per resignationem Henrici de Turr' fuit provisum [501] Guidoni de Turre xix kalendas Februarii anno supra-

dicto; [502] non est notum in ecclesia Eboracensi quod dictus Henricus ibidem prebendam habuit.

Item de prebenda in ecclesia Suthwellensi, de qua per obitum Henrici de Edenstowe fuit provisum Petro de Gildesburgh' xvi[mo] kalendas Februarii anno supradicto; [495] Dominus Henricus de Ingleby tenet eam iure regio ut supra.

Item fuit dispensatum cum Willelmo Vyolesseye (Whittelsy) ut parochialem ecclesiam de Patwatton' (Patrington) alias Pringeston', de qua nuper ei provisum fuerat, insimul cum archidiaconatu quem obtinebat in ecclesia Lincolniensi voluit eam obtinere iii[tio] idus Maii anno Clementis x[mo]; [503] non invenitur quod dictus Willelmus habuerat archidiaconatum in ecclesia Lincolniensi, nec contra talis ecclesia in diocesi Eboracensi invenitur.[504]

(fol. 88) Item de thesauraria ecclesia Eboracensis, de qua per obitum episcopi Tusculanensis cardinalis fuit provisum Johanni de Wynewyk' iiii[to] idus [505] Junii anno supradicto; [506] dictus cardinalis nunquam habuit dictam thesaurariam set idem Johannes habet eam iure regio, quo iure contentus, prohibitionem impetravit ne primi fructus exigerentur.

Item de prebenda Altaris Sancte Katerine (Saint Katherine's Altar) in ecclesia Beverlacensi, de qua per obitum Willelmi Aberwyk' acceptatio facta per Johannem de Aula fuit eidem confirmata xix[mo] kalendas Decembris anno supradicto,[507] non habet effectum quia prius fuit confirmata Ricardo de Meux, qui solvit ut supra in recepta.

Item de prebenda de Barneby (Barmby on the Marsh) in ecclesia de Hoveden' (Howden), de qua per obitum Walteri Purdhomme [508] acceptatio facta per Ricardum Drax fuit eidem confirmata x[mo] kalendas Februarii anno supradicto,[509] non habuit effectum quia Magister Thomas de Nevill' tenet eam virtute cuiusdam gratie sibi facte de anteriori data.

Item de prebenda in ecclesia Suthwellensi, de qua per obitum Elie Pelegrini et Henrici de Welteby fuit provisum Willelmo de Aragon' secundo idus Februarii anno supradicto; [510] Dominus Thomas de Brembr' occupavit dictam prebendam post mortem dictorum Elie et Henrici iure regio, et est prohibitum.

Item de prebenda in ecclesia Eboracensi, de qua per resignationem Guidonis de Turr' fuit provisum Domino Bernardo tituli Sancti Eustachii diaconi cardinalis xix[mo]

---

[502] 14 January 1351.
[503] 13 May 1352. *Cal. Pap. Regs. Petitions*, i, 208.
[504] Only the tops of the letters of the last four words appear in my photostat. I have not been able to examine the original to see whether they are cut away in the manuscript.
[505] Followed by *Julii* deleted by a line.
[506] 10 June 1351.
[507] 13 November 1351.
[508] Following by *fuit* deleted by a line.
[509] 23 January 1352.
[510] 12 February 1352.

---

[496] 5 May 1351.
[497] Followed by *quod* deleted by a line.
[498] 12 May 1351.
[499] Presumably for *possessionem*.
[500] 13 May 1351.
[501] Followed by *qu* deleted by a line.

kalendas Martii anno supradicto,[511] non habuit effectum quia dictus Guido prebendam in dicta ecclesia non habuit, nec per consequens cardinalis.

Item de prebenda in ecclesia Suthwellensi, de qua per obitum Henrici de Wlteby fuit provisum Thome Fastolf' vi[to] nonas Martii anno supradicto;[512] Dominus Thomas de Brembr' tenuit eam iure regio, ut supradictum est.

Item de prebenda in ecclesia Eboracensi, de qua per obitum Bernardi de Novo Campo fuit provisum Johanni de Appelby ii[do] idus Augusti anno xi[mo],[513] non habet effectum quia prius fuit confirmata Simoni de Brisele, qui eam tenet prout continetur in arreragiis supra.

(fol. 88[v]) Item de ecclesia de Brumpton' (Brompton), de qua per obitum archiepiscopi Eboracensis, vel alias quovis modo, fuit provisum Johanni de Appelby vii[mo] kalendas Novembris anno supradicto,[514] et Johanni Provano iiii[to] nonas Novembris eodem anno,[515] non habuit effectum quia cardinalis de Turr'[516] habuit eam, et ipse non.

Item de prebenda de Osbaldewyk' (Osbaldwick) in ecclesia Eboracensi, de qua per consecrationem Gilberti de Welton' episcopi Karliolensis fuit provisum Ricardo de Kilvyngton' secundo idus Maii anno supradicto;[517] prius fuerat provisum Simoni de Brisele per mortem Bernardi de Novo Dampno qui eam tenet, et ponitur in arreragiis[518] supra.

Item de prebenda in ecclesia Eboracensi, in cuius iure quod competebat Simoni de Brusele fuit subrogatus Willelmus de Latton' xiii[mo] kalendas Decembris anno supradicto,[519] non habuit effectum quia dictus Simon tunc vivebat et vivit adhuc.

Item de prebenda de Stranxale (Strensall) quam episcopus Londoniensis obtinebat in ecclesia Eboracensi, de qua fuit provisum Raynaldo Sancti Adriani diacono cardinali viii[mo] kalendas Martii.[520] non habuit effectum quia prius fuerat provisum cardinali Albanensi, qui eam tenet.

### (fol. 89) Dunolmensis

De prebenda in ecclesia de Langecestr' (Lanchester), de qua per resignationem Hugonis Pelegrini fuit provisum Willelmo Gavyny, non habet effectum quia dictus Hugo nunquam resignavit.

Item de ecclesia de Seggefeld' (Sedgefield), de qua per obitum Johannis de Whithchurch' fuit provisum Waltero Mairyn v[to] idus Octobris anno viii[vo],[521] non habuit effectum quia dictus Johannes tunc vivebat.

Item de ecclesia de Acton' (Haughton-le-Skerne), de qua per obitum Johannis Giffard' fuit provisum Radulpho de Kelleby xii[mo] kalendas Decembris anno supradicto;[522] Dominus Henricus de Ingelby tenet eam [523] iure regio, et est prohibitum.

Item de hospitale de Bolton' (Boulton), de quo per obitum Roberti de Baldesby fuit provisum Johanni de Assebourn' iiii[to] nonas Maii anno Clementis nono;[524] dictus Johannes non fuit gratiam suam prosecutus quia hospitale non vacavit in curia et Alex' de Nevill' tenet eam collatione ordinaria.

Item de ecclesia de Robury (Rothbury), de qua per obitum ultimi rectoris fuit provisum Johanni de Asseburn' et secum dispensatum ut archidiaconatum Bukingham insimul posset possidere, non habet effectum quia quidam Johannes Mareshal tenet eam auctoritate ordinaria.

Item de [525] prebenda in ecclesia Beate Marie de Derlyngton' (Darlington), de qua per resignationem ex causa permutationis Thome de Newyle fuit provisum Garcie de Galardo iiii[to] idus Julii Domini Innocentii anno iiii[to],[526] non habet effectum [527] quia dictus Thomas non resignavit, ymo tenet.

### (fol. 89[v]) Karleolensis

De archidiaconatu Karleolensi cum ecclesia sibi annexa, de quibus per obitum Willelmi Trifolean' fuit provisum Willelmo de Samyaco nonas Maii pontificatus Domini Clementis anno viii[vo],[528] non habuit effectum quia dictus Dominus Willelmus non fuit gratiam suam prosecutus.[529]

### SECOND ACCOUNT OF HUGH PELEGRINI
### 1358-1363

(fol. 91)[1] Rationes Hugonis Pelegrini, olim in Anglia camere apostolice collectoris, de pecuniis et aliis causis per ipsam in dicta collectoria nomine dicte camere apostolice receptis ac etiam solutis, assignatis et expensis ac etiam de restis dicte camere debitis, a die prima mensis Junii anno domini M° CCC° LVIII° usque ad primam diem mensis Septembris anno domini M° CCC° LXIII°, prout in presenti libro compotorum continetur.[2]

---

[511] 12 February 1352.
[512] 2 March 1352.
[513] 12 August 1352.
[514] 26 October 1352.
[515] 2 November 1352.
[516] Bernard de la Tour d'Auvergne, deacon of S. Eustachio.
[517] 12 May 1353: Cal. Pap. Regs. Petitions, i, 247.
[518] Followed by ut deleted by a line.
[519] 19 November 1352.
[520] Year omitted in MS.
[521] 11 October 1349.

[522] 20 November 1349.
[523] eum, MS.
[524] 4 May 1351.
[525] Followed by ecc deleted by a line.
[526] 12 July 1356.
[527] Followed by d deleted by a line.
[528] 7 May 1350; Trifolean is Briseban elsewhere.
[529] Folio 90 is blank on both recto and verso.
[1] This folio is the original parchment cover of this report.
[2] Below this title are written in contemporary hand the names of the following dioceses: Vigorniensis, Bangorensis, Assavensis, Menevensis. In the upper left hand corner are written in a modern hand the following numbers: In. 6, 1358, 1363, 833. The last is probably the number given to this report in the series of Collectorie as they were formerly numbered in the Vatican Archives.

(fol. 93, i)[3] Hic est compotus Hugonis Pelegrini, nuper apostolice sedis in partibus Anglie, Wallie et Hibernie nuntii deputati, de omnibus et singulis per eum seu alios nomine dicte sedis receptis, liberatis, assignatis et expensis, de quibuscumque obventionibus ad ecclesiam Romanam in dictis partibus qualitercumque expectantibus, a primo die Junii anno domini millesimo CCC° LVIII°, quo die de receptis, assignatis et expensis cum camera computavit, usque ad primum diem mensis Septembris anno domini millesimo CCC° LXIII°.

Sequitur recepta arreragiorum denariorum Beati Petri per supradictum Hugonem dimissorum primo die Junii anno domini millesimo CCC° LVIII°, quo die cum camera apostolica computavit [4]

De archidiaconatu Surie dimisso in arreragiis supradicto primo die Junii pro annis LIIII°, LV°, LVI° et LVII°, pro quolibet anno v li. xiii s. iiii d., xxii li. xiii s. iiii d.

De archidiaconatu Essexie dimisso in arreragiis pro annis LV°, LVI° et LVII°, pro quolibet anno v li. x s., xvi li. x s.

De episcopo Batoniensi dimisso pro annis LVI° et LVII°, pro quolibet anno xi li. v s., xxii li. x s.

De episcopo Norwycensi dimisso pro annis LV°, LVI° et LVII°, pro quolibet anno xxi li. x s., lxiiii li. x s.

De episcopo Lincolniensi dimisso pro annis LV° ii li. et pro LVI° et LVII°, pro quolibet anno xlii li., iiii^xx vi li.[5]

(fol. 93^v) De archiepiscopo Eboracensi dimisso pro annis LVI° et LVII°, pro quolibet anno xi li. x s., xxiii li.

De archidiacono Midelsexie dimisso pro anno LVII° v li. x s.

De episcopo Exoniensi dimisso pro anno LVII° ix li. v s.

De episcopo Saresburiensi dimisso pro anno LVII° xvii li.

De archidiacono Roffensi dimisso pro anno LVII° v li. xii s.

De archidiacono Wyntoniensi dimisso pro anno LVII° xi li. xiii s. iiii d.

De episcopo Cicestrensi dimisso pro anno LVII° viii li.

De episcopo Conventrensi et Lichfeldensi dimisso pro anno LVII x li. v s.

De episcopo Hereffordensi dimisso pro anno LVII° vi li.

De episcopo Wygorniensi dimisso pro anno LVII° x li. v s.

De archidiacono Eliensi dimisso pro anno LVII° v li.

Summa totalis recepte dictorum precedentium arreragiorum iii° xxiii li. xiii s. viii d. Approbatum.

Sequitur recepta denariorum Beati Petri a supradicto die Junii anno domini millesimo CCC° LVIII° usque ad primum diem Septembris anno LXIII°

De archidiacono Surie pro annis LVIII, LIX, LX, et LXI°, pro quolibet anno v li. xiii s. iiii d., xxii li. xiii s. iiii d.

De archidiacono Essexie pro annis LVIII°, LIX°, LX°, LXI°, et LXII°, pro quolibet anno v li. x s., xxvii li. x s.

De episcopo Batoniensi pro annis LVIII°, LIX°, LX°, et LXI°, pro quolibet anno xi li. v s., xlv li.

De episcopo Norowycensi pro annis LVIII°, LIX° et LX°, pro quolibet anno xxi li. x s., lxiiii li. x s.

De episcopo Lincolniensi pro annis LVIII°, LIX°, LX° et LXI°, pro quolibet anno xlii li., clxviii li.

De archiepiscopo Eboracensi pro anno LVIII° xi li. x s.

De archidiacono Midelsexie pro annis LVIII° et LIX°, pro quolibet anno v li. x s., xi li.

Summa a precedenti citra [6] iii° l li. iii s. iiii d. Approbatum.

(fol. 94, ii) De episcopo Exoniensi pro annis LVIII°, LIX° et LX°, pro quolibet anno ix li. v s., xxvii li. xv s.

De episcopo Saresbiriensi pro annis LVIII°, LIX°, LX°, et LXI°, pro quolibet anno xvii li., lxviii li.

De archidiacono Roffensi pro annis LVIII°, LIX°, LX°, LXI° et LXII°, pro quolibet anno v li. xii s., xxviii li.

De archidiacono Wyntoniensi pro annis LVIII° et LIX°, pro quolibet anno xi li. xiii s. iiii d., xxiii li. vi s. viii d.

De episcopo Cicestrensi pro annis LVIII°, LIX° et LX° pro quolibet anno viii li., xxiiii li.

De episcopo Conventrensi et Lichfeldensi pro annis LVIII° et LIX°, pro quolibet anno x li. v s., xx li. x s.

De episcopo Hereffordensi pro annis LVIII°, LIX° et LX°, pro quolibet anno vi li., xviii li.

De episcopo Wygorniensi pro annis LVIII°, LIX° et LX, pro quolibet anno x li. v s., xxx li. xv s.

De archidiacono Cantuariensi pro annis LVIII°, LIX°, LX°, LXI° et LXII°, pro quolibet anno viii li., xl li.

De archidiacono Colcestr' pro annis LVIII°, LIX°, LX°, LXI° et LXII°, pro quolibet anno v li. x s., xxvii li. x s.

De archidiacono Eliensi pro annis LVIII°, LIX°, LX° et LXI°, pro quolibet anno v li., xx li.

Summa presentis pagine iii° xxvii li. xvi s. viii d. sterlingorum.[7] Approbatum.

Summa totalis recepte dictorum denariorum Beati Petri tam arreragiorum in ultimo compoto dimissorum

---

[3] Folio 91 verso, the inside of the cover, is the face of a notarial document dated 7 December 1335. It contains an inventory of the goods of a deceased bishop assigned by William Coste, canon of Agde, to John Pasagia, rector of Gajan in the diocese of Mirepois, on the order of the camerarius and the treasurer. Folio 92 is blank on recto and verso. The original foliation of this report is retained on account of several references to *infra* and *supra*.

[4] At the head of the folio in the right-hand corner is the caption: *Recepta arayratgorum.*

[5] The phrase *summa a prece* is written at the foot of the page, but no amount is given.

[6] Written over *in margine* deleted by a line.

[7] In the margin, the same sum in the text having been deleted by a line.

quam aliorum receptorum post usque ad dictum primum diem Septembris anno LXIII° mi li. xiii s. viii° d. sterlingorum.[7] Approbatum.

(fol. 94ᵛ) Sequitur recepta arreragiorum annui census dimissorum primo die Junii anno LVIII° supradicto.

De priore de Bodmyne dimisso in arreragiis pro annis LVI°, et LVII°, pro quolibet anno ii s., iiii s.

De abbate de Faverestham dimisso pro anno LVII° xiii s. iiii d.

De abbate Sancti Albani dimisso pro anno LVII° xiii s. iiii d.

De priore Karliolensi dimisso pro anno LVII° in xiii s. iiii d., xiii s. iiii d.

De abbitissa Sancte Clare dimissa pro anno [8] LVII in vi d., vi d.

Summa xliiii s. vi d. Approbatum

Sequitur recepta dicti annui census a dicto primo die Junii anno LVIII° usque ad primum diem Septembris anno LXIII°

De priore de Bodmyne pro annis LVIII°, LIX°, LX° et LXI°, pro quolibet anno ii s. viii s.

De abbate de Faveresham pro annis LVIII°, LIX°, LX° et LXI°, pro quolibet anno xiii s. iiii d., liii s. iiii d.

De abbate Sancti Albani pro annis LVIII°, LIX°, LX°, LXI° et LXII°, pro quolibet anno xiii s. iiii d., lxvi s. viii d.

De priore Karliolensi pro annis LVIII°, LIX°, LX° et LXI°, pro quolibet anno xiii s. iiii d., liii s. iiii d.

De abbate de Malmesbur' pro annis LVIII°, LIX°, LX°, LXI° et LXII°, pro quolibet anno xiii s. iiii d., iii li. vi s. viii d.

De custode de Skardeburgh' pro annis LVIII°, LIX°, LX°, LXI°, et LXII°, pro quolibet anno xv d., vi s. iii d.

De abbate de Charteseye pro annis LVIII°, LIX°, LX°, LXI° et LXII° pro quolibet anno viii s., xl s.

Summa a precedenti summa usque hic xiiii li. xiiii s. iii d.

(fol. 95, iii) De priore de Tunbrug' pro annis LVIII°, LIX°, LX°, LXI° et LXII°, pro quolibet anno xiii s. iiii d., iii li. vi s. viii d.

De priore de [9] Chaucumbe pro annis LVIII°, LIX°, LX°, LXI°, LXII°, pro quolibet anno xv d., vi s. iii d.

De priore de Angleseye pro annis LVIII°, LIX° et LX°, pro quolibet anno ii s., vi s.

De abbate Sancti Edmundi de Bury pro annis LVIII°, LIX°, LX°, LXI et LXII°, pro quolibet anno xiii s. iiii d., iii li. vi s. viii d.

Summa usque hic vii li. v s. vii d. sterlingorum.

Summa totalis recepte tam arreragiorum quam ordinariorum censuum receptorum post usque ad dictum

primum diem Septembris anno LXIII° xxiiii li. iiii s. iiii d. sterlingorum.[10] Approbatum.

Sequitur recepta legatorum ad Terram Sanctam a dicto die primo Junii anno LVIII° usque ad primum diem Septembris anno LXIII°

De Isabella de Vito uxori quondam Johannis Kata per manus episcopi Londoniensis, cui fuit commissum quia cum ipsa super quibusdam votis dispensaret, l s.

De Domino Johanne de Welburne, prebendario de Hustweyt (Husthwaite) in ecclesia Eboracensi, qui cum camera composuit pro fructibus male perceptis pro ducentis fl. in subsidium Terre Sancte xxx li.

De Henrico de Exennale pro legato Johannis Holleston' et Petronille uxoris eius Eboracensis diocesis xl s.

De executore Domini Johannis [11] Wake militis Wellensis diocesis xx s.

De executore Domini Johanni de Ekesale quondam canonici Londoniensis xx s.

De Johanne Merchaunt' de Bordon' (Borden) Cantuariensis diocesis egeno et paupere cum quo fuit dispensatum super voto Sancti Jacobi iii li. vi s. viii d.

Summa pagine a precedenti summa usque hic xxxix li. xvi s. viii d.

(fol. 95ᵛ) De executore Domini Willelmi de Alcestr' Wygorniensis diocesis v s.

De Rogero de Berwyco Lincolniensis diocesis ii s.

De parte Johannis de Midildon' Eboracensis diocesis xx s.

⟨Summa pa⟩gine usque ⟨hic⟩ xxvii s.[12]

Summa totalis legatorum dicto tempore xli li. iii s. viii d. Approbatum

Summa universalis omnium precedentium receptarum mlxvii li. i s. viii d.

Sequitur recepta arreragiorum quorundam beneficiorum per Dominum Hugonem supradicto primo die Junii anno LVIII° dimissorum.[13]

## Cantuariensis

De prioratu de Folkeston' (Folkestone), cuius collatio facta Willelmo Medici per suum abbatem fuit eidem confirmata per Clementem antequam dictus Hugo esset nuntius, et fuit dimissus in arreragiis supradicto die in xv li. xiii s. iiii d.; solvit in partem vii li.; de residuo rendetur infra in arreragiis.

De ecclesia de Maydestan' (Maidstone), taxata cvi li. xiii s. iiii d., de qua fuit per obitum cardinalis Tusculani provisum Hugoni Pelegrini per Clementem vii idus Septembris anno x°,[14] qui fuit dimissus in arreragiis pro fructibus dicte ecclesie cvi li. xiii s. iiii d.

---

[7] [footnote reference]
[8] Followed by *in* not deleted.
[9] Followed by *Angleseye* deleted by a line.
[10] Follows the same sum deleted by a line.
[11] Followed by *de Ekesale quondam canonici Londoniensis* deleted by a line.
[12] In the margin, which is cut too close.
[13] In the margin opposite this heading is the caption *Recepta arrayratgiorum*.
[14] 7 September 1351.

De ecclesia de Stokebury (Stockbury), taxata xxvii li. vi s. viii d., que fuit appropriata priori et conventui de Ledes (Leeds) per Clementem viii° idus Augusti anno xi°,[15] et dimissa in arreragiis in xvii li. xiii s. iiii d., solvit x li. vi s. viii d.

De ecclesia de Ikham (Ickham), taxata xxx li., de qua per resignationem Roberti de Bourn' fuit provissum Rogero de Wye per Innocentium ii° kalendas Decembris anno iiii°,[16] et fuit dimissa in arreragiis in solidis [17] fructibus, nichil hic, eo quod non habuit effectum, quia iste Rogerus non habuit possessionem, sed Magister Willelmus de Hertelbury auctoritate ordinaria, qui diu cum eodem Rogero litigavit et optinuit deffinitivam sententiam in palatio apostolico contra ipsum. Iuravit magister dictus Rogero sibi fuisse de hoc sibi factam fidem et se vidisse sententias xxiiii die Maii, et evicit eam G. Eltherii qui eam possedit.[18]

Summa pagine a precendenti summa usque hic cxxiiii li.

(fol. 96, iiii) [19] De ecclesia de Buclond (Buckland), taxata ix li. vi s. viii d., de qua ex causa permutationis facta cum Johanne de Stok fuit provisum Johanni de Horton' per Innocentium viii [20] kalendas Augusti anno primo,[21] pro resta dimissa iiii li. xiii s. iiii d.

De ecclesia de Wyvelesbergh' (Woodnesborough), taxata xvi li. xiii s. iiii d., appropriata per Clementem abbatie Sancti Augustini Cantuariensis, que fuit dimissa in arreragiis, nichil hic sed ponitur infra in arreragiis. Respondetur infra in arreragiis.[18]

### Roffensis

De ecclesia de Eynesfford (Eynsford), taxata xx li., de qua per resignationem Viviani de Blankeford' fuit provisum Johanni de Croso per Clementem xviii° kalendas Februarii anno x°,[22] non habuit effectum quia iste Vivianus fuit privatus per sententiam diu ante istam resignationem, et provisum alteri per ordinarium. Constat per litteras Domini Symonis archiepiscopi Cantuariensis quod Vivianus fuit diu ante provisionem per sententiam diffinitivam [23] privatus per predecessorem ipsius domini archiepiscopi, et ab ipso ordinario provisum Willelmo de Bradele; et fuit facta dicta privatio xxviii die mensis Aprilis anno XLVI et collatio eodem anno ii° nonas Junii.[18]

### Londoniensis

De prebenda de Kenteston' (Kentish Town) in ecclesia Londoniensi, dimissa in arreragiis in xxx s. iiii d.,

de qua fuit provisum Rogero Holm; [24] idem Rogerus de ista summa et aliis pro diversis beneficiis suis camere in curia satisfecit.

De archidiaconatu Midelsexie in ecclesia Londoniensi, non taxato, cuius acceptatio fuit Andree de Offord confirmata per Clementem xv kalendas Junii anno vii° vel viii°,[25] dimisso in arreragiis pro medietate, x li. ii s. ii d.

De prebenda de Herleston' (Harlesden in Willesden) in ecclesia Londoniensi, taxata iii li. vi s. viii d., dimissa in arreragiis, de qua per obitum Johannis de Ambresbury acceptatio facta per Johannem Wada fuit sibi confirmata per Clementem iiii° idus Maii anno ix°,[26] iii li. vi s. viii d.

De ecclesia de Ests (Hayes), taxata xxiii li. vi s. viii d., dimissa in arreragiis, de qua per resignationem Magistri Ricardi Drax fuit provisum Willelmo Durandi per Clementem v° nonas Martii anno vii°,[27] xxiii li. vi s. viii d.

De decanatu ecclesie Londoniensis, taxato lviii li. xiii s. vi d., inclusis v li. viii s. x d. pro temporalibus obmissis in ultimo compoto quia tunc non constabat, de quo fuit provisum Ricardo de Hilyngton' per Innocentium v° idus Aprilis anno ii°,[28] dimisso in arreragiis in xx li., solvit additos v li. viii s. x d., pro dictis temporalibus obmissis, xxv li. vii s. x d.

Summa pagine lxvi li. xvi s. viii d.

(fol. 96ᵛ) De prebenda de Isoldon' (Islington) in ecclesia Londoniensi, taxata v li. vi s. viii d., que fuit confirmata Willelmo de Lughtburgh' per Innocentium vii° kalendas Junii anno vii,[29] dimissa, v li. vi s. viii d.

De ecclesia de Kelleveden' (Kelvedon), taxata xxvi li. xiii s. iiii d., dimissa in arreragiis, unio cuius facta per ordinarium monasterio Westmonasterii fuit confirmata per Clementem anno ix°,[30] xxvi li. xiii s. iiii d.

De capella seu ecclesia de Stamfford (Stanford le Hope), taxata xxvi li. xiii s. iiii d., nichil hic sed ponitur infra in arreragiis.

De ecclesia de Brayle (Rayleigh), non taxata, dimissa in arreragiis, de qua per obitum Johannis de Hynton' fuit provisum Ricardo Broun per Innocentium xi° kalendas Februarii anno quarto,[31] certificatum est per officialem Londoniensem quod ipse Ricardus nunquam habuit possessionem, quia rex contulit cuidam Nicholao de Horton' ratione temporalium prioratus de Pretoella (Prittlewell) existentium in manu sua tempore guerre.

### Cicestrensis

De prebenda de Ferynges (Ferring) in ecclesia Cicestrensi, taxata xxx li. et dimissa in arreragiis in viii li.

---

[15] 6 August 1352.
[16] 30 November 1356.
[17] *solidum*, MS.
[18] The last sentence is in the margin.
[19] At the top of the folio over the left margin is the heading: *Recepta arrayratgiorum.*
[20] Followed by *lk* apparently deleted by a line.
[21] 25 July 1353.
[22] 15 January 1352.
[23] A stain renders the portion of the word after *diff* illegible.

[24] *Homl*, MS.
[25] 18 May 1349 or 1350.
[26] 12 May 1351.
[27] 3 March 1349.
[28] 9 April 1354.
[29] 26 May 1359.
[30] 5 May 1351: *Cal. Pap. Regs. Petitions*, i, 386.
[31] 22 January 1356.

xiii s. iiii d., de qua per resignationem Symonis Godwyn fuit provisum Johanni de Acton' per Clementem antequam dictus Hugo esset nuntius, non debuisset fuisse dimissa nisi in vii li., quia respondetur in supradicto compoto reddito primo die Junii anno LVIIIº de xxiii li., et vii li. ponuntur infra in arreragiis.

De decanatu Cicestrensi, taxato liiii li. vi s. viii d., dimisso in [32] xxx li., de quo per obitum Walterii Segrave fuit provisum Willelmo de Lynne per Clementem iiii kalendas Junii anno viii,[33] in partem dictarum xxx li., xv li. De residuo respondetur in arreragiis.

De thesauraria Cicestrensi, taxata xlvi li. xiii s. iiii d., et prebenda de Sydelstham (Sidlesham) in ecclesia Cicestrensi, taxata xxx li., dimissa in xii li. ii s. ix d., de qua per obitum Bernardi del Fau fuit provisum Waltero Gest per Clementem xiiº kalendas Decembris anno viiiº,[34] infra in arreragiis de prebenda quia de thesauraria est in plenum satisfactum.

Summa pagine xlvii li.

(fol. 97, v)[35] De prebenda de Walton' in ecclesia collegiata de Bosham, taxata xxxiii li. vi s. viii d., dimissa in arreragiis, que fuit confirmata Ottoni de Northwode per Clementem vi idus Aprilis anno viiiº,[36] in partem dicte taxe xxiiii li.

De archidiaconatu Lewensi, dimisso in arreraygiis, non taxato, collatio cuius facta Willelmo de Lutghteburgh' fuit eidem confirmata per Clementem iiº idus Augusti anno xiº,[37] ponitur infra in arreraygiis.

De prebenda de Sutton' in ecclesia Cicestrensi, taxata xxvi li. xiii s. iiii d., de qua per consecrationem Michaelis in episcopatum Londoniensem fuit provisum Michaeli de Northburgh', ponitur infra in arreragiis.

De archidiaconatu Cicestrensi, non taxato, dimisso in arreraygiis, qui fuit confirmatus Ade de Houton' per Clementem anno viiiº,[38] iii li. vi s. viii d.

De prebenda in ecclesia Cicestrensi, taxata xxvi li. xiii s. iiii d., dimissa, de qua per obitum Thome de London' fuit provisum Ricardo Drax per Innocentium viº idus Februarii anno secundo,[39] xxvi li. xiii s. iiii d.

De prebenda de Colleworth' (Colworth) in ecclesia Cicestrensi, de qua per consecrationem Thome episcopi Norwycensis fuit provisum Henrico de Walton', dimissa in arreraygiis, respondetur infra in fine arreraygiorum inter beneficia dicti Henrici pro quibus simul se obligavit.

Item de prebenda de Sidlestham (Sidlesham) in ecclesia Cicestrensi, taxata ad xxx li., de qua per obitum Walteri Gest fuit provisum Johanni de Bishopheston'

per Innocentium viº idus Februarii anno secundo,[39] dimissa in arreragiis xv li. Non debuisset fuisse dimissa nisi in xv li., quia de aliis xv li. est responsum in aliis compotis.[40]

De precentoria ecclesie Cicestrensis, taxata liii li. vi s. viii d., de qua per obitum cardinalis de Mota[41] fuit provisum[42] cardinali de[43] Gordonio (Gourdon)[44] et dimissa in solidis fructibus, ponitur infra in arreragiis.

## Wyntoniensis

De ecclesia de Westmunes (West Meon), taxata xx li., que fuit confirmata Johanni de Kenigton' per Clementem idus Maii anno viiiº,[45] dimissa in vi li., nichil hic sed ponitur infra in arreraygiis.

Summa pagine lxix li.

(fol. 97ᵛ) Hospitale Sancte Crucis, dimissum, ponitur infra in arreraygiis.

Rectoria sive custodia domus Sancti Nicholay de Portesmuth' (Portsmouth), dimissa, ponitur infra in arreraygiis.

Archidiaconatus Surie, dimissus, ponitur in arreraygiis.

De ecclesia de Laverstok (Laverstoke), taxata xiiii li., in qua et ad omne ius quod competebat Johanni Crom fuit subrogatus Johannes Banbury per Clementem iiº idus Aprilis anno ixº,[46] dimissa in arreraygiis in xii li., solvit ix li. De residuo respondetur infra in arreraygiis.

De prebenda in ecclesia monialium de Warwell' (Wherwell), dimissa, nichil hic, sed ponitur in arreraygiis.

De prioratu de Apellorciomb' (Appuldurcombe), dimisso, nichil, sed infra in arreraygiis.

## Saresbiriensis

De ecclesia de Elyngden' (Elingdon), taxata xxxiii li. vi s. viii d., dimissa in arreraygiis, de qua per resignationem Rogeri Holm fuit provisum Jacobo Beufort per Clementem viº idus Novembris anno viiº vel viiiº,[47] quia simul fuerunt missi, xxxiii li. vi s. viii d.

De archidiaconatu Saresbiriensi, taxato xxxiii li. vi s. viii d., dimisso, de quo per obitum Roberti de Luffenham et de canonicatu et prebenda eiusdem ecclesie vacantibus per obitum Jacobi Hovent' acceptatio facta per Rogerum de Kynton' fuit eidem confirmata per Clementem vº kalendas Martii anno,[48] xxxiii li. vi s. viii d.

---

[32] Followed by *arreragiis* deleted by a line.
[33] 29 May 1349.
[34] 20 November 1349.
[35] At the top of the folio over the left margin is the heading: *Recepta arayratgiorum.*
[36] 8 April 1350.
[37] 12 August 1352.
[38] 8 May 1350: *Cal. Pap. Regs. Letters*, iii, 336.
[39] 8 February 1354.

[40] In the margin: *visum est.*
[41] Gaillard de Mota, deacon of St. Lucy in Silice.
[42] Followed by *cardinali per obitum* deleted by a line.
[43] Followed by *Mota* deleted by a line.
[44] William Farinier, priest of Ss. Marcellino e Pietro.
[45] 15 May 1350.
[46] 12 April 1351.
[47] 8 November 1348 or 1349.
[48] 25 February 1350: *Cal. Pap. Regs. Letters*, iii, 356.

De ecclesia de Kyveleye (Keevil), taxata xxvi li. xiii s. iiii d., et dimissa in x li., de qua per obitum Roberti le Umbles fuit provisum Magistro Thome Tromipsale per Clementem antequam dictus Hugo esset nuntius, in partem dictarum x li., iii li. vi s. viii d.

De prebenda de Swaclive (Swallowcliffe) in ecclesia collegiata de Hestredebneth' (Heytesbury), taxata vi li. xiii s. iiii d., et dimissa in lxvi s. viii d., de qua fuit provisum Roberto Baker per obitum Thome de Littilton' per Clementem antequam dictus Hugo esset nuntius, iii li. vi s. viii d.

Summa pagine lxxxii li. vi s. viii d.

(fol. 98, vi)[49] De prebenda de Wermynstre (Warminster) in ecclesia Saresbiriensi, que fuit dimissa in v li., nichil hic, sed infra in arreraygiis.

De prebenda de Dysamynstr' (Yetminster) in ecclesia Saresbiriensi, dimissa in xxvi li. xiii s. iiii d., de qua fuit provisum Henrico de Walton', respondetur infra in fine tam in recepta quam in arreraygiis, quia iste Henricus fuit pro ista prebenda et pro aliis diversis beneficiis simul obligatus, ut ibi patet.

De prebenda in ecclesia Saresbiriensi, de qua per obitum Thome de Astele fuit provisum Reginaldo de Brian per Clementem nonas Maii anno viii°,[50] dimissa, ponitur infra in arreraygiis.

De prebenda de Northnuwynton' (North Newnton) in ecclesia monialium de Wilton', taxata xiii li. vi s. viii d., que Johanni de Vienna fuit confirmata per Clementem xiiii kalendas Junii anno viii°,[51] dimissa in arreragiis in viii li. vi s. viii d., viii li. vi s. viii d. Declaretur quia reperitur dimissa ratione confirmationis facte dicto Johanni in dicta summa.[52]

De ista prebenda fuit provisum per mortem istius Johannis de Vienna Guillelmo de Meltborna per Clementem iii° idus Maii pontificatus sui anno ix°,[53] et sic cum confirmatione precedenti est infra annum et non debetur nisi una annonata.

Item de eadem prebenda fuit provisum Ricardo de Wylington' per Clementem nonas Junii anno xi°,[54] sed non habuit effectum talis provisio, quia per dictum Guillielmum de Meltborna fuit evicta.

Et est sciendum quod per dictum obitum fuit provisum Willelmo de Melburn' de eadem prebenda per Clementem nonas Maii anno ix°,[55] qui evicit eam a dicto Ricardo et prefata solutio fuit eidem Willelmo allocata.

De prebenda de Netherhaven' (Netheravon) in ecclesia Saresbiriensi, taxata xx li, de qua per obitum ultimi prebendarii fuit provisum Willelmo de Melburn' per

Clementem iii° nonas Maii anno ix°,[56] que fuit dimissa in arreraygiis in vi li. xiii s. iiii d., vi li. xiii s. iiii d.

De prebenda de Netherber' (Netherbury) in ecclesia Saresbiriensi nichil hic, sed infra in arreraygiis.

De prebenda de Cheseyburn' (Chisenbury) in ecclesia Saresbiriensi, dimissa in solidis fructibus, nichil hic, sed infra in arreraygiis.

Summa pagine xv li.

(fol. 98ᵛ) De prebenda de [57] Byshopeston' (Bishopstone), dimissa, nichil hic, sed infra in arreragiis.

De prebenda de Heword (Highworth) in ecclesia Saresbiriensi, taxata c li., de qua per obitum Walteri de London' fuit provisum Raymundo Pelegrini per Clementem xiii° kalendas Junii anno ix°,[58] de qua per regem fuit provisum Henrico de Walton', et fuit prohibitum per regem ne dictus Raymundus se intromiteret de dicta prebenda, et dicto Hugoni ne dictos primos fructus exigeret, et tandem idem Raymundus dimissit prebendam de Hengestrega (Henstridge) in ecclesia Wellensi, et sic habuit dictam prebendam. Ideo deliberet camera quid agendum. liii li. vi s. viii d. Restat xlvi li. xiii s. iiii d. de quibus facit dubium.[59]

De ecclesia de Scorcombe (Corscombe), de qua acceptatio facta per Johannem Brokeland fuit eidem confirmata, nichil hic, sed infra in arreraygiis.

De prebenda de Wermynstr' (Warminster), dimissa, nichil hic, sed infra in arreraygiis.

De prebenda de Hull' (Hill Deverill) in ecclesia de Hredbur' (Heytesbury), taxata vi li. xiii s. iiii d., de qua per obitum Magistri Roberti Tresk fuit provisum Bartholomeo Patricii per Clementem vii° idus Martii anno ix°,[60] in partem iii li. vi s. viii d. De residuo respondetur infra in arreragiis.[59]

De prebenda de Preston' in ecclesia Saresbiriensi, taxata xvi li. xiii s. iiii d., de qua per obitum Roberti Tresk fuit provisum Johanni Goud per Clementem viii° idus Martii anno ix°,[61] que fuit dimissa in arreraygiis xvi li. xiii s. iiii d.

De [62] prebenda de Northnewenton' (North Newnton) in ecclesia monialium de Wylton' (Wilton), de qua per obitum Johannis de Vienna fuit provisum Willelmo de Melbourn', respondetur supra in eodem folio circa medium alterius pagine, quia per obitum dicti Johannis fuit provisum duobus, ut patet ibi.

Summa pagine lxxviii li. vi s. viii d.

(fol. 99, vii)[63] De ecclesia de Wyteburn' Fakelan' (Winterborne Stickland), taxata iiii li. vi s. viii d., nichil hic, sed infra in arreraygiis.

---

[49] At the left side of the top of the page is abbreviated the heading: *Recepta arreraygiorum.*
[50] 7 May 1350.
[51] 19 May 1349.
[52] This sentence is in the margin.
[53] 13 May 1351.
[54] 5 June 1352.
[55] 7 May 1351.

[56] 5 May 1351.
[57] Followed by *Heword* deleted by a line.
[58] 20 May 1350.
[59] The last sentence is in the margin.
[60] 9 March 1351.
[61] 8 March 1351.
[62] Followed by *prebenda* deleted by a line.
[63] At the top of the page over the left margin is the heading: *Recepta arreraygiorum.*

De prebenda de Streton' (Stratton) in ecclesia Saresbiriensi, de qua ex causa permutationis fuit provisum Johanni Thwrsteyn', nichil hic, sed infra in arreragiis.

De archidiaconatu Dorcestr' cum ecclesia de Gussugh' (Gussage), dimisso in arreraygiis, nichil hic, sed infra in arreraygiis.

De prebenda de Aulton' (Alton) Sancti Pancratii in ecclesia Saresbiriensi, taxata viii li., que fuit confirmata Willelmo de Nassyngton' per Innocentium xi° kalendas Novembris anno iiii°,[64] dimissa, viii li.

De prebenda de Bymynstre (Beminster) in ecclesia Saresbiriensi, dimissa, taxata xiii li. vi s. viii d., que fuit confirmata Petro de Whopnton' per Innocentium xi° kalendas Novembris anno iiii°,[64] xiii li. vi s. viii d.

De thesauraria ecclesie Saresbiriensis, taxata iiii\*\* vi li. xiii s. iiii d., dimissa in arreraygiis in lvii li. xv s. vii d., de qua per obitum cardinalis de Mota [65] fuit provisum cardinali de Florentia [66] per Innocentium iiii° kalendas Januarii anno iiii°,[67] lvii li. xv s. vii d.

De subdecanatu ecclesie Saresbiriensis et prebenda eidem annexa nichil hic, sed in arreraygiis.

De prioratu de Ledres (Loders), dimisso, nichil hic, sed infra in arreraygiis.

## Exoniensis

De thesauraria ecclesie Exoniensis, taxata xx li., nichil hic, sed infra in arreraygiis.

De archidiaconatu Barnastapol', non taxato, dimisso, qui fuit confirmatus Johanni de Reynham, nichil hic, sed infra in arreraygiis.

De prebenda Exoniensi, taxata iiii li., dimissa in arreraigiis, que fuit confirmata Nycholao Terere per Clementem vi° nonas Aprilis anno viii°,[68] iiii li.

De ecclesia de Eymystr' (Axminster), taxata xvii li. vi s. viii d., dimissa in vi li., de qua per obitum Henrici de Calmyngton' fuit provisum Nicholao Teret per Clementem iiii° kalendas Aprilis anno nono,[69] vi li.

Summa pagine lxxxix li. ii s. iii d.[70]

(fol. 99v) De prebenda in ecclesia Exoniensi, taxata iiii li. et dimissa in arreraygiis, que per obitum Johannis Pipert' fuit confirmata Jacobo de Mildon' per Clementem iiii° kalendas Martii anno ix°,[71] iiii li.

De decanatu Exoniensi et prebenda, taxatis lxii li. xiii s. iiii d. et dimissis in lii li. xiii s. iiii d., de quibus per obitum Richardi de Brayle, fuit provisum Reginaldo

de Bogwell' per Clementem xv kalendas Octobris anno x°,[72] in partem dicte reste xx li.

De prebenda ecclesie Exoniensis, taxata iiii li., dimissa, de qua per obitum Henrici de Brathele fuit provisum Henrico de Walton', infra in arreraygiis.

De vicaria de Holmton' (Yealmpton?), non taxata, dimissa, infra in arreraygiis.

De prebenda in ecclesia Exoniensi, taxata iiii li., que fuit confirmata Thome David, infra in arreraygiis.

De prioratu de Ortington' (Otterton), taxato iiii\*\* vi li. xiii s. iiii d., dimisso in arreraygiis, qui fuit Thome Sedile confirmatus per Innocentium ii° kalendas Februarii anno iiii°,[73] in partem dicte taxe lv li.

## Wygorniensis

De ecclesia de Estlegh' (Astley), dimissa in viii li. pro resta, infra in arreragiis.

De ecclesia Sanctorum Philipi et Jacobi Bristoll', non taxata, infra in arreraygiis.

De ecclesia de Kynghtwich' (Knightwick), taxata iiii li. vi s. viii d., dimissa in xxxiii s. iiii d., infra in arreraygiis. Ymo fuit dimissa in solidis fructibus licet non debuisset.

## Bathoniensis et Wellensis

De prebenda de Harpetre (East Harptree) in ecclesia Wellensi, dimissa in iiii li., infra in arreraygiis.

De ecclesia de Hyngham (High Ham), taxata xviii li., de qua per assecutionem ecclesie de Beniton' (Donnington) fuit provisum Johanni Farendon' per Clementem anno vii°,[74] dimissa in xviii li., xviii li.

Summa pagine xcvii li.

(fol. 100, viii)[75] De prebenda de Wyvewescomule (Wiveliscombe) in ecclesia Wellensi nichil hic, sed infra in arreraygiis.

De decanatu Wellensi, taxato c li., de quo per obitum Walteri de London' fuit provisum Johanni de Karloton' per Clementem v° kalendas Junii anno viii°,[76] dimissa in lx li., lx li.

De cancellaria ecclesie Wellensis, taxata xlvi li. xiii s. iiii d., de qua per assecutionem decanatus Wellensis fuit provisum Johanni de Horsyngton' per Clementem kalendas Junii anno vii°,[77] dimissa in xx li. xii s., in partem vi li.

De prioratu Montis Acuti (Montacute), taxato ad cxxxiii li. vi s. viii d., de quo per obitum Johannis la Porta fuit provisum per Clementem Johanni la Porta, dimissa in cviii li. vi s. viii d., in partem xxxiii li. vi s. viii d.

---

[64] 22 October 1356.
[65] Gaillard de Mota, deacon of St. Lucy in Silice.
[66] Francis de Aptis, priest of S. Marco.
[67] 29 December 1356.
[68] 8 April 1350. It should be *vi idus: Cal. Pap Regs. Petitions.* i, 195.
[69] 29 March 1351.
[70] In the margin opposite this item: *Hic incipiunt concordarum summe paginarum.*
[71] 26 February 1351.

[72] 17 September 1351.
[73] 31 January 1356.
[74] 15 July 1348: *Cal. Pap. Regs. Petitions,* i, 135.
[75] At the top of the page over the left margin is the heading: *Recepta arreraygiorum.*
[76] 28 May 1349.
[77] 1 June 1348.

De prebenda de Welliscumbe (Wiveliscombe) in ecclesia Wellensi, dimissa, non taxata, que fuit confirmata Thome de Bekton' per Clementem iiii° idus Maii anno nono,[78] xl s.

De thesauraria ecclesie Wellensis, taxata ad xxxiii li. vi s. viii d., que fuit confirmata Richardo de Thormerton' per Clementem idus Novembris anno xi°,[79] que fuit dimissa in xxxiii li. vi s. viii d., solvit in partem xiii li. vi s. viii d.

De archdiaconatu Wellensi cum prebenda sibi annexa, taxatis lxvi li. xiii s. iiii d., de quibus per consecrationem episcopi Menevensis fuit provisum Domino Willelmo episcopo Tusculano per Innocentium nonas Januarii anno primo,[80] fuit dimisso in arreragiis in xliiii li. viii s. xi d., solvit xliiii li. viii s. xi d.

De precentoria Wellensi et prebenda Cumbe (Combe) quinte, de quibus respondetur in ultimo compoto de vi li. xiii s. iiii d., et dimittitur in arreragiis in xliiii li. vi s. viii d., ac si taxaretur ad li li., sicut per errorem taxe in libro taxe subponendo quod ecclesia de Quyell' (Yeovil) sit eidem precentorie annexa, quod non est verum, ymmo est rector in eadem et taxata per se xxv li. xiii s. iiii d., et sic vera taxa dictarum precentorie et prebende est xxv li. vi s. viii d., de quibus est reponsum in dicto compoto de vi li. xiii s. iiii d., et solvit in plenum xviii li. xiii s. iiii d. Vidi super hoc litteram certificatoriam Domini Bathoniensis episcopi sub data anni LXII et xxiii die Maii.[81]

Summa pagine clxxvii li. xv s. vii d.

(fol. 100ᵛ) De prebenda de Wytchurche (Whitchurch) in ecclesia Wellensi, dimissa, nichil hic, sed infra in arreraygiis.

De prebenda de Asselberche (Haslebury Plucknet) in ecclesia Wellensi, taxata ad x li., de qua per obitum Gilberti de Brueria fuit provisum Transmontano Raycabordi per Innocentium iiii° nonas Decembris anno iiii°,[82] dimissa in arreragiis, x li.

De ecclesia de Melles (Mells), taxata xxiii li. vi s. viii d., que fuit Andree de Wormynstr' confirmata per Innocentium xv° kalendas Martii anno iiii°,[83] dimissa in arreragiis, xxiii li. vi s. viii d.

De ecclesia de Preston', taxata ad iiii li. v s. iiii d., de qua per assecutionem alterius beneficii fuit provisum Johanni Atthowell' per Innocentium ii° nonas Maii anno iiii°,[84] dimissa in arreraygiis, iiii li. v s. iiii d.

### Hereffordensis

De prebenda de Morton' (Moreton) in ecclesia Hereffordensi nichil hic, sed infra in arreraygiis.

De vicaria de Lodebur' (Ledbury), taxata viii li., de qua per assecutionem archidiaconatus Menevensis factam per Richardum de Cleangle fuit provisum Roberto Michaelis per Clementem v° idus Octobris,[85] dimissa in arreraygiis, viii li.

De portione prebendali Elie de Ludeber',[86] dimissa, nichil hic, sed infra in arreraygiis.

De parochiali ecclesia de Monte Gomeri (Montgomery), de qua fuit provisum Nicholao de Upton' per Innocentium viii idus Septembris anno primo,[87] qui pro fructibus eiusdem convenit cum camerario xvii kalendas Februarii pontificatus Domini Innocentii anno primo [88] in xii li., dimissa in arreraygiis in viii li. xiii s. iiii d., viii li. xiii s. iiii d.

De prebenda de Euthyngton' (Ewithington), taxata x li., de qua per obitum Edmundi de Gremmesby fuit provisum Thome Greffyn viii° kalendas Octobris anno secundo,[88a] in partem dicte taxe xl s.

Summa pagine lvi li. v s. iiii d.

(fol. 101, ix)[89] De prebenda de Bolyngehope (Bullinghope) in ecclesia Hereffordensi, taxata ad xvi li., de qua per obitum Stephani de Ledebur' fuit provisum Willelmo de Dalton', et dimissa in arreraygiis, non habuit effectum quia fuit confirmata Willelmo Wroth per Innocentium idus Octobris anno iii°,[90] et de ista confirmatione respondetur in proxima pagina.

De ecclesia Kynggeslond (Kingsland), taxata xx li., de qua Willelmo de Penbrygg' fuit de novo provisum per Innocentium iiii° kalendas Martii anno ii°,[91] dimissa in arreraygiis, xx li.

De prebenda de Bolynghope (Bullinghope) in ecclesia Hereffordensi, taxata ad xvi li., collatio cuius facta Willelmo Wroth fuit eidem confirmata per Innocentium idus Octobris anno iii°,[90] dimissa, xvi li.

De prebenda de Preston' in ecclesia Hereffordensi, taxata [92] iii li. ii s. ix d., que fuit Petro de Whoton' confirmata per Innocentium xi° kalendas Novembris anno iiii°,[93] dimissa in arreraygiis, iii li. ii s. ix d.

### Norwycensis

De ecclesia de Branfford (Bramford), taxata xlvi li. xiii s. iiii d., que fuit unita monasterio de Bello Cicestrensis diocesis per Clementem vi° idus Jullii anno ix°,[94] dimissa in arreraigiis, xlvi li. xiii s. iiii d.

De prioratu de Castellacre (Castle Acre), de quo fuit

[78] 12 May 1351.
[79] 13 November 1352.
[80] 5 January 1353.
[81] This sentence is in the margin.
[82] 2 December 1356.
[83] 16 February 1356.
[84] 6 May 1356.
[85] 11 October 1349: *Cal. Pap. Regs. Petitions*, i, 179.
[86] Followed by *nichil hic* deleted by a line.
[87] 6 September 1353.
[88] 16 January 1353.
[88a] 24 September 1354.
[89] At the top of the page at the left margin is the heading: *Recepta arreraygiorum.*
[90] 15 October 1355.
[91] 26 February 1354.
[92] Followed by *ad xvi* deleted by a line.
[93] 22 October 1356.
[94] 10 July 1350.

ex causa de novo provisum Willelmo de Warrenna antequam dictus Hugo esset nuntius, et sibi dimissa, ponitur infra in arreraygiis.

De ecclesia de Herdwyke (Hardwick), taxata v li. vi s. viii d., infra in arreraygiis. Nichil hic, sed infra in arreraygiis dimititur in resta liii s. iiii d.[95]

De ecclesia de Hulmo [96] (Holme), dimissa in x li., taxata xl li., nichil hic, sed infra in arreraygiis.

De ecclesia de Pulham, taxata liii li. vi s. viii d., de qua per obitum Johannis de Hildresse fuit provisum Michaeli de Northburgh' per Clementem ii° nonas Septembris anni vii°,[97] que fuit dimissa in arreraygiis in xvii li. ii s. v d., xvii li. ii s. v d.

Summa pagine cii li. xviii s. vi d.

(fol. 101ᵛ) De prioratu Sancte Fidis Hortham (St. Faith, Horsham), taxato c iiiixx iiii li., de quo per obitum Pontii de Serveria fuit provisum Bertrando Iori per Clementem viii° kalendas Octobris anno vii° vel viii°,[98] quia simul missi, dimisso in arreraygiis, in partem xxvi li. xiii s. iiii d.

De ecclesia de Redegrave (Redgrave), taxata xxvi li. xiii s. iiii d., acceptatio cuius facta per Willelmum de Brunstere fuit eidem confirmata per Clementem v° kalendas Martii anno vii°,[99] fuit dimissa in iiii li., iiii li.[100]

De ecclesia de Derham (East Dereham), dimissa, nichil hic, sed infra in arreraygiis.

De ecclesia de Elvedene (Elveden), taxata xiii li. vi s. viii d., de qua per resignationem Richardi de Hemesbi fuit provisum Willelmo Symonis per Innocentium xiii° kalendas Januarii anno primo,[101] que fuit dimissa pro resta in vii li. xiii s. iiii d., vii li. xiii s. iiii d.

De ecclesia de Turston' (Thurston), taxata xx li., de qua fuit provisum Roberto Torp per Innocentium xviii° kalendas Junii anno ii°,[102] dimissa in vi li. xiii s. iiii d., vi li. xiii s. iiii d.

### Eliensis

De prioratu de Suavesheye (Swavesey), de quo Stephano Bertrand fuit provisum per Clementem antequam dictus Hugo esset nuntius, et sibi dimisso in x li., solvit in partem vi li.

### Lincolniensis

De prioratu de Cogges, qui fuit confirmatus Willelmo Hamonis per Clementem antequam dictus Hugo esset nuntius, et sibi dimisso in viii li., solvit in partem liii s. iiii d.

De vicaria ecclesie de Wodfford (Watford), taxata iiii li. xiii s. iiii d., de qua,[103] lis pendens [104] in palatio inter Ricardum filium Ade Blakwyne et Walterum de Lodenay, fuit provisum Roberto de Cherpgat' per Clementem antequam dictus Hugo esset nuntius, et eidem dimissa in arreraygiis, iiii li. xiii s. iiii d.

Summa pagine lviii li. vi s. viii d.

(fol. 102, x)[105] De ecclesia de Hungerston' (Hungarton), taxata xxiii li. vi s. viii d., unita Beate Marie Leycestrie per Clementem nonas kalendas Martii anno x°,[106] dimissa in arreraygiis, xxiii li. vi s. viii d.

De prebenda de Ketene (Ketton) in ecclesia Lincolniensi, taxata lxvi li. xiii s. iiii d., que ex causa permutationis fuit Willelmo de Dalton' confirmata per Clementem iiii° kalendas Novembris anno xi°,[107] dimissa, lxvi li. xiii s. iiii d.

De prebenda de Farendon' (Farndon) in ecclesia Lincolniensi, taxata liii li. vi s. viii d., de qua per obitum Francici de Ursinis fuit provisum Thome de Badby per Clementem antequam dictus Hugo esset nuntius, pro resta dimissa, xiii li. vi s. viii d.

De prebenda de Sutton' (Sutton cum Buck.) in ecclesia Lincolniensi, taxata iiᶜ lx m., de qua per resignationem Baldrati de Malabayla fuit provisum Thome de Brembr' per Clementem iii° kalendas Maii anno vi°,[108] dimissa in arreraygiis, quo tempore camera debebat habere taxam vel residuum et portare honera in casu quo ille cui erat provisum vellet dimittere totum, et sic fecit iste, quia tempore mortalitatis tandem fuit compositum in lxvi li. xiii s. iiii d., solvit lxvi li. xiii s. iiii d.

De prebenda de Langefford (Langford) in ecclesia Lincolniensi, taxata lx li., que fuit Magistro Johanni Leth' confirmata per Clementem kalendas Septembris anno vii° vel viii°,[109] quia simul missi, pro resta dimissa, xv li.

De decanatu Lincolniensi, taxato iiᶜ lxvi li. xiii s. iiii d., de quo per obitum Johannis electi Cantuariensis fuit provisum Symoni de Bryseleye per Clementem vi° idus Octobris anno vii° vel viii°,[110] quia simul missi, dimisso in arreraygiis in c iiiixx vi li. xiii s. iiii d., solvit in partem cxxvii li. vi s. viii d.

De ecclesia de Ketering' (Kettering), taxata xxiii li. vi s. viii d., de quibus est responsum, que fuit confirmata Johanni Wade et fructus male percepti remissi, pro quibus debet dare ex compositione facta cum camera in subsidium contra Turcos iiᶜ florenos, infra in arreraygiis.

Summa pagine iiiᶜ xii li. vi s. viii d.

---

[95] This sentence is in the margin.
[96] Follows *Ulmo* deleted by a line.
[97] 4 September 1348.
[98] 24 September 1348 or 1349.
[99] 25 February 1349.
[100] Noted in the margin is *corigatur nomen*. The name elsewhere is le Breustere: *Cal. Pap. Regs. Letters*, iii, 349.
[101] 20 December 1353.
[102] 15 May 1354.

[103] *quas*, MS. *Cf.* p. 98 above.
[104] *pendebat*, MS.
[105] At the top of the page over the left margin is the heading: *Recepta arreraygiorum*.
[106] 22 February 1352.
[107] 29 October 1352.
[108] 29 April 1348.
[109] 1 September 1348 or 1349.
[110] 10 October 1348 or 1349.

(fol. 102[v]) De prebenda de Badefford Maiore (Bedford Maior) in ecclesia Lincolniensi, taxata viii li., que fuit confirmata Willelmo de Wytlestye per Clementem viii[o] idus Maii anno vii[o], vel viii[o],[111] quia simul missi, dimissa, renditur infra in arreraygiis.

De archidiaconatu Bukynghamie in ecclesia Lincolniensi, non taxato, de quo per obitum cardinalis Tusculani fuit provisum Johanni de Asseburn' per Clementem idus Novembris,[112] infra in arreraygiis.

De subdecanatu ecclesie Lincolniensi, taxato xl li., qui fuit confirmatus Hamoni Belers per Clementem iii[o] kalendas Maii anno ix[o],[113] dimisso in arreraygiis in xxv li., solvit in partem xv li.

De archidiaconatu Norhampton', non taxato, de quo per obitum Johannis cardinalis Portuensis fuit provisum Johanni de Bukyngham per Clementem anno ix[o],[114] dimisso in arreraygiis pro medietate, deductis procurationibus, solvit xl li.

De prebenda de Greton' (Gretton) in ecclesia Lincolniensi, taxata xlvi li. xiii s. iiii d., de qua per uxorationem Aymerici de Cursorno seu dimissionem fuit provisum Johanni de Bukyngham per Clementem xii[o] kalendas Maii anno ix[o],[115] de qua respondetur in supradicto compoto de xxx li., et solvit pro [116] resta xvi li. xiii s. iiii d.[117]

De prebenda Walton' Rival' (Welton Rivall) in ecclesia Lincolniensi, taxata xxxiii li. vi s. viii d., de qua per obitum Johannis de Hatton' fuit provisum Johanni de Asseburn' per Clementem iiii[o] nonas Maii anno nono,[118] dimissa in arreraygiis, non habuit effectum quia per dictum obitum fuit confirmata Johanni Lamberti, qui in palatio apostolico obtinuit tres sententias contra dictum Johannem de Asseburn', et pro dicta confirmatione respondetur infra in alia recepta post receptionem istorum arreraygiorum.[119]

De prebenda de Skarles (South Scarle) in ecclesia Lincolniensi, taxata xl li., de qua per obitum Thome de Crosse fuit provisum Johanni de Kyrkeby per Clementem iiii[o] nonas Maii anno ix[o],[120] dimissa [121] in xx li., solvit in partem vii li. xvii s. i d.

Summa pagine lxxix li. x s. v d.

(fol. 103, xi)[122] De media portione de Seggebork' (Sedgebrook), taxata xii li. vi s. viii d., de qua per

obitum ultimi rectoris fuit provisum Roberto de Seggebork' per Clementem xi[o] kalendas Augusti anno x[o],[123] dimissa in ii li. xiii s. iiii d., infra in arreraygiis.

De ecclesia de Folkesworth' (Folksworth), taxata vi li. xiii s. iiii d., de qua per obitum Henrici de Wotteby fuit provisum Symoni [124] Spark' per Clementem vi[o] kalendas Februarii anno x[o],[125] dimissa in v li., solvit v li.

De ecclesia Grefford (Greatford), taxata xiiii li. xiii s. iiii d., de qua fuit ⟨unita⟩ monasterio Beate Marie Wyntoniensis per Clementem iii[o] idus Jullii anno xi[o],[126] dimissa, ponitur infra in arreraygiis.

De prebenda de Cliston' (Clifton) in ecclesia Lincolniensi, dimissa, nichil hic, sed infra in arreraygiis.

De ecclesia de Edelesburgh' (Edlesborough), taxata xxx li., de qua per obitum Johannis de Wellde fuit provisum Johanni de Skynstede per Clementem ii[o] nonas Octobris anno xi[o],[127] dimissa in xx li., solvit xx li.

De prebenda de Bokeden' (Buckden) in ecclesia Lincolniensi, taxata xl li., de qua fuit provisum Eddwardo le Bothelier antequam dictus Hugo esset nuntius, dimissa in arreraygiis, xl li.

De ecclesia de Custon' (Owston), taxata xl li., unio cuius facta priori et conventui de Novo Burgo (Newburgh) fuit confirmata per Clementem viii[o] kalendas Junii anno xi[o],[128] dimissa in arreraygiis, xl li.

De ecclesia de Melcheburn' (Melchbourne), taxata v li. vi s. viii d., de qua per obitum Bartholomei de Drayton' fuit provisum Rodulpho de Ulnhale per Innocentium vi[o] kalendas Februarii anno ii[o],[129] nichil hic, sed infra in arreraygiis.

De prebenda de Carleton' et Turleby (Carlton le Moorland cum Thurlby) in ecclesia Lincolniensi, dimissa, nichil hic, sed infra in arreraygiis.

Summa pagine cv li.

(fol. 103[v]) De prebenda Sancti Martini in ecclesia Lincolniensi, taxata vi li. xiii s. iiii d., de qua per obitum Henrici de Chadesden' fuit provisum Roberto de Burton' per Innocentium ix[o] kalendas Februarii anno ii[o],[130] dimissa in arreyragiis, vi li. xiii s. iiii d.

De ecclesia de Stykeneye (Stickney), taxata xviii li. xiii s. iiii d., de qua per assecutionem alterius beneficii fuit provisum Johanni Anntel per Innocentium v[o] kalendas Februarii anno ii[o],[131] dimissa in arreragiis, xviii li. xiii s. iiii d.

De ecclesia de Hornecastr' (Horncastle), taxata xxxiii li. vi s. viii d., que fuit confirmata Johanni de Kyrkeby per Innocentium kalendas Februarii anno ii[o],[132] dimissa in xviii li. vi s. viii d., xviii li. vi s. viii d.

---

[111] 8 May 1349 or 1350.
[112] 13 November 1350: *Cal. Pap. Regs. Letters*, iii, 413.
[113] 29 April 1351.
[114] 19 May 1350 to 18 May 1351.
[115] 20 April 1351.
[116] *pro* repeated MS.
[117] Note in the margin: *videatur taxa. Visa est et bona est.*
[118] 4 May 1351.
[119] In the margin: *vide sententias et exequtoriam sub data anni LVIII pontificatus domini nostri anno vi° die iii menssis Julii.*
[120] 4 May 1351.
[121] Followed by *in li. xxx* deleted by a line.
[122] At the top of the page over the left margin is the heading: *Recepta arreraygiorum.*

[123] 22 July 1351.
[124] Followed by *Sp* deleted by a line.
[125] 27 January 1352.
[126] 13 July 1352.
[127] 6 October 1352.
[128] 25 May 1352.
[129] 27 January 1354.
[130] 24 January 1354.
[131] 28 January 1354.
[132] 1 February 1354.

Ista ecclesia taxatur ad maiorem summam in libro taxe, sed archiepiscopus Cantuariensis qui nunc est, tunc rector dicte ecclesie, fecit eam [133] retaxare ad taxam supradictam.

De ecclesia de Bukenhill' (Bucknell), taxata ad x li., ad quam obtinendam Laurentius Breto fuit abilitatus et de eadem sibi de novo provisum per Innocentium xi° kalendas Junii anno iii°,[134] dimissa in arreraygiis, x li.

De ecclesia de Pekebrak' (Polebrooke), taxata viii li., de qua per obitum Johannis de Wircle fuit provisum Willelmo de Estenden' per Innocentium ii° kalendas Junii anno iiii°,[135] dimissa in arreyragiis, viii li.

De ecclesia de Kyrkebybayn (Kirkby on Bain), taxata viii li., de qua per obitum Willelmi de Corbrugge fuit provisum Thome de Selep per Innocentium nonas Augusti anno ii°,[136] dimissa in arreyragiis, viii li.

De prebenda de Crospery (Cropredy) in ecclesia Lincolniensi, taxata lxvi li. xiii s. iiii d., de qua ex causa permutationis cum Guidono de Pestello pro prebenda ecclesie Cestrensis super Stratam (Chester-le-Street) fuit provisum Willelmo de Rothewell' per Innocentium iii° nonas Decembris anno vi°,[137] dimissa in arreyragiis, lxvi li. xiii s. iiii d.

### Conventrensis et Lichfeldensis

De archidiaconatu Conventrensi, non taxato, et prebenda de Langedon' (Longdon) in ecclesia Lichfeldensi, taxata xx li., de quibus fuit provisum Humfredo de Hastynges per Clementem antequam dictus Hugo esset nuntius, et in arreyragiis dimissis; de isto archidiaconatu et prebenda [138] (fol. 104, xii)[139] de quibus etiam fuit provisum per obitum Humfredi Willelmo de Sallwe, per cuius obitum fuit provisum Willelmo de Cruce, et per obitum istius Willelmi fuit provisum Willelmo de Dryffeld de dicto archidiaconatu, qui pro ista provisione satisfecit, et respondetur infra in principio secunde pagine; et de prebenda fuit provisum Waltero de Dalby, qui pro ista provisione et duabus precedentibus, quantum ad prebendam, de quibus nichil fuerat solutum, composuit cum camera in iii^e lviii fl. solvendum in vii annis, incipiendo in festo nativitatis domini anno LIX, scilicet l fl., et sic de anno in annum usque ad plenam solutionem, sed in ultimo anno debet solvere lviii fl.; de istis solvit pro iiii^or terminis pro ii^e fl. xxx li. De residuo respondetur infra in arreyragiis.[140]

De ecclesia de Hodynet (Hodnet), de qua per consecrationem Domini Radulphi episcopi Batoniensis fuit provisum Nicholao [141] de Heth', nichil hic, quia pro ista ecclesia et pro diversis aliis beneficiis suis composuit cum camera, ut continetur infra in fine recepte et etiam in arreyragiis.

De ecclesia de Legh' (Leigh), dimissa in arreyragiis de tempore antequam dictus Hugo esset nuntius in v li., nichil hic, sed infra in arreyragiis.

De ecclesia de Northwerth' (Northenden), dimissa in arreyragiis in x s., x s.

De archidiaconatu Conventrensi et prebenda de Langedon' in ecclesia Lichfeldeni, de quibus per obitum Humfredi de Astynges fuit provisum Willelmo de Sallowe, dimissis in arreyragiis, supra continetur in fine precedentis pagine et in principio istius pagine.

De prebenda in ecclesia Licheffeldensi, de qua per obitum Willelmi Appelltre fuit provisum Thome [142] Attehull' per Clementem antequam dictus Hugo esset nuntius, nichil hic, sed infra in arreyragiis.

De decanatu Lichfeldensi cum prebenda sibi annexa, taxato ad xl li., de quo per assecutionem decanatus Lincolniensis per Symonem de Brysleye fuit provisum Johanni de Bokyngham antequam dictus Hugo esset nuntius,[143] dimissa in arreyragiis, nichil hic, sed infra in arreyragiis sequentibus.

Summa pagine xxx li. x s.

(fol. 104^v) De archidiaconatu Stafford' in ecclesia Lichfeldensi, non taxato, qui fuit confirmatus Ricardo de Brinemyngham per Clementem ii° idus Decembris anno ii°,[144] dimisso in arreyragiis, xx s. Officialis dicti archidiaconatus iuravit quod plus non valuit medietas, exceptis procurationibus.

De prebenda in ecclesia collegiata Sancti Sedde Sallopie (St. Chad Shrewsbury), de qua per obitum Willelmi Appeltre fuit provisum Roberto Subgrave per Clementem iii° idus Decembris anno viii°,[145] fuit dimissa, sed non habuit effectum quia Dominus Hugo Opas eam possidet iure regio adhuc hodie iure regio.

De precentoria Lichfeldensi, taxata xl li., collatio cuius facta per ordinarium fuit Thome de Badeby confirmata per Clementem iiii° idus Maii anno ix°,[146] dimissa in arreyragiis in xiii li. vi s. viii d., xiii li. vi s. viii d.

De prebenda de Ulton' (Ufton) in ecclesia Lichfeldensi, taxata iiii li. i m., de qua per resignationem Johannis de Wynwyke fuit provisum Johanni de Melborn', que fuit dimissa in arreyragiis per errorem, nichil hic, quia responsum est in ultimo compoto per dictum Hugonem.[147]

De prebenda de Ecleshale (Eccleshall) in ecclesia Lichfeldensi, de qua per resignationem Johannis de

---

[133] Followed by *prossessit* deleted by a line.
[134] 22 May 1355.
[135] 31 May 1356.
[136] 5 August 1354.
[137] 3 December 1358.
[138] At the bottom of the page: *Summa pagine cxxxvi li. vi s. viii d.*
[139] At the top of the page over the left margin is the heading: *Recepta arreraygiorum.*
[140] The last sentence is in the margin.

[141] *Nicholar*, MSS.
[142] Followed by *Athe* deleted by a line.
[143] Followed by *dim* deleted by a line.
[144] 12 December 1343.
[145] 11 December 1349.
[146] 12 May 1351.
[147] In the margin: *responsum est ut hic continetur.*

Meleborn' fuit provisum Johanni de Wynwyk', nichil hic, sed infra in arreyragiis.

De ecclesia de Codyngton' (Coddington), taxata vi li. xiii s. iiii d., de qua per resignationem Johannis Charnels ex causa permutationis fuit provisum Philipo Dryn' per Clementem xi° kalendas Augusti anno x°,[148] dimissa in arreyragiis, vi li. xiii s. iiii d.

De prebenda de Berkwich' (Berkswick) in ecclesia Lichfeldensi, taxata xx li., de qua per obitum [149] Tidonis Varesio fuit provisum Willelmo Clavyla per Innocentium vii° kalendas Maii anno primo,[150] que fuit dimissa in arrayragiis, nichil quia non habuit effectum, nec dictus Willemus unquam fuit [151] prosecutus.[152]

Summa pagine xxi li.

(fol. 105, xiii)[153] De prebenda de Langedon' (Longdon) in ecclesia Lichfeldensi, de qua per obitum Willelmi Crosse fuit provisum Waltero Dalby per Innocentium xi° kalendas Octobris anno primo,[154] dimissa in arreyragiis, sed pro ista provisione et aliis composuit cum camera ut patet in principio pagine precedentis carte seu folii.

De prebenda de Walveya (Wolvey) in ecclesia Lichfeldensi, taxata vi li. xiiii ⟨s.⟩ iiii d., de qua fuit provisum Johanni Bernere, dimissa, ponitur infra in arreyragiis.

De archidiaconatu Conventrensi in ecclesia Lichfeldensi, non taxato, de quo per obitum Willelmi de Cruce fuit provisum Willelmo de Dryffeld per Innocentium viii° kalendas Februarii anno ix°,[155] dimisso in arreyragiis, pro medietate xiii li. vi s. viii d.

De ecclesia de Wynewik (Winwick), dimissa, nichil hic, sed infra in arreyragiis.

De decanatu ecclesie Sancti Johannis Cestrie, simul taxato cum omnibus prebendis, de quo per assecutionem alterius beneficii per Hugonem de Trikyngham fuit provisum Alexandro de Dalby per Innocentium ii° nonas Octobris anno ii°,[156] dimisso in arreyragiis, pro parte taxe ipsum contingente xxvi li. xiii s. iiii d.

De prebenda de Tervyn (Tarvin) in ecclesia Lichfeldensi, taxata xxxiii li. vi s. viii d., provisio cuius facta per Clementem Petro de Gildesburgh' fuit sibi confirmata per Innocentium xiii° kalendas Martii anno v°,[157] dimissa, xxxiii li. vi s. viii d.

De prebenda in ecclesia collegiata Sancti Johannis Cestrie, de qua fuit provisum Guidoni de Pestello ex causa permutationis, et dimissa hic in arreyragiis, que

non deberet esse, quia prebenda non est in dicta ecclesia sed in ecclesia collegiata Cestrie super stratam (Chester-le-Street) Dunolmensis diocesis, et ibi respondetur.

De ecclesia de Walton' nichil hic, sed infra in arreyragiis, et fuit dimissa in xiiii li.

### Assavensis

De prebenda in ecclesia Assavensi, taxata iii li., de qua per obitum Richardi Hernag'[158] fuit provisum Richardo de Midelton' per Clementem iiii° nonas [159] Maii anno nono,[160] dimissa, iii li.

De ecclesia de Dynbygh' (Denbigh) cum capella infra in arreyragiis.

Summa pagine lxxvi li. vi s. viii d.

### (fol. 105ᵛ) Bangorensis

De prebenda in ecclesia Bangorensi, taxata v li. vi s. viii d., de qua per obitum Roberti Tresk' fuit provisum Hugoni de Melton' per Clementem viii idus Martii anno nono,[161] dimissa in arreyragiis, v li. vi s. viii d.

### Menevensis

De ecclesia de Lambanglorath' (Llanfihangel ar Arth), non taxata, de qua per obitum Ricardi Aprovanseys fuit provisum Ludovico Cauncey, non habuit effectum, quia dictus Ludovicus non prosecutus est gratiam et mortuus est. Vidi super hoc litteras certificatorias officialis Menevensis sub data xxi die Maii anno M° CCC° LXI°.[162]

De prebenda de Langenten (Llanganten), que ecclesia in registro vocatur, taxata iiii li. vi s. viii d., de qua per mortem Gryffiny de Canton' fuit provisum Martino Monlich' per Innocentium xiii° kalendas Octobris anno iiii°,[163] pro resta dimissa vi s. viii d.

De ecclesia de Weston' (Wiston), non taxata, de qua per resignationem Rogeri Johannis fuit provisum Willelmo de Neuton', infra in arreyragiis.

De ecclesia Sancti Bernachii (Llanfyrnach), taxata vi li. xiii s. iiii d., de qua primo fuit provisum Willelmo de Renhale per Innocentium xix kalendas Junii anno iiii°,[164] dimissa in arreyragiis, non habuit effectum quia dictus Willelmus non est prosecutus; sed per obitum Johannis de Chanton' fuit provisum Ricardo de Chaunton' per Innocentium ii° kalendas Jullii anno vii°,[165] respondetur infra in arreyragiis ultimis. Vidi super hoc litteras certificatorias officialis Menevensis sub data diei xxi mensis Maii anno LXI°.[166]

[148] 22 July 1351.
[149] Followed by *Titodus* deleted by a line.
[150] 25 April 1353.
[151] Followed by *prosequ* deleted by a line.
[152] In the margin opposite this item: *doce*.
[153] At the top of the page over the left margin is the heading: *Recepta arreyragiorum*.
[154] 21 September 1353.
[155] The year should be 3 Innocent VI, making the date 25 January 1355: *Cal. Pap. Regs. Petitions*, i, 270.
[156] 6 October 1354.
[157] 17 Febraury 1357.
[158] Apparently it should be Hering: *Cal. Pap. Regs. Letters*, iii, 364.
[159] Followed by *Ap* deleted by a line.
[160] 4 May 1351.
[161] 8 March 1351.
[162] This sentence is repeated in the margin.
[163] 19 September 1356.
[164] 14 May 1356.
[165] 30 June 1359.
[166] This sentence is in the margin.

Eboracensis

De prebenda de Wetewang' (Wetwang) in ecclesia Eboracensi, taxata cx li., de qua per Clementem fuit provisum Domino Anibaldo cardinali [167] per obitum Georgii de Saluriis, dimissa in lvii li. xi s.; dictus cardinalis nunquam habuit possessionem nec fuit prosecutus; nec etiam Dominus Willelmus de Vayraco cui etiam per dictum obitum fuit provisum; sed rex contulit iuri suo Johanni de Mesburn', sed antequam haberet possessionem fuerunt levate xxx li, de quibus est responsum per Dominum Raymundum Pelegrini in compotis suis et per dictum Hugonem xxii li. ix s., de quibus est responsum. Vidi super hoc litteras regis sub die xiiii Septembris anno regni Anglie regis Edwardi tertii xxv°.[168]

Summa pagine v li. xiii s. iiii d.

(fol. 106, xiiii)[169] De prebenda de Mastham (Masham) in ecclesia Eboracensi, taxata ad novam taxam iiii^xx li., de qua per obitum Johannis de Ufford fuit provisum Reginaldo de Brian per Clementem, dimissa in arreyragiis per dictum Dominum Raymundum; et de eadem prebenda per consecrationem dicti Reginaldi in episcopatum Arevenensem (St. David) fuit provisum Andree de Ufford per Clementem xvii° kalendas Jullii anno vii° vel viii°,[170] quia simul missi; et fuit scriptum per cameram quod facta fuit plena informatio quod iste due vacationes fuerunt infra annum, et quod nisi fructus unius annate exigerentur, de qua annata est responsum in ultimo compoto de xli li. xiii s. iiii d. et solvit pro resta xxxviii li. vi s. viii d. Vidi litteras dominorum camerarii et thesaurarii datas xxvii Aprilis anno LIX°.[168]

De ecclesia de Branthyngham (Brantingham), taxata xx li., de qua per obitum cardinalis de Gardia [171] fuit provisum Edmundo Kankesgate per Clementem antequam dictus Hugo esset nuntius, dimissa in iii li., iii li.

De archidiaconatu Richemondie in ecclesia Eboracensi, taxato ii^c li., de quo per obitum domini Portuensis cardinalis fuit provisum Henrico de Walton', dimisso in solidis fructibus; est erratum quia dictus Hugo respondet in compoto suo reddito de xxxiii li. vi s. viii d., et sic est resta clxvi li. xiii s. iiii d., pro quibus et quibusdam aliis beneficiis est simul obligatus, ut patet infra in fine recepte et etiam in fine arreyragiorum.[172]

De prebenda de Dunham in ecclesia collegiata Suthwell', taxata xxxvi li. xiii s. iiii d., de qua per obitum Henrici de Harwedon' fuit provisum Adde de Everyngham per Clementem iiii° nonas Maii anno vii° vel viii°,[173]

quia simul missi, pro resta dimissa xxvi li. xiii s. iiii d.

De prebenda de Mastham (Masham) in ecclesia Eboracensi, de qua per consecrationem electi Menevensis fuit provisum Andree de Ufford ut supra in principio presentis pagine, et ibi respondetur.[174]

De prebenda in ecclesia collegiata Beverlacensi, taxata xvi li, acceptatio cuius facta per Alanum de Wynfilete fuit eidem confirmata per Clementem ii° kalendas Augusti anno x°,[175] pro resta dimissa viii li.

Summa pagine lxxvi li.

(fol. 106^v) De prebenda de Sarwe (Sharow) in ecclesia collegiata Ripponensi, taxata v li, que per obitum Willemi Aleberwyk' fuit provisum Johanni de Donygton' per Clementem iii° idus Maii anno ix°,[176] dimissa, hic nichil, sed infra in arreyragiis.

De prebenda de Torp' (Thorpe) in ecclesia collegiata de Hoveden' (Howden), taxata xxx li., de qua per obitum Roberti de Tresk' fuit provisum Ade Robelyn per Clementem viii° idus Martii anno ix°,[177] in partem xii li. restantium dimissarum vi li. De residuo repondetur infra in arreyragiis.[178]

De prebenda de Westward (Husthwaite) in ecclesia Eboracensi, de qua fuit de novo provisum Johanni de Welburn', dimissa in ii^c fl., infra in arrayragiis.

De ecclesia de Walton', taxata xxvi li. xiii s. iii d., que fuit confirmata Henrico de Gateggarg' per Clementem ii° kalendas Augusti anno x°,[179] pro resta dimissa xx li.

De prebenda in ecclesia collegiata de Suthwell', de qua per consecrationem Gilberti episcopi Karlionensis Thome Gryffyn fuit provisum, nichil hic, sed infra in arreyragiis.

De prebenda in ecclesia Eboracensi, de qua per consecrationem electi Tirwycensis fuit provisum Frederico Salampi, dimissa in arreyragiis; ignoratur qui sunt isti, quia certificatum est quod non sunt tales qui habuerunt in ecclesia Eboracensi, et ponitur in arreyragiis.[179a]

De ecclesiis de Waumpti (Wharram Percy), taxata xxiii li. vi s. viii d., et de Eltele (Kirk Ella), taxata xlvi li. xiii s. iiii d.,[180] que fuerunt unite monasterio de Hautemprise (Haltemprice) per Clementem idus Junii anno ii°,[181] pro resta dimissa, xxxv li.

De prebenda de Esbaldewyk' (Osbaldwick), dimissa, nichil hic, sed infra in arreyragiis.

Summa pagine lxi li.

(fol. 107, xv)[182] De ecclesia Sancte Trinitatis Ebor-

---

[167] Bishop of Tusculum.
[168] This sentence is in the margin.
[169] At the top of the page over the left margin is the heading: *Recepta arreyragiorum.*
[170] 15 June 1349.
[171] Gerard Domar, priest of S. Sabina.
[172] In the margin: *constat de errore per compotum ultimum Magistri Hugonis.*
[173] 4 May 1349.

[174] In the margin: *in presenti pagina et in principio respondetur.*
[175] 31 July 1351.
[176] 13 May 1351.
[177] 8 March 1351.
[178] This sentence is in the margin.
[179] 31 July 1351.
[179a] See *Cal. Pap. Regs. Letters,* iii, 425.
[180] Followed by *de* deleted by a line.
[181] 13 June 1343.
[182] At the top of the page over the left margin is the heading: *Recepta arreyragiorum.*

aci, non taxata, de qua per obitum Roberti Sutton' fuit provisum Willelmo de Roycelby per Innocentium xi° kalendas Aprilis anno ii°,[183] dimissa in arreyragiis, iiii li. x s.

De prebenda de Munketon' (Monkton) in ecclesia collegiata Ripponensi, de qua per consecrationem Michaelis episcopi Londoniensis fuit provisum Johanni de Wellbek', dimissa, nichil hic, sed infra in arreyragiis.

De prebenda de Stranxale (Strensall) in ecclesia Eboracensi, de qua fuit provisum domino cardinali Petragoricensi,[184] infra in arreyragiis.

De ecclesia de Rudestan (Rudston), taxata xxvi li. xiii s. iiii d., de qua Ade de Thirmenton' fuit de novo provisum per Innocentium vi° idus Junii anno iii°,[185] dimissa in arreyragiis, xxvi li. xiii s. iiii d.

De prebenda de Richehill' (Bickhill) in ecclesia Eboracensi, taxata xx li., de qua per renuntiationem Garcie de Galhardo fuit provisum Thome de Novill' per Innocentium iiii° idus Jullii anno quarto,[186] dimissa in arreyragiis, xx li.

De prebenda in ecclesia collegiata Ripponensi, de qua per resignationem Ricardi de Thoresby fuit provisum ex causa permutationis cum prebenda Beverlacensi Bertrando de Cardalhaco xiii° [187] kalendas Novembris anno iiii°,[188] non habuit effectum, quia antequam haberet effectum fuit promotus in episcopum Montis Albani (Montauban), per cuius promotionem fuit provisum alteri ut infra in arreyragiis.

De prebenda altaris ecclesie Sancti Andree in ecclesia collegiata Beverlacensi, taxata xxvii li., de qua per resignationem Bertrandi de Cardalhaco ex causa permutationis cum prebenda in ecclesia collegiata Ripponensi fuit provisum Richardo de [189] Thuresby per Innocentium xiiii kalendas Octobris anno iiii°,[190] dimissa in arreyragiis, xxvii li.

Summa pagine lxxviii li. iii s. iiii d.

(fol. 107ᵛ) De ecclesia Beati Wlffrydi de Kyrcham (St. Wilfrid Kirkham), de qua permutatio facta inter Adam de Chestreffeld cum rectore ecclesie de [191] Anywell' (Hanwell) et capella de Braynfford' (Brentford) Londoniensis diocesis fuit confirmata x° kalendas Novembris per Innocentium anno viii°,[192] ponitur in arreyragiis.

De prebenda ad altare Sancti Petri in ecclesia collegiata Beverlacensi, taxata xxv li., in qua et ad omne ius quod competebat Richardo Drax fuit subrogatus Ricardus Suglworth' per Innocentium nonas Januarii anno x°,[193] qui quidem Ricardus Drax obtinuit tres sententias contra Johannem Klybury, nichil hic, sed infra in arreyragiis.

De [194] ecclesia de Catton', de qua institutio facta in personam Johannis de Exestre fuit sibi confirmata per Innocentium viii° kalendas Februarii anno iiii°,[195] taxata xl li., xl li.

## Dunolmensis

De prioratu de Tynemuta (Tynemouth), de quo per assecutionem abbatie monasterii Sancti Albani factam per Thomam priorem dicti prioratus de quo fuit sibi data [196] potestas providendi per Clementem anno vii° vel viii°,[197] quia simul missi, non est prioratus sed custodia temporalis, prout placet abbati. Vidi inhibitoriam regis scriptam Domino Raymundo quod nichil exigeret cum sit temporale sub data xx die Octobris anno regni sui xxiiii°ʳ.

De hospitali de Greham (Gretham), non taxato, de quo per obitum Johannis de Stoks fuit provisum Thome Johannis de Bredbarke per Clementem ii° idus Decembris,[198] in partem medietatem valoris, dimisso in arreyragiis, iii li. vi s. viii d.

De prebenda in ecclesia collegiate Langecestr' (Lanchester), de qua per resignationem Henrici de Exton' fuit provisum Galfrido de Cornezano per Innocentium xv° kalendas Decembris anno primo,[199] nomine prebende ignorante quia in dicta ecclesia alique prebende non habunt certum nomen, infra in arreyragiis.

Summa pagine xliii li. vi s. viii d.

(fol. 108, xvi) [200] De prebenda in dicta ecclesia vocata Assh' (Esh), taxata viii li. xiii s. iiii d., de qua per promotionem Michaelis episcopi Londoniensis fuit provisum Johanni de Burton' per Innocentium xix° kalendas Januarii anno primo,[201] pro resta dimissa iiii li. vi s. viii d.

De prebenda in ecclesia collegiata Cestrie super stratam (Chester-le-Street) vocata Lamseley (Lamesley), taxata xx li., de qua per promotionem Thome electi Norwicensis fuit provisum Willelmo de Lutheburgh' per Innocentium vi° idus Februarii anno ii°,[202] nichil hic, sed infra in arreyragiis.

De prebenda in dicta ecclesia taxata xx li., de qua per resignationem Willelmi de Rothwell' fuit provisum Guidoni de Pestello per Innocentium iii° nonas Decembris anno v°,[203] que fuit dimissa in arreyragiis, in partem x li.

---

[183] 22 March 1354.
[184] Talleyrand de Périgueux, bishop of Albano.
[185] 8 June 1355.
[186] 12 July 1356.
[187] Followed by *k* deleted by a line.
[188] 20 October 1356.
[189] Followed by *Trus* deleted by a line.
[190] 18 September 1356.
[191] Followed by *Ay Anyll* deleted by a line.
[192] 23 October 1360.

[193] 5 January 1362.
[194] Followed by *prebenda de* deleted by a line.
[195] 25 January 1356.
[196] Followed by *potates* deleted by a line.
[197] 11 August 1349: *Cal. Pap. Regs. Letters*, iii, 314.
[198] 12 December 1350: *Cal. Pap. Regs. Petitions*, i, 208.
[199] 17 November 1353.
[200] At the top of the page over the left margin is the heading: *Recepta arreyragiorum*.
[201] 14 December 1353.
[202] 8 February 1354.
[203] 3 December 1357.

### Karliolensis

De ecclesia de Crostwayt' (Crosthwaite), in qua et in iure quod competebat Willelmo de Selario fuit subrogatus Johannes Henry per Innocentium ii° Idus Januarii anno x°,[204] taxata xxx li. xiii s. iiii d., dimissa, nichil hic, sed infra in arreyragiis.

### Hibernia
### Dublinensis

De decanatu ecclesie Dublinensis, de quo fuit provisum Matheo de Brysele, dimisso in arreyragiis in xiii li. vi s. viii d., nichil hic, sed infra in arreyragiis.

De thesauraria ecclesie Sancti Patricii Dublinensis et prebenda de Galmoram (Ballymore) in eadem, de quibus collatio facta Johanni Attegate fuit sibi confirmata per Clementem viii idus Maii anno viii°,[205] dimissa, nichil hic, sed infra in arreyragiis.

De decanatu ecclesie Dublinensis, de quo per obitum Mathey de Bryseley fuit provisum Johanni Bryan per Clementem anno viii°,[206] taxata xli li., infra in arreyragiis pro resta dimissa.

Summa pagine xiiii li. vi s. viii d.

(fol. 108v) De prebenda de H'uute (Howth) in ecclesia Dublynensi, taxata ad antiquam taxam xxiii li. vi s. viii d., de qua per consecrationem Stephani Lawell' episcopi Lymiracensis (Limerick) fuit provisum Willelmo de Keleseye per Innocentium vii° idus Aprilis anno ii°,[207] dimissa in arreyragiis, solvit in partem xiii li. vi s. viii d. De residuo respondetur in arreyragiis.[208]

De cancellaria Dublinensi, taxata xl li., de qua collatio facta Johanni de Troye fuit eidem confirmata per Innocentium iiii° kalendas Junii anno ii°,[209] in xxxiii li. vi s. viii d., in partem dicte reste dimisse vi li. xiii s. iiii d. Debit cancellarius [210] quia infra; ponitur in sequenti recepta.[211]

### Fernensis

De prebenda de Taghmon' in ecclesia Fernensis, de qua per obitum Johannis de Sutton' et ecclesia [212] de Colstryf' (Coolstuffe) dicte diocesis per obitum Thome Michaelis fuit provisum Johanni Strond, in episcopum Fernensem electum, ne ⟨in⟩ oprobrium episcopi haberet mendicare, per Clementem xvi° kalendas Martii anno xi°,[213] dimissa, nichil, sed infra in arreyragiis.

Item de prebenda de Homl (Clone) in ecclesia Fernensi, de qua per ingressum religionis aut mortem vel alio modo Hugonis de Burgh' fuit provisum Ricardo Radulphi per Clementem anno xi°,[214] dimissa in arreyragiis, taxata iii li. vi s. viii d., solvit iii li. vi s. viii d.

De ecclesia de Veteri Rose (Old Ross), de qua ex causa permutationis fuit provisum Johanni de Welewik per Innocentium xvi° kalendas Augusti anno ii°,[215] nichil hic, sed infra in arreyragiis.

Summa pagine xvi li. xiii s. iiii d.[216]

Summa universalis recepte omnium precedentium arrayragiorum beneficiorum collatorum in Anglia ii^m cxv li. ii s. i d. Approbatum.

Summa generalis omnium precedentium receptarum in universso iii^m clxxxii li. iii s. ix d.

(fol. 109, xvii) Sequitur recepta primorum fructum a primo die Junii anno LVIII° ultra arreyragias tunc dimissas de quibus respondetur supra.

### Cantuariensis

De ecclesia de Fysyngdon' (Frittenden), taxata x li., de qua Thome Askeby fuit per cardinalem Urgelensem [217] de novo provisum, x li.

De vicaria ecclesie Beate Marie de Sandwico (Sandwich), taxata iiii li., confirmata [218] Henrico Yngg' per Clementem iiii° idus Februarii anno v°,[219] iiii li.

De prepositora de Wyngham (Wingham), taxata xl li., in qua et ad ius quod competebat Roberto de Sudbur' fuit subrogatus Johannes de Severley per Innocentium pridie idus Februarii anno vii°,[220] xl li.

### Roffensis

De ecclesia de Mepham (Meopham), taxata xxvi li. xiii s. iiii d., de qua Johanni de Brygham fuit per cardinalem Petragoricensem [221] de novo provisum, xxiii li. vi s. viii d.

De ecclesia de Eynesford (Eynsford), taxata xx li., de qua fuit confirmatio facta Johanni de Wantham per Innocentium vii° kalendas Junii anno vii°,[222] in partem vi li. xiii s. iiii d.

### Londoniensis

De ecclesia Beate Marie Magdalene in veteri piscaria Londonie (St. Mary Magdalen, Old Fish Street), taxata vi li. xiii s. iiii d., de qua Johanni Blythe per cardinalem Urgellensem [217] fuit de novo provisum, vi li. xiii s. iiii d.

De ecclesia Sancti Dyonisii Londonie, non taxata, de

---

[204] 12 January 1362.

[205] 8 May 1350.

[206] 13 August 1349. The day of the month is taken from *Cal. Pap. Regs. Petitions*, i, 203, where the year is given as 9 Clement VI.

[207] 7 April 1354.

[208] The last sentence is in the margin.

[209] 29 May 1354.

[210] *cancellari*, MS.

[211] The whole item is deleted by lines, except the last sentence which is in the margin.

[212] Followed by *et* deleted by a line.

[213] The date is incorrect. It should be 17 July 1352: *Cal. Pap. Regs. Petitions*, i. 231.

[214] 12 August 1352: *ibid.*, i, 233.

[215] 17 July 1354.

[216] Follows *xvii li. vi s. viii d.* deleted by a line.

[217] Nicholas de Capucio, bishop of Urgel, cardinal priest of S. Vitale.

[218] *confirmato*, MS.

[219] 10 February 1347.

[220] 12 February 1359.

[221] Elias Talleyrand de Périgueux, bishop of Albano.

[222] 26 May 1359.

qua per obitum Ade de Trensgeston' fuit provisum Willelmo de Langeton' per Innocentium ii° kalendas Jullii anno v°,[223] in partem de vi li. pro medietate, iiii li.

De archidiaconatu Londoniensi, non taxato, permutatio facta per Johannem Berneta de eodem fuit eidem confirmata per Innocentium iii° idus Maii anno vi°,[224] pro medietate xxvi li. xiiii s. iiii d.

Summa pagine cxxi li. vi s. viii d.

(fol. 109ᵛ) De ecclesia de Purle (Purleigh), taxata xii li., de qua Johanni Philipi cardinalis Urgellensis de novo providit, in partem vi li.

De ecclesia Beate Marie de Monte Alto (St. Mary Mounthaw), que non taxatur, de qua cardinalis Petragoricensis Willelmo de Ewerdon' de novo providit, xx s.

De prebenda de Fynesbury (Finsbury), taxata xiii li. vi s. viii d., de qua acceptatio facta per Ricardum de Aston' fuit eidem confirmata per Innocentium iii° idus Maii anno vi°,[224] xiii li. vi s. viii d.

De ecclesia Sancti Edmundi Londonie, non taxata, de qua per resignationem Radulphi de Debery fuit provisum Willelmo de Cheleston' per Innocentium xi° kalendas Novembris anno v°,[225] viii li.

De ecclesia de Matheselon' Londonie (Whitechapel), non taxata, de qua per resignationem Johannis Schillyng' fuit provisum David Doyer per Innocentium vii° idus Aprilis anno vii°,[226] in partem xx s., vi s. viii d.

### Cicestrensis

De ecclesia de Upmerdon' (Up Marden), taxata xiii li. vi s. viii d., de qua per obitum Willelmi Haket fuit provisum Willelmo Chesterbyr' per Innocentium iii° nonas Septembris anno v°,[227] xiii li. vi s. viii d., xiii li. vi s. viii d.

De vicaria de Hoo (Hooe), taxata iiii li. xiii s. iiii d., de qua fuit Willelmo nato Roberto Hull' per cardinalem Petragoricensem de novo provisum, in partem xlvi s. viii d.

De ecclesia Mereston' (Merston), taxata vi li. xiii s. iiii d., de qua Hugo Lawe fuit per cardinalem Petragoricensem de novo provisum, vi li. xiii s. iiii d.

De decanatu ecclesia collegiate de Malyng' (South Malling), taxato xl li., qui fuit Johanni de Ethyngham confirmatus per Innocentium vi° idus Maii anno v°,[228] xl li.

De thesauraria Cicestrensi, taxata xlvi li. xiii s. iiii d., confirmata Willelmo de Lughtburgh' per Innocentium v° kalendas Januarii anno vi°,[229] in partem xxx li.

Summa pagine cxxi li.

---

[223] 30 June 1357.
[224] 13 May 1358.
[225] 22 October 1357.
[226] 7 April 1359.
[227] 3 September 1357.
[228] 10 May 1357.
[229] 28 December 1358.

(fol. 110, xviii) Wyntoniensis

De ecclesia de Langgefeld (Lingfield), taxata xxvi li. xiii s. iiii d., de qua fuit Amando Ferylhyng' per cardinalem Petragoricensem de novo provisum, xxvi li. xiii s. iiii d.

De ecclesia de Clopham (Clapham), taxata ix li. vi s. viii d., de qua fuit ex causa permutationis Thome de Bredon' provisum per Innocentium xi° kalendas Decembris anno v°, ix li. vi s. viii d.

De ecclesia de Chayham (Cheam), taxata xxiii li. vi s. viii d., de qua fuit Johanni Attelowenill' per cardinalem Petragoricensem de novo provisum, in partem xix li. vi s. viii d.

### Saresbiriensis

De ecclesia de Merhulla (Marnhull), taxata xvi li. xiii s. iiii d., de qua fuit rectori eiusdem per cardinalem Urgellensem de novo provisum, xvi li. xiii s. iiii d.

De ecclesia de Broghton' (Broughton), taxata x li., de qua fuit Johanni de Pourbyk' de novo provisum per Innocentium xi° kalendas Decembris anno v°,[230] x li.

De prebenda de Horynhgtham (Horningsham), taxata v li., de qua fuit Radulpho de Ringested per cardinalem Petragoricensem de novo provisum, v li.

De ecclesia de Warfeld (Warfield), taxata viii li., de qua fuit Symoni de Tocale per cardinalem Petragoricensem de novo provisum, viii li.

De ecclesia de Watreton' (Water Eaton?), taxata vii li. vi s. viii d., de qua fuit Henrico Forestier per cardinalem Petragoricensem de novo provisum, vii li. vi s. viii d.

De ecclesia Beate Marie de Yalmested (Yattendon?), taxata vi li. xiii s. iiii d., de qua fuit Johanni Knave per cardinalem Urgellensem de novo provisum, vi li. xiii s. iiii d.

De vicaria ecclesie de Pydelton' (Puddlehinton), taxata v li., de qua fuit Ricardo Ensthache per cardinalem Petragoricensem de novo provisum, v li.

Summa pagine cxiii li.

(fol. 110ᵛ) De vicaria de Poterne (Potterne), taxata xx li., de qua fuit per cardinalem Urgellensem Johanni de Holy de novo provisum, in partem xviii li.

De vicaria de Gillyngham (Gillingham), taxata vi li. xiii s. iiii d., de qua fuit Willelmo Thomer per cardinalem Petragoricensem de novo provisum, in partem iiii li.

De prebenda de Upebury (Yetminster Prima) in ecclesia Saresbiriensi taxata viii li. xiiii s. iiii d., de qua per resignationem Dalmacii magistri de Monte Floro fuit [231] Philipo Bernardini provisum per Innocentium vii° kalendas Junii anna vi°,[232] viii li. xiii s. iiii d.

De prebenda de Ratffen (Rotefen) in ecclesia Saresbiriensi, taxata vi li. xiii s. iiii d., de qua ex causa per-

---

[230] 21 November 1357.
[231] Followed by *provisum* deleted by a line.
[232] 26 May 1358.

mutationis cum Willelmo Driffeld fuit provisum P. de Gildesburgh' per Innocentium kalendas Junii anno v°,[233] in partem iii li. vi s. viii d.

### Exoniensis

De vicaria ecclesie de Seventon' (Seaton), taxata iiii li., de qua fuit vicario eiusdem per cardinalem Urgellensem de novo provisum, iiii li.

De prebenda Sancti Karentoci (Crantock), taxata xxx s., de qua prebendario eiusdem per dictum Urgellensem fuit de novo provisum, xxx s.

De vicaria de Rethewell' (Bickleigh), non taxata, de qua Johanni Day per dominum Urgellensem fuit de novo provisum, pro medietate iii li. vi s. viii d.

De ecclesia Sancti Martini Exonie, non taxata, de qua rectori eiusdem fuit per dominum Petragoricensem de novo provisum, pro medietate xl s.

De vicaria de Wallyngton' (Walkhampton), non taxata, de qua fuit Ade de Thon' per dominum Urgellensem de novo provisum, xl s.

De prebenda Bursaly ecclesie de Tydyngton' (Tiverton), non taxata, de qua prebendario eiusdem fuit per dominum Urgellensem de novo provisum, xxxix s.

De archidiaconatu [234] Barnastopal', non taxato, de quo ex causa permutationis cum Johanni Darky fuit provisum Willelmo Muge per Innocentium iiii° nonas Septembris anno vi°,[235] in partem vi li. xiii s. iiii d.

Summa pagine lv li. ix s.

(fol. 111, xix) De prebenda in ecclesia Exoniensi, taxata iiii li., quam Johannes de Norwod obtinuit, de qua Radulpho de Rynggeste fuit provisum per Innocentium idus Martii anno iii°,[236] iiii li.

De ecclesia de Stoke, taxata vii li. vi s. viii d., collatio cuius facta per episcopum Rogero de Ynkepenne fuit eidem confirmata per Innocentium iii° idus Februarii anno vi°,[237] vii li. vi s. viii d.

De archidiaconatu de Totenes, non taxato, et canonicatu et prebenda ecclesie Exoniensis taxata iiii li., de quibus per obitum Johannis de Norwod fuit provisum Petro de Gildesburgh' per Clementem anno vii°,[238] de dicta prebenda est responsum de iiii li., et solvit de archidiaconatu x li.

De ecclesia de Lansant (Lezant), taxata v li., de qua per obitum Thome de Word fuit provisum Willelmo Dary per Innocentium ii° idus Decembris anno v°,[239] v li.

De ecclesia de Cliste (Clyst), non taxata, de qua fuit Thome [240] Tanteffer per Cardinalem Petragoricensem de novo provisum xxxv s.

De vicaria ecclesie de Brygham (Brixham), taxata vi li., collatio cuius facta Johanni Wodeman fuit sibi confirmata per Innocentium ix° kalendas Octobris anno vii°,[241] vi li.

De vicaria de Alestyngton' (Ilsington), non taxata, de qua fuit Thome Brugges per cardinalem Urgellensem de novo provisum, iii li. vi s. viii d.

De prebenda in ecclesia collegiata Sancti Endolien' (St. Endellion), taxata iiii li. ii s., de qua per obitum Willelmi Donne fuit provisum Symoni Wythull' per Innocentium iiii° nonas Jullii anno vi°,[242] iiii li. ii s.

De ecclesia de Gryddestowe (Bridestow), taxata xii li., collatio cuius facta per ordinarium Henrico Pyk fuit eidem confirmata per Innocentium kalendas Junii anno nono,[243] xii li.

Summa pagine liii li. x s. iiii d.

(fol. 111ᵛ) De prebenda Exoniensi, taxata iiii li., de qua per obitum Thome David fuit provisum Johanni Seye per Innocentium xi° kalendas Junii anno ix°,[244] iiii li.

De prebenda Exoniensi, taxata iiii li., collatio cuius facta per episcopum Henrico Pik fuit eidem confirmata per Innocentium kalendas Junii anno ix°,[245] in partem xl s.

De prebenda in ecclesia collegiata de Credynton' (Crediton), taxata iii li., de qua per obitum Johannis Colst' fuit provisum Willelmo de Banitton' per Innocentium iiii° idus Augusti anno ix°,[246] iii li.

### Wygorniensis

De ecclesia de Honyniton' (Honington), taxata x li., de qua fuit Luce Willelmi, rectori eiusdem, per cardinalem Petragoricensem de novo provisum, x li.

De ecclesia Sancti Schuythyny (Swithin) Wygornie, taxata vi li. vi s. viii d., de qua rectori eiusdem fuit per cardinalem Petragoricensem de novo provisum, vi li. vi s. viii d.

De ecclesia de Boutiston' (Beverstone), taxata x li., de qua Waltero de Evesham per cardinalem Petragoricensem de novo fuit provisum, x li.

De ecclesia de Merston' (Long Marston), taxata x li., de qua rectori eiusdem cardinalis Petrogoricensis de novo providit, x li.[247]

De vicaria de Haukesbury (Hawkesbury), taxata iiii ⟨li.⟩ vi s. viii d., de qua Johanni de Oly fuit per cardinalem Wrgellensem de novo provisum, iiii li. vi s. viii d.

De vicaria de Campeden' (Campden), non taxata, de

---

[233] 1 June 1357.
[234] Followed by *Ba* deleted by a line.
[235] 2 September 1358.
[236] 15 March 1355.
[237] 11 February 1358.
[238] 4 May 1349: *Cal. Pap. Regs. Petitions*, i, 156.
[239] 12 December 1357.
[240] Followed by *Temf* deleted by a line.

[241] 23 September 1359.
[242] 4 July 1358.
[243] 1 June 1361.
[244] 22 May 1361.
[245] 1 June 1361.
[246] 10 August 1361.
[247] Against this and the next three items the following note appears in the margin: *Non sunt in registro mihi dato per cameram.*

qua Gilberto Darling' fuit per cardinalem Urgellensem de novo provisum, v li.

De ecclesia de Elyngton' (Ekington), de qua Symoni de Blockele fuit per cardinalem Petragoricensem de novo provisum, taxata vi li. xiii s. iiii d., vi li. xiii s. iiii d.

Summa pagine lxi li. vi s. viii d.

(fol. 112, xx) De ecclesia de Northfeld (Northfield), taxata xvi li., de qua Roberto Meryweder per cardinalem Petragoricensem fuit de novo provisum, xvi li.

De prebenda in ecclesia collegiata de Westbury, taxata vi li. xiii s. iiii d., de qua ex causa permutationis fuit Bernardo Ritherii provisum per Innocentium xi° kalendas Maii anno v°,[248] vi li. xiii s. iiii d.

### Batoniensis et Wellensis

De vicaria Pypminister' (Pitminster), taxata iiii li. vi s. viii d., de qua Matheo Palmel fuit per cardinalem Petragoricensem provisum, iiii li. vi s. viii d.

De prebenda bursaly in ecclesia Wellensi, taxata v li. vi s. viii d., de qua per obitum Johannis Cok' fuit provisum Pontio Weyreriis per Innocentium ix° kalendas Junii anno vi°,[249] v li. vi s. viii d.

De vicaria de Wyllescumbe (Winscombe), taxata iiii li. vi s. viii d., de qua Willelmo de Wyndesor' fuit per cardinalem Urgellensem de novo provisum, iiii li. vi s. viii d.

### Hereffordensis

De ecclesia de Lanoran' (Llanwarne), taxata vi li. xiii s. iiii d., de qua Philipo Kalffodes cardinalis Petragoricensis de novo providit, vi li. xiii s. iiii d.

### Norwycensis

De ecclesia de Fordelle (Fordley), taxata iiii li. vi s. viii d., de qua Johanni de Stortesham fuit per cardinalem Petragoricensem provisum, iiii li. vi s. viii d.

De ⟨ecclesia⟩ de Askeby (Ashby), taxata vi li., de qua Petro Alani fuit per cardinalem Petragoricensem de novo provisum, vi li.

De ecclesia de parva Bradlyng' (Little Bradley), taxata v li. vi s. viii d., de qua Thome de Bradley fuit per cardinalem Urgellensem provisum, v li. vi s. viii d.

Summa pagine lix li.

(fol. 112ᵛ) De ecclesia de Wodnorton' (Wood Norton), taxata iiii li., de qua Johanni de Ellefford fuit per cardinalem Petragoricensem de novo provisum, in partem xv s.[250]

De ecclesia de Weston', taxata xxvi li. xiii s. iiii d., de qua Johanni Dirby fuit ex causa permutationis cum Willelmo Mugge provisum per Innocentium iiii° nonas Septembris,[251] in partem xii li. xiii s. iiii d.

De archidiaconatu Northffolch' in ecclesia Norowcensi, non taxato, per obitum Magistri Roberti de Wfflete collatio facta Willelmo de Blithe fuit eidem confirmata per Innocentium vii° kalendas Junii anno vii°,[252] vi li. xiii s. iiii d.

### Eliensis

De archidiaconatu Eliensi, taxato xii li. vi s. viii d., de quo fuit provisum cardinali Aragonie[253] per Innocentium xli. li. vi s. viii d.

De ecclesia de Wovre (Over), taxata xxxv li. vi s. viii d., de qua per obitum Andree de Wfford fuit provisum Thome de Clispton' per Innocentium iiii° nonas Decembris anno vi°,[254] in partem xx li. xiii s. iiii d.

### Lincolniensis

De ecclesia de Eddilla (Evenley?), taxata xiii li. vi s. viii d., de qua per dominum Petragoricensem fuit Willelmo de[255] Otton' provisum, xiii li. vi s. viii d.

De prebenda de Welton' Rivaus (Welton Rivall) in ecclesia Lincolniensi, taxata xxxiii li. vi s. viii d., de qua per obitum Johannis de Acton' acceptatio facta per Johannem Lamberti fuit eidem confirmata per Clementem iiii° idus Maii anno nono,[256] in partem xxix li. v s. ii d.

De prebenda de Coryngham (Corringham) in ecclesia Lincolniensi, taxata xiˣˣ vi li. xiii s. iiii d., de qua per obitum cardinalis Anibaldi[257] fuit provisum Raymundo Pelegrini per Clementem vii° idus Septembris anno nono,[258] quo anno fuerint omnes domus, grangie, blada et omnia animalia per infortunium aliunde veniens combusta, liii li. vi s. viii d. De residuo est paratus stare iudicio camere.

De vicaria ecclesie de Wodfford (Woodford), non taxata, de qua Ricardo de Wodfford fuit per cardinalem Urgellensem de novo provisum, iii li.[259]

Summa pagine clxxxii li. v s. ii d.

(fol. 113, xxi) De prebenda de Leghton' Manerii (Leighton Manor) in ecclesia Lincolniensi, taxata xlvi li. xiii s. iiii d., de qua per promotionem electi Ruensis (Rieux) fuit provisum Francisco de Sancto Maximo per Innocentium vi° kalendas Februarii anno iiii°,[260] xlvi li. xiii s. iiii d.

De ecclesia de Saxelby, taxata v li., de qua Thome filio Nicholai de Gormund per cardinalem Petragoricensem ⟨fuit⟩ de novo provisum, v li.[259]

De vicaria ecclesie de Multon' (Moulton), taxata xxxiii li. vi s. viii d., de qua Johanni de Casterton' fuit

---

[248] 21 April 1357.
[249] 24 May 1358.
[250] Opposite this item in the margin is noted: *Non est in regestro mihi tradito per cameram.*
[251] 2 September 1358: *Cal. Pap. Regs. Petitions*, i, 309.

[252] 26 May 1359.
[253] Nicholas Roselli, priest of S. Sisto.
[254] 2 December 1358.
[255] Followed by *V* deleted by a line.
[256] 12 May 1351.
[257] Anibaldus de Ceccano, bishop of Tusculum.
[258] 7 September 1350.
[259] In the margin opposite this item is noted: *Non est in regestro camere mihi tradito.*
[260] 27 January 1356.

per cardinalem Petragoricensem de novo provisum, xxxiii li. vi s. viii d.[261]

De prebenda de Bannebury (Banbury) in ecclesia Lincolniensi, taxata xxx li., de qua per resignationem Johannis de Parma fuit provisum ⟨Johanni⟩ de Stratele per Innocentium v° kalendas Septembris anno ii°,[262] xxx li.

De ecclesia parva de Kynnewell' (Little Kimble), taxata iiii li. xiii s. iiii d., de qua Johanni de Kargth' per cardinalem Petragoricensem fuit de novo provisum, iiii li. xiii s. iiii d.

De ecclesia de Dynggeley (Dingley), taxata iiii li. xiii s. iiii d., de qua Thome de Dynggeleye fuit per cardinalem Petragoricensem de novo provisum, in partem xl s.

De ecclesia de Flethergate (Fleet),[263] taxata liii li. vi s. viii d., de qua per obitum Johannis de Suldham fuit provisum Ade de Kanaresburgh' per Innocentium iii° idus Augusti anno ix°;[264] de ista ecclesia prior de Castelacre recepit duas partes et pro ipsis facit onera, et rector pro tertia parte, cuius pars quo ad taxam est xvii li. xv s. vi d. obolus, solvit in partem iii li. vi s. viii d.

De ecclesia Beate Marie de Trop iuxta Lylylleburn' (Catthorpe near Lilbourne), non taxata, de qua Roberto Chanel fuit per cardinalem Urgellensem provisum, vi li.[261]

De vicaria ecclesie de Wathfford (Watford), taxata iiii li. xiii s. iiii d., de qua per resignationem Rogeri Waldesthef fuit provisum Willelmo de Waldegrave per Innocentium ix° kalendas Augusti anno ⟨viii⟩,[265] iiii li. xiii s. iiii d.

Summa pagine cxxxv li. xiii s. iiii d.

(fol. 113ᵛ) De ecclesia de Ycelep (Islip), taxata x li. xiii s. iiii d., de qua Ade de Picham fuit per cardinalem Petragoricensem de novo provisum, x li. xiii s. iiii d.

De ecclesia de Berkhamsted (Little Berkhampstead), taxata vi li., de ⟨qua⟩ Willelmo de Wauton' fuit per cardinalem Petragoricensem de novo provisum, vi li.[266]

De vicaria ecclesie de Stropmunndevile (Stoke Mandeville), non taxata, de qua Willelmo Dalby fuit per cardinalem Petragoricensem de novo provisum, xl s.

De ecclesia de Stangrond (Standground), taxata xx li., de qua Thome de Clipton' fuit per cardinalem Petragoricensem de novo provisum, in partem xiii li. vi s. viii d.

De ecclesia de Schother (Scotter), taxata xxx li.,

de qua Thome Resen fuit per cardinalem Petragoricensem de novo provisum, xxx li.[267]

De ecclesia de Lughteburgh' (Ludborough), taxata xxv li. xiii s. iiii d., de qua per resignationem Thome de Bertwell' ex causa permutationis cum vicaria Sancti Michaelis Conventur' (Coventry) fuit provisum Willelmo Antonii per Innocentium vii° kalendas Junii anno vi°,[268] in partem xix li. xiii s. iiii d.

De ecclesia de Wythenhale (Witherley), taxata xii li. vi s. viii d., de qua Johanni de Melburn' fuit per cardinalem Petragoricensem de novo provisum, xii li. vi. s. viii d.

De vicaria ecclesie de Fryseby (Frisby on the Wreake), non taxata, de qua Willelmo Clement' fuit provisum per cardinalem Petragoricensem, v li.

De vicaria ecclesie de Thurleburn', alias Turbeley ut in currente,[269] alias vocata Therlibriy (Thurlby) et melius, taxata x li., de qua Johanni de Hastyng' fuit per cardinalem Petragoricensem provisum, in partem v li.[270]

De prebenda Sancte Crucis (Spaldwick) in ecclesia Lincolniensi, taxata x li., que non invenitur, missa per cameram, de qua fuit provisum Johanni[271] de Selby, in partem v li.

De ecclesia de Harworthyngham (Hagworthingham), taxata xii li., de qua per assecutionem ecclesie de Wetynffed[272] (Wetheringsett) Norowcensis diocesis auctoritate litterarum apostolicarum factam, fuit provisum Henrico Romelon per Innocentium iiii° nonas Maii anno nono,[273] in partem iii li.

Summa pagine cxii li.

## (fol. 114, xxii) Conventrensis et Lichfeldensis

De ecclesia de Malo Passu (Malpas), taxata xiii li. vi s. viii d., de qua Edemundo de Bothelher fuit per cardinalem Petragoricensem de novo provisum, xiii li. vi s. viii d.

De ecclesia de Watton' (Wootton), taxata vi li. xiii s. iiii d., de qua Jordano de [274] Hulmo fuit per cardinalem Petragoricensem de novo provisum, vi li. xiii s. iiii d.

De vicaria ecclesie de Merston' (Merston-upon-Dove), taxata iiii li. xiii s. iiii d., de qua Henrico de Merston, fuit per cardinalem Petragoricensem de novo provisum, iiii li. xiii s. iiii d.[275]

---

[261] Against this item is noted in the margin: *Non est in regestro camere mihi tradito.*

[262] 28 August 1354.

[263] The priory of Castle Acre had the rectories of two churches in the diocese of Lincoln. Of these Fleet is the one assessed at the above figure in *Taxatio Ecclesiastica . . . P. Nicholai IV*, p. 62.

[264] 11 August 1361.

[265] The date is 24 July 1360.

[266] Bracketed against this and the next four items is the note in the margin: *Non sunt in registris camere mihi traditis.*

[267] Although this item is included in the bracket, the following note appears opposite it in the margin: *Non est in registro camere mihi tradito.*

[268] 26 May 1358.

[269] Followed by *taxata* deleted by a line.

[270] In the margin opposite this item is noted: *Non est in registro camere michi tradito.*

[271] Followed by *S* deleted by a line.

[272] Followed by *fuit provisum* deleted by a line.

[273] 12 May 1361.

[274] Followed by *Ulmo* deleted by a line.

[275] In the margin opposite this item is the note: *nec ista.* It refers to the note opposite the preceding item.

De ecclesia Beate Marie de Sutton' (Sutton-Cold-field), taxata xiii li. vi s. viii d., de qua Symoni Basset per cardinalem Petragoricensem fuit de novo provisum, vi li. vi s. viii d. Ista ecclesia est de patronatu laycali, et Symon obiit, quare plus levari non potuit.

De cantoria in ecclesia Sancti Michaelis, non taxata, de qua Henrico de Stanffeld fuit per cardinalem Petragoricensem de novo provisum, xl s.[276]

De vicaria de Wynwyk' (Winwick), taxata xxvi li. xiii s. iiii d., de qua Willelmo de Ormby fuit per cardinalem Petragoricensem de novo provisum, et de eadem fuit Roberto de Trusswell' etiam ⟨provisum⟩ per Innocentium viii° kalendas Februarii anno iiii°,[277] totum infra annum, xxvi li. xiii s. iiii d.

De ⟨ecclesia⟩ de Weston' super Trentam (Weston-upon-Trent), taxata xii li., de qua ex causa permutationis cum Thoma de Bredon' de parochiali ecclesia de Champham (Clapham) Wyntoniensis diocesis fuit provisum Nicholao [278] de Limbergh per Innocentium ii° idus Februarii anno vi°,[279] in partem viii li.

De ecclesia de Egmandon' (Edgmond), taxata xii li., in qua et ad omne ius quod competebat Willelmo [280] Cherleton' fuit subrogatus Hugo Karles per Innocentium ix° kalendas Augusti anno viii°,[281] xii li.

De ecclesia de Standich' (Standish), taxata xiii li. vi s. viii d., de qua Willelmo de Standich' fuit per cardinalem Petragoricensem de novo provisum, in partem vi li. xiii s. iiii d.

Summa pagine lxxxvi li. vi s. viii d.

(fol. 114ᵛ) De archidiaconatu [282] Stahefford in ecclesia Lichfeldensi, non taxato, de quo per obitum Willelmi Apoltre fuit provisum Rogero Doylyng' per Clementem ii° idus Decembris anno viii°,[283] xx s. Iste archidiaconatus consistit in visitationibus et procurationibus, et per iuramentum officialis eiusdem medietas plus non valuit ultra visitationes et procurationes predictas, et dicto die fuit confirmatus dicto Rogero in diocesi Lincolniensi, sed debet esse in Lichfeldensi.[284]

De dicto archidiaconatu Stahfford, non taxato ut supra, de quo per obitum Rogerii Dorkyng' fuit provisum Willelmo de Crombrygh' per Innocentium ii° kalendas Februarii anno ii° [285] modo quo in proximo [286] supra xx s.

De vicaria Sancti Michaelis (Coventry), taxata c s., de qua fuit ex causa permutationis provisum Thome de Bretwell' per Innocentium viii° kalendas Junii anno vi°,[287] l s.

De vicaria ecclesie de Alb'ton (Albrighton), non taxata, de qua Henrico Fabri fuit per cardinalem Petragoricensem de novo provisum, iiii s. iiii d.[288]

De prebenda de Humdesacr' (Handsacre), taxata xiii li. vi s. viii d., de qua fuit provisum et confirmatio facta Ricardo Rowel ex causa permutationis per Innocentium vii° kalendas Jullii anno vi°,[289] xiii li. vi s. viii d.

De archidiaconatu Stafford' et prebenda de Byshope-hull' (Bishopshull) in ecclesia Lichfeldensi, non taxatis, de quibus collatio facta auctoritate ordinaria Johanni de Sulgrave fuit [290] eidem confirmata per Innocentium vii° kalendas Julii anno vii°,[291] pro archidiaconatu xx s. et pro prebenda liii s. iiii d., iii li. xiii s. iiii d.

Summa pagine xxiiii li. iii s. iiii d.

(fol. 115, xxiii) De ecclesia parochiali de Worthyn' (Worthen) Hereffordensis diocesis ac prebenda et sacristia ecclesie Lichfeldensis fuit dispensatum cum Ricardo de Stafford ut eas valeat licite retinere per Innocentium iii° nonas Junii anno vii°;[292] sacristiam nunquam obtinuit sed prebendam in ecclesia collegiata de Pentrych' (Pentrich), de quibus composuit pro iiiixx i li. x s. viii d. certis terminis solvendis contentis infra in arreyragiis, xx li.

### Assavensis

De ecclesia de Escynyok (Yscifiog), taxata vii li., ut dicit cancellarius episcopi quia non invenitur in registro taxationum, de qua per assecutionem decanatus Assevensis fuit provisum fuit provisum David de Graston' per Innocentium iii° nonas Septembris anno v°,[293] in partem iiii li. vi s. viii d., iiii li. vi s. viii d.

### Bangorensis

De ecclesia Sancte Marie Lannar (Llannor), taxata iiii li. x d., de qua Johanni nato Gryffyni fuit per cardinalem Petragoricensem de novo provisum, iiii li. x d.

### Menevensis

De archidiaconatu Breconie in ecclesia Menevensi, taxato xxi li., de quo fuit archidiacono eiusdem per cardinalem Urgellensem de novo provisum, xxi li.[294]

De ecclesia de Prendylgast' (Prendergast), non taxata, fuit per cardinalem Petragoricensem rectori eiusdem provisum, iii li. vi s. viii d.

---

[276] In the margin bracketed against this item and the next is the note: *Non est in registro camere michi tradito.*

[277] 25 January 1356.

[278] *Nicholau*, MS.

[279] 12 February 1358.

[280] Followed by *Eh* deleted by a line.

[281] 24 July 1360.

[282] Followed by *Staff'* deleted by a line.

[283] 12 December 1349.

[284] The following note appears in the margin opposite this item: *dicit dictus Rogerus quod secundum litteras sibi missas non est intentio camere de talibus procurationibus et visitationibus aliquid recipere.*

[285] 31 January 1354.

[286] *proproximo*, MS.

---

[287] 25 May 1358.

[288] In the margin opposite this item is noted: *Non est in registro camere michi tradito.*

[289] 25 June 1358.

[290] *fuerunt*, MS.

[291] 25 June 1359.

[292] 3 June 1359.

[293] 3 September 1357.

[294] In the margin: *non est in registro camere mihi tradito.*

De ecclesia de Bredell' (Bridell), non taxata, de qua rectori eiusdem fuit per cardinalem Petragoricensem provisum, iii li. vi s. viii d.

De ecclesia de Lancodemaur' (Llangoedmore), taxata vi li., de qua rectori eiusdem fuit provisum per cardinalem Petragoricensem de novo, liii s. iiii d.

Summa pagine lviii li. xiiii s. ii d.

(fol. 115ᵛ) De prebenda de Lanbeudy (Llanboidy) de Landelbeybreyvi (Llandewi Brefi), taxata v li., de qua per resignationem cardinalis Cesaragustemensis (Saragossa [295]) fuit provisum Johanni Gouch' per Innocentium vᵒ idus Jullii anno vᵒ,[296] v li.

De vicaria ecclesie Thome de Abdogmale (St. Dogmells), non taxata, de qua Philipo Henrico fuit per cardinalem Petragoricensem de novo provisum, xxxiii s. iiii d.

### Eboracensis

De archidiaconatu [297] Clyffland' in ecclesia Eboracensi, taxato xxxvi li., acceptatio cuius facta per Willelum de Fereby ex causa permutationis cum ecclesia de Lympax (Kippax) fuit eidem confirmata per Innocentium xᵒ kalendas Augusti anno vᵒ,[298] xxxvi li.

De ecclesia Sancti Romaldi (Romaldkirk), taxata xx li., de qua rectori eiusdem fuit per cardinalem Petragoricensem de novo provisum, xx li.[299]

De prebenda Sancte Marie et Sanctorum Angelorum Eboraci, taxata vi li. xiii s. iiii d., de qua fuit dispensatum cum Johanne de Atum ut, non [300] obstante quod scripserat sententiam furis condempnati ad mortem, per Clementem idus Novembris anno xiᵒ,[301] vi li. xiii s. iiii d.

De ecclesia Sancte Crucis in Eboraco, taxata v li., de qua Willelmo de Houdon' fuit per cardinalem Petragoricensem de novo provisum, v. li.[302]

De ecclesia de Slynggeby (Slingsby), taxata xiii li. vi s. viii d., de qua per obitum Nicholay de Fereby fuit provisum Johanni Lyom per Innocentium iiiiᵒ nonas Augusti anno vᵒ,[303] xiii li. vi s. viii d.

De prebenda de Rugthorp' (Bugthorpe) in ecclesia Eboracensi, taxata xl li., de qua per obitum Bernardi de Rapistangno fuit provisum Willelmo de Rapistangno per Innocentium ixᵒ kalendas Junii anno sexto,[304] xl li.

Summa pagine cxxvii li. xiii s. iiii d.

(fol. 116, xxiiii) De vicaria de Tykyll' (Tickhill), taxata xx li., de qua per cardinalem Petragoricensem

fuit Rolgo de Slamiteburn' de novo provisum, in partem v li.[302]

De ecclesia de Appelden' in Ridal (Appleton le Street), taxata xx li. ad novam taxam, unita monasterio Sancti Albani Lincolniensis diocesis per Clementem xviiiᵒ kalendas Jullii anno viiᵒ vel viiiᵒ,[305] quia simul missi, xx li.

De ecclesia de Lyvene (Leven), taxata xiii li. vi s. viii d., de qua per assecutionem subdecanatus ecclesie Saresbiriensis per Nicholaum de Mordffeld fuit provisum Petro de Steopellton' per Innocentium xixᵒ kalendas Septembris anno viᵒ,[306] xiii li. vi s. viii d.

De medietate ecclesie de Houtonbussell' (Hutton Bushel), taxata iuxta novam taxam ad iiii li., de qua Nicholao [307] de Wytteby fuit per cardinalem Petragoricensem de novo provisum, iiii li.[308]

De prebenda de Trop (Thorpe) in ecclesia Ripponensi, taxata secundum novam taxam ad vi li. xiii s. iiii d., de qua collatio facta auctoritate ordinaria ex causa permutationis cum Domino Willelmo de Cusantiis fuit Willelmo de Dalton' confirmata per Innocentium xiᵒ kalendas Octobris anno viᵒ,[309] vi li. xiii s. iiii d.

De prebenda de Fynton' (Fenton) in ecclesia Eboracensi, taxata liii li. vi s. viii d., quam obtinet Robertus de Walkynton', fuit confirmatum per Innocentium vᵒ kalendas Februarii anno vᵒ,[310] liii li. vi s. viii d.[311]

De prebenda de Donyngton' (Dunnington) in ecclesia Eboracensi, taxata x li., de qua collatio et provisio auctoritate ordinaria facte Willelmo de Fereby fuerunt [312] eidem confirmate per Innocentium xiiiiᵒ kalendas Decembris anno viiᵒ,[313] x li.

De prebenda altaris Sancte Katerine in ecclesia Beverlacensi, taxata vi li. xiii s. iiii d., vacante per obitum Willelmi de Abirwylli, fuit Johanni de Aula confirmata per Innocentium viᵒ nonas Octobris anno viᵒ,[314] vi li. xiii s. iiii d.

De ecclesia de Thormerby (Thornaby), taxata iiii li., de qua Ade de Bolton' fuit per cardinalem de [315] de novo provisum, in partem xl s.

De prebenda de Osbaldewyk' (Osbaldwick) in ecclesia Eboracensi, taxata xxvi li. i m., de qua per obitum Bernardi de Novo Dapno fuit provisum Symoni de Brisele per Clementem nonas Jullii anno xiᵒ,[316] in par-

---

[295] William d'Aigrefeuille, priest of S. Maria in Trastevere.
[296] 11 July 1357.
[297] Followed by *Eboracensi* deleted by a line.
[298] 23 July 1357.
[299] In the margin opposite this item is the note: *Non est in registro per cameram mihi tradito.*
[300] Followed by *ne* deleted by a line.
[301] 13 November 1352.
[302] Opposite this item in the margin: *Non est in dicto regestro.*
[303] 2 August 1357.
[304] 24 May 1358.

[305] 14 June 1348 or 1349.
[306] 14 August 1358.
[307] *Nicholau*, MS.
[308] In the margin opposite this item: *Non est in registro mihi per cameram tradito.*
[309] 21 September 1358.
[310] 28 January 1357.
[311] Opposite this item in the margin is the note: *Non est in registro mihi per cameram tradito.*
[312] *fuit*, MS.
[313] 18 November 1359.
[314] 2 October 1358.
[315] A blank space is left in the manuscript for the name.
[316] 7 July 1352.

tem per manus Domini Henrici de Barton' qui possidet, vi li. xiii s. iiii d.

Summa pagine cxxvii li. xiii s. iiii d.

(fol. 116ᵛ) De vicaria de Cotom (West Coatham), taxata v li., de qua Johanni Myemoie fuit provisum de novo per dominum Petragoricensem, v li.[317]

De ecclesia de Bolton' Percy, taxata xl li., collatio et institutio facte [318] auctoritate ordinaria Johanni de Irfford fuerunt [319] eidem confirmate per Innocentium viᵒ idus Junii anno viiᵒ,[320] in partem xxvi li. xiii s. iiii d.

De custodia sacristie capelle Beate Marie et Sanctorum Angelorum Eboraci collatio et provisio facte auctoritate ordinaria Johanni de Waltham fuerunt sibi confirmate per Innocentium viiᵒ kalendas Jullii anno viiᵒ,[321] taxata xxxiii li. vi s. viii d., xxxiii li. vi s. viii d.

De ecclesia de Holtesby (Holtby), taxata v li. vi s. viii d., de qua Willelmo de Dryffeld fuit provisum per dominum Petragoricensem, in partem iii li. vi s. viii d.[322]

De vicaria ecclesie de Walkyngham (Walkeringham), taxata viii li., de qua ex causa permutationis fuit Willelmo Zarwell' provisum per Innocentium xiiiiᵒ kalendas Decembris anno viiᵒ,[323] in partem iiii li.

De ecclesia de [324] Claworth' (Clayworth), taxata xxiii li. vi s. viii d., de qua Nicholao [325] Daubeney fuit ex causa permutationis per Innocentium provisum xiiiiᵒ kalendas Decembris anno viiᵒ,[326] in partem xi li. xiii s. iiii d.

De ecclesia Sancti Wlfeydy Eboraci (St. Wilfrid, York), taxata iiii li., permutatio facta per Ricardum de Wyntryngham cum Gerlaco de Clare de ecclesia de Langeton' (Langton) fuit dicto Ricardo confirmata per Innocentium ixᵒ kalendas Septembris anno ixᵒ,[327] in partem xl s.

De prebenda de Sharwe (Sharow) in ecclesia collegiata Ripponensi, taxata v li., que Johanni de Donyngton' fuit confirmata per Clementem iiᵒ idus Maii anno ixᵒ,[328] v li.

De ecclesia de Brantyngham (Brantingham), taxata lxvi li. xiii s. iiii d., de qua, vacante per obitum Magistri Thome de Novill', fuit provisum Willelmo Strode per

Innocentium xviᵒ kalendas Septembris anno,[329] in partem xiii li. vi s. viii d.

Summa pagine ciiii li. vi s. viii d.

(fol. 117, xxv) De prebenda de Amplefford (Ampleforth) in ecclesia Eboracensi, taxata xl li., de qua Willelmo de Curtenay fuit provisum per Innocentium iiiᵒ idus Augusti anno ixᵒ,[330] in partem xx li.

De ecclesia de Brampton', (Brompton), taxata liii li. vi s. viii d., de qua, vacante per obitum cardinalis de Turre,[331] fuit provisum Thome de Mounte de Wycham, qui dimittet ecclesiam de Alglisto (Halstow) quam obtinet, per Innocentium iiiiᵒ kalendas Januarii anno ixᵒ,[332] in partem xxxii li. xiii s. iiii d.

De ecclesia de Patrikbruntton' (Patrick Brompton), taxata xx li., quam Willelmus Storde obtinet, vacante, alias dum vacabit, per assecutionem parochialis ecclesie de Brantyngham (Brantingham), fuit provisum Roberto Palmer per Innocentium iiiᵒ idus Martii anno ixᵒ,[333] in partem vi li. xiii s. iiii d.

De vicaria [334] ecclesie Ponteffracti (Pontefract), taxata xvi li., que ex causa permutationis facte cum Johanne de Beck' fuit confirmata Hugoni de Raston' per Innocentium ixᵒ kalendas Septembris anno viᵒ,[335] in partem xii li.

De ecclesia de Slyngesby (Slingsby), taxata vi li. xiii s. iiii d. ad novam taxam, de qua per resignationem Bartholomey Sydey fuit provisum Thome de Bryseleye per Innocentium nonas Martii anno decimo,[336] vi li. xiii s. iiii d.

### Dunelmensis

De prebenda in ecclesia collegiata de Norton', taxata vi li., de qua Hugoni de Wymondeswold fuit provisum ⟨per⟩ cardinalem Urgellensem de novo,[337] vi li.[338]

### Karliolensis

De ecclesia de Ryvers (Bowness?), taxata secundum novam taxam iii li., de qua rectori eiusdem fuit per cardinalem Petragoricensem de novo provisum, iiii li.

Summa pagine lxxxviii li.

### (fol. 118, xxv)[339] Hibernia

De prebenda de Holy (Clone) in ecclesia Fernensi, taxata iii li. vi s. viii d., de qua per ingressum religionis Hugonis de Burgh' fuit provisum Ricardo Radulphi

---

[317] In the margin opposite this item is the note: ⟨Non⟩ est in ⟨registr⟩o mihi per ⟨ca⟩meram ⟨tra⟩dito. The margin has been clipped too close.
[318] factis, MS.
[319] fuit, MS.
[320] 8 June 1359.
[321] 25 June 1359.
[322] In the margin opposite this item is the note: Non est in dicto registro.
[323] 18 November 1359.
[324] Followed by Cba deleted by a line.
[325] Nicholau, MS.
[326] 18 November 1359.
[327] 24 August 1361.
[328] 14 May 1351.

[329] 17 August 1361. The year, which is lacking in the manuscript, is supplied from Cal. Pap. Regs. Petitions, i, 321.
[330] 11 August 1361.
[331] Bernard de la Tour d'Auvergne, deacon of S. Eustachio.
[332] 29 December 1361.
[333] 13 March 1361.
[334] Followed by Pont' deleted by a line.
[335] 24 August 1358.
[336] 7 March 1362.
[337] provisum is repeated in the manuscript.
[338] In the margin opposite this item is noted: non est in registro mihi tradito.
[339] Folio 117ᵛ is blank. The second folio numbered xxv.

per Innocentium idus Augusti anno vi°,[340] iii li. vi s. viii d.

De thesauraria ecclesie Dublinensis, taxata xx li., de qua per resignationem Johannis Gate fuit provisum Hugoni Tesdale per Innocentium ii° idus Februarii anno vii°,[341] in partem vii li.

De archidiconatu Richemondye, taxato ii° li., et prebenda [342] de Midelton (Middleton) in ecclesia Cicestrensi, taxata v li., de Deygmynstr' (Yetminster) in ecclesia Saresbiriensi, taxata xxvi li. xiii s. iiii d., que summe se extendunt [343] ad ii° xxxi li. xiii s. iiii d., de quibus respondetur in compoto reddito supradicto primo die Junii anno LVIII pro dicto archidiaconatu de xxxiii li. vi s. viii d., et tunc restabant de dictis beneficiis c iiii^xx xviii li. vi s. viii d., de quibus Dominus Henricus de Walton', cui fuit provisum videlicet de archidiaconatu per obitum domini cardinalis Portuensis episcopi per Clementem iiii° idus Aprilis anno viii°,[344] et de prebenda Saresbiriensi per eumdem Clementem antequam dictus Hugo esset nuntius per promotionem Johannis de Wfford, et de prebenda Cicestrensi per promotionem episcopi Norwycensis per Innocentium vi° idus Februarii anno primo,[345] simul pro omnibus se obligavit, post cuius obligationem solvit cxxviii li. vi s. viii d. Et lxx li. restantes ponuntur infra in arreyragiis.

De cancellaria Dublinensi, taxata xl li. ad antiquam taxam, cuius collatio facta Johanni de Troy fuit eidem confirmata iiii kalendas Junii anno ii°,[346] in partem reste de xxxiii li. vi s. viii d., vi li. xiii s. iiii d.

Summa pagine cxlv li. vi s. viii d.[347]

(fol. 118ᵛ) De subdecanatu Eboracensi, taxato liii li. vi s. viii d., de quo fuit provisum seu confirmatio facta Willelmo de [348] Radfford' [349] per Innocentium vi° kalendas Decembris anno vii°,[350] et prebenda de Grantham in ecclesia Saresbiriensi, taxata liii li. vi s. viii d., fuit simili modo confirmata, et de prebenda de Rothynchel (Rathmichael) in ecclesia Dublinensi, taxata xiii li. vi s. viii d., de Clypston (Clifton) in ecclesia Lincolniensi, taxata x li., de Cheswyk' (Chiswick) in ecclesia Londoniensi, taxata vi li., de Ranton' (Rampton) in ecclesia collegiata Suthwell' Eboracensis diocesis, taxata xx li., quequid prebende fuerunt etiam per Dominum Innocentium confirmate, et est summa taxe omnium clvi li., de quibus solvit in partem iiii^xx xvii li. x s. Et lviii li. x s. restantes ponuntur infra in arreyragiis.

De ecclesia de Hodenet (Hodnet) Lichefeldensis diocesis et prebenda [351] de Farendon' (Faringdon ) in ecclesia Saresbiriensi, de Mota (Moorfields in St. Giles Cripplegate, London) in ecclesia Londoniensi, de Hundreton' (Hunderton) in ecclesia Hereffordensi et de Ledebury (Ledbury) Hereffordensis diocesis, pro quibus omnibus Nicholaus Heth', cui fuit provisum, composuit cum camera in curia pro primis fructibus dictorum beneficiorum in viii° l fl. ponderis camere, solvendis videlicet c. fl. in festo nativitatis domini anno LIX° et eodem modo in subsequentibus festis nativitatis, in quolibet c fl., quousque de iiii° fl. fuerit satisfactum, et residuos [352] iiii° l fl. in proximo festo dicte nativitatis post ultimam solutionem dictorum iiii° fl. solvere debet de premissis, solvit pro tribus primis terminis iii° fl., xlvi li. xiii s. iiii d.

Summa pagine cxliiii li. iii s. iiii d.

(fol. 119, xxvi) De cancellaria Saresbiriensi, taxata iiii^xx viii li., de qua per consecrationem Symonis episcopi Londoniensis fuit provisum Johanni de Norton' per Innocentium vii° kalendas Decembris anno ix°,[353] et de prebenda de Huve (Hove) in ecclesia Cicestrensi, taxata xx li., de qua per consecrationem Willelmi episcopi Roffensis fuit provisum dicto Johanni per Innocentium vii° kalendas Decembris anno ix°,[353] pro istis duobus beneficiis dictus Johannes est simul obligatus in cviii li., solvit xxxvi li. Et lxxii li. restantes ponuntur infra in arreyragiis.

Summa pagine xxxvi li.

Summa universalis omnium receptorum de beneficiis collatis et missis per cameram post dicta compota m ix° lvii li. xviii s. viii d. Approbatum.

Summa summarum omnium precedentium receptorum vᵐ cxl li. ii s. v d. sterlingorum.

(fol. 120, xxvii)[354] Secuntur assignationes facte in Romana curia et extra de mandato camere cum expensis a primo die Junii anno LVIII° usque ad primum diem Septembris anno LXIII

Et est sciendum quod supradictus Hugo a primo die Junii anno domini millesimo CCC° LVIII° cum camera computavit et in conclusione compoti tenebatur eidem Hugoni in vii° lxii li. xiii s. iiii d.

Item xxiiii° die Augusti anno LIX° assignavit dictus Hugo prefate camere per manus Raymundi de Sancto Claro iiiᵐ. fl., precii fl. iii s. i d., iiii° lxii li. x s.

Item xxvi die Novembris anno supradicto assignavit et liberavit Londonie regi Francie de mandato domini nostri per bullam iiiᵐ fl., solutus pro fl. ii s. xi d., iiii° xxxvii li. x s. Fecit fidem de mandato per bullam Domini Innocentii sub data xviii kalendas Jullii anno vii°,[355] et de quietantia per litteras regis Francie qui

[340] 13 August 1358.
[341] 12 February 1359.
[342] prebendar, MS.
[343] extedunt, MS.
[344] 10 April 1350.
[345] 8 February 1353.
[346] 29 May 1354.
[347] Followed by an entry deleted by lines which reads as follows: Summa pagine usque ad ultimam provisionem exclusive xlii li.
[348] Followed by Raf deleted by a line.
[349] Followed by per obitum deleted by a line.
[350] 26 November 1359.

[351] prebendar, MS.
[352] Followed by iiii° fl. deleted by a line.
[353] 25 November 1361.
[354] Folio 119ᵛ is blank.
[355] 14 June 1359.

confitetur se recepisse in anno LX° per litteras datas x die Februarii anno lxiii°.

Item mense Augusti anno domini M° CCC° LX assignavit prefate camere idem Hugo v^m fl., solutus pro fl. iii s. i d., vii^c lxx li. xvi s. viii d.

Item mense Martii anno domini M° CCC° LXII° assignavit prefate camere per manus societatis de Malabayla iiii^m fl., solutus pro fl. iii s., vi^c li.

Item penultimo die Decembris anno supradicto misit dicte camere unam litteram per quam societas de Malabaylis debuit eidem assignare iiii^m fl., solvit pro fl. iii s., vi^c li. Dicit dominus R. solutionem fuisse factam per societatem de Provanis in duabus parcellis, dictam summam in duabus parcelllis, quare una fuit de [356] ii^m fl. ponderis fortis xxiii die Decembris et alia de aliis duobus milibus iiii die Januarii anno LXIIII°.

(fol. 120^v) Item xviii° die Aprilis anno LXIII° assignavit sepedicte camere per manus societatis Albertorum Antiquorum v^m fl., solvit pro fl. iii s., vii^c 1 li.

Item xxiiii° die Augusti anno supradicto assignavit dicte camere per manus dicte societatis iiii^m fl., solvit pro fl. iii s., vi^c li.

Summa universalis omnium precedentium asignationum iiii^m ix^c lxxxiii li. x s. sterlingorum. Approbatum.

(fol. 121, xxviii) Sequuntur expensi tempore supradicto

Libravit dictus Hugo Petro Picardi cursori mense Maii anno LXI° de mandato camere xl s.[357]

Item eidem cursori mense Octobris anno LXI°, istuc iterum, misso pro negotiis subcidii xlii s.

Item xxi° die Decembris anno supradicto eidem cursori, istuc remisso cum litteris apostolicis super positione decime, libravit, de mandato domini camerarii, x li.

Item duobus famulis cum duobus equis conducentibus dictum cursorem ad archiepiscopum Cantuariensem et ab ipso usque ad mare xxxvi s. viii d.

Item pro diversis nuntiis missis per Angliam et ad Hiberniam et ad curiam Romanam, pergameno, papiro et cera dicto quinquenio xxv li.[358]

Item solutum pro c arcubus, pro iiii^c cordis, iiii^m ii^c sagitis, mlxii capitibus ferri pro ousdem sagitis xxviii li. xii d.

Item pro sex coffinis faciendis pro premissis, imponedo panno, in cereato ad coperendum et cordulo ad ligandum xxx s. iiii d.

Summa pagine lxx li. x s.

Summa summarum omnium assignationum et ex-

pensorum, de quibus tamen non docet, sed promitit stare rationi et verificare tam assignationes quam espensos, alias super eis stare ordinationi camere, non facta tamen aliqua mentione de loquerio hospitii pro quo pro quinque annis computabat xxxiii li. vi s. viii d., videlicet pro quolibet anno vi li. xiii s. iiii d., v^m liiii li.

Quibus detractis de summa universali recepte que est de v^m cxl li. ii s. v d., restat quod debet iiii^xx vi li. ii s. v d., quas realiter igitur solvit.

(fol. 122, xxix)[359] Sequuntur arrayragia debita camere apostolice in Anglia dimissa per supradictum Hugonem primo die Septembris anno domini millesimo CCC° LXIII°

### Denarii Beati Petri

De archidiacono Surrye pro anno LXII° v li. xiii s. iiii d.[360]

Episcopus Bathoniensis et Wellensis pro anno LXII° xi li. v s.[361]

Episcopus Norwicensis pro annis LXI° et LXII°, pro quolibet xxi li. x s., xliii li.[360]

Episcopus Lincolniensis pro anno LXII° xlii li.

Archiepiscopus Eboracensis pro annis LIX°, LX°, LXI°, et LXII°, pro quolibet anno xi li. x s., xlvi li.[362]

Archidiaconus Middelssexie pro annis LX°, LXI°, et LXII°, pro quolibet v li. x s., xvi li. x s.

Episcopus Exoniensis pro annis LXI° et LXII°, pro quolibet ix li. v s., xviii li. x s.

Archdiaconus Wyntoniensis pro annis LX°, LXI°, et LXII°, pro quolibet xi li. xiii s. iiii d., xxxv li.

Episcopus Cicestrensis pro annis LXI° et LXII°, pro quolibet viii li., xvi li.

Episcopus Lichefeldensis pro annis LX°, LXI° et LXII°, pro quolibet x li. v s., xxx li. xv s.

Episcopus Hereffordensis pro annis LXI° et LXII°, pro quolibet vi li., xii li.

Episcopus Wigorniensis pro annis LXI° et LXII°, pro quolibet x li. v s., xx li. x s.

Archidiaconus Elyensis pro anno LXII v li.

Summa pagine restantium de denariis Beati Petri iii^c ii l. iii s. iiii d.

(fol. 122^v) Arreyragia annui censis

Abbatissa Sancte Clare [363] pro annis LVIII°, LIX°, LX°, LXI° et LXII, pro quolibet anno vi d., ii s. vi d.

Prior de Anglesey pro annis LXI° et LXII°, pro quolibet anno ii s., iiii s.

Prior de Bodemyn' pro anno LXII° ii s.

Prior Karliolensis pro anno LXII° xiii s. iiii d.

---

[356] Followed by *d.* deleted by a line.

[357] In the left margin, bracketed against this and the next four items is the note: *Repellantur nisi doceat*. In the right margin, opposite this and the next two items, is the note: *doce. Docuit per litteras istius camere et depositionem cursoris*.

[358] In the margin opposite this item is the additional note: *doce; per partes camera noluit admittere*.

[359] Folio 121^v is blank.

[360] Opposite this item in the margin is the note: *solvit*.

[361] In the margin opposite this item: *Promisit G. Derby, canonicus Wellensis, solvere infra quindennam purificationis*.

[362] Followed by *x s.* deleted by a line. This is followed by the entry: *Episcopus Exoniensis pro annis LXI* deleted by a line.

[363] Followed by *de* in MS.

Abbas de Fraverham pro anno LXII° xiii s. iiii d. Summa arreragiorum censum xxxv s. ii d.

(fol. 123, xxx) Sequntur arreyragia primorum fructuum, et primo in qualibet dyocesi ponuntur primo dimissa supradicto primo die Junii anno LVIII° et subsequenter alia. Et est sciendum quod taxe et provisiones subsequentium beneficiorum que non inveniuntur expresse hic continentur supra in recepta.

### Cantuariensis

De prioratu de Folkeston' (Folkestone) ordinis Sancti Benedicti, cuius collatio facta Willelmo Medici fuit eidem confirmata, debet pro resta viii li. xiii s. iiii d.

De ⟨ecclesia⟩ de Stokebury (Stockbury) appropriata priori et conventui de Ledes (Leeds) pro resta vii li. vi s. viii d.[364]

De ecclesia de Ikham (Ickham), taxata xxx li., de qua fuit provisum, per resignationem Roberti de Bouton', Rogero de Wye per Innocentium ii° kalendas Decembris anno iiii°,[365] non habuit effectum quia iste Rogerus non habuit possessionem sed Magister Willelmus de Hertelbury auctoritate ordinaria, qui diu litigavit cum dicto Rogero, obtinuit diffinitivam sententiam in palatio apostolico contra ipsum Rogerum, de qua sententia fecit fidem.[366]

De ecclesia de Wyvelesbergh' (Woodnesborough), taxata xvi li. xiii s. iiii d., appropriata abbatie Sancti Augustini Cantuarie per Innocentium ii° kalendas Decembris anno primo,[367] xvi li. xiii s. iiii d.

De ecclesia de Bokelond (Buckland), taxata xiii li. vi s. viii d., appropriata abbati et conventui Sancti Augustini Cantuarie per Innocentium modo quo supra, xiii li. vi s. viii d.

Summa pagine xlvi li.

(fol. 123ᵛ) De ecclesia de Chartham, taxata xxvi li. xiii s. iiii d., que fuit confirmata Waltero de Bruton' per Innocentium vi° kalendas Junii anno vi°,[368] xxvi li. xiii s. iiii d. Non habuit effectum.[369]

De eadem ecclesia de Chartham, taxata ut immediate, de qua per obitum Willelmi de Bradleye fuit provisum Ricardo de Unggbred per Innocentium vii° idus Julii anno ix°,[370] xxvi li. xiii s. iiii d.

De ecclesia de Bisshopesburn' (Bishopsbourne), taxata xxxiii li. vi s. viii d., de qua per obitum Johannis Thurstayn' fuit provisum Roberto Pres per Innocentium iiii° idus Augusti anno vii° vel viii°,[371] quia simul missi,

xxxiii li. vi s. viii d. Pro dicta summa fuit obligati dictus Robertus Pres et Nicholaus Heth'.

De ecclesia de [372] Croydon', nundum missa, taxata xl li., de qua fuit provisum per consecrationem Ade episcopi Menevensis Ade Robelyn per Innocentium iii° kalendas Novembris anno ix°,[373] xl li.

De capella libera de Bokinefeld (Bockingfold), de qua per obitum Willelmi de Brandley fuit provisum David Wyngham per Innocentium iii° idus Augusti anno ix°.[374]

### Roffensis

De ecclesia de Eynesford (Eynsford), taxata xx li., de qua per resignationem Viviani de Blankefford fuit provisum Johanni de Croso per Clementem xviii° kalendas Februarii anno x°,[375] non habuit effectum quia iste Vivianus fuit privatus per sententiam domini ante istam resignationem et pro alteri. Non habuit effectum.[369]

(fol. 124, xxxi) De ecclesia de Mepham (Meopham), taxata xxvi li. xiii s. iiii d., fuit provisum Johanni de Brygham, per dominum Petragoricensem de novo provisum, pro resta iii li. vi s. viii d.

De eadem ecclesia, ut immediate, de qua per obitum Johannis Blod fuit provisum Johanni de Kyrkeby per Innocentium iiii° nonas Julii anno ix°,[375a] xxvi li. xiii s. iiii d.[376]

De supradicta ecclesia de Eynefford, taxata xx li., collatio et provisio auctoritate ordinaria Johanni de Wyngham fuerunt eidem confirmate per Innocentium viii° kalendas Junii anno vi°,[377] xiii li. vi s. viii d.

Concessum fuit regi Anglie ut episcopi Wyntoniensis et Eliensis possent unire [378] unum vel plura beneficia ad patronatum dicti regis [379] exspectantia mense priorisse et conventui monasterii sororum de ordine predicatorum et in dictis beneficiis vicarios instituere per Innocentium iii° idus Maii anno primo.[380]

Item eisdem quod possint unire dictis sororibus unum, duo aut plura beneficia quorum redditus c li. secundum decimam non excedant.

### Londoniensis

De prebenda de Kentiston' (Kentish Town) in ecclesia Londoniensi, taxata vi li. xiii s. iiii d., de qua per obitum Ade Merymouth' fuit provisum Rogero Holm per Clementem VI°, antequam dictus Hugo esset nuntius, que fuit dimissa in xxxiii s. iiii d., nichil quia dictus Rogerus pro ista summa et diversis aliis beneficiis

---

[364] In the margin opposite this item is the note: *in arayragiis*. The following entry which is deleted by a line reads: *De ecclesia de Bokelond pro resta cuius taxa et provisio supra in recepta ii li. vi s. viii d.*

[365] 30 November 1356.

[366] Opposite this item in the margin is noted: *inutilis est*.

[367] 30 November 1353.

[368] 27 May 1358.

[369] This sentence is in the margin.

[370] 9 July 1361.

[371] 10 August 1359 or 1360.

[372] Followed by *Crod* deleted by a line.

[373] 30 October 1361.

[374] 11 August 1361.

[375] 15 January 1352.

[375a] 4 July 1361.

[376] In the margin opposite this item is noted: *in arayragiis*.

[377] 25 May 1358.

[378] *uniri*, MS.

[379] *ragis*, MS.

[380] 13 May 1353.

camere in curia se obligavit, et debet adhuc x li. nisi per acquitationem vel libros camere aliud appareat.[381]

(fol. 124ᵛ) De capella seu ecclesia de Staunfford (Stanford le Hope), taxata xxvi li. xiii s. iiii d., de qua per obitum Edmundi de Gremesby fuit provisum Johanni de Torksaye per Innocentium viiiᵒ idus Octobris anno iiᵒ,[382] xxvi li. xiii s. iiii d.[376]

De ecclesia de Brayle (Rayleigh), non taxata, dimissa in arreyragiis, de qua obitum Johannis de Hyrton' fuit provisum Ricardo Broun' per Innocentium xiᵒ kalendas Februarii anno iiiiᵒ,[383] certificatum est per officialem quod iste Ricardus nunquam fuit possessionem assecutus, quia rex contulit cuidam Nicholao de [384] Horton', ratione temporalitatis prioratus de Pretwell' (Prittlewell) existentis in manu sua tempore guerre,[385] quia dicta ecclesia est de patronatu prioris de Pretwell' predicti.[386]

De ecclesia Sancte Trinitatis Londonie, non taxata, de qua fuit dispensatum cum Thoma Balle presbytero ut non obstante deffectu natalium posset eam retinere per Innocentium xiiᵒ kalendas Junii anno [387] ixᵒ,[388] medietas.[376]

De ecclesia de Herlaume (Harlow), taxata xiii li. vi s. viii d., fuit provisum per obitum Ricardi Drax' Johanni Parker per Innocentium xiᵒ kalendas Junii anno,[389] xiii li. vi s. viii d.[376]

De prioratu Sancte Crucis Londonie,[390] non taxato, qui fuit confirmatus Johanni Bury per Innocentium xiiᵒ kalendas Junii anno xᵒ,[391] medietas.[376]

De archidiaconatu Milddelsexie, de quo fuit provisum domino cardinali Rothomagensi (Rouen)[392] per Innocentium xiiii kalendas Decembris anno viᵒ.[393]

De ecclesia de Sabacheswroth' (Sawbridgeworth) diocesis Londoniensis, appropriata monasterio [394] de Wastmonasterio dicte diocesis per Clementem iiiᵒ nonas Maii anno ixᵒ,[395] taxata xlvi li. xiii s. iiii d., pro taxa integra xlvi li. xiii s. iiii d.[376]

(fol. 125, xxxii) De ecclesia de Purle (Purleigh), cuius taxa et provisio supra in recepta, pro resta vi li.

De ecclesia Sancti Sthwythini Londonie, non taxata, que fuit confirmata Radulpho Nichol' de Bury per

Innocentium vᵒ kalendas Octobris anno xᵒ,[396] medietas, De ista ecclesia ut patet in litteris missis per cameram fuit provisum [397] quinque personis infra annum.

De ecclesia Sancti Dyonisii, que non taxatur, pro resta ii li.[398]

De prebenda de Wallokesbern' (Wenlock's Barn, St. Giles) in ecclesia Londoniensi, taxata v li., que per consecrationem Domini Radulphi de Bury in episcopatum Dunelmensem acceptatio facta per Johannem de Branketree fuit eidem confirmata per Inncentium iiiiᵒ kalendas Julii anno viiiᵒ,[399] v li.

De ecclesia de Matfelon (Whitechapel) Londonie, non taxata, cuius provisio supra in recepta, pro resta xiii s. iiii d.[400]

De thesauraria quam **Johannes Cok** obtinebat **in** ecclesia Londoniensi fuit provisum Petro cardinali Rothomagensi iiiᵒ idus Maii anno viᵒ per Innocentum,[401] nichil hic, sed quia in camera satisfecit.[402]

Hic deficit unum beneficium, sed ponitur infra folio lvi[403]

Cicestrensis

De prebenda de Ferryng' (Ferring) in ecclesia Cicestrensi, taxata xxx li., de qua per resignationem Symonis Godwyn fuit provisum Johanni de Acton' per Clementem, dimissa in viii li. xiii s. iiii d., fuit erratum quia respondetur in recepta de xxiii li., et sic restant dumtaxat vii li.[404]

De decanatu Cicestrensi, cuius taxa et provisio supra in recepta, pro resta xv li.[405]

De prebenda de Sillesham (Sidlesham) in ecclesia Cicestrensi, taxata xxx li., de qua per obitum Edmundi de Arundell' fuit provisum Waltero Gest per Clementem xiiᵒ kalendas Decembris anno viiiᵒ,[406] pro resta pro qua Dominus Johannes de [407] Bissopeston' nunc prebendarius est obligatus xii li. ii s. ix d.[376]

De thesauraria Cicestrensi, cuius taxa et provisio supra in recepta, pro resta xvi li. xiii s. iiii d.[376]

(fol. 125ᵛ) De prebenda de Walton' in ecclesia collegiata de Bossham (Bosham), cuius taxa et provisio continentur supra in recepta, ix li. vi s. viii d.[376]

De archidiaconatu Levensi (Lewes), non [408] taxato, qui fuit confirmatus Willelmo de Lugthdeburgh' per Clementem iiᵒ idus Augusti anno xiᵒ,[409] medietas.[376]

---

[381] In the margin opposite this item is the note: *videatur in camera*.

[382] 8 October 1354.

[383] 22 January 1356.

[384] *et*, MS.

[385] Followed by *sue* deleted by a line.

[386] In the margin opposite this item is noted: *inutilis*.

[387] Followed by *xᵒ* deleted by a line.

[388] 21 May 1361.

[389] 22 May 1361. The year which is lacking in the manuscript is supplied from *Cal. Pap. Regs. Petitions*, i, 319.

[390] A house of Crutched Friars.

[391] 21 May 1362.

[392] Peter de la Forêt, priest of Ss. XII Apostoli.

[393] 18 November 1358. In the margin: *in arayragiis*.

[394] Followed by *de* deleted by a line.

[395] 5 May 1351.

[396] 27 September 1362.

[397] Followed by *v* deleted by a line.

[398] In the margin is noted *in recepta*.

[399] 28 June 1360.

[400] In the margin is noted: *pars in arayragiis*.

[401] 13 May 1358.

[402] In the margin is noted: *satisfecit camere*.

[403] Below, p. 162.

[404] In the margin opposite this item: *in arayragiis totum*.

[405] In the margin opposite this item: *solvit*.

[406] 20 November 1349.

[407] Followed by *Bis* deleted by a line.

[408] Followed by *taxatt* deleted by a line.

[409] 12 August 1352.

De prebenda de Sutton' in ecclesia Cicestrensi, taxata xxvi li. xiii s. iiii d., de qua per consecrationem Michaelis de Northburgh' in episcopum Londoniensem fuit provisum Michaeli de Northburgh', consanguineo suo, per Innocentium xv° kalendas Junii anno primo,[410] xxvi li. xiii s. iiii d.

De precentoria Cicestrensi, taxata liii li. vi s. viii d., de qua per obitum cardinalis de Mota [411] fuit provisum cardinali de Gordonio [412] per Innocentium viii° kalendas Novembris anno iiii°,[413] satisfactum est in curia ut est scriptum.[414]

De prebenda de Midelton' (Middleton) in ecclesia Cicestrensi, cuius taxa et provisio continentur supra in recepta, respondetur infra in fine arreyragiorum inter beneficia que fuerunt Henrici de Walton'.[376]

De vicaria de Hoe (Hooe), taxata iiii li. xiii s. iiii d., de qua Willelmo nato Roberti Hull' fuit provisum per cardinalem Petragoricensem,[415] pro resta xlvi s. viii d.

De ecclesia de Bukstede (Buxted), taxata xxxii li., de qua per assecutionem prepositure de Wyngham (Wingham) per Johannem de Beverle fuit provisum Waltero Seton' per Innocentium iii° kalendas Aprilis anno vi°,[416] xxxii li.[376]

De archidiaconatu Cicestrensi, non taxato, permutatio facta cum decanatu ecclesie collegiate Cestrie super stratam (Chester-le-Street) Dunelmensis diocesis fuit Johanni de Skwlthorp' confirmata per Innocentium v° kalendas Januarii anno vi°,[417] medietas.[376]

(fol. 126, xxxiii)[418] De prebenda de Waltham in ecclesia Cicestrensi, taxata x li., de qua per consecrationem Roberti episcopi Conventrensis et Lichfeldensis fuit provisum Ade de Hilton' per Innocentium x° kalendas Januarii anno viii°, x li.[419]

De prebenda de Colleword (Colworth) in ecclesia Cicestrensi, taxata xxvi li. xiii s. iiii d., de qua per obitum Ricardi Drax fuit provisum Johanni de Stretheleye per Innocentium vii° kalendas Junii anno ix°,[420] xxvi li. xiii s. iiii d.[421]

De prebenda de Ippethorn' (Upthorne) in ecclesia Cicestrensi, taxata vi li. xiii s. iiii d., de qua per obitum Thome David fuit provisum Philipo de Cortenay per

Innocentium x° kalendas Jullii anno ix°,[422] vi li. xiii s. iiii d.[421]

De prebenda de Thornhy (West Thorney) in ecclesia Cicestrensi, taxata x li., per obitum Johannis Thurstayn fuit provisum Willelmo de Cherchull' per Innocentium iii° idus Jullii anno ix°,[423] x li.

De percentoria et prebenda ecclesie Cicestrensis, taxatis liii li. vi s. viii d., de quibus per obitum cardinalis de Cordonio [412] fuit provisum cardinali Aquensi [424] per Innocentium vi° kalendas Octobris anno ix°,[425] liii li. vi s. viii d.[426]

De decanatu Cicestrensi, nondum per cameram misso, taxato cum prebenda sibi annexa liii li. vi s. viii d., de quo per consecrationem Domini Willelmi episcopi Cicestrensis fuit provisum Magistro Willelmo de Pothoowe per Innocentium anno primo,[427] liii li. vi s. viii d.[421]

Hic deficiunt tria beneficia que ponuntur infra folio lvi°.[403]

### Wyntoniensis

De ecclesia de Westmines (West Meon), taxata xx li., que fuit confirmata Johanni de Kynyngton' per Clementum idus Maii anno viii°,[428] pro resta vi li.[429]

(fol. 126ᵛ) De hospitali Sancte Crucis, non taxato, confirmato Johanni de Edyndon' per Clementem xviii° kalendas Junii anno viii°,[430] vii li. iii s. vi d.[421]

De ecclesia sive custodia domus Sancti Nicholay de Portesmouth' (Portsmouth), non taxata, confirmata Johanni de Edyndon' per Clementem v° kalendas Martii anno viii°,[431] x li.

De archidiaconatu Sureye, taxato iiiixx li, confirmato Johanni de Edyndon' per Clementem ii° idus Februarii anno xi°,[432] iiiixx li.

De ecclesia de Laverstok' (Laverstoke), taxata xiiii li., in qua et ad jus quod competebat Johanni Crom' fuit subrogatus Johannes de Bannebury per Clementem ii° idus Jullii anno x°,[433] pro resta iii li.[421]

De prebenda de Midelton' (Middleton) in ecclesia monialium de Warwell' (Wherwell), taxata xxvi li. xiii s. iiii d., de qua fuit provisum Johanni Brankerre per Innocentium v° kalendas Januarii anno primo,[434] xxvi li. xiii s. iiii d.[421]

---

[410] 18 May 1353.
[411] Gaillard de Mota, deacon of St. Lucy in Silice.
[412] William Farinier of Gourdon, priest of Ss. Marcellino e Pietro.
[413] 25 October 1356.
[414] In the margin opposite this item: *videatur*.
[415] Talleyrand de Périgueux, bishop of Albano.
[416] 30 March 1358.
[417] 28 December 1358.
[418] At the beginning of the folio is the following item canceled by lines: *De ecclesia de Wp'ndon'* (Up Marden), *taxata xii li. vi s. viii d., de qua per obitum Willelmi Habret' fuit provisum Willelmo de Chestreton' per Innocentium iiii° nonas Septembris anno v°* (2 September 1357) *xii li. vi s. viii d.*
[419] 23 December 1360.
[420] 26 May 1361.
[421] In the margin opposite this item: *in arayragiis*.

[422] 22 June 1361.
[423] 13 July 1361.
[424] Peter Itherii of Périgueux, bishop of Dax, priest of Ss. Quattro Coronati.
[425] 26 September 1361.
[426] In the margin opposite this item: *videatur camera, si sit satisfactum*.
[427] 1353.
[428] 15 May 1350.
[429] Followed by *iii s. vi d.* deleted by a line. In the margin opposite this item is the note: *in arayragiis*.
[430] 15 May 1350.
[431] 25 February 1350.
[432] 12 February 1352. It should be anno x: *Cal. Pap. Regs. Petitions*, i, 225.
[433] 14 July 1352.
[434] 28 December 1353.

De prioratu de Appellorccomb (Appuldurcombe), taxato xxx li. xvii s., confirmato Johanni Ozanna per Clementem v° kalendas Martii anno viii°,[431] xxx li. xvii s.[435]

De vicaria ecclesia de Shalfford (Shalford), taxata x li. xiii s. iiii d., de qua ex causa permutationis cum vicaria de Bampton' fuit provisum Roberto de Hepp' per Innocentium xi° kalendas Decembris anno v°,[436] x li. xiii s. iiii d.[437]

De ecclesia de Waltham, taxata xx li., de qua per obitum Guilberti David fuit provisum Hugoni de Crastr' per Innocentium iiii° nonas Jullii anno ix°,[438] xx li.[435]

De vicaria ecclesie Omnium Sanctorum de Skynggeston' (Kingston on Thames), taxata v li. vi s. viii d., de qua ex causa permutationis cum vicaria de Pottern' (Potterne) fuit provisum Johanni Doyle per Innocentium viii° kalendas Octobris anno ix°,[439] v li. vi s. viii d.

De ecclesia de Chayham (Cheam), cuius taxa et provisio supra in recepta, pro resta iiii li.[421]

(fol. 127, xxiiii) De ecclesia de Havante (Havant), taxata xxvi li. xiii s. iiii d., de qua per obitum Johannis Noion fuit provisum Johanni Uppehulle per Innocentium iiii° nonas Jullii anno ix°,[440] xxvi li. xiii s. iiii d.[435]

### Sarresbiriensis

De ecclesia de Kyveleye (Keevil), cuius taxa et provisio supra in recepta, pro resta vi li. xiii s. iiii d.[426]

De prebenda de Wermynstr' (Warminster) in ecclesia Saresbiriensi, taxata v li., de qua per obitum Johannis de Aberebury fuit provisum Thome de Stranghall' per Clementem, v li[421]

De prebenda de Dynynstr' (Yetminster), de qua per promotionem Johannis de Wfford fuit provisum Henrico de Walton', ponitur in fine arreyragiorum.[421]

De prebenda in ecclesia Saresbiriensi vocata de Netherburyn (Netherbury), de qua per obitum Thome de Asteleye fuit provisum Reginaldo de [441] Bryan per Clementem nonas Maii anno viii°.[442]

De prebenda de Norwynton' (North Newnton) in ecclesia monialium de Wylton' (Wilton), taxata xiii li. vi s. viii d., que fuit confirmata Johanni de Vienna xiii° kalendas Junii per Clementem anno viii°,[443] et dimissa in resta in viii li., et infra ratione collationis facte Willelmo de Medburin' per obitum dicti Johannis est etiam dimissa in solidis fructibus, non debuit esse, quia dicte confirmatio et provisio fuerunt infra annum, et de dictis viii li. vi s. viii d. respondetur supra in recepta.

De prebenda de Nothersuny (Netherbury) in ecclesia Saresbiriensi, de qua per obitum Thome de Laco fuit confirmata Reginaldo Bryan per Clementem xvi° kalendas Septembris anno viii°,[444] taxata lx li., lx li.[445] Executio debet fieri contra executorem dicti Reginaldi quondam episcopi Wygoriensis et non contra Hugonem Pelegrini prebendarium.

De prebenda de Cheresenburn' (Chisenbury) in ecclesia Saresbiriensi, taxata xx li., de qua per obitum Roberti de Horton' fuit provisum Thome de Edyndon' per Clementem kalendas Februarii anno viii°,[446] xx li.

(fol. 127ᵛ) De prebenda de Byssopeston' (Bishopstone) in ecclesia Saresbiriensi, taxata xx li., de qua per obitum Petri Raymundi de Rapistangno fuit provisum [447] Raymundo Pelegrini per Clementem kalendas Februarii anno viii°,[446] non debuisset fuisse dimissa quia non habuit effectum, eo quod rex contulit Willelmo de Okeburun' qui possidet.[448]

De ecclesia de Scorcumbe (Corscombe), taxata xi li., que fuit confirmata Johanni Brokelond viii° idus Junii per Clementem anno ix°,[449] xi li.[450]

De prebenda de Wermynstr' (Warminster) in ecclesia Saresbiriensi, taxata v li., de qua per obitum Baldewyni de Moyn acceptatio facta per Bartholomeum de Bronden' fuit sibi confirmata per Clementem v° idus Septembris anno ix°,[451] v li.[421]

De prebenda de Hull' (Hill Deverill) in ecclesia collegiata de Hertelbury (Heytesbury), taxata vi li. xiii s. iiii d., de qua per obitum Roberti Trek' fuit provisum Thome Patricii per Clementem viii° idus Maii anno ix°,[452] pro resta in iii li. vi s. viii d., iii li. vi s. viii d.[453]

De prebenda de Norowynton' (North Newnton), xiii li. vi s. viii d., de qua per obitum Johannis de Vyenna fuit confirmata Willelmo Richardi de Wyllyngton', et ante fuit provisum de eadem Willelmo de Melbburn' per Clementem nonas Maii anno ix°; [454] iste Johannes evicit istam prebendam a dicto Willelmo Ricardi et ista collatio et confirmatio in principio istius folii ex alia parte sunt infra annum, ideo non debentur fructus nisi pro una annata, de qua respondetur ut supra in dicto principio folii.[455]

De ecclesia de Wyntreburen' Fekelen' (Winterborne

---

[435] In the margin opposite this item: *pars in arayragiis.*

[436] 21 November 1357.

[437] In the margin opposite this item: *non habuit effectum.*

[438] 4 July 1361.

[439] 24 September 1361.

[440] 4 July 1361.

[441] *et*, MS.

[442] 7 May 1350.

[443] 20 May 1349.

[444] 17 August 1349.

[445] Opposite this sentence in the margin is the note: *doce proximo.*

[446] 1 February 1350.

[447] *provisum* repeated in MS.

[448] In the margin opposite this item: *in arayragiis; non habuit effectum.*

[449] 6 June 1350.

[450] In the margin opposite this item: *inutilis est.*

[451] 9 September 1350.

[452] 8 May 1351.

[453] In the margin opposite this item: *in arayragiis.*

[454] 7 May 1351.

[455] In the margin opposite this item: *non debet quia infra annum.*

Stickland), taxata iiii li. vi s. viii d., de qua per resignationem Willelmi de Cheston' fuit provisum Thome Henrico per Innocentium xiiii° kalendas Jullii anno primo,[456] iiii li. vi s. viii d.[453]

(fol. 128, xxxv) De prebenda de Streton' (Stratton) in ecclesia Saresbiriensi, taxata xiii li. vi s. viii d., de qua [457] ex causa permutationis fuit provisum Johanni Thurstayn per Innocentium idus Martii anno iii°,[458] xiii li. vi s. viii d.

De archidiaconatu Dorcestr' in ecclesia Saresbiriensi, taxato lxiii li., de quo per obitum cardinalis Albiensis (Albi)[459] fuit provisum cardinali Autisidiorensi (Auxerre)[460] per Innocentium iii° idus Februarii anno iii°,[461] lxiii li.[462]

De subdecanatu Saresbiriensi cum prebenda annexa, taxato iiii li. vi s. viii d., collatio cuius facta Radulpho de Querendon' fuit sibi confirmata per Innocentium ii° kalendas Februarii anno iiii°,[463] iiii li. vi s. viii d.

De prioratu de Ledres (Loders), taxato xxvi li., provisio cuius facta Symoni de Clouda fuit sibi confirmata per Innocentium ii° kalendas Februarii anno tertio,[464] xxvi li.

De prebenda vocata Ratfen (Rotefen) in ecclesia Saresbiriensi, cuius taxa et provisio supra in recepta, pro resta iii li. vi s. viii d.

De prebenda de Hussoheburn'et Borbach' (Husseburn and Burbage), taxata liii li. vi s. viii d., de qua vacante per obitum Johannis de Wythcherch' acceptatio facta per Saladinum de Fallet' fuit eidem confirmata per Innocentium kalendas Junii anno vi°,[465] liii li. vi s. viii d.[453]

De prebenda de Bedmynstr'[466] (Bedminster) in ecclesia Saresbiriensi, taxata xiii li. vi s. viii d., de qua per resignationem Willelmi Hale fuit provisum Thome de Clypston' per Innocentum idus Decembris anno vi°,[467] xiii li. vi s. viii d.[453]

De vicaria de [468] Portan' (Potterne), taxata xx li., de qua vicario eiusdem fuit per cardinalem Urgellensem de novo provisum, pro resta xl s.[453]

(fol. 128ᵛ) De vicaria de Gillyngham (Gillingham), taxata vi li. xiii s. iiii d., de qua Willelmo Thomer cardinalis Petragoricensis de novo providit, pro resta liii s. iiii d.

De prebenda Saresbiriensi acceptatio cuius facta per Johannem de Wfford Norowycensis diocesis fuit eidem confirmata per Innocentium vii° kalendas Jullii anno vii°;[469] iste Johanes nunquam habuit prebendam in dicta ecclesia nec cognoscitur ibidem.[470]

De prebenda de Calme (Calne) et thesauraria in ecclesia Saresbiriensi, de quibus per obitum Cardinalis de Florentia [471] fuit provisum cardinali Nemausenensi [472] per Innocentium xiii° kalendas Octobris anno ix°,[473] taxata iiiixx vi li. xiii s. iiii d., iiiixx vi li. xiii s. iiii d.[453]

De ecclesia Sancti Petri de Wartham (Warham), taxata iiii li. vi s. viii d., de qua per resignationem Thome de Berneby fuit provisum Henrico Worth' per Innocentium v° idus Octobris anno ix°,[474] iiii li. vi s. viii d.[453]

De prebenda de Netterbury (Netherbury) in ecclesia Saresbiriensi, taxata xiii li. vi s. viii d., de qua Johanni de Blibury fuit confirmata ex causa permutationis facta cum Roberto de Bourton' per Innocentium ix° kalendas Junii anno vi°,[475] xiii li. vi s. viii d.

De ecclesia de Assehebury (Ashbury), taxata xxvi li. xiii s. iiii d., de qua per obitum Walteri Moryn fuit provisum Thome de Bisshopesbury per Innocentium iiii° kalendas Octobris anno ix°,[476] xxvi li. xiii s. iiii d.[477]

De vicaria ecclesie Sancte Marie de Potern' (Potterne), taxata xx li., de qua ex causa permutationis cum Johanne Dayle pro vicaria ecclesie Omnium Sanctorum de Kynggeston' (Kingston on Thames) Wyntoniensis diocesis fuit provisum Thome West per Innocentium viii° kalendas Octobris anno ix°,[478] xx li.[477]

(fol. 129 xxxvi) De cancellaria ecclesie Saresbiriensis, taxata iiiixx viii li., de qua per consecrationem Symonis episcopi Londoniensis fuit provisum Johanni de Norton' per Innocentium xvii° kalendas Decembris anno ix°;[479] de ista cancellaria et prebenda de Huce (Hove) in ecclesia Cicestrensi respondetur simul supra in fine recepte et etiam infra in fine arreyragiis.[453]

De ecclesia de Corff (Corfe Castle), taxata x li., de qua per assecutionem precentorie Saresbiriensis factam per Philipum de Cotfford fuit provisum Symoni Thebaut per Innocentium iii° kalendas Novembris anno ix°,[480] x li.[470]

De prebenda de Remynstr' (Bedminster)[481] in ecclesia Saresbiriensi, taxata xiii li. vi s. viii d., de qua per obitum Ricardi de Norowyco fuit confirmatio facta

---

456 18 June 1353.

457 Followed by *per resignationem* deleted by a line.

458 15 March 1355.

459 Bernard d'Albi, bishop of Porto.

460 Peter de Croso, priest of Ss. Silvestro e Martino ai Monti.

461 11 February 1355.

462 In the margin opposite this item: *scriptum est quod non fiat executio.*

463 31 January 1356.

464 31 January 1355.

465 1 June 1358.

466 In John de Cabrespino's report the prebend is said to be located outside the diocese of Salisbury: below, p. 190.

467 13 December 1358.

468 Followed by *Portenrn' Portra* deleted by a line.

469 25 June 1359.

470 In the margin opposite this item: *non habuit possessionem.*

471 Francis de Aptis, priest of S. Marco.

472 John de Blanzac, priest of S. Marco, bishop of Nimes.

473 19 September 1361.

474 11 October 1361.

475 24 May 1358.

476 28 September 1361.

477 In the margin opposite this item: *pars in arayragiis.*

478 24 September 1361.

479 15 November 1361.

480 30 October 1361.

481 See above on this page and *Cal. Pap. Regs. Petitions*, i, 413.

Henrico de Wynton' per Innocentium xi° kalendas Februarii anno decimo,[482] xiii li. vi s. viii d.[453]

De prebenda de Wedefford (Woodford), taxata xvi
li. xiii s. iiii d., ac archidiaconatu Dorcestrie in ecclesia
Saresbiriensi, taxato lxii li., de quibus per obitum cardinalis Autisidorensis (Auxerre)[483] fuit provisum cardinali de Canilhaco episcopo Penestrino[484] per Innocentium iiii° idus Martii anno x°,[485] lxxix li. xiii s.
iiii d.[453]

De prebenda de Ratffen' (Rotefen) in ecclesia Saresbiriensi, cuius taxa et provisio supra in recepta, pro
resta iii li. vi s. viii d.[486]

Hic deficit unum benefficium et ponitur infra folio lvi°.

### Exoniensis

De[487] thesauraria ecclesie Exoniensis, taxata xx li.,
acceptatio[488] cuius per Robertum de Mildelond fuit
eidem confirmata per Clementem xv° kalendas Junii
anno vii°,[489] xx li.[490]

De archidiaconatu Barnastapoll', non taxato, qui fuit
confirmatus Johanni de Reynham per Clementem vi°
nonas Aprilis anno viii°,[491] xiii li. vi s. viii d.[492]

De archidiaconatu Barnastapoll' in ecclesia Exoniensi,
non taxato, qui composuit ad xx m., de quo ex causa
permutationis fuit provisum Willelmo Mugge per Innocentium iiii° nonas Septembris anno vi°,[493] pro resta vi
li. xiii s. iiii d.[492]

(fol. 129ᵛ) De decanatu Exoniensi, cuius taxa et
provisio supra in recepta, pro resta xxxii li. xiii s.
iiii d.[490]

De prebenda Exoniensi, taxata iiii li., de qua per
obitum Henrici de Brathele fuit provisum Henrico de
Walton' per Innocentium iiii° kalendas Martii anno
primo,[494] iiii li.[490]

De prebenda Exoniensi, taxata iiii li., que fuit confirmata Henrico Pik per Innocentium kalendas Junii
anno vi°,[495] pro resta xl s.

De vicaria de[496] Yalmston' (Yealmpton), non
taxata, in qua et ad ius quod competebat Johanni[497] de
Conuwbe fuit subrogatus Robertus Gervasii per Innocentium ii° idus Octobris anno ii°.[498]

De prebenda Exoniensi, taxata iiii li., que fuit confirmata Thome David per Clementem viii° idus Maii
anno x°,[499] iiii li.[490]

De prioratu de Hotrenton' (Otterton), taxato iiiixx
vi li. xiii s. iiii d., qui fuit confirmatus Thome Sedile per
Innocentium ii° kalendas Februarii anno iii°,[500] pro resta
xxxi li. xiii s. iiii d.

⟨Qu⟩od[501] hic deficit de ⟨dic⟩ta[501] dyocesi require
infra folio lv°. ⟨Unum⟩ debet hic poni et alia duo benefficia que defficiunt require folio lvi°.

### Wygoriensis

De ecclesia de Estelegh' (Astley), taxata xi li. vi s.
viii d., de qua per obitum Henrici de Stowe fuit provisum Henrico de Askeby et etiam subrogatus in iure
quod dicto Henrico competebat, qui super hoc litigans
in curia decessit tempore Domini Clementis, pro resta
viii li. Sed ista non habuit effectum quia Thomas
Leghe, rector dicte ecclesie, exhibuit vi° die Jullii anno
LIX° sententiam diffinitivam pro Johanne Gogke de
Burlyngham contra dictum Henricum de Stowe et etiam
contra Henricum de Askeby per quam constitit quod
idem Henricus nullum ius habuit et per consequens
provisio nulla.[502]

(fol. 130, xxxvii) De ecclesia Sanctorum Philipi et
Jacobi Brystoll', non taxata, de qua[503] fuit per obitum
Roberti Reve provisum Nicholao[504] de Dyngton' per
Clementem; ista ecclesia non sufficit pro victu simplicis
capellani, ymo rector est quasi mendicans, pro medietate
xx s.[490]

De ecclesia de Kynthwich' (Knightwick), taxata iiii
li. vi s. viii d., de qua ex causa permutationis fuit provisum Johanni de Charneux per Innocentium anno
primo, pro resta xxxiii s. iiii d.[490]

De hospitali Sancti Wlstani Wygornie, non taxato,
de quo per resignationem Petri Francici fuit provisum
Johanni de Hareswell', canonico Sancti Martini Londonie, per Innocentium v° kalendas Jullii anno v°,[505]
medietas.[490]

De ecclesia de Clyve Episcopi (Bishop's Cleeve),
taxata xl li., acceptatio et provisio facte Ricardo de
Drayton' fuerunt eidem confirmate per Innocentium vii°
kalendas Jullii anno ix°,[506] xl li.[490]

### Bathoniensis et Wellensis

De prebenda de Harpetre (East Harptree) in ecclesia
Wellensi, de qua consecrationem Ludovici episcopi

---

[482] 22 January 1362.
[483] Peter de Croso, priest of Ss. Silvestro e Martino ai Monti.
[484] Raymond de Canillac, bishop of Palestrina.
[485] 12 March 1362.
[486] In the margin opposite this item: *superius est eadem.*
[487] Followed by *prebenda* deleted by a line.
[488] *taxatio*, MS.
[489] 18 May 1349.
[490] In the margin opposite this item: *in arayragiis.*
[491] 8 April 1350. It should be 6 ides: *Cal. Pap. Regs. Peti-tions*, i, 195.
[492] In the margin: *pars in arayragiis.*
[493] 2 September 1358.
[494] 26 February 1355.
[495] 1 June 1358.
[496] Followed by *Yl* deleted by a line.
[497] *Jolp'*, MS.
[498] 14 October 1354.

[499] 8 May 1352.
[500] 31 January 1355.
[501] These letters, supplied above conjecturally, have been lost by trimming the margin too close.
[502] In the margin: *non habuit effectum.*
[503] Followed by *per* deleted by a line.
[504] *Nicholau*, MS.
[505] 27 June 1357.
[506] 25 June 1361.

Dunelmensis fuit ⟨provisum⟩ Henrico de Hacweden' per Clementem et dimissa per Dominum Raymundum Pelegrini, pro resta iiii li.

De prebenda de Wyvelescumbe (Wiveliscombe), taxata xxvi li. xiii s. iiii d., de qua per obitum Johannis de Ufford et etiam in vita sua cum vacaret per consecrationem suam in archiepiscopum Cantuariensem fuit provisum Willelmo de Bergmemey per Clementem, pro resta xiii li. vi s. viii d.[490]

De cancellaria ecclesie Wellensis ac prebenda de Cdumpton (Compton Dundon) eidem annexa, taxata xlvi li. xiii s. iiii d., de qua per assecutionem decanatus Wellensis per Johannem de Carleton' fuit provisum Johanni de Hostyngton' per Clementem kalendas Junii anno viii[o],[507] pro resta xiiii li. xii s.[490]

(fol. 130[v]) De thesauraria Wellensi, taxata xxxiii li. vi s. viii d., que fuit Ricardo de Thormenton' confirmata per Clementem, idus Novembris anno xi[o],[508] pro resta xx li.[490]

De [509] prebenda de Wychurche (Whitchurch) in ecclesia Wellensi, taxata viii li., de qua per obitum Roberti de Luffenham, acceptatio facta per Ricardum de Thormenton' fuit eidem confirmata per Innocentium iii[o] kalendas Februarii anno ii[o],[510] que quidem prebenda per dictum obitum fuit collata Thome de Edyndon' per Clementem v[o] kalendas Maii anno ix[o],[511] et iste obtinet qui evicit eam a dicto Roberto, viii li.

De prioratu Montis Acuti (Montacute), taxato cxxxiii li. vi s. viii d., provissio cuius supra in recepta, pro resta lxxv li.

De vicaria Sancti Cuthberti Wellensis, taxata vi li. xiii s. iiii d., acceptatio cuius fuit Roberto Stax confirmata per Innocentium vi[o] kalendas Junii anno vii[o],[512] vi li. xiii s. iiii d.[490]

De succentoria eccelsie Wellensis, taxata v li. vi s. viii d., collatio ordinaria facta Willelmo de Cokham fuit eidem confirmata per Innocentium xi[o] kalendas Maii anno v[o],[513] v li. vi s. viii d.

De prepositura Wellensi, taxata xl li., de qua per obitum Andree de Wfford fuit provisum ⟨Ade⟩ de Hiliton' per Innocentium iii[o] nonas Februarii anno vii[o],[514] xl li.[490]

De prebenda de Holcumbe (Holcombe) in ecclesia Wellensi, taxata xxvi li. xiii s. iiii d., de qua vacante aut cum vacabit per assecutionem canonicatus et prebende per Thomam de Barton' fuit provisum Waltero Moryn per Innocentium xix[o] kalendas Septembris anno viii[o],[515] xxvi li. xiii s. iiii d.[490]

(fol. 131, xxxviii) De prebenda ac archidiaconatu Wellensibus, taxatis lxvi li. xiii s. iiii d., de quibus per obitum Domini Willelmi episcopi Tusculani cardinalis fuit provisum [516] cardinali Carcassonensi [517] per Innocentium vii[o] kalendas Octobris anno ix[o],[518] lxvi li. xiii s. iiii d.[490]

De prebenda de Honggsteyg' (Henstridge) in ecclesia Wellensi, taxata xvi li. xiii s. iiii d., de qua per resignationem Symonis Thebaut fuit provisum Johanni Thebaut per Innocentium ix[o] kalendas Januarii anno ix[o],[519] xvi li. xiii s. iiii d.[490]

De prepositura Wellensi, taxata xl li., de qua per obitum Ade de Hylton' fuit provisum Willelmo de Wytham per Innocentium nonas Januarii anno x,[520] xl li.[490]

De prebenda Bursali in ecclesia Wellensi, taxata v li. vi s. viii d., de qua per obitum Johannis Thurstayn fuit provisum Johanni Corf' ⟨per⟩ Innocentium v[o] nonas Maii anno x[o],[521] v li. vi s. viii d.[490]

Hic deficit unum benefficium et ponitur infra folio lvi[o].

## Hereffordensis

De prebenda de Morton' (Moreton Magna) in ecclesia Hereffordensi, taxata xx li., de qua per obitum Thome de Stauntton' fuit provisum Symoni de Sudbury per Clementem iiii[o] nonas Jullii anno vii[o], vel viii[o],[522] pro resta xiii s. iiii d.[490]

De portione prebendali de Ledbury et aliis beneficiis, de quibus fuit [523] provisum [524] Nicholao [525] Heth' respondetur supra in fine recepte quia composuit cum camera ut ibi.[490]

De prebenda de Ethyngton' (Ewithington) in ecclesia Hereffordensi, cuius taxa et provisio supra in recepta, pro resta viii li.

De prebenda de Prato, non taxata, de qua per obitum Willemi de Fowohop fuit confirmata Baudowyno de Wytteneye per Innocentium vii[o] kalendas Junii anno iiii[o]; [526] ista prebenda consistit dumtaxat in una trossa feni, trossa feni.

Hic deficiunt tria benefficia que ponuntur infra folio lvi[o].

## (fol. 131[v]) Norwycensis

De prioratu de Castellacr' (Castle Acre), de quo ex causa [526a] fuit provisum de novo Willelmo de Waren' per Clementem anno antequam dictus Hugo esset nuntius, debentur iiii[c] iiii[xx] li. xix s. vii d.[490]

[507] 1 June 1349.
[508] 13 November 1352.
[509] Followed by *ecclesia* deleted by a line.
[510] 30 January 1354.
[511] 27 April 1351.
[512] 27 May 1359.
[513] 21 April 1357.
[514] 3 February 1359.
[515] 14 August 1360.

[516] *provisum* repeated in MS.
[517] Stephen Aubert, bishop of Carcassonne, deacon of S. Maria in Aquiro.
[518] 25 September 1361.
[519] 24 December 1361.
[520] 5 January 1362.
[521] 3 May 1362.
[522] 4 July 1349: *Cal. Pap. Regs. Petitions*, i, 169.
[523] *de quibus fuit* repeated in MS.
[524] Followed by *Symoni de Sudbury per Clementem* deleted by a line.
[525] *Nicholau*, MS.
[526] 26 May 1356.
[526a] *permutationis* is lacking, MS.

De ecclesia de Herdwyk' (Hardwick), taxata v li. vi s. viii d., de qua fuit provisum Radulpho de Suttholst' per Clementem, pro resta liii s. iiii d.

De ecclesia de Ulmo (Holme), taxata xl li., de qua per resignationem Villelmi de Merton' fuit provisum Thome Michel' per Clementem antequam dictus Hugo esset nuntius, pro resta x li.[490]

De prioratu Sancte Fidis de Horsham, cuius taxa et provisio supra in recepta folio,[527] pro resta clvii li. vi s. viii d.[528]

De ecclesia de Derham (East Dereham), taxata lxxiii li. vi s. viii d., de qua per obitum Alani de Hotvin fuit provisum Symoni Thebaud, nunc episcopo Londoniensi, per Clementem iiiº kalendas Aprilis anno xº,[529] pro resta xl li. xvi s. viii d.[490]

De precentoria Wellensi cum prebenda sibi annexa et ecclesia de Gevele (Yeovil), taxatis ut in libro taxe apparet xlv li. xiii s. iiii d., de quibus fuit provisum Edwardo Gourney, et de residuo respondetur tam in compoto Domini Hugonis quam Domini Raymundi, xx li. vi s. viii d.[490]

De medietate ecclesie de Westwalton' (West Walton), taxata xii li., collatio cuius facta per ordinarium Jacobo de Heraygtoft' fuit eidem confirmata per Innocentium iiº [530] nonas Septembris anno ixº,[531] xii li.[532]

De ecclesia de Weston', taxata xxvi li. xiii s. iiii d., provisio cuius continetur supra in recepta, pro resta xiiii li.[533]

De ecclesia de Estbylneye (East Bilney), taxata iiii li. vi s. viii d., que fuit Thome de Walton' confirmata per Innocentium viº kalendas Jullii anno sexto,[534] iiii li. vi s. viii d.[533]

(fol. 132, xxxix) De ecclesia de Lacfford (Lackford) taxata xx li., de qua per dimissum Ricardi de Walkeleyn' fuit provisum Johanni de Stokeny per Innocentium iiiiº idus Octobris anno viiiº,[535] xx li.[528]

De decanatu rurali Linie (Lynn), non taxato, de quo ex causa permutationis fuit provisum Ade Thebaud per Innocentium xviiº kalendas Septembris anno viiiº,[536] medietas.[533]

De ecclesia de Wadnorton' (Wood Norton), de qua Johanni de Elford cardinalis Petragoricensis de novo providit, taxata iiii li., pro resta xl s.[533]

De decanatu de Hunlyard (Humbleyard), non taxato, de quo per resignationem Walteri de Kakton' fuit pro-

visum Symoni de Sudbur' per Innocentium iiiº kalendas Jullii anno vº,[537] medietas.[533]

De archidiaconatu Sudburie in ecclesia Norwycensi non plus scribitur in literis missis per cameram.[538]

De ecclesia de magna Cressyngham (Great Cressyngham), taxata xiiii li., provisio auctoritate ordinaria facta Johanni de Stolle fuit eidem confirmata per Innocentium ixº kalendas Januarii anno ixº,[539] xiiii li.

De ecclesia de Macham (Marsham), taxata xvi li. xiii s. iiii d., de qua per assecutionem cancellarie Saresbiriensis per Johannem de Norton fuit provisum Ricardo Amcotes per Innocentium iiº nonas Junii anno xº,[540] xvi li. xiii s. iiii d.[528]

De ecclesia Sancti Georgii de Sudbur', non taxata, de qua per assecutionem cancellariatus in ecclesia Londoniensi fuit provisum Thome de Baketon' per Innocentium iiiiº idus Martii anno xº,[541] medietas.[533]

De ecclesia de Chemonton' (Chevington), taxata xvi li. xiii s. iiii d., que fuit Hugoni de Nepol confirmata per Innocentium xiº kalendas Februarii anno x,[542] xvi li. xiii s. iiii d.[533]

De archidiaconatu Sudburie, non taxato, vacante per obitum Henrici la Souch' in Romana curia defuncti, fuit provisum Johanni de Humbleton' per Innocentium iiiº nonas Martii anno xº.[543]

Hic deficit unum beneficium et ponitur infra folio lviiº.

## (fol. 132ᵛ) Elyensis

De prioratu de Suaveseye (Swavesey), de quo fuit provisum Stephano Brand per Clementem antequam dictus Hugo esset nuntius, pro resta iiii li.[533]

De ecclesia de Overe (Over), cuius taxa et provisio supra in recepta, xiiii li. xiii s. iiii d.[528]

De dicta ecclesia, de qua per obitum dicti Thome de Clipston' fuit provisum Rogero de Stamfford per Innocentium iiiº idus Augusti anno ixº,[544] xxxv li. vi s. viii d.[528]

## Lincolniensis

De prioratu de Cogges, cuius provisio seu confirmatio supra in recepta, pro resta v li. vi s. viii d.[533]

De ecclesia de Humbeyston' (Humberstone), taxata xvi li. vi s. viii d., appropriata monasterio Beate Marie [545] Leycestr' per Clementem ixº kalendas Martii anno xº,[546] xvi li. vi s. viii d.

De decanatu Lincolniensi, cuius taxa et provisio supra in recepta, pro resta lviiii li. vi s. viii d.[533]

De ecclesia de Keteringi (Kettering), que fuit con-

---

[527] A space is left blank for the number.
[528] In the margin: *pars in arayragiis*.
[529] 30 March 1352.
[530] Followed by *kalendas* deleted by a line.
[531] 4 September 1361.
[532] In the margin: *non habuit effectum*.
[533] In the margin: *in arayragiis*.
[534] 26 June 1358.
[535] 12 October 1360.
[536] 16 August 1360. *viiiº* is followed by *medietas* deleted by a line.

[537] 29 June 1357.
[538] In the margin: *infra ponitur*.
[539] 24 December 1361.
[540] 4 June 1362.
[541] 12 March 1362 (St. Gregory's church).
[542] 22 January 1362.
[543] 5 March 1362. In the margin: *in arayragiis*.
[544] 11 August 1361.
[545] Followed by *Lest* deleted by a line.
[546] 22 February 1352.

firmata Johanni Wade pro fructibus cuius satisfecit et est responsum ratione istius confirmationis, sed pro fructibus male perceptis debet dari in subsidium contra Turcos ii° fl.

De prebenda de Redfford maiori (Bedford Maior) in ecclesia Lincolniensi, taxata viii li., que fuit Willelmo Wyntreleseye, nunc episcopo [547] Roffensi, confirmata per Clementem viii° idus Maii anno vii° vel viii°,[548] quia simul missi, viii li.[533]

(fol. 133, xl) De archidiaconatu Bukynghamye in ecclesia Lincolniensi, non taxato, de quo vacante per obitum cardinalis Anibaldi [549] fuit provisum Johanni de Assecheburn' per Clementem idus Novembris anno ix°,[550] medietas.[533]

De subdecanatu Lincolniensi, cuius taxa et provisio supra in recepta, pro resta x li.

De prebenda de Walton Rivaus (Welton Rivall) in ecclesia Lincolniensi, taxata xxxiii li. vi s. viii d. de qua per obitum Johannis de Acton' acceptatio per Johannem Lamberti fuit eidem confirmata per Clementem iiii° idus Maii anno ix°,[551] et subsequenter ex causa permutationis facte cum isto Johanne fuit provisum Ricardo de Daventre per Innocentium vii° kalendas Maii anno v°,[552] et sic duplices fructus, pro resta [553] xxxvii li. viii s. ii d. Pro quibus dictus Willelmus de Navesby, canonicus Londoniensis et etiam Lincolniensis est obligatus in libro folio,[554] et residuo respondetur in recepta Magistri Ramundi folio xx.

De prebenda de Suthscarle (South Scarle), cuius taxa et provisio supra in recepta, pro resta xii li. ii s. xi d.[533]

De medietate ecclesie de Seggbrok' (Sedgebrook), taxata xii li. vi s. viii d., de qua per obitum ultimi rectoris fuit provisum Roberto de Seggebrok' per Clementem xi° kalendas Augusti anno decimo,[555] pro resta liii s. iiii d.[533]

(fol. 133ᵛ) De ecclesia de Trefford (Greatford), taxata xiiii li. xiii s. iiii d., que unita ⟨fuit⟩ monasterio Beate Marie Wyntonie per Clementem iii° idus Jullii anno xi°,[556] xiiii li. xiii s. iiii d.[533]

De prebenda de Clifton' in ecclesia Lincolniensi, taxata xx li., acceptatio cuius facta per Stephanum de Ravensheye fuit eidem confirmata per Clementem vi° kalendas Augusti anno xi°,[557] xx li.[533]

De ecclesia de Meleheburn' (Melchbourne), taxata v li. vi s. viii d., de qua per obitum Bartholomey de Dray-

ton' fuit provisum Radulpho de Ulnhale per Innocentium vi° kalendas Februarii anno ii°,[558] v li. vi s. viii d.[559]

De prebenda de Carleton' Thurkely (Carleton le Moorland cum Thurlby), cuius taxa xxvi li. xiii s. iiii d., ⟨de qua⟩ per consecrationem Nicholay episcopi Wrgellensis (Urgel) fuit provisum Roberto de Wyngeworth' per Innocentium ix° kalendas Maii anno primo,[560] pro resta xvi li. xiii s. iiii d.[533]

De ecclesia de Dynggeley (Dingley), cuius taxa et provisio supra in recepta, pro resta liii s. iiii d.[533]

De ecclesia de Luthghteburgh' (Ludborough), taxata xxvi li. xiii s. iiii d., cuius provisio supra in recepta vii li.

De vicaria de Therluby (Thurlby), cuius taxa et provisio supra in recepta, pro resta v li.[533]

De prebenda Sancte Crucis (Spaldwick) in ecclesia Lincolniensi, cuius taxa et provisio supra in recepta, pro resta v li.[561]

(fol. 134, xli) De prebenda de Carleton cum Thurleby in ecclesia Lincolniensi, taxata xxvi li. xiii s. iiii d., de qua per resignationem Willemi de Walcote fuit provisum Edwardo de Scherdestoke per Innocentium kalendas Martii anno vito,[562] xxvi li. xiii s. iiii d.[533]

De prebenda de Scarle (South Scarle) in ecclesia Lincolniensi, taxata xl li., de qua per resignationem Willelmi de Kyrkeby fuit provisum Johanni de Appely per Innocentium iii° idus Jullii anno vito,[563] xl li.[533]

Le ecclesia de Cosynton' (Cossington), taxata vi li. xiii s. iiii d., que Johanni de Melburn' fuit confirmata per Innocentium vii° kalendas Jullii anno vii°,[564] vi li. xiii s. iiii d.[533]

De ecclesia de Hogthon' (Houghton Regis), taxata xvi li. xiii s. iiii d., de qua presentatio et institutio facte per diocesanum fuerunt Hugoni Sparkyng' confirmate per Innocentium ix° kalendas Septembris anno vii° vel viii°,[565] quia simul missi, xvi li. xiii s. iiii d.[533]

De ecclesia de Eydon', taxata iiii li. xiii s. iiii d., de qua per resignationem Walteri de Heynoworth' fuit provisum Roberto de Deyworth' per Innocentium ii° idus Decembris anno viii°,[566] iiii li. xiii s. iiii d.[533]

De ecclesia de Hagworlyngham (Hagworthingham), taxa cuius et provisio supra in recepta, pro resta ix li.[561]

De prebenda de Norton' (Bishop Norton), taxata xxxiii li. vi s. viii d., et archidiaconatu Lincolniensi, non taxato, de quibus per obitum Thome de Northwod fuit provisum Hugoni Abbati per Innocentium vii° idus Maii anno primo,[567] et xii° kalendas Martii proximo

[547] episcopus, MS.
[548] 8 May 1350; Cal. Pap. Rtgs. Petitions, i, 196.
[549] Anibaludus de Ceccano, bishop of Tusculum.
[550] 13 November 1350.
[551] 12 May 1351.
[552] 25 April 1357.
[553] Followed by xxxvii li. viii s. ii d. deleted by a line.
[554] A blank space is left for the number in the manuscript.
[555] 22 July 1351.
[556] 18 July 1352.
[557] 27 July 1352.

[558] 27 January 1354.
[559] In the margin: non habuit effectum.
[560] 23 April 1353.
[561] In the margin: pars in arayragiis.
[562] 1 March 1358.
[563] 13 July 1358.
[564] 25 June 1359.
[565] 24 August 1359 or 1360.
[566] 12 December 1360.
[567] 9 May 1353.

sequentes [568] per resignationem eiusdem Hugonis fuit provisum cardinali Magalonensi,[569] et scriptum per cameram quod ibidem erat compositum et quod hic nichil exigeretur.[570]

(fol. 134ᵛ) De prebenda de Nasington' (Nassington) in ecclesia Lincolniensi, quam obtinet Ludovicus de Charlton' fuit eidem confirmata per Innocentium iii° kalendas Februarii anno ix°.[571]

De capellania perpetua ecclesie parochialis de Cleti (Clee) fuit Johanni de Walton' per obitum ultimi capellani seu vicarii provisum per Innocentium xi° kalendas Julii anno ix°,[572] non taxata, medietas.[533]

De prebenda de Hempyngham (Empingham), taxata xxxli li. xiii s. iiii d., de qua per obitum Willelmi de Dune fuit provisum Willelmo de Funeby per Innocentium xi° kalendas Junii anno ix°,[573] xxxvi li. xiii s. iiii d.[559]

De ecclesia de Felthergate (Fleet), cuius taxa et provisio supra in recepta.

De [574] prebenda de Milton' Ecclesia,[575] taxata xl li., et archidiaconatu Oxonie cum ecclesia [575] de Issteleya (Iffley), taxata xiiii° li. xiii s. iiii d., eidem annexa, in ecclesia Lincolniensi, de quibus per obitum cardinalis de Gordonio [576] fuit provisum cardinali Aquensi [577] per Innocentium iiii° idus Augusti anno ix°,[578] liiii li. xiii s. iiii d.[579] Advertendum si de archidiaconatu qui per se non taxatur sit aliquid exigendum.

De vicaria ecclesie de Clee, taxata x li., de qua per obitum Johannis de Elveye fuit provisum Johanni Alayn per Innocentium iii° kalendas Maii anno x°,[580] x li.[561]

De ecclesia de Stangrunde (Standground), taxata xx li., de qua ex causa permutationis cum ⟨ecclesia⟩ de Rypton' (Abbots Ripton) fuit provisum Johanni de Wynton' per Innocentium vii° kalendas Octobris anno ix°,[581] xx li.[579]

De dicta ecclesia de Ripton' Abbatis ex predicta causa fuit provisum Thome de Clipton' dicto die, taxata xxiii li. vi s. viii d., xxiii li. vi s. viii d.[579]

(fol. 135, xlii) De prebenda de Glatton' in ecclesia Lincolniensi, taxata iiii li. vi s. viii d., de qua per obitum Ade de Hilton' fuit provisum Johanni de Sutton' per

Innocentium iiii° kalendas Martii anno x°,[582] iiii li. vi s. viii d.[583]

De medietate ecclesie de Stkell' (East Keal?)[584] taxata xix li., de qua ex causa permutationis fuit provisum Galfredo Trethepayn per Innocentium idus Aprilis anno x°,[585] xix li.

De ecclesia de Coltesworth' (Colsterworth), taxata xxi li. vi s. viii d., fuit provisum Roberto de Hynkole per Innocentium idus Aprilis anno x°,[585] plus non continetur in littera missa, xxi li. vi s. viii d.[561]

De capella Sancti Thome ad Pontem Stamfford (Stamford), non taxata, in qua Johannes de Lewes fuit subrogatus Edmundo Wrthwell' super lite in palatio pendente per Innocentium iiii° idus Maii anno decimo,[586] medietas.[579]

De ecclesia de Strangrunde (Standground), cuius taxa et provisio supra in recepta, pro resta vi li. xiii s. iiii d.[579]

Hic deficiunt iiii°ʳ beneficia que ponuntur infra folio lvii°.

### Conventrensis et Lichfeldensis

De archidiaconatu Conventrensi, non taxato, et prebenda de Langedon' (Longdon), taxata xx li., in eccclesia Lichfeldensi, de quibus fuit de novo provisum Humfrido de Astyng', dimissis in arrayragiis per Dominum Raymundum Pelegrini, debentur fructus archidiaconatus ut infra, etiam et in recepta continetur quod Dominus Walterus Dalby puro ista vacatione quantum ad prebendam et duabus aliis vacationibus composuit cum camera.[579]

De ecclesia de Hodynet (Hodnet), de qua per consecrationem Radulphi episcopi Bathoniensis fuit provisum Nicholao [587] de Heth'; idem Nicholaus pro ista ecclesia et quibusdam aliis beneficiis suis composuit cum camera ut supra in recepta in fine.[588]

(fol. 135ᵛ) De ecclesia de Legh' (Leigh), dimissa per Dominum Raymundum Pelegrini in ix li. xiii s. iiii d., de qua fuit de novo provisum [589] Johanni de Holond, respondetur supra in prima recepta de iiii li. xiii s. iiii d., et plus levari non potest quia de patronatu laicali.[590]

De archidiaconatu Conventrensi, non taxato, et prebenda de Langtdon' (Longdon) in ecclesia Lichfeldensi, taxata xx li., de quibus post obitum Humfrydy de

[568] 18 February 1354.
[569] Audoin Aubert, bishop of Maguelone, priest of Ss. Giovanni e Paolo.
[570] In the margin: *doce quod nihil exigetur*.
[571] 30 January 1361. In the margin: *in arayragiis*.
[572] 21 June 1361.
[573] 22 May 1361.
[574] Followed by *ecclesia* deleted by a line.
[575] *ecclesie*, MS.
[576] William Farinier of Gourdon, priest of Ss. Marcellino e Pietro.
[577] Peter Itherii, bishop of Dax, priest of Quattro Coronati.
[578] 10 August 1361.
[579] In the margin: *in arayragiis*.
[580] 29 April 1362.
[581] 25 September 1361.

[582] 26 February 1362.
[583] Glatton does not appear to have been a prebend of Lincoln, and the church of Glatton was assessed at £21 3s. 4d. The collation of Adam de Hilton to Glatton was confirmed by the pope in 1360: *Cal. Pap. Regs. Petitions*, i, 315. In the margin opposite this item: *in arayragiis*.
[584] The church in question is apparently East Keal, whose tax was xviii li. xiii s. iv d., for which see below page 235.
[585] 13 April 1362.
[586] 12 May 1362.
[587] *Nicholau*, MS.
[588] In the margin: *videatur compositio*.
[589] *de novo* repeated in MS.
[590] In the margin: *attende*.

Astyng' fuit provisum Willelmo Sallowe per Clementem iiii° nonas Septembris anno viii°,[591] dimissis in arreyragiis in xxvi li. xiii s. iiii d. Walterus Dalby composuit [592] cum camera ut supra ex alia parte istius folii, et sic restant pro archidiaconatu xiii li. vi s. viii d.[579]

De prebenda Lichfeldensi, de qua per obitum Willelmi Apeltre fuit provisum Thome Attehull' per Clementem xi° kalendas Julii anno viii°,[593] debentur fructus, medietas.[579]

De decanatu Lichfeldensi, taxato xl li., de quo per assecutionem decanatus Lincolniensis per Symonem de Brysekeye fuit provisum Johanni de Bukyngham nonas Novembris per Clementem anno viii°,[594] pro resta xx li.[579]

De archidiaconatu Staffordie in ecclesia Lichfeldensi, qui fuit confirmatus Ricardo de Byrmyngham per Clementem ii° idus Decembris anno viii°;[595] Nicholaus Heth' ut supra in recepta respondet [596] nomine Rogerii Deyking' cui etiam eodem die fuit provisum.[579]

De prebenda in ecclesia collegiata Sancti Sedde Sallopie (St. Chad, Shrewsbury), de qua per obitum Willelmi Apeltre fuit provisum Roberto de Sulgrave per Clementem iii° idus Decembris anno viii°,[597] dimissa et in advertentia, eo quod non habuit effectum quia Dominus Hugo Opas tenet eam iure regio.[579]

(fol. 136, xliii) De prebenda de Wlton' (Ufton) in ecclesia Lichfeldensi, de qua per resignationem Johannis de Wynwyk' fuit provisum Johanni de Melburn' per Clementem xviii° kalendas Februarii,[598] taxata iiii li. xiii s. iiii d., de quibus respondetur in recepta, et ideo non debuisset fuisse dimissa hic in arreyragiis.[599]

De prebenda de Keleshale (Eccleshall), taxata lxvi li. xiii s. iiii d., de qua per resignationem Johannis de Melburn' fuit provisum Johanni de [600] Wynwyk's per Clementem xvii° idus Februarii anno decimo,[601] lxvi li. xiii s. iiii d.[579]

De prebenda de Berkwyth' (Berkswick) in ecclesia Lichfeldensi, taxata xx li., de qua per obitum Tydonis de Varesio fuit provisum Willelmo Claville per Innocentium vii° kalendas Maii anno primo;[602] non habuit effectum, nec unquam dictus Willelmus fuit prosecutus.[579]

De prebenda de Langedon' (Longdon) in ecclesia Lichfeldensi, cuius taxa et provisio et compositio cum camera supra in recepta, de qua compositione restant clviii fl. solvendum videlicet l in festo nativitatis domini proximo et sic quolibet anno in dicto festo et in ultimo plus viii fl.[603]

De prebenda de Wolveye (Wolvey) in ecclesia Lichfeldensi, taxata vi li. xiii s. iiii d., de qua per consecrationem Michaelis electi Londoniensis fuit provisum Johanni Barnere per Innocentium nonas Octobris anno secundo,[604] vi li. xiii s. iiii d.

De ecclesia de Wynwyk' (Winwick), taxata xxvi li. xiii s. iiii d., de qua per obitum Johannis de Clesenhale fuit provisum Roberto de Cresswell' per Innocentium viii° kalendas Februarii anno iiii°,[605] xxvi li. xiii s. iiii d.[606]

(fol. 136ᵛ) De ecclesia de Walton', taxata xliiii li., de qua fuit provisum Magistro Johanni de Bulkynton' iii° nonas Decembris anno v° per Innocentium,[607] pro

De ecclesia de Weston' super Trentam (Weston-upon-Trent), taxata xii li., ex causa permutationis cum Thoma de Braydon' de parochiali ecclesia de Champham (Clapham) Wyntoniensis diocesis fuit provisum Nicholao de Lymberch' per Innocentium ii° idus Februarii anno vi°,[608] pro resta iiii li.[579]

De ecclesia de Standich' (Standish), taxata xiii li. vi s. viii d., de qua Willelmo de Standich cardinalis Petragoricensis de novo providit, pro resta vi li. xiii s. iiii d.[579]

De vicaria Sancti Michaelis Conventarie, cuius taxa et provisio supra in recepta, l s.[579]

De prebenda in ecclesia collegiata Sancti Johannis Cestrie, taxata iiii li., de qua ex causa permutationis fuit confirmata Ricardo Boulle per Innocentium vii° kalendas Jullii anno vii°,[609] iiii li.

De capellania Sancti Michaelis scita in castro de Clederhoy (Clitheroe), non taxata, fuit per devolutionem provisum Johanni de Borton' per Innocentium iiii° kalendas Junii anno vi°,[610] medietas.[579]

De ecclesia de Codyngton' (Coddington), taxata vi li. xiii s. iiii d., de qua per assecutionem ecclesie de Wynton' (Burton-in-Winhale) per Johannem Charneux fuit provisum Waltero Lyngge per Innocentium iiii° nonas Junii anno vi°,[611] vi li. xiii s. iiii d.[579]

De vicaria ecclesie Sancti Michaelis Conventrie fuit provisum per dominum Petragoricensem cardinalem Willelmo Anth' vi° kalendas Septembris anno LVII°, pro taxa.[579]

(fol. 137, xliiii) De prioratu de Kyrkeby (Monks

---

[591] 2 September 1349.
[592] Followed by *in* deleted by a line.
[593] 21 June 1349.
[594] 5 November 1349.
[595] 12 December 1349.
[596] *respondetur*, MS.
[597] 11 December 1349.
[598] 15 January 1352: *Cal. Pap. Regs. Petitions*, i, 224.
[599] In the margin: *non debet esse*.
[600] Followed by *Uy* deleted by a line.
[601] 16 January 1352.
[602] 25 April 1353.

[603] In the margin: *pars in arayragiis*.
[604] 7 October 1354.
[605] 25 January 1356.
[606] In the margin: *solvit integre H. Pelegrino*. This item is followed by the item, deleted by lines: *De ecclesia de Walton' super Trentam, taxata xii li., ex causa permutationis cum Thoma Cat.*
[607] 3 December 1357.
resta xiiii li.[579]
[608] 12 February 1358.
[609] 25 June 1359.
[610] 29 May 1358.
[611] 2 June 1358.

Kirby), taxato iiii<sup>xx</sup> i li. x s. viii d., de quo per assecutionem prioratus de Veteri Belismo (Vieux Belesme) Sagiensis (Séez) diocesis per Oliverum de Desertis fuit provisum Willelmo de Grauleriis per Innocentium xiii° kalendas Martii anno vii°,[612] iiii<sup>xx</sup> i li. x s. viii d.[579]

De ecclesia de Wrothyn (Worthen) et aliis beneficiis de quibus fuit dispensatum cum Richardo de Stafford modo quo continetur supra in recepta folio,[613] debet pro resta lviii li. xiii s. iiii d. De quibus debuit solvisse in festo Beati Johannis anno LXIII° x li., et in festo Beati Michaelis tunc proximo sequente x li., et sic de anno in annum quousque integre fierit satisfactum sic quod in ultimo termino solvet viii li. xiii s. iiii d.[603]

De prebenda de Wulveveye (Wolvey) in ecclesia Lichfeldensi, que [614] fuit confirmata dicto Ricardo, comprehenditur in compositione predicta.[603]

De ecclesia de Erkalawe parva (Child's Ercall), non taxata, que Stephano de Eyncheton' fuit confirmata per Innocentium vii° kalendas Junii anno vii°,[615] vi li. xiii s. iiii d., pro quibus Willelmus Saltto, qui eam possidet, se obligavit.[579]

De ecclesia de Erkelawe, non taxata, que fuit Stephano Eyncheton' per cardinalem Urgellensem collata, fuit eidem per Innocentium ix° kalendas Octobris anno viii° [616] confirmata, vi li. xiii s. iiii d.[579]

De ecclesia de [617] Midle (Middle), taxata xx li., de qua per obitum Roberti de Conventr' fuit provisum Johanni de Ygg' per Innocentium x° kalendas Januarii anno ix°,[618] xx li.

De prebenda de Termini (Tarvin) in ecclesia Lichfeldensi, taxata xxxiii li. vi s. viii d., de qua per obitum Willelmi de Dryffeld fuit provisum Nicholao de Hetth' per Innocentium iii° idus Augusti anno ix°,[619] xxxiii li. vi s. viii d.[620]

Predicta prebenda fuit confirmata dicto Willelmo per Innocentium iii° ⟨idus⟩ Augusti anno ix° supradicto, ideo virtute istius confirmationis nichil debetur.[620]

(fol. 137ᵛ) De capella de [621] Clyderhowe (Clitheroe), non taxata, in qua fuit subrogatus David Martini, fuit Johanni de Burton', qui de eadem litigabat, provisum [622] ix° kalendas Januarii anno ix°,[623] medietas.[620]

De parochiali ecclesia Burnhull' (Burnhill), de qua per dominum cardinalem Petragoricensem fuit provisum Hugoni de Pambuton'.[620]

De prebenda in ecclesia collegiata de Penbryth' (Penkridge), de qua per obitum Thome Michael fuit provisum Thome Eltonhed per Innocentium vii° idus Aprilis anno x°,[624] debentur fructus.[620]

De capella ecclesie Sancti Michaelis de Clyderhow (Clitheroe), in qua in omni iure quod competebat Johanni de Borton' fuit subrogatus Johannes de Pork per Innocentium vii° kalendas Februarii anno x°,[625] medietas.[620]

Hic deficiunt tria benefficia et ponuntur infra folio lvii°.

### Assavensis

De prebenda ecclesie Assavensis, taxa cuius et provisio supra in recepta, pro resta vi s. viii d.[620]

De ecclesia de Dynkyglh' (Denbigh), taxata vi li. xiii s. iiii d., de qua vacante [626] de iure, ut asseritur, fuit provisum Willelmo de Snyderlond per Clementem idus Novembris anno ix°; [627] alius possidet iure ordinario et litigat in curia.[620]

De ecclesia de Escyvyok (Yscifiog), cuius taxa et provisio supra in recepta, de resta liii s. iiii d.[620]

Hic deficiunt quinque beneficia que ponuntur infra folio lvii°.

### Menevensis

De ecclesia de Lambanglarath' (Llanfihangel ar Arth), non taxata, de qua per obitum Ricardi Aprovanses fuit provisum Ludovico Taunton' per Clementem antequam dictus Hugo esset nuntius, et dimissa in arrayragiis, sed nunquam habuit quia dictus Ludovicus nunquam [628] habuit possessionem et mortuus est.[620]

(fol. 138, xlv) [629] De ecclesia de Weston' (Wiston), non taxata, de qua per resignationem Rogeri dicti Johannis fuit provisum Willelmo de [630] Neuhawe per Innocentium xix° kalendas Junii anno iiii<sup>to</sup>.[631] medietas.

De ecclesia Sancti Bernachi super Taff' (Llanfyrnach), taxata vi li. xiii s. iiii d., de qua fuit provisum Willelmo de Neuhwo per Innocentium xix° kalendas Junii anno iiii°; [631] ista provisio non habuit effectum, sed per obitum Johannis de Champton' fuit provisum Ricardo de Champton' vi li. xiii s. iiii d.

De archidiaconatu de Kermerdyn' (Carmarthen) in ecclesia Menevensi cum ecclesia de Laman (Llanrhian) et prebenda eidem annexis, taxatis xx li. xiii s. iiii d., collatio cuius facta auctoritate ordinarii Hawlayno ap David fuit eidem confirmata per Innocentium xii° kalendas Jullii anno v°,[632] xx li. xiii s. iiii d.

Advertendum est si de archidiaconatu, qui per se non taxatur, sit aliquid exigendum.

---

[612] 17 February 1359.
[613] A blank space is left for the number.
[614] *qui*, MS.
[615] 26 May 1359.
[616] 23 September 1360.
[617] Followed by *Midel* deleted by a line.
[618] 23 December 1361.
[619] 11 August 1361.
[620] In the margin: *in arrayragiis.*
[621] Followed by *Ch* deleted by a line.
[622] *subrogatus*, MS.
[623] 24 December 1361.

[624] 7 April 1362.
[625] 26 January 1362.
[626] Followed by *per* deleted by a line.
[627] 13 November 1350.
[628] Followed by *fuit* deleted by a line.
[629] At the top of the page over the left margin is noted: *omnes huius pagine in arrayragiis.*
[630] Followed by *Newneh* deleted by a line.
[631] 14 May 1356.
[632] 20 June 1357.

De cantaria ecclesie de Arberwyll' (Abergwili), taxata vi li. xiii s. iiii d., seu ecclesia de Lambetyn' (Lampeter Pont Stephen), taxata v li., quam obtinet David de Sancto Claro fuit provisum Cook de Averefford per Innocentium vi° idus Martii anno vi^to,[633] vi° li. xiii s. iiii d.

De ecclesia de Langdemar (Llangoedmore), cuius taxa et provisio supra in recepta, pro resta iii li. vi s. viii d.

De archidiaconatu de Kermerdyn in ecclesia Menevensi, taxato xx li. xiii s. iiii d. cum annexis, in quo et ad ius quod competebat Haweyno ap David fuit subrogatus David Martini per Innocentium vi^to kalendas Decembris anno viii°,[634] xx li. xiii s. iiii d.

De prebenda de Rayn (Royll) in ecclesia de Abberwill', collatio cuius facta Ade de Hauton' fuit eidem confirmata per Innocentium iii° kalendas [635] Septembris anno viii°.[636]

(fol. 138^v)[637] De hospitali Sancti David Confessoris Swynness' (Swansea), collatio cuius facta David Martini fuit eidem confirmata per Innocentium iii° kalendas Februarii anno nono.[638]

De prebenda in ecclesia Menevensi, de qua per obitum Thome David fuit provisum David Wagham per Innocentium xi° kalendas Jullii anno nono.[639]

De prebenda de Landewybrev (Llandewi Brefi) in ecclesia Menevensi, de qua per obitum Gryffyni de Caunton' fuit provisum Willelmo de Eserdon' per Innocentium ii° nonas Novembris anno quinto.[640]

De portione seu prebenda in ecclesia Sancti Mauritii de Haberwiyll' (Abergwili), de qua per obitum Willelmi de Deybradk' fuit provisum Waltero de Fenton' per Innocentium iiii° nonas Jullii anno ix°.[641]

De prebenda de Marther' (Mathry) in ecclesia Menevensi, de qua cum vacabit per consecrationem Ade electi Menevensi fuit mandatum provideri Philipo de [642] Hauton' per Innocentium iii° kalendas Novembris anno nono.[643]

De prebenda quam dominus electus obtinebat in ecclesia de Arberwiyll' (Abergwili), cum vacabit ut supra, fuit mandatum provideri Philipo Martini per Innocentium iii° kalendas Novembris anno ix°.[643]

De prebenda de Landevaylolt' (Llangyfelach) in ecclesia collegiata de Arbewyll' (Abergwili), que tanto tempore vacavit quod eius collatio est sedi apostolice devoluta, fuit provisum Alexandro Millokt', debentur fructus.

### (fol. 139, xlvi) Eboracensis

De prebenda Wetewang' (Wetwang) in ecclesia Eboracensi, taxata iiii^xx x li., de qua per obitum Georgii de Saluriis fuit provisum Domino Anibaldo cardinali [644] per Clementem, et dimissa [645] arrayragiis per Dominum Raymundum Pelegrini in lvii li. xi s.; dictus Anibaldus nunquam habuit possessionem nec fuit prosecutus, quia rex contulit Ricardo de Wynwyk' qui adhuc possidet dictam prebendam; ideo nichil levari potest.[646]

De prebenda de Massham (Masham) in ecclesia Eboracensi, taxata secundum novam taxam iiii^xx li., de qua fuit provisum per obitum Magistri Johannis de Wfford Reginaldo de Bryan per Clementem antequam dictus Hugo esset nuntius, et per consecrationem dicti Reginaldi in episcopum Menevensem fuit de eadem prebenda provisum Andree de Wfford xviii° kalendas Jullii anno vii° vel viii°,[647] quia simul missi, fuit scriptum per cameram quod facta fuit plena informatio quod iste due provisiones fuerunt infra annum et quod nisi fructus unius annate exigerentur, de quibus superius in recepta ante compotum est responsum de xli. li xiii s. iiii d. et in recepta istius de xxxviii li. vi s. viii d.[648]

De archidiaconatu Richemondie in ecclesia Eboracensi et aliis beneficiis, de quibus fuit provisum Henrico de Walton' pro quibus est simul obligatus, respondetur supra de receptis in fine recepte, et infra de arreyragiis in fine arreyragiorum.[646]

De prebenda Massham ut supra in [649] presenti folio.[650]

De prebenda de [651] Thorp (Thorpe) in ecclesia de Hoveden (Howden), cuius taxa et provisio supra in recepta, pro resta vi li.

(fol. 139^v) De prebenda de Hustwarth' (Husthwaite) in ecclesia Eboracensi, taxata xxx li., de qua fuit provisum Johanni de Wlburn' de novo, et fructus male percepti remissi pro quibus debet dare ii^c fl. in subsidium contra Turcos per Clementem xii° kalendas Jullii [652] anno x°,[653] solvit xxx li. pro annata [654] et respondetur supra in recepta, et debet ii^c fl.[646]

De prebenda de Eton' (Eaton) in ecclesia collegiata Suthwell', taxata vi li. xiii s. iiii d., de qua per consecrationem Gilberti episcopi Karliolensis [655] fuit pro-

[633] 10 March 1358.
[634] 26 November 1360.
[635] Followed by *Februarii anno ix°* deleted by a line.
[636] 30 August 1360.
[637] At the head of the page is the note: *omnes huius pagine in arayragiis.*
[638] 30 January 1361.
[639] 21 June 1361.
[640] 4 November 1357.
[641] 4 July 1361.
[642] Followed by *Huton'* deleted by a line.
[643] 30 October 1361.

[644] Bishop of Tusculum.
[645] Followed by *Ary* deleted by a line.
[646] In the margin: *in arayragiis.*
[647] 14 June 1349: *Cal. Pap. Regs. Petitions*, i, 178.
[648] In the margin: *satisfecit in resta Domini Raymundi Pelegrini.*
[649] Followed by *in precedenti folio* deleted by a line. *In* is repeated in the manuscript.
[650] In the margin: *supra est eadem.*
[651] Followed by *Trop* deleted by a line.
[652] Followed by *an.*
[653] 20 June 1351.
[654] *anna*, MS.
[655] *Karbonensis*, MS.

visum Ade Gryffyn per Clementem x° kalendas Junii anno x°,[656] vi li. xiii s. iiii d.[646]

De prebenda in ecclesia Eboracensi, de qua per consecrationem electi Terwynensis fuit provisum Frederíco Salamay ignoratur qui sunt isti, et certifficatum est non habuerunt nec habent prebendam in dicta ecclesia.[646]

De prebenda de Osbaldewyk' (Osbaldwick) in ecclesia Eboracensi, cuius taxa et provisio supra in recepta, pro resta xx li.

De prebenda de Monketon' (Monkton) in ecclesia collegiata Ripponensi, taxata xiii li. vi s. viii d., de qua per consecrationem Michaelis episcopi Londoniensis fuit provisum Johanni de Wynwyk' per Innocentium xv° kalendas Junii anno ii°,[657] xiii li. vi s. viii d.

De prebenda de Stranxale (Strensall) in ecclesia Eboracensi, taxata liii li. vi s. viii d., de qua per consecrationem Michaelis episcopi Londonensis fuit provisum cardinali Petragoricesnsi per Innocentium ii° idus Octobris anno ii°,[658] liii li. vi s. viii d.[646]

De ecclesia Sancte Trinitatis Eboracensis, cuius taxa et provisio supra in recepta, pro resta xl s.

(fol. 140, xlvii) De prebenda de Sharowe (Sharow) in ecclesia collegiata Ripponensi, taxata v li. ad novam taxam, de qua per resignationem Ricardi de Thoresby fuit provisum ex causa permutationis Bertrando de Cardilhaco per Innocentium xiii° kalendas Novembris anno iiii°,[659] non habuit effectum hic quia antequam haberet possessionem fuit promotus in episcopus Montis Albani (Montauban) per cuius promotionem fuit provisum alteri ut infra in pagina presenti.[660]

De prebenda altaris Sancti Petri in ecclesia collegiata Beverlacensi, taxata xxvi li., de qua per obitum Willelmi de Fereby fuit provisum Johanni Blebur' per Innocentium xix° kalendas Februarii anno iiii°,[661] non habuit effectum quia Magister Andreas de Ufford, qui eam possidebat, evicit [662] ipsam, per cuius obitum fuit provisum Ricardo Drax ut infra, et de provisione facta dicto Andree respondetur in compoto precedenti Domini Hugonis.[663]

De vicaria de Tykyll' (Tickhill), de qua Rogero de Slateburn' Dominus Petragoricensis de novo providit, que taxatur xx li., pro resta xv li.

De medietate ecclesie de Houtton' Bussell' (Hutton Bushel), taxata xii li., de qua Dominus Petragoricensis de novo providit Nicholao de Wilteby, pro resta viii li.[664]

De ecclesia de Bolton (Bolton Percy), cuius taxa et confirmatio supra in recepta, pro resta xiii li. vi s. viii d.

De ecclesia de Holteby (Holtby), taxa cuius et provisio supra in recepta, pro resta xl s.

De vicaria ecclesie de Waltryngham (Walkeringham), cuius taxa et provisio supra in recepta, pro resta iiii li.

De prebenda de Skarwe (Sharow), in ecclesia collegiata Ripponensi, taxata ad novam taxam v li., de qua per munus consecrationis Bertrandi de Cardilhaco episcopi Montis Albani (Montauban) fuit provisum Willelmo de Esonden' per Innocentium vi° idus Martii anno vi[to],[665] v li.

(fol. 140[v]) De ecclesia de Claworth (Clayworth), cuius taxa et provisio supra in recepta, pro resta.

De ecclesia de Hoggescoth', non taxata, de qua per cardinalem Urgellensem fuit Willelmo Gilberlot' de novo provisum, medietas.[646]

De ecclesia de Colksby (Cowesby), taxata v li., de qua per dominum Urgellensem fuit Rythero de [666] Holperby de novo provisum, v li.[663]

De vicaria Pontisfracti (Pontefract), cuius taxa et provisio supra in recepta, pro resta iiii li.

De ecclesia Sancti Wolfridi (York), cuius taxa et provisio supra in recepta, pro resta xl s. Istam tenet Ricardus de Otrynton'.

De ecclesia de Thormotby (Thornaby), taxata iiii li., de qua per dominum Petragoricensem fuit Ade de Bolton' de novo provisum, pro resta xl s.

De ecclesia de Brantyngham (Brantingham), cuius taxa et provisio supra in recepta, liii li. vi s. viii d.[667]

De prebenda de Amplefford (Ampleforth) in ecclesia Eboracensi, cuius taxa et provisio supra in recepta, pro resta xx li.

De ecclesia de Pat'brumpton' (Patrick Brompton), cuius taxa et provisio supra in recepta, pro resta xiii li. vi s. viii d.

De [668] ecclesia de Brumpton (Brompton), cuius taxa et provisio supra in recepta, pro resta xx li. xiii s. iiii d.

De prebenda de Sharwe (Sharow) in ecclesia collegiata Ripponensi, taxata v li., de qua per obitum Willelmi Aberwill' fuit provisum [669] Johanni de Donynton' per Clementem iii° idus Maii anno ix°,[670] v li.[671]

(fol. 141, xlviii) De vicaria ecclesie de Gillyng' (Gilling), que ex causa permutationis facte cum Gerlaco de [672] Clave fuit Johanni de Reok' confirmata per Innocentium ix° kalendas Septembris anno viii,[673] taxata ad novam taxam x li.

De ecclesia Sancti Wlffridy [674] (York), taxata iiii li.,

[656] 23 May 1351.
[657] 18 May 1354.
[658] 14 October 1354.
[659] 20 October 1356.
[660] In the margin: *non debet esse.*
[661] 14 January 1356.
[662] Followed by *eam* deleted by a line.
[663] In the margin: *non habuit effectum.*
[664] In the margin: *satisfecit in resta Domini Raymundi.*

[665] 10 March 1358.
[666] Followed by *Her* deleted by a line.
[667] In the margin: *pars in arayragiis.*
[668] Followed by *prebenda de* deleted by a line.
[669] Followed by *confirmata* not deleted.
[670] 13 May 1351.
[671] Follows *v li.* deleted by a line.
[672] Followed by *E* not deleted.
[673] 24 August 1360.
[674] Followed by *in ecclesia* deleted by a line.

que ex causa permutationis cum Gerlaco de Clave fuit Ricardo de Wryntyngham confirmata per Innocentium ix° kalendas Septembris anno viii°,[673] iiii li.

De ecclesia de Langedon' (Langton), taxata x li. ad novam taxam, que ex causa permutationis facte cum Ricardo de Wyntryngham fuit confirmata Gerlaco de Clave per Innocentium ix° kalendas Septembris anno viii°,[673] x li.

De vicaria de Gyllyng', in qua Johannes Parker fuit subrogatus in omni iure quod competebat Gerlaco de Clave Sepnensis (Speier) diocesis per Innocentium ix° kalendas Maii anno ix°,[675] x li. ad novam taxam.[646]

De prebenda de Masham in ecclesia Eboracensi, taxata ad novam taxam iiiixx li., de qua per obitum [676] Andree Offord fuit provisum Cardinali Magalonensi (Maguelone)[677] per Innocentium xiiii kalendas Decembris anno vi°.[678]

De ecclesia de Aghton' (Aughton), de qua iure devoluto fuit provisum Hugoni de Bolton' per Innocentium kalendas Februarii anno nono.[679]

De prebenda in ecclesia Sancti Johannis Beverlaci ad altare Beate Marie, taxata vi li., de qua per obitum Ricardi Junioris nati Radulfi de Thormerton' fuit provisum Willelmo de Dalton' iiii° nonas Jullii anno ix°,[680] xvi li.[681]

De capella de Bokynffold (Bockingfold), non taxata de qua per obitum Willemi de Braylle fuit provisum Ricardo de Hormyngton' per Innocentium iii° nonas Julii anno nono.[682]

(fol. 141ᵛ) De ecclesia Omnium Sanctorum Eboraci, taxata v li. vi s. viii d., de qua per obitum Simonis Warde fuit provisum David [683] Morton alias Orort' per Innocentium iiii° nonas Jullii anno ix°,[680] v li. vi s. viii d.[646]

De ecclesia de Langedon' (Langton), taxata, de qua per obitum Gerlaci de Clave fuit provisum Thome Mart' per Innocentium xii° kalendas Jullii anno ix°,[684] x li.

De prebenda ecclesie collegiate Ripponensis vocata Mounkton' (Monkton), taxata ad novam taxam xiii li. vi s. viii d., in qua et omni iure quod competebat Thome de Clipston' fuit subrogatus Willelmus Ronde per Innocentium vi° idus Jullii anno ix°,[685] xiii li.

De prebenda de Amplefford (Ampleforth) in ecclesia Eboracensi, taxata xl li., de qua per obitum Henrici

la Souch' fuit provisum Willelmo Curteneye per Innocentium iii° idus Augusti anno ix°,[686] xx li.[687]

De prebenda de Wystowe (Wistow) in ecclesia Eboracensi, taxata c li., et archidiaconatu eiusdem ecclesie, non taxato, de quibus per obitum domini cardinalis Penestrensis [688] fuit provisum domino cardinali Carcassonensi (Carcassonne)[689] per Innocentium xiii° kalendas Octobris anno ix°,[690] c li. pro prebenda.[691]

De prebenda de Dryffeld (Driffeld) in ecclesia Eboracensi, taxata c li., de qua per obitum Willelmi de Sancto Martiali fuit provisum Domino Hugoni de Sancto Martiali cardinali [692] per Innocentium xiii° kalendas Octobris anno nono,[690] c li.[691]

De prebenda de Bolui (Bole) in ecclesia Eboracensi, taxata xvi li., de qua per obitum Thome de Nevill' fuit provisum domino cardinali Cluniacensi [693] per Innocentium xiiii° kalendas Octobris anno ix°,[694] xvi li.[691]

De prebenda in ecclesia collegiata Beverlacensi, de qua per obitum R. Letormentor' fuit provisum Petro La Sage per Innocentium xi kalendas Jullii anno nono.[695]

(fol. 142, xlix) De [696] ecclesia de Hugate (Hugate), taxata xxiii li. vi s. viii d. ad novam taxam, cuius collatio facta auctoritate ordinaria Johanni Herneys fuit eidem confirmata per Innocentium iii° kalendas Januarii anno ix°,[697] xxiii li. vi s. viii d.

De prebenda ad altare Sancti Petri in ecclesia collegiata Beverlacensi, taxata xxv li., in qua fuit subrogatus Ricardus Suggworth' in omni iure quod competebat Ricardo Drax contra Johannem de Blybur', tres sententias diffinitivas reportavit, per Innocentium nonas Januarii anno x°,[698] xxv li.[699]

Hic deficiunt octo beneficia que ponuntur infra foliis lvii° et viii°.

## Dunelmensis

De prioratu de Tynemuta (Tynemouth), de quo per assecutionem abbatie Sancti Albani per Thomam priorem dicti prioratus, de quo fuit sibi data potestas providendi per Clementem anno viii°,[700] non habuit effectum quia non est prioratus perpetuus, sed custodia temporalis ad voluntatem abbatis.[699]

De hospitali de Gretham, non taxato, de quo per obitum Johannis de Stoketon' fuit provisum Thome

---

[675] 23 April 1361.
[676] Followed by *Auditor'* underlined by a line.
[677] Audoin Aubert, priest of Ss. Giovanni e Paolo.
[678] 18 November 1358. In the margin: *scriptum quod composuit cum camera.*
[679] 1 February 1361. In the margin: *non habuit effectum.*
[680] 4 July 1361.
[681] In the margin: *in arayragiis*; also *scriptum quod composuit cum camera* deleted by a line.
[682] 5 July 1361. In the margin: *in arayragiis.*
[683] Followed by *alias Orort'* deleted by a line.
[684] 20 June 1361.
[685] 10 July 1361.

[686] 11 August 1361.
[687] In the margin: *supra est eadem.*
[688] Peter des Prés, bishop of Palestrina.
[689] Stephen Aubert, deacon of S. Maria in Aquiro.
[690] 19 September 1361.
[691] In the margin: *in arayragiis.*
[692] Deacon of S. Maria in Portico.
[693] Androin de la Roche, abbot of Cluny, priest of S. Marcello.
[694] 18 September 1361.
[695] 21 June 1361. In the margin: *in arayragiis.*
[696] Followed by *prebenda* deleted by a line.
[697] 30 December 1360.
[698] 5 January 1362.
[699] In the margin: *non habuit effectum.*
[700] 11 August 1349: above, p. 131.

Johannis de Brydkyrk' per Clementem ii° idus Octobris anno nono,[701] debetur medietas exceptis iii li. vi s. viii d., de quibus supra in recepta [702] respondetur.[691]

De prebenda in ecclesia collegiata Langescestr' (Lanchester), de qua ex causa permutationis cum Henrico de Exton' fuit provisum Galfrido de Cornesyo per Innocentium xv kalendas Decembris anno primo,[703] debentur fructus. Nomen prebende et taxa ignoratur, quia in dicta ecclesia prebende non habent certa nomina. Medietas.[691]

De prebenda de Lymley (Lamesley) ecclesie collegiate Cestrie super stratam (Chester-le-Street), taxata xx li., de qua per promotionem electi Norowycensis fuit provisum Willelmo de Lugtheburgh' per Innocentium vi° idus Februarii anno ii°,[704] xx li.[691]

(fol. 142ᵛ) De prebenda de dicta ecclesia Cestrie vocata Lamley (Lamesley), taxa cuius et provisio supra in recepta, pro resta x li.[705] Debet fieri executio contra executores Willelmi de Rothewell' in diocesi Lincolniensi, qui habuit fructus virtute sequestri sibi commissi et est obligatus.

De vicaria de Wytyngham (Whittingham), taxata x li., de qua per obitum Willelmi de Arbally fuit provisum Johanni de Wodefford per Innocentium xv° kalendas Augusti anno vᵗᵒ,[706] x li.[705]

De decanatu ecclesie collegiate Cestrie super stratam permutatio facta auctoritate ordinaria cum Johanne de Sculthorp pro archidiaconatu Cicestrensi per Adam de Houton' fuit eidem confirmata per Innocentium kalendas Junii anno vi°,[707] in libro taxe non invenitur decanatus sed vicaria taxata xxxiii li. vi s. viii d., xxxiii li. vi s. viii d.[703]

De vicaria de Newton' in Clendale (Kirknewton), de qua per obitum Roberti de Jarmy fuit provisum Roberto Hepp' per Innocentium nonas Septembris anno vii°,[708] taxata xx, xx li.[705]

De prioratu dicto Sella Sancte Rege (St. Bees), collatio facta auctoritate ordinaria Willelmo de Sluynesbur' fuit eidem confirmata per Innocentium ix° kalendas Septembris anno viii°.[709]

De ecclesia de Routhebury (Rothbury), in qua et ad omne ius quod competebat Willelmo de Emldon' fuit Johannes de Apeilby subrogatus per Innocentium xvi° kalendas Februarii anno ix°,[710] taxata ad novam taxam lxvi li. xiii s. iiii d., lxvi li. xiii s. iiii d.[705] De ista ecclesia pendet adhuc lis in curia.

De prebenda in ecclesia collegiata de Norton', de qua per obitum Thome Drax fuit provisum Bernardo de Lynar Avinionie per Innocentium vii° kalendas Maii anno ix°,[711] prebende in dicta ecclesia non habent certa nomina, debentur fructus, medietas.[712]

(fol. 143, 1) De prebenda ecclesie collegiate de Haukelond (Auckland), de qua per obitum Thome de Brydekyrk' fuit provisum Waltero de Wykham per Innocentium ii° idus Augusti anno ix°,[713] ista prebenda non habet certum nomen, medietas.

De ecclesia de Stanhop' (Stanhope), taxata xl s. ad novam taxam, de qua per obitum Thome Brydekyrk' fuit provisum Willelmo de Norowyco per Innocentium viii° kalendas Septembris anno nono [714] xl s.

De prebenda ecclesie collegiate de Haukelond (Auckland), de qua per obitum dicti Thome fuit provisum Roberto de Strautton' per Innocentium xvi° kalendas Septembris,[715] non habet certum nomen ut supra, medietas.

De capella seu ecclesia libera de [716] Jesumouth' (Jesmond), collatio facta auctoritate ordinaria Thome de Ponteh' fuit eidem confirmata per Innocentium ix° idus Januarii anno ix°,[717] non reperitur taxa, medietas.

De ecclesia de Stanhop' (Stanhope), nove taxe xl s., collatio facta autoritate ordinaria Ricardo de Wylingtton' per obitum Thome de Bridekyrk' fuit eidem Ricardo confirmata per Innocentium iiii° kalendas Januarii anno ix°,[718] xl s.

De prebenda ecclesie collegiate de Norton', de qua per consecrationem Domini Johannis Wygorniensis episcopi fuit provisum Willelmo Ilberd per Innocentium iiii° idus Martii anno x°.[719] Prebende in ista ecclesia non habent certa nomina.

De capella de Jesimouth' (Jesmond), vacante per obitum Henrici Beuffamit, fuit provisum Matheo de Bolton' per Innocentium xiii° kalendas Februarii anno x°,[720] non reperitur taxa.[721]

De vicaria ecclesie de Newenton' in Clendale (Kirknewton), taxata xx li., collatio facta auctoritate ordinaria Johanni de Castro Bernardi fuit eidem confirmata per Innocentium iiii° idus Maii anno x°,[722] xx li.

(fol. 143ᵛ) De ecclesia de Stanhop' (Stanhope), nove taxe xl s., collatio cuius facta auctoritate ordinaria Ricardo de Welyngton' per obitum Thome de Bryde-

---

[701] 14 October 1350.
[702] Followed by *re* deleted by a line.
[703] 17 November 1353.
[704] 8 February 1354.
[705] In the margin: *in arayragiis*.
[706] 18 July 1357.
[707] 1 June 1358.
[708] 5 September 1359.
[709] 24 August 1360. In the margin: *in arayragiis*.
[710] 17 January 1361.

[711] 25 April 1361.
[712] In the margin: *in arayragiis*.
[713] 12 August 1361.
[714] 25 August 1361.
[715] 17 August 1361: *Cal. Pap. Regs. Petitions*, i, 321.
[716] Followed by *Js* not deleted.
[717] 24 December 1361. It should be *kalendas: ibid.*, i, 323.
[718] 29 December 1361.
[719] 12 March 1362.
[720] 20 January 1362.
[721] In the margin opposite this item: *omnes huius pagine usque huc in arayragiis*.
[722] 12 May 1362.

kyrk' fuit eidem Ricardo confirmata per Innocentium iiii° idus Maii anno x°,[722] xl s. [723]

## Karliolensis

De ecclesia de Crostwayt' (Crosthwaite), taxata xxx li. xiii s. iiii d., in qua et ad omne ius quod competebat Willelmo de Selario fuit subrogatus Johannes Henrici per Innocentium ii° idus Januarii anno quinto,[724] non habuit effectum quia iste Johannes ⟨non⟩ habuit, nec est [725] prosecutus, nec unquam possessionem assecutus.[726]

De vicaria de Brampton', de qua ex causa permutationis cum vicaria de Schaldifford (Shalford) Wynttoniensis diocesis fuit provisum Johanni Hamyll' per Innocentium xi° kalendas Septembris anno v°,[727] taxata viii li., viii li.[723]

De ecclesia de Musgrave, vacante per obitum Johannis de Storton', fuit provisum Roberto Kerrot' per Innocentium ii° kalendas Martii anno v°,[728] taxata xiii li. vi s. viii d., xiii li. vi s. viii d.[723]

De ecclesia de Kerkelond (Kirkland), vacante ex eo quod Johannes de Kerkeby ipsam unacum [729] ecclesia de Wysck' (Ousby) per mensem et amplius detinuit paciffice et sine dispensatione aliqua, fuit provisum Johanni de Kerkeby per Innocentium viii° kalendas Novembris anno vii°,[730] taxata xl li., xl li.[731]

De vicaria ecclesia de Treswayt' (Crosthwaite), taxata xx li., provisio auctoritate apostolica facta Willelmo de Esyngdon' clerico fuit eidem confirmata per Innocentium ii° kalendas Jullii anno viii°,[732] xx li.[731]

## (fol. 144, li) Hibernia

De decanatu ecclesie Dublinensis, taxato xli li., de quo fuit provisum Matheo de Brysseleye per Clementem antequam dictus Hugo esset nuntius, pro resta dimissa xiiii li. xiii s. iiii d.[733]

De thesauraria ecclesie Dublinensis et prebenda de Balimo (Ballymore), collatio facta Johanni de Gate fuit eidem confirmata per Clementem viii° idus Maii anno viii°,[734] taxata xx li. debentur xx li.[735]

De decanatu ecclesie Dublinensis, taxato xli li., de quo per obitum Mathey de Brysseley fuit provisum Johanni Bryon, pro resta dimissa xx li.[735]

De cancellaria ecclesie Dublinensis, taxata xl li., collatio facta Johanni de Troy fuit eidem confirmata per

Innocentium iiii° kalendas Junii anno ii°,[736] pro resta dimissa xxvi li. xiii s. iiii d.[735]

De prebenda ecclesie Dublinensis, de qua per consecrationem Johannis electi Dublinensis fuit provisum Willelmo Roberti per Clementem nonas kalendas Januarii anno viii°,[737] debentur fructus.[735]

De prebenda ecclesie Dublinensis, de qua per consecrationem episcopi Lymiricensis fuit provisum Ricardo Drax per Innocentium xvi° kalendas Maii anno ii°,[738] debentur fructus.[739]

De prebenda ecclesie Dublinensis, taxata xxiii li. vi s. viii d., de qua per obitum Willelmi de Kelsey fuit provisum Johanni de Luddeley per Innocentium iii° kalendas Maii anno vi°,[740] xxiii li. vi s. viii d.[739]

De decanatu ecclesie [741] Carkagensis (Cork), de quo per provisionem factam Geraldo de Bury ad episcopatum Carkagensem fuit provisum Georgio de Ruppe canonico Carkegensi per Innocentium ii° nonas Februarii anno vii°.[742]

(fol. 144ᵛ) De archidiaconatu ecclesie Cassillensis (Cashel) collatio auctoritate ordinaria facta Johanni Carada fuit eidem confirmata per Innocentium vi° idus Junii anno vii°.[743]

De archidiaconatu Colnensi (Cloyne) collatio facta per episcopum Rogero de Braybrok' fuit sibi confirmata per Innocentium idus Augusti anno vii°.[744]

De decanatu ecclesie Waterffordensis ellectio facta de Waltero Reve ad dictum decanatum fuit eidem confirmata per Innocentium iiii° kalendas Junii anno ix°.[745]

De thesauraria ecclesie Dublinensis taxata xx li. ad antiquam taxam, quia novam ignoro, de qua per resignationem Johannis Lymberd, procuratoris Johannis Gate, dicte ecclesie thesaurarii, fuit provisum Hugoni de Thesdale Eboracensis diocesis per Innocentium ii° idus Februarii anno vii°,[746] pro resta xiii li.[747]

De decanatu ecclesie de Duacensi (Kilmacduagh), de quo per munus consecrationis impensum N. episcopo Duacensi fuit provisum Johanni Megillekeaby, qui se obtulit paratum ⟨resignare⟩ thesaurariam eiusdem ecclesie dum et cetera, per Innocentium ii° nonas Aprilis anno vii°.[748]

De prebenda de Houth' (Howth) in ecclesia Dublinensi, taxata xxiii li. vi s. viii d., collatio facta auctoritate apostolica Waltero Moryn fuit eidem confirmata

---

[723] In the margin: *in arayragiis*.
[724] 12 January 1357.
[725] *est* repeated, MS.
[726] In the margin: *pars in arayragiis*.
[727] 22 August 1357.
[728] 28 February 1357.
[729] Followed by *de* not deleted.
[730] 25 October 1359.
[731] In the margin: *in arayragiis*.
[732] 30 June 1360.
[733] In the margin: Dublinensis. *Omnes inscripte huius diocesis sunt in arayragiis*.
[734] 8 May 1350.
[735] In the margin: *Dublinensis*.

[736] 29 May 1354.
[737] 24 December 1349.
[738] 16 April 1354.
[739] In the margin: *Dublinensis*.
[740] 29 April 1358.
[741] Followed by *K* deleted by a line.
[742] 4 February 1359. In the margin: *Carkagensis*.
[743] 8 June 1359. In the margin: *Cassellensis*.
[744] 13 August 1359. In the margin: *Colnensis*.
[745] 29 May 1361. In the margin: *Waterffordensis*.
[746] 12 February 1359.
[747] In the margin: *Dublinensis*.
[748] 4 April 1359. In the margin: *Duacensis*.

per Innocentium ii° idus Octobris anno viii°,[749] sed in proximo providetur alteri et ibi habet effectum.[750]

De prebenda de Houth' in ecclesia Dublinensi, cuius taxa et provisio supra in recepta secundum antiquam taxam x li.[750]

De eadem prebenda de qua eadem causa fuit provisum Thome [751] Gryk, ideo non habet effectum.[750]

(fol. 145, lii) De prebenda ecclesie Dublinensis, de qua per obitum Walteri Moryn fuit provisum Ade Robelyn per Innocentium kalendas Januarii anno nono,[752] debentur fructus.[750]

## Fernensis

De prebenda de Taghomon (Taghmon) in ecclesia Fernensi (Ferns), de qua per obitum Johannis de Sutton' fuit provisum Johanni Gate Galteryn per Clementem iii° idus Jullii anno xi°.[753]

De prebenda de Taghomom in ecclesia Fernensi per obitum Johannis Sutton' et parochiali ecclesia de Colsteuf' (Coolstuffe) dicte ⟨diocesis⟩ per obitum Thome Michel fuit ⟨provisum⟩ Domino J. Estruord in episcopatum Fernensem electum ne habeat in obprobrium episcopi mendicare per Clementem xvii° kalendas Augusti anno xi°.[754]

De ecclesia de Veteri Rose (Old Ross), de qua ex causa permutationis cum Nicholao Dystart fuit provisum Johanni de Welwek per Innocentium xvi° kalendas Augusti anno ii°.[755]

De prebenda de Taghomon in ecclesia Fernensi, de qua per obitum Johannis Sutton' fuit provisum Johanni Galtryn per Innocentium vi° idus Martii anno vi°.[756]

De prebenda de [757] Taghomon in ecclesia Fernensi, in qua et ad omne ius quod competebat Johanni Castri fuit subrogatus Walterius de Dodendale per Innocentium iiii° idus Septembris anno vii°.[758]

## Osoriensis

De prebenda de Wylmodowak (Kilmacdonagh) in ecclesia Osoriensi (Ossory), de qua per consecrationem Thome archiepiscopi Tuamensis fuit provisum Ricardo Radulphy per Clementem ii° idus Augusti anno xi°.[759]

De decanatu ecclesie Osoriensis, electio facta de Thoma de Wyntton' fuit eidem confirmata per Innocentium vi° kalendas Februarii anno ii°,[760] taxa non reperitur in libro, debentur fructus.

De prebenda ecclesie Lymiricensis, de qua per obitum Thome de Corkebay fuit provisum Johanni Cate per Innocentium xi° kalendas Januarii anno secundo.[761]

De prebenda de Disert' in ecclesia Lymyricensi, de qua per provisionem factam Stephano de Walle de archidiaconatu dicte ecclesie fuit provisum David Baucout' vi° idus Maii anno vi°.[762]

De decanatu ecclesie Lymyricensis, de quo per obitum Thome de Borkele fuit provisum Stephano de Walle per Innocentium ii° idus Decembris anno vᵗᵒ.[763]

De thesauraria ecclesie Lymyricensis de qua per obitum Ade Hunt' fuit provisum Goltero Godheyn per Innocentium vi° idus Martii anno viᵗᵒ.[764]

De precentoria ecclesie Lymiricensis, de qua eo quod Adam Craddok' ipsam cum ecclesia de Noutton' (Newtown) per tres annos detinuit fuit provisum Philipo Braybocok' per Innocentium v° idus Martii anno vi°.[765]

De decanatu Lymiricensi, de quo per munus consecrationis impensum Domino Stephano electo Lymiricensi fuit provisum Henrico Albo sive Vytlo', canonico dicte ecclesie, per Innocentium xviii° kalendas Junii anno viii°.[766]

De decanatu ecclesie Lymiricensis, vacante per obitum Henrici Wyth' fuit provisum Ade With' per Innocentium iii° idus Augusti anno ix°.[767]

De cancellaria ecclesie Lymiricensis, de qua per consecrationem Domini Stephani Lawele episcopi Lymiricensis fuit provisum Bartholomeo Dullart per Innocentium xiii° kalendas Januarii anno ix°.[768]

## Dunensis

De prioratu ecclesie Dunensis (Down), cum vacabit per consecrationem Ricardi electi Dunensis fuit mandatum provideri Nicholao Langton' per Innocentium v° idus Decembris anno primo,[769] taxa non reperitur in libro taxe.[770]

## (fol. 146, liii) Lismonensis (Lismore)

De ecclesia de Dunggeyen (Dungarvan), de qua ex causa permutationis cum decanatu rurali de Lynne (Lynn) Norwycensis diocesis cum [771] Adam Thebaut' fuit provisum Henrico de Wyntryngton' per Innocentium viii° kalendas Novembris anno viii°.[772]

---

[749] 14 October 1360.

[750] In the margin: *Dublinensis.*

[751] Followed by *Gy* deleted by a line.

[752] 1 January 1361.

[753] 13 July 1352. In the margin: *inscripte huius diocesis sunt in arayragiis.*

[754] 16 July 1352.

[755] 17 July 1354.

[756] 10 March 1358.

[757] Followed by *Th* deleted by a line.

[758] 10 September 1359.

[759] 12 August 1352.

[760] 27 January 1354.

[761] 22 December 1354. In the margin: *inscripte huius diocesis sunt in arayragiis.*

[762] 10 May 1358.

[763] 12 December 1357.

[764] 10 March 1358.

[765] 11 March 1358.

[766] 15 May 1360.

[767] 11 August 1361.

[768] 20 December 1361.

[769] 9 December 1353.

[770] In the margin: *in arayragiis.*

[771] Followed by *Johanne* deleted by a line.

[772] 25 October 1360. In the margin, bracketed against this and the next item: *in arayragiis.*

De prebenda Lismorensi, de qua per obitum Johannis de Balstot' fuit provisum Thome Lovestok per Innocentium anno v°,[773] debentur fructus.

De archidiaconatu Richemondie in ecclesia Eboracensi et prebenda de Myldelton' (Middleton) in ecclesia Cicestrensi et de Dymynstre (Yetminster) in ecclesia Saresbiriensi, quorum beneficiorum taxa et provisio continentur supra in fine recepte, et restant de eisdem beneficiis lxx li.[774]

Et est sciendum quod dictus Henricus de Wallton' fuit dimissus in compoto reddendo primo die Junii anno LVIII in c iiii$^{xx}$ xviii li. vi s. viii d., de quibus solvit ante obitum suum xl li., et dividendum residum pro resta debebantur de archidiaconatu cxxxvi li. xiii s. iiii d., de quibus solvit archidiaconus qui nunc est iiii$^{xx}$ viii li. vi s. viii d., de quibus et xv li. solutis post dictum compotum respondetur supra in recepta, et debentur adhuc in partem reste dictarum lxx li. xlviii li. vi s. viii d., et de prebenda Cicestrensi iii li. vi s. et de dicta prebenda Saresbiriensi xviii li. v s.

De subdecanatu Eboracensi et prebenda [775] de Grantham in ecclesia Saresbiriensi, de Rythemell' (Rathmichael) in ecclesia Dublinensi, de Clippton' (Clifton) in ecclesia Lincolniensi, de Cheswyk' (Chiswick) in ecclesia Londoniensi, de Rampton' in ecclesia collegiata Suthwellensi Eboracensis diocesis, quorum beneficiorum taxa et provisio continentur supra in ultimo folio recepte, pro resta lviii li. x s.

Quas debet solvere in quolibet festo Beati Johannis Baptiste et nativitatis domini xix li. x s. sterlingorum quousque fuerit satisfactum.

(fol. 146$^v$). De ecclesia de Hodneth' (Hodnet) Lychefeldensis diocesis et prebenda de Farendon' (Faringdon) in ecclesia Saresbiriensi, de Mora (Moorfields, St. Giles Cripplegate) in ecclesia Londoniensi, de Hundreton' (Hunderton) in ecclesia Hereffordensi et de Ledebury (Ledbury) in diocesi Hereffordensi, pro quorum beneficiorum primis annatis [776] Nicholaus [777] Beth' composuit cum camera in curia pro viii° 1 fl. ponderis camere solvendis videlicet in terminis contentis supra in ultimo folio xxvi recepte, de quibus solvit ut supra iii$^c$ fl. et debet pro resta v$^c$ 1 fl.

De cancellaria Saresbiriensi et prebenda de Huve (Hove) in ecclesia Cicestrensi, quarum taxa et provisio continentur supra in recepta, pro resta lxxii li.

Solvit xxxvi li in libro recepte folio;[778] residuum debet solvere a festo Beati Johannis Baptiste in unum annum, videlicet anno LXV°.

## Adhuc Hibernia

De prebenda de Coleneay (Cooliney) in ecclesia Calonensi (Cloyne), de qua ex [779] causa permutationis cum Johanne de Welwich' fuit provisum Nicholao Disert per Innocentium xvi° kalendas Augusti anno ii°.[780]

De prebenda in ecclesia Cassallensi quam obtinebat Thomas Matormagham fuit provisum Willelmo Vyolet' per Innocentium ii° nonas Novembris anno v$^{to}$.[781]

De vicaria perpetua in Thahendesyng' (Tashinny) Ardakensis (Ardagh) diocesis, de qua per obitum Augustini Osyn fuit provisum Thome Margeoyd per Innocentium ii° idus Septembris anno viii°.[782]

De prebenda de Disert' in ecclesia Lymiricensi, de qua per obitum Stephani Germon' fuit provisum Johanni de Madam per Innocentium xi° kalendas Februarii anno x°.[783]

(fol. 147, liiii) De prebenda de [784] Cullomen (Cooliney) in ecclesia Clonensi (Cloyne), de qua per obitum Thome episcopi Lismorensis fuit provisum Ricardo de Gate per Innocentium iiii° nonas Junii anno vi°.[785]

De prioratu monasterii Sancte Katerine Weterffordensis diocesis (St. Catherine Waterford), de quo per obitum fratris Philipi prioris eiusdem et reservationem fuit provisum fratri David canonico eiusdem monasterii iiii° nonas Jullii anno vi° per Innocentium.[786]

Ellectio facta de Waltero Reve ad decanatum Watraffordensem (Waterford) in Ibernia, vacantem [787] per mortem Ade Lok, fuit confimata per Innocentium iiii° kalendas Junii anno vi°.[788]

Sequntur beneficia collata per dominos cardinales Petragoricensem et Urgellensem de quibus nichil est recepta. Alia vero de quibus recepta est in toto vel in parte ponuntur supra in recepta et in arreyragiis.

## Saresbiriensis

De prioratu seu officio nuncupato de Noyone et de Novo Mercato (Neufmarché),[789] de quo fuit provisum Nicholao Bomin per cardinalem Petragoricensem, debentur fructus.

## Wygorniensis

De ecclesia de Honyngtton' (Honington), de qua Luce filio Willelmi fuit per cardinalem Urgellensem de novo provisum, nichil, quia eidem fuit provisum per

---

[773] 1357.

[774] In the margin: *quatuor proximo sequentes superius sunt in eorum locis.*

[775] Followed by *in* deleted by a line.

[776] *prime annate*, MS.

[777] *Nicholao*, MS.

[778] A blank is left in the manuscript for the number of the folio.

[779] *et*, MS.

[780] 17 July 1354.

[781] 4 November 1357.

[782] 12 September 1360.

[783] 22 January 1362.

[784] Followed by *Cullomeiy* deleted by a line.

[785] 2 June 1358.

[786] 4 July 1358.

[787] *vacat*, MS.

[788] 29 May 1358.

[789] The prior and the abbot of Neufmarché had property in Fittleton, Wilts: *Reg. Simonis de Gandavo*, i, 374.

cardinalem Petragoricensem [790] de eadem et virtute istius provisionis respondetur in recepta.

## Norwycensis

De ecclesia Omnium Sanctorum de Katellerston' (Kettlestone), taxata xiii li. vi s. viii d., de qua Johanni de Arderndon' cardinalis Urgellensis de novo providit, xiii li. vi s. viii d.

(fol. 147ᵛ) De ecclesia Sancte Marie de Westwyngg' (West Winch?), de qua Paulo Attewod de Midelton' cardinalis Urgellensis de novo providit, debentur fructus.

## Lincolniensis

De prebenda de Bonnebury (Banbury) in ecclesia Lincolniensi, taxata xxx li., de qua Magistro Johanni de Streteleye cardinalis Petragoricensis de novo providit, xxx li.

De ecclesia de Asheby parva (Little Ashby) taxata iiii li. xiii s. iiii d., de qua Willelmo Edele de Skynton' cardinalis Petragoricensis de novo providit, iiii li. xiii s. iiii d.

De vicaria ecclesie de Belyngton' (Bullington), non taxata, de qua Johanni de Derlton' cardinalis Petragoricensis de novo providit, debetur medietas.

De ecclesia de Longhous (Laughton) fuit provisum per dominum Petragoricensem Waltero de Bernak'.

De ecclesia Sancti Clementis de Wylouby (Willoughby) fuit provisum per dominum Petragoricensem Hugoni de Kusase, taxata xxiii li. vi s. viii d., debentur xxiii li. vi s. viii d.

De rectoria medietatis ecclesie de Baghenderby (Bag Enderby) fuit provisum per dominum Urgellensem Willelmo nato Roberti, iii li., iii li.

## Exoniensis

De cantaria perpetua Sancte Anne scita in ecclesia Omnium Sanctorum Exonie fuit provisum per dominum Urgellensem Alexandro Sporeman, non taxata, debetur.

## Lichfeldensis

De ecclesia de Aldesley (Alderley) fuit provisum per dominum Petragoricensem Johanni Raston', taxata viii li., viii li.

De ecclesia de Burnehull' (Burnhill) fuit provisum per dominum Petragoricensem Hugoni de Pemberton', non taxata, medietas.

(fol. 148, 1v) De vicaria ecclesie de Derset' magna (Great Dassett) fuit provisum per dominum Petragoricensem Willemo de Wy de Westebury, non taxata, medietas.

## Bangorensis

De ecclesia de Dlanbrugian' (Llangian) fuit provisum per dominum Petragoricensem David nato Johannis.

## Menevensis

De ecclesia de Kenneythmaur' (Cenarth) fuit provisum per dominum Petragoricensem Roberto Le Despenser, non taxata, medietas.

De ecclesia de Prendelgast (Prendergast) fuit provisum per dominum Urgellensem Thome Balymor'; alteri fuit provisum et respondetur supra in recepta.

## Eboracensis

De ecclesia de Foston' fuit provisum per dominum Petragoricensem Johanni Norffeld.

De ecclesia de Hokisgorthe fuit provisum per dominum Urgellensem cardinalem Willelmo Sibthorp iiiiᵒ kalendas Octobris anno LVIIᵒ.[791]

De ecclesia de Colwesbi (Cowesby) fuit provisum per dominum Urgellensem Richardo de Helperby.

Quod sequitur debet continuari in diocesi Exoniensi supra folio xxxvi, quia ibi deficit.

## Exoniensis continuatur

De vicaria ecclesie de Columpton' (Collumpton), non taxata, de qua per obitum Petri Moleys fuit provisum Thome de Pylton' per Innocentium iiiᵒ idus Maii anno viᵒ,[792] pro medietate vi li. xiii s. iiii d.

De ecclesia de Lansant (Lezant), collatio cuius facta Johanni de Brokelond, taxata iiii li., fuit [793] eidem confirmata per Innocentium xiᵒ kalendas Octobris anno viᵒ,[794] iiii li.

De prebenda ecclesie collegiate de Credyngton' (Crediton), in qua prebende non habent certa nomina, fuit per obitum [795] Thome David provisum Thome Andree per Innocentium xiᵒ kalendas Jullii anno ixᵒ, debentur fructus.

(fol. 148ᵛ) De prebenda ecclesie collegiate Sancte Thete (St. Teath), taxata iiii li., de qua per obitum Thome David fuit provisum Johanni Braker per Innocentium xiᵒ kalendas Jullii anno ixᵒ,[796] iiii li.

De portione parochialis ecclesie Sancte Endolient' (St. Endellion), de qua per obitum Willelmi Donne fuit provisum Symoni Wythull' per Innocentium iiiiᵒ nonas Jullii anno ixᵒ,[797] debentur fructus.

De prebenda ecclesie Exoniensis taxata iiii li., de qua per obitum Ricardi de Tormerton' et per mortem Willelmi de Bradelle fuit provisum Ade de Hilton' per Innocentium iiiiᵒ nonas Jullii anno ixᵒ,[798] iiii li.

De ecclesia de Basth', de qua, ex eo quod Henricus de Monte dictam ecclesiam vnacum alia pluribus annis tenuit et in presbyterium non promotus, fuit provisum

---

[790] *provisum* repeated MS.

[791] 28 September 1357.
[792] 13 May 1358.
[793] Over a word erased with a heavy line.
[794] 21 September 1358.
[795] Followed by *D* deleted by a line.
[796] 21 June 1361.
[797] 4 July 1361.
[798] 4 July 1361.

Crenezerio de Lauk' per Innocentium vi° kalendas Jullii anno nono.[799] Talis ecclesia non reperitur in ista diocesi.

De archidiaconatu Cornubie in ecclesia Exoniensi, non taxato, de quo per obitum Thome David fuit provisum Alexandro de Nevill' per Innocentium x° kalendas Septembris anno ix°,[800] medietas.

De prebenda ecclesie collegiate de Credyngton' (Crediton) de qua per obitum Johannis Colstere fuit provisum Willelmo de Bampton' per Innocentium iii° idus Augusti anno nono,[801] non habet proprium nomen.

De prebenda Sancti Karentoci (Crantock), que est ecclesia collegiata et non habet proprium nomen, collatio cuius facta Rogero de Stamfford fuit eidem confirmata per Innocentium x° kalendas Novembris anno ix°.[802]

De prebenda ecclesie collegiate Sancti Karentoci, et non habet certum nomen, cuius collatio facta Johanni de Holond fuit eidem confirmata per Innocentium iii° idus Maii anno ix°.[803]

De ecclesia Sancti Petri Exoniensis, collatio cuius fuit Johanni More confirmata per Innocentium iiii° nonas Maii [804] anno x°,[805] non taxata.

(fol. 149, lvi) Summa omnium arreyragiorum.[806]

Sequentia continuantur cum arrayragiis supra positis, quilibet in sua dyocesi.

### Londoniensis

De archidiaconatu Essexie [807] in ecclesia Londoniensi, non taxato, de quo collatio facta Willelmo Rothewelle fuit eidem confirmata per Innocentium iii° idus Februarii anno vi°,[808] medietas fructuum.

### Cicestrensis

De archidiaconatu Lewensi in ecclesia [809] Cicestrensi, quem Willelmus de Lughteburgh' obtinebat, vacante eo quod idem Willelmus thesaurariam dicte ecclesie fuit assecutus, fuit provisum Thome Bronwen per Innocetium vii° idus Septembris anno sexto,[810] debetur medietas fructuum.

De prebenda de Saleseya (Selsea) in ecclesia Cicestrensi, de qua per obitum Johannis Leth' fuit provisum Roberto de Askeby per Innocentium anno nono,[811] pro taxa xxi li. vi s. viii d.

De prebenda de Waltham in eadem ecclesia, taxata

x li., de qua per obitum Ade de Hilton' fuit provisum Waltero de Multon' per x li.

### (fol. 149ᵛ) Saresbiriensis

De prebenda de Preston' in ecclesia Saresbiriensi, taxata xvi li. xiii s. iiii d., de qua fuit provisum Thome de Setton' per Innocentium xi kalendas Novembris anno quinto,[812] xvi li. xiii s. iiii d.

### Exoniensis

De ecclesia Sancti Ylgani (Illogan) Exoniensis diocesis, de qua fuit provisum Nicholao de Lynbergh' per Innocentium xi° kalendas Decembris anno v°,[813] pro taxa viii li.

De prebenda Sancte Columbe minoris in ecclesia collegiata Sancti Karentoci (Crantock) fuit subrogatus in omni iure quod competebat David Mynard Johannes Crosiley, magister in artibus, per Innocentium nonas Maii anno vii°,[814] pro taxa.

### Bathoniensis et Wellensis

De vicaria Sancti Cuthberti Wellensis, de qua per resignationem Philipi Hente fuit provisum Willelmo Massyngham per Innocentium ii° nonas Septembris anno v°,[815] pro taxa vi li. xiii s. iiii d.

### Herefordensis

De prebenda in ecclesia Herefordensi quam Adam electus Menevensis obtinebat provisum fuit Johanni de Caven per Innocentium [816] iii° kalendas Novembris anno nono.[817]

De prebenda quam Symon episcopus Londoniensis obtinebat in eadem ecclesia fuit provisum Thome Thebaud per Innocentium iii° idus Decembris anno nono.[818]

De decanatu ecclesie Herefordensis quem obtinebat Thomas Trollek, in decanum Londoniensem electus, fuit provisum Willelmo de Remyngham per Innocentium vii° idus Aprilis anno x°,[819] pro taxa xxxi li. viii s. v [820] d.

### (fol. 150, lvii) Norwicensis

De ecclesia de Polham (Pulham), taxata liii li. vi s. viii d., de qua per obitum Willelmi de Kylleseye fuit provisum Ricardo Michael per Innocentium vi° idus Februarii anno vi°,[821] liii li. vi s. viii d.

---

[799] 26 June 1361.
[800] 23 August 1361.
[801] 11 August 1361.
[802] 23 October 1361.
[803] 13 May 1361.
[804] Followed by *non taxata* deleted by a line.
[805] 4 May 1362.
[806] Blank in MS.
[807] Repeated in the manuscript and deleted by a line.
[808] 11 February 1358.
[809] *ecclesie*, MS.
[810] 7 September 1358.
[811] *nona*, MS. 1361.

[812] 22 October 1357.
[813] 21 November 1357.
[814] 7 May 1359.
[815] 4 September 1357.
[816] Followed by *iiii* deleted by a line.
[817] 30 October 1361.
[818] 11 December 1361.
[819] 7 April 1362.
[820] Over *iiii* deleted by a line.
[821] 8 February 1358.

## Lincolniensis

De ecclesia parva Kynewell' (Little Kimble), taxata iiii li. xiii s. iiii d., de qua per assecutionem ecclesie de Gesyngton' (Garsington) per Stephanum de Gesyngton' fuit provisum Johanni Rocelli per Innocentium vi° idus Martii anno vi°,[822] iiii li. xiii s. iiii d.

De prebenda Lincolniensi, de qua per obitum [823] Jacobi de Borelay fuit provisum Domino G. episcopo Tusculano [824] per Innocentium xv kalendas Septembris anno vi°.[825]

De officio capelle seir [826] in altare Sancti Petri in ecclesia Lincolniensi, non taxato, vacante per assecutionem ecclesie de Ovre (Over) factam per Thomam de Clypston', fuit provisum Willelmo de Byston' per Innocentium iiii° nonas Decembris anno vi°,[827] medietas fructuum.

De ecclesia de Haughton' (Houghton) presentatio et institutio facte Hugoni de Spabyng' fuerunt [828] eidem auctoritate apostolica confirmate vel provisum de novo per Innocentium xviii° kalendas Septembris anno viii°.[829]

## Licheffeldensis

De prebenda de Wesford (Weeford) in ecclesia Lichfeldensi, de qua in omni iure quod competebat Antonio de Monte Peliologo fuit subrogatus Thomas Michael per Innocentium x° kalendas Junii anno v°.[830]

De prebenda de Sterfold (Stotfold) in ecclesia Lichfeldensi, taxata x li., de qua per liberam resignationem Raymundi de Sancto Claro fuit provisum Johanni de Sancto Claro xiii° kalendas Maii anno vi° per Innocentium,[831] x li.

(fol. 150ᵛ) De cantaria ecclesie Lichfeldensis quam Thomas de Badeby debuit dimittere per assecutionem canonicatus et prebende ecclesie Lincolniensis fuit provisum.[832]

## Assavensis

De ecclesia de Landrineawe (Llandrinio), taxata vii li., que fuit confirmata Griffino de Challeton' per Innocentium iii° nonas Maii anno ix°,[833] vii li.

De ecclesia de Dynerth' (Denbigh), taxata xv li. vi s. viii d., de qua per obitum Willelmi de Sundurlund fuit provisum Willelmo Harden per Innocentium ix° kalendas Maii anno ix°,[834] xv li. vi s. viii d.

De ecclesia de Denbech' (Denbigh), vacante per obitum dicti Willelmi fuit provisum Hugoni de Craft per Innocentium iiii° kalendas Maii anno ix°.[835]

De ecclesia de Kylkeyn (Kilken), taxata vii li., et capella eidem ⟨annexa⟩, de qua per obitum Willelmi [836] ultimi rectoris eiusdem fuit provisum Waltero Freystrop' per Innocentium xi° kalendas Jullii anno ix°,[837] vii li.

De ecclesia de Meyvoc (Meifod), de qua per consecrationem Ludovici episcopi Herefordensis fuit provisum Willelmo de Challeton' per Innocentium iiii° kalendas Octobris anno nono.[838]

## Eboracensis

De prebenda de Hoveden' (Howden), taxata xxxiii li. vi s. viii d., de qua per obitum Johannis de Metha fuit provisum Ricardo Drax per Innocentium vii° idus Junii anno v°,[839] xxxiii li. vi s. viii d.[840]

De prebenda de Northewell' (Norwell), taxata xxxvi li. xiii s. iiii d., in qua in omni iure quod competebat Johanni de Denton' fuit subrogatus Thomas [841] per Innocentium vi° kalendas Augusti anno v°,[842] xxxvi li. xiii s. iiii d.

(fol. 151, lviii) De prebenda de Domygton' (Dunnington), taxata x li., de qua fuit provisum Ricardo Drax, eo quod Michael de North'burgh' minus iuste dicebatur obtinere, per Innocentium x° kalendas Novembris anno v°,[843] x li.

De prebenda in ecclesia collegiata Ripponensi vocata de Nonwyk (Anwyke), taxata xlv m., acceptatio, collatio et provisio facte Thome de Clypston' fuerunt eidem confirmate per Innocentium vii° kalendas Jullii anno vii°,[844] xxx li.

De vicaria ecclesie de Newerk (Newark), de qua per obitum fratris Thome de Weston' fuit provisum Willelmo de Thorald per Innocentium xiii° kalendas Februarii anno vii°.[845]

De capella sive capellania alias dicta cantoria de Wentbrigg' (Wentbridge), de qua per obitum Thome Attemore fuit provisum Roberto de Wyk per Innocentium xi° kalendas Decembris anno vii°.[846]

De archidiaconatu de Estridyng' in ecclesia Eboracensi, non taxato, vacante eo quod Guillelmus de Walcote qui ipsum obtinebat aliam ecclesiam extitit assecutus, fuit provisum Waltero de Skyrlawe per Innocentium ii° kalendas Decembris anno vii°,[847] medietas.

---

[822] 10 March 1358.
[823] Followed by *Johannis* deleted by a line.
[824] William de Court.
[825] 18 August 1358.
[826] The editor of *Cal. Pap. Regs. Petitions* translates the phrase *capelle seir* as chaplaincy: i, 307.
[827] 2 December 1358.
[828] *fuit*, MS.
[829] 15 August 1360.
[830] 23 May 1357.
[831] 19 April 1358.
[832] Left blank in MS.
[833] 5 May 1361.
[834] 23 April 1361.

[835] 28 April 1361.
[836] Followed by a blank space in MS.
[837] 21 June 1361.
[838] 28 September 1361. In the margin: *scribe*.
[839] 7 June 1357.
[840] In the margin: *scribe totum usque ad finem*.
[841] Followed by a blank space in MS.
[842] 27 July 1357.
[843] 23 October 1357.
[844] 25 June 1359.
[845] 20 January 1359.
[846] 21 November 1359.
[847] 30 November 1359.

De custodia seu sacristia capelle Beate Marie et Sanctorum Angelorum Eboracensis provisio et collatio facte auctoritate ordinaria Johanni de Waltham fuerunt eidem auctoritate apostolica confirmate vel provisum de novo per Innocentium ix° kalendas Januarii anno ix°,[848] iiii^xx viii li. vii s. viii d.

(fol. 152)[849] Infrascripta benefficia extracta sunt de regestris beneficiorum collatorum in Anglia et Ybernia tam per sancte memorie Clementem papam VI^m quam Innocentium, a prima die menssis Augusti anno M° CCC° XLIX°, quo tempore Dominus Hugo Pelegrini in illis partibus nuntiationis officium sucepit, usque ad primam diem menssis Septembris anno domini M° CCC° LXIII°, quo tempore dictus Hugo prefatum officium dimisit, de quibus in aliquibus rationibus suis nullam facit penitus mentionem.

### Licheffeldensis

De parochiali ecclesia de Danyton' (Donington) dyocesis Licheffeldensis, per resignationem Johannis de Pentrich', fuit provisum Thome de Pentrich' xi kalendas Jullii pontificatus Domini Clementis anno viii°.[850]

### Lincoliensis

De canonicatu et prebenda ecclesie Lincoliensis similiter, videlicet per munus consecrationis fuit provisum Johanni de Columpna vi° nonas Iulii pontificatus Domini Clementis anno supradicto.[851]

### Wynthoniensis

In iure et ad omne ius quod competebat Edmunddo de Chynbury in parochiali ecclesia de Laver de Bostok (Laverstoke), Wynthoniensis diocesis fuit subrogatus Thomas de Entham quinto kalendas Iulii pontificatus Domini Clementis anno supradicto.[852]

### Menevensis

De canonicatu et prebenda ecclesie Menevensis, vacantibus pro eo quod Reginaldus de Brian nunc electus dicte ecclesie fuit aliam pingulorem asequtus, fuit provisum Johanni Guanigre ii kalendas Octobris pontificatus Domini Clementis anno supradicto,[853] sed de ista fuit provisum anno secundo Innocentii sexti xv kalendas Novembris[854] et pro illa respondetur.

### Cantuariensis

Fuit dispenssatum cum Adam de Derghengton' ut ecclesiam de Wilkham (Wickham) diocesis Cantuariensis, simonia si quam commisit in aliquo non obstante, valeat licite retinere, et remissi fructus quos percepit ex eadem, set dabit sextam partem fructuum in subssidium contra Turchos ydus Octobris pontificatus Domini Clementis anno supradicto.[855]

### Londoniensis

De canonicatu et prebenda Londoniensi, simili modo vacantibus, fuit provisum eidem Michaeli xiii kalendas Decembris pontificatus Domini Clementis anno predicto.[856]

### (fol. 152ᵛ) Exoniensis

Item de canonicatu et prebenda ecclesie de Criditon' (Crediton) Exoniensis diocesis per obitum Johannis Huppeville nonas Decembris pontificatus Domini Clementis anno supradicto.[857]

### Licheffeldensis

Collatio facta de archidiaconatu Staffordie in ecclesia Licheffelddensi Ricardo Beningham fuit eidem confirmata ii ydus Decembris pontificatus Domini Clementis anno supradicto.[858] Ista provisio ponitur inter araytgia in libro suo, sed non in libro camere; respondetur tamen in ultimis computis suis, sed non concordant date.

### Dublinensis

De canonicatu et prebenda ecclesie Dublinensis, vacantibus per consecrationem Domini Johannis electi Dublinensis, fuit provisum Willelmo Rotberti ix kalendas Januarii pontificatus Domini Clementis supradicto.[859]

### Exoniensis

Collatio facta de archidiaconatu Exonie, canonicatibus et prebendis in ecclesia Cicestreni, de Walton' in ecclesia collegiata de Bosham eiusdem diocesis, necnon in ecclesiis collegiatis Sancte Thethe (St. Teath), Sancti Thome Clayseneye (Glasnay), Sancte Marie de Otherii (Ottery) Exoniensis per ordinarium Othonii de Norhwodde vi ydus Aprilis pontificatus Domini Clementis anno supradicto.[860] De ecclesia Sancte Marie de Othery non respondetur; de aliis respondetur; sed dicit quod est capella libera regis.

### Cicestrensis

Item Ade de Houton' de archidiaconatu Cicestrensi; de ista respondetur in ultimis computis.

De anno nono pape Clementis

---

[848] 24 December 1361.
[849] Folio 151ᵛ is blank.
[850] 21 June 1349. In the margin: *per resignationem* (two words rendered illegible by a stain) *fuit provisum Thome de Melburn'* (word illegible) *Domini Innocentii.*
[851] 2 July 1349. In the margin: *inperfecte poni⟨tur⟩.* The last letters are obsecured by a stain.
[852] 27 June 1349.
[853] 30 September 1349.
[854] 18 October 1354. Followed by *anno* deleted by a line.

[855] 15 October 1349.
[856] 19 November 1349.
[857] 5 December 1349.
[858] 12 December 1349.
[859] 24 December 1349.
[860] 8 April 1350.

### Eboracensis

De canonicatu et prebenda Sancti Michaelis in ecclesia collegiata Sancti Johannis Beverlacensi, vacantibus per obitum Gryffini alias Griffredi de Groppo, fuit provisum Rotberto de Beverlaco xv kalendas Junii pontificatus Domini Clementis anno ix°.[861]

### Cicestrensis

De canonicatu et prebenda Cicestrensi, vacantibus per obitum Symonis Sapiti, de quibus fuit provisum Willelmo de Albussato, per cuius consecrationem in episcopum Foroiuliensem (Fréjus) fuit provisum postmodum Domino Nicolao in Via Lata presbytero (fol. 153) cardinali, per cuius resignationem fuit provisum Michaeli de Northburgh' iiii° nonas Junii pontificatus Domini Clementis anno ix°.[862]

### Lincoliensis

De canonicatu et prebenda ecclesie Lincoliensis, vacantibus per obitum cardinalis Tusculani[863] fuit provisum Raymundo Pelegrini viii° ydus Septembris anno supradicto.[864]

### Rossensis Ybernia[865]

Item de Santio de Kikbos ad decanatum ecclesie Rossensis quinto ydus Septembris pontificatus Domini Clementis anno ix°.[866]

Item Johanni Albroyot de cancellaria unacum canonicatu et prebenda ecclesie Rossensis per assequtionem decanatus ipsius ecclesie factam per Alexandrum quinto ydus Septembris pontificatus Domini Clementis anno ix°.[866]

### Lincoliensis

Fuit concessum abbati et conventui monasterii de Neuhous (Newhouse) Premostratensis ordinis diocesis Lincoliensis ut upsi in vicariis ecclesiarum parochialium quas ad presens optinent et optinebunt possint per ordinarium loci canonicos expresse professos in vicarios facere collocari usque ad sex, ydus Novembris pontificatus Domini Clementis anno supradicto.[867]

### Saresbiriensis

Item Willelmo Mullebourn' de parochiali ecclesia de Bratton' Saresbiriensis diocesis iiii° kalendas Martii pontificatus Domini Clementis anno ix°.[868]

### Lincoliensis

Item Johanni Garriz de prioratu conventuali Beate

Marie Thykfford (Thetford) Lincoliensis diocesis[869] et Guillelmo Conqueteire de prioratu de Villa Berffeud (Villeberfol) Carnotensis (Chartres) diocesis quinto nonas Martii pontificatus Domini Clementis anno supradicto.[870]

### (fol. 153ᵛ) Wellensis

Fuit facta gratia domino episcopo Wellensi ut duas dignitates vel perssonatus vacantes vel vacaturi in dicta ecclesia, ad collationem ipsius alias pertinentes, auctoritate appostolica perssonis quibus videtur[871] valeat providere xv kalendas Maii pontificatus Domini Clementis anno ix°.[872]

### Londoniensis et Wellensis

Item per Johannem Thoursteyn de prebenda Wellensi per obitum Henrici de Carleton' et de prebenda Londoniensi per obitum Walteri de Londonis iii° ydus Maii pontificatus Domini Clementis anno supradicto.[873] De prima prebenda respondetur, set non de ultima, scilicet de Londonia.

### Non est nomen diocesis

Item Johanni de Croso de parochiali ecclesia de Arpalhamtis diocesis iii° ydus Maii pontificatus Domini Clementis anno ix°.[873]

### Lincoliensis

Item Hugoni de Wymundewold de prebenda ecclesie Lincoliensis per obitum Johannis de Bredon' iii° ydus Maii pontificatus Domini Clementis anno ix°.[873]

Item Galtero de Quentre de canonicatu et prebenda ecclesie Dunkeldensis (Dunkeld) per obitum Johannis de Rokelburw iiii° ydus Maii pontificatus Domini Clementis anno supradicto.[874]

### De anno decimo pape Clementis

### Lincoliensis

Parochialis ecclesia de Gibbeteye, alias de Siweseye vulgaliter nuncupata, (Sibsey) Lincoliensis diocesi fuit unita mensse prioris et conventus monasterii de Spalding dicte diocesis, reservato,[875] vicario perpetuo ibi instituendo, xii kalendas Iulii pontificatus Domini Clementis pape sexti anno decimo.[876]

### (fol. 154) Eboracensis

Provisio facta et permutatio postea subsequta per Rotbertum de Askeby et Walterum Woldhouse de

---

[861] 18 May 1351.
[862] 2 June 1350.
[863] Anibaldus de Ceccano.
[864] 6 September 1350.
[865] Heading repeated against the next item.
[866] 9 September 1350.
[867] 13 November 1350. In the margin: *videatur si debetur aliquid camere.*
[868] 26 February 1351.

[869] It should be the diocese of Norwich.
[870] 3 March 1351.
[871] *vident*, MS.
[872] 17 April 1351.
[873] 13 May 1351.
[874] 12 May 1351. In the margin: *notatur quod dicitur, quia nimis obscure ponitur.*
[875] *reservata*, MS.
[876] 20 June 1351.

canonicatibus et prebendis in ecclesia Eboracensi fuit confirmata per Clementem pontificatus sui anno decimo vii ydus Septembris.[877]

### Rossensis Ybernia

Item Johanni Senescalli de subdecanatu ecclesie Rossensis per Clementem ix kalendas Decembris anno predicto.[878]

### Eboracensis

Item Henrico de Ingelby de prebenda de Oxton' et Crepul' (Oxton and Cropwell Bishop) in ecclesia Beate Marie de Suthwell' diocesis Eboracensis per collationem archiepiscopi Eboracensis ix° kalendas Decembris pontificatus Domini Clementis anno predicto.[878]

### Licheffeldensis

De canonicatu et prebenda de Ulton' (Ufton) in ecclesia Licheffeldensi per resignationem Johannis de Wynewyk ac parochiali ecclesia de Stamfford (Stanford on Avon) per resignationem ipsius fuit provisum Johanni de Melbont per Clementem xviii kalendas Februarii anno x.[879] Respondetur de prebenda sed non de parochiali ecclesia.

### Lincoliensis

De canonicatu Lincoliensis ecclesie et prebenda de Cropy (Cropredy) per obitum domini cardinalis Hostiensis (Ostia)[880] fuit provisum Guidoni de Pestello decretorum doctori per Clementem iiii° nonas Aprilis anno predicto.[881]

Item Johanni Astynges de parochiali ecclesia de Werketon' (Warkton) Lincoliensis diocesis per resignationem Nicholay de Merton' per Clementem viii ydus Maii anno predicto.[882]

### De anno xi° Clementis

Unio facta priori et conventui monasterio de Novoburgo (Newburgh) Eboracensis diocesis de parochiali ecclesia de Custon' (Owston) Lincoliensis diocesis fuit confirmata, reservatione non obstante, vii kalendas Junii.[883]

### Saresbiriensis

Provisio facta Galffrido Mordak' de parochiali ecclesia de Brinekevorhe (Brinkworth) Saresbiriensis diocesis fuit confirmata ydus Junii.[884]

### Cicestrensis

Item per Adam Hoton' de archidiaconatu Cicestrensi per obitum ultimi archidiaconi xv kalendas Iulii.[885]

### Wellensis

Item per Adam de Trewellove de canonicatu et prebenda Cumba septima (Combe Septima), vacantibus in ecclesia Wellensi per obitum Thome de Donfford, ix kalendas Iulii.[886]

Item per Johannem de Hardrio de vicaria perpetua parochialis ecclesie de Mildenhale (Mildenhall) Norwicensis diocesis ix kalendas Iulii.[886]

De canonicatu et prebenda de Taghtinon' (Taghmon) in ecclesia Fernensi in Ybernia per obitum Johannis de Synton' fuit provisum Johanni Gate, thesaurario Dublinensis diocesis, iii ydus Iulii.[887]

### (fol. 154ᵛ) Eboracensis

Parochiales ecclesie de Wanumpycy (Wharram Percy) et de Eiveley (Kirk Ella) Eboracensis diocesis fuerunt unite priori monasterii de Hautenpresey (Haltemprice) ydus Iunii,[888] que taxantur lxxiii li. vi s. viii d., de quibus non respondetur nisi de lxx li., et sic deficiunt iii li. vi s. viii d.[889]

### Saresbiriensis

Parochialis ecclesia de Bosteldon' (Basildon) Saresbirienesis diocesis fuit unita collegio Sancti Johannis Baptiste (in Basildon) vel cantorie unius custodis et cappellanorum et ministrorum in ibi servientium viii kalendas Augusti.[890]

De canonicatu et prebenda de Kilmodowuok (Kilmacdonagh) in ecclesia Clonensi (Cloyne) per consecrationem Thome archiepiscopi Tuanensis (Tuam) fuit provisum Richardo Radulphi.

### Eboracensis

Fuit dispenssatum cum Johanne de Akun ut, non obstante furem et condempnationem mortis,[891] canonicatum et prebendam non curatos[892] in capella Sancte Marie et Sanctorum Angelorum Eboraci valeat retinere ydus Novembris.[893]

### De anno primo Domini Innocentii pape sexti

### Lincoliensis

Item simili modo eidem episcopo de canonicatu et

---

[877] 7 September 1351.
[878] 23 November 1351.
[879] 15 January 1352.
[880] Bertrand de Pouget.
[881] 2 April 1352.
[882] 8 May 1352.
[883] 26 May 1352.
[884] 13 June 1352.

[885] 17 June 1352.
[886] 23 June 1352.
[887] 13 July 1352.
[888] 13 June 1352.
[889] In the margin: *tam in recepta quam in arayragiis.*
[890] 25 July 1352.
[891] Presumably the clause should read non obstante furis condempnatione ad mortem.
[892] *canonicatuum et prebendarum curatorum*, MS.
[893] 13 November 1352.

prebenda ecclesie Lincoliensis cum vacaverint per consecrationem ut supra iii nonas Januarii.[894]

## Cantuariensis

Item fuit provisum Willelmo de Coston' de parochiali ecclesia de Wimbelden' (Wimbledon) Cantuariensis diocesis, vacante per obitum bone memorii Domini Adhemarii nuper sancte Romane ecclesie cardinalis,[895] viiᵒ ydus Martii.[896]

## Aichadiensis in Ybernia

De canonicatu et prebenda Aichadiensibus (Aghadoe), vacantibus per obitum Altherii, fuit provisum Andree Pantaleonis viiiᵒ kalendas Augusti.[897]

## Non est diocesis

De parochiali ecclesia de Salwode (Saltwood), vacante per liberam resignationem Symonis se Suberia fuit provisum Ricardo de Emesby v kalendas Augusti.[898] Nescitur de qua diocesi sit et ideo est incerta.

## Nescit ubi sit.

De prioratu ecclesie Dunensis (Down) cum vacabit per consecrationem Ricardi electi Dunensis fuit provisum Nicholao Langton' v ydus Decembris.[899]

Anno secundi Domini Innocentii

## Menevensis

In iure quod competebat Thome Melyn dum vivebat super parochialem ecclesiam de Ynebeya (Tenby) Menevensis diocesis fuit subrogatus Guido de Bryone baro iiiiᵒ kalendas Martii.[900]

## Exoniensis

De canonicatu et prebenda ecclesie Exoniensis vacantibus per liberam resignationem Willelmi de Cusantia fuit provisum Johanni de Sauceyo xi kalendas Aprilis.[901]

## Dublinensis

De canonicatu et prebenda ecclesie Sancti Patricii Dublinensis, vacantibus per consecrationem episcopi Lymeriscensis (Limerick), fuit provisum Ricardo de Drax xvi kalendas Maii.[902]

## (fol. 155) Lincoliensis

Motu proprio fuit provisum Hugoni Alberti de

canonicatu et prebenda ac archidiaconatu ecclesie Lincoliensis, vacantibus per obitum ultimi archidiaconi viii ydus Maii.[903] De ista respondetur in initio arayragiorum ulteriarum suarum rationum.

## Colonensis et Fernensis

De canonicatu et prebenda de Coleneny (Cooliney) in ecclesia Colonensis (Cloyne), per resignationem Johannis de Wellewyl, fuit provisum Nicholao Disaard et dicto Johanni fuit provisum de ecclesia de Veteri Rosse (Old Ross) Fernensis diocesis xvi kalendas Augusti.[904]

## Dunellmensis

De portione ecclesie de Nortan' (Norton) Dunelmensis diocesis, vacante per promotionem M. electi Londoniensis, fuit provisum Willelmo de Esenden' xi kalendas Januarii.[905]

De anno tertio Domini Innocentii

## Osoriensis

Electio facta de Thoma de Wauton' ad decanatum ecclesie Osoriensis fuit eidem confirmata vi kalendas Februarii.[906]

## Lincoliensis

De canonicatu et prebenda ecclesie Lincoliensis, vacantibus per obitum Henrici de Chaddesdene fuit provisum Thome de Madestayne viii kalendas Februarii.[907] De ista per mortem eiusdem providetur Thome de Burton' ix kalendas Februarii anno iiᵒ,[908] et de ista responditur in [909] recepta ulteriorum computorum. Collatio facta auctoritate appostolica de canonicatu et prebenda ecclesie Lincoliensis Johanni de Wellorurne fuit eidem confirmata v kalendas Februarii.[910]

## Eboracensis

Prebenda de Fenton' quam optinet in ecclesia Eboracensi Rotbertus de Walkyton' fuit eidem confirmata v kalendas Februarii.[910]

## Exoniensis

De archidiaconatu Cornubie in ecclesia Exoniensi, vacante per consecrationem episcopi Dublinensis fuit provisum Thome David vii ydus Februarii.[911]

## Lincoliensis [912]

Acceptationes et provisiones facte ex causa permu-

---

[894] 3 January 1353.
[895] Aymar Robert, priest of S. Anastasia.
[896] 9 March 1353.
[897] 25 July 1353.
[898] 28 July 1353.
[899] 9 December 1353.
[900] 26 February 1354.
[901] 22 March 1354.
[902] 16 April 1354.

[903] 8 May 1354.
[904] 17 July 1354.
[905] 22 December 1354.
[906] 27 January 1355.
[907] 25 January 1355.
[908] 24 January 1354.
[909] Followed by *arayragiis vel* deleted by a line.
[910] 28 January 1355.
[911] 7 February 1355.
[912] The heading is repeated before the next item.

tationis Willelmo de Dalton' et Willemo Hugata de canonicatibus et prebendis in ecclesia Lincoliensi auctoritate ordinaria fuerunt eisdem confirmate per papam iiii° kalendas Augusti.[913] De istis provisionibus respondetur in recepta et in arayragiis, sed sunt de tempore Clementis.

De novo fuit provisum J. de M. de parochiali ecclesia de W. diocesis Lincoliensis quam alter simoniace tenebat vii ydus Novembris.[914] Ista provisio datur inperfecte, et ex testu [915] ipsius non potest perfectus censsus [916] elici, et alias fuit data inter inutiles quia non ponitur nomen ecclesie nec nomen provisi.

De anno quarto Domini Innocentii

### (fol. 155ᵛ) Licheffeldensis

De canonicatu et prebenda de Welvey (Wolvey), quos in ecclesia Licheffeldensi optinebat episcopus Londoniensis, fuit provisum Symoni de Suberia vii kalendas Martii.[917]

### Saresbiriensis

De canonicatu et prebenda de Huldeverel (Hill Deverill) Saresbiriensis diocesis, vacantibus per obitum Bartholomei Patricii, fuit provisum Amautio Patricii ii nonas Maii.[918]

### Waterffordensis in Ybernia

Provisio facta auctoritate ordinaria de decanatu ecclesie Waterffordensi Nicholao Disaard fuit confirmata ii kalendas Iulii.[919]

### Fernensis in Ybernia

Collatio facta auctoritate ordinaria de canonicatu et prebenda de [920] Killaaygi (Killigney) in ecclesia Fernensi et ecclesia de [921] Caustdoff' (?) eisdem canonicatui et prebende annexa Nicolao Disaarde fuit eidem confirmata iiii ydus Julii.[922]

### Dublinensis

Dispenssatum fuit cum Johanne de Sutsham quod possit canonice retinere canonicatum et prebendam de Tamothin (Timothan) in ecclesia Sancti Patricii Dublinensis secundo kalendas Iulii.[919]

### Lincoliensis

De parochiali ecclesia de Ewordde (Epworth) Lin-

coliensis diocesis, vacante per obitum Willelmi de Clyve, fuit provisum Thome de Clipston' ii ydus Septembris.[923]

### Dublinensis

De canonicatu et prebenda ecclesie Sancti Patricii Dublinensis in Ybernia, vacantibus per obitum [924] Johannis de Balscote, fuit provisum Ricardo Gate ii ydus Septembris.[923]

### Menevensis

De canonicatu et prebenda ecclesie de Aberwyly (Abergwili) Menevensis diocesis, taxatis iiii li. vi s. viii d., vacantibus per obitum Griffini de Camdton' fuit provisum Martino de Monlisth' xiii kalendas Octobris.[925] Pro ista respondetur in recepta de iiii li. et non ponitur in arayragiis ubi debet poni pro vi. s. viii d.

### Lismorensis

In omni iure quod competebat dum vivebat Egidio Longus in parochiali ecclesia de Dungarvan et cappellania eidem annexa Lismorensis diocesis fuit subrogatus Adam Thebaut ix kalendas Decembris.[926]

De anno quinto Domini Innocentii

### Exoniensis

De archidiaconatu Tottonie in ecclesie Exoniensi Ricardo de Sbumton' v kalendas Novembris.[927]

### Cassellensis

De canonicatu et prebenda Cassellensi in Ybernia Willelmo Violetii nonas Novembris.[928]

De media rectoria parochialis ecclesie de Hoton' Bussill' (Hutton Bushel, Yorks), per duos solita gubernari rectores, Nicholao de Wyteby vi kalendas Augusti.[929]

### Cantuariensis

De perpetua vicaria parochialis ecclesie de Northbornrue (Northbourne) Cantuariensis diocesis Guillelmo Dreye ii kalendas Septembris.[930]

(fol. 156) De anno sexto Domini Innocentii

### Menevensis

De canonicatu et prebenda de Llannarth' (Llanarth) in ecclesia de Llandewabrevy (Llandewi Brefi) Menevensis diocesis, qui tanto tempore vacavit quod est

---

[913] 29 July 1355.
[914] 7 November 1355.
[915] For *textu*.
[916] For *sensus*.
[917] 24 February 1356.
[918] 6 May 1356.
[919] 30 June 1356.
[920] *doky*, MS.
[921] *de* repeated MS.
[922] 12 July 1356.

[923] 12 September 1356.
[924] Followed by *Griffini* deleted by a line.
[925] 19 September 1356.
[926] 23 November 1356.
[927] 28 October 1357.
[928] 4 November 1357.
[929] 27 July 1357. This Item is followed by the heading *De anno sexto Domini Innocentii* which is deleted by a line.
[930] 31 August 1357.

devoluta, fuit provisum Galffrido Iarden iii ydus Februarii.[931]

## Eboracensis

De canonicatu et prebenda ecclesie Beverllacensis Eboracensis diocesis, vacantibus per obitum Andree Offord alias le Moyne, fuit provisum Ricardo de Drax legum doctori quarto nonas Decembris.[932]

## Menevensis

Item collatio et provisio facte per Dominum Nicholaum tituli Sancti Vitalis presbyterum cardinalem appostolice sedis nuntium Philipo Elkyas, Menevensis diocesis magistro in artibus, de precentoria ecclesie Landavensis fuerunt eidem confirmate et sibi de novo provisum si sit vel fuerit reservata ydus Decembris.[933]

De anno septimo Domini Innocentii

## Cantuariensis

Reservata fuit parochialis ecclesia de Buxtede (Buxted) Cantuariensis diocesis confferenda Waltero Potyn cum vacabit per asequtionem preposature ecclesie collegiate de Wyngham (Wingham), de qua dominus noster papa providit Johanni de Scuerly iii kalendas Aprilis.[934]

## Menevensis

Item collatio et provisio facte per cardinalem Urgellensem Philipo Elays, Menevensis diocesis magistro in artibus, de precentoria ecclesie Londoniensis quam possidet fuerunt eidem confirmate auctoritate appostolica et sibi de novo provisum vii kalendas Iullii.[935]

De anno octavo Domini Innocentii

## Lincoliensis

De parochiali ecclesia in Karselowe (Creslow) Lincoliensis diocesis fuit provisum Roberto de Mancestre, presbytero Licheffeldensis diocesis, v kalendas Februarii.[936]

## Cicestrensis

Dispenssatum fuit cum Waltero de Strathon presbytero quod licite possit retinere perpetuam vicariam ecclesie parochialis de Iklesham (Icklesham) Cicestrensis diocesis ii ydus Januarii.[937]

## Cantuariensis

De parochiali ecclesia de Bekstede (Buxted) Cantuariensis diocesis, vacante per adeptationem ipsius preposature, fuit provisum Waltero de Tradynton' v kalendas Februarii.[938]

Ex causa permutationis fuit provisum Johanni Dich' de cappellania perpetua Beati Petri de Wollen' (Woolley) Eboracensis diocesis et Henrico Nundy de parochiali ecclesia Beate Marie de Herefford' (Hertford) Lincoliensis ⟨diocesis⟩. Ponuntur inter extracta per me.

## (fol. 156ᵛ) Lincoliensis et Norwicensis

Simili modo fuit provisum Rogero de Burton de parochiali ecclesia Detfford (Denford) Lincoliensis diocesis et Johanni de Ylglam de parochiali ecclesia Sancti Georgii de Suberi (Sudbury) Norwicensis.

## Lincoliensis

Eodem modo fuit provisum Henrico de Lalt' de cantoria seu cappellania [939] perpetua iuxta pontem ville de Elnestowe (Elstow) Lincoliensis diocesis et Johanni Manssatgier de vicaria perpetua Sancti Michaelis iuxta villam Sancti Albani dicte diocesis y kalendas Aprilis.[940]

## Eboracensis

Presentatio, institutio et inductio auctoritate ordinaria facte Thome Cissill' de Hoveden' de perpetua vicaria parochialis ecclesie de Estyngton' (Eastrington) Eboracensis diocesis fuerunt eidem confirmate et provisum de novo iii kalendas Aprilis.[941]

## Norwicensis

Presentatio per patronum laicum et institutio per episcopum Norwicensem facte ⟨Johanni⟩ de Wfforde de parochiali ecclesia de Hoynigham (Hingham) Norwicensis diocesis fuerunt eidem confirmate et provisum de novo xi kalendas Maii.[942]

## Dunelmensis

De hospitali pauperum Sancti Egidii de Kypute (Kepier) Dunelmensis diocesis, vacante per obitum Petri de Toersby, fuit provisum Johanni de Appelby, legum doctori, viii kalendas Maii.[943]

## Londoniensis

De parochiali ecclesia de Halawe (Harlow) Londoniensis diocesis fuit ⟨provisum⟩ Magistro Ricardo Anglici, cum vacabit per asequtionem archidiaconatus Tottonie in ecclesia Exoniensi, vi ydus Maii.[944]

## Lincoliensis

Collatio et provisio auctoritate ordinaria facte Ade de Hilton' de parochiali ecclesia de Glaton' (Glatton) Lincoliensis diocesis et postmodum collatio et provisio

[931] 11 February 1358.
[932] 2 December 1358.
[933] 13 December 1358.
[934] 30 March 1359.
[935] 25 June 1359.
[936] 28 January 1360.
[937] 12 January 1360.
[938] 28 January 1360.

[939] *cappllania*, MS.
[940] 28 March 1360.
[941] 30 March 1360.
[942] 21 April 1360.
[943] 24 April 1360.
[944] 10 May 1360.

auctoritate appostolica facte eidem Ade de prepositura
ecclesie Wellensis ac etiam de canonicatu et prebenda
eiusdem ecclesie eidem prepositure unitis fuerunt eidem
confirmate et provisum de novo iiii[to] kalendas Julii.[945]

### De anno ix° Domini Innocentii

Presentatio et institutio facte per episcopum et patronum laicum Johanni de Wfford de parochiali ecclesia
de Hyngham (Hingham) fuerunt eidem confirmate vel
provisum de novo et etiam super etate dispenssatum
xiii kalendas Februarii.[946]

### Lincoliensis

Collatio et provisio auctoritate ordinaria facte Willelmo Percehaye de Spaldewe de canonicatu et prebenda
ecclesie Sancte Crucis in ecclesia Lincoliensis, quos
Rotbertus de Streton episcopus Licheffeldensis in dicta
ecclesia optinebat, fuerunt eidem Willelmo auctoritate
appostolica confirmate et sibi provisum de novo iii nonas
Maii.[947]

### (fol. 157) Exoniensis

De canonicatu et prebenda ecclesie Exoniensis per
obitum Thome David fuit provisum Johanni de Seys
xi kalendas Iulii.[948]

### Assavensis

Item de parochiali ecclesia de Kalkem (Kilken) cum
capella eidem annexa Assavensis diocesis, vacante per
obitum Willelmi ultimi rectoris eiusdem, fuit provisum
Waltero Freystrop', et est paratus dimittere parochialem
ecclesiam de parva Hardas (Lower Hardres) Cantuariensis diocesis, xi kalendas Iulii.[948]

### Lincoliensis

De canonicatibus et prebendis ecclesiarum Narbonensis
(Narbonne) et Lincoliensis, vacantibus per obitum
quondam Willelmi de Theminis, fuit provisum Raynaldo
de Theminis, clerico Caturcensis (Cahors) diocesis, xi
kalendas Iulii.[948]

### Norwicensis

Parochialis ecclesia Dereham (East Dereham) Norwicensis, quam optinet Dominus Symon de Suberia
electus Londoniensis, per consecrationem ipsius fuit
reservata conferenda Bartholomeo Sedey iurisperito iii
kalendas Novembris.[949]

### Wellensis

Motu proprio fuit provisum Domino Petro cardinali
Aquensi (Dax)[950] de canonicatu et prebenda ac thesauraria ecclesie Wellensis, vacantibus per obitum

Ricardi de Tormenton' cenioris in Romana curia defuncti, ii ydus Novembris.[951]

### De anno decimo Domini Innocentii

### Norwicensis

De decanatu rurali sine cura de Fordham Norwicensis
diocesis, vacante per obitum Johannis Hoppe in Romana
curia defuncti, fuit provisum Waltero Palmer, presbytero diocesis Hereffordensis, v nonas Maii.[952]

### Cantuariensis

Item collatio et provisio facte per cardinalem Petragoricensem, tunc in partibus Anglie appostolice sedis
legatum, Wyllelmo Dreye de perpetua vicaria parochialis
ecclesie de Northburn' (Northbourne) Cantuariensis
diocesis, tunc vacante per liberam resignationem factam
per Johannem Stannfford in manibus dicti domini
cardinalis, fuerunt [953] eidem Willelmo auctoritate apostolica confirmate et sibi provisum de novo iiii ydus
Maii.[954]

### Limiricensis

Electio facta per capitulum ecclesie Limiricensis de
Magistro Philipo Leuffannt, canonico dicte ecclesie, ad
decanatum ipsius ecclesie, vacantem per promotionem
et consecrationem Stephani episcopi Limiricensis, fuit [955]
auctoritate apostolica confirmata [956] et sibi provisum
de novo.

### Leghlinensis (Leighlin) Ybernia

Electio facta per precentorem et capitulum ecclesie
Leghlinensis in Ybernia de Thoma Mastaffu ad decana-
tum ipsius ecclesie, vacantem per consecrationem
Willelmi Grispini episcopi Leghlinensis, fuit auctoritate
appostolica confirmata et sibi provisum de novo kalendas
Junii.[957]

### Londoniensis

De canonicatu et prebenda ecclesie Londoniensis,
vacantibus per liberam resignationem Henrici dicti Lem-
brech vel procuratoris sui, fuit provisum Banavato
Castellionis iii ydus Iunii.[958]

### (fol. 157[v]) Lincoliensis

De canonicatu et prebenda ecclesie Lincoliensis, vacantibus per liberam resignationem attornatoris cardinalis Carcassonensis,[959] fuit provisum Amaneno de
Uffabarneto, clerico diocesis Burdegalensis (Bordeaux),
x kalendas Iulii.[960]

[945] 28 June 1360.
[946] 20 January 1361.
[947] 5 May 1361 (prebend of Spaldwick).
[948] 21 June 1361.
[949] 30 October 1361.
[950] Peter Itherii, bishop of Dax, priest of Ss. Quattro Coronati.
[951] 12 November 1361.
[952] 3 May 1362.
[953] *fuit*, MS.
[954] 12 May 1362.
[955] *fuerint*, MS.
[956] *confirmate*, MS.
[957] 1 June 1362.
[958] 11 June 1362.
[959] Stephen Aubert, bishop of Carcassonne, deacon of S. Maria in Aquiro.
[960] 22 June 1362.

## Imelatensis Ybernia

De archidiaconatu ecclesie Imelatensis (Emly), vacante per obitum Henrici Albi in Romana curia defuncti, fuit provisum Henrico Ricard Imelatensis diocesis v kalendas Iulii.[961]

## Exoniensis

De canonicatu et prebenda ecclesie Exoniensis, vacantibus per obitum Ade de Hulthon' in curia Romana defuncti, fuit provisum Willelmo de Bremingham, sacre teulogie professori, ydus Iulii.[962]

## Saresbiriensis

Subrogatus fuit Arnaldus Garini presbyter in omni iure et ad omne ius quod competebat Arnaldo Pelegrini, clerico dicte diocesis extra Romanam curiam deffuncto, in et super canonicatu et prebenda de Bisstoppton' (Bishopstone) in ecclesia Saresbiriensi, super quibus idem Arnaldus Pelegrini diu in palatio appostolico litigavit contra Willelmo de Obeburn' Saresbiriensis diocesis, et pro se et contra dictum Willelmum tres sententias super possessione reportavit, ydus Iulii.[963]

## Wellensis

De decanatu ecclesie Wellensis, que dignitas electiva existit, reservato, vacante per obitum Johannis de Carlton' extra Romanam curiam defuncti, fuit provisum

Thome de Paxton, sacri palatii appostolici auditori kalendas Augusti.[964]

## Corkagensis

De decanatu ecclesie Corkagensis (Cork), vacante per consecrationem Georgii episcopi Cassallensis (Cashel), fuit provisum Thome Eliot'.

## Menevensis

Item Willelmo de Boldwyn' Menevensis diocesis de archidiachonatu de Kermendyn (Carmarthen) in ecclesia Menevensi, vacante per obitum David Martini in Romana curia defuncti, nonas Augusti.[965]

## Cicestrensis

De prioratu conventuali Lewensi, ordinis Cluniascensis, Cicestrensis diocesis, cum vacabit per asequtionem pacificam administrationis bonorum monasterii Ternothen' (Tournus) Cabilonensis (Châlon-sur-Saône) diocesis faciendam per fratrem Hugonem de Chincriato ultimum priorem dicti prioratus, fuit provisum Geraldo Bothoms, monacho bacallario in decretis, xvii kalendas Septembris.[966]

---

[961] 27 June 1362.
[962] 15 July 1362.
[963] 15 July 1362.

[964] 1 August 1362.
[965] 5 August 1362.
[966] 16 August 1362. The remainder of the codex contains a list of papal provisions to benefices in Scotland during the pontificates of Clement VI and Innocent VI and Urban V (fols. 158-177ᵛ) and the account of William de Grenlaw, papal collector in Scotland during the pontificate of Innocent VI (fols. 178-193).

# ACCOUNTS OF JOHN DE CABRESPINO COLLECTOR FROM 1363 TO 1371

Vatican Archives, Collectorie 11, fols. 1-71ᵛ (first copy of account for 1363 and 1364), 74-137ᵛ (second copy of the same),[1] 138-96ᵛ (account for period from 1364 to 1366), 202-62ᵛ (second copy of the same),[2] Collectorie 12, fols. 1-57 (1366 to 1368), 58-139 (1368 to 1370).

## FIRST ACCOUNT 1363-1364

(fol. 2)[3] Iste sunt rationes Johannis de Cabrespino, doctoris decretorum canonici Narbonensis in partibus Anglie et Ybernie appostolice sedis nuntii, de omnibus et singulis receptis, habitis et levatis per eum vel alios, traditis, expenssis et asignatis tam de restis arayratgiorum denariorum Beati Petri, censsuum ecclesie Romane, beneficiorum collatorum in illis partibus per Romanos pontiffices diverssos successive quam de quibuscumque aliis obventionibus sive emolumentis ad Romanam ecclesiam in illis partibus qualitercumque spectantibus a prima die menssis Septembris anno MCCCLXIIIᵒ usque ad ultimam diem menssis Martii anno domini Mᵒ CCCᵒ LXIIIIᵒ. Et primo ponitur recepta arayratgiorum denariorum Beati Petri, secundo recepta ordinaria dictorum denariorum, tertio recepta arayratgiorum annui censsus ecclesie Romane in illis partibus debitis, quarto ordinaria recepta dicti censsus et legatorum in subssidium Terre Sancte,[4] quinto recepta arayratgiorum beneficiorum collatorum in illis partibus per felicis recordationis Clementem Benedictum et Innocentium, sexto ordinaria recepta dictorum beneficiorum per iam dictos Romanos pontifices in illis partibus collatorum, ultimo recepta beneficiorum collatorum per Dominum Urbanum papam quintum et alie quedam extraordinarie recepte, ut in sequentibus per ordinem aparebit.

Sequitur recepta arayratgiorum denariorum Beati Petri per Dominum Raymundum Pelegrini nomine Domini Hugonis Pelegrini, fratris sui olim in Anglia appostolici sedis nuntii, mihi [5] traditorum a prima die menssis Septembris anno LXIIIᵒ usque ad ultimam diem menssis Martii anno LXIIIIᵒ.

Primo recepi ab exequtoribus bone memorie Domini Rotberti episcopi Cicestrensis pro denariis Beati Petri per eum debitis de anno LXIᵒ viii li. sterlingorum.

### xxi die Octobris

Item a domino nunc episcopo Cicestrensi pro eisdem denariis pro anno LXIIᵒ viii li.

Item a domino episcopo Herefordensi pro eisdem denariis dimissis in arayratgiis pro annis LXI et LXIIᵒ pro quolibet in sex libris, xii li.

### iiiiᵃ die Novembris

Item recepi a domino archidiacono Wynthoniensi, dimisso in arayratgiis pro dictis denariis pro annis LX, LXI et LXIIᵒ, pro quolibet dictorum annorum in xi li. xiii s. iiiiᵒʳ d., que summe ascendunt in summa xxxv li., in partem dicte summe xxiii li. vi s. viii d.[6] (fol. 2ᵛ) Restat quod debet pro uno anno, videlicet LXIIᵒ xi li. xiii s. iiii d.[7]

### Prima die Decembris

Item recepi ab archidiacono Surreie, dimisso in arayratgiis pro dictis denariis pro anno LXIIᵒ in v li. xiii s. iiii d., v li. xiii s. iiii d.

### xii die Decembris

Item recepi a domino episcopo Norwicensi pro eisdem denariis Beati Petri pro annis LXI et LXIIᵒ, pro quolibet xxi li. x s., xliii li.

### xii die Januarii

Item recepi a domino Wygorniensi episcopo, qui debebat pro resta de dictis denariis annis LXI et LXIIᵒ, pro quolibet x li. v s., in summa xx li. x s.

### xiii die Januarii

Item a domino episcopo Exoniensi, dimisso in arayratgiis pro dictis denariis pro annis LXIᵒ et LXIIᵒ, pro quolibet in ix li. et v s., xviii li. x s.

### xvii die Januarii

Item a Domino Rotberto episcopo Conventrensi et Lichfeldensi, dimisso in arayratgiis pro dictis denariis pro annis LXᵒ, LXIᵒ et LXIIᵒ, pro quolibet anno x li. v s., in plenam solutionem xxx li. xv s.

### quinta die Februarii

Item a domino archiepiscopo Eboracensi, dimisso in arayratgiis pro dictis denariis pro annis LIXᵒ, LXᵒ, LXIᵒ et LXIIᵒ, pro quolibet xi li. x s., in plenum xlvi li.

---

[1] For convenience the first copy is designated as **a** and the the second as **b**. Variations in the spelling of proper names are noted, unless the variation has no significance in relation to the identification of the person or place. For this purpose it seems superfluous to note, for example, that the form is *Lichfeldensis* in one copy and *Licheffeldensis* in the other. Variations in the spelling of other words are not noted unless one form or the other seems to be uncommon.

[2] The first copy is designated as **a** and the second as **b**.

[3] Folio 1 is blank. According to the original foliation, which has to be kept as far as it goes on account of references to above and below, this is folio i.

[4] In **b**, fol 76, mention of the legacies is omitted under *quarto*.

[5] Om. **b**.

[6] At the foot of the page: *Summa pagine li li. vi s s viii d.*

[7] In the margin: *Resta.*

sexta die Februarii

Item a domino episcopo Bathoniensi et Wellensi pro dictis denariis de anno LXII° xi li. v s.

xv die Februarii

Item a domino episcopo Sarisberiensi pro dictis denariis pro anno LXII° per manus Domini Raymundi Pelegrini xvii li.

Summa pagine usque hic cxcii li. xiii s. iiii d.

Summa universalis omnium precedentium arayratgiorum ii° xliiii li.

Recepta denariorum Beati Petri facta de tempore meo, videlicet a dicta prima die Septembris anno LXIII° citra

xxvi die Octobris

Primo a domino episcopo Sarisberiensi pro anno LXIII° in plenam solutionem xvii li.

Item ab archidiacono Colcestrie Londoniensis diocesis pro dictis denariis pro anno LXIII° in plenam satisfactionem v li. x s.

Summa a precedenti summa usque hic xxii li. x s.

Summa generalis tam omnium precedentium arayratgiorum quam ordinariorum denariorum Beati Petri ii° lxvi li. x s.

(fol. 3, ii) Recepta annui censsus de tempore mei Johannis de Cabrespino dicto anno M° CCCLXIII°

die xii Octobris

Primo recepi a custode ecclesie de Scaudeburgh' diocesis Eboracensis xv d. sterlingorum.

die xviii Octobris

Item ab abbate Sancti Albani diocesis Lincoliensis xiii s. iiii d.

die xxiii Octobris

Item ab abbate Sancti Edmundi Norwicensis diocesis xiii s. iiii d.

Item ab abbate de Corteseye viii s.

Item ab abbate Sancti Aldemi Malbesbury xiii s. iiii d.

Item a priore de Tenebrigg' xiii s. iiii d.

Summa recepte predicti censsus [8] iii li. ii s. vii d.

(fol. 3ᵛ) Recepta de arayratgiis per Dominum Raymundum Pelegrini michi dimissis, et primo ponuntur beneffica per Dominum Hugonem Pelegrini, olim in Anglia collectorem, in ultimis suis rationibus in curia redditis de anno LVIII° in arayratgiis dimissa, et subsequenter alia postmodum collata

Diocesis Cantuariensis

Primo recepi de prioratu de Folkeston' ordinis Sancti Benedicti, cuius collatio facta Guillelmo Medici fuit

eidem confirmata per Clementem, et dimisso in arayragiis in viii° li. xiii s. iiii d., viii li.   xiii s. iiii d.[9]

folio xxxvii

Item de ecclesia de Wynelesbergh' (Woodnesborough), taxata xvi li. xiii s. iiii d., appropriata [10] abbatie [11] Sancti Augustini Cantuariensis per Innocentium ii° kalendas Decembris pontificatus sui anno primo,[12] in plenam solutionem xvi li. xiii s. iiii d.

folio xli

Item de ecclesia de Brokelond' (Brookland), taxata xiii li. vi s. viii d. appropriata abbati et conventui Sancti Augustini Cantuariensis per Innocentium anno quo supra, in plenam solutionem xiii li. vi s. viii d.

Sequitur recepta benefficiorum collatorum post computa dicti Hugonis civitatis et diocesis antedicte.

folio xxxiiii

De ecclesia de Chertham (Chartham) diocesis Cantuariensis, taxata xxvi li. xiii s. iiii d., de qua per obitum Willelmi de Brandeleye fuit provisum Ricardo de Suggorgh' per Innocentium vii° ydus Julii anno ix°,[13] xxvi li. xiii s. iiii d.

folio xxxvii

De ecclesia de Bishopesburn' (Bishopsbourne), taxata xxxiii li. vi s. viii d., de qua per obitum Johannis Turstayn' fuit provisum Rotberto Pres per Innocentium iiii° ydus Augusti anno vii° vel viii°,[14] quia simul missi, in plenam solutionem xxxiii li. vi s. viii d.

folio xxxix

De ecclesia de Croydon', nondum missa, taxata xl li., de qua per consecrationem Adde episcopi Menevensis fuit provisum Adde Robelyn per Innocentium secundo kalendas Novembris anno ix°,[15] in plenam solutionem xl li.

Summa pagine cxxxviii li. xiii s. iiii d.

(fol. 4, iii) Roffensis diocesis
folio xxxv

De ecclesia de Mepham (Meopham), taxata xxvi li. xiii s. iiii d., de qua per dominum cardinalem Petragoricensem fuit provisum Johanni de Brigham, dimissa in arrayragiis in iii li. vi s. et viii d., in plenam solutionem iii li. vi s. viii d.

folio xxxv

De eadem ecclesia, de qua per obitum Johannis Blode

---

[9] In the margin of a: *iii li. recepte folio xxxvi.*

[10] *appropriate,* a, b.

[11] abbatisse, a, b.

[12] 30 November 1353. Date om. b except *anno primo.*

[13] 9 July 1361.

[14] 10 August 1359 or 1360.

[15] 31 October 1361.

[8] *senssus,* b.

fuit provisum Johanni de Kyrkeby per Innocentium iiii° nonas Iulii anno ix°,[16] et taxatur xxvi li. xiii s. iiii d. ut supra, in partem dicte taxe xvi li. xiii s. iiii d. Restat quod debet adhuc x li quas iuravit solvere in proximo festo Beati Michaelis sub pena excommunicationis late in scriptis.[17]

### folio xxxv

De ecclesia de Eneyfford (Eynsford), taxata xx li., cuius collatio et provisio auctoritate ordinaria facte Johanni de Wyngham fuerunt eidem confirmate per Innocentium viii° kalendas Junii anno vii°,[18] dimissa in arrayratgiis in xiii li. vi s. viii d., in plenam solutionem xiii li. vi s. viii d.

### Londoniensis et post dicta computa
### folio xxxviii°

De ecclesia Sancte Trinitatis Londonie, non taxata, ratione dispenssationis facte cum Thoma Balle presbytero ut, non obstante defectu natalium quem patiebatur, posset eam retinere per Innocentium xii kalendas Junii anno ix°,[19] qui iuravit quod omnes obventiones dicte ecclesie, nullis deductis expensis, non valent communiter ultra x li., in partem dicte medietatis camere debite ii li. x s. Restat quod debet ii li. x s., de quibus iuravit solvere medietatem in festo Pasche proximo lapsso et aliam medietatem in festo Beati Michaelis proximo venienti sub pena excommunicationis late in scriptis.[20]

### folio xli

De ecclesia Sancti Dyonisii Londonie, cuius provisio supra in recepta Domini Hugonis Pelegrini folio xvii°, dimissa in arrayratgiis in ii li., ii li.

### folio xxxix

De prebenda vocata Sancti Pancratii in ecclesia Londoniensi, taxata xlii si vi d., ratione provisionis facte Bonanato Castillionis per Innocentium iii ydus Maii[21] anno x°,[22] in plenam solutionem dicte taxe ii li. ii s. vi d.[23]

Summa pagine xxxix li. xix s. ii d.

### (fol. 4ᵛ) folio xl

De ecclesia de Purle (Purleigh) cuius taxa et provisio supra in recepta dicti Domini Hugonis folio xvii°, dimissa in arrayratgiis in vi li., in plenam satisfactionem vi li.

### folio xxxix

De ecclesia Sancti Schwythyni (St. Swithin) Londonie, non taxata, que fuit confirmata Radulpho Nicholay de Bury per [24] Innocentium v kalendas Octobris anno ix°,[25] de qua Johannes Burthon' nunc rector composuit ad vi m. pro medietate et iuravit quod omnes obventiones unius anni, nullis deductis expensis, ultra xii m. communiter non ascendunt, pro medietate in eius plenam satisfactionem iiii li.

### folio xxxix°

De prebenda de Wallekasbern' (Wenlock's Barn, St. Giles) in ecclesia Londoniensi, taxata v li., que, vacans [26] per consecrationem Radulphy de Bury in episcopatum Dunulnensem, fuit accepta per Johannem de Brankenee et eidem confirmata per Innocentium iiii kalendas Iulii anno viii°,[27] in plenam solutionem v li.

### folio xl

De ecclesia de Matffelon [28] (Whitechapel) Londonie, non taxata, cuius provisio supra in recepta Domini Hugonis folio xvii°, dimissa in arrayratgiis in xiii s. iiii d., in partem dicte reste vi s. viii d. Restat quod debet vi s. viii d. quos debuit solvere in feste Pasche proximo lapsso.[29]

### folio xxxix

De ecclesia de Sabricheswrth' (Sawbridgeworth) Londonie, taxata xlvi li. xiii s. iiii d., appropriata monasterio de Wastmostier (Westminster) per Clementem iii nonas Maii anno ix°,[30] in partem dicte taxe xxxiii li. vi s. viii d. Restat quod debet xiii li. vi s. viii d. quas debet solvere in proximo festo Beati Johannis Baptiste et habeo obligationem conventus.[31]

### Cicestrensis dyocesis
### folio xxxv

De decanatu Cicestrensi, cuius taxa et provisio in recepta dicti Domini Hugonis folio v, dimisso in arrayratgiis in xv li., in plenam solutionem xv li.

### folio xli

De cancellaria Sarisberiensi et prebenda de Huvia (Hove) in ecclesia Cicestrensi, dimissis in arrayratgiis in lxxii li. ratione provisionis facte Johanni de Northon,' in partem xxxvi li. Restat quod debet xxxvi li. quas debet solvere in festo Beati Johannis anno LXV.[32]

Summa pagine xcix li. xiii s. iiii d.

---

[16] 4 July 1361.
[17] In the margin: *Resta.*
[18] 25 May 1359.
[19] 21 May 1361.
[20] In the margin: *Resta.*
[21] *Junii,* **b.**
[22] 13 May or 11 June 1362.
[23] In the margin: *non est in arrayratgiis.*

[24] *per* is blotted and repeated in **a.**
[25] 27 September 1361.
[26] *que vacans* om. **b** and in its place *cuius provisio supra in recepta Domini Hugonis.*
[27] 28 June 1360.
[28] *Matsselon',* **b.**
[29] In the margin: *Resta.*
[30] 5 May 1351.
[31] In the margin of **a**: *noviter reperta.*
[32] In the margin of **a**: *Resta.*

(fol. 5, iiii) folio xxxiiii

De prebenda de Sutthon' (Sutton) in ecclesia Cicestrensi, taxata xxvi li. xiii s. iiii d., de qua per consecrationem Michaelis de Northeburgh' in episcopatum Londoniensem fuit provisum Michaeli de Northeburgh', consanguineo suo, per Innocentium xv kalendas Iunii anno primo,[33] in plenam solutionem xxvi li. xiii s. iiii d.

folio xxxiiii

De prebenda de Effeld' (Heathfield) in ecclesia Cicestrensi, taxata xxvi li. xiii s. iiii d., ratione provisionis facte Johanni de Lutham, in plenam solutionem xxvi li. xiii s. iiii d.[34]

Sequitur recepta benefficiorum collatorum post computa

folio xxxiii

De vicaria de Heo (Hooe), taxata iiii li. xiii s. iiii d., de qua fuit provisum Guillelmo nato Rotberti Hall' per cardinalem Petragoricensem, dimissa in arrayratgiis in xlvi s. viii d., in plenam solutionem xlvi s. viii d.

folio xxxiiii

De prebenda de Waltham in ecclesia Cicestrensi, taxata x li., de qua per consecrationem Rotberti episcopi Convetrensis et Lichfeldensis fuit provisum Waltero de Hylthon' per Innocentium nonas[35] Januarii anno x°,[36] in plenam satisfactionem x li.

folio xxxiiii

De prebenda de Torneye (Thorney) in ecclesia Cicestrensi, taxata x li., de qua per obitum Johannis Turstayn fuit provisum Willelmo de Cherchill' per Innocentium iiii° ydus Iulii anno ix°,[37] in plenam solutionem x li.

folio xlii°

De prebenda de Seleseya (Selsey) in ecclesia Cicestrensi, de qua per obitum Johannis Leth fuit provisum Rotberto de Askeby per Innocentium anno ix°,[38] et taxatur xxi li. vi s. viii d., in partem dicte taxe x li. Restat quod debet xi li. vi s. viii d. quas iuravit solvere in proximo venienti festo Omnium Sanctorum et dedit fideiussores.[39]

Wynthoniensis diocesis
folio xl

De ecclesia sive custodia domus Sancti Nicholay de Portesmouth', non taxata, confirmata Johanni de Edyn-

don' per Clementem v kalendas Martii anno viii°,[40] dimissa in resta in x li., in plenam solutionem x li.
Summa pagine xcv li. xiii s. iiii d.

(fol. 5ᵛ) folio xxxvi

De archidiaconatu Surreie, taxato lxxx li., confirmato Johanni de Edyndon' per Clementem ii ydus Februarii anno xi,[41] in plenam solutionem lxxx li.

folio xli° [42]

De ecclesia de Waltham, taxata xx li., de qua per obitum Gilberti David fuit provisum Hugoni de Craft' per Innocentium iiii° nonas Iulii anno ix°,[43] in partem dicte taxe iiii li. Restat quod debet xvi li. quas iuravit solvere in proximo venienti festo Omnium Sanctorum sub pena excommunicationis late in scriptis.[44]

folio xxxvii°

De prioratu de Apellorecomb' (Appuldurcombe), taxata xxx li. xvii s., confirmato Johanni Ozanna per Clementem v kalendas Martii anno viii°,[45] in partem dicte taxe v li. Restat quod debet xxv li. xvii s.[44]

folio xxxviii

De vicaria ecclesie Omnium Sanctorum de Kyngeston' (Kingston on Thames), taxata v li. vi s. viii d., de qua ex causa permutationis cum vicaria de Potern' (Potterne) fuit provisum Johanni Doyle per Innocentium viii° kalendas Octobris anno ix°,[46] in plenam satisfactionem v li. vi s. viii d.

folio xxxvii

De ecclesia de Havunte (Havant), taxata xxvi li. xiii s. iiii d., de qua per obitum Johannis Noion fuit provisum Johanni Uppewll' per Innocentium iiii° nonas Iulii anno ix°,[47] in partem dicte taxe vi li. xiii s. iiii d. Restat quod debet xx li., nec habet certum terminum ad solvendum quia rector non fuit repertus nec plures fructus inventi.[48]

Sarrisberiensis diocesis
folio xlii

De prebenda de Notherburyn (Netherbury in Ecclesia) in ecclesia Sarisberiensi, de qua per obitum Thome de Luce fuit confirmata Reginaldo Brian per Clementem xvi kalendas Septembris anno viii°,[49] taxata lx li., in plenam solutionem dicte taxe lx li.

---

[33] 18 May 1353.
[34] In the margin of a: *non fuit dimissa in arrayratgiis.*
[35] Over *x kalendas* deleted by dots, a.
[36] 5 January 1362.
[37] 12 July 1361.
[38] 1361.
[39] In the margin of a: *Resta.*

[40] 25 February 1350.
[41] 12 February 1352: *Cal. Pap. Regs. Petitions,* i, 225.
[42] *folio xxxvii,* b.
[43] 4 July 1361.
[44] In the margin: *Resta.*
[45] 25 February 1350.
[46] 24 September 1361.
[47] 4 July 1361.
[48] In the margin: *resta.*
[49] 17 August 1349.

### folio xlii

De prebenda de Starton' (Stratton) in ecclesia Sarisberiensi, de qua fuit provisum Johanni Hanneye ad presentationem regis Anglie per dominum Vigorniensem episcopum vigore gratie dicto regi concesse per Innocentium, pro taxa xiii li. vi s. viii d.

Summa pagine clxxiiii li. vi s. viii d.

### (fol. 6, v) folio xxxvi

De prebenda de Cheresenbury' (Chisenbury) in ecclesia Sarisberiensi, taxata xx li., de qua per obitum Rotberti de Horthon' fuit provisum Thome de Edyndon' per Clementem kalendas Februarii anno viii°,[50] in plenam solutionem xx li.

### folio xli

De subdecanatu Sarisberiensi cum prebenda annexa, taxato iiii li. vi s. viii d., cuius [51] collatio facta Radulpho de Querendon' fuit sibi confirmata per Innocentium ii° kalendas Februarii anno iii°,[52] cuius fructus adeo sunt tenues et exiles quod vix sufficiunt ad suportationem onerum, ut constat per certificatorium episcopi iiii li. vi s. viii d.

### folio xxxvi

De prioratu de Ledres (Loders), taxato xxvi li., cuius provisio facta Symoni de Clouda fuit sibi confirmata per Innocentium ii kalendas Februarii anno iii°,[53] in plenam solutionem xxvi li.

Recepta beneefficiorum collatorum post dicta computa

### folio xli

De prebenda de Ratffen (Rotefen) in ecclesia Sarisberiensi, cuius taxa et provisio in recepta dicti Hugonis folio xviii°, dimissa in arrayratgiis in iii li. vi s. viii d., in plenam solutionem iii li. vi s. viii d.

### folio xli

De vicaria de Gillyngham (Gillingham), taxata vi li. xiii s. iiii d., de qua fuit provisum Willelmo Tormer per cardinalem Petragoricensem, dimissa in arrayratgiis in ii li. xiii s. iiii d., in plenam solutionem ii li. xiii s. iiii d.

### folio xxxv

De prebenda de Nettebury [54] in Terra (Netherbury in Terra) in ecclesia Sarisberiensi, taxata xiii li. vi s. viii d., que fuit confirmata Johanni de Blyburi ex causa permutationis facte [55] cum Rotberto de Bourthon' per

Innocentium ix kalendas Iunii anno sexto,[56] in plenam [57] solutionem [58] dicte taxe xiii li. vi s. viii d.[59]

### folio xxxiii

De ecclesia de Asscheburi (Ashbury), taxata xxvi li. xiii s. iiii d., de qua per obitum Walteri Moryn fuit provisum Thome de Bisopesbury per Innocentium iiii kalendas Octobris anno ix,[60] in partem dicte taxe x li. Restat quod debet xvi,[61] li. xiii s. iiii d. quas debet solvere in medio Augusti sub pena excommunicationis late.[62]

Summa pagine lxxix li. xiii s. iiii d.

### (fol. 6ᵛ) folio xxxiii

De vicaria Sancte Marie de Poterna (Potterne), taxata xx li., de qua ex causa permutationis cum Johanne Doyle pro vicaria ecclesie Omnium Sanctorum de Kyngeston' (Kingston on Thames) Wynthoniensis diocesis fuit provisum Thome West' per Innocentium viii° kalendas Octobris anno ix°,[63] in partem dicte taxe v li. Restat quod debet xv li.[64]

### Exoniensis dyocesis
### folio xli

De archidiaconatu Barnastapol' in ecclesia Exoniensi, non taxato, de quo ex causa permutationis cum Johanne Darby fuit provisum Willelmo Muge per Innocentium iiii° ⟨nonas⟩ [65] Septembris anno vi°,[66] et dimisso in arrayratgiis ratione istius provisionis in vi li. xiii s. iiii d., et ratione alterius provisionis vel confirmationis de eodem archidiaconatu facte Johanni de [67] Reyntham per Clementem vi nonas Aprilis anno viii°,[68] de qua debetur medietas, que ascendit ex compositione facta ad xiii li. vi s. iiii d., et sic debentur ratione istarum duarum provisionum xxᵗⁱ li., in partem dicte summe x li. Restat quod debet Willelmus Muge nunc archidiaconus x li., quas debuit solvere in proximo lapsso festo Pasche sub pena excommunicationis late in scriptis.[69]

### folio xxxvi

De prebenda Exoniensi, taxata iiii li., que fuit confirmata Henrico Pik per Innocentium kalendas Iunii

---

[50] 1 February 1350.
[51] Followed by *provisio et,* b.
[52] 31 January 1355.
[53] 31 January 1355.
[54] Followed by *taxata xxvi li. xiii s. iiii d.* deleted by a line, a.
[55] *facta,* MSS.

[56] 24 May 1358.
[57] Over *partem* deleted by a line, a.
[58] Followed by *partem* deleted by a line, b.
[59] Follows the same sum deleted by a line, a. It is followed by *Restat quod debet vi li. xiii s. iiii d.* deleted by a line, a.
[60] 28 September 1361.
[61] *xviii,* a.
[62] In the margin: *attende* and *Resta,* a.
[63] 24 September 1361.
[64] In the margin: *Resta,* a.
[65] Supplied from *Cal. Pap. Regs. Petitions,* i, 332.
[66] 2 September 1358.
[67] *de* repeated, a.
[68] 8 April 1350. It should be *vi idus: ibid.,* i, 195.
[69] In the margin: *Resta,* a.

anno ix°,[70] dimissa in arrayratgiis in xl s., in plenam solutionem dicte reste ii li.

### folio xxxix [71]

De vicaria de Yalmyston' (Yealmpton), non taxata, in qua ad ius quod competebat Johanni de Cornube fuit subrogatus Rotbertus Gervasii per Innocentium ii° ydus Octobris pro vero valore medietatis dicte vicarie que est, ut certificavit episcopus, xl s., in plenam solutionem ii li.

### folio xxxiiii [72]

De prioratu de Otruthon' (Otterton), taxato lxxxvi li. xiii s. iiii d., dimisso in arayratgiis in xxxi li. xiii s. iiii d., ratione confirmationis facte Thome Sedile per Innocentium ii° kalendas Februarii anno ii°,[73] in plenam solutionem xxxi li. xiii s. iiii d.

### folio xxxix [74]

De prebenda ecclesie collegiate Credingthon' (Crediton), de qua per obitum Thome David fuit provisum Thome Andree per Innocentium xi kalendas Iulii anno ix°,[75] que non taxatur, pro medietate fructuum, salvo iure super maiori valenti si [76] reperiatur,[76] ii li. x s.

### folio xxxiiii

De prebenda ecclesie Exoniensis, taxata iiii li., de ⟨qua⟩ per obitum Thome David fuit provisum Johanni Seys per Innocentium xi kalendas Iulii anno ix°,[77] iiii li.

Summa pagine lvii li. iii s. iiii d.

### (fol. 7, vi) Bathoniensis et Wellensis
### folio xli

De prebenda de Arpetre (East Harptree) in ecclesia Wellensi, de qua per consecrationem Ludovici episcopi Dunelmensis fuit provisum Henrico de Hatweden' per Clementem, dimissa in arayratgiis in iiii li., in plenam solutionem dicte reste iiii li.

### folio xl

De prebenda de Wycurche (Whitchurch) in ecclesia Wellensi, taxata viii li., de qua per obitum Rotberti de Luffenham acceptatio facta per Ricardum de Tormenton' fuit eidem confirmata per Innocentium iiii kalendas Februarii anno secundo,[78] que quidem prebenda per dictum obitum fuit collata Thome de Edyndon' per Clementem v kalendas Maii ix,[79] et iste optinet

qui evicit eam a dicto Rycardo, in plenam solutionem dicte taxe viii li.

### folio xxxiiii

De prioratu Montis Acuti (Montacute), taxato cxxxiii li. vi s. viii d., cuius provisio in recepta dicti Hugonis folio viii°, dimisso in arayratgiis in lxxv li., in plenam solutionem dicte reste lxxv li.

Recepta beneficiorum collatorum post computa.

### folio xl

De succentoria ecclesie Wellensis, taxata v li. vi s. viii d., cuius collatio auctoritate ordinaria facta Willelmo de Bokham fuit eidem confirmata per Innocentium xi kalendas Maii anno quinto,[80] in plenam solutionem dicte taxe v li. vi s. viii d.

### folio xl

De prebenda burssali in ecclesia Wellensi, taxata v li. vi. s. viii d., de qua per obitum Johannis Turstayn fuit provisum Johanni Couff' per Innocentium quinto nonas Maii anno x°,[81] in partem dicte taxe ii li. xiii s. iiii d. Restat quod debet ii li. xiii s. iiii d. quas debet solvere in festo ascenssionis sub pena excommunicationis.

### Hereffordensis dyocesis
### folio xxxviii

De prebenda de Prato, non taxata, que per obitum Willelmi de Sowoph' fuit confirmata Baudoyno de Wytenee per Innocentium viii° kalendas Iunii anno iiii°,[82] que prebenda consistit dumtaxat in una trossa feni, pro cuius medietate solvit in plenam xii d. et iuravit quod alios redditus non habet.

### folio xlii

De prebenda de Wynghton', alias Evthyngthon' (Ewithington) in ecclesia Hereffordensi, cuius taxa et provisio in recepta dicti Hugonis folio viii°, dimissa in arayratgiis in viii° li., in plenam solutonem dicte reste viii li.

Summa pagine ciii li. i s.

### (fol. 7ᵛ)[83] Norwicensis dyocesis
### folio xxxvii

De ecclesia de Herdwyko (Hardwick), taxata v li.

---

[70] 1 June 1361.
[71] *xxiiii*, **b.**
[72] *xxxix*, **b.**
[73] 31 January 1354.
[74] *xxxviii*, **b.**
[75] 21 June 1361.
[76] Om. **b.**
[77] 21 June 1361.
[78] 29 January 1354.
[79] 27 April 1351.

[80] 21 April 1357.
[81] 3 May 1362.
[82] 25 May 1356.
[83] The following item at the top of the folio in **a** is deleted by lines. *De decanatu ecclesie Herffordensis, taxato xxxi li. viii s. v d., vacante per liberam resignationem Thome Trillec fuit provisum Willelmo de Bermingham per Dominum Urbanum pontificatus sui anno primo vii kalendas Februarii* (26 January 1363), *in partem dicte taxe vi li. xiii s. iiii d. Restat quod debet xxiiii li. xv s. i d. quas debet solvere videlicet medietatem in festo Pasche preterito, aliam medietatem in sequenti festo Beati Michaelis. Item debet aliam annatam ratione alterius provisionis ut in arayratgiis aparet.* In the margin: *cancellatur quia infra ponitur cum beneficiis collatis per Dominum Urbanum* and *Resta.*

vi s. viii d., ratione provisionis facte Rodulpho de Suttholst' et dimissa in arayratgiis in ii li. xiii s. iiii d., in plenam solutionem dicte reste ii li. xiii s. iiii d.

### folio xxxvii

De prioratu Sancte Fidis de Horssham (Horsham), cuius taxa et provisio supra in recepta dicti Hugonis folio ix°, dimissa in arrayratgiis in clvii li. vi s. viii d., in partem dicte reste xxxvi li. Restat quod debet cxxi li. vi s. viii d.[84]

Recepta beneficiorum collatorum post dicta computa

### folio xxxv

De ecclesia de Lacfford[85] (Lackford), taxata xx li., de qua per dimissionem Ricardi de Walkeleyn' fuit provisum Johanni de Stoekeney[86] per Innocentium iiii° ydus Octobris anno viii°,[87] in partem dicte taxe x li. Restat quod debet x[88] li. quas iuravit solvere in festo beati Michaelis sub pena excommunicationis late.[89]

### folio xxxv

De ecclesia de Magna Cresyngham (Great Cressingham), taxata xiiii li., cuius provisio auctoritate ordinaria facta Johanni de Stoks fuit eidem confirmata per Innocentium ix kalendas Januarii anno ix°,[90] in plenam solutionem xiiii li.

### folio xxxviii

De ecclesia de Macham (Marsham), taxata xvi li. xiii s. iiii d., de qua per asequtionem cancellarie Sarisberiensis per Johannem de Northon' fuit provisum Ricardo Amcotos per Innocentium nonas Januarii anno x°,[91] in partem dicte taxe viii li. Restat quod debet viii li. xiii s. iiii d. quas debet solvere in proximo festo[92] Omnium Sanctorum sub pena excommunicationis late in scriptis.

Summa pagine lxx li. xiii s. iiii d.

### (fol. 8, vii) Eliensis diocesis
### folio xxxvii

De ecclesia de Overe (Over), cuius taxa et provisio in recepta dicti Hugonis folio xx, dimissa in arrayratgiis ratione dicte provisionis in xiiii li. xiii s. iiii d., et ratione alterius provisionis de eadem ecclesia facte Rogero de Stanfford' per Innocentium iii° ydus Augusti anno ix°,[93] de qua debetur tota taxa que est xxxv li. vi s. viii d., que summe ascendunt in summa l li., in partem dicte

summe xxxvii li. x s. Restat quod debet xii li. x s. quas debet solvere in proximo festo Beati Michaelis sub pena excommunicationis late in scriptis.[94]

### Lincoliensis diocesis
### folio xli

De cappellania perpetua iuxta pontem ville de Elnestoue (Elstow), non taxata, de qua ex causa permutationis fuit provisum Henrico de Lalt' per Innocentium v kalendas Aprilis anno viii,[95] in plenam solutionem xxvi s. viii d.

### folio xxxviii

De ecclesia de Humberstayn (Humberstone), taxata xvi li. vi s. viii d., appropriata monasterio Beate Marie Leycestr' per Clementem ix kalendas Martii anno x,[96] in plenam satisfactionem xvi li. vi s. viii d.

### folio xxxvi

De subdecanatu Lincoliensi, cuius taxa et provisio in recepta dicti Hugonis folio x°, dimissa in arrayratgiis in x li., in plenam solutionem x li.

### folio xlii

De prebenda de Walthon' Rival' (Welton Rivall) in ecclesia Lincoliensi, taxata xxxiii li. vi s. viii d., de qua per obitum Johannis de Acton' acceptatio facta per Johannem Lamberti fuit eidem confirmata per Clementem iiii° ydus Maii anno ix°,[97] et subsequenter ex causa permutationis facte cum isto Johanne fuit provisum Ricardo Daventre per Innocentium vii kalendas Maii anno quinto[98] et sic debentur duplices fructus, dimissa in arrayratgiis in xxxvii li. viii° s. ii d., in partem dicte reste iiii li. i s. vi d.[99] Restat quod debet xxxiii li. vi s. viiii d.

### folio xl

De ecclesia de Denfford' (Denford), taxata xx li., de qua ex causa permutationis fuit provisum Rogero de Bonithon' per Innocentium v kalendas Aprilis anno viii°,[100] in partem x li.[101]

Recepta beneficiorum collatorum post dicta computa

### folio xl

De ecclesia de Lutghteburgh' (Ludborough), taxata xxvi li. xiii s. iiii d., cuius provisio in recepta dicti Hugonis folio xxi, dimissa in arrayratgiis in vii li., in plenam solutionem vii li.

---

[84] In the margin: *Resta.*
[85] *Lafford'*, b.
[86] *Stokeney*, b.
[87] 12 October 1360.
[88] *xx*, a.
[89] In the margin: *resta*, a.
[90] 24 December 1361.
[91] 5 January 1362.
[92] Followed by *Beati* deleted by a line, a.
[93] 11 August 1361.

[94] In the margin: *Resta.*
[95] 28 March 1360.
[96] 22 February 1352.
[97] 12 May 1351.
[98] 25 April 1357.
[99] In the margin: *Resta.*
[100] 28 March 1360.
[101] In the margin: *Resta*, a.

### folio xxxiii

De prebenda Sancte Crucis in ecclesia Lincoliensi (Spaldwick), cuius taxa et provisio in recepta dicti Hugonis folio xxi, dimissa in arrayratgiis in v li., in partem dicte reste ii li. x s. Restat quod debet ii li. x s. quas debuit solvere in festo Pasche proximo lapsso.[102]

Summa pagine lxxxviii li. xiiii s. x d.

### (fol. 8ᵛ) folio xxxiii

De ecclesia de Hagworlyngham (Hagworthingham), cuius taxa et provisio in recepta dicti Hugonis folio xxi, dimissa in arrayratgiis in ix li., in partem dicte reste dimisse vi li. Restat quod debet iii li.[102]

### folio xli

De ecclesia de Fethelgathe (Fleet), cuius taxa et provisio in recepta dicti Hugonis folio xxiº, dimissa in arrayratgiis in xiiii li. viii s. x d. obolo, in plenam solutionem xiiii li. viii s. x d. ob.

### folio xxxviii

De vicaria ecclesie de Clee, taxata x li., de qua per obitum Johannis de Elneye fuit provisum Johanni Alayn per Innocentium iii kalendas Maii anno xº,[103] in partem dicte taxe v li. Restat quod debet v li. quas debet solvere in proximo festo Ascentionis sub pena excommunicationis late in scriptis.[102]

### folio xl

De ecclesia de Coltesworth (Colsterworth), taxata xxi li, vi s. viii d., de qua fuit provisum Rotberto de Lynkole per Innocentium ydus Aprilis anno xº,[104] in partem dicte [105] taxe x li. xiii s. iiii d.[106] Restat quod debet x li. xiii s. iiii d. quas debet solvere in festo Beati Michaelis proximo venienti.[102]

De ecclesia de Aseby [107] (Ashby) parva, taxata iiii li. xiii s. iiii d., de qua Willelmo Edelet [108] de Skyton' cardinalis Petragoricensis providit, nichil quia ponitur in arrayratgiis.

### folio xxxvii

De vicaria ecclesie de Bolyngton' (Bullington), non taxata, de qua Johanni de Dalton [109] cardinalis Petragoricensis de novo providit, de qua dictus Johannes iuravit quod non valet communiter ultra c s., et super hoc est commissa inquisitio, pro medietate dicti valoris ii li. x s.

### folio xli

De rectoria medietatis ecclesie de Baghenderby (Bag Enderby), taxata iii li., de qua per dominum cardinalem Urgellensem fuit provisum Willelmo nato Rotberti, in plenam solutionem iii li.

### Convetrensis et Licheffeldensis
### folio xxxix

De prebenda de Langnedon' (Longdon) et archidiaconatu Convetrensi in ecclesia Lichfeldensi, cuius taxa et provisio ac compositio cum camera in recepta dicti Hugonis folio xii et xiiiº, dimissis in arrayratgiis in clviii fl. solvendis temporibus et terminis ibidem designatis in partem dicte summe 1 floreni fortes.

### folio xxxix

De prebenda de Wolveye (Wolvey) in ecclesia Lichfeldensi, taxata vi li. xiii s. iiii d., de qua per consecrationem Michaelis electi Londoniensis fuit provisum Johanni Barnete per Innocentium nonas Octobris anno iiº,[110] in plenam solutionem dicte taxe vi li. xiii s. iiii d.

Summa pagine xlviii li. v s. vi d. ob. Item 1 fl. fortes.

(fol. 9, viii) Recepta benefficiorum collatorum post dicta computa

### (fol. xxxiii)

De prebenda in ecclesia collegiata Sancti Johannis Cestrie, taxata iiii li., de qua ex causa permutationis fuit confirmata Ricardo Boulle per Innocentium vii kalendas Iulii anno viiº,[111] in plenam solutionem dicte taxe iiii li.

### folio xxxiii

De parochiali ecclesia de Worthyn (Worthen) Herffordensis diocesis ac aliis benefficiis expressatis in libro recepte dicti Hugonis folio xxii, ratione dispensasationis facte cum Ricardo de Stafford ut dicta beneffica simul posset retinere per Innocentium iiiiº kalendas Iunii anno viiº,[112] dimissis in arrayratgiis in lviii li. xiii s. et iiii d., de quibus debuit solvere in festo Beati Johannis anno lxiiiº x li., et in festo Beati Michaelis tunc sequenti x li., et sic de anno in annum quousque de dicta summa fuerit integraliter satisfactum, sic quod in ultimo termino solvet viiiº li. xiii s. iiii d., pro terminis Beati Johannis et Beati Michaelis proximis preteritis [113] xx li. Restat quod debet xxxviii li. xiii s. iiii d.[114]

### folio xlii

De ecclesia de Audle (Middle), taxata xx li., de qua per obitum Rotberti de Conventren' fuit provisum

---

[102] In the margin: *Resta*.
[103] 29 April 1362.
[104] 13 April 1362.
[105] Followed by *resta* deleted by a line, **a**.
[106] In the margin: *non est in regestro camere*, **a**.
[107] *Aselny*, **b**.
[108] *Debet*, **b**.
[109] *Derlton*, **b**.

[110] 7 October 1354.
[111] 25 June 1359.
[112] 29 May 1359.
[113] *predictis*, **b**.
[114] In the margin: *Resta*.

Johanni Deygg' per Innocentium x kalendas Januarii anno ix°,[115] in plenam solutionem dicte taxe xx li.

### folio xxxviii

De prebenda de Sterffold [110] (Stotfold) in ecclesia Lichfeldensi, taxata x li., de qua per liberam resignationem Raymundi de Sancto Claro fuit provisum Johanni de Sancto Claro xiii kalendas Martii per Innocentium anno vi,[117] in plenam solutionem dicte taxe x li.

### Eboracensis dyocesis
### folio xxxvii

De prebenda de Strop (Thorpe) in ecclesia de Hovedon' (Howden), cuius taxa et provisio in recepta dicti Hugonis folio xiii°, dimissa in arrayratgiis in vi li., in plenam solutionem dicte reste vi li.

### folio xxxvii

De vicaria Pontisfracti (Pontefract), taxata xvi li., dimissa in resta in iiii li. ratione confirmationis facte Hugoni de Raston' per Innocentium ix kalendas Septembris anno vi°,[118] iiii li.

### folio xxxiii

De prebenda de Oswaldewyk' (Osbaldwick) in ecclesia Eboracensi, cuius taxa et provisio in recepta dicti Hugonis folio xxiii°, dimissa in arrayratgiis in xx li., in plenam solutionem dicte reste xx li.

### folio xl

De prebenda de Monkethon' (Monkton) in ecclesia collegiata Ripponensi, taxata xiii li. vi s. viii d., de qua per consecrationem M. episcopi Londoniensis fuit provisum Johanni de Wynwyk' per Innocentium xv kalendas Maii anno secundo,[119] in plenam solutionem dicte reste xiii li. vi s. viii d.[120]

### folio xlii

De prebenda de Chawe (Sharow) in ecclesia collegiata Ripponensi, de qua per consecrationem B de Cardalhaco in episcopatum Montis Albani (Montauban) fuit provisum Guillelmo de Esenden' per Innocentium vi ydus Martii anno vii°,[121] et taxatur v li., v li.

---

[115] 23 December 1361.
[116] *Steford*, b.
[117] 17 February 1358.
[118] 24 August 1358.
[119] 17 April 1354.
[120] In the margin of a: *De subdecanatu Eboracensi et aliis beneficiis de quibus per confirmationem fuit provisum G de Radfford per Innocentium vi kalendas Decembris anno vii°* (26 November 1359), *dimissa in arrayratgiis in lviii li. et x s., solvit in partem xix li. x s.* The item is deleted by lines with the following explanation: *Cancellatur quia infra folio ii° ponitur magis plene.* The item is omitted in b, but the explanation appears in the margin deleted by lines.
[121] 10 March 1359.

### folio xlii

Item de eadem prebenda ratione confirmationis facte Johanni de Donynton' per Clementem iii ydus Maii anno ix°,[122] v li.
Summa pagine cvii li. vi s. viii d.

### (fol. 9ᵛ) folio xl

De ecclesia Sancte Trinitatis Eboraci, cuius taxa et provisio in recepta dicti Hugonis folio xiiii, dimissa in arrayratgiis in xl s., in plenam solutionem dicte reste ii li.

### folio xxxvi

De ecclesia de Brumpton' (Brompton), taxata liii li. vi s. viii d., de qua per obitum cardinalis de Turre [123] fuit provisum Thome de Monte de Wykcham per Innocentium iiii kalendas Januarii anno ix°,[124] dimissa in arrayratgiis in xx li. xiii s. iiii d., xx li. xiii s. iiii d.

Recepta benefficiorum collatorum post computa

### folio xxxvi

De vicaria de Tikyllis (Tickhill), de qua Rogero de Salteburn' dominus cardinalis Petragoricensis de novo providit, que taxatur [125] xx li., et fuit dimissa in resta in xv li., in plenam solutionem dicte reste xv li.

### folio xl [126]

De ecclesia de Bolthon' (Bolton Percy), cuius taxa et confirmatio in recepta dicti Hugonis folio xxiiii°, dimissa in arrayratgiis in xiii li. vi s. viii d., in plenam solutionem dicte reste xiii li. vi s. viii d.

### folio xxxv

De ecclesia de Holtheby (Holtby), cuius taxa et provisio supra in recepta dicti Hugonis folio xxiiii°,[127] dimissa in arrayratgiis in ii li., in plenam solutionem dicte reste ii li.

### folio xxxvi

De vicaria ecclesie de Waltyngham (Walkeringham), cuius taxa et provisio in recepta dicti Hugonis, dimissa in arrayratgiis in iiii li., in plenam solutionem dicte reste iiii li.

### folio xxxvi

De ecclesia de Claworth (Clayworth), cuius taxa et provisio in recepta dicti Hugonis folio xxiiii°, dimissa in arrayratgiis in xi li. xiii s. iiii d., in plenam solutionem dicte reste xi li. xiii s. iiii d.

### folio xxxv

De ecclesia Sancti Wlffridi (York), cuius taxa et

---

[122] 13 May 1351.
[123] Bernard de la Tour d'Auvergne, deacon of S. Eustachio.
[124] 29 December 1361.
[125] Om. b.
[126] *xxxv*, b.
[127] *xiiii°*, b.

provisio in recepta dicti Hugonis, dimissa in arrayratgiis in ii li, in plenam solutionem dicte reste ii li.

### folio xxxix

De ecclesia de Tornotby (Thornaby), taxata iiii li., de qua per Dominum Petragoricensem fuit provisum Adde de Balthon',[128] dimissa in [129] arrayratgiis in ii li., in plenam solutionem dicte reste ii li.

### folio xlii

De ecclesia de Bratyngham (Brantingham), cuius taxa et provisio in recepta dicti Hugonis folio xxiiii°, dimissa in arrayratgiis in liii li. vi s. viii d., in partem dicte reste xiii li. vi s. viii d. Restat quod debet xl li., videlicet xiii li. vi s. viii d. in festo Pasche proximo lapsso et residuum in festo Beati Michaelis proximo venienti.[130]

### folio xxxviii

De prebenda de Amplefford (Ampleforth) in ecclesia Eboracensi, cuius taxa et provisio in recepta dicti Hugonis folio xxiiii, dimissa in arrayratgiis in xx li., in plenam solutionem dicte reste xx li.

Summa pagine cvi li.

### (fol. 10, ix) folio xxxiii

De ecclesia de Pat' Brumthon' (Patrick Brumpton), cuius taxa et provisio in recepta dicti Hugonis folio xxiiii°, dimissa in arrayratgiis in xiii li. vi s. viii d., in plenam solutionem dicte reste xiii li. vi s. viii d.

### folio xl

De vicaria ecclesia de Gelynig' (Gilling), que ex causa permutationis facte cum Gerlaco de Clave fuit Johanni de Reoko [131] confirmata per Innocentium ix kalendas Septembris anno viii°,[132] que taxatur ad novam taxam x li., in plenam solutionem dicte taxe x li.

### folio xxxv

De ecclesia de Langedon' (Langton), taxata x li., de qua per obitum Gerlaci de Clave fuit provisum Thome Morc' [133] per Innocentium xii kalendas Iulii anno ix°,[134] in plenam solutionem dicte taxe x li.

De prebenda de Amplefford (Ampleforth) in ecclesia Eboracensi, taxata xl li., de qua per obitum Henrici la Sauch' fuit provisum Willelmo Curteneye per Innocentium iiii ydus Augusti anno ix°,[135] nichil hic quia supra ponitur in precedenti pagina.[136]

### folio xl

De ecclesia de Hugate (Huggate), taxata xxiii li. vi s. viii d. ad novam taxam, cuius collatio facta auctoritate ordinaria Johanni Herneys [137] fuit eidem confirmata per Innocentium iii kalendas Januarii anno ix°,[138] in plenam solutionem dicte taxe xxiii li. vi s. viii d.

### folio xlii

De archidiaconatu Astridyng' in ecclesia Eboracensi, non taxato, de quo, vacante per asequtionem alterius benefficii, fuit provisum Waltero de Skirlaue [139] per Innocentium ii kalendas Decembris anno vii°,[140] de quo idem Walterus iuravit quod quedam ecclesia dicto archidiaconatui annexa non valet communiter ultra 1 m., pro parte medietatis dictarum 1 marcham viii li. Restat quod debet xiii m., que valent viii li. xiii s. iiii d., quas iuravit in proximo ⟨festo⟩ venienti Omnium Sanctorum ⟨solvere⟩.[141]

### Dunelmensis dyocesis post dicta computa folio xlii

De prebenda ecclesie collegiate de Northon' (Norton), de qua per consecrationem Johannis Vigorniensis episcopi fuit provisum Willelmo Ylberde per Innocentium iiii° ydus Martii anno x,[142] que prebende non habunt certa nomina, et taxata ad vi li., in partem dicte taxe iii li. Restat quod debet iii li.[143]

Summa pagine lxvii li. xiii s. iiii d.

### (fol. 10ᵛ) folio xlii

De vicaria ecclesie de Newethon' in Clendale (Kirknewton), taxata xx li., de [144] qua collatio facta auctoritate ordinaria Johanni de Castro Bernardi fuit eidem confirmata per Innocentium iiii° ydus Maii anno x°,[145] in plenam solutionem dicte taxe xx li.

### folio xxxix

De subdecanatu Eboracensi et prebendis de Grantham in ecclesia Sarisberiensi, de Rithemell' (Rathmichael) in ecclesia Dublinensi,[146] de Clipthon' (Clifton) in ecclesia Lincoliensi, de Cheswyk' (Chiswick) in ecclesia Londoniensi, de Rampton' [147] in ecclesia collegiata Suthwellensi Eboracensis diocesis, quorum [148] beneffi-

---

[128] *Walton'*, **b.**
[129] Followed by *ay* deleted by a line, **a**
[130] In the margin: *Resta.*
[131] *Recho*, **b.**
[132] 24 August 1360.
[133] *moic'*, **b.**
[134] 20 June 1361.
[135] 10 August 1361.
[136] In the margin: *vacat*, **a.**

[137] *Heneys*, **b.**
[138] 30 December 1360 is probably wrong: *Cal. Pap. Regs., Petitions*, p. 384 gives date as 4 Kal. Jan. which was 29 December 1361.
[139] Skinlaue, **b.**
[140] *anno viii*, **b.** 30 November 1359 or 1360.
[141] In the margin: *Resta.*
[142] 12 March 1362.
[143] In the margin: *Resta*, **a.**
[144] Om. **b.**
[145] 12 May 1362.
[146] *Dunelmensis*, **a**; *Dunlinensis*, **b.**
[147] *Ramptonen'*, **b.**
[148] *que*, **b.**

ciorum taxe et provisiones continentur in recepta dicti Hugonis folio xxv, dimissis in arrayratgiis in lviii li. et x s., de quibus debet solvere quolibet festo nativitatis Beati Johannis Baptiste et nativitatis domini xix li. et x s. quousque fuerit integraliter satisffactum, de dicta festa pro termino nativitatis domini anno LXIII° xix li. x s. Restat quod debet xxxix li. solvendas ut supra.[149]

## Kareolensis dyocesis
### folio xliii

De ecclesia de Crostwyt (Crosthwaite), taxata xxx li. xiii s. iiii d., in qua ad omne ius quod competebat Guillelmo de Solario fuit subrogatus Johannes Henrici per Innocentium ii ydus Januarii anno v,[150] in partem dicte taxe iiii li., quas solvit Thomas de Eskihewed [151] nunc incumbens, et dicit quod iste Johannes Henrici nunquam habuit possessionem dicte rectorie set vicarie eiusdem, tamen quam dicit esse taxatam ad novam taxam ad iiii li., et super hoc produxit unam litteram testimonialem sigillo regis Anglie sigillatam extractam de regestero scakarii sui, super quo ad maiorem securitatem habendam fuit commissa inquisitio episcopo, qui debet certificare huic ad festum Beati Michaelis proximum venturum, et ulterius dictus Thomas obligavit se ad solvendum in dicto festo Beati Michaelis illud quod aparebit ipsum debere pro dicta vicaria de Crostwayt, et ecclesia si reperiatur de ea dicto Johanni Henrici provisum et ipsum dicte ecclesie possessionem habuisse.

Summa pagine xliii li. x s.

Summa generalis omnium precedentium arrayratgiorum benefficiorum m iii° xx li. vii s. ii d. ob. Item l fl. fortes.

(fol. 11, x) Recepta benefficiorum collatorum per Dominum Urbanum

### Herffordensis xxvi [152] Octobris

De decanatu ecclesie Herffordensis, vacante per liberam resignationem Thome Trillec, de quo fuit provisum Magistro Willelmo de Bermingham, qui taxatur xxxi li. viii s.[153] v d., per Dominum Urbanum septimo kalendas Februarii anno primo,[154] in partem dicte taxe vi li. xiii s. iiii d. Restat quod debet xxiiii li. xv s. i d., de quibus debet solvere medietatem in festo Pasche proximo lapsso et aliam [155] medietatem in festo Beati Michaelis. Item debet aliam annatam ratione alterius provisionis facte per Innocentium ut infra in arrayratgiis aparebit.[156]

### Cicestrensis xvi Novembris

De decanatu Cicestrensi, taxata liii li. vi s. viii d., de quo fuit Magistro Nicholao de Aston, magistro in sacra pagina,[157] per Dominum Urbanum xi kalendas Decembris anno primo,[158] in partem dicte taxe v li. Restat quod debet xlviii li vi s. viii d. quas debet solvere terminis infrascriptis, videlicet xii li. in dominica de quinquagesima proxima lapssa et alias xii in festo Beati Johannis [159] proximo venienti, et alias xii li. in sequenti festo Omnium Sanctorum, et residuas xii li. vi s. et viii d. in dominica de quinquagessima tunc sequenti sub pena excommunicationis late in scriptis.[160]

### Wynthoniensis xxviii Novembris

De ecclesia de Dumtesfold (Dunsfold) Wynthoniensis diocesis, taxata ad xx<sup>ti</sup> m., que valent xiii li. vi s. viii d., de qua per obitum Willelmi de Charsteston' fuit provisum Johanni de Lewes per Dominum Urbanum xix kalendas Februarii anno primo,[161] in partem dicte taxe vi li. xiii s. iiii d. Restat quod debet vi li. xiii s. iiii d. quas iuravit solvere in festo Omnium Sanctorum proximo venienti sub pena excommunicationis late in scriptis.[160]

Summa pagine xviii li. vi s. viii d.

### (fol. 11ᵛ) Roffensis iiª Decembris

De ecclesia de Ston' (Stone) Roffensis diocesis, taxata xx li., de qua fuit provisum Johanni Pays eo quod [162] Magistro Nicholao de Aston' fuit provisum de decanatu Cicestrensi per Dominum Urbanum xi kalendas Decembris anno primo,[163] in partem dicte taxe x li. Restat quod debet x li. quas debet solvere in festo Beati Johannis proximo venienti.[160]

### Exoniensis xii Januarii

De ecclesia de Morcestr' Episcopi (Morchard Bishop) diocesis Exoniensis, in qua fuit subrogatus Johannes Leye in omni iure quod competebat Rotberto Donslond super qua invicem litigabant, taxata vi li. xiii s. iiii d., in partem dicte taxe iii li. vi s. viii d. Restat quod debet iii li. vi s. viii [164] d. quas debet solvere in festo assumptionis Beate Marie proximo venienti sub pena excommunicationis late in scriptis.[160]

Summa pagine xiii li. vi s. viii d.

Summa universalis benefficiorum collatorum per Dominum Urbanum xxxi li. xiii s. iiii d.

(fol. 12, xi) Recepta quorumdam extraordinariorum
x die Novembris

Recepi pro quodam calice mihi tradito per Dominum

---

[149] In the margin: *Resta*, **a**.
[150] 12 January 1357.
[151] *Eskichwed*, **b**.
[152] *xxv*, **b**.
[153] Followed by *viii* deleted by a line, **a**.
[154] 26 January 1363.
[155] *ecclesiam*, **b**.
[156] In the margin: *Resta*.

[157] *patra pagana*, **b**.
[158] 21 November 1362.
[159] Om. **b**.
[160] In the margin: *Resta*.
[161] 14 January 1363.
[162] *quod* repeated, **a**.
[163] 21 November 1362.
[164] *iiii*, **b**.

Raymundum Pelegrini ponderanti 1 libram et v on-ssas [165] ad pondus Anglie, fracto in pede, et ponderato et extimato per Anthonium de Valle et Raynerium [166] Dominici mercatorum habitatorum Londonie, xxxvi s.

### v Februarii

Item recepi pro fructibus reservatis prebende de Massham (Masham) in ecclesia Eboracensi quam olim in dicta ecclesia optinuit Dominus Maglonensis cardinalis [167] pro tempore vacationis xlv li. xi s. vi d.

Item recepi a Domino Johanne de Wylthon' canonico Sarisberiensi pro medietate obventionum [168] subdecanatus Sarisberiensis pro anno LXI, quo tempore vacavit per mortem Magistri Nicholay de Marchisfeld in curia defuncti, quarum obventionum medietas dicitur ad cameram pertinere et alia medietas ad dominum cardinalem de Urssinis [169] decanum Sarisberiensem, salvo iure camere super maiori summa si reperiatur fuisse recepta ix li. v s. viii d.

Item recepi a Domino Raymundo Pelegrini, solvente nomine Domini Hugonis Pelegrini, fratris sui olim in Anglia sedis appostolice collectoris, pro resta omnium in quibus per finem computorum suorum, de omnibus per eum ex quacumque causa in dictis partibus nomine [170] camere appostolice receptis, camere appostolice teneri, computatis asignatis, solutis et espenssis per eum, prout in rationibus suis in xxvii foliis poni scriptis clarius et plenius continetur, lxxxvi li. ii s. v d.

Summa pagine cxlii li. xv s. vii d.

Summa universalis omnium precedentium receptarum m viic lxiiii li. viii s. viii d. ob. sterlingorum. Approbatum.[171]

(fol. 12v) Sequitur mihi tradita per Dominum Raymundum Pelegrini nomine fratris sui ultra computa predicta superius scripta die x Novembris anno domini Mo CCCLXIIIo

Primo unum librum continentem taxam benefficiorum Anglie cum postibus cohopertis de pelle alba.

Item unum parvum librum cohopertum de pergameno continentem taxam antiquam benefficiorum Ybernie.

Item xcii bullas diverssorum Romanorum pontificum super diverssis materiis emanatas.[172]

Item unum librum magnum cohopertum de pelle rubea continentem taxationes benefficiorum Anglie olim missum per cameram ad corrigendum.

Item unum calicem argenti cum pathena fractum in

pede deauratum, cuius pondus, exstimatio et [173] venditio in principio precedentis pagine.

Item unam casulam antiquam de diaspro operato cum avibus coloris viridis, alba, stola, manipulo, amictu cum operatibus, modici valde [174] valoris.

Item unam culcitram cum pulvinari de pluma.

Item duo cartularia [175] seu tabularia cum uno scamno [176] sive banqueto.

Item unam capssiam et unum scrinium cum barris ferreis, item duo alia scrinia sive cofretos, item unam rotam fusteam, que omnia quasi nullius sunt valoris.

Omnia autem premissa dimissa sunt in hospitio Raynerii Dominici, factoris Albertorum Antiquorum excepto libro taxe quem dimisi subcollectori.

(fol. 14, xiii) [177] Sequntur expensse facte per me Johannem de Cabrespino ad regna Anglie et Ybernie et non nullas provincias regni Francie per cameram missum pro dictis negotiis camere exequendis

Et est sciendum quod anno domini Mo CCCo LXIIIo et prima die menssis Augusti ego exivi de Avinionia pro dictorum negotiorum exequtione et fui in civitate Londonie xxviii die dicti menssis, quia, propter moram quam feci Brugis (Bruges) pro negotiis camere, et in Calesyo (Calais) quia non poteram transsire mare quia habebam ventum contrarium, citius ibi venire non potui, in quo spatio sunt xxviiio dies, cum sex equis. Item exivi de Anglia pro redeundo ad curiam [178] ad reddendum rationes et ad faciendum relationem de negotiis vi die Martii et intravi curiam xii die Aprilis, in quo spatio sunt xxxvi dies.

Expendi xxviii die Augusti pro uno famulo misso Domino Raymundo Pelegrini ut veniret Londonie ut ibi sibi presentarem comissiones meas xii d. sterlingorum.

Item die xiii Septembris misi Berengarium Ferrarii, clericum meum, Brugis cum comissione mea facta Domino P. de Marchinell',[179] curato de [180] Bibre,[181] ut faceret inventarium nomine camere de bonis Domini Guiraudi de Marssenacho, quondam in provincia Remensi (Reims) camere appostolice collectoris, qui tunc [182] in illis partibus diem suum clauserat [183] extremum, et dictum officium interim regeret quousque esset aliud per cameram ordinatum, et stetit per x dies xx s. viii d.

Item misi eundem xvi die Octobris domino Cantuariensi archiepiscopo cum processibus factis contra illos

---

[165] Presumably for *uncias.*
[166] *Raymundum,* **b.**
[167] Audoin Aubert, bishop of Maguelone, bishop of Ostia.
[168] *obvenientia,* **b.** Followed by *eiusdem* deleted by a line, **a.**
[169] Raynaldus Orsini, deacon of S. Adriano.
[170] *ratione,* **b.**
[171] Only part of this entry appears in **a,** and it is partially erased and illegible
[172] *emanatis,* **b.**

[173] *exstima,* **a.**
[174] Om. **b.**
[175] *cantulatona,* **a.**
[176] *scano,* **a.**
[177] Folio 13 (xii) is blank on the recto and verso.
[178] *cameram,* **b.**
[179] Followed by *r* apparently deleted by a dot, **a.** Perhaps the scribe started to write *rectori.*
[180] Om. **b.**
[181] *libre,* **b.** It might be Bevere-lés-Audenarde, Beveren-lés-Roulers or Beveren-Waes in Belgium.
[182] *tunc* with a line of abbreviation over the whole word, **a.**
[183] *clausit,* **b.**

qui erant camere obligati ut ipsos exequeretur, et stetit per iiii[or] dies vi s. vi d.

Item ultima die Octobris misi dominis episcopis Convetrensi et Licheffeldensi ac Karleolensi processus contra omnes dictarum diocesum camere debitorum per Willelmum curssorem Londonie, et debuit portare responsionem [184] de receptione dictorum processum, et habuit pro salario suo xii s.

Summa xl s. ii d.

(fol. 14[v]) Item die iii Novembris pro plicandis et ligandis arcubus et flechis traditis per Magistrum Raymundum Pelegrini et ipsis portandis ad portum Tamizie et inde Brugis (Bruges) xvi s. iiii d.

Item pro plicandis pannis emptis pro pynhota [185] de mandato domini thesaurarii ii s. viii d.

Item pro uno libro ad scribendum computa et tribus quaternis [186] papiri iiii s.

Item expendi pro uno famulo qui vi die Decembris portavit secundos processus agravatorios domino archiepiscopo Eboracensi [187] vii s.

Item expendi pro uno famulo qui xii die Decembris portavit secundos processus agravatorios officiali Bathoniensi et Wellensi iii s. iiii d.

Item expendi pro uno famulo qui vi die Januarii portavit secundos processus agravatorios episcopo Sarisberiensi iii s. viii d.

Item expendi pro uno famulo qui viii[o] die Januarii ⟨portavit⟩ processus factos contra vicarium Bathoniensem ut solveret denarios Beati Petri pro annos LXI et LXII[o] iii s. iiii d.

Item dedi uni nuntio qui portavit domino thesaurario litteras super cambio per me facto cum Albertis Antiquis de quinque milibus florentis primo missis iiii s. vi d.

Item pro pergameno, papiru, cera et aliis multis minutis expensis xxvi s.

Item pro copiandis computis et diverssis aliis scriptis xiiii [188] s. ii d. obolus.

Item pro loquario [189] hospitii conssueverunt collectores in Anglia pro singulis annis computare vi li. xiii s. iiii d.

Item Magister R. de Campo Anibaldo, notarius suus, aserit se expendisse ultra premissa pro pergameno, papiro et diverssis aliis minutis expensis usque ad summam viii[o] fl.

Summa pagine x li. xviii s. iiii d. ob.

Summa universalis omnium expensarum xii li. xviii s. vi d. ob.

Item plus xxiiii s. et sic pro toto xiiii li. ii s. vi d. ob.[190]

Item pro expensino [191] facto lxiiii diebus eundo et redeundo vi[xx] fl.[190]

(fol. 15[v])[192] Sequntur asignationes per me facte camere [193] de omnibus per me receptis in Anglia nomine ipsius a dicta prima die menssis Septembris anno LXIII[o] usque ad ultimam diem Martii anno LXIIII[o]

Primo asignavi de mandato camere per bullam michi facto ix die menssis Decembris anno LXIII[o] Raynerio Dominici, factori societatis Albertorum Antiquorum Londonie comoranti, pro quinque milibus florenis fortibus, computato quolibet floreno pro tribus solidis sterlingorum, qui ascendunt in summam vii[c] l li. sterlingorum.

Item die decima menssis Februarii anno LXIII[o] secundum computationem Anglie tradidi et assignavi de mandato domini thesaurarii, episcopi Nemausensis (Nîmes), licteratorie michi facto pro Comite Dalphinio et [194] conssociis suis, Johanni Petherii, burgensi Londoniensi, cxciii li. xiii s. iiii d. sterlingorum.

Item die xxii Februarii tradidi et assignavi dicto Raynerio Dominici, factori predicte societatis Albertorum Antiquorum de Florentia, in civitate Londonie commoranti, pro quinque milibus florenis cugni domini nostri pape novi et noviter in curia Romana currentis assignandis camere xxii die menssis Aprilis anno LXIIII[o], computato quolibet de dictis florenis pro tribus solidis et obolo, qui ascendunt in summam vii[c] lx li. viii s. iiii d. sterlingorum.

Summa m vii[c] iiii li. i s. viii d. sterlingorum [195] Approbatum.[195]

Item pro expensis itinerum et processum et aliorum tangentium cameram fuerunt sibi taxate pro omnibus expensis dicto tempore factis xxxii li. ii s. x d. ob.[196]

Et sic est summa totalis omnium assignatorum et expensarum tempore predicto [197] m vii[c] xxxvi li. iiii s. vi d. ob.

Factis vero deductione et compenssatione de receptis et levatis ad assignationes ⟨et⟩ expenssas factis per dictum collectorem, que recepta fuit m vii[c] lxiiii li. viii s. viii d. ob., l fl. fortes, cl fl. crosete quas receperit a camera, et assignationes et expenssas que fuerunt im vii[c] xxxvi li. iiii s. vi d. ob., aparet dictum collectorem debere camere, omnibus compenssatis, pro tempore suprascripto xxviii li. iiii s. ii d. sterlingorum; valent clxxxiiii fl. medietas camere, computato floreno pro tribus solidis in pretio. Item l fl. fortes, cl fl. crosete.

---

[191] Petty expenditure?

[192] Folio 15 (xiiii) recto is blank. In **b** the *compotus brevis*, which comes at the end of **a**, is placed here following the expenses.

[193] Om. **b**.

[194] *et* repeated, **a**.

[195] Lacking **a**. The following items preceding those on folio 17 are found only in **b**, fol. 92.

[196] In the margin bracketed against this and the next two items: *approbatur*.

[197] *est* repeated, MS.

---

[184] *respontionem*, MSS.

[185] *pinho*, **b**.

[186] *caternis*, **b**.

[187] Over *Cantuariensi* deleted by a line, **a**.

[188] *xxiiii*, **b**.

[189] Presumably for *locario: loquerio*, **b**.

[190] Item lacking, **a**.

(fol. 17, xvi)[198] Sequntur benefficia collata dominis cardinalibus in Anglia, pro quibus debentur primi fructus camere appostolice, dimissa in arrayratgiis per Dominum Hugonem Pelegrini prima die Septembris anno domini Mº CCCº LXIIIº.

### Primo : Londoniensis

De archidiaconatu Midelsexie, de quo fuit provisum domino cardinali Rothomagensi [199] per Innocentium xiiiiº kalendas Decembris anno viº.[200]

### Sarisberiensis

De prebenda de Calne et thesauraria in ecclesia Sarisberiensi, de quibus per obitum cardinalis de Florentia [201] fuit provisum domino cardinali Nemausensi (Nimes)[202] per Innocentium xiiiº kalendas Octobris anno ixº,[203] pro taxa lxxxvi li. xiii s. iiii d.

De prebenda de Wodefforde (Woodford), taxata xvi li. xiii s. iiii d., et archidiaconatu Dorcestrie in ecclesia Sarisberiensi, taxato lxii li., de quibus per obitum domini cardinalis Autisiodorensis [204] fuit provisum domino cardinali de Canilhaco, episcopo Penestrino [205] per Innocentium iiiiº ydus Martii anno xº,[206] lxxix li. xiii s. iiii d.

De archidiaconatu Dorcestrye in ecclesia Sarisberiensi, taxato lxiii li. de quo per obitum domini cardinalis Albiensis [207] fuit provisum domino cardinali Autisiodorensi (Auxerre)[208] per Innocentium iii ydus Februarii anno iiiº,[209] lxiii li.[210]

### Wellensis

De prebenda et archidiaconatu Wellensi, de quibus per obitum domini Tusculani cardinalis [211] fuit provisum domino cardinali Carcassonensi,[212] pro taxa lxvi li. xiii s. iiii d.

Summa restarum presentis pagine iiᶜ xxxiii li.[213]

### (fol. 17ᵛ) Lincholiensis

De prebenda de Milton' in ecclesia Lincolniensi,[214]

taxata xl li., et archidiaconatu Exoniensi (Oxford) in ecclesia Lincholiensi cum ecclesia de Isteleye [215] (Iffley), taxata xiiii li. xiii s. iiii d., de quibus per obitum domini cardinalis de Gordonio (Gourdon)[216] fuit provisum domino cardinali Aquensi (Dax)[217] per Innocentium iiiiº ydus Augusti anno ixº,[218] pro toto liiii li. xiii s. iiii d. Et est advertendum si de archidiaconatu qui per se non taxatur est aliquid exigendum.

De prebenda Lincholiensi de qua per obitum Jacobi de Borelay fuit provisum Domino Guillelmo episcopo Tusculanensi.

De prebenda de Northon (Bishop Norton), taxata xxxiii li. vi s. viii d., et archidiaconatu Lincoliensi, non taxato, de quibus per obitum Thome de Northwod fuit provisum Hugoni Alberti per Innocentium vii ydus Maii anno primo,[219] et [220] xii kalendas Martii anno sequenti [221] per resignationem eiusdem Hugonis fuit provisum domino cardinali Magalonensi (Maguelone),[222] nichil hic quia scriptum est per cameram quod ibidem erat compositum et quod hic nichil exhigeretur.[223]

### Eboracensis

De prebenda de Stranxale (Strensall) in ecclesia Eboracensi, de qua per consecrationem Michaelis episcopi Londoniensi fuit provisum domino cardinali Petragoricensi [224] per Innocentium pridie ydus Octobris anno iiº,[225] pro taxa liii li. vi s. viii d.

De prebenda de Wystowe (Wistow) in ecclesia Eboracensi, de qua per obitum domini cardinalis Penestrini [226] fuit provisum domino cardinali Carcassonensi (Carcassonne),[227] pro prebenda pro taxa c li. Advertatur si debet aliquod pro archidiaconatu qui non taxatur.

Summa restarum pagine iiᶜ viii li.[228]

(fol. 18, xvii)[229] De prebenda de Bohuc' (Bole) in eadem ecclesia, de qua per obitum Thome de Nevill' fuit provisum domino cardinali Cluniacensi [230] per Inno-

---

[198] The recto and verso of folio 16 are blank.
[199] Peter de la Forêt, priest of Ss. XII Apostoli.
[200] 18 November 1358.
[201] Francis de Aptis, priest of S. Marco.
[202] John de Blanzac, priest of S. Marco.
[203] 19 September 1361.
[204] Peter de Croso, priest of Ss. Silvestro e Martino ai Monti.
[205] Raymond de Canillac.
[206] 12 March 1362.
[207] Bernard d'Albi, bishop of Porto—but apparently a mistake for Cardinalis Sabinensis.
[208] Peter de Croso, priest of Ss. Silvestro e Martino ai Monti.
[209] 11 February 1355; p. 96.
[210] In the margin: *scriptum est per dominos camerarium et thesaurarium quod non fiat exequtio pro dicta taxa camere debita.*
[211] William de Court.
[212] Stephen Aubert, deacon of S. Maria in Aquiro.
[213] Item only in **b**, fol. 92ᵛ.
[214] *Sarisberiensi*, MSS.

[215] *Yseleye*, **b**.
[216] William Farinier, priest of Ss. Marcellino e Pietro.
[217] Peter Itherii, priest of Ss. Quattro Coronati.
[218] 10 August 1361.
[219] 9 May 1353.
[220] Follows *et* blotted and deleted, **a**.
[221] 18 February 1354.
[222] Audoin Aubert, priest of Ss. Giovanni e Paolo.
[223] In the margin: *vidi litteras domini camerarii et domini Eduensis* (Autun) *episcopi, olim thesauarii, sub data anni LV et iiii die menssis Decembris hoc continentes.*
[224] Elias Talleyrand de Périgueux, bishop of Albano.
[225] 14 October 1354.
[226] Peter des Prés, bishop of Palestrina.
[227] Stephen Aubert, deacon of S. Maria in Aquiro.
[228] Item only in **b**, fol. 93.
[229] The first item, which follows, is deleted by lines in **a**; omitted in **b**. *De prebenda de Diffeld in dicta ecclesia Eboracensi, de qua per obitum Thome de Nevill' fuit provisum domino cardinali Cluniascensi per Innocentium xiiii kalendas Octobris anno ix* (18 September 1361).
[230] Androin de la Roche, priest of S. Marcello.

centium xiiii° kalendas Octobris anno ix°,[231] pro taxa xvi li.

De prebenda de Dirffeld' (Driffeld) in ecclesia Eboracensi, taxata c li., de qua per obitum G. de Sancto Martiali fuit provisum domino Hugoni de Sancto Martiali cardinali [232] per Innocentium xiii kalendas Octobris anno ix°,[233] c li.

### Wellensis

De prebenda et thesauraria Wellensibus, de qua per obitum Ricardi de Tornenton' senioris, in Romana curia defuncti, fuit provisum domino cardinali Aquensi (Dax)[234] per Innocentium ii ydus Novembris anno ix°.[235]

Summa restarum pagine cxvi li. et i benefficium non taxatum.[236]

Summa restarum debitarum per dominos cardinales v^c lvii li.[236]

(fol. 20, xix)[237] Sequntur arrayratgia dimissa in Anglia de denariis Beati Petri.

Archidiaconus Cantuariensis pro anno LXIII° viii li.
Archidiaconus Roffensis pro anno LXIII° v li. xii s.
Episcopus Cicestrensis pro anno LXIII° viii li.
Archidiaconus Exssexie pro anno LXIII° v li. x s.
Archidiaconus Middelsexie pro annis LX°, LXI°, LXII° et LXIII°, pro quolibet v li. et x s., xxii li.
Archidiaconus Wynthoniensis pro anno LXIII° [238] xi li. xiii s. iiii d.
Archidiaconus Surreie pro anno LXIII° v li. xiii s. iiii d.
Episcopus Bathoniensis et Wellensis pro anno LXIII° xi li. v s.
Episcopus Exoniensis pro anno LXIII° ix li. v s.
Archidiaconus Eliensis pro annis LXII° et LXIII°, pro quolibet quinque libre, x li.
Episcopus Norwicensis pro anno LXIII° xxi li. x s.
Episcopus Lincholiensis pro annis LXII° et LXIII°, pro quolibet xlii li., lxxxiiii li. De istis debet solvere dominus Cantuariensis archiepiscopus pro anno LXII°, quo anno spiritualitas ecclesie Lincoliensis in manibus suis fuit ratione vacationis xlii li., et credo quod iam sint solute.

Summa restarum pagine ii^c ii li. viii s. viii d.[239]

(fol. 20^v) Episcopus Convetrensis et Licheffeldensis pro anno LXIII° x li. v s.
Episcopus Hereffordensis pro anno LXIII° vi li.
Episcopus Wygorniensis pro [240] anno LXIII° x li. v s.

---
[231] 18 September 1361.
[232] Deacon of S. Maria in Portico.
[233] 19 September 1361.
[234] Peter Itherii, priest of Ss. Quattro Coronati.
[235] 12 November 1361.
[236] Item found only in **b**, fol. 93^v.
[237] Folios 18 verso 19 verso are blank.
[238] *annis LXII° et LXIII°*, **b**.
[239] Items in **b** only, fols. 94-95.
[240] *pro* repeated, **a**.

Archiepiscopus Eboracensis pro anno LXIII° xi li. x s.
Summa pagine xxxviii li.[239]
Summa restarum denariorum Beati Petri ii^c xl li. viii s. viii d.[239]

(fol. 21, xx) Sequntur arrayratgia annui censsus

Abbas de Faveresham pro annis LXII° et LXIII°, pro quolibet xiii s. iiii d., xxvi s. viii d.
Prior de Tenebrug' pro anno LXIII° xiii s. iiii d.
Abbas de Corteseye Wyntoniensis diocesis pro anno LXIII° viii s.
Abbas Sancti Edmundi Norwicensis diocesis pro anno LXIII° xiii s. iiii d.
Prior de Bodmyne pro annis LXII et LXIII°, pro quolibet ii s., iiii s.
Abbas Sancti Albani pro anno LXIII° xiii s. iiii d.
Abbas Sancti Adelmi Malmesbur' pro anno LXIII° [241] xiii s. iiii d.
Abbatissa Sancte Clare Londonie, que facit singulis annis i libram cere pro qua solvit vi d., pro annis LVIII°, LIX°, LX, LXI, LXII° [242] et LXIII° iii s.
Prior de Chaucombe pro anno LXIII° xv d.
Prior de Angleseya pro annis LXI, LXII° et LXIII°, pro quolibet ii s., vi s.
Custos de Skardeburchg' pro anno LXIII° xv d.
Prior ecclesie Karliolensis pro annis LXII° et LXIII°, pro quolibet xiii s. iiii d., xxvi s. viii d.
Summa pagine vi li. ix s. viii d.[239]

(fol. 27)[243] Reste arrayragiorum dimissorum per Dominum Hugonem Pelegrini, olim sedis apostolice in partibus Anglie, Wallie et Hibernie nuntium, Domino Johanni de Cabrespino, decretorum doctori eius successori in officio predicte nuntiationis, tradite per dictum Dominum Johannem nunc nuntium religioso viro Dompno Johanni de Caroloco, priori de Bermundeseye Wyntoniensis diocesis eius subcollectori, locumtenenti et commissario in dictis partibus deputato.

### De diocesi Cantuariensi

Ecclesia de Stokebury [244] (Stockbury) que fuit appropriata priori et conventui de Ledes (Leeds) per Clementem viii° idus Augusti anno xi,[245] que taxatur ad xxvii li. vi s. viii d., dimissa in arrayragiis pro resta vii li. vi s. viii d. Fructus dicte ecclesie presentes et futuri fuerunt sequestrati usque ad dictam summam, ut constat per certificatorium domini Cantuariensis archiepiscopi.[246]

Capella libera de Bokineffeld' (Bockingfold), de qua per obitum Willelmi de Bradley fuit provisum David

---
[241] *LXIIII*, **b**.
[242] *LXI°*, **a**.
[243] Folios 21^v to 26^r inclusive are blank.
[244] *Stoburo*, **b**.
[245] 6 August 1352.
[246] Followed by *datum* deleted by a line, **a**.

Wigham per Innocentium [247] iii° idus Augusti anno decimo,[248] fuit dimissa in solidis fructibus.[249]

### (fol. 27ᵛ) Roffensis

Ecclesia de Mepham (Meopham), taxata ad xxvi li. xiii s. iiii d. de qua per obitum Johannis Blode fuit provisum Johanni de Kyrkeby per Innocentium [247] iiiiᵗᵒ nonas [250] Julii anno ix,[251] debet de resta x li. De dictis decem libris habet terminum hinc ad festum Sancti Michaelis proximum, pro quibus solvendum dicto termino Willelmus Nel, nomine proprio et ut procurator dicti rectoris se obligavit sub pena excommunicationis late in scriptis et iuravit die xiiii Octobris anno domini Mᵐᵒ CCCᵒ LXIIItio.

### De tempore Domini Urbani

De ecclesia de Stone, quam obtinere solebat Nicolaus de Aston', magister in theologia, fuit provisum Johanni Pays xi kalendas Decembris per Dominum Urbanum papam V anno primo,[252] taxata xx li., pro resta x li. Habet terminum.

Summa pagine xx li.[253]

### (fol. 28) Londoniensis

Ecclesia seu capella de Stamford' (Stanford le Hope), de qua per obitum Edmundi de Gremesby fuit provisum Johanni de Torkesey [254] per Innocentium [255] viii idus Octobris anno iiᵈᵒ,[256] pro taxa xxvi li. xiii s. iiii d. De ista capella nichil penitus factum fuit, quamvis processus fuerunt emanati, quare de novo fiat processus et procedatur contra ipsam, et perquiratur in quo decanatu est, decanus enim de Hertlawe [257] (Harlow) dicit,[258] in suo certificatario quod non reperitur in decanatu suo vel alibi.[259]

Ecclesia Sancte Trinitatis Londonie, non taxata, de qua fuit dispensatum cum Thoma Ball' presbytero ut, non obstante defectu natalium, possit eam retinere per Innocentium [255] xii kalendas Junii anno ixᵒ,[260] dimissa in solidis fructibus et composita medio iuramento ad c s., debet pro resta ii li. x s. Secunda die Decembris anno quo supra dictus Thomas promisit et iuravit solvere medietatem in festo Pasche et alteram medietatem in festo Sancti Michaelis proximo futuro et se obligavit sub pena excommunicationis late in scriptis.

Ecclesia de Herlawe (Harlow), de qua per obitum Ricardi Drax fuit provisum Johanni Parker [261] per Innocentium [255] xi kalendas Junii anno ixᵒ,[262] pro taxa xiii li. vi s. viii d. Fructus fuerunt sequestrati, ut constat per certificatorium officialis Londoniensis, et fuit probatum per quinque testes quod ante x annis citra non fuit aliquis rector in illa ecclesia ita nominatus.

Prioratus Sancte Trinitatis Londonie, qui non taxatur, de quo [263] fuit provisum Johanni de Buri [264] et est eidem confirmata per Innocentium [265] xii kalendas Junii anno x,[266] dimissus in solidis fructibus.

Archidiaconatus Midelsexie, de quo provisum fuit domino cardinali Rothomagensi (Rouen)[267] per Innocentium [265] xiiii kalendas Decembris anno viᵗᵒ,[268] dimissus.[269]

Summa pagine xlii li. x s.[270]

(fol. 28ᵛ)[271] Ecclesia de Matfelon [272] (Whitechapel) Londonie, non taxata, de qua per resignationem Johannis Schillyng' fuit provisum David Doyer per Innocentum [265] vii idus Aprilis anno vii,[273] dimissa in xiii s. iiii d., debet de resta vi s. viii d. Habet terminum in festo Pasche.

Archidiaconatus Essexie in ecclesia Londoniensi, non taxatus, qui fuit confirmatus Willelmo Rothewelle per Innocentium iii idus Februarii anno viᵗᵒ,[274] fuit dimissus in solidis fructibus.

Ista que sequntur non fuerunt tradita in arrayragiis per dictum Dominum Hugonem Pelegrini.

De ecclesia de Herlawe (Harlow) Londoniaria, de qua per assecutionem archidiaconatus Tetonie (Totnes) fuit provisum Magistro Ricardo Anglici per Innocentium vi idus May anno viii,[275] pro taxa xiii li. vi s. viii d. A retro in precedenti pagina est iterato pro alia provisione et sunt fructus sequestrati per officialem Londoniensem.

De ecclesia de Sabrichesword' (Sawbridgeworth) diocesis Londoniensis, que fuit unita monasterio Westmonasterii iuxta Londoniam per Clementem iiiᵗⁱᵒ nonas Maii anno ix,[276] pro resta xiii li. vi s. viii d. Habunt terminum ad festum proximum Beati Johannis Baptiste

[247] For *per Innocentium* **b** has *pro anno.*
[248] 11 August 1362.
[249] In the margin: *fiat processus.* At the foot of the page in **b** (fol. 97): *summa patet.*
[250] *idus,* **b.**
[251] 4 or 12 July 1361.
[252] 21 November 1362.
[253] Item in **b** only, fol. 97ᵛ.
[254] *Dorkesey,* **b.**
[255] *pro anno,* **b.**
[256] 8 October 1354.
[257] *Hertalwe,* **b.**
[258] *dicto,* **b.**
[259] In the margin: *perquiratur.*
[260] 21 May 1361.

[261] *Parbey,* **b.**
[262] 22 May 1361.
[263] *qua,* **a, b.**
[264] *Duro,* **b.**
[265] *pro anno,* **b.**
[266] 21 May 1362.
[267] Peter de la Forêt, priest of Ss. XII Apostoli.
[268] 18 November 1358.
[269] In the margin: *cardinalis.*
[270] Item in **b** only, fol 98.
[271] The caption *Londoniensis* is repeated at the top of the page.
[272] *Matphelon,* **b.**
[273] 7 April 1359.
[274] 11 February 1358.
[275] 10 May 1360.
[276] 5 May 1351.

et sunt obligati prior et conventus per litteras traditas dicto priori de Bermundeseye.

Summa pagine xxvii li.[277]

(fol. 29)[278] Sequentes sunt de tempore Domini Urbani

De ecclesia sive capella de Alswik' (Alswick), de qua ex causa permutationis fuit provisum Roberto Franceys per dictum dominum nostrum iii$^{tio}$ nonas Januarii anno primo,[279] fructus.

De ecclesia de Langdon' (Langdon Hills), de qua ex simili causa fuit provisum Willelmo de Swiffeld' dicto die, fructus.

De ecclesia Sancti Botolphi extra Lagathe (St. Botolph, Aldgate) Londonie collatio et provisio et pacifica administratio facte Radulpho de Cantebriggia, presbytero canonico regulari domus Sancte Trinitatis Londonie, expresse per priorem et conventum dicte domus fuerunt auctoritate apostolica confirmate v nonas Martii anno predicto[280] fructus.

De prebenda Sancti Pancratii in ecclesia Sancti Pauli Londonie fuit ex causa permutationis provisum Radulpho de Davyntre[281] v nonas Martii anno predicto,[280] pro taxa xlii s. vi d.

De prebenda de Kentiford' (Kentish Town) in ecclesia Londoniensi, taxata vi li. xiii s. iiii d., de qua per obitum Ade Mermouth' fuit provisum Rogero Holm, debet de resta tam pro ista quam pro diversis aliis beneficiis suis pro quibus partes satisfecit in camera x li. Nisi appareat per libros vel acquietantiam camere ex toto solvisse.

Summa pagine xii li. ii s. vi d.[282]

### (fol. 29$^{v}$)  Cicestrensis

Prebenda de Ferryng'[283] (Ferring) in ecclesia Cicestrensi, de qua per resignationem Simonis Godwyn fuit provisum Johanni de Acton' per Clementem, dimissa in vii li.

Prebenda de Sillesham[284] (Sidelsham) in ecclesia Cicestrensi, de qua per obitum Edmundi de Arundell' fuit provisum Waltero Gest per Clementem xii kalendas Decembris anno viii,[285] taxata in xxx li., fuit dimissa in xii li. ii s. ix d.

Archidiaconatus Lewensis, non taxatus, qui fuit confirmatus Willelmo Lugtheburgh'[286] per Clementem ii idus Augusti anno xi,[287] in solidis fructibus.

Idem, de quo fuit provisum Thome Bronwen[288]

per Innocentium ii idus Septembris anno sexto,[289] eo quod Willelmus predictus fuit assecutus thesaurarie dicte ecclesie, dimisso in aliis solidis fructibus.

Ecclesia de Bukstede (Buxted), de qua per assecutionem prepositure de Wyngham (Wingham) per Johannem de Beverle fuit provisum Waltero Sutton' per Innocentium iiii$^{to}$ kalendas Aprilis anno vi,[290] pro taxa xxxii li.

De archidiaconatu Cicestrensi, non taxato, permutatio facta cum decanatu ecclesie collegiate Cestrie super Stratam (Chester-le-Street) Dunelmensis diocesis fuit Johanni de Skwlthorp'[291] confirmata per Innocentium v kalendas Januarii anno vi,[292] fructus.

Summa pagine li li. ii s. ix d.[293]

(fol. 30)[294] De prebenda de Waltham in ecclesia Cicestrensi, taxata x li., de qua per consecrationem Roberti episcopi Conventrensis fuit provisum Ade de Hilton' per Innocentium x kalendas Januarii anno viii,[295] dimissa pro taxa in x li.

De prebenda de Colleword (Colworth) in ecclesia Cicestrensi, de qua per obitum Ricardi Drax fuit provisum Johanni de Streteleye per Innocentium vii kalendas Junii anno ix,[296] pro taxa xxvi li.

De prebenda le Ippethorn' (Ipthorne) in ecclesia Cicestrensi, de qua per obitum Thome David fuit provisum Philipo de Cortenay[297] per Innocentium x kalendas Julii anno ix$^{o}$,[298] pro taxa vi li. xiii s. iiii d.

De thesauraria Cicestrensi ratione confirmationis facte Willelmo de Lugtheburgh' pro resta xvi li. xiii s. iiii d.

De archidiaconatu Lewensi in ecclesia Cicestrensi, quem Willelmus de Lughtburgh' predictus obtinebat, vacante per assecutionem dicte thesaurarie, fuit provisum Thome Bronwen per Innocentium vii idus Septembris anno vi,[299] dimisso in solidis fructibus.

De prebenda de Walton' in ecclesia collegiata de Bosinham (Bosham), cuius taxa et provisio continentur supra in recepta, ix li. vi s. viii d.

Summa pagine lxix li. vi s. viii d.[300]

(fol. 30$^{v}$)[301] De prebenda de Seleseya (Selsey) in ecclesia Cicestrensi, de qua per obitum Johannis Leth' fuit provisum Roberto de Askby[302] per Innocentium anno ix,[303] dimissa[304] pro resta xi li vi s. viii d.

---

[277] Item in **b** only, fol. 98$^{v}$.
[278] The caption *Londoniensis* is repeated at the top of the page.
[279] 3 January 1363.
[280] 3 March 1363.
[281] *Camtre*, **b**.
[282] Item in **b** only, fol. 99.
[283] *Feyyng'*, **b**.
[284] *Gilhesham*, **b**.
[285] 20 November 1349.
[286] *Luttheburgen'*, **b**.
[287] 12 August 1352.
[288] *Donroneven*, **b**.

[289] 12 September 1358.
[290] 29 March 1358.
[291] *Scwelthorp*, **b**.
[292] 28 December 1358.
[293] Item in **b** only, fol. 99$^{v}$.
[294] The caption *Cicestrensis* is repeated at the top of the page.
[295] 23 December 1360.
[296] 26 May 1361.
[297] *Crathenay*, **b**.
[298] 22 June 1361.
[299] 7 September 1358.
[300] Item in **b**, fol. 100.
[301] The heading *Cicestrensis* is repeated at the top of the page.
[302] *Aslly*, **b**.
[303] 1361.
[304] Followed by *pro taxa* deleted by a line, **a**.

Ista que sequntur non fuerunt tradita in arrayragiis per dictum Dominum Hugonem Pelegrini

De vicaria ecclesie de Ilkesham [305] (Icklesham), de qua fuit dispensatum cum Waltero de Stratton' presbytero quod eam posset licite retinere per Innocentium ii idus Januarii anno viii,[306] pro taxa xvi li. xiii s. iiii d.

De prioratu conventuali Lewensi ordinis Cluniacensis, vacante per assecutionem monasterii Trenerthen' (Tournus) Cabilionensis (Châlon-sur-Saône) diocesis factam per fratrem Hugonem de Chuccrato [307] ultimi prioris dicti prioratus, fuit provisum fratri Geraldo Rothonis, monacho baculario in decretis, pro taxa.

Summa pagine xxviii li.[308]

(fol. 31)[309] Sequentia beneficia fuerunt collata de tempore Domini Urbani

De decanatu ecclesie Cicestrensis et canonicatu et prebenda sibi annexis, vacantibus per consecrationem Willelmi episcopi Cicestrensis, fuit provisum Nicholao de Aston', magistro in sacra pagina, xii kalendas Decembris anno primo,[310] pro resta [311] xlviii li. vi s. viii d. Habet terminum ad solvendum xii li. dominica in quinquagesima proxima venienti, et alias xii li. in festo Beati Johannis Baptiste, et alias xii in festo Omnium Sanctorum, et residuas xii li. vi s. viii d. in sequenti dominica de quinquagesima, et ad hoc Johannes de Aston', procurator dicti Magistri Nicholai, se obligavit et iuravit die xvi Novembris anno LXIII.

Summa patet.[312]

(fol. 31ᵛ) Wyntoniensis

De ecclesia de Westmines (West Meon), taxata ad xx li., que fuit confirmata Johanni de Kenyngton' [313] per Clementem idus Maii anno viii,[314] pro resta dimissa vi li. Bona et fructus dicte ecclesie sequestrati fuerunt per episcopum Wyntoniensem ut per eius certificatorium clare constat.

De hospitali Sancte Crucis, non taxato, confirmato Johanni de Edyngdon' per Clementem xviii kalendas Junii anno viii,[315] dimissa in vii li. iii s. vi d. Archidiaconus Surreie qui dictum hospitale tenet habet terminum ad solvendum in festo Beati Johannis Baptiste.

De ecclesia de Lavertok' (Laverstoke), taxata ad xiiii li., in qua fuit subrogatus Johannes de Banneburi, dimissa in resta iii li. Allegavit excusationem, fuit citatis et non comparuit.

De prebenda de Midelton (Middleton) in ecclesia

monialium de Warwell' (Wherwell), de qua fuit provisum Johanni Branketre per Innocentium v kalendas Januarii anno primo,[316] pro taxa dimissa xxvi li. xiii s. iiii d. Bona et fructus dicte ecclesie sunt per dictum episcopum sequestrata ut constat per eius certificatorium.

De prioratu de Appulburtorp' (Appuldurcombe), confirmato Johanni Osanna per Clementem v kalendas Martii anno viii,[317] dimisso in xxx li. xvii s., ad quas taxatur, pro resta xxv li. xvii s. Bona et fructus ut supra sunt sequestrata.

De ecclesia de Waltham, taxata xx li. et dimissa, de qua per obitum Gilberti David fuit provisum Hugoni Craft' per Innocentium iiiiᵗᵒ nonas Julii anno ix,[318] pro resta xvi li. Habet terminum in festo Omnium Sanctorum.

De ecclesia de Chayham (Cheam), cuius taxa et provisio supra in recepta, pro resta iiii li.

Summa pagine lxxxvii li. xii s. x d.[319]

(fol. 32)[320] De ecclesia de Havunte (Havant), taxata xxvi li. xiii s. iiii d., de qua per obitum Johannis Noion fuit provisum Johanni Uppehull' per Innocentium iiiiᵗᵒ nonas Julii anno ixᵒ,[318] debet pro resta xx li. Non habet terminum sed fructus sunt sequestrati.

Sequentia beneficia non fuerunt tradita in arreragiis per Dominum Hugonem

De ecclesia de Derham (East Dereham), quam obtinuit Dominus Simon de Sudbur' episcopus Londoniensis, que reservata conferenda Bertholomei Sidey per Innocentium iii idus Decembris anno ixᵒ.[321]

Item sequentia beneficia collata tempore Domini Urbani

De ecclesia de Drynteffeld (Dunsfold), taxata xiii li. vi s. viii d., de qua per obitum Willelmi de Charsterston' fuit provisum Johanni de Lewes xix kalendas Februarii anno primo,[322] pro resta vi li. xiii s. iiii d. Habet terminum ad festum Omnium Sanctorum et fuit monitus sub pena excommunicationis late in scriptis.

De ecclesia de Newton' [323] (Newington by Lambeth), taxata iii li. vi s. viii d., dum vacabit per consecrationem Thome electi Dublinensi fuit provisum Thome de Elselse [324] xii kalendas Aprilis dicto anno,[325] iii li. vi s. viii d.[326]

Item de eadem ecclesia fuit provisum Willelmo de

---

[305] *Islesham*, **b.**
[306] 12 January 1360.
[307] *Curcrato*, **b.**
[308] Item in **b** only, fol. 100ᵛ.
[309] The heading *Cicestrensis* is repeated at the head of the page.
[310] 20 November 1362.
[311] Over *taxa* deleted by a line, **a.**
[312] Item in **b** only, fol. 101.
[313] *Keyyngton*, **b.**
[314] 15 May 1350.
[315] 15 May 1350.

[316] 28 December 1353.
[317] 25 February 1350.
[318] 4 July 1361.
[319] Item in **b** only, fol. 101ᵛ.
[320] The heading *Wyntoniensis* is repeated at the top of the page.
[321] *iii idus Septembris*, **b.** 11 September or 11 December 1361. In the margin: *Fiat processus.*
[322] 14 January 1363.
[323] *Neffton*, **b.**
[324] *Elphelse*, **b.** In the margin: *fiat processus.*
[325] 21 March 1363.
[326] In the margin bracketed against this item and the next: *infra annum.*

Brukill' xvii kalendas Maii dicto anno.[327] Ista ecclesia est in iurisdictione exempta domini archiepiscopi Cantuariensis, quare fiat processus.

Summa pagine xxx li.[328]

### (fol. 32ᵛ) Saresburiensis

Fructus beneficiorum huius diocesis sunt sequestrati tam presentes quam futuri, ut constat per certificatorium domini episcopi Saresburiensis.

De ecclesia de Kyveleye [329] (Keevil), de qua fuit provisum Magistro Thome Trompsale, taxata ad xxvi li. xiii s. iiii d., pro resta dimissa vi li. xiii s. iiii d.

De prebenda de Wermynstr' (Warminster) in ecclesia Saresburiensi, de qua per obitum Johannis de Barebury [330] fuit provisum Thome de Scraghull' per Clementem, pro taxa v li. De ista et sequenti certificavit episcopus quod vidit acquietantiam, sed nondum fecit fidem Domino Johanni de Cabrispino.

Item de eadem, de qua per obitum Baldewyni de Moyn acceptatio facta per Bartholomeum de Bradden' fuit confirmata per Clementem v idus Septembris anno ix,[331] pro taxa v li.

De prebenda de Hull' (Hill Deverill) in ecclesia collegiata de Haltebury (Heytesbury), taxata vi li. xiii s. iiii d., de qua per obitum Roberti Trek fuit provisum Thome Patricii per Clementem viii idus Martii anno ix°,[332] pro resta [332a] dimissa iii li. vi s. viii d.

De ecclesia de Wyntreburn' Fakelan' (Winterborne Stickland), de qua per resignationem Willelmi de Cheston' fuit provisum Thome Henrico per Innocentium xiiii kalendas Julii anno primo,[333] pro taxa iiii li. vi s. viii d.

De prebenda de Streton' (Stratton) in ecclesia Saresburiensi, de qua ex causa permutationis fuit provisum Johanni de Turstayn per Innocentium idus Martii anno iiitio,[334] pro taxa xiii li. vi s. viii d. Sunt sequestrati fructus, sed Johannes Hanney nunc prebendarius allegavit istam provisionem minime effectum habuisse, et fuit sibi datus terminus ad probandum hunc ad festum assencionis domini.

De prebenda de Bischopeston' (Bishopstone) in ecclesia Saresburiensi, taxata xx li., de qua per obitum Petri Raymundi de Rappistangno fuit provisum Raymundo Pelegrini per Clementem kalendas Februarii anno viii°.[335] Dicit Dominus Hugo in rationibus suis quod non habuit effectum eo quod rex contulit Willelmo

de Okburn qui [336] possidet.[336] De hoc non fecit fidem, quare perquiratur.

Summa pagine xxxvii li. xiii s. iiii d.[337]

(fol. 33) [338] De prebenda de Husthburn' et Borbach' (Husseburn and Burbage), de qua per obitum Johannis de Withecherch' fuit confirmata Saladino de Fallet' per Innocentium kalendas Junii anno vi,[339] pro taxa liii li. vi s. viii d. Episcopus rescripsit quod situata est extra diocesi et decanatu Saresburiensi, quare exploretur de ea et fiat executio.[340]

De prebenda de Bedmynstr' [341] (Bedminster) in ecclesia Saresburiensi, de qua per resignationem Willelmi Hale fuit provisum Thome de Clipston' per Innocentium idus Decembris [342] anno vi,[343] pro taxa xiii li. vi s. viii d. Idem ut in precedenti.

De vicaria de Potern (Potterne) pro resta xl s.

Item de eadem ab alia parte ratione provisionis ex causa permutationis facte Thome West per Innocentium viii kalendas Octobris anno ix,[344] pro resta xv li.

De prebenda Saresburiensi, acceptatio facta per Johannem de Wffordi Norwicensis diocesis fuit eidem confirmata per Innocentium vii kalendas Julii anno vii,[345] fructus. Episcopus scripsit quod nunquam iste Johannes habuit prebendam in dicta ecclesia, quare [346] exploretur.[347]

De prebenda de Colme (Calne) et thesauraria in dicta ecclesia, de quibus fuit provisum domino cardinali Nemausenensi [348] per Innocentium iii kalendas Octobris anno ix,[349] pro taxa iiiixx vi li. xiii s. iiii d.[350]

De ecclesia Sancti Petri de Wartham (Warham), de qua per resignationem Thome de Berneby fuit provisum Henrico de Worth' per Innocentium v idus Octobris anno ix,[351] pro taxa iiii li. vi s. viii d.

Summa pagine ultra debitum cardinalis lxxxviii li.[352]

(fol. 33ᵛ) [353] De ecclesia de Ascheburi (Ashbury), taxata xxvi li. xiii s. iiii d., de qua per obitum Walteri Moryn fuit provisum Thome de Bischoppesbury per

---

[327] 15 April 1363.
[328] Item in **b** only, fol. 102.
[329] *Kunbern*, **b**.
[330] *Batebury*, **b**.
[331] 9 September 1350.
[332] 8 March 1351.
[332a] *post restam*, **b**.
[333] 18 June 1353.
[334] 15 March 1355.
[335] 1 February 1350.

[336] Om. **b**.
[337] Item in **b** only, fol. 102ᵛ.
[338] The heading *Saresburiensis* is repeated at the top of the page.
[339] 1 June 1358.
[340] In the margin: *fiat executio*.
[341] *Bmynstr'*, **b**.
[342] *Sebtembris*, **b**.
[343] 13 September or December 1358.
[344] 24 September 1361.
[345] 25 June 1359.
[346] *quare* repeated and deleted by a line, **a**.
[347] In the margin: *exploretur*.
[348] John de Blanzac, priest of S. Marco, bishop of Nimes.
[349] 29 September 1361.
[350] In the margin: *Cardinalis Nemausenensis*. In **b** only: *summa summatur inter dominos cardinales*.
[351] 11 October 1361.
[352] Item in **b** only, fol. 103.
[353] The heading *Saresburiensis* is repeated at the top of the page.

Innocentium iiii kalendas Octobris anno ix,[354] pro resta xvi li. xiii s. viii d. Habet terminos ad solvendum videlicet vi li. xiii s. iiii d. in festo Pasche et residuum in festo Beate Marie Augusti proximis futuris, et ita iuravit et promisit dictus Dominus T. die xvi Octobris.

De ecclesia de Corf' [355] (Corfe Castle), de qua per assecutionem precentorie Saresburiensis per Philipum Cotffordi [356] fuit provisum Simoni Thebaud per Innocentium iii kalendas Novembris anno ix,[357] pro taxa x li. Episcopus certificavit quod nunquam habuit possessionem; exploretur de hoc.[358]

De prebenda de Bemynstr' (Bedminster)[359] in ecclesia Saresburiensi, de qua per obitum Ricardi de Norwico fuit facta confirmatio Henrico de Wynton' per Innocentium xi kalendas Februarii anno xi [360] pro taxa xiii li. vi s. viii d. In primo processu misso episcopo rescripsit se non invenisse que et qualis esset illa prebenda dicto Henrico confirmata, tamen in dicto processu non erat nomen prebende; etiam exploretur.[361]

De prebenda de Wedeford' (Woodford), taxata xvi [362] li., xiii s., iiii d., et archidiaconatu Dorcestr' in dicta ecclesia, taxato lxii li., de quibus fuit provisum domino cardinali de Canilhaco, episcopo Penestrino, per Innocentium iiii idus Martii anno ixo,[363] lxxxix [364] li. xiii s. iiii d.[365]

De prebenda de Preston' in ecclesia Saresburiensi, de qua fuit provisum Thome de Sotton' [366] per Innocentium xi kalendas Novembris anno v,[367] pro taxa xvi li. xiii s. iiii d.

Summa pagine excluso debito domini cardinalis lvi li. xiii s. iiii d.[368]

(fol. 34)[369] Sequentia beneficia non fuerunt tradita in arrayragiis per Dominum Hugonem Pelegrini.

De prebenda de Bischopston' (Bishopstone) in ecclesia Saresburiensi, in qua in omni iure quod competebat Arnaldo Pelegrini fuit subrogatus Arnaldus Garini presbyter [370] per Innocentium idus Julii anno decimo,[371] pro taxa xx li.

Item sequentia beneficia collata tempore Domini Urbani

De prebenda quam Johannes de Bokyngham, nunc episcopus Lyncolniensis, obtinebat in ecclesia Saresburiensi fuit provisum Roberto Sumpter, legum doctori diocesis Exoniensis, ii nonas Decembris anno primo.[372] Certificatum est de ista per episcopum quod non habuit effectum nec dictus Robertus umquam habuit possessionem, quia dominus rex dictam prebendam et alia beneficia dicti episcopi contulisse dicitur Johanni Hanneye; exploretur tamen.[373]

De prebenda de Horton' in ecclesia Saresburiensi, de qua per obitum Ricardi de Tormerton' fuit provisum Willelmo de Laughebergh' kalendas Januarii.[374] Certificatum est quod extra diocesim et decanatum Saresburiensis situatur; exploretur et fiat processus compulsorius.[375]

De prebenda de [376] in ecclesia Saresburiensi, vacante per obitum Willelmi de Farlee, collatio facta fuit Nicholao de Luda, thesaurario domini regis, fuit confirmata, etiam si alio quovismodo vacet vel sit reservata valeat, ac si vacasset solomodo per mortem dicti Willelmi.

De ecclesia de Donnintton' (Downton), collatio et provisio eiusdem facte Thome de Edyngdon' fuerunt auctoritate apostolica confirmate vel provisum de novo decimo septimo kalendas May,[377] pro taxa lxvi li. xiii s. iiii d. Episcopus scripsit quod sequestravit fructus repertos usque ad valorem xl m.

Summa pagine lxxxvi li. xiii s.[378]

(fol. 34v)[379] De prebenda in ecclesia Saresburiensi quam Ricardus de Norwico per nonnullas annos pacifice possedit, etiam si alio quovismodo vacet,[380] provisio facta Henrico Wynterton', baccallario in legibus, fuit confirmata vel provisum de novo v nonas Martii.[381] Episcopus rescripsit quod explorare nequivit que et qualis sit dicta prebenda, et ideo exploretur.[382]

De officio subdecanatus ecclesie Saresburiensis, de quo per obitum Nicholai de Mardfeld' [383] fuit provisum Willelmo de Slinton' nonas Decembris anno predicto.[384] Fructus proventi sunt sequestrati.

## (fol. 35) Exoniensis

De thesauraria ecclesie Exoniensis, acceptatio cuius

[354] 28 September 1361.
[355] Chorf', b.
[356] Cothford', b.
[357] 30 October 1361.
[358] In the margin: exploretur, a.
[359] See above, p. 146.
[360] 22 January 1361.
[361] In the margin: exploretur.
[362] vi, b.
[363] 12 March 1361.
[364] lxxix, b.
[365] In the margin: Cardinalis de Canilhaco.
[366] Setton, b.
[367] ix kalendas, b. 22 or 24 October 1357.
[368] Item in b only, fol. 103.
[369] The heading Saresburiensis is repeated at the top of the page.
[370] Omitted in b.
[371] 15 July 1362.

[372] 4 December 1362.
[373] In the margin: exploretur.
[374] 1 January 1363.
[375] In the margin: fiat processus.
[376] A blank space for the name is left in a and b.
[377] 15 April 1363.
[378] Item in b only, fol. 104.
[379] The heading Saresburiensis is repeated at the top of the page.
[380] vacaverit, b.
[381] 3 March 1363.
[382] In the margin: exploretur.
[383] Martffelt, b.
[384] 5 December 1362.

per Robertum de Midlond' [385] fuit eidem confirmata per Clementem xv kalendas Junii anno vii,[386] pro taxa xx li. Fructus sunt sequestrati per episcopum, prout in eius certificatorio continetur.

De archidiaconatu Barnastapol', pro resta duarum provisionum, unius facte Johanni de Reynham et alterius Willelmo Mugge nunc archidiacono, x li. Dictus archidiaconus promisit et iuravit solvere infra octabas Pasche, et fuit monitus sub pena excommunicationis late in scriptis.

De decanatu Exoniensi, de quo per obitum Ricardi de Brayle fuit provisum Reginaldo de Bogwell' per Clementem xv kalendas Octobris anno xi,[387] qui taxatur ad lxii li. xiii s. iiii d., pro resta xxxii li. xiii s. iiii d. Obligatus est coram Domino Hugone Pelegrini in libro obligationum folio,[388] et nichilominus fructus dicti decanatus sunt, ut constat per certificatorium episcopi, sequestrati.

De prebenda Exoniensi, taxata iiii li., que fuit confirmata Thome David per Clementem viii idus May anno x°,[389] iiii li.[390] Episcopus rescripsit quod fructus sunt sequestrati.

De prebenda Exoniensi, de qua per obitum Henrici de Brathele fuit provisum Henrico de Walton' per Innocentium iiii kalendas Martii anno primo,[390a] pro taxa iiii li. Episcopus rescripsit quod nescit dictum Henricum re aut nomine posessorem, quare de hoc exploretur.[391]

De vicaria ecclesie de Columpton (Collumpton), non taxata, de qua per obitum Petri Moleys fuit provisum Thome de Pylton' per Innocentium iii idus May anno vi^to,[392] dimissa pro medietate in vi li. xiii s. iiii d. Nichil rescripsit episcopus super hoc se fecisse, quare rescribatur.[393]

Summa pagine lxxiii li. vi s. viii d.[394]

(fol. 35^v)[395] De ecclesia de Lansant (Lezant), collatio cuius facta fuit Johanni de Broklond' et fuit eidem confirmata per Innocentium xi kalendas Octobris anno vi,[396] pro taxa iiii li. Episcopus rescripsit quod tandus alter est iste rector.

De prebenda ecclesie Sancte Tethe (St. Teath), de qua per obitum Thome David fuit provisum Johanni Braker per Innocentium xi kalendas Julii anno ix^no [397] pro taxa iiii li. Episcopus rescripsit quod non est ecclesia collegiata, sed in duas tantum portiones cum

vicaria divisa, et nullum possessorem ad monendum invenit, sed sequestrum interposuit.

De portione parochialis ecclesie Sancte Endoliente (St. Endellion), de qua per obitum Willelmi Donne fuit provisum Simoni Withull' per Innocentium iiii nonas Julii anno ix°.[398] Episcopus rescripsit quod nescit valorem fructuum nec detentorem, sed certificatum est sibi quod satisfactum est Domino Hugoni Pelegrini.

De prebenda ecclesie Exoniensis, de qua per obitum Ricardi de Tormerton' et Willelmi de Braddeley fuit provisum Ade de Hilton' [399] per Innocentium iiii nonas Julii anno ix°,[398] pro taxa iiii li. Sequestrati sunt fructus.

De ecclesia de Basch', de qua, ex eo quod Henricus de Monte dictam ecclesiam unacum alia pluribus annis tenuit et in presbyterio non promotus, fuit provisum Crenezerio de Lauff' per Innocentium vi kalendas Julii anno ix°.[400] Non reperitur in diocesi ut episcopus rescripsit; tamen exploretur.[401]

De archidiaconatu Cornubie in ecclesia Exoniensi, non taxato, de quo per obitum Thome David fuit provisum Alexandro de Nevill' per Innocentium x kalendas Septembris[402] anno nono.[403] Nichil pertinens[404] episcopus rescripsit super hoc, sed dicit quod dictus archidiaconus de eo non curat sed eum contempnit.

Summa pagine xii li.[405]

(fol. 36)[406] De prebenda Sancti Karentoci (Crantock), que est in ecclesia collegiata et non habet proprium nomen, collatio cuius facta Rogero de Stamford fuit eidem confirmata per Innocentium x kalendas Novembris anno ix^no,[407] Obligatus est in lx s. coram Domino Hugoni Pelegrini in libro obligationum folio[408] et sunt fructus sequestrati.[409]

De ecclesia Sancti Petri Exonie, collatio cuius fuit Johanni More confirmata per Innocentium iiii nonas May anno decimo.[410] Episcopus rescripsit quod vix sufficit ad sustentationem proprii sacerdotis et nil aliud pertinens.

De prebenda in eadem ecclesia cuius collatio facta Johanni de Holond' fuit confirmata per Innocentium iiii idus May anno nono.[411] Sequestrati sunt fructus.

De prebenda Sancte Columbe minoris (St. Columb

---

[385] *Mitlond'*, **b**.
[386] 18 May 1349.
[387] 17 September 1352.
[388] A blank space for the number is left in MSS.
[389] 8 May 1352.
[390] Sum om. **b**.
[390a] 26 February 1353.
[391] In the margin: *exploretur*.
[392] 13 May 1358.
[393] In the margin: *rescribatur*.
[394] Item in **b** only, fol. 105.
[395] The heading *Exoniensis* is repeated at the top of the page.
[396] 21 September 1358.
[397] 21 June 1361.

[398] 4 July 1361.
[399] *Chilton'*, **b**.
[400] 26 June 1361.
[401] In the margin: *exploretur*.
[402] Written over *Julii* deleted by a line, **a**.
[403] 23 August 1361.
[404] *Nichil pertinens* is written over *Non reperitur in diocesi ut* deleted by a line, **a**.
[405] Item in **b** only, fol. 105^v.
[406] The heading *Exoniensis* is repeated at the top of the page.
[407] 23 October 1361.
[408] A blank space for the number is left in MSS.
[409] This item is bracketed with the next two and opposite each in the margin is a letter. Against this item is *a*, against the second *c* and against the third *b*.
[410] 4 May 1362.
[411] 12 May 1361.

Minor) in ecclesia Sancti Karentoci fuit subrogatus in omni iure quod competebat David Maynardi Johannes Truseley, magister in artibus, per Innocentium nonas May anno vii,[412] pro taxa. Nullus processus fuit adhuc super hoc emanatus.

Sequentia non fuerunt tradita in arrayragiis per Dominum Hugonem Pelegrini

De archidiaconatu Tottonie (Totnes) in ecclesia Exoniensi, de quo fuit provisum Ricardo de Slunton' per Innocentium v kalendas Novembris anno v<sup>to</sup>.[413] Nondum fuit factus processus.

De prebenda Exoniensi, de qua per obitum Ade de Hilton' fuit provisum Willelmo de Bermyngham per Innocentium idus Julii anno x°.[414] Nec de isto fuit adhuc factus processus.

(fol. 36<sup>v</sup>)[415] Sequentia beneficia sunt collata per Dominum Urbanum

De ecclesia de Morchestr' Episcopi (Morchard Bishop), taxata vi li. xiii s. iiii d., in qua in omni iure quod competebat Roberto Bonuslond' fuit subrogatus Johannes de Leye xviii kalendas Februarii,[416] pro resta iii li. vi s. viii d. Habet terminum ad solvendum in festo assumptionis Beate Marie et fuit monitus sub pena excommunicationis late in scriptis xii [417] die Januarii.
Summa patet.[418]

### (fol. 37) Wigorniensis

De ecclesia de Estelegh' (Astley), taxata xi li. vi s. viii d., de qua per obitum Henrici de Stowe fuit provisum Henrico de Askeby et etiam [419] subrogatus in iure quod dictto [420] Henrico competebat, qui super hoc litigans in curia decessit tempore Domini Clementis, pro reste viii li. In rationibus Magistri Hugonis continetur quod ista provisio non habuit effectum, quia Thomas Leghe, rector dicte ecclesie exhibuit vi die Julii anno domini LIX [421] sententiam diffinitivam pro Johanne Gogle de Burkyngham contra dictum Henricum de Stowe [422] et etiam contra Henricum de Askeby per quam constitit [423] quod idem Henricus nullum ius habuit et per consequens provisio nulla.

De ecclesia Sanctorum Philipi et Jacobi Bristoll', non taxata, de qua per obitum Roberti Reve fuit provisum Nicholao de Dynghton' per Clementem, xx s. Continetur in rationibus Domini Hugonis quod est paupera quasi mendicans.

De ecclesia de Kyntwich' (Knightwick), taxata iiii li. vi s. viii d., de qua ex causa permutationis fuit provisum Johanni [424] de Charneaux per Innocentium anno primo,[425] pro resta dimissa xxxiii s. iiii d.

De hospitali Sancti Wlstani Wigornie, non taxato, de quo per resignationem Petri Francisci fuit provisum Johanni de Hareswell', canonici Sancti Martini Londonie, per Innocentium v kalendas Julii anno v,[426] fructus.

De ecclesia de Clyve Episcopi (Bishop's Cleeve), taxata xl li., acceptatio et provisio facte Ricardo de Draxton' fuerunt eidem confirmate per Innocentium vii kalendas Julii anno ix°,[427] xl li. Die xxix Novembris anno domini LXIII Magister Johannes Brian, possidens nunc istam ecclesiam super qua litigat in curia cum dicto Ricardo, promisit solvere dictas xl li. in casu quo dicta ecclesia ab eo [428] evincatur, obligavit se et bona ac beneficia presentia et futura et iuravit.
Summa pagine l li. xiii s. iiii d.[429]

### (fol. 37<sup>v</sup>) Batoniensis et Wellensis

De prebenda de Wyvelescombe (Wiveliscombe), taxata xxvi li. xiii s. iiii d., de qua per obitum Johannis de Ufford', et etiam in vita sua cum vacaret per consecrationem suam in archiepiscopum Cantuariensem, fuit provisum Willelmo Bergviney per Clementem, pro resta xiii li. vi s. viii d. Fructus sunt sequestrati per custodem spiritualitatis civitatis et diocesis Bathoniensis et Wellensis presentes et futuri.

De cancellaria ecclesie Wellensis et prebenda de Sumpton' (Compton Dundon) eidem annexa, taxata xlvi li. xiii s. iiii d., de qua per assecutionem decanatus Wellensis fuit provisum Johanni de Horsyngton' per Clementem kalendas Junii anno viii°,[430] pro resta xiiii li. xii s. Sunt fructus sequestrati ut supra.

De thesauraria Wellensi, taxata xxxiii li. vi s. viii d., que fuit Ricardo de Tormerton' confirmata per Clementem idus Novembris anno undecimo,[431] pro resta xx li. Sunt fructus sequestrati ut supra.

De vicaria Sancti Cutberti Wellensis, acceptatio fuit cuius Roberto Stax confirmata per Innocentium vi kalendas Junii anno vii,[432] pro taxa vi li. xiii s. iiii d. Sunt fructus sequestrati ut supra.[433]

De prepositura Wellensi, de qua per obitum Andree de Ufford' fuit provisum Ade de Hilton' per Inno-

---

[412] *anno vi°*, **b**, 7 May 1359.
[413] 28 October 1357.
[414] 15 July 1362.
[415] The heading *Exoniensis* is repeated at the top of the page.
[416] 15 January 1363.
[417] *xiii*, **b**.
[418] Item in **b** only, fol. 106<sup>v</sup>.
[419] Over *ecclesiam* deleted by a line, **a**.
[420] *dictus*, **b**.
[421] *LX*, **b**.
[422] This name omitted in **b**.
[423] *constat*, **b**.

[424] Followed by *de Hareswell', canonici Sancti Martini Londonie, per Innocentium v kalendas Julii anno v* deleted by a line, **a**.
[425] 1353.
[426] 27 June 1357.
[427] 25 June 1361.
[428] ab eo om. in **b**.
[429] Item in **b** only, fol. 107.
[430] 1 June 1349.
[431] 13 November 1352.
[432] 27 May 1359.
[433] Item om. **b**.

centium iii nonas Februarii anno viiº,[434] pro taxa xl li. Sunt fructus sequestrati ut supra.

De prebenda de Holcumbe (Holcombe) in ecclesia Wellensi, de qua vacante aut cum [435] vacabit per assecutionem canonicatus et prebende de [436] per Thomam de Barton, fuit provisum Waltero Moryn per Innocentium xixº kalendas Septembris anno viii,[437] xxvi li. xiii s. iiii d. Sunt fructus sequestrati ut supra.

Summa pagine cxiiii li. xiii s. iiii d.[438]

(fol. 38)[439] De prebenda et archidiaconatu Wellensibus, de quibus per obitum domini episcopi Tusculani [440] fuit provisum cardinali Carcassonensi [441] per Innocentium vii kalendas Octobris anno ixº, pro taxa [442] xvi li. xiii s. iiii d.[443]

De prebenda de Honggesteyg' (Henstridge) in ecclesia Wellensi, de qua per resignationem Simonis Thebaud fuit provisum Johanni Thebaud per Innocentium vii kalendas Octobris anno ixº, pro taxa [442] lxvi li. xiii s. iiii d. Sunt fructus sequestrati ut supra.

De prepositura Wellensi, de qua per obitum Ade de Hilton' fuit provisum Willelmo de Wikham per Innocentium nonas Januarii anno ixº,[445] pro taxa xl li. Sunt fructus sequestrati ut supra.[446]

De prebenda Bursali in ecclesie Wellensi, taxata v li. vi s. viii d., de qua per obitum Johannis Turstayn fuit provisum Johanni Corf' per Innocentium v nonas May anno xº,[447] pro resta liii s. iiii d. Habet terminum ad festum Ascencionis domini et ita iuravit.

De vicaria Sancti Cuthberti Wellensis, de qua per resignationem Philipi Honte fuit provisum Willelmo Massyngham per Innocentium iiº nonas Novembris anno v,[448] pro taxa vi li. xiii s. iiii d. Sunt fructus sequestrati ut supra.[449]

Sequentia sunt reperta que non sunt in arrayragiis traditis per Dominum Hugonem Pelegrini

De prebenda et thesauraria Wellensibus, de quibus fuit provisum domino cardinali Aquensi [450] per obitum

Ricardi de Tomerton' per Innocentium ii idus Novembris anno ixº,[451] pro taxa xxxiii li. vi s. viii d.[452]

Summa pagine lxvi li. excluso cardinali.[453]

(fol. 38ᵛ)[454] De decanatu Wellensi, qui dignitas electiva existit, vacante et reservata per obitum Johannis de Carlton' fuit provisum Thome de Paxton', sacri palatii auditori, per Innocentium kalendas Augusti anno xº,[455] pro taxa.[456] Litigatur in curia inter Dominum Stephanum Pempol, legum doctorem et dicti decanatus possessorem, et dictum Dominum Thomam, qui fuit facta provisio sub conditione que nondum extitit purificata; ideo fuit supercessum ab executione.

## De tempore Domini Urbani

De prioratu conventuali Montisacuti (Montacute), ordinis Cluniacensis, vacante per motionem Geraldi Rothonis ad priorem Lewensem fuit provisum Francisco de Barghiato iii [457] Januarii anno primo,[458] pro taxa cxxxiii li. vi s. viii d. Habet terminum ad solvendum in festis Beati Johannis Baptiste et Omnium Sanctorum proximis futuris et in festis Ascencionis domini et Sancti Michaelis extunc proximis secuturis [459] per equales portiones, videlicet in quolibet termino xxxiii li. vi s. viii d. Est obligatus et monitus sub pena excommunicationis late in scriptis.

Summa pagine patet.[460]

## (fol. 39) Herfordensis

De prebenda de Morton' (Moreton Magna) in ecclesia Herfordensi, taxata xx li., de qua per obitum Thome de Stanton' fuit provisum Simoni de Sudbur' per Clementem iiii nonas Julii anno viii,[461] pro resta xiii s. iiii d.[462]

De prebenda in eadem ecclesia Herfordensi quam obtinebat Adam electus Menevensis fuit provisum Johanni de Caney per Innocentium iii kalendas Novembris anno ixº.[463]

De portione prebendali de Ledebury (Ledbury), respondetur infra in fine arayratgiorum cum aliis benefficiis Nicholay Heth.

---

[434] 3 February 1359.
[435] Om. **b**.
[436] A blank space for the name is left in MSS.
[437] 14 August 1360.
[438] Item in **b** only, fol. 107ᵛ.
[439] The heading *Bathoniensis et Wellensis* is repeated at the top of the page.
[440] William de Court.
[441] Stephen Aubert, deacon of S. Maria in Aquiro.
[442] 25 September 1361.
[443] In the margin: *Cardinalis Carcassonensis*.
[444] 24 December 1361.
[445] 5 January 1361.
[446] In the margin: *Wykham, et dicitur quod habuit ex collatione regis*.
[447] 3 May 1362.
[448] 4 November 1357.
[449] In the margin: *iterato supra in precedenti pagina*.
[450] Peter Itherii, bishop of Dax, priest of Ss. Quattro Coronati.

[451] 12 November 1361.
[452] In the margin: *Cardinalis Aquensis*.
[453] Item in **b** only, fol. 108.
[454] The heading *Bathoniensis et Wellensis* is repeated at the top of the page.
[455] 1 August 1362.
[456] No sum is given in either MS.
[457] A blank space is left for idus, nonas or kalendas.
[458] 30 December 1362, or 3 or 11 January 1363.
[459] Om. **b**.
[460] Item in **b** only, fol. 108ᵛ.
[461] 4 July 1349.
[462] The item which follows in **a** is deleted by lines and has *solvit* against it in the margin. *De prebenda de Ethynton' (Ewithington) in eadem, de qua per obitum Edmundi de Grymmisby fuit provisum Thome Griffyn per Innocentium viii kalendas Octobris anno ii* (24 September 1354), *que taxatur ad x li., pro resta viii li.*
[463] 30 October 1361.

De prebenda de Morton (Moreton Magna), de qua per [464] promotionem Symonis Thebaud in episcopum Londoniensem fuit provisum Thome Thebaud per Innocentium iiiº idus Decembris anno ixº,[465] pro taxa xx li.

De decanatu ecclesie Herfordensis, quem obtinebat Thomas Trelek in decanum Londoniensem electus, fuit provisum Willelmo de Remyngham [466] per Innocentium viiº idus Aprilis anno xº,[467] pro taxa xxxi li. viii s. v d.[468]

De eodem [469] decanatu per resignationem dicti Thome fuit provisum dicto Willelmo de Remyngham [466] per Urbanum vii kalendas Februarii anno primo,[470] pro resta xxiiii li. xv s. i d. Habet terminum ad solvendum dictas xxiiii li. xv s. i d. medietatem in festo Pasche et aliam in festo Sancti Michaelis.

Summa pagine lxxvii li. viii s. ii d.[471]

### (fol. 39ᵛ) Norwicensis

De prioratu de Castelacr' (Castle Acre), de quo ex causa fuit provisum Willelmo de Warenn' per Clementem anno primo,[472] pro taxa iiiiᶜ iiiiˣˣ li. xix s. vii d. Est obligatus viribus camere cum aliis de conventu sub publico instrumento sigillo conventus sigillato; etiam fructus fuerunt mandati sequestrari usque ad summam iiiiˣˣ li. dumtaxat per errorem.

De ecclesia de Hulmo (Holme), taxata xl li., de qua per resignationem Willelmi de Merton' fuit provisum Thome Michel per Clementem, pro resta x li. Episcopus certificavit quod istud beneficium est litigiosum et nulli fructus fuerunt ad sequestrandum reperti.

De prioratu Sancte Fidis de Horsham, taxato c iiiiˣˣ iiii li., de quo per obitum Pontii de Serveria fuit provisum Bernardo Jori per Clementem viii kalendas Octobris anno vii vel viii,[473] pro resta cxxi li. vi s.[474] viii d.[474] Fructus sunt sequestrati.

De ecclesia de Weston', taxata xxvi li. xiii s. iiii d., de qua Johanni Derby fuit, ex causa permutationis cum Willelmo Muge, provisum per Innocentium iiii nonas Septembris anno vi,[475] pro resta xiiii li. Fructus sunt sequestrati.

De ecclesia de Estbilneye (East Bilney), taxata iiii li. vi s. viii d., que fuit Thome de Walton' confirmata per Innocentium vi kalendas Julii anno viᵗᵒ,[476] iiii li. vi s. viii d. Episcopus rescripsit se nullos fructus ad

sequestrandum reperisse et quod dictus Thomas mortuus est et dimisit executorem Willelmum Broun de Bilneye.

Summa pagine viᶜ xxx li. xii s. xi d.[477]

(fol. 40)[478] De ecclesia de Derham (East Dereham), de qua per obitum Alani de Hotbin fuit provisum Simoni Thebaud, nunc episcopo Londoniensi, per Clementem iii kalendas Aprilis anno xº,[479] pro resta xl li. xvi s. viii d. Nichil per episcopum quo ad executionem processum est, quia rescripsit quod rector iam incumbens est unus de secretariis regis et nullus est ausus secure ingredi rectoriam ad sequestrandum

De eadem fuit per promotionem dicti Symonis in episcopum Londoniensem provisum Bartholomeo Sydei iurisperito per Innocentium vii kalendas Decembris anno ixº,[480] xl li. vi s. viii d.

De ecclesia de Lacfford (Lackford), taxata xx li., de qua per dimissionem Ricardi de Walkeleyn fuit provisum Johanni de Stokeney per Innocentium iiii idus Octobris anno viiiº,[481] pro resta x li. Habet terminum ad festum Sancti Michaelis in quo termino iuravit solvere et fuit monitus sub pena excommunicationis late in scriptis.

De decanatu rurali Linie (Lynn), non taxato, de quo ex causa permutationis fuit provisum Ade Tebaud per Innocentium xviiº kalendas Septembris anno viiiº,[482] fructus. Nulli fructus sunt reperti ad sequestrandum.

De ecclesia de Wadenorton' (Wood Norton), de qua Johanni de Elford' cardinalis Petragoricensis de novo providit, pro resta xl s. Fructus sunt sequestrati.

De decanatu de Humhard' (Humbleyard), non taxato, de quo per resignationem Walteri de Bakton' fuit provisum Simoni de Sudbur' per Innocentium iiiº kalendas Julii anno vº,[483] fructus. Episcopus rescripsit quod iste Simon nunquam habuit possessionem nec aliquid percepit.

De ecclesia de Masham (Marsham), taxata xvi li. xiii s. iiii d., de qua per assecutionem cancellarie Saresburiensis factam per Johannem de Norton' fuit provisum Ricardo Amcotes per Innocentium ii nonas Januarii anno xº,[484] pro resta viii li. xiii s. iiii d. Habet terminum in festo Omnium Sanctorum in quo promisit et iuravit solvere et fuit monitus sub pena excommunicationis late in scriptis.

De precentoria Wellensi cum prebenda sibi annexa in ecclesia de Beverele (Yeovil), taxatis ut in libro taxe apparet xlv li. xiii s. iiii d., de quibus fuit provisum

---

[464] Followed by *mortem* deleted by a line, **a**.
[465] *Sebtenbris*, **b**. 11 December 1361.
[466] *Bemyngham*, **b**.
[467] 7 April 1362.
[468] In the margin, bracketed against this item and the next: *videatur si sint due annate vel eadem*.
[469] *eadem*, MSS.
[470] 26 January 1363.
[471] Item in **b** only, fol. 109.
[472] 19 May 1342 to 18 May 1343.
[473] 24 September 1348 or 1349.
[474] Om. **a**.
[475] 2 September 1358.
[476] 26 June 1358.

[477] Item in **b** only, fol. 109ᵛ. Followed in **b** by two items and two pages (fol. 110 recto and verso) from the diocese of Lincoln which are deleted by lines because they appear on following pages.
[478] The heading *Norwicensis* is repeated at the top of the page.
[479] 30 March 1352.
[480] 25 November 1361.
[481] 12 October 1360.
[482] 16 August 1360.
[483] 29 June 1357.
[484] 4 January 1362.

Edmundo Gourney, et de residuo respondetur tam in compotis Domini Hugonis quam Domini Raymundi, pro resta xx li. vi s. viii d.[485]

Summa pagine lxxxi li. vi s. viii d.[486]

(fol. 40v)[487] De ecclesia <Sancti> Georgii de Sudbur', non taxata, de qua per assecutionem cancellariatus in ecclesia Londoniensi fuit provisum Thome de Bakton' per Innocentium iiii° idus Martii anno x°,[488] fructus. Episcopus rescripsit quod dictus Thomas nunquam habuit possessionem dicte ecclesie.

De ecclesia de Chevyngton' (Chevington), que fuit Hugoni Nepol confirmata per Innocentium xi kalendas Februarii anno x°,[489] pro taxa xvi li. xiii s. iiii d. Non clare rescripsit episcopus super executione istius.

De archidiaconatu Sudburie, vacante per obitum Henrici la Souche fuit provisum Johanni de Humbletton' per Innocentium iii nonas Martii anno x°,[490] fructus. Fiat processus contra eum.[491]

De ecclesia de Polham (Pulham), de qua per obitum Willelmi de Kylleseye fuit provisum Ricardo Michel per Innocentium vi° idus Februarii anno sexto,[492] pro taxa liii li. vi s. viii d. Fiat processus.[491]

Extra arrayragia Magistri Hugonis

De decanatu rurali de Fordham, vacante per obitum Johannis Hope fuit provisum Waltero Palmer per Innocentium v nonas Maii anno x°,[493] fructus. Fiat processus.[491]

De ecclesia Sancti Georgii de Sudbur',[494] de qua ex causa permutationis cum Rogero de Burton' fuit provisum Johanni de Hegham per Innocentium v° nonas May anno x°,[495] fructus. Fiat processus.[491]

Summa pagine lxx li.[496]

(fol. 41) Norwicensis de tempore Domini Urbani

De ecclesia de Holme, de qua per obitum Domini Michel fuit provisum Roberto de Grymeston' xviii kalendas Januarii anno primo,[497] pro taxa xl li.

Item eadem die per obitum eiusdem Thome fuit provisum Johanni Bathe. Fiat processus pro una annata tantum.[498]

De ecclesia de Multon' (Moulton), de qua per obitum Edmundi de Witewell' fuit provisum Hamoni de Deval presbytero Lincolniensis diocesis ii idus Martii anno predicto.[499] Fiat processus.[491]

Summa pagine patet.[500]

(fol. 41v) Eliensis

De prioratu de Suaveseye (Swavesey), de quo fuit provisum Stephano Bertrandi per Clementem, pro resta iiii li.

De ecclesia de Ovre[501] (Over), taxata xxxv li. vi s. viii d., de qua per obitum Thome de Clipston' fuit provisum Rogero de Stanford', pro resta xii li. x s. Habet terminum ad festum Sancti Michaelis et in dicto termino iuravit solvere et fuit monitus sub pena excommunicationis late in scriptis.

Summa pagine xvi li. x s.[502]

(fol. 42) Lincolniensis

De prioratu de Cogges, qui fuit confirmatus Willelmo Hamonis per Clementem, pro resta v li. s. viii d. Fructus sunt sequestrati per episcopum.

De decanatu Lincolniensi, taxato cclxvi[503] li. xiii s. iiii d., de quo per obitum Johannis electi Cantuariensis fuit provisum Symoni de Briseleye per Clementem vi idus Octobris anno vii vel viii,[504] pro resta lix li. vi s. viii d. De executione in hac parte quo ad sequestrationem fructuum episcopus rescripsit quod fructus sunt in diocesibus Eboracensi, Conventrensi et Lichfeldensi.[505]

De ecclesia de Ketering'[506] (Kettering), que fuit confirmata Johanni Wade, pro fructibus satisfecit, sed pro fructibus male perceptis debet dare in subsidium Terre[507] Sancte[507] contra Turcos cc fl. Ostendit acquietantiam Domini Bertrandi de Cosnaco, prioris Brive quondam domini pape thesaurarii, cuius copiam habemus, sed dicitur quod est falsa, quare videatur in registris camere si satisfecit.[508]

De prebenda de Bedeford maiore (Bedford Major) in ecclesia Lincolniensi, que fuit Willelmo Wynttelesseye,[509] nunc episcopo Roffensi, confirmata per Clementem viii° idus Maii anno vii vel octavo,[510] pro taxa viii li. Fructus sunt sequestrati.

De archidiaconatu Bukynghamie in ecclesia Lincolniensi, non taxato, de quo vacante per obitum cardinalis Aynibaldi[511] fuit provisum Johanni de Ascheburn' per

---

[485] In the margin: *videatur utrum sit in ista diocesi vel in diocesi Bathoniensi et Wellensi.*

[486] Item in **b** only, fol. 111.

[487] The heading *Norwicensis* is repeated at the top of the page.

[488] 12 March 1362. (St. Gregory's church)

[489] 22 January 1362.

[490] *anno ix°*, **b**. 5 March 1361 or 1362.

[491] In the margin: *fiat processus.*

[492] 8 February 1358.

[493] *anno ix°*, **b**. 3 May 1361 or 1362.

[494] *Sotburg'*, **b**.

[495] 3 May 1362.

[496] Item in **b** only, fol 111v.

[497] 15 December 1362.

[498] In the margin bracketed against this and the preceding item: *iste due provisiones sunt infra annum ac fiat processus pro una annata tantum.*

[499] 14 March 1363.

[500] Item in **b** only, fol. 112.

[501] Over *Toure* deleted by a line, **a**.

[502] Item in **b** only, fol. 112v.

[503] *lxvi*, **b**.

[504] 10 October 1348.

[505] *Lincoliensi*, **b**.

[506] *Ketingis*, **b**.

[507] Omitted in **a**.

[508] In the margin of **a**: *videat an sit vera dicta quitatio.*

[509] Wyteleysey, **b**.

[510] 8 May 1349 or 1350.

[511] Bishop of Tusculum.

Clementem idus Novembris anno ix°,[512] fructus. Nulli fructus fuerint inventi ad sequestrandum.

De prebenda de Walton' Rivaus (Welton Rivall) in ecclesia Lincolniensi, de qua ex causa permutationis cum Johanne de Acton'[513] fuit provisum Ricardo de Davyntr' per Innocentium vii kalendas May anno v°,[514] pro taxa xxxiii li. vi s. viii d. Fructus sunt sequestrati et Dominus Willelmus de Navesby est obligatus in libro obligationum nigro[515] folio lxxiiii.

Summa pagine cvi li.[516]

(fol. 42ᵛ)[517] De prebenda de Suthscarle[518] (South Scarle) in ecclesia Lincolniensi, taxata xl li., de qua per obitum Thome de Crosse fuit provisum Johanni de Kirkeby per Clementem iiii nonas Maii anno ix,[519] pro resta xii li. ii s. xi d. Alias vocatur de Clifton' et non habet fructus suos in diocesi Lincolniensi sed in diocesi Eboracensi, ut constat per certificatorium episcopi Lincolniensis.

De medietate ecclesie de Seggebrok (Sedgebrook), taxata xii li. vi s. viii d., de qua fuit provisum Roberto de Seggesburg per Clementem xi kalendas Augusti anno x°,[520] pro resta liii s. iiii d. Nulli fructus fuerunt reperti ad sequestrandum.

De ecclesia de Greffordi (Greatford), que fuit unita monasterio Beate Marie Wintonie per Clementem iii idus Julii anno xi,[521] pro taxa xiiii li. xiii s. iiii d. Episcopus rescripsit quod non est in eius diocesi et ideo exploretur in qua diocesi est.[522]

De prebenda de Clifton' in ecclesia Lincolniensi, acceptatio cuius facta per Stephanum de Ravenseya fuit eidem confirmata per Clementem vi kalendas Augusti anno xi°,[523] pro taxa xx li. Episcopus rescripsit quod in diocesi Eboracensi habet fructus suos et redditus et non in diocesi Lincolniensi.

De prebenda de Carleton' Thurleby (Carlton le Moorland cum Thurlby), taxata xxvi li. xiii s. iiii d., de qua per consecrationem Nicholay episcopi Urgellensis (Urgel) fuit provisum Roberto de Wyngeworth per Innocentium ix° kalendas May anno primo,[524] pro resta xvi li. xiii s. iiii d. Nichil quo ad executionem processum est quia allegavit solutionem quam non ostendit.

De ecclesia de Dyngeleye (Dingley), de qua Thome

de Dyngeleye cardinalis Petragoricensis providit, pro resta liii s. iiii d. Fructus sunt sequestrati.

Summa lxviii li. xvi s. ii d.[525]

(fol. 43)[526] De vicaria de Thurlebry (Thurlby), taxata x li., de qua per cardinalem Petragoricensem fuit provisum Johanni de Hastyng', pro resta v li.

De prebenda Sancte Crucis (Spaldwick) in ecclesia Lincolniensi, taxata x li., de qua fuit provisum Johanni de Selby, pro resta ii li. x s. Debet solvere in festo Pasche.

De prebenda de Carleton' cum Thurleby in ecclesia Lincolniensi, de qua per resignationem Willelmi de Walcote fuit provisum Edwardo de Scherdestoke per Innocentium kalendas Martii anno vi°,[527] pro taxa xxvi li. xiii s. iiii d. Fructus sunt sequestrati.

De prebenda de Scarle (South Scarle) in ecclesia Lincolniensi, de qua per resignationem Willelmi de Kirkeby fuit provisum Johanni de Appilby per Innocentium iii idus Julii anno vi,[528] pro taxa xl li. Iterato est ut supra in primo precedentis pagine, et non habet fructus in diocesi Lincolniensi sed in Eboracensi.

De ecclesia de Cosyngton' (Cossington), que Johanni de Melburn' fuit confirmata per Innocentium vii kalendas Julii anno vii,[529] pro taxa vi li. xiii s. iiii d. Rescripsit episcopus quod non est in eius diocesi, quare exploretur de ea.[522]

De ecclesia de Haghton' (Houghton Regis), que fuit Hugoni Sperkyng' confirmata per Innocentium ix° kalendas Septembris anno vii,[530] pro taxa xvi li. xiii s. iiii d. Similiter non est in diocesi et ideo exploretur.[522]

De ecclesia de Eydon', taxata iiii li. xiii s. iiii d., de qua per resignationem Walteri de Heyneworth' fuit provisum Roberto de Deyeworth' per Innocentium ii idus Decembris anno viii,[531] iiii li. xiii s. iiii d.[532] Fructus sunt sequestrati.

Summa pagine xciiii li. i s.[533]

(fol. 43ᵛ)[526] De ecclesia de Hagoworthynham (Hagworthingham), taxata xii li., de qua per assecutionem ecclesie de Wentyngsted' (Wetheringsett) Norwicensis diocesis auctoritate litterarum apostolicarum fuit provisum Henrico Remelon per Innocentium iiii nonas Maii anno ix°,[534] pro resta iii li.

De prebenda de Nasyngton'[535] (Nassington) in ecclesia Lincolniensi, taxata c li., que fuit confirmata Lodowico de Carlton' fuit eidem confirmata per Inno-

---

[512] 13 November 1350.
[513] *Agthon*, **b.**
[514] 25 April 1357.
[515] Om. **b.**
[516] Item only in **b**, fol. 113.
[517] The heading *Lincolniensis* is repeated at the top of the page.
[518] *Sutharle*, **b.**
[519] 4 May 1351.
[520] 22 July 1351.
[521] *anno ix°*, **b.** 13 July 1350 or 1352.
[522] In the margin: *exploratur*, **a.**
[523] 27 July 1352.
[524] *iii kalendas*, **b.** 23 or 29 April 1353.

[525] Item in **b** only, fol. 113ᵛ.
[526] The heading *Lincolniensis* is repeated at the top of the page.
[527] 1 March 1358.
[528] *anno vii°*, **b.** 13 July 1358 or 1359.
[529] 25 June 1359.
[530] 24 August 1359.
[531] 12 December 1360.
[532] *xiii li. iiii s. iiii d.*, **b.**
[533] Item in **b** only, fol. 114.
[534] 4 May 1361.
[535] *Nashinton'*, **b.**

centium iii° kalendas Februarii anno x°,[536] pro taxa c li. Fuit dictus nuntius prohibitus per breve regium ne faceret executionem contra nunc incumbentem ad presentationem dicti ragis, sed contra dictum Lodovicum, qui est nunc episcopus Herfordensis, et dictus nuntius scripsit litteras clausas super hoc dicto episcopo, et debet rescribere, et fuerunt tradite littere Magistro Ricardo de Ravensore, clerico regis, qui eas debet facere presentari.

De capellania perpetua ecclesie parochialis de Cleti (Clee) fuit provisum Johanni de Walton' per Innocentium xi kalendas Julii anno ix°,[537] non taxata, fructus. Episcopus rescripsit quod non reperitur talis in sua diocesi, et ideo exploratur.[522]

De prebenda de Multon' ecclesia (Milton Ecclesia), taxata xl li., et de archidiaconatu Oxonie cum ecclesia de Isteleye (Iffley), taxata xiiii li. xiii s. iiii d., in in ecclesia Lincolniensi, de quibus per obitum cardinalis de Gordonio [538] fuit provisum cardinali Aquensi [539] per Innocentium quarto idus Augusti anno ix°,[540] liiii li. xiii s. iiii d.[541] Est advertendum si de archidiaconatu qui per se non taxatur sit aliquid exigendum.

De vicaria de Clee, taxata x li., de qua per obitum Johannis de Elveye fuit provisum Johanni Alayn per Innocentium iii° kalendas May anno decimo,[542] pro resta v li. Habet terminum ad festum Assentionis et est monitus sub pena excommunicationis late in scriptis.

Summa pagina exclusa provisione de cardinali cviii li.[543]

(fol. 44)[526] De ecclesia de Stangrunde (Standground), de qua ex causa permutationis cum ecclesia de Rypton' (Abbots Ripton) fuit provisum Johanni de Wynton' per Innocentium vii kalendas Ostobris anno ix°,[544] pro taxa xx li. Fructus sunt sequestrati.

Item de eadem ecclesia, de qua per cardinalem Petragoricensem fuit provisum Thome de Clipston', pro resta vi li. xiii s. iiii d. De ista non est adhuc certificatum.[545]

De ecclesia de Ripton' Abbatis (Abbots Ripton), de qua ex causa permutationis fuit provisum Thome de Clipston' per Innocentium vii kalendas Octobris anno ix°,[546] pro taxa xxiii li. vi s. viii d. Fructus sunt sequestrati.

De prebenda de Clatton' (Glatton) in ecclesia Lincolniensi, de qua per obitum Ade de Hilton' fuit provisum Johanni de Sutton', pro taxa iiii li. vi s. viii d. Fuit scriptum episcopo super ista similiter cum aliis et

fuit erratum in nomine Johannis, loco cuius fuit positus Rogerus, et fuit rescriptum quod dictus Rogerus non habebat prebendam in dicta ecclesia. Fiat ergo processus de novo.[547]

De medietate ecclesie de Sterkell' (East Keal?), de qua ex causa permutationis fuit provisum Galfredo Trenthepani per Innocentium idus Aprilis anno x°,[548] pro taxa xix li. Fructus sunt sequestrati.

De ecclesia de Coltesword' (Colsterworth), de qua fuit provisum Roberto de Hinkole per Innocentium idus Aprilis anno x°, pro taxa xxi li. vi s. viii d., pro resta x li. xiii s. iiii d. Habet terminum ad festum Beati Michaelis, quo termino Johannes de Brina, rector nunc ipsius ecclesie, iuravit solvere, et fuit monitus sub pena excommunicationis late in scriptis.

Summa pagine lxxxiiii li.[549]

(fol. 44ᵛ)[526] De capella Sancti Thome ad pontem Stamford', non taxata, in qua Johannes de Lewes fuit subrogatus Edmundi Withwell' super lite in palatio pendente per Innocentium iiii° idus May anno x°.[550] fructus. Sequestrati sunt fructus.

De ecclesia de parva Kynewell' (Little Kimble), de qua per assecutionem ecclesie de Gesyngton' (Garsington) per Stephanum de Gesyngton' fuit provisum Johanni Rocelli per Innocentium vi idus Martii anno vi,[551] pro taxa iiii li. xiii s. iiii d.[552]

De prebenda Lincolniensi, de qua per obitum Jacobi de Borelay fuit provisum G. episcopo Tusculano [553] per Innocentium xv kalendas Septembris anno vi°.[554]

De officio capelle sere in altare Sancti Petri in ecclesia Lincolniensi, non taxata, vacante per assecutionem ecclesie de Ovre (Over) factam per Thomam de Clipston', fuit provisum Willelmo de Biston per Innocentium iiii nonas Decembris anno vi°,[555] fructus.

De ecclesia de Haghton' [556] (Houghton Regis) presentatio et institutio facte Hugoni de Sparkyng' fuerunt eidem auctoritate apostolica confirmate [557] vel provisum de novo per Inocentium xviii kalendas Decembris anno viii°.[558]

Summa patet.[559]

(fol. 45) Lincolniensis; extra arrayragia Domini Hugonis Pelegrini.

De ecclesia de Kyrselawe (Creslow), de qua fuit pro-

---

[536] 30 January 1362.
[537] 21 June 1361.
[538] William Farinier of Gourdon, priest of Ss. Marcellino e Pietro.
[539] Peter Itherii, bishop of Dax, priest of Ss. Quattro Coronati.
[540] 10 August 1361.
[541] In the margin of b: *cardinalis.*
[542] 29 April 1362.
[543] Item in b only, fol. 114ᵛ
[544] 25 September 1361.
[545] *Fructus sunt sequestrati,* b.
[546] 25 September 1361.

[547] in the margin: *processus,* a.
[548] 13 April 1362.
[549] Item in b only, fol. 115.
[550] 12 May 1362.
[551] 10 March 1358.
[552] In the margin: *de sequentibus nondum est certificatum.*
[553] William de Court.
[554] 18 August 1358. In the margin: *Cardinalis Tusculanus.*
[555] 2 December 1358.
[556] *Haugton',* b.
[557] *confirmata,* MSS.
[558] 14 November 1360.
[559] Item in b only, fol. 115ᵛ.

visum Roberto de Mamcestr' [560] per Innocentium v⁰ kalendas Februarii anno vii^mo.[561]

De ecclesia Beate Marie Herfordie (Hertford), de qua ex causa permutationis cum Johanne Dich' fuit provisum Henrico Midy per Innocentium v⁰ kalendas Aprilis anno viii⁰.[562]

De vicaria perpetua Sancti Michaelis iuxta villam Sancti Albani dicte diocesis, de qua ex causa permutationis cum Henrico de Lalt fuit provisum Johanni [563] de Massyng' kalendis et anno quibus supra.

De ecclesia de Derford' (Denford), de qua ex causa permutationis cum Johanne de Higham fuit provisum Rogero de Burton' [564] kalendis et anno predictis, taxa xx li., pro resta x li. Habet terminum ad festum Omnium Sanctorum.

De prebenda de Languestowe (Stowe Longa) in ecclesia Lincolniensi, de qua fuit provisum Reginaldo de Theminis per Innocentium xi kalendas Julii anno ix⁰,[565] pro taxa xlii li. vi s. viii d.

De prebenda de Stoke (East Stoke) in ecclesia Lincolniensi, taxata iiii^xx vi li. xiii [566] s. iiii d., de qua per obitum Johannis de Northwod fuit provisum Hugoni Pelegrini per Clementem iiii⁰ nonas May anno vii⁰,[567] de qua dictus Magister Hugo non respondet in compotis suis nisi de xxxiii li. vi s. viii d., debet de resta liii li. vi s. viii d. Dicit quod fuit in anno mortalitatis et plus levari non potuit, et fuit remissus depositioni camere, et pro eo Raynerius Domenici respondit in casu quo erit determinatum per cameram.

Summa pagine cv li. xiii s. iiii d.[568]

(fol. 45^v) [526] De prebenda de Coryngham (Corringham) in ecclesia Lincolniensi, taxata ad vi^xx vi li. xiii s. iiii d., de qua fuit provisum domino Raymundo Pelegrini per Clementem iiii nonas May anno vii⁰,[567] pro resta lxxiii li. vi s. viii d. De ista facit dubium ut de precedenti et fuit ut in precedenti ordinatum.

### De tempore Domini Urbani

De prebenda in ecclesia Lincolniensi intitulata E in ecclesia collegiata Beate Marie iuxta castrum Leycestr' (Leicester, St. Mary the less in Castle) fuit ex causa permutationis provisum Henrico de Lymbergh' v nonas Martii anno primo.[569] Episcopus rescripsit quod iste Henricus nondum habuit possessionem, quare exploretur si et quando recipiet.[570]

De magistratu de Burton Sancti Lazari (Burton Lazars), collatio facta per Dominum Philipum patriarcham Jerosolomeni auctoritate ordinaria Galfrido de Chaddesdene, militi dicti hospitalis, fuit [571] eidem auctoritate apostolica confirmata,[572] et nichilominus subrogatus dictus Galfridus in omni iure quod competebat Roberto Haliday v⁰ nonas Martii dicto anno.[573] Fructus sunt sequestrati.

De prebenda ecclesie Lincolniensis vacanta [574] per obitum Willelmi Spaldewell' fuit provisum Johanni de Kyrkeby, regis Anglie clerico, xiii⁰ kalendas Maii [575] anno predicto.[576] Episcopus rescripsit quod iste Johannes non habet prebendam adhuc in dicta ecclesia, quare exploretur si et quando habebit.[570]

Summa pagine patet.[577]

### (fol. 47) [578] Conventrensis et Lichefeldensis

De archidiaconatu Conventrensi, non taxato, de quo fuit provisum Humfrido de Hastyng', fructus.

De eodem archidiaconatu et prebenda de Langdon' (Longdon) in ecclesia Lichfeldensi, taxata xx li., de quibus post obitum Humfridi de Hastyng' fuit provisum Willelmo de Sallow per Clementem iii nonas Septembris anno viii⁰,[579] pro quibus Walterus Dalby dicitur composuisse cum camera, pro resta archidiaconatus xiii li. vi s. viii d.

De prebenda Lichfeldensi, de qua per obitum Willelmi Apeltre fuit provisum Thome atte Hull' per Clementem xi kalendas Julii anno viii⁰,[580] fructus. Fructus sunt per episcopum sequestrati.

De decanatu Lichfeldensi, taxato xl li., de quo per assecutionem decanatus Lincolniensis per Simonem de Bryseleye fuit provisum Johanni de Bokyngham per Clementem nonas Novembris anno viii⁰,[581] pro resta xx li. Fructus sunt per episcopum sequestrati.

De prebenda in ecclesia collegiata Sancti Sedde Saloppie (St. Chad, Shrewsbury), de qua per obitum Willelmi Apeltr' fuit provisum Roberto de Sulgrave per Clementem iii idus Decembris anno viii⁰.[582] Dicit Dominus Hugo quod non habuit effectum, quia Dominus Hugo Opas eam tenet iure regio.

De prebenda de Keleshale (Eccleshall), de qua per resignationem Johannis de Melburn' fuit provisum Johanni de Wynwik [583] per Clementem xvii idus Feb-

---

[560] *Mayncestr'*, **b.**
[561] 28 January 1359.
[562] 28 March 1360.
[563] *Johanne*, **a.**
[564] *Burdon'*, **b.**
[565] *Junii*, **b.** 22 May or 21 June 1361.
[566] *iiii*, **b.**
[567] 4 May 1349.
[568] Item in **b** only fol. 116.
[569] 3 March 1363.
[570] In the margin: *exploretur.*

[571] *fuerunt*, MSS.
[572] *confirmate*, MSS.
[573] 3 March 1363.
[574] *vacantem*, **a.**
[575] *Martii*, **b.**
[576] 17 February or 19 April 1363.
[577] Item in **b** only, fol. 116^v.
[578] Folio 46 recto and verso is blank.
[579] 3 September 1349.
[580] 21 June 1349.
[581] 5 November 1349.
[582] 11 December 1349.
[583] *Wynwile.* **b.**

ruarii anno ix°,[584] pro taxa lxvi li. xiii s. iiii d. Fructus sunt per episcopum sequestrati.

De ecclesia de Legh' (Leigh), dimissa in arayragiis per Dominum Raymundum Pelegrini in ix li. xiii s. iiii d., de qua fuit de novo provisum Johanni de Holdon', respondetur in recepta dicti Raymundi de iiii li. xiii s. iiii d., et plus levari non potest quia est de patronatu laycali.[585]

Summa pagine c li.[586]

(fol. 47ᵛ)[587] De prebenda de Berkwik' (Berkswick) in ecclesia Lichfeldensi, taxata xx li., de qua per obitum Tidonis de Varesio fuit provisum Willelmo Caville per Innocentium vii kalendas Maii anno primo,[588] xx li. Continetur in compoto Magistri Raymundi quod numquam habuit effectum nec dictus Willelmus prosecutus est.

De prebenda de Langdon' (Longdon) in ecclesia Lichfeldensi pro resta ratione compositionis facte cum camera per Walterum de Dalby cviii fl. Habet terminos in festo nativitatis domini proximo futuro ad solvendum l fl. et in alio festo nativitatis domini lviii fl. restantes.

De ecclesia de Walton', de qua fuit provisum Magistro Johanni de Bolkynton' iii nonas Decembris anno v per Innocentium,[589] pro resta xliiii li., ad quas taxatur, xiiii li. Fructus futuri sunt sequestrati.

De ecclesia de Weston' super Trentam (Weston-upon-Trent), taxata xii li., de qua ex causa permutationis fuit provisum Nicholao de Lymbergh' per Innocentium ii idus Februarii anno vi°,[590] pro resta iiii li. Solvit episcopo ut constat per certificatorium suum.

De ecclesia de Standych' (Standish), taxata xiii li. vi s. viii d. de qua Willelmo de Standich' cardinalis Petragoricensis de novo providit, pro resta vi li. xiii s. iiii d. Nulli fructus fuerunt reperti ad sequestrandum.

De vicaria Sancti Michaelis Conventrensis, taxata c s., de qua ex causa permutationis fuit provisum Thome de Bertwell' per Innocentium vii kalendas Junii anno vi,[591] pro resta l s. Nichil penitus de ista per episcopum certificatur.

Summa pagine xlvii li. iii s. iiii d. Item cviii fl.[592]

(fol. 48)[587] De capellania Sancti Michaelis sita in castro de Cliderwe (Clitheroe), non taxata, fuit per devolutionem provisum Johanni de Burton'[593] per Innocentium iiii° kalendas Junii anno vi°,[594] fructus. Epis-

copus rescripsit quod non potest fieri per cum executio quia est in manus domini.

De ecclesia de Codyngton' (Coddington), de qua per assecutionem ecclesie de Wynton' (Burton-in-Winhale) per Johannem Charneux fuit provisum Waltero Kyngge[595] per Innocentium iiii nonas Junii anno vi,[596] pro taxa vi li. xiii s. iiii d. Episcopus rescripsit quod non sunt ibi fructus nec potest ibi fieri executio citra festum[597] Sancti Petri ad Vincula.

De vicaria ecclesie Sancti Michaelis Conventrensis, de qua per Dominum Petragoricensem cardinalem fuit provisum Willelmo Anthonii, pro taxa c s. Nichil de ista per episcopum certificatur.

De prioratu de Kyrkeby (Monks Kirby), de quo per assecutionem prioratus de Veteri Belismo (Vieux Belesme) Sagiensis (Séez) diocesis per Oliverium de Desertis fuit provisum Willelmo de Grauleriis per Innocentium xiii° kalendas Martii anno vii°.[598] pro taxa iiiiˣˣ i li. x s. viii d. Episcopus rescripsit quod non audet exequi propter metum mortis et cruciatum corporis, tamen incumbens est, ut dicitur, in curia[599] Romana et est obligatus coram Domino Hugoni Pelegrini in libro piloso folio.[600]

De ecclesia de Erklawe (Child's Ercall), que fuit Stephano Byncheton' collata per cardinalem Urgellensem et confirmata per Innocentium ix kalendas Octobris anno viii,[601] pro compositione facta per eum vi li. xiii s. iiii d. Est obligatus coram Domino Hugoni Pelegrini in libro piloso folio[600] et nichil fructus sunt per episcopum sequestrati.

Item est alia confirmatio facta eidem Stephano per dictum Dominum Innocentium vii kalendas Junii anno viiᵐᵒ.[602] Videatur si debentur due annuate vel non.

Summa pagine xcix li. xvii s. iiii d.[603]

(fol. 48ᵛ)[587] De prebenda de Termyn (Tarvin) in ecclesia Lichfeldensi, de qua per obitum Willelmi de Dryffeld' fuit provisum Nicholao de Heth' per Innocentium iii idus Augusti anno ix°,[604] pro taxa xxxiii li. vi s. viii d. Continetur in compotis Domini Hugonis Pelegrini quod dicta prebenda fuit confirmata dicto Willelmo iii[605] Augusti anno ix° et ideo dicit quod virtute istius confirmationis nichil debetur, tamen iste Nicholaus et Robertus Pres sunt obligati pro dicta summa solvenda penes dictum Dominum Hugonem in libro piloso folio[606] et termini solutionum sunt lapsi

---

[584] 16 January 1351.
[585] In the margin: nichil.
[586] Item in b only fol. 118.
[587] The heading Conventrensis et Lichfeldensis is repeated at the top of the page.
[588] 25 April 1353.
[589] 3 December 1357.
[590] 12 February 1358.
[591] 26 May 1358.
[592] Item in b only, fol. 118ᵛ.
[593] Burpton', b.
[594] 29 May 1358.

[595] Lyngge, b.
[596] 2 June 1358.
[597] festum repeated a.
[598] 17 February 1359.
[599] copia, b.
[600] No number is given in MSS.
[601] 23 September 1360.
[602] 26 May 1359.
[603] Item in b only, fol. 119.
[604] 11 August 1361.
[605] A blank space follows iii in MSS.
[606] A blank space is left in MSS

Episcopus enim certificavit quod non sunt fructus et possessor est in curia Romana.

De capella de Chederhowe (Clitheroe), non taxata, in qua fuit subrogatus David Martini Johanni de Burton', qui de eadem litigabat, ix° kalendas Januarii per Innocentium anno ix°,[607] fructus. Sed responsum est quod episcopus rescripsit se non posse facere executionem quia est in manus domini.

De prebenda in ecclesia collegiata de Penbrych' (Penkridge), de qua per obitum Thome Michel fuit provisum Thome de Eltonhed' per Innocentium vii idus Aprilis anno x°,[608] fructus. Rescripsit episcopus se non potuisse sequestrare propter breve regis, quia dominus rex pretendit se habere ius conferendi dictam prebendam.

De predicta capella Sancti Michaelis de Cliderowe (Clitheroe), in qua in omni iure quod competebat Johanni de Burton' fuit subrogatus Johannes de Pork' per Innocentium vii kalendas Februarii anno x°,[609] fructus. De ista supra est responsum.[610]

De prebenda de Wefford' (Weeford) in ecclesia Lichfeldensi, de qua in omni iure quod competebat Anthonio de Monte Peliologo fuit subrogatus Thomas Michiel per Innocentium x kalendas Junii anno v°.[611] Nondum est factus processus contra eum.[612]

Summa pagine patet.[613]

(fol. 49)[587] De cantaria ecclesie Lichfeldensis quam Thomas de Badeby[614] debuit dimittere per assecutionem canonicatus et prebende ecclesie Lincolniensis fuit provisum.[615]

### De tempore Domini Urbani

De prebenda de Sou Gnowsale (Gnosall) in ecclesia Lichfeldensi, de qua provisio et collatio facte auctoritate ordinaria Hugoni de Carle fuerunt eidem auctoritate apostolica confirmate vel provisum de novo v° nonas Martii anno primo.[616]

De prebenda in ecclesia Lichfeldensi, de qua per obitum Willemi de Dryfeld' in curia defuncti fuit provisum Alexandro de Dalby iiii nonas Januarii anno predicto.[617]

De ecclesia de Worthyn (Worthen) et aliis beneficiis de quibus fuit dispenssatum cum Ricardo de Stafford', modo quo continetur supra in recepta Domini Hugonis folio xxii, debet pro resta lviii li. xiii s. iiii d., de quibus debuit solvisse in festo Beati Johannis anno LXIII x li. et in festo Beati Michaelis tunc proximo sequenti x li.

et sic de anno in annum quousque integre fuerit satisfactum sic quod in ultimo termino solvet viii li. xiii s. iiii d., in qua compositione includitur prebenda de Wulveveye (Wolvey) in ecclesia Licheffeldensi dicto Ricardo confirmata, ut in libro recepte dicti Hugonis continetur, de qua supra summa solvit xx li., restat quod debet adhuc xxxviii li. xiii s. iiii d., secundum restam supra in prenoto datam xxxviii li. xiii s. iiii d.[618] Supra debet poni ante collata per Dominum Urbanum.

Summa pagine patet.[619]

### (fol. 49ᵛ) Assavensis

De prebenda ecclesie Assavensis, cuius taxa et provisio superius ⟨in⟩ recepta, pro resta vi s. viii d.

De ecclesia de Dynbygh' (Denbigh), de qua, vacante de iure ut asseritur, fuit provisum Willelmo Snydirlond' per Clementem idus Novembris anno ix,[620] pro taxa vi li. xiii s. iiii d. Continetur in compotis Domini Hugonis quod alius possidet iure regio et litigat[621] in curia.

De ecclesia de Landryneawe (Llandrinio), taxata vii li., que fuit confirmata Giffrino de Challeton' per Innocentium iii nonas May anno ix,[622] vii li.

De ecclesia de Denerth' (Denbigh), de qua per obitum Willelmi de Sundurlund' fuit provisum Willelmo Harden per Innocentium ix kalendas Maii anno ix°,[623] xv li. vi s. viii d.

De ecclesia de Dymbech (Denbigh), vacante per obitum dicto Willelmi fuit provisum Hugoni de Craft' per Innocentium iiii kalendas Maii anno ix°.[624]

De ecclesia de Kylkeyn (Kilken) et capella eidem annexa, de qua per obitum ultimi rectoris eiusdem fuit provisum Waltero Freystrop' per Innocentium xi° kalendas Julii anno ix°,[625] pro taxa vii li.

De ecclesia de Meyvot (Meifod), de qua per consecrationem Ludovici episcopi Herfordensis fuit provisum Willelmo de Clableton' per Innocentium iiii kalendas Octobris anno nono,[626] pro taxa xxiiii li. xiii s. iiii d. Est obligatus coram Domino Hugoni Pelegrini, ut continetur in libro obligationum folio,[627] et sunt lapsi termini.

De ecclesia de Escyvyck (Yscifiog), cuius taxa et provisio supra in recepta, pro resta liii s. iiii d.

Summa pagine lvi li. xiii s. iiii d.[628]

---

[607] 24 December 1361.
[608] 7 April 1362.
[609] 26 January 1362.
[610] In the margin: *Supra pro alia provisione.*
[611] 23 May 1357.
[612] In the margin: *fiat processus.*
[613] Item in **b** only, fol. 119ᵛ.
[614] *Badelin*, **b.**
[615] Left blank in MSS.
[616] 3 March 1363.
[617] 2 January 1363.

[618] Follows *lviii li. xiii s. iiii d.* deleted by a line, **a.**
[619] Item in **b** only, fol. 120.
[620] 13 November 1350.
[621] *litigant*, **a.**
[622] 5 May 1361.
[623] 23 April 1361.
[624] 28 April 1361.
[625] 21 June 1361.
[626] 28 September 1361.
[627] Blank space in MSS.
[628] Item in **b** only, fol. 120ᵛ.

#### (fol. 50) Menevensis

De ecclesia de Lambanglarath' (Llanfihangel ar Arth), non taxata, de qua per obitum Ricardi Aprovanses fuit provisum Ludovico Taunton' per Clementem. Continetur in compotis Domini Hugonis quod numquam habuit effectum quia mortuus est ante adeptam [629] possessionem.

De ecclesia de Weston' (Wiston), non taxata, de qua per resignationem Rogeri dicti Johanni fuit provisum Willelmo de Neuhawe per Innocentium xix kalendas Junii anno iiii°,[630] fructus.

De ecclesia Sancti Bernachii super Taff' (Llanfyrnach), de qua fuit provisum Willelmo de Newhaw per Innocentium xix kalendas Junii anno iiii°,[630] pro taxa vi li. xiii s. iiii d.

De archidiaconatu de Kermerdyn (Carmarthen) in ecclesia Menevensi cum ecclesia de Laman (Llanrhian) et prebenda eidem annexa taxatis xx li. xiii s. iiii d., collatio cuius facta auctoritate ordinaria Hawlano ab David fuit eidem confirmata per Innocentium xii kalendas Julii anno v^to,[631] xx li. xiii s. iiii d. Advertendum est si de archidiaconatu qui per se non taxatus sit aliquid exigendum.

De cantaria ecclesie de Arberwill' (Abergwili), taxata vi li. xiii s. iiii d., seu ecclesia de Lambetyn (Lampeter Pont Stephen), taxata v li., quam obtinet David de Sancto Claro fuit provisum Ceok' de Avereford' per Innocentium vi° idus Martii anno vi°,[632] vi li. xiii s. iiii d.

De ecclesia de Langdemar (Llangoedmore), taxata vi li., de qua rectori eiusdem per cardinalem Petragoricensem fuit provisum, pro resta iii li. vi s. viii d.

Summa pagine xxxvii li. vi s. viii d.[633]

(fol. 50^v)[634] De archidiaconatu de Kermerdyn in ecclesia Menevensi cum annexa taxata xx li. xiii s. iiii d., de quo ad omne ius quod competebat Hawlayno Abdavit fuit subrogatus David Martini per Innocentium vi kalendas Decembris anno viii°,[635] xx li. xiii s. iiii d.

De prebenda de Rayn (Royll) in ecclesia de Alberwill' (Abergwili), collatio cuius facta Ade de Houton' fuit eidem confirmata per Innocentium ii idus Septembris anno viii°.[636]

De prebenda Sancti David confessoris Swynness' (Swansea), collatio cuius facta David Martini fuit eidem confirmata per Innocentium iii kalendas Februarii anno ix°.[637]

De prebenda in ecclesia Menevensi, de qua per obitum Thome David fuit provisum David Wagham per Innocentium xi kalendas Julii anno ix.[638]

De prebenda de Landewibrev (Llandewi Brefi) in ecclesia Menevensi, de qua per obitum Griffini de Caunton' fuit provisum Willelmo de Eserdene per Innocentium ii nonas Decembris anno v.[639]

De prebenda seu portione in ecclesia Sancti Martini de Harberwill' (Abergwili), de qua per obitum Willelmi de Deybradle fuit provisum Waltero de Fenton' per Innocentium iiii nonas Julii anno ix°.[640]

De prebenda de Marthery (Mathry) in ecclesia Menevensi, de qua cum vacabit per consecrationem Ade electi Menevensis fuit provisum Philipo de Hauton' per Innocentium iii kalendas Novembris anno ix°.[641] Iste electus resignavit antequam haberet temporalitatem et sic dicitur quod non habuit effectum quia rex contulit alteri ratione temporalitatis in manu sua existentis.[642]

Summa pagine patet.[643]

(fol. 51)[634] De prebenda quam dictus electus obtinebat in ecclesia de Arberwill' (Abergwili) dum vacabit [644] ut supra fuit mandatum provideri Philipo Martini per Innocentium iiii kalendas Novembris anno ix.[645]

De prebenda de Landevaylok' (Llangyfelach) in ecclesia collegiata de Arberwill', que tanto tempore vacavit quod eius collatio est sedi apostolice devoluta, fuit provisum Alexandro Millok'.

Extra compota sive arraragia Domini Hugonis Pelegrini

De archidiaconatu de Kermerdyn in ecclesia Menevensi, de quo per obitum David Martini fuit provisum Willelmo Blodwyn per Innocentium nonas Augusti anno x°,[646] pro taxa xx li. xiii s. iiii d.

Summa pagine patet.[647]

#### (fol. 51^v) Eboracensis

De prebenda de Hustward' (Husthwaite) in ecclesia Eboracensi, taxata xxx li., de qua fuit [648] provisum Johanni de Ulburn' [649] de novo et fructus male percepti remissi pro quibus debet dare cc fl. in subsidium contra Thurcos per Clementem xii kalendas Julii anno x,[650] pro resta cc fl. Fiat processus contra eum.[651]

De prebenda de Etton' (Eaton) in ecclesia collegiata

---

[629] *adheptam*, **a.**
[630] 14 May 1356.
[631] 20 June 1357.
[632] 10 March 1358.
[633] Item only in **b**, fol. 121.
[634] The heading *Menevensis* is repeated at the top of the page.
[635] 26 November 1360.
[636] 12 September 1360.
[637] 30 January 1361.

[638] 21 June 1361.
[639] *Septembris*, **b.**  4 December 1357.
[640] 4 July 1361.
[641] 30 October 1361.
[642] *existenti*, MSS.
[643] Item in **b** only, fol. 121^v.
[644] *vacabunt*, MSS.
[645] 29 October 1361.
[646] 5 August 1362.
[647] Item in **b** only, fol. 122.
[648] *fuit* repeated, **a.**
[649] *Ulbrunn'*, **b.**
[650] 20 June 1351.
[651] In the margin of **b**: *Isti ii° fl. sunt computati ut soluti in ultimis computis Domini Hugonis Pelegrini inter receptas legatorum in subsidium Terre Sancte, ideo debetur cancellari.*

Suthwell', de qua per consecrationem Gilberti episcopi Karliolensis fuit provisum Ade Griffyn per Clementem x° kalendas Junii anno x°,[652] pro taxa vi li. xiii s. iiii d. Archiepiscopus Eboracensis rescripsit quod nescitur quis possidet quia lis pendet, ut dicitur, in curia Romana super ea. Fructus enim proventuri [653] sunt sequestrati.

De prebenda in ecclesie Eboracensi, de qua per consecrationem electi Terwynensis fuit provisum Federico Salamay. Archiepiscopus rescripsit quod prefatam numquam prebendam habuerunt in dicta ecclesia.

De prebenda de Stransall (Strensall) in ecclesia Eboracensi, de qua per consecrationem Michaelis episcopi Londoniensis fuit provisum cardinali Petragoricensi per Innocentium ii° idus Octobris anno ii°,[654] pro taxa liii li. vi s. viii d.[655]

De ecclesia de Hoggescoth', non taxata, de qua per cardinalem Urgellensem fuit provisum Willelmo Gibbelete, fructus. Archiepiscopus rescripsit quod non est in eius diocesi.

De vicaria de Gillyng' (Gilling), in qua Johannes Parker fuit subrogatus in omni iure quod competebat Gerlaco de Clave per Innocentium ix kalendas May anno ix,[656] pro taxa x li. Cum alia provisione facta de eadem Johanni de Reck' per Innocentium ix kalendas Septembris anno viii,[657] pro qua solvit, videtur infra annum; videatur si est infra vel extra.

Summa pagine exclusa provisione domini cardinalis xvi li. xiii s. iiii d.[658]

(fol. 52)[659] De ecclesia de Brantyngham (Brantingham), taxata lxvi li. xiii s. iiii d., de qua vacante per obitum Magistri Thome de Nevill' fuit provisum Willelmo Strode per Innocentium xvi kalendas Septembris,[660] pro resta liii li. vi s. viii d. Habet terminum ad solvendum xxiiii die Februarii xiii li. vi s. viii d., et totidem in festo Pasche proximo futuro, et residuum in festo Sancti Michaelis, pro quibus est obligatus et iuravit et fuit monitus sub pena excommunicationis late in scriptis. Pro duobus primis terminis Nicholaus Rocelli de Florentia, mercator [661] habitator Londonie, est obligatus.

De prebenda in ecclesia Sancti Johannis Beverlaci ad altare Beate Marie, de qua per obitum Ricardi [662] nati [662] Ricardi de Tormerton' fuit provisum Willelmo de Dalton' iiii nonas Julii anno ix,[663] per Innocentium,

pro taxa xvi li. Magister Willelmus Wikam possidet istam prebendam prout constat per certificatorium domini archiepiscopi; sunt enim fructus proventuri sequestrati.

De capella de Bekynfeld' (Bockingfold), non taxata, de qua per obitum Willelmi de Brayle fuit provisum Ricardo de Hormyngton' per Innocentium iiii nonas Julii anno ix.[663] Rescripsit archiepiscopus quod non est in eius diocesi, et ideo exploretur ubi est.[664]

De ecclesia Omnium Sanctorum Eboraci, de qua per obitum Simonis Warde fuit provisum David Mort' sive Martini per Innocentium iiii nonas Julii anno ix°,[663] pro taxa v li. vi s. viii d. Allegavit Robertus Hug' litis pendentis super antecedente ecclesia in curia Romana, et quia ipsam non poterat probare, deposuit dictam pecuniam penes Raynerum Dominici, factorem Albertorum Antiquorum in civitate Londonie. Et habet terminum ad faciendum fidem de lite pendente et eo cautione ad debite cavendum ad medium mensis Aprilis; alias qua pecunia predicta cedat camere insolutum.

Summa pagine lxxiiii li. xiii s. iiii d.[665]

(fol. 52ᵛ)[659] De prebenda de Monkton' in ecclesia collegiata Riponensi, in qua in omni iure quod competebat Thome de Clypston' fuit subrogatus Willelmus Roude per Innocentium vi idus Julii anno ix°,[666] pro taxa ad novam taxam xiii li. vi s. viii d. Fuit sibi datus terminus ad solvendum in festo purificationis Beate Marie in unum annum, pro quibus se obligavit et iuravit et fuit monitus sub pena excommunicationis late in scriptis.

De prebenda de Woystowe (Wistow) in ecclesia Eboracensi et archidiaconatu eiusdem ecclesie, non taxato, de quibus per obitum cardinalis Penestrini (Palestrina)[667] fuit provisum cardinali Carcasonensi (Carcassonne),[668] pro taxa prebende c li.[669]

De prebenda de Dryffeld (Driffeld) in dicta ecclesia, de qua per obitum Willelmi [670] de Sancto Martiali fuit provisum cardinali de Sancto Martiali,[671] pro taxa c

De prebenda de Bolum (Bole) in eadem, de qua per obitum Thome de Nevill' fuit provisum cardinali Cluniacensi,[673] pro [670] taxa [670] xvi li.[674]

De prebenda in ecclesia collegiata Sancti [670] Johannis Beverlaci, de qua per obitum Ricardi de Tormerton' fuit provisum Petro le Sage per Innocentium xi kalendas

---

[652] 23 May 1351.
[653] Omitted in **b**.
[654] 14 October 1354. Year omitted in **b**.
[655] In the margin: *Cardinalis Petragoricensis*.
[656] 23 April 1361.
[657] 24 August 1360.
[658] Item in **b** only, fol. 122ᵛ.
[659] The heading *Eboracensis* is repeated at the top of the page.
[660] 17 August 1361: *Cal. Pap. Regs. Petitions*, i. 321.
[661] *marcator*, **a**.
[662] Om. **b**.

[663] 4 July 1361.
[664] In the margin: *Exploretur*, **a**.
[665] Item in **b** only, fol. 123.
[666] 10 July 1361.
[667] Peter des Prés.
[668] Stephen Aubert, deacon of S. Maria in Aquiro.
[669] In the margin: *Cardinalis Carcasonensis*.
[670] Om. **b**.
[671] Hugo de Sancto Martiali, deacon of S. Maria in Portico. li.[672]
[672] In the margin: *Cardinalis Sancti Martialis*.
[673] Androin de la Roche, priest of S. Marcello.
[674] In the margin: *Cardinalis Cluniacensis*.

Julii anno ix°.[675] Non reperitur in diocesi Eboracensi, ut constat per literas archiepiscopi.

De prebenda de Hoveden' (Howden) in ecclesia Eboracensi, de qua per obitum Johannis de Metha fuit provisum Ricardo Drax per Innocentium vii idus Junii anno v°,[676] pro [677] taxa [677] xxxiii li. vi s. viii d. Fuit mandatum archiepiscopo fructus sequestrari et rescripsit quod dictus Ricardus numquam dictam prebendam obtinuit, quare fuit supercessum.

De prebenda de Northhill' (Norwell) in ecclesia Suthwellensi, in qua in omni iure competebat Johanni de Denton' fuit subrogatus [678] Thomas de [679] per Innocentium vi kalendas Augusti anno v,[680] pro taxa xxxvi li. xiii s. iiii d.[681] Sciatur cum Domino Raymundo Pelegrini cognomen subrogati, et fiat de novo processus quia in primis processibus nesciebatur cognomen subrogati.[682]

Summa pagine lxxxiii li. vi s. viii d.[683]

(fol. 53)[659] De capella sive cantaria de Wentebrigg' (Wentbridge), de qua per obitum Thome atte More fuit provisum Roberto de Wik' per Innocentium xi kalendas Decembris anno vii°.[684] Fructus sunt sequestrati, proventuri tamen, quia alii reperti non fuerunt.

De archidiaconatu de Eastriddyng' in ecclesia Eboracensi cum ecclesia de Mapelton' (Mappleton), non taxata, sibi annexa, vacantibus eo quod Willelmus Walcote qui ipsum obtinebat aliam ecclesiam extitit assecutus, fuit provisum Waltero de Scirlaw per Innocentium ii kalendas Decembris anno vii,[685] composuit medio iuramento,[686] salvo iure pluris, ad [687] pro ecclesia xvi li. xiii s. iiii d. De archidiaconatu vero dicit quod nullos habet redditus nisi procurationes et correctiones de quibus non debetur annata determinet camera. Promisit et iuravit solvere medietatem in mense Februarii anno LXIII et residuum in festo Omnium [688] Sanctorum.

De custodia seu sacristia capelle Beate Marie et Sanctorum Angelorum Eboraci, provisio et collatio facte auctoritate ordinaria Johanni de Waltham fuerunt eidem auctoritate apostolica confirmate vel provisum de novo per Innocentium ix kalendas Januarii anno ix°,[689] pro taxa iiiixx viii li. viii s. viii d.

Extra arreragia Domini Hugonis

---

De capellania perpetua Beati Petri de Wolvey, de qua ex causa permutationis cum Henrico Nudy fuit provisum Johanni Dich' per Innocentium v kalendas Aprilis anno octavo.[690] Non est in diocesi prout archiepiscopus rescripsit.

De vicaria de Estyng' (Eastrington) presentatio et inductio facte auctoritate ordinaria de Thoma de Sissill' fuerunt eidem auctoritate apostolica confirmate vel provisum de novo per Innocentium iii° kalendas Aprilis anno viii.[691] Fructus sunt sequestrati presentes et futuri.

Summa pagine cv li. ii s.[692]

(fol. 53ᵛ) Eboracensis de tempore Domini Urbani

De portione ecclesie de Hotton' Bussell' (Hutton Bushel), vacante per obitum Nicholai de Witheby [693] fuit provisum Johanni Pol de Clifford' xvi kalendas Februarii anno primo,[694] pro taxa ad novam taxam iiii li.

De eadem portione que fuit eodem anno xiii kalendas Maii [695] confirmata Alano de Hake clerico.[696] Non debetur nisi una annata, et sunt fructus sequestrati, ut constat per certificatorium archiepiscopi.

De vicaria ecclesie de Kildewik' (Kildwick), collatio et provisio auctoritate ordinaria ex causa permutationis facte Rogero de Slateburn', non obstante quod tempore huius collationis esset excommunicatus, fuerunt eidem auctoritate apostolica confirmate vel de novo provisum v nonas Martii,[697] pro taxa xii li. Fructus presentes usque ad valorem v m. et proventuri usque ad integram summam sunt sequestrati.

De canonicatu et prebenda ecclesie Beverlacensis Eboracensis diocesis, vacantibus per obitum Andree Offord' alias le Moyne fuit provisum Ricardo de Drax, legum doctori, iiii° ydus Novembris.[698] Ista fuit noviter extracta de corectione regestri camere et hic posita.[699]

Restam archidiaconatus Richmundie require infra in fine cum aliis benefficiis.

Summa pagine xvi li.[700]

(fol. 54) Dunelmensis

Omnes fructus et redditus beneficiorum infrascriptorum presentes et futuri huius diocesis, illorum tamen qui in diocesi reperti sunt, fuerunt sequestrati, ut constat per litteras episcopi certificatorias.

De hospitali de Gretham, non taxato, de quo per obitum Johannis de Stoketon' fuit provisum Thome Johannis de Bridkirk' per Clementem ii idus Octobris

---

[675] 21 June 1361.
[676] 7 June 1357.
[677] Om. **b**.
[678] *obligatus*, **b**.
[679] Blank space in MSS. The lacking name is Mount of Wytham.
[680] 27 July 1357.
[681] In the margin: *non est in regestro camere.*
[682] In the margin: *fiat processus.*
[683] Item only in **b**, fol. 123ᵛ.
[684] 21 November 1359.
[685] 30 November 1359; date om. **b**.
[686] Followed by *ad*, **a**; clause om. **b**.
[687] Blank space in MSS. It should read: *pro ecclesia ad.*
[688] *Omnium* repeated and deleted by dots, **a**.
[689] 24 December 1361.

[690] 28 March 1360.
[691] 30 March 1360.
[692] Item in **b** only, fol. 124.
[693] *Withely*, **b**.
[694] 17 January 1363.
[695] 19 April 1363.
[696] Om. **b**.
[697] 3 March 1363.
[698] 10 November 1362.
[699] Followed in **a** by the item: *De canonicatu et prebenda ecclesie collegiate de Northon!* which is deleted by lines.
[700] Item in **b** only, fol. 124ᵛ.

anno ix,[701] debetur medietas extra iii li. vi s. viii d. quibus Dominus Hugo computat in receptis, fructus extra iii li. vi s. viii d. Fructus presentes et futuri sunt sequestrati.

De prebenda in ecclesia collegiata Langecestr' (Lanchester), de qua ex causa permutationis cum Henrico de Exton' fuit provisum Galfrido de Cornesio per Innocentium xv° kalendas Decembris anno primo,[702] fructus.

De prebenda de Lymley (Lamesley) ecclesie collegiate Cestrie super Stratam (Chester-le-Street), de qua per electionem electi Norwicensis fuit provisum Willelmo de Lughteburgh' per Innocentium vi idus Februarii anno secundo,[703] pro taxa xx li.

De prebenda in eadem ecclesia vocata Lamseley (Lamesley), taxata xx li., de qua per obitum Willelmi de Rothwell' fuit provisum Guidoni de Pestello per Innocentium iii nonas Decembris anno v[to],[704] pro resta x li.

De vicaria de Witingham (Whittingham), de qua per obitum Willelmi Arbalbi fuit provisum Johanni de Wodeford' per Innocentium xv kalendas Augusti anno v,[705] x li.

De decanatu ecclesie collegiate Cestrie super Stratam (Chester-le-Street), permutatio facta auctoritate ordinaria cum Johanne de Sulthorp' pro archidiaconatu Cestrie per Adam de Houton' fuit eidem confirmata per Innocentium kalendas Junii anno vi°,[706] qui [706a] decanatus taxatur ad xxxiii li. vi s. viii d.

De vicaria de Newton' in Glendale (Kirknewton), de qua per obitum Roberti de Jarmy fuit provisum Roberto Hepp' per Innocentium nonas Septembris anno vii,[707] pro taxa xx li.

Summa pagine xciii li. vi s. viii d.[708]

(fol. 54[v])[709] De prioratu dicto sella Sancte Rege (St. Bees), collatio facta auctoritate ordinaria Willelmo de Swynesburi fuit eidem confirmata per Innocentium ix kalendas Septembris anno viii°.[710] Episcopus rescripsit quod iste prioratus non est in eius diocesi. Est tamen in diocesi Eboracensi in archidiaconatu Richmundie et fiat processus.[711]

De ecclesia de Rowtheburi (Rothbury), in qua et ad omne ius quod competebat Willelmo de Emeldon' fuit Johannes Appilby subrogatus per Innocentium xvi kalendas Februarii anno ix°,[712] pro taxa ad novam

taxam lxvi li. xiii s. iiii d. De ista pendet adhuc lis in curia et est obligatus Domino Hugoni Pelegrini si evincatur.

De prebenda in ecclesia de Norton', de qua per obitum Thome Drax fuit provisum Bernardo de Lynar' Avinionie per Innocentium vii kalendas Maii anno ix°,[713] Episcopus rescripsit quod non reperitur talis in dicta ecclesia.[714]

De prebenda ecclesie collegiate de Hauklond' (Auckland), de qua per obitum Thome de Bridekyrk' fuit provisum Waltero de Wikam per Innocentium ii idus Augusti anno ix°.[715]

De ecclesia de Stanhop' (Stanhope), de qua per obitum Thome de Bridekyrk' fuit provisum Willelmo de Norwico per Innocentium viii kalendas Septembris anno ix,[716] pro taxa xl s.

De eadem ecclesia, collatio facta auctoritate ordinaria Ricardo de Wylyngton' per obitum prefati Thome fuit eidem confirmata per Innocentium iiii° kalendas Januarii anno ix°,[717] pro taxa xl s. Ista provisio cum precendenti sunt infra annum.

Item de eadem ecclesia, collatio predicta dicto Ricardo facta fuit confirmata per dictum Dominum Innocentium iiii idus Maii anno x°.[718] Magister Willelmus Strode, rector ecclesie de Brantyngham (Brantingham) Eboracensis diocesis est obligatus pro solvendo xl s. quum dictus Ricardus, qui pro dicta ecclesia in curia Romana litigat cum Domino Johanne Blane, obtinebit pacificam possessionem.

Summa pagine lxx li. xiii s. iiii d.[719]

(fol. 55)[709] De prebenda ecclesie collegiate de Hauklond (Auckland), de qua per obitum dicti Thome fuit provisum Roberto de Stratton' per Innocentium xvi kalendas Septembris anno.[720] Episcopus rescripsit quod in sua diocesi non reperitur talis.

De capella libera de Jesmouth' (Jesmond), collatio facta auctoritate ordinaria Thome de Ponth' fuit eidem confirmata per Innocentium ix° idus Januarii anno ix°.[721]

De eadem, vacante per obitum Henrici Beuffamut, fuit provisum Matheo de Bolton' per Innocentium xiii kalendas Februarii anno x°.[722]

De prebenda ecclesie collegiate de Norton', de qua per consecrationem Domini Johannis episcopi Wigorniensis [723] fuit provisum Willelmo Ilkerd' per Innocen-

---

[701] 14 October 1350.
[702] 17 November 1353.
[703] 8 February 1354.
[704] 3 December 1357.
[705] 18 July 1357.
[706] 1 June 1358.
[706a] que, a.
[707] 5 September 1359.
[708] Item in b only, fol. 125.
[709] The heading *Dunelmensis* is repeated at the top of the page.
[710] 24 August 1360.
[711] In the margin: *fiat processus*.
[712] 17 January 1361.

[713] 25 April 1361.
[714] Over *diocesi* deleted by a line, a. In the margin: *non est in regestro camere*.
[715] 12 August 1361.
[716] 25 August 1361.
[717] 29 December 1361.
[718] 12 May 1362.
[719] Item b only, fol. 125[v].
[720] 17 August 1361: *Cal. Pap. Regs. Petitions*, i, 321.
[721] 24 December 1361: above, p. 157.
[722] 20 January 1362.
[723] Om. b.

tium iii idus Martii anno xº,[724] que taxatur vi li., pro resta iii li.

Extra compota Domini Hugonis.

De hospitali pauperum Sancti Egidii de Kypitr' (Kepier), de quo per obitum Petri de Thoersby fuit provisum Johanni de Appilby per Innocentium viiiº kalendas Maii anno viiiº.[725] Nondum est factus processus.[726]

De tempore Domini Urbani

De ecclesia de Routhebury (Rothbury), presentatio, institutio et inductio facte auctoritate ordinaria Johanni Marescalli fuerunt eidem auctoritate apostolica confirmate vel de novo provisum v nonas Martii anno primo,[727] pro taxa lvi li. xiii s. iiii d.

De canonicatu et prebenda ecclesie collegiate de Northon' (Norton) Dunelmensis diocesis, vacantibus per obitum Thome de Drax' fuit provisum Bernardo de Lutane clerico per Clementem anno viiiº vii kalendas Maii.[728] Supra debet poni ante provisiones Domini Urbani. Ista est noviter extracta de corectione regestri camere et hic posita.

Summa pagine lix li. xiii s. iiii d.[729]

### (fol. 55ᵛ) Karliolensis

De ecclesia de Crostwayt (Crosthwaite), in qua in omni iure competenti Johanni de Selario fuit subrogatus Johannes Henrici per Innocentium ii idus Januarii anno v,[730] pro taxa xxx li. xiii s. iiii d. Continetur in compotis Domini Hugonis quod non habuit effectum nec iste Johannes est prosecutus nec possessionem adeptus;[731] fructus tamen sunt sequestrati, ut constat per certificatorium episcopi.

De vicaria de Brampton', de qua ex causa permutationis cum vicario de Schaldeford' (Shalford) Wyntoniensis diocesis fuit provisum Johanni Amyll' per Innocentium xi kalendas Septembris anno v,[732] pro taxa viii li., viii li. Fructus presentes et futuri sunt sequestrati, ut constat per certificatorium episcopi.

De ecclesia de Musgrave,[733] vacante per obitum Johannis de Stocton' fuit provisum Roberto Kenet per Innocentium ii kalendas Martii anno v,[734] pro taxa xiii li. vi s. viii d. Dicit Ricardus Upton', nunc rector dicte ecclesie, quod dicta provisio non habuit effectum, et super hoc produxit unum testem super hoc clare deponentem, et fuit scriptum episcopo ut certificet huic ad festum Sancti Michaelis, et dictus Ricardus obligavit

se ad solvendum in casu quo reperietur ipsum teneri dicta die seu in quindena, et fuit supercessum ab executione usque ad illam diem.

De vicaria ecclesie de Crostwait (Crosthwaite), provisio facta Willelmo de Esyngdon' fuit eidem confirmata per Innocentium iiº kalendas Julii anno viiiᵛᵒ,[735] xx li. Fructus presentes et futuri sunt sequestrati, ut constat per certificatorium episcopi.

De ecclesia de Kyrkelond (Kirkland), de qua, ex eo quod Johannes de Kerkebi unacum ecclesia de Wyllesey (Ousby) per menssem et amplius detinuit, fuit provisum Johanni de Kerkebi per Innocentium viii kalendas Novembris anno viiº,[736] taxata xl li., xl li.

Summa pagine cxii li. iiii d.[737]

(fol. 56) Beneficia collata per dominos cardinales in Anglia que tamen ponuntur supra in arrayragiis suis locis appetentibus

#### Saresburiensis

De prioratu seu officio nuncupato de Noyone et de Novo Mercato (Neufmarché), de quo fuit provisum Nicholao Bomin per cardinalem Petragoricensem, debentur fructus.

#### Wigorniensis

De ecclesia de Honyngton' (Honington), de qua Luce filio Willelmi fuit per cardinalem Urgellensem provisum.

#### Norwicensis

De ecclesia Omnium Sanctorum de Katellerston' (Kettlestone), taxata xiii li. vi s. viii d., de qua Johanni de Arderndon' cardinalis Urgellensis de novo providit, pro taxa xiii li. vi s. viii d.

De ecclesia Sancte Marie de Westwyngg' (West Winch?), de qua Paulo de atte Wod de Middelton' cardinalis Urgellensis de novo providit, fructus.

Summa pagine patet.[738]

### (fol. 56ᵛ) Lincolniensis

De prebenda de Boneburi (Banbury) in ecclesia Lincolniensi, taxata xxx li., de qua Magistro Johanni de Streteleye cardinalis Petragoricensis de novo providit, xxx li.

De ecclesia de Ascheby parva (Little Ashby), taxata iiii li. xiii s. iiii d., de qua Willelmo Edele de Skynton' cardinalis Petragoricensis de novo providit, iiii li. xiii s. iiii d.

De ecclesia de Longhous [739] (Laughton) fuit provisum per dominum Petragoricensem Waltero Bernark'.

De ecclesia Sancti Clementis de Wilouby (Willoughby) fuit provisum per dominum Petragoricensem Hugoni de Kusase, taxata xxiii li. vi s. viii d., xxiii li. vi s. viii d.

---

[724] 12 March 1362.
[725] 24 April 1360.
[726] In the margin of a: *fiat processus.*
[727] 3 March 1363.
[728] 25 April 1350.
[729] Item in b only, fol. 126.
[730] 12 January 1357.
[731] *adheptus,* a.
[732] 22 August 1357.
[733] *Mansgrave,* b.
[734] 28 February 1357.

[735] 30 June 1360.
[736] 25 October 1359.
[737] Item in b only, fol. 126ᵛ.
[738] Item in b only, fol. 127.
[739] *Longhouis,* b.

### Exoniensis

De cantaria perpetua Sancte Anne sita in ecclesia Omnium Sanctorum Exonie fuit provisum per dominum Urgellensem Alexandro Sporeman, non taxata de qua Summa pagine lviii li.[740]

### (fol. 57) Lichfeldensis

De ecclesia de Aldesley [741] (Alderley) fuit provisum per cardinalem Petragoricensem Johanni Raston', taxata viii li., viii li.

De ecclesia de Burnehull' (Burnhill) fuit provisum per dominum Petragoricensem Hugoni de Pamberton', non taxata, medietas fructus.

De vicaria ecclesie de Dorset magna (Great Dassett) fuit provisum per dominum Petragoricensem Willelmo de Wy de Westeburi, non taxata, medietas.

### Bangorensis

De ecclesia de Dlanbrugian (Llangian) fuit provisum per dominum Petragoricensem David nato Johannis.

### Menevensis

De ecclesia de Kemarthmaure (Cenarth) fuit provisum per dominum Petragoricensem Roberto le Despenser, non taxata, medietas.

Summa pagine patet.[742]

### (fol. 57ᵛ) Eboracensis

De ecclesia de Foston' fuit per dominum Petragoricensem provisum Johanni Norffeld'.

De ecclesia de Holisgarth' fuit provisum per dominum Urgellensem cardinalem Willelmo Sibthorp' iiii kalendas Octobris anno domini LXVII.[743]

De ecclesia de Colwesby (Cowesby) fuit provisum per dominum Urgellensem Ricardo de Helperby.[744]

### (fol. 58) Hibernia; Dublinensis diocesis

De decanatu ecclesie Dublinensis, taxato xli li., de quo fuit provisum Matheo de Briseleye per Clementem antequam Dominus Hugo Pelegrini esset collector, pro resta xiiii li. xiii [745] s. iiii d.

De thesauraria ecclesie Dublinensis et prebenda de Balimo (Ballymore), collatio facta Johanni de Grace fuit eidem confirmata per Clementem viii idus Maii anno octavo,[746] pro taxa xx li.

De decanatu ecclesie Dublinensis, taxato xli li. de quo per obitum Mathei de Briseley fuit provisum Johanni Brian, pro resta xx li.

De cancellaria ecclesie Dublinensis, taxata xl li., collatio facta Johanni de Troy [747] fuit eidem confirmata per Innocentium iiii kalendas Junii anno iiº,[748] pro resta xxvi li. xiii s. iiii d.

De prebenda ecclesie Dublinensis, de qua per consecrationem Domini Johannis electi Dublinensis fuit provisum Willelmo Roberti per Clementem nono kalendas Januarii anno viii,[749] debentur fructus.

De prebenda ecclesie Dublinensis, de qua per consecrationem episcopi Lincolniensis fuit provisum Ricardo Drax per Innocentium xvi kalendas Maii anno iiº,[750] fructus.

Summa pagine lxxxi li. xi s. viii d.[751]

(fol. 58ᵛ) De prebenda ecclesie Dublinensis, taxata xxiii li. vi s. viii d., de qua per obitum Willelmi de Kelseye fuit provisum Johanni de Luddeleye per Innocentium xiii kalendas Maii anno vi,[752] pro taxa xxiii li. vi s. viii d.

### Corkagensis

De decanatu ecclesie Kargagensis, de quo per provisionem factam [753] Geraldo de Buri ad episcopatum Kargagensem fuit provisum Georgio de Rupe, canonico Cargagensi, per Innocentium iiº nonas Februarii anno viiiº.[754]

### Cassalensis

De archidiaconatu ecclesie Cassalensis, collatio auctoritate ordinaria facta Johanni Carada fuit eidem confirmata per Innocentium vii idus Junii anno vii.[755]

### Colnensis

De archidiaconatu Colnensi, collatio facta per episcopum Rogero de Braybrok' fuit sibi confirmata per Innocentium idus Augusti anno vii.[756]

### Waterffordensis

De decanatu ecclesie Waterfordensi, electio facta de Waltero Reve ad dictum decanatum fuit eidem confirmata per Innocentium iiii kalendas Junii anno ix.[757]

Summa pagine patet.[758]

### (fol. 59) Dublinensis

De thesauraria ecclesie Dublinensis, taxata xx li. ad antiquam taxam, de qua per resignationem Johannis Lymberd', procuratoris Johannis [759] Gate, dicte ecclesie

---

[740] Item in **b** only, fol. 127ᵛ.

[741] *Adesbey*, **b**.

[742] Item in **b** only, fol. 128.

[743] 28 September 1367.

[744] In the margin bracketed against the last three items: *non sunt in registro per cameram tradito.*

[745] *xviii*, **b**.

[746] 8 May 1350.

[747] *Trop*, **b**.

[748] 29 May 1354.

[749] 24 December 1349.

[750] 16 April 1354.

[751] Item in **b** only, fol. 129.

[752] 19 April 1358.

[753] *facta*, MSS.

[754] 4 February 1360.

[755] 7 June 1359.

[756] 13 August 1359.

[757] 29 May 1361.

[758] Item in **b** only, fol. 129ᵛ.

[759] Followed by *atte* deleted by a line.

thesaurarii, fuit provisum Hugoni de Thesdale Eboracensis diocesis per Innocentium ii idus Februarii anno vii,[760] pro resta xiii li.

### Duacensis

De decanatu ecclesie Duacensis (Kilmacduagh), de quo per munus consecrationis impensum N. episcopo Duacensi fuit provisum Johanni Megillekeaby, qui se obtulit paratum ⟨resignare⟩ thesaurariam eiusdem ecclesie dum et cetera, per Innocentium ii nonas Aprilis anno vii.[761]

### Dublinensis

De prebenda de Houth' (Howth) in ecclesia Dublinensi, taxata xxiii li. vi s. viii d., collatio facta auctoritate apostolica Waltero Moryn fuit eidem confirmata per Innocentium ii idus Octobris anno viii.[762]

De prebenda de Houth in ecclesia Dublinensi, taxata xxiii li. vi s. viii d., de qua per consecrationem Stephani Lawell' episcopi Lymiricensis fuit provisum Willelmo de Kelesey per Innocentium vii idus Aprilis anno ii,[763] debet pro resta x li.

Summa pagine patet xxiii li.[764]

### (fol. 59ᵛ) Fernensis diocesis

De prebenda de Taghomon (Taghmon) in ecclesia Fernensi, de qua per obitum Johannis de Sutton' fuit provisum Johanni Gote [765] Calteryn per Clementem iii idus Julii anno xi.[766]

De prebenda de Taghomon in ecclesia Fernensi, de qua per obitum Johannis de Sutton' et parochiali ecclesia de Colstoufr' (Coolstuffe) dicte ⟨diocesis⟩ per obitum Thome Michel fuit ⟨provisum⟩ Domino J. de Estruord', in episcopatum Fernensem electum, ne habeat in opprobrium episcopi mendicare, per Clementem xvii [767] kalendas Augusti anno xi.[768]

De ecclesia de Veteri Rose (Old Ross), de qua ex causa permutationis cum Nicholao Distart fuit provisum Johanni de Welwek' per Innocentium xvi kalendas Augusti anno iiᵒ.[769]

De prebenda de Taghomon in ecclesia Fernensi, de qua per obitum J. Sutton' fuit provisum Johanni Galtryn per Innocentium vi idus Martii anno viᵗᵒ.[770]

De prebenda de Taghomon in ecclesia Fernensi, in qua et ad omne ius quod competebat Johanni Castri fuit subrogatus Walterus de Dodendale per Innocentium iiii idus Septembris anno octavo.[771]

### (fol 60) Osoriensis diocesis

De prebenda de Wilmodewak' (Kilmacdonagh) in ecclesia Osoriensi, de qua per consecrationem Thome archiepiscopi Tuamensis fuit provisum Ricardo Radulphi per Clementem ii idus Augusti anno xi.[772]

De decanatu ecclesie Osoriensis, electio facta de Thoma de Wynton' fuit eidem confirmata per Innocentium vii kalendas Februarii anno iiᵒ,[773] fructus.

De canonicatu et prebenda ecclesie Ossoriensis, cum vacabunt per consecrationem Thome electi Dublinensis fuit provisum Nicholao de Chedelington' per Dominum Urbanum v kalendas Aprilis.[774]

De portione de Castro Canok (Castle Knock) in ecclesia Dublinensi, collatio et provisio facte auctoritate ordinaria per obitum Johannis Dene quondam Ade de Lyngeston' quam per xxiiiiᵒʳ annos vel circiter possedit et adhuc possidet fuerunt eidem auctoritate appostolica confirmate vel provisum de novo, non obstante quod tempore collationis huius ordinarius esset excommunicatus, per Urbanum v nonas Martii anno primo.[775]

### Limiricensis

De prebenda ecclesie Lymiricensis, de qua per obitum Thome de Corkbay fuit provisum Johanni Cate per Innocentium xi kalendas Januarii anno ii.[776]

De prebenda de Disertis (Disert) in ecclesia predicta, de qua per provisionem factam Stephano de Walle de archidiaconatu dicte ecclesie fuit provisum David Baucoutr' vi idus Martii anno viᵗᵒ.[777]

De decanatu [778] ecclesie Lymiricensis predicte, de quo per obitum Thome de Borkele fuit provisum Stephano de Valle per Innocentium ii idus Decembris anno v.[779]

De thesauraria ecclesie Limiricensis, de qua per obitum Ade Hunt' fuit provisum Gilberto Godheyn per Innocentium vi idus Martii anno vi.[780]

(fol. 60ᵛ) De precentoria ecclesie Limiricensis, de qua ex eo quod Adam Craddok' ipsam cum ecclesia de Noutton' (Newtown) per tres annos detinuit fuit provisum Johanni [781] Braybrok' per Innocentium v idus Martii anno vi.[782]

De decanatu [783] Limiricensi, de quo per munus consecrationis impensum Domino Stephano electe Limericensis fuit provisum Henrico Albo sive Wrth', canonico dicte ecclesie, per Innocentium xviii kalendas Junii anno viiiᵒ.[784]

De decanatu ecclesie Limericensis, vacante per obitum

---

[760] 12 February 1359.
[761] 4 April 1359.
[762] 14 October 1360.
[763] 7 April 1354.
[764] Item in **b** only, fol. 130.
[765] *Gorte*, **b**.
[766] 13 July 1352.
[767] *vii*, **b**.
[768] 16 July 1352.
[769] 17 July 1354.
[770] 10 March 1358.
[771] 10 September 1356.

[772] 12 August 1352.
[773] 26 January 1354.
[774] 28 March 1363.
[775] 3 March 1363.
[776] 22 December 1354.
[777] 10 March 1358; above, p. 159.
[778] *canonicatu*, **b**.
[779] 12 December 1357.
[780] 10 March 1358.
[781] *Philipo*, above, p. 159.
[782] 11 March 1358.
[783] *canonicatu*, **b**.
[784] 15 May 1360.

Henrici With' fuit provisum Ade With' per Innocentium iii idus Augusti anno ix°.[785]

De cancellaria ecclesie Limiricensis, de qua per consecrationem Domini Stephani Lowele episcopi Limiricensis fuit provisum Bartholomeo Dullard per Innocentium xiii kalendas Januarii anno ix°.[786]

## Dunensis [787] diocesis

De prioratu ecclesie Dunensis (Down), cum vacabit per consecrationem Ricardi electi Dunensis, fuit mandatum provideri Nicholao Langton' per Innocentium v idus Decembris anno primo,[788] fructus.

## Lismonensis [789] (Lismore) diocesis

De ecclesia de Dunggrian (Dungarvan), de qua ex causa permutationis cum decanatu rurali de Lynne (Lynn) Norwicensis diocesis cum Adam Thebaud fuit provisum Henrico de Wyntryngton' per Innocentium viii° kalendas Novembris anno viii°.[790]

De prebenda Lismoricensis, de qua per obitum Johannis de Balstok' fuit provisum Thome Lovestok' per Innocentium anno quinto,[791] debentur fructus.

(fol. 61) Sequentia beneficia iiii°ʳ debent poni superius in arrayragiis et sunt diverse benefficia pro quibus ea obtinentes nunc sunt obligati [792] promiscue pro eisdem

De archidiaconatu Richmundie in ecclesia Eboracensi, prebenda de Midelton' (Middleton) in ecclesia Cicestrensi et de Dymynstr' [793] (Yetminster) in ecclesia Saresburiensi, de quibus fuit provisum Henrico de Walton', pro resta lxx li. Est obligatus coram Domino Hugone Pelegrini ad solvendum et habet terminos.

De subdecanatu Eboracensi, et prebenda de Grantham in ecclesia Saresburiensi, de Rithemall' (Rathmichael) in ecclesia Dublinensi, de Clipston' (Clifton) in ecclesia Lincolniensi, de Cheswik, (Chiswick) in ecclesia Londoniensi, de Rompton' (Rampton) in ecclesia collegiata Suthwell' Eboracensis diocesis fuit provisum seu confirmatio facta Willelmo de Radfford' per Innocentium vii kalendas Decembris anno viii°,[794] pro resta xxxix li. Quas debet solvere in festo nativitatis Beati Johannis Baptiste proximo futuro xix [795] li. x s. et residuum in festo nativitatis domini proximo sequturo.

Summa pagine cx li.[796]

(fol. 61ᵛ) De ecclesia de Hodeneth' (Hodnet) Lich-

feldensis diocesis, et prebenda de Farendon' (Faringdon) in ecclesia Saresburiensi, de Mora (Moorfields, St. Giles, Cripplegate) in ecclesia Londoniensi, de Hundreton' (Hunderton) in ecclesia Herfordensi et de Ledeburi (Ledbury) in diocesi Herfordensi, de quibus fuit provisum Nicholao Heth et composuit cum camera in curia pro primis fructibus dictorum beneficiorum pro viii° 1 fl. ponderis camere, debet de resta vᶜ 1 fl. Est obligatus coram Domino Hugoni Pelegrini et termini solutionum iam transacti.

De cancellaria Saresburiensi et prebenda de Huve (Hove) in ecclesia Cicestrensi, de quibus fuit provisum Johanni de Norton' per consecrationem Simonis episcopi Londoniensis per Innocentium vii kalendas Decembris anno ix,[797] pro resta xxxiiii li.[798] Habet terminum a festo Beati Johannis Baptiste proximo futuro in unum annum quo curret annus LXV.

Summa pagine xxxvi li. Item v° 1 fl.[799]

Summa universalis omnium arrayratgiorum premissorum de restis et annatis benefficiorum, exclusis benefficiis dominorum cardinalium, iiiiᵐ cxlv li. Item [800] viᶜ lvii fl.

Summa restarum debitarum per dominos cardinales vᶜ lviii li.

Summa restarum denariorum Beati Petri iiᶜ xl li. viii s. viii d.

Summa restarum annui censsus vi li. ix s. vi d.

Summa universsalis omnium precedentium [801] restarum iiiiᵐ ixᶜ xlviii li. xviii s. ii d. sterlingorum. Item viᶜ lviii fl. Approbatum.

(fol. 62) Exploretur pro iure camere de infrascriptis concessionibus [802] et mandatis utinam effectum habuerunt necne et si aliquid dicte camere debeatur.[803]

## Roffensis

Mandatum fuit quod episcopi Wyntoniensis et Eliensis possynt unire unum vel plura beneficia ad patronatum regis Anglie spectantia mense priorisse et conventus monasterii sororum de ordine predicatorum et in dictis beneficiis vicarios instituere per Innocentium iii idus Maii anno.[804]

Item eisdem quod possint unire dictis monialibus unum, duo aut plura beneficia quorum redditus c li. secundum decimam non excedant per.[804]

## Wigorniensis

Concessum fuit episcopo Wigorniensi ut vi beneficia ecclesiastica curata, dum vacabunt, in sua diocesi, etiam

---

[785] 11 August 1361.
[786] 20 December 1361.
[787] In the margin: *Dymenensis*, **a.**
[788] 9 December 1353.
[789] *Lismoricensis*, **b.**
[790] 25 October 1360.
[791] 1357.
[792] Followed by *simul* deleted by a line, **a.**
[793] *Dymgnstr'*, **b.**
[794] 25 November 1360.
[795] *xxix*, **b.**
[796] Item in **b** only, fol. 132.

[797] 25 November 1361.
[798] Follows *lxxii li.* deleted by a line, **a**; *xxxvi li.*, **b.**
[799] This and the following sums are found only in **b**, fol. 132ᵛ.
[800] Followed by *mclviii fl.* deleted by a line.
[801] *precendentium*, MS.
[802] *cessionibus*, **b.**
[803] *debeatis*, **b.**
[804] Left blank in MSS.

si ad collationem apostolicam spectarent, posset conferre per.[804]

### Eliensis

Una ex parochialibus ecclesiis de Hadenham (Haddenham) et de Leveryngton' (Leverington), cum vacabunt, quam episcopus Eliensis elegerit, fuerit unita [805] mense sue per.[804]

### Londoniensis

Fuit data potestas episcopo Londoniensi ut parochialem ecclesiam de Oremell' (Orwell) Eliensis diocesis unire valeat auctoritate apostolica monasterio de Sempringham.

Fuit data potestas Thome episcopo Eliensi ut parochialem ecclesiam de Hynton' (Cherry Hinton) uniat domui collegii scolarium Sancti Petri universitatis Cantebrigie per.[804]

### (fol. 62ᵛ) Lincolniensis

Unio facta de ecclesia de Turkliston' (Thurcaston), de Belgrave, Bifeld' (Byfield) Lincolniensis diocesis monasterio Sancti Ebrulffy (St. Evroul) Exoniensis diocesis fuit per papam confirmata, videlicet illam quam magister elegerit.

Fuit concessum abbati et conventui monasterii de Seuhos (Newhouse) Primostratensis ordinis Lincolniensis diocesis ut [806] ipsi [806] in vicariis ecclesiarum quas ad proprios usus [807] obtinent et obtinebunt possint per ordinarium loci canonicos expresse professos in vicariis facere collocari usque ad vi.

Ecclesie de Hombreston' (Humberstone) et de Hungeston (Hungarton) fuerunt unite monasterio Beate Marie Leycestrie, et de ecclesia de Hungeston' est satisfactum, et de alia est inquirendum si habet adhuc effectum.

Exploretur de parochiali ecclesia de Warisleye (Waresley) Lincolniensis diocesis ad presentationem custodis et scolarium aule de Valence Marie universitatis Cantebrigie Eliensis diocesis unita et appropriata auctoritate apostolica per episcopum Londoniensem predictis [808] custodi et scolaribus.

Item de ecclesiis de Saxthorp' (Saxthorpe), de Tilney, de Wareslee (Waresley) parochialibus Norwicensis et Lincolniensis diocesium appropriatis predictis custodi et scolaribus.

(fol. 64)[809] Benefficia infrascripta data fuerunt michi Johanni de Cabrespino per Dominum Raymundum Pelegrini nomine Domini Hugonis Pelegrini, olim in Anglia camere appostolice collectoris, in computis suis ultimis redditis in [810] Londonia anno domini Mᵒ CCCᵒ LXIIIᵒ et prima die menssis Septembris in arrayratgiis, que non habuerunt effectum rationibus contentis in quolibet ipsorum breviter et non ad plenum, que quidem benefficia idem Johannes tradit et assignat camere inter inutiles provisiones quia de eis nichil penitus habuit, levavit vel recepit.

### Cantuariensis

De ecclesia de Ikham (Ickham), taxata xxx li., de qua fuit provisum per resignationem Roberti de Bouton' Rogero de Wye per Innocentium ii kalendas Decembris anno iiiiᵒ,[811] non habuit effectum quia iste Rogerius non habuit possessionem, sed Magister Willelmus de Hertelbury auctoritate ordinaria, qui dyu litigavit cum dicto Rogero et optinuit diffinitivam sententiam in palatio appostolico contra ipsum Rogerum, de qua sententia fecit fidem Domino Raymundo sub data xxiiii die Maii.

De ecclesia de Chartham, taxata xxvi [812] li. xiii s. iiii d., que fuit confirmata Waltero de Burton' per Innocentium vi kalendas Iunii anno viᵒ,[813] non habuit effectum quia constat per litteras clausas domini archiepiscopi Cantuariensis quod anno domini M CCC LIIIIᵒ viiiᵒ kalendas Januarii [814] de dicta ecclesia fuit provisum Magistro Willelmo de Brandelee, familiari dicti domini archiepiscopi, et ex tunc idem Magister Willelmus permanssit rector continue usque ad mortem suam, qui in curia Romana decessit, et per eius mortem fuit provisum Ricardo de Bugbred', et de ista respondetur.

### Roffensis

De ecclesia de Eynefforde (Eynsford), taxata xx li., de qua per resignationem Viviani de Blakefford fuit provisum Johanni de Croso per Clementem xviii kalendas Februarii anno xᵒ,[815] non habuit effectum quia iste Vivianus fuit privatus per sententiam dyu ante istam resignationem, et provisum alteri, et ita idem Dominus Raymundus mihi respondit, ut continetur in libro per ipsum mihi dato.

Concessum fuit regi Anglie ut episcopi Wynthoniensis et Eliensis possint unire unum vel plura benefficia ad patronatum dicti regis spectantia mensse et priorisse conventus monasterii sororum de ordine predicatorum et in dictis benefficiis vicarios instituere per Innocentium iii ydus Maii anno primo.[816]

Item eisdem quod possint unire dictis sororibus unum, duo aut plura benefficia quorum redditus c li. secundum decimam non excedant; de istis duobus est inquirendum an sit aliquid deductum ad effectum.

---

[805] *fuerint unite*, MSS.
[806] Om. **b.**
[807] *predicta*, MSS.
[808] *predictum*, MSS.
[809] Folio 63 contains items of arrears of census deleted by lines and with the marginal note: *cancellantur quia supra ponuntur plenius*. On folio 63ᵛ Peter's pence is treated in the same manner with the same explanation.

[810] Over two words erased with a heavy line, **a.**
[811] 30 November 1356.
[812] *xvi*, **b.**
[813] 27 May 1358.
[814] 25 December.
[815] 15 January 1352.
[816] 13 May 1353.

## (fol. 64ᵛ) Londoniensis

De prebenda de Kentiston' (Kentish Town) in ecclesia Londoniensi, taxata vi li. xiii s. iiii d., de qua per obitum Ade Merymouth' fuit provisum Rogero Holm per Clementem VIº antequam dictus Hugo esset nuntius, que fuit dimissa in xxxiii s. iiii d., nichil quia dictus Rogerus pro ista summa et diverssis aliis benefficiis camere in curia se obligavit, et dicit Dominus Raymundus Pelegrini quod ipse fuit presens, set pro resta debet adhuc x li., nisi per aquitantiam vel libros camere aliud compareat, quia mihi ostendit quitantiam Domini Reginaldi, tunc thesaurarii domini nostri pape, de xxx m. cum dimidia sterlingorum solutis camere in cxxxv fl. xiii s. iiii d. monete Avinionie sub data xiiii die Februarii anno LV, pontificatus domini nostri anno tertio, et asserit se residuum solvisse.

De ecclesia de Brayle (Rayleigh), non taxata, dimissa in arrayragiis, de qua per obitum Johannis de Horthon' fuit provisum Ricardo Broun' per Innocentium xi kalendas Februarii anno iiiiº,[817] non habuit effectum quia certificatum est per officialem quod iste Ricardus nunquam fuit possessionem assequtus, quia rex contulit cuidam Nicholao de Horton' ratione temporalitatis prioratus de Pretwell' (Prittlewell) existentis in manu sua tempore guerre, quia dicta ecclesia est de patronatu prioris de Pretwell' predicti.

## Cicestrensis

De prebenda [818] de Walton' in ecclesia collegiata de Bosham, cuius taxa et provisio continentur [819] supra in recepta, ix li. vi s. viii d., non habuit effectum quia probatum fuit per testes, videlicet per Dominum Johannem de Northon, Robertum de Muskham, Ricardum de Hoyton' quod ista prebenda est capella libera regis Anglie ad eius omnimodam dispositionem pertinens, de qua per dominum nostrum papam nichil conssuevit recipi vel levari, et sic nichil habui sed nichilominus dedi ecclesiam in arrayragiis.

De precentoria Cicestrensi, taxata liii li. vi s. viii d., de qua per obitum cardinalis de Mota [820] fuit provisum cardinali de Gordonio [821] per Innocentium viii kalendas Novembris anno iiiiº,[822] nichil quia dicitur fuisse satisfactum in curia, et vide litteras domini camerarii sub data ultima die Januarii anno LXIIº.[823]

De prebenda et precentoria ecclesie Cicestrensis, taxatis ut supra proximo, de quibus per obitum cardinalis de Gordonio fuit provisum cardinali Aquensi [824]

per Innocentium vi kalendas Octobris anno ixº,[825] nichil quia fuit scriptum per dominos camerarium et thesaurarium quod supersedeatur per [826] litteras eorum sub data ultima die Januarii anno LXIIº, et ideo nichil factum fuit.[827]

## Wynthoniensis

De vicaria ecclesie de Schalfford' (Shalford), taxata x li. xiii s. iiii d., de qua ex causa permutationis cum vicaria de Bampton' fuit provisum Roberto de Hepp per Innocentium xi kalendas Decembris anno vº,[828] non habuit effectum quia iste Robertus nunquam habuit possessionem, ut fui certificatus per dominum episcopum Wynthoniensem, ut in suo certificatorio continetur, et per iiiiᵒʳ alios testes fidedignos, rectores et cappellanos eiusdem dyocesis.

## (fol. 65) Saresburiensis

De prebenda de Norwynton' (North Newnton) in ecclesia monialium de Wylton' (Wilton), taxata xiii li. vi s. viii d., que fuit confirmata Johanni de Vyenna [829] xiii kalendas Iunii per Clementem anno viiiº,[830] et dimissa in resta in viii li., ratione collationis facte Willelmo de Melburn' per obitum dicti Johannis est etiam dimissa in solidis fructibus, sed non debuit esse quia dicta confirmatio et provisio fuerunt infra annum, et de dictis viiiº li. vi s. et viii d. responssum fuit in recepta dicti Hugonis.

De ecclesia de Scorcumbe (Corscombe), taxata xi li., que fuit confirmata Johanni Brokelond' viiiº ydus Iunii per Clementem anno ixº,[831] non habuit effectum quia dictus Johannes nunquam habuit possessionem dicte ecclesie, ut constat per litteras episcopi Saresburiensis, sed quidam alius in eisdem litteris nominatus, et ego retinui dictas litteras.

De prebenda de Norowynton' (North Newnton), taxata xiii li. vi s. viii d., de qua per obitum Johannis de Vienna fuit confirmata Willelmo Ricardi de Wyllyngton', et ante de eadem fuit provisum Guillelmo de Melburn' per Clementem nonas Maii anno ixº; [832] iste Johannes evicit istam prebendam a dicto Guillelmo Ricardi, et ista collatio et confirmatio cum quadam alia supra posita in principio istius pagine sunt infra annum, et ideo non debentur fructus nisi pro una annata, de qua responssum est ut supra in principio pagine.

De archidiaconatu Dorcestris in ecclesia Saresburiensi, taxata lxiii li., de quo per obitum cardinalis Albiensis (Albi)[833] fuit provisum cardinali Autissi-

---

[817] 22 January 1356.
[818] *ecclesia*, b.
[819] *continetur*, MSS.
[820] Gaillard de Mota, deacon of St. Lucy in Silice.
[821] William Farinier of Gourdon, priest of Ss. Marcellino e Pietro.
[822] 25 October 1356.
[823] In the margin: *cardinalis*.
[824] Peter Itherii of Périgueux, bishop of Dax, priest of Ss. Quattro Coronati.

[825] 26 September 1361.
[826] Om. b.
[827] In the margin: *cardinalis* and *attende*.
[828] 21 November 1357.
[829] *vicania*, b.
[830] 20 May 1349.
[831] 6 June 1350.
[832] 7 May 1351.
[833] Bernard d'Albi, bishop of Porto.

diorensi (Auxerre)[834] per Innocentium iii° ydus Februarii anno iii°;[835] scriptum est per dominos camerarium et thesaurarium quod non fiat exequtio.

De cancellaria Saresburiensi, taxata iiii[xx] viii li., de qua per consecrationem Simonis episcopi Londoniensis fuit provisum Johanni de Northon' per Innocentium xvii kalendas Decembris anno ix°;[836] de ista cancellaria et prebenda respondetur inter alia beneffica in fine arayratgiorum[837] et hic ponitur dumtaxat ad memoriam, quia non ponitur in ordine arayratgiorum istius diocesis.

### Norwicensis

De medietate ecclesie de West Walton', taxata xii li., cuius collatio facta per ordinarium Jacobo de Heraygtoft' fuit eidem confirmata per Innocentium secundo nonas Septembris anno ix°,[838] non habuit effectum quia fuit amotus per sententiam,[839] ut patet in cedula in libro meo annexa.

### Lincoliensis

De prebenda de Northon' (Bishop Norton), taxata xxxiii li. vi s. viii d., et archidiaconatu Lincoliensi non taxato, de quibus per obitum Thome de Northword fuit provisum Hugoni Abbati per Innocentium vii ydus Maii anno primo,[840] et xii kalendas Martii proxime sequentes[841] per resignationem eiusdem Hugonis fuit provisum cardinali Magalonensi,[842] et scriptum per cameram quod ibidem erat compositum et pro hic nichil exigeretur, super quo vide litteras dominorum camerarii et thesaurarii sub data iiii[a] die menssis Decembris anno LV° predictam continentes.

(fol. 65[v]) De prebenda de Empyngham (Empingham), taxata xxxvi li. xiii s. iiii d., de qua per obitum Willelmi de Dune fuit provisum Guillelmo de Funeyby per Innocentium xi kalendas Iunii anno ix°,[843] non habuit effectum quia iste Willelmus de Funeyby ante adeptam possessionem decessit, ut patet per litteras regias et regestrum camere, per cuius mortem fuit provisum Johanni de Ludham per Innocentium iii ydus Decembris anno ix°,[844] qui Johannes de Ludham fuit privatus per sententiam regis Anglie, ratione temporalitatis in manu sua existentis, et provisus de ea Ricardo de Ravesere, clerico regis, qui eam possidet, et fui prohibitus per regem ne de hac provisione me intromitterem, quas sententiam et prohibitionem retinui.

De ecclesia de Melcheburn' (Melchbourne), taxata v li. vi s. viii d., de qua per obitum Bartholomei de Draython' fuit provisum Radulffo de Ulnhale per Innocentium vi kalendas Februarii anno secundo;[845] fuit allegatum quod dicta provisio nullum habuit effectum et habuit terminum usque ad festum purificationis Beate Marie ad faciendum de hoc fidem, alias quod solvat summam prelibatam, et sunt obligati Dominus Rogerus Grene, rector dicte ecclesie, Magister Willelmus de Burgho diocesis Lincolniensis, Symon Patyn eiusdem diocesis et Vigellus de Hauckynton' de Londonia; certificavit episcopus Lincoliensis infra predictum terminum quod dicta provisio non habuit effectum, ut in certificatorio dicti episcopi continetur.

### Conventrensis et Licheffeldensis

De ecclesia de Hodynet (Hodnet), de qua per consecrationem Domini Radulphi episcopi Bathoniensis fuit provisum Nicholao Heth'; pro ista provisione et aliis Nicholaus predictus composuit cum camera et de illa respondetur in fine arayratgiorum et ideo in ista diocesi non debuit poni.

De archidiaconatu Stafford' in ecclesia Licheffeldensi, qui fuit confirmatus Ricardo Byrymigham per Clementem secundo ydus Decembris anno viii°;[846] de isto fuit eadem die alteri provisum, de qua provisio respondetur in recepta dicti Hugonis.

### Eboracensis

De prebenda de Watewang' (Wetwang) in ecclesia Eboracensi, taxata iiii[xx] et x li., de qua per obitum Georgii de Salitis fuit provisum Domino Anibaldo cardinali[847] per Clementem, et dimissa in arayragiis per Dominum Raymundum Pelegrini in lvii li. et xi s., non habuit effectum quia Anibaldus nunquam habuit possessionem nec fuit prosequtus quia rex contulit Ricardo de Wynwyk, qui adhuc possidet dictam prebendam, et ideo nichil levari potest.

De prebenda de Massham (Masham) in ecclesia Eboracensi, taxata secundum novam taxam iiii[xx] li., de qua fuit provisum per obitum Magistri Johannis de Wfford' Reginaldo de Brian per Clementem antequam dictus Hugo esset nuntius, et per consecrationem dicti Reginaldi in episcopum Menevensem fuit de eadem prebenda provisum Audree de Wfforde xviii° kalendas Julii anno (fol. 66) septimo vel viii°,[848] quia simul missi; fuit scriptum per cameram quod facta fuit plena informatio quod iste due provisiones fuerunt infra annum et quod non exigerentur fructus nisi unius annate, de quibus superius in recepta ante computum in rationibus predicti Hugonis est responssum, et ideo non debet dimitti in arayragiis.

---

[834] Peter de Croso, priest of Ss. Silvestro e Martino ai Monti.
[835] 11 February 1355.
[836] 15 November 1361.
[837] The remainder of the sentence, except *istius diocesis* om. **b**.
[838] 4 September 1361.
[839] It could also be extended *simoniam*.
[840] 9 May 1353.
[841] 18 February 1354.
[842] Audoin Aubert, bishop of Maguelone, priest of Ss. Giovanni e Paolo.
[843] 22 May 1361.
[844] 11 December 1361.

[845] 27 January 1354.
[846] 12 December 1349.
[847] Bishop of Tusculum.
[848] 14 June 1348 or 1349.

De prebenda de Scharowe (Sharow) in ecclesia collegiata Ripponensi, taxata v li. ad novam taxam, de qua per resignationem Richardi de Torresby fuit provisum ex causa permutationis Bertrando de Cardalhaco per Innocentium xiii kalendas Novembris anno iiiiº,[849] non habuit effectum hoc quia antequam haberet possessionem fuit promotus in episcopum Montis Albani (Montauban), per cuius promotionem fuit provisum alteri, de qua respondetur in recepta mea.

De ecclesia de Colksby (Cowesby), taxata v li., de qua per dominum Urgellensem fuit provisum Rithero de Helperby,[850] non habuit effectum ut constat per litteras Eboracensis archiepiscopi.

De ecclesia de Langedon', taxata x li. ad novam taxam, que ex causa permutationis facte cum Ricardo de Wyntryngham fuit confirmata Gerlhaco de Clave per Innocentium ix kalendas Septembris anno viii;[851] ista provisio non habuit effectum quia alteri fuit provisum de eadem infra annum, et pro illa responssum est in recepta mea.

De prebenda de Massham (Masham) in ecclesia Eboracensi, taxata lxxx li. ad novam taxam, de qua per obitum Andree Offorde fuit provisum cardinali Magalonensi (Maguelone)[852] per Innocentium xiiii kalendas Decembris anno viº;[853] et super ista provisione vide litteras dominorum camerarii et thesaurarii sub data ii die Novembris quod composuerat in curia ad solvendum ibi.

De ecclesia de Agthon' (Aughton), de qua iure devoluto fuit provisum Hugoni de Bloten' per Innocentium kalendas Februarii anno ixº;[854] ista provisio non habuit effectum, nec iste Hugo de Boltena unquam habuit possessionem dicte ecclesie, sed est unita priori et conventui monasterii de Elerton'[855] (Ellerton) dicte Eboracensis diocesis, ut constat per litteras domini archiepiscopi Eboracensis in modum instrumenti publici confectas sub anno domini MCCCLIIII et die xix Octobris, sigillatas dicti archiepiscopi sigillo, et signis Henrici de Bagworth', Michaelis Hamule, Rogeri [856] de Clone, notariorum appostolicorum, signatas.

## Dymelniensis

De prioratu de Tynemuta (Tynemouth), de quo per asequtionem abbatie Sancti Albani per Thomam priorem dicti prioratus, de quo fuit sibi data potestas providendi per Clementem anno viiiº;[857] non habuit effectum quia non est prioratus perpetuus sed custodia temporalis ad voluntatem abbatis.

## Dublinensis

De prebenda ecclesie Dublinensis, de qua per obitum Walteri Moryn fuit provisum Ade Robelyn per Innocentium kalendas Januarii anno ixº;[858] non habuit effectum quia de eadem prebenda ex eadem causa fuit provisum Thome Gryk.

(fol. 70)[859] Compotus brevis[860] redditus camere apostolice per Dominum Johannem de Caprespino, canonicum Narbonensem (Narbonne), in Anglia camere apostolice collectorem, de receptis, levatis et assignatis et expensis per eum a die prima mensis Augusti[861] anni LXIII usque ad diem xii mensis Aprilis[862] anni LXIIII[ti].

Et primo computat se recepisse de arayratgiis sibi dimissis per Dominum Raymundum Pelegrini nomine Domini Hugonis fratris sui de denariis Beati Petri ii<sup>c</sup> xliiii li. sterlingorum.

Item computat se recepisse de tempore suo de denariis Beati Petri xxii li. x s.

Item computat se recepisse de censu annuo de tempore suo iii li. vi s. vii d.

Item computat se recepisse de arrayragiis sibi dimissis per dictos Dominos Raymundum et Hugonem ratione beneficiorum debitorum m iii<sup>c</sup> xx li. vii s. ii d. ob., 1 fl. fortes.

Item computat se recepisse de tempore suo pro annalibus beneficiorum collatorum tempore Domini Urbani xxxi li. xiii s. iiii d.

Item computat se recepisse de quibusdam extraordinariis sive diversis cxlii li. xv s. vii d.

Summa totalis omnium et singulorum receptorum per Dominum Johannem predictum tam de arrayratgiis Dominorum Raymundi et Hugonis Pelegrini quam aliis per ipsum receptis rationibus, et ex causis suprascriptis est m vii<sup>c</sup> lxiiii li. viii s. viii d. ob.,[863] 1 fl. fortes.[863] Item plus cl fl. de croseta quos habuit a camera anno LXIII de mense Julii.[864]

(fol. 70ᵛ) De quibus computat se assignasse anno LXIII diversis diebus et personis nomine camere apostolice m vii<sup>c</sup> iiii<sup>or</sup> li. i s. viii d. sterlingorum.

Item computat ipsum fuisse in itinere tam eundo quam redeundo lxiiii<sup>or</sup> dies cum sex equitaturis;[865] fuit ordinatum quod valeat cxx fl. solutos[866] in xviii li.

Item computat se expendisse in diversis expensis in libro rationum suarum contentis particulariter, videlicet pro processibus faciendis et nuntiis mittendis xii li. xviii s. vi d. ob.

---

[849] 20 October 1356.
[850] *Chelporby,* **b.**
[851] 24 August 1360.
[852] Audoin Aubert, priest of Ss. Giovanni e Paolo.
[853] 18 November 1358.
[854] 1 February 1361.
[855] *Erlaton',* **b.**
[856] Rogero, MSS
[857] 19 May 1349 to 18 May 1350

[858] 1 January 1361
[859] Folios 66ᵛ to 69ᵛ inclusive are blank
[860] In **b** the *compotus brevis* is placed between the expenses and the assignments. See above, p. 184, note 192.
[861] *Septembris,* **b.**
[862] *diem ultimam mensis Martii,* **b.**
[863] Lacking, **a.**
[864] Item lacking, **a.**
[865] The remainder of the item is lacking in **a.**
[866] Reading doubtful.

Item computat ultra predictam clericum suum expendisse tam in pergamenis quam papiru et cera xxiiii s. iiii d.[867]

Summa expensarum predictarum xxxii li. ii s. x d. ob. Valent ccxiiii fl.

Summa vero omnium assignatorum et expensarum tempore predicto est m vii<sup>c</sup> xxxvi li. iiii s. vi d. ob. Approbatum.

Facta vero deductione de receptis et levatis per dictum collectorem in dicto tempore, que sunt in summa m vii<sup>c</sup> lxiiii li. viii s. viii d. ob., l fl. fortes, cl fl. crosete, ad assignationes et expensas, que sunt in summa m vii<sup>c</sup> xxxvi li. iiii s. vi d. ob., aparet dictum collectorem debere camere, omnibus compensatis et deductis, xxviii li. iiii s. ii d.; valent clxxxiiii fl. cum dimidio camere i floreno pro iii s. in pretio computato. Item l fl. fortes. Item cl fl. de croseta.

(fol. 71)[868] Sequuntur episcopatus Anglie de quibus recepit dictus Dominus Johannes de censibus et denariis Beati Petri et annatis.

Et primo episcopatus Cantuariensis, Roffensis, Londoniensis, Cicestrensis, Wynthoniensis, Saresburiensis, Exoniensis, Bathoniensis et Wellensis [869] uniti, Herfordensis, Norwicensis, Eliensis, Lincoliensis, Convetrensis et Licheffeldensis uniti, Eboracensis, Dunelmensis, Karleolensis.

De istis nichil recepit quia non venerunt, sed sunt excommunicati per processus, videlicet

Vigorniensis, Bangorensis, Assavensis, Menevensis.

(fol. 71<sup>v</sup>) Sequuntur episcopatus Hibernie in quibus non fuit ausus ire, nec habuit tempus, videlicet

Hibernia, Fernensis, Clonensis, Limiricensis, Dunensis, Lilmonensis (Lismore?).[870]

Item datum in restis denariorum Beati Petri debitas per diverssas perssonas ii<sup>c</sup> xl li. viii s. viii d. sterlingorum.

Item annui censsus vi li. ix s. vi d.

Item pro beneficiis collatis dominis cardinalibus v<sup>c</sup> lvii li.

Item de restis et annatis beneficiorum collatorum aliis iiii<sup>m</sup> cxlv li. Item vi<sup>c</sup> lviii fl.

Item sunt quedam beneficia non taxata de quibus non potest poni certa summa prout in libro particulariter aparet.

Et sic est summa universalis omnium premissarum restarum iiii<sup>m</sup> ix<sup>c</sup> xlviii li. xviii s. viii d. vel circa. Item vi<sup>c</sup> lviii fl. Approbatur.

(fol. 74)[871] Compotus sive rationes Johannis de Cabrespino,[872] collectoris in regno Anglie [873] a [874] die [874] ⟨pri⟩ma Septembris anni LXIII usque ad diem penultimam Februarii [874] anni ⟨L⟩XIIII et a dicta die penultima Februarii anni [875] usque ad diem mensis Maii anni LXVI, et [876] patet [877] in libro et est [876] copie rationum per ipsum in cameram [878] redditurum.

Prime et secunde rationes [878]

(fol. 75)[879] Rationes prime Johannis de Cabrespino collectoris Anglie [880]

## SECOND ACCOUNT OF JOHN DE CABRESPINO 1364-1366

(fol. 138)[1] Rationes reddite camere appostolice per Johannem de Cabrespino, doctorem decretorum collectorem Anglie, de omnibus receptis, asignatis et expensis per Dominum Johannem de Caroloco, locumtenentem suum in dicto officio, vel ipsum Johannem, de quibuscumque peccuniis in dictis partibus ad cameram appostolicam pertinentibus a penultima die menssis Februarii anno M<sup>o</sup> CCCLXIIII<sup>o</sup> usque ad xx<sup>am</sup> diem Maii anno LXVI<sup>o</sup>, prout in presente libro particulariter continetur, ac etiam de restis debitis dicte camere.

(fol. 139)[2] Rationes secunde Johannis de Cabrespino, collectoris Anglie.

(fol. 140)[3] Sequuntur computa et rationes Johannis de Cabrespino, doctoris decretorum, in Anglia et Ybernia sedis apostolice nuntii et collectoris, de omnibus et singulis receptis, expensis et assignatis per Dominum Johannem de Caroloco, priorem Lewensem locumtenentem suum, de quibuscumque obventionibus et

---

[867] The remainder of the account to the list of bishoprics is found only in **b**, fols. 88<sup>v</sup>, 89.

[868] Here **a** and **b** become duplicates again.

[869] *Licheffeldensis*, **a**; *Lichefeldensis* deleted by a line, **b**.

[870] The remainder of the account appears only in **b**.

[871] Folios 72 to 73<sup>v</sup> are blank. Folio 74 is the original cover of this report. The skin has been left rough, it has been much rubbed, and in places it is stained. In the upper left corner is

noted in modern hand *1364, 680*. The latter is probably the number given to the report in the Archives when it was a separate volume.

[872] The name is conjectural because the manuscript is rubbed. There are probably two more illegible words, which may be *doctoris decretorum*.

[873] Followed by three or four words which are illegible.

[874] Conjectural.

[875] The year is illegible excepting an initial *L*. Presumably it is *LXIIII*. It is followed by one or two illegible words.

[876] Several words, probably four or five, are illegible.

[877] The word may be *ponitur* or *ponuntur*.

[878] One or more subsequent words are illegible.

[879] Folio 74<sup>v</sup> is blank.

[880] This heading is preceded by a note of which the early portion is rendered illegible by a stain. The legible portion reads *ii<sup>c</sup> xxxiii li. Item in qua* (or *quo*) *xx li. iiii s.* The heading is followed by the note in a modern hand: *Urb. V.*

Folio 75<sup>v</sup> is blank. On folio 76 begins the second copy of the account given above. Variants in the second copy are noted in accordance with the principles stated above, p. 172.

[1] The roughly finished original parchment cover of the account. In a modern hand at the top: *64-66*.

[2] Folio 138<sup>v</sup> is blank. On folio 139 in a modern hand: *Urb. V. 1364 ad 1366*; *873*. The last is presumably the number of the account in the series of Collectorie before it was bound in the present volume.

[3] Folio 139<sup>v</sup> is blank.

emolumentis in dictis partibus spectantibus ad cameram apostolicam quovis modo a penultima die mensis Februarii anni domini MCCCLXIIII[ti], quo tempore dictus Johannes de Cabrespino de Anglia exivit et recessit, usque ad xx[am] diem mensis Maii anni MCCCLXVI[ti], quo tempore presentes rationes fuerunt per dictum Dominum Johannem, priorem Lewensem, misse Avinionie dicto Domino Johanni de Cabrespino, inclusa in presentibus computis assignatione facta camere apostolice per dictum Johannem de Cabrespino de xi milibus florenis ponderis camere diversis diebus et mensibus anno LXVI°, ut infra in ultima assignatione apparet post diem presentis conclusionis.

Sequitur recepta arayragiorum de denariis Beati Petri in primis computis dimissorum.

Primo a domino episcopo Lincoliensi, dimisso in arayragiis pro anno [4] LXII° pro dictis denariis in xlii li., xlii li.

Item ab archidiacono Wynthoniensi dimisso in arayragiis in xi li. xiii s. iiii d.

Item ab archidiacono Eliensi, dimisso in arayragiis pro anno LXII° in v li., v li.

Summa pagine xlvii li.

(fol. 140[v]) Sequitur recepta ordinaria census denariorum Beati Petri.

De archidiacono Cantuariensi [5] pro annis LXIII et IIII[to], pro quolibet viii li., xvi li.

De archidiacono Essexie pro anno LXIII° v li. x s.

De archidiacono Surreie pro annis LXIII° et IIII°, pro quolibet v li. xiii s. iiii d., xi li. vi s. viii d.

De episcopo Exoniensi pro annis LXIII°, LXIIII° et LXV°, pro quolibet ix li. v s., xxvii li. xv s.

De archidiacono Eliensi pro anno LXIII° v li.

De episcopo Norwicensi pro annis LXIII° et LXIIII°, pro quolibet xxi li. x s., xliii li.

De episcopo Lincoliensi pro anno LXIII° xlii li.

De episcopo Convetrensi et Lichefeldensi pro anno LXIII° x li. v s.

De episcopo Herfordensi pro annis LXIII° et LXIIII°, pro quolibet vi li., xii li.

De episcopo Wygorniensi pro anno LXIIII°, et debet pro tertio,[6] x li. v s.

De archiepiscopo Eboracensi pro anno LXIII° xi li. x s.

Summa pagine cxciiii li. xi s. viii d.

Summa totalis denariorum Beati Petri ii[c] xli li. xi s. viii d.

(fol. 141) Sequitur recepta annui census

### Cantuariensis

De abbate de Faversham, dimisso in arayragiis pro anno LXII° et postea pro anno LXIII°, pro quolibet xiii s. iiii d., xxvi s. viii d.

### Roffensis

De priore de Tonnebrigg' pro annis LXIII et LXIIII°,[7] pro quolibet xiii s. iiii d., xxvi s. viii d.

### Wynthoniensis

De abbate de Chertesey pro anno LXIII° et LXIIII°, pro quolibet viii s., xvi s.

### Norwicensis

De abbate Sancti Edmundi de Bury pro annis LXIIII° et LXV°, pro quolibet xiii s. iiii d., xxvi s. viii d.

### Exoniensis

De priore de Bodmyn, dimisso pro anno LXII° et postea pro annis LXIII°, LXIIII° [8] et LXV°, pro quolibet ii s., viii s.

### Lincoliensis

De abbate Sancti Albani pro annis LXIIII° et LXV°, pro quolibet xiii s. iiii d., xxvi s. viii d.

### Saresburiensis

De abbate Sancti Aldelmy Malmesbury pro annis LXIIII° et LXV°, pro quolibet xiii s. iiii d., xxvi s. viii d.

### Londoniensis

De abbatissa et sororibus Sancte Clare Londoniensis, dimissis pro annis LVIII, LIX, LX, LXI et LXII° et postea pro LXIII° et LXIIII°, pro quolibet vi d., iii s. vi d.

### Eliensis

De priore de Anglesey, dimisso pro annis LXI° et LXII° et postea pro annis LXIII° et LXIIII°, pro quolibet ii s., viii s.

### Eboracensis [9]

De custode de Scardeburgh' pro anno LXIII° xv d. Summa pagine viii li. x s. i d.

(fol. 141[v]) Sequitur recepta arayragiorum primorum fructuum dimissorum per me, Johannem de Cabrespino, collectorem Anglie, domino priori Lewensi camere apostolice in Anglia subcollectori,[10] distincta per dioceses

### Cantuariensis nichil

### (fol. 142) Roffensis

De ecclesia de Mepham (Meopham), taxata xxvi li. xiii s. iiii d., de qua per obitum Johannis Bolde fuit provisum Johanni de Kirkeby per Innocentium iiii° nonas Julii anno ix°,[11] dimissa in arayragiis in x li. **pro duabus provisionibus, in plenam solutionem x li.**

---

[4] *annis,* MSS.
[5] *Cantuarensi* is repeated and deleted by dots, **a.**
[6] *et debet pro tertio* lacking, **b.**

[7] *LXIIII[to] et LXV,* **b.**
[8] *XLIIII,* **a.**
[9] Followed by *de custo* deleted by dots, **a.**
[10] *in Anglia subcollectori* lacking, **a.**
[11] 4 July 1361.

De ecclesia de Ston' (Stone) Roffensis diocesis, quam obtinere solebat Nicholaus de Aston', magister in teulogia, fuit provisum Johanni Pays x kalendas Decembris per Dominum Urbanum papam quintum anno primo,[12] taxata [13] xx li., in partem dicte taxe v li.

Summa pagine et diocesis xv li.

### (fol. 142ᵛ) Londoniensis

De ecclesia Sancte Trinitatis Londonie, non taxata, de qua fuit dispensatum cum Thoma Balle ut ipsam posset licite retinere non obstante defectu natalium, de qua composuit pro medietate ad c s., de quibus solvit in aliis computis l s., in partem dicte reste xxv s.[14]

De ecclesia de Matfelon' (Whitechapel), non taxata, de qua fuit provisum David Doyer per [15] Innocentium vii idus Aprilis anno viiⁿ,[16] dimissa in arayragiis in vi s. viii d., vi s. viii d.

De archdiaconatu Essexie in ecclesia Londoniensi, non taxato, qui fuit confirmatus Willelmo de Bothewell' per Innocentium iiiⁿ idus Februarii anno viⁿ,[17] in partem certorum fructuum et proventuum lvi s. viii d.

De ecclesia de Sabrigesworth' (Sawbridgeworth), que fuit unita monasterio Westmonasterii iuxta Londoniam per Clementem iii [18] nonas Maii anno ixⁿ,[19] dimissa in arayragiis in xiii li. vi s. viii d., in complementum dicte reste xiii li. vi s. viii d.

De ecclesia de Langedon' (Langdon Hills), non taxata, de qua ex causa permutationis fuit provisum Willelmo de Swilfolde per Dominum Urbanum iii nonas Januarii anno primo,[20] qui composuit pro medietate fructuum medio iuramento in xl s., solvit in partem dicte compositionis xiii s. iiii d.[21]

Summa pagine et diocesis xviii li. viii s. iiii d.

### (fol. 143) Cicestrensis

De prebenda de Feryng' (Ferring) in ecclesia Cicestrensi, de qua fuit provisum Johanni de Acton', dimissa in arayragiis in vii li., in complementum dicte reste vii li.

De prebenda de Sidelesham (Sidlesham) in ecclesia Cicestrensi, de qua ⟨per obitum⟩ Edmundi [22] de Arundell' fuit provisum Waltero Gest per Clementem xii kalendas Decembris anno viiiⁿ,[23] dimissa in arayragiis in xii li. li s. ix d., in plenam solutionem dicte reste xii li. ii s. ix d.

De ecclesia de Bucstede (Buxted), de qua per assecu-

tionem prepositure de Wyngham (Wingham) fuit provisum Johanni de Strettley per Innocentium vii kalendas Aprilis anno viⁿ,[24] dimissa in arayragiis in xxxii li., in partem dicte reste xx li.[25]

De prebenda de Colleworth' (Colworth) in ecclesia Cicestrensi, de qua per obitum Ricardi Drax fuit provisum Johanni de Strettley per Innocentium vii kalendas Junii anno nono,[26] dimissa in arayragiis in xxvi li. xiii s. iiii d. in plenam solutionem dicte reste xxvi li. xiii s. iiii d.

De thesauraria Cicestrensi ratione confirmationis facte Willelmo de Lughteburg', dimissa in arayragiis in xvi li. xiii s. iiii d., in partem dicte reste vi li. xiii s. iiii d.[27]

De vicaria de Iklesham (Icklesham), de qua fuit dispensatum cum Waltero de Straton' presbytero quod eam [28] posset licite retinere per Innocentium ii idus Januarii anno viiiⁿ,[29] dimissa in arayragiis pro tota taxa in xvi li. xiii s. iiii d., in partem dicte reste sive taxe x li.[30]

De ecclesia de Horstedekeynes (Horsted Keynes), de qua fuit provisum Johanni de Middonhull', taxata xiii li. vi s. viii d., in plenam solutionem dicte taxe xiii li. vi s. viii d.[31]

Summa pagine et diocesis iiiiˣˣ xv li. xvi s. i d.

### (fol. 143ᵛ) Wynthoniensis

De ecclesia de Lavertok' (Laverstoke), taxata xiiii li., in qua ad ius quod competebat Johanni Crom fuit subrogatus Johannes de Banbury, dimissa in arayragiis in iii li., in plenam solutionem dicte reste iii li.

De prebenda de Midelton (Middleton) in ecclesia monialium de Warwell' (Wherwell), taxata xxvi li. xiii s. iiii d., de qua fuit provisum Johanni de Branketre per Innocentium v kalendas Januarii anno primo,[32] dimissa in arayragiis in tota predicta taxa, in partem dicte taxe sive reste vi li. xiii s. iiii d.[33]

De ecclesia de Waltham, taxata xx li., de qua per obitum Gilberti David fuit provisum Hugoni Crast' per Innocentium iiiⁿ nonas Julii anno ixⁿ,[34] dimissa in arayragiis in xvi li., in plenam solutionem xvi li.

De ecclesia de Havunte (Havant), taxata xxvi li. xiii s. iiii d., de qua per obitum Johannis Noion fuit provisum Johanni de Upelhull' per Innocentium iiiiⁿ nonas Julii anno ixⁿ,[35] dimissa in arayragiis in xx li., in partem dicte reste xiii li. vi s. viii d.[36]

Summa pagine et diocesis xxxix li.

---

[12] 22 November 1362.
[13] *taxate*, MSS.
[14] In the margin: *resta xxv s.*
[15] Om. **a.**
[16] 7 April 1359.
[17] 11 February 1358.
[18] *in,* **a.**
[19] 5 May 1351.
[20] 3 January 1363.
[21] In the margin: *resta xxvi s. viii d.*
[22] *Emd',* MSS.
[23] 20 November 1349.

[24] 30 March 1358.
[25] In the margin: *resta xii li.*
[26] 26 May 1361.
[27] In the margin: *resta x li.*
[28] *eum,* **a.**
[29] 12 January 1360.
[30] In the margin: *resta vi li. xiii s. iiii d.*
[31] In the margin: *Ista non fuit in regestris nec in arayragiis.*
[32] 28 December 1353.
[33] In the margin: *resta xx li.*
[34] 5 July 1361.
[35] 4 July 1361.
[36] In the margin: *resta vi li. xiii s. iiii d.*

## (fol. 144) Saresburiensis

De ecclesia de Wyntteburn' Stikelan (Winterborne Stickland), taxata iiii li. vi s. viii d., de qua per resignationem Willelmi de Cheston' fuit provisum Thome Henrici per Innocentium xiiii kalendas Julii anno primo,[37] dimissa in arayragiis in dicta taxa, in partem dicte taxe sive reste xx s.[38]

De vicaria de Poterna (Potterne), taxata xx li., de qua vicario eiusdem fuit per cardinalem Urgellensem provisum, dimissa in arayragiis in xl s., in plenam solutionem dicte reste xl s.

De eadem vicaria de Poterna, ratione provisionis ex causa permutationis facte cum Johanne Dayle pro vicaria ecclesie Omnium Sanctorum de Kyngeston, (Kingston on Thames) Wyntoniensis diocesis fuit provisum Thome West per Innocentium viiio kalendas Octobris anno ixo,[39] dimissa in arayragiis in xv li., in plenam solutionem dicte reste xv li.

De ecclesia de Assebury (Ashbury), taxata xxvi li. xiii s. iiii d., de qua per obitum Walteri Moryn fuit provisum Thome de Buzopesbury per Innocentium iiii kalendas Octobris anno ix,[40] dimissa in arayragiis in xvi li. xiii s. iiii d., in partem dicte reste vi li. xiii s. iiii d.[41]

De officio subdecanatus Saresburiensis et ecclesia[42] de[43] Candelhaddon' (Caundle Stourton) eidem annexa, taxata iiii li. vi s. viii d., de quo per obitum Nicolai de Mordefeld' fuit provisum Willelmo de Slynton' per Dominum Urbanum nonas Decembris anno primo,[44] in complementum dicte taxe ecclesie iiii li. vi s. viii d.

Summa pagine et diocesis xxix li.

## (fol. 144v) Exoniensis

De thesauraria Exoniensi, acceptatio cuius facta per Robertum de Midelond fuit eidem confirmata per Clementem xv kalendas Julii anno viio,[45] taxata xx li., dimissa in arayragiis in tota taxa, in plenam solutionem dicte taxe xx li.

De archidiaconatu Barnastapolie, non taxato, pro resta duarum provisionum, unius facte Johanni de Reynham per Clementem xv kalendas Julii anno viio,[45] et alterius Willelmo Mucgge per Innocentium iiiio nonas Septembris anno vio,[46] dimisso in arayragiis in x li., in plenam solutionem dicte reste x li.

De decanatu Exoniensi, de quo per obitum Ricardi de Brayle fuit provisum Reginaldo de Buggewell, per Clementem xv kalendas Octobris anno xio,[47] et taxata

xlii li. xiii s. iiii d., dimisso in arayragiis in xxxii li. xiii s. iiii d., in plenam solutionem dicte reste xxxii li. xiii s. iiii d.

De vicaria ecclesie de Columpton' (Collumpton), non taxata, de qua per obitum Thome de Melyns fuit provisum Thome de Pilton' per Innocentium iii idus Maii anno vio,[48] dimissa in arayragiis pro medietate fructuum in vi li. xiii s. iiii d., in plenam solutionem dicte reste vi li. xiii s. iiii d.

De ecclesia de Lanssant (Lezant), cuius collatio facta Johanni de Brokelond' fuit eidem confirmata per Innocentium xi kalendas Octobris anno vio,[49] et taxata iiii li., dimissa in arayragiis pro tota taxa, in complementum ipsius taxe iiii li.

Summa pagine lxxiii li. vi s. viii d.

(fol. 145)[50] De prebenda ecclesie collegiate Sancte Tethe (St. Teath) taxata iiii li., de qua per obitum Thome David fuit provisum Johanni Braker per Innocentium xi kalendas Julii anno ixo,[51] dimissa in arayragiis pro tota taxa, in plenam solutionem ipsius iiii li.

De prebenda Sancti Karenttoci[52] (Crantock) que est in ecclesia collegiata et non habet proprium nomen, collatio cuius facta Rogero de Stanford' fuit eidem confirmata per Innocentium x kalendas Novembris anno nono,[53] taxata xxx s., et dimissa in arayragiis in tota taxa, in plenam solutionem ipsius xxx s.

De prebenda in eadem ecclesia, cuius collatio facta Johanni de Holond' fuit eidem confirmata per Innocentium iiiio idus Maii anno nono,[54] taxata in lx s., dimissa in arayragiis in solidis fructibus, in plenam solutionem dicte taxe lx s.

De ecclesia Sancti Petroceri (St. Peter) Exonie, non taxata, cuius collatio facta Johanni More fuit eidem confirmata per Innocentium iiiio nonas Maii anno xo,[55] dimissa in arayragiis in solidis fructibus, in partem eorum lxvi s. viii d. Episcopus certificavit quod non valet tamen annuatim.

De prebenda Exoniensi, de qua per obitum Ade de Hilton' fuit provisum Willelmo de Bermyngham per Innocentium idus Julii anno xo,[56] et taxata iiii li., in plenam solutionem dicte taxe iiii li.

Summa pagine xv li. xvi s. viii d.

Summa totius istius diocesis tam istius pagine quam precendentis iiiixx ix li. iii s. iiii d.

## (fol. 145v) Wigoriensis

De ecclesia Sanctorum Philipi et Jacobi Bristoll', non taxata, de qua per obitum Roberti Rove fuit provisum

---

[37] 18 June 1353.
[38] In the margin: *resta iii li. vi s. viii d.*
[39] 24 September 1361.
[40] 28 September 1361.
[41] In the margin: *resta x li.*
[42] *ecclesie*, a.
[43] *et ecclesie de* repeated, MSS.
[44] 5 December 1362.
[45] 17 June 1348.
[46] 2 September 1358.
[47] 17 September 1352.

[48] 13 May 1358.
[49] 21 September 1358.
[50] The heading *Exoniensis* is repeated at the top of the page.
[51] 21 June 1361.
[52] *Karenton*, a.
[53] 23 October 1361.
[54] 12 May 1361.
[55] 4 May 1362.
[56] 15 July 1362.

Nicolao de Dygthon' per Clementem, que vix sufficit ad victus sumptum [57] sacerdotis, ymo sacerdos est quasi mendicans, dimissa [58] in arayragiis pro medietate fructuum in xx s., in plenam solutionem dicte reste xx s.

Summa pagine et diocesis xx s.

### (fol. 146) Bathoniensis et Wellensis

De cancellaria ecclesie Wellensis et prebenda de Brompton' (Compton Dundon) eidem annexa, taxatis xlvi li. xiiii s. iiii d., de quibus per assecutionem decanatus Wellensis fuit provisum Johanni de Horsyngthon' per Clementem kalendas Junii anno viii°,[59] dimissa in arayragiis in xiiii li. xii s., in plenam solutionem dicte reste xiiii l. xii s.

De prebenda et archidiaconatu Wellensibus, de quibus per obitum domini episcopi Tusculani cardinalis [60] fuit provisum cardinali Carcassonensi [61] per Innocentium vi kalendas Octobris anno ix°,[62] taxatis lxvi [63] li. xiii s. iiii d., dimissa in arayragiis in tota predicta taxa, in partem ipsius xxv li. vii s. i d. ob.[64]

De prebenda bursali in ecclesia Wellensi, taxata v li. vi s. viii d., de qua per obitum Johannis Torstayn, fuit provisum Johanni Coffr' per Innocentium v° nonas Maii anno x°,[65] dimissa in arayragiis in liii s. iiii d., in plenam solutionem dicte reste liii s. iiii d.

De vicaria Sancti Cuthberti Wellensis, taxata vi li. xiii s. iiii d., de qua per resignationem Philipi Honte fuit provisum Willelmo Massyngham per Innocentium ii nonas Novembris anno v°,[66] dimissa in arayragiis in plenam taxam, in partem ipsius taxe sive reste iii li. vi s. viii d.[67]

De prebenda et thesauraria Wellensi, taxata xxxiii li. vi s. viii d., de qua fuit provisum domino cardinali Aquensi [68] per obitum Ricardi de Thornenthon' senioris in Romana curia defuncti per Innocentium ii idus Novembris anno nono,[69] dimissa in arayragiis pro tota taxa, in partem ipsius reste xii li. xvi s. viii d. ob.[70]

De prioratu conventuali Montisacuti (Montacute) ordinis Cluniacensis, taxato cxxxiii li. vi s. viii d., de quo per promotionem Geraldi Rothonis ad prioratum

Lewensem fuit provisum Francisco de Barchiato iii [71] Januarii per Dominum Urbanum anno primo, dimisso in tota taxa, in plenam solutionem ipsius taxe cxxxiii li. vi s. viii d.

Summa pagine et diocesis cxcii li. ii s. vi d.

### (fol. 146ᵛ) Herfordensis

De prebenda in ecclesia Herfordensi, quam Adam electus Menevensis obtinebat, fuit provisum Johanni de Canney per Innocentium iii kalendas Novembris anno nono,[72] que fuit dimissa in arayragiis in solidis fructibus, in partem dictorum fructuum xl s.

De decanatu ecclesie Herfordensis, de quo per resignationem Thome Trulek' fuit provisum Willelmo de Bemyngham per Dominum Urbanum vii kalendas Februarii anno primo,[73] qui taxatur xxxi li. viii s. v d., dimisso in arayragiis in tota taxa, in partem ipsius reste xxii li. xv s.[74]

De ecclesia de Wordyn (Worthen) et aliis beneficiis de quibus fuit dispensatum cum Ricardo de Stanford' ut ea valeat licite retinere, de resta debita per confessionem propriam, quia nec ponitur in registris camere nec in computis Domini Hugonis Pelegrini, xxxviii li. xiii s. iiii d., de quibus solvit xx li.[75]

Summa pagine et diocesis xliiii li. xv s.

### (fol. 147) Norwicensis

De prioratu Sancte Fidis de Horsham, taxato clxxxiiii li., de quo per obitum Pontii de Serveria fuit provisum Benedicto Jory per Clementem viii kalendas Octobris anno vii° vel viii°,[76] dimisso in arayragiis in cxxi li. vi s. viii d., in partem dicte reste li li.[77]

De ecclesia de Weston' taxata xxvi li. xiii s. iiii d., de qua Johanni de Derby fuit ex causa permutationis cum Willelmo Mugge provisum per Innocentium iiii° nonas Septembris anno vi,[78] dimissa in arayragiis in xiiii li., in plenam solutionem dicte reste xiiii li.

De ecclesia de Estbylney (East Bilney), taxata iiii li. vi s. viii d., que fuit Thome de Walton' confirmata per Innocentium vi kalendas Julii anno vi°,[79] dimissa in arayragiis pro tota taxa predicta, in partem ipsius xliii s. iiii d.[80]

De ecclesia de Lacceford' (Lackford), taxata xx li., de qua per dimissionem Ricardi de Walkeles fuit provisum Johanni de Sokeney per Innocentium iiii idus

---

[57] *sumptis*, MSS.
[58] Lacking, **a.**
[59] 1 June 1349.
[60] William de Court.
[61] Stephen Aubert, deacon of S. Maria in Aquiro.
[62] 26 September 1361.
[63] After the same figure deleted, **a.**
[64] In the margin: *Resta xli li. vi s. ii d. ob.* In the margin of **a** only: *Ista summa fuit recepta pro fructibus qui venerunt tempore vacationis et iam ponitur in arayragiis pro integra taxa, set non debet fieri quia dicti fructus non fuerant reservati tempore Innocentii.*
[65] 3 May 1362.
[66] 4 November 1357.
[67] In the margin: *Resta iii li. vi s. viii d.*
[68] Peter Itherii, bishop of Dax, priest of Ss. Quattro Coronati.
[69] 12 November 1361.
[70] In the margin: *Resta xx li. ix s. xi d. ob.*

[71] A blank space is left in MSS. 30 December 1362. Given as 3 Kal. Jan. in *Cal. Pap. Regs. Petitions*, i, 393.
[72] 30 October 1361.
[73] 26 January 1363.
[74] In the margin: *Resta viii li. xiii s. v d.*
[75] In the margin: *Resta xviii li. xiii s. iiii d., et non ponitur in registris camere nec in computis Domini Hugonis.*
[76] 24 September 1348 or 1349.
[77] The part payment was 51 pounds and so in the margin: *Resta lxx li. vi s. viii d.*
[78] 2 September 1358.
[79] 26 June 1358.
[80] In the margin: *Resta xliii s. iiii d.*

Octobris anno viii°,[81] dimissa in arayragiis in x li., in plenam solutionem dicte reste x li.

De decanatu rurali Linie (Lynn), non taxato, de quo ex causa permutationis fuit provisum Ade Thebaud per Innocentium xvii kalendas Septembris anno viii°,[82] dimissa in arayragiis in solidis fructibus, in partem ipsorum xxxiii s. iiii d.[83]

De ecclesia de Masham (Marsham), taxata xvi li. xiii s. iiii d., de qua per assecutionem cancellarie Saresburiensis factam per Johannem de Nortton' fuit provisum Ricardo Comites per Innocentium ii nonas Januarii anno x°,[84] dimissa in arayragiis in viii li. xiii s. iiii d., in complementum dicte reste viii li. xiii s. iiii d.

De ecclesia Sancti Gregorii de Subur', non taxata ut dicitur, de qua per assecutionem cancellarie in ecclesia Londoniensi fuit provisum Thome de Balthon' per Innocentium iiii° idus Martii anno x°,[85] dimissa in arayragiis in solidis [86] fructibus, et reperitur taxata in xxv m. que [87] valent xvi li. xiii s. iiii d., in partem dicte reste vi li. xiii s. iiii d.[88]

Summa pagine et diocesis xciiii li. iii s. iiii d.

### (fol. 147ᵛ) Eliensis

De ecclesia de Overe (Over), taxata xxxv li. vi s. viii d., de qua per obitum Thome de Clipston' fuit provisum Rogero de Stamford' per Innocentium iii° idus Augusti anno nono,[89] dimissa in arayragiis in xii li. x s., in plenam solutionem dicte reste xii li. x s.

Summa pagine et diocesis xii li. x s.

### (fol. 148) Lincoliensis

De prioratu de Cogges, qui fuit confirmatus Willelmo Hamonis per Clementem, dimisso in arayragiis in v li. vi s. viii d. in partem reste iiii li.[90]

De archidiaconatu Bukyngham in ecclesia Lincoliensi, non taxato, de quo per obitum cardinalis Aynibaldi [91] fuit provisum Johanni de Ascheburn' per Clementem idus Novembris anno ix°,[92] dimisso in arayragiis in solidis fructibus, pro quibus composuit medio iuramento pro xx li., de quibus solvit in partem dicte compositionis xiii li. vi s. viii d.[93]

De prebenda de Suthscarle (South Scarle) in ecclesia Lincoliensi, taxata xl li., de qua per obitum Thome Crosse fuit provisum Johanni de Kirkeby per Clemen-

tem iiii° nonas Martii anno nono,[94] dimissa in arayragiis in xii li. ii s. xi d., in partem dicte reste vi li. i s. vi d.[95]

De prebenda de Carlethon' cum Turleby (Carleton le Moorland cum Thurlby), de qua per consecrationem Nicholai episcopi Urgellensis (Urgel) fuit provisum Rothberto de Wyngeworth' per Innocentium ix kalendas Maii anno primo,[96] taxata xxvi li. xiii s. iiii d., dimissa in arayragiis in xvi li. xiii s. iiii d., in partem dicte reste iii li. vi s. viii d.[97]

De vicaria de Therlebury (Thurlby), taxata x li., de qua per cardinalem Petragoricensem fuit provisum Johanni de Asting', dimissa in arayragiis in v li., in complementum dicte reste v li.

Summa pagine xxxi li. xiiii s. x d.

(fol. 148ᵛ)[98] De ecclesia de Hoghton' (Houghton Regis), que fuit Hugoni de Sparkyngio confirmata per Innocentium ix° kalendas Septembris anno vii°,[99] dimissa in arayragiis in xvi li. xiii s. iiii d., in partem dicte reste xii li.[100]

De ecclesia de Eydon', taxata iiii li. xiii s. iiii d., de qua per resignationem Walteri de Heyreworth' fuit provisum Rotberto de Deyworth' per Innocentium ii idus Decembris anno viii°,[101] dimissa in arayragiis in tota taxa, in complementum dicte reste iiii li. xiii s. iiii d.

De ecclesia de Hagworthyngham (Hagworthingham), taxata xii li., de qua per assecutionem ecclesie de Wyninyngstede (Wetheringsett) Norwicensis diocesis auctoritate litterarum apostolicarum fuit provisum Henrico Romelon per Innocentium iiii° nonas Maii anno nono,[102] dimissa in arayragiis in iii li., in complementum dicte reste iii li.

De vicaria de Cloee (Clee), taxata x li., de qua per obitum Johannis Olney fuit provisum Johanni Aleyn per Innocentium iii kalendas Maii anno x°,[103] dimissa m arayragiis in v li., in complementum dicte reste v li.

Summa pagine xxiiii li. xiii s. iiii d.

(fol. 149)[98] De ecclesia de Strangrond' (Standground), de qua per cardinalem Petragoricensem fuit provisum Thome de Clipston', taxata xx li., dimissa in arayragiis in vi li. xiii s. iiii d., in complementum dicte reste vi li. xiii s. iiii d.

De prebenda de Glatton' in ecclesia Lincoliensis, de qua per obitum Ade de Hilton' fuit provisum Rogero de Sutton' per Innocentium iiii° kalendas Martii anno x°,[104] et taxata iiii li. vi s. viii d., dimissa in arayragiis

---

[81] 12 October 1360.
[82] 16 August 1360.
[83] In the margin: *Resta xxxiii s. iiii d.* In **b** only: *taxa x m.*
[84] 4 January 1362.
[85] 12 March 1362.
[86] Followed by *fuit* deleted by dots, **a**.
[87] *qui*, **a**.
[88] In the margin: *Resta x li.*
[89] 11 August 1361.
[90] In the margin: *Resta xxvi s. viii d.*
[91] Bishop of Tusculum.
[92] 13 November 1350.
[93] In the margin: *Resta vi li. xiii s. iiii d.*

[94] 4 March 1351.
[95] In the margin: *Resta vi li. i s. v d.*
[96] 23 April 1353.
[97] In the margin: *Resta xiii li. vi s. viii d.*
[98] At the top of the page: *Adhuc Lincoliensis.*
[99] 24 August 1359.
[100] In the margin: *Resta iiii li. xiii s. iiii d.*
[101] 12 December 1360.
[102] 4 May 1361.
[103] 29 April 1362.
[104] 26 February 1362.

pro tota taxa, in complementum ipsius iiii li. vi s. viii d.[105]

De medietate ecclesie de Sukel (East Keal?), taxata xix li., de qua ex causa permutationis fuit provisum Galfrido Trenthapan per Innocentium idus Aprilis anno x°,[106] dimissa in arayragiis pro tota taxa, in partem dicte reste ix li. vi s. viii d.[107]

De ecclesia de Coltesworth' (Colsterworth), taxata xxi li. vi s. viii d., de qua fuit provisum Rotberto de Hinkele per Innocentium idus Aprilis anno x°,[108] dimissa in arayragiis in x li. xiii s. iiii d., in complementum dicte reste x li. xiii s. iiii d.

De ecclesia de Kirsselawe (Creslow), taxata iiii li. xiii s. iiii d., de qua fuit provisum Rotberto de Mamcestr' per Innocentium v kalendas Februarii anno vii°,[109] dimissa in arayragiis pro tota taxa, in complementum ipsius iiii li. xiii s. iiii d.

De vicaria perpetua Sancti Michaelis iuxta villam Sancti Albani (Kingsbury) dicte diocesis, de qua ex causa permutationis cum Henrico de Lake fuit provisum Johanni Massetger per Innocentium v kalendas Aprilis anno viii°,[110] et non taxatur, solvit in partem fructuum xx s.

Summa pagine xxxvi li. xiii s. iiii d.

(fol. 149ᵛ)[98] De ecclesia de Denfford' (Denford), taxata xx li., de qua ex causa permutationis cum Philipo[111] Hygham fuit provisum Rogero de Brinton' kalendis et anno quibus supra, dimissa in arayragiis in x li., in complementum dicte reste x li.

Summa pagine x li.
Summa totius diocesis Lincoliensis ciii li. i s. vi d.

### (fol. 150) Conwetrensis et Licheffeldensis

De prebenda Langedon' (Longdon) in ecclesia Licheffeldensi, cuius taxa est xx li., pro qua et quibusdam aliis beneficiis composuit cum camera Walterus Dalby, composuit in iii° lviii fl., dimissa in arayragiis in c et viii° fl., in partem dicte reste pro 1 fl., quolibet predictorum florenorum pro iii s. ii d. computato, vii li. xviii s. iiii d.[112]

De ecclesia de Weston' super Trentham (Weston-upon-Trent), taxata xii li., de qua ex causa permutationis fuit provisum Nicholao de Homberkh' per Innocentium ii idus Februarii anno vi°,[113] dimissa in arayragiis in iiii°r li., in complementum dicte reste iiii li.

De ecclesia de Standich (Standish), taxata xiii li. vi s. viii d., de qua Gilberto de Standich' cardinalis Petragoricensis de novo providit, dimissa in arayragiis in vi li. xiii s. iiii d., in complementum dicte reste vi li. xiii s. iiii d.

De vicaria seu capellania Sancti Michaelis Convetrensis, taxata v li., de qua ex causa permutationis fuit provisum Thome de Brokwell' per Innocentium vii kalendas Junii anno vi°,[114] dimissa in arayragiis in l s., in complementum dicte reste ii li. x s.

De eadem vicaria Sancti Michaelis Convetrensis, de qua per dominum cardinalem Petragoricensem fuit provisum Willelmo Anthonii, dimissa in arayragiis in tota taxa, in complementum dicte reste sive taxe v li.

De ecclesie de Erkelwe (Child's Ercall), non taxata, que fuit Stephano Eyncheton' collata per dominum cardinalem Urgellensem et confirmata per Innocentium ix kalendas Octobris anno viii°,[115] pro compositione facta per eum ad vi li. xiii s. iiii d., et dimissa in arayragiis in tota dicta summa, in complementum dicte reste vi li. xiii s. iiii d.[116]

Summa pagine et diocesis xxxii li. xv s.,[117] inclusis vii li. xviii s. iiii d. receptis pro 1 fl.

### (fol. 150ᵛ) Assavensis

De ecclesia de Meyvot (Meifod), taxata xxv li. vi s. viii d., dimissa in arayragiis in tota taxa, de qua per consecrationem Ludovici episcopi Herffordensis fuit provisum Willelmo de Charleton' per Innocentium iiii° kalendas Octobris anno nono,[118] in complementum dicte reste xxv li. vi s. viii d.

Summa pagine et diocesis xxv li. vi s. viii d.

### (fol. 151) Menevensis

De archidiaconatu de Kermerdyn (Carmarthen) in ecclesia Menevensi cum ecclesia de Laman (Llanrhian) et prebenda eidem annexa, taxato xx li. xiii s. iiii d., collatio cuius facta auctoritate ordinaria Haulayno ap David fuit eidem confirmata per Innocentium xii kalendas Julii anno v,[119] dimisso in arayragiis pro tota taxa, in complementum ipsius xx li. xiii s. iiii d.

De hospitali Sancti David de Sweynesey (Swansea), collatio cuius facta David Martini fuit eidem confirmata per Innocentium iii kalendas Februarii anno ix°,[120] dimisso in arayragiis in solidis fructibus quia non taxatur, in partem ipsorum fructuum xl s.

Summa pagine et diocesis xxii li. xiii s. iiii d.

---

[105] In the margin: *non est prebenda sed est ecclesia parochialis in diocesi Lincoliensi et taxata xxi li. iii s. iiii d., et ideo debet xvi li. xvi s. viii d.*
[106] 13 April 1362.
[107] In the margin: *Resta ix li. xiii s. iiii d.*
[108] 13 April 1362.
[109] 28 January 1359.
[110] 28 March 1360.
[111] *Johanne,* **b.**
[112] In the margin: *Resta lviii fl.*
[113] 12 February 1358.

[114] 26 May 1358.
[115] 23 September 1360.
[116] In the margin: *confirmatio fuit facta eidem per Innocentium sed est infra annum.*
[117] The remainder of the item lacking, **b.**
[118] 28 September 1361.
[119] 20 June 1357.
[120] 30 January 1361.

(fol. 151ᵛ) Eboracensis

De prebenda de Eton' (Eaton) in ecclesia collegiata Sutthwellensi, de qua per consecrationem Gilberti episcopi Karleolensis fuit provisum Thome Gryffyn per Clementem x kalendas Junii anno xᵒ,[121] et est taxata vi li. xiii s. iiii d., dimissa in arayragiis in tota taxa predicta, in complementum ipsius vi li. xiii s. iiii d.

De ecclesia de Brantyngham (Brantingham), taxata lxvi li. xiii s. iiii d., de qua vacante per obitum Magistri Thome de Nevill' fuit provisum Willelmo Storde per Innocentium xvi kalendas Septembris,[122] dimissa in arayragiis in xl li., in partem dicte reste xxxiii li. vi s. viii d.[123]

De prebenda de Munketon' (Monkton) in ecclesia collegiata Ripponensi, in qua in omni iure quod competebat Thome de Clipston' fuit subrogatus Willelmus Ronde per Innocentium vi idus Julii anno nono,[124] taxata ad novam taxam xiii li. vi s. viii d., dimissa in arayragiis pro tota taxa, in complementum ipsius xiii li. vi s. viii d.

De vicaria de Estyngton' (Eastrington), presentatio et inductio cuius facte [125] auctoritate ordinaria Thome de Sissill' fuerunt eidem auctoritate apostolica confirmate per Innocentium iii kalendas Aprilis anno viiiᵒ,[126] pro resta dimissa v li.

De portione ecclesie de Hoton' Buschell' (Hutton Bushel), vacante per obitum Nicholai de Owyteby, fuit provisum Johanni Poll' de Clifford xvi kalendas Februarii anno primo,[127] dimissa in arayragiis in iiii li., in complementum dicte reste iiii li.

De eadem portione vacanti ut supra fuit provisum eodem anno xiii kalendas Maii [128] Alano Akae clerico, et utraque est infra annum.[129]

Summa pagine lxii li. vi s. viii d.

(fol. 152)[130] De vicaria ecclesie de Kildewyk (Kildwick), cuius collatio et provisio facte [131] auctoritate ordinaria ex causa permutationis Rogero de Slateburn', non obstante quod tempore huiusdem collationis esset excommunicatus, fuerunt eidem auctoritate apostolica confirmate vel provisum de novo v nonas Martii anno primo per Urbanum,[132] taxata xii li., dimissa in arayragiis in tota taxa, sed dicitur quod non taxatur nisi

ad iii li. vi s. viii d., et apparet in libro taxarum, solvit iii li. vi s. viii d.[133]

Summa pagine iii li. vi s. viii d.

Summa totius diocesis Eboracensis lxv li. xiii s. iiii d.

(fol. 152ᵛ) Dunelmensis

De prebenda de Lamseby (Lamesley), taxata xx li., de qua per obitum Willelmi de Rothewell' fuit provisum Guidoni de Pestell' per Innocentium iii nonas Decembris anno vᵒ,[134] dimissa in arayragiis in x li., pro complemento ipsius reste x li.

De vicaria de Whityngham (Whittingham), taxata x li., de qua per obitum Willelmi de Arkelby fuit provisum Johanni de Worddefford' per Innocentium xv kalendas Augusti anno vᵒ,[135] dimissa in arayragiis in x li., pro complemento dicte reste x li.

De decanatu ecclesie collegiate Cestrie super Stratam (Chester-le-Street), et decanatus non invenitur taxatus, sed vicaria taxatur xxxiii li. vi s. viii d., cuius permutatio facta auctoritate ordinaria cum Johanne de Sculthorp' pro archidiaconatu Cicestrensi per Adam de Howenton' fuit eidem confirmata per Innocentium kalendas Junii anno viᵒ,[136] dimissa in arayragiis in tota taxa predicta, in partem ipsius reste xvi li. xiii s. iiii d.[137]

De prebenda ecclesie collegiate de Northon' (Norton), taxata vi li., de qua per consecrationem Domini Johannis episcopi Wygorniensis fuit provisum Willelmo Ilbert' per Innocentium iiiiᵒ idus Martii anno xᵒ,[138] dimissa in arayragiis in iii li., in complementum dicte reste iii li.

Summa pagine et diocesis xxxix li. xiii s. iiii d.

(fol. 153) Landavensis

De precentoria Landavensi, de qua fuit provisum Magistro Philipo Enyas per Innocentium, taxata ut apparet in regestro v li. xiii s. iiii d., dimissa in arayragiis in tota taxa, in partem dicte reste xl s.[139]

Summa pagine et diocesis patet.

(fol. 153ᵛ) Sequentes iiiiᵒʳ sunt obligati pro diversis beneficiis que sunt in diversis diocesibus et cadunt supra in arayragiis.

De archidiaconatu Richmondie in ecclesia Eboracensi et prebenda de Middelton' (Middleton) in ecclesia Cicestrensi et de Vamynstr' alias Dymynstr' (Yetminster) in ecclesia Saresburiensi, de quibus fuit provisum Henrico de Walthon', dimissa in arayragiis in lxx li., in partem dicte reste vi li. xiii s. iiii d.[140]

---

[121] 23 May 1351.
[122] 17 August 1361: above, p. 203.
[123] In the margin: *Resta vi li. xiii s. iiii d.*
[124] 10 July 1361.
[125] *facta,* **a.**
[126] 30 March 1360.
[127] 17 January 1363.
[128] 19 April 1363.
[129] Item lacking, **b.**
[130] The heading *Eboracensis* is repeated at the top of the page.
[131] *facta,* **a.**
[132] 3 March 1363.

[133] In the margin: *Resta si sit data (recta,* **b)** *prima taxa viii li. xiii s. iiii d.; alias nichil restat.*
[134] 3 December 1357.
[135] 18 July 1357.
[136] 1 June 1358.
[137] In the margin of **b** only: *Resta xvi li. xiii s. iiii d.*
[138] 12 March 1362.
[139] In the margin: *Resta iii li. xiii s. iiii d.*
[140] In the margin: *Resta lxiii li. vii (vi,* **b)** *s. viii d.*

De subdecanatu Eboracensi et prebenda de Chartham (Grantham) in ecclesia Saresburiensi, de Bithemell' (Rathmichael) in ecclesia Dublinensi, de Cliston (Clifton) in ecclesia Lincolniensi, de Cheswyk' (Chiswick) in ecclesia Londoniensi, de Rompton' (Rampton) in ecclesia collegiata Suthewell' Eboracensis diocesis, de quibus fuit provisum seu confirmatio facta Willelmo de Rottoford' per Innocentium vii kalendas Decembris anno viii°,[141] dimissis in arayragiis in xxxix li., pro complemento dicte reste xxxix li.

De ecclesia de Houdenerth (Hodnet) Lichefeldensis diocesis et prebenda de Farendon' (Faringdon) in ecclesia Saresburiensi, de Mora (Moorfields, St. Giles Cripplegate) in ecclesia Londoniensi, de Hondreston' (Hunderton) in ecclesia Herffordensi, de Ledbury in diocesi Herffordensi, de quibus fuit provisum Nicolao Heeth' et composuit pro omnibus predictis beneficiis cum camera pro viii° l fl. ponderis camere, dimissis in arayragiis in v° l fl., solvit in partem dicte reste, videlicet pro ecclesia de Hodeneth' vi li. xiii s. iiii d. Valent, computato floreno pro iii s., xliiii fl. xvi sterlingi.[142]

De cancellaria Saresburiensi, prebenda de Huvite (Hove) in ecclesia Cicestrensi, de quibus fuit provisum Johanni de Northon' per consecrationem Simonis episcopi Londoniensis per Innocentium vii kalendas Decembris anno x°,[143] dimissis in arayragiis in xxxvi li., solvit in partem dicte reste xxxiiii li.[144]

Summa pagine iiii^xx vi li. vi s. viii d.,[145] inclusis vi li. xiii s. iiii d. pro xliiii fl. xvi sterlingis.

(fol. 154) Sequentia duo beneficia fuerunt collata in Anglia per dominos cardinales et tertium per Dominum Urbanum [146] que inter arayragias suis locis competentibus et diocesibus

### Norwicensis

De ecclesia Sancte [147] Marie de Westwynch' (West Wynch), de qua Paulo Antewode Middelton' cardinalis Urgellensis de novo providit, pro taxa dimissa v li. vi s. viii d.

### Eboracensis

De ecclesia de Foston', de qua per dominum cardinalem Petragoricensem fuit provisum Johanni de Nesseffolde, pro taxa ad novam taxam vi li. xiii s. iiii d.

De portione ecclesie de Houton' Bussell' (Hutton Bushel), vacante per obitum Nicolay de Whyteby fuit provisum Johanni Poll' de Clifford' per Urbanum xvi kalendas Februarii anno primo,[148] et dicitur quod

taxatur ad xii li. secundum antiquam taxam et secundum novam ad iiii^or li., tamen solvit viii li.[149]

Summa pagine xx li.

Summa universalis recepte arayratgiorum primorum fructuum benefficiorum collatorum per sedem appostolicam mxxviii li. viii s. v d., inclusis xiiii li. xi s. viii d. receptis pro xcv fl. camere, que diminuunt summam florenorum dimisam in arreyragiis aliorum compotorum.[150]

(fol. 154^v) Sequitur recepta de beneficiis collatis et confirmatis in regno Anglie per Dominum Urbanum papam V a vi die Martii anno MCCCLXIII secundum computationem Anglie usque ad xx diem Maii [151] anno LXVI°

### Roffensis

Ex causa permutationis fuit provisum Johanni Sacombe de Eton' de vicaria perpetua parochialis ecclesie Sancti Nicolai Roffensis, non taxata, xiii kalendas Novembris anno ii°; [152] composuit pro fructibus medio iuramento in iiii li., iiii li.

Et de vicaria parochialis ecclesie de Shom' (Shorne), de qua ex simili causa fuit provisum Johanni Thome, et continentur iste due provisiones in una in regestro, in partem taxe xl s.

Summa pagine et diocesis vi li.

### (fol. 155) Londoniensis

De parochiali ecclesia Sancti Martini in Vineria (St. Martin Vintry) Londonie, cuius collatio et provisio facte auctoritate ordinaria Nicolao de Drayton', bacallario in legibus, quam possidet pacifice, fuerunt eidem [153] confirmate vel provisum de novo per Urbanum viii° idus Julii anno primo,[154] et non taxata, sed composuit medio iuramento pro xiii li. vi s. viii d., solvit in partem dicte compositionis xl s.[155]

De parochiali ecclesia Omnium Sanctorum de Bredstret' (All Hallows, Breadstreet) Londonie cuius collatio et provisio facte auctoritate ordinaria ad presentationem patroni Johanni de Cliston', presbytero iurisdictionis imedietate curie Cantuariensis, fuerunt eidem confirmate vel provisum de novo xiii kalendas Octobris anno ii°,[156] et taxata viii li., solvit pro complemento dicte taxe viii li.

Summa pagine et diocesis x li.[157]

### (fol. 155^v) Wynthoniensis

De canonicatu et prebenda de Tymberbury (Tims-

---

[141] 25 November 1360.
[142] In the margin: *Resta v° v fl. xx sterl.*
[143] 25 November 1362.
[144] In the margin: *Resta ii li.*
[145] Remainder of the sentence om. **b.**
[146] *Urbanum* repeated and deleted by a line, **a.**
[147] Over *Sancte* deleted by dots, **a.**
[148] 17 January 1363.

[149] In the margin: *Resta secundum antiquam taxam iiii li. secundum novam nichil.*
[150] Entry in **a** only.
[151] Follows *Martii* deleted by a line, **a.**
[152] 20 October 1364.
[153] *fuit*, MSS.
[154] 8 July 1363.
[155] In the margin: *Resta xi li. vi s. viii d.*
[156] 19 September 1364.
[157] *et diocesis* om. **a.**

bury) in ecclesia monialium de Romeseye (Romsey) ordinis Sancti Benedicti Wynthoniensis diocesis, vacantibus per obitum Willelmi de Farbeth' extra curiam defuncti, cuius collatio et provisio auctoritate ordinaria facte Waltero de Sevenhinton' fuerunt eidem confirmate vel provisum de novo et subrogatus in iure quod eidem Willelmo et quondam Andree de Offord in eisdem competebat per Urbanum vii idus Julii anno primo,[158] in partem taxe que est xxviii li. xiii s. iiii d., xl s.

Summa pagine patet.

### (fol. 156) Saresburiensis

De parochiali ecclesia de Wayboyouse (Way Baieuse) diocesis Saresburiensis, taxata viii li., cuius collatio facta per episcopum Saresburiensem Johanni Pikerell', presbytero Lincoliensis diocesis, fuit eidem confirmata vel provisum de novo, non obstante defectu natalium quem patitur de presbytero genitus et soluta, et fuit habilitatus per Urbanum ii kalendas Septembris anno primo,[159] in partem dicte taxe xxvi s. viii d.[160]

De precentoria in ecclesia Saresburiensi, que dignitas curata existit, taxata xxxiii li. vi s. viii d., vacante et reservata per mortem Philipi de Codefford extra curiam Romanam defuncti, collata Rotberto de Waltham per Urbanum viii° idus Novembris anno tertio,[161] et debet dimittere decanatum libere capelle infra castrum de Wallingfford diocesis Saresburiensis, in partem dicte taxe xiii li. vi s. viii d.[162]

Summa pagine et diocesis xiiii li. xiii s. iiii d.

### (fol. 156ᵛ) Exoniensis

De collatione et provisione ex causa permutationis factis [163] Willelmo Seerel de archidiaconatu Tattonie in ecclesia Exoniensi, non taxato, pro ecclesia parochiali de Daddyngton' (Doddington) Lincoliensis diocesis sibi confirmatis [164] vel provisum de novo per Urbanum vii° kalendas Maii anno primo,[165] ex compositione facta medio iuramento pro mediis fructibus exceptis procurationibus pro xxxi li. x s., in partem dicte compositionis xi li. x s.[166]

De decanatu, canonicatu et prebenda ecclesie Exoniensis, cuius acceptatio, collatio et provisio facte vigore litterarum apostolicarum per Rotbertum [167] Sumpt', legum doctorem, dum vacarent per obitum Rotberti Hemeward et Reginaldi de Begwell' extra curiam Romanam defunctorum [168] fuerunt confirmate vel provisum de novo per Urbanum iii idus Octobris anno

primo,[169] decanatus taxatur ad lxii li. xiii s. iiii d. et prebenda ad iiii li., de quibus solvit in partem dictarum taxarum xxii li. iiii s. v d. ob.[170]

Summa pagine xxxiii li. xiiii s. v d. ob.

### (fol. 157) Wygorniensis

De parochiali ecclesia Sancte Wereburge Bristol', de qua per resignationem Hugonis de Penbrgh' fuit provisum Johanni de Aldebury per Urbanum v idus Junii anno ii°,[171] pro taxa iiii li. vi s. viii d.

Summa pagine patet.[172]

### (fol. 157ᵛ) Lincoliensis

De vicaria perpetua parochialis ecclesie de Chirkebury (Charlbury), de qua ex causa permutationis cum vicaria de Offynton' (Uffington) fuit provisum Rotberto Frankeley per Urbanum xiii kalendas Aprilis anno ii°,[173] in partem taxe dicte vicarie v li.[174]

De parochiali ecclesia de Frysby iuxta Waynfflet (Firsby near Wainfleet) Lincoliensis diocesis ex causa permutationis fuit provisum Johanni Attewade de Hannewoth' iii kalendas Augusti anno ii°,[175] que taxatur xii li. xvi s. viii d., in partem dicte taxe vi li. iii s. iiii d.[176]

De vicaria de Fiskenay (Friskney), de qua ex causa permutationis fuit provisum Rogero de Slatoburn', taxata v li., in partem ii li. x s.[177]

Summa pagine xiii s. iiii d.

### (fol. 158) Eboracensis

De canonicatu et prebenda in capella Sanctorum Marie et Angelorum Eboraci, vacantibus in curia per obitum Nicholai de Whyteby, cuius collatio facta per ordinarium auctoritate apostolica Thome de Middelton', presbytero Lincoliensis diocesis, fuit eidem confirmata per Urbanum iii kalendas Maii anno primo,[178] pro taxa v li.

De parochiali ecclesia de Stretton' (Sturton) Eboracensis diocesis, cuius institutio, admissio et inductio facte de Richardo de Redfford', iurisperto, qui eam per xv annos tenuit et adhuc tenet pacifice, fuerunt eidem confirmate per Urbanum ii kalendas Maii anno primo,[179] in partem taxe que est xliiii li., xi li.[180]

De vicaria perpetua parochialis ecclesie de Sutton' in Galtrys (Sutton in Galtres) Eboracensis diocesis, taxata ad novam taxam v li., vacante per obitum Henrici

---

[158] 9 July 1363.
[159] 31 August 1363.
[160] In the margin: *Resta vi li. xiii s. iiii d.*
[161] 6 November 1364.
[162] In the margin: *Resta xx li.*
[163] *facte*, b.
[164] *confirmata*, b.
[165] 25 April 1363.
[166] In the margin: *Resta xx li.*
[167] Follows *Willelmum* deleted by dots.
[168] *defuncti*, a.

[169] 13 October 1363.
[170] In the margin: *Resta xliiii li. viii s. x d. ob.*
[171] 9 June 1364.
[172] Sentence om. b.
[173] 20 March 1364.
[174] In the margin: *Resta.*
[175] 30 July 1364.
[176] In the margin: *Resta vi li. xii s. viii d.*
[177] In the margin: *Resta ii li. x s.*
[178] 29 April 1363.
[179] 30 April 1363.
[180] In the margin: *Resta xxxiii li.*

de Burton', ultimi vicarii eiusdem, cuius presentatio, institutio et inductio in possessionem facte auctoritate ordinaria Willelmo de Hirton', priori prioratus de Merton' (Marton) ordinis Sancti Augustini Eboracensis diocesis, fuerunt eidem confirmate vel provisum de novo per Urbanum iii kalendas Junii anno primo,[181] in plenam solutionem dicte taxe v li.

Dispensatum fuit cum Johanne Daygnie, clerico Wygorniensis diocesis ut parochialem ecclesiam de Ilkelay (Ilkley) Eboracensis diocesis, quam pacifice possidet, licite possit obtinere, non obstante defectu natalium quem patitur de soluto genitus et soluta, que taxatur ad novam taxam xxvi m., que valent xvii li. vi s. viii d., in partem dicte taxe vi li. xiii s. iiii d.[182]

De perpetua vicaria parochialis ecclesie de Donkastre (Doncaster), non taxata, vacante per obitum Johannis de Gisbourn' fuit provisum Alano de Rosen per Urbanum xv kalendas Octobris anno iiº,[183] in partem fructuum composuit xvi li. xiii s. iiii d., viii li. vi s. viii d.[184]

Summa pagine et diocesis xxxvi li.

Summa precendentium beneficiorum collatorum per Dominum Urbanum tempore suprascripto cxx li. vii s. ix d. ob.

(fol. 158ᵛ) Sequitur recepta de quibusdam beneficiis existentibus in manibus camere tempore vacationis.

De decanatu Eboracensi et prebenda de Strenssal' (Strensal) in ecclesia Eboracensi, vacantibus per obitum domini cardinalis Petragoricensis, qui obiit xvii die Januarii anno LXIIIIº secundum computationem ecclesie Romane, videlicet pro primo anno vacationis iiiiᶜ lx li.

Item de [185] eodem decanatu in partem fructuum secundi [186] anni vacationis per obitum dicti domini cardinalis iiᶜ li.[187]

Item de prebenda de Thame in ecclesia Lincoliensi, vacante per obitum dicti domini cardinalis pro primo anno vacationis cxlviii li. vi s. viii d.

Summa pagine de fructibus beneficiorum existentium in manibus camere [188] viiiᶜ viii li. vi s. viii d.

(fol. 159) De legatis ad Terram Sanctam
Item recepte [189] fuerunt de legatis ad subsidium Terre Sancte x li.
Summa pagine patet.

Sequitur recepta facta per me post computa mea de quibusdam restis certorum beneficiorum Dominorum Raymundi et Hugonis Pelegrini

---

[181] 30 May 1363.
[182] In the margin: *Resta x li. xiii s. iiii d.*
[183] 17 September 1364.
[184] In the margin: *Resta viii li. vi s. viii d.*
[185] *de* repeated, **a.**
[186] *secundi* repeated and deleted, **a.**
[187] In the margin: *Resta iiᶜ li.*
[188] *de fructibus . . . camere* om. **b.**
[189] *recepti*, **b.**

## Lincoliensis

Primo de prebenda de Coringham (Corringham) in ecclesia Lincoliensi, taxata viˣˣ vi li. xiii s. iiii d., collata Domino Raymundo Pelegrini, dimissa pro complemento taxe in arayragiis in lxxiii li. vi s. viii d., pro complemento lxxiii li. vi s. viii d.

## Saresburiensis

Item de prebenda de Heword (Highworth) in ecclesia Saresburiensi, taxata c li., collata Domino Raymundo Pelegrini, dimissa in arayragiis pro complemento taxe in xlvi li. xiii s. iiii d., xlvi li. xiii s. iiii d.

Item de prebenda de Stok (East Stoke) in ecclesia Lincoliensi, taxata lxxxvi li. xiii s. iiii d., collata Domino Hugoni Pelegrini, reperta remanere in arayragiis pro complemento taxe in liii li. vi s. viii d., pro complemento liii li. s. viii d.

Summa premissarum trium restarum solutarum clxxiii li. vi s. viii d.

(fol. 159ᵛ) Summa omnium receptarum particularium
Summa de denariis Beati Petri tam de arayragiis quam de aliis iiᶜ xli li. xi s. viii d.

Summa de annuo censu tam pro arayragiis quom pro aliis viii li. x s. i d.

Summa de arayragiis beneficiorum mˡᵉ xxviii li. viii s. v d.

Summa de annatis beneficiorum collatorum post ultima computa cxx li. vii s. ix d. ob. sterlingorum.

Summa de vacationibus beneficiorum existentium in manibus camere viiiᶜ viii li. vi s. viii d. sterlingorum.

Summa de legatis ad Terram Sanctam x li.

Summa universalis omnium premissarum summarum iiᵐ iiᶜ xvii li. iiii s. vii d. ob.

Summa arayragiorum beneficiorum Dominorum Hugonis et Raymundi Pelegrini, de quibus in precedenti pagina clxxiii li. vi s. viii d.

Et sic est summa universalis omnium receptorum tam per me quam per Dominum Johannem de Caroloco, locumtenentem meum post ultima computa iiᵐ iiiᶜ xc li. xi s. iii d. ob. sterlingorum,[190] inclusis xiiii li. xi s. viii d. receptis pro xcv fl. camere que diminuunt summam florenorum dimissam in arreragiis precedentibus. Approbatum.

(fol. 160) Secuntur assignationes facte per Johannem de Cabrespino, doctorem decretorum canonicum Narbonensem, de quibuscumque pecuniis per eum vel per Dominum Johannem de Caroloco, priorem Lewensem locumtenentem suum in officio collectorie Anglie, ad cameram apostolicam spectantibus, quovismodo receptis, habitis et levatis, a penultima die mensis Februarii anno domini MCCCLXIIIIᵗᵒ secundum computationem ecclesie Romane, quo tempore dictus Johannes de Anglia recessit, usque ad xx diem mensis Maii anno domini

---

[190] The remainder of the entry om. **b.**

MCCCLXVI<sup>to</sup>, quo tempore presentes rationes fuerunt de Anglia eidem Johanni misse, inclusis ii<sup>m</sup> fl. ponderis camere signatis die xxii mensis Junii, et iiii<sup>m</sup> fl. eiusdem ponderis assignatis die iii mensis Julii, et quinque milia assignatis ix die eiusdem mensis Julii, ut in principio sequentis pagine patet

Primo assignavit camere apostolice per manus Nicolai Lambertesqui, de Florentia, factoris et procuratoris Domini Nicolai Jacobi de Albertis Antiquis, militis de Florentia, anno domini MCCCLXIIII° et die xxvii mensis Novembris iii<sup>c</sup> lxii [191] li. viii s. iiii d. sterlingorum [192] in ii<sup>m</sup> viii<sup>c</sup> xxiiii fl. camere xx s. monete Avinionie.

Item anno domini MCCCLXV et die iii mensis Januarii in propria persona in mille fl. ponderis camere, quolibet floreno pro tribus s. et ii d. computato, clviii li. vi s. viii d. sterlingorum.

(fol. 160<sup>v</sup>) Item assignavit camere antedicte die xxii mensis Junii anno predicto LXVI<sup>to</sup> duo milia fl. Item assignavit iii die Julii anni predicti iiii<sup>or</sup> milia fl. ponderis camere. Item assignavit ix die Julii anno predicto quinque milia fl. ponderis antedicti. Que summe florenorum predictorum ascendunt in universo xi<sup>m</sup> fl. ponderis antedicti, qui floreni valent in summa, quolibet eorum pro tribus solidis sterlingorum computato, prout factum fuit cambium predictum cum Albertis Antiquis, mercatoribus de Florentia, vel cum sociis et factoribus ipsorum m vi<sup>c</sup> l li. sterlingorum.

Item assignavit in aurisiis [193] emptis pro domino nostro papa, traditis Domino Bernardo de Sancto Stephano, anno predicto die xxv Septembris lx li. [194]

Summa omnium assignatorum mm<sup>lia</sup> cccxxx [195] li. xv s. sterlingorum,[196] inclusis xiiii li. xi s. viii d. receptis pro xcv fl. camere, que diminuunt summam florenorum dimissam in arreragiis precedentibus,[197] que quidem summa fuit assignata in xiiii<sup>m</sup> viii<sup>c</sup> et xxiiii fl. xx s. monete Avinionie et inclusis lx li. sterlingorum in sua specie.

Secuntur expense facte tam pro certis aurifriziis emptis quam pro aliis negotiis cameram tangentibus ab ultimis computis citra.[198]

Item tradidit dictus Johannes de Caroloco, locumtenens meus, Berengario Ferarii pro veniendo ad curiam et redeundo pro expensis suis ad denuntiandum arrestum appositum in pecuniis camere et ad sciendum voluntatem camere [199] si pecunie eidem camere debite in Anglia reciperentur sub predicto arresto vel dimitterentur in manibus debitorum et pro quibusdam aliis viatgiis per ipsum factis occasione predicta, prout particulariter declarabit dictus Johannes de Caroloco et Berengarius predictus, ix li.[200]

Item solvit dictus Dominus Johannes de Caroloco pro quibusdam necessariis emptis pro officio, videlicet pergameno, papiro, cera et aliis iii li. vi s. viii d.

Item pro expensis diversorum nuntiorum per ipsum, Dominum Johannem de Caroloco, missorum ad diversas partes pro negotiis cameram tangentibus xv s. vi d.

Summa pagine xiii li. ii s. ii d.[201]

(fol. 161<sup>v</sup>) Item anno domini MCCCLXV tradidi Berengario Ferarii, quem misi ad Angliam pro negotiis camere, videlicet cum regestris beneficiorum in Anglia collatorum et bullis certis directis prelatis Anglie super executionem faciendum vigorose pro debitis camere et quibusdam aliis scripturis cameram tangentibus, pro expensis suis viii francos. Valent xxvi s. viii d. sterlingorum.[202]

Item pro uno roncino sibi empto xii fl camere. Valent xxxvi s. sterlingorum.

Item pro loquerio hospitii pro duobus annis, pro quolibet vi li. xiii s. iiii d., prout semper consuevit computari, xiii li. vi s. viii d.

Summa pagine xvi li. xix [203] s. iiii d.[204]

Summa expensarum est xxx li. i s. vi d. Approbatum.

Et sic est summa omnium assignatorum et expensarum [205] ii<sup>m</sup> iii<sup>c</sup> lx li. xv s. Approbatum.

Factis vero deductione et compenssatione de receptis et levatis, qui sunt in summa ii<sup>m</sup> iii<sup>c</sup> xc li. et xi s. iiii d. ob., ad assignationes, solutiones et expenssas, que sunt in summa ii<sup>m</sup> iii<sup>c</sup> lx li. xv s. sterlingorum, aparet dictum collectorem debere camere pro predicto tempore xxix li. xvi s. iii d. ob. sterlingorum.

### (fol. 162) Anglia [206]

Compotum Domini Johannis de Cabrespino, collectoris Anglie, abreviatum et assummatum de omnibus emolumentis nomine camere apostolice in dicta collectoria tam per se quam per Dominum Johannem de Caroloco, priorem Lewensem locumtenentem suum in

---

[191] iiii<sup>c</sup> lxii, **b.**
[192] The remainder of the sentence, om. **b.**
[193] For aurifriziis.
[194] Item om. **b.**
[195] mm<sup>lia</sup> ccixx, **b.**
[196] The remainder of the entry om. **b.**
[197] In the margin: approbatum.
[198] The first item in **a** is deleted by lines and has noted against it in the margin: cancellatur quia supra ponitur inter assignationes. It reads: Primo expendi de mandato domini thesaurarii pro certis aurifriziis emptis pro domino nostro papa lx li. The item is not deleted in **b.**
[199] Followed by s deleted by a line, **a.**
[200] The following entry, which is deleted by lines in **a**, reads: Item tradidit dictus Johannes de Caroloco dicto Berengario pro expensis factis in recipienda possessionem (possessione, a) prebende de Stranssal' (Strensal) pro domino cardinali Ostiensi (Elias de S. Eredio) que ad manus camere tenetur et dicto domino cardinali de vi<sup>c</sup> fl. auri annis singulis pro ea, licet tamen non valeat, respondetur vii li. x s. The item is not deleted in **b.**
[201] lxxx li. xii s. ii d., **b.**
[202] Sentence om. **a.**
[203] ix, **b.**
[204] The next three items om. **b.**
[205] est repeated, **a.**
[206] The following abbreviated account is placed at the end of **b** on folios 260 to 262<sup>v</sup>.

dicta collectoria, receptis et levatis et expensis et assignationibus, prout in libro compotorum suorum dicte camere assignato plenius sive seriosius continetur, videlicet a penultima die mensis Februarii de anno domini M° CCC° LXIIII° usque ad xx diem mensis Maii de anno domini M° CCC° LXVI^to

Et primo de receptis titulorum sequentium

De arrayragiis denariorum Beati Petri in aliis precedentibus suis compotis dimissorum xlvii li.

De recepta ordinaria census dictorum denariorum Beati Petri cxciiii li. xi s. viii d.

Summa totalis tam de arrayragiis quam de ordinariis dictorum denariorum ii^c xli li. xi s. viii d.

Summa pagine ii^c xli li. xi s. viii d.

(fol. 162^v) De annuis censibus viii li. x s. i d.

De arrayragiis primorum fructuum beneficiorum collatorum seu confirmatorum per sedem apostolicam et eius auctoritate mille xxviii li. viii s. v d.,[207] inclusis xiiii li. xi s. viii d. receptis pro xcv fl. camere.

De annatis beneficiorum collatorum post eius ultima compota cxx li. vii s. ix d. ob.

De fructibus beneficiorum existentium in manu camere viii^c viii li. vi s. viii d.

De legatis in subsidium Terre Sancte x li.

De quibusdam restis quorumdam beneficiorum Dominorum Hugonis et Raymundi Pelegrini quas idem collector post ultima sua compota levavit clxxiii li. vi s. viii d.

Summa universalis omnium scriptarum receptarum tam per se quam per dictum eius locumtenentem in dicto tempore levatarum ii^m iii^c xc li. xi s. iii d. ob. sterlingorum,[207] inclusis xiiii li. xi s. viii d. receptis pro xcv fl. camere, que [208] diminuunt summam florenorum dimissam in arreyragiis precedentibus. Approbatum.

Item aparet ultra predictam dictum(?) debere per finem aliorum compotorum xxviii li. iiii s. ii d. 1 fl. fortes cl fl. de croseta.[209]

(fol. 163) Secundo computat idem collector de assignatis per eum seu alios suo nomine a dicta die penultima Februarii dicti anni MCCCLXIIII^ti usque ad xx diem Maii anni suprascripti MCCCLXVI^ti, inclusis ii^m florenis ponderis camere assignatis die xxii mensis Junii et iiii^m fl. eiusdem ponderis assignatis die iii mensis Julii et v^m assignatis ix die predicti mensis Julii, ut infra continentur [210] in principio sequentis pagine.

Primo assignavit apostolice camere per manus Nicholai Lambertesqui de Florentia, factoris Domini Nicholai Jacobi de Albertis Antiquis, militis de Florentia, anno domini M° CCC° LXIIII^to die xxvii Novembris iiii^c lxii li. viii s. iiii d. Approbatum.[211]

Item anno domini millesimo trecentesimo LXV^to die iii mensis Januarii in persona sua in mille fl. ponderis camere, quolibet pro tribus solidis et ii denariis computato [212] clviii li. vi s. viii d.

(fol. 163^v) Item assignavit dicte camere dicto anno domini millesimo CCC° LXVI^to die xxii mensis Junii duo milia fl.

Item die iii Julii anni eiusdem quatuor milia et die ix mensis Julii et anni predicti v^m fl. ponderis predicti que summe faciunt xi^m fl. dicti ponderis, qui floreni valent in summa, quolibet computato pro tribus solidis sterlingorum, m^le vi^c 1 li. sterlingorum.

Item assignavit in aurifriziis emptis pro domino nostro papa, traditis Domino Bernardo de Sancto Stephano anno predicto die xxv Septembris lx li.[211]

Summa omnium assignatorum a dicta die penultima Februarii de anno domini millesimo CCC° LXIIII^to usque ad predictam xx diem mensis Maii de anno domini millesimo CCC° LXVI^to, de quo tempore facit conclusionem quo ad receptas et expensas et etiam usque ad predictam ix diem Julii de anno predicto LXVI in quo termino facit conclusionem quo ad assignationes pecuniarum, est ii^m iii^c xxx li. xv s.[213] sterlingorum,[210] inclusis xiiii li. xi s. viii d. receptis pro xcv fl. camere, que diminuunt summam florenorum dimissam in arreyragiis precedentibus, que quidem summa fuit assignata camere in xiiii^m viii^c xxiiii fl. camere xx s. monete Avinionie et lx li. sterlingorum in sua specie.

(fol. 164) Tertio collector predictus computat de expensis factis [214]

Item [215] pro denuntiando camere arrestum appositum in pecuniis tam in mittendo de [216] Anglia ad curiam quam in reditu nuntii ix li.[217]

Item pro pargamenis, papiro, cera et quibusdam aliis iii li. vi s. viii d.

Item pro diversis nuntiis missis ad diversas partes collectorie xv s. vi d.

Item pro mittendis in Angliam regestris beneficiorum viii francos; valent xxxvi s. viii d.

Item pro uno roncino xii fl; valent xxxvi s.

Item computat de duabus annatis pro loquerio hospitii xiii li. vi s. viii d.

Summa xxx li. i s. vi d.[218]

---

[212] *computatoto,* **a.**
[213] *ii^m cclxx li. xv s. sterlingorum* **b.**
[214] Followed by *tam pro emptione quorumdam aurifrisiorum quam aliis, ut sequuntur* deleted by a line. The first item, deleted by lines, in **a,** reads: *Primo dicit se expendisse de mandato domini thesaurarii pro emendis certis aurifrisiis lx li.* In the margin *supra ponitur inter assignationes.*
[215] In the margin: *primo,* **a.**
[216] *in,* **a.**
[217] The next item, which is deleted by lines in **a,** reads: *Item pro recipienda possessione prebende de ⟨Stranssal'⟩ pro domino cardinali Ostiensi vii li. x s.*
[218] The sum is repeated twice and deleted by a line once, **a;** om. **b.**

[207] The remainder of the item om. **b.**
[208] Followed by *quod valent* deleted by a line.
[209] Item om. **b.**
[210] The remainder of the sentence om. **b.**
[211] Om. **b.**

(fol. 164ᵛ) Summa omnium predictorum expensorum xxx li. sterlingorum.²¹⁹

Summa universalis omnium assignatorum et expensorum, ut predicitur, iiᵐ iiiᶜ lx li. xv s.²¹⁹Approbatum.²²⁰

Factis vero deductione et compenssatione de receptis et levatis, qui sunt in summa iiᵐ iiiᶜ xc li. xi s. iiii d. ob., ad assignata, soluta et expenssas, que sunt in summa iiᵐ iiiᶜ lx li. xv s. sterlingorum per dictum collectorem, aparet ipsum debere camere quia plus recepit quam assignavit xxix li. xvi s. iii d. ob.²²¹

(fol. 165)²²² Item dat in restis de denariis Beati Petri debitas per diversas perssonas viᶜ viii l. xvi s. iiii d.²²³

Item de annuo censsu ix li. xi s. ix d.²²⁴

Item de annatis benefficiorum, ut in libro particulariter aparet, iiiᵐ vᶜ lxi li. v s. viii d. ob., vel circa; etiam vᶜ lxiii fl. xx d. sterlingorum.

Et sic est summa universalis omnium restarum premissarum iiiiᵐ clxxix li.²²⁵ xiii s. ix d. ob. sterlingorum vel circa; vᶜ lxiii fl., xx d. sterlingorum. Approbatum.

(fol. 166)²²⁶ Secuntur reste arrayragiorum denariorum Beati Petri

Archidiaconus Cantuariensis pro annis LXV et LXVI, pro quolibet viii li., xvi li.

Archidiaconus Roffensis pro annis LXIII, LXIIII, LXV et LXVI, pro quolibet v li. xii s., xxii li. viii s.

Archidiaconus Colcestrie pro annis LXIIIIᵒ, LXV et LXVI, pro quolibet v li. x s., xvi li. x s.²²⁷

Episcopus Cicestrensis pro annis LXIII, LXIIII, LXV et LXVI, pro quolibet viii li., xxxii li.

Archidiaconus Exssey pro annis LXIIII, LXV et LXVIᵒ, pro quolibet v li. x s., xvi li. x s.

Archidiaconus Midelssexie pro annis LX, LXI, LXII et LXIII, LXIIII, LXV et LXVI, pro quolibet v li. x s. xxxviii li. x s.²²⁸

Archidiaconus Wyntoniensis pro annis LXII, LXIII, LXIIII, LXV et LXVI, pro quolibet xi li. xiii s. iiii d., lviii li. vi s. viii d.

Archidiaconus Surreie pro annis LXV et LXVIᵒ, pro quolibet v li. xiii s. iiii d., xi li. vi s. viii d.

Episcopus Saresburiensis pro annis LXIIII, LXV et LXVI, pro quolibet xvii li., li li.

Episcopus Bathoniensis et Wellensis pro annis LXIII, LXIIII, LXV et LXVI, pro quolibet xi li. v s., xlv li.
Summa pagine iiiᶜ vii li. xi s. iiii d.²²⁹

(fol. 166ᵛ)²³⁰ Episcopus Exoniensis pro anno LXVI ix li. v s.

Archidiaconus Eliensis pro annis LXIIIIᵒ, LXV et LXVI, pro quolibet v li., xv li.

Episcopus Norwicensis pro annis LXV et LXVI, pro quolibet xxi li. x s., xliii li.

Episcopus Lincoliensis pro annis LXIIII, LXV et LXVI, pro quolibet xlii li., cxxvi li.

Episcopus Convetrensis pro annis LXIIII, LXV et LXVI, pro quolibet x li. v s., xxx²³¹ li. xv s.

Episcopus Herffordensis pro annis LXV et LXVI, pro quolibet vi li., xii li.

Episcopus Wigorniensis pro annis LXV et LXVI et debet pro tertio,²³² pro quolibet x li. v s., xxx li. xv s.²³³

Archiepiscopus Eboracensis pro annis LXIIII, LXV et LXVI, pro quolibet xi li. x s., xxxiiii li. x s.
Summa pagine iiiᶜ i li. v s.²³⁴

Summa universalis restarum omnium denariorum Beati Petri viᶜ viii li. xvi s. iiii d.²³⁵

(fol. 167) Reste de annuo censu
Abbas de Faveresham Cantuariensis diocesis pro annis LXIIII, LXV et LXVI, pro quolibet xiii s. iiii d., ii li.

Prior Tenebrib' pro anno LXVI xiii s. iiii d.

Abbas de Cortestye pro annis LXV et LXVI, pro quolibet viii s., xvi s.

Abbas Sancti Edmundi Norwicensis diocesis pro anno LXVI xiii s. iiii d.

Prior de Bodmyne pro anno LXVI ii s.

Abbas Sancti Albani Lincoliensis diocesis pro anno LXVI xiii s. iiii d.

### Saresburiensis

Abbas Sancti Aldelmy Malesbury pro anno LXVI xiii s. iiii d.

### Londoniensis

Abbatissa et sorores Sancte Clare Londonie, que dant annuatim i li. cere et solvunt pro ea vi d., pro annis LXV et LXVI, pro quolibet vi d., xii d.

Prior de Chaucombe pro annis LXIII, LXIIII, LXV et LXVI, pro quolibet xv d., v s.

Prior de Angleseye, qui dat quolibet anno ii s., pro annis LXV et LXVI iiii s.

---

²¹⁹ The sum is omitted in **b**.
²²⁰ Om. **b**.
²²¹ Item om. **b**.
²²² The items on this folio are lacking in **b**.
²²³ Follows *viᶜ xvi li. vi s. iiii d.* deleted by a line.
²²⁴ Follows *viii li. xviii s. v d.* deleted by a line.
²²⁵ Followed by *v s. v d.* deleted by a line.
²²⁶ Folio 165ᵛ is blank.
²²⁷ *xxii li.,* **b**.
²²⁸ Followed in **a** by an entry which reads: *Item, idem pro annis LX, LXI, LXII, pro quolibet v li. x s.,—xvi li. x s.* and this entry is deleted by a line. In **b**, where the folio is numbered 226, there are two separate entries for this item; one for years LXIII, LXIV, LXV, LXVI for £22, and one for years LX, LXI, LXII for £16 10s.

²²⁹ *iiiᶜ xiii li. i s. iiii d.,* **b**.
²³⁰ At the top of the page is the heading: *De denariis Beati Petri.*
²³¹ *xxxi,* **b**.
²³² *et debet pro tertio* om. **b**.
²³³ *xx li. x s.,* **b**.
²³⁴ *iiᶜxcii li.,* **b**.
²³⁵ Follows *viᶜ xv li. xi s. iiii d.,* deleted by a line, in **a**; but the sum is given in **b** as *vᶜ lxxxviii li. xi s. iiii d.*

Custos ecclesie de Scandeburgh' pro annis LXIIII, LXV et LXVI, pro quolibet xv d., iii s. ix d.

Prior ecclesie Karliolensis pro annis LXII,[236] LXIII, LXIIII, LXV et LXVI, pro quolibet xiii s. iiii d., iii li. vi s. viii d.[237]

Summa pagine ix li. xi s. ix d.[238]

(fol. 167ᵛ) Reste arrayragiorum dimissorum in aliis computis de annatis beneficiorum.[239]

### Cantuariensis

De ecclesia de Stokebury (Stockbury), que fuit appropriata priori et conventui de Lodes (Leeds) per Clementem viii idus Augusti anno xi,[240] taxata xxvii li. vi s. viii d., vii li. vi s. viii d.

De cappella libera de Bokineffeld' (Bockingfold), cuius taxa et provisio in aliis computis, fructus.

### Roffensis

De ecclesia de Staton' (Stone) Roffensis diocesis, cuius taxa et provisio in aliis arayragiis, dimissa in x li., de quibus solvit v li., restant v li.

### Londoniensis

De capella seu ecclesia de Stafford' (Stanford le Hope), le qua per obitum Edmundi de Grymmesby fuit provisum ⟨Johanni⟩ de Torkesey per Innocentium viii idus Octobris anno iiᵒ,[241] pro taxa xxvi li. xiii s. iiii d.[242]

De ecclesia Sancte Trinitatis Londonie, non taxata, de qua fuit dispensatum cum Thoma Ball' ut, non obstante defectu natalium, possit eam retinere per Innocentium xi kalendas Junii anno nono,[243] qui composuit pro mediis fructibus ad v li., dimissa in arayragiis in l s., de quibus solvit xxv s., restant xxv s.

Summa pagine xl li. v s. Item i beneficium non taxatum.

(fol. 168) De ecclesia de Herlawe (Harlow), de qua per obitum Ricardi Drax fuit provisum Johanni Paker per Innocentium xi kalendas Junii anno nono,[243] pro tota taxa xiii li. vi s. viii d.

De prioratu Sancte Crucis Londonie (Holy Cross, London), non taxato, qui fuit confirmatus Johanni Burys per Innocentium xii kalendas Junii anno xᵒ,[244] fructus.

De archidiaconatu de Midelsseye, de quo fuit pro-

visum cardinali Rothomagensi [245] per Innocentium xiiii kalendas Decembris anno vi,[246] fructus.

De archidiaconatu Exexie in ecclesia Londoniensi, non taxato, qui composuit pro mediis fructibus in v li. xiii s. iiii d., de quibus solvit lvi s. viii d., restant lvi s. viii d.

De ecclesia de Herlawe (Harlow), de qua per assecutionem archidiaconatus Tortonie (Totnes) fuit provisum Ricardo Anglici per Innocentium vii idus Maii anno viii,[247] pro taxa xiii li. vi s. viii d.

De ecclesia sive capella de Delswik (Alswick), de qua ex causa permutationis fuit provisum Rotberto Franceys per Urbanum iii nonas Januarii anno primo,[248] composuit pro medietate fructuum, quia non taxatur, xxxiii s. iiii d.

De ecclesia de Langedon' (Langdon Hills), de qua ex simili causa fuit provisum Willelmo Swifferd' [249] dicto die, composuit medio iuramento ad xl s., de quibus solvit xiii s. iiii d., debet xxvi s. viii d.

De ecclesia Sancti Batolphi extra Delgate (St. Botolph, Aldgate) Londonie, collatio et provisio facte Radulpho de Cantabrigia, presbytero, canonico regularium domus Sancte Trinitatis Londonie, expresse professo per priorem et conventum dicte domus, fuerunt auctoritate apostolica confirmate v nonas Martii anno primo,[250] debentur fructus.[251]

Summa pagine xxxii li. x s. Item iii beneficia non taxantur.

(fol. 168ᵛ) De prebenda Sancti Pancratii in ecclesia Sancti Pauli Londonie fuit ex causa permutationis provisum Radulpho de Daventr' per Urbanum v nonas ⟨Martii⟩ anno primo,[252] pro taxa xlii s. vi d.

De ecclesia de Kynteston' [253] (Kentish Town) in ecclesia Londoniensi, taxata vi li. xiii s. iiii d., de qua per obitum Ade Murymouth' fuit provisum Rogero Holm' tam pro resta istius provisionis quam pro diversis aliis beneficiis, pro quibus partem satisfecit in camera, x li.[254]

### Cicestrensis

De archidiaconatu Lewensi, non taxato, qui fuit confirmatus Guillelmo de Lugteburgh' per Clementem ii idus Augusti anno xi,[255] fructus.

Item de eodem fuit provisum Thome Brenwen' per

---

[236] Om. b.
[237] ii li. xiii s. iiii d., b.
[238] viii li. xviii s. v d., b.
[239] de annatis beneficiorum om. b.
[240] 6 August 1352.
[241] 8 October 1354.
[242] In the margin: non habuit effectum quia dictus Johannes nunquam fuit rector.
[243] 22 May 1361.
[244] 21 May 1362.

[245] Peter de la Forêt, priest of Ss. XII Apostoli.
[246] 18 November 1358.
[247] 9 May 1360.
[248] 3 January 1363.
[249] Swiffeld', b.
[250] 3 March 1363.
[251] In the margin: non habuit effectum quia iste provisus omni iuri sibi competenti in dicta ecclesia, et iuravit ad sacra dei evangelia quod nunquam sibi fuit aliqua provisio facta, et est super hoc certificatorium episcopi.
[252] 3 March 1363.
[253] Over Kenaston' deleted by a line, a.
[254] In the margin of a: ostendit gratiam domini thesaurarii domini nostri pape.
[255] 12 August 1352.

Innocentium vii idus Septembris anno vi,[256] eo quod Guillelmus predictus fuit assecutus thesaurariam dicte ecclesie, fructus.

De ecclesia de Bukstede (Buxted), de qua per assecutionem prepositure de Wyngham (Wingham) per Johannem de Severle fuit provisum Valtero Sotton' per Innocentium iiii kalendas Aprilis anno [257] vi,[258] dimissa in arayragiis in xxxii li., de quibus solvit xx li., restant xii li.

De archidiaconatu Cicestrensi, non taxato, permutatio facta cum decanatu ecclesie collegiate Cestr' [259] super Stratam (Chester-le-Street) Dunelmensis [260] diocesis fuit Johanni de Skulthorp confirmata per Innocentium v kalendas Januarii anno primo,[261] fructus.

De prebenda de Waltham in ecclesia Cicestrensi, taxata x li., de qua per consecrationem Rotberti episcopi Conventrensi fuit provisum Ade de Hilton' x kalendas Januarii anno viii°,[262] x li.

Summa pagine xxxiiii li. ii s. vi d. Item ii beneficia. (fol. 169) De prebenda Iptorn' (Upthorne) in ecclesia Cicestrensi, de qua per obitum Thome David fuit provisum Philipo de Courtenay per Innocentium x kalendas Julii anno ix°,[263] pro taxa vi li. xiii s. iiii d.

De thesauraria Cicestrensi, ratione confirmationis facte Willelmo de Lugteburg, dimissa in arayragiis in xvi li. xiii s. iiii d., de quibus solvit vi li. xiii s. iiii d. restant x li.[264]

De prebenda de Sylox' (Selsey) in ecclesia Cicestrensi, de qua per obitum Johannis Leth fuit provisum Rotberto Deskely per Innocentium anno ix°,[265] pro resta dimissa xi li. vi s. viii d.

De vicaria de Iklesham (Icklesham), de qua fuit dispensatum cum Valtero de Straton' presbytero quod eam possit licite retinere per Innocentium ii idus Januarii [266] anno viii°,[267] dimissa in arayragiis in xvi li. xiiii s. iiii d. de quibus solvit x li., restant vi li. xiii s. iiii d.

De prioratu conventuali Lewensi ordinis Cluniacensis, vacante per assecutionem monasterii Trenothien' (Tournus) Cabilonensis (Châlon-sur-Saône) diocesis fac-

tam [268] per fratrem Hugonem de Chyncerato ultimi prioris dicti prioratus, fuit provisum fratri Geraldo Bothonis, monacho bachallario in decretis, fructus.[269]

De decanatu ecclesie Cicestrensi et canonicatu et prebenda sibi annexis, vacantibus [270] per consecrationem Willelmi episcopi Cicestrensis, fuit provisum Nicholao de Deston', magistro in sacra pagina, xi kalendas Decembris per Urbanum anno primo,[271] xlviii li. vi s. viii d.

Summa pagine lxxxiii li. Item ii beneficia.

### (fol. 169ᵛ) Wynthoniensis

De ecclesia de Westmunies (West Meon), taxata xx li., que fuit confirmata Johanni de Kenygton' per Clementem idus Maii anno viii°,[272] pro resta vi li.

De hospitali Sancte Crucis, non taxato, confirmato [273] Johanni de Edynghton' per Clementem xviii kalendas Junii anno viii,[274] vii li. iii s. vi d.

De prebenda de Midelton' (Middleton) in ecclesia monialium de Worwell' (Wherwell), de qua fuit provisum Johanni de Brenketre per Innocentium v kalendas Januarii anno primo,[275] dimissa in arayragiis in xxvi li. xiii s. iiii d. de quibus solvit vi li. xiii s. iiii d., restat xx li.

De prioratu de Apelburethorp' (Appuldurcombe) confirmato Johanni de Osanna per Clementem v kalendas Martii anno viii°,[276] xxv li. xvii s.

De ecclesia de Hovunte (Havant), taxata xxvi li. xiii s. iiii d., de qua per obitum Johannis Noion fuit provisum Johanni Wpewll' per Innocentium iiii° nonas Julii anno ix°,[277] dimissa in arayragiis in xx li., de quibus solvit xiii li. vi s. viii d., restant vi li. xiii s. iiii d.[278]

De ecclesia de Dinnteffaude (Dunsfold), taxata xiii li. vi s. viii d., de qua per obitum Guillelmi de Chasreton' fuit provisum Johanni de Bewos xix kalendas Februarii anno primo,[279] vi li. xiii s. iiii d.

De ecclesia de Newton' (Newington by Lambeth), taxata xiiii [280] li. vi s. viii d., dum vacabit per conse-

---

[256] 7 September 1358.

[257] Om. **a**.

[258] 29 March 1358.

[259] *Cicestrensis,* **a**.

[260] *Lincoliensis,* MSS.

[261] 28 December 1353; *anno vi°,* **b**.

[262] 23 December 1360.

[263] 22 June 1361.

[264] Followed by the item deleted by lines: *De archidiaconatu Lewensi in ecclesia Cicestrensi, quem Willelmus de Lutthenburgh predictus obtinebat, vacante per assecutionem dicte thesaurarie, fuit provisum Thome Bronwen per Innocentium vii idus Septembris anno vi°, fructus.* In the margin: *in precedenti pagina ponitur et ideo hic cancellatur.* In **b** the item is not deleted.

[265] 1361.

[266] Follows *Junii* not deleted, **a**.

[267] 12 January 1360.

[268] *facte,* MSS.

[269] In the margin of **b** only: *non habuit effectum, ut dicitur, quia vigore illius provisionis non fuit admissus, quia est de patronatu laicali.*

[270] Om. **a**.

[271] 21 November 1362.

[272] 15 May 1350.

[273] *confirmata,* MSS.

[274] 15 May 1350.

[275] 28 December 1353.

[276] 25 February 1350.

[277] 4 July 1361.

[278] The next item, which is deleted by lines in **a**, reads: *De ecclesia de Dertham (East Dereham), quam obtinuit Simon de Subur', episcopus Londoniensis, que fuit reservata conferenda Bartholomeo Sidey per Innocentium iii idus Decembris anno ix°, fructus vel taxa.* In the margin: *Debet esse in diocesi Norwicensi, et est et ideo hic cancellatur.*

[279] 14 January 1363.

[280] *iii li.,* **b**.

crationem [281] electi Dublinensis fuit provisum Thome de Eltesle per Urbanum xii kalendas Aprilis anno primo [282] xiiii [280] li. xiii s. iiii d.

De eadem ecclesia fuit provisum Guillelmo de Brink-hill' xvii kalendas Maii dicto anno,[283] que provisio non valet quia infra annum.

Summa pagine lxxv li. xiii s. x d. Item i beneficium.

### (fol. 170) Saresburiensis

De ecclesia de Kyvelegh' (Keevil), de qua fuit provisum Magistro Thome de Thrompeshawe, taxata xxvi li. xiii s. iiii d., pro resta dimissa vi li. xiii s. iiii d.

De prebenda de Wermynstr' (Warminster) in ecclesia Saresburiensi, de qua per obitum Johannis de Brambury fuit provisum Thome de Scraghull' per Clementem, v li.

Item de eadem prebenda par obitum Baldewyny de Morryn acceptatio facta per Bartholomeum de Brandon' fuit confirmata per Clementem vi idus Septembris anno ix°,[284] v li.

De prebenda de Hull' (Hill Deverill) in ecclesia collegiata de Hertelbury (Heytesbury), taxata vi li. xiii s. iiii d., de qua per obitum Rotberti Trek' fuit provisum Thome Patricii per Clementem viii idus Martii anno ix°,[285] iii li. vi s. viii d.

De ecclesia de Wynterburnn' Sakelan (Winterborne Stickland), de qua per resignationem Willelmi de Cheston' fuit provisum Thome Henrici per Innocentium xiiii kalendas Julii anno primo,[286] dimissa in arayragiis in iiii li. vi s. viii d., de quibus solvit xx s., restant iii li. vi s. viii d.

De prebenda de Stretton' (Stratton) in ecclesia Saresburiensi, de qua ex causa permutationis fuit provisum Johanni Turstayn per Innocentium idus Martii anno iii,[287] xiii li. vi s. viii d.

De prebenda de Hussebourn' et Brokach' (Husseburn and Burbage), de qua per obitum Johannis de Whitchurche fuit confirmata Saladino de Fallet' per Innocentium kalendas Junii anno vi,[288] liii li. vi s. viii d.

De prebenda de Bedmynstr' (Bedminster) in ecclesia Saresburiensi, de qua per resignationem Willelmi Hale fuit provisum Thome de Clipston' per Innocentium idus Decembris anno vi°,[289] xiii li. vi s. viii d.

De prebenda Saresburiensi acceptatio facta per Johannem Ufford Norwicensis diocesis fuit eidem confirmata per Innocentium vii kalendas Julii anno vii,[290] fructus.

Summa pagine ciii li. vi s. viii d. Item i beneficium.

(fol. 170ᵛ) [291] De prebenda de Clone (Calne) et thesauraria in dicta ecclesia, de quibus fuit provisum [292] cardinali Nemausenensi [293] lxxxvi li. xiii s. iiii d.

De ecclesia Sancti Petri de Wortham (Warham), de qua per resignationem Thome de Barneby fuit provisum Henrico Worth' per Innocentium v idus Octobris anno ix°,[294] iiii li. vi s. viii d.

De ecclesia de Assebury (Ashbury), taxata xxvi li. xiii s. iiii d., de qua obitum Walteri Motyn fuit provisum Thome de Biscopesbury per Innocentium iiii kalendas Octobris anno ix°,[295] de quibus solvit vi li. xiii s. iiii d., restant xvi li. xiii s. iiii d.[296]

De ecclesia de Corff' (Corfe Castle), de qua per assecutionem prepositure Saresburiensis per Philipum Coddefford' fuit provisum Simoni Thebaud' per Innocentium iii kalendas Novembris anno ix°,[297] x li.

De prebenda de Bedmynstr' (Bedminster) in ecclesia Saresburiensi, de qua per obitum Ricardi de Norwico fuit confirmata [298] Henrico de Wynton' per Innocentium xi kalendas Februarii anno xi°,[299] xiii li. vi s. viii d.

De prebenda de Roddeford' (Woodford), taxata xvi li. xiii s. iiii d., et archidiaconatu de Cestr' (Dorchester) in dicta ecclesia, taxato lxii [300] li., de quibus fuit provisum cardinali de Canilhaco, episcopo Penestrino, per Innocentium iiii idus Martii anno x°,[301] lxxviii [302] li. xiii s. iiii d.

De prebenda de Preston' in ecclesia Saresburiensi, de qua fuit provisum Thome de Sotton' per Innocentium xi kalendas Novembris anno v,[303] xvi li. xiii s. iiii d.

De prebenda de Biscopeston' (Bishopstone) in ecclesia Saresburiensi, de qua in omni iure quod competebat Arnaldo Pelegrini fuit subrogatus Arnaldus Gauryny presbyter per Innocentium idus Julii anno x°,[304] xx li.

De prebenda quam Johannes de Brukyngham, nunc episcopus Lincolyensis, obtinebat in ecclesia Saresburiensi fuit provisum Rotberto Sumpt', legum doctori, ii nonas Decembris per Urbanum anno primo,[305] fructus vel taxa.

De prebenda de Horton' in ecclesia Saresburiensi, de qua per obitum Ricardi de Tormenton' fuit provisum

---

[281] Follows *electionem* deleted by dots, **a**.
[282] 21 March 1363.
[283] 15 April 1363.
[284] 8 September 1350.
[285] 8 March 1351.
[286] 18 June 1353.
[287] 15 March 1355.
[288] 1 June 1358.
[289] 13 December 1358.
[290] 25 June 1359.
[291] The heading *Saresburiensis* is repeated at the top of the page.
[292] Followed by *the* deleted by a line, **a**.
[293] John de Blanzac, priest of S. Marco, bishop of Nimes.
[294] 11 October 1361.
[295] 28 September 1361.
[296] In the margin: *error est in taxa, quia non taxatur nisi ad xv m. (xxv m., b) ut patet in libro taxarum.*
[297] 30 October 1361.
[298] *confirmato*, **a**.
[299] 22 January 1361 or 1362. Presumably a mistake for ix or x.
[300] Follows the same sum deleted, **a**.
[301] 12 March 1362.
[302] *lxxix*, **b**.
[303] 22 October 1357.
[304] 15 July 1362.
[305] 4 December 1362.

Willelmo de Laugeberch' per Urbanum kalendas Januarii anno primo,[306] fructus vel taxa.

Summa pagine ii$^c$ xlvii li. vi s. viii d. Item duo beneficia.

(fol. 171)[291] De prebenda in ecclesia Saresburiensi, vacante per obitum Willemi Farleagh', collatio facta Nicolao de Luda, thesaurario domini regis, fuit eidem confirmata etiam si alio quovismodo vacet vel sit reservata valeat ac si vacasset per mortem dicti Guillelmi per Urbanum, fructus.[307]

De ecclesia de Doniton' (Downton), collatio et provisio eiusdem facte Thome de Edingndon' fuerunt eidem auctoritate apostolica confirmate vel provisum de novo xvii kalendas Maii per Urbanum,[308] lxvi li. xiii s. iiii d.

De prebenda in ecclesia Saresburiensi, videlicet Bedmynstr' (Bedminster), quam Ricardus de Norwico per nonnullos annos possedit, etiam si alio quovismodo vacet, provisio facta Henrico de Wynton', bacallario in legibus, fuit eidem confirmata vel provisum de novo v nonas Martii per Urbanum,[309] fructus.

### Exoniensis

De prebenda Exoniensi, taxata iiii li., que fuit confirmata Thome David per Clementem viii idus Maii anno x°,[310] iiii li.[311]

De prebenda Exoniensi, de qua per obitum Henrici de Bratheler fuit provisum Henrico de Walton' per Innocentium iiii kalendas Martii anno primo,[312] iiii li.

De portione parochialis ecclesie Sancte Endoliente (St. Endellion), de qua per obitum Willelmi Donne fuit provisum Simoni Whithull' per Innocentium iiii nonas Julii anno ix°,[313] fructus.[314]

De prebenda ecclesie Exoniensis, de qua per obitum Ricardi de Tormenton' et Willelmi de Brakdeley fuit provisum Ade de Ilton' per Innocentium iiii nonas Julii anno ix°, pro taxa iiii li.

Summa pagine lxxviii li. xiii s. iiii d. Item iii beneficia.

(fol. 171$^v$)[315] De ecclesia de Basch, de qua, ex eo quod Henricus de Monte dictam ecclesiam una cum alia pluribus annis tenuit etiam in presbyterum non promotus, fuit provisum Crenezeno de Lauf' per Innocentium vi kalendas Julii anno ix°,[316] fructus.[317]

De archidiaconatu Cornubie in ecclesia Exoniensi, non

taxato, de quo per obitum Thome David fuit provisum Alexandro Nevyll' per Innocentium x kalendas Septembris anno ix°.[318]

De prebenda Sancte Columbe minoris (St. Columb Minor) in ecclesia Sancti Karentoci (Crantock) fuit subrogatus in omni iure quod competebat David Maynard' Johannes Tursseley, magister in artibus, per Innocentium nonas Maii anno vii,[319] pro taxa.

De archidiaconatu Tottonie in ecclesia Exoniensi, de quo fuit provisum Ricardo de Svunton' per Innocentium v kalendas Novembris anno v.[320]

De ecclesia de Morchefer' episcopi (Morchard-Bishop), taxata vi li. xiii s. iiii d., in qua in omni iure quod competebat Rotberto Douffold' fuit subrogatus Johannes de Leye [321] xviii kalendas Februarii,[322] iii li. vi s. viii d.

### Wygorniensis

De ecclesia de Ostlegh' (Astley), taxata xi li. vi s. viii d., de qua per obitum Henrici de Stowe fuit provisum Henrico de Diskeby et etiam subrogatus in iure quod dicto Henrico competebat, qui super hoc litigans in curia decessit tempore Domini Clementis, viii li.

De ecclesia de Kirthwich' (Knightwick), taxata iiii li. vi s. viii d. de qua ex causa permutationis fuit provisum Johanni de Chareneux per Innocentium anno primo,[323] xxxiii s. iiii d.

De hospitali Sancti Walfstuni Wigorniensi, non taxato, de quo per resignationem Petri Francisci fuit provisum Johanni de Hareswell', canonico Sancti Martini Londonie, per Innocentium v kalendas Julii anno v.[324]

De ecclesia de Clive Episcopi (Bishop's Cleeve), taxata xl li., cuius acceptatio et provisio facte Ricardo de Drayton' fuerunt eidem confirmate per Innocentium vii kalendas Julii anno ix°,[325] xl li.

Summa pagine liii li. Item v beneficia.

### (fol. 172) Bathoniensis et Wellensis

De prebenda de Wyvescombe (Wivelescombe), taxata xxvi li. xiii s. iiii d., de qua [326] per obitum Johannis de Ufforde, etiam si in vita sua vacaret per consecrationem suam in archiepiscopum Cantuariensem, fuit provisum Willelmo de Bergeney per Clementem, xiii li. vi s. viii d.

De thesauraria Wellensi, taxata xxxiii li. vi s. viii d., que fuit Ricardo Tormerton confirmata per Clementem idus Novembris anno xi°,[327] xx li.

De vicaria Sancti Cuthberti Wellensi, acceptatio cuius

---

[306] 1 January 1363.
[307] Om. **b.**
[308] 15 April 1363.
[309] 3 March 1363; *fructus* om. **b.**
[310] 8 May 1352.
[311] In the margin of **a**: *debet respondere Dominus Hugo Pelegrini, quia exibitum est quantum et qualiter ipse recepit.*
[312] 26 February 1353.
[313] 4 July 1361.
[314] *fructus* om. **b.** In the margin: *ostendit quittantiam Domini Hugonis Pelegrini de solutio.*
[315] The heading *Exoniensis* is repeated at the top of the page.
[316] 26 June 1361.
[317] Om. **b.**

[318] 23 August 1361.
[319] 7 May 1359.
[320] 28 October 1357.
[321] *Beye*, **b.**
[322] 15 January 1363.
[323] 1353.
[324] 27 June 1357.
[325] 25 June 1361.
[326] *quo*, **a.**
[327] 13 November 1352.

facta per Rotbertum Stali fuit eidem confirmata per Innocentium vi kalendas Junii anno vii,[328] pro taxa vi li. xiii s. iiii d.

De prepositura Wellensi, de qua fuit provisum Ade de Hilton' [329] per obitum Andree de Wfford per Innocentium iiii nonas Februarii anno vii,[330] pro taxa xl li.

De prebenda de Holkomb' (Holcombe) in ecclesia Wellensi, de qua vacante aut cum vacabit per assecutionem alterius prebende [331] per Thomam de Barthon' fuit provisum Waltero Moryn per Innocentium xix kalendas Septembris anno viii,[332] xxvi li. xiii s. iiii d.

De archidiaconatu Wellensi cum prebenda, de quibus per obitum domini episcopi Tusculani cardinalis [333] fuit provisum cardinali Carcassonensi [334] per Innocentium vii kalendas Octobris anno ix°,[335] dimissis in arayragiis pro tota taxa que est lxvi li. xiii s. iiii d., de quibus solvit xxv li. vii s. i d. ob., restant xli li. vi s. ii d. ob.

De prebenda de Hengstrug' (Henstridge) in ecclesia Wellensi, de qua per resignationem Simonis Thebaudi fuit provisum Johanni Thebaudi per Innocentium ix kalendas Januarii anno ix°,[336] pro taxa xvi li. xiii s. iiii d.

De prepositura Wellensi, de qua per obitum Ade de Hilton fuit provisum Willelmo de Wycham per Innocentium nonas Januarii anno x°,[337] pro tota [338] taxa xl li.

Summa pagine iic iiii li. xiii s. iiii d.

(fol. 172ᵛ)[339] De vicaria Sancti Cuberti Wellensi, de qua per resignationem Philipi Hente fuit provisum Willelmo Massyngham per Innocentium ii nonas Novembris anno v,[340] dimissa in arayragiis in vi li. xiii s. iiii d., de quibus solvit iii li. vi s. viii d., restant iii li. vi s. viii d.

De prebenda et thesauraria Wellensibus, de quibus fuit provisum cardinali Aquensi [341] per obitum Ricardi de Tomerton' per Innocentium ii idus Novembris anno ix°,[342] dimissis in arayragiis in xxxiii li. vi s. viii d., de quibus solvit xii li. xvi s. viii d. ob., restant xx li. ix s. xi d. ob.

De decanatu Wellensi, que dignitas electiva existit, vacante et reservata per obitum Johannis de Carleton', fuit provisum Thome de Paxton', sacri palatii auditori,

per Innocentium kalendas Augusti anno x°,[343] taxa, taxa.[344]

### Herffordensis

De prebenda de Morthon (Moreton Magna) in ecclesia Herffordensi, taxata xx li., de qua per obitum Thome de Starumpton' fuit provisum Simoni de Subr' per Clementem iii nonas Julii anno viii°,[345] pro resta xiii s. iiii d.[346]

De prebenda in ecclesia Herffordensi, quam Adam electus Menevensis obtinebat, fuit provisum Johanni de Cauney per Innocentium iii kalendas Novembris anno ix°,[347] dimissa in arayragiis in solidis fructibus, solvit in partem eorum xl s., et habet terminos ad docendum de valore et ad solvendum si teneatur.

De prebenda de Motton' (Moreton Magna), de qua per promotionem Simonis Thebaudi in episcopum Londoniensem fuit provisum Thome Thebaudi per Innocentium iii idus Novembris anno ix°,[348] pro taxa xx li.

Summa pagine xliiii [349] li. ix s. xi d. ob.

(fol. 173)[350] De decanatu ecclesie Herffordensis, quem obtinebat Thomas Trulek' in decanatu Londoniensi electus, fuit provisum Willelmo de Bermyngham per Innocentium vii idus Aprilis anno x°,[351] pro taxa xxxi li. vi s. viii d.[352]

De eodem decanatu per resignationem dicti Thome fuit provisum dicto Willelmo per Urbanum vii kalendas Februarii anno primo,[353] dimisso in arayragiis in xxiiii li. xv s. i d., de quibus solvit xxii li. xv s., restant xl s. i d.[354]

### Norwicensis

De prioratu de Castelachre (Castle Acre), de quo fuit provisum Willelmo de Waren' per Clementem anno primo,[355] pro taxa iiiic lxxx li. xix s. vii d.'

De ecclesia de Hulmo (Holme), taxata xl li., de qua per resignationem Willelmi de Merton' fuit provisum Thome Michrel per Clementem, x li.

De prioratu Sancte Fidis de Horsham, taxata c iiiixx iiii [356] li., de quo per obitum Pontii de Serveria fuit provisum Benedicto Jori per Clementem viii° kalendas

---

[328] 27 May 1359.

[329] Hilthona, **b**.

[330] 2 February 1359.

[331] Followed by a blank space in MSS.

[332] 14 August 1360.

[333] William de Court.

[334] Stephen Aubert, deacon of S. Maria in Aquiro.

[335] 25 September 1361.

[336] 24 December 1361.

[337] 5 January 1362.

[338] Om. **b**.

[339] The heading *Bathoniensis et Wellensis* is repeated at the top of the page.

[340] 4 November 1357.

[341] Peter Itherii, bishop of Dax, priest of Ss. Quattro Coronati.

[342] 12 November 1361.

[343] 1 August 1362.

[344] In the margin of **b** only: *non habuit effectum quia Stephanus Pampel, doctor legum, ipsum decanatum optinuit per dominum Urbanum.*

[345] 5 July 1349.

[346] Follows the same sum deleted by dots, **a**.

[347] 30 October 1361.

[348] 11 November 1361.

[349] *xxiiii*, **b**.

[350] The heading *Herffordensis* is repeated at the top of the page.

[351] 7 April 1362.

[352] *ii li. i d.*, **a**.

[353] 26 January 1363.

[354] In the margin of **a** only: *ambe provisiones fuerunt uno anno et ideo non debetur nisi una annata.*

[355] 19 May 1342 to 18 May 1343.

[356] *cxxiiii*, **b**.

Octobris anno vii vel viii°,[357] dimisso in arayragiis in cxxi li., de quibus solvit li li., restant lxx li.

De ecclesia de Estbylney (East Bilney), taxata iiii li. vi s. viii d., que fuit Thome de Walton' confirmata per Innocentium vi kalendas Julii anno vi^to,[358] pro taxa dimissa in arayragiis in iiii li. vi s. viii d., de quibus solvit xliii s. iiii d., restant ii li. iii s. iiii d.

Summa pagine v^c xcvi [359] li. ix s. viii d.

(fol. 173^v)[360] De ecclesia Dereham (East Dereham), de qua per obitum Alani de Houcomb fuit provisum Simoni Thebaud', nunc episcopo Londoniensi, per Clementem iii kalendas Aprilis anno x°,[361] xl li. xvi s. viii d.

De eadem ecclesia per promotionem dicti Simonis in episcopum Londoniensem fuit provisum Bartholomeo Sidey iurisperito per Innocentium vii kalendas Decembris anno ix°,[362] pro taxa xl li. xvi s. viii d.

De decanatu rurali Linie (Lynn), non taxato, de quo ex causa permutationis fuit provisum Ade Thebaud' per Innocentium xvii kalendas Septembris anno viii°,[363] dimisso in arayragiis in iii li. vi s. viii d., de quibus solvit xxxiii s. iiii d., restant xxxiii s. iiii d.

De ecclesia de Wadnorton' (Wood Norton), de qua Johanni Elfford' cardinalis Petragoricensis de novo providit, xl s.

De decanatu de Humkard' (Humbleyard), non taxato, de quo per resignationem Walteri de Walton' fuit provisum Simoni de Subur' per Innocentium iii kalendas Julii anno v°,[364] fructus.[365]

De precentoria [366] Wellensi cum prebenda sibi annexa et ecclesia de Gevole (Yeovil), taxatis xlv li. xiii s. iiii d., de quibus fuit provisum Edmundo Gourney xx li. vi s. viii d.[367]

De ecclesia Sancti Gregorii de Sudbur', de qua per assecutionem cancellarie in ecclesia Londoniensi fuit provisum Thome de Bakton' per Innocentium iiii idus Martii anno x°,[368] que taxatur xxv m., dimissa in arayragiis pro tota taxa, de quibus solvit vi li. xiii s. iiii d., restant x li.[369]

Summa pagine cxvi li. vi s. viii d.

(fol. 174)[360] De ecclesia de Chevyngton' (Chevington), que fuit Hugoni Nepoll' confirmata per Innocen-

tium vii kalendas Februarii anno x°,[370] pro taxa xvi li. xiii s. iiii d.

De archidiaconatu Sudburie, vacante per obitum Henrici Lasouche, fuit provisum Johanni de Humbleton' per Innocentium iii nonas Martii anno vi°,[371] fructus.

De ecclesia de Poleham (Pulham), de qua per obitum Guillelmi de [372] Kerleffey fuit provisum Ricardo Michael' per Innocentium vi idus Februarii anno vi,[373] pro taxa liii li. vi s. viii d.[374]

De decanatu rurali de Fordham, vacante per obitum Johannis Hoppe, fuit provisum Waltero Palm' per Innocentium v nonas Maii anno x°,[375] fructus.[376]

De ecclesia Sancti Gregorii de Sudbur', de qua ex causa permutationis cum Rogero de Burton' fuit provisum Johanni de Herham per Innocentium v nonas Maii anno x°,[375] taxata xxv m., restant xvi li. xiii s. iiii d. vel xxv m.[377]

De ecclesia de Holm (Holme), de qua per obitum Thome Michiel fuit provisum Rotberto de Grymeneston' xviii kalendas Januarii anno primo,[378] pro taxa xl li.

Item de eadem per obitum eiusdem Thome fuit provisum Johanni Bathe.

De ecclesia de Multon' (Moulton), de qua per obitum Edmundi de Wihrewell' fuit provisum Hamoni de Deval, presbytero Lincoliensis diocesis, ii idus Martii per Urbanum anno primo,[379] pro taxa xxvi li. xiii s. iiii d.

### Eliensis

De prioratu de Suaveseye (Swavesey), de quo fuit provisum Stephano Bertrandi per Clementem, pro resta iiii li.

Summa pagine cxxx li. xiii s. iiii d.

### (fol. 174^v) Lincoliensis

De prioratu de Coges (Cogges), qui fuit Willelmo Admonis dimissus in arayragiis in v li. vi s. viii d., de quibus solvit iiii li., restat xxvi s. viii d.

De decanatu Lincoliensi, taxato ii^c lxvi li. xiii s. iiii d., de quo per obitum Johannis electi Cantuariensis fuit provisum Simoni de Briseley per Clementem vi idus Octobris anno vii vel viii°,[380] pro resta lix li. vi s. viii d.

De ecclesia de Keteryng' (Kettering), que fuit confirmata Johanni Wade, qui pro fructibus satisfecit sed pro fructibus male perceptis debet dare ii^c fl. contra Turchos ii^c fl.[381]

---

[357] 24 September 1348 or 1349.

[358] 26 June 1358.

[359] *iiii^c xcvi*, **b**.

[360] The heading *Norwicensis* is repeated at the top of the page.

[361] 30 March 1352.

[362] 25 November 1361.

[363] 16 August 1360.

[364] 29 June 1357.

[365] Om. **b**.

[366] Over *prioratu* deleted by a line, **a**.

[367] In the margin of **a**: *de hoc fuit computum in ultimis computis Domini Hugonis Pelegrini et ideo non debuit poni in arraragiis set cancellari.*

[368] 12 March 1362.

[369] Followed by *xiii s. iiii d.* deleted by a line **a**; not deleted **b**.

[370] 26 January 1362.

[371] 5 March 1358.

[372] Followed by *Kerkel* deleted, **a**.

[373] 8 February 1358.

[374] In the margin of **a**: *inutilis est.*

[375] 3 May 1362.

[376] Om. **b**.

[377] In the margin of **a**: *ista est inutilis quia eodem anno fuit provisum et solutum, ut patet in recepta.*

[378] 15 December 1362.

[379] 14 March 1363. The remainder of the term om. **b**.

[380] 10 October 1349.

[381] In the margin: *Iste ostendit in partibus aquitantiam domini*

De prebenda de Redfford maion' (Bedford Maior) in ecclesia Lincoliensi, que fuit Willelmo de Wynchelesey, nunc episcopo Roffensi, confirmata per Clementem viii idus Maii anno vii vel viii,[382] pro taxa viii li.

De archidiaconatu Bukyngham in ecclesia Lincoliensi, non taxato, de quo, vacante per obitum cardinalis Aynibaldi,[383] fuit provisum Johanni de Asscheburn' per Clementem idus Novembris anno x°,[384] dimisso in arayragiis in solidis fructibus, pro quibus composuit medio iuramento pro medietate ad xx li., de quibus solvit xiii li. vi s. viii d., restant vi li. xiii s. iiii d.

De prebenda de Welton Riveus (Welton Rivall) in ecclesia Lincoliensi, de qua ex causa permutationis cum Johanne de Sutton' fuit provisum Radulpho vel Ricardo Daventr' per Innocentium vii kalendas Maii anno v°,[385] pro taxa xxxiii li. vi s. viii d.

De prebenda de Suthscharle (South Scarle) in ecclesia Lincoliensi, taxata xl li., de qua per obitum Thome de Crosse fuit provisum Johanni de Kyrkeby per Clementem iiii nonas Maii anno ix°,[386] dimissa in arayragiis in xii li. ii s. xi d., de quibus solvit vi li. i s. vi d., restant vi li. i s. v d.

Summa pagine cxiiii li. xiiii s. ix d.

(fol. 175)[387] De medietate ecclesie de Segesbork' (Sedgebrook), taxata xii li. vi s. viii d., de qua fuit provisum Rotberto Sotge de Bercotes per Clementem xi kalendas Augusti anno x°,[388] pro resta dimissa ii li. xiii s. iiii d.

De ecclesia de Trefford' (Greatford), que fuit unita monasterio Beate Marie Wynton' per Clementem iii idus Julii anno xi°,[389] pro taxa xiiii li. xiii s. iiii d.

De prebenda de Cliston (Clifton) in ecclesia Lincoliensi, acceptatio cuius facta per Stephanum See de Ravensser' fuit eidem confirmata per Clementem vi kalendas Augusti anno xi°,[390] pro taxa xx li.

De prebenda de Karleton' cum Turleby (Carlton le Moorland cum Thurlby), taxata xxvi li. xiii s. iiii d., de qua per consecrationem N. episcopi Urgellensis (Urgel) fuit provisum Rotberto de Wyngeworth' per Innocentium ix kalendas Maii anno primo,[391] dimissa in arayragiis in xvi li. xiii s. iiii d., de quibus solvit iii li. vi s. viii d. restant xiii li. vi s. viii d.

De ecclesia de Dyngeley (Dingley), de qua Thome de Dyngeley[392] cardinalis Petragoricensis providit, ii li. xiii s. iiii d.

De prebenda Sancte Crucis (Spaldwick) in ecclesia Lincoliensi, taxata x li., de qua fuit provisum Johanni de Selby, ii li. x s.

De prebenda de Carleton' cum Turleby in ecclesia Lincoliensi, de qua per resignationem Willelmi de Walcote fuit provisum Ewardo de Scherdestoke per Innocentium ix kalendas Martii anno vi°,[393] pro taxa xxvi li. xiii s. iiii d.

De prebenda de Scharle alias vocata Southsharle (South Scarle) in ecclesia Lincoliensi, de qua per resignationem Willelmi de Kirkeby fuit provisum Johanni de Appilley per Innocentium iii idus Julii anno vi°,[394] pro taxa xl li.

De ecclesia de Cosingthon' (Cossington), que Johanni de Melburn' fuit confirmata per Innocentium ix kalendas Septembris anno vii°,[395] pro taxa vi li. xiii s. iiii d.

Summa pagine cxxix li. iii s. iiii d.

(fol. 175ᵛ)[387] De ecclesia de Hoghton' (Houghton Regis), que fuit Hugoni Spathyng' confirmata per Innocentium ix kalendas Septembris anno vii°,[396] dimissa in arayragiis in xvi li. xiii s. iiii d., de quibus solvit xii li., restant iiii li. xiii s. iiii d. Ista ecclesia in registro non taxatur nisi ad xviii m. in toto et sic esset integre satisfactum.[397]

De prebenda ecclesia de Nassingthon' (Nassington) in ecclesia Lincoliensi, taxata c li., que fuit confirmata Ludovico de Charletona per Innocentium iii kalendas Februarii anno x°,[398] pro taxa c li.

De capellania perpetua ecclesie parochialis de Clee, de qua fuit provisum Johanni de Walthon' per Innocentium xi kalendas Julii anno ix°,[399] non taxata, fructus.[400]

De prebenda de Multon' ecclesie (Milton Ecclesia), taxata xl li., et archidiaconatu ⟨Oxonie cum⟩ ecclesia[401] de Isteley (Iffley), taxata xiiii li. xiii s. iiii d., in ecclesia Lincoliensi, de quibus per obitum cardinalis de Gordonio[402] fuit provisum cardinali Aquensi[403] per Innocentium iiii idus Augusti anno ix°,[404] liiii li. xiii s. iiii d.

De ecclesia de Stagrunde (Standground), de qua ex causa permutationis cum ecclesia de Ripton' (Abbots Ripton) fuit provisum Johanni de Digton' per Innocentium vii° kalendas Octobris anno x,[405] pro taxa xx li.

---

thesaurarii post recessum Johannis de Cabrespino, de soluto cuius copia fuit posita in regestris et ideo debet cancellari.

[382] 8 May 1349 or 1350.
[383] Bishop of Tusculum.
[384] 13 November 1351.
[385] 25 April 1357.
[386] 4 May 1351.
[387] The heading Lincoliensis is repeated at the top of the page.
[388] 22 July 1351.
[389] 13 July 1352.
[390] 27 July 1352.
[391] 23 April 1353.
[392] Followed by fuit deleted by dots, a.

[393] 21 February 1358.
[394] 13 July 1358.
[395] 24 August 1359.
[396] 24 August 1359.
[397] In the margin of a deleted by lines: non taxatur nisi ad xii li. preter portionem vicarii et ideo solvit totum, nec debuit poni in arreragiis.
[398] 30 January 1362.
[399] 21 June 1361.
[400] Fructus om. b. In the margin of a: Ista provisio non habere hic (reading doubtful) debet quia bis fuit provisum in anno.
[401] ecclesie, MSS.
[402] William Farinier of Gourdon, priest of Ss. Marcellino e Pietro.
[403] Peter Itherii, bishop of Dax, priest of Ss. Quattro Coronati.
[404] 10 August 1361.
[405] 25 September 1362.

De ecclesia de Ripton' Abbatis (Abbots Ripton), de qua ex causa permutationis fuit provisum Thome de Clopton' per Innocentium vii⁰ kalendas Octobris anno x⁰,[405] pro taxa xxiii li. vi s. viii d.

De prebenda de Glatton' in ecclesia Lincoliensi, de qua per obitum Ade de Hilton' fuit provisum Rogero de Sutton', pro taxa iiii li. vi s. viii d.[406] Satisfactum est sed post istam solutionem factam compertum est quod ista non est prebenda in ecclesia Lincoliensi sed est ecclesia parochialis de Glatton' et taxatur xxi li. iii s. iiii d., et sic debentur pro resta xvi li. xvi s. viii d.

Summa pagine cancellata iiii li. vi s. viii d., positis in ultima provisione et additis xvi li. xvi s. viii d., que debet esse vera resta ii⁰ xix li x s. viii d.[407]

(fol. 176)[387] De medietate ecclesie de Strikel (East Keal?), de qua ex causa permutationis fuit provisum Galfrido Trenthapan per Innocentium idus Aprilis anno x⁰,[408] de quibus solvit ix li. vi s. viii d, restant ix li. xiii s. iiii d. Sed episcopus certificat quod ambo portionarii, videlicet tota ecclesia non taxatur nisi ad xxviii m., et quod duo portionarii percipiunt fructus equis portionibus et est satisfactum de xiiii m. pro dicta medietate, et sic nichil debet pro resta si sit ita.

De capella Sancti Thome ad pontem Stafford' (Stamford), non taxata, in qua Johannes de Lowes fuit subrogatus Edmundo Wyrtewell' super lite in palatio per Innocentium iiii idus Maii anno x⁰.[409]

De ecclesia de parva Kynewell' (Little Kimble), de qua per assecutionem ecclesie de Gesyngton' (Garsington) fuit provisum Johanni Rocell' per Innocentium vi idus Martii anno vi,[410] pro taxa iiii li. xiii s. iiii d.

De prebenda Lincoliensi, de qua per obitum Jacobi de Botelay fuit provisum Domino Willelmo episcopo Tusculano per Innocentium xv kalendas Septembris anno vi,[411] taxa vel fructus.[412]

De officio capelle soye in altare Sancti Petri in ecclesia Lincoliensi, non taxato, vacante per assecutionem ecclesie de Ovre (Over) factam per Thomam de Clipston, fuit provisum Willelmo de Beston' per Innocentium iiii nonas Decembris anno vi⁰,[413] fructus.[414]

De ecclesia de Hohgton' (Houghton Regis) presentatio et institutio facte Hugoni de Sparkyng' fuerunt eidem confirmate vel provisum de novo per Innocentium

xviii kalendas Decembris anno viii⁰,[415] fructus vel taxa.[416]

De ecclesia Beate Marie Herefford' (Hertford), de qua ex causa permutationis fuit provisum Henrico Midy per Innocentium v kalendas Aprilis anno viii⁰,[417] fructus vel taxa.[416]

De prebenda de Langestowe (Stowe Longa) in ecclesia Lincoliensi, de qua fuit provisum Reginaldo de Theminis per Innocentium xi kalendas Julii anno ix⁰,[418] pro taxa xlii li. vi s. viii d.

Summa pagine lvi li. xiii s. iiii d. Item ii [419] beneficia.

(fol. 176ᵛ)[420] Prebenda in ecclesia Lincoliensi intitulata E in ecclesia collegiata Beate Marie iuxta castrum Leycestr' (Leicester, St. Mary the less in Castle) fuit ex causa permutationis provisum Henrico de Lymbergh' per Urbanum nonas Maii anno primo.[421]

De magistratu de Berton' Sancti Lazari (Burton Lazars), collatio facta per Dominum Philipum patriarcham Jerosolitanensem auctoritate ordinaria Galfredo de Chaddesden', militi dicti hospitalis, fuit [422] eidem auctoritate apostolica confirmata,[423] et nichilominus ⟨subrogatus⟩ dictus Galfridus in omni iure quod competebat Rotberto Halday v nonas Martii dicto anno.[424]

De prebenda ecclesie Lincoliensis, vacante per obitum Willelmi Spaldewell',[425] fuit provisum Johanni de Kyrkeby, regis Anglie clerico, per Urbanum kalendas Maii anno primo.[426]

## Conwetrensis et Lichfeldensis

De archidiaconatu Convetrensi, non taxato, de quo fuit provisum Humfrido de Astingis.

De eodem archidiaconatu et prebenda de Langedon' (Longdon) in ecclesia Lichfeldensi, taxata xx li., de quibus per obitum Humfridi de Astingis fuit provisum Willelmo de Salow per Clementem iii⁰ nonas Septembris anno viii⁰,[427] pro quibus Walterus de Dalby dicitur

---

[406] In the margin of **a**: *ecclesia est, non prebenda.*
[407] *viii d.* om. **b.**
[408] 13 April 1362.
[409] 12 May 1362.
[410] 10 March 1358.
[411] 18 August 1358.
[412] *taxa vel fructus,* om. **b.**
[413] 2 December 1358.
[414] *fructus* om **b.** In the margin of **a**: *Episcopus certificat quod non sunt fructus pertinentes officio nec altari nec pretio capellani dum celebrat, et ideo nichil debetur.*

[415] 14 November 1360.
[416] *fructus vel taxa,* om. **b.**
[417] 28 March 1360.
[418] 21 June 1361.
[419] *vii,* **b.**
[420] The heading *Lincoliensis* is repeated at the top of the page. The following entries which appear only in **b** (folio 236ᵛ) are deleted by lines. *De prebenda de Stoke* (East Stoke) *in ecclesia Lincoliensi, taxata lxxxvi li. xiii s. iiii d., de qua per obitum Johannis de Northwode fuit provisum Hugoni Pelegrini per Clementem iiii nonas Maii anno vi* (4 May 1348) *solutum est hic in curia et ideo cancellatur. De prebenda de Cotyngham* (Corringham) *in ecclesia Lincoliensi, taxata cxxvi li. xiii s. iiii d., solutum est.*
[421] 7 May 1363.
[422] *fuerunt,* MSS.
[423] *confirmate,* **b.**
[424] 3 March 1363.
[425] *Sraldewell',* **a.**
[426] 1 May 1363.
[427] 3 September 1349.

composuisse cum camera, pro resta archidiaconatus xiii li. vi s. viii d.

Summa pagine xiii li. vi s. viii d. Item iii beneficia.

(fol. 177)[428] De prebenda Lichfeldensi, de qua per obitum Willelmi Apeltr' fuit provisum Thome Atohull' per Clementem xi kalendas Julii anno viii,[429] fructus.[430]

De decanatu Lichfeldensi, taxato xl li., de quo per assecutionem decanatus Lincoliensis per Simonem de Bryzoley fuit provisum Johanni de Bokyngham per Clementem nonas Novembris anno viiio,[431] pro resta xx li.

De prebenda in ecclesia collegiata Sancte Cadde Salopp' (St. Chad, Shrewsbury), de qua per obitum Willelmi Alpetr' fuit provisum Rotberto de Sulgrave per Clementem ii idus Decembris anno viiio,[432] fructus vel taxa.[433]

De prebenda de Ekleshale (Eccleshall), de qua per resignationem Johannis de Melburn' fuit provisum Johanni de Wynwyk' per Clementem vii idus Februarii anno ixo,[434] pro taxa lxvi li. xiii s. iiii d.

De prebenda de Berkewyk' (Berkswick) in ecclesia Lichfeldensi, taxata xx li., de qua per obitum Guidonis de Voresio fuit provisum Willelmo Cavunle per Innocentium vii kalendas Maii anno primo,[435] xx li.

De prebenda de Langedon' (Longdon) in ecclesia Lichfeldensi, pro resta ratione compositionis facte cum camera per Walterum Dalby, dimissa in arayragiis in cviii fl., de quibus l fl., restant lviii fl.

De ecclesia de Walton', de qua fuit provisum Magistro Hugoni de Bokyngtton' iii nonas Decembris anno v per Innocentium,[436] xiiii li.

De capellania Sancti Michaelis sita in castro de Cliderow (Clitheroe), non taxata, fuit per devolutionem provisum Johanni de Borton' per Innocentium iiii kalendas Junii anno vio,[437] fructus vel taxa.[433]

De ecclesia de Codigniton' (Coddington), de qua per assecutionem ecclesie de Wyngton' (Burton-in-Win-hale) per Johannem Charnexx fuit provisum Waltero Lyngge per Innocentium iii nonas Junii anno vio,[438] pro taxa vi li. xiii s. iiii d.

Summa pagine cxxvii li. vi s. viii d. Item lviii[439] fl. Item iii beneficia.

(fol. 177v)[428] De prioratu de Kyrkeby (Monks Kirby), de quo per assecutionem prioratus de Veteri Bexsmo (Vieux Belesme) Saginensis (Séez) diocesis

per Oliverum de Desertis fuit provisum Willelmo de Grauleriis per Innocentium xiii kalendas Martii anno vio,[440] pro taxa lxxxi li. x s. viii d.

De prebenda de Teryn alias de Tervyn (Tarvin) in ecclesia Lichfeldensi, de qua per obitum Willelmi de Dirffoldd' fuit provisum Nicholao de Lath per Innocentium iii idus Augusti anno ixo,[441] pro taxa xxxiii li. vi s. viii d.

De capellania de Cliderowe (Clitheroe), non taxata, in qua fuit subrogatus David Martini Johanni de Botarii,[442] (qui de eadem litigabat, ix kalendas Januarii)[443] per Innocentium anno ixo.[444]

De prebenda in ecclesia collegiata de Penkigh' (Penkridge), de qua per obitum Thome Michiel fuit provisum Thome de Eltonheved per Innocentium vii idus Aprilis anno xo.[445]

De capellania Sancti Michaelis de Clyderowe (Clitheroe), in qua in omni iure quod competebat Johanni de Botton' fuit subrogatus Johannes Park' per Innocentium vii kalendas Februarii, anno xo.[446]

De prebenda de Wyfford' (Weeford) in ecclesia Lichfeldensi, de qua in omni iure quod competebat Anthonio de Mortepologio fuit subrogatus Thomas Michiel per Innocentium x kalendas Junii anno vo.[447]

De cantoria ecclesie Lichfeldensis, quam Thomas de Badeby debuit dimittere per assecutionem canonicatus et prebende ecclesie Lincoliensis fuit provisum.

De prebenda in ecclesia Lichfeldensi, de qua per obitum Willelmi de Duffeldd' fuit provisum Alexandro de Dalby iiii nonas Januarii anno primo.[448]

De prebenda de Gonssale (Gnosall) in ecclesia Lichfeldensi, de qua collatio et provisio facte auctoritate ordinaria Hugoni de Garles fuerunt eidem auctoritate apostolica confirmate vel de novo provisum per Urbanum v nonas Martii anno primo.[449]

Summa pagine cxiiii li. xvii s. iiii d. Item vii beneficia.

(fol. 178) Assavensis

De ecclesia de Dynbegh' (Denbigh), vacante de iure, ut asseritur, fuit provisum Willelmo de Sunderlond' per Clementem idus Novembris anno ixo,[450] pro taxa vi li. xiii s. iiii d.

De ecclesia de Landryneawe (Llandrinio), taxata vii li., que fuit confirmata Griffino de Charleton' per Innocentium iii nonas Maii anno xo,[451] vii li.

De ecclesia de Dynbegh' (Denbigh), de qua per

---

[428] The heading *Conwetrensis* appears at the top of the page.
[429] 21 June 1349.
[430] Om. **b.**
[431] 5 November 1349.
[432] 12 December 1349.
[433] *fructus vel taxa*, om. **b.**
[434] 7 February 1351.
[435] 25 April 1353.
[436] 3 December 1357.
[437] 29 May 1358.
[438] 3 June 1358.
[439] l instead of lviii, in **b.**

[440] 17 February 1358.
[441] 11 August 1361.
[442] *Bolton'*, **b.**
[443] The clause in brackets is omitted in **a.**
[444] 24 December 1361.
[445] 7 April 1362.
[446] 26 January 1362.
[447] 23 May 1357.
[448] 2 January 1363.
[449] 3 March 1363.
[450] 13 November 1350.
[451] 5 May 1362.

obitum Willelmi de Synndelond' fuit provisum Guillelmo de ⟨Harden⟩ per Innocentium ix kalendas Maii anno ixᵒ,[452] xv li. vi s. viii d.

De eadem ecclesia fuit provisum H⟨ugoni⟩ de Castr' iiii kalendas Maii anno predicto,[453] sed ambo sunt infra annum.

De ecclesia de Klkeyn (Kilken) et capella eidem annexa, de qua per obitum ultimi rectoris eiusdem fuit provisum Waltero Fraystorp per Innocentium xi kalendas Julii anno xᵒ,[454] pro taxa vii li.

De ecclesia de Meyvioyt (Meifod), de qua per assecutionem Ludovici episcopi Herffordensis fuit provisum Willelmo de Cherleton' per Innocentium iiii kalendas Octobris anno ixᵒ,[455] pro taxa xxiiii li. xiii s. iiii d.[456]

## Menewensis

De ecclesia de Lamhanglarath' (Llanfihangel ar Arth), de qua per obitum Ricardi Aprovansses fuit provisum Ludovico Counton' per Clementem.

De ecclesia de Weston' [457] (Wiston), de qua per resignationem Rogeri dicti Johannis fuit provisum Willelmo de Newhawe per Innocentium xix kalendas Junii anno iiiiᵒ.[458]

Summa pagine lx li. xiii s. iiii d. Item duo beneficia.

(fol. 178ᵛ)[459] De ecclesia Sancti Bermethii super Taff' (Llanfyrnach), de qua fuit provisum Willelmo de Newhawe, alias Ricardo de Caunton' et melius, per Innocentium xix kalendas Junii anno iiiiᵒ,[458] pro taxa vi li. xiii s. iiii d.

De cantoria ecclesie de Arberwill' (Abergwili), taxata vi li. xiii s. iiii d., seu ecclesia de Lampetr' Talbot Stevene (Lampeter Pont Stephen), taxata v li., quam obtinet David de Sancto Claro, fuit provisum Cook' de Averefford' per Innocentium vi idus Martii anno viᵒ,[460] vi li. xiii s. iiii d.

De ecclesia de Langdemore (Llangoedmore), taxata vi li., de qua Willemo de Aperaoniens per cardinalem Petragoricensem fuit provisum iii li. vi s. viii d.

De archidiaconatu de Kermerdyn (Carmarthen) in ecclesia Menevensi cum annexa, taxato xx li. xiii s. iiii d., quo ad omne ius quod competebat Haulayno apDavid fuit subrogatus David Martini per Innocentium vi kalendas Decembris anno viii,[461] xx li. xiii s. iiii d.

De prebenda de Roil (Royll) in ecclesia de Arberwyll' (Abergwili), collatio cuius facta Ade de Horton'

fuit eidem confirmata per Innocentium ii idus Septembris anno viii.[462]

De prebenda Sancti David Confessoris de Swymesen (Swansea), collatio cuius facta David Martini fuit eidem confirmata per Innocentium iii kalendas Februarii anno ix,[463] pro resta xl s.[464]

De prebenda in ecclesia Menevensi, de qua per obitum David fuit provisum David Waham per Innocentium xi kalendas Julii anno ixᵒ.[465]

De prebenda de [466] Landewybrevn (Llandewi Brefi) in ecclesia Menevensi, de qua per obitum Griffini de Camton' fuit provisum Willelmo de Ossenden' per Innocentium ii nonas Decembris anno v.[467]

De prebenda seu portione in ecclesia Sancti Martini de Harlerwill (Abergwili), de qua per obitum Willelmi de Dynbrayk' fuit provisum Waltero de Fenton' per Innocentium iiii nonas Julii anno ixᵒ.[468]

Summa pagine xxxvii li. vi s. viii d. Item iiii beneficia.

(fol. 179)[459] De prebenda de Marthir (Mathry) in ecclesia Menevensi, de qua cum vacabit per consecrationem Ade electi Menevensis fuit provisum Philipo de Houthon' per Innocentium iiiiᵗᵒ kalendas Novembris anno x.[469]

De prebenda quam dictus electus ⟨obtinebat⟩ in ecclesia de Arberwyll' (Abergwili), dum vacabit ut supra, fuit mandatum provideri Philipo Martini per Innocentium iii kalendas Novembris anno ix.[470]

De prebenda de Landevaylok' (Llangyfelach) in ecclesia collegiata de Arberwyill', que tanto tempore vacavit quod eius collatio est sedi appostolice devoluta, fuit provisum Alexandro Millok'.

De archidiaconatu de Chermerdyn (Carmarthen) in ecclesia Menevensi, de quo per obitum David Martini fuit provisum Willelmo de Boldewyn per Innocentium ydus Augusti anno x,[471] pro taxa xx li. xiii s. iiii d.

## Eboracensis

De prebenda de Hustwayt (Husthwaite) in ecclesia Eboracensi, de qua fuit provisum Johanni de Welborun' per Clementem xiii kalendas Julii anno decimo,[472] qui composuit ad iiᶜ fl. contra Turcos et cetera.[473]

---

[452] 23 April 1361.
[453] 28 April 1361.
[454] 21 June 1362.
[455] 28 September 1361.
[456] In the margin: *solutum est*. The item is deleted by lines in both **a** and **b**.
[457] *Wosten'*, **a**.
[458] 14 May 1356.
[459] The heading *Menewensis* is repeated at the top of the page.
[460] 10 March 1358.
[461] 26 November 1360.

[462] 12 September 1360.
[463] 30 January 1361.
[464] In the margin: *solutum est*. In **b** the item is incomplete.
[465] 21 June 1361.
[466] *dor*, **a**.
[467] 4 December 1357.
[468] 4 July 1361.
[469] 29 October 1362. This date is wrong.
[470] 30 October 1361.
[471] 13 August 1362.
[472] 19 June 1351.
[473] Item deleted by lines, **a**. In the margin: *soluti sunt in ultimis computis Domini Hugonis inter legata Terre Sancte in xxx li. sterlingorum*.

De prebenda in ecclesia Eboracensi, de qua per consecrationem electi Terwynensis fuit provisum Frederico Salaman, fructus.[474]

De prebenda de Stranssal' (Strensall) in ecclesia Eboracensi, de qua per consecrationem Michaelis episcopi Londoniensis fuit provisum cardinali Petragoricensi per Innocentium ii ydus Octobris anno secundo,[475] pro taxa liii li. vi s. viii d.

De ecclesia de Hoggescarth', non taxata, de qua per cardinalem Urgellensem fuit provisum Willelmo Gibbelot'.

Summa pagine lxxiiii li.  Item vi beneficia.

(fol. 179ᵛ)[476] De vicaria de Gylingis (Gilling), de qua Johannes Parker fuit subrogatus in omni iure quod competebat Gerlaco de Clave per Innocentium x kalendas Maii anno ix,[477] pro taxa x li.[478]

Item de eadem fuit provisum Johanni de Beck' per Innocentium ix kalendas Septembris anno viii°.[479]

De ecclesia de Brantyngham (Brantingham), taxata lxvi li. xiii s. iiii d., de qua vacante per obitum Magistri Thome de Newill'[480] fuit provisum Willelmo Stord' per Innocentium xvi kalendas Septembris,[481] dimissa in arayragiis et male in liii li. vi s. et viii d., licet non debuit dimitti nisi in xl li., quia in aliis computis meis respondetur de xiii li. vi s. viii d. et sic est vera resta xl li., de quibus solvit xxxiii li. vi s. viii d., et sic restant vi li. xiii s. iiii d.

De prebenda in ecclesia Sancti Johannis Beverloci ad altare Beate Marie, de qua per obitum Ricardi de Tormerton' fuit provisum Guillelmo de Dalton' iiii nonas Julii anno ix° per Innocentium,[482] pro taxa xvi li.

De prebenda de Bokynffeld' (Bockingfold), non taxata, de qua per obitum Willelmi de Braddele fuit provisum Ricardo de Hormyngthon' per Innocentium iiii^to nonas Julii anno ix°.[482]

De ecclesia Omnium Sanctorum Eboraci, de qua per obitum Symonis Warde fuit provisum David Mort sive[483] Martini per Innocentium iiii nonas Julii anno ix°,[482] pro taxa v li. vi s. viii d.[484]

De prebenda de Wystowe (Wistow) in ecclesia Eboracensi et archidiaconatu eiusdem ecclesie, non taxato, de quibus per obitum cardinalis Penestrini[485]

fuit provisum cardinali Carcassonnensi,[486] pro taxa prebende c li.

De prebenda de Dyrffeld' (Driffeld) in dicta ecclesia, de qua per obitum Guillelmi de Sancto Martiali fuit provisum cardinali de Sancto Martiali,[487] pro taxa c li.

Summa pagine iiᶜ xxxviii li.  Item i benefficium.

(fol. 180)[476] De prebenda de Bolmi (Bole) in eadem de qua per obitum Thome de Newill' fuit provisum cardinali[488] Cluniacensi,[489] pro taxa xvi li.

De prebenda in ecclesia collegiata Beverlaci, de qua per obitum Ricardi de Tormenton' fuit provisum Johanni le Sage per Innocentium xi kalendas Julii anno ix.[490]

De prebenda de Hoveden' (Howden) in ecclesia Eboracensi, de qua per obitum Johannis de Metheham fuit provisum Ricardo Drax per Innocentium vii ydus Julii anno v,[491] pro taxa xxxiii li. vi s. viii d.

De prebenda de Notthwell' (Norwell) in ecclesia collegiata Suthwell', in qua in omni iure quod competebat Johanni de Deiton' fuit subrogatus Thomas Montt de Wikham per Innocentium vi kalendas Augusti anno v,[492] pro taxa xxxvi li. xiii s. iiii d.

De capella sive cantoria de Wertebrig' (Wentbridge), de qua per obitum Thome atte More fuit provisum Rotberto de Wyk' per Innocentium kalendas Decembris anno vii°.[493]

De archidiaconatu de Efforddyng' (East Riding) in ecclesia Eboracensi cum ecclesia de Mapeldon' (Mappleton), non taxata, sibi annexa, vacante ex eo quod Willelmus Walcote qui ipsum optinebat aliam ecclesiam extitit asequtus, fuit provisum Waltero de Skirlawe per Innocentium ii kalendas Decembris anno vii°,[494] composuit medio iuramento, salvo iure pluris, pro ecclesia ad xvi li. xiii s. iiii d.

De custodia seu sacristia capelle Beate Marie et Sanctorum Angelorum Eboracensis, provisio et collatio cuius facte auctoritate ordinaria Johanni de Valtham fuerunt eidem auctoritate appostolica confirmate per Innocentium ix kalendas Januarii anno ix,[495] pro taxa lxxxviii li. viii s. viii d.

De capellania perpetua Beati Petri de Wolvey, de qua ex causa permutationis cum Henrico Mydy fuit provisum Johanni Dich' per Innocentium v kalendas Aprilis anno viii°.[496]

De canonicatu et prebenda ecclesie Beverlaci Eboracensis diocesis, vacantibus per obitum Andree Lefford alias le Moyne fuit provisum Ricardo Drag, legum

---

[474] Om. **b.**
[475] 14 October 1354.
[476] The heading *Eboracensis* is repeated at the top of the page.
[477] 22 April 1361.
[478] In the margin of **a**: *solvit in primis computis pro prima annata.*
[479] 24 August 1360.  In the margin: *est infra annum.*
[480] *Stewill',* **b.**
[481] 17 August 1361.
[482] 4 July 1361.
[483] *ssyve,* **a**; *sye,* **b.**
[484] In the margin: *incumbens habet sententiam diffinitivam pro se et contra dictum David.*
[485] Peter des Prés.

[486] Stephen Aubert, deacon of S. Maria in Aquiro.
[487] Hugo de Sancto Martiali, deacon of S. Maria in Portico.
[488] Followed by *Petragoricensi* deleted by a line, **a.**
[489] Androin de la Roche, priest of S. Marcello.
[490] 21 June 1361.
[491] 9 July 1357.
[492] 27 July 1357.
[493] 1 December 1359.
[494] 30 November 1359.
[495] 24 December 1361.
[496] 28 March 1360.

doctori, iiii^to ydus Novembris.[497] Ista fuit noviter extracta de corectione regestri camere et hic posita.

Summa pagine cxci li. ii s. Item iii benefficia.

### (fol. 180^v) Dunelmensis

De hospitali de Giretham (Gretham), non taxato, de quo per obitum Johannis de Bridkyrk' per Clementem ii ydus Octobris anno ix°,[498] debetur medietas exceptis tribus libris vi s. viii d., de quibus Dominus Hugo computat in recepta.

De prebenda in ecclesia collegiata Langestr' (Lanchester), de qua ex causa permutationis cum Henrico de Exton' fuit provisum Galffrido de Cornesio per Innocentium xv kalendas Decembris anno primo.[499]

De prebenda de Lumley (Lamesley) in ecclesia collegiata Cestr' super stratam (Chester-le-Street), de qua per electionem electi Norwicensis fuit provisum Willelmo de Bughteburg' per Innocentium vi° ydus Februarii anno ii,[500] pro taxa xx li.

De decanatu ecclesie collegiate Cestr' super stratam, permutatio facta auctoritate ordinaria cum Johanne de Sculthorp' pro archidiaconatu Cicestrensi per Adam de Houton' fuit eidem confirmata per Innocentium kalendas Junii anno vi,[501] et taxatur xxxiii li. vi s. viii d., de quibus solvit xvi li. xiii s. iiii d., restant xvi li. xiii s. iiii d.

De vicaria de Newenton' in Glendale (Kirknewton), de qua per obitum Rotberti de Jarnni fuit provisum Rotberto Hoppe' per Innocentium nonas Septembris anno vii°,[502] pro taxa xx li.

De prioratu dicto celle Sancte Rege (St. Bees), collatio facta auctoritate ordinaria Willelmo de Weynesbury fuit eidem confirmata per Innocentium ix kalendas Septembris anno viii°.[503]

De ecclesia de Routhebury (Rothbury), in qua ad omne ius quod competebat Willelmo de Emeldon' fuit Johannes Alpelby subrogatus per Innocentium xvi kalendas Februarii anno ix,[504] taxata ad novam taxam lxvi li. xiii s. iiii d.

De prebenda in ecclesia de Northon' (Norton), de qua per obitum Thome Drax' fuit provisum Bernardo de Linar' per Innocentium vii kalendas Maii anno ix.[505]

Summa pagine cxxiii li. vi s. viii d. Item iiii benefficia.

(fol. 181)[506] De prebenda in ecclesia Hauklande (Auckland), de qua per obitum Thome de Bridkik' fuit

provisum Willelmo de Wikham per Innocentium ii ydus Augusti anno x.[507]

De ecclesia de Stanhopp' (Stanhope), de qua per obitum Thome de Bridkik' fuit provisum Willelmo de Norwico per Innocentium viii kalendas Septembris anno ix°,[508] pro taxa xl s.

De eadem ecclesia, collatio facta auctoritate ordinaria Richardo de Wynghton' per obitum prefati Thome fuit eidem confirmata per Innocentium iiii kalendas Januarii anno x°,[509] xl s.

De eadem ecclesia, collatio predicta dicto Richardo facta fuit confirmata per Innocentium iiii ydus Maii anno x,[510] pro taxa xl s.

De prebenda ecclesie collegiate de Haukelond' (Auckland), de qua per obitum dicti Thome fuit provisum Rotberto de Straton'.

De capella libera de Jesmouth' (Jesmond), collatio facta auctoritate ordinaria Thome de Pemek' fuit eidem confirmata per Innocentium ix ydus Januarii anno ix°,[511]

De eadem, vacante per obitum Henrici Beufaunt fuit provisum Matheo de Bolton' per Innocentium xiiii kalendas Februarii anno x.[512]

De hospitali pauperum Sancti Egidii de Kuptr' (Kepier), de quo per obitum Petri de Toresby fuit provisum Johanni de Appilby per Innocentium viii kalendas Maii anno viii.[513]

De ecclesia de Routhebury (Rothbury), presentatio et institutio facte auctoritate ordinaria Johanni Marescalli fuerunt eidem auctoritate apostolica confirmate vel provisum de novo per Urbanum v nonas Martii anno primo.[514]

De canonicatu et prebenda ecclesie collegiate de Northon' (Norton), vacantibus per obitum Thome Drax' fuit provisum Benedicto de Lucano clerico per Clementem anno viii vii kalendas Maii.[515]

Summa pagine vi li. Item vi benefficia.

### (fol. 181^v) Karliolensis

De ecclesia de Crostwayt (Crosthwaite), in qua in omni iure competenti Johanni de Salario fuit subrogatus Johannes Henrici per Innocentium ii ydus Januarii anno quinto,[516] pro taxa xxx li. xiii s. iiii d.

De vicaria de Bamthon' (Brampton), de qua ex causa permutationis cum vicaria de Schaldefford' (Shalford) Winthoniensis diocesis fuit provisum Johanni

[497] 10 November (1362).
[498] 14 October 1350.
[499] 17 November 1353.
[500] 8 February 1354.
[501] 1 June 1358.
[502] 5 September 1359.
[503] 24 August 1360.
[504] 17 January 1361.
[505] 25 April 1361.
[506] The heading *Dunelmensis* is repeated at the top of the page.

[507] 12 August 1362.
[508] 25 August 1361.
[509] 29 December 1361. See above, p. 205.
[510] 12 May 1362.
[511] 24 December 1361. See above, p. 157.
[512] 19 January 1362.
[513] 24 April 1360.
[514] 3 March 1363.
[515] 25 April 1350. In the margin of **a**: *ista est noviter extracta de corectione regestri camere et hic posita.*
[516] 12 January 1357.

Amyle per Innocentium xi kalendas Septembris anno v,[517] pro taxa viii li.

De ecclesia de Musgrave, vacante per obitum Johannis de Stokton'[518] fuit provisum Rotberto Kenok' per Innocentium ii kalendas Martii anno v,[519] pro taxa xiii li. vi s. viii d.

De vicaria de Crostewayt (Crosthwaite), provisio cuius facta Willelmo de Esenden' fuit eidem confirmata per Innocentium ii kalendas Junii anno viii,[520] pro taxa xx li.

De ecclesia de Kukelonde (Kirkland), de qua, ex eo quod Johannes de Kerkeby una cum ecclesia de Wyllesey (Ousby) per menssem et amplius detinuit, fuit provisum Johanni de Kerkeby per Innocentium viii kalendas Novembris anno vii [521] xl li.

Summa pagine lxxii li.

(fol. 182) Sequentes [522] sunt obligati pro diversis benefficiis que cadunt supra suis debitis locis

De archidiaconatu Richemundie in ecclesia Eboracensi, prebenda de Midelton' (Middleton) in ecclesia Cicestrensi et de Dynemynstr' (Yetminster) in ecclesia Saresburiensi, de quibus fuit provisum Henrico de Walthon', dimissis in arayragiis pro archidiaconatu xlviii li. vi s. viii d., pro prebenda de Midelthon' iii li. vi s. viii d. et pro prebenda Dynemynstr' xviii li. vi s. viii [523] d., que omnia ascendunt ad lxx li., de quibus solvit vi li. xiii s. iiii d., restant lxiii li. vi s. viii d.

De ecclesia de Hodeneth' [524] (Hodnet) Lichfeldensis diocesis et prebenda de Farendon' (Faringdon) in ecclesia Saresburiensi, de Mora (Moorfields, St. Giles Cripplegate) in ecclesia Londoniensi, de Humbrethon' (Hunderton) in ecclesia Herffordensi, de Ledbury in diocesi Herffordensi, de quibus fuit provisum Nicholao Heth' et composuit cum camera pro omnibus in viii$^c$ l fl. ponderis camere, dimissis in arayragiis in v$^c$ l fl., de quibus solvit vi li. xiii s. iiii d. qui valent, computato floreno pro tribus s. sterlingorum, xliii fl. et xvi d. sterlingorum, restat quod debet v$^c$ et v fl. xx d. sterllingorum.

Summa pagine lxiii li. vi s. viii d. Item v$^c$ et v fl. xx d. sterllingorum.

(fol. 182$^v$) Sequntur arayratgia benefficiorum collatorum in Anglia per dominos cardinales.

### Saresburiensis

De prioratu seu officio de Noion alias de Novo Mer-

cato (Neufmarché), de quo fuit provisum Nicholao Romeri per cardinalem Petragoricensem.

### Wygorniensis

De ecclesia de Honyngton' (Honington), de qua Luce filio Guillelmi fuit per cardinalem Urgellensem de novo provisum.[525]

### Norwicensis

De ecclesia Omnium Sanctorum de Carleston (Kettlestone), de qua Johanni Ardern' cardinalis Urgellensis de novo providit, pro taxa xiii li. vi s.[526] viii d.[526]

### Lincoliensis

De prebenda de Bonbury (Banbury) in ecclesia Lincoliensi, de qua Magistro Johanni de Streteley cardinalis Petragoricensis de novo providit, pro taxa xxx li.

De ecclesia de Ascheby parva (Little Ashby), de qua Willelmo Edele de Slyndon' cardinalis Petragoricensis de novo providit, pro taxa iiii li. xiii s. iiii d.

De ecclesia de Longhous (Laughton), de qua fuit provisum Waltero Bernak' per cardinalem Petragoricensem.

De ecclesia Sancti Clementis de Wylouby (Willoughby) fuit provisum per dominum cardinalem Petragoricensem Hugoni de Kipasse, pro taxa xxiii li. vi s. viii d.

### Exoniensis

De cantoria perpetua Sancte Anne sita in ecclesia Omnium Sanctorum Exonie fuit provisum per dominum Urgellensem Alexandro Sporeman'.

### Licheffeldensis

De ecclesia de Asdeby (Alderley), de qua per cardinalem Petragoricensem fuit provisum Johanni de Baston', pro taxa viii li.

De ecclesia de Burnhull' (Burnhill), de qua per dominum Petragoricensem fuit provisum Hugoni de Pamberton', non taxata.

Summa pagine lxxix li. vi s. viii d. Item v benefficia.

(fol. 183) De vicaria ecclesie de Dorsete magna (Great Dassett), de qua per dominum cardinalem Petragoricensem [527] fuit provisum Guillelmo Wy de Westbury, non taxata.

### Bangorensis

De ecclesia de Damburgham (Llangian) fuit provisum per dominum cardinalem Petragoricensem David nato Johannis.

### Menevensis

De ecclesia de Kemerthmaur' (Cenarth), de que

[517] 22 August 1357.
[518] Stolaton', **b.**
[519] 28 February 1357.
[520] 31 May 1360.
[521] 25 October 1359.
[522] Followed by two words so heavily deleted by lines as to be illegible, **a.**
[523] *iiii*, **b.**
[524] Follows *Hode* blotted, **a.**

[525] In the margin of **a**: *computatum fuit et solutum in computis suis ultimo rendatis.*
[526] Om. **a.**
[527] Om. **b.**

cardinalis Petragoricensis providit Rotberto le Despensser, vi li. xiii s. iiii d.[528]

De ecclesia de Houbescarth', de qua per dominum cardinalem Urgellensem fuit provisum Willelmo Sibbethop' iiii kalendas Octobris.[529] Non habuit effectum quia episcopus certificat quod non est in sua diocesi.[530]

De ecclesia de Kouseby (Cowesby), de qua per dominum Urgellensem fuit provisum Henrico de Herpelby.[531]

Summa universalis restarum denariorum Beati Petri est vi$^c$ viii li. xvi s. iiii d.

Summa vero restarum annui census est ix li. xi s. ix d.

Summa restarum de annatis beneficiorum iii$^m$ v$^c$ lxi li. v s. viii d. ob. vel circa. Item v$^c$ lxiii fl. xx d. sterlingorum.

Et sic est summa universalis omnium precedentium restarum iiii$^m$ clxxix li. xiii s. ix d. ob. vel circa, v$^c$ lxiii fl. xx d. sterlingorum. Approbatum

(fol. 183$^v$) Exploretur pro iure camere de infrascriptis concessionibus et mandatis si effectum habuerunt vel non et si aliquid dicte camere debeatur.[532]

### Roffensis

Mandatum fuit quod episcopi Wynthoniensis et Eliensis possint unire unum vel plura benefficia ad patronatum regis Anglie spectantia mense [533] priorisse et conventus monasterii sororum de ordine predicatorum et in dictis benefficiis vicarios instituere per Innocentium iii ydus Maii anno primo.[534]

Item eisdem quod possint unire dictis monialibus unum, duo aut plura benefficia quorum redditus c li. secundum decimam non excedant.

### Wygorniensis

Concessum fuit episcopo Wygorniensi ut sex benefficia ecclesiastica curata, dum vacabunt, in sua diocesi, etiam si ad collationem appostolicam spectarent, posset conferre.

### Eliensis

Una ex parochialibus ecclesiis de Hadenham (Haddenham) et de Leveryngton' (Leverington), cum vacabunt, quam episcopus Eliensis elegerit, fuerit unita [535] mensse sue.

Fuit data potestas episcopo Londoniensi ut parochialem ecclesiam de Dromell' (Orwell) Eliensis diocesis unire valeat auctoritate appostolica monasterio de Sempringham.

Fuit data potestas Thome episcopo Eliensi ut parochialem ecclesiam de Hynton' (Cherry Hinton) uniat domui collegiate scolarium Sancti Petri universsitatis Canthebrigie.

Unio facta de ecclesia de Turbilston' (Thurcaston), de Belgrave, Difeld (Byfield) Lincoliensis diocesis monasterio Sancti Ebrulff (St. Evroul) Exoniensis diocesis fuit per papam confirmata, videlicet illa quam magister elegerit.

Fuit concessum abbati et conventui monasterii de Seuhous (Newhouse) Premostratensis ordinis Lincoliensis diocesis ut ipsi in vicariis ecclesiarum quas ad proprios usus [536] obtinent et obtinebunt possint per ordinarium loci canonicos expresse professos in vicariis facere collocari usque ad sex.

(fol. 184) Ecclesie de Humbreston' (Humberstone) et de Hungeston' (Hungarton) fuerint unite monasterio Beate Marie Leycestr', et de ecclesia de Hungeston' est satisfactum et de alia est inquirendum si habuit effectum.

Exploretur de parochiali ecclesia de Waresleye (Waresley) Lincoliensis diocesis ad presentationem custodis et scolarium aule de Valencie Marie universsitatis Canthebrigie Eliensis diocesis unita et appropriata auctoritate appostolica per episcopum Londoniensem predictis custodi et scholaribus

Item de ecclesiis de Saxthorp' (Saxthorpe), de Tilney et de Waresle (Waresley) parochialibus Norwicensis et Lincoliensis diocesium appropriatis predictis custodi et scolaribus.

### Ybernie

Item dat pro arayratgiis omnia benefficia Ybernie data pro arayratgiis in aliis computis de quibus nichil recepit.

### Anglie et Ybernie

Item dat pro arayratgiis omnia benefficia collata per dominum nostrum Urbanum sive in Anglia sive in Ybernia a iii kalendas Maii pontificatus sui anno primo [537] usque ad viii kalendas Februarii anno tertio,[538] exceptis positis supra in recepta, et dicta pro arayratgiis data infra singulariter et distincte designantur.

(fol. 185) [539] Sequntur arayratgia benefficiorum collatorum et missorum in Anglia per sanctissimum patrem dominum Urbanum papam quintum a iii kalendas Maii pontificatus sui anno primo [537] citra.

### Eliensis

De parochiali ecclesia de Ebesworth' (Elsworth) Eliensis diocesis, vacatura cum Johannes de Merthon' dignitatem, personatum vel officium curatum in ecclesia Lichfeldensi fuerit pacifice assecutus, fuit provisum

---

[528] Sum om. **a.**
[529] 28 September 1357.
[530] This sentence lacking, **b.**
[531] The remaining items on this folio are lacking in **b.**
[532] In the margin of **a**: *attende*
[533] *messe*, MSS.
[534] 13 May 1353.
[535] *fuerint unite*, MSS.

[536] *pus* with a general sign of abbreviation, MSS.
[537] 29 April 1363.
[538] 25 January 1365.
[539] Folio 184$^v$ is blank.

Thome Eltesle, clerico dicte Eliensis diocesis, bacallario in utroque iure, iii kalendas Maii.[540]

### Nortwycensis

Collatio et provisio facte auctoritate ordinaria Waltero de Reddenesse, clerico Eboracensis diocesis, de parochiali ecclesia de Kokkling (Blickling) Nortwicensis diocesis, vacante ex eo quod Willelmus de Swanifler archidiaconatum Norwicensem est pacifice assecutus, fuerunt confirmate vel provisum de novo,[541] pro taxa x li. xiii s. iiii d.

Item collatio et provisio facte fratri Stephano Johannis [542] indito Stephani de prepositura monasterii Sancte Marie Nortonen' ordinis Sancti Benedicti, vacante per promotionem abbatis dicti monasterii, fuerunt confirmate vel provisum de novo v nonas Martii.[543]

Item ordinatio facta per bone memorie Dominum Ottonem,[544] tunc in partibus Anglie apostolice sedis legatum, de uno perpetuo vicario in parochiali ecclesia de Morton' dicte diocesis fuit confirmata vel provisum de novo.

### Exoniensis

Item collatio et provisio ex causa permutationis, et est Willelmo Sirel de archdiaconatu Tottonensi in ecclesia Exoniensi pro ecclesia parochiali de Dodington (Doddington) Lincolniensis diocesis, fuerunt [545] confirmate vel provisum de novo vii kalendas Maii.[546] Composuit medio iuramento pro xxxi li. x s., de quibus solvit xi li. x s., restant xx li.

### Lincolniensis

Motu proprio fuit provisum cardinali Morinensi [547] de canonicatu et prebenda ac archidiaconatu Lincolniensibus, vacantibus per obitum cardinalis Magalonensis,[548] v idus Maii.[549] Non habuit effectum quia rex contulit Wycham.

De perpetua vicaria parochialis ecclesie de Haringwhrth' (Harringworth) Lincolniensis diocesis, vacante per obitum Simonis Alten in Romana curia defuncti, fuit provisum Johanni Cosin, presbytero dicte diocesis.[550]

### (fol. 185[v]) Lichefeldensis

Item Johanni de Dytthon', clerico Lichefeldensis diocesis, de canonicatu et prebenda quos Willelmus Askeby, sedis apostolice capellanus, in ecclesia Lincolniensis obtinuit, vacantibus per resignationem ipsius in manibus [551] ordinarii aut per assecutionem alterius prebende in dicta.

### Saresburiensis

Item Waltero de Childerle parva, presbytero Eliensis diocesis, de parochiali ecclesia de Brodesydelyng' (Sydling St. Nicholas) Saresburiensis diocesis, vacante per mortem Nicholai de Englysey, que tanto tempore vacavit quod eius collatio est ad sedem apostolicam devoluta.

### Lincolniensis

Item Johanni Anneston', presbytero Lincolniensis diocesis, de parochiali ecclesia de Hokclive (Hockliffe) ⟨Lincolniensis⟩ diocesis, vacante in curia per obitum Johannis Wyndhull', vii kalendas Maii.[552]

Item Petro Newbold, bacallario in legibus, de canonicatu et prebenda ecclesie collegiate de Rippon' et prebenda de Munketon' (Monkton) in eadem ecclesia, vacantibus per obitum Johannis de Wynewyk.

### Eboracensis

Item Johanni de Estsex, presbytero, de parochiali ecclesia de Rustan' (Rudston) Eboracensis diocesis, vacante per cessionem vel resignationem liberam ultimi rectoris eiusdem a tanto tempore quod eius collatio est ad sedem apostolicam legitime devoluta.

### Herfordensis

Item Johanni Brekenhull', presbytero Herfordensis diocesis, de perpetua vicaria parochialis ecclesie de Borydon' (Burrington) dicte diocesis, vacante per resignationem Ade de Abbatia in manibus ordinarii.

### Dunelmensis

Item Thome de Penreth', presbytero Karleolensis diocesis, de parochiali ecclesia de Wythesurgion' (Washington) Dunelmensis diocesis, vacante ex eo quod Robertus de Warthtop', patiens defectum natalium de soluto hinc et inde genitus, eam per duos annos et ultra detinuit nulla dispensatio super hoc obtenta.

### Bangorensis

Item Theodorico filio Johannis Appoweyn, clerico Bangorensis diocesis, de dimidia ecclesia parochiali de Laddinan (Llandinam), seu eiusdem ecclesie dimidia portione, dicte Bangorensis diocesis, vacante ex eo quod episcopus Bangorensis eandem, tanquam illicitus detentor, per triennium occupavit, iiii kalendas Maii.[553]

### Cantuariensis

De parochiali ecclesia de Boxele (Boxley) Cantuariensis diocesis, vacante per obitum Domini Vitalis

---

[540] 29 April.
[541] The remainder of the sentence, om. **b**.
[542] Om. **b**.
[543] 3 March.
[544] *Ottonum*, MSS.
[545] *fuit*, MSS.
[546] 25 April.
[547] Giles Ecelin de Montaigue, priest of St. Martin in Montibus.
[548] Audoin Aubert, bishop of Maguelone, bishop of Ostia.
[549] 11 May
[550] In the margin of **a**: *Lichefeldensis* deleted by a line.

[551] Om. **a**.
[552] 25 April.
[553] 28 April.

Sancti Martini in Montibus cardinalis, fuit provisum Thome Sanville, clerico Cantuariensis diocesis, ii nonas Maii.[554]

### (fol. 186) Eboracensis

Collatio facta per archiepiscopum Eboracensem auctoritate apostolica de canonicatu et prebenda in ecclesia Sanctorum Marie et Angelorum Eboracensi Thome de Middelton', presbytero Lincolniensis diocesis, vacantibus per obitum Nicholai de Wyteby in Romana curia defuncti, fuit auctoritate apostolica confirmata vel provisum de novo.

Institutio, admissio et inductio facte de Ricardo de Redforde, iurisperito, al parochialem ecclesiam de Stretton' (Sturton) Eboracensis diocesis, quam per xv annos vel circa tenuit et adhuc tenet pacifice, fuerunt confirmate vel provisum de novo; solvit in partem taxe xi li., restat xxxiii li.[555]

### Saresburiensis

Item subrogatus fuit Wilelmus de Okerbon' in omni iure quod competebat quondam Arnaldo Pagena in canonicatu et prebenda de Buschrepton' (Bishopstone) in ecclesia Saresburiensi,[556] quos idem Willelmus per octo annos et amplius tenuit, super quibus dictus quondam Arnaldus contra ipsum Willelmum litem movit et postmodum regno Anglie decessit, vii idus Maii.[557]

### Lichefeldensis

De canonicatu ecclesie Lichefeldensis et prebenda de Prees in ipsa ecclesia, vacantibus per resignationem Petri alias Johannis de Aleston', fuit provisum Roberto de Stratton', legum doctori, auditori palatii, xvi kalendas Junii.[558]

### Eliensis

Collatio et provisio facte auctoritate ordinaria, iure devoluto, de prioratu seu administratione prioratus de Swaveseye (Swavesey) Eliensis diocesis, a monasterio Sanctorum Sergi et Bachi Andegadvensis (Angers) dependente, ordinis Sancti Benedicti, per unum religiosum dicti monasterii solito gubernari, fratri Johanni Walkelin, monacho monasterii Westmonasterii, monasterii Londoniensis diocesis, fuerunt[559] confirmate vel provisum de novo, xvi kalendas Junii.[560]

### Cicestrensis

Unita fuit et annexa ecclesia parochialis de Lannsing (Lancing) Cicestrensis diocesis mense et usui ministri et fratrum hospitalis Sancte Trinitatis de Modyndenn

(Muttinden) Cantuariensis ⟨diocesis⟩ servata portione compteni pro vicario dicte ecclesie, v kalendas Junii.[561]

De archidiaconatu ecclesie Landavensis, vacante per resignationem Thome de Eltesle Eliensis diocesis, in utroque iure bacallarii, fuit eidem Thome provisum, kalendas Junii.[562]

### Dunelmensis

De canonicatu et prebenda sive portione vel Byres (Byers) in ecclesia collegiata de Aukelond (Auckland) Dunelmensis diocesis, vacantibus per mortem Rogeri de Blanner, (fol. 186v) Romana curia defuncti, fuit provisum Rogero de Slateburn, presbytero Eboracensis diocesis, v idus Junii.[563]

### Carkagensis, Ybernia

De canonicatu ecclesie Carkagensis, vacante per consecrationem Georgii electi Cassellensis, fuit provisum Willelmo Bulla, clerico Laoniensis diocesis in Ybernia, v idus Junii.[563]

### Ymlacensis, Ybernia

De rectoria curata de Tirpararus (Tipperary) Ymlacensis diocesis, vacante per consecrationem David Penlyn electi Ymlacensis, fuit provisum Oddoni Ohogan, clerico Cassellensis diocesis.

### Menevensis

Item Thome de Therford', clerico Lincolniensis diocesis, de canonicatu et prebenda ecclesie Sancti Mauritii de Abrewely (Abergwili) Menevensis diocesis, vacantibus per resignationem Johannis de Waltham.

### Eboracensis

Item Rogero de Ulran, presbytero Eboracensis diocesis, de beneficio ecclesiastico, videlicet de ecclesia parochiali Sancte Helene in Sebynegaut' (Stonegate, York) Eboracensis diocesis, per mortem Johannis de Botere, v idus Junii.[564]

### Cicestrensis

De parochiali ecclesia de Westechenor (West Ichenor), Cicestrensis diocesis, vacante per mortem Rogeri de Lyndon, ultimi rectoris eiusdem, extra Romanam curiam defuncti, que tanto tempore vacavit quod eius collatio est ad sedem apostolicam legitime devoluta, fuit provisum Roberto Amye de Brendbrogton', presbytero[565] Lincolniensis diocesis, v kalendas Junii.[566]

### Eboracensis

De vicaria perpetua parochialis ecclesie de Slypton' in Craven' (Skipton in Craven) dicte diocesis, vacante

---

[554] 6 May.
[555] Sum om. **b**. In the margin of **a**: *taxata xliiii li.*
[556] Followed by *diocesis*, MSS.
[557] 9 May.
[558] 17 May.
[559] *fuit*, MSS.
[560] 17 May.

[561] 28 May.
[562] 1 June.
[563] 9 June.
[564] 9 June.
[565] *bresbytero*, MSS.
[566] 28 May.

per mortem Willelmi de Dragton', ultimi vicarii eiusdem, a tanto tempore quod eius collatio est ad sedem apostolicam legitime devoluta, fuit provisum Thome filio Johannis filii Matilde Achaliate de Shirburn' in Elmeto Eboracensis diocesis.

Collatio et provisio facte auctoritate ordinaria Nicholai de Chedelyngton' de cancellaria ecclesie Dublinensis, vacante ex eo quod Johannes de Troye, dictam cancellariam obtinens, prebenda de Wardes (Swords) in ipsa ecclesia fuit pacifice assecutus etiam si dictus ordinarius tempore collationis esset excommunicatus, fuerunt confirmate vel sibi provisum de novo.

### Eboracensis

Item Roberto de Brompton', presbytero Eboracensis diocesis, de parochiali ecclesia de Kayingham (Keyingham) dicte diocesis, vacante per resignationem sive dimissionem Willelmi de Brokeleby, que tanto tempore vacavit quod eius collatio est ad sedem apostolicam legitime devoluta.

### Saresburiensis

Item Willelmo Person, presbytero Saresburiensis diocesis, de parochiali ecclesia de Swyndon' (Swindon) dicte Saresburiensis diocesis, que per cessionem vel dimissionem [567] Nicholai Hamnan, (fol. 187) ultimi rectoris eiusdem, tanto tempore vacavit quod eius collatio est ad sedem apostolicam legitime devoluta.

### Dunelmensis

Item Waltero Jabes, presbytero Dunelmensis diocesis, de vicaria ecclesie parochialis de Nernham (Norham) dicte diocesis, vacante per mortem Willelmi de Elwik', ultimi vicarii eiusdem extra Romanam curiam defuncti, quam frater Ricardus Cave, monachus et apostata ordinis Cisterciensis per duos annos et amplius occupavit pacifice indebite.

### Eboracensis

Item Johanni de Boldeston', clerico Eboracensis diocesis, de parochiali ecclesia de Mysen (Misson) dicte diocesis, vacante per resignationem seu [568] dimissionem Johannis de Sulthorp a tanto tempore quod eius collatio est ad sedem apostolicam devoluta.

### Eboracensis

Item Willelmo de Wincornik', presbytero Eboracensis diocesis, de parochiali ecclesia de Manfeld (Manfield) dicte diocesis, vacante per resignationem vel obitum [569] quondam Willelmi de Scruttewill', [570] ultimi rectoris eiusdem, a tanto tempore quod eius collatio est ad sedem apostolicam legitime devoluta.

### Eboracensis

Item Roberto de Wadyngham, clerico Lincolniensis diocesis, de parochiali ecclesia Kayingham (Keyingham) Eboracensis diocesis vacante per resignationem Willelmi de Brokeslesby in manibus ordinarii a tanto tempore quod eius collatio est ad sedem apostolicam legitime devoluta.

### Eboracensis

Item Willelmo de Rippon', clerico Eboracensis diocesis, de parochiali ecclesia Sancti Martini in Mikilgate (Micklegate) Eboracensis civitatis, vacante per obitum quondam Thome de Bretby in Romana curia defuncti, iiii idus Junii. [571]

### Eboracensis

De parochiali ecclesia de Elkesley Eboracensis diocesis, vacante per mortem Johannis Cambok a tanto tempore quod eius collatio est ad sedem apostolicam legitime devoluta, fuit provisum Roberto de Overe, clerico Eliensis diocesis.

### Lichefeldensis

De parochiali ecclesia de Bodile (Baddiley) Lichefeldensis diocesis, vacante per resignationem Willelmi de Hunkele, ultimi rectoris eiusdem, in manibus ordinarii a tanto tempore [572] quod eius collatio est ad sedem apostolicam legitime devoluta, fuit provisum Rogero de Wodemorton', presbytero Nortwycensis diocesis.

### Lichefeldensis

Item Rogero de Wodenoton', presbytero Norwycensis diocesis, de ecclesia de Gaddele (Baddiley) Lichefeldensis diocesis, que valet xxv m. sterlingorum secundum communem extimationem annuatim.

### Eboracensis

Item Roberto de Marton' de officio seu beneficio non curato in ecclesia collegiata Sancti Johannis Beverlaci Eboracensis diocesis, valet annuatim vi m. sterlingorum.

### (fol. 187ᵛ) Eboracensis

Item Roberto de Sochowe, presbytero Eboracensis diocesis, de ecclesia de Aghton' (Aughton), valet secundum communem extimationem xl li. sterlingorum.

### Eliensis

Item Roberto de Svere, clerico [573] Eliensis diocesis de ecclesia de Elkesley, que taxatur ad xl m. sterlingorum.

### Eboracensis [574]

Item Johanni Ulram, presbytero, de parochiali ec-

---

[567] Followed by *R* deleted, **a.**
[568] Followed by *dis* deleted by a line, **a.**
[569] *obitus*, **b.**
[570] *Souttewill*, **b.**

[571] 10 June. In the margin of **a**: *taxata iiii li.*
[572] *tempore* repeated **a.**
[573] Over *presbytero* deleted, **a.**
[574] In the manuscripts the heading is repeated before each of the next six items.

clesia de Usegate (All Saints Pavement in Ousegate) in civitate Eboraci, que taxatur ad xv m. per annum.

Item Ade de Thornton', presbytero Eboracensis diocesis, de canonicatu et prebenda ecclesie de Rippon' et prebende de Munketon' (Monkton) in eadem ecclesia, quorum fructus xlvi li. xiii s. iiii d. secundum taxam non excedunt, iii nonas Julii.[575]

De parochiali ecclesia Omnium Sanctorum in Usegat' Eboraci, vacante in Romana curia per obitum Simonis Varde, fuit provisum Johanni de Verram, presbytero Eboracensis diocesis.

Item Roberto de Brompton, presbytero Eboracensis diocesis, de parochiali ecclesia in Kayingham (Keyingham) dicte diocesis, vacante per resignationem Willelmi de Brokeslewyn a tanto tempore quod eius collatio est ad sedem apostolicam legitime devoluta.

Item Johanni de Otrynham, presbytero Eboracensis diocesis, de parochiali ecclesia de Cotom (Cotham) dicte diocesis, vacante per resignationem Radulphi de Jacwell' a tanto tempore quod eius collatio est ad sedem apostolicam devoluta.

De parochiali ecclesia de Qwylan (Whixley) Eboracensis diocesis, que per obitum Nicholai Sesan tanto tempore vacavit quod eius collatio est ad sedem apostolicam legitime devoluta, fuit provisum Johanni de Torkeseye, bacallario in legibus, vii idus Julii.[576]

### Menevensis

Collatio et provisio auctoritate ordinaria dudum facte Johanni de Lese ordinis Sancti Benedicti de prioratu de Brecconia (Brecon) Menevensis, quem per xiiii annos et ultra possedit, vacante per obitum Nicholai Wardeden ultimi prioris eiusdem, fuerunt confirmate vel provisum de novo.[577]

### Eboracensis

Item collatio et provisio facte per Johannem archiepiscopum Eboracensem Thome de Middelton', vigore concessionis[578] facte ordinariis per felicis recordationis Innocentium papam VI super beneficiis conferendis sine cura que xv li. Turonensium parvorum secundum taxationem decime non excederent, de canonicatu et prebenda in capella Beate Marie et Sanctorum Angelorum Eboracensi, vacantibus per obitum Nicholai Wytheby, fuerunt confirmate de novo.

### (fol. 188) Imelacensis

De archidiaconatu ecclesie Imelacensis, vacante in Romana curia per consecrationem Willelmi episcopi Imelacensis, fuit provisum Johanni Sautton', clerico Imelacensis diocesis.

### Eboracensis

Dispensatum cum Johanne Baupyne, clerico Wygorniensis diocesis, ut parochialem ecclesiam de Ildelay (Ilkley) Eboracensis diocesis, quam pacifice possidet, licite valeat retinere non obstante defectu natalium quem patitur de soluto genitus et soluta, taxata xvii li. vi s. viii d., de quibus solvit vi li. xiii s. iiii d., restat x li. xiii s. iiii d.

### Londoniensis

Item institutio, collatio et provisio facte auctoritate ordinaria, Nicholao de Drayton', bacallario in legibus, de parochiali ecclesia Sancti Martini in Vinetria (St. Martin Vintry) Londoniensi, quam possidet pacifice, fuerunt confirmate vel provisum de novo, qui composuit medio iuramento pro xiii li. vi s. viii d., de quibus solvit ii li., restat xi li. vi s. viii d.

### Lymericensis

Collatio facta auctoritate ordinaria Geraldo Laweles, presbytero Limericensis diocesis, de thesauraria ecclesie Limericensis, vacante per obitum Ade Hunete in partibus defuncti, fuit auctoritate apostolica confirmata vel provisum de novo, vii idus Julii.[579]

### Exoniensis et Landavensis [580]

Ex causa permutationis fuit provisum Martino de Neuton' de parochiali ecclesia de Kiltingan (St. Mary Hill) et Henrico de Stanton' de canonicatu et prebenda ecclesie collegiate de Glausne (Glasnay) Exoniensis et Landavensis [580] diocesium.

### Lincolniensis

Item Rogero de Slareburn' de perpetua vicaria parochialis ecclesie de Friskenay (Friskney) Lincolniensis diocesis et Willelmo Glayne de Podyngton' de vicaria perpetua parochialis ecclesie de Kaldewyk (Kildwick) Eboracensis diocesis.

### Londoniensis

Item Ade Tebaud' de libera capella de Chelmesforde (Chelmsford) Londoniensis diocesis et Thome Thebaud filio Roberti Thebaud' de Jewwya de decanatu [581] rurali Leninne (Lynn) Norwycensis diocesis.

### Nortwycensis

De decanatu [581] rurali de Bodenhal (Redenhall) Nortwicensis diocesis, vacante per liberam resignationem Willelmi Tamworth', clerici Londoniensis diocesis, fuit provisum Thome de Dayton' Lincolniensis diocesis.

---

[575] 5 July.

[576] 9 July.

[577] In the margin of **a**: *taxa xx li.*

[578] *commissionis,* **b**.

[579] 9 July.

[580] In **a** the first *n* is deleted by dots; in **b** the word is *Lodoniensis.*

[581] *canonicatu,* MSS.

## Wyntoniensis

Collatio et provisio facte auctoritate ordinaria Waltero de Sevenhampton', magistro in artibus, de canonicatu et prebenda de Tymberbury (Timsbury) in ecclesia monasterii monialium de Romeseye (Romsey) ordinis Sancti Benedicti Wyntoniensis diocesis, vacantibus per obitum Willelmi de Farlegh' extra curiam defuncti, fuerunt confirmate vel provisum de novo et fuit surrogatus in iure quod eidem Willelmo et quondam Andree de Offord in eisdem competebat, idus Julii,[582] solvit in partem taxe xl s. Restat.[583]

## (fol. 188ᵛ) Elfinensis in Ybernia

De prioratu de Innocentia iuxta Atheluayn (Athlone) ordinis Cluniacensis Elfinensis diocesis in Ybernia, vacante per obitum Mathei ultimi prioris eiusdem, fuit provisum fratri Willelmo Otomoltens, monacho et cancellario dicte prioratus, vi idus Augusti.[584]

## Eboracensis

De parochiali ecclesia de Hornesee (Hornsea) Eboracensis, vacante apud sedem apostolicam per obitum Domini Raymundi de Fargiis quondam cardinalis,[585] fuit provisum[586] Nicholao de Lonayns,[587] iii idus Augusti.[588]

## Eboracensis

Motu proprio fuit provisum Domini Guillelmi cardinalis Cesaraugustanensis (Saragossa)[589] de canonicatu ecclesie Eboracensis et prebenda de Masham in eadem[590] ecclesia, vacante per obitum cardinalis Magolonensis.[591]

## Bangorensis

De parochiali ecclesia Sanctorum Sirici et Julitte Languile (Llanerfyl?) Bangorensis diocesis, vacante per obitum ultimi rectoris eiusdem extra Romanam curiam defuncti, et quia tanto tempore vacavit quod eius collatio secundum statuta Lateranensis concilii est ad sedem apostolicam legitime devoluta, fuit provisum Reginaldo de Suynemere, presbytero dicte diocesis.

## Limericensis

De vicaria perpetua ecclesie parochialis de Kylkyde[592] (Killkeedy) Limericensis diocesis, vacante per obitum Thome, ultimi vicarii eiusdem extra Romanam curiam defuncti, a tanto tempore vacavit quod eius collatio est

ad sedem apostolicam legitime devoluta, fuit provisum Thome de Burge, presbytero Imelacensis diocesis.

## Londoniensis

Collatio facta per episcopum Cantuariensem Thome Yonge, officiali curie Cantuariensis, de cancellaria ecclesie Londoniensis, que dignitas est, fuit confirmata vel provisum de novo, et dimittet prebendam Wellensem vel prebendam in capella regia de Wymbernemister' (Wimborne Minster) Saresburiensis diocesis, xii kalendas Septembris.[593]

## Eboracensis

De vicaria perpetua parochialis ecclesie de Kukeham (Kirkham) Eboracensis diocesis, vacante per resignationem Willelmi de Slaiteburn' factam in manibus ordinarii, que tanto tempore vacavit quod eius collatio est ad sedem apostolicam legitime devoluta, vel alio quovismodo vacante, fuit provisum Symoni de Tonebrigge, presbytero Roffensis diocesis, et dimittet parochialem ecclesiam de Excete Cicestrensis diocesis.

## Eboracensis

De perpetua vicaria ecclesie parochialis de Chilling' (Gilling) Eboracensis diocesis, vacante ex eo quod Gerlacus de Clave, clericus Spirensis (Speyer) diocesis, eam detinuit occupatam in presbyterum non promotus infra tempus debitum, vel alio quovismodo, fuit provisum Thome filio Johannis de Briston', clerico Norwycensis diocesis.

## Saresburiensis

Item Roberto de Folby, clerico Eboracensis diocesis, de parochiali ecclesia Sancte Marie de Wynterburne Stakelane (Winterborne Stickland) Saresburiensis diocesis, vacante per mortem Thome Henrici de Chestr' in Romana curia defuncti.

## (fol. 189) Eboracensis [594]

Item fuit provisum Johanni de Ulram, presbytero Eboracensis diocesis, de parochiali ecclesia curata Omnium Sanctorum in Usegate (All Saints Pavement in Ousegate) Eboraci, vacante in curia per mortem Simonis Warde.

Item Roberto de Magon', clerico Eboracensis diocesis, de parochiali ecclesia de Tresk' (Thirsk) dicte diocesis, vacante per mortem ultimi possessoris eiusdem, et tanto tempore vacavit quod eius collatio est secundum statuta Lateranensis concilii ad sedem apostolicam legitime devoluta, et dimittet ecclesiam de Trichewell' (Titchwell) super qua litigat in palatio apostolico.

Item Reginaldo de Swynemore, presbytero Bangorensis diocesis, de parochiali ecclesia de Mollyng'

---

[582] 15 July.
[583] In the margin of **a**: *taxa xxviii li. xiii s. iiii d.*
[584] 8 August.
[585] Deacon of S. Maria Nuova.
[586] Followed by *R* deleted by a line, **a**.
[587] *Lenoyns*, **b**. Cf. *Cal. Pap. Lett., Petitions* i, 446; M-H. Laurent, *Urbain V, Lettres Communes*, no. 2613.
[588] 11 August.
[589] William d'Aigrefeuille, priest of S. Maria in Trastevere.
[590] Followed by *can* deleted by a line, **a**.
[591] Audoin Aubert, bishop of Maguelone, bishop of Ostia.
[592] *Kynlkyde*, **b**.

[593] 21 August. In the margin of **a**: *taxa xxxi li.*
[594] In the manuscripts this heading is repeated before the next two items.

(Melling) Eboracensis diocesis, vacante per mortem sive liberam resignationem eiusdem, et tanto tempore vacavit quod eius collatio est ad sedem apostolicam legitime devoluta, etiam si alio quovismodo vacante.

### Assavensis

Item Lewelmo de Brechonia, canonico [595] Menevensi, de parochiali ecclesia Sancti Eudelani (Dolwyddelan) Assevensis diocesis, vacante per liberam resignationem seu dimissionem factam per Theodorum natum Johannis Eweyn, ultimi rectoris eiusdem, vi kalendas Septembris.[596]

### Saresburiensis

Confirmata fuit auctoritate apostolica unio facta auctoritate ordinaria [597] de consensu capituli de parochiali ecclesia de Harewille (Harwell) Saresburiensis diocesis, que de patronatu Edwardi primogeniti regis Anglie Wallie principis existebat et ipsius principis infra castrum suum de Wallyngford (Wallingford) dicte diocesis, iii kalendas Septembris.[598]

De parochiali ecclesia de Roddegrave (Redgrave) dicte diocesis, vacante per obitum Johannis de Eye, ultimi rectoris eiusdem, extra Romanam curiam defuncti, que tanto tempore vacavit quod eius collatio est ad sedem apostolicam legitime devoluta, etiam si alio quovismodo vacante, fuit provisum Rogero Ry de Wodenorton', presbytero Nortwycensis.

### Norwycensis

Item Willelmo de Malteby, presbytero Eboracensis diocesis, de parochiali ecclesia in Snterleye (Blakeney or Glandford) Norwycensis diocesis, vacante per mortem ultimi rectoris eiusdem, et que tanto tempore vacavit quod eius collatio est ad sedem apostolicam legitime devoluta.

### Norwycensis

Item Andree de Burwille, presbytero Norwycensis diocesis, de parochiali ⟨ecclesia⟩ in Sniterlee (Blakeney or Glandford) dicte diocesis, vacante per obitum Walteri Mayney de Silneye extra Romanam curiam defuncti, que tanto tempore vacavit quod eius collatio est ad sedem apostolicam legitime devoluta, vel alio quovismodo, et dimittet parochialem ecclesiam de Rishull' (Rishangles) dicte diocesis.

### (fol. 189ᵛ) Norwycensis

Item Thome Draper, presbytero Londoniensis diocesis, de parochiali ecclesia de Frange (Frenze) Norwycensis diocesis, vacante per liberam resignationem Willelmi de Colneye in manibus ordinarii factam, et

tanto tempore vacavit quod eius collatio est ad sedem apostolicam devoluta, xi kalendas Septembris.[599]

### Dunelmensis

Item Ade de Thornithon', presbytero Eboracensis diocesis, de canonicatu et prebenda seu portione ecclesie collegiate de Derhengton' (Darlington) Dunelmensis diocesis, vacante per obitum quondam Willelmi de Kyldesby extra Romanam curiam defuncti, etiam si in tanto tempore vacavit quod eius collatio est sic ad sedem apostolicam devoluta.

### Eliensis

Surrogatus fuit Walterus de Baketon', magister in artibus, in omni iure quod competebat quondam Henrico de Harwedon' in ecclesia parochiali de Hadenham (Haddenham) dicte Eliensis diocesis, super qua dum viveret in[600] Romana curia litigabat, et dimittet parochialem ecclesiam de Wygoresham (Wittersham) Cantuariensis diocesis, et unum [601] beneficium infrascriptum, videlicet prebendam Cicestrensem vel canonicatum sub expectatione prebende ecclesie Sancti Johannis Beverlaci Eboracensis diocesis, xi kalendas Octobris.[602]

### Eboracensis

Unio et incorporatio dudum facte per archiepiscopum Eboracensem de parochiali de Colston', communiter Kercolston' nuncupata, (Car-Colston) conventui et monasterio de Radesforda, communiter Wirkesop' nuncupata (Worksop), ordinis Sancti Augustini Eboracensis diocesis, fuerunt confirmate vel provisum de novo, vii idus Octobris.[603]

### Exoniensis

Gratia, acceptatio, collatio et provisio facte vigore litterarum acceptarum Roberto Sumpter, clerico Exoniensis diocesis legum doctori de canonicatu et prebenda ecclesie Exoniensis, vacantibus per obitum Roberti Heyzeward', cum decanatu Exoniensi, vacante per obitum Reginaldi de Rogwill' extra Romanam curiam defuncti, fuerunt confirmate vel provisum de novo. Decanatus taxatur lxii li. xiii s. iiii d. et prebenda iiii li., de quibus solvit xxii li. iiii s. v d. ob., restant xliii li. viii s. x d. ob.

### Herfordensis

De canonicatu et prebenda de Murthon magna (Moreton Magna) in ecclesia Herfordensi, vacantibus per consecrationem Simonis de Sudebiria electi Londoniensis, fuit provisum Johanni Godewik', clerico Norwicensis diocesis, bacallario in legibus xiiii kalendas Novembris.[604]

---

[595] *canonicatu*, MSS.
[596] 27 August.
[597] *apostolica*, **b.**
[598] 30 August.
[599] 22 August.
[600] *qua veniet in*, MSS. For the above reading see below p. 285.
[601] *duum*, **a.**
[602] 21 September.
[603] 9 October.
[604] 19 October.

### Eboracensis

Unio et incorporatio facte per archiepiscopum Eboracensem de parochiali ecclesia de Hemyngburgh' (Hemingborough) Eboracensis diocesis priori et capellano Dunelmensibus fuerunt auctoritate apostolica confirmate vel provisum de novo, xi kalendas Novembris.[605]

### Saresbiriensis

Collatio facta per episcopum Saresbiriensem Johanni Pikerel, presbytero Lin (fol. 190) colniensi diocesis, de parochiali ecclesia de Waybaxhouse (Upway) Saresbiriensis diocesis, fuit confirmata vel provisum de novo, non obstante defectu natalium quem patitur de presbytero genitus et soluta, et fuit habilitatus. Solvit xxvi s. viii d., restat.

### Eboracensis

Item collatio facta Johanni Beaupyre, clerico Wygorniensis diocesis, de parochiali ecclesia de Ilkelay (Ilkley) Eboracensis diocesis, fuit confirmata vel provisum de novo, ⟨non⟩ obstante defectu natalium quem patitur de presbytero genitus et soluta.

### Limericensis

Collatio et provisio auctoritate ⟨ordinaria⟩ facte Philipo de Walle, clerico Limericensis diocesis, de archidiaconatu[606] ecclesie Artfertensis, que dignitas curata in eadem ecclesia existit, vacante per obitum Bernardi Ythothnus extra curiam Romanam defuncti, fuerunt confirmate vel provisum de novo.

### Wellensis

Item collatio et provisio facte auctoritate ordinaria per episcopum Wellensem Johanni Benoit, presbytero Saresburiensis diocesis, de canonicatu et prebenda ecclesie Wellensis fuerunt confirmate vel provisum de novo, ii kalendas Septembris.[607]

### Wellensis

Item collatio auctoritate ordinaria facta per episcopum Wellensem et Bathoniensem Johanni Benoit, presbytero, de canonicatu et prebenda Combe tertie decime in ecclesia Wellensi fuit auctoritate apostolica confirmata vel provisum de novo, ii kalendas Septembris.[607]

Secuntur beneficia collata in Anglia anno secundo

### Menevensis

Primo de canonicatu ecclesie collegiate de Landewybrevy[608] (Llandewi-Brefi) et prebenda de Lannarth' (Llanarth) in eadem Menevensi diocesi, vacante per

mortem Ricardi Wrote[609] extra Romanam curiam defuncti, fuit provisum Petro de Belgrave, clerico Lincolniensis diocesis, nisi sit alteri jus quesitum, vii idus Novembris.[610]

### Waterfordiensis

Electio facta per canonicos capituli[611] seu conventus prioratus Beate Katerine iuxta Waterfordia, Waterfordiensis diocesis ordinis Sancti Augustini, de fratre David Bossher in priorem dicte prioratus, vacantem per obitum fratris Andree Eduard ultimi prioris eiusdem extra Romanam curiam defuncti, fuit confirmata vel provisum de novo, vi idus Novembris.[612]

### Londoniensis

De ecclesia parochiali et curata Sancti Leonardi in Estchepe (St. Leonard, Eastcheap) Londonie, vacante ex eo quod quidam Johannes Tavern' de Lichefeld aliam ecclesiam parochialem et curatam de Bromlee (Bromley) Roffensis diocesis extitit pacifice assecutus, aut alio quovismodo vacante, fuit provisum Ricardo Cauthon clerico Menevensis diocesis, et dimittet parochialem ecclesiam Sancti Bernarchi super Taf' (Llanfyrnach) dicte Menevensis diocesis, iiii idus Novembris.[613]

### (fol. 190ᵛ) Leoniensis in Ybernia

De archidiaconatu Leoniensis diocesis in Ybernia, vacante per consecrationem Domini Thome episcopi Leoniensis, seu alio quovismodo, fuit provisum Mauricio Okahil, presbytero Fynoborensis diocesis, et dimittet archidiaconatum Duacensem.

### Corkagensis in Ybernia

De canonicatu et prebenda ecclesie Corkagensis[614] de Kyllapowlr' Molane (Kilaspugmullane) in eadem Corkagensi ecclesia, vacantibus per mortem Willelmi Espeworth' extra Romanam curiam[615] defuncti, qui tanto tempore vacaverunt quod eorum collatio est ad sedem apostolicam legitime devoluta, fuerunt provisum David Gower, presbytero Lymoricensis diocensis.

Item Ricardo de Valle, clerico Corgensis (Cork) diocesis de thesauraria ecclesie Limericensis, vacante per mortem Roberti Godyn in Romana curia defuncti.

### Imlacensis in Ybernia

Item Edmundo Prayneg', clerico Imlacensis diocesis, de canonicatu et prebenda de Dysirt Lamen (Isert Laurence) in ecclesia cathedrali Imlacensis diocesis,

---

[605] 22 October.
[606] Followed by *dicta* deleted by dots, **a**.
[607] 31 August.
[608] Followed by *Beate Katerine* deleted by a line, **a**.

[609] *Wyote*, **b**.
[610] 7 November.
[611] *capitulum*, MSS.
[612] 8 November.
[613] 10 November.
[614] Followed by *ecclesia* deleted by a line, **a**.
[615] Om. **a**.

vacantibus per consecrationem Domini David de Foynlyn electi Imlacensis, pridie idus Novembris.[616]

### Norwycensis

De parochiali ecclesia de Sudbiria (Sudbury) Norwycensis diocesis, vacante ex eo quod Henricus de Campedene cancellariam ecclesie Londoniensis est pacifice assecutus, fuit provisum Thome de Kaketon', bacallario in legibus, x kalendas Decembris.[617]

### Saresburiensis

De canonicatu et prebenda ecclesie de Wilston' (Wilton) Saresburiensis diocesis, vacantibus per consecrationem Thome Trillek', electi Cicestrensis, fuit ⟨provisum⟩ Thome de Paxton', legum doctori auditori palatii apostolici, vii kalendas Decembris.[618]

### Wellensis

De canonicatu et prebenda ecclesie Wellensis, vacantibus per consecrationem Thome de Trellenk' electi Cicestrensis, fuit provisum Roberto de Stratton', legum doctori, et dimittet prebendam ecclesie collegiate Auclandie (Auckland) Dunelmensis diocesis, quos nondum possidet.

### Lincolniensis

Motu proprio fuit provisum Domini Johanni, tituli Sancti Martini presbytero cardinali, de parochiali ecclesia de Eburgbury (Adderbury) Lincolniensis diocesis, vacante prout supra.

### Herfordensis

De canonicatu et prebenda ecclesie Herfordensis, vacantibus per consecrationem Thome electi Cicestrensis, fuit provisum Nicholao de Chaddesdey, legum doctori, et dimittet prebendam Lichefeldensem, vi kalendas Decembris.[619]

(fol. 191) De canonicatu et prebenda ecclesie Herfordensis, vacantibus per consecrationem prout supra, fuit provisum Willelmo Bell', scholari in legibus.

### Exoniensis

De parochiali ecclesia de Niwaton' Sancti Cirici (Newton, St. Cyres) Exoniensis diocesis, que, post liberam resignationem Johannis Lynham, ultimi rectoris eiusdem, in manibus episcopi Exoniensis factam, tanto tempore vacavit quod eius collatio est ad sedem apostolicam legitime devoluta, licet per Willelmum de Molton', qui se gerit pro vicario eiusdem, ipsam detineat indebite occupatam, fuit provisum Johanni [620] Denis, presbytero Lincolniensis diocesis.

### Londoniensis

De decanatu ecclesie Londoniensis, vacante per consecrationem Domini Thome episcopi Cicestrensis, fuit provisum Johanni Appelby, legum doctori in Romana curia advocato, et dimittet parochialem ecclesiam de Wytteburn (Whitburn) Dunelmensis diocesis ac hospitale pauperum de Kipier (Kepier) et parochialem ecclesiam de Routhebury (Rothbury) que non dum possidet, et super hiis noscitur in palatio apostolico litigari.

### Exoniensis

De parochiali ecclesia curata de Essewat' (Ashwater) Exoniensis diocesis, vacante per mortem Magistri Ricardi Giffard, cuius collatio est secundum statuta Lateranensis concilii ad sedem apostolicam legitime devoluta, fuit provisum Willelmo de Todeworth', clerico dicte diocesis bacallario in legibus, iiii kalendas Decembris.[621]

### Cantuariensis

De parochiali ecclesia de Bissopysburn (Bishopsbourne) Cantuariensis diocesis, vacante ex eo quod quidam Willelmus de Tingull', ipsam nuper obtinens, aliud beneficium incomparabile [622] in ecclesia Wellensi est, ut dicitur, auctoritate apostolica pacifice assecutus, fuit provisum Johanni Digg', presbytero Cantuariensis diocesis, iii nonas Decembris.[623]

### Saresburiensis

De canonicatu et prebenda ecclesie monasterii monialium de Wilton' Saresburiensis diocesis, vacantibus per consecrationem Thome electi Cicestrensis, fuit provisum Waltero de Multon' presbytero, et dimittet parochialem ⟨ecclesiam⟩ Chevele (Cheveley) Norwycensis diocesis, vi idus Decembris.[624]

### Dunelmensis

De parochiali ecclesia de Wyteburn (Whitburn) Dunelmensis, vacante cum Johannes de Appelby de canonicatu Londoniensi fuit pacifice assecutus, fuit provisum [625] Ricardo de Wynchecumbe Wygorniensis diocesis, xix kalendas Januarii.[626]

### (fol. 191ᵛ) Dunelmensis

De parochiali ecclesia de Wermow Episcopi (Bishop-Wearmouth) Dunelmensis diocesis, vacante ex eo quod Willelmus Newipart eandem ecclesiam curatam et ecclesiam parochialem de Spefford (Spofforth) Eboracensis diocesis non unitas aut annexas sed diversas occupavit et possedit,[627] simul per ii annos et amplius contra

---

[616] 12 November.
[617] 22 November.
[618] 25 November.
[619] 26 November.
[620] *Johannis*, **a**.

[621] 28 November.
[622] Presumably for *incompatibile*.
[623] 3 December.
[624] 8 December.
[625] Followed by *Johanne* deleted by a line, **a**.
[626] 14 December.
[627] *detinuit*, **b**.

constitutionem *execrabilis*, fuit provisum Willelmo de Arderne, magistro in artibus Lincolniensis diocesis, et dimittet parochialem ecclesiam de Chesdon' (Chesterton) dicte Lincolniensis diocesis, xv kalendas Januarii.[628]

## Lincolniensis

De parochiali ecclesia in Hagworthinghan (Hagworthingham) Lincolniensis diocesis, vacante ex eo quod Johannes de Swyneshevede, olim rector [629] eiusdem, ecclesiam parochialem de Werthrynsete (Wetheringsett) Norwycensis diocesis est pacifice assecutus, fuit provisum Thome de Thetford', clerico dicte diocesis, pridie nonas ⟨Januarii⟩.[630]

## Londoniensis

De parochiali ecclesia de Hakeneye (Hackney) Londoniensis diocesis, vacante cum Thomas de Paxton', auditor palatii apostolici, de canonicatu Wellensi fuit pacifice assecutus, fuit provisum [631] Thome de Wormenhale, licentiato in utroque iure, vi idus Januarii.[632]

## Lichefeldensis

De parochiali ecclesia de Estlemyngton alias Lemyngton' Hastyng' (Leamington Hastings) Lichefeldensis diocesis, vacante per obitum ultimi rectoris eiusdem extra Romanam curiam defuncti, que tanto tempore vacavit quod eius collatio est ad sedem apostolicam devoluta, fuit provisum Ricardo de Thisho, bacallario in decretibus, et dimittet parochialem ecclesiam de Herthelegh' (Hartley) Roffensis diocesis, iiii [633] idus Januarii.[634]

## Herfordensis

De perpetuo beneficio, prebenda seu portione wlgariter nuncupata in ecclesia parochiali de Holegode (Holdgate) Herfordensis diocesis, vacante per consecrationem Thome electi Cicestrensis, fuit provisum Ricardo de Tornecombe, clerico Wyntoniensis diocesis, iiii idus Januarii.[634]

## Lincolniensis

Ex causa permutationis fuit provisum Johanni Hasting de vicaria perpetua parochialis ecclesie de Offynton' (Uffington) et Roberto Frankelyn, presbytero Lincolniensis diocesis, de perpetua vicaria parochialis ecclesie de Cherlebury (Charlbury) dicte diocesis, solvit in partem taxe vicarie de Cherlebury, v li., iii idus Januarii,[635] restat.[636]

## Menevensis

De canonicatu et prebenda ecclesie collegiate de Aburgwyly (Abergwili) Menevensis diocesis vacantibus per resignationem Philipi Bellicampo, fuit provisum Ricardo Piger, clerico Lincolniensis diocesis, pridie kalendas Februarii.[637]

## Exoniensis

Collatio et provisio facte Johanni de Mounceaux, presbytero, de parochiali (fol. 192) ecclesia Sancti Brioci de Nanstenez (St. Breoke) Exoniensis diocesis fuerunt confirmate vel provisum de novo, non obstante defectu natalium quem patitur de presbytero genitus et soluta, vii kalendas Martii.[638]

## Lichefeldensis

Acceptatio et collatio, vigore litterarum apostolicarum facte Hugoni Carles, clerico Lichefeldensis diocesis, de canonicatu et prebenda ecclesie de Langevaylaugh (Llangyfelach) in ecclesia de Abregvilly (Abergwili) Menevensis diocesis, vacantibus per mortem Willelmi H. a tanto tempore quod eorum collatio est ad sedem apostolicam legitime devoluta, fuerunt confirmate vel provisum de novo, et dimittet parochialem ecclesiam de Egemundon' (Edgmond) vel canonicatum et prebendam de Goswesale (Gnosall) dicte Lichefeldensis diocesis.

## Norwycensis

De parochiali ecclesia de Snerterle (Blakeney or Glandford) Norwycensis diocesis, vacante per obitum Walteri Mayn' de Tilneye, que tanto tempore vacavit quod eius collatio est ad sedem apostolicam legitime devoluta, fuit provisum Willelmo Bell', et dimittet parochialem ecclesiam de Stanforde (Stanford) Saresburiensis diocesis ac canonicatum et prebendam Herfordensis nuper sibi collatos, v nonas Martii.[639]

## Eboracensis [640]

De parochiali ecclesia de Brantingham Eboracensis diocesis, vacante ex eo quod Willelmus Strode ipsam per annum et ultra, cessante legitimo impedimento canonicata dispensatione non obtenta, detinuit in presbyterum non promotus, fuit provisum Johanni de Thoresby, legum doctori, et dimittet parochialem ecclesiam de Lilleford' (Lilford) Lincolniensis diocesis, xvi kalendas Aprilis.[641]

## Lincolniensis et Saresburiensis

Ex causa permutationis fuit provisum Johanni Hasting', Lincolniensis diocesis presbytero, de vicaria per-

---

[628] 18 December.
[629] *rectoris*, **a.**
[630] 4 January.
[631] The manuscripts read: *fuit provisum pacifice assecutus fuit.*
[632] 8 January.
[633] Om. **b.**
[634] 10 January.
[635] 11 January.
[636] In the margin of **a**: *taxa x li. vicaria de Cherlebury.*

[637] 31 January.
[638] 24 February.
[639] 3 March.
[640] Followed by *Ebo* deleted by a line. **a.**
[641] 17 March.

petua de Osynton' (Uffington) Saresburiensis diocesis et Roberto Frankeleyn, presbytero Lincolniensis diocesis, de vicaria perpetua parochialis ecclesie de Cherlebury (Charlbury) dicte Lincolniensis diocesis, solvit pro vicaria ultima supra xxv li.

### Eboracensis

Communicatur auditori cause pendentis [642] in palatio apostolico inter Ricardum de Derby, presbyterum Lichfeldensem, et Johannem de Brinkeles super archidiaconatu Nothingie (Nottingham) in ecclesia Eboracensi ut si dictus se in eodem jus habere docere non poterit ipsum archidiaconatum prefato Ricardo adiudicet et sibi provideat de, xi kalendas Aprilis.[643]

### Dunelmensis

De capellania sive hospitali Sancti Edmundi Regis (fol. 192ᵛ) et martiris in Gareshed (Gateshead) Dunelmensis diocesis, vacante per mortem quondam Walteri Fawtonberge extra Romanam curiam defuncti, fuit provisum Ade de Fenroter, clerico dicte diocesis, nonas Aprilis.[644]

### Lichefeldensis

De parochiali ecclesia de Weyngton' (Warrington) Lichefeldensis diocesis, vacante per ⟨obitum⟩ quondam Johannis de Stanfordham extra Romanam curiam defuncti, a tanto tempore quod eius collatio est ad sedem apostolicam legitime devoluta, fuit provisum Johanni de Par seniori, clerico dicte diocesis, pridie nonas Aprilis.[645]

### Menevensis

De parochiali [646] ecclesia de Langladewen (Llanglydwen) Menevensis diocesis, vacante per obitum Johannis Sampsonis [647] ultimi rectoris eiusdem in Romana curia defuncti, fuit provisum Philipo Loyde alias dicto Priton'.[648]

### Dunelmensis

De canonicatu ecclesie de Aukeland (Auckland) et prebenda de Bires (Byers) in eadem ecclesia Dunelmensis diocesis, vacante per obitum Rogeri de la Blaynere in Romana curia defuncti, fuit provisum Thome Cokyn, clerico dicte diocesis.

### Eboracensis

Item Willelmo Wasselyn, clerico Lincolniensis diocesis, de parochiali ecclesia de Feriby (North Ferriby) Eboracensis diocesis, vacante per obitum Roberti de

Bridelington', ultimi rectoris eiusdem extra Romanam curiam defuncti, que tanto tempore vacavit quod eius collatio est secundum Lateranensis concilii statuta [649] ad sedem apostolicam legitime devoluta.

### Norwycensis

Provisio facta auctoritate apostolica ex causa permutationis Johanni de Heyngham de parochiali ecclesia **Sancti Gregorii de Sudbury Norwycensis diocesis,** etiam si per habilitatem [650] ipsius Johannis sibi ius non competat ex eo quod aliam parochialem ecclesiam teneat infra tempus debitum ad sacerdotium non promotus, fuit auctoritate apostolica confirmata vel provisum de novo, **x kalendas Junii.**[653]

### Lincolniensis

De vicaria parochialis ecclesie de Eyton' iuxta Milton Mombray (Eaton near Melton Mowbray) fuit provisum ex causa permutationis Johanni de Stevenach' et Rogero Judde de parochiali ecclesia de Esthwell' (Eastwell) Lincolniensis diocesis, vii kalendas Junii.[654]

### Medensis in Ybernia

Collatio et provisio auctoritate ordinaria facte Philipo Whit' Medensis diocesis de archidiaconatu Lismorensi in Ybernia, vacante per obitum Magistri Thome Walche alias Leynaff', ultimi archidiaconi eiusdem extra Romanam curiam defuncti, fuerunt confirmate vel provisum de novo, iiii kalendas Junii.[655]

### Roffensis in Ybernia (?)

De archidiaconatu Roffensi per resignationem Willelmi Reed fuit provisum Willelmo Wenlok', et dimittet ecclesiam parochialem de Horton' Roffensis diocesis et prebendas capelle Beate Marie Magdalene de Brig (fol. 193) genorth' (Bridgenorth) et capelle [656] Sancti Johannis in Witlesfordbrigge (St. John on the Bridge, Whittlesford), nonas Junii.[657]

### Londoniensis

De novo fuit provisum Johanni de Lingesdon' de parochiali ecclesia de Alta Rothing (High Roding) Londoniensis diocesis, quam per annum et ultra pacifice tenuit in presbyterum non promotus, et fuit habilitatus,[658] xviii kalendas Julii.[659]

De prioratu monasterii Salopie (Shrewsbury),

---

[642] *pendenti,* **a.**
[643] 22 March.
[644] 5 April.
[645] 4 April.
[646] Followed by *ex* deleted by a line, **a.**
[647] *Sampsonig,* **b.**
[648] *Poriton,* **b.**

---

[649] Om. **a.**
[650] *pro habilitate,* **b.** There are no footnotes numbered 651 and 652.
[653] 23 May.
[654] 26 May.
[655] 29 May.
[656] *capella,* MSS.
[657] *Julii,* **b.** 5 June or 7 July.
[658] *inhabilitatus,* MSS.
[659] 14 June.

vacante per obitum Rogeri de Cufraston' quondam prioris eiusdem in Romana curia defuncti, fuit provisum Johanni Perle, monacho dicti monasterii, xii kalendas Julii.[660]

### Exoniensis

De canonicatu et prebenda bursaria vulgariter nuncupata in ecclesia collegiata Sancte Crucis Criditon' (Crediton) Exoniensis diocesis, vacantibus ex eo quod Walterus de Bamiton' ipsam prebendam obtinens aliam prebendam in dicta ecclesia est pacifice assecutus, et quia tanto tempore vacaverunt quod eorum collatio est ad sedem apostolicam legitime devoluta fuit provisum Rogero Payn, clerico Exoniensis ⟨diocesis⟩ ix kalendas Junii.[661]

### Wellensis

Acceptatio facta vigore litterarum apostolicarum per Willelmum Tingel, in utroque iure doctorem, et collatio subsecuta de archidiaconatu Taunton' in ecclesia Wellensi, cui prebenda est annexa, vacante per obitum Roberti Hereward extra Romanam curiam defuncti, fuerunt [662] confirmate vel provisum de novo, et dimittet parochialem ecclesiam de Bissopisburne (Bishopsbourne) Cantuariensis diocesis, ac canonicatum et prebendam ecclesie Sancti Karenthoci (Crantock) Exoniensis diocesis, vi idus Augusti.[663]

### Lincolniensis

Ex causa permutationis fuit provisum Johanni Attewode de Anneworth' a parochiali ecclesia de Frisby iuxta Waynflet (Firsby near Wainfleet) Lincolniensis diocesis et Willelmo nato Willelmi de Wadyngton' de Hanneworth' de parochiali ecclesia de Syweldby (Shoby) dicte diocesis, iii kalendas Augusti.[664]

### Lincolniensis

Ex causa permutationis fuit provisum Roberto de Wysingser' de perpetua vicaria de Hugton' (Luton) Lincolniensis diocesis et Willelmo de Haddon' de libera capella in Temeford (Chelmsford) Londoniensis diocesis, viii idus Augusti.[665]

### Herfordensis

De canonicatu et prebenda de Hunderton' in ecclesia Herfordensi, vacantibus per privationem Nicholai Hethe per dominum papam factam propter pluralitatem et multitudinem nimian beneficiorum que obtinebat, fuit provisum Nicholao de Drayton', bacallario in legibus, iiii kalendas Septembris.[666]

### (fol. 193ᵛ) Dunelmensis

Collatio facta ex causa permutationis Roberto de Warthcopp' de parochiali ecclesia in Wssington (Washington) Dunelmensis diocesis auctoritate ordinaria, non obstante defectu natalium quem patitur de soluto genitus et soluta, fuit confirmata vel provisum de novo, xiii kalendas Octobris.[667]

### Lincolniensis

De parochiali ecclesia de Slapton' Lincolniensis diocesis, vacante cum Matheus de Assheton' canonicatum et prebendam ecclesie Eboracensis fuit pacifice assecutus, fuit provisum Ricardo de Croxton', clerico Eliensis diocesis.

### Dunelmensis

Item Johanni de Swetehop', clerico Dunelmensis diocesis, canonicatu et prebenda ecclesie de Narton' (Norton) ⟨dicte⟩ diocesis, vacantibus per obitum Thome Peleyn alias dicti Drax in Romana curia defuncti, kalendas Octobris.[668]

### Lincolniensis

Item Johanni de Stevenach' alias de Whist, presbytero Lincolniensis diocesis, de parochiali ecclesia de Sitheston' (Syston) dicte diocesis, vacante per obitum Willelmi Wertington' extra Romanam curiam defuncti, a tanto tempore quod eius collatio est ad sedem apostolicam legitime devoluta.

### Roffensis

Collatio et provisio per viam permutationis auctoritate ordinaria facte Johanni de Alsthawe de parochiali ecclesia de Snrthelond (Snodland) Roffensis diocesis fuerunt confirmata vel provisum de novo.

### Lincolniensis

Motu proprio fuit provisum Domino H. cardinali Ostiensi [669] de canonicatu et prebenda ecclesie Lincolniensis vacantibus per obitum cardinalis Petragoricensis, xi kalendas Novembris.[670]

### Dunelmensis

Ex causa permutationis fuit provisum Nicholao Hunggeford de canonicatu Carleolensi et vicaria de Witingham (Whittingham) Dunelmensis diocesis ab ecclesia Carleolensi dependente et Johanni de [671] Forde de prioratu Sancte Fredeswid' (St. Frideswide) ordinis Sancti Augustini Lincolniensis diocesis, iii kalendas Novembris.[672]

---

[660] 20 June.
[661] 24 May.
[662] *fuit*, MSS.
[663] 8 August.
[664] 30 July.
[665] 6 August.
[666] 29 August.

[667] 19 September.
[668] 1 October.
[669] Elias de S. Eredio.
[670] 22 October.
[671] *de* repeated, MSS.
[672] 30 October.

### Londoniensis

Collatio et provisio facte auctoritate apostolica Thome de Baketon', bacallario in legibus, de parochiali ecclesia Sancti Gregorii de Sudbir' tunc vacante ex eo quod Henricus de Compender ipsam obtinens cancellariam ecclesie Londoniensis fuit pacifice assecutus etiam si per simplicem resignationem dicti H. vacavit, fuerunt confirmate vel provisum de novo, vii kalendas Novembris.[673]

### Saresburiensis

De canonicatu et prebenda de Neweton' (North Newnton) wlgariter nuncupata in ecclesia de Wilton' Saresburiensis diocesis, vacantibus per consecrationem Thome Trillek' episcopi Roffensis, fuit provisum Rogero de Freton', legum doctori, et dimittet parochialem ecclesiam de Ratlefden' (Rattlesden) Norwycensis diocesis et prebendam ecclesie collegiate (fol. 194) de Bromierd' (Bromyard) Herfordensis diocesis, nonas Novembris.[674]

### Roffensis

Collatio et provisio facte auctoritate apostolica Willelmo Wenlok' de archidiaconatu Roffensi, etiam per constitutionem *execrabilis* vacaverit, fuerunt confirmate vel provisum de novo, vii kalendas Novembris.[673]

### Eboracensis

De vicaria de Kerneteby (Carnaby) vel dicta Fraysthorp' (Fraisthorpe) Eboracensis diocesis, vacante per obitum quondam Willelmi de Appelby extra Romanam curiam defuncti, fuit provisum Johanni de Skilling' de Heldon', presbytero dicte diocesis, pridie kalendas Novembris.[675]

### Exoniensis

De parochiali ecclesia de Essewat' (Ashwater) Exoniensis diocesis, vacante per obitum Ricardi Giffard extra Romanam curiam defuncti, fuit provisum Willelmo Todeworth', clerico dicte diocesis, nisi sit alteri specialiter jus quesitum.

Completum est de anno secundo

Beneficia collata et confirmata in Anglia per dominum nostrum Dominum Urbanum papam V pontificatus sui anno tertio.

### Saresburiensis

Et primo de precentoria in ecclesia Saresburiensi, que dignitas est curata, vacante et reservata per mortem Philipi de Codeford extra Romanam curiam defuncti, fuit provisum Roberto de Walsham, et dimittet decanatum libere capelle infra castrum de Wallingford dicte Saresbiriensis diocesis, viii idus Novembris.[676] Solvit in partem dicte taxe xiii li. vi s. viii d. Restat.

### Roffensis

De parochiali ecclesia de Clyve (Clyffe) Roffensis diocesis, vacante per privationem Johannis de Bisshipeston' per dominum papam factam, fuit provisum Roberto de Trimeston', clerico Norwicensis diocesis, et dimittet parochialem ecclesiam de Holme, super qua litigat.

### Saresburiensis

De canonicatu et prebenda ecclesie Saresburiensis, vacante per mortem Philipi de Codeforde extra Romanam curiam defuncti, fuit provisum Johanni Gurmunchestr', presbytero, xv kalendas Decembris.[677]

### Dunelmensis

De parochiali ecclesia de Wermow episcopi (Bishop-Wearmouth) Dunelmensis diocesis, vacante per lapsum temporis concessi Willelmo de Newport de ipsa retinenda cum quadam parochiali ecclesia, fuit provisum Willelmo de Arderne, magistro in artibus, et dimittet parochialem ecclesiam de Chesterton' Lincolniensis diocesis, xv kalendas Decembris.[678]

### (fol. 194ᵛ) Dublinensis in Ybernia

De hospitali Sancti Johannis Baptiste extra portam civitatis Dublinensis in Ybernia, quem illicite detinet Guillelmus Gerardi, frater dicti hospitalis, fuit provisum Henrico Randelf presbytero dicti hospitalis.

### Lincolniensis

De canonicatu et prebenda ecclesia Lincolniensis, vacantibus per privationem Raymundi Pelegrini per dominum papam factam, fuit provisum Henrico le Despenser Lincolniensis diocesis, bacallario in legibus, et dimittet parochialem ecclesiam de Besseworth' (Market Bosworth) Lincolniensis diocesis ac prebendas Saresbiriensem et Landavensem, iii nonas Decembris.[679]

### Londoniensis

De parochiali ecclesia de Hakenay (Hackney) Londoniensis diocesis, vacatura cum Thomas de Paxton', sedis apostolice capellanus, dignitatem in ecclesia Wellensi fuerit pacifice assecutus, fuit provisum Waltero de Multon', presbytero Norwycensis diocesis, et dimittet parochialem ecclesiam de Chivele (Cheveley) Norwycensis diocesis, vii idus Decembris.[680]

### Wellensis

Surrogatus fuit [681] Stephanus Pempel, legum doctor, in omni iure quod competebat Thome de Paxton', audi-

[673] 26 October.
[674] 5 November.
[675] 31 October.
[676] 6 November.

[677] 17 November.
[678] 17 November.
[679] 3 December.
[680] 7 December.
[681] Followed by *Wellensis* deleted by dots, **a**.

tori palatii apostolici, in decanatu ecclesie Wellensis, qui super eo contra dictum Stephanum, ad eundem decanatum auctoritate ordinaria electum, litem movit, qui quidem Thomas postmodum iuri sibi in eo competenti expresse renuntiavit, et dimittet prebendas Exoniensem ac collegiatarum Sancti Thome martiris de Glasney (Glasnay) Exoniensis diocesis et de Abirwyli (Abergwili) Menevensis diocesis ecclesiarum, x kalendas Januarii.[682]

### Eboracensis

Motu proprio fuit provisum Domino H. cardinali Ostiensi [683] de canonicatu et prebenda ecclesie Eboracensis vacantibus per obitum cardinalis Petragoricensis, iii nonas Januarii.[684]

### Wyntoniensis

De archidiaconatu Sutrye (Surrey) in ecclesia Wyntoniensi, vacante per mortem Johannis de Hedington' extra Romanam curiam defuncti, fuit provisum Thome de Paxton', legum doctori, et dimittet parochialem ecclesiam de Hakenay (Hackney) Londoniensis diocesis, iiii nonas Januarii.[685]

Dispensatur cum Radulpho de Tregrisyon, bacallario in legibus, rectore parochialis ecclesie de Dulo (Duloe) Exoniensis diocesis, ut in quacunque universitate vel studio generali insistendo, audiendo vel legendo iura civilia hinc ad biennium ratione dicte sue ecclesie non teneatur se facere ad ordinem presbyteratus promoveri, nonas Januarii.[686]

### Saresburiensis

Provisio auctoritate apostolica facta Henrico de Wynterton', bacallario in legibus, de canonicatu et prebenda ecclesie Saresbiriensis, quos Ricardus de (fol. 195) Norwico defunctus per nonnullos annos pacifice possederat, etiam si vacent per obitum Thome de Clipston' in Romana curia defuncti,[687] fuit confirmata vel provisum de novo, nonas Januarii.[688]

### Elphinensis

Postulatio facta per viam compromissi de fratre Mauricio Magneyill', canonico monasterii Sancti Augustini de Cluamcuarsgut nafynam (Clontuskert Omanny) Aroucensis ordinis Elphinensis diocesis, in priore dicti monasterii fuit confirmata vel provisum de novo, pridie nonas Januarii.[689]

### Elphinensis

Postulatio facta per viam compromissi de fratre Donato Magseyrad, canonico professo monasterii canonicorum regularium Sancti Augustini Roscoman (Roscommon) Arouacensis ordinis Elphinensis diocesis, de presbytero religioso et soluta genito, ad monasterium predictum, vacantem per obitum fratris Thome eiusdem monasterii prioris conventualis, fuit confirmata vel provisum de novo, nonas Januarii.[688]

### Midensis

De prioratu conventuali Sancti Petri Noveville (Newtown) iuxta Trym (Trim) Midensis diocesis ordinis Sancti Augustini, cum vacabit per assecutionem possessionis pacifice monasterii Thome martiris prope civitatem Dublinensem faciendam per abbatem dicti monasterii, fuit provisum fratri Thome Bertram, canonico dicti monasterii, viii idus Januarii.[690]

### Menevensis

De canonicatu et prebenda ecclesie collegiate de Aberwili (Abergwili) Menevensis diocesis, vacantibus vel vacaturis si vel cum Stephanus Pempel decanatum ecclesie Wellensis fuit pacifice assecutus, fuit provisum Thome de Eltesle, presbytero Eliensis diocesis, conferendam sibi certa forma reservata, viii idus Januarii.[690]

### Exoniensis

De canonicatu et prebenda ecclesie Exoniensis, vacantibus vel vacaturis prout supra, fuit provisum Roberto de Guneston', bacallario in legibus, et dimittet parochialem ecclesiam in Cleve (Clyffe) Roffensis diocesis, nuper per dominum papam sibi collatam, et parochialem ecclesiam de Holme dicte Norwycensis diocesis, super qua litigat, vii kalendas Februarii.[691]

### Saresburiensis

De archidiaconatu Barkschire in ecclesia Saresbiriensi diocesi, vacante per mortem Edmundi de Lambeth extra curiam defuncti, fuit provisum Thome de Paxton', legum doctori, auditori palatii, et dimittet parochialem ecclesiam de Hakeneye (Hackney) Londoniensis diocesis, vii kalendas Februarii.[691]

### (fol. 195ᵛ) Elphinensis in Ybernia

Electio canonica [692] facta et confirmata [693] per episcopum subsequta de Thoma Mannirgoassa, canonico ecclesie Elphinensis, ad decanatum dicte ecclesie, vacantem per obitum Nicholai ultimi decani eiusdem, fuerunt confirmate vel provisum de novo, nonas Februarii.[694]

---

[682] 23 December.
[683] Elias de S. Eredio.
[684] 3 January.
[685] 2 January.
[686] 5 January. In the margin: *non debetur annata quia non est nec collata nec provisum.*
[687] *fuerunt,* b.
[688] 5 January.
[689] 4 January.

[690] 6 January.
[691] 26 January.
[692] *canonice,* MSS.
[693] *confirmato,* MSS.
[694] 5 February.

## Exoniensis

De canonicatu et prebenda ecclesie collegiate de Glayssenay (Glasnay) Exoniensis diocesis, vacaturis cum Stephanus Pempell' decanatum ecclesie Wellensis fuerit pacifice assecutus, fuit provisum Thome Worderove, presbytero Eboracensis diocesis, bacallario in decretis, vi idus Februarii.[695]

## Lincolniensis

Item collatio et provisio facte auctoritate apostolica Thome de Tetfforde, clerico Lincolniensis diocesis, de parochiali ecclesia in Hagworthingham Lincolniensis diocesis, vacante per assecutionem parochialis ecclesie de Wethertrigsete (Wetheringsett) Norwycensis diocesis collate Johanni de Swyneshevede, quam dictus Thomas possedit diu pacifice, licet felicis recordationis Dominus Innocentius papa VI$^{tus}$ quondam Hervico [696] Romelon, clerico Cameracensis (Cambrai) diocesis de dicta ecclesia sic vacante providit, qui litteris super hoc non confectis extra Romanam curiam decessit, fuerunt confirmate vel provisum de novo.

## Landavensis

De archidiaconatu ecclesie Landavensis, vacante per liberam resignationem Magistri Thome de Eltisle, fuit provisum Thome de Southam, clerico Lichefeldensis diocesis, xvi kalendas Martii.[697]

## Corkagensis

Collatio et provisio facte auctoritate ordinaria Nicholao Barri de archidiaconatu Corkagensi, quem per annos et dies possedit pacifice, etiam si tanto tempore vacavit quod eius collatio fuerit ad sedem apostolicam legitime devoluta, fuerunt confirmate et provisum de novo, xii kalendas Martii.[698]

## Cicestrensis

De custodia hospitalis domus Beate Marie Cicestrensis, vacante per privationem Johannis de Domyton', clerici dicte diocesis, per dominum papam factam, fuit provisum Simoni Batere, presbytero Lincolniensis ⟨diocesis⟩, nonas Martii.[699]

## Exoniensis

De canonicatu et prebenda ecclesie collegiate Beati Thome martiris Glesneye (Glasnay) Exoniensis diocesis, vacaturis cum Stephanus Pempell' ipsos dimiserit, fuit provisum Petro Crugov, presbytero dicte diocesis, et dimittet parochialem ecclesiam Sancti Wylololay (Landewednack) dicte diocesis, nonas Martii.[700]

## Menevensis

Item Ricardo Treveninn, clerico Exoniensis diocesis, de canonicatu et prebenda ecclesie collegiate de Aberwili (Abergwili) Menevensis diocesis, vacantibus ut supra, viii idus Martii.[701]

## (fol. 196) Elphinensis in Ybernia

Confirmatio facta per Karolum episcopum [702] Elphinensem de Thoma Matumgossa, electo ad decanatum Elphinensem fuit confirmata; supra in principio pagine ponitur iterato, xvi kalendas Aprilis.[703]

## Eliensis

De parochiali ecclesia de Ditton' (Fen Ditton) Eliensis diocesis vacatura dum Nicholai de Bagthorp dignitatem, personatum vel officium in ecclesia Exoniensi fuerit pacifice assecutus, fuit provisum Thome de Hornynggisherd' Norwicensis diocesis, legum doctori, xvi kalendas Aprilis.[703]

## Eliensis

De parochiali ecclesia de Balthesden' (Rattlesden) Norwycensis diocesis, vacatura dum Rogerus de Freton' canonicatum et prebendam de Neweton' (North Newnton) in ecclesia de Wilton' Sarisbiriensis diocesis fuerit pacifice assecutus, fuit provisum Thome Worderove, presbytero Eboracensis ⟨diocesis⟩, et dimittet canonicatum et prebendam ecclesie collegiate de Glesney (Glasnay) per dominum papam nuper sibi collatas.[704]

## Cantuariensis

Collatio et provisio auctoritate ordinaria facte Willelmo Reed' de prepositura ecclesie collegiate de Wyngham (Wingham) Cantuariensis diocesis, vacante per mortem Johannis de Terverley [705] extra Romanam curiam defuncti, fuerunt confirmate vel provisum de novo, xv kalendas Maii.[706]

De archidiaconatu Leoniensi, vacante ex eo quod Thomas Otormachaym beneficium incompassibile una cum dicto archidiaconatu, dispensatione legitima non obtenta, contra canonum statuta tenuit tanto tempore quod eius collatio est ad sedem apostolicam legitime devoluta, fuit provisum [707] Donato Otytyrd, et dimittet prebendas dicte ecclesie et Cassellensis, xi kalendas Maii.[708]

## Dunelmensis

Acepptatio, collatio et provisio facte vigore litterarum apostolicarum Matheo de Balthon' de vicaria paro-

---

[695] 8 February.
[696] *Herco'vico*, MSS.
[697] 14 February.
[698] 18 February.
[699] 7 March.
[700] 7 March.

[701] 8 March. In the margin: *supra certificatum est in alia provisione.*
[702] *episcopi*, MSS.
[703] 17 March.
[704] *collatam*, **b.**
[705] Gerverley, **b.**
[706] 17 April.
[707] Followed by *F* deleted by dots, **a.**
[708] 21 April.

chialis ecclesie Beati Nicholai Novicastri (Newcastle upon Tyne) Dunelmensis diocesis, vacante per obitum ultimi rectoris seu [709] vicarii eiusdem extra Romanam curiam defuncti, quam per x annos possedit pacifice, reservationibus non obstantibus, fuerunt confirmate vel provisum de novo, xi kalendas Maii.[708]

### Lincolniensis

Acceptatio, collatio et provisio facte vigore litterarum apostolicarum Thome de Eltesle, presbytero Eliensis diocesis, de prebenda ecclesie Lincolniensis, vacante per obitum Johannis de Edyngton, extra Romanam curiam defuncti, fuerunt confirmate vel provisum de novo, xi kalendas Maii.[708]

### Saresbiriensis

Johanni Turk', presbytero Wellensis diocesis de vicaria perpetua de Jatmystre (Yetminster) Saresbiriensis diocesis et Willelmo Bonenffant de vicaria perpetua de Stanniton' Drew (Stanton Drew) dicte Wellensis diocesis.

### (fol. 196ᵛ) Eboracensis

Item collatio et provisio facte vigore litterarum appostolicarum felicis recordationis Domini Clementis pape VI Johanni de Newham, presbytero de parochiali ecclesia de Marthon in Crawen' (Marton in Craven) Eboracensis diocesis, fuerunt confirmate et provisum de novo, ix kalendas Mayi.[710]

### Lincolniensis

Item acceptatio et collatio facte auctoritate litterarum appostolicarum per Henricum de Dumeston', clericum Norwicensis diocesis, de parochiali ecclesia de Horwode magna (Great Horwood) Lincolniensis diocesis fuerunt auctoritate appostolica confirmate vel provisum de novo, ix kalendas Maii.[711]

### THIRD ACCOUNT OF JOHN DE CABRESPINO 1366 TO 1368

(Collectorie 12, fol. 1)[1] Computa seu rationes reddite tertio per Dominum Johannem de Cabrespino, collectorem Anglie, videlicet a die xx mensis Maii anni LXVI usque ad xviii diem mensis Februarii anni LXVIII quo ad receptus, licet [2] computa fuerint reddita [3] et finita mense Augusti et ibi sic similis conclusa. Tertie rationes

(fol. 2)[4] Tertie rationes facte per dominum Computa seu rationes Johannis de Cabrespino, collectoris Anglie, data camere appostolice anno domini Mᵒ CCCᵒ LXVIII de mensse Julii

(fol. 2ᵛ) Denarius Beati Petri solvitur quolibet anno in Anglia per perssonas infrascriptas et pro quotis infrascriptis, et ascendit in summam quolibet anno cxcix li. v s. iiii d.

Archiepiscopus Eboracensis xi li. x s.
Episcopus Saresbiriensis xvii li.
Episcopus Cicestrensis viii li.
Episcopus Wygorniensis x li. v s.
Episcopus Convetrensis et Lichfeldensis x li. v s.
Episcopus Lincoliensis xlii li.
Episcopus Exoniensis ix li. v s.
Episcopus Herffordensis vi li.
Episcopus Norwicensis xxi li. x s.
Episcopus Bathoniensis et Wellensis xi li. v s.
Archidiaconus Cantuariensis viii li.
Archidiaconus Roffensis v li. xii s.
Archidiaconus Middelssexie v li. x s.
Archidiaconus Wynthoniensis xi li. xiii s. iiii d.
Archidiaconus Surreie [5] v li. x s.
Archidiaconus Colcestr' v li. x s.
Archidiaconus Exessexie v li. x s.
Archidiaconus Eliensis v li.

Censsus ordinarius [6] solvitur in Anglia per infrascriptas perssonas et ascendit quolibet anno iiii li. xv s.

Abbas de Faversham xiii s. iiii d.
Abbas de Cortesey' viii s.
Abbas Sancti Edmundi de Bury xiii s. iiii d.
Abbas de Malmesbury xiii s. iiii d.
Abbas Sancti Albani xiii s. iiii d.
Prior de Tenebrigiis xiii s. iiii d.
Prior de Bodmyn ii s.
Prior de Anglisey' ii s.
Prior Karleolensis xiii s. iiii d.
Prior de Caucombus xv d.
Abbatissa Sancte Clare Londoniensis vi d.
Custos de Scardeburg' xv d.

(fol. 3, i)[7] Sequuntur computa sive rationes Johannis de Cabrespino, doctoris decretorum canonici Narbonensis in Anglia apostolice camere nuntii et collectoris, de omnibus et singulis per eum et per Dominum Johannem de Caroloco, priorem Lewensem, seu alios quoscumque nomine dicte camere receptis, liberatis, assignatis et expensis, tam de denariis Beati Petri, annuo censu, restis et annatis beneficiorum ac quibuscumque aliis obventionibus ad ecclesiam Romanam

---

[709] rectoris seu, om. **a.**
[710] 23 April.
[711] 23 April. Folios 197 to 201ᵛ are blank. Folios 202 to 262ᵛ duplicate folios 140 to 196ᵛ.
[1] The original rough parchment cover of this account.
[2] Reading doubtful on account of the roughness of the parchment.
[3] Followed by *in mense* deleted by a line.

[4] Folio 1ᵛ is blank.
[5] *Saresbiriensis*, MS.; i. e. Sar—.
[6] Followed by *Beati Petri* deleted by a line.
[7] The Arabic numeral is the modern foliation and the Roman the original foliation.

qualitercumque spectantibus a xx die mensis Maii anno domini M CCCᵒ LXVIᵗᵒ, quo tempore ultimo cum camera computavit, usque ad xviiiᵃᵐ diem Februarii anni LXVIII secundum computationem ecclesie Romane et sexagesimi septimi secundum computationem ecclesie Anglicane.

### Primo de denariis Beati Petri

De archiepiscopo Eborinii pro annis LXIIIIᵒ, quinto et sexto, pro quolibet xi li. x s., xxxiiii li. x s.

De episcopo Saresbiriensi pro anno LXIIIIᵒ xvii li.

De episcopo Cycestrensi pro annis LXIIIᵒ, quarto et quinto, pro quolibet viii li., xxiiii li.

De episcopo Wygorniensi, dimisso [8] in arayragiis pro annis LXIII, sexagesimo quinto et sexagesimo sexto, licet de LXIIIIᵗᵒ in ultimis computis fuerit computatum, pro quolibet dictorum trium annorum x li. v s., xxx li. xv s.

De episcopo Convetrensi et Licheffeldensi pro annis LXIIIIᵗᵒ et LXVᵗᵒ, pro quolibet x li., v s., xx li. x s.

De episcopo Lincoliensi pro annis LXIIIIᵗᵒ, quinto et sexto, pro quolibet xlii li., cxxvi li.

Summa pagine iiᶜ lii li. xv s.

(fol. 3ᵛ) De episcopo Exoniensi pro anno LXVI ix li. v s.

De episcopo Hereffordensi pro annis LXV et sexto, pro quolibet vi li., xii li.

### Bathoniensis et Wellensis [8a]

De episcopo Eliensi, solvente pro ecclesia Bathoniensi et Wellensi, cui prefuit immediate, pro annis LXIIIIᵒ, quinto et sexto licet pro LXIIIᵒ adhuc debeatur, pro quolibet dictorum trium annorum xi li. v s., xxxiii li. xv s.

De archidiacono Cantuariensi pro annis LXVᵗᵒ et sexto, pro quolibet viii li., xvi li.

De archidiacono Roffensi pro annis LXIII et LXIIIIᵒ, pro quolibet v li. et xii s., xi li. iiii s.

De archidiacono Midelssexie in ecclesia Londoniensi, quem dimisit Dominus Hugo Pelegrini in arayragiis pro annis LX, LXI et LXII, sed ostendit quitationem dicti Domini Hugonis LX, solvit pro LXIᵒ, LXIIᵒ, LXIIIᵒ et LXIIIIᵒ, pro quolibet dictorum iiiiᵒʳ annorum v li. x s., xxii li.[9]

De archidiacono Wynthoniensi pro annis LXII et LXIII, pro quolibet xi li. xiii s. iiiiᵒʳ d., xxiii li. vi s. viii d.

De archidiacono Surreie pro annis LXVᵒ et sexto, pro quolibet v li. xiii s. iiii d., xi li. vi s. viii d.

De archidiacono Colcestr' pro annis LXIIIIᵒ et quinto, pro quolibet v li. x s., xi li.

De archidiacono Exessye pro anno LXIIIIᵗᵒ v li. x s.

Summa pagine clv li. vii s. iiii d.

Summa maior recepte arreyragiorum denariorum Beati Petri est iiiiᶜ viii li. ii s. iiii d.

(fol. 4, ii)  Recepta de annuo censu

De abbate de Faversham pro annis LXIIIIᵒ, Vᵗᵒ et sexto, pro quolibet xiii s. iiii d., xl s.

De priore de Tenebrig' pro annis LXVI et septimo, pro quolibet xiii s. iiii d., xxvi s. viii d.

De abbate de Corthesey pro annis LXV et sexto, pro quolibet viii s., xvi s.

De abbate de Malmesbury pro annis LXVIᵒ et septimo, pro quolibet xiii s. et iiii d., xxvi s. viii d.

De priore de Bodmyn pro annis LXVI et septimo, pro quolibet ii s., iiii s.

De abbate Sancti Edmundi de Bury pro annis LXVI et septimo, pro quolibet xiii s. iiii d., xxvi s. viii d.

De abbate Sancti Albani pro annis LXVI et septimo, pro quolibet xiii s. iiii d., xxvi s. viii d.

De custode de Schardeburgh' pro annis LXIIIIᵒ, LXVᵒ, sexto et septimo, pro quolibet xv d., v s.

De abbatissa Sancte Clare Londonie pro annis LXVᵒ, LXVIᵒ et LXVII, pro quolibet vi d., xviii d.

Summa pagine viii li. xiii s. ii d., de quibus sunt v li xvi s. i d. de restis dicti census dimissis in precedentibus computis, et lvii s. i d. de recepta ordinaria dicti census, videlicet de anno LXVII.

(fol. 4ᵛ)  Sequitur recepta primorum fructum

### De diocesi Canturiensi nichil.

### De diocesi Roffensi

De vicaria de Shorn' (Shorne), taxata vi li. xiii s. iiii d., ratione provisionis facte ex causa permutationis Johanni Thome per Urbanum xiii kalendas Novembris anno ii,[10] dimissa in arayragiis pro iiii li. xiii s. et iiii d., pro complemento dicte reste iiii li. xiii s. iiii d.

De ecclesia de Ston' (Stone), taxata [11] xx li., ratione provisionis facte per Urbanum Johanni Pays x kalendas Decembris anno primo,[12] dimissa in arayragiis in v li., pro complemento dicte reste v li.

Summa pagine ix li. xiii s. iiii d.

(fol. 5, iii) Londoniensis

De archydiaconatu Essey', non taxato, ratione confirmationis facte Willelmo de Rothewell' per Innocentium iii idus Februarii anno viᵒ,[13] qui composuit medio iuramento pro mediis fructibus pro x li. xiii s. iiii d., dimisso in arayragiis pro vii li. xvi s. viii d., pro complemento dicte reste vii li. xvi s. viii d. Licet in araragiis aliorum computorum, non fuit nisi pro lvi s. viii d.; residuum fuit solutum pro incertis proventibus dicti archidiaconatus.

De ecclesia sive capella de Alswyk (Alswick), non taxata, ratione provisionis facte Rotberto Franceys per

---

[8] *dimissis*, MS.
[8a] In the margin.
[9] In the margin: *Dominus Hugo debet solvere pro anno LXᵒ.*

[10] 20 October 1364.
[11] Followed by *de* deleted by lines.
[12] 22 November 1362.
[13] 11 February 1358.

Urbanum iii nonas Januarii anno primo,[14] qui composuit medio iuramento pro medietate veri valoris, nullis deductis expensis, pro xxxiii s. iiii d., solvit pro complemento xxxiii s. iiii d.

De ecclesia Sancte Trinitatis Londonie, non taxata, ratione dispensationis facte cum Thoma Ball' quod, non obstante defectu natalium, posset illam retinere per Innocentium xi kalendas Junii anno ixº,[15] dimissa in arayragiis in xxv s., pro complemento dicte reste xxv s.

De ecclesia Sancti Martini in Vinetira Londonie, non taxata, ratione confirmationis facte Nicholao de Drayton', bachalario in legibus, per Urbanum vii idus Julii anno primo,[16] qui composuit medio iurato pro medietate veri valoris et cetera pro xiii li. vi. s. viii d., dimissa in arayragiis pro xi li. vi. s. viii d., pro complemento dicte reste xi li. vi. s. viii d.

De cancellaria Londoniensi, taxata xxxi li., ratione confirmationis facte Thome Jong, officiali curie Cantuariensis, per Urbanum xii kalendas Septembris anno primo,[17] pro complemento dicte taxe xxxvi li.

Summa pagine liii li. i s. viii d.

(fol. 5ᵛ)[18] De ecclesiis Sanctorum Stephani et Olavi in Colomastret et Veteri Iudisura (St. Stephen, Coleman St. and St. Olave, Old Jewry, London), non taxatis, ratione provisionis facte Radulpho de Daventer' per Urbanum vii kalendas Junii anno iiiiº,[19] qui composuit pro medietate veri valoris et cetera pro xv li., in partem dicte summe x li.[20]

De prioratu Sancte Crucis fratrum mendicantium (Holy Cross, London), non taxato, ratione confirmationis facte Johanni de Burs per Innocentium xii kalendas Junii anno x,[21] qui composuit pro medietate et cetera pro iii li. vi. s. et viii d., solvit pro complemento iii li. vi. s. viii d.

De decanatu Londonie, taxato liii li. vi. s. viii d., ratione provisionis facte Johanni Appelby per Urbanum iii nonas Decembris anno secundo,[22] in partem dicte taxe xiii li. vi. s. et viii d.[23]

Summa pagine xxvi li. xiii s. iiii d.

### (fol. 6, iiii) De diocesi Cicestrensi

De prebenda de Waltham in ecclesia Cicestrensi, taxata x li., ratione provisionis facte Ade de Hilton' per consecrationem Rotberti episcopi Cicestrensis per

Innocentium x kalendas Januarii anno viiiº,[24] pro complemento taxe x li.

De prebenda de Sillosey (Selsey) in eadem ecclesia, taxata xxi li. vi. s. viii d., ratione provisionis facte Rotberto de Askeby per obitum Johannis Leth' per Innocentium anno ixº,[25] dimissa in arayragiis pro xi li. vi. s. et viii d., pro complemento dicte reste xi li. vi. s. viii d.

De ecclesia de Bukstede (Buxted), de qua per assecutionem prepositure de Wyngham (Wingham) per Johannem de Beverle fuit provisum Waltero Sotton' per Innocentium iiii kalendas Aprilis anno viº,[26] et taxatur xxxii li., dimissa in arayragiis pro xii li., in complementum dicte reste xii li.

De precentoria Cicestrensi, taxata liii li. vi. s. viii d., de qua per obitum cardinalis de Gordonio [27] fuit provisum cardinali Aquensi [28] per Innocentium vi kalendas Octobris anno ixº,[29] in partem dicte taxe xxi li. xiii s. iiii d.[30]

Summa pagine lv li.

### (fol. 6ᵛ) De diocesi Wynthoniensi

De ecclesia de Newton' (Newington by Lambeth), taxata xiiii li. xiii s. iiii d., de qua per consecrationem Thome electi Dublinensis fuit provisum Thome de Eltosle per Urbanum xii kalendas Aprilis anno primo,[31] et secundo fuit provisum de eadem Willelmo de Brynkhill' xvii kalendas Maii per Urbanum eodem anno,[32] et sic non debetur nisi una annata, quia ambe sunt infra annum, pro ultima provisione et pro complemento dicte taxe xiiii li. xiii s. iiii d.[33]

De ecclesia de Dunteffaud' (Dunsfold), taxata xiii li. vi. s. viii d., de qua per obitum Willelmi de [34] Chateston' fuit provisum Johanni de Lewes per Urbanum xix kalendas Februarii anno primo,[35] dimissa in arayragiis pro vi li. xiii s. iiii d., in partem dicte reste iii li. vi. s. viii d.[36]

De prebenda de Tymberbury (Timsbury) in ecclesia monialium de Bomesey (Romsey), taxata xxviii li. xiii s.[37] iiii d., ratione confirmationis et provisionis de novo aut subrogationis facte Waltero de Semenhinton' per

---

[14] 3 January 1363.
[15] 22 May 1361.
[16] 9 July 1363.
[17] 21 August 1363.
[18] The heading *Adhuc Londoniensis* appears at the top of the page.
[19] 26 May 1366.
[20] In the margin: *resta v li.*
[21] 21 May 1362.
[22] 3 December 1363.
[23] In the margin: *resta xl li.*

[24] 23 December 1360.
[25] 1361.
[26] 29 March 1358.
[27] William Farinier of Gourdon, priest of Ss. Marcellino e Pietro.
[28] Peter Itherii, bishop of Dax, priest of Ss. Quattro Coronati.
[29] 26 September 1361.
[30] In the margin: *resta xxxi li. xiii s. iiii d.*
[31] 21 March 1363.
[32] 15 April 1363.
[33] In the margin: *Ista ecclesia non fuerat dimissa in arayragiis nisi pro iii li. vi. s. viii d.*
[34] Followed by *Cath* deleted by a line.
[35] 14 January 1363.
[36] In the margin: *resta iii li. vi. s. viii d.*
[37] Followed by *xii* deleted by a line.

Urbanum idus Julii anno primo,[38] dimissa in arayragiis pro xxvi li. xiii s. iiii d., in partem dicte reste xx li.[39]

De prebenda de Midelthon' (Middleton) in ecclesia monialium de Warwell' (Wherwell), taxata xxvi li. xiii s. iiii d., ratione provisionis facte Johanni Branketre per Innocentium quinto kalendas Januarii anno primo,[40] dimissa in arayragiis in xx li., in partem dicte reste v li.[41]

Summa pagine xliii li.

### (fol. 7, v) De diocesi Saresbiriensi

De prebenda de Husbourn' et Burbach' (Hurstbourne and Burbage) in ecclesia Saresbiriensi, taxata liii li. vi s. viii d., de qua per obitum Johannis de Whitchirbe fuit provisum Saladino de Falletis per Innocentium kalendas Junii anno sexto,[42] pro complemento taxe liii li. vi s. viii d.

De prebenda de Yamynser' (Yetminster) in ecclesia Saresbiriensi ratione provisionis facte Henrico de Walton', dimissa in arayragiis inter iiii^or obligatos cum archidiaconatu Richemundie in ecclesia Eboracensi et prebenda de Midelton' (Middleton) in ecclesia Cicestrensi in lxx li., de quibus pro ista debentur xviii li. vi s. viii d., de quibus solvit in ultimis computis vi li. xiii s. iiii d., pro complemento reste xi li. xiii s. iiii d.

De prebenda de Newenton' (North Newnton) in ecclesia monialium Wilton', taxata xx li, de qua per consecrationem Thome Trivok episcopi Roffensis fuit provisum Rogero de Freton', legum doctori, per Urbanum nonas Novembris anno secundo,[43] pro complemento taxe xx li.

De ecclesia de Wynterburn' Stikelan (Winterborne Stickland), taxata iiii li. vi s. viii d., de qua per resignationem Willelmi de Cheston' fuit provisum Thome Henrici per Innocentium xiiii kalendas Julii anno primo,[44] dimissa in arayragiis pro iii li. vi s. viii d., pro complemento dicte reste iii li. vi s. viii d.

De ecclesia de Wayboxhousse (Way Baieuse), taxata viii li., ratione confirmationis facte Johanni Pikerel quod non obstante defectu natalium quem patitur de presbytero genitus et soluta per Urbanum xi kalendas Novembris anno primo,[45] dimissa in arayragiis in vi li. xiii s. iiii d., pro complemento dicte reste vi li. xiii s. iiii d.

De prebenda de Shaftebury (Shaftesbury), que consistit in ecclesia de Gyllyngham (Gillingham) Saresbiriensis diocesis, taxata xxx li., de qua per obitum Raymundi Pelegrini fuit provisum Ricardo de Newen-

ton' per Urbanum xi kalendas Januarii anno iiii,[46] in partem dicte taxe x li.[47]

Summa pagine cv li.

(fol. 7^v)[48] De prebenda de Byscopeston' (Bishopstone) in ecclesia Saresbiriensi, taxata xx li., ratione subrogationis facte Willelmo de Okebourn' in iure quod competebat quondam Arnaldo Pagani per Urbanum vii idus Maii anno primo,[49] pro complemento dicte taxe xx li.

De vicaria de Osynton' (Uffington), non taxata, ratione provisionis facte ex causa permutationis Johanni de Astyngis per Urbanum xiii kalendas Aprilis anno ii°,[50] qui composuit pro medietate fructuum et cetera pro vi li. xiii s. iiii d. in partem dicte summe iii li. vi s. viii d.[51]

De precentoria Saresbiriensi, taxata xxxiii li. vi s. viii d., de qua vacante per mortem Philipi de Odefforde fuit provisum Rotberto de Walsham per Urbanum idus Novembris anno iii°,[52] dimissa in arayragiis in xx li., pro complemento dicte reste xx li.

De ecclesia de Stokton' (Stockton), taxata vi li. xiii s. iiii d., de qua, cum vacaret ex eo quod Johannes de Bokyngham parochialem ecclesiam de [53] Aiwe (Harrow) Londoniensis diocesis esset pacifice assecutus, fuit provisum Waltero Mally per Urbanum xii kalendas Decembris anno iiii,[54] in partem dicte taxe iii li. vi s. viii d.[55]

Summa pagine xlvi li. xiii s. iiii d.

### (fol. 8, vi) De diocesi Exoniensi

De prebenda bursali in ecclesia Sancte Crucis de Crediton', non taxata, de qua, vacante ex eo quod Walterus de Braunton' ipsam prebendam obtinens aliam prebendam in dicta ecclesia est assecutus pacifice, que tanto tempore vacavit et cetera, fuit provisum Rogero Payn per Urbanum x kalendas Julii anno ii,[56] pro integra medietate fructum ii li.

De decanatu ecclesie Exoniensis, taxato lxii li. xiii s. iiii d., et prebenda in eadem ecclesia, taxata iiii li., de quibus per obitum Raynaldi de Bugwell' et Rotberto Herward' fuit confirmatio facta vel provisum de novo Rotberto Sumpt', legum doctori, iii idus Octobris anno primo,[57] dimissis in arayragiis in xliiii li. viii s. x d. ob., in complementum dicte reste xliiii li. viii s. x d. ob.

De ecclesia de Morchiende Episcopi (Morchard-

---

[38] 15 July 1363.
[39] In the margin: *resta vi li. xiii s. iiii d.*
[40] 28 December 1353.
[41] In the margin: *resta xv li.*
[42] 1 June 1358.
[43] 5 November 1364.
[44] 18 June 1353.
[45] 22 October 1363.

[46] 22 December 1365.
[47] In the margin: *resta xx li. Ista est de annatis.*
[48] At the top of the page: *Adhuc Saresbiriensis.*
[49] 9 May 1363.
[50] 20 March 1364.
[51] In the margin: *resta iii li. vi s. viii d.*
[52] 13 November 1364.
[53] Followed by *Awe* deleted by a line.
[54] 20 November 1365.
[55] In the margin: *resta iii li. vi s. viii d. Ista est de annatis beneficiorum collatorum post alia computa secunda.*
[56] 22 June 1364.
[57] 13 October 1363.

Bishop), taxata vi li. xiii s. iiii d., ratione subrogationis facte de Johanne de Leye in omni iure competenti Rotberto de Dimslonde per Urbanum xviii kalendas Februarii anno primo,[58] dimissa in arayragiis pro iii li. vi s. viii d., in complementum dicte reste iii li. vi s. viii d.

De archidiaconatu Tottonie, non taxato, ratione compositionis facte pro medietate veri valoris medio iuramento per Willelmum Stoel, cui fuit confirmatus per Urbanum vii kalendas Maii anno primo,[59] dimisso in arayragiis pro xx li., in partem dicte reste x li.[60]

De prebenda collegiate ecclesie de Glausney' (Glasnay) Exoniensis diocesis, non taxata, ratione provisionis facte Henrico de Stacthon' per Urbanum vii idus Julii anno primo,[61] pro medietate veri valoris eiusdem xxvi s.

De ecclesia de Nanssant (St. Breoke), taxata iiii li. vi s. viii d., ratione confirmationis facte Johanni de Mountene per Urbanum vii kalendas Martii anno ii°,[62] iiii li. vi s. viii d.

De prebenda Sancte Crucis de Creditton', de qua, vacante per resignationem Philipi de Bellocampo, fuit provisum Johanni Mer', de cuius taxa vel valore nondum constat, in partem taxe vel fructuum ii li. x s.[63]

Summa pagine lxvii li. xviii s. ii d. ob.

### (fol. 8ᵛ) De diocesi Wygorniensi

De ecclesia de Hanyngthon' (Honington), taxata x li., de qua Luce filio Willelmi cardinalis Petragoricensis vel Urgellensis de novo providit, fuit computum in ultimis computis Domini Hugonis Pelegrini et solutum.

### Bathoniensis et Wellensis

De vicaria Sancti Cuberti Wellensi ratione in arayragiis in iii li. vi s. viii d. ratione provisionis facte Willelmo de Massyngham per Innocentium ii nonas Novembris anno v°,[64] pro complemento dicte reste iii li. vi s. viii d.

De thesauraria Wellensi, taxata xxxiii li. vi s. viii d. ratione provisionis facte Ricardo de Tormenton, sive confirmationis per Clementem idus Novembris anno xi,[65] dimissa in arayragiis in xx li., in partem dicte reste xv li.[66]

De decanatu Wellensi, taxato c li., ratione provisionis facte sive subrogationis Stephano Pampel, legum doctori, in omni iure quod competebat Thome de Paxthon', palatii apostolici auditori, per Urbanum x kalendas Januarii anno tertio,[67] in partem dicte taxe xx li.[68]

De prebenda de Honggesttong' (Henstridge) in ec-

clesia Wellensi, taxata xvi li. xiii s. iiii d., ratione provisionis facte Johanni Thebaut per Innocentium ix kalendas Januarii anno ix,[69] in complemento dicte taxe xvi li. xiii s. iiii d.

Summa pagine lv li.

### (fol. 9, vii) De diocesi Herfordensi

De ecclesia de Worthyn (Worthen) et aliis beneficiis de quibus fuit dispensatum cum Ricardo de Staforde ut ea possit licite retinere per Innocentium iii kalendas Novembris anno ix,[70] non dimissa in arayragiis nec missa per cameram sed explorata, dimissa in arayragiis pro xviii li. xiii s. iiii d. in ultimis computis meis, pro complemento dicte reste xviii li. xiii s. iiii d.[71]

De prebenda de Morton' minori [72] (Moreton Minor) in ecclesia Herffordensi, taxata x li., ratione provisionis facte Waltero Bell', scolari in legibus, per Urbanum vi kalendas Decembris anno ii,[73] in partem dicte taxe iiii li.[74]

De prebenda de Wynthyngton' (Withington Parva) in ecclesia Herffordensi, quam Adam electus Menevensis obtinuit, taxata iii li. x s., ratione provisionis facte Johanni Carrewe per Innocentium iii kalendas Novembris anno nono,[75] dimissa in arayragiis in xxx s., pro complemento dicte reste i li. x s.

Summa pagine xxiiii li. iii s. iiii d.

### (fol. 9ᵛ) De diocesi Norwicensi

De ecclesia de Estbilney (East Bilney), taxata iiii [76] li. vi s. viii d., ratione confirmationis facte Thome de Walton' per Innocentium vi kalendas Julii anno vi,[77] dimissa in arayragiis pro xliii s. iiii d., pro complemento dicte reste xliii s. iiii d.

De prioratu Sancte Fidis de Horsham, taxato clxxxiiii li., ratione provisionis facte Benedicto Jori per obitum Pontii Servera per Clementem viii kalendas Octobris anno vii°, vel viii°,[78] dimissa in arayragiis in lxx li., in partem dicte reste xxx li.[79]

De archidiaconatu Sudbur', non taxato, ratione provisionis facte Johanni de Humbleton' per Innocentium iii nonas Martii anno x,[80] qui composuit et solvit pro mediis fructibus v li.

De ecclesia Omnium Sanctorum de Keteleston' (Kettlestone), taxata xiiii li., ratione provisionis facte per cardinalem Urgellensem Johanni de Ardendon', pro complemento dicte taxe xiiii li.

De ecclesia Sancti Georgii de Sudburo, taxata xvi li.

---

[58] 15 January 1363.
[59] 25 April 1363.
[60] In the margin: *resta x li.*
[61] 9 July 1363.
[62] 24 February 1364.
[63] In the margin: *ista est de annatis et non de restis.*
[64] 4 November 1357.
[65] 13 November 1352.
[66] In the margin: *resta v li.*
[67] 23 December 1364.
[68] In the margin: *resta lxxx li.*

[69] 24 December 1361.
[70] 30 October 1361.
[71] In the margin: *Explorata.*
[72] Over *minori* deleted by a line.
[73] 26 November 1363.
[74] In the margin: *resta vi li.*
[75] 30 October 1361.
[76] Followed by *v* deleted by a line.
[77] 26 June 1358.
[78] 24 September 1348 or 1349.
[79] In the margin: *resta xl li.*
[80] 5 March 1362.

xiii s. iiii d., ratione provisionis facte Thome de Balthon' per Innocentium iii idus Martii anno x,[81] dimissa [82] in arayragiis in x li., pro complemento dicte reste x li.

De decanatu rurali Lynnye (Lynn) taxato iii li. vi s. viii d., ratione provisionis racte de eodem Ade Thebaud per Innocentium xvii [83] kalendas Septembris anno viii°,[84] dimisso in arayragiis in xxxiii s. iiii d., pro complemento dicte reste xxxiii s. iiii d.

De ecclesia de Bokling' (Blickling) dicte diocesis, taxata x li. xiii s. iiii d., ratione provisionis facte Waltero de Reddenesse per Urbanum iii kalendas Maii anno primo,[85] in partem dicte taxe v li. vi s. viii d.[86]

De ecclesia de Wadnorthon' (Wood Norton), ratione provisionis facte Johanni de Elforde per cardinalem Petragoricensem, pro complemento reste dimisse ii li.

Summa pagine lxx li. iii s. iiii d.

### (fol. 10, viii) De diocesi Lincoliensi

De archidiaconatu de Bukkyngham, non taxato, ratione provisionis facte Johanni de Ascheburn' per Clementem idus Novembris anno ix,[87] qui composuit pro mediis fructibus pro xx li., dimisso in arayragiis in vi li. xiii s. iiii d., pro complemento dicte taxe vi li. xiii s. iiii d.

De ecclesia de Edyndon' (Eydon), ratione provisionis facte Rotberto de Deyworth' per Innocentium ii idus Decembris anno ix°,[88] que data fuit esse taxata in secundis computis et etiam in restis primi computi in iiii li. xiii s. iiii d., quia computum est postea per libros taxarum et alios ipsam esse taxatam ad viii li., pro complemento dicte taxe iii li. vi s. iiii d.

De prebenda de Sutharle (South Scarle), ratione provisionis facte Johanni de Kyrkeby per Clementem iii nonas Maii anno ix,[89] per obitum Thome de Crosse, dimissa in arayragiis in vi li. i s. v d., pro complemento dicte reste vi li. i s. v d.

De vicaria de Therlebury (Thurlby), taxata x li., ratione provisionis facte Rotberto Frankeleyn per Urbanum iii idus Januarii anno ii.,[90] dimissa in arayragiis in v li., pro complemento dicte reste v li.

De prebenda de Clifton' taxata xx li., ratione confirmationis facte Stephano de Ravensere per Clementem vi kalendas Augusti anno xi,[91] pro complemento dicte taxe xx li.

De prioratu de Cogges, dimisso in arayragiis per Dominum Hugonem Pelegrini in arayragiis [92] in v li. vi

s. viii d., ratione confirmationis facte Willelmo Hamonis per Clementem, de quibus per me respondetur in aliis computis de iiii li., et dimittitur in arayragiis in xxvi s. viii d., pro complemento dicte reste xxvi s. viii d.

Summa pagine xlii li. viii s. i d.

(fol. 10ᵛ)[93] De ecclesia de Askeby [94] parva (Ashby Parva), taxata iiii li. vii s. iiii d., licet alias fuerit data taxa in iiii li. xiii s. iiii d. per errorem, ratione provisionis facte per cardinalem Petragoricensem Willelmo Odele de Slyndon', in complementum dicte taxe iiii li. vii s. iiii d.

De prebenda de Carleton' cum Turleby (Carlton le Moorland cum Thurlby) in ecclesia Lincoliensi, taxata xxvi li. xiii s. iiii d., de qua per consecrationem Nicholai episcopi Urgellensis (Urgel) fuit provisum Rotberto de Wyngeworth' per Innocentium ix kalendas Maii anno primo,[95] dimissa in arayragiis in xiii li. vi s. viii d., pro complemento dicte reste xiii li. vi s. viii d.

Item de eadem prebenda, taxata xxvi li. xiii s. iiii d., ratione provisionis facte Edwardo de Sherdestok' per Innocentium kalendas Martii anno vi,[96] in partem dicte taxationis xiii li. vi s. viii d.[97]

De vicaria de Eyton' iuxta Melton' Mowbray (Eaton near Melton Mowbray), non taxata, ratione provisionis facte per Urbanum Johanni de Stevenasch' vii kalendas Junii anno ii°,[98] pro qua composuit pro medietate veri valoris medio iuramento pro xxvi s. quia pauperrima est, pro complemento dicte compositionis xxvi s. viii d.

De vicaria de Haryngworth' (Harringworth), non taxata, ratione provisionis facte Johanni Cosyn per Urbanum v idus Maii anno primo,[99] qui composuit pro mediis fructibus pro x li., x li.

De ecclesia Dyngeley (Dingley), dimissa in arayragiis in ii li. xiii s. iiii d., ratione provisionis facte per cardinalem Petragoricensem Thome Dyngeley, in complementum dicte reste ii li. xiii s. iiii d.

De vicaria de Friskenay (Friskney), taxata v li., ratione provisionis facte Rogero de Slatebourn' per Urbanum vii idus Julii anno primo,[100] dimissa in arayragiis in l s., in complementum dicte reste ii li. x s.

Summa pagine xlvii li. x s. viii d.

(fol. 11, ix)[101] De ecclesia de Sitheston' (Syston), non dimissa in arayragiis per Dominum Hugonem Pelegrini nec missa per cameram, sed explorata ratione appropriationis facte auctoritate apostolica priori et conventui de Ulvescroft' (Ulverscroft), pro taxa xii li.[102]

De ecclesia de Fryseby iuxta Waynflete (Firsby near

---

[81] 13 March 1362.

[82] *dimisso*, MS.

[83] Followed by *S* deleted by lines.

[84] 16 August 1360.

[85] 29 April 1363.

[86] In the margin: *resta v li. vi s. viii d.*

[87] 13 November 1350.

[88] 12 December 1361.

[89] 5 May 1351.

[90] 11 January 1364.

[91] 27 July 1352.

[92] Followed by *v* deleted by a line.

[93] At the top of the page: *Lyncoliensis*.

[94] Follows *Asch* deleted by a line.

[95] 23 April 1353.

[96] 1 March 1358.

[97] In the margin: *resta xiii li. vi s. viii d.*

[98] 26 May 1364.

[99] 11 May 1363.

[100] 9 July 1363.

[101] At the top of the page: *Lincoliensis*.

[102] In the margin: *explorata*.

Wainfleet), taxata xii li. xvi s. viii d., ratione provisionis facte ex causa permutationis Johanni Attewod per Urbanum iii kalendas Augusti anno ii,[103] dimissa in arayragiis in vi li. xiii s. iiii d., pro complemento dicte reste vi li. xiii s. iiii d.

De decanatu Lyncoliensi, taxato ii[c] lxvi li. xiii s. iiii d., ratione provisionis facte Symoni de Bryseley per Clementem idus Octobris anno vii° vel viii°,[104] dimissa in arayragiis in lix li. vi s. viii d., in partem dicte reste xliiii li. xiii s. iiii d.[105]

De vicaria ecclesie Sancti Mychaelis de Kyngesbury iuxta villam Sancti Albani (Kingsbury), non taxata, de qua ex causa permutationis fuit provisum Johanni Messatger per Innocentium v kalendas Aprilis anno viii,[106] pro qua composuit pro iii li. vi s. viii d., dimissa in arayragiis in xlvi s. viii d., pro complemento dicte reste xlvi s. viii d.

De medietate ecclesie de Seggebrok' (Sedgebrook), dimissa in arayragiis in liii s. iiii d. per Dominum Hugonem Pelegrini ratione provisionis facte Rotberto Sagge de Bercotes per Clementem xi kalendas Augusti anno x°,[107] pro complemento reste dimisse liii s. iiii d.

De vicaria de Coddesdone (Cuddesdon), taxata v li. vi s. viii d., ratione provisionis facte Waltero de Schitborn' per Urbanum iii idus Augusti anno iii,[108] pro complemento dicte taxe v li. vi s. viii d.[109]

De ecclesia de Estuwellis (Eastwell), taxata viii li., ratione provisionis facte Rotgero Judde per Urbanum vii kalendas Junii anno ii,[110] in partem dicte taxe ii li.[111]

Summa pagine lxxv li. xiii s. iiii d.

(fol. 11ᵛ)[101] De prebenda de Cosyngham (Corringham) in ecclesia Lincoliensi, taxata cxxvi li. xiii s. iiii d., ratione provisionis facte per obitum Raymundi Pelegrini domino cardinali Aquensi[112] per Urbanum iiii° nonas Septembris anno iii,[113] per manus Willelmi Nawesby, firmarii dicte prebende, tam pro parte dicte taxe quam pro fructibus qui venerunt tempore vacationis, qui sunt pauci, xxxvii li. viii s. vii d. ob.[114]

Item de eadem per manus eiusdem ex eisdem causis xlv li.

De prebenda de Thame in ecclesia Lincoliensi, taxata clxviii m., que valent cxii li., de qua fuit provisum domino cardinali Hostiensi[115] per obitum cardinalis Petragoricensis per Urbanum xi° kalendas Novembris

anno ii,[116] tam pro parte dicte taxe quam pro parte fructuum pertinentium camere apostolice pro tempore vacationis per mortem dicti domini cardinalis Hostiensis, qui non sunt certi nec divisi, per manus Willelmi de Nawesby, firmarii dicte prebende lxxv li.[117]

Item recepi de eadem prebenda ex premissis causis per manus Berengarii Ferrarii et pro totali resta firme dicte prebende anni LXVI, que erat l li. sed retinuit pro pensione sua sibi per dictum dominum cardinalem constituta et expensis x li., restat quod tradidit michi xl li.

De prebenda de Midelthon' (Milton Ecclesia), in ecclesia Lincoliensi, taxata xl li., et archidiaconatu Oxonie, non taxato, cum ecclesia de Ystelelya (Iffley) eidem archidiaconatu annexa, que taxatur xiiii li. xiii s. iiii d., ratione provisionis facte per mortem cardinalis de Gordonio[118] domino cardinali Aquensi[119] per Innocentium iiii idus Augusti anno ix°,[120] pro complemento dictarum taxarum et pro medietate veri valoris dicti archidiaconatus, pro quo solvit xviii li. xiii s. iiii d., lxxiii li. vi s. viii d.

Summa pagine ii[c] lxx li. xv s. iii d. ob.

## (fol. 12, x) De diocesi Convetrensi et Licheffeldensi

De prebenda de Langedon' (Longdon) in ecclesia Licheffeldensi, pro qua Walterus de Dalby composuit cum camera, dimissa in arayragiis pro lviii fl., pro complemento dicte reste, computato floreno pro iii s. et i d. sterlingorum, viii li. xviii s. x d. ob. sterlingorum.

De prebenda de Tervyn (Tarvin), dimissa in arayragiis per Dominum Hugonem Pelegrini in xxxiii li. vi s. viii d. ratione provisionis facte Nicolao Heth' per Innocentium iii idus Augusti anno ix°,[121] in partem dicte reste viii li. xvii s. ii d.[122]

De prioratu de Kyrkeby (Monks Kirby), dimisso in arayragiis in lxxxi li. x s. viii d. ratione provisionis facte Willemo de Grauleriis per Innocentium iii kalendas Martii anno vii,[123] in partem dicte reste xl li.[124]

De prebenda de Ekleshale (Eccleshall), taxata lxvi li. xiii s. iiii d., que fuerat dimissa in arreragiis pro totali,[125] sed quia ab antiquo auctortate apostolica divisa fuit in tres partes equales, ut patet per divisionem vel per instrumentam divisionis, cuius copia remanet penes registrum officii, et extunc non fuit in aliqua

---

[103] 30 July 1364.
[104] 15 October 1348 or 1349.
[105] In the margin: *Resta xiiii li. xiii s. iiii d.*
[106] 28 March 1360.
[107] 22 July 1351.
[108] 11 August 1365.
[109] In the margin: *ista est de annatis quia non est in arreragiis.*
[110] 26 May 1364.
[111] In the margin: *resta vi li.*
[112] Peter Itherii, bishop of Dax, priest of Ss. Quattro Coronati.
[113] 2 September 1365.
[114] In the margin: *resta xliiii li. iiii s. viii d. ob.* Followed by *non computata secunda recepta* deleted by a line.
[115] Elias de S. Eredio.

[116] 22 October 1364.
[117] In the left margin: *resta xxvii li. pro taxa et ultra fructus vacationis.* In the right margin: *ista summa non ponitur in conclusione set stat inpendenti pro videndo ad quem pertinet.* This note may relate to the next item.
[118] William Farinier of Gourdon, priest of Ss. Marcellino e Pietro.
[119] Peter Itherii, bishop of Dax, priest of Ss. Quattro Coronati.
[120] 10 August 1361.
[121] 11 August 1361.
[122] In the margin: *resta xxiiii li. ix s. vi d.*
[123] 27 February 1359.
[124] In the margin: *resta xli li. x s. viii d.*
[125] Added in the margin by another hand.

parte certa taxa limitata, pro tertia parte prime taxe debita camere ratione provisionis facte Johanni de Wynnewik' per Clementem vii idus Februarii anno x,[126] xxii li. iiii s. v d. quartus.

De ecclesia de Walthon' (Walton), taxata xliiii li., ratione provisionis facte Magistro Hugoni de Bokyngton' per Innocentium iii nonas Decembris anno v,[127] dimissa in arayragiis in xiiii li., in partem dicte reste vii li.[128]

De decanatu Licheffeldensi, taxato xl li., de quo per assecutionem decanatus Lincoliensis per Symonem de Bryseley fuit provisum Johanni de Bokingham per Clementem nonas Novembris anno viii,[129] dimissa in arayragiis in xx li., in plenam solutionem dicte reste xx li.

### De diocesi Assavensi nichil

Summa pagine cvii li. v d. et quartus.

### (fol. 12ᵛ) De diocesi Menevensi

De archidiaconatu de Kermerdyn (Carmarthen), taxato xx li. xiii s. iiii d., ratione provisionis sive subrogationis facte David Martini in omni iure competenti Hauleyno ap David per Innocentium vi kalendas Decembris anno viiiᵒ,[130] pro complemento dicte taxe xx li. xiii s. iiii d.

De eodem archidiaconatu, dimisso ut supra ratione provisionis facte Willelmo Boldewy per Innocentium nonas Augusti anno x,[131] pro complemento dicte taxe xx li. xiii s. iiii d.

De prebenda in ecclesia de Aberwill' (Abergwili), non taxata, quam dimisit Stephanus Pompel per assecutionem decanatus Wellensis, de qua[132] fuit provisum Thome de Elteslee per Urbanum viii idus Januarii anno tertio,[133] qui composuit et solvit pro mediis fructibus pro iii li. vi s. viii d., iii li. vi s. viii d.

De ecclesia de Kenethenaur' (Cenarth), taxata vi li. xiii s. iiii d., ratione provisionis facte per cardinalem Petragoricensem Rotberto Spenser vi li. xiii s. iiii d.

De hospitali Sancti David cum ecclesia Sancti David de Swynesey (Swansea) sibi annexa, taxato x li., cuius tertia pars pertinet ad vicarium dicte ecclesie, ratione confirmationis facte David Martini per Innocentium iii kalendas Februarii anno ixᵒ,[134] dimisso in arayragiis in xl s., ii li.

De ecclesia Sancti Bernachii super Taff' (Llanfyrnach), taxata vi li. xiii s. iiii d., non dimissa in arayragiis ⟨per⟩ Dominum Hugonem nec missa per cameram,

ratione provisionis facte Ricardo de Caunton' per Innocentium, nescio tamen quo anno, vi li. xiii s. iiii d.[135]

De ecclesia de Langladewen' (Llanglydwen), taxata xl s., ratione provisionis facte Philipo Lond', alias dicto Priton', per mortem Johannis Samssonis per Urbanum ii idus Aprilis anno iiᵒ,[136] in partem dicte taxe x s.[137]

De prioratu de Breconia (Brecon), taxato xx li., ratione provisionis facte Johanni de Losa per Urbanum vii idus Julii anno primo,[138] pro complemento taxe xx li.

Summa pagine lxxx li. x s.

### (fol. 13, xi) De diocesi Eboracensi

De ecclesia Sancti Martini in Mikelgate Eboraci (St. Martin in Micklegate, York), taxata iiii li. xiii s. iiii d., ratione provisionis facte Willelmo de Rippon' per Urbanum iiii idus Junii anno primo,[139] iiii li. xiii s. iiii d.

De archidiaconatu Richemundie in ecclesia Eboracensi, ratione provisionis facte Henrico de Walton', dimisso inter iiiiᵒʳ obligatos cum prebenda de Midelton (Middleton) in ecclesia Cicestrensi et prebenda de Yatmynstr' (Yetminster) in ecclesia Saresbiriensi in arayragiis in lxx li, de quibus de isto archidiaconatu debebantur xlviii li. vi s. viii d., in complementum dicte reste xlviii li. vi s. viii d.

De ecclesia de Sutton', taxata xliiii li., ratione provisionis seu confirmationis facte Ricardo de Retefford' per Urbanum ii nonas Maii anno primo,[140] dimissa in arayragiis in xxxiii li., pro complemento dicte reste xxxiii li.

De vicaria de Doncastr' (Doncaster), non taxata, ratione provisionis facte Alano de Raseyn per Urbanum xv kalendas Novembris anno iiᵒ,[141] qui composuit pro medietate pro xvi li. xiii s. iiii d., dimissa in arayragiis in viii li. vi s. viii d., pro complemento dicte reste viii li. vi s. viii d.

De ecclesia de Ylkelay (Ilkley), taxata xvii li. vi s. viii d., ratione confirmationis facte Johanni Benpeny per Urbanum vii idus Julii anno primo,[138] dimissa in arayragiis in x li. xiii s. iiii d., in partem dicte reste v li. vi s. viii d.[142]

De ecclesia de Brantyngham (Brantingham), taxata lxvi li. xiii s. iiii d., ratione provisionis facte Willelmo Storde per mortem magistri Thome de Newyll' per Innocentium xvi kalendas Septembris,[143] in plenam satisfactionem dicte taxe vi li. xiii s. iiii d.

Summa pagine cvi li. vi s. viii d.

### (fol. 13ᵛ)[144] De perpetua vicaria parochialis ecclesie

---

[126] 7 February 1352.
[127] 3 December 1357.
[128] In the margin: *resta vii li.*
[129] 5 November 1349.
[130] 26 November 1360.
[131] 5 August 1362.
[132] *quo,* MS.
[133] 6 January 1365.
[134] 30 January 1361.

[135] In the margin: *explorata.*
[136] 12 April 1364.
[137] In the margin: *resta xxx s.*
[138] 9 July 1363.
[139] 10 June 1363.
[140] 6 May 1363.
[141] 18 October 1364.
[142] In the margin: *resta v li. vi s. viii d.*
[143] 17 August 1361.
[144] At the top of the page: *Eboracensis.*

de Clive (Cliff of Cliffe), non taxata, ratione provisionis facte Willelmo de Cammon' per Urbanum nonas Februarii anno v,[145] pro qua composuit medio iuramento pro c s., v li.[146]

Summa pagine patet.

### (fol. 14, xii) De diocesi Dunelmensi

De prebenda in ecclesia collegiata de Northon' (Norton), taxata vi li., de qua per obitum Thome de Peleyn alias Drax' fuit provisum Johanni Swetopp' per Urbanum kalendas Octobris anno ii⁰,[147] vi li.

De ecclesia de Owytebern' (Whitburn), taxata xl li., ratione provisionis facte Ricardo de Wynchecomb' per Urbanum xix kalendas Januarii anno ii,[148] in partem dicte taxe vi li. xiii s. iiii d.[149]

De ecclesia Sancti Nicolai Novi Castri (Newcastle-upon-Tyne) Dunelmensis diocesis, taxata secundum novam taxam x li., ratione provisionis facte Matheo de Balthon' per Urbanum xi kalendas Maii anno iii⁰,[150] in partem dicte taxe v li.[151]

Summa pagine xvii li. xiii s. iiii d.

Summa universalis receptarum de arreyragiis beneficiorum dimissis in aliis computis et annatis beneficiorum postea collatorum m iii^c ix li. iiii s. iiii d. quartus,[152] inclusis cum ista summa xxvi li. iii s. iiii d. que sunt recepte de beneficiis post dicta arreragia collatis, inclusis etiam viii li. xviii s. x d. sterlingorum receptis pro lviii fl. camere, computato floreno camere pro iii s. i d. sterlingorum, qui diminuunt summam florenorum dimissam in aliis computis.

(fol. 14ᵛ) Sequentes summe recepte sunt de diversis vacantium beneficiorum infrascriptorum, videlicet de fructibus qui veniunt tempore vacationis.

Et primo de decanatu Eboracensi, dimisso in arayragiis pro secundo anno vacationis per obitum domini cardinalis Petragoricensis incipientis xxiii die Februarii anno domini M⁰ CCC⁰ LXIIII^to, dimisso in arayragiis in ii^c li., in plenam solutionem dicte reste ii^c li.[153]

Item de prebenda de Stranssal (Strensall) in ecclesia Eboracensi, per obitum eiusdem vacante, pro secundo anno vacationis incipientis ut supra per compositionem factam cum capitulo Eboracensi quod capitulum fructus dicte prebende receperat, lxxv li. x s.

Item de eadem prebenda, existente in manu camere, licet de ea esset domino H. tunc cardinali Hostiensi [154] provisum, in partem solutionis firme tertii anni xxxiii li. vi s. viii d.

Item de eadem prebenda, collata dicto domino cardinali Hostiensi, pro qua camera rendebat dicto domino cardinali in festo nativitatis domini vi^c fl. et camera recipiebat fructus eiusdem, licet tantum non valeret pro ultima solutione firme dicte prebende anni LXVI, que fuit l m., que [155] valent xxxiii li. vi s. viii d., et prima solutione anni LXVII, que fuit de eadem [156] per manus Guillelmi de Merffelde et Rogerii Bennaborg', firmiarorum dicte prebende, lxvi li. xiii s. iiii d.

Item de capitulo Eboracensi in plenam satisfactionem fructuum qui obvenerunt de prebenda de Mastham (Masham) in ecclesia Eboracensi tempore vacationis per mortem domini cardinalis Magalonensis [157] reservatorum et per capitulum ipsum receptorum, et etiam prebende de Stranssal in eadem ecclesia per mortem cardinalis Petragoricensis ex compositione inde facta pro eisdem, inclusis xl li. quas dictum capitulum recepit a firmariis dicti domini cardinalis Petragoricensis, c li.

Item de decanatu Eboracensi arrendato per cameram appostolicam pro tertio et ultimo anno vacationis per mortem domini cardinalis Petragoricensis pro iiii^c xx^ti li. sterlingorum, quo anno fuit provisum domini cardinali Avinionie [158] de eodem per Urbanum viii⁰ kalendas Octobris anno iiii^to,[159] de qua peccunia fuerunt per cameram adiudicate predicto domino cardinali Avinionie pro parte ipsum contingente trescente et quindecim libre sterlingorum, recepi pro iiii^ta parte dicte firme camere appostolice debita cv li.[160]

Summa pagine v^c lxxx li. x s.

### (fol. 15, xiii) Recepta extraordinaria de certis censibus debitis ecclesie Romane

Item recepi a magistro et fratribus ordinis Sancti Gilberti de Sempyngham (Sempringham) diocesis Lincoliensis per manus fratris Guillelmi de Beverlaco, canonici eiusdem ordinis, pro censu unius marche auri quam singulis bienniis tenentur solvere ecclesie Romane, pro qua consueverunt solvere lxiiii^or fl. auri ponderis camere, ut videtur contineri in ultima quitatione dicti census eis concessa per Dominum Gaucelmum,[161] tunc episcopum Nemausensem (Nimes) nunc vero Magalonensis (Maguelone), domini nostri pape thesaurarium, sub anno domini M⁰ CCC⁰ LXIII die xiiii mensis Octobris indictione prima pontificatus Domini Urbani pape V anno primo, pro duobus terminis sive bienniis

---

[145] 5 February 1367.
[146] In the margin: *de annatis.*
[147] 1 October 1364.
[148] 14 December 1363.
[149] In the margin: *resta xxxiii li. vi s. viii d.*
[150] 21 April 1365.
[151] In the margin: *resta v li.*
[152] In the margin: *approbatum.*
[153] The following note with regard to this item is deleted by lines: *Item de eodem decanatu in plenam solutionem tertii anni vacationis per obitum eiusdem incipientis ut supra iiii⁰ xx li.* In the margin: *cancellatur quia statim ponitur pro rata solutionis cameram contingente.*

[154] Elias de S. Eredio.
[155] *qui,* MS.
[156] Followed by *supra* deleted by a line.
[157] Audoin Aubert, bishop of Maguelone, bishop of Ostia.
[158] Anglicus Grimoard, priest of S. Pietro in Vincoli.
[159] 24 September 1366.
[160] In the margin: ⟨a⟩diudicata fuerunt eidem domino cardinali pro rata temporis ipsum contingente ⟨per⟩ cameram.
[161] Followed by *e* deleted by lines.

completis et terminatis in festo apostolorum Petri et Pauli proximo preterito, videlicet anno domini M⁰ CCC⁰ LXVII pro dictis duabus marchis, seu lxiiii fl. predictis pro qualibet marcha, computato fl. camere pro iii s. sterlingorum, xix li. iiii s.

Item recepi a magistro et fratribus hospitali Sancte Trinitatis de Santingheveld (Saint-Inglevert) Morinensis (Thérouanne) diocesis pro censu annuo c allecium qui dicti magister et fratres tenentur ecclesie Romane annis singulis pro xxv annis inceptis anno domini M⁰ CCC⁰ XLII⁰ et die iii mensis Julii quibus cessaverunt solvere et terminatis iii die dicti mensis anno LXVII⁰, computato quolibet miliari dictorem allecium pro x franchis auri cugni Francie, xxv franchos.

Summa pagine xix li. iiii s., xxv franchos.

Et sic est summa totalis omnium et singulorum receptorum [162] per dictum Dominum Johannem collectorem tam de denariis Beati Petri, de annuo censu, de beneficiis collatis post alia computa et arreragiis beneficiorum in aliis compotis dimissorum ac etiam de fructibus tempore vacationis, obventionibus quam aliis duabus receptis extraordinariis iiᵐ iiiᶜ xxv li. xiii s. x d. i quartus, xxv franchi,[163] inclusis in summa viii l. xviii s. x d. sterlingorum receptis pro lviii fl. camere, computato floreno camere pro iii s. i d. sterlingorum, que diminuunt summam florenorum in aliis computis dimissis. Approbatum.

(fol. 15ᵛ) Sequntur asignationes, solutiones, traditiones et liberationes facte per dictum collectorem de quibuscumque peccuniis per eum seu alios suo nomine receptis de sua collectoria ad cameram appostolicam pertinentibus quovismodo a vicesima die menssis Maii anni sexagesimi sexti usque ad ⟨xviii diem⟩ [164] menssis ⟨Februarii⟩ [164] anni sexagesimi octavi.

Primo asignavit anno domini M⁰ CCC⁰ LXVI⁰ die xv menssis Decembris in iiiᶜ li. sterlingorum, computato floreno camere pro iii s. dicte monete, duo milia fl. camere.

Item liberavit, solvit seu asignavit de mandato camere per bullam sibi factam nobili uno Beraudo, dalphino Alvernie, anno a nativitate domini M⁰ CCC⁰ LXVII⁰ die xiiii menssis Februarii in trescentis viginti duabus libris decem et octo solidis iiiiᵒʳ d. sterlingorum, computato quolibet franco boni ponderis et cungni regis Francie pro tribus solidis ii d. ob. et pitta sive uno ferlino dicte monete, duo milia franchos.

Item assignavit camere anno predicto ix die menssis Aprilis in centum quinquaginta li. sterlingorum, computato quolibet fl. camere pro tribus s. dicte monete, mille florenos camere.

Item asignavit camere anno predicto die decima

octava Junii in ducentis viginti quinque li. sterlingorum, computato fl. camere ut supra, mille quingintos fl. camere.[165]

Item restituit thesaurario Cicestrensi vi li. xiii s. iiii d. quas ab eodem indebite receperat et in precedentibus computis camere asignaverat ratione confirmationis facte de dicta thesauraria Willelmo de Lugtheburgh', que confirmatio non habuit effectum nec fuit in eius odium impetrata, ut aparet ex productis per eundem thesaurarium, vi li. xiii s. iiii d. sterlingorum.

Summa asignatorum pagine miiii li. xi s. viii d.[166]

(fol. 16, xiiii) Item asignavit camere appostolice die vii menssis Augusti anno sexagesimo octavo in perssona propria in sex milibus fl. camere, computato quolibet dictorum florenorum pro tribus solidis et tribus pittis sive tribus ferlinis sterlingorum, ix⁰ xviii li. xv s. sterlingorum in viᵐ fl., quolibet fl. pro tribus s. et tribus pittis sterlingorum computato.

Summa omnium assignatorum predictorum est m ixᶜ xxiii li. vi s. viii d.

(fol. 16ᵛ) Sequntur expensse facte infra predictum tempus tam per Dominum Johannem de Caroloco, subcollectorem Anglie, quam per dictum collectorem pro dicto officio collectorie et aliis.

Primo expendit dictus Johannes Caroloco, subcollector, pro diverssis nuntiis misis tam ad partes Ybernie quam Anglie cum commissionibus missis diversis perssonis ad levandum fructus benefficiorum vacantium per consecrationem Domini Guillelmi de Wykham in episcopum Wyntoniensem et pro certis scriptis habitis pro expeditione officii in curia regis xxvi s. viii d.

Item dedi viii die menssis Novembris ⟨nuntio⟩ qui iverat ad portum de Sanduich ad recuperandum certas litteras et scriptas tangentes officium dicte collectorie et benefficia que fuerant illuc missa, que omnia fuerant per custodes dicti portus arestata et capta, iiii s..

Item solvi pro uno nuntio qui portavit litteras meas clausas domino episcopo Lincoliensi ne impediret commissarium deputatum ad recipiendum fructus archidiaconatus Lincoliensis vacantis per consecrationem episcopi Wynthoniensis quos dictus episcopus ad se aserit pertinere iii s. vi d.

Item uni nuntio qui portavit processus cancellario studii de Cantabrigia contra archidiaconum Midelsexie in ecclesia Londoniensi pro denariis Beati Petri iiii s. vi d.

---

[162] *singudarum*, MS.

[163] In the margin: *et restant deberi camere per finem aliorum compotorum suorum lviii li. v d. ob. sterlingorum, l fl. fortes, cl fl. croseti.*

[164] A blank space in MS.

[165] The following item, deleted by lines, reads: *Item asignavit Domino Anglico cardinali Avinionie* (priest of S. Pietro in Vincoli) *pro rata vel in deductionem rate ipsum contingentis de fructibus tertii et ultimi anni vacationis eiusdem decanatus collati predicto domino cardinali per Urbanum viiiᵒ kalendas Octobris pontificatus sui anno quarto* (24 September 1366) *in sua specie centum libros sterlingorum.* In the margin: *ista cancellatur quia dicto domino cardinali Avinionie adiudicate fuerunt per cameram pro parte ipsum contingente de dicta annata iiiᵒ et xv li., ut aparet per litteras domini camerarii.*

[166] A repetition of this item is deleted by a line.

Item uni famulo qui xvi die Novembris portavit litteras capitulo Eboracensi ut solveret restas prebende de Massaham (Masham) et de Stranssal' (Strensall) vi s. vi d.

Item uni famulo qui portavit viii die Decembris processus contra eos qui non solvebant vi s.

Item pro pergameno et cera et aliis xii s.

Item uni nuntio qui portavit litteras Avinionie dominis patriarche et thesaurario pro amparatione certorum negotiorum tangentium custodiam civitatis Avinionie et comitatus Venayssini iii s. iiii d.

Item pro loquerio hospitii trium annorum, computando pro quolibet anno vi li. xiii s. iiii d., prout alii collectores computare conssueverunt, xx li.
Summa omnium expensarum predictarum est xxiii li. vi s. vi d. sterlingorum.[167]

(fol. 17) Compotus brevis redditus per Dominum Johannem de Cabrespino, canonicum Narbonensem in Anglia camere apostolice collectorem, de receptis, levatis et assignatis et expensis per eum seu per alios suo nomine a xx die mensis Maii anni domini M CCC° LXVI usque ad xviii diem mensis Februarii anni LXVIII secundum computationem ecclesie Romane et LXVII secundum computationem ecclesie Anglicane. Quantum ad receptas.

Et primo computat se recepisse de restis seu arreragiis denariorum Beati Petri in aliis computis dimissis, que fuerunt in summa vi<sup>c</sup> viii li. xvi s. iiii d., iiii<sup>c</sup> viii li. ii s. iiii d. sterlingorum.

Item computat se recepisse de restis seu areragiis annui census, que erant in summa ix li. xi s. ix d. sterlingorum, v li. xvi s. i d. sterlingorum.

Item de recepta ordinaria dicti census de anno LXVII ii li. xvii s. i d. sterlingorum.

Et sic est summa totius recepte annui census in dicto tempore viii li. xiii s. ii d. sterlingorum.

(fol. 17<sup>v</sup>) Item computat se recepisse de restis seu arreragiis beneficiorum in aliis computis dimissis, que fuerunt in summa iii<sup>m</sup> v<sup>c</sup> lxi li. v s. viii d. ob. sterlingorum, v<sup>c</sup> lxiii fl., xx d. sterlingorum, m ii<sup>c</sup> lxxxiii li. xii d. quartum sterlingorum.

Item computat se recepisse de annatis beneficiorum collatorum usque ad pridiem ydus Julii pontificatus Domini Urbani anno v<sup>to</sup> [168] xxvi li. iii s. iiii d.

Et sic est summa totalis recepte tam de arreragiis seu restis quam annatis beneficiorum in predicto tempore collatorum ut supra proximo patet m iii<sup>c</sup> ix li. iiii s. iiii d. quartus sterlingorum. In qua summa includuntur viii li. xviii s. x d. sterlingorum que recepte fuerunt pro lviii fl. camere, computato fl. camere pro iii s. uno d. sterlingorum, que diminuunt summam florenorum dimissam in areragiis in precendentibus compotis.

Item computat se recepisse de fructibus sertorum beneficiorum in libro rationum suarum nominatorum qui obvenerunt tempore vacationis v<sup>c</sup> lxxx li. x s.

Item computat se recepisse de extraordinariis, videlicet [169] pro duabus marchis auri receptis a magistro et fratribus ordinis Sancti Gilberti de Sempingnam diocesis Lincoliensis pro ii terminis seu quattuor [170] annis iam elapsis xix li. iiii s. sterlingorum.[171]

(fol. 18) Item computat se recepisse extraordinarie a magistro et fratribus hospitalis Sancte Trinitatis de Santingheveld (Saint-Inglevert) Morinensis (Thérouanne) diocesis pro censu annuo centum allecium debitorum pro xxv annis, computando pro quolibet miliari dictorum allecium x francos, valent in summa xxv francos

Et sic est summa universalis omnium et singularum receptarum precendentium tam de denariis Beati Petri et annuo censu quam de arreragiis et annatis beneficorum et de fructibus tempore vacationis obventionibus et etiam duabus receptis extraordinariis ii<sup>m</sup> iii<sup>c</sup> xxv li. xiii s. x d. quartus strelingorum, xxv franci, inclusis in ista summa viii li. xviii s. x d. sterlingorum receptis pro lviii fl. camere, computato fl. camere pro iii s. uno d. sterlingorum, que diminuunt summam florenorum in aliis computis dimissam. Approbatum.

Item aparet apud finem aliorum duorum computorum suorum precedentium ipsum debere camere apostolice lviii li. v d. ob. sterlingorum, l fl. fortes, cl fl. de croseta, quos habuit a camera in abeundo.[172]

Et sic est summa universalis omnium receptorum levatorum, inclusis que debentur [173] per finem aliorum compotorum suorum precedentium, ut patet supra proximo, ii<sup>m</sup> iii<sup>c</sup> lxxxiii li. xiiii s. iii d. iii quartos sterlingorum, xxv franquos, l fl. fortes, cl fl. crosete. Approbatum.

(fol. 18<sup>v</sup>) Secundo idem collector computatat se assignasse,[174] solvisse et tradidisse seu liberasse tam camere apostolice quam aliis eius certo mandato tam per se quam per Dominum Johannem de Caroloco locumtenentem eiusdem a ix die mensis Julii anni LXVI usque ad diem xviii mensis Februarii anni LXVIII, prout fidem fecit, mille iiii li. xi s. viii d. sterlingorum, videlicet in iiii<sup>m</sup> v<sup>c</sup> fl. camere, ii<sup>m</sup> francis auri, vi li. xiii s. iiii d. sterlingorum in sua specie, floreno quolibet pro tribus solidis computato, et franco pro tribus solidis et tribus pittis computato.

Item assignavit idem dominus collector die vii mensis Augusti anno LXVIII per manus suas proprias camere apostolice in sex milibus fl. camere, computato fl. camere pro tribus s. et tribus pittis sive ferlinis, ix<sup>c</sup> xviii li. xv

---

[167] The sum is repeated in the manuscript.
[168] 14 July 1367.

[169] Followed by *a magistro* deleted by a line.
[170] Over *ii* deleted by a line.
[171] In the margin: *attende quia visitatio biennalis.*
[172] *abivien*, MS.
[173] Followed by *per ipsum* deleted by a line.
[174] Followed by *camere apostolice* deleted by a line.

s. sterlingorum in vi$^m$ fl., quolibet fl. pro iii s. et tribus pittis sterlingorum computato.

Summa omnium assignatorum precedentium m ix$^c$ xxiii li. vi s. viii d.

(fol. 19) Tertio idem collector computat tam ipsum quam locumtenentem suum expendisse infra predictum tempus tam pro diversis nuntiis missis pro negotiis camere seu collectorie ad Yberniam et per Angliam cum diversis commissionibus, litteris et processibus quam pro certis scripturis officium tangentibus, ut patet particulariter in libro suarum rationum, iii li. vi s. vi d. sterlingorum.

Item computat pro loquerio hospitii trium annorum, prout consuetum est per predecessores suos pro quolibet anno vi li. xiii s. iiii d. sterlingorum, assendunt in summam xx li. sterlingorum.

Summa expensarum in dicto tempore xxiii li. vi s. vi d. sterlingorum.[175] Approbatum.

Et sic est summa totalis omnium assignatorum et expensarum in predicto tempore m ix$^c$ xlvi li. xiii s. ii d. sterlingorum.

Item fuerunt sibi colloquate et deducte pro expensis per ipsum factis ratione cuiusdem commissionis sive ambaxiate facte ad regem Anglie et principem Wallie et ducem Lencastrie pro certis negotiis expediendis cum eisdem ultra centum florenos quos a camera receperat quum illuc ivit xxxiiii li. x s. sterlingorum.

Item quia in dicto itinere amisit duos equos qui decostiterant sibi centum et x fl. fuerunt sibi colloquate xvi li. x s. sterlingorum, quolibet floreno pro tribus s. computato.

Et sic est summa omnium assignatorum et expensarum ac collocatorum ratione ambaxiate predicte m ix$^c$ xcvii li. xiii s. ii d. Approbatum.[176]

(fol. 19$^v$) Factis vero deductione et compensatione de receptis, levatis et restatis per ipsum deberi per finem aliorum suorum compotorum [177] ac etiam inclusis xxv franchis pro iiii$^{or}$ li. ix d., quolibet pro tribus s. ii d. iii pittis, ac 1 fl. fortibus pro vi li. v s., quolibet pro ii s. ix d. sterlingorum computato, que omnia ascendunt ii$^m$ iii$^c$ xciiii li.[178] iii quartos sterlingorum, cl fl. crosete quos habuit a camera, ad expensas, asignatas et collocata, que sunt m ix$^c$ xcvii li. xiii s. ii d. sterlingorum, aparet ipsum debere, omnibus compenssatis et deductis, iii$^c$ xcvi li. vi s. x d. iii quartos sterlingorum. Que omnia predicta fuerunt ⟨soluta⟩ manualiter et realiter ⟨per dictum Dominum Johannem⟩ Domino Geraldo Maurelli vicetezaurario domini nostri pape in ii$^m$ v$^c$ lxxxviii fl. ii tertiis de floreno i d. iii quartis sterlingorum die xvi Augusti anni LXVIII. Approbatum.

Resta debetur per eum cl fl. crozete quos recepit a camera et pro istis est scriptus in libro extracto de notis Domini Johannis Palasini pre solvendo in Avinione vel alias concordando cum camera semel [179] primum [180] et hic et in libro predicto dicti Domini Johannis Palasini debet liberari et quitari.

(fol. 20) Item quarto idem collector dat et assignat in restis seu arreragiis de denariis Beati Petri debitis per diversas personas seu prelatos ⟨prout⟩ in suis computis clarius continetur v$^c$ xcix li. iiii s. viii d. sterlingorum.

Item de annuo censu x li. viii s. vii d. sterlingorum.

Item de annatis beneficiorum antiquorum in summa ii$^m$ ix$^c$ ii li. ii s. vi d. sterlingorum, v$^c$ v fl. cum dimidio, ii d. sterlingorum.

Item dat in restis de annatis beneficiorum collatorum per Dominum Urbanum a iii$^o$ kalendas Maii pontificatus sui anno primo usque ad pridie ydus Julii pontificatus sui anno quinto [181] ii$^o$ lxxix li. x s. sterlingorum.

Et sic est summa universalis omnium precedentium restarum sive arreragiorum beneficiorum tam antiquorum quam de tempore Domini Urbani iii$^m$ clxxxi li. xii s. vi d. sterlingorum, v$^c$ v fl. cum dimidio, ii d. sterlingorum.

(fol. 20$^v$) Summa vero universalis omnium precedentium restarum seu arreragiorum tam de denariis Beati Petri, annuo censu quam annatis omnium beneficiorum collatorum usque ad pridie ydus Julii pontificatus Domini Urbani anno quinto est iii$^m$ vii$^c$ xci li. v s. ix d. sterlingorum, v$^c$ v fl. cum dimidio, ii d. sterlingorum.

Item dat in restis plura beneficia de quibus ignorat taxam quarum non potest certas summas assignare seu nominare, prout in libro rationum suarum particulariter describuntur.

Item etiam sunt multa beneficia inutilia que non habuerunt effectum provisiones rationibus in suo libro declaratur.

(fol. 21) Et sic est summa universalis omnium assignatorum et expensarum in predicto tempore m ix$^c$ xlvi li. xiii s. ii d. sterlingorum.

Item fuerunt sibi collocate et deducte ratione cuiusdam commissionis sive ambaxiate per ipsum facte ad regem Anglie et principem Wallie ac ducem [182] Lencastrie pro certis negotiis expediendum cum eisdem ultra centum fl. quos a camera receperat quum ivit illuc xxxiiii li. x s. sterlingorum.

Item quia in dicto itinere amisit duos equos qui decostiterant sibi centum et x fl. fuerunt sibi collocate pro dictis equis xvi li. x s. sterlingorum.

Et sic est summa universalis omnium assignatorum,

---

[175] This item is repeated at the foot of the page.

[176] At the bottom of the page: *folium* preceded by a word, apparently of three or four letters, which I can not decipher.

[177] Followed by *que sunt in summa* deleted by a line.

[178] Followed by *xix s. viii* deleted by a line.

[179] Followed by *debet* deleted by a line.

[180] Extension doubtful. The word appears to be *pm* with the general sign of abbreviation.

[181] 29 April 1363 to 14 July 1367.

[182] *duci*, MS.

expensarum, collocatorum ratione predicte ambaxiate m ix^e xcvii li. xiii s. ii d.[183]

Factis vero deductione et compensatione de receptis, levatis ac restatis per ipsum deberi per finem aliorum suorum computorum, et inclusis xxv franchis pro iiii^or li. ix d., quolibet pro tribus s. ii d. iii pittis computato, ac l fl. fortibus [184] pro vi li. v s., quolibet pro ii s. ix d. sterlingorum computato, que omnia assendunt ii^m iii^c xciiii li. iii quartos sterlingorum, cl fl. crosete quos habuit a camera, ad assignata, expenssa ac collocata, que sunt m ix^c xcvii li. xiii s. ii d. sterlingorum, aparet dictum Dominum Johannem de Cabraspina debere camere, omnibus deductis et compenssatis iii^c xcvi li. vi s. x d. iii quartos sterlingorum. Que predicta fuerunt soluta realiter per dictum Dominum Johannem Domino Geraldo Maurelli vicetezaurario domini nostri pape in ii^m v^c lxxxviii fl. ii tertiis de floreno i d. iii quartis sterlingorum die xvi Augusti anni LXVIII.

Et sic resta debetur per ipsum Dominum Johannem cl fl. crosete.[185]

(fol. 22, xvi) [186] Sequntur arayratgia denarioum Beati Petri, censuum et antiquarum provisionum factarum per Dominum Clementem papam VI et Dominum Innocentium in regno Anglie et Ybernie tradita camere apostolice per Johannem de Cabrespino, in dictis partibus dicte camere collectorem, anno domini M° CCC° LXVIII° die.

## De denariis Beati Petri

Archiepiscopus Eboracensis pro annis LXVII° et LXVIII°, pro quolibet xi li. et x s., xxiii li.

Episcopus Saresbiriensis pro annis LXV, sexto et septimo et octavo, pro quolibet xvii li., lxviii li.

Episcopus Cicestrensis pro annis LXVI, septimo et octavo, pro quolibet viii li., xxiiii li.

Episcopus Wygorniensis pro annis LXVII° et LXVIII°, pro quolibet x li. et v s., xx li. x s.

Episcopus Conventrensis et Licheffeldensis pro annis LXVI°, VII° et LXVIII°, pro quolibet x li. v s., xxx li. xv s.

Episcopus Lincoliensis pro annis LXVII° et VIII°, pro quolibet xlii li., lxxxiiii li.

Episcopus Exoniensis pro annis LXVII° et VIII°, pro quolibet ix li. v s., xviii li. x s.

Episcopus Hereffordensis pro annis LXVII° et VIII°, pro quolibet vi li., xii li.

Episcopus Bathoniensis et Wellensis pro annis LXIII°, LXVII° et LXVIII°, quia de LXIIII°, LXV°

et LXVI° est satisfactum, pro quolibet xi li. v s., xxxiii li. xv s.

Archidiaconus Cantuariensis pro annis LXVII° et VIII°, pro quolibet viii li., xvi li.

Archidiaconus Roffensis pro annis LXV°, sexto, septimo et VIII°, pro quolibet v li. xii s., xxii li. viii s.

Summa pagine iii^c lii li. xviii s.

(fol. 22^v) Archdiaconus Midelxey' pro annis LXV, sexto, VII° et VIII°, pro quolibet v li. s., xxii li.[187]

Archidiaconus Wynthoniensis pro annis LXIIII°, V°, VI°, VII° et LXVIII°, pro quolibet xi li. xiii s. iiii d., lviii li. vi s. viii d.

Archidiaconus Surreie pro annis LXVII° et LXVIII°, pro quolibet v li. x s., xi li.

Archidiaconus Colcestrensis pro annis LXVI°, VII° et LXVIII°, pro quolibet v li. x s., xvi li. x s.

Archidiaconus Exsxoxie pro annis LXV°, LXVI°, VII° et LXVIII°, pro quolibet v li. x s., xxii li.

Archidiaconus Eliensis pro annis LXIIII°, LXV, LXVI, LXVII et LXVIII°, pro quolibet v li., xxv li.

Episcopus Norwicensis pro annis LXV°, LXVI, LXVII et LXVIII°, pro quolibet xxi li. x s., lxxxvi li.

Summa pagine ii^c xlvi li. vi s. viii d.

Summa universalis omnium precedentium arayratgiorum de denariis Beati Petri est v^c xcix li. iiii s. viii d.

De quibus sunt de arreragiis in aliis compotis dimissis ii^c li. xiiii s. et pro annis LXVII et LXVIII, pro quolibet cxcix li. v s. iiii d., valent iii^c xcviii li. x s. viii d.

(fol. 23, xvii) Arrayratgia de annuo censu.

Abbas de Faversham pro annis LXVII et VIII°, pro quolibet xiii s. iiii d., xxvi s. viii d.

Prior de Tenebrig' pro anno LXVIII° xiii s. iiii d.

Abbas de Chertesey' pro annis LXVII° et VIII°, pro quolibet viii s., xvi s.

Abbas Sancti Edmundi de Bury pro anno LXVIII° xiii s. iiii d.

Abbas de Malmesbury pro anno LXVIII xiii s. iiii d.

Prior de Bodmyn pro anno LXVIII° ii s.

Abbas Sancti Albani pro anno LXVIII° xiii s. iiii d.

Abbatissa Sancte Clare Londonie pro anno LXVIII° vi d.

Custos de Schardeburgh' pro anno LXVIII° xv d.

Prior de Anglesey pro annis LXV°, LXVI°, LXVII° et LXVIII°, pro quolibet ii s., viii s.

Prior ecclesie Carliolensis pro annis LXII°, LXIII, LXIIII LXV, LXVI, LXVII et LXVIII°, pro quolibet xiii s. iiii d., iiii li. xiii s. iiii d.

Prior de Chaucomb' pro annis LXIII°, LXIIII°, LXV, LXVI, LXVII° et LXVIII°, pro quolibet xv d., vii s. vi d.

Summa pagine x li. viii s. vii d.

Quarum sunt iii li. xv s. viii d. de arreragiis in aliis computis et pro

---

[183] In the margin *Approbatum* is bracketed against this and the next item.
[184] Followed by *que* deleted by a line.
[185] In the margin *resta*.
[186] The summary on folios 17 to 20 was inserted between folios xiiii and xv of the original account. Folio xv is folio 21 in the modern enumeration, but the number either was not placed upon it in the original foliation or it has been cut away. Folio 21^v is blank.

[187] In the margin: *Item debet Dominus Hugo Pelegrini pro anno LX ratione archidiaconatus Midelxey v li. x s.*

(fol. 23ᵛ) De annatis beneficiorum arreragia antiqua

## Cantuariensis

De ecclesia de Stokebury [188] (Stockbury), taxata xxvi li. vi s. viii d., que fuit appropriata priori et conventui de Ledes (Leeds) per Clementem viii idus Augusti anno xiᵒ,[189] dimissa in arayratgiis pro vii li. vi s. viii d. Iste vii li. vi s. viii d. sunt de pensione quia de taxa ecclesie est satisfactum, sed quia simul ponuntur taxa et pensio ideo fuit error.

De capella de Bokenffelde (Bockingfold), de qua per obitum Willelmi de Braydeley fuit provisum David Wygham per Innocentium iii idus Augusti anno xᵒ,[190] fructus. Nunquam potui habere aliquod certificatorium bonum de isto beneficio, et est alia provisio facta de eodem per obitum eiusdem Guillelmi Ricardo de Homyngton' per Innocentium iiii nonas Julii anno ixᵒ.[191]

## Londoniensis

De ecclesia seu capella de Stafford (Stanford le Hope), de qua per obitum Edmundi de Grymnesby fuit provisum Johanni de Torkesey per Innocentium viiiᵒ idus Octobris anno iiᵒ,[192] dimissa pro taxa xxvi li. xiii s. iiii d. Nunc incumbens allegat quod nunquam fuit ibi rector dictus Johannes de Torkesey nec Edmundus de Grymnesby.

De archidiaconatu Midelsey', de quo fuit provisum cardinali Rothomagensi [193] per Innocentium xiiii kalendas Decembris anno vi,[194] fructus.

De ecclesia de Herlawe (Harlow) Londoniensis diocesis, de qua per assecutionem archidiaconatus Totton' fuit provisum Magistro Ricardo Anglici alias Drax' per Innocentium vii idus Januarii anno viii,[195] pro taxa xiii li. vi s. viii d. Allegatur quod ista provisio non habuit effectum et pendet terminus ad probandum.

Summa pagine xlvii li. vi s. viii d. Item ii beneficia.

(fol. 24, xviii) [196] De ecclesia de Langedon' (Langdon Hills), de qua ex causa permutationis fuit provisum Willelmo de Swyffeld' per Urbanum iii nonas Januarii anno primo,[197] non taxata, sed composuit pro xl s., debet pro resta xxvi s. viii d.[198]

De prebenda Sancti Pancratii in ecclesia Londoniensi, de qua ex causa permutationis fuit provisum Radulpho de Davent' per Urbanum v nonas Martii anno primo,[199] pro taxa xlii s. vi d.

## Cicestrensis

De archidiaconatu Lewensi, non taxato, qui fuit confirmatus Guillelmo de Lughteburgh' per Clementem ii idus Augusti anno xi,[200] fructus.

Item de eodem archidiaconatu fuit provisum Thome Bronwen per Innocentium vii idus Septembris anno viᵒ,[201] eo quod predictus Willelmus est assecutus thesaurariam dicte ecclesie, fructus.

De archidiaconatu Cicestrensi, non taxato, permutatio cuius facta cum decanatu ecclesie collegiate Cestr' super stratam (Chester-le-Street) Dunelmensis diocesis fuit Johanni de Skulthop' confirmata per Innocentium v kalendas Januarii anno vi,[202] fructus.

De prebenda de Ippethorn' (Upthorne) in ecclesia Cicestrensi, de qua per obitum Thome David fuit provisum Philipo de Courtenay per Innocentium xᵒ kalendas Julii anno ixᵒ,[203] pro taxa vi li. xiii s. iiii d.

De vicaria de Iklesham (Icklesham), de qua fuit dispensatum cum Waltero de Stratton' presbytero quod eam posset licite retinere per Innocentium ii idus Januarii anno viii,[204] pro parte taxe que est xvi li. xiii s. iiii d., vi li. xiii s. iiii d.

De prioratu Lewensi ordinis Cluniacensis et cetera datur inter inutiles provisiones ex causa ibi contenta.

De precentoria Cicestrensi, taxata liii li. vi s. viii d., de qua per obitum cardinalis de Gordonio [205] fuit provisum cardinali Aquensi [206] per Innocentium vi kalendas Octobris anno ixᵒ,[207] pro resta xxxi li. xiii s. iiii d.

De decanatu ecclesie Cicestrensis ac canonicatu et prebenda sibi annexis, vacantibus per consecrationem Willelmi episcopi Cicestrensis, fuit provisum Nicolao de Aston', magistro in sacra pagina, per Urbanum xi kalendas Decembris anno primo,[208] xlviii li. vi s. viii d.[209]

De prebenda de Midelton (Middleton) in ecclesia Cicestrensi, de qua cum archidiaconatu Richmundie et aliis beneficiis contentis inter iiiiᵒʳ obligatos, pro resta dicte prebende pro qua debebantur pro dicta prebenda xviii li. vi s. viii d., debet pro resta iii li. vi s. viii d.

Summa pagine c li. ii s. vi d. Item iii beneficia.

## (fol. 24ᵛ) Wynthoniensis

De ecclesia de Westmunres (West Meon), taxata xx li., que fuit confirmata Johanni de Kenyngton' per Clementem idus Maii anno viii,[210] vi li.

De hospitali Sancte Crucis, non taxato, confirmato

---

[188] Followed by *xv* deleted by a line.
[189] 6 August 1352.
[190] 11 August 1362.
[191] 4 July 1361.
[192] 8 October 1354.
[193] Peter de la Forêt, priest of Ss. XII Apostoli, archbishop of Rouen.
[194] 18 November 1358.
[195] 7 January 1360.
[196] The heading *Londoniensis* is repeated at the top of the page.
[197] 3 January 1363.
[198] In the margin: *de tempore Domini Urbani.*
[199] 3 March 1363.

[200] 12 August 1352.
[201] 7 September 1358.
[202] 28 December 1358.
[203] 22 June 1361.
[204] 12 January 1360.
[205] William Farinier of Gourdon, priest of Ss. Marcellino e Pietro.
[206] Peter Itherii, bishop of Dax, priest of Ss. Quattro Coronati.
[207] 26 September 1361.
[208] 21 November 1362.
[209] In the margin: *de tempore Domini Urbani.*
[210] 15 May 1350.

Johanni de Edyngdon' per Clementem xviii kalendas Junii anno viii°,[210] vii li. iii s. vi d.

De prebenda de Midelton' (Middleton) in ecclesia monialium de Warwell' (Wherwell), de qua fuit provisum ⟨Johanni⟩ de Branketre per Innocentium v kalendas Januarii anno primo,[211] xv li.

De prioratu de Appulburthorp' (Appuldurcombe) confirmato Johanni de Osanna per Clementem v kalendas Maii anno viii,[212] xxv li. xvii s.[213]

De ecclesia de Havunte (Havant), taxata xxvi li. xiii s. iiii d., de qua per obitum Johannis de Noion' fuit provisum Johanni de Uppeull' per Innocentium iiii nonas Julii anno ix°,[214] pro resta vi li. xiii s. iiii d.

De ecclesia de Duntesfaude (Dunsfold), taxata xiii li. vi s. viii d., de qua per obitum Willelmi de Charteston' fuit provisum Johanni de Lewes per Urbanum xix kalendas Februarii anno primo,[215] pro resta iii li. vi s. viii d.[216]

### Sarresbiriensis diocesis

De ecclesia de Kyvelegh' (Keevil), de qua fuit provisum Magistro Thome de Trompeshawe, taxata xxvi li. xiii s. iiii d., pro resta dimissa vi li. xiii s. iiii d.

De prebenda de Wermynstr' (Warminster) in ecclesia Saresbiriensi, de qua per obtium Johannis de Bambury fuit provisum Thome de Straghull' per Clementem, pro taxa v li.

Item de eadem prebenda fuit per obitum Baldewyni de Mori acceptatio facta per Bartholomeum de Bradon' fuit [217] confirmata per Clementem vii idus Septembris anno ix°,[218] pro taxa v li.

De prebenda de Hull' (Hill Deverill) in ecclesia collegiata de Hertelbury (Heytesbury), taxata vi li. xiii s. iiii d., de qua per obitum Rotberti Trek' fuit provisum Thome Patricii per Clementem viii idus Martii anno ix,[219] pro resta iii li. vi s. viii d.

Summa pagine lxxxiiii li. vi d.

(fol. 25, xix)[220] De prebenda de Stratton' in ecclesia Saresbiriensi, taxata xiii li. vi s. viii d., de qua ex causa permutationis fuit provisum Johanni Turstayn per Innocentium idus Martii anno iii,[221] pro taxa xiii li. vi s. viii d. Allegatur quod ista provisio non habuit effectum et ad hoc probandum habet terminum.

De prebenda de Rodmynstr' (Bedminster) in ecclesia Saresbiriensi, taxata xiii li. vi s. viii d., de qua per

resignationem Guillelmi de Hale fuit provisum Thome de Cliston' per Innocentium idus Decembris anno vi,[222] pro taxa xiii li. vi s. viii d. Episcopus semper certificat quod nunquam habuit possessionem et est in diocesi Bathoniensi et in fine istius diocesis providetur alteri.

De prebenda Saresbiriensi acceptatio cuius facta per Johannem Wfford Norwicensis diocesis fuit eidem confirmata per Innocentium vii kalendas Julii anno vii,[223] fructus. In omnibus certificatoriis episcopus rescribit quod nunquam habuit prebendam in ecclesia.

De prebenda de Calme (Calne) in ecclesia Saresbiriensi ac thesauraria in eadem ecclesia, de quibus fuit provisum domino cardinali Nemausenensi [224] per Innocentium iii kalendas Octobris anno ix°,[225] pro taxa lxxxvi li. xiii s. iiii d.[226]

De ecclesia de Wartham (Warham), de qua per resignationem Thome de Barneby fuit provisum Henrico de Worth' per Innocentium v idus Octobris anno x,[227] pro taxa iiii li. vi s. viii d. Fuit allegatum quod ista provisio non habuit effectum, et commissum episcopo quod de hoc informari et referret, qui retulit verum esse quod non habuerat effectum, et ideo debet cancellari.

De prebenda de Redfforde (Woodford), taxata xvi li. xiii s. iiii d., et archidiaconatu Dorcestr' in dicta ecclesia, taxato lxii li., de quibus fuit provisum cardinali de Canilhaco, episcopo Penestrino, per Innocentium iii idus Martii anno x,[228] pro taxa lxxviii li. xiii s. iiii d.

De prebenda de Preston' in ecclesia Saresbiriensi, de qua fuit provisum Thome de Sotton' per Innocentium xi kalendas Novembris anno v,[229] pro taxa xvi li. xiii s. iiii d. Episcopus semper certificat quod non habuit effectum.

De prebenda de Horton' in ecclesia Saresbiriensi, de qua per obitum Ricardi de Tormenton' fuit provisum Willelmo de Langebergh' kalendas Januarii anno primo per Urbanum,[230] debentur fructus.[231] Dominus Nicholaus de Luda ipsam tenet, ut patet in sequenti provisione; ideo debet ista cancellari.

Summa pagine ii[c] xiii li. Item ii beneficia.

(fol. 25[v])[220] De prebenda in ecclesia Saresbiriensi vocata de Horton; vacante per obitum Guillelmi de Fralegh', collatio facta Nicolao de Luda, thesaurario domini regis, fuit eidem confirmata etiam si quovis alio modo vacet vel sit reservata valeat ac si vacavisset per mortem dicti Willelmi, fructus.

De ecclesia de Dountton' (Downton), cuius collatio et provisio facte Thome de Edyandon' fuerunt [232] eidem

---

[211] 28 December 1353.
[212] 27 April 1350.
[213] In the margin: *Ministri regis totum occupant quia debitor suus est.*
[214] 4 July 1361.
[215] 14 January 1363.
[216] In the margin: *de tempore Domini Urbani.*
[217] *fuit* repeated, MS.
[218] 7 September 1350.
[219] 8 March 1351.
[220] The heading *Sarresbiriensis* is repeated at the top of the page.
[221] 15 March 1355.

[222] 13 December 1358.
[223] 25 June 1359.
[224] John de Blanzac, bishop of Nimes, priest of S. Marco.
[225] 29 September 1361.
[226] In the margin: *cardinalis.*
[227] 11 October 1362.
[228] 12 March 1362.
[229] 22 October 1357.
[230] 1 January 1363.
[231] In the margin: *vacat.*
[232] *fuit*, MS.

auctoritate apostolica confirmate vel provisum de novo per Urbanum xvii kalendas Maii anno primo,[233] pro taxa lxvi li. xiii s. iiii d.

De prebenda de Redmynstr' (Bedminster) in ecclesia Saresbiriensi, taxata xiii li. vi s. viii d., quam Ricardus de Norwico per nonnullus annos possedit, etiam si alio quovismodo vacet, provisio facta Henrico de Wynton', bachalario in legibus, fuit eidem confirmata vel provisum de novo per Urbanum v nonas Martii anno primo,[234] fructus. Iste nunquam habuit possessionem quia Willelmus de Chiletton, ipsam possidet, et est in diocesi Bathoniensi et Wellensi, et ideo debet cancellari. Data est inter inutiles.

De prebenda de Biscopeston' (Bishopstone) in ecclesia Saresbiriensi, taxata xx li. de qua per obitum Petri Raymundi de Rapistagno fuit provisum Raymundo Pelegrini per Clementem kalendas Februarii anno viii,[235] pro taxa xx li. Credo quod ista provisio fuit facta Arnaldo Pelegrini, qui, lite pendente inter ipsum et Willelmum Okeborun', obiit, et alius subrogatus fuit in iure dicti Arnaldi per Innocentium idus Julii anno x°,[236] que provisio posita est inter inutiles.

### Exoniensis

De prebenda ecclesie Exoniensis, de qua per obitum Henrici de Brandeley fuit provisum Henrico de Walton' per Innocentium iiii kalendas Martii anno primo,[237] pro taxa iiii li.

De prebenda ecclesie Exoniensis, de qua per obitum Ricardi de Tarmenthon' et Guillelmi de Braydeley fuit provisum Ade de Ilthone per Innocentium iiii nonas Julii anno ix°,[238] pro taxa iiii li.

De ecclesia de Basch', de qua vacante ex eo quod Henricus de Monte dictam ecclesiam pluribus annis tenuit in presbyterum non promotus fuit provisum Cornesio de Lauf' per Innocentium vii kalendas Julii anno ix,[239] pro taxa, fructus.

Summa pagine xciiii li. xiii s. iiii d. Item unum beneficium.

(fol. 26, xx)[240] De archidiaconatu Cornubie, non taxato, de quo per obitum Thome David fuit provisum Alexandro Nevil per Innocentium x kalendas Septembris anno ix°,[241] composuit conditionaliter quia litigat, fructus.

De prebenda Sancte Columbe minoris (St. Columb Minor) in ecclesia Sancti Karentoci (Crantock) fuit subrogatus in omni iure quod competebat David May-

nard' Johannes Truseley, magister in artibus, per Innocentium nonas Martii anno vii°,[242] fructus vel taxa.

De archidiaconatu Tonton' in ecclesia Exoniensi, de quo fuit provisum Ricardo Desbunton' per Innocentium v kalendas Novembris anno v.[243] Alia est provisio facta Willelmo Steel de eodem, pro qua partem solvit et pars remanet non soluta, ut patet in recepta et in arayratgiis novarum collationum Urbani, sed dicit quod ista non habuit effectum.

### Wygorniensi

De ecclesia de Esthelegh' (Astley), taxata xi li. vi s. viii d., de qua per obitum Henrici de Stowe fuit provisum Henrico de Askeby et etiam subrogatus in iure quod competebat dicto Henrico, qui super hoc litigans in curia decessit tempore Domini Clementis, pro resta viii li. Dominus Hugo Pelegrini dicit in rationibus suis istam provisionem non habuisse effectum et ego idem invenio. Ideo debet cancellari.

De ecclesia de Kynewich (Knightwick), taxata iiii li. vi s. viii d., de qua ex causa permutationis fuit provisum Johanni Charneuy per Innocentium anno primo,[244] pro resta xxxiii s. iiii d.

De hospitali Sancti Wulstani, non taxato, de quo per resignationem Petri Francici fuit provisum Johanni de Harewell', canonico Sancti Martini Londonie per Innocentium v kalendas Julii anno v,[245] fructus. Est hospitale pauperum et ministri eius vovent castitatem et abdicationem proprietatis et obedientiam et vivunt de mendicitate, ideo et cetera, nec habent decimas nec ecclesias, ideo.

De ecclesia de Clif' Episcopi (Bishop's Cleeve), taxata xl li., acceptatio et provisio eius facte Ricardi de Dayton' fuerunt eidem confirmate per Innocentium vii kalendas Julii anno ix,[246] pro taxa xl li.

Summa pagine xlix li. xiii s. iiii d.

### (fol. 26ᵛ) Bathoniensis et Wellensis

De prebenda de Wyvelescumbe (Wivelescombe), taxata xxvi li. xiii s. iiii d., de qua per obitum Johannis de Wfforde, etiam si in vita sua vacaverit, fuit provisum Willelmo de Bageney per Clementem, pro resta xiii li. vi s. viii d.

De thesauraria Wellensi, taxata xxxiii li. vi s. viii d., que fuit Rogero de Brounton' confirmata per Clementem idus Novembris anno xi°,[247] pro resta v li.

De prepositura Wellensi, de qua fuit per obitum Andree de Wfforde provisum Ade de Ilton' per Innocentium iii nonas Februarii anno vii,[248] pro taxa xl li. Post per obitum dicti Ade provisum fuit Domino

[233] 15 April 1363.
[234] 3 March 1362.
[235] 1 February 1350.
[236] 15 July 1362.
[237] 26 February 1353.
[238] 4 July 1361.
[239] 25 June 1361.
[240] The heading *Exoniensis* is repeated at the top of the page.
[241] 23 August 1361.
[242] 7 March 1359.
[243] 28 October 1357.
[244] 1353.
[245] 27 June 1357.
[246] 25 June 1361.
[247] 13 November 1352.
[248] 3 February 1359.

Willelmo de Wykeham, qui usque ad consecrationem suam ipsam tenuit, ut infra patet.

De prebenda de Holcombe in ecclesia Wellensi, de qua, vacante aut cum vacabit per assecutionem canonicatus et prebende per Thomam de Boston', fuit provisum Waltero Mayn per Innocentium xix kalendas Septembris anno viii,[249] pro resta xxvi li. xiii s. iiii d. Incumbens allegavit quod nunquam habuit[250] possessionem nec provisio habuit effectum, et fuit commissum episcopo ut de hoc se informaret, qui, facta inquisitione, certificavit dictam provisionem non habuisse effectum, ut in litteris suis, que sunt penes registrum, continetur. Ideo debet cancellari.

De prebenda et archidiaconatu Wellensibus, de quibus per obitum domini episcopi Tusculani cardinalis fuit provisum cardinali Carcassonensi[251] per Innocentium vii idus Octobris anno ix°,[252] pro taxa lxvi li. xiii s. iiii d. De tempore vacationis per obitum dicti domini cardinalis Tusculani recepte fuerunt ab executoribus domini episcopi Bathoniensis xxv li. vii s. ii d. ob., de quibus responsum est in aliis computis.

De prepositura Wellensi, de qua per obitum Ade de Ylton' fuit provisum Willelmo de Wyktham per Innocentium nonas Januarii anno ix°,[253] pro taxa xl li.

De prebenda et thesauraria Wellensibus, de quibus fuit provisum cardinali Aquensi[254] per obitum Ricardi de Tormenton' per Innocentium ii idus Novembris anno ix°,[255] pro taxa xxxiii li. vi s. viii d. De tempore vacationis fuerunt recepte xii li. xvi s. et viii d., de quibus respondetur in aliis computis et datur pro recepta, et videatur si pertinent camere.

Summa pagine ii⁣ᶜ xxv li.

### (fol. 27, xxi) Herffordensis

De prebenda de Metton' (Moreton Magna) in ecclesia Herffordensi, taxata xx li., de qua per obitum Thome de Stratton' fuit provisum Symoni de Sudbur' per Clementem iii nonas Julii anno viii,[256] pro resta xiii s. iiii d.

De prebenda de Metton', de qua per promotionem supradicti Symonis in episcopum Londoniensem fuit provisum Thome Thebaud per Innocentium iii idus Decembris anno ix°,[257] pro taxa xx li.

De decanatu Herffordensi, taxato xxxi li. vi s. viii d., de quo per resignationem Thome Trelek' episcopi Roffensis fuit provisum Waltero de Bermyngham per Urbanum vii kalendas Februarii anno primo,[258] pro

resta xl s. i d. Alia fuit provisio eidem Gualtero facta per Innocentium vii idus Aprilis anno x,[259] sed ambe sunt infra annum et ideo non debetur nisi una annata.

### Norwicensis

De prioratu de Castelacre (Castle Acre), de quo ex causa permutationis fuit provisum Willelmo de Waren' per Clementem anno primo,[260] pro taxa iiii⁣ᶜ lxxx li. xix s. vii d. Antiqua est provisio et nunquam aliquid potuit habere quia de patronatu est laicali, et statim fuit exclusus quia bastardus erat et dissipator prioratus.

De ecclesia de Holm (Holme), taxata xl li., de qua per resignationem Guillelmi de Merton, fuit provisum Thome Michel per Clementem, pro resta x li.

De prioratu Sancte Fidis de Horsham, taxata clxxxiiii li., de quo per obitum Pontii de Servera fuit provisum Benedicto Jori per Clementem viii idus Octobris anno vii vel viii,[261] pro resta xl li.

De ecclesia Derham (East Dereham), de qua per obitum Alani de Hotton' alias Howton' fuit provisum Symoni Thebaud, nunc episcopo Londoniensi, per Clementem iii kalendas[262] Aprilis anno x°,[263] pro resta xl li. xvi s. viii d.

Item de eadem fuit per promotionem dicti Symonis provisum Bartholomeo Sydey iurisperito per Innocentium vii kalendas Decembris anno ix°,[264] pro taxa lxxiii li. vi s. viii d. Tamen non habuit effectum quia rex contulit eam Thome Kynes.

Summa pagine vi⁣ᶜ lxvii li. xvi s. iiii d.

(fol. 27ᵛ)[265] De decanatu de Humbard (Humbleyard), non taxato, de quo per resignationem Walteri de Bakton' fuit provisum Symoni de Sudbur' per Innocentium iii kalendas Julii anno v°,[266] fructus.

De ecclesia de Cherynton' (Chevington), taxata xvi li. xiii s. iiii d., que fuit Hugoni Nepell' confirmata per Innocentium vii kalendas Februarii anno x,[267] pro taxa xvi li. xiii s. iiii d.

De decanatu rurali de Sorham (Fordham), vacante per obitum Johannis Hoppe, fuit provisum Waltero Palmer per Innocentium v nonas Martii anno x,[268] fructus.

De ecclesia de Holm (Holme), de qua per obitum Thome Michel fuit provisum Rotberto de Grymmeston' per Urbanum xviii kalendas Januarii anno primo,[269] pro taxa xl li.[270]

---

[249] 14 August 1360.
[250] Followed by *provisionem* deleted by a line.
[251] Stephen Aubert, deacon of S. Maria in Aquiro.
[252] 9 October 1361.
[253] 5 January 1361.
[254] Peter Itherii, bishop of Dax, priest of Ss. Quattro Coronati.
[255] 12 November 1361.
[256] 5 July 1349.
[257] 11 December 1361.
[258] 26 January 1363.
[259] 7 April 1362.
[260] 19 May 1342 to 18 May 1343.
[261] 8 October 1348 or 1349.
[262] Follows *idus* deleted.
[263] 30 March 1352.
[264] 25 November 1361.
[265] The heading *Norwicensis* is repeated at the top of the page.
[266] 29 June 1357.
[267] 26 January 1362.
[268] 3 March 1362.
[269] 15 December 1362.
[270] In the margin bracketed against this item and the next: *de tempore Domini Urbani.*

Item de eadem per obitum eiusdem Thome fuit provisum Johanni Bache eadem die, sed non debetur nisi una annata.

De ecclesia de Multton' (Moulton), de qua per obitum Edmundi de Wyhtewell' fuit provisum Hamoni de Wall', presbytero Lichefeldensis diocesis, per Urbanum ii idus Martii anno primo,[271] pro taxa xxvi li. xiii s. iiii d.

### Eliensis

De prioratu de Swavesey, de quo fuit provisum Stephano Bertrandi per Clementem, pro resta dimissa iiii li.

### Lincoliensis

De decanatu Lincoliensi, taxato iiᶜ lxvi li. xiii s. iiii d., de quo per obitum Johannis electi Cantuariensis fuit provisum Symoni de Bryseley per Clementem vi idus Octobris anno vii vel viii°,[272] pro resta xiiii li. xiii s. iiii d.

De prebenda de Radfford maiori (Bedford Maior) in ecclesia Lincoliensi, que fuit Guillelmo de Wyttesley confirmata per Clementem viii idus Maii anno vii vel viii,[273] pro taxa viii li.

De prebenda de Walton' Rivaus (Welton Rivall) in ecclesia Lincoliensi, de qua ex causa permutationis cum Johanne de Atton' fuit provisum Rotberto de Daventr' per Innocentium vii kalendas Maii anno v,[274] pro taxa xxxiii li. vi s. viii d.

Summa pagine cxliii li. vi s. viii d. Item ii beneficia.

(fol. 28, xxii)[275] De ecclesia de Trefford (Greatford) que fuit unita monasterio Beate Marie Wynthonie per Clementem iii idus Julii anno xi°,[276] pro taxa xiiii li. xiii s. iiii d. Episcopus certificat quod non est in diocesi Lincoliensi.

De prebenda Sancte Crucis (Spaldwick) in ecclesia Lincoliensi, taxata x li., de qua fuit provisum Johanni de Selby, pro resta l s.

De prebenda de Carleton' cum Turleby (Carlton le Moorland cum Thurlby) in ecclesia Lincoliensi, de qua per resignationem Guillelmi de Walcote fuit provisum Edwardo de Sherdestok' per Innocentium kalendas Martii anno vi,[277] que taxatur xxvi li. xiii s. iiii d., pro resta xiii li. vi s. viii d.

De prebenda de Suthecarle (South Scarle) in ecclesia Lincoliensi, de qua per resignationem Guillelmi de Kyrkebi fuit provisum Johanni de Appilby per Innocentium iii idus Julii anno vi°,[278] pro taxa xl li.

De ecclesia de Cosyngton (Cossington), que fuit Johanni de Melburn' confirmata per Innocentium vii

kalendas Julii anno vii,[279] pro taxa vi li. xiii s. iiii d. Episcopus certificat quod non est in sua diocesi.

De prebenda de Nasington' (Nassington) in ecclesia Lincoliensi, taxata c li., que fuit confirmata Ludovico de Charleton' per Innocentium iii kalendas Februarii anno ix[280] pro taxa c li.

De ecclesia de Stagrunde (Standground), de qua ex causa permutationis cum ecclesia Rippon' (Abbots Ripton) fuit provisum Johanni de Acton' per Innocentium vii kalendas Octobris anno ix,[281] pro taxa xx li.

De ecclesia de Rippton' Abbatis, de qua ex causa permutationis fuit provisum Thome de Clopton' per Innocentium vii kalendas Octobris anno ix°,[281] pro taxa xxiii li. vi s. viii d.

De prebenda de Glauton' (Glatton) in ecclesia Lincoliensi, de qua per obitum Ade de Ylton' fuit provisum Rogero de Sutton', dimissa pro taxa in iiii li. vi s. et viii d., de quibus fuit responsum in aliis computis, sed quia est ecclesia et taxatur ad xxi li. iii s. iiii d. et est in decanatu de Iavesle (Yaxley), debet adhuc xvi li. xvi s. viii d.[282]

De ecclesia de parva Kynewell (Little Kimble), de qua per assecutionem ecclesie de Gesyngton' (Garsington) fuit provisum Johanni Rocell' per Innocentium vi idus Martii anno vi,[283] pro taxa iiii li. xiii s. iiii d. Episcopus semper certificat quod non est talis in sua diocesi nec rector ita nominatus.

De prebenda Lincoliensi, de qua per obitum Jacobi de Borlay fuit provisum Domino Guillelmo episcopo Tusculano per Innocentium xv kalendas Septembris anno vi°,[284]

De ecclesia de Hogthon' (Houghton Regis), taxata xii li., que fuit Hugoni de Spackyng' confirmata per Innocentium xviii kalendas Decembris anno viii,[285] fructus vel taxa.

Summa pagine iiᶜ xlii li. Item ii beneficia.

(fol. 28ᵛ)[275] De ecclesia Beate Marie Herefford' (Hertford), de qua ex causa permutationis cum Johanne Dich' fuit provisum Henrico Mydy per Innocentium v kalendas Aprilis anno viii°,[286] fructus.

De prebenda de Langestowe (Stowe Longa) in ecclesia Lincoliensi, de qua fuit provisum Raynaldo de Temynis per Innocentium xi kalendas Julii anno ix,[287] pro taxa xlii li. vi s. viii d.

De prebenda in ecclesia Lincoliensi intitulata E. in ecclesia collegiata Beate Marie iuxta castrum Leycestr' (St. Mary the Less in Castle, Leicester) fuit ex causa

[271] 14 March 1363.
[272] 10 October 1348 or 1349.
[273] 8 May 1349 or 1350.
[274] 25 April 1357.
[275] The heading *Lincoliensis* is repeated at the top of the page.
[276] 13 July 1352.
[277] 1 March 1358.
[278] 13 July 1358.
[279] 25 June 1359.
[280] 30 January 1361.
[281] 25 September 1361.
[282] In the margin: *est ecclesia, non prebenda.*
[283] 10 March 1358.
[284] 18 August 1358. In the margin: *cardinalis.*
[285] 14 November 1360.
[286] 28 March 1360.
[287] 21 June 1361.

permutationis provisum Henrico de Lymbergh' per Urbanum v nonas Maii anno primo.[288]

De magistratu de Burton' Sancti Lazari (Burton Lazars), collatio facta per Dominum Philipum patriarcham Jhrosolimitanum auctoritate ordinaria Galffrido de Chadesden', militi dicti hospitalis, fuit [289] eidem auctoritate apostolica confirmata,[290] et nichilominus subrogatus dictus Galffridus in omni iure quod competebat Rotberto Haliday v nonas Martii dicto anno.[291]

De prebenda de Cosingham (Corringham) in ecclesia Lincoliensi, taxata cxxvi li. xiii s. iiii d., per obitum Raymundi Pelegrini fuit provisum cardinali Aquensi [292] per Urbanum iiii[to] nonas Septembris anno tertio,[293] pro resta dicte taxe xliiii li. iiii s. viii d. ob.

De prebenda ecclesie Lincoliensis vacante per obitum Guillelmi de Spaldewell', que vocatur prebenda Sancte Crucis (Spaldwick), fuit provisum Johanni de Kurkeby, clerico regis Anglie, per Urbanum xiii kalendas Maii anno primo.[294] Johannes de Selby ipsam tenet ex collatione regis et sic debentur l s. de eadem ex causa provisionis.

### Conwetrensis et Licheffeldensis

De archidiaconatu Convetrensi, non taxato, de quo fuit provisum Humfrido de Astyng', fructus.

Item de eodem archidiaconatu et prebenda de Langedon' (Longdon) in ecclesia Licheffeldensi, taxata xx li., de quibus post obitum Humfridi de Astyng' fuit provisum Willelmo de Salow per Clementem iiii[o] nonas Septembris anno viii,[295] de quibus Walterus Dalby dicitur composuisse cum camera pro resta archidiaconatus xiii li. vi s. viii d.

De prebenda de Lichefeldensi, de qua per obitum Guillelmi de Apeltr' fuit provisum Thome Attehull' per Clementem xi kalendas Julii anno viii[o],[296] fructus vel taxa.

De prebenda in ecclesia collegiata Sancte Sedde Saloppie (St. Chad, Shrewsbury), de qua per obitum Guillelmi Apeltr' fuit provisum Rotberto de Sulgrave per Clementem iii idus Decembris anno viii,[297] fructus. Non habuit effectum quia Hugo Espas ipsam tenuit et adhuc tenet iure regio.

Summa pagine lv li. xiii s. iiii d. Item v beneficia.

(fol. 29, xxiii)[298] De prebenda de Berkewik' (Berkswick) in ecclesia Licheffeldensi, taxata xx li., de qua per obitum Guidonis de Varesio fuit provisum Willelmo Cammule' per Innocentium vii[o] kalendas Maii anno primo,[299] pro taxa xx li.

De ecclesia de Walton', de qua fuit provisum Magistro Hugoni alias Johanni de Bolkyngton' iii nonas Decembris [300] anno v per Innocentium,[301] pro resta vii li.

De capellania Sancti Michaelis sita in castro de Cliderow (Clitheroe), non taxata, de qua fuit per devolutionem provisum Johanni de Burtton' per Innocentium iiii kalendas Junii anno vi.[302] Episcopus certificat quod non possit fieri executio quia est de patronatu laicali, videlicet ducis Lancastrie et regis Anglie, et est sine cura dependens ab ecclesia de Whalheya (Whalley) Licheffeldensis diocesis, que olim fuit plebana sed postea fuit ibi debite translatum monasterio Loci Benedicti de Stanlaw Cisterciensis ordinis dicte diocesis, propter maris innundationem, de auctoritate et littera Nicolai pape iiii[ti], sub data Rate (Rieti) x[o] kalendas Augusti pontificatus sui anno ii,[303] et postea predicta fuerit confirmata per Innocentium papam VI sub data vii kalendas Septembris pontificatus sui anno vii[o],[304] et pro ista appropriatione fuit lata sententia in curia de arcubus anno LXV die xxii Junii. Et de ista capellania fuerunt facte due subrogationes, isti Johanni de Borton', una per Innocentium ix kalendas Januarii anno ix [305] de David Martini et alia de Johanne Park' per Innocentium vii kalendas [306] anno x, que, licet posite fuerunt in aliis arrayragiis, hic tamen non ponuntur quia nichil valent, et sunt posite inter inutiles, et cetera.

De ecclesia de Codyngton (Coddington), de qua per assecutionem ecclesie de Wynthon' (Burton-in-Winhale) per Johannem Charnexux fuit provisum Waltero Lyngge per Innocentium iii nonas Junii anno vi,[307] pro taxa vi li. xiii s. iiii d.

De prioratu de Kyrkeby (Monks Kirby), de quo per assecutionem prioratus de Vetibelismo (Vieux Belesme) Saginensis (Séez) diocesis per Oliverum de Sertis fuit provisum Guillelmo de Grauleriis per Innocentium xiii kalendas Martii anno vii,[308] et taxatur lxxxi li. x s. viii d., debet de resta xli li. x s. viii d.

De ecclesia de Erklawe (Child's Ercall), que fuit confirmata Stephano de Synthethon' per Innocentium vii kalendas Julii anno vii[o],[309] pro taxa vi li. xiii s. iiii d.

De prebenda de Torvyn (Tarvin) in ecclesia Lycheffeldensi, de qua per obitum Guillelmi de Dyrffeld' fuit provisum Nicolao de Heth' per Innocentium iii idus Augusti anno x,[310] pro resta xxiiii li. ix s. vi d.

[288] 3 May 1363.
[289] fuerunt, MS.
[290] confirmate, MS.
[291] 3 March 1363.
[292] Peter Itherii, bishop of Dax, bishop of Albano.
[293] 2 September 1365.
[294] 19 April 1363.
[295] 2 September 1349.
[296] 21 June 1349.
[297] 11 December 1349.
[298] The heading Convetrensis et Licheffeldensis is repeated at the top of the page.

[299] 25 April 1353.
[300] Follows Octobris deleted by a line.
[301] 3 December 1357.
[302] 29 May 1358.
[303] 23 July 1289.
[304] 26 August 1359.
[305] 24 December 1361.
[306] A blank space is left in MS.
[307] 3 June 1358.
[308] 17 February 1359.
[309] 25 June 1359.
[310] 11 August 1362.

De prebenda in ecclesia collegiata de Penkyrgh' (Penkridge), de qua per obitum Thome Mychael fuit provisum Thome de Eltonheved' per Innocentium vii° idus Aprilis anno x,[311] fructus vel taxa.

De cantoria ecclesie Licheffeldensis, quam Thomas de Badeby debuit dimittere per assecutionem canonicatus et prebende ecclesie Lincoliensis fuit provisum. Nondum dimisit, ymo adhuc tenet.

De prebenda in ecclesia Lichenfeldensi, de qua per obitum Guillelmi de [312] Dyrffeld' in curia defuncti fuit provisum Alexandro de Dalby per Urbanum iiii nonas Januarii anno primo.[313] Episcopus certificat quod ista prebenda vocatur de Tervyn (Tarvin), et credo quod verum sit quia supra providetur Nicolao Heth' per obitum dicti Guillelmi, qui ipsam in presenti optinet et solvit ibi partem.

Summa pagine cvi li. vi s. x d.

(fol. 29ᵛ)[298] De prebenda de Goionssale (Gnosall) in ecclesia Lichefeldensi, de qua collatio et provisio facte auctoritate ordinaria Hugoni de Carles fuerunt eidem auctoritate apostolica confirmate vel provisum de novo per Urbanum v nonas Martii anno primo,[314] fructus vel taxa. Episcopus certificat quod est prebenda de Morenhal (Morehall) in ecclesia collegiata de Gnossall' et quod dictus Hugo nunquam possessionem ⟨habuit⟩.

### Assawensis

De ecclesia de Dyngkgh' (Denbigh), de qua, vacante de iure, ut asseritur, fuit provisum Guillelmo de Sunndelond' per Clementem idus Novembris anno ix°,[315] pro taxa vi li. xiii s. iiii d.

De ecclesia de Landrymeawe (Llandrinio), taxata vii li., que fuit confirmata Griffno de Charleton' per Innocentium iii nonas Maii anno ix°,[316] pro taxa vii li.

De ecclesia de Dyngkegh' (Denbigh), vacante per obitum Guillelmi de Sunnderlond', fuit provisum Guillelmo de Ardern' per Innocentium ix° kalendas Maii anno ix°,[317] xv li. vi s. viii d. Credo quod ista taxa non sit bona quia supra non taxatur nisi vi li. xiii s. et iiii d.

Item de dicta ecclesia, vacante per obitum dicti Guillelmi fuit provisum Hugoni Croft' per Innocentium iiiiᵗᵒ kalendas Maii anni ix°.[318]

De ecclesia de Kylkeyn (Kilken) et capella eidem annexa, de qua per obitum ultimi rectoris eiusdem fuit provisum Waltero de Freyysthorp' per Innocentium xi kalendas Julii anno ix,[319] pro taxa vii li., vii li.

### Menewensis

De ecclesia de Lamhanglarath' (Llanfihangel ar Arth), non taxata, de qua per obitum Aprovansses fuit provisum Ludovico Caunnton' per Clementem. Episcopus ceritficat quod est de patronatu principis Wallie; ideo non habuit effectum.

De ecclesia de Weston' (Wiston), non taxata, de qua per resignationem Rogeri dicti Johannis fuit provisum Guillelmo de Newehaw per Innocentium xix° kalendas Junii anno iiii°,[320] fructus.

De ecclesia de Langdemore (Llangoedmore) taxata vi li., de qua Guillelmo de Apromeiis per cardinalem Petragoricensem fuit provisum, pro resta iii li. vi s. viii d.

De prebenda in ecclesia Menevensi de qua per obitum Thome David fuit provisum David Wagham per Innocentium xi kalendas Julii anno ix°,[321] fructus vel taxa.

Summa pagine xxxix li. vi s. viii d. Item iii beneficia.

(fol. 30, xxiiii)[322] De prebenda de Landewiheim (Llandewi Brefi) in ecclesia Menevensi, de qua per obitum Griffini de Cauntton' fuit provisum Guillelmo de Osenden' per Innocentium ii nonas Decembris anno vᵗᵒ.[323] Non est prebenda in ecclesia Menevensi que vocetur Landewihem, sed ecclesia de Landewiheim et est collegiata per se, et non illa vacavit.

De prebenda seu portione in ecclesia Sancti Martini de Harberwill' (Abergwili), de qua per obitum Willelmi de Doybrayk' fuit provisum Waltero de Fenton' per Innocentium iiii° nonas Julii anno ix°,[324] fructus vel taxa.

### Landavensis

De precentoria Landavensi, non dimissa in arrayragiis nec missa per cameram, de qua fuit provisum Magistro Philipo de Enyas ut ipse confitetur, et dixit se teneri [325] camere pro primis fructibus dicte precentorie in v li. xiii s. iiii d., de quibus in alia recepta respondetur de xl s., debet pro resta iii li. xiii s. iiii d.

### Eboracensis

De prebenda in ecclesia Eboracensi de qua per consecrationem electi Terwynensis fuit provisum Frederico Saleman. Archiepiscopus rescribit quod alias non audivit de talibus prebendariis, quorum nichil est solutum.

De prebenda de Stranssal (Strensall) in ecclesia Eboracensi, de qua per consecrationem Michaelis episcopi Londoniensis fuit provisum cardinali Petragoricensi per Innocentium ii idus Octobris anno ii°,[326] pro taxa liii li. vi s. viii d.[327]

---

[311] 7 April 1362.
[312] Followed by *dis* deleted by a line.
[313] 2 January 1363.
[314] 3 March 1363.
[315] 13 November 1350.
[316] 5 May 1361.
[317] 23 April 1361.
[318] 28 April 1361.
[319] 21 June 1361.

[320] 14 May 1356.
[321] 21 June 1361.
[322] The heading *Menevensis* is repeated at the top of the page.
[323] 4 December 1357.
[324] 4 July 1361.
[325] *teni*, MS.
[326] 14 October 1354.
[327] In the margin: *attende quod notificetur camere quia in Anglia non sunt bona quia exigantur de iure capituli. Cardinalis.*

De vicaria de Gillyng' (Gilling), in qua Johannes Puker fuit subrogatus in omni iure quod competebat Gerlaco de Clave per Innocentium x kalendas Maii anno ix°,[328] pro taxa x li.

Item de eadem fuit provisum Johanni de Bock' per Innocentium ix kalendas Septembris anno viii°,[329] pro qua solvit x li.[330]

Summa pagine lxvii li. Item iii beneficia.

(fol. 30ᵛ)[331] De prebenda de Wistowe (Wistow) in ecclesia Eboracensi et archidiaconatu eiusdem, non taxato, de quibus per obitum cardinalis Penestrini[332] fuit provisum cardinali Carcassonnensi,[333] pro taxa prebende c li.[334]

De prebenda de Dirffeld' (Driffeld) in dicta ecclesia, de qua per obitum Guillelmi de Sancto Martiali fuit provisum cardinali de Sancto Martiali,[335] pro taxa c li.[334]

De prebenda de Bolm (Bole) in eadem ecclesia, de qua per obitum Thome de Newell' fuit provisum cardinali Cluniacensi,[336] pro taxa xvi li.[334]

De prebenda de Nortwell' (Norwell) in ecclesia collegiata de Sutwell' (Southwell), in qua in omni iure quod competebat Johanni de Dontton' fuit subrogatus Thomas Mount de Wyktham per Innocentium vi kalendas Augusti anno v,[337] pro taxa xxxvi li. xiii s. iiii d.

De capella sive cantoria de Wentebug' (Ferrybridge), de qua per obitum Thome Datemore fuit provisum Rotberto de Wyk' per Innocentium xi kalendas Octobris anno vii°,[338] Archiepiscopus certificat quod non sit talis capella in sua diocesi quod sciatur.

De archidiaconatu de Estriddyngg' in ecclesia Eboracensi cum ecclesia de Mapelton' (Mappleton) non taxata sibi annexa, vacante ex eo quod Guillelmus Walcor', qui ipsum optinebat, aliam ecclesiam extitit assecutus, fuit provisum Waltero de Skyrlawe per Innocentium ii kalendas Decembris anno vii,[339] composuit medio iuramento et salvo iure pluris, pro ecclesia ad xvi li. xiii s. iiii d. Lis pendet in curia et creditur quod ordinarius optinebit. De archidiaconatu vero dicit quod nullos habet redditus nisi procurationes et correctiones.

De custodia seu sacristia capelle Beate Marie et Sanctorum Angelorum Eboraci, collatio et provisio cuius facte auctoritate ordinaria Johanni de Waltham fuerunt eidem auctoritate apostolica confimate vel provisum de novo per Innocentium ix kalendas Januarii anno ix°,[340] pro taxa lxxxviii li. viii s. viii d.

De capellania perpetua Beati Petri de Wolvey, de qua ex causa permutationis cum Henrico Midi fuit provisum Johanni Dich' per Innocentium v kalendas Aprilis anno viii°,[341] fructus seu taxa. Archiepiscopus et eius officialis semper rescribunt quod non est talis in diocesi.

Summa pagine iiiᶜ lvii li. xv s. iiii d. Item ii beneficia.

### (fol. 31, xxv) Dunelmensis

De hospitali de Gretham, non taxato, de quo per obitum[342] Johannis de Stokton' fuit provisum Thome Johannis de Brydkyrk' per Clementem ii idus Octobris anno ix,[343] debetur medietas exceptis iii li. vi s. viii d. de quibus Dominus Hugo computat in receptis suis.

De prebenda in ecclesia collegiata Langcestr' (Lanchester), de qua ex causa permutationis cum Henrico de Exton' fuit provisum Galfrido de Cornesio per Innocentium xv kalendas Decembris anno primo,[344] fructus. Episcopus certificat quod nunquam habuit illam prebendam.

De prebenda de Dumley (Lamesley), in ecclesia collegiata Cestr' super stratam (Chester-le-Street), de qua per electionem electi Norwicensis fuit provisum Guillelmo de Lughtesburg' per Innocentium vi idus Februarii anno ii,[345] pro taxa xx li.

De decanatu ecclesie collegiate Cestr' super stratam permutatio facta auctoritate ordinaria cum Johanne de Scultherp' pro archidiaconatu Cicestrensi per Adam de Houtton' fuit eidem confirmata per Innocentium kalendas Junii anno vi,[346] decanatus taxatur ad xxxiii li. vi s. viii d., debet de resta xvi li. xiii s. iiii d.

De vicaria de Newton' en Glendale (Kirknewton), de qua per obitum Rotberti de Jarum fuit provisum Rotberto Hoppe per Innocentium nonas Septembris anno vii,[347] pro taxa xx li. Episcopus certificat quod nunquam habuit possessionem nec provisio effectum.

De prebenda in ecclesia de Northon' (Norton), de qua per obitum Thome Drax fuit provisum Bernardo de Lynariis per Innocentium vii kalendas Maii anno ix.[348] Episcopus certificat quod non est talis prebendarius in ecclesia nec unquam fuit quod sciatur.

De prebenda in ecclesia collegiata Aukland (Auckland), de qua per obitum Thome de Bridkik' fuit provisum Willelmo de Wiktham' per Innocentium[349] ii idus Augusti anno ix°,[350] fructus.

De ecclesia de Stanopp' (Stanhope), de qua per obitum Thome de Bridkik' fuit provisum Guillelmo de

---

[328] 22 April 1361.
[329] 24 August 1360.
[330] In the margin: *solvit.*
[331] The heading *Eboracensis* is repeated at the top of the page.
[332] Peter des Prés.
[333] Stephen Aubert, deacon of S. Maria in Aquiro.
[334] In the margin: *cardinalis*
[335] Hugo de Sancto Martiali, deacon of S. Maria in Portico.
[336] Androin de la Roche, priest of S. Marcello.
[337] 27 July 1357.
[338] 21 September 1359.
[339] 30 November 1359.
[340] 24 December 1361.

[341] 28 March 1360.
[342] Followed by *cardinalis* deleted by a line.
[343] 14 October 1350.
[344] 17 November 1353.
[345] 8 February 1354.
[346] 1 June 1358.
[347] 5 September 1359.
[348] 25 April 1361.
[349] Followed by *I* deleted by a line.
[350] 12 August 1361.

Norwico [351] per Innocentium viii kalendas Septembris anni ix°,[352] pro taxa xl s.

Item de eadem ecclesia collatio facta auctoritate ordinaria Ricardo de Wlyngthton' per obitum prefati Thome fuit eidem confirmata per Innocentium iiii° kalendas Januarii anno ix,[353] pro taxa xl s. Infra annum et prohibitus sit per regem ne faciat executionem contra incumbentem auctoritate regia.

Item de eadem ecclesia collatio predicta dicto Ricardo facta fuit confirmata per Innocentium iiii^to idus Maii anno x°,[354] pro taxa xl s.

De prebenda ecclesie collegiate de Houkeland' (Auckland), de qua per obitum dicti Thome fuit provisum Rotberto Stratton' per Innocentium xvi kalendas Septembris.[355] De ista prebenda providetur supra eadem pagina Guillelmo de Wykeham.

Summa pagine lxii li. xiii s. iiii d. Item iiii beneficia.

(fol. 31^v)[356] De capella libera de Jesmouh' (Jesmond), collatio facta auctoritate ordinaria Thome de Penreth' fuit eidem confirmata per Innocentium ix idus Januarii anno ix°.[357]

Item de eadem vacante per obitum Henrici Beufaunt fuit provisum Matheo de Bolthon' per Innocentium xiii kalendas Februarii anno x°.[358]

De hospitali pauperum Sancti Egidii de Kiptis (Kepier), de quo per obitum Petri de Toresby fuit provisum Johanni de Apilby per Innocentium viii kalendas Maii anno viii°.[359]

De ecclesia de Rothebury (Rothbury), presentatio, institutio et inductio facte auctoritate ordinaria Johanni Marescalli fuerunt eidem auctoritate apostolica confirmate vel de novo provisum per Urbanum v nonas Martii anno primo,[360] pro taxa lxvi li. xiii s. iiii d.

De canonicatu et prebenda ecclesie collegiate de Norton', vacantibus per obitum Thome Drax fuit provisum Bernardo de Lucano [361] clerico per Clementem anno viii vii kalendas Maii,[362] fructus.

## Kareolensis alias Karliolensis

De ecclesia de Crostwayt (Crosthwaite), in qua in omni iure competenti Johanni de Salario fuit subrogatus Johannes Henrici per Innocentium ii idus Januarii anno v,[363] pro taxa xxx li. xiii s. iiii d. In rationibus Magistri

Hugonis Pelegrini continetur quod non est prosecutus gratiam nec possessionem adeptus.

De vicaria de Bampton' (Brampton), de qua ea causa permutationis cum vicaria de Schaldefford (Shalford) Wyntoniensis diocesis fuit provisum Johanni Amyl per Innocentium xi kalendas Septembris anno v,[364] pro taxa viii li.

De vicaria de Crostoanwayt (Crosthwaite), provisio cuius facta Guillelmo de Esenden' fuit eidem confirmata per Innocentium ii kalendas Julii anno viii,[365] pro taxa xx li.

De ecclesia de Kerkelond (Kirkland), vacante ex eo quod Johannes de Kerkeby ipsam cum ecclesia de Wysohopp' (Ousby) per mensem et amplius detinuit pacifice et sine dispensatione, fuit provisum Johanni de Kerkeby per Innocentium viii kalendas Novembris anno vii,[366] pro taxa xl li.

Summa pagine clxv li. vi s. viii d. Item iii beneficia.

(fol. 32, xxvi) Sequntur reste de iiii^or obligatis

De ecclesia de Hodonet (Hodnet) Licheffeldensis diocesis et prebenda de Farendon' (Faringdon) in ecclesia Saresbiriensi, de Mora (Moorfields, St. Giles Cripplegate) in ecclesia Londoniensi, de Hundreton' (Hunderton) in ecclesia Herffordensi, et de Leddebury (Ledbury) in diocesi Herffordensi, de quibus fuit provisum Nicolao Heth', et composuit cum camera in curia pro primis fructibus dictorum beneficiorum pro viii^c l fl. ponderis camere, de qua summa sunt recepte in aliis secundis computis pro ecclesia de Hodonet vi li. xiii s. iiii d., que valent xliiii fl. et medium minus ii d. sterlingorum, computato floreno camere pro iii s. sterlingorum. Restat quod debet, detractis iii^c fl. de quibus respondit Dominus Hugo Pelegrini in suis ultimis computis, v^c v fl. et medium et ii d. sterlingorum.

Et est sciendum quod alii tres obligati totum solverunt excepta prebenda de Midelton' (Middleton) in ecclesia Cicestrensi, pro qua debentur iii li. vi s. viii d., que posita est in suo loco in diocesi Cicestrensi, et ideo hic non debet esse, sed ponitur pro memoriali tantum.

Sequntur arrayratgia beneficiorum collatorum per dominos cardinales

### Saresbiriensis

De prioratu seu officio de Noion alias de Novo Mercato (Neufmarché), de quo fuit provisum Nicolao Rom per cardinalem Petragoricensem, fructus.

### Lincoliensis

De prebenda de Rombury (Banbury) in ecclesia Lincoliensi, de qua Magistro Johanni de Strekeley cardinalis Petragoricensis providit, pro taxa xxx li.

De ecclesia de Longonis (Laughton), de qua fuit

---

[351] Followed by *viii* deleted by a line.
[352] 25 August 1361.
[353] 29 December 1361.
[354] 12 May 1362.
[355] 17 August.
[356] The heading *Dunelmensis* is repeated at the top of the page.
[357] 24 December 1361. In the margin bracketed against this item and the next: *Prohibitum per breve regium ne faciam executionem contra nunc incumbentem ex collatione regis.*
[358] 20 January 1362.
[359] 24 April 1360. In the margin: *Prohibitum est ut supra.*
[360] 3 March 1363.
[361] Followed by *per Clementem* not deleted.
[362] 25 April 1350.
[363] 12 January 1357.

[364] 22 August 1357.
[365] 30 June 1360.
[366] 25 October 1359.

provisum Waltero Benak' per cardinalem Petragoricensem. Episcopus certificat quod non est [367] in sua diocesi.

De ecclesia Sancti Clementis [368] de Wylowby (Willoughby) fuit provisum per cardinalem Petragoricensem Hugoni de Kipas, pro taxa xxiii li. vi s. viii d.

### Exoniensis

De cantoria perpetua Sancte Anne sita in ecclesia Omnium Sanctorum Exonie fuit provisum per dominum Urgellensem Alexandro Spereman'. Episcopus certificat quod non est in sua diocesi.

Summa pagine liii li. vi s. viii d., v<sup>c</sup> v fl. et medium et ii d. sterlingorum.

Summa areragiorum usque hic ii<sup>m</sup> vii<sup>c</sup> lxxiiii li. viii s. ii d., v<sup>c</sup> v fl. cum dimidio.

### (fol. 32<sup>v</sup>) Licheffeldensis

De ecclesia de Asdeby (Alderley), de qua per cardinalem Petragoricensem fuit provisum Johanni Baston', pro taxa viii li. Episcopus certificat quod non est talis rector nec ecclesia in sua diocesi.

De ecclesia de Burnhull' (Burnhill), de qua per dominum Petragoricensem cardinalem fuit provisum Hugoni de Pamberton', non taxata.[369]

De vicaria ecclesie de Dorssete magna (Great Dassett), de qua per dominum Petragoricensem fuit provisum Guillelmo Wy de Westbury, non taxata.

### Bangorensis

De ecclesia de Danburgham (Llangian) fuit provisum per dominum Petragoricensem David nato Johannis.

De ecclesia de Kouseby (Cowesby), de qua per dominum Urgellensem fuit provisum Henrico de Helperby.

### (fol. 33, xxvii) Sequntur arrayratgia antique Ybernie.

### Dublinensis

De decanatu ecclesie Dublinensis fuit provisum Matheo de Drysoley, qui taxatur xli li., pro resta xiiii li, xiii s. iiii d.

De thesauraria ecclesie Dublinensis et prebenda de Balliris (Ballymore), collatio facta Johanni de Cate fuit eidem confirmata per Clementem viii idus Maii anno viii,[370] pro taxa ix li.

De decanatu ecclesie Dublinensis, taxato xli li., de quo per obitum Mathei de Duseley' fuit provisum Johanni Briani, pro resta xx li.

De cancellaria ecclesie Dublinensis, taxata xl li., collatio facta Johanni de Troy fuit eidem confirmata

per Innocentium iiii° kalendas Julii anno ii,[371] pro resta xxvi li. xiii s. iiii d.

De prebenda ecclesie Dublinensis, de qua per consecrationem Johannis electi Dublinensis fuit provisum Guillelmo Rotberti per Clementem ix kalendas Januarii anno viii°,[372] fructus.

De prebenda ecclesie Dublinensis, de qua per consecrationem episcopi Lulucensis (Lincoln) fuit provisum Ricardo Drax' per Innocentium xvi kalendas Maii anno ii,[373] fructus.

De prebenda ecclesie Dublinensis, taxata xxiii li. vi s. viii d., de qua per obitum Wyli de Kelsey fuit provisum Johanni de Luddeley per Innocentium xiii° kalendas Maii anno vi,[374] xxvi li. vi s. viii d.

### Carkagensis

De decanatu ecclesie Carkagensis, de quo per provisionem factam Geraldo de Dury de episcopatu Carkagensi provisum Georgio de Rupe, canonico Carkagensi, per Innocentium ii nonas Februarii anno vii°.[375]

### Cassalensis

De archidiaconatu ecclesie Cassalensis collatio auctoritate ordinaria facta Johanni Tarada fuit eidem confirmata per Innocentium vii° idus Junii anno vii°.[376]

De archidiaconatu Colnensi (Cloyne) collatio facta per episcopum Rogero de Draybroyk fuit eidem confirmata per Innocentium idus Augusti anno vii°.[377]

De decanatu ecclesie Waterffordensis electio facta de Waltero Rene ad dictum decanatum fuit eidem confirmata per Innocentium iiii kalendas Junii anno ix°.[378]

### Dublinensis

De thesauraria ecclesie Dublinensis, taxata xx li. ad antiquam taxam, de qua per resignationem Johannis Gathe fuit provisum Hugoni de Testale per Innocentium ii idus Februarii anno vii°,[379] pro resta xiii li.

Summa pagine cix li. xiii s. iiii d. Item vi beneficia.

### (fol. 33<sup>v</sup>) Duacensis

De decanatu ecclesie Duascensis de quo per consecrationem Nicolai episcopi Duacensis fuit provisum Johanni Muggilkeaby per Innocentum ii nonas Aprilis anno vii°.[380]

### Dublinensis

De prebenda de Houth' (Howth) in ecclesia Dublinensi, taxata xxiii li. vi s. viii° d., collatio facta Waltero

---

[367] *sunt*, MS.
[368] Followed by *in* deleted by a line.
[369] In the margin bracketed against this item and the next: *sunt de patronatu laicali, et est prohibitum per breve regium ne exigantur.*
[370] 8 May 1350.

[371] 28 June 1354.
[372] 24 December 1349.
[373] 16 April 1354.
[374] 19 April 1358.
[375] 4 February 1359.
[376] 7 June 1359.
[377] 13 August 1359.
[378] 29 May 1361.
[379] 12 February 1359.
[380] 4 April 1359.

Matyn fuit confirmata per Innocentium idus Octobris anno viii°.[381]

De eadem de qua fuit provisum per consecrationem Stephani episcopi Limericensis Waltero de Kelesey per Innocentium vii idus Aprilis anno ii°,[382] pro resta x li.

De eadem ex eadem causa fuit provisum Thome Drik'; non habet effectum.

De prebenda ecclesie Dublinensis de qua per obitum Walteri Moryn fuit provisum Ade Robelyn per Innocentium kalendas Januarii anno ix°.[383]

De portione de Castro Canok (Castle Knock) in ecclesia Dublinensi, collatio et provisio facte auctoritate ordinaria per obitum Johannis Dene quondam de Kyngeston', quam per xxiiii°ʳ annos vel circiter [384] pocedit, fuerunt eidem auctoritate appostolica confirmate vel provisum de novo, non obstante quod tempore collationis huiusdem ordinarius esset excommunicatus, per Urbanum v nonas Martii anno.[385]

### Fernensis

De prebenda de Tagmon' (Taghmon) in ecclesia Fernensi, de qua per obitum Johannis de Sutton' fuit provisum Johanni Cote Galteryn per Clementem iii° idus Julii anno xi°.[386]

De prebenda de Thagmon' in ecclesia Fernensi per obitum Johannis de Sutton' et parochiali ecclesia de Colteiffer (Coolstuffe), de quibus per obitum Thome Michiel fuit provisum Domino Johanni Efornord, in episcopum Fernensem electo, ne habeat in opprobrium mendicare, per Clementem vii idus Augusti anno xi°.[387]

De ecclesia de Veterosia (Old Ross), de qua ex causa permutationis cum Nicholao Distart fuit provisum Johanni de Welwek' per Innocentium xvi kalendas Augusti anno ii.[388]

### Fernensis

De prebenda de Taghmon in ecclesia Fernensi, de qua per obitum Johannis de Sutton fuit provisum Johanni Galteryn per Innocentium vi idus Martii anno vi°.[389]

De prebenda de Taghmon in ecclesia Fernensi, in qua in omni iure quod competebat Johanni Castri fuit subrogatus Walterus de Dondale per Innocentium iiii idus Septembris anno viii°.[390]

### Osoriensis

De prebenda de Walmowak (Kilmacdonagh) in ecclesia Osoriensi, de qua per consecrationem [391] Thome

archiepiscopi Duanensis (Tuam) fuit provisum Ricardo Radulphi per Clementem ii idus Augusti anno xi.[392]

De decanatu ecclesie Osoriensis electio facta de Thoma de Wynton' fuit eidem confirmata per Innocentium vi idus Februarii anno ii.[393]

De canonicatu et prebenda Osoriensibus dum vacabunt per consecrationem Thome electi Dublinensis fuit provisum Nicholao de Chedelington' per Urbanum v kalendas Aprilis.[394]

### Limericensis

De prebenda ecclesie Limericensis, de qua per obitum Thome de Corkelay fuit provisum Johanni Cautte per Innocentium xi kalendas Januarii anno ii°.[395]

De prebenda de Disert alias Osert in ecclesia Limericensi, de qua per provisionem factam Stephano de Valle de archidiaconatu dicte ecclesie fuit provisum David Bauconiti vi idus Maii anno vi°.[396]

Summa pagine patet x li.

(fol. 34, xxviii)[397] De thesauraria ecclesie Limericensis, de qua per obitum Ade Hunt fuit provisum Guillelmo Godwyn per Innocentum vi idus Decembris anno vi°.[398]

De decanatu ecclesie Limericensis, de quo per obitum Thome de Torkele fuit provisum Stephano de Valle per Innocentium ii idus Decembris anno vi°.[399]

De precentoria ecclesie Limericensis, de qua, eo quod Adam Card' ipsam cum ecclesia de Noutton' (Newtown) per tres annos retinuit, fuit provisum Philipo Draykok per Innocentium v idus Martii anno vi.[400]

De decanatu Limericensi, de quo per munus consecrationis impressum Stephano episcopo Limericensi fuit provisum Henrico Albo, canonico dicte ecclesie, per Innocentium xviii kalendas Junii anno viii°.[401]

De eodem decanatu, vacante per obitum Henrici, fuit provisum Ade Wyh' per Innocentium iii° idus Augusti anno ix°.[402]

De cancellaria ecclesie Limericensis, de qua per consecrationem Domini Stephani Lowels episcopi Limericensis fuit provisum Bartholomeo Dullart per Innocentium xiii° kalendas Januarii anno ix°.[403]

### Dunensis

De prioratu ecclesie Dunensis, cum vacabit per consecrationem Ricardi electi Dunensis, fuit mandatum

---

[381] 15 October 1360.
[382] 7 April 1354.
[383] 1 January 1361.
[384] Followed by *pocessid* deleted by a line.
[385] 3 March.
[386] 13 July 1352.
[387] 7 August 1352.
[388] 17 July 1354.
[389] 10 March 1358.
[390] 10 September 1360.
[391] Over *resignationem* deleted by a line.

[392] 12 August 1352.
[393] 8 February 1354.
[394] 28 March.
[395] 22 December 1354.
[396] 10 May 1358.
[397] The caption *Limericensis* is repeated.
[398] 8 December 1358.
[399] 12 December 1358.
[400] 11 March 1358.
[401] 15 May 1360.
[402] 11 August 1361.
[403] 20 December 1361.

provideri Nicolao Langton' per Innocentium v idus Octobris anno primo.[404]

De ecclesia de Dungervan (Dungarvan), que ex causa permutationis cum decanatu rurali de Lynie (Lynn) Norwycensis diocesis cum Adam Thebaud fuit provisum Henrico de Wyterton' alias Wynthrigham per Innocentium viii° kalendas Novembris anno viii°.[405]

### Limericensis

De prebenda Limericensi, de qua per obitum Johannis de Balstok' fuit provisum Thome Lavestoke per Innocentium anno v°.[406]

Summa omnium precedentium arrayratgiorum de annatis est ii^m ix^c ii li. ii s. vi d., v^c v fl. et medium, ii d. sterlingorum.

(fol. 34^v) Infrascripte sex provisiones extracte fuerunt de regestris camere de anno primo Domini Urbani que non erant misse nec tradite collectori Anglie, que debent in suis locis debitis collocari, et de eis responderi in sequentibus computis

### Eliensis

Motu proprio fuit provisum A. cardinali Cluniacensi [407] de canonicatu, prebenda ac archidiaconatu ecclesie Eliensis, vacantibus per obitum cardinalis de Gordonio,[408] per Urbanum iii ydus Novembris anno primo.[409]

### Limericensis

De perpetua vicaria de Kildyn (Kildimma) Limericensis diocesis, vacante per mortem David de Yncourt in Romana curia defuncti, fuit provisum Johanni Pastyn, presbytero Laonensis diocesis de Ybernia, per Urbanum vii kalendas Februarii anno primo.[410]

Collatio facta auctoritate ordinaria ex causa permutationis Johanni de Midelton' presbytero de parochiali ecclesia de Kirleby Ravenwasch' (Kirkby Ravensworth) fuit eidem auctoritate appostolica confirmata vel provisum de novo et tenetur concordare cum camera de fructibus et cetera, xii kalendas Aprilis per Urbanum anno primo.[411]

### Licheffeldensis, Londoniensis, Saresbiriensis, Menevensis

Concessum fuit episcopis Wythoniensi et Vygorniensi ut ipsi et quilibet eorum ad nominationem regis Anglie possint providere quinque perssonis ydoneis de de-

canatu ecclesie Licheffeldensi, que dignitas curata et electiva maior post episcopalem existit, necnon canonicatibus et prebendis Londoniensis, Saresbiriensis, Menevensis ac collegiate de Abberwill' (Abergwili) Menevensis diocesis ecclesiarum, cum vacabunt per consecrationem Johannis de Bokyngham electi Lincoliensis per Urbanum iiii^to ydus Aprilis anno primo.[412]

### Karleolensis

Collatio et provisio facte per episcopum Karleolensem de parochiali ecclesia de Caldebek' (Caldbeck) Karleolensis diocesis etiam si sit reservata fuerunt auctoritate appostolica confirmate vel provisum de novo Guillelmo de Rugenhill' per Urbanum v nonas Martii anno primo.[413]

### Limericensis

De canonicatu et prebenda ac archidiaconatu ecclesie Limericensis, vacantibus per obitum Petri Godini, ultimi archidiaconi eiusdem, extra Romanam curiam defuncti, de quibus ordinarius excommunicatus propter debita camere appostolice non potuit ordinare etiam si alio quovismodo vaccent, fuit provisum Ade Cradok, in utroque iure perito,[414] et dimittet prebendam et precentoriam [415] Imelacensem per Urbanum viii kalendas Maii anno primo.[416]

(fol. 35, xxix) Sequntur arrayratgia beneficiorum collatorum in regno Anglie per sanctissimum in Christo patrem Dominum Urbanum papam quintum a iii° kalendas Maii pontificatus sui anno primo usque ad pridie idus Julii anno quinto,[417] quia de ulteriori tempore in Anglia beneficia nondum sunt recepta nec de ⟨eisdem⟩ computatur in rationibus nunc camere assignatis

### Dublinensis

Collatio et provisio facte auctoritate ordinaria Nicolao de Chedelyngton' de cancellaria ecclesie Dublinensis, vacante ex eo quod Johannes de Troye, dictam cancellariam obtinens, prebendam de Swordes (Swords) in ipsa ecclesia fuit pacifice assecutus etiam si dictus ordinarius tempore collationis esset excommunicatus, fuerunt sibi confirmate vel provisum de novo v nonas Martii anno primo.[418] Iterum et per eundem modum providetur eidem v kalendas Julii anno primo,[419] que [420] hic in arrayratgiis non ponitur quia utraque est infra annum.

### Eliensis

De parochiali ecclesia de Elloswort (Elsworth) Eliensis, vacatura cum Johannes de Morthon' digni-

---

[404] 11 October 1353.
[405] 25 October 1360.
[406] 1357.
[407] Androin de la Roche, abbot of Cluny, priest of S. Marcello.
[408] William Farinier of Gourdon, priest of Ss. Marcellino e Pietro.
[409] 11 November 1362.
[410] 26 January 1363.
[411] 21 March 1363.

[412] 10 April 1363.
[413] 3 March 1363.
[414] *pervecto*, MS.
[415] Follows *thesaurariam* deleted by a line.
[416] 24 April 1363.
[417] 29 April 1363 to 14 July 1367.
[418] 3 March 1363.
[419] 27 June 1363.
[420] Followed by *habet* deleted by a line.

tatem, personatum vel officium curatum in ecclesia Lichfeldensi fuerit pacifice assecutus, fuit provisum Thome Eltesle, clerico dicte Eliensis diocesis bachalario in utroque iure, iii° kalendas Maii anno primo.[421] Infra providetur alteri per eandem vacationem xi kalendas Februarii anno iiii[to].[422]

## Norwicensis

Collatio et provisio facte auctoritate ordinaria Waltero de Redenesse, clerico Eboracensis diocesis, de parochiali ecclesia de Keklyng alias Bleklyk (Blickling), taxata x li. xiii s. iiii d., Norwicensis diocesis, vacante ex eo quod Willelmus de Swynflet archidiaconatum Norwici est pacifice assecutus, fuerunt confirmate vel provisum de novo, pro resta dicte taxe v li. vi s. viii d., iii kalendas Maii.[423]

Item collatio et provisio facte fratri Stephano Je indito Stephani de prepositura monasterii Sancte Marie Nortton' ordinis Sancti Benedicti, vacante per promotionem abbatis dicti monasterii, fuerunt confirmate vel provisum de novo, fructus.

Item ordinatio facta per bone memorie dominum decanum (Otto), tunc in partibus Anglicanis apostolice sedis legatum, de uno perpetuo vicario in parochiali ecclesia de Merton' (Morton) dicte diocesis fuit confirmata vel provisum de novo.

## Exoniensis et Lincoliensis

Item collatio et provisio ex causa permutationis facte Willelmo Seerl de archidiaconatu Tottonensi in ecclesia Exoniensi pro ecclesia parochiali de Doddyngton' (Doddington) Lincoliensis diocesis fuerunt confirmate vel provisum de novo per Urbanum vii° kalendas Maii anno primo,[424] pro resta ratione compositionis facte medio iuramento pro medietate fructuum x li.

Summa pagine xv li. vi s. viii d. Item iiii beneficia.

## (fol. 35ᵛ) Anno primo

## Lincoliensis

Motu proprio fuit provisum cardinali Morinensi [425] de canonicatu et prebenda ac archidiaconatu Lincoliensibus, vacantibus per obitum cardinalis Magalonensis [426] v idus Maii.[427] Sed non habuit effectum quia rex contulit totum iure suo Willelmo de Wiktham et ideo ponitur inter inutiles provisiones.

Item Johanni de Ditton', clerico Licheffeldensis diocesis, de canonicatu et prebenda quam Willelmus de Askeby, sedis apostolice capellanus, que vocatur Bedfir' minori (Bedford Minor) in ecclesia Lincoliensi, optinuit, vacante per resignationem ipsius in manibus

ordinarii aut per assecutionem alterius prebende in dicta ecclesia v idus Maii.[427]

## Saresbiriensis

Item Waltero de Chiderle parvo, presbytero Eliensis diocesis, de parochiali ecclesia de Bradesydoling' (Sydling St. Nicholas) Saresbiriensis diocesis, vacante per mortem Nicolai de Englisch', que tanto tempore vacavit quod eius collatio est ad sedem apostolicam devoluta. Sed est appropriata monasterio de Midelton' (Milton) eiusdem diocesis, et nunquam habebit possessionem, ideo ponitur inter inutiles.

## Lincoliensis

Item Johanni de Doneston', presbytero Lincoliensis diocesis, de parochiali ecclesia de Hokelive (Hockliffe) dicte diocesis, taxata viii li., vacante in curia per obitum Johannis de Wynhull', vii kalendas Maii.[424]

Item Petro de Newbald', bachalario in legibus, de canonicatu et prebenda ecclesie collegiate de Rippon' et prebenda de Muketon' (Monkton) in eadem, vacantibus per obitum Johannis de Winnewik', vii idus Maii.[428] Sed fuit prohibitum per regem ne fiat aliqua executio contra incumbentem, et lis pendet in curia, et infra providetur alteri iii kalendas Julii anno primo.[429]

## Herffordensis

Item Johanni Brinkehull', presbytero Herffordensis diocesis, de vicaria perpetua parochialis ecclesie de Bortton' (Burrington) dicte diocesis, vacante per resignationem Ade de Abbatia in manibus ordinarii, vii idus Maii.[428]

## Dunellmensis

Item Thome de Penreth', presbytero Karliolensis diocesis, de ecclesia de Wesyntton' (Washington) Dunellmensis diocesis, vacante ex eo quod Rotbertus de Warthecopp', patiens defectum natalium de soluto et inde genitus, iam per duos annos et ultra tenuit, nulla dispensatione super hoc obtenta, vii idus Maii.[428]

## Licheffeldensis

De canonicatu ecclesie Licheffeldensis et prebenda de Prees in eadem, vacantibus per resignationem Petri, alias dicti Johannis, de Alerston', fuit provisum Rotberto de Straton', legum doctori, auditori palatii apostolici, xvii kalendas Junii anno primo,[430] sed allegatur quod non habuit effectum.

## (fol. 36, xxx)[431] Eliensis

Collatio et provisio facte auctoritate ordinaria iure devoluto de prioratu seu administratione prioratus de

---

[421] 29 April 1363.
[422] 22 January 1366.
[423] 29 April.
[424] 25 April 1363.
[425] Giles Ecelin de Montaigue, priest of St. Martin in Montibus.
[426] Audoin Aubert, bishop of Maguelone, bishop of Ostia.
[427] 11 May 1363.

[428] 9 May 1363.
[429] 29 June 1363.
[430] 16 May 1363.
[431] The heading *Anno primo* is repeated at the top of the page.

Swaveseye (Swavesey) Eliensis diocesis, a monasterio
Sanctorum Sergi et Bachi Andegavensis (Angers)
dependente, ordinis Sancti Benedicti, per unum religiosum dicti monasterii solito gubernari, fratri Johanni
Wakelyn, monacho monasterii Westmonasterii, monasterii Londoniensis diocesis fuerunt confirmate vel provisum de novo per Urbanum xvi kalendas Junii anno
primo.[432]

### Cicestrensis

Unita fuit et annexa ecclesia parochialis de Lamoyng'
(Lancing) Cicestrensis diocesis mense et usui ministri
et fratrum hospitalis Sancte Trinitatis de Modynden'
(Muttinden) Cantuariensis, servata portione competenti pro vicario dicte ecclesie per Urbanum anno primo
v kalendas Junii.[433]

### Landavensis

De archidiaconatu ecclesie Landavensis, vacante per
resignationem Thome de Eltesby Eliensis diocesis, in
utroque iure bachalario, fuit eidem Thome provisum
per Urbanum anno primo kalendas Junii.[434]

### Dunellmensis

De canonicatu et prebenda seu portione de Bires
(Byers) in ecclesia collegiata de Arkesland (Auckland)
Dunellmensis diocesis, vacante per mortem Rotgeri de
Blamer' in Romana curia defuncti, fuit provisum Ragero
de Slateborne, presbytero Eboracensis diocesis, per
Urbanum anno primo v idus Junii.[435] Ista prebenda
nichil valet propter guerras, licet taxetur ad xvi li.

### Corkagensis in Ybernia

De canonicatu [436] ecclesie Corkagensis, vacante per
consecrationem Georgii electi Cassellensis, fuit provisum Willelmo Bulla, clerico Inliacensis [437] diocesis in
Ybernia, per Urbanum anno primo v idus Junii.[435]

### Imlacensis in Ybernia

De rectoria curata de Typerar' (Tipperary) Ymlacensis diocesis, vacante per consecrationem David
Penlyn electi Imlacensis, fuit provisum Odoni Ohogan,
clerico Cassalensis diocesis, v idus Junii.[435]

### Menevensis

Item Thome de Terfford', clerico Lincoliensis diocesis, de canonicatu et prebenda in ecclesia Sancti
Mauricii de Abbewill' (Abergwili) Menevensis diocesis,
vacante per resignationem Johannis de Watham, v idus
Junii.[435]

### Eboracensis

Item Rotgero de Ulram, presbytero Eboracensis
diocesis, de beneficio ecclesiastico, videlicet parochiali
ecclesia Sancte Helene in Stayngat' (Stonegate, York)
Eboracensis diocesis, vacante per mortem Johannis de
Rator' per Urbanum anno primo v idus Junii.[435]

### Cicestrensis

De parochiali ecclesia de West Ichenor Cicestrensis
diocesis, vacante per mortem Rogeri Lydon', ultimi
rectoris eiusdem, extra Romanam curiam, que tanto
tempore vacavit quod eius collatio est ad sedem apostolicam legitime devoluta, fuit provisum Rotberto Amys
de Brendbroghton', presbytero Lincoliensis diocesis, per
Urbanum anno primo v kalendas Julii.[438]

### (fol. 36ᵛ)[439] Eboracensis

De vicaria perpetua parochialis ecclesie de Skipton'
in Crasve (Skipton in Craven) dicte diocesis,[440] vacante
per mortem Willelmi de Draghton', ultimi vicarii eiusdem, a tanto tempore quod eius collatio est ad sedem
apostolicam legitime devoluta, fuit provisum Thome
Johannis filio [441] Matilde Achaliate de Shirburn' in
Elneto Eboracensis diocesis, v kalendas Julii.[438]

### Saresbiriensis

Item Guillelmo Persone, presbytero Saresbiriensis
diocesis, de parochiali ecclesia de Swyndon' (Swindon)
dicte diocesis Saresbiriensis, que per cessionem vel
dimissionem Nicolai Homan, ultimi rectoris eiusdem,
tanto tempore vacavit quod eius collatio est ad sedem
apostolicam legitime devoluta, v kalendas Julii.[438]

### Dunellmensis

Item Waltero Johannis, presbytero Dunellmensis
diocesis, de vicaria ecclesie parochialis de Nornham
(Norham) dicte diocesis, vacante per mortem Guillelmi
de Elwyk, ultimi vicarii eiusdem, extra Romanam
curiam defuncti, quam [442] frater Nicolaus Cave, monachus et apostata ordinis Cisterciensis per duos annos
et ultra occupavit indebite, v kalendas Julii.[438]

### Eboracensis

Item Johanni de Baldeston, clerico Eboracensis diocesis, de parochiali ecclesia de Mysen (Misson) dicte
diocesis, vacante per resignationem seu dimissionem
Johannis de Schorlehorp a tanto tempore quod eius
collatio est ad sedem apostolicam legitime devoluta, v
kalendas Julii.[438]

Item Willelmo de Wyncornwik, presbytero Eboracensis, de parochiali ecclesia de Manfeld (Manfield)

---

[432] 17 May 1363.
[433] 28 May 1363.
[434] 1 June 1363.
[435] 9 June 1363.
[436] *decanatu* is written above *canonicatu* and neither is deleted.
[437] *Laoniensis*, above, p. 243.

[438] 27 June 1363.
[439] The heading *Anno primo* is repeated at the top of the page.
[440] Followed by *Eboracensis* deleted by a line.
[441] filii, MS.
[442] *quem*, MS.

dicte diocesis, vacante per resignationem vel dimissionem quondam Guillelmi de Struttewill', ultimi rectoris eiusdem, a tanto tempore quod eius collatio est ad sedem apostolicam legitime devoluta, v kalendas Julii.[438]

Item Rotberto de Wadyngham, clerico Lincoliensis diocesis, de parochiali ecclesia de Kayngham (Keyingham) Eboracensis diocesis, vacante per resignationem Guillelmi de Brokelesby in manibus ordinarii a tanto tempore quod eius collatio est ad sedem apostolicam legitime devoluta, v kalendas Julii.[438]

De parochiali ecclesia de Elkesley Eboracensis diocesis, vacante per mortem Johannis Chambroch a tanto tempore quod eius collatio est ad sedem apostolicam legitime devoluta, fuit provisum Rotberto de Overe, clerico Eliensis diocesis, taxata xl m., v kalendas Julii.[438]

### Licheffeldensis

De parochiali ecclesia de Badile (Baddiley) Licheffeldensis diocesis, vacante per resignationem Guillelmi de Hynkele, ultimi rectoris eiusdem, in manibus ordinarii a tanto tempore quod eius collatio est ad sedem apostolicam legitime devoluta, fuit provisum Rotgero de Wadnorton', presbytero Norwicensis diocesis, per Urbanum anno primo iii nonas Julii.[443]

Item Rotgero de Wadnorton', presbytero Norwicensis diocesis, de ecclesia de Gabile (Baddiley) Licheffeldensis diocesis, que valet xxv m. sterlingorum secundum communem extimationem annuatim, iii nonas Julii.[444]

### (fol. 37)[439] Eboracensis

Item Rotberto de Sochowe, presbytero Eboracensis diocesis, de ecclesia de Agthon' (Aughton), valet secundum communem extimationem xl li. sterlingorum, iiiº nonas Julii.[443]

Item Johanni Ulram, presbytero, de parochiali ecclesia de Usegate (All Saints Pavement in Ousegate) in civitate Eboraci, que taxatur ad xv m. sterlingorum, iiiº nonas Julii. In hoc loco provisionum est alia collatio facta eidem de eadem ecclesia per mortem eiusdem et sub eadem data et eodem anno. Et subsequenter est alia provisio facta eidem de eadem xviii kalendas Maii anno iiiiº,[445] et neuter istarum valet quia ille qui nunc eam tenet ostendit diffinitionem contra illum per cuius mortem impetratur. Ideo ponitur inter inutiles.

Item Ade de Thornton' presbytero Eboracensis diocesis, de canonicatu et prebenda ecclesie de Rippon' et prebenda de Mukton' (Monkton) in eadem ecclesia, quorum fructus lxvi li. xiii s. et iiii d. secundum taxam non excedunt, per Urbanum anno primo iiiº nonas Julii.[443] De ista prebenda supra providetur alteri vii kalendas Maii eodem anno,[446] et est prohibitum per regem ne fiat aliqua executio.

Item Johanni de Othyngham, presbytero Eboracensis diocesis, de parochiali ecclesia de Corom' (Cotham) dicte diocesis, vacante per resignationem Radulphi de Yarwell' a tanto tempore quod eius collatio est ad sedem apostolicam devoluta, xiii kalendas Augusti.[447]

De parochiali ecclesia de Otnylay (Whixley) Eboracensis diocesis, que per obitum Nicolai Sesay tanto tempore vacavit quod eius collatio est ad sedem apostolicam devoluta, fuit provisum Johanni Torkesey, bachalario in legibus, vii idus Julii.[448]

Dispensatum fuit cum Johanne Raugine, clerico Wygorniensis diocesis, ut parochialem ecclesiam de Ilkelay (Ilkley) Eboracensis diocesis, taxata xvii li. vi s. viii d., quam pacifice possidet, licite valeat obtinere[449] non obstante defectu natalium quem patitur de soluto genitus et soluta, que taxatur ad novam taxam xxvi m., que valent xvii li. vi s. viii d., debet pro resta v li. vi s. viii d.[450]

### Limericensis

Collatio facta auctoritate ordinaria Gerardo Laweles, presbytero Limericensis diocesis, de thesauraria ecclesie Limericensis, vacante per obitum Ade Hunnte in partibus defuncti, fuit auctoritate apostolica confirmata vel provisum de novo, vii idus Julii.[448]

### Eboracensis

Ex causa permutationis fuit provisum Willelmo Glayne de Podyngton' de vicaria parochialis ecclesie de Kyldewik' (Kildwick) Eboracensis diocesis, vii idus Julii.[448]
Summa pagine v li. vi s. viii d.

### (fol. 37ᵛ)[439] Landavensis

Ex causa permutationis fuit provisum Martino de Relerynton' de parochiali ecclesia de Kykyngan (St. Mary Hill) diocesis Landavensis cum prebenda ecclesie collegiate de Glausne (Glasnay) Exoniensis diocesis, de qua est satisfactum.

### Londoniensis et Norwycensis

Item Ade Thebaud de libera capella de Chelmeforde (Chelmsford) Londoniensis diocesis et Thome Thebaud filio Rotberti Thebaudo de Jewewya de decanatu rurali Lynnie (Lynn) Norwicensis diocesis, vii idus Julii.[448]

### Norwicensis

De decanatu rurali de Rodenhal (Redenhall) Norwicensis diocesis vacante per liberam resignationem Guillelmi de Thamworth' olim Londoniensis diocesis, fuit provisum Thome de Drayton Lincoliensis diocesis, vii idus Julii.[448]

---

[443] 5 July 1363.
[444] 5 July 1363. In the margin: *Eadem est collatio.*
[445] 14 April 1366.
[446] 25 April 1363.

[447] 20 July 1363.
[448] 9 July 1363.
[449] Ove *retinere* deleted by dots.
[450] In the margin deleted by lines: *De archidiaconatu ecclesie Imelacensis, vacante in curia per consecrationem episcopi Imelacensis, fuit provisum Johanni.*

## Wynthoniensis

Collatio et provisio facte auctoritate ordinaria Waltero de Sevenhampton', magistro in artibus, de canonicatu et prebenda de Tymberbury (Timsbury), taxata xxviii li. xiii s. iiii d., que est in ecclesia monialium de Rameseye (Romsey) ordinis Sancti Benedicti Wyntoniensis diocesis, per obitum Willelmi de Farlegh' extra curiam defuncti, fuerunt confirmate [451] vel provisum de novo, et fuit subrogatus in iure quod eidem Guillelmo et quondam Andree de Offord' in eisdem competebat, anno primo idus Julii,[452] pro resta vi li. xiii s. iiii d.

## Elphinensis

De prioratu de Innocentia iuxta Atheluam (Athlone) ordinis Cluniacensis Elfinensis diocesis in Ybernia, vacante per obitum Mathei ultimi prioris eiusdem, fuit provisum fratri Guillelmo Stanelays, monacho ac cellerario dicti [453] prioratus, vi idus Augusti.[454]

De parochiali ecclesia de Hornesse (Hornsea) Eboracensis diocesis, vacante apud sedem apostolicam per obitum Domini Raymundi de Fargiis, quondam cardinalis,[455] fuit provisum Nicolao de Lonays, iii idus Augusti.[456]

Motu proprio fuit provisum Domino Guillelmo cardinali Cesaraugustanensi (Saragossa)[457] de canonicatu ecclesie Eboracensis et prebenda de Masham in eadem, vacantibus per obitum cardinalis Magalonensis,[458] xvii kalendas Septembris.[459]

## Inliacensis

De archidiaconatu [460] ecclesie Inliacensis, vacante in curia Romana per consecrationem Willelmi episcopi Inliacensis, fuit provisum Johanni Stantton', clerico Inliacensis diocesis, xvii kalendas Septembris.[459]

## Bangorensis

De parochiali ecclesia Sanctorum Cirici et Julite Lanquile (Llanerfyl?) Bangorensis diocesis, vacante per obitum ultimi rectoris eiusdem extra Romanam curiam defuncti, et que tanto tempore vacavit quod eius collatio est ad sedem apostolicam devoluta, fuit provisum Reginaldo de Swynemere, presbytero dicte diocesis, xvii kalendas Septembris.[459]

Summa pagine vi li. xiii s. iiii d.

---

[451] *fuit confirmata*, MS.
[452] 15 July 1363.
[453] Followed by *monasterii* deleted by a line.
[454] 8 August 1363.
[455] Deacon of S. Maria Nuova.
[456] 11 August 1363.
[457] William d'Aigrefeuille, priest of S. Maria in Trastevere.
[458] Audoin Aubert, bishop of Maguelone, bishop of Ostia.
[459] 16 August 1363.
[460] Over *decanatu* deleted by a line.

## (fol. 38, xxxii)[461] Limericensis

De vicaria perpetua de Kiwide (Killkeedy) Limericensis diocesis, vacante per mortem Thome ultimi rectoris eiusdem extra Romanam curiam defuncti, a tanto tempore quod eius collatio est ad sedem apostolicam legitime devoluta, fuit provisum Thome de Burgo, presbytero Imliacensis diocesis, xi kalendas Septembris.[462]

## Eboracensis

De vicaria perpetua parochialis ecclesie de Kulenham (Kirkham) Eboracensis diocesis, vacante per resignationem Guillelmi de Slayteburn' factam in manibus ordinarii, que tanto tempore vacavit quod eius collatio est ad sedem apostolicam legitime devoluta vel alio quovis modo vacet, fuit provisum Symoni de Tonbreog', presbytero Roffensis diocesis, et dimittet parochialem ecclesiam de Excete Cicestrensis diocesis, xi kalendas Septembris.[462]

De perpetua vicaria ecclesie parochialis de Gyllyngis (Gilling) Eboracensis diocesis, vacante ex eo quod Gerlacus de Clave, clericus Spirensis (Speyer) diocesis eam detinuit occupatam in presbyterum non promotus infra tempus debitum vel alio quovis modo, fuit provisum Thome filio Johannis de Briston', clerico Norwicensis diocesis, xi kalendas Septembris.[462]

## Saresbiriensis

Item Rotberto Falky, clerico Eboracensis diocesis, de parochiali ecclesia Sancte Marie de Wynterburn' Stikelan (Winterborne Stickland) Saresbiriensis diocesis, vacante per mortem Thome Henrici de Chelstr' in Romana curia defuncti, xi kalendas Septembris.[462]

## Eboracensis

Item fuit provisum Johanni Ulram, presbytero Eboracensis diocesis, de parochiali ecclesia curata Omnium Sanctorum in Usegate (All Saints Pavement in Ousegate, York) Eboracensis diocesis, vacante in curia per mortem Symonis Wardde, xi kalendas Septembris.[462] De ista ecclesia supra providetur bis eidem sub data viiº idus Julii.[448]

## Assawensis

Item Awelmo de Brecon', canonico Menevensi, de parochiali ecclesia Sancti Ewdelani (Dolwyddelan) Assavensis diocesis, vacante per liberam resignationem seu dimissionem factam per Theodorum natum Johannis Oweyn, ultimi rectoris eiusdem, xi kalendas Septembris.[462]

## Saresbiriensis

Confirmata fuit auctoritate apostolica unio facta auctoritate ordinaria de consensu capituli de parochiali ecclesia de Harewell' (Harwell) Saresbiriensis diocesis,

---

[461] The heading *Anno primo* is repeated at the top of the page.
[462] 22 August 1363.

que de patronatu Edwardi primogeniti regis Anglie, Wallie principis, existebat et ipsius principis infra castrum suum de Walyngford' (Wallingford) dicte diocesis, iii kalendas Septembris.[463]

## Norwicensis

Item Willelmo Malteby, presbytero Eboracensis diocesis, de parochiali ecclesia de Sinterle [464] (Blakeney or Glandford) Norwicensis diocesis, vacante per mortem ultimi rectoris eiusdem, que tanto tempore vacavit quod eius collatio est ad sedem apostolicam devoluta, xi kalendas Septembris.[462]

Item Andree de Buewellis, presbytero Norwicensis diocesis, de parochiali ecclesia de Sniterle (Blakeney or Glandford) dicte diocesis, vacante per mortem Walteri Moyner' de Salney extra Romanam curiam defuncti, que tanto tempore vacavit et cetera vel alio quovis modo, et dimittet parochialem ecclesiam de Risehugll' (Rishangles) dicte diocesis, xi kalendas Septembris.[465]

(fol. 38ᵛ)[466] Item Thome Draper, presbytero Londoniensi, de parochiali ecclesia de Freng' (Frenze) Norwicensis diocesis, vacante per liberam resignationem Willelmi de Calneye in manibus ordinarii factam, que tanto tempore vacavit quod eius collatio est ad sedem apostolicam devoluta, xi kalendas Septembris.[462]

## Dunelmensis

Item Ade de Torington', presbytero Eboracensis diocesis, de canonicatu et prebenda seu portione ecclesie collegiate de Dorington' (Darlington) Dunelmensis diocesis, vacante per obitum quondam Guillelmi de Kyldesby extra Romanam curiam defuncti, etiam si tanto tempore vacavit quod eius collatio sit ad sedem apostolicam devoluta, xi kalendas Septembris.[462]

## Eliensis

Subrogatus fuit Walterus de Baketon', magister in artibus, in omni iure quod competebat quondam Henrico de Harwedon' in ecclesia parochiali de Harwedon' [467] (Haddenham) diocesis Eliensis, super qua dum viveret in Romana curia litigabat, et dimittet parochialem ecclesiam de Wigeresham (Wittersham) Cantuariensis diocesis et unum beneficium de infrascriptis, videlicet prebendam Cicestrensem vel canonicatum sub expectatione prebende ecclesie Sancti Johannis Beverlaci Eboracensis diocesis, xi kalendas Septembris.[462]

## Eboracensis

Unio et incorporatio dudum facte per archiepiscopum Eboracensem de parochiali ecclesia de Colston', com-

muniter Kerkelston nuncupata (Car-Colston), conventui et monasterio de Radescord', communiter Werkesop' nuncupato (Worksop), ordinis Sancti Augustini Eboracensis diocesis, fuerunt confirmate vel provisum de novo, vii idus Octobris.[468]

## Herfordensis

De canonicatu et prebenda de Morthon' magna (Moreton Magna) in ecclesia Herffordensi, vacante per consecrationem Symonis de Sudbur' electi Londoniensis, fuit provisum Johanni Galdewyk', clerico Norwicensis diocesis bachalario in legibus, xiiii kalendas Novembris.[469]

## Eboracensis

Unio et incorporatio facte [470] per archiepiscopum Eboracensem de parochiali ecclesia de Henynglourgh' (Hemingborough) Eboracensis diocesis priori et capitulo Dunelmensibus fuerunt auctoritate apostolica confirmate vel provisum de novo, xvi kalendas Novembris.[471]

## Limericensis

Collatio et provisio auctoritate ordinaria facte Philipo de Valle, clerico Limericensis diocesis, de archidiaconatu ecclesie Arefredensis (Ardfert) qui dignitas curata in eadem ecclesia existit, vacante per obitum Bernardi Ytonithyni extra Romanam curiam defuncti, fuerunt confirmate vel provisum de novo, xi kalendas Novembris.[472]

## Wellensis

Item collatio et provisio facte auctoritate ordinaria per episcopum Wellensem se Bathoniensem Johanni Bennoyt, presbytero Saresbiriensis diocesis, de canonicatu et prebenda ecclesie Wellensis fuerunt confirmate vel provisum de novo, ii kalendas Septembris.[473]

Item collatio et provisio auctoritate ordinaria facte per episcopum Wellensem Johanni Beneyt, presbytero, de canonicatu et prebenda de Cumba tertiadecima in ecclesia Wellensi fuerunt auctoritate apostolica confirmate vel provisum de novo, ii kalendas Septembris.[474]

(fol. 39, xxxiii) Sequuntur beneficia collata anno secundo Domini Urbani

## Waterfordensis

Electio facta per canonicos et capitulum seu conventum prioratus Sancte Katherine iuxta Wareffordam Waterfordensis diocesis ordinis Sancti Augustini de fratre David Bassher in priorem dicti prioratus, vacante per obitum fratris Andree Cadward', ultimi prioris

---

[463] 30 August 1363.
[464] Follows *Stlne* deleted by a line.
[465] 22 August 1363. In the margin: *Eadem est ecclesia.*
[466] The headings *Anno primo* and *Norwicensis* are repeated at the top of the page.
[467] Followed by *dicte* deleted by a line.

[468] 9 October 1363.
[469] 19 October 1363.
[470] *facta*, MS.
[471] 17 October 1363.
[472] 22 October 1363.
[473] 31 August 1363.
[474] In the margin: *Eadem est provisio et eadem die facta.*

eiusdem extra Romanam curiam defuncti, fuit confirmata vel provisum de novo, vi idus Novembris.[475]

## Leoniensis, Ybernia

De archidiaconatu Leoniensi in Ybernia, vacante per consecrationem Domini Thome episcopi Leoniensis vel alio quovis modo, fuit provisum Mauricio Hakaill', presbytero Sunaworensis (Fenabore or Kilfenoragh) diocesis, et dimittet archidiaconatum Duacensem (Kilmacduagh).

## Corkagensis

De canonicatu et prebenda ecclesie Corkagensis de Killaspawlrualit (Kilaspugmullane) in eadem Corkagensi ecclesia, vacante per mortem Guillelmi de Espewerth' extra Romanam curiam defuncti, qui tanto tempore vacavit quod eorum collatio est ad sedem apostolicam devoluta, fuit provisum David Gower, presbytero Limericensis diocesis, iiii idus Novembris.[476]

## Limericensis

Item Ricardo de Valle, clerico Corkagensis diocesis, de thesauraria ecclesie Limericensis, vacante per mortem Rotberti Godym in Romana curia defuncti, iiii idus Novembris.[476]

## Imlacensis, Ybernia

Item Admundo Prayneg, clerico Imlacensis diocesis, de canonicatu et prebenda de Dysep, Laman (Isert Laurence) in ecclesia Imlacensi, vacantibus per consecrationem Domini David Feynlyn, ii idus Novembris.[477]

## Norwicensis

De parochiali ecclesia de Subur' (Sudbury) Norwicensis diocesis, vacante ex eo quod Henricus de Campeden' cancellariam ecclesie Londoniensis est pacifice assecutus, fuit provisum Thome de Bokton', bachalario in legibus, x kalendas Septembris.[478]

## Wellensis

De canonicatu et prebenda ecclesie Wellensis, vacaturis per consecrationem Thome de Trellek electi Cicestrensis, fuit provisum Rotberto de Stratton', legum doctori, et dimittet prebendam ecclesie collegiate Aucland' (Auckland) Dunelmensis diocesis, quos nondum possidet, vii kalendas Decembris.[479]

## Lincoliensis

Motu proprio fuit provisum Domino Johanni titulo Sancti Marci presbytero cardinali de parochiali ecclesia de Edburbury (Adderbury) Lincoliensis diocesis, vacatura prout supra, vi kalendas Decembris.[480]

## Hereffordensis

De canonicatu et prebenda ecclesie Herffordensis vocata de Morthon minori (Moreton Minor), taxata x li., vacatura, per consecrationem Domini Thome electi Cicestrensis, fuit provisum Willelmo Bell', scolari in legibus, vi kalendas Decembris.[480] Et de eadem eadem data fuit provisum Nicolao de Chasdesden' que provisio datur inter inutiles quia non habuit effectum.

## (fol. 39ᵛ)[481] Exoniensis

De parochiali ecclesia de Newenton' Sancti Cirici (Newton, St. Cyres) Exoniensis diocesis, que post liberam resignationem Johannis Lynham, ultimi rectoris eiusdem, in manibus episcopi Exoniensis factam tanto tempore vacavit quod eius collatio est ad sedem apostolicam legitime devoluta, licet per Willelmum de Malton', qui se gerit pro vicario eiusdem, ipsam detineat indebite occupatam, fuit provisum Johanni Deyns, presbytero Lincoliensis diocesis, iiii kalendas Decembris.[482]

## Londoniensis

De decanatu ecclesie Londoniensis, taxato liii li. vi s. viii d., vacaturo per consecrationem Thome episcopi Roffensis, fuit provisum Johanni Appelby, legum doctori, in Romana curia advocato, et dimittet parochialem ecclesiam de Witeburne' (Whitburn) Dunelmensis diocesis ac hospitale pauperum de Kipier (Kepier) et parochialem ecclesiam de Routhebury (Rothbury) quem nondum possidet, et super hiis noscitur in palatio apostolico litigari, pro resta dicte taxe xl li., iii nonas Decembris.[483]

## Exoniensis

De parochiali ecclesia curata de Essewatere (Ashwater) Exoniensis diocesis, vacante per mortem Magistri Ricardi Griffarde, cuius collatio est secundum statuta Lateranensis concilii ad sedem apostolicam legitime devoluta, fuit provisum Willelmo Coddeworth', clerico dicte diocesis bachalario in legibus, xviii kalendas Januarii.[484]

## Cantuariensis

De parochiali ecclesia de Biscopesburn' (Bishopsbourne) Cantuariensis diocesis, vacante ex eo quod quidam Guillelmus de Tynghull' ipsam nuper optinens aliud beneficium incompatibile in ecclesia Wellensi est, ut dicitur, auctoritate apostolica pacifice assecutus, fuit provisum Johanni de Digg', presbytero Cantuariensis diocesis, nonas Decembris.[485]

## Dunelmensis

De parochiali ecclesia de Wyhnteburn' (Whitburn) Dunelmensis diocesis, taxata xl li., vacatura cum Jo-

[475] 8 November 1363.
[476] 10 November 1363.
[477] 12 November 1363.
[478] 22 November 1363. It should be Decembris: above, p. 249.
[479] 25 November 1363.
[480] 26 November 1363.

[481] The heading *Anno secundo* appears at the top of the page.
[482] 28 November 1363.
[483] 3 December 1363.
[484] 15 December 1363.
[485] 5 December 1363.

hannes de Appelby decanatum Londoniensem fuerit pacifice assecutus, fuit provisum Ricardo de Wthecombe, presbytero Wygorniensis diocesis, pro resta xxxiii li. vi s. viii d., xix kalendas Januarii.[486]

De parochiali ecclesia de Wormouth' Episcopi (Bishop-Wearmouth) Dunelmensis diocesis, vacante ex eo Willelmus Neupport eandem ecclesiam curatam et ecclesiam parochialem de Spaford' (Spofforth) Eboracensis diocesis, non unitas aut annexas sed diversas, occupavit et possedit simul per duos annos et amplius contra constitutionem *Execrabilis*, fuit provisum Willelmo de Arderne, magistro in artibus Lincoliensis diocesis, et dimittet parochialem ecclesiam de Chesterton' eiusdem diocesis, xv kalendas Januarii.[487]

De ista ecclesia providetur eidem xv kalendas Decembris anno tertio,[488] et nondum habet effectum quia de ea in curia litigatur inter David Wlorth', qui eam possidet et impetrantem impedit.

Summa pagine xl li.

### (fol. 40, xxxiiii)[481] Lincoliensis

De parochiali ecclesia de Hagworthingham Lincoliensis diocesis, vacante ex eo quod Johannes de Sweysheved, olim rector eiusdem ecclesie, ecclesiam parochialem de Werelynsete (Wetheringsett) Norwicensis diocesis est pacifice assecutus, fuit provisum Thome de Thodford, clerico dicte diocesis, ii nonas Januarii.[489]

### Licheffeldensis

De parochiali ecclesia de Estlymyngton' alias Bemyngton Laseyng' (Leamington Hastings) Lichfeldensis diocesis, vacante per obitum ultimi rectoris extra Romanam curiam defuncti, que tanto tempore vacavit quod eius collatio est ad sedem apostolicam legitime devoluta, fuit provisum Ricardo de Thiso, bachalario in decretibus, et dimittet parochialem ecclesiam de Herbegh' (Hartley) Roffensis diocesis, iiii idus Januarii.[490]

### Lincoliensis

Ex causa permutationis fuit provisum Johanni de Astings de vicaria perpetua parochialis ecclesie de Osyngton' (Uffington), non taxata, sed composuit pro mediis fructibus ad vi li. xiii s. iiii d., debet pro resta iii li. vi s. viii d., iii idus Januarii.[491]

### Menevensis

De canonicatu et prebenda ecclesie collegiate de Aberwill' (Abergwili) Menevensis diocesis, que vocatur Lannewyth' (Llandygwydd), vacante per resignationem

Philipi de Bello Campo, fuit provisum Ricardo Pagher, clerico Lincoliensis diocesis, ii kalendas Februarii.[492]

### Norwicensis

De parochiali ecclesia de Snynterlee [493] (Blakeney or Glandford), Norwicensis diocesis, vacante per obitum Walteri Wayn' de Tylneis, que tanto tempore vacavit quod eius collatio est ad sedem apostolicam legitime devoluta, fuit provisum Willelmo Bell', et dimittet parochialem ecclesiam de Stanford Saresbiriensis diocesis et canonicatum et prebendam Herfordenses nuper sibi collatos, v nonas Martii.[494] De ista ecclesia sunt alie due provisiones simul et successive supra, sub data xiº kalendas Septembris anno primo,[495] et neuter ipsarum habuit effectum, ut certificat episcopus.

### Eboracensis

De parochiali ecclesia de Brattyngham (Brantingham) Eboracensis diocesis, vacante ex eo quod Willelmus Stord' ipsam per annum et ultra, cessante legitimo impedimento canonicata dispensatione non obtenta, detinuit, in presbyterum non promotus, fuit provisum Johanni de Toresby, legum doctori, et dimittet parochialem ecclesiam de Lilliefford' (Lilford) Lincoliensis diocesis, xvi kalendas Aprilis.[496]

Communicatur auditori cause pendentis in palatio apostolico inter Ricardum de Derby, presbyterum Lincoliensis diocesis, et Johannem de Brinkelee super archidiaconatu Notingham', taxato xlii li. x s., in ecclesia Eboracensi ut si dictus Johannes ius in eodem habere docere non possit, ipsum archidiaconatum prefato Ricardo adiudicet et provideat de eodem, xi kalendas Aprilis.[497]

Summa pagine iii li. vi s. viii d.

### (fol. 40ᵛ)[481] Dunelmensis

De capellania sive hospitali Sancti Edmundi regis et Martiris in Garthed' (Gateshead) Dunelmensis diocesis, vacante per mortem quondam Walteri Francomberg' extra curiam Romanam defuncti, fuit provisum Ade Fenreter, clerico eiusdem diocesis, xi kalendas Aprilis.[497]

### Licheffeldensis

De parochiali ecclesia de Warington' (Warrington) Licheffeldensis diocesis, taxata xiii li. vi s. viii d., vacante per mortem quondam Johannis de Stanfordham extra Romanam curiam defuncti, a tanto tempore quod eius collatio est ad sedem apostolicam legitime devoluta, fuit provisum Johanni Par seniori, clerico dicte diocesis,

[486] 14 December 1363.
[487] 18 December 1363.
[488] 17 November 1364.
[489] 4 January 1364.
[490] 10 January 1364.
[491] 11 January 1364.

[492] 31 January 1364.
[493] Follows *Sw* deleted by a line.
[494] 3 March 1364.
[495] 22 August 1363.
[496] 17 March 1364.
[497] 22 March 1364.

nonas Aprilis.[498] Iste propter potentiam ducis Lancastrie non est ausus possessionem intrare, et sibi opponitur qui est apostata et inhabilis ad beneficium.

### Menevensis

De parochiali ecclesia de Langladewen' (Llanglydwen) Menevensis diocesis, taxata xl s., vacante per mortem Johannis Sampsonis, ultimi rectoris eiusdem, in Romana curia defuncti, fuit provisum Philipo Layde alias dicto Priten, pro resta dicte taxe xxx s., ii nonas Aprilis.[499]

### Dunelmensis

De canonicatu de Arkcelande (Auckland) et prebenda de Bires (Byers) in eadem Dunelmensis diocesis, vacantibus per obitum Rogeri de Blamer' in Romana curia defuncti, fuit provisum Thome Coker, clerico dicte diocesis, ii nonas Aprilis.[499] Sed ista provisio non habuit effectum quia ante fuit provisum alteri v idus Junii anno primo,[500] et est pauperima et quasi nichil valet.

### Eboracensis

Item Willelmo Waselyn, clerico Lincoliensis diocesis, de ecclesia parochiali de Foreby (North Ferriby) Eboracensis diocesis, vacante per obitum Rotberti de Gridolynton', ultimi rectoris eiusdem, extra Romanam curiam defuncti, que tanto tempore vacavit quod secundum statuta Lateranensis concilii est ad sedem apostolicam legitime devoluta, ii nonas Aprilis.[499] Sed iste non fuit gratiam prosequutus; ymo ei renuntiavit.

### Kareolensis

De parochiali ecclesia de Wiggeston' (Wigton) Kareolensis diocesis, vacante per obitum quondam Gilberti de Wyngton' extra curiam defuncti, etiam si tanto tempore vacaverit quod eius collatio sit ad sedem apostolicam legitime devoluta, fuit provisum Ricardo de Tyrneby, presbytero dicte diocesis, qui dimittet vicariam parochialis ecclesie de Neuburn' (Newburn) Dunelmensis diocesis, ii idus Maii.[501]

De parochiali ecclesia de Esthwell'[502] (Eastwell), taxata viii li., Lincoliensis diocesis fuit provisum ex causa permutationis cum vicaria parochialis ecclesie de Eyton' iuxta Mekton' (Eaton near Melton Mowbray) Rogero Jude, pro resta dicte taxe vi li., vii° kalendas Junii.[503]

Summa pagine vii li. x s.

### (fol. 41, xxxv)[481] Lismorensis

Collatio et provisio auctoritate ordinaria facte Philipo Whyt Minendensis diocesis de archidiaconatu Lismorensi in Ybernia, vacante per obitum Magistri Thome Wlasche alias Leynas, ultimi archidiaconi eiusdem[504] extra Romanam curiam defuncti, fuerunt confirmate vel provisum de novo, iiii kalendas Junii.[505]

### Londoniensis

De novo fuit provisum Johanni de Langeston' de parochiali ecclesia de alta Roddyng' (High Roding) Londoniensis diocesis, quam per annum et ultra tenuit pacifice in presbyterum non promotus, et fuit habilitatus, xviii kalendas Julii.[506]

### Convetrensis et Licheffeldensis

De prioratu monasterii Salopp' (Shrewsbury), vacante per obitum Rogeri de Emfraston', quondam prioris eiusdem in Romana curia defuncti, fuit provisum Johanni Perch, monacho dicti monasterii, xii kalendas Julii.[507] Iste est prioratus claustralis et nichil valet quia est solum officium et non habet aliud nec aliquantulum maiorem portionem in mensa.

### Wellensis

Acceptatio facta vigore litterarum apostolicarum per Willelmum Tynggill', in utroque iure doctorum, et collatio subsequuta de archidiaconatu de Taunton' in ecclesia Wellensi, cui prebenda est annexa, vacante per obitum Rotberti Hereward' extra Romanam curiam defuncti, fuerunt confirmate vel provisum de novo, et dimittet parochialem ecclesiam de Bissopebourn' (Bishopsbourne) Cantuariensis diocesis ac canonicatum et prebenda ecclesie Sancti Karentoci (Crantock) Exoniensis diocesis, vi idus Augusti.[508] De isto pendet lis in curia et incumbens habuit pro se diffinitivam sententiam.

### Lincoliensis

Ex causa permutationis fuit provisum Willelmo nato Willelmi de Vadigton' de Hanieworth' de parochiali ecclesia de Suweldeby (Shoby) diocesis Lincoliensis, iii° kalendas Augusti.[509]

### Lincoliensis et Londoniensis

Ex causa permutationis fuit provisum Rotberto de Wysyngere de perpetua vicaria de Lyngdon (Luton) Lincoliensis diocesis et Willelmo Hoddon' de libera capella de Chelmeford' (Chelmsford) Londoniensis diocesis, viii idus Augusti.[510]

### Herffordensis

De canonicatu et prebenda de Hundreton' (Hunderton) in ecclesia Herffordensi, vacantibus per priva-

---

[498] 5 April 1364.
[499] 4 April 1364.
[500] 9 June 1363.
[501] 14 May 1364.
[502] Follows *Eth* deleted by a line.
[503] 26 May 1364.

[504] Followed by *rectoris* not deleted.
[505] 29 May 1364.
[506] 14 June 1364.
[507] 20 June 1364.
[508] 8 August 1364.
[509] 30 July 1364.
[510] 6 August 1364.

tionem Nicolai Heth' per dominum papam factam propter pluralitatem et multitudinem beneficiorum que optinebat, fuit provisum Nicolao de Draytton', bachalario in legibus, iii kalendas Septembris.[511]

### Dunelmensis

Collatio facta ex causa permutationis Rotberto de Warcomp' de parochiali ecclesia de Wesyngton' (Washington) Dunelmensis diocesis auctoritate ordinaria, non obstante defectu natalium quem patitur de soluto genitus et soluta, fuit confirmata vel provisum de novo, xiiii° kalendas Octobris.[512] Supra ponitur alia provisio de eadem ii nonas Maii anno primo,[513] pro qua habuit terminos.

### (fol. 41ᵛ)[481] Lincoliensis

De parochiali ecclesia de Slapton' Lincoliensis diocesis, vacante cum Matheus de Asschton' canonicatum et prebendam ecclesie Eboracensis fuerit pacifice assecutus, fuit provisum Ricardo de Crexton', clerico Eliensis diocesis, kalendas Octobris.[514]

### Roffensis

Collatio et provisio per viam permutationis auctoritate ordinaria facte Johanni de Aschewade de parochiali ecclesia de Snedlond' (Snodland) Roffensis diocesis fuerunt confirmate vel provisum de novo, ii kalendas Octobris.[515] Alia est subrogatio facta eidem ii kalendas Julii anno iiiiᵗᵒ.[516]

### Lincoliensis

Motu proprio fuit provisum Domino H. cardinali Hostiensi[517] de canonicatu et prebenda in ecclesia Lincoliensi vacantibus per obitum cardinalis Petragoricensis, xi kalendas Novembris.[518]

### Norwicensis et Londoniensis

Collatio et provisio facte auctoritate apostolica Thome de Bakthon', bachalario in legibus, de parochiali ecclesia Sancti Gregorii de Sudbur', tunc vacante ex eo quod Henricus de Compender' ipsam optinens cancellariam ecclesie Londoniensis fuit pacifice assecutus, etiam si per simplicem resignationem dicti H. vacaverit, fuerunt confirmate vel provisum de novo, vii kalendas Novembris.[519] Supra ponitur alia confirmatio eidem facta x kalendas Decembris eodem anno,[520] et utraque est infra annum.

---

[511] 30 August 1364.
[512] 18 September 1364.
[513] 6 May 1363.
[514] 1 October 1364.
[515] 30 September 1364.
[516] 30 June 1366.
[517] Elias de S. Eredio.
[518] 22 October 1364. In the margin: *cardinalis*.
[519] 26 October 1364.
[520] 22 November 1363.

### Eboracensis

De vicaria de Keterby (Carnaby) alias dicta Fraysthorp' (Fraisthorpe) Eboracensis diocesis, vacante per obitum quondam Willelmi de Appelby extra Romanam curiam defuncti, fuit provisum Johanni de Skirling' de Heldon', presbytero dicte diocesis, ii kalendas Novembris.[521]

### Exoniensis

De parochiali ecclesia de Essewat' (Ashwater) Exoniensis diocesis, vacante per obitum Ricardi Grifford' extra Romanam curiam defuncti, fuit provisum Willelmo de Coddesworth', clerico dicte diocesis, nisi sit alteri specialiter ius quesitum, ii nonas Novembris.[522] Ante providetur eidem eodem anno xviii kalendas Januarii,[523] et ambe sunt infra annum, et ideo debet ista cancellari quia pro illa recepit terminos.

(fol. 42, xxxvi) Sequuntur beneficia collata anno tertio per Dominum Urbanum papam modernum

### Saresbiriensis

De canonicatu et prebenda ecclesie Saresbiriensis, taxata xii m., vacantibus per mortem Philipi Codefforde extra Romanam curiam defuncti, fuit provisum Johanni de Gymoncestr' presbytero, debet pro taxa viii li., xv kalendas Decembris.[524]

### Dunelmensis

De parochiali ecclesia de Wermout Episcopi (BishopWearmouth) Dunelmensis diocesis, vacante per lapsum temporis concessi Willelmo de Newpport' de ipsa retinenda cum quadam alia parochiali ecclesia, fuit provisum Willelmo de Arden', magistro in artibus, et dimittet ecclesiam parochialem de Chesterton' Lincoliensis diocesis, xv kalendas Decembris.[524] Supra est alia provisio de eadem eidem xv kalendas Januarii anno ii°,[525] et tertia est infra xiii kalendas Decembris anno quinto,[526] et neuter earum habet adhuc effectum quia David Wlcort', clericus regis, litigat in curia contra istum impetrantem et credo quod ipse optinebit.

### Dunelmensis

De hospitali Sancti Johannis Baptiste extra portam civitatis Dunelmensis in Ybernia quod illicite detinet Willelmus Gerard', frater dicti hospitalis, fuit provisum Henrico Baudulff', fratri dicti hospitalis, xv kalendas Decembris.[524] Episcopus certificat quod non est in sua diocesi tale hospitale, sed credo quod debet esse Dublinensis quia est in Ybernia.

---

[521] 31 October 1364.
[522] 4 November 1364.
[523] 15 December 1363.
[524] 17 November 1364.
[525] 18 December 1363.
[526] 19 November 1366.

### Londoniensis

De parochiali ecclesia de Hakeney (Hackney) Londoniensis diocesis, vacatura cum Thomas de Paxton', sedis apostolice capellanus, dignitatem in ecclesia Wellensi fuerit assecutus, fuit provisum Waltero de Multon', presbytero Norwicensis diocesis, et dimittet parochialem ecclesiam de Chyrvele (Cheveley) Norwicensis diocesis, vii idus Octobris.[527] Nondum habet effectum.

### Wellensis, Exoniensis

Subrogatus fuit Stephanus Pampel, legum doctor, in omni iure quod competebat Thome de Paxton', auditori palatii apostolici, in ecclesie Wellensis decanatu, qui super eo contra Stephanum ad eundem decanatum auctoritate ordinaria electum litem movit, qui quidem Thomas postmodum iuri sibi in eo competenti expresse renuntiavit, et dimittet prebendam Exoniensem ac collegiatarum Sancti Thome martiris de Glasweye (Glasnay) Exoniensis diocesis et de Abergwik' (Abergwili) Menevensis diocesis ecclesiarum, x kalendas Januarii.[528] Decanatus taxatur c li. et debet pro resta lxxx li.

### Eboracensis

Motu proprio fuit provisum Domini H. cardinali Hostiensi [517] de canonicatu et prebenda ecclesia Eboracensis, vacantibus per obitum cardinalis Petragoricensis, iii nonas Januarii.[529]

Summa pagine lxxxviii li.

### (fol. 42ᵛ) [530] Saresbiriensis

Provisio facta auctoritate apostolica Henrico de Wynterton', bachalario in legibus, de canonicatu et prebenda ecclesie Saresbiriensis, quos Ricardus de Norwico defunctus per nonnullos annos possederat, etiam si vacent per obitum Thome de Clipston' in Romana curia defuncti, fuit confirmata vel provisum de novo, nonas Januarii.[531] Ista prebenda vocatur Bemynstr' (Beaminster), et sunt due provisiones de eadem in antiquis arrayratgiis facte diversis personis, et neuter earum, ut dicitur, habuit effectum.

### Elphinensis

Postulatio facta per viam compromissi de fratre Mauricio Magneill', canonico monasterii Sancti Augustini de Clunncuaysgrit Masynaa (Clontuskert Omanny) Arouacensis ordinis Elphinensis diocesis, in priorem dicti monasterii fuit confirmata vel provisum de novo, ii nonas Januarii.[532]

Postulatio facta per viam compromissi de fratre Donato Merseyrad', canonico professo monasterii canonicorum regularium Sancti Augustini Roscoman (Roscommon) Arouacensis ordinis Elphinensis diocesis, de presbytero religioso et soluta genito, ad monasterium predictum, vacantem per obitum fratris Thome eiusdem monasterii prioris conventualis, fuit confirmata vel provisum de novo, nonas Januarii.[531]

### Midensis

De prioratu conventuali Sancti Petri Nove Ville (Newtown) iuxta Tryn (Trim) Midinensis diocesis ordinis Sancti Augustini, cum vacabit per assecutionem possessionis pacifice monasterii Sancti Thome martiris prope civitatem Dunelmensem (Dublin) faciendam per abbatem dicti monasterii, fuit provisum fratri Thome Berthon, canonico dicti monasterii, viii idus Januarii.[533]

### Exoniensis

De canonicatu et prebenda ecclesie Exoniensis, vacantibus vel vacaturis prout supra, fuit provisum Rotberto de Guneston', bachalario in legibus, et dimittet parochialem de Cleve (Clyffe) Roffensis diocesis nuper per dominum papam sibi collatam et parochialem ecclesiam de Olme (Holme) Norwicensis diocesis super qua litigat in curia, vii kalendas Februarii.[534] Ista provisio nondum habuit effectum quia iste non vult [535] dimittere ecclesiam de Holm, que valet xl li., quam tenet pro prebenda que non [536] valet nisi iiiiᵒʳ li. absenti.

### Elphinensis

Electio canonica [537] facta et confirmatio per episcopum subsequuta Thome de Munnirgoassa, canonico Elphinensi, ad decanatum ipsius ecclesie, vacantem per obitum Nicolai ultimi decani eiusdem, fuerunt confirmate vel provisum de novo, nonas Februarii.[538]

### (fol. 43, xxxvii) [530] Exoniensis

De canonicatu et prebenda ecclesie collegiate de Glesenay (Glasnay) Exoniensis diocesis, vacaturis cum Stephanus Pampel decanatum ecclesie Wellensis fuerit pacifice assecutus, fuit provisum Thome Waderowe, clerico Eboracensis diocesis, bachalario in legibus, vi idus Februarii.[539]

### Lincoliensis

Collatio et provisio auctoritate apostolica facte Thome de Tetteforde, clerico Lincoliensis diocesis, de parochiali ecclesia in Hagworthyngham (Hagworthingham) Lincoliensis diocesis, vacante per assecutionem parochialis ecclesie de Wetlingsete (Wetheringsett) Norwicensis diocesis collate Johanni de Swyneshevede, quam dictus

---

[527] 9 October 1365.
[528] 23 December 1364.
[529] 3 January 1365. In the margin: *cardinalis.*
[530] The heading *Anno tertio* is repeated at the top of the page.
[531] 5 January 1365.
[532] 4 January 1365.
[533] 6 January 1365.
[534] 26 January 1365.
[535] *wlt,* MS.
[536] Followed by *habet* deleted by a line.
[537] *canonice,* MS.
[538] 5 February 1365.
[539] 8 February 1365.

Thomas possedit diu pacifice, licet felicis recordationis Dominus Innocentius papa VI quondam Hewrico Romelyn, clerico Camircensis (Cambrai) diocesis, de dicta ecclesia sic vacante providet, qui, litteris super hoc non confectis, extra Romanam curiam decessit, fuerunt confirmate vel provisum de novo, xv kalendas Martii.[540] Est alia provisio sibi facta de eadem ii nonas Januarii anno ii,[541] pro qua recepit terminos.

### Corkagensis

Collatio et provisio auctoritate ordinaria facte Nicolao de Bary de archidiaconatu Corkagensi, quem per annos et dies possedit pacifice, etiam si tanto tempore vacavit quod eius collatio et cetera, fuerunt confirmate vel provisum de novo, xii kalendas Martii.[542]

### Cicestrensis

De custodia hospitalis domus Beate Marie Cicestrensis, vacante per privationem Johannis de Domintton', clerici [543] dicte diocesis, per dominum papam factam, fuit provisum Symoni Bate, presbytero Lincoliensis diocesis, nonas Martii.[544]

### Exoniensis

De canonicatu et prebenda ecclesie collegiate Beati Thome martiris Glausney' (Glasnay) diocesis Exoniensis, vacantibus cum Stephanus Pampel ipsos dimiserit, fuit provisum Petro Amgov, presbytero dicte diocesis, et dimittet parochialem ecclesiam Wynwolay (Landewednack) dicte diocesis, nonas Martii.[544]

### Eliensis

De parochiali ecclesia de Ditton' (Fen Ditton) Eliensis diocesis, vacatura dum Nicolaus de Bapthorp' dignitatem, personatum vel officium in ecclesia Exoniensi fuerit pacifice assecutus, fuit provisum Thome de Hornyngysherd' Norwicensis diocesis, legum doctori, xvi kalendas Aprilis.[545]

De parochiali ecclesia de Stroham (Stretham) Eliensis diocesis, vacatura dum Rotbertus de Stratton', auditor palatii apostolici, dignitatem, personatum vel officium in ecclesia Lincoliensi fuerit pacifice assecutus, fuit provisum Rotberto de Fordham, presbytero Norwicensis diocesis, ydus Martii.[546]

### (fol. 43ᵛ)[530] Karliolensis

De parochiali ecclesia de Wiggeton' (Wigton) Kariolensis diocesis, vacante per obitum quondam Gilberti de Wiggeton' extra Romanam curiam defuncti, etiam

si tanto tempore vacavit quod eius collatio et cetera, fuit provisum Ricardo de Tyrneby, presbytero dicte diocesis, qui dimittet vicariam parochialis ecclesie de Neuburn' (Newburn) Dunelmensis diocesis, ii idus Maii.[547]

### Norwicensis

De parochiali ecclesia de Barlesden (Rattlesden) Norwicensis diocesis, vacatura dum Rogerus de Freton' canonicatum et prebendam de Newton' (North Newnton) in ecclesia [548] de Wilton' Saresbiriensis diocesis fuerit pacifice assecutus, fuit provisum Thome Woderore, presbytero Eboracensis diocesis, et dimittet canonicatum et prebendam ecclesie collegiate de Glasenay (Glasnay) per dominum nostrum papam nuper sibi collatos, vi idus Aprilis.[549]

### Cantuariensis

Collatio et provisio auctoritate ordinaria facte Willelmo Redd' de prepositura ecclesie collegiate de Wyngham (Wingham) Cantuariensis diocesis, vacante per mortem Johannis de Teverleye extra Romanam curiam defuncti, fuerunt confirmate vel provisum de novo, xv kalendas Maii.[550]

De archidiaconatu Laonensi, vacante ex eo Thomas Othormachaym beneficium incompatibile una cum dicto archidiaconatu, dispensatione legitima non optenta, contra canonum statuta tenuit tanto tempore quod eius collatio et cetera, fuit provisum Donato Ocreynd', et dimittet prebendas dicte ecclesie et Cassellensis, xi kalendas Maii.[551]

### Dunelmensis

Acceptatio, collatio et provisio facte vigore litterarum apostolicarum Matheo de Bolton' de vicaria parochialis ecclesie Beati Nicolai Novicastri (Newcastle upon Tyne) Dunelmensis diocesis, taxata x li., vacante per obitum ultimi vicarii eiusdem extra curiam defuncti, quam per x annos possedit pacifice reservationibus non obstantibus, fuerunt confirmate vel provisum de novo, x kalendas Maii,[552] pro resta v li.

### Saresbiriensis et Wellensis

Ex causa permutationis fuit provisum Johanni Turk, presbytero Wellensis diocesis, de vicaria perpetua de Jatmynstr' (Yetminster) Saresbiriensis diocesis et Willelmo Rouenffaunt de vicaria perpetua ecclesie de Stanenton' D'w (Stanton Drew) dicte Wellensis diocesis, ix kalendas Junii.[553]

### Eboracensis

Collatio et provisio facte vigore litterarum apostoli-

---

[540] 15 February 1365.
[541] 4 January 1364.
[542] 18 February 1365.
[543] *clerico*, MS.
[544] 7 March 1365.
[545] 17 March 1365.
[546] 15 March 1365.

[547] 14 May 1365.
[548] *in ecclesia* repeated MS.
[549] 8 April 1365.
[550] 17 April 1365.
[551] 21 April 1365.
[552] 22 April 1365.
[553] 24 May 1365.

carum felicis recordationis Clementis pape VI[ti] Johanni de Newham, presbytero, de parochiali ecclesia de Marton' in Crowen' (Craven) Eboracensis diocesis fuerunt confirmate vel provisum de novo, v kalendas Maii.[554]

## Lincoliensis

Acceptatio, collatio et provisio facte vigore litterarum apostolicarum per Henricum Dunston', clericum Norwicensis diocesis, de parochiali ecclesia de Orwode magna (Great Horwood) Lincoliensis diocesis fuerunt auctoritate apostolica confirmate vel provisum de novo, ix kalendas Maii.[555] Ista provisio non habuit effectum quia Johannes Skyret alias Bokyngham evicit eam in curia per sententiam diffinitivam et optinuit exequutionem sub bulla sub data viii idus Maii pontificatus Domini Urbani anno iiii.[556] Ideo datur inter Inutiles et his debet cancellari.

Summa pagine v li.

### (fol. 44, xxxviii)[530] Lincoliensis

Ex causa permutationis fuit provisum Ricardo de Barnewik, presbytero Eboracensis diocesis, de parochiali ecclesia Sancti Nicolai in Calesio (Calais) Morinensis (Thérouanne) diocesis et Thome de Tanffelde, presbytero Eboracensis diocesis, de archidiaconatu Glyndelacensi (Glendalough) in ecclesia Sancti Patricii Dublinensis in Ybernia, taxato x m., viii kalendas Augusti.[557] Prima est extra nuntiationem meam.

## Saresbiriensis

Ex causa permutationis fuit provisum Willelmo de Lerenth' Saresbiriensis diocesis de parochiali ecclesia de Statton' (Staunton) cum vicaria de Codesdon' (Cuddesdon), pro qua, scilicet ultima, est satisfactum in computis meis, iii idus Augusti.[558]

## Lincoliensis

De prebenda ecclesie Lincoliensis, vacante per obitum Raymundi Pelegrini, collectoris apostolici, fuit provisum Petro episcopo Albani cardinali, iiii[to] nonas Septembris.[559]

## Eboracensis

Collatio et provisio facte Johanni de Metheley, monacho de prioratu Sancti Johannis Ewangeliste de Ponte fracto (Pontefract) Cluniacensis ordinis Eboracensis diocesis, licet aliquando habitum suum, non tamen animo apostatandi sed causa solaciandi, dimiserit, fuerunt confirmate vel provisum de novo, iiii idus Septembris.[560] Ista provisio nondum habuit effectum,

nec credo quod habebit quia dux Lankastrie, de cuius fundatione est, introduxit alium ad presentationem abbatis Cluniacensis per devolutionem, quia prior de Caritate (La Charité-sur-Loire), ad cuius collationem pertinet, non contulit, ut dicitur, infra tempus iuris.

## Londoniensis

De parochiali ecclesia de Harwe (Harrow) Londoniensis, vacante per obitum Raymundi Pelegrini extra Romanam curiam defuncti, collectoris apostolici, fuit provisum Johanni de Bokyngham, et dimittet parochialem ecclesiam de Stolton' (Stockton) Saresbiriensis diocesis, ii idus Septembris.[561] Itero providetur eidem de eadem ecclesia iiii[ti] idus Augusti anno iiii[to].[562]

(fol. 44[v]) Sequntur beneficia collata per Dominum Urbanum papam modernum anno quarto

## Saresbiriensis

De parochiali ecclesia de Statton' (Stockton) Saresbiriensis diocesis, taxata vi li. xiii s. iiii d., vacante cum Johannes de Bokyngham parochialem ecclesiam de Harwe (Harrow) Londoniensis diocesis fuerit pacifice assecutus, fuit provisum Waltero Malby, clerico Exoniensis diocesis, xii kalendas Decembris,[563] pro resta dimissa iii li. vi s. viii d.

## Herffordensis

De canonicatu et prebenda ecclesie collegiate de Bromyerd (Bromyard) Herffordensis diocesis, vacantibus vel vacaturis[564] dum Rogerus de Freton' canonicatum et prebendam de Newton' (North Newnton) Wlgariter nuncupata in ecclesia collegiata de Wilton' Saresbiriensis diocesis fuerit pacifice assecutus, vel alio quovis modo, fuit provisum Laurencio de Harpele, presbytero Norwicensis diocesis, iiii nonas Decembris.[565]

## Saresbiriensis

De canonicatu et prebenda ecclesie Saresbiriensis, vacantibus per obitum Raymundi Pelegrini, collectoris apostolici, fuit provisum Thome de Paxton', auditori palatii apostolici, et dimittet archidiaconatum Barkschire in dicta ecclesia quem nondum possidet, v idus Decembris.[566]

De archidiaconatu Barkschire fuit provisum Johanni de Harowell', et dimittet archidiaconatum Wygorniensem, iiii idus Decembris.[567]

## Exoniensis

De canonicatu et prebenda ecclesie Sancti Karentoci (Crantock) Exoniensis diocesis, vacante cum Willelmus

---

[554] 27 April 1365.
[555] 23 April 1365.
[556] 8 May 1366.
[557] 25 July 1365.
[558] 11 August 1365.
[559] 2 September 1365.
[560] 10 September 1365.

[561] 12 September 1365.
[562] 10 August 1366.
[563] 20 November 1365.
[564] *vacatura*, MS.
[565] 2 December 1365.
[566] 9 December 1365.
[567] 10 December 1365.

Tynchull' canonicatum et prebendam ac dignitatem vel officium aut personatum in ecclesia Wellensi fuerit pacifice assecutus, fuit provisum Thome Cride, idus Decembris.[568]

De uno beneficiorum infrascriptorum, videlicet thesaurarie ac canonicatus et prebende ecclesie Exoniensis ac canonicatuum et prebendarum ecclesiarum Wellensis et Menevensis vacaturo[564] dum Rotbertus de Middelonde prebendam ecclesie Eboracensis fuerit pacifice assecutus, fuit provisum Ricardo de Tische, presbytero bachalario in decretis, et dimittet medietatem ecclesie de Wlton' (Ufton), que in ecclesia Licheffeldensi prebenda dicitur, supra qua litigat in palatio, vel parochialem ecclesiam de Hertelegh' (Hartley) Roffensis diocesis, xiiii kalendas Januarii.[569]

### Saresbiriensis

De canonicatu et prebenda de Shaftebiron (Shaftesbury) Saresbiriensis diocesis, taxatis xxx li., vacantibus per obitum Raymundi Pelegrini, collectoris apostolici, fuit provisum Ricardo de Neuenton', clerico Licheffeldensis diocesis, xi kalendas Januarii,[570] pro resta dimissa xx li.

De parochiali ecclesia de Stekton' (Stockton) Saresbiriensis diocesis, vacante ex eo quod Johannes de Bokyngham' ultimus rector eiusdem, ecclesiam de Harwe (Harrow) Londoniensis diocesis est pacifice assecutus, fuit provisum Johanni de Hetton' presbytero, et dimittet parochialem ecclesiam de Hodelene (West Hoathley) Cicestrensis diocesis, ii idus Januarii.[571] Ista tamen provisio non habet effectum quia supra in principio huius pagine providetur alteri qui eam tenet et partem solvit; ideo cancelletur quia datur inter Inutiles.

Summa pagine xxiii li. vi s. viii d.

### (fol. 45, xxxix)[572] Londoniensis

De canonicatu et prebenda ecclesie Londoniensis, vacantibus per obitum Raymundi Pelegrini, capellani et collectoris apostolici extra Romanam curiam defuncti, fuit provisum Johanni Bonlegh', clerico dicte diocesis, iiii[to] nonas Januarii.[573]

### Dunelmensis

De perpetua vicaria parochialis ecclesie de Northam (Norham) Dunelmensis diocesis, per clericos seculares consueta ab olim gubernari, vacante per mortem quondam Willelmi Elwik, licet quidam frater Richardus de Sores, monachus professus monasterii de Kynlose (Kinloss) Moroniensis (Moray) diocesis ordinis Cisterciensis, habitu dicti ordinis derelicto, ipsam per tres

annos et amplius occupavit indebite et iniuste, fuit provisum Johanni Mores, presbytero Licheffeldensis diocesis, et dimittet magisterium Sancti Bartholomei de Twedmth' (Tweedmouth), iiii[to] nonas Januarii.[574]

### Leoniensis

De regimine et administratione domus Sancti Johannis Baptiste iuxta Lanonath' (Nenagh) ordinis Sancti Augustini Leoniensis diocesis in Ybernia, vacante per obitum fratris Laurencii, ultimi prioris eiusdem, etiam si fuerit reservata, fuit provisum fratri Johanni Passelyn, presbytero, dicte domus canonico, ii kalendas Januarii.[575]

### Cassallensis

De archidiaconatu ecclesie Cassallensis, vacante per[576] consecrationem Johannis episcopi Tuanensis, fuit provisum Geraldo Omoltorkera, clerico Limericensis diocesis in Ybernia, nonas Januarii.[577]

### Dublinensis

De canonicatu et prebenda ecclesie Dublinensis, vacantibus per obitum Raymundi Pelegrini, capellani et collectoris apostolici extra Romanam curiam defuncti, fuit provisum Alexandro de Puellesden', clerico Wygorniensis diocesis, vi idus Januarii.[578]

### Dunelmensis

De vicaria perpetua parochialis ecclesie de Northam (Norham) Dunelmensis diocesis, per clericos seculares solita gubernari, vacante per mortem quondam Guillelmi de Elwik, ultimi vicarii eiusdem, fuit provisum Johanni de Lewik', presbytero dicte diocesis, licet Ricardus de Sores, monachus monasterii de Kynglosse (Kinloss) Moranensis (Moray) diocesis ordinis Cicterciensis, ipsam per tres annos et amplius indebite et iniuste occupaverit, xiiii kalendas Februarii.[579] Supra eadem pagina providetur alteri iiii nonas Januarii.[580]

### Eliensis

De parochiali ecclesia de Elesworthe (Elsworth) Eliensis diocesis, vacatura dum Johannes de Morton' dignitatem, personatum vel officium curatum in ecclesia Licheffeldensi fuerit pacifice assecutus, necnon de canonicatu et prebenda ecclesie Licheffeldensis vacaturis dum Johannes de Waltham canonicatum et prebendam ecclesie Lincoliensis fuerit pacifice assecutus, fuit provisum Guillelmo de Wetharisdale presbytero, et dimittet parochialem ecclesiam de Stanfforde (Stanford) et prebendam Herffordensem et provisionem sibi factam de parochiali ecclesia de Snitterle (Blakeney or

[568] 13 December 1365.
[569] 19 December 1365.
[570] 22 December 1365.
[571] 12 January 1366.
[572] The heading *Anno quarto* is repeated at the top of the page.
[573] 2 January 1366.

[574] 2 January 1366. In the margin: *statim ponitur iterato*.
[575] 31 December 1365.
[576] Followed by *obitum* deleted by a line.
[577] 5 January 1366.
[578] 8 January 1366.
[579] 19 January 1366.
[580] 2 January 1366.

Glandford), Norwicensis diocesis, xi kalendas Februarii.[581] De ista ecclesia fuit provisum alteri supra iiii° kalendas Maii anno primo.[582]

### (fol. 45ᵛ)[572] Wygorniensis

De parochiali ecclesia de Clve episcopi (Bishops Cleeve) Wygorniensis diocesis, super qua Ricardus de Dranthon' clericus et Johannes de Brian diu in palatio apostolico litigaverunt, vacante per privationem dicti Johannis, fuit provisum Ricardo predicto, xi kalendas Februarii.[581]

### Saresbiriensis

De canonicatu et prebenda ecclesie monasterii monialium de Wylton' (Wilton) diocesis Saresbiriensis, vacantibus per amotionem Rotgerii de Chestrefold', fuit provisum Edwardo de Cherdestok', presbytero Saresbiriensis diocesis, et dimittet parochialem ecclesiam de Entel (East Knoyle) dicte diocesis, xi kalendas Februarii.[581]

### Wygorniensis

De archidiaconatu ecclesie Wygorniensis, vacaturo dum Johannes de Harewell' archidiaconatum Barchir' in ecclesia Saresbiriensi fuerit pacifice assecutus, fuit provisum Symoni Clement' presbytero, et dimittet parochialem ecclesiam de Pimperne Saresbiriensis diocesis, iiii kalendas Februarii.[583] Archidiaconatus iste habet annexam ecclesiam de Claverdon', que taxatur xv m. et mediam, et non habet alios certos redditus.

### Exoniensis

De canonicatu et prebenda ecclesia collegiate de Criditon' (Crediton) Exoniensis diocesis, vacantibus per resignationem Philipi de Bello Campo, fuit provisum Johanni More, clerico diocesis Saresbiriensis, vi idus Februarii.[584] Iste solvit l s. in partem taxe, de qua nondum constat ut patet in ultimis computis.

### Eboracensis

Collatio et provisio facte Ade de Eboraco presbytero auctoritate ordinaria de precentoria ecclesie Eboracensis, quam possidet pacifice, fuerunt confirmate vel provisum de novo.

### Lincoliensis

De parochiali ecclesia de Paston' Lincoliensis diocesis, vacatura dum Johannes Thome dignitatem, personatum vel officium in ecclesia Saresbiriensi fuerit pacifice assecutus, fuit provisum Guillelmo Graule, clerico Lincoliensis diocesis, xv kalendas Aprilis.[585]

### Landavensis

Collatio et provisio facte per principem Wallie Rotberto de Walsham de archidiaconatu ecclesie Landavensis, vacante tempore vacationis episcopatus Landavensis, licet post lapsum sex mensium a tempore vacationis sibi collatus fuit, et per Thomam de Elteslee, cui de eo per sedem apostolicam provisum extitatur, in manibus domini cardinalis Vabrensis (Vabres)[586] apud sedem apostolicam fuisset resignatus, et tamquam de sic vacanti provisum fuisset per dominum papam Thome de Southam, qui ipsum postmodum in manibus domini cardinalis Lemovicensis (Limoges)[587] apud eandem sedem resignavit, etiam si alio quovis modo vacet, fuerunt confirmate vel provisum de novo, et taxatur xxi li., v idus Aprilis.[588]

### (fol. 46, xl)[572] Eboracensis

Subrogatus fuit Thomas de Tettefford', subdiaconus Lincoliensis diocesis, in omni iure et ad omne ius quod competebat Johanni de Waltham, presbytero Lincoliensis diocesis, in et super parochiali ecclesia de Herdsham (Heversham) Eboracensis diocesis, super qua lis pendet in palatio apostolico inter dictum Johannem de Waltham et Nicolaum de Feribus, clericum Eboracensis diocesis, qua lite pendente prefatus Johannes parochialem ecclesiam de Lingford (Langford) Saresbiriensis diocesis, auctoritate ordinaria collatam, fuit pacifice assecutus, et dimittet canonicatum et prebendam ecclesie collegiate de Abrewyly (Abergwili) Menevensis diocesis ac litem quam habet super parochiali ecclesia de Hagworthyngham (Hagworthingham) Lincoliensis diocesis, v idus Aprilis.[588]

### Assawensis

De canonicatu et prebenda ecclesie Assavensis in Wallia, de quibus, dudum vacantibus per obitum Ricardi de Midelton' in curia defuncti, dominus Innocentius papa VIᵘˢ providit Johanni Carold, qui, possessione ipsorum non habita, ipsos in manibus episcopi Assavensis libere resignavit, et subsequenter de ipsis, qui tanto tempore vacaverant per resignationem huiusmodi quod eorum collatio fuerat ad sedem apostolicam legitime devoluta, idem dominus Innocentius Johanni Guifundum clerico per certos executores provideri mandavit, qui antequam sibi provisum extitisset extra curiam decessit, fuit provisum Symoni Latchebury, presbytero Limericensis diocesis, xviii kalendas Maii.[589]

### Eboracensis

De parochiali ecclesia Sancte Helene in Staynegate in Eboraco (St. Helen in Stonegate, York), vacante per mortem Thome de Langecoste in Romana curia

---

[581] 22 January 1366.
[582] 28 April 1363.
[583] 29 January 1366.
[584] 8 February 1366.
[585] 18 March 1366.

[586] William Bragose, elect of Vabres, priest of S. Lorenzo in Lucina.
[587] Nicholas de Bessia, deacon of S. Maria in Via Lata.
[588] 9 April 1366.
[589] 14 April 1366.

defuncti, fuit provisum Henrico de Hugat', presbytero Eboracensis diocesis, xviii kalendas Maii.[589] Ante est alia provisio et neuter habuit effectum.

Item Johanni de Londe, presbytero Eboracensis diocesis, de parochiali ecclesia Omnium Sanctorum super pavimentum in Eboraco (All Saints in the Pavement, York), vacante per obitum Symonis Walde in Romana curia defuncti, xviii kalendas Maii.[589] Ante providetur de eadem bis vel ter iii° nonas Julii anno primo,[590] et neuter earum habuit effectum quia incumbens habet sentenciam diffinitivam contra illum per cuius mortem impetratur. Et ideo hic debet cancellari et datur inter inutiles, et est inter inutiles.

### Licheffeldensis

De canonicatu et prebenda ecclesie de Maithall' (Morehall) in ecclesia collegiata de Gnoushale (Gnosall) Licheffeldensis diocesis, vacantibus per privationem Nicolai Heth' propter pluralitatem beneficiorum que optinebat, fuit provisum Johanni Daniel, clerico Licheffeldensis diocesis, xvi kalendas Maii.[591] Ista provisio non habuit effectum quia impetrans non fuit gratiam prosecutus ex causa.

### Norwicensis

Subrogatus fuit Hamo de Deval presbyter in omni iure quod competebat Michaeli de Hauthon' in parochiali ecclesia de Multon' (Moulton) Norwicensis diocesis, super qua inter dictum Hamonem et Michaelem lis pendebat in palatio apostolico, qua lite pendente, dictus Michaelis decessit extra curiam, v nonas Maii.[592]

### (fol. 46ᵛ)[572] Lincoliensis

Collatio et provisio facte auctoritate ordinaria Johanni Skynet de Bukyngham de parochiali ecclesia de Horwode magna (Great Horwood) Lincoliensis diocesis, etiam si fuerit devoluta vel reservata, fuerunt confirmate vel provisum de novo iiiⁱᵗᵒ nonas Maii.[593] Ista provisio nondum habuit effectum et post providetur alteri per dimissionem istius iiii idus Augusti.[594]

### Lincoliensis et Londoniensis

Ex causa permutationis fuit provisum Radulpho de Dalbentr' de parochiali ecclesia Sanctorum Stephani et Olavi in Colmmastret et veteri Judismo (St. Stephen, Coleman St. and St. Olave, Old Jewry) et Johanni de Leyham de parochiali ecclesia Sancti Benedicti de Graschurche (St. Benet Gracechurch) Londonie, vii kalendas Junii.[595] Prima ecclesia non taxatur, sed composuit pro xv li., de quibus satisfecit de x li., ut patet in ultimis computis, restat quod debet v li. Item pro

secunda, quia non taxatur, est facta compositio pro viii li., de quibus nichil solvit.

### Menevensis

De canonicatu et prebenda Sancti Mauricii de Aberwill (Abergwili) Menevensis diocesis, vacatura dum Thomas de Tettefforde parochialem ecclesiam Haversham (Heversham) fuerit pacifice assecutus, fuit provisum Johanni Kell', clerico Eboracensis diocesis, vii kalendas Junii.[595]

### Roffensis

Subrogatus fuit Johannes de Althawe in omni iure quod competebat cuidam impetranti in parochiali ecclesia de Suthelond' (Snodland) Roffensis diocesis, super qua cum ipsam esset auctoritate ordinaria causa permutationis assecutus dictus impetrans in palatio apostolico eidem Johanni litem movit, et extunc apud sedem apostolicam decessit, ii kalendas Julii.[596]

### Darensis

De prioratu conventuali Sancte Marie de Connall' (Connel) Darensis diocesis ordinis Sancti Augustini, vacante per privationem factam fratri Willelmo Wyk de ecclesia Dunensi, fuit provisum Waltero Tirell' de Ybernia nato, canonico monasterii Sancti Thome martiris prope Dublin' dicti ordinis, xvi kalendas Augusti.[597]

### Limericensis

Collatio et provisio facte auctoritate ordinaria Mauricio filio Petri clerico de archidiaconatu ecclesie Limericensis, tempore felicis recordationis Domini Innocentii pape VI vacante, quem possedit diu prout possidet pacifice, etiam si reservatus fuerit vel devolutus, fuerunt confirmate vel provisum de novo, xvii kalendas Augusti.[598]

Summa pagine v li.

### (fol. 47, xli)[572] Saresbiriensis

De canonicatu et prebenda in ecclesia Saresbiriensi, vacaturis dum Fortanerius de Calvomonte prioratum, canonicatum et prebendam ecclesie Sancte Redagundis Pictavensis (Poitiers) fuerit pacifice assecutus, fuit provisum Johanni Strattford', Saresbiriensis diocesis clerico, et dimittet parochialem ecclesiam de Chymark' (Chilmark) dicte diocesis, xii kalendas Augusti.[599]

### Exoniensis

Collatio et provisio facte auctoritate apostolica Rogero Payn de canonicatu et prebenda ecclesie de Creditton' (Crediton) Exoniensis diocesis et prebenda busaria

---

[590] 5 July 1363.
[591] 16 April 1366.
[592] 3 May 1366.
[593] 4 May 1366.
[594] 10 August 1366.

[595] 26 May 1366.
[596] 30 June 1366.
[597] 17 July 1366.
[598] 16 July 1366.
[599] 21 July 1366.

nuncupata in ecclesia predicta, vacantibus, ut credebatur, quia eam optinens aliam prebendam inibi fuerat pacifice assecutus, et cuius collatio erat devoluta, non obstante quod assertum fuerit ipsum studuisse in iure civili per quinque annos et non studuerat nisi per quatuor, xi kalendas Augusti.[600]

De canonicatu ecclesie Sancte Crucis de Credigton' (Crediton) Exoniensis diocesis et de prebenda de Carswille (Kerswell) in eadem ecclesia, vacantibus ex eo quod Johannes Perour, se[601] gerens pro canonico dicte ecclesie, ipsam prebendam de Carswille optinens, aliam certam prebendam wlgariter nuncupatam bursariam auctoritate ordinaria fuit pacifice assecutus, etiam si devoluta fuerit vel alio quovis modo vacet, fuit provisum Johanni Cheyney, clerico Exoniensis diocesis, iii kalendas Augusti.[602]

Dublinensis

Collatio et provisio facte auctoritate ordinaria ex causa permutationis Thome de Bath', Limericensis diocesis cancellario, de altera prebenda de Lursk' (Lusk) in ecclesia Dublinensi, quam possidet pacifice etiam si reservata sit vel devoluta, fuerunt confirmate vel provisum de novo, vii idus Augusti.[603]

Archadiensis

Item electio concorditer facta de Patricio Orator' ad decanatum Archadiensem, que dignitas curata et electiva existit, vacantem per mortem Christoferi Ophearghila extra curiam defuncti, et confirmatio auctoritate ordinaria subsecuta, fuerunt confirmate vel provisum de novo, vii idus Augusti.[603]

(fol. 47v)[572] Londoniensis

De novo fuit provisum Johanni de Bokyngham de parochiali ecclesia de Arowe alias Harwe (Harrow) Londoniensis diocesis, vacante et reservata per obitum Raymundi Pelegrini, quem prius asserverat esse capellanum sedis apostolice et pro certo tempore Domini Innocentii pape V dictam capellaniam resignavit, iiii idus Augusti.[604] Supra providetur bis et omnes sunt infra annum.

Lincoliensis et Eboracensis

De canonicatu et prebenda de Chastre (Caistor) in ecclesia Lincoliensi, vacantibus vel vacaturis per privationem Henrici Ingelby fuit provisum Johanni Cheyne, etiam si eos causa permutationis vel alio quovis modo dimiserit, et dimittet parochialem ecclesiam de Kyrkeby Mipperton' (Kirkby Misperton) Eboracensis diocesis, iii idus Septembris.[605]

Eboracensis

De canonicatu et prebenda ecclesie collegiate de Howeden' (Howden) Eboracensis diocesis, quos Jacobus de Multton' in dicta ecclesia solebat optinere, vacantibus de iure, quos Guillelmus Dimby presbyter vigore gratie sibi facte de canonicatu sub expectatione prebende dicte ecclesie acceptavit, tacito in dicta gratia defectu natalium quem patitur de presbytero genitus et soluta, et in ipsis est intrusus de facto, de ipsis fuit provisum Guillelmo predicto, ii idus Septembris.[606]

Motu proprio fuit provisum Domino Anglico cardinali Avinionensi[607] de canonicatu et prebenda ac decanatu ecclesie Eboracensis vacantibus per obitum cardinalis Petragoricensis, viii kalendas Octobris.[608]

Lincoliensis

Provisio facta vigore litterarum apostolicarum Benedicto de Masingham, presbytero diocesis Norwicensis, de perpetua vicaria parochialis ecclesie de Littone (Luton) Lincoliensis diocesis, quam possidet licet dicatur vacasse et vacare ex eo quod quondam Rotbertus de Wyssinglote, cui de ipsa vacante in curia ex causa permutationis provisum fuerat, antequam eius possessionem haberet, aliam parochialem ecclesiam fuit pacifice assecutus, et sic mandatum apostolicum non videtur ad plenum executum, fuit confirmata vel provisum de novo, v kalendas Octobris.[609]

Eboracensis

De canonicatu et prebenda ecclesie collegiate de Southwell' Eboracensis diocesis, ⟨vacantibus⟩ per Henrici de Engelby ac canonicatu et prebenda ecclesie Saresbiriensis ⟨vacantibus⟩ per Johannis Welboren' privationes et amotiones per dominum papam factas propter multitudinem beneficiorum, fuit provisum Johanni Cheyne, clerico Licheffeldensis diocesis, et dimittet parochialem ecclesiam de Kyrkeby Misporton' (Kirkby Misperton) et gratiam sibi factam de canonicatu et prebenda quos idem Henricus dicitur ⟨tenere⟩ in ecclesia Lincoliensis, iii idus Octobris.[610]

Dunelmensis

De capellania seu[611] magisterio hospitalis de Scehoborn' (Sherburn) Dunelmensis diocesis, vacante per amotionem Alani de Scherehington', fuit provisum Waltero de Wadesborgh', ix° kalendas Novembris.[612]

(fol. 48, xlii) Sequntur beneficia collata per Dominum Urbanum anno suo quinto

[600] 22 July 1366.
[601] *de*, MS.
[602] 30 July 1366.
[603] 7 August 1366.
[604] 10 August 1366.
[605] 11 September 1366.
[606] 12 September 1366.
[607] Anglicus Grimoard, priest of S. Pietro in Vincoli.
[608] 24 September 1366.
[609] 27 September 1366.
[610] 13 October 1366.
[611] *sul*, MS.
[612] 24 October 1366.

De canonicatu et prebenda ecclesie Johannis de Beverlaco, vacantibus per privationem Johannis Belbury fuit provisum Rogero de Frethon', legum doctori, ii idus Novembris.[613]

### Dunelmensis

De parochiali ecclesia de Wermouth' (Bishop Wearmouth) Dunelmensis diocesis, ad quam vacantem per obitum Willelmi Neuport David de Wlhorth' fuit presentatus et auctoritate ordinaria institutus, vacante per privationem dicti David facta per dominum papam, fuit provisum Thome Cloynaus, clerico Eboracensis diocesis, xiii kalendas Decembris.[614] Supra sunt due provisiones de eadem, videlicet xv kalendas Januarii anno ii⁰ [615] et xv kalendas Decembris anno tertio,[616] et neuter earum adhuc habuit effectum quia dictus David, qui est principalis in cancellaria regis eam possidet et super hoc hodie in curia litigat.

### Eboracensis

De prioratu Beate Marie de Lanchastria (Lancaster). Eboracensis diocesis, qui consistit in ecclesie Beate Marie Lanchastrie qui taxatur lxxx li., a monasterio Sancti Martini Saginensis (Séez) ordinis Sancti Benedicti dependente, vacante per promotionem Petri abbatis dicti monasterii ad ipsum monasterium, fuit provisum Willelmo Raymbaut, monacho dicti monasterii, et dimittet officium baylivie dicti monasterii, vii kalendas Decembris.[617]

### Londoniensis

De parochiali ecclesia Sancti Martini de Vinetria (St. Martin Vintry) Londoniensis diocesis, vacatura dum Nicolaus Drayton' beneficium ad collationem episcopi Wygorniensis fuerit pacifice assecutus, fuit provisum Rotberto Cantello, presbytero Wellensis diocesis, vi kalendas Decembris.[618]

### Lincoliensis

De parochiali ecclesia de Surfflet (Surfleet) Lincoliensis diocesis, vacante per amotionem Guillelmi de Kywell', fuit provisum Johanni Skireth de Bokyngham dicte diocesis, et dimittet parochialem ecclesiam de Horwoud' magna (Great Horwood), nonas Decembris.[619]

De capella perpetua sive [620] rectoria leprosarie Sancti Juliani iuxta Sanctum Alanum (St. Julian, Hertford) Lincoliensis diocesis, vacatura dum Johannes de Kyrlynburgh' dignitatem, personatum vel officium ecclesie Lincoliensis fuerit pacifice assecutus, fuit provisum

Hugoni de Pringthon', presbytero dicte diocesis, iiii idus Decembris.[621]

### Saresbiriensis

De archidiaconatu [622] Bakschirie, qui dignitas est in ecclesia Saresbiriensi, vacante per consecrationem Johannis de Harwell' electi Bathoniensis, fuit provisum Alexandro de Darby, clerico Licheffeldensis diocesis, taxato liiii li., xix kalendas Februarii.[623]

Summa pagine lxxx li.[624]

### (fol. 48ᵛ) [625] Lincoliensis

Item eidem Alexandro de canonicatu et prebenda ecclesie Lincoliensis, vacaturis prout supra, et dimittet decanatum curatum ecclesie Sancti Johannis Cestrie (Chester) Licheffeldensis diocesis et expectationem ad prebendam Eboracensem et litem quam habet super prebenda de Tervym (Tarvin) in ecclesia Licheffeldensi qui taxatur xl li., xix kalendas Februarii.[623] De quo decanatu fuit provisum Johanni de Wodehaus, vii kalendas Januarii.[626]

### Wellensis

De canonicatu et prebenda ecclesie Wellensis vacaturis per consecrationem electi Bathoniensis fuit provisum Johanni Brompton' clerico, xvi kalendas Januarii.[627]

### Licheffeldensis

De canonicatu et prebenda ecclesie collegiate Sancti Johannis Cestrie Licheffeldensis diocesis, vacaturis per amotionem Johannis de Wynelty, fuit provisum Thome de Eltonhed, clerico dicte diocesis, xvi kalendas Januarii.[627]

De canonicatu et prebenda ecclesie Licheffeldensis, vacantibus per amotionem Hugonis de Wimodeswold', fuit provisum Thome Aleyn presbytero, xiiii kalendas Januarii.[628]

### Lincoliensis

De parochiali ecclesia de Harwode magna (Great Horwood) Lincoliensis diocesis, vacatura dum Johannes de Bokyngham parochialem ecclesiam de Sceflet (Surfleet) dicte diocesis fuerit pacifice assecutus, fuit provisum Johanni Skiret, et dimittet parochialem ecclesiam de Lilingeston' (Lillingstone), iii nonas Januarii.[629] De ista est alia provisio supra iiiiᵗᵒ nonas Maii anno iiiiᵗᵒ.[630]

---

[613] 12 November 1366.
[614] 19 November 1366.
[615] 18 December 1363.
[616] 17 November 1364.
[617] 25 November 1366.
[618] 26 November 1366.
[619] 5 December 1366.
[620] Followed by *un* deleted by a line.

[621] 10 December 1366.
[622] Followed by *Bakchschi* deleted by a line.
[623] 14 January 1367.
[624] Followed by *Summa arreyragiorum* deleted by a line.
[625] The heading *Anno quinto* appears at the top of the page.
[626] 26 December 1366.
[627] 17 December 1366.
[628] 19 December 1366.
[629] 3 January 1367.
[630] 4 May 1366.

### Wygorniensis

Collatio facta auctoritate ordinaria Thome Spret, legum doctori, de perpetua vicaria parochialis ecclesie Sancti Nicolai Bustollie (Bristol) Wigorniensis diocesis quam possidet pacifice, etiam si reservata vel devoluta fuerit, fuit confirmata vel provisum de novo, xiiii kalendas Februarii.[631]

### Dunelmensis

De archidiaconatu Dunelmensi (Down), vacante per consecrationem Guillelmi Mercier episcopi Conwotrensis (Connor), fuit provisum Johanni Domengan qui dimittet parochialem ecclesiam de Cannelyn (Camclyn?) dicte Dunelmensis (Down) diocesis, xv kalendas Februarii.[631a]

### Eboracensis

De canonicatu et prebenda ecclesie collegiate de Hawedon' (Howden) Eboracensis diocesis, vacantibus ex eo quod Henricus Swyth', non graduatus, ipsos cum beneficiis aliis, videlicet ecclesiam parochialem de Wndele (Oundle) Lincoliensis ⟨diocesis⟩ canonicatus et prebendas ecclesiarum Lincoliensis, Londoniensis et Menevensis, alias Abenwilk (Abergwili) optinens, ipsa beneficia et eorum valores iuxta constitutionem domini pape editam non dedit, aut per privationem seu alio quovis modo, fuit provisum Ricardo Sufflet, iii kalendas Februarii.[632] Nichil valet quia non est gratiam prosecutus ex causa certa et rationabili.

### (fol. 49, xliii)[625] Dunelmensis

Item Nicolao Suffled' de canonicatu et prebenda ecclesie collegiate Cestr' (Chester-le-Street) diocesis Dunelmensis, ex eo quod David Wulors plura beneficia que optinet cum eisdem et valores ipsorum secundum constitutionem domini pape non traditit, etiam si per amotionem ipsius vacent vel alio quovis modo, iii kalendas Februarii.[632] Non fuit prosecutus ex causa supradicta.

### Eboracensis

Item Georgio Sicilie de Hewden' de canonicatu et prebenda ecclesie de Rippon' Eboracensis diocesis, quos Willelmus Dalton' tempore constitutionis predicte cum nonnullis beneficiis optinens ipsam et eorum valores secundum constitutionem predictam non traditit, si ex eo aut alio quovis modo vacent, iii kalendas Februarii.[632] Non fuit prosecutus gratiam ex causa supradicta.

### Exoniensis

De canonicatu et prebenda ecclesie collegiate Sancti Tuoci alias Karontoci (Crantock) Exoniensis diocesis, per amotionem Thome Leynis propter pluralitatem beneficiorum que optinebat, fuit provisum Philipo

Hoynie Lincoliensis diocesis, iii kalendas Aprilis.[633] Non habuit effectum quia ante amotionem fuerat mortuus.

### Lincoliensis

Motu proprio mandatur provideri domino Anglico cardinali Avinionensi [634] de canonicatu et prebenda ecclesie Lincoliensis vacaturis per consecrationem Guillelmi de Wykeham electi Wyntoniensis, ii idus Julii.[635]

Motu proprio fuit provisum Domino Nicolao titulo Sancte Marie in via [636] lata diacono cardinali [637] de canonicatu et prebenda ecclesie Lincoliensis vacantibus per obitum Petri episcopi Albanensis,[638] ii idus Julii.[635]

Motu proprio fuit provisum Guillelmo titulo Sanctorum Johannis et Pauli presbytero cardinali [639] de canonicatu et prebenda ecclesie Lincoliensis vacantibus per obitum domini H. cardinalis Hostiensis,[640] ii idus Julii.[635]

### Eboracensis

Item eodem motu fuit provisum Marcho cardinali Viterbiensi [641] de canonicatu et prebenda ecclesie Eboracensis, vacantibus per mortem Domini H. cardinalis Hostiensis, ii idus Julii.[635]

Summa arreragiorum beneficiorum collatorum per Dominum Urbanum a tertio kalendas Maii anno suo primo [642] usque ad pridie idus Julii anno v [635] iie lxxix li. x s.

Summa vero universalis omnium arreragiorum beneficiorum antiquorum et beneficiorum collatorum per Dominum Urbanum iii^m clxxxi li. xii s. vi d., v^c v fl. cum dimidio ii d. sterlingorum.

(fol. 49^v) Summa universsalis omnium restarum precedentium tam de denariis Beati Petri, annuo censsu quam annatarum omnium benefficiorum collatorum in dictis partibus usque ad pridie ydus Julii pontificatus Domini Urbani anno quinto est iii^m vii^c xci li. v s. ix d., v^c v fl. medius ii d. sterlingorum.

Item plura benefficia quorum taxa non ponitur ut superius sunt descripta.

(fol. 50, xliiii) Collationes et provisiones beneficiorum infrascriptorum date fuerunt per Dominum Hugonem Pelegrini, olim in Anglia camere apostolice collectorem, Domino Johanni de Cabrespino, decretorum doctori nunc dicte camere in eisdem partibus collectori, in arrayratgiis anno LXIII de mense Septembris que non videntur habere effectum nec habent, rationibus et causis in qualibet earum breviter et succincter subscriptis, et

---

[631] 19 January 1367.
[631a] 18 January 1367.
[632] 30 January 1367.

[633] 30 March 1367.
[634] Anglicus Grimoard, bishop of Albano.
[635] 14 July 1367.
[636] *vio*, MS.
[637] Nicholas de Bessia.
[638] Peter Itherii, bishop of Dax.
[639] William Sudre, bishop of Marseille.
[640] Elias de S. Eredio.
[641] Mark de Viterbo, priest of S. Prassede.
[642] 29 April 1363.

sunt etiam alique provisiones beneficiorum collatorum per Dominum Urbanum papam V usque ad iii kalendas Maii anno primo,[642] que collationes et provisiones per eundem Dominum Johannem dantur pro inutilibus et non habentibus effectum ut sibi videtur.

### Cantuariensis

De prioratu de Horton' (Monks Horton) ordinis Cluniacensis, vacante ex eo quod fratri Petro de Tenolio ipsum optinenti fuit provisum de alio benefficio et dimitet dictum prioratum, fuit provisum fratri Dyonisio de Opton' per Urbanum vii ydus Februarii anno primo.[643] Ista provisio non habuit effectum quia noluit dictam gratiam acceptare et paulo post habuit prioratum de Breum'dis' (Prittlewell)

### Roffensis

De canonicatu et prebenda de Newch' (Newerch) in ecclesia Roffensi (Ross) et Roskwyn (Rosskeen), de quibus per obitum Andree de Busche collatio et provisio facte auctoritate ordinaria Johanni de Cromdole, decretorum doctori, fuerunt auctoritate appostolica confirmate vel provisum de novo per Urbanum ydus Novembris anno primo.[644] Non habuit effectum quia in dicta ecclesia sunt monachi et non canonici.

### Londoniensis

De ecclesia de Herlawe (Harlow), de qua per obitum Ricardi Drax' fuit provisum Johanni Parker per Innocentium xi⁰ kalendas Junii anno ix⁰,[645] xiii li. vi s. viii d. Ista provisio non habuit effectum quia rex contulit eam, ratione temporalitatis abbatis Sancti Edmundi, de cuius collatione est, in suis manibus existentis, Domino Willelmo de Molsso, decano Sancti Martini Londonie, et ita fuit probatum et ita verum esse asserit dominus cancellarius domini regis Anglie.

Item de eadem ecclesia per assecutionem archidiaconatus Totton' (Totnes) fuit provisum Ricardo Anglici per Innocentium vii⁰ idus Maii anno viii⁰,[646] xiii li. vi s. viii d. Ista provisio non habuit effectum ex causa supra proxima scripta.

De ecclesia Sancti Rotholphi' extra Algate (St. Botolph by Aldgate) Londonie collatio et provisio et pacifica possessio ac administratio facte Radulpho de Cantabrigia, presbytero canonico regulari domus Sancte Trinitatis Londonie expresse professo, per priorem et conventum dicte domus, fuerunt auctoritate apostolica confirmate, v nonas Martii anno primo.[647]

Ista provisio non habuit effectum quia dictus Radulphus ex ista causa citatus renuntiavit omni iuri sibi competenti in dicta ecclesia et iuravit ad sancta dei

ewangelia corporaliter tacta quod nunquam fuit sibi aliqua collatio nec provisio vel adminstratio facta nisi ad certum tempus, videlicet quod prior posset eum removere ad placitum et voluntatem suam. Et illud idem certificat episcopus cui super hoc fuit commissa inquisitio facienda.

De prioratu de Petruwill' (Prittlewell) ordinis Cluniacensis, vacante per asequtionem prioratus Montis Acuti (Montacute) factam per fratrem Franciscum de Bargiaco, fuit provisum fratri P. de Tenolio, priori de Horthona (Monks Horton) dicti ordinis, per Urbanum vii kalendas Februarii anno primo.[648] Ista provisio non habuit effectum quia dictus P. nunquam voluit dictam gratiam acceptare, nec alii in ista translatione expressi.

### (fol. 50ᵛ) Inutiles

### Cicestrensis

De thesauraria Cicestrensi ratione confirmationis facte Guillelmo de Lughtheburgh' pro resta xvi li. xiii s. iiii d. Ista provisio non habuit effectum quia nunquam fuit per ipsum impetrata nec per alium, eo sciente, mandante vel ratum habente, et ita iuravit ad sancta dei ewangelia coram testibus et notario publico, et quum primum audivit de ea fieri mentionem ei renuntiavit expresse, ut patet per instrumentum publicum cuius copiam authenticam penes me habeo, et successor repetit quod indebite est solutum propter defectum probationis propter metum excommunicationis pro [649] eadem.

De prioratu Lewensi [650] ordinis Cluniacensis, vacante per assecutionem monasterii de Ternothien' (Tournus) Cabilonensis (Châlon-sur-Saône) diocesis factam per fratrem Hugonem de Chyceraco, ultimi prioris dicti prioratus, fuit provisum fratri Geraldo Bothonis, monacho bachalario in decretis.

Ista provisio non habuit effectum quia est de patronatu laicali, videlicet comitis Waren' et modo domini comitis Arunndelli, ubi debet prior poni et institui sub certa forma in fundatione apposita, et isti etiam non fuit provisum sed mandatum provideri et papa mortuus fuit ante aliquam provisionem sibi factam per suum executum, et nichilominus iste predicte gratie re integra renuntiavit, et ita probatur per testes et instrumenta ac libros.

### Saresbiriensis

De ecclesia de Corff' (Corfe), de qua per assecutionem prepositure Saresbiriensis per Philipum Coddeford' fuit provisum Symoni Thebaud per Innocentium iii kalendas Novembris anno ix⁰,[651] pro taxa x li. Ista provisio non habuit effectum quia iste Symon nunquam habuit possessionem et ita certificat semper episcopus, et idem deponit episcopus Londoniensis, et probavit incumbens per ydoneos testes.

---

[643] 7 February 1363.
[644] 13 November 1362.
[645] 22 May 1361.
[646] 9 May 1360.
[647] 3 March 1363. In the margin: *de tempore domini Urbani.*

[648] 26 January 1363.
[649] Follows *de* deleted by a line.
[650] Follows *Lewellin* deleted by a line.
[651] 30 October 1361.

De prebenda de Redmynstr' (Bedminster) in ecclesia Saresbiriensi, de qua per obitum Ricardi de Norwico facta fuit confirmatio Henrico de Wynton' per Innocentium xi° kalendas Februarii anno xi°,[652] pro taxa xiii li. vi s viii d. Ista provisio non habuit effectum quia nunquam habuit possessionem et ista certificat episcopus quotiens super hoc ei scribitur.

De prebenda de Bischopeston' (Bishopston) in ecclesia Saresbiriensi, de qua in omni iure quod competebat Arnaldo Pelegrini fuit subrogatus Arnaldus Garini presbyter per Innocentium idus Julii anno x°,[653] pro taxa xx li. Ista provisio non habuit effectum quia Guillelmus de Okebuorn' ipsam tenet iure regio et de ea habuit confirmationem, pro qua solvit ut patet in istis rationibus meis [654] in receptis beneficiorum.

(fol. 51, xlv) [655] De prebenda vocata Stretton' (Stratton), quam Johannes de Bukyngham, nunc episcopus Lincoliensis, optinuit in ecclesia Saresbiriensi, fuit provisum Rotberto Sumpt', legum doctori, ii nonas Decembris per Dominum Urbanum anno primo.[656] Non habuit effectum quia rex contulit eam Johanni Hanney qui istam possidet.[657]

De prebenda in ecclesia Saresbiriensi quam Ricardus de Norwico per nonnullos annos pacifice possedit, etiam si quovis modo vacet, provisio facta Henrico de Wynton', bachalario in legibus, fuit eidem confirmata vel provisum de novo per Urbanum v° nonas Martii anno primo.[658] Non habuit effectum quia nunquam habuit possessionem, et Willelmus de Charleton' ipsam possidet, et vocatur Bedmynstr' (Bedminster) et est in diocesi Bathoniensi et Wellensi.

## Bathoniensis et Wellensis

De vicaria Sancti Cuberti Wellensis, acceptatio cuius facta per Rotbertum Stuti fuit confirmata per Innocentium vi° kalendas Junii anno vii°,[659] pro taxa vi li. xiii s. iiii d. Ista confirmatio non habuit effectum quia fuit impetrata lite pendente inter Dominum Rotbertum et Guillelmum de Masyngham, qui etiam habuit istam vicariam ex provisione apostolica pro qua solvit, qui Guillelmus habuit sententiam diffinitivam contra [660] dictum Rotbertum.[661]

De decanatu Wellensi, qui dignitas electiva existit, vacante et reservato per obitum Johannis de Carleton', fuit provisum Thome de Paxton', auditori sacri palatii, per Innocentium kalendas Augusti anno x°.[662] Ista provisio non habuit effectum quia Stephanus Pampel optinuit contra ipsum in curia et hic constat per provisionem Domini Urbani x kalendas Januarii anno tertio,[663] ubi dictus Thomas iuri suo renuntiavit.

## Norwicensis

De ecclesia de Poltham (Pulham), de qua per obitum Guillelmi de Kelslesey fuit provisum Ricardo Michael per Innocentium vi idus Februarii anno vi°,[664] pro taxa liii li. vi s. viii d. Ista provisio non habuit effectum quia iste Ricardus nunquam habuit possessionem eo quod dominus rex contulit eam iure suo Willelmo de Wykeham, nunc episcopo Wyntoniensi.

De ecclesia Sancti Gregorii de Subur', de qua ex causa permutationis cum Rotgero de Burton' fuit provisum Johanni de Herham' per Innocentium v nonas Maii anno x°.[665] Ista provisio non habuit effectum quia de ista ecclesia fuit provisum eodem anno iiii° idus Martii [666] Thome de Balton', qui solvit ut patet in computis meis, qui adhuc tenet eam et habet ulterius confirmationem de ea ut patet in novis provisionibus.

## (fol. 51ᵛ) [667] Lincoliensis

De capella Sancti Thome ad pontem Stafford' (Stamford Bridge), non taxata, in qua Johannes de Lewes fuit subrogatus Edmundo Whitewell' super lite in palatio per Innocentium iiii° idus Maii anno x°.[668] Nichil valet quia non habet aliquas receptas nec iste de ea curavit propter eius paupertatem.

## Licheffeldensis

De capellania Sancti Mychaelis sita in castro de Childerow (Clitheroe), non taxata, fuit per devolutionem provisum Johanni de Borthon' per Innocentium iiii kalendas Junii anno vi°.[669] Ista provisio non habuit effectum quia ista capellania est capella sive cura dependens et annexa monasterio de Whalleya (Whalley) ordinis Cisterciensis Licheffeldensis diocesis, que ecclesia olim fuit plebania et modo est ibi debite translatum monasterio Loci Benedicti de Stanlawe (Stanlaw) Cisterciensis ordinis dicte diocesis propter maris inundationem, et dicta annexio fuit facta per Nicolaum papam IIIItum sub data Reate (Rieti) x° kalendas Augusti pontificatus sui anno ii°,[670] et confirmata per Innocentium papam VItum sub data viii kalendas Septembris pontificatus sui anno vii°,[671] et pro ista appropriatione fuit lata sententia in curia de archubus anno

---

[652] 22 January 1362(?). Richard of Norwich died October 1361 (Emden, ii, 1376).
[653] 15 July 1362.
[654] Followed by *ultimis* deleted by a line.
[655] The headings *Inutiles* and *Saresbiriensis* are repeated at the top of the page.
[656] 4 December 1362.
[657] In the margin: *de tempore Domini Urbani*.
[658] 3 March 1363.
[659] 27 May 1359.
[660] Followed by *illum* deleted by a line and dots.
[661] *Ricardum*, MS. In the margin: *ut patet in receptis*.

[662] 1 August 1362.
[663] 23 December 1364.
[664] 8 February 1358.
[665] 3 May 1362.
[666] 12 March 1362.
[667] The heading *Inutiles* is repeated at the head of the page.
[668] 12 May 1362.
[669] 29 May 1358.
[670] 23 July 1289.
[671] 25 August 1359.

LXV die xxi Junii, et de ista capellania est una sub-1ogatio facta David Martini per obitum Johannis de Borthon' per Innocentium ixº kalendas Januarii anno ix,[672] et alia de Johanne Pork per Innocentium vii kalendas Februarii anno xº,[673] et omnes nichil valent.[674]

De prebenda de Wfford' (Weeford) in ecclesia Licheffeldensi, de qua in omni iure quod competebat Anthonio de Montepologio fuit subrogatus Thomas Michel per Innocentium xº kalendas Junii anno v.[675] Non habuit effectum quia Magister Johannes de Statton', prebendarius dicte prebende habuit diffinitivam sententiam contra istum Thomam in vita sua, cuius copia remanet penes registrum.

## Menevensis

De cantoria ecclesie de Arberwill' (Abergwili), taxata vi li. xiii s. iiii d., seu ecclesia Sancti Lampetr' Talbot Stevene (Lampeter Pont Stephen), taxata v li., que optinet David de Sancto Claro, fuit provisum Cook' de Averefford' per Innocentium viº idus Martii anno viº.[676] Ista provisio non habuit effectum quia mortuus fuit antequam habuit possessionem vel potuerit habere, et ita probatum fuit per plures testes in libro dicti domini collectoris nominatos.

De prebenda de Royl in ecclesia de Arberwill', collatio cuius facta Ade de Hotton' fuit eidem confirmata per Innocentium ii idus Septembris anno viiiº.[677] Ista provisio non habuit effectum quia iuravit episcopus quod dicta confirmatio non fuit impetrata ipso mandante, sciente vel ratum habente, et etiam fuit factus episcopus antequam aliquid de hoc sciverit.

(fol. 52, xlvi)[678] De prebenda de Marthir (Mathry) in ecclesia Menevensi, de qua cum vacabit per consecrationem Ade electi Menevensis fuit provisum Philipo de Howton' per Innocentium iiiiº kalendas Novembris anno ixº.[679] Ista provisio non habuit effectum quia rex eam contulit ratione temporalitatis episcopatus Menevensis existentis in manu sua.

De prebenda de Landevaylok' (Llangyfelach) in ecclesia collegiata de Aberwill', que tanto tempore vacavit quod eius collatio est ad sedem apostolicam devoluta, fuit provisum Alexandro Milok'. Ista provisio non habuit effectum nec potuit habere quia est, et ab antiquis temporibus fuit, appropriata mense episcopi Menevensis, et impetrans mortuus est.

De prebenda quam Adam electus Menevensis optine-bat, vocata Royl, in ecclesia de Alberwill', dum vacabit ut supra, fuit mandatum provideri Philipo Martini per Innocentium iiiº kalendas Novembris anno ixº.[680] Ista provisio non habuit effectum quia rex contulit eam ratione temporalitatis ecclesie Menevensis existentis in manibus suis, et ita semper certificat episcopus et deposuit in presentia mea.

## Eboracensis

De ecclesia de Hoggestarth', non taxata, de qua per cardinalem Urgellensem fuit provisum Guillelmo Gibelot. Episcopus semper certificat quod non sit talis in sua diocesi.

De prebenda Sancti Johannis Beverlaci ad altare Beate Marie, de qua per obitum Ricardi nati Ricardi de Cymenton' fuit provisum Guillelmo de Dalton' iiiiº nonas Julii anno ixº, per Innocentium.[681] Ista provisio non habuit effectum quia rex contulit eam Willelmo de Wykeham, nunc episcopo Wyntoniensi, qui eam retinuit usque ad tempus sue promotionis et hic constat et de ipsa per promotionem suam providetur alteri.

De ecclesia Omnium Sanctorum Eboraci, de qua per obitum Symonis Warde fuit provisum David Mort' sive Martini per Innocentium iiiiº nonas Julii anno ixº,[681] taxata v li. vi s. viii d. Non habuit effectum quia incumbens ostendit diffinitivam sententiam latam in curia contra dictum David, et episcopus certificat quod nunquam fuit in possessionem.

De prebenda Sancti Johannis Beverlaci, de qua per obitum Ricardi de Tormenton' fuit provisum Johanni le Sage per Innocentium xiº kalendas Julii anno ixº.[682] Non habuit effectum quia rex contulit eam Guillelmo de Wykham ut supra eadem pagina est dictum.

De ecclesia de Appilton' in Wyndale (Appleton in Rydale), de qua per mortem Walteri Flameng' fuit provisum Thome Torp de Ventewang' per Urbanum xiii kalendas Aprilis,[683] pro taxa nova xx li. Ista provisio non habuit effectum quia est unita abbati et conventui Montis Albani (St. Albans) ordinis Sancti Benedicti per Clementem iii ydus Augusti anno viiiº.[684]

(fol. 52ᵛ)[685] De prebenda de Hoveden' (Howden) Eboracensis (est ecclesia collegiata per se et debet esse in diocesi Eboracensi), de qua per obitum Johannis de Metheham fuit provisum Ricardo Drax' per Innocentium vii idus Julii anno v,[686] pro taxa xxxiii li. vi s. viii d. Ista provisio non habuit effectum quia iste Johannes de Metheburn' adhuc hodie vivit et tenet dictam prebendam et dictus Ricardus cui providetur mortuus est.

---

[672] 24 December 1361.

[673] 26 January 1362.

[674] In the margin deleted by lines: *de prebenda de Ebeleshae, de qua per resignationem Johannis de Melburn fuit provisum Johanni de Winwyk per Clementem vii idus Februarii anno xº* (7 February 1352).

[675] 23 May 1357.

[676] 10 March 1358.

[677] 12 September 1360.

[678] The headings *Inutiles* and *Menevensis* are repeated at the top of the page.

[679] 29 October 1361.

[680] 30 October 1361.

[681] 4 July 1361.

[682] 21 June 1361.

[683] 20 March 1363.

[684] 11 August 1349.

[685] The headings *Inutiles* and *Eboracensis* are repeated at the top of the page.

[686] 9 July 1357.

## Dunelmensis

De prioratu celle Sancte Brege (St. Bees) collatio facta auctoritate ordinaria Guillelmo de Swynesbury fuit eidem confirmata per Innocentium ix kalendas Septembris anno viii°.[687] Iste prioratus non est in diocesi Dunelmensi sed est in diocesi Eboracensi, et non habuit effectum ut patet per bullam factam super revocatione dicte gratie, cuius copia remanet penes registrum collectorie.

De ecclesia de Routheburyn (Rothbury), in qua et ad omne ius quod competebat Guillelmo de Emeldon' fuit [688] Johannes Appelby subrogatus per Innocentium xvi kalendas Februarii anno ix°,[689] taxata ad novam taxam lxvi li. xiii s. iiii d. Iste, lite pendente super dicta ecclesia, et ipsius possessione non habita, fuit assecutus decanatum Londoniensem, et sic nunquam habuit dictam ecclesiam.

## Karliolensis

De ecclesia de Musgrave, vacante per obitum Johannis de Stokton', fuit provisum Rotberto Kerok' per Innocentium ii kalendas Martii anno v.[690] pro taxa xiii li. vi s. viii d. Fuit allegatum per Ricardum de Urston' quod dicta provisio non habuit effectum, et commissa inquisitio episcopo qui rescripsit quod nunquam habuit effectum, ut in hoc obligationum folio vi° in principio latius continetur.

De ecclesia de Caldebek (Caldbeck) collatio et provisio facte auctoritate ordinaria per Dominum Gilbertum Kareolensem episcopum Guillelmo de Ragenhill' fuerint eidem auctoritate apostolica confirmate vel de novo provisum vii kalendas Septembris per Urbanum anno primo.[691] Sed non habuit effectum quia ante habitam confirmationem dictus episcopus decessit, et rex, ratione temporalitatis ecclesie Karliolensis, contulit eam prout apparet per litteras dicti regis et archiepiscopi Cantuariensis ac episcopi Karliolensis, quarum copie remanent penes registrum collectorie.

(fol. 53, xlvii) Sequntur quedam collationes et provisiones quorumdam beneficiorum facte per sanctissimum in Christo patrem Dominum Urbanum papam Vᵘᵐ a vᵗᵒ kalendas Aprilis pontificatus sui anno primo [692] usque ad ii idus Julii pontificatus sui anno vᵗᵒ,[693] que non habent effectum rationibus in qualibet earum breviter assignatibus, quas collationes et provisiones dominus collector Anglie dat et tradit camere apostolice pro inutilibus et non habentibus effectum, salva semper ipsius camere determinatione.

## Lincoliensis

Motu proprio fuit provisum cardinali Morinensi (Thérouanne)[694] de canonicatu, prebenda et archidiaconatu ecclesie Lincoliensis, vacantibus per obitum cardinalis Magalonensis (Maguelone)[695] per Urbanum vii kalendas Maii anno primo.[696] Ista provisio est data in arrayragiis, sed non habuit effectum quia rex contulit predicta beneficia iure suo Willelmo de Wiktham, nunc episcopo Wyntoniensi et cancellario suo, per cuius promotionem providetur alteri, ut patet in provisionibus domini nostri anni vi sui pontificatus.

## Saresbiriensis

Item Waltero de Chiderle parva, presbytero Eliensis diocesis, de parochiali ecclesia de Brodesydeling' (Sydling St. Nicholas) Saresbiriensis diocesis, vacante per mortem Nicolai de Snglisch', que tanto tempore vacavit quod eius collatio est ad sedem apostolicam devoluta, per Urbanum v idus Maii anno primo.[697] Ista est appropriata abbati de Midelton' (Milton) eiusdem diocesis et nunquam habuit possessionem nec creditur quod possit habere.

## Eboracensis

Item Johanni Essey' presbytero de parochiali ecclesia de Rustane (Rudston) Eboracensis diocesis, vacante per cessionem vel resignationem liberam ultimi rectoris eiusdem a tanto tempore quod eius collatio et cetera vii kalendas Maii per Urbanum anno primo.[696] Non habet effectum quia est appropriata abbati et monasterio Beate Marie Cantuarie.

## Bangorensis

Item Theodorico filio Johannis Apprelbyn, clerico Bangorensis diocesis, de parochiali ecclesia de Laddinan (Llandinam) seu eiusdem ecclesie dimidia portione dicte Bangorensis diocesis, vacante ex eo quod episcopus Bangorensis eam, tamquam illicitus detentor, per triennium occupavit. Ista provisio non habet effectum. Ostense sunt littere provisionis facte per episcopum Bangorensem Guillelmo de Loryng', qui nunc tenet eam, sub data ix° kalendas Decembris anno LXII° et littere sui predecessoris sub data xvi kalendas Septembris anno LVIII° et instrumentum publicum continens quod iste Theodoricus iuravit super sancta dei ewangelia in dicta ecclesia non habere ius et dicte gratie renuntiavit, tamquam subrepticie et male, sub data ix die Aprilis anno LXIII°.

(fol. 53ᵛ) Inutiles anno primo Domini Urbani

## Cantuariensis

De parochiali ecclesia Doxele (Boxley) Cantuariensis diocesis, vacante per obitum Domini Vitalis Sancti

---

[687] 24 August 1360.
[688] Followed by *provisum* deleted by a line.
[689] 17 January 1361.
[690] 28 February 1357.
[691] 26 August 1363.
[692] 28 March 1363.
[693] 14 July 1367.

[694] Giles Ecelin de Montaigue, priest of St. Martin in Montibus.
[695] Audoin Aubert, bishop of Ostia.
[696] 25 April 1363.
[697] 11 May 1363.

Martini in Montibus cardinalis, fuit provisum Thome Caville, clerico Cantuariensis diocesis, per Urbanum, pridie nonas Maii anno primo.[698] Ista provisio non habuit effectum nec umquam habuit possessionem, et post mortem istius cardinalis fuerunt iiii<sup>or</sup> rectores in eadem, et hoc fuit probatum.

### Eboracensis

Collatio facta per archiepiscopum Eboracensem auctoritate apostolica de canonicatu et prebenda in ecclesia Sanctorum Marie et Angelorum Eboraci Thome de Midelton', presbytero [699] Lincoliensis diocesis, vacantibus per obitum Nicolai de Whyteby in Romana curia defuncti, fuit auctoritate apostolica confirmata vel provisum de novo per Urbanum vii idus Maii.[700] Ista provisio non habet effectum quia supra iii kalendas Maii eodem anno [701] providetur eidem pro qua provisione satisfecit, ut patet in computis meis, et infra providetur eidem iterato de eisdem vii idus Julii eodem anno,[702] et omnes provisiones sunt infra annum.

### Dublinensis

Collatio et provisio facte auctoritate ordinaria Nicolao de Cherdelington' de cancellaria ecclesie Dublinensis, vacante ex eo quod Johannes de Trohe dictam cancellariam optinens prebendam de Wertes (Swords) in ipsa ecclesia fuit pacifice assecutus, etiam si dictus ordinarius tempore collationis esset excommunicatus, fuerunt confirmate vel sibi provisum de novo per Urbanum v kalendas Julii anno primo.[703] Iterum providetur eidem supra v nonas Martii eodem anno,[704] que provisio data est in arrayragiis et utraque est infra annum et non debetur nisi una annata.

### Eboracensis

Item Rotberto de Brompton', presbytero Eboracensis diocesis, de parochiali ecclesia de Kayngham (Keyingham) dicte diocesis, vacante per resignationem sive dimissionem Guillelmi de Broklesby, que tanto tempore vacavit quod eius collatio et cetera, per Urbanum iiii<sup>to</sup> idus Junii anno primo.[705] Ista provisio non habuit effectum quia est appropriata abbatti de Melssa (Meaux), cuius approbriationis copia remanet penes registrum collectorie, et iterato fuit provisum eidem de eadem iii° nonas Julii eodem anno.[706]

Item Rotberto de Morthon' de officio seu beneficio non curato in ecclesia collegiata Sancti Johannis Beverlaci Eboracensis diocesis, quod valet annuatim vi m.

sterlingorum, per Urbanum iii nonas Julii anno primo.[706] Ista provisio non habuit effectum quia Willelmus de la Mare, prepositus tunc dicte collegiate ecclesie Sancti Johannis Beverlaci, dictum officium seu beneficium contulit Hugoni de Trylyngham, qui adhuc hodie vivit anno domini M° CCC° L die xx Octobris, ut constat per litteras sue collationis per ipsum exhibitas et productas.

(fol. 54, xlviii)[707] Item Rotberto de Over', clerico Eliensis diocesis, de ecclesia de Elkesley, que taxatur xl m. sterlingorum. De ista ecclesia fuit iterato provisum eidem v kalendas Julii eodem anno,[703] et pro illa datur in arayragiis quia utraque est infra annum et non debetur nisi una annata.

De parochiali ecclesia curata Omnium Sanctorum in Usgate (All Saints Pavement in Ousegate) Eboraci,[708] vacante in curia per obitum Symonis Warde, fuit provisum Johanni de Werram, presbytero Eboracensis diocesis, per Urbanum iii nonas Julii.[706] De ista fuit provisum eidem per Urbanum iii nonas Julii eodem anno,[706] et pro illa provisio datur in arayragiis quia non debetur nisi una annata, et de eadem providetur eidem xviii kalendas Maii anno iiii<sup>to</sup>,[709] et nulla earum habet effectum quia ille qui nunc tenet dictam ecclesiam habet diffinitivam sententiam contra istum.

Item Rotberto de Brampton' presbytero Eboracensis diocesis, de parochiali ecclesia de Kayngham (Keyingham) dicte diocesis, vacante per resignationem Guillelmi de Torkelesby a tanto tempore quod eius collatio et cetera per Urbanum iii nonas Julii.[706] De ista prius, videlicet v kalendas Julii eodem anno,[703] providetur eidem et per eumdem modum, et pro illa datur in arayragiis, quia non debetur nisi una annata quia sunt infra anno.

Item collatio et provisio facte per Johannem archiepiscopum Eboracensem Thome de Midelton', vigore concessionis facte ordinariis per felicis recordationis Innocentium papam VI<sup>um</sup> super beneficiis conferendis sine cura que xv li. Turonensium parvorum secundum taxam decime [710] non excederent, et canonicatu et prebenda in capella Beate Marie et Sanctorum Angelorum Eboraci, vacantibus per obitum Nicolai de Wyteby, fuerunt confirmate vel provisum de novo per Urbanum vii idus Julii anno primo.[702] De ista prebenda fuit provisum eidem antea bis, videlicet iii kalendas Maii per Urbanum anno primo,[701] et pro illa solvit ut patet in secundis computis collectoris, et postea iterato ii nonas Maii eodem anno,[711] et tertio hic, et omnes sunt infra annum et non debetur nisi una annata.

Item Rotberto de Northon', clerico Eboracensis diocesis, de parochiali ecclesia de Tresk' (Thirsk) dicte

---

[698] 6 May 1363.
[699] Followed by *diocesis* deleted by a line.
[700] 9 May 1363.
[701] 29 April 1363.
[702] 9 July 1363.
[703] 27 June 1363.
[704] 3 March 1363.
[705] 10 June 1363.
[706] 5 July 1363.

[707] The headings *Inutiles anno primo* and *Eboracensis* are repeated.
[708] Followed by *diocesis* deleted by a line.
[709] 14 April 1366.
[710] Followed by *valoris* deleted by a line.
[711] 6 May 1363.

diocesis, vacante per mortem ultimi predecessoris eiusdem, et que tanto tempore vacavit quod eius collatio et cetera, et dimittet ecclesiam de Stikwoll' (Stixwould) super qua litigat in palatio apostolico. Ista est appropriata a xx annis citra priori et conventui de Novo Burgo (Newburgh) eiusdem diocesis, et ita semper certificat archiepiscopus.

(fol. 54ᵛ)[707] Item Reginaldo de Swynesmor', presbytero Bangorensis diocesis, de parochiali ecclesia de Moling' (Melling) Eboracensis diocesis, vacante per mortem sive liberam resignationem ⟨ultimi rectoris⟩ eiusdem et tanto tempore vacavit quod eius collatio est ad sedem apostolicam legitime devoluta, etiam si quovis alio modo vacet, per Urbanum xii kalendas Septembris anno primo.[712] Ista est appropriata abbati de Crosgton' (Croxton) Lincoliensis diocesis.

### Norwicensis

De parochiali ecclesia de Rodegrave (Redgrave) dicte diocesis, vacante per obitum Johannis de Eye, ultimi rectoris eiusdem, extra Romanam curiam defuncti, que tanto tempore vacavit quod eius collatio et cetera, etiam si quovis alio modo vacet, fuit provisum Rotgero Ny, presbytero de Wodenorthon' (Wood Norton) Norwicensis diocesis, per Urbanum iii kalendas Septembris anno primo.[713] Ista provisio non habuit effectum quia Johannes Crouch nunc incumbens optinuit in curia Romana diffinitivam sententiam contra istum impetrantem, ut constat per instrumentum publicum dicte sentencie late per P. Flandrini, tunc electum Cusentini (Cosenza) et auditorem palacii apostolici, anno domini Mᵒ CCCᵒ LXVᵗᵒ die Lune x Martii.

### Herffordensis

De canonicatu et prebenda de Mertton' maiori alias magna (Moreton Magna) in ecclesia Herffordensi, vacantibus per consecrationem Symonis episcopi Londoniensis, fuit provisum Johanni Goldewik', clerico Norwicensis diocesis bachalario in legibus, per Urbanum xiiii kalendas Novembris anno primo.[714] Ista provisio nondum habuit effectum quia Johannes de Bicepsthon tenet eam iure regio.

### Eboracensis

Item collatio facta Johanni de Aupter' alias Aupere, clerico Wygorniensis diocesis, de parochiali ecclesia de Ylkelay (Ilkley) Eboracensis diocesis fuit confirmata vel provisum de novo, non obstante defectu natalium quem patitur de presbytero genitus, per Urbanum xiiiiᵒ kalendas Novembris anno primo.[714] Isti fuit facta alia confirmatio de eadem ecclesia vii idus Julii eodem

anno,[702] pro qua in parte satisfecit, et non debetur nisi una annata quia ambe sunt infra annum.

Inutiles anno secundo

### Menevensis

Primo de canonicatu ecclesie collegiate de Landdewybryvi (Llandewi-Brefi) et prebenda de Lamarth' (Llanarth) in eadem Menevensis diocesis, vacantibus per mortem Ricardi Wrote extra Romanam curiam defuncti, fuit provisum Petro de Delegrave, clerico Lincoliensis diocesis, nisi sit alteri ius quesitum per Urbanum vii idus Novembris anno iiᵒ.[715] Ista provisio non habuit effectum quia appropriata est mense episcopi Menevensis et ita fuit probatum.

### Londoniensis

De parochiali ecclesia et curata Sancti Leonardi in Estchepe Londoniensis diocesis, vacante ex eo quod quondam Johannes Taverner de Lichefeld aliam ecclesiam[716] parochialem et curatam de Bromlegh' (Bromley) Roffensis diocesis extitit pacifice assecutus, aut alio quovis modo vacet, fuit provisum Ricardo Caniton', clerico Menevensis diocesis, et dimittet parochialem ecclesiam Sancti Bernachii super Staf' (Llanfyrnach) dicte Menevensis diocesis, per Urbanum iiii idus Novembris anno ii.[717] Ista provisio nondum habuit effectum, nec habebit ut credo, quia captus fuit et dicitur quod renuntiavit gratie.

### (fol. 55, xlix)[718] Saresbiriensis

De canonicatu et prebenda ecclesie de Wilthon' Saresbiriensis diocesis, vacantibus in curia per consecrationem Thome electi Cicestrensis, fuit provisum Thome de Paxton', legum doctori auditori palatii, per Urbanum vii kalendas Decembris anno secundo.[719] Ista prebenda vocata Newenthon' (North Newnton), et fuit provisum de eadem eodem[720] anno nonas Novembris[721] Rogero de Freton', pro qua provisione solvit, ut patet in recepta, et de eadem providetur alteri eodem anno vi idus Decembris,[722] et non debetur nisi una annata quia omnes sunt infra annum.

### Herffordensis

De canonicatu et prebenda ecclesie Hereffordensis, vacantibus per consecrationem Thome electi Cicestrensis fuit provisum Nicholao de Chadesden', legum doctori, viiᵒ kalendas Decembris per Urbanum anno iiᵒ,[723] et dimittet prebenda Licheffeldensem. Istam pro-

---

[712] 21 August 1363.
[713] 30 August 1363.
[714] 19 October 1363.

[715] 7 November 1363.
[716] *ecclesiam* repeated MS.
[717] 10 November 1363.
[718] The heading *Inutiles anno secundo* is repeated at the top of the page.
[719] 25 November 1363.
[720] After *eodem* deleted by a line.
[721] 5 November 1364.
[722] 8 December 1363.
[723] 25 November 1363.

visio non habuit effectum quia sub eadem data eodem anno fuit provisum Guillelmo Bello, qui partem taxe iam solvit.

## Saresbiriensis

De canonicatu et prebenda ecclesie monasterii monialium de Wylton' Saresbiriensis diocesis, vacaturis per consecrationem Thome electi Cicestrensis, fuit provisum G(ualtero) de Moulton' presbytero per Urbanum vi idus Decembris anno ii⁰,[724] et dimittet parochialem ecclesiam de Chevelet (Cheveley) Norwicensis diocesis. Ista provisio non habuit effectum quia eodem anno iii nonas Novembris [725] fuit provisum de eadem Rotgero de Freton', qui pro sua provisione solvit, et iterum ponitur supra in principio huius pagine.

## Londoniensis

De parochiali ecclesia de Hakeney (Hackney) Londoniensis diocesis, vacatura cum Thomas de Paxton', auditor palatii apostolici, decanatum Wellensem fuerit pacifice assecutus, fuit provisum Thome de Wormenhale, licentiato in utroque iure, per Urbanum vi idus Januarii anno ii⁰,[726] Ista provisio nondum habuit effectum quia dictus T. adhuc tenet eam quia non habuit decanatum predictum, ymo Stephanus Pampel, ut patet in beneficiis collatis per Urbanum x kalendas Januarii anno tertio.[727]

## Herfordensis

De perpetuo beneficio, prebenda seu portione wlgariter nuncupata in ecclesia parochiali de Holgode (Holdgate) Herffordensis diocesis, vacante per consecrationem Thome electi Cicestrensis, fuit provisum Ricardo de Tornecombe, clerico Wyntoniensis diocesis, per Urbanum v idus Januarii anno ii⁰.[728] Ista provisio non habuit effectum quia iste impetrans fuit minor annis et non admissus ad eam, sed renuntiavit gratie et episcopus contulit alteri.

## Menevensis

Acceptatio et collatio vigore litterarum apostolicarum facte Hugoni Carles, clerico Licheffeldensi diocesi, de canonicatu et prebenda ecclesie de Langevaylaugh' (Llangyfelach) in ecclesia de Abrewill' (Abergwili) Menevensis diocesis, vacantibus per mortem Guillelmi H. a tanto tempore quod eius collatio et cetera, fuerunt confirmate vel provisum de novo per Urbanum vii⁰ kalendas Martii anno ii⁰,[729] et dimittet parochialem ecclesiam de Ogomondon' (Edgmond) vel canonicatum et prebendam de Glauswesale (Gnosall) Licheffeldensis diocesis. Ista provisio non habuit effectum quia appropriata est ab antiquo mense episcopi, et ista fuit probatum.

(fol. 55ᵛ)[718] Saresbiriensis et Lincoliensis

Ex causa permutationis fuit provisum Johanni de Astyng', presbytero Lincoliensis diocesis, de vicaria perpetua de Asynton' (Uffington) Saresbiriensis diocesis et Rotberto de Frankelagn, presbytero dicte diocesis de perpetua vicaria ecclesie parochialis de Cherlebury (Charlbury) dicte Lincoliensis diocesis per Urbanum xiii kalendas Aprilis anno secundo.[730] De istis eisdem beneficiis et personis fuit provisum per Urbanum iii idus Januarii anno ii⁰,[731] et sunt infra annum, et est satisfactum de vicaria de Cherlebury in plenum et de alio de medietate, et pro illa resta ponitur in arayragiis.

## Norwicensis

Provisio facta auctoritate apostolica ex causa permutationis Johanni de Heyngham de parochiali ecclesia Sancti Gregorii de Sudbury Norwicensis diocesis, etiam si per inhabilitatem ipsius Johannis sibi ius non competat ex eo quod aliam parochialem ecclesiam tenuerat infra tempus debitum ad sacerdotum non promotus, fuit auctoritate apostolica confirmata vel provisum de novo per Urbanum x⁰ kalendas Junii anno ii⁰.[732] Ista provisio non habuit effectum quia de ea fuit provisum Thome de Bakton' per Innocentium iiii idus Martii anno x⁰,[733] et per Urbanum x kalendas Septembris anno ii⁰,[734] et pro prima provisione est satisfactum in ⟨plenum⟩ ut patet in recepta collectoris.

## Roffensis

De archidiaconatu Roffensi, vacante per resignationem Guillelmi Red, fuit provisum Guillelmo Venlok', et dimittet ecclesiam parochialem de Horton' Roffensis diocesis et prebendas capelle Beate Marie Magdalene de Briggenorth' (Bridgenorth) et capellam Sancti Johannis in Witlesfordbrigg' (Whittlesford) per Urbanum nonas Junii anno ii⁰.[735] Ista provisio non habuit effectum quia noluit gratiam acceptare quia minus perdebat in dimissione aliorum beneficiorum que plus valent in duplo, et est alia provisio facta de eodem eidem vii kalendas Novembris eodem anno.[736]

## Lincoliensis

Item Johanni de Stevenach' alias de Wihist' Lincoliensis diocesis de parochiali ecclesia de Sitheston' (Syston) dicte diocesis, vacante per obitum Guillelmi Welprohyngton' extra Romanam curiam defuncti a tanto tempore quod eius collatio et cetera, per Urbanum kalendas Octobris anno ii⁰.[737] Ista provisio non habet

---

[724] 8 December 1363.
[725] 3 November 1364.
[726] 8 January 1364.
[727] 23 December 1364.
[728] 9 January 1364.
[729] 24 February 1364.

[730] 20 March 1364.
[731] 11 January 1364.
[732] 23 May 1364.
[733] 12 March 1362.
[734] 23 August 1364.
[735] 5 June 1364.
[736] 26 October 1364.
[737] 1 October 1364.

effectum quia est appropriata priori de Ulvescroft' (Ulverscroft) eiusdem diocesis, et pro appropriatione est satisfactum ut patet in recepta collectoris.

## Dunelmensis et Lincoliensis

Ex causa permutationis fuit provisum Nicolao de Humgreford' de canonicatu Carleolensi et vicaria de Whytyngham (Whittingham) Dunelmensis diocesis ab ecclesia Carleolensi dependente et Johanni de Ford de prioratu Sancte Fredeswide (St. Frideswide) Exoniensis diocesis ordinis Sancti Augustini Lincoliensis diocesis per Urbanum iii kalendas Novembris anno ii°.[738] Ista provisio non habuit effectum quia non verace fuit optenta et papa totum cassavit et priorem, ut dicitur, et constat per litteras domini cardinalis Nemausensis (Nîmes)[739] sub data xi die Martii anno domini M° CCC° LXV.

(fol. 56, 1) Inutiles anno secundo et tertio

## Roffensis

Collatio et provisio facte auctoritate apostolica Guillelmo Wenlok' de archidiaconatu Roffensi, etiam si per constitutionem *execrabilis* vacaverit, fuerunt confirmate vel provisum de novo per Urbanum vii° kalendas Novembris anno ii°.[736] Ista provisio non habuit effectum quia noluit gratiam acceptare ex causa in precedenti pagina super eadem provisione expressa.

De parochiali ecclesia de Clyve (Cliffe) Roffensis diocesis per privationem Johannis de Bischospeton' per dominum papam factam fuit provisum Rotberto de Nynveston', clerico Norwicensis diocesis, per Urbanum xvi kalendas Decembris anno tertio,[740] et dimittet parochialem ecclesiam de Holme super qua litigat. Ista provisio non habuit effectum quia renuntiavit gratie ex causa et cetera.

## Lincoliensis

De canonicatu et prebenda ecclesie Lincoliensis, vacantibus per privationem Raymundi Pelegrini per dominum papam factam fuit provisum Henrico le Despensser Lincoliensis diocesis, bachalario in legibus, et dimittet parochialem ecclesiam de Resseworth' (Market Bosworth) Lincoliensis diocesis et prebendas Saresbiriensem et Landavensem, per Urbanum xv kalendas Decembris anno iii°.[741] Ista provisio non habuit effectum quia dicta privatio non fuit executa sed per mortem dicti Raymundi fuit provisum de ea cardinali Aquensi,[742] qui ipsam tenuit usque ad mortem suam, et nunc per mortem illius habet eam cardinalis Lemovicensis.[743]

## Wyntoniensis

De archidiaconatu Surreie in ecclesia Wyntoniensi, vacante per mortem Johannis de Edyngdon' extra Romanam curiam defuncti, fuit provisum Thome de Paxton, legum doctori, et dimittet parochialem ecclesiam de Hakeney' (Hackney) Londoniensis diocesis per Urbanum iiii° nonas Januarii anno iii°.[744] Ista provisio non habet effectum quia adhuc vivit dictus Johannes et est archidiaconus.

## Saresbiriensis

De archidiaconatu Baskchire in ecclesia Saresbiriensi, vacante per mortem Edmundi de Lamboth' extra curiam defuncti, fuit provisum Thome de Paxton', legum doctori auditori palatii, et dimittet parochialem ecclesiam de Hakeneye Londoniensis diocesis. Ista provisio non habuit effectum quia iste Thomas nunquam fuit ausus prosequi gratiam istam, sed Dominus Johannes de Harowill' nunc episcopus Bathoniensis fuit subrogatus in omni iure competenti dicto Thome per Urbanum iiii idus Decembris anno iiii°,[745] de qua subrogatione debet dictus episcopus respondere, et de isto archidiaconatu fuit alteri provisum per consecrationem dicti episcopi fuit provisum Alexandro de Dalby per Urbanum xix kalendas Februarii anno quinto.[746]

(fol. 56ᵛ) Inutiles anno tertio

## Landavensis

De archidiaconatu Landavensi, vacante per liberam resignationem Magistri Thome de Eltesle, fuit provisum Thome de Southam Licheffeldensis diocesis per Urbanum xvi° kalendas Martii anno tertio.[747] Ista provisio non habuit effectum quia ante habitam possessionem resignavit et fuit provisum per principem Wallie Rotberto de Waltham, et dicta provisio confirmata per Urbanum v idus Aprilis anno iiii,[748] que provisio habet effectum.

## Menevensis

Item Ricardo Tervemini, clerico Exoniensis diocesis, de canonicatu et prebenda ecclesie collegiate de Abergwili Menevensis diocesis, vacantibus per dimissionem Stephani Pampel. Ista provisio non habuit effectum quia alteri[749] fuit provisum per Urbanum viii idus Januarii anno tertio,[750] pro qua provisione est satisfactum.

## Elphinensis

Confirmatio facta per episcopum Elphinensem de Thoma Matumgrossa, electo ad decanatum Elphinen-

---

[738] 30 October 1364.
[739] John de Blanzac, priest of S. Marco.
[740] 16 November 1364.
[741] 17 November 1364.
[742] Peter Itherii, bishop of Dax, bishop of Albano.
[743] Nicholas de Bessia, deacon of S. Maria in Via Lata.

[744] 2 January 1365.
[745] 10 December 1365.
[746] 14 January 1367.
[747] 14 February 1365.
[748] 9 April 1366.
[749] *alii*, MS.
[750] 6 January 1365.

sem, fuit confirmata per Urbanum xvi kalendas Aprilis anno tertio.[751] Non habet effectum quia est alia confirmatio eidem facta eodem anno nonas Februarii,[752] pro qua datur in arayragiis.

### Lincoliensis

Item acceptatio, collatio et provisio facte vigore litterarum apostolicarum Thome de Eltesle, presbytero Eliensis diocesis, de prebenda ecclesie Lincoliensis, vacante per obitum Johannis de Edyndon' extra curiam defuncti, fuerunt confirmate vel provisum de novo per Urbanum ix kalendas Maii anno tertio.[753] Ista provisio non habet effectum quia facta fuit de dicto beneficio vacante per mortem Johannis de Edyndon', qui tamen Johannes anno LXVII die xxv mensis Januarii erat sanus et vivus et mihi exhibitus et monstratus loquens, iens, comedens et libens in civitate Londonie et ultra hanc date sunt alie rationes per quas etiam dicta provisio, etiam si dictus Johannes mortuus esset, non posset habere effectum, que remanent penes registrum collectorie.

### Lincoliensis

Acceptatio, collatio et provisio facte vigore litterarum apostolicarum per Henricum de Duniston', clericum Norwicensis diocesis, de parochiali ecclesia de Horwode magna (Great Horwood) Lincoliensis diocesis fuerunt confirmate vel provisum de novo per Urbanum xiii kalendas Julii anno iii°.[754] Ista provisio non habuit effectum quia Johannes Kyret alias Bokyngham eam evicit in curia per diffinitivam sententiam et habuit exequutionem sub bulla sub data viii idus Maii pontificatus Domini Urbani pape anno iiii[to].[755]

De prebenda ecclesie Lincoliensis, vacante per obitum Raymundi Pelegrini, collectoris apostolici extra Romanam curiam defuncti, fuit provisum Petro episcopo Albanensi cardinali per Urbanum iiii nonas Septembris anno iii°.[756] Ista est data in arayragiis et non debet hic poni inter inutiles.

(fol. 57, li)Inutiles anno quarto.

### Saresbiriensis

De parochiali ecclesia de Stokton' (Stockton) Saresbiriensis, vacante ex eo quod Johannes de Bokyngham, ultimus rector eiusdem, ecclesiam de Harwe (Harrow) Londoniensis diocesis est pacifice assecutus, fuit provisum Johanni de Horton' presbytero, et dimittet parochialem ecclesiam de Hodelene (West Hoathley) Cicestrensis diocesis, per Urbanum ii kalendas Januarii anno iiii[to].[757] Ista provisio non habet effectum quia de

eadem fuit provisum Waltero Malbly per Urbanum xii kalendas Decembris eodem anno,[758] qui eam possidet et partem solvit.

### Londoniensis

De canonicatu et prebenda ecclesie Londoniensis, vacantibus per obitum Raymundi Pelegrini, apostolice sedis nuntii extra curiam defuncti, fuit provisum Alexandro de Dalby, et dimittet canonicatum et prebendam ecclesie Licheffeldensis, super quibus litigat, per Urbanum idus Januarii anno iiii[to].[759] Ista provisio non habet effectum quia de ea fuit provisum Johanni Boulegh', qui eam tenet, per Urbanum iiii° nonas Januarii eodem anno.[760]

### Eboracensis

Item Johanni de Hynde, presbytero Eboracensis diocesis, de parochiali ecclesia Omnium Sanctorum super pavimentum in Eboraco, vacante per obitum Symonis Ward' in Romana curia defuncti, per Urbanum xviii kalendas Maii anno iiii[to].[761] Ista provisio et quedam alia facta Johanni Ulram per Urbanum vii° idus Julii anno primo [762] non habunt effectum quia incumbens habet diffinitivam sententiam contra illum per cuius mortem impetratur.

FOURTH ACCOUNT OF JOHN DE CABRESPINO
1368 TO 1370

(fol. 58)[1] Computa seu rationes [2] Johannis de Cabrespino, doctoris [2] decretorum [2] ⟨in⟩[4] ⟨          ⟩[3] regno Anglie camere apostolice nuntii [2] ⟨et⟩[4] collectoris a xviii die mensis Februarii anni [2] ⟨a⟩[4] nativitate domini MCCCLXVIII usque ad festum Omnium Sanctorum anni a nativitate domini MCCCLXX.[2]

(fol. 59[v])[5] Denarii Beati Petri qui solvuntur in Anglia ascendunt pro quolibet anno cxcix li. v s. iiii d. Et solvuntur per xviii personas infrascriptas, ut sequitur:

Archiepiscopus Eboracensis xi li. x s.
Episcopus Saresbiriensis xvii li.
Episcopus Cicestrensis viii li.
Episcopus Wigorniensis x li. v s.
Episcopus Conwetrensis et Licheffeldensis x li. v s.
Episcopus Lincolniensis xlii li.

[751] 17 March 1365.
[752] 5 February 1365.
[753] 23 April 1365.
[754] 19 June 1365.
[755] 8 May 1366.
[756] 2 September 1365.
[757] 31 December 1365.

[758] 20 November 1365.
[759] 13 January 1366.
[760] 2 January 1366.
[761] 14 April 1366.
[762] 9 July 1363.
[1] The original rough parchment cover of this account. It is badly rubbed. Folio 57 verso is blank.
[2] Conjectural in part.
[3] One or two words are illegible.
[4] Illegible.
[5] Folios 58 verso and 59 recto are blank.

Episcopus Exoniensis ix li. v s.
Episcopus Herffordensis vi li.
Episcopus Bathoniensis et Wellensis xi li. v s.
Episcopus Norwicensis xxi li. x s.
Archidiaconus Cantuariensis viii li.
Archidiaconus Roffensis v li. xii s.
Archidiaconus Mydelsexie v li. x s.
Archidiaconus Wynthoniensis xi li. xiii s. iiii d.
Archidiaconus Surreie [6] v li. x s.
Archidiaconus Colcestrie v li. x s.
Archidiaconus Excessie v li. x s.
Archidiaconus Eliensis v li.
Summa cxcix li. v s. iiii d.

(fol. 60) Census ordinarius qui solvitur in Anglia ascendit pro quolibet anno iiii li. xv s. Et solvitur per personas infrascriptas:

### Abbates

Abbas de Faversham xiii s. iiii d.
Abbas de Courtesey viii s.
Abbas Sancti Edmundi de Bury xiii s. iiii d.
Abbas de Malmesbury xiii s. iiii d.
Abbas Sancti Albani xiii s. iiii d.

### Priores

Prior de Tenebrig' xiii s. iiii d.
Prior de Bodmin ii s.
Prior de Angley ii s.
Prior Karleolensis xiii s. iiii d.
Prior de Chamcombus xv d.
Abbatissa Sancte Clare Londoniensis vi d.
Custos de Scamdebrig' xv d.
Summa iiii li. xv s.

(fol. 60ᵛ) Memorandum quod ego, Johannes de Cabrespino, collector Anglie, dimisi et dedi camere apostolice anno LXVIIIº, cum ultimo cum eadem camera de mense Augusti computavi in Monteflaschone (Montefiascone), in restis sive arrayrargiis de denariis Beati Petri ibi debitis pro tempore preterito et toto anno LXVIIIº predicto in summa vᶜ xcix li. iiii s. viii d., licet debuerim dimittere vᶜ xcix li. xi s. iiii d. quia archidiaconus Saresbiriensis [7] per errorem non fuit dimissus in arrayrargiis pro annis LXVIIº et LXVIIIº nisi in xi li. pro dictis duobus annis, et debuit dimitti in xi li. vi s. viii d., quia pro quolibet anno solvit v li. xiii s. iiii d., et de tanto fuit responsum in aliis dictis computis, et sic fuit vera resta dictorum denariorum Beati Petri vᶜ xcix li. xi s. iiii d.

De qua resta dictorum denariorum do in recepta presentium computorum eidem camere traditorum iiiiᶜ lxxi li. xi s. viii d.

Item do adhuc eidem camere de premissis restis in

arrayrargiis, incluso dicto anno LXVIIIº dumtaxat, cxxvii li. xix s. viii d.

Et sic est summa recepte et arrayrargiorum vᶜ xcix li. xi s. iiii d.

(fol. 61) Item memorandum quod in restis sive arrayrargiis de anno censu, incluso dicto anno LXVIIIº dumtaxat, x li. viii s. vii d.

De qua resta dicti census [8] do camere apostolice in recepta presentium computorum eidem camere traditorum iii li. xii s. i d.

Item do adhuc eidem camere de premissis restis in arrayrargiis, incluso dicto anno LXVIIIº, vi li. xvi s. vi d.

Et sic est summa receptorum et arrayrargiorum x li. viii s. vii d.

(fol. 61ᵛ) Item memorandum quod dimisi in arrayrargiis de annatis beneficiorum collatorum per Dominos Clementem, Innocentium ac Urbanum usque ad iiiº kalendas Maii pontificatus sui anno primo [9] ultra restam archidiaconatus Midelsex in ecclesia Londoniensi collati domino cardinali Rothomagensi [10] et hospitalis Sancti David in ecclesia Menevensi collati David Martini, que beneficia fuerunt dimissa pro non taxatis, iiᵐ ixᶜ ii li. ii s. vi d., licet non debuerim dimittere nisi iiᵐ ixᶜ ii li. i s. et vi d., quia precentoria Cicestrensi collata domino cardinali Aquensi [11] fuit dimissa in arrayrargiis in xxxi li. xiiii s. iiii d. et non debet esse nisi xiii s. iiii d., quia ad plus non taxatur, et sic fuit vera resta dictorum beneficiorum iiᵐ ixᶜ ii li. i s. vi d.

De qua resta do in recepta presentium computorum eidem camere traditorum ultra dicta beneficia non taxata et ultra explorata quorum exploratum et non taxatorum summa recepte est cxxxiiiiᵒʳ li. x s. x d. ob.

Inclusis tamen in dicta recepta xlv [12] li. xvi s. viii d. sterlingorum receptis pro iiiᶜ fl. camere de resta vᶜ et quinque fl. et medii et ii d., pro beneficiis Nicholay Heth, que resta fuit posita inter quatuor obligatos, ccccclxxxviii li. xvi s. viii d.

Item do adhuc eidem camere de premissis restis in arrayrargiis iiᵐ iiiiᶜ ii li. vi s. x d.

Et de beneficiis Ybernie que includebantur in premissa resta, que post conclusionem predictam fuerunt tradita novo collectori ibidem creato cxix li. xiii s. iiii d.

Et sic est summa dicte recepte et arrayrargiorum, omnibus inclusis excepta recepta exploratorum et non taxatorum iiiᵐ x li. xvi s. x d.

(fol 62) De qua summa que summam reste dimisse excedit detrahuntur pro iiiᶜ fl. camere receptis in diminutionem reste florenorum dimisse, que resta fuit vᶜ quinque fl. medius ii d., quorum fl. quilibet de iiᶜ eorum

---

[6] *Saresbiriensis*, MS.
[7] Probably a mistake for Surrey: above, pp. 239, 273.

[8] *ccensus*, MS.
[9] 29 April 1363.
[10] Peter de la Forêt, priest of Ss. XII Apostoli.
[11] Peter Itherii, bishop of Dax, priest of Ss. Quattro Coronati.
[12] Follows *xv* deleted by a line.

constat iii s. et i d. sterlingorum et quilibet de aliis centum constat iii s. dicte monete, pro summa eorum xlv li. xvi s. viii d.

Item pro resta prebende de Nasynghon (Nassington) in ecclesia Lincolniensi collate domino cardinali Carcassonensi,[13] que non fuit michi dimissa in arrayrargiis nec per me camerae data liii li. ii s.

Item pro resta archidiaconatus Eboracensis eidem domino cardinali collati, non data michi in arrayrargiis nec per me camere dimissa, v li. x s.

Item pro vicaria de Impryngthon' (Impington) Eliensis diocesis, etiam michi non data in arrayrargiis nec per me camere data, tam pro recepta ipsius que est xliii s. iiii d., quam pro resta eiusdam que est eitam xliii s. iiii d., iiii li. vi s. viii d.

Summa istarum detractionum cviii li. xv s. iiii d.

Quibus omnibus detractis de summa recepte et arrayrargiorum precedentium restat quod summa receptorum et arrayrargiorum predictorum in aliis computis dimissorum est ii$^m$ ix$^c$ ii li. i s. vi d.

(fol. 62$^v$) Item memorandum quod dimisi in arrayrargiis de annatis beneficiorum collatorum per Dominum Urbanum a iii$^o$ kalendas Maii pontificatus sui anno primo[14] usque ad pridie ydus Julii pontificatus sui anno quinto,[15] quia tunc de ulteriori tempore non fuit computatum in beneficiis in quibus tunc taxa eorum fuit expressa ac declarata, que beneficia patent in aliis computis, cclxxix li. x s.

De qua resta do in recepta presentium computorum eidem camere traditorum ccxlix li. x s.

Item do adhuc eidem camere de premissis restis in arrayrargiis de decanatu[16] Wellensi confirmato Stephanio Pampel, legum doctori, xx li.

Et de prioratu Beate Marie Lancastrie (Lancaster) diocesis Eboracensis collato Willelmo Raymbaut x li.

Et sic est summa pro dictis duobus beneficiis xxx li.

Et sic apparet quod est summa receptorum et arrayrargiorum immediate premissorum beneficiorum cclxxix li. x s.

(fol. 63) Sequntur computa et rationes Johannis de Cabrespino, doctoris decretorum canonici Narbonensis in regno Anglie appostolice sedis nuncii et collectoris, de omnibus et singulis per eum et dominum Johannem de Caroloco, priorem Lewensem, seu alios quoscumque nomine dicte camere receptis, liberatis, assignatis et expenssis, tam de denariis Beati Petri, annuo censsu, restis et annatis beneficiorum, fructibus pro tempore vacationis, legatis camere appostolice et Terre Sancte et quibuscumque aliis obventionibus ad cameram predictam in eodem regno qualitercumque spectantibus, a xviii die menssis Februarii anni a nativitate domini

MCCCLXVIII usque ad festum Omnium Sanctorum anni a nativitate domini M$^o$CCCLXX.

Primo de arayratgiis denariorum Beati Petri

De archiepiscopo Eboracensi, dimisso in arayratgiis pro annis LXVII$^o$ et octavo, pro quolibet in xi li. et x s., recepte fuerunt pro complemento dicte reste xxiii li.

Item de episcopo Saresbiriensi, dimisso in arayratgiis pro annis LXV$^o$, LXVI$^o$, septimo et octavo, pro quolibet in xvii li. recepte fuerunt ab eodem pro annis sexagesimo quinto, sexto et septimo li li.[17]

Summa pagine lxxiiii li.

Item de episcopo Cicestrensi, dimisso in arayratgiis pro annis LXVI$^{to}$, septimo et octavo, pro quolibet in viii$^{to}$ li., recepte fuerunt ab eodem pro complemento dictorum trium annorum xxiiii li.

Item de episcopo Wygorniensi, dimisso in arayratgiis pro annis LXVII$^o$ et octavo, pro quolibet in x li. et v s., recepte fuerunt ab eodem pro complemento dicte reste xx li. x s.

Item de episcopo Conwetrensi et Licheffeldensi, dimisso in arayratgiis pro annis LXVI$^{to}$, septimo et octavo, pro quolibet in x li. et v s., recepte fuerunt ab eodem pro complemento dicte reste xxx li. xv s.

Item de episcopo Lincoliensi, dimisso in arayratgiis pro annis LXVII$^o$ et octavo, pro quolibet in xlii li., recepte fuerunt ab eodem pro parte dicte reste lxxx li.[18]

Item de episcopo Exoniensi, dimisso in arayratgiis pro annis LXVII$^o$ et octavo, pro quolibet in ix li. v s., recepte fuerunt ab eodem pro complemento dicte reste xviii li. x s.

Item de episcopo Norwicensi, dimisso in arayratgiis pro annis LXV$^{to}$, sexto, septimo et octavo, pro quolibet in xxi li. x s., recepte fuerunt ab eodem pro complemento dicte reste lxxxvi li.

Summa pagine cclix li. xv s.

(fol. 64) Item de episcopo Bathoniensi et Wellensi, dimisso in arayratgiis pro annis LXIII$^o$, LXVII$^o$ et LXVIII$^o$, quia de annis LXIIII$^{to}$, quinto et sexto fuit in ultimis meis computis computatum, pro quolibet dictorum trium annorum in xi li. et v s., et sic pro dictis tribus annis in xxxiii li. xv s., recepte fuerunt ab eodem in partem dicte reste, videlicet in partem anni LXIII v li.[19]

Item de episcopo Herffordensi, dimisso in arayratgiis pro annis LXVII$^o$ et VIII$^o$, pro quolibet in vi li., nichil.[20]

Item de archidiacono Cantuariensi, dimisso in arayratgiis pro annis LXVII$^o$ et octavo, pro quolibet in viii$^o$ li., recepte fuerunt pro complemento dicte reste xvi li.

---

[13] Stephen Aubert, bishop of Carcassonne, deacon of S. Maria in Aquiro.

[14] 29 April 1363.

[15] 14 July 1367.

[16] Followed by *Cu* deleted by a line.

[17] In the margin: *et de xvii li. pro anno LXVIII$^o$ respondetur in arayratgiis.*

[18] In the margin: *et de residuis iiii$^{or}$ li. respondetur in arayratgiis.*

[19] In the margin: *de residuis xxviii li. xv s. respondetur in arayratgiis.*

[20] In the margin: *de dictis xii li. respondetur in arayratgiis.*

Item de archidiacono Roffensi, dimisso in arayratgiis pro annis LXV^to, sexto, septimo et octavo, pro quolibet v li. xii s., nichil hic.[21]

Item de archidiacono Midelssexie, dimisso in arayratgiis pro annis sexagesimo, LXV^to, sexto, septimo et octavo, quia de aliis annis est responssum, pro quolibet in v li. x s., recepte fuerunt pro complemento dicte reste, inclusis v li. x s. receptis per me a Domino Hugone Pelegrini, xxvii li. x s.

Summa pagine xlviii li. x s.

(fol. 64^v) Item de archidiacono Wynthoniensi, dimisso in arayratgiis pro annis LXIIII^to, quinto, sexto, septimo et octavo, pro quolibet in xi li. xiii s. iiii d., et sic pro dictis quinque annis in lviii li. vi s. viii d., recepte fuerunt ab eodem in partem dicte reste, videlicet pro annis LXIIII^to, quinto et VI^to, xxxv li.[22]

Item de archidiacono Surreie,[23] dimisso in arayratgiis pro annis LXVII^o et octavo, pro quolibet in v li. x s., et sic pro dictis duobus annis in xi li.,[24] licet debuisset dimiti in xi li. vi s. viii d., videlicet pro quolibet dictorum annorum v li. xiii s. iiii d., quia tantum solvit et de tanto fuit responssum in recepta aliorum computorum, recepte fuerunt pro complemento dicte reste xi li. vi s. viii d.

Item de archidiacono Colcestrie, dimisso in arayratgiis pro annis LXVI^o, septimo et octavo, pro quolibet in v li. x s., et sic pro dictis tribus annis in xvi li. x s., recepte fuerunt in partem dicte reste, videlicet pro annis LXVI et VII^o xi li.[25]

Item de archidiacono Exessie, dimisso in arayratgiis pro annis LXV^to, sexto, septimo et octavo, pro quolibet in v li. x s., et sic pro dictis iiii^or annis in xxii li., recepte fuerunt pro complemento dicte reste xxii li.

Summa pagine lxxix li. vi s. viii d.

(fol. 65) Item de archidiacono Eliensi, dimisso in arayratgiis pro annis LXIIII^to, quinto, sexto, septimo et octavo, pro quolibet in v li., et sic pro dictis quinque annis in xxv li., recepte fuerunt in partem dicte reste, videlicet pro annis LXIIII^to et LXV^to x li.[26]

Summa pagine patet.

Summa universalis totius recepte predictorum denariorum dimissorum in arayratgiis est cccclxxi li. xi s. viii d. Approbatum.

Summa restarum predictorum arayratgiorum est cxxvii li. xix s. viii d.[27]

(fol. 65^v) Sequitur ordinaria recepta dictorum denariorum Beati Petri.

De archiepiscopo Eboracensi pro anno LXIX^o xi li. x s.

Item de episcopo Cicestrensi pro anno LXIX^o viii li.

Item de episcopo Conwetrensi et Lichfeldensi pro anno LXIX^o x li. v s.

Item de episcopo Exoniensi pro anno LXIX^o ix li. v s.

Item de archidiacono Midelssexie pro anno LXIX^o v li. x s.

Summa pagine et totius ordinarie recepte denariorum Beati Petri est xliiii li. x s. Approbatum.

Summa universalis omnium precedentium receptarum est v^c xvi li. i s. viii d. Approbatum.

(fol. 66) Sequitur recepta arayratgiorum annui censsus.

De abbate de Faversham', dimisso in arayratgiis pro annis LXVII^o et octavo, pro quolibet in xiii s. iiii d., nichil hic.[28]

De abbate de Corthesey', dimisso in arayratgiis pro annis LXVII^o et VIII^o, pro quolibet viii s., nichil hic.[29]

De abbate Sancti Edmundi de Bury, dimisso in arayratgiis pro anno LXVIII^o in xiii s. iiii d., recepti fuerunt pro complemento dicte reste xiii s. iiii d.

De abbate de Malmesbury, dimisso in arayratgiis pro anno LXVIII^o in xiii s. iiii d., recepti fuerunt dicti xiii s. iiii d.

De abbate Sancti Albani Lincoliensis dyocesis, dimisso in arayratgiis pro anno LXVIII^o in xiii s. iiii d., recepti fuerunt dicti xiii s. iiii d.

De priore de Tenebrig', dimisso in arayratgiis pro anno LXVIII^o in xiii s. iiii d., recepti fuerunt dicti xiii s. iiii d.

De priore de Bodmyn dimisso in arayratgiis pro anno LXVIII^o in ii s., recepti fuerunt dicti ii s.

Summa recepte pagine ii li. xv s. iiii d.

(fol. 66^v) De priore de Anglesey Eliensis diocesis, dimisso in arayratgiis pro annis LXV, sexto, septimo et octavo, pro quolibet in ii s., recepti fuerunt pro complemento dicte reste viii s.

De priore Karleolensi, dimisso in arayratgiis pro annis LXII^o, tertio, iiii^to, v^to, vi^to, vii^o et octavo, pro quolibet in xiii s. iiii d., nichil hic.[30]

De priore de Chaucombus, dimisso in arayratgiis pro annis LXIII^o, quarto, quinto, sexto, septimo et octavo, pro quolibet in xv d., recepti fuerunt in complemento dicte reste vii s. vi d.

De abbatissa Sancte Clare Londonie, dimissa in arayratgiis pro anno LXVIII in vi d., nichil hic.[31]

De custode de Scandeburgh', dimisso in arayratgiis pro anno LXVIII in xv d., recepti fuerunt dicti xv d.

Summa recepte pagine xvi s. ix d.

---

[21] In the margin: *De xxii li. viii s. respondetur in arayratgiis.*
[22] In the margin: *de residuis xxiii li. vi s. viii d. respondetur in arayratgiis.*
[23] Blotted and over it has been written *Saresbiriensi.*
[24] Followed by *vi s. viii d.* deleted by a line.
[25] In the margin: *de residuis v li. x s. respondetur in arayratgiis.*
[26] In the margin: *de residuis xv li. respondetur in arayratgiis.*
[27] In the margin: *Resta.*

[28] In the margin: *respondetur in arayratgiis de xxvi s. viii d.*
[29] In the margin: *respondetur in arayratgiis de xvi s.*
[30] In the margin: *De iiii li. xiii s. iiii d. respondetur in arayratgiis.*
[31] In the margin: *respondetur in arayratgiis de vi d.*

Summa universalis recepte arayratgiorum annui cen-ssus est iii li. xii s. i d.[32]

Summa restarum predictorum arayratgiorum annui censsus est vi li. xvi s. vi d.

(fol. 67) Sequitur ordinaria recepta annui censsus.

De abbate Sancti Edmundi de Bury pro annis LXIX° et LXX°, pro quolibet xiii s. iiii d., xxvi s. viii d.

De abbate de Malmesbury Saresbiriensis diocesis pro anno LXIX° xiii s. iiii d.

De abbate Sancti Albani Lincoliensis diocesis pro annis LXIX° et LXX°, pro quolibet xiii s. iiii d., xxvi s. viii d.

De priore de Tenebrig, pro anno LXIX° xiii s. iiii d.

De priore de Bodmyn pro annis LXIX° et LXX°, pro quolibet ii s., iiii s.

De priore de Anglesey Eliensis diocesis pro anno LXIX° ii s.

De priore de Chaucombus pro annis LXIX° et LXX°, pro quolibet xv d., ii s. vi d.

De custode de Scandeburgh pro annis LXIX° et LXX°, pro quolibet xv d., ii s. vi d.

Summa recepte pagine iiii li. xi s.

Summa tam extraordinarie quam ordinarie recepte annui censsus est viii li. iii s. i d. Approbatum.

(fol. 67ᵛ) Sequitur recepta arayratgiorum de annatis beneficiorum in aliis computis dimissorum, collatorum per Dominos Clementem, Innocentium et Urbanum usque ad iii° kalendas Maii pontificatus sui anno primo.[33]

### Dyocesis Cantuariensis

De vicaria de Nortburn' (Northbourne), taxata vi li. xiii s. iiii d., non dimissa in arayratgiis nec data per cameram sed explorata, de qua fuit provisum de novo per cardinalem Petragoricensem Villelmo Droyde de Munigham ii kalendas Septembris pontificatus Domini Innocentii pape sexti[34] anno quinto,[35] pro taxa vi li. xiii s. iiii d.[36]

### Londoniensis

De archidiaconatu Midelssexie, de quo fuit provisum domino cardinali Rothomagensi[37] per Innocentium xiiii kalendas Decembris pontificatus sui anno vi°,[38] dimisso in arayratgiis pro medietate fructuum quia non taxatur, recepte fuerunt pro complemento dictorum fructuum viii li. v s. i d. Fructus ascendunt secundum computum archidiaconi ad xvi li. x s. ii d.[39]

Summa recepte pagine tam de explorata quam de non taxata xiiii li. xviii s. v d.

### (fol. 68) Cicestrensis

De vicaria de Iklesham (Icklesham), taxata xvi li. xiii s. iiii d., de qua fuit dispenssatum cum Waltero de Stratthon' presbytero quod eam posset retinere per Innocentium ii ydus Januarii anno viii°,[40] dimissa in arayratgiis in vi li. xiii s. iiii d., recepte fuerunt pro complemento dicte reste vi li. xiii s. iiii d.

### Wynthoniensis

De ecclesia de Westmines (West Meon), taxata xx li., que fuit confirmata Johanni de Cheryngthon' per Clementem ydus Maii anno viii°,[41] dimissa in arayratgiis in vi li., recepte fuerunt pro complemento dicte reste vi li.

De ecclesia de Havunte (Havant), taxata xxvi li. xiii s. iiii d., de qua per obitum Johannis de Noion fuit provisum Johanni de Uppewll' per Innocentium iiii° nonas Julii anno ix°,[42] dimissa in arayratgiis in vi li. xiii s. iiii d., recepte fuerunt dicte vi li. xiii s. iiii d.

De ecclesia Duntesfaud' (Dunsfold), taxata xiii li. vi s. viii d., de qua per obitum Willelmi de Chartesthon' fuit provisum Johanni de Lewes per Urbanum xix kalendas Februarii anno primo,[43] dimissa in arayratgiis in iii li. vi s. viii d., recepte fuerunt dicte iii li. vi s. viii d.

Summa recepte pagine xxii li. xiii s. iiii d.

### (fol. 68ᵛ) Saresbiriensis

De prebenda de Wermystr' (Warminster) in ecclesia Saresbiriensi, taxata v li., dimissa in arayratgiis in v li., de qua vacante per obitum Baldewyn de Moryn accaptatio facta per Bartholomeum de Braddon' fuit confirmata per Clementem vii ydus Septembris anno ix°,[44] recepte fuerunt pro complemento dicte reste v li.

De vicaria de Witewatham (White Waltham), non taxata nec dimissa in arayratgiis camere ratione provisionis facte de eadem per cardinalem Petragoricensem Henrico Coyn xviii kalendas Octobris pontificatus Domini Innocentii anno quinto,[45] recepte fuerunt pro medietate fructuum, informatione habita medio iuramento, iii li. vi s. viii d.[46]

De prebenda de Hull' (Hill Deverill) in ecclesia collegiata de Hertelbury (Heytesbury), taxata vi li. xiii s. iiii d., de qua per obitum Rotberti Trek' fuit provisum Thome Patricii per Clementem viii° ydus Martii anno ix°,[47] dimissa in arayratgiis in iii li. vi s. viii d., recepte fuerunt dicte iii li. vi s. viii d.

---

[32] In the margin bracketed against this item and the next: *Approbatum.*
[33] 29 April 1363.
[34] *quinti*, MS.
[35] 31 August 1357.
[36] In the margin: *explorata.*
[37] Peter de la Forêt, archbishop of Rouen, priest of Ss. XII Apostoli.
[38] 18 November 1358.
[39] In the margin: *non fuit dimissus pro beneficio taxato.*

[40] 12 January 1360.
[41] 15 May 1350.
[42] 4 July 1361.
[43] 14 January 1363.
[44] 7 September 1350.
[45] 14 September 1357.
[46] In the margin: *non est in arayratgiis camere.*
[47] 8 March 1351.

## Exoniensis

De prebenda ecclesie Exoniensis de qua per obitum Willemi de Brachele fuit provisum Henrico de Walthon' per Innocentium iii kalendas Martii anno primo,[48] dimissa in arayratgiis pro taxa ipsius in iiii li., recepte fuerunt dicte iiii li.

Summa recepte pagine xv li. xiii s. iiii d., quarum sunt de exploratis iii li. vi s. viii d.

(fol. 69) De prebenda ecclesie Exoniensis de qua per obitum Richardi de Tormenthon' et Willelmi de Brayley fuit provisum Adde de Ylton' per Innocentium iiii[to] nonas Julii anno nono,[49] dimissa in arayratgiis pro taxa ipsius in iiii li., recepte fuerunt dicte iiii li.

## Wygorniensis

De ecclesia de Kyrcchwich' (Knightwick), taxata iiii li. vi s. viii d., de qua ex causa permutationis fuit provisum ⟨Johanni⟩ de Chareneux' per Innocentium anno primo,[50] dimissa in arayratgiis in xxxiii s. iiii d., recepti fuerunt dicti xxxiii s. iiii d.

De ecclesia de Wylarddesey' (Willersey), de qua, vacante ex eo quod Johannes dictus Massan de Wynchecombe vicarum de Belbury (Blewbury) Saresbiriensis diocesis extitit asequtus, fuit provisum per cardinalem Petragoricensem Rotberto de Aldyngthon' iii kalendas Januarii pontificatus Domini Innocentii anno vi°,[51] et taxatur tota ecclesia ad vi li. xiii s. iiii d., et divisa fuit ipsa ecclesia in tres partes, quarum rector eius non recepit nisi unam partem que se extendit ad xliiii s. v d. ob., et non fuit dimissa in arayratgiis quia non fuerat data per Dominum Hugonem Pelegrini nec missa per cameram, set fuit postea explorata, recepti fuerunt in plenam satisfactionem dicti debiti xliiii s. v d. ob.[52]

Summa recepte pagine vii li. xvii s. ix d. ob. quarum sunt de exploratis ii li. iiii s. v d. ob.

(fol. 69[v]) De ecclesia de Clyve episcopi (Bishop's Cleeve) taxata xl li., acceptatio et collatio cuius facte per Richardum de Drayton' fuerunt eidem confirmate per Innocentium vii° kalendas Julii anno ix°,[53] dimissa in arayratgiis pro taxa ipsius in xl li., recepte fuerunt pro complemento dicte reste xl li.

## Bathoniensis et Wellensis

De vicaria de Hengstyng' (Henstridge), de cuius taxa adhuc non constat, de qua, vacante ex eo quod Rotbertus Thome, vicarius eiusdem, ecclesiam de Gylingham (Gillingham) Saresbiriensis diocesis fuit pacifice asequtus, fuit provisum per cardinalem Petragoricensem Radulpho Thome vi° kalendas Februarii pontificatus

Domini Innocentii anno vi°,[54] non dimissa in arayratgiis sed noviter explorata, recepte fuerunt in partem dicte taxe iiii li. vi s. viii d.[55]

De prebenda de Wyvelescombe (Wivelescombe), taxata xxvi li. xiii s. iiii d., de qua per obitum Johannis de Ufford, vel etiam si in vita sua vacaret, fuit provisum Willelmo de Bergeney per Clementem, dimissa in arayratgiis in xiii li. vi s. viii d., recepte fuerunt dicte xiii li. vi s. viii d.

De thesauraria Wellensi, taxata xxxiii li. vi s. viii d., confirmata Rotgero de Brompton' per Clementem ydus Novembris (fol. 70)[56] anno xi°,[57] dimissa in arayratgiis in v li., recepte fuerunt pro complemento dicte reste v li.

De prebenda et thesauraria Wellensibus, taxatis xxxiii li. vi s. viii d., de quibus per obitum Richardi de Tormenthon' fuit provisum cardinali Aquensi[58] per Innocentium ydus Novembris anno ix°,[59] dimissis in arayratgiis in dicta taxa, recepte fuerunt pro complemento ipsius xxxiii li. vi s. viii d.

De prebenda de Coy (Curry) in ecclesia Wellensi, taxata xx s., de qua nuper vacante per obitum Thome de Beuffort' fuit provisum Willelmo de Odecombe per cardinalem Petragoricensem nonas Julii pontificatus Domini Innocentii anno quinto,[60] non dimissa in arayratgiis sed postea explorata, recepti fuerunt dicti xx s.[61]

De prebenda et archidiaconatu Wellensibus, taxatis lxvi li. xiii s. iiii d., de quibus per obitum domini episcopi Tuschulani cardinalis[62] fuit provisum cardinali Carcassonensi[63] per Innocentium vii° kalendas Octobris anno ix°,[64] dimissis in arayratgiis pro taxa ipsius, recepte fuerunt pro complemento dicte taxe lxvi li. xiii s. iiii d.

## Norwicensis

De prioratu Sancte Fidis de Horsham, taxato clxxxiiii li., de quo per obitum Pontii de Cervera fuit provisum Benedicto Jory per Clementem viii kalendas Octobris anno vii° vel octavo,[65] dimisso in arayratgiis in xl li., recepte fuerunt pro complemento dicte reste xl li.

Summa recepte pagine cxlvi li. quarum sunt de exploratis xx s.

(fol. 70[v]) De ecclesia de Chemyngthon' (Chevington), taxata xvi li. xiii s. iiii d., que fuit confirmata Hugoni Impol per Innocentium vii° kalendas Februarii

---

[48] 27 February 1353.
[49] 4 July 1361.
[50] 1353.
[51] 30 December 1357.
[52] In the margin: *non est in arayratgiis camere.*
[53] 25 June 1361.
[54] 27 January 1358.
[55] In the margin: *non est in arayratgiis camere.*
[56] At the bottom of fol. 69[v]: *Summa recepte pagine lvii li. xiii s. iiii d. quarum sunt de exploratis iiii li. vi s. viii d.*
[57] 13 November 1352.
[58] Peter Itherii, bishop of Dax, priest of Ss. Quattro Coronati.
[59] 13 November 1361.
[60] 7 July 1357.
[61] In the margin: *non est in arayratgiis camere.*
[62] William de Court.
[63] Stephen Aubert, deacon of S. Maria in Aquiro.
[64] 25 September 1361.
[65] 24 September 1348 or 1349.

anno x°,⁶⁶ dimissa in arayratgiis in xvi li. xiii s. iiii d., **recepte fuerunt in partem dicte reste x li.⁶⁷**

### Eliensis

De vicaria de Ympryngthon' (Impington), taxata iiii li. vi s. viii d., ratione provisionis facte de eadem per cardinalem Petragoricensem Richardo de Shelford xiii kalendas Decembris pontificatus Domini Innocentii anno quinto,⁶⁸ non dimissa in arayratgiis sed explorata, recepte in partem dicte taxe ii li. iii s. iiii d.⁶⁹

### Lincoliensis

De decanatu Lincoliensi, taxato iiᶜ lxvi li. xiii s. iiii d., de quo per obitum Johannis electi Cantuariensis fuit provisum Symoni de Bryseley' per Clementem ydus Octobris anno viiº vel viiiº,⁷⁰ dimisso in arayratgiis in xiiii li. xiii s. iiii d., recepte fuerunt dicte xiiii li. xiii s. iiii d.

De prebenda de Longstow (Stowe Longa) in ecclesia Lincoliensi, taxata xlii li. vi s. viii d., de qua fuit provisum Reginaldo de Theminis per Innocentium xi kalendas Julii anno ixº,⁷¹ dimissa in arayratgiis pro taxa ipsius in xlii li. vi s. viii d., recepte fuerunt in partem dicte reste xxii li. x s.⁷²

Summa recepte pagine xlix li. vi s. viii d. quarum sunt de exploratis ii li. iii s. iiii d.

(fol. 71) De prebenda de Glatton' in ecclesia Lincoliensi, de qua per obitum Ade de Ylthon' fuit provisum Rotgero de Sutthon', dimissa in arayratgiis Domini Hugonis Pelegrini in iiii li. vi s. viii d., de quibus fuit per me responssum in aliis computis, set quia non est prebenda set ecclesia apellata de Glatthon' et taxatur xxi li. iii s. iiii d., dimissa per me in arayratgiis in xvi li. xvi s. viii d., recepte fuerunt pro complemento dicte reste xvi li. xvi s. viii d.

De ecclesia de Gordyngthon' (Godington), taxata iiii li. vi s. viii d., de qua vacante per obitum Thome de Bamborgh' fuit per cardinalem Petragoricensem provisum Rotberto Olmer' xvi kalendas Januarii pontificatus Domini Innocentii anno sexto,⁷³ non data michi in arayratgiis nec per me camere quia tunc nesciebam, set fuit postea explorata, recepte fuerunt pro complemento dicte taxe iiii li. vi s. viii d.⁷⁴

De prebenda de Bambury (Banbury) in ecclesia Lincoliensi, taxata xxx li., de qua per cardinalem Petra-

goricensem fuit provisum ⁷⁵ de Sterkeley, dimissa in arayratgiis in xxx li, recepte fuerunt pro complemento dicte reste xxx li.

De prebenda de Nasyngthon' (Nassington) in ecclesia Lincoliensi, taxata c li., ratione provisionis facte de eadem domino cardinali Carcassonensi,⁷⁶ recepte fuerunt in partem dicte taxe xlvi li. xviii s.⁷⁷

**Summa recepte pagine xcviii li. i s. iiii d.** quarum sunt de exploratis li li. iiii s. viii d.

(fol. 71ᵛ) De prebenda de Carlethon' cum Turleby (Carlton le Moorland cum Thurlby), taxata xxvi li. xiii s. iiii d., de qua fuit provisum Edwardo de Sherdestok' per resignationem Willelmi de Walcote per Innocentium kalendas Martii anno viº,⁷⁸ dimissa in arayratgiis in xiii li. vi s. viii d., recepte fuerunt in partem dicte reste vi li. xiii s. iiii d.⁷⁹

### Conwetrensis et Lichfeldensis

De ecclesia de Walton', taxata xliiii li., de qua fuit provisum Magistro Hugoni alias Johanni de Bolkyntton' per Innocentium iii nonas Decembris anno quinto,⁸⁰ dimissa in arayratgiis in vii li., recepte fuerunt pro complemento dicte reste vii li.

De ecclesia de Fylyngley' (Fillongley) ratione confirmationis facte de eadem priori et conventui de Maxstok' (Maxstoke), non dimissa in arayratgiis, recepte fuerunt pro taxa ipsius, que est xvi m. que valent x li. xiii s. iiii d., pro complemento dicte taxe x li. xiii s. iiii d.⁸¹

De ecclesia de Hodeneth (Hodnet) Lichfeldensis dyocesis, prebenda de Farendon (Faringdon) in ecclesia Saresbiriensi, de Mora (Moorfields, St. Giles Cripplegate) in ecclesia Londoniensi, de Hamdreton' (Hunderton) in ecclesia Herffordensi et de Ledbury in diocesi Herffordensi, de quibus fuit provisum Nicholao Heth', dimissis in arayratgiis in vᶜ et quinque fl. et medio et ii d. inter iiiiᵒʳ obligatos, recepte fuerunt in partem (fol. 72)⁸² dicte reste pro iiᶜ fl. camere, computando quolibet fl. pro iii s. et i d., xxx li. xvi s. viii d., et pro c fl. camere, quolibet eorum pro iii s. computato, xv li., et sic recepte fuerunt in summa pro dictis iiiᶜ fl. xlv li. xvi s. viii d.⁸³

---

⁶⁶ 26 January 1362.
⁶⁷ In the margin: *de residuis vi li. xiii s. iiii d. respondetur in arayratgiis.*
⁶⁸ 19 November 1357.
⁶⁹ In the margin: *non est in arayratgiis camere. De aliis xliii s. iiii d. respondetur in arayratgiis.*
⁷⁰ 15 October 1348 or 1349.
⁷¹ 21 June 1361.
⁷² In the margin: *de residuis xix li. xvi s. viii d. respondetur in arayratgiis.*
⁷³ 17 December 1358.
⁷⁴ In the margin: *non est in arayratgiis camere.*

⁷⁵ The Christian name is not given.
⁷⁶ Stephen Aubert, deacon of S. Maria in Aquiro.
⁷⁷ In the margin: *non est in libris meis nec camere quia michi non fuit data. De residuis liii li. ii s. respondetur in arayratgiis.*
⁷⁸ 1 March 1358.
⁷⁹ In the margin: *de residuis vi li. iii s. iiii d. respondetur in arayratgiis.*
⁸⁰ 3 December 1357.
⁸¹ In the margin: *non est in libris camere, set prior michi misit, nec dicit per quem factam fuit confirmationem nec quo tempore.*
⁸² At the end of fol. 71ᵛ: *Summa pagine xxiiii li. vi s. viii d. quarum sunt de exploratis x li. xiii s. iiii d.*
⁸³ In the margin: *de residuis iiᶜ v fl. medio et ii d. respondetur in arayratgiis.*

## Landawensis

De precentoria Landawensi, taxata v li. xiii s. iiii d., non dimissa michi in arayratgiis nec missa per cameram, ratione provisionis facte de eadem Magistro Philipo de Enyas per Innocentium ut ipse confitetur et dicit se teneri camere pro primis fructibus dicte precentorie in v li. xiii s. iiii d., de quibus responssum fuit in secundis computis meis de xl s., recepte fuerunt pro complemento dictorum fructuum iii li. xiii s. iiii d.

## Assawensis

De ecclesia de Dynlegh' (Denbigh), de qua, vacante de iure ut asseritur, fuit provisum Willelmo de Surderlond' per Clementem ydus Novembris anno ix,[84] dimissa in arayratgiis in vi li. xiii s. iiii d., recepte fuerunt in partem dicte reste iiii li. x s.[85]

## Menwensis

De hospitali Sancti David quondam regis quod concistit in ecclesia de Swynesey' (Swansea), taxata x li., cuius magister percipit duas partes et vicarius tertiam partem, confirmato David Martini per Innocentium iii kalendas Februarii anno ix°,[86] non dimissa in arayratgiis quia ipsius taxa non fuerat reperta, set (fol. 72ᵛ)[87] composuerat cum priore Lewensi pro medietate fructuum in iiii li., que fuerunt solute in aliis ultimis computis meis, recepte fuerunt in complemento taxe dictarum duarum partium, que taxa est vi li. xiii s. iiii d., videlicet ii li. xiii s. iiii d.[88]

## Eboracensis

De prebenda de Scharow (Sharow) in ecclesia collegiata Ripponensi, de qua, in Romana curia vacante per obitum Willelmi de Dirffelde, fuit provisum Thome de Hakton', non dimissa in arayratgiis quia nec michi data fuerat, recepte fuerant pro nova taxa ipsius v li.[89]

De eadem prebenda, taxata ad novam taxam v li., de qua per resignationem Richardi de Torresby fuit provisum ex causa permutationis B. de Cardalhaco per Innocentium xiiii kalendas Novembris anno quarto,[90] recepte fuerunt in complementum dicte taxe v li.[91]

De prebenda de Wystowe (Wistow) in ecclesia Eboracensi, taxata c li., et archidiaconatu eiusdem non

taxato, de quibus per obitum cardinalis Penestrini[92] fuit provisum cardinali Carcassonensi,[93] dimissis in arayratgiis pro taxa prebende in c li. et pro archidiaconatu in fructibus, recepte fuerunt in partem taxe dicte prebende lxxviii li. iii s. iiii d.[94]

Et in partem fructuum archidiaconatus, qui consistit in ecclesia de Mobesburch (Mexborough), procurationibus et synodalibus ac denariis Beati Petri, que omnia valent, ut patet per regestrum, lxvii li., recepte fuerunt in partem dictorum fructuum et reste dimisse xxviii li.[95]

Summa recepte pagine cxviii li. xvi s. viii d. quarum sunt de exploratis et non dimissis in arayratgiis xl li. xiii s. iiii d.

### (fol. 73) Dunelmensis

De ecclesia de Routhebury (Rothbury), taxata ad novam taxam lxvi li. xiii s. iiii d., cuius presentatio, institutio et in possessionem inductio auctoritate ordinaria facte de Johanne Marshall' fuerunt auctoritate appostolica eidem confirmate vel provisum de novo per Urbanum quinto nonas Martii anno primo,[96] dimissa in arayratgiis in dicta taxa, recepte fuerunt in partem dicte reste x li.[97]

Summa pagine patet.

Summa universalis predicte recepte de annatis benefficiorum precedentium, inclusis in ea xlv li. xvi s. viii d. receptis pro iiiᵉ fl. camere, est viᶜ xix li. vii s. vi d. ob., quarum sunt de exploratis vel non dimissis in arayratgiis cxxx li. x s. x d. ob.[98] Approbatum.

Summa arayratgiorum benefficiorum collatorum per Clementem, Innocentium et Urbanum usque ad iii kalendas Maii pontificatus sui anno primo[99] est iiᵐ iiiiᶜ ii li. vi s. x d. Item iiᶜ v fl. medius ii d. sterlingorum.

(fol. 74)[100] Sequitur recepta arayratgiorum de annatis benefficiorum collatorum per Dominum Urbanum in Anglia a tertio kalendas Maii pontificatus sui anno primo usque ad ii ydus Julii pontificatus sui anno quinto,[101] que arayratgia fuerunt per me in ultimis computis meis dimissa, et de aliis benefficiis postea collatis respondebitur infra.

### De diocesi Roffensi

De parochiali ecclesia de Sutdelond' (Snodland) Roffensis diocesis, taxata x li., de qua collatio et provisio ex causa permutationis auctoritate ordinaria facte

---

[84] 13 November 1350.
[85] In the margin: *de aliis ii li. iii s. iiii d. respondetur in arayratgiis.*
[86] 30 January 1361.
[87] At the foot of fol. 72: *Summa recepte pagine liiii li.* This is followed by the following deleted by lines: *xvi s. viii d. quarum sunt de non dimissis iii li. xiii s. iiii d.*
[88] In the margin: *non fuit dimissa in arayratgiis quia credebat integre fuisse satisfactum.*
[89] In the margin: *non est in arayratgiis camere.*
[90] 19 October 1356.
[91] In the margin: *non fuit data in arayratgiis, quia Dominus Hugo dixerat in suis arayratgiis quod non habuerat effectum ex causa in eis contenta.*

[92] Peter des Prés.
[93] Stephen Aubert, deacon of S. Maria in Aquiro.
[94] In the margin: *de residuis xxi li. xvi s. viii d. respondetur in arayratgiis.*
[95] In the margin: *michi non fuit dimissus pro beneffficio taxato. De residuis v li. x s. respondetur in arayratgiis.*
[96] 3 March 1363.
[97] In the margin: *de residuis lvi li. xiii s. iiii d. respondetur in arayratgiis.*
[98] Follows *cxxxiiii li. iii (?) s. xi d. ob.* deleted by lines.
[99] 29 April 1363.
[100] Folio 73ᵛ is blank.
[101] 14 July 1367.

Johanni de Abschaw fuerunt auctoritate appostolica confirmate vel provisum de novo per Urbanum ii kalendas Octobris anno secundo,[102] dimissa in arayratgiis pro dicta taxa, recepte fuerunt in complementum ipsius taxe et reste x li.[103]

## Londoniensis

De ecclesiis Sanctorum Stephani et Olavi in veteri Judeismo (St. Stephen, Coleman St. and St. Olave, Old Jewry) Londonie, non taxate, set composuit medio iuramento pro xv li., ratione provisionis facte de eiusdem ex causa permutationis cum Johanne de Loyham fuit provisum Raddulpho de Davwetr' per Urbanum vii kalendas Maii anno quarto,[104] dimissis in arayratgiis in v li., recepte fuerunt per complementum dicte reste v li.[105]

De ecclesia Sancti Benedicti de Greschirch' (St. Benet Gracechurch) Londonie, non taxata, ratione provisionis facte de eadem ex eadem causa permutationis cum supradictis ecclesiis Sanctorum Stephani et Olavi Johanni (fol. 74ᵛ)[106] de Lexam per Urbanum eadem die, qui composuit medio iuramento pro viii li., recepte fuerunt pro complemento dicte compositionis viii l.[103]

De decanatu ecclesie Londoniensis, taxato liii li. vi s. viii d., de quo vacato consecrationem Thome episcopi Roffensis, fuit provisum Johanni Appelby, legum doctori in Romana curia advocato, per Urbanum iii nonas Decembris anno secundo,[107] et debet dimittere parochialem ecclesiam de Whytheburn' (Whitburn) Dunelmensis diocesis ac hospitale pauperum de Kypren (Kepier) et parochialem ecclesiam de Routhebury (Rothbury), que nondum possidet et super quibus noscitur in palatio appostolico litigare, dimisso in arayratgiis in xl li, recepte fuerunt pro complemento dicte reste xl li.[108]

## Wynthoniensis

De prebenda de Tymberbury (Timsbury) in ecclesia monialium de Ramesey' (Romsey) ordinis Sancti Benedicti Wyntoniensis diocesis, taxata xxviii li. xiii s. iiii d., de qua, vacante per obitum Willelmi de Franleeh' extra Romanam curiam defuncti, fuit auctoritate ordinaria provisum Waltero de Sevenhuton', magistro in artibus, et subrogatus in omni iure quod competebat in ea Willelmo de Franleeh' et Andree de Wfford' per Urbanum ydus Julii anno primo,[109] dimissa in arayratgiis in vi li. xiii s. iiii d., recepte fuerunt pro complemento dicte reste vi li. xiii s. iiii d.[108]

Summa recepte pagine liiii li. xiii s. iiii d. quarum sunt de non taxatis viii li.

## (fol. 75) Saresbiriensis

De archidiaconatu Bakschir', qui dignitas est in ecclesia Saresbiriensi, taxato liiii li., de quo, vacante per consecrationem Johannis de Harwell' electi Bathoniensis, fuit provisum Alexandro de Dalby, clerico Lichfeldensis dyocesis, per Urbanum xix kalendas Februarii anno quinto,[110] dymissio in arayratgiis in liiii li. pro taxa ipsius, recepte fuerunt in partem dicte reste x li.[111]

De prebenda de Aulton inferiori alias Nortbury (North Alton) in ecclesia Saresbiriensi, taxata viii li., de qua, vacante per mortem Philipi de Codefford extra Romanam curiam defuncti, fuit provisum Johanni de Gymonchestr' presbytero per Urbanum xvi kalendas Decembris anno tertio,[112] dimissa in arayratgiis in dicta taxa, recepte fuerunt ab eodem in complementum dicte reste et taxe viii li.[108]

De perpetua vicaria parochialis ecclesie de Orffynthon' (Uffington) Saresbiriensis diocesis, non taxata, de qua ex causa permutationis fuit provisum Johanni de Astyng' per Urbanum iii ydus Januarii anno secundo,[113] dimissa in arayratgiis in iii li. vi s. viii d., recepte fuerunt pro complemento dicte reste iii li. vi s. viii d.[108]

De parochiali ecclesia de Stokton' (Stockton) Saresbiriensis diocesis, taxata vi li. xiii s. iiii d., de qua, vacante cum Johannes de Bokyngham parochialem ecclesiam de Harwe (Harrow) Londoniensis diocesis fuit pacifice asequtus, fuit provisum Waltero Malby per [114] (fol. 75ᵛ) Urbanum xii kalendas Decembris anno quarto,[115] dimissa in arayratgiis in iii li. vi s. viii d., recepte fuerunt pro complemento dicte reste iii li. vi s. viii d.[108]

De canonicatu et prebenda de Shaftesbury Saresbiriensis diocesis, que concistit in ecclesia de Gylyngham (Gillingham) eiusdem diocesis, taxata xxx li., de qua vacante per obitum Raymundi Pelegrini, collectoris appostolici, fuit provisum Richardo de Newton', clerico Lichfeldensis diocesis, per Urbanum xi kalendas Januarii anno quarto,[116] dimissa in arayratgiis in xx li., recepte fuerunt pro complemento dicte reste xx li.[108]

De prebenda de Durenfford (Durnford) in ecclesia Saresbiriensi, taxata xli li. xiii s. viii d., de qua, vacante dum Fortanerius de Calvomonte prioratum, canonicatum et prebendam ecclesie Sancte Radegundis (Poitiers) pacifice fuerit asequtus, fuit provisum Johanni de Stafford', clerico Saresbiriensis diocesis, per Ur-

---

[102] 30 September 1364.
[103] In the margin: *de non taxatis*.
[104] 25 April 1366.
[105] In the margin: *de taxatis*.
[106] At the foot of folio 74: *Summa recepte pagine xv li. quarum sunt de non taxatis x li.*
[107] 3 December 1363.
[108] In the margin: *de taxatis*.
[109] 15 July 1363.

[110] 14 January 1367.
[111] In the margin: *de non taxatis. De residuis xliiii li. respondetur in arayratgiis.*
[112] 16 November 1364.
[113] 11 January 1364.
[114] At the bottom of the page: *Summa recepte pagine xxi li. vi s. viii d. quarum sunt de non taxatis x li.*
[115] 20 November 1365.
[116] 22 December 1365.

banum xii kalendas Augusti anno quarto,[117] et debet dimittere parochialem ecclesiam de Chimarch' (Chilmark) eiusdem diocesis, dimissa in arayratgiis in dicta taxa, recepte fuerunt in partem dicte reste et taxe viii li. vi s. viii d.[118]

### Exoniensis

De archidiaconatu Totthonie in ecclesia Exoniensi, non taxato, cuius collatio et provisio facte ex causa permutationis cum ecclesia de Dodyngthon' (Doddington) Lincoliensis diocesis Willelmo Stel fuerunt eidem confirmate vel provisum de novo per Urbanum vii kalendas Maii anno primo,[119] dimisso in arayratgiis ratione archidiaconatus predicti in x li., recepte fuerunt pro complemento dicte reste x li.[108] Restat quod debetur annata pro dicta ecclesia de Dodyngthon'.

Summa recepte pagine xli li. xiii s. iiii d. quarum sunt de non taxatis viii li. vi s. viii d.

(fol. 76) De canonicatu et prebenda ecclesie Exoniensis, taxata iiii li., de quibus, vacantibus vel vacaturis dum Stephanus Panpel, legum doctor, decanatum Wellensem fuerit pacifice asequtus, fuit provisum Rotberto de Gymston', bacallario in legibus, per Urbanum vii kalendas Februarii anno tertio,[120] et debet dimittere parochialem ecclesiam de Clive (Cliffe) Roffensis diocesis nuper ei collatum et parochialem ecclesiam de Clive (Holme) dicte Norwicensis diocesis super qua litigat in curia, dimissa in arayratgiis pro taxa dicte prebende vel fructibus, recepte fuerunt pro complemento taxe ipsius prebende iiii li.[121]

De parochiali ecclesia de Essewatr' (Ashwater) Exoniensis diocesis, taxata xii li., de qua, vacante per mortem Magistri Richardi Griffardi, que tanto tempore vacavit quod eius collatio est ad sedem appostolicam legitime devoluta, fuit provisum Willelmo de Coddeworth', clerico[122] diocesis predicte bacallario in legibus, per Urbanum xviii kalendas Januarii anno secundo,[123] dimissa in arayratgiis in taxa vel fructibus, recepte fuerunt pro complemento dicte reste xii li.[121]

### Wygorniensis

De vicaria perpetua parochialis ecclesie Sancti Nicholay Brystolie, taxata v li., de qua collatio facta auctoritate ordinaria Thome Sprech', legum doctori, quam possidet pacifice etiam si reservata vel devoluta fuerit, fuit confirmata vel provisum de novo per Urbanum xiiii kalendas Februarii anno quinto,[124] dimissa in arayratgiis

in taxa vel fructibus, recepte fuerunt pro complemento dicte reste v li.[121]

Summa recepte pagine xxi li. de non taxatis.

(fol. 76ᵛ) De archidiaconatu Wygorniensi, non taxato, et ecclesia de Clamerdon' (Claverdon') eidem annexa, taxata x li. vi s. viii d., de quo, vacante eo quod Johannes Harwell' archidiaconatum Basckyrie (Berkshire) fuit pacifice asequtus, fuit provisum Symoni Clementis per Urbanum iii kalendas Februarii anno quarto,[125] et dimittet parochialem ecclesiam de Pymperne (Pimperne) Saresbiriensis diocesis, dimisso in arayratgiis in taxa vel fructibus, recepte fuerunt in partem fructuum archidiaconatus et taxe ecclesie xv li. iii s. iiii d.[121]

### Bathoniensis et Wellensis

De canonicatu et prebenda Wellensibus, que prebenda apellatur Yatton', taxata xxx li., de quibus vacaturis per consecrationem Thome de Mikllik' electi Cicestrensis fuit provisum Rotberto de Stratton', legum doctori, per Urbanum vii kalendas Decembris anno secundo,[126] et tenetur dimittere prebendam ecclesie collegiate de Aucheland' (Auckland) Dunelmensis diocesis, quam nondum possidet, dimissis in arayratgiis in dicta taxa vel fructibus, recepte fuerunt pro complemento dicte taxe xxx li.[121]

De decanatu ecclesie Wellensis, taxato c li., in quo subrogatus fuit Stephanus Pampel, legum doctor, in omni iure quod competebat Thome de Paxton, auditori palatii apostolici, qui super eo contra dictum Stephanum ad eundem auctoritate ordinaria electum litem movit, qui quidem Thomas postea iuri sibi competenti in eo expresse renuntiavit, per Urbanum x kalendas Januarii anno tertio,[127] et tenetur dimittere prebendas Exoniensem ac collegiatarum ecclesiarum Sancti Thome martiris de Glasweye (Glasnay) Exoniensis diocesis et de Abergwyll' (Abergwili) Menevensis,[128] dimisso in arayratgiis in lxxx li., recepte fuerunt in partem dicte reste lx li.[129]

Summa recepte pagine cv li. iii s. iiii d. quarum sunt de non taxatis xlv li. iii s. iiii d.

(fol. 77) De prebenda de Comba tertiadecima in ecclesia Wellensi, taxata v li. vi s. viii d., cuius collatio et provisio auctoritate ordinaria facte Johanni Beneit fuerunt eidem confirmate vel provisum de novo per Urbanum ii kalendas Septembris anno primo,[130] dimissa in arayratgiis in taxa vel in fructibus, recepte fuerunt in complementum dicte reste v li. vi s. viii d.[121]

### Herffordensis

De prebenda de Bromyerd (Bromyard), taxata viii

---

[117] 21 July 1366.
[118] In the margin: *de non taxatis. De aliis viii li. vi s. viii d. respondetur in arayratgiis.*
[119] 25 April 1363.
[120] 26 January 1365.
[121] In the margin: *de non taxatis.*
[122] Followed by *Lincoliensis* deleted by dots.
[123] 15 December 1363.
[124] 19 January 1367.

[125] 30 January 1366.
[126] 25 November 1363.
[127] 23 December 1364.
[128] *ecclesiarum* is repeated, MS.
[129] In the margin: *de taxatis. De aliis xx li. respondetur in arayratgiis.*
[130] 31 August 1363.

li., de qua, vacante vel vacatura dum Rotgerus de Frethon' canonicatum et prebendam de Newenton vulgariter nuncupata (North Newnton) in ecclesia de Wylton' Saresbiriensis diocesis fuerit pacifice assequtus vel alio quovis modo, fuit provisum Laurentio de Harppele, presbytero Norwicensis diocesis, per Urbanum iiii^to nonas Decembris anno quarto,[131] dimissa in arayratgiis in dicta taxa, recepte fuerunt pro complemento dicte reste viii li.[121]

### Norwicensis

De ecclesia de Bliklyng' (Blickling), taxata x li. xiii s. iiii d., cuius collatio et provisio auctoritate ordinaria facte Waltero de Reddenes fuerunt eidem confirmate per Urbanum iii kalendas Maii anno primo,[132] dimissa in arayratgiis pro parte taxe in v li. vi s. viii d., recepte fuerunt pro complemento dicte reste v li. vi s. viii d.[133]

De parochiali ecclesia de Barlesden' (Rattlesden), taxata xx li., de qua, vacante vel vacatura dum Rotgerus de Frethon' canonicatum et prebendam [134] de Newenthon' in ecclesia de Walthon' (Wilton) (fol. 77^v)[135] Saresbiriensis diocesis pacifice assequtus, fuit provisum Thome de Waderone, presbytero Eboracensis diocesis, per Urbanum vi ydus Aprilis anno tertio,[136] et tenetur dimittere canonicatum et prebendam ecclesie collegiate de Gleseney' (Glasnay) per dominum papam nuper ei collatas, dimissa in arayratgiis in taxa vel in fructibus, recepte fuerunt in partem dicte reste x li.[137]

### Lincoliensis

De parochiali ecclesia de Estwell' (Eastwell), taxata viii li., de qua fuit provisum ex causa permutationis cum vicaria parochialis ecclesie de Eython' iuxta Mekton' (Eaton near Melton Mowbray) Rogero Jude per Urbanum vii kalendas Junii anno secundo,[138] dymissa in arayratgiis in vi li., recepte fuerunt pro complemento dicte reste vi li.[133]

De parochiali ecclesia de Hokelme (Hockliffe), taxata viii li., de qua vacante in curia per obitum Johannis de Wynhull' fuit provisum Johanni de Armeston, presbytero per Urbanum vii kalendas Maii anno primo,[139] dimissa in arayratgiis in taxa vel fructibus, recepte fuerunt pro complemento dicte taxe viii li.[121]

De parochiali ecclesia de Hagwortyngham (Hagworthingham) taxata xii li., de qua, vacante ex eo quod Johannes de Sweysheved olim rector dicte ecclesie ecclesiam parochialem de Werelynsete (Wetheringsett)

Norwicensis diocesis est pacifice assequtus, fuit provisum Thome de Totfford' per Urbanum ii nonas Januarii anno secundo,[140] dimissa in arayratgiis in taxa vel fructibus, recepte fuerunt pro parte dicte taxe viii li.[141]

De prebenda de Milthon' (Milton Ecclesia) in ecclesia Lincoliensi, taxata xl li., de qua vacante vel vacatura per consecrationem Johannis de Harwell' electi in episcopum Bathoniensem fuit provisum Alexandro de Dalby (fol. 78)[142] per Urbanum xix kalendas Februarii anno quinto,[143] et tenetur dimittere decanatum curatum ecclesie Sancti Johannis Cestrie Lichfeldensis diocesis et expectationem ad prebendam Eboracensem et litem quam habet super prebenda de Termyn (Tarvin) in ecclesia Lichfeldensi, que taxatur xl li., dimissa in arayratgiis in taxa vel in fructibus, recepte fuerunt in complementum dicte taxe et reste xl li.[121]

### Conwetrensis et Lichfeldensis

De decanatu Sancti Johannis Cestrie, taxato xxvi li. xiii s. iiii d., de quo vacante per consecrationem Johannis de Harwell' electi Bathoniensis, fuit provisum Johanni de Wodehousse per Urbanum vii kalendas Januarii anno quinto,[144] dimisso in arayratgiis in taxa vel in fructibus, recepte fuerunt in partem dicte reste sive taxe xiii li. vi s. viii d.[145]

### Landavensis

De archidiaconatu ecclesie Landawensis, taxato xxi li., cuius collatio et provisio facte per principem Wallie Rotberto de Walsham eo quod vacabat tempore vacationis episcopatus Landawensis, licet post lapssum sex menssium a tempore vacationis sibi collatus fuerit, et per Thomam de Elteslee cui de eo per sedem appostolicam provisum extiterat in manibus domini cardinalis Wabrensi (Vabres)[146] apud sedem appostolicam fuisset resignatus, et tanquam de sic vacanti provisum fuisset per dominum papam Thome de Senthon', qui ipsum postmodum in manibus domini cardinalis Lemovicensis (Limoges)[147] apud eandem sedem resignavit, etiam si alio quovis modo vaccet, fuerunt confirmate vel provisum de novo per Urbanum v ydus Aprilis anno iiii^to,[148] dimisso in arayratgiis in taxa et cetera, recepte fuerunt pro complemento dicte reste xxi li.[121]

Summa recepte pagine lxxiiii li. vi s. viii d. de non taxatis.

---

[131] 2 December 1365.

[132] 29 April 1363.

[133] In the margin: *de taxatis*.

[134] Followed by *Norwicensis* deleted by dots.

[135] At the foot of folio 77: *Summa recepte pagine xviii li. xiii s. iiii d. quarum sunt de non taxatis xiii li. vi s. viii d.*

[136] 8 April 1365.

[137] In the margin: *de non taxatis. De aliis x li. respondetur in arayratgiis.*

[138] 26 May 1364.

[139] 25 April 1363.

[140] 4 January 1364.

[141] In the margin: *de non taxatis. De aliis iiii li. respondetur in arayratgiis.*

[142] At the bottom of folio 77^v: *Summa recepte pagine xxxii li. quarum sunt de non taxatis xxvi li.*

[143] 14 January 1367.

[144] 26 December 1366.

[145] In the margin: *de non taxatis. De aliis xiii li. vi s. viii d. respondetur in arayratgiis.*

[146] William Bragose, priest of S. Lorenzo in Lucina.

[147] Nicholas de Bessia, deacon of S. Maria in Via Lata.

[148] 9 April 1366.

(fol. 78ᵛ) Menevensis

De prebenda in ecclesia Sancti Mauricii de Alwewyll' (Abergwili), taxata xxxiii s. iiii d., de qua vacante per resignationem Johannis de Waltham fuit provisum Thome de Tettefford' per Urbanum quinto ydus Junii anno primo,[149] dimissa in arayratgiis in taxa vel fructibus, recepti fuerunt pro complemento dicte reste xxxiii s. iiii d.[121]

De ecclesia de Langladewen' (Llanglydwen), taxata xl s., de qua vacante per mortem Johannis Samssonis, ultimi rectoris eiusdem, in Romana curia defuncti, fuit provisum Philipo Layde alias dicti Pryton per Urbanum ii nonas Aprilis anno secundo,[150] dimissa in arayratgiis in xxx s., recepti fuerunt pro complemento dicte reste xxx s.[133]

### Eboracensis

De ecclesia de Ylkelay (Ilkley), taxata xvii li. vi s. viii d. iuxta novam taxam, de qua fuit dispenssatum cum Johanne Baugine, clerico Wygorniensis diocesis, ut ipsam possit licite retinere non obstante defectu natalium quem patitur de soluto genitus et soluta per Urbanum vii ydus Julii anno primo,[151] dimissa in arayratgiis in v li. vi s. viii d., recepte fuerunt pro complemento dicte reste v li. vi s. viii d.[133]

De prioratu Beate Marie Lancastrie, qui concistit in ecclesia Beate Marie Lancastrie, que taxatur lxxx li., a monasterio Sancti Martini Saginensis (Séez) ordinis Sancti Benedicti deppendente, de quo vacante per promotionem Petri abbatis dicti monasterii ad ipsum monasterium fuit provisum Willelmo Raymbaut, monacho dicti monasterii, per Urbanum vii kalendas Decembris anno quinto,[152] et tenetur dimitere officium baylivie dicti monasterii, dimisso in arayratgiis in lxxx li., recepte fuerunt in partem dicte reste lxx li.[153]

Summa recepte pagine lxxviii li. x s. quarum sunt de non taxatis i li. xiii s. iiii d.

(fol. 79) De archidiaconatu Northyngham in ecclesia Eboracensi, taxato xlii li. x s., de quo commissum fuit auditori cause pendentis in palatio appostolico inter Richardum Darby, presbyterum Lincoliensis diocesis, et Johannem de Brynkele ut, si dictus Johannes ius in eodem habere non possit, ipsum archidiaconatum preffato Richardo adiudicet et provideat de eodem per Urbanum xi kalendas Aprilis anno secundo,[154] dimisso in arayratgiis in taxa vel fructibus, recepte fuerunt pro complemento dicte reste xvii li. x s.[121]

De ecclesia Sancti Martini in Mikelgate (Micklegate, York), de qua ex causa permutationis cum ecclesia de Aldyngham (Addingham) fuit provisum Johanni Stayff,

per Urbanum xix kalendas Januarii anno quinto,[155] non dimissa in arayratgiis quia ipsam non habebam, recepte fuerunt pro taxa iiii li. xiii s. iiii d.[121]

De ecclesia de Aldyngham proxime dicta, de qua ex simili causa permutationis cum ecclesia supradicta Sancti Martini fuit provisum Willelmo de Rippon' eadem die, non dimissa in arayratgiis ex causa premissa, recepte fuerunt pro complemento taxe dicte ecclesie, que est x li.,[156] x li.[121]

De vicaria de Kernetby (Carnaby) alias dicta Fraysthorp (Fraisthorpe), taxata x li., de qua vacante per obitum quondam Willelmi de Appelby extra Romanam curiam defuncti fuit provisum Johanni de Skylling' per Urbanum ii kalendas Novembris anno secundo,[157] dimissa in arayratgiis in taxa vel fructibus, recepte fuerunt pro complemento taxe x li.[121]

### Dunelmensis

De vicaria parochialis ecclesie Sancti Nicholay Novi Castri (Newcastle) Dunelmensis diocesis, taxata x li. iuxta novam taxam, de qua, vacante per obitum ultimi vicarii eiusdem extra Romanam curiam deffuncti, acceptatio, collatio et provisio facte vigore litterarum appostolicarum (fol. 79ᵛ)[158] Matheo de Bolthon', qui eam per x annos possedit pacifice, reservationibus non obstantibus, fuerunt confirmate vel provisum de novo per Urbanum xi kalendas Maii anno tertio,[159] dimissa in arayratgiis in v li., recepte fuerunt pro complemento dicte reste v li.[133]

De cappellania seu hospitali Sancti Edmundi regis et martiris de Gatesheved' (Gateshead) Dunelmensis diocesis, taxata iii li. vi s. viii d., de qua per mortem quondam Walteri Francoberg' extra Romanam curiam defuncti fuit provisum Adde de Fenrothr' per Urbanum xi kalendas Aprilis anno secundo,[154] dimissa in arayratgiis in taxa vel fructibus, recepte fuerunt in complementum ipsius taxe et reste iii li. vi s. viii d.[121]

De ecclesia de Wesyngthon' (Washington) Dunelmensis diocesis, taxata xxxiii li. vi s. viii d. secundum antiquam taxam et secundum novam xxii li. x s., de qua, vacante ex eo quod Rotbertus de Wardetop' patiens defectum natalium de soluto genitus et soluta eam per duos annos et ultra tenuit nulla dispenssatione super hoc optenta, fuit provisum Thome de Pentech', presbytero Karleolensis diocesis, per Urbanum vii kalendas Maii anno primo,[160] dimissa in arayratgiis in dicta taxa, recepte fuerunt pro complemento dicte nove taxe, reservata potestate exigendi antiquam taxam si debeatur, xxii li. x s.[133]

---

[149] 9 June 1363.
[150] 4 April 1364.
[151] 9 July 1363.
[152] 25 November 1366.
[153] In the margin: *de taxatis. De aliis x li. respondetur in arayratgiis.*
[154] 22 March 1364.

[155] 14 December 1366.
[156] Followed by *dicte* deleted by a line.
[157] 31 October 1364.
[158] At the foot of fol. 79: *Summa recepte pagine de non taxatis xlii li. iii s. iiii d.*
[159] 21 April 1365.
[160] 25 April 1363.

Summa recepte pagine xxx li. xvi s. viii d. quarum sunt de non taxatis xxv li. xvi s. viii d.

Summa universalis recepte istorum benefficiorum collatorum per Dominum Urbanum tempore supradicto est v^c xxxv li. vi s. viii d. quarum sunt de benefficiis non dimissis pro taxa ii^c lxxxv li. xvi s. viii d. Approbatum. Et de taxatis ii^c xlix li. x s.[161]

(fol. 80^v)[162] Sequitur recepta de annatis benefficiorum collatorum in Anglia per Dominum Urbanum a ii ydus Julii pontificatus sui anno quinto[163] usque ad viii^o kalendas Martii pontificatus sui anno viii^o[164] quia de ulteriori tempore benefficia a camera non recepi.

### Londoniensis

De archidiaconatu Exessie, non taxato, ratione provisionis facte de eodem Henrico de Wynterton, in utroque iure bacallario, per Urbanum xv kalendas Februarii anno vi^o,[165] qui computavit pro fructibus omnibus dicti archidiaconatus preter procurationes vi li. x s., recepte fuerunt pro medietate dictorum fructuum iii li. v s. Istam provisionem non habeo in benefficiis michi datis per cameram set reformationem gratie sub data xiiii kalendas Julii anno vi^o.[166]

De parochiali ecclesia Sancti Benedicti de Graschirche (St. Benet Gracechurch) Londonie, non taxata, ratione confirmationis facte Johanni de Lexham, qui eam per annum et ultra possedit pacifice, etiam si fuerit reservata vel devoluta, per Urbanum viii kalendas Junii anno vi^o,[167] qui composuit medio iuramento pro medietate veri valoris in viii li., recepte fuerunt in partem dicte compositionis vi li.[168]

De parochiali ecclesia de Alta Botyng' (High Roding), taxata xii li., de qua ex causa permutationis cum ecclesia de Norwolde (Northwold) Norwicensis diocesis fuit provisum Benedicto de[169] Sauter' per Urbanum xi kalendas Martii anno vi^o,[170] recepte fuerunt in partem dicte taxe vi li.[171]

Summa recepte pagine xv li. v s.

### (fol. 81) Saresbiriensis

De prebenda de Fordygnthon' (Fordington), taxata xvi li. xiii s. iiii d., de que vacante per consecrationem Willelmi de Wykeham episcopi Wynthoniensis fuit provisum Reginaldo de Cobham per Urbanum xiii kalendas

Februarii anno vi^o,[172] recepte fuerunt pro complemento dicte taxe xvi li. xiii s. iiii d.

De vicaria parochialis ecclesie de Wermynstr' (Warminster), taxata v li., de qua ex causa permutationis cum ecclesia de Templecombe Wellensis diocesis fuit provisum Thome Hotyngis per Urbanum xix kalendas Januarii anno vi^o,[173] recepte fuerunt pro complemento dicte taxe v li.

### Norwicensis

De ecclesia de Nortwod' (Northwold), taxata xli m. que valent xxvii li. vi s. viii d., de qua ex causa permutationis cum ecclesia de Altabotyng' (High Roding) Londoniensis diocesis fuit provisum Johanni de Glatton' per Urbanum xi kalendas Martii anno sexto, recepte fuerunt in partem dicte taxe xiiii li.[174]

De ecclesia de Fornham, taxata viii li., cuius collatio facta vigore litterarum appostolicarum in forma communi Willelmo Adany, presbytero Norwicensis diocesis, super qua lis pendebat inter Willelmum Treswelle, tunc possessorem auctoritate ordinaria, qua lite pendente idem Willelmus extra Romanam curiam decessit, fuit confirmata vel provisum de novo et subrogatus in omni iure competenti dicto defuncto per Urbanum viii kalendas Martii anno vi^o,[175] recepti fuerunt in partem dicte taxe xxvi s. viii d.[176]

Summa recepte pagine xxxvii li.

(fol. 81^v) De ecclesia de Turston' (Thurston), taxata xx li., de qua acceptatio et provisio facte vigore litterarum appostolicarum per Rotbertum de Fordham, presbyterum Norwicensis diocesis, per obitum Rotberti de Torpp', ultimi rectoris eiusdam, licet in impetratione dicte gratie mentionem non fecisset de quadam gratia sibi facta de parochiali ecclesia de Stretham Eliensis diocesis certo modo vacatura, fuerunt confirmate vel provisum de novo per Urbanum x kalendas Februarii anno septimo,[177] recepte fuerunt in partem dicte reste x li.[178]

### Lincoliensis

De vicaria de Kerdyngthon' (Cardington), non taxata, de qua ex causa permutationis cum vicaria de Stokffeld' (Stotfold?) fuit provisum Thome Sunych per Urbanum vii ydus Martii anno vi^o,[179] qui composuit medio iuramento pro mediis fructibus in xl s., recepti fuerunt pro complemento dicte compositionis xl s.

De vicaria de Stokffelde (Stotfold?) predicta, non taxata, de ⟨qua⟩ ex simili causa fuit provisum Rad-

---

[161] In the margin: *de aliis xxx li. respondetur in arayratgiis.*
[162] The recto of folio 80 is blank.
[163] 14 July 1367.
[164] 22 February 1370.
[165] 18 January 1368.
[166] 18 June 1368.
[167] 25 May 1368.
[168] In the margin: *de aliis ii li. respondetur in arayratgiis.*
[169] Followed by *S* deleted by a dot.
[170] 20 February 1368.
[171] In the margin: *de aliis vi li. respondetur in arayratgiis.*

[172] 20 January 1368.
[173] 14 December 1367.
[174] In the margin: *de aliis xiii li. vi s. viii d. respondetur in arayratgiis.*
[175] 23 February 1368.
[176] In the margin: *de aliis vi li. xiii s. iiii d. respondetur in arayratgiis.*
[177] 23 January 1369.
[178] In the margin: *de aliis x li. respondetur in arayratgiis.*
[179] 9 March 1368.

dulpho de Berefford', recepti fuerunt in partem fructuum xiii s. iiii d.

De archidiaconatu Oxonie, non taxato, et ecclesia de Ystele (Iffley) eidem annexa, taxata xiiii li. xiii s. iiii d., de quo vacante per obitum domini cardinalis Aquensis [180] fuit provisum Magistro Thome de Southam per Urbanum viii ydus Augusti anno quinto,[181] recepte fuerunt in partem solutionis primorum fructuum archidiachonatus et taxe ecclesie x li.

De ecclesia de Barawell' (Barwell), taxata xxiii li. vi s. viii d., de qua collatio et provisio auctoritate ordinaria facte Laurentio de Ibstok', presbytero Lincoliensis diocesis, fuerunt eidem confirmate vel provisum de novo per Urbanum xi kalendas Februarii anno viiⁿ,[182] recepte fuerunt in partem dicte taxe xiii li. vi s. viii d.[183]

Summa recepte pagine xxxvi li.

### (fol. 82) Assawensis

De vicaria parochialis ecclesie de Cogitva (Cegidfa or Guilsfield), non taxata, de qua collatio et provisio dudum facte auctoritate ordinaria Johanni de Apiorwerth', quamvis ipsam per tres mensses antequam xxv etatis sue annum atigisset possederat, fructus ex ea percipiendo, fuerunt confirmate vel provisum de novo et mandatum fuit ipsum habilitari per Urbanum ydus Martii anno sexto,[184] recepte fuerunt in partem fructuum iii li. vi s. viii d.

### Eboracensis

De prebenda in ecclesia collegiata Sancti Johannis Beverlaci, videlicet ad altare Beate Marie, taxata xvi li., de qua nuper vacante per consecrationem Wyllelmi de Wykeham episcopi Wynthoniensis fuit provisum Philipo de Weston' per Urbanum xiii kalendas Februarii anno viⁿ,[185] recepte fuerunt in complementum dicte taxe xvi li.

De prebenda de Wygthon' (Weighton) in ecclesia Eboracensi, taxata xl li., de qua vacante per obitum Thome de Bukthon' et reservata fuit provisum Willelmo de Ganthorp' per Urbanum xiii kalendas Februarii anno sexto,[185] recepte fuerunt in complementum dicte taxe xl li.

De prebenda Dunham in ecclesia collegiata de Sutwell' Eboracensis diocesis, taxata xxxvi li. xiii s. iiii d., de qua vacante per consecrationem Willelmi de Wykeham episcopi Wynthoniensis fuit provisum Johanni de Capeden' per Urbanum xiii kalendas Februarii anno sexto,[185] recepte fuerunt pro complemento dicte taxe xxxvi li. xiii s. iiii d.

Summa recepte pagine xcvi li.

(fol. 82ᵛ) De prioratu de Kertmellis (Cartmel) ordinis Sancti Augustini, taxato xi li. vi s. viii d. iuxta novam taxam, ad quem prioratum vacantem per liberam resignationem et cetera electio concorditer facta ad eundem de fratre Richardo de Kellet, canonico eiusdem ecclesie, et confirmatio auctoritate ordinaria subsequta fuerunt confirmate vel provisum de novo per Urbanum nonas Martii anno septimo,[186] recepte fuerunt in partem [187] dicte taxe vi li.[188]

De prebenda de Lagthon' in Mortyng' (Laughton en le Morthen) in ecclesia Eboracensi, taxata c et x m. que valent lxxiii li. vi s. viii d., de qua vacante per consecrationem Willelmi de Wykeham episcopi Wynthoniensis fuit provisum Johanni de Bokyngham per Urbanum xiii kalendas Februarii anno vi,[185] recepte fuerunt pro complemento dicte taxe lxxiii li. vi s. viii d.

### Dunelmensis

De prebenda in ecclesia collegiata de Langcestr' (Lanchester), taxata vi li. xiii s. iiii d., de qua vacante per obitum Johannis Nesbyt in Romana curia defuncti fuit provisum Johanni de Babyngle per Urbanum iii kalendas Decembris anno viⁿ,[189] recepte fuerunt in partem taxe iiii li.[190]

Summa recepte pagine lxxxiii li. vi s. viii d.

Summa universalis de annatis beneficiorum collatorum per Dominum Urbanum a ii ydus Julii pontificatus sui anno quinto [191] usque ad viii [192] kalendas Martii pontificatus eiusdem anno viiiⁿ [193] quia de ulteriori tempore non recepi cclxvii li. xi s. viii d. Approbatum.

(fol. 83) Summa maior et universsalis totius recepte de annatis beneficiorum collatorum per dominos Clementem, Innocentium et Urbanum usque ad octavo kalendas Martii pontificatus sui anno octavo [193] est mccccxxii li. v s. x d. ob. sterlingorum Approbatum.

Quarum sunt de arayratgiis dominorum Clementis et Innocentii ac Urbani usque ad tertio kalendas Maii pontificatus sui anno primo [194] cccclxxxviii li. xvi s. viii d.

Et de exploratis et non taxatis de tempore supradicto cxxx li. x s. x d. ob.

Et de beneficiis collatis per Dominum Urbanum a tertio kalendas Maii pontificatus sui anno primo [194] usque ad ii ydus Julii pontificatus sui anno quinto [191] dimissis pro taxa ccxlix li. x s.

Et de eisdem beneficiis in quibus taxa non fuit expressa cclxxxv li. xvi s. viii d.

---

[180] Peter Itherii, bishop of Dax, bishop of Albano.
[181] 6 August 1367.
[182] 22 January 1369.
[183] In the margin: *de aliis x li. respondetur in arayratgiis.*
[184] 15 March 1368.
[185] 20 January 1368.

[186] 7 March 1369.
[187] Follows *complementum* deleted by a line.
[188] In the margin: *de aliis v li. vi s. viii d. respondetur in arayratgiis.*
[189] 29 November 1367.
[190] In the margin: *de aliis ii li. xiii s. iiii d. respondetur in arayratgiis.*
[191] 14 July 1367.
[192] *vii*, MS.
[193] 22 February 1370.
[194] 29 April 1363.

Et de benefficiis collatis per Dominum Urbanum a ii ydus Julii pontificatus sui anno quinto [191] usque ad octavo kalendas Martii pontificatus sui anno octavo [193] cclxvii li. xi s. viii d.

(fol. 83[v]) Sequitur recepta de fructibus obvenientibus tempore vacationis.

De thesauraria ecclesie Wellensis, vacante per obitum cardinalis Aquensis,[195] recepte fuerunt in partem solutionis fructuum qui venerunt tempore vacationis eiusdem thesaurarie, que modicum vacavit quia statim rex eam contulit iure regalie, vii li. iiii s. ob. Reservata potestate exigendi a thesaurario dicte thesaurarie iiii li. pro conssimilibus fructibus eidem venditis per Magistrum Thomam de Chepthon, firmarium dicte thesaurarie.

De archidiaconatu Exonie (Oxford) pro fructibus obvenientibus tempore vacationis eiusdem per obitum Domini Petri cardinalis Aquensis recepte fuerunt per manus domini episcopi Lincoliensis [196] xxi li. vii s.

De archidiaconatu Lincoliensi pro fructibus obvenientibus tempore vacationis eiusdem per consecrationem Willelmi de Wykham episcopi Wynthoniensis recepte fuerunt a domino episcopo Lincoliensi xvii li.

Summa recepte pagine xlv li. xi s. ob. Approbatum.

(fol. 84) Sequitur recepta de legatis ad Terram Sanctam et cameram appostolicam

De exequtoribus testamenti Magistri Thome de Bukthon' pro bonis Domini Willelmi de Braydeley' in testamento dicti Magistri Thome legatis xx li.

De exequtoribus testamenti domini episcopi Exoniensis nuper deffuncti pro ii[c] fl. legatis camere appostolice xxxi li. xiii s. iiii d.

De primario domini episcopi Lincoliensis in recompenssationem expenssarum et oblationum quas Matildis Gilbos, que votum suum de visitando limina appostolorum propter corporis debilitatem non potuit adimplere, in eundo et reddeundo et offerendo fecisset iuxta litteram domini primarii super hoc directtam recepti [197] fuerunt xxvii s.

Summa recepte pagine liii li. iiii d. Approbatum.

Summa universsalis omnium premissarum receptarum denariorum Beati Petri, annui censsus, de annatis befficiorum, fructibus venientibus tempore vacationis et legatis camere appostolice et Terre Sancte est ii[m] xlv li. ii s. Item ultra predicta fuerunt recepte ad nomen Hugonis Pelegrini ex causis in breveto contentis viii li. ii s. Approbatum.

(fol. 84[v]) Sequntur expensse facte ratione officii tempore supradicto

Primo fuerunt expensse in tribus annis iam transactis pro diverssis nuntiis missis ad diverssos prelatos Anglie cum diverssis processibus tangentibus negotia eiusdem camere et diverssis vicibus viii li. iiii s. iiii d.

Item anno LXIX[o] de mensse Maii ego, exeuns Brugis, misi pro negotiis camere unum familiarem meum ad faciendum et procurandum quod de pecuniis ibidem recollectis pro camera antedicta fieret cambium propter guerram de qua tunc in illis partibus timebatur, quia nondum receperam mandatum de tradendis dictis pecuniis Albertis Antiquis nec ipsi habebant mandatum a magistris suis recipiendi easdem, et stetit tam in eundo, stando quam redeundo per xvi dies, et expendit tam pro transsitu maris quam pro aliis expensis ii li. x s. sterlingorum.

Item eodem anno de mensse Augusti recepi commissiones domini nostri pape et domini camerarii ad levandum certa specialia debita in Anglia, et ad levandum annatas de benefficiis per impetrantes acceptatis, et ad levandum peccunias levatas de procurationibus contra prohibitionem pape, et certa benefficia in illis partibus collata, que omnia ter feci copiari propter viarum pericula, et misi ad Angliam interdum per Albertos, interdum per alios, propter predicta pericula, et expendi pro omnibus, videlicet pergamenis, scriptoribus sive notariis, cordonibus, cera et nuntiis iii li.

Item feci copiari receptas et asignationes meas de toto tempore meo de collectoria Anglie quas misi domino camerario ut mandabat et constitit quod fuerunt duplicate iii s. sterlingorum.

Summa expenssarum pagine xiii li. xvii s. iiii d. sterlingorum.

(fol. 85) Item misi anno LXVIII de mensse Novembris ad Angliam benefficia collata in illis partibus et dedi uni famulo mercatorum ut illa fideliter traderet vi s. sterlingorum.

Item misi anno LXX[o] de mensse Januarii ad Angliam ad faciendum copiari taxas benefficiorum iuxta mandatum domini camerarii, et dedi famulo iii fl. qui valent ix s. sterlingorum.

Item pro loquerio hospitii collectoris et genitum suarum sive substitutorum, pro quo, cum nichil aliud a camera recipiat, conssuevit computare pro quolibet anno vi li. xiii s. iiii d., pro tribus annis inceptis xviii die Februarii anno a nativitate domini et cetera LXVIII et transactis eadem die eiusdem menssis anno LXXI[o] xx li.

Summa pagine xx li. xv s.

Summa maior dictarum expenssarum xxxiiii li. xii s. iiii d.

(fol. 85[v]) Sequntur asignationes facte camere appostolice de pecuniis supradictis

Primo fuerunt asignate camere appostolice in Viterbio anno domini MCCCLXIX[o] die ultima menssis Augusti per manus Philipi Astacii et Bernardi de Podissano de Luca in iii[m] v[c] fl. ponderis camere, quolibet dictorum florenorum pro iii s. et i d. sterlingorum computato, v[c] xxxix li. xi s. viii d. sterlingorum.[198]

---

[195] Peter Itherii, bishop of Dax, bishop of Albano.
[196] *episcopi* repeated MS.
[197] *recepte*, MS.

[198] Bracketed against this and the other items on this page: *docuit de istis omnibus per litteras camere.*

Item fuerunt asignate camere appostolice die xxiiii menssis Januarii anno LXX° per Johannem Bandini, factorem societatis Albertorum Antiquorum, mercatorum de Florentia, in m ix^c lxx fl. camere et ii s. monete Avinionie, quolibet dictorum fl. pro iii et tribus quartis unius denarii sterlingorum computato, ccc li. sterlingorum.

Item fuerunt asignate camere appostolice Rome die xx Martii anno LXX° per manus Justi Bonaviti, factoris societatis Albertorum Antiquorum, mercatorum de Florentia, in m iiii^c xiiii fl. ponderis camere xxiii s. iiii d. monete Avinionie, quolibet dictorum fl. ut supra computato, ccxv li. ix s. ii d. sterlingorum.

Item fuerunt assignate camere appostolice die quinta menssis Septembris anno LXX° per manus Thome Moris, factoris societatis Albertorum Antiquorum, mercatorum de (fol. 86)[199] Florentia, in mcccclxxxxiiii fl.[200] auri ponderis camere xiii s. et iii d. monete Avinionie, quolibet dictorum fl. pro iii s. et ob. sterlingorum cum xiii partibus ducentarum lxxviii partium unius sterlingi computato, ii^c xxvi li. i s. ii d. ob. sterlingorum.

Item fuerunt asignate camere appostolice in Avinionia die xiii menssis Februarii anno LXXI° per manus Albertorum Antiquorum predictorum, me presente, in m v^c fl. camere, quolibet dictorum fl. pro iii s. et i d. sterlingorum computato, ii^c xxxi li. v s. sterlingorum.[201]

Item fuerunt restitute Johanni de Wedlynburgh', thesaurario Cicestrensi, virtute cuiusdam commissionis domini camerarii, que ab eodem indebite fuerant recepta ratione cuiusdam ficte et simulate confirmationis dicte thesaurarie impetrate maliciose pro predecessore suo, qui ea non indigebat nec eam habuit ratam vel gratam; ymo ei quum primum ad eius devenit notitiam cum instrumento publico renuntiavit, xxx li. sterlingorum.[202]

Item fuerunt assignate camere appostolice in Avinionia die ultima menssis Februarii anno LXXI° per manus Albertorum Antiquorum, mercatorum de Florentia, in ii^m cccxci fl. ponderis camere et xxv s. monete Avinionie, quolibet dictorum fl. (fol. 86^v)[203] pro tribus s. et i d. sterlingorum computato, iii^c lxviii li. xv s.[201]

Item fuerunt asignate eidem camere appostolice per predictum Dominum Johannem in Avinionia die xxix menssis Martii anno LXXI° in vii^c fl. camere, quolibet eorum pro tribus s. et i d. sterlingorum computato, cvii li. xviii s. iiii d.[201]

Summa pagine iiii^c lxxvi li. xiii s. iiii d. Approbatum.

Summa universalis omnium predictorum assignatorum et restitutiorum est ii^m xix li. iiii^or d. ob. Approbatum. In xii^m ix^c lix fl. camere iii li. iii s. vii monete

Avinionie et in xxx li. sterlingorum in sua specie restitutis.[204]

(fol. 87) Computus brevis redditus camere appostolice per Dominum Johannem de Cabrespino, canonicum Narbonensem in regno Anglie preffate camere collectorem, anno domini M° CCC° LXXI° de mensse Aprilis de omnibus receptis, levatis, expenssis, solutis et asignatis tam per eum quam per suos substitutos de dicta collectoria ad cameram predictam pertinentibus a xviii die menssis Februarii anni domini M° CCCLXVIII usque ad festum Omnium Sanctorum anni domini M CCC° LXX

Et est sciendum quod predictus Dominus Johannes per finem et conclusionem ulteriorum computorum suorum prefate camere appostolice redditorum in Monteflaschone (Montefiascone) anno domini MCCCLXVIII de mensse Augusti remanssit debens eidem camere cl fl. de crozeta, quos ab eadem camera receperat anno LXIII° cum primo ad Angliam fuit missus, qui quidem (fol. 87^v) cl fl. in libris camere inter mutua ipsius etiam sunt scripti ubi debent cancellari prout tunc tempus fuit ordinatum, sed debent solvi hic prout ipse computat in finem.

Postquam idem Dominus Johannes computat primo se recepisse de restis sive arayratgiis denariorum Beati Petri in aliis predictis computis dimissis, que reste sive arayratgia fuerunt in summa vera v^c xcix li. xi s. iiii d., iiii^c lxxi li. xi s. viii d. sterlingorum. Approbatum.

Et sic restat adhuc deberi de dictis arayratgiis prout infra data in restis cxxvii li. xix s. viii d. Approbatum.[205]

Item computat se recepisse de recepta ordinaria dictorum denariorum postea contingente, videlicet de annis LXIX° et LXX°, xliiii li. x s. Approbatum.

(fol. 88) Et sic aparet adhuc deberi de ordinaria recepta dictorum annorum LXIX et LXX, prout infra in restis datur, iii^c liiii li. viii d.[205]

Et sic est summa totius recepte denariorum Beati Petri v^c xvi li. i s. viii d. sterlingorum. Approbatum.

Summa vera restarum dictorum denariorum est iiii^c lxxxii li. iiii d. Approbatum.[205]

(fol. 88^v) Item computat se recepisse de restis sive arayratgiis annui censsus, que reste sive arayratgia fuerunt in summa, incluso anno LXVIII° dumtaxat, x li. viii s. vii d., iii li. xii s. i d. Approbatum.

Et sic restat adhuc deberi de dictis restis, prout infra datur, vi li. xvi s. vi d. Approbatum.[205]

Item computat se recepisse de ordinaria recepta dicti censsus postea contingente, videlicet de annis LXIX et LXX°, iiii li. xi s. Approbatum.

Et sic restat adhuc deberi de annuo censsu pro dictis duobus annis LXIX et LXX° iiii li. xix s.[205]

Et sic est summa totius recepte annui censsus viii li. iii s. i d. Approbatum.

---

[199] At the foot of fol. 85^v: *Summa pagine mlv li. x d. Approbatum.*

[200] *fl.* repeated MS.

[201] In the margin: *docuit.*

[202] In the margin: *docuit de comissione, informatione et restitutione.*

[203] At the foot of fol. 86: *Summa pagine iiii^c lxxxvii li. vi s. ii d. ob. Approbatum.*

[204] *restititutis*, MS.

[205] In the margin: *resta.*

Summa vero restarum annui censsus est, ut infra datur, non incluso anno LXXIᵒ, xi li. xv s. vi d. Approbatum.

(fol. 89) Item computat se recepisse de restis sive arayratgiis beneffciorum collatorum per Dominos Clementem et Innocentium ac Urbanum usque ad iiiᵒ kalendas Maii pontificatus sui anno primo [206] ultra restam archidiaconatus Midelssexie in ecclesia Londoniensi collati domino cardinali Rothomagensi [207] et restam hospitalis Sancti David in ecclesia Menwensi collati David Martini, que duo beneffcia fuerunt dimissa pro non taxatis, que resta vera fuit iiᵐ ixᶜ ii li. i s. vi d., iiiiᶜ lxxxviii li. xvi s. viii d. Approbatum.

In qua summa includuntur iiiᶜ fl. camere recepti de resta florenorum dimissa, que fuit vᶜ v fl. medius camere ii d. sterlingorum in xlv li. xvi s. viii d. dicte monete, quolibet de iiᶜ fl. predictus pro iii s. i d. et quolibet fl. de aliis c pro tribus s. steringorum computato.

Et restat adhuc deberi de eisdem restis sive arayratgiis, inclusis restis prebende de Nasyngthon' (Nassington) in ecclesia Lincoliensi collate domino cardinali Carcassonensi [208] et archidiaconatus Eboracensis collati eidem et vicarie de Ympryngthon' (Impington) diocesis Eliensis, que (fol. 89ᵛ) beneffcia non erant in libris camere quia sibi data non fuerant, prout infra datur in restis, iiᵐ iiiiᶜ ii li. vi s. x d., iiᶜ v fl. medium ii d. sterlingorum.[205]

In qua resta non includuntur beneffcia Ybernie que michi debantur in resta antiqua, quia postea fuerunt tradita novo collectori ibidem deputato, ut infra dicetur, quorum summa fuit cxix li. xiii s. iiii d.[209]

Item computat se recepisse de beneffciis exploratis et non contentis in libris camere et predictis duobus beneffciis non taxatis cxxx li. x s. x d. Approbatum.

Item computat se recepisse de restis sive arayratgiis beneffciorum collatorum per Dominum Urbanum a tertio kalendas Maii pontificatus sui anno primo usque ad pridie ydus Julii pontificatus sui anno quinto,[210] in quibus tunc tempus taxa fuit expressa, que reste fuerunt in summa iiᶜ lxxix li. x s., iiᶜ xlix li. x s. Approbatum.

Et sic restat adhuc deberi de eisdem restis pro decanatu Wellensi collato Stephano Pampel xx li. et pro prioratu Beate Marie Lancastrie x li., et sic in summa xxx li. Approbatum.[205]

(fol. 90) Item computat se recepisse de annatis beneffciorum tempore predicto collatorum in quibus tunc tempus taxa non fuit expressa iiᶜ lxxxv li. xvi s. viii d. Approbatum.

Item computat se recepisse de annatis beneffciorum collatorum per Dominum Urbanum a ii ydus Julii

pontificatus sui anno quinto usque ad viiiᵒ kalendas Martii pontificatus sui anno octavo,[211] quia de ulteriori tempore non computat quia beneffcia alia a paucis diebus citra dicit se recepisse, iiᶜ lxvii li. xi s. viii d. Approbatum.

Et sic est summa totalis recepte tam de arayratgiis sive restis quam de annatis beneffciorum quorumcumque tempore supradicto collatorum, inclusis iiiᶜ fl. camere receptis de resta florenorum dimissa ut superius est expressum, m iiiiᶜ xxii li. v s. x d. ob. sterlingorum, Approbatum.

Item computat se recepisse de fructibus obvenientibus tempore vacationis de certis beneffciis in libro contentis xlv li. xi s. ob. sterlingorum. Approbatum.

(fol. 90ᵛ) Item computat se recepisse de legatis ad Terram Sanctam et cameram appostolicam liii li. iiii d. Approbatum.

Item computat se recepisse extraordinarie a Domino Hugone Pelegrini, olim in dicto regno camere appostolice collectore, pro taxa prebende Exoniensis confirmate Thome David per Clementem viii ydus Maii anno x [212] iiii li. et pro portione parochialis ecclesie Sancte Endolientis (St. Endellion) Exoniensis diocesis collata Symoni Wyll' per Clementem iiii nonas Julii anno ixᵒ [213] iiii li. ii s., quas pecunias fuit probatum ipsum recepisse tempore suo et sic in summa viii li. ii s. Approbatum.

Et sic est summa universsalis omnium et singularum receptarum precedentium tam de denariis Beati Petri, annuo censsu, arayratgiis et annatis beneffciorum, fructibus obvenientibus tempore vacationis, legatis Terre Sancte et camere appostolice quam de ultima extraordinaria recepta, inclusis in eadem recepta iiiᶜ fl. camere receptis in xlv li. xvi s. viii d. sterlingorum, ut in precedentibus est declaratum, iiᵐ liii li. iiii s. sterlingorum. Approbatum.

(fol. 91) Secundo idem collector computat se asignasse, solvisse seu liberasse tam camere appostolice quam aliis eius certo mandato, tam per se quam per alios certos mercatores solventes pro ipso et Domino Johanne de Caroloco, priore Lewensi locumtenente suo, a die xvi menssis Augusti anni domini MCCCLXVIII, qua die fuit conclusum cum eo in aliis computis quo ad asignationes licet non quo ad receptas, usque ad diem xxix menssis Martii inclusive anni LXXI, ut fidem fecit de omnibus pecuniis, infrascriptas, videlicet iiᵐ xix li. iiii d. ob. sterlingorum in xiiᵐ ixᶜ lix fl. camere, iii li. iii s. vii d. monete Avinionie, et in xxx li. sterlingorum in sua specie restitutis. Approbatum.

Quorum florenorum quilibet de viiiᵐ xci constat iii s. i d. sterlingorum, et quilibet de iiiᵐ iiiᶜ lxxxiiiiᵒʳ fl. constat iii s. et iii ferlinos sive tres quartas unius denarii sterlingorum et quilibet de m iiiiᶜ lxxxiiiiᵒʳ fl. predictis constat iuxta conventiones camere iii s. ob. cum xiii

[206] 29 April 1363.
[207] Peter de la Forêt, priest of Ss. XII Apostoli.
[208] Stephen Aubert, deacon of S. Maria in Aquiro.
[209] In the margin: *Attende quod de ista summa debet respondere collector Ybernie.*
[210] 14 July 1367.

[211] 22 February 1370.
[212] 8 May 1352.
[213] 4 July 1350.

partibus ducentorum lxxviii partium unius sterlingi. Approbatum.

De predictis omnibus fides fiat per litteras ut patet aparere in libro rationum dicti Domini Johannis.

(fol. 91ᵛ) Tertio idem collector computat tam ipsum quam substitutos suos expendisse pro negotiis camere pro pergameno et cera, ut in libro patet, in tribus annis xiiii li. xii s. iiii d.[214]

Item computat pro loquerio hospitii, prout ipsemet et alii predecessores sui computare, habere et recipere conssueverunt, pro tribus annis inceptis die xviii Februarii anno domini MCCCLXVIII et terminatis die xviii eiusdem menssis anni LXXI, computando pro quolibet anno vi li. xiii s. iiii d., prout ipse et alii computare conssueverunt, in summa xx li.

Summa omnium predictarum expenssarum xxxiiii li. xi s. iiii d. sterlingorum.

Summa universalis omnium premissarum asignationum et expenssarum iiᵐ liii li. xii s. viii d. ob. sterlingorum.

(fol. 92) Facta autem reductione et compenssatione de levatis et receptis que sunt in summa iiᵐ liii li. iiii s. sterlingorum ad soluta, asignata et expenssa que sunt in summa iiᵐ liii li. xii s. viii d. ob. dicte monete, aparet ipsum collectorem plus asignasse, solvisse et expendisse quam recepisse viii s. viii d. ob. sterlingorum.

Ipse autem collector debet camere appostolice predictos cl fl. de crozeta a camera prefata, ut dictum est, receptos, et in libris eiusdem inter mutua scriptos, et etiam in conclusione dictorum suorum computorum positos.

(fol. 93)[215] Quarto idem collector dat et asignat in restis sive arayratgiis de denariis Beati Petri, incluso in dictis restis anno LXXᵒ dumtaxat, iiiiᶜ lxxxii li. iiii d., quarum sunt de restis antiquis cxxvii li. xix s. viii d.

Item de annuo censsu, incluso etiam anno LXXᵒ dumtaxat, xi li. xv s. vi d., quarum sunt de restis antiquis vi li. xvi s. vi d.

Item dat de annatis beneficiorum collatorum per Dominos Clementem, Innocentium et Urbanum usque ad iii kalendas Maii pontificatus sui anno primo,[216] inclusis in ipsa resta restis [217] prebende de Nasyngthon' (Nassington) in ecclesia Lincoliensi et archidiaconatus Eboracensis collatorum domino cardinali Carcassonensi [218] et vicarie de Ympryngthon' (Impington) diocesis Eliensis, que beneficia non erant in libris camere quia ei non fuerant (fol. 93ᵛ) data nec per ipsum camere, et que in summa reste dictorum beneffi-

ciorum non includebantur, exclusis beneficiis Ybernie, iiᵐ iiiiᶜ ii li. vi s. x d., iiᶜ v fl. medium, ii d. sterlingorum, et aliqua beneficia non taxata.[219]

Item de annatis beneficiorum collatorum per Dominum Urbanum a tertio kalendas Maii pontificatus sui anno primo usque ad viiiᵒ kalendas Martii pontificatus sui anno viiiᵒ,[220] quia de ulteriori tempore non computat, quia a paucis diebus citra beneficia aliqua alia in collectoria sua per prefatum Dominum Urbanum collata de camera habuit et recepit et nondum fuerunt in partibus presentata, iiᶜ xl li. xviii s. Item multa beneficia in quibus taxa non ponitur que in libro patent clare et distincte.

Summa universsalis restarum sive arayratgiorum omnium beneficiorum collatorum per Dominos Clementem, Innocentium et Urbanum tempore supradicto (fol. 94) in quibus taxa ponitur et exprimitur est iiᵐ viᶜ xliii li. iiii s. x d. sterlingorum, iiᶜ v fl. medius, ii d. sterlingorum.

Et sic est summa universsalis omnium arayratgiorum sive restarum tam denariorum Beati Petri, annui censsus, incluso tamen pro istis duabus restis anno LXXᵒ dumtaxat, quam de annatis beneficiorum quorumcumque ibidem collatorum usque ad viiiᵒ kalendas Martii pontificatus Domini Urbani pape quinti anno viiiᵒ est iiiᵐ cxxxvii li. viii d. sterlingorum, iiᶜ v fl. medius camere, ii d. sterlingorum, et plura beneficia in quibus taxa non ponitur ut in libro particulariter et clare sunt distincta et descripta.

(fol. 95)[221] Sequntur reste sive arayratgiarum denariorum Beati Petri dimisse per Johannem de Cabrespino, collectorem Anglie camere apostolice, anno domini Mᵒ CCCᵒ LXXI die et cetera.

Primo debet archiepiscopus Eboracensis pro anno LXXᵒ xi li. x s.

Item episcopus Saresbiriensis debet pro annis LXVIIIᵒ, nono et LXXᵒ, pro quolibet xvii li., et sic pro dictis tribus annis li li.

Item episcopus Cicestrensis debet pro anno LXXᵒ viii li.

Item episcopus Wygorniensis debet pro annis LXIXᵒ et LXXᵒ, pro quolibet x li. v s., et sic pro dictis duobus annis xx li. x s.

Item episcopus Conwetrensis et Licheffeldensis debet pro anno LXXᵒ x li. v s.

Item episcopus Lincolniensis debet pro resta anni LXVIII iiii li. et pro annis LXIXᵒ et LXXᵒ, pro quolibet xlii li., et sic debet lxxxviiiᵒ li.

Item episcopus Exoniensis debet pro anno LXXᵒ ix li. v s.

Item episcopus Herffordensis debet pro annis

---

[214] In the margin: *potest docere per libros, ut dicit, particulariter, et post vide iterato id agendum.*

[215] Folio 92ᵛ is blank.

[216] 29 April 1363.

[217] *restas,* MS.

[218] Stephen Aubert, deacon of S. Maria in Aquiro.

[219] In the margin: *iste reste precedentes usque hic dantur superius in receptis, sed, ut reperiuntur infimus, ponuntur hic cum aliis.*

[220] 22 February 1370.

[221] Folio 94ᵛ is blank.

LXVII°, octavo, IX° et LXX°, pro quolibet vi li., et sic debet pro dictis iiii°ʳ annis xxiiii li.

Summa pagine ii͏ᶜ xxii li. x s. quarum sunt de restis antiquis xxxiii li. Approbatum.

(fol. 95ᵛ) Item episcopus Bathoniensis et Wellensis debet de resta anni LXIII vi li. v s. et pro annis LXVII°, VIII° nono et LXX°, pro quolibet xi li. v s., et sic debet pro totali resta supradicta li li. v s.

Item episcopus Norwicensis debet pro annis LXIX° et LXX°, pro quolibet xxi li. x s., et sic debet pro dictis duobus annis xliii li.

Item archidiaconus Cantuariensis debet pro annis LXIX° et LXX°, pro quolibet viii li., et sic pro dictis duobus annis xvi li.

Item archidiaconus Roffensis debet pro annis LXVᵗᵒ, VI°, VII°, VIII°, IX° et LXX°, pro quolibet v li. et xii s., et sic debet pro dictis vi annis xxxiii li. xii s.

Item archidiaconus Middelsey' debet pro anno LXX° v li. x s.

Item archidiaconus Wynthoniensis debet pro annis LXVII°, VIII°, nono et LXX°, pro quolibet xi li. xiii s. iiii d., et sic debet pro dictis iiii°ʳ annis xlvi li. xiii s. iiii d.

Item archidiaconus Surreie [222] debet pro annis LXIX° et LXX°, pro quolibet v li. x s., et sic pro dictis duobus annis xi li.

Item archidiaconus Colcestr' debet pro annis LXVIII°, nono et LXX°, pro quolibet v li. x s., et sic pro dictis tribus annis debet xvi li. x s.

Summa pagine ii͏ᶜ xxiii li. x s. iiii d. quarum sunt de restis antiquis lxxix li. xix s. viii d.

(fol. 96) Item archidiaconus Excessie debet pro annis LXIX° et LXX°, pro quolibet v li. x s., et sic pro dictis duobus annis debet xi li.

Item archidiaconus Eliensis debet pro annis LXVI°, VII°, VIII°, nono et LXX°, pro quolibet v li., et sic pro dictis quinque annis debet xxv li.

Summa pagine xxxvi li. quarum sunt de restis antiquis xv li.

Summa universalis omnium precedentium restarum denariorum Beati Petri est iiii͏ᶜ lxxxii li. iiii d. quarum sunt de restis antiquis cxxvii li. xix s. viii d. Approbatum.

(fol. 96ᵛ) Sequntur reste annui census de tempore supradicto

Primo abbas de Faverscham debet pro annis LXVII°, VIII°, nono et LXX°, pro quolibet xiii s. iiii d., et pro dictis quatuor annis debet ii li. xiii s. iiii d.

Item abbas de Corthesey debet pro annis LXVII°, octavo, nono et LXX°, pro quolibet viii s.,[223] et sic pro dictis iiii°ʳ annis debet xxxii s.

Item abbas de Malmesbury debet pro anno LXX° xiii s. iiii d.

Item prior de Tenebrig' debet pro anno LXX° xiii s. iiii d.

Item prior de Anglesey debet pro anno LXX° ii s.

Item prior Karleolensis debet pro annis LXII°, tertio, quarto, quinto, VI°, septimo, octavo, nono et LXX° pro quolibet xiii s. iiii d., et sic pro dictis novem annis vi li.

Item abbatissa Sancte Clare Londoniensis debet pro annis LXVIII°, nono et LXX°, pro quolibet vi d., et sic pro dictis tribus annis xviii d.

Summa pagine xi li. xv s. vi d. quarum sunt de restis antiquis vi li. xvi s. vi d. Approbatum.

(fol. 97) Sequntur arayratgia sive reste de annatis beneficiorum collatorum per Dominos Clementem, Innocentium et Urbanum usque ad iii° kalendas Maii pontificatus sui anno primo [224] dimisse camere apostolice tempore supradicto

## Cantuariensis diocesis

De ecclesia de Stokbury (Stockbury) Cantuariensis diocesis, taxata xxvi li. vi s. viii d., que fuit appropriata priori et conventui de Ledes (Leeds) per Clementem viii° ydus Augusti anno xi°,[225] pro resta dicte taxe vii li. vi s. viii d. Sed iste vii li. vi s. viii d. sunt de pensione quia de taxa ecclesie est satisfactum, sed quia simul ponitur taxa ecclesie et pensionis ideo fuit error.

De ecclesia de Bokenffeld' (Bockingfold), de qua per obitum Willelmi de Braydeley fuit provisum David Wyngham per Innocentium iii° ydus Augusti anno x°,[226] taxa vel fructus. Nunquam potui habere aliquod notificatorium bonum de isto beneficio, et est alia provisio facta de eadem per obitum eiusdem Willelmi Ricardo de Hemyngthon' per Innocentium iiii° nonas Julii anno ix°.[227]

## Londoniensis

De ecclesia seu capella de Stafford' (Stanford le Hope), de qua per obitum Edmundi Grynnesby fuit provisum Johanni de Torkesby per Innocentium viii ydus Octobris anno secundo,[228] pro taxa ipsius xxvi li. xiii s. iiii d. Nunc incumbens allegat quod nunquam fuit ibi rector dictus Johannes nec Edmundus de Grymnesby.

De ecclesia de Herlawe (Harlow) Londoniensis diocesis, de qua per assequtionem archidiaconatus Tothon' (Totnes) fuit provisum Magistro Ricardo Anglici alias Drax per Innocentium vii ydus Januarii anno viii°,[229] pro taxa ipsius xiii li. vi s. viii d. Allegatum tamen est quod ista provisio non habuit effectum.

Summa pagine xlvii li. vi s. viii d. et unum beneficium non taxatum.

---

[222] *Saresbiriensis*, MS., i. e. Sar'.
[223] Followed by *viii d.* deleted by a line.

[224] 29 April 1363.
[225] 6 August 1352.
[226] 11 August 1362.
[227] 4 July 1361.
[228] 8 October 1354.
[229] 7 January 1360.

(fol. 97ᵛ) De ecclesia de Longedon' (Langdon Hills), non taxata, de qua ex causa permutationis fuit provisum Willelmo de Swyffeld' per Urbanum iiiᵒ nonas Januarii anno primo,[230] qui composuit pro medietate fructuum in xl s., debet pro resta xxvi s. viii d.

De ecclesia Sancti Pancratii in ecclesia Londoniensi, de qua ex causa permutationis fuit provisum Radulpho de Doventis per Urbanum quinto nonas Martii anno primo,[231] pro taxa ipsius xlii s. vi d.

## Cicestrensis diocesis

De archidiaconatu Lewensi, non taxato, qui fuit confirmatus Willelmo de Lutheburgh' per Clementem pridie ydus Augusti anno xiᵒ,[232] fructus.

Item de eodem archidiaconatu ratione provisionis facte de eodem Thome Bronwen' eo quod predictus Guillelmus assequtus est thesaurariam dicte ecclesie per Innocentium viiᵒ ydus Septembris anno viᵒ,[233] fructus.

De archidiaconatu Cicestrensi, non taxato, permutatio cuius facta cum decanatu ecclesie collegiate Cestr'[234] super stratam (Chester-le-Street) Dunelmensis diocesis fuit Johanni de Slinothop' confirmata per Innocentium quinto kalendas Januarii anno sexto,[235] fructus.

De prebenda de Ypthorn' (Upthorne) in ecclesia Cicestrensi, de qua per obitum Thome David fuit provisum Philipo de Correnoy per Innocentium xᵒ kalendas Julii anno ixᵒ,[236] pro taxa vi li. xiii s. iiii d.

De precentoria Cicestrensi, taxata liii li. vi s. viii d., de qua vacante per obitum cardinalis de Gordonio[237] fuit provisum cardinali Aquensi[238] per Innocentium viᵒ ydus Octobris anno nono,[239] de resta xxxi li. xiii s. iiii d.

De decanatu Cicestrensi, taxato liii li. vi s. viii d., et canonicatu et prebenda (fol. 98)[240] sibi annexis, de quibus vacantibus per consecrationem Guillelmi episcopi Cicestrensis fuit Nicholao de Aston' provisum, magistro in sacra pagina, per Urbanum xi kalendas Decembris anno primo,[241] pro resta xlviii li. vi s. viii d.

De prebenda de Midelton' (Middleton) in ecclesia Cicestrensi, de qua cum archidiaconatu Richmundie et aliis beneficiis contentis inter quatuor obligatos, pro resta iii li. vi s. viii d.

---

[230] 3 January 1363.
[231] 3 March 1363.
[232] 12 August 1352.
[233] 7 September 1358.
[234] Follows *Cestr'* blotted and deleted by a line.
[235] 28 December 1358.
[236] 22 June 1361.
[237] William Farinier of Gourdon, priest of Ss. Marcellino e Pietro.
[238] Peter Itherii, bishop of Dax, priest of Ss. Quattro Coronati.
[239] 10 October 1361.
[240] At the foot of folio 97ᵛ: *Summa pagine xli li. xv s. x d.; tria beneficia non taxata.*
[241] 21 November 1362.

## Wynthoniensis

De hospitali Sancte Crucis, non taxato, confirmato Johanni de Edyngdon' per Clementem xviiiᵒ kalendas Julii anno viiiᵒ,[242] pro resta vii li. iii s. vi d.

De prebenda de Midelthon' (Middleton) in ecclesia monialium de Werwell' (Wherwell), taxata xxvi li. xiii s. iiii d., de qua fuit provisum Johanni de Braketre per Innocentium v kalendas Januarii anno primo,[243] pro resta xv li.

De prioratu de Appelburthorp' (Appuldurcombe), taxato xxx li. xvii s., confirmato Johanni de Ozanna per Clementem quinto kalendas Maii anno viiiᵒ,[244] pro resta xxv li. xvii s. Sed ministri regis totum occupant quia debitor suus erat.

## Saresbiriensis

De ecclesia de Kirvelegh' (Keevil), taxata xxvi li. xiii s. iiii d., de qua fuit provisum Magistro Thome de Trompesawe per Clementem, pro resta vi li. xiii s. iiii d.
Summa pagine cvi li. vii s. ii d.

(fol. 98ᵛ) De prebenda de Wermynstr' (Warminster) in ecclesia Saresbiriensi, taxata v li., de qua per obitum Johannis de Bambury fuit provisum Thome de Strangull' per Clementem, pro resta v li.

De prebenda de Stretthon' (Stratton) in ecclesia Saresbiriensi, taxata xiii li. vi s. viii d., de qua ex causa permutationis fuit Johanni Turstayn provisum per Innocentium ydus Martii anno iiiᵒ,[245] pro taxa xiii li. vi s. viii d. Sed allegatur quod ista provisio non habuit effectum.

De prebenda de Redmiminstr' (Bedminster) in ecclesia Saresbiriensi, taxata xiii li. vi s. viii d., de qua per resignationem Willelmi de Hale fuit provisum Thome de Clipston' per Innocentium ydus Decembris anno sexto,[246] pro taxa xiii li. vi s. viii d. Sed episcopus semper certificat quod nunquam habuit possessionem, et est in diocesi Bathoniensi, et infra in fine istius diocesis providetur alteri.

De prebenda Saresbiriensi acceptatio cuius facta per Johannem Ubfforde Norwicensis diocesis fuit eidem confirmata per Innocentium viii kalendas Julii anno viiᵒ,[247] fructus. Sed episcopus in omnibus certificatoriis litteris rescribit quod dictus Johannes nunquam habuit in dicta ecclesia prebendam.

De prebenda de Calme (Calne) in ecclesia Saresbiriensi et thesauraria in eadem, de quibus fuit provisum cardinali Nemausenensi[248] per Innocentium iiiᵒ kalendas Octobris anno nono,[249] pro taxa ipsius lxxxvi li. xiii s. iiii d.

---

[242] 14 June 1349.
[243] 28 December 1353.
[244] 27 April 1350.
[245] 15 March 1355.
[246] 13 December 1358.
[247] 24 June 1359.
[248] John de Blanzac, bishop of Nimes, priest of S. Marco.
[249] 29 September 1361.

De ecclesia de Wartham (Warham), taxata iiii⁰ʳ li. vi s. viii d., de qua per resignationem Thome de Barneby fuit provisum Thome de Worth' per Innocentium v⁰ ydus Octobris anno decimo,[250] iiii li. vi s. viii d. Sed fuit allegatum quod ista provisio non habuit effectum, et episcopo commissum quod de hoc se informaret et referret, qui retulit verum esse quod non habuit effectum, ideo debet cancellari.

Summa pagine cxxii li. xiii s. iiii d. et unum beneficium non taxatum.

(fol. 99) De prebenda de Pedfford' (Woodford), taxata xvi li. xiii s. iiii d., et archidiaconatu Dordestron' (Dorset) in dicta ecclesia, taxato lxii li., de quibus fuit provisum cardinali[251] de Canilhaco, episcopo Penestrino, per Innocentium iiii⁰ ydus Martii anno x⁰,[252] lxxviii li. xiii s. iiii d.

De prebenda de Pestron' (Preston) in ecclesia Saresbiriensi, de qua fuit provisum Thome de Stocthon' per Innocentium xi⁰ kalendas Novembris anno quinto,[253] pro taxa xvi li. xiii s. iiii d. Sed episcopus semper certificat quod non habet effectum.

De prebenda de Horthona (Horton) in ecclesia Saresbiriensi, de qua per obitum Willelmi Diffroclegh' collatio facta Nicholao de Luda, thesaurario domini regis Anglie, fuit eidem confirmata, etiam si alio quovis modo vacet vel sit reservata valeat, ac si vacasset per mortem dicti Willelmi, per Urbanum iiii⁰ nonas Januarii anno primo,[254] fructus.

De ecclesia de Dounton' (Downton), cuius collatio et provisio facte auctoritate ordinaria Thome de Edyndon' fuerunt[255] eidem auctoritate apostolica confirmate[256] vel provisum de novo, pro taxa ipsius lxvi li. xiii s. iiii d.

De prebenda de Biscopethon' (Bishopstone) in ecclesia Saresbiriensi, taxata xx li., de qua per obitum Petri Raymundi de Rapistagno fuit provisum Raymundo Pelegrini[257] per Clementem kalendas Februarii anno viii⁰,[258] pro taxa xx li. Credo quod ista provisio fuit facta Arnoldo Peregrini, qui, lite pendente inter ipsum et Willelmum Okeburn', obiit, et alius subrogatus fuit[259] in iure dicti Arnoldi per Innocentium ydus Julii anno x⁰,[260] que provisio fuit posita inter inutiles quia dictus Willelmus de Okeburn' eam tenet iure regio, ut patet in provisionibus inutilibus camere datis.

Exoniensis

De ecclesia de Bascher, de qua, vacante eo quod Henricus de Monre pluribus annis tenuit eam in presbyterum non promotus, fuit provisum Cornesio de Laustr' per Innocentium (fol. 99ᵛ)[261] vii⁰ kalendas Julii anno nono,[262] fructus.

De archidiaconatu Cornubie, non taxato, de quo per obitum Thome David fuit provisum Alexandro Nevill' per Innocentium x⁰ kalendas Septembris anno ix⁰,[263] fructus.

De prebenda Sancte Columbe minoris (St. Columb Minor) in ecclesia Sancte Karentoci (Crantock), in quo fuit subrogatus in omni iure quod competebat David Maynardi Johannes Ruseley, magister in artibus, per Innocentium nonas Maii anno vii⁰,[264] fructus.

De archidiaconatu Tothon' in ecclesia Exoniensi, de quo fuit provisum Ricardo Desbuntton' per Innocentium quinto kalendas Novembris anno quinto,[265] fructus. Sed alia est provisio facta de eodem Willelmo Streel ex causa permutationis cum parochiali ecclesia de Dodyngthon' (Doddington) Lincolniensis diocesis per Urbanum vii⁰ kalendas Maii anno primo,[266] pro qua provisione pars fuit soluta in aliis computis, de residuo respondetur in istis, sed dicitur quod dicta provisio facta Ricardo Desbuntton' non habuit effectum.

Wygorniensis

De ecclesia de Estolegh' (Astley), taxata xi li. vi s. viii d., de qua per obitum Henrici de Stowe fuit provisum Henrico de Askeby et etiam subrogatus in omni iure quod dicto Henrico competebat, qui super hoc litigans in curia decessit tempore Domini Clementis, pro resta viii li. Sed Dominus Hugo Pegrini dicit in rationibus suis quod ista provisio non habuit effectum, et ego idem invenio, et ideo debet cancellari.

De hospitali Sancti Wulstani (Worcester), non taxato, de quo per resignationem Petri Francisci fuit provisum Johanni de Harewell', canonico Sancti Martini Londoniensis, per[267] Innocentium v⁰ kalendas Julii anno quinto,[268] fructus. Sed est hospitale pauperum et ministri eius vovent castitatem, abdicationem proprietatis et obedientiam et vivunt de mendicitate, nec habent decimas nec ecclesias, ideo et cetera.

Summa pagine viii li. et quinque beneficia non taxata.

(fol. 100) Bathoniensis et Wellensis

De vicaria de Henstingh' (Henstridge), de cuius taxa adhuc non constat, de qua, vacante ex eo quod

---

[250] 11 October 1362.
[251] Followed by *Aquensi* deleted by a line.
[252] 12 March 1362.
[253] 22 October 1357.
[254] 2 January 1363.
[355] *fuit*, MS.
[256] *confirmata*, MS.
[257] *Pegrini*, MS.
[258] 1 February 1350.
[259] Follows *est* deleted by a line.
[260] 15 July 1362.

[261] At the end of folio 99: *Summa pagine clxxxii li., et unum beneficium non taxatum.*
[262] 25 June 1361.
[263] 23 August 1361.
[264] 7 May 1359.
[265] 28 October 1357.
[266] 25 April 1363.
[267] *per* repeated MS.
[268] 27 June 1357.

Robertus Thome vicarius eiusdem ecclesiam de Gilyngham (Gillingham) Saresbiriensis diocesis fuit pacifice assequtus, fuit provisum per cardinalem Petragoricensem Radulpho Thome vi kalendas Februarii anno vio,[269] non dimissa in arayratgiis sed explorata, pro qua provisione fuerunt recepte iiii li. vi s. viii d. Restat quod debet.

De prepositura Wellensi, de qua vacante per obitum Andree de Wfford' fuit provisum Ade de Ylthon' per Innocentium nonas Februarii anno viio,[270] pro taxa ipsius xl li. Et per obitum dicti Ade fuit provisum Domino Willelmo de Wykham nunc episcopo Wynthoniensis, qui eam usque ad consecrationem suam tenuit, ut patet infra eadem pagina.

De prebenda de Holcombe in ecclesia Wellensi, de qua, vacante aut cum vacabit per assequtionem canonicatus et prebende per Thomam de Baston', fuit provisum Waltero Mayn per Innocentium xixo kalendas Septembris anno viiio,[271] pro resta xxvi li. xiii s. iiii d. Incumbens allegat quod nunquam habuit possessionem nec provisio habuit effectum, et fuit commissum episcopo ut de hoc se informaret, qui, facta inquisitione, certificavit dictam provisionem non habuisse effectum, ut in litteris suis, que sunt penes registrum, continetur, ideo debet cancellari.

De prepositura Wellensi, de qua per obitum Thome de Ylthon' fuit provisum Willelmo de Wykham per Innocentium nonas Januarii [272] anno ixo,[273] pro resta vel taxa xl li.

Summa pagine cvi li. xiii s. iiii d.

### (fol. 100ᵛ) Herffordensis

De prebenda de Metton' (Moreton Magna) in ecclesia Herffordensi, taxata xx ⟨li.⟩, de qua per obitum Thome de Stantton' fuit provisum Symoni de Subur' per Clementem iiio nonas Julii anno viiio,[274] pro resta xiii s. iiii d.

De prebenda de Motton' (Moreton Magna) predicta, de qua per promotionem dicti Symonis in episcopum Londoniensem fuit provisum Thome Thebaud' per Innocentium iiio ydus Decembris anno nono,[275] pro taxa xx li.

De decanatu Herffordensi, taxato xxxi li. vi s. viii d., de quo per resignationem Thome Trelek' episcopi Roffensis fuit provisum Waltero de Bernigham per Urbanum viio kalendas Februarii anno primo,[276] pro resta xl s. i d. Alia fuit provisio eidem Waltero [277]

facta de eodem per Innocentium vii ydus Aprilis anno [278] xo,[279] sed ambe sunt infra annum, et ideo non debetur nisi una annata.

### Norwicensis

De prioratu de Castelacre (Castle Acre), de quo ex causa permutationis fuit provisum Willelmo de Warenis per Clementem anno primo,[280] pro taxa iiiio lxxx li. xix s. vii d. Ista provisio est antiqua et nunquam potuit aliquid haberi quia de patronatu est laycali, et statim fuit exclusus quia bastardus et dissipator prioratus erat.

De ecclesia de Holm (Holme), taxata xl li., de qua per resignationem Willelmi de Morthon' fuit provisum Thome Michel per Clementem, pro resta x li.

De ecclesia Derham (East Dereham), de qua per obitum Alani de Hotton' fuit provisum Symoni Thebaud nunc episcopo Londoniensi per Clementem iiio kalendas Aprilis anno xo,[281] pro resta xl li. xvi s. viii d.

Summa pagine vᶜ liiii li. ix s. viii d.

(fol. 101) Item de eadem fuit per promotionem dicti Symonis provisum Bartholomeo Sydey per Innocentium viio kalendas Decembris anno nono,[282] pro taxa ipsius lxxiii li. vi s. viii d. Ista provisio non habuit effectum quia rex contulit eam Thome Kynes.

De decanatu de Hombard' (Humbleyard), non taxato, de quo per resignationem Walteri de Bokron fuit provisum Symoni de Subur' per Innocentium iiio kalendas Julii anno quinto,[283] fructus.

De ecclesia de Cherintthon' (Chevington), taxata xvi li. xiii s. iiii d., que fuit Hugoni Nepell' confirmata per Innocentium viio kalendas Februarii anno xo,[284] pro resta vi li. xiii s. iiii d.

De decanatu rurali de Fordham, de quo vacante per obitum Johannis Hoppe fuit provisum Waltero Palmer' per Innocentium vo nonas Martii anno xo,[285] fructus.

De ecclesia de Holm (Holme), de qua per obitum Thome Michel fuit provisum Roberto de Grymneston' per Urbanum xviiio kalendas Januarii anno primo,[286] xl li.

Item de eadem per obitum Thome eiusdem fuit provisum Johanni Bache eadem die sed non debetur nisi una annata.

De ecclesia de Mithethon' (Moulton), de qua per obitum Edmundi de Wythtewell' fuit provisum Haymoni de Wall', presbytero Licheffeldensis diocesis, per Urbanum pridie ydus Martii anno primo,[287] pro taxa xxvi li. xiii s. iiii d.

---

[269] 27 January 1358.
[270] 5 February 1359.
[271] 14 August 1360.
[272] Follows *Februarii* deleted by a line.
[273] 5 January 1361.
[274] 5 July 1349.
[275] 11 December 1361.
[276] 26 January 1363.
[277] *Willelmo*, MS.

[278] Followed by *primo* deleted by a line.
[279] 7 April 1362.
[280] 19 May 1342 to 18 May 1343.
[281] 30 March 1352.
[282] 25 November 1361.
[283] 29 June 1357.
[284] 26 January 1362.
[285] 3 March 1362.
[286] 15 December 1362.
[287] 14 March 1363.

Eliensis diocesis

De prioratu de Subavesevy (Swavesey), de quo fuit provisum Stephano Bertrandi per Clementem, pro resta iiii li.

Summa huius pagine est cl li. xiii s. iiii d. et duo beneficia non taxata.

(fol. 101ᵛ) De archidiaconatu, canonicatu et prebenda ecclesie Eliensis, de quibus, vacantibus per obitum cardinalis de Cordonio,[288] motu proprio fuit provisum domino A. cardinali Cluniacensi [289] per Urbanum iiiᵒ ydus Novembris anno primo,[290] taxa vel fructus.

De vicaria de Ympryngthon' (Impington), taxata iiii li. vi s. viii d., de qua per cardinalem Petragoricensem fuit provisum Ricardo de Chelfford' xiii kalendas Decembris pontificatus Domini Innocentii anno quinto,[291] pro resta xliii s. iiii d.

## Lincolniensis

De prebenda de Radfford' maiori (Bedford Maior) in ecclesia Lincolniensi, taxata viii li., que fuit Willelmo de Wytesley confirmata per Clementem ydus Octobris anno viiᵒ vel octavo,[292] pro taxa viii li.

De prebenda de Walthon' Ryvaus (Welton Rivall) in ecclesia Lincolniensi, de qua ex causa permutationis cum Johanne de Hotthon' fuit provisum Roberto Daventr' per Innocentium viiᵒ kalendas Maii anno quinto,[293] pro taxa ipsius xxxiii li. vi s. viii d.

De ecclesia de Trefforde (Gretford), que fuit unita monasterio Beate Marie Wynthoniensis per Clementem iiiᵒ ydus Julii anno xiᵒ,[294] pro taxa ipsius xiiii li. xiii s. iiii d. Episcopus certificat quod ista ecclesia non est in diocesi Lincolniensi.

De prebenda Sancte Crucis (Spaldwick) in ecclesia Lincolniensi, de qua fuit ⟨provisum⟩ Johanni de Selby, pro resta ii li. x s.

De prebenda de Carlethon' cum Turleby (Carlton le Moorland cum Thurlby) in ecclesia Lincolniensi, de qua nuper per resignationem Willelmi de Waltochi fuit provisum Eduardo de Schrdestok' per Innocentium kalendas Martii anno viᵒ,[295] pro resta vi li. xiii s. iiii d.

De prebenda de Suthscarle (South Scarle) in ecclesia Lincolniensi, de qua per resignationem (fol. 102)[296] Willelmi de Barkeby fuit provisum Johanni de Appelby per Innocentium iiiᵒ ydus Julii anno viᵒ,[297] pro taxa xl li.

De ecclesia de Cosyngthon' (Cossington), que fuit

Johanni de Melburn' confirmata per Innocentium viiᵒ kalendas Julii anno viiᵒ,[298] pro taxa vi li. xiii s. iiii d. Sed episcopus certificat quod non est in sua diocesi.

De prebenda de Nesyngthon' (Nassington) in ecclesia Lincolniensi, taxata c li., que fuit confirmata Ludovico de Carlethon' per Innocentium kalendas Februarii anno ixᵒ,[299] pro taxa c li.

Item de eadem prebenda ratione provisionis facte de ea domino cardinali Carcassonensi,[300] pro resta taxa liii li. ii s.

De ecclesia de Stragund (Standground), de qua ex causa permutationis cum ecclesia Rippon' (Abbots Ripton) fuit provisum Johanni de Acton' per Innocentium viiᵒ kalendas Octobris anno ixᵒ,[301] pro taxa xx li.

De ecclesia de Ripthon' abbatis (Abbots Ripton), de qua ex causa permutationis fuit provisum Thome de Clipton' per Innocentium viiᵒ kalendas Octobris anno ixᵒ,[301] pro taxa xxiii li. vi s. viii d.

De ecclesia de parva Kynewell' (Little Kimble), de qua per assequtionem ecclesie de Gesynthon' (Garsington) fuit provisum Johanni Rocelli per Innocentium viᵒ ydus Martii anno viᵒ,[302] pro taxa iiii li. xiii s. iiii d. Sed episcopus certificat quod non est talis in sua diocesi, nec rector taliter nominatus.

De prebenda in ecclesia Lincolniensi, de qua per obitum Jacobi de Borlay fuit provisum Domino Guillelmo episcopo Tusculano per Innocentium xvᵒ kalendas Septembris anno viᵒ,[303] taxa vel fructus.

De ecclesia de Hoghton' (Houghton Regis), taxata xii li., quo fuit confirmata Hugoni de Spabrigham per Innocentium xviiᵒ kalendas Decembris anno viiiᵒ,[304] fructus.

De ecclesia Beate Marie Herffordensis (Hertford), de qua ex causa permutationis cum Johanne (fol. 102ᵛ)[305] Dich' fuit provisum Henrico Midi per Innocentium quinto kalendas Aprilis anno viiᵒ,[306] taxa vel fructus.

De prebenda de Langhestow (Stowe Longa), taxata xliiii li. vi s. viii d., in ecclesia Lincolniensi, de qua fuit provisum Reginaldo de Theminis per Innocentium vi kalendas Julii anno ixᵒ,[307] pro resta xix li. xvi s. viii d.

De prebenda in ecclesia Lincolniensi intitulata E. in ecclesia collegiata Beate Marie iuxta castrum Leycestrensem (St. Mary the Less in Castle, Leicester), de qua fuit ex causa permutationis provisum Henrico de Kynbergh' per Urbanum quinto nonas Martii anno primo,[308] taxa vel fructus.

---

[288] William Farinier of Gourdon, priest of Ss. Marcellino e Pietro.
[289] Androin de la Roche, abbot of Cluny, priest of S. Marcello.
[290] 11 November 1362.
[291] 19 November 1357.
[292] 15 October 1348 or 1349.
[293] 25 April 1357.
[294] 13 July 1352.
[295] 1 March 1358.
[296] At the foot of fol. 101ᵛ: *Summa pagine est lxvii li. vi s. viii d., et unum beneficium non taxatum.*
[297] 13 July 1358.

[298] 25 June 1359.
[299] 1 February 1361.
[300] Stephen Aubert, deacon of S. Maria in Aquiro.
[301] 25 September 1361.
[302] 10 March 1358.
[303] 18 August 1358.
[304] 15 November 1360.
[305] At the foot of fol. 102: *Summa pagine iiᵒ xlvii li. xv s. iiii d. et duo beneficia non taxata.*
[306] 28 March 1359.
[307] 26 June 1361.
[308] 3 March 1363.

De magistratu de Burthon' Sancti Lazari (Burton Lazars), cuius collatio facta per Willelmum Philipum patriarcham Jherosolimitanam auctoritate ordinaria Gedfrido de Chadesven', militi dicti hospitalis, fuit eidem confirmata auctoritate apostolica, et nichilominus subrogatus in omni iure quod competebat Roberto de Haldam, per Urbanum quinto nonas Martii anno primo,[308] taxa vel fructus.

De prebenda ecclesie Lincolniensis, que vocatur Sancte Crucis (Spaldwick), de qua vacante per obitum Willelmi de Spadewell' fuit provisum Johanni de Barleby, clerico regis Anglie, per Urbanum xiii° kalendas Maii anno primo,[309] taxa vel fructus. Sed Johannes de Solby eam tenet et possidet ex collatione regis Anglie, et supra debentur 1 s. de eadem pro alia provisione.

### Conwetrensis et Licheffeldensis

De archidiaconatu Conwetrensi, non taxato, de quo fuit provisum Humffrido de Astyng', fructus.

Item de eodem archidiaconatu et prebenda de Langhedon' (Longdon) in ecclesia Licheffeldensi, taxata xx li., de quibus post obitum Humffridi de Astyng' fuit provisum Willelmo de Salow per Clementem iiii° nonas Septembris anno viii°,[310] de quibus Willelmus Dalby dicitur composuisse cum camera pro resta archidiaconatus xiii li. vi s. viii d.

Summa pagine xxxiii li. iii s. iiii d. et v beneficia non taxata.

(fol. 103) De prebenda Licheffeldensi, de qua per obitum Willelmi Appeltr' fuit provisum Thome Attewell' per Clementem xi kalendas Julii anno viii°,[311] taxa vel fructus.

De prebenda in ecclesia collegiata Sancte Sedde Saloppie (St. Chad, Shrewsbury), de qua per obitum Willelmi Alpetr' fuit provisum Roberto de Sulgrave per Clementem iii° ydus Decembris anno viii°,[312] taxa vel fructus. Sed non habuit effectum quia Hugo Espas ipsam tenuit et adhuc tenet iure regio.

De prebenda de Berkewyk (Berkswick) in ecclesia Licheffeldensi, taxata xx li., de qua per obitum Guidonis de Waresio fuit provisum Willelmo Camube per Innocentium vii° kalendas Maii anno primo,[313] pro taxa xx li.

De capellania Sancti Michaelis sita in castro de Childewort alias de Childerow (Clitheroe), non taxata, de qua fuit provisum per devolutionem Johanni de Sutton' per Innocentium iiii°[314] kalendas Junii anno vi°,[315] fructus. Sed episcopus certificat quod non possit fieri exequtio quia est de patronatu laicali, videlicet regis Anglie et ducis Lancastrie, et sine cura dependens ab ecclesia de Whalleya (Whalley) Lichfeldensis dio-

cesis, que olim fuit plebana, sed postea fuit ibi translatum debite monasterio Loci Benedicti de Stanlaw Cisterciensis ordinis dicte diocesis, propter maris inundationem, de licentia et auctoritate Domini Nicholai pape iiii[ti], sub data Reute (Rieti) x° kalendas Augusti pontificatus sui anno secundo,[316] et subsequentur dicta fuerunt confirmata per Innocentium papam sextum sub data vii° kalendas Septembris anno vii°,[317] et pro ista appropriatione fuit lata sententia de arcubus anno LXV die xxii Junii, et de ista capella fuerunt facte due subrogationes isti Johanni de Borthon', una per Innocentium ix° kalendas Januarii anno nono[318] de David Martini, et alia de Johanne Park' per Innocentium vii° kalendas[319] anno x°, que tamen hic non ponuntur quia nichil valent, et in aliis computis ponuntur, date fuerunt inter inutiles.

De ecclesia de Codyngthon' (Coddington), de qua per assequtionem ecclesie de Wyngthon' (Burton-in-Winhale) per Johannem de Charneyny fuit provisum Waltero Linge per Innocentium (fol. 103)[320] nonas Junii anno sexto,[321] pro taxa ipsius vi li. xiii s. iiii d.

De prioratu de Kyrkeby (Monks Kirby), taxato lxxxi li. x s. viii d., de quo per assequtionem prioratus de Veteribelismo (Vieux Belesme) Saginensis (Séez) diocesis per Oliverum de Sertis fuit provisum Guillelmo de Grauleriis per Innocentium xiii° kalendas Martii anno vii°,[322] pro resta xli li. x s. viii d.

De ecclesia de Herkelave (Child's Ercall), que fuit confirmata Stephano de Syntthethon' per Innocentium vii° kalendas Julii anno vii°,[323] pro resta vi li. xiii iiii d.

De prebenda de Tarvyn (Tarvin) in ecclesia Licheffeldensi,[324] de qua per obitum Willelmi de Dirfeld fuit provisum Nicholao Heth' per Innocentium iii° ydus Augusti anno x°,[325] pro resta xxiiii li. ix s. vi d.

De prebenda in ecclesia collegiata de Pynkyrgh' (Penkridge), de qua per obitum Thome Michael' fuit provisum Thome de Heltonhevede per Innocentium vii° ydus Aprilis anno x°,[326] taxa vel fructus.

De cantoria ecclesie Licheffeldensis[327] quam Thomas de Kyrdeby debuit dimittere per assequtionem canonicatus et prebende ecclesie Lincolniensis fuit provisum et cetera. Nondum[328] dimisit sed adhuc eam tenet.

De prebenda in ecclesia Licheffeldensi de qua per obitum Willelmi de Dyrffeld' in curia defuncti fuit provisum Alexandro de Dalby per Urbanum iiii° nonas

---

[308] 19 April 1363.
[310] 2 September 1349.
[311] 21 June 1349.
[312] 11 December 1349.
[313] 25 April 1353.
[314] Follows v deleted by a dot
[315] 29 May 1358.

[316] 23 July 1289.
[317] 26 August 1359.
[318] 24 December 1361.
[319] A blank space is left in MS.
[320] At the foot of folio 103: *Summa pagine xx li. et iii beneficia non taxata.*
[321] 5 June 1358.
[322] 17 February 1359.
[323] 25 June 1359.
[324] Over *Lincolniensi* deleted by a line.
[325] 11 August 1362.
[326] 7 April 1362.
[327] Over *Lincolniensis* deleted by a line.
[328] *Nundum*, MS.

Januarii anno primo [329] taxa vel fructus. Episcopus certificat quod ista prebenda vocatur de Tarvyn (Tarvin), et credo quod verum sit quia supra eadem pagina providetur Nicholao Heth' per obitum Willelmi qui ipsam in presenti obtinet et pro ea partem solvit.

De prebenda de Gonssale (Gnosall) in ecclesia Licheffeldensi,[324] de qua collatio et provisio facte auctoritate ordinaria Hugoni de Carles fuerunt eidem auctoritate apostolica confirmate vel provisum de novo per Urbanum quinto nonas Martii anno primo,[330] taxa vel fructus. Episcopus certificat quod est prebenda de Morenhal (Morehall) in ecclesia collegiata de Gonssale et quod dictus Hugo nunquam habuit possessionem.

Summa pagine lxxix li. vi s. x d. et tria beneficia non taxata.

### (fol. 104) Assawensis

De ecclesia de Dynkegh' (Denbigh), de qua, vacante de iure ut asseritur, fuit provisum Willelmo de Sumderlond' per Clementem ydus Novembris anno ix°,[331] pro resta ii li. iii s. iiii d.

De ecclesia de Landrimeawe (Llandrinio), taxata vii li., que fuit confirmata Griffino de Charleton' per Innocentium iii° nonas Maii anno ix°,[332] pro dicta taxa vii li.

De ecclesia de Dynkegh', de qua vacante per obitum Willelmi de Sumdelond' fuit provisum Willelmo Arden' per Innocentium ix° kalendas Maii anno nono,[333] pro taxa xv li. vi s. viii d. Sed credo quod ista taxa non sit bona quia supra proximo non taxatur nisi vi li. xiii s. iiii d.

Item de eadem ecclesia, vacante per obitum dicti Willelmi, fuit provisum Hugoni Croft' per Innocentium iiii^to kalendas Maii anno nono,[334] taxa.

De ecclesia de Kyklkeyn (Kilken) et capella eidem annexa, de qua per obitum ultimi rectoris eiusdem fuit provisum Waltero de Fraystorpp' per Innocentium xi° kalendas Julii anno nono,[335] pro taxa vii li.

### Menewensis

De ecclesia de Lamhanglarath' (Llanfihangel ar Arth), non taxata, de qua per obitum Ricardi Approvanss' fuit provisum Ludovico Cauntthon' per Clementem, taxa vel fructus. Sed episcopus certificat quod est de patronatu principis Wallie et ideo non habuit effectum.

Summa pagine xxxi li. x s. et unum beneficium non taxatum.

(fol. 104^v) De ecclesia de Weston' (Wiston), non taxata, de qua per resignationem Rogeri dicti Johannis

fuit provisum Willelmo de Newawe per Innocentium xix° kalendas Junii anno iiii°,[336] fructus.

De ecclesia de Langdomor' (Llangoedmore), taxata vi li. xiii s. iiii d., de qua Guillelmo de Appromes' fuit provisum per cardinalem Petragoricensem, iii li. vi s. viii d.

De prebenda in ecclesia Menewensi, de qua per obitum Thome David fuit provisum David Wagham per Innocentium xi kalendas Julii anno nono,[335] taxa vel fructus.

De prebenda de Landewybremy (Llandewi Brefi) in ecclesia Menewensi, de qua per obitum Griffini de Campthon' fuit provisum Willelmo de Ossenden' per Innocentium pridie nonas Decembris anno quinto,[337] taxa vel fructus. Sed episcopus certificat quod non est prebenda in ecclesia Menewensi que sic vocetur, sed ecclesia de Landewybremy et est collegiata per se, et illa non vacavit.

De prebenda seu portione in ecclesia Sancti Martini de Harlewell' (Abergwili), de qua per obitum Willelmi Daxbrayk' fuit provisum Waltero de Frethon' per Innocentium iiii° nonas Julii anno nono,[338] taxa vel fructus.

### Eboracensis

De prebenda in ecclesia Eboracensi de qua per consecrationem electi Terwynensis fuit provisum Federico Salenan, taxa vel fructus. Archiepiscopus rescribit quod nunquam audivit loqui de talibus prebendariis.

De prebenda de Stranssale (Strensall) in Eboracensi ecclesia, de qua per consecrationem Michaelis episcopi Londoniensis fuit provisum cardinali Petragoricensi per Innocentium pridie ydus Octobris anno secundo,[339] pro taxa liii li. vi s. viii d.

De vicaria de Gylbyng' (Gilling), in qua Johannes Park' fuit subrogatus in omni iure quod (fol. 105)[340] competebat Gerlaco de Clave per Innocentium x° kalendas Maii anno ix°,[341] pro taxa x li.

Item de eadem fuit provisum Johanni Beek' per Innocentium nono kalendas Septembris anno viii°,[342] taxa vel fructus.

De prebenda de Wystowe (Wistow), taxata c li., in ecclesia Eboracensi et archidiaconatu eiusdem ecclesie, non taxato, de quibus per obitum cardinalis Penestrini[343] fuit provisum cardinali Carcassonensi,[344] pro resta taxe prebende xvi li. xvi s. viii d., et pro resta archidiaconatus v li. x s.

De prebenda de Driffeld' in ecclesia Eboracensi, de

---

[329] 2 January 1363.
[330] 3 March 1363.
[331] 13 November 1350.
[332] 5 May 1361.
[333] 23 April 1361.
[334] 28 April 1361.
[335] 21 June 1361.

[336] 14 May 1356.
[337] 4 December 1357.
[338] 4 July 1361.
[339] 14 October 1354.
[340] At the foot of fol. 104^v: *Summa pagine lvi li. xiii s. iiii d. et quinque beneficia non taxata.*
[341] 22 April 1361.
[342] 24 August 1360.
[343] Peter des Prés.
[344] Stephen Aubert, deacon of S. Maria in Aquiro.

qua per obitum Willelmi de Sancto Martiali fuit provisum cardinali de Sancto Martiali,[345] pro taxa c li.

De prebenda de Bolin (Bole) in ecclesia Eboracensi, de qua per obitum Thome de Newell' fuit provisum cardinali Cluniacensi,[346] pro resta xvi li.

De prebenda de Newell' (Norwell) in ecclesia collegiata de Suthwell', in qua in omni iure quod competebat Johanni de Dotthon' fuit subrogatus Thomas de Moynut de Wycham per Innocentium vi° kalendas Augusti anno quinto,[347] pro taxa xxxvi li. xiii s. iiii d.

De capella sive cantoria de Wentebrig' (Ferrybridge), de qua per obitum Thome Attemor' fuit provisum Roberto de Wyk' per Innocentium xi kalendas Decembris anno vii°,[348] taxa vel fructus. Archiepiscopus certificat quod non est talis capella in sua diocesi quod sciatur.

De archidiaconatu de Estridyg' in ecclesia Eboracensi [349] cum ecclesia de Mapelthon' (Mappleton), non taxata, sibi annexa, de quo [350] vacante eo quod Willelmus Walcore, qui ipsum [351] obtinebat, aliam ecclesiam extitit assequtus, fuit provisum Waltero Eskorlawe per Innocentium pridie kalendas Decembris anno vii°,[352] qui composuit medio iuramento et salvo iure pluris, pro ecclesia xvi li. xiii s. iiii d. De archidiaconatu vero dicitur quod nullos habet redditus preter visitationes et correctiones.

De custodia sive sacristia capelle Beate Marie et Sanctorum Angelorum Eboraci, cuius collatio et provisio auctoritate ordinaria facte Johanni de Wykham fuerunt (fol. 105ᵛ)[353] eidem auctoritate apostolica confirmate vel provisum de novo per Innocentium ix° kalendas Januarii anno primo,[354] pro taxa lxxxviii li. viii s. viii d.

De capellania Beati Petri de Wolvey, de qua ex causa permutationis cum Henrico Myd' fuit provisum Johanni Dich' per Innocentium quinto kalendas Aprilis anno viii°,[355] taxa vel fructus. Sed archiepiscopus et eius officialis semper rescribunt quod non est talis in diocesi sua.

### Dunelmensis

De hospitali de Gretham, non taxato, de quo per obitum Johannis de Stokthon' fuit provisum Thome Johannis de Brydekyrk' per Clementem pridie ydus Octobris anno ix°,[356] fructus. Exceptis iii li. vi s. viii

d., de quibus Dominus Hugo Peregrini in suis rationibus respondet.

De prebenda in ecclesia collegiata Langcestr' (Lanchester), de qua ex causa permutationis cum Henrico de Exthon' fuit provisum Galfrido de Cornesio per Innocentium xv kalendas Decembris anno primo,[357] fructus. Sed archiepiscopus certificat quod nunquam habuit illam prebendam.

De prebenda de Dumley (Lamesley) in ecclesia collegiata Cestrie super Stratam (Chester-le-Street), de qua per obitum electi Norwicensis fuit provisum Willelmo de Sugteburg' per Innocentium ydus Februarii anno secundo,[358] pro taxa xx li.

De decanatu ecclesie collegiate Cestr' super stratam, cuius permutatio facta auctoritate ordinaria cum Johanne Schultorpp' pro archidiaconatu Cicestrensi per Adam de Hotton' fuit eidem confirmata per Innocentium kalendas Julii anno vi°,[359] et decanatus taxatur xxxiii li. vi s. viii d., pro resta xvi li. xiii s. iiii d.

De vicaria de Newthon' englendale (Kirknewton), de qua per obitum Roberti de Jarun fuit provisum Roberto Hepp' per Innocentium nonas Septembris anno vii°,[360] pro taxa xx li. Sed episcopus certificat quod nunquam habuit possessionem nec provisio habuit effectum.

Summa pagine cxlv li. ii s. et tria beneficia non taxata.

(fol. 106) De prebenda in ecclesia de Northon' (Norton), de qua per obitum Thome Drax' fuit provisum Bernardo de Lyneriis per Innocentium vii° kalendas Maii anno ix°,[361] taxa vel fructus. Sed episcopus certificat quod non est talis prebendarius in ecclesia nec umquam fuit quod sciatur.

De prebenda in ecclesia collegiata Haukland' (Auckland), de qua per obitum Thome de Brydkyrk fuit provisum Willelmo de Wycham per Innocentium pridie ydus Augusti anno ix°,[362] taxa vel fructus.

De ecclesia de Stanopp' (Stanhope), de qua per obitum Thome de Brydkyk fuit provisum Willelmo de Norwico per Innocentium viii kalendas Septembris anno ix°,[363] pro taxa xl s.

De eadem ecclesia collatio facta auctoritate ordinaria Ricardo de Wulyngthon' per obitum prefati Thome fuit eidem confirmata per Innocentium iiii° kalendas Januarii anno ix°,[364] pro taxa xl s. Sed iste due provisiones sunt infra annum et prohibitus fui per regem ne facerem exequtionem contra incumbentem auctoritate regia.

Item de eadem collatio predicta dicto Ricardo facta

---

[345] Hugo de Sancto Martiali, deacon of S. Maria in Portico.
[346] Androin de la Roche, priest of S. Marcello.
[347] 27 July 1357.
[348] 21 November 1359.
[349] Followed by *d* deleted by a dot.
[350] *qua*, MS.
[351] *ipsam*, MS.
[352] 30 November 1359.
[353] At the end of fol. 105: *Summa pagine ii° vi li. xiii s. iiii d. et duo beneficia non taxata.*
[354] 24 December 1353.
[355] 28 March 1360.
[356] 14 October 1350.

[357] 17 November 1353.
[358] 13 February 1354.
[359] 1 July 1358.
[360] 5 September 1359.
[361] 25 April 1361.
[362] 12 August 1361.
[363] 25 August 1361.
[364] 29 December 1361.

fuit confirmata per Innocentium iiii° ydus Maii anno x°,[365] pro taxa xl s.

De prebenda ecclesia collegiata de Houkeland (Auckland), de qua per obitum dicti Thome fuit provisum Roberto de Stratton per Innocentium xvi° kalendas Septembris.[366] Sed de ista prebenda providetur supra eodem folio Willelmo de Wycham.

De capella libera de Jesmenth' (Jesmond), cuius collatio facta auctoritate ordinaria Thome de Penreth fuit eidem confirmata per Innocentium nono ydus Januarii anno ix°,[367] taxa vel fructus.

Item de eadem,[368] vacante per obitum Henrici Beuffaunt, fuit provisum Matheo de Bolthon' per Innocentium xiiii° kalendas Februarii anno x°,[369] taxa vel fructus. Sed prohibitum est per breve regium ne fiat exequtio contra nunc incumbentem auctoritate regia.

Summa pagine vi li. et quinque beneficia non taxata.

(fol. 106ᵛ) De hospitali pauperum Sancti Egidii de Kyptor' (Kepier), de quo per obitum Petri de Cortesby fuit provisum Johanni de Appelby per Innocentium ix° kalendas Maii anno viii°,[370] taxa vel fructus. Sed prohibitum est per breve regium ut supra.

De ecclesia de Roukbury (Rothbury), de qua [371] presentatio, institutio, inductio facte auctoritate ordinaria Johanni Marescalli fuerunt auctoritate apostolica confirmate vel provisum de novo per Urbanum quinto nonas Martii anno primo,[372] que taxatur lxvi li. xiii s. iiii d., pro resta lvi li. xiii s. iiii d.

De canonicatu et prebenda ecclesie collegiate de Northon' (Norton), de quibus vacantibus per obitum Thome Drax' fuit provisum Bernardo de Luchonie clerico per Clementem vii° kalendas Maii anno viii°,[373] taxa vel fructus. Sed supra per obitum eiusdem providetur alteri.

### Karleolensis

De ecclesia Crostwayt (Crosthwaite), in qua in omni iure competenti Johanni de Solario fuit subrogatus Johannes Henrici per Innocentium pridie ydus Januarii anno quinto,[374] pro taxa xxx li. xiii s. iiii d. In rationibus Magistri Hugonis Peregrini continetur quod non est prosequtus gratiam nec possessionem adeptus.

De vicaria de Rampton' (Brampton), de qua ex causa permutationis cum vicaria de Scaldefford (Shalford) Wynthoniensis diocesis fuit provisum Johanni Amyl per Innocentium xi kalendas Septembris anno quinto,[375] pro taxa viii li.

De vicaria de Costwayt (Crosthwaite), de qua provisio facta Willelmo de Eseneden fuit eidem confirmata per Innocentium pridie kalendas Julii anno viii°,[376] pro taxa xx li.

Summa pagine cxv li. vi s. viii d. et duo beneficia non taxata.

(fol. 107) De ecclesia de Kerkelonden (Kirkland), de qua, vacante ex eo quod Johannes de Kerkeby ipsam cum ecclesia de Wissopp' (Ousby) per mensem et amplius detinuit pacifice et sine dispensatione, fuit provisum Johanni de Kerkeby per Innocentium viii° kalendas Novembris anno vii°,[376a] pro taxa xl li.

De parochiali ecclesia de Kaldebek' (Caldbeck) Karleolensis diocesis, de qua collatio et provisio facte auctoritate ordinaria per episcopum Karleolensem Willelmo Rugenhill' fuerunt confirmate, etiam si reservata foret, per Urbanum quinto nonas Martii anno primo,[372] taxa vel fructus. Sed ista provisio non habuit effectum, quia ante istam confirmationem episcopus decessit et rex contulit eam ratione temporalitatis dicti episcopatus in suis manibus existentis.

Summa istius pagine xl li. et unum beneficium non taxatum.

### Sequitur resta de quatuor obligatis

De ecclesia de Hodenell' (Hodnet) Lichfeldensis diocesis et prebenda de Farendon' (Faringdon) in ecclesia Saresbiriensi, de Mora (Moorfields, St. Giles Cripplegate) in ecclesia Londoniensi, de Humdreeton' (Hunderton) in ecclesia Herffordensi, de quibus fuit provisum Nicholao Heth' et composuit cum camera pro primis fructibus dictorum beneficiorum in viiiᶜ fl. et 1 fl., pro resta iiᶜ v fl. et medius, ii d. sterlingorum.

Et est sciendum quod alii tres totum solverunt excepta prebenda de Middelton' (Middleton) in ecclesia Cicestrensi, pro qua debentur iii li. vi s. viii d., que posita est pro resta in suo loco in diocesi Cicestrensi, et ideo hic non ponitur nisi pro memoriali.

Summa istius pagine xl li., item iiᶜ v fl. medius ii d. sterlingorum, et unum beneficium.

(fol. 107ᵛ) Sequuntur reste beneficiorum collatorum per dominos cardinales.

### Saresbiriensis

De prioratu seu officio de Noion alias de Novo Mercato (Neufmarché), de quo fuit provisum Nicholao Rem per cardinalem Petragoricensem, fructus.

### Lincolniensis

De ecclesia de Logonis (Laughton), de qua nuper fuit provisum Waltero Lenake per cardinalem Petragoricensem, fructus.

De ecclesia Sancti Clementis de Willowby (Willoughby) fuit provisum per cardinalem Petragoricensem

---

[365] 12 May 1362.
[366] 17 August.
[367] 24 December 1361. See above, p. 157.
[368] *eodem*, MS.
[369] 19 January 1362.
[370] 23 April 1360.
[371] *quo*, MS.
[372] 3 March 1363.
[373] 25 April 1350.
[374] 12 January 1357.
[375] 22 August 1357.

[376] 30 June 1360.
[376a] 25 October 1359.

Hugoni de Kypas, pro taxa xxiii li. vi s. viii d. Sed episcopus certificat quod non est in sua diocesi.

### Exoniensis

De cantoria perpetua Sancte Marie sita in ecclesia Omnium Sanctorum Exoniensis diocesis fuit provisum per dominum Urgellensem Alexandro Speremon', taxa vel fructus. Sed episcopus certificat quod non est in sua diocesi.

### Licheffeldensis [377]

De ecclesia de Asdeby (Alderley), de qua per cardinalem Petragoricensem fuit provisum Johanni Baston', pro taxa viii li.

De ecclesia de Burhull' (Burnhill), de qua per cardinalem Petragoricensem fuit provisum Hugoni de Pankeston', fructus. Sed ista est de patronatu laicali et est prohibitum per regem ne aliquid exigatur.

De vicaria ecclesie de Dorsette magna (Great Dassett), de qua per dominum cardinalem Petragoricensem fuit provisum Willelmo de Westbury, fructus. Sed est prohibitum ut in precedenti ex eadem causa.

### Bangorensis

De ecclesia de Damburgham (Llangian) fuit provisum per eundem cardinalem David nato Johannis, taxa vel fructus.

Summa pagine xxxi li. vi s. viii d. et quatuor beneficia non taxata

### (fol. 108) Bangorensis

De ecclesia de Bouseby (Cowesby) fuit provisum per cardinalem Urgellensem Henrico de Helperby, fructus.

De vicaria de Impryngthon' (Impington), taxata iiii li. vi s. viii d., de qua per cardinalem Petragoricensem fuit provisum Ricardo de Schelfford xii° kalendas Decembris pontificatus Domini Innocentii anno iiii°,[378] pro resta xliii s. iiii d.

Summa istius patet quia xliii s. iiii d. et unum beneficium non taxatum.

Summa universalis omnium arrayratgiorum sive restarum de annatis beneficiorum collatorum per Dominos Clementem, Innocentium et Urbanum usque ad iiii kalendas Maii pontificatus sui anno primo [379] ii^m iiii^c ii li. vi s. x d.; item ii^c v fl. medius ii d. sterlingorum. Approbatum.

### (fol. 108^v) Anno primo

Sequuntur reste arrayratgiorum beneficiorum collatorum per dominum nostrum papam Urbanum in Anglia a iii° kalendas Maii pontificatus sui anno primo [380] usque ad pridie ydus Julii pontificatus sui anno quinto [381] de quo tempore in aliis computis arayratgia dedi.

### Eliensis

De pariochiali ecclesia de Elleworth (Elsworth) Eliensis diocesis, vacatura cum Johannes de Morthon' dignitatem, personatum vel officium curatum in ecclesia Licheffeldensi fuerit pacifice assecutus, fuit provisum Thome Eltesle, clerico dicte Eliensis diocesis bacallario in utroque iure, per Urbanum iii° kalendas Maii anno primo,[380] taxa vel fructus. Sed infra providetur alteri per eamdem vacationem xi kalendas Februarii anno quarto.[382]

### Norwicensis

De collatione et provisione factis [383] Stephano Je Judicis Stephani de prepositura monasterii Sancte Marie de Morthon' ordinis Sancti Benedicti, vacante per promotionem abbatis dicti monasterii, que fuerunt eidem confirmate vel provisum de novo per Urbanum iii° kalendas Maii anno primo,[380] taxa vel fructus.

### Norwicensis

De ordinatione facta per bene memorie dominum decanum (Otto), tunc in partibus Anglicanis apostolice sedis legatum, de uno perpetuo vicario in parochiali ecclesia de Metthon' (Morton) dicte diocesis, que fuit confirmata [384] vel provisum de novo per Urbanum iii° kalendas Maii anno primo,[380] taxa vel fructus.

### Exoniensis et Lincolniensis [385]

De collatione et provisione ex causa permutationis factis [386] Willelmo Stel de archidiaconatu Totthon' in ecclesia Exoniensi pro ecclesia parochiali de Dedyngdon' (Doddington) Lincolniensis diocesis, que fuerunt eidem confirmate vel provisum de novo per Urbanum vii° kalendas Maii anno primo,[387] pro quo archidiaconatu est in totum satisfactum; restat quod debetur annata pro dicta ecclesia de Dodyngdon' Lincolniensis diocesis, taxa vel fructus.

### (fol. 109) [388] Lincolniensis

De provisione facta Johanni de Ditton', clerico Licheffeldensis diocesis, de canonicatu et prebenda quam Willelmus de Askeby, sedis apostolice capellanus, que vocatur Redsir' minori (Bedford Minor) in ecclesia Lincolniensi, vacante per resignationem ipsius in manibus ordinarii aut per assequtionem alterius prebende in dicta ecclesia, taxa vel fructus.

### Lincolniensis

De provisione facta Petro de Newuald', bacallario in legibus, de canonicatu et prebenda ecclesie collegiate

[377] Lincolniensis, MS.
[378] 20 November 1356.
[379] 28 April 1363.
[380] 29 April 1363.
[381] 14 July 1367.
[382] 22 January 1366.
[383] facta, MS.
[384] fuerunt confirmate, MS.
[385] Follows Eliensis et Lincolniensis deleted by a line.
[386] facte, MS.
[387] 25 April 1363.
[388] The heading Anno primo is repeated at the top of the page.

de Rippin' et prebenda do Mikethon' (Monkton) in eadem, vacante per obitum Johannis de Wymewyk' per Urbanum vii° kalendas Maii anno primo,[387] taxa vel fructus. Sed de ista lis pendet in curia, et fuit prohibitum per regem ne fiat aliqua exequtio contra incumbentem, et infra providetur de eadem alterii iii° kalendas Julii anno primo.[389]

## Herffordensis

De provisione facta Johanni de Brinkhull', presbytero Herffordensis diocesis, de vicaria perpetua parochialis ecclesie de Bertton' (Burrington) dicte diocesis, vacante per resignationem Ade de Abbatia factam in manibus ordinarii, per Urbanum vii kalendas Maii anno primo [387] taxa vel fructus.

## Licheffeldensis

De canonicatu ecclesie Licheffeldensis et prebenda de Pices (Prees) in eadem ecclesia, vacantibus per resignationem Petri alias dicti Johannis de Alaston', fuit provisum Roberto do Straton, legum doctori auditori palatii apostolici, per Urbanum xvii° kalendas Junii anno primo,[390] taxa vel fructus. Sed allegatur quod non habuit effectum.

## Eliensis

De collatione et provisione factis [391] auctoritate ordinaria iure devoluto de prioratu seu administratione prioratus Swaveseye Eliensis diocesis, monasterii Sanctorum Sergii et Bachi Andegavensis (Angers) dependentis, ordinis Sancti Benedicti, per unum religiosum dicti monasterii solito [392] gubernari, fratri Johanni Wakelyn, monacho monasterii Westmonasterii, monasterii Londoniensis diocesis, que fuerunt confirmate vel provisum de novo per Urbanum xvi° kalendas Junii anno primo,[393] taxa vel fructus.

## (fol. 109ᵛ) [388] Cicestrensis

De parochiali ecclesia de Lamoygh' (Lancing) Cicestrensis diocesis, unita et annexa mense et usui ministri et fratrum hospitalis Sancte Trinitatis de Modyngdon' (Muttinden) Cantuariensis diocesis, servata portione competenti pro vicaria dicte ecclesie, per Urbanum quinto kalendas Junii anno primo,[394] taxa vel fructus.

## Landawensis

De archidiaconatu ecclesie Landawensis, vacante per resignationem Thome de Eltesby Eliensis diocesis, in utroque iure bacallario, fuit eidem provisum Thome per Urbanum kalendas Junii anno primo,[395] taxa vel fructus.

---

[389] 29 June 1363.
[390] 16 May 1363.
[391] *facta*, MS.
[392] *solitum*, MS.
[393] 17 May 1363.
[394] 28 May 1363.
[395] 1 June 1363.

## Dunelmensis

De canonicatu et prebenda seu portione de Bures (Byers) in ecclesia collegiata de Arkesland (Auckland) Dunelmensis diocesis, per mortem Rogeri de Blamer' in Romana curia defuncti, fuit provisum Rogero de Slatobue, presbytero Eboracensis diocesis, per Urbanum v° ydus Junii anno primo,[396] taxa vel fructus. Sed ista prebenda non valet propter guerras, licet taxatur ad xvi li.

## Eboracensis

De beneficio ecclesiastico, videlicet parochiali ecclesia Sancte Helene in Stayngat' (Stonegate, York) Eboracensis diocesis, de qua vacante per mortem Johannis de Rastore fuit provisum Rogero Ulram, presbytero Eboracensis diocesis, per Urbanum v° ydus Junii anno primo,[396] taxa vel fructus.

## Cicestrensis

De parochiali ecclesia de Westichnor (West Ichenor) Cicestrensis diocesis, de qua vacante per mortem Rogeri Lyndon', ultimi rectoris eiusdem, extra Romanam curiam defuncti, que tanto tempore vacavit quod eius collatio est ad sedem apostolicam legitime devoluta, fuit provisum Roberto Amys de Brentbrogthon', presbytero Lincolniensis diocesis, per Urbanum quinto kalendas Julii anno primo,[397] taxa vel fructus.

## Eboracensis

De vicaria perpetua parochialis ecclesie de Skipton' in Crasve (Skipton in Craven) dicte Eboracensis diocesis, de qua vacante per mortem Willelmi de Dragthon', ultimi rectoris eiusdem, et tanto tempore quod eius collatio est ad sedem apostolicam legitime devoluta, fuit provisum Thome Johannis filii Marild' Archaliate de Schirbturn' in Elmeto Eboracensis diocesis per Urbanum quinto kalendas Julii anno primo,[397] taxa vel fructus.

## (fol. 110) [388] Saresbiriensis

De parochiali ecclesia de Swynden (Swindon) Saresbiriensis diocesis, que per cessionem vel dimissionem Nicholai de Hoeman, ultimi rectoris eiusdem, que tanto tempore vacavit quod eius collatio est ad sedem apostolicam legitime devoluta, fuit collata Willelmo Persone, presbytero dicte diocesis, per Urbanum quinto kalendas ⟨Julii⟩ anno primo,[397] taxa vel fructus.

## Dunelmensis

De vicaria parochiali ecclesie de Nornham (Norham) Dunelmensis diocesis, vacante per mortem Willelmi de Elwyk', ultimi vicarii eiusdem extra Romanam curiam defuncti, quam frater Ricardus monachus et apostata [398]

---

[396] 9 June 1363.
[397] 27 June 1363.
[398] *apastata*, MS.

ordinis Cisterciensis per duos annos et amplius occupavit indebite, fuit provisum Waltero Johannis, presbytero Dunelmensis diocesis, per Urbanum quinto kalendas Julii anno primo [397] taxa vel fructus.

### Eboracensis [899]

De parochiali ecclesia de Missey' (Misson) Eboracensis diocesis, de qua vacante per resignationem seu dimissionem Johannis de Scharlehorpp' tanto tempore quod eius collatio est ad sedem apostolicam legitime devoluta, fuit provisum Johanni de Baldeston', clerico dicte diocesis, per Urbanum quinto kalendas Julii anno primo,[397] taxa vel fructus.

De parochiali ecclesia de Manffeld (Manfield) Eboracensis diocesis, de qua vacante per resignationem vel dimissionem quondam Willelmi de Strattowill', ultimi rectoris eiusdem, a tanto tempore quod eius collatio est ad sedem apostolicam legitime devoluta, fuit provisum Willelmo de Wyntornwyk', presbytero Eboracensis diocesis, per Urbanum quinto kalendas Julii anno primo,[397] taxa vel fructus.

De parochiali ecclesia de Bayngham (Keyingham) Eboracensis diocesis, de qua vacante per resignationem Willelmi de Brokelesby in manibus ordinarii a tanto tempore quod eius collatio est ad sedem apostolicam legitime devoluta, fuit provisum Roberto de Wadyngham, clerico Lincolniensis diocesis, per Urbanum quinto kalendas Julii anno primo,[397] taxa vel fructus.

De parochiali ecclesia de Elkesley Eboracensis diocesis, de qua, vacante per resignationem Johannis Cambrith a tanto tempore quod eius collatio est et cetera, fuit provisum Roberto de Outre, clerico Eliensis diocesis, per Urbanum v° kalendas Julii anno primo,[397] taxa vel fructus.

### Licheffeldensis

De parochiali ecclesia de Bradyle (Baddiley) Licheffeldensis diocesis, de qua, vacante per resignationem Willelmi de Hynkele, ultimi rectoris eiusdem, in manibus ordinarii a tanto tempore quod (fol. 110ᵛ) [888] eius collatio est ad sedem apostolicam legitime devoluta, fuit provisum Rogero de Wadnorthon', presbytero Norwicensis diocesis, per Urbanum iii° nonas Julii anno primo,[400] taxa vel fructus. In arayratgiis aliis ultimis dimissis est alia provisio facta eidem de eadem eadem die et eodem anno que hic non ponitur quia eadem est provisio.

### Eboracensis

De provisione facta Roberto de Sochow, presbytero Eboracensis diocesis, de ecclesia de Agthon' (Aughton) Eboracensis diocesis, que valet secundum communem extimationem xl li. sterlingorum, per Urbanum iii° nonas Julii anno primo,[400] taxa vel fructus.

De parochiali ecclesia de Usegate (All Saints Pavement in Ousegate) in civitate Eboraci, que taxatur ad xv m. sterlingorum, de qua fuit Johanni Ulram provisum per Urbanum iii° nonas Julii anno primo,[400] taxa vel fructus. Sed in libro provisionum est alia provisio et collatio facte eidem de eadem ecclesia per mortem eiusdem et sub eadem data eodem anno, et subsequenter est alia provisio facta eidem de eadem xviii° kalendas Maii anno iiiiᵗᵒ,[401] et neutra istarum valet quia ille qui eam nunc tenet ostendit diffinitivam sententiam contra illum per cuius mortem impetratur, et ideo pro istis duabus provisionibus posita fuit inter inutiles et pro prima etiam poni debet ex causa predicta.[402]

De provisione facta Ade de Thotton', presbytero Eboracensis diocesis, de canonicatu et prebenda ecclesie de Rippon' et prebenda [403] de Mukthon' (Monkton) in eadem ecclesia, quarum fructus lxvi li. xiii s. iiii d. secundum taxationem valorem annuum non excedunt, per Urbanum iii° nonas Julii anno primo,[400] taxa vel fructus. Sed de ista prebenda supra providetur alteri vii° kalendas Maii anno ⟨primo⟩,[404] et est prohibitum per regem ne aliqua fiat exequtio contra incumbentem.

De parochiali ecclesia de Cotom' (Cotham) Eboracensis diocesis, de qua, vacante per resignationem Radulphi de Gerwell' a tanto tempore quod eius collatio est ad sedem apud sedem apostolicam devoluta, fuit provisum Johanni de Otyngham, presbytero Eboracensis diocesis, per Urbanum xiii° kalendas Augusti anno primo,[405] taxa vel fructus.

(fol. 111) [888] De parochiali ecclesia de Ottulay (Whixley) Eboracensis diocesis, de qua, vacante per obitum Nicholai Cessay tanto tempore quod eius collatio est ad sedem apostolicam devoluta, fuit provisum Johanni de Torkeseys, bacallario in legibus, per Urbanum vii° ydus Julii anno primo,[406] taxa vel fructus.

De provisione facta ex causa permutationis Willelmo Glayne de Podyngthon' de vicaria parochialis ecclesie de Kyldesbyk (Kildwick) Eboracensis diocesis per Urbanum vii° ydus Julii anno primo,[406] taxa vel fructus.

### Landawensis et Exoniensis

De provisione facta ex causa permutationis Martino de Neryngthon' de parochiali ecclesia de Kylyngham (St. Mary Hill) Landawensis diocesis cum prebenda ecclesie collegiate de Glausite (Glasnay) Exoniensis diocesis pro qua est satisfactum.

### Londoniensis et Norwicensis

De provisione facta ex causa permutationis Ade Thebaud' de libera capella de Chelmesford (Chelmsford)

---

[899] This heading is repeated before each of the next three items.

[400] 5 July 1363.

[401] 14 April 1366.

[402] The next four items are each preceded by the heading *Eboracensis.*

[403] *prebende,* MS.

[404] A blank space is left in MS. 25 April 1363.

[405] 20 July 1363.

[406] 9 July 1363.

Londoniensis diocesis et Thome Thebaud' filio Roberti Thebaud de Jewewya de decanatu rurali Lynie (Lynn) Norwicensis diocesis per Urbanum vii° ydus Julii anno primo,[406] taxa vel fructus.

## Norwicensis

De decanatu rurali de Rodenhal (Redenhall) Norwicensis diocesis, de quo, vacante per liberam resignationem Willelmi de Thanworth', clerici Londoniensis diocesis, fuit provisum Thome Drayton' Lincolniensis diocesis per Urbanum vii° ydus Julii anno primo,[406] taxa vel fructus.

## Eboracensis

De parochiali ecclesia de Ornesee (Hornsea) Eboracensis diocesis, de qua, vacante apud sedem apostolicam per obitum Domini Raymundi de Fargiis quondam cardinalis,[407] fuit provisum Nicholao de Lovanys per Urbanum iii° ydus Augusti anno primo,[408] taxa vel fructus.

## (fol. 111ᵛ)[388] Eboracensis

De canonicatu ecclesie Eboracensis et prebenda de Missham (Masham) in eadem, de quibus vacantibus per obitum cardinalis Maglonensis[409] fuit provisum Domino Guillelmo Cesaraugustanensi[410] motu proprio per Urbanum xvii° kalendas Septembris anno primo,[411] taxa vel fructus.

## Bangoriensis

De parochiali ecclesia Sanctorum Evitici et Julite Lanquile (Llanerfyl?) Bangorensis diocesis, de qua, vacante per obitum ultimi rectoris eiusdem extra curiam defuncti et que tanto tempore vacavit quod eius collatio est ad sedem apostolicam legitime devoluta, fuit provisum Reginaldo de Wynemere, presbytero dicte diocesis, per Urbanum xvii° kalendas Septembris anno primo,[411] taxa vel fructus.

## Eboracensis[412]

De parochialis ecclesiae vicaria perpetua de Kulenham (Kirkham) Eboracensis diocesis, de qua, vacante per resignationem Willelmi de Slayteburn' factam in manibus ordinarii, que tanto tempore vacavit quod eius collatio est ad sedem apostolicam legitime devoluta, vel alio quovis modo vacet, fuit provisum Symoni de Tenebrig', presbytero Roffensis diocesis, et dimittet parochialem ecclesiam de Exete (Excete) Cicestrensis diocesis, per Urbanum xi° kalendas Septembris anno primo,[413] taxa vel fructus.

De vicaria perpetua parochialis ecclesie de Gyling' (Gilling) Eboracensis diocesis, de qua, vacante ex eo quod Gerlacus de Clave, clericus Spirensis (Speyer) diocesis, eam detinuit occupatam in presbyterum non promotus infra tempus debitum, vel alio quovis modo vacet, fuit provisum Thome filio Johannis Briston', clerico Norwicensis diocesis, per Urbanum xi kalendas Septembris anno primo,[413] taxa vel fructus.

## Saresbiriensis

De parochiali ecclesia Beate Marie de Wynterbura' Stikolan (Winterborne Stickland) Saresbiriensis diocesis, de[414] qua vacante per mortem Thome Henrici de Chelstr' in Romana curia defuncti fuit provisum Roberto Falky, clerico Eboracensis diocesis, per Urbanum xi kalendas Septembris anno primo,[413] taxa vel fructus.

## Eboracensis

De parochiali ecclesia curata Omnium Sanctorum in Uregate (All Saints Pavement in Ousegate, York) Eboracensis diocesis, de qua vacante in curia per mortem Symonis Warde fuit provisum Johanni Ulram, presbytero (fol. 112)[388] Eboracensis diocesis, per Urbanum xi° kalendas Septembris anno primo,[413] taxa vel fructus. De ista ecclesia supra providetur eidem sub data vii° kalendas Julii.[415]

## Assawensis

De parochiali ecclesia Sancti Ewdelani (Dolwyddelan) Assawensis diocesis, de qua, vacante per liberam resignationem seu dimissionem factam per Theodorum natum Johannis Owyn, ultimum rectorem[416] eiusdem, fuit provisum Awelmo de Brechon', canonico Menewensi, per Urbanum xi° kalendas Septembris anno primo,[413] taxa vel fructus.

## Saresbiriensis

De parochiali ecclesia de Ayewell' (Harwell) Saresbiriensis diocesis, que est de patronatu Edduardi primogeniti regis Anglie Wallie principis et ipsius principis infra castrum suum de Walyngfford' (Wallingford) dicte diocesis, unita auctoritate ordinaria de consensu capituli, que unio[417] fuit confirmata per Urbanum iii° kalendas Septembris anno primo,[418] taxa vel fructus.

## Norwicensis

De parochiali ecclesia de Sniterle (Blakeney or Glandford) Norwicensis diocesis, de qua, vacante per mortem ultimi rectoris eiusdem, que tanto tempore vacavit quod eius collatio est ad sedem apostolicam legitime devoluta, fuit provisum Willelmo Maltheby per Urbanum xi°

---

[407] Deacon of S. Maria Nuova.
[408] 11 August 1363.
[409] Audoin Aubert, bishop of Maguelone, bishop of Ostia.
[410] William d'Aigrefeuille, priest of S. Maria in Trastevere.
[411] 16 August 1363.
[412] This heading is repeated before the next item.
[413] 22 August 1363.

[414] *de* repeated MS.
[415] 25 June 1363.
[416] *ultimi rectoris*, MS.
[417] Followed by *q* deleted by a line.
[418] 30 August 1363.

kalendas Septembris anno primo,[413] taxa vel fructus.

Item Andree de Burwell', presbytero Norwicensis diocesis, fuit provisum de parochiali ecclesia de Sniterle dicte diocesis, vacante per mortem Walteri Moyner' de Salnen' extra Romanam curiam defuncti, que tanto tempore vacavit quod eius collatio et cetera, vel alio quovis modo, et dimittet parochialem ecclesiam de Restull' (Rishangles) dicte diocesis, per Urbanum x° kalendas Septembris anno primo,[419] taxa vel fructus.[420]

### Norwicensis

De parochiali ecclesia de Freng' (Frenze) Norwicensis diocesis, de qua, vacante per liberam resignationem Willelmi de Cotlneye in manibus ordinarii factam, que tanto tempore vacavit quod eius collatio est ad sedem apostolicam legitime devoluta, fuit provisum Thome Drapier, presbytero Londoniensis diocesis, per Urbanum xi° kalendas Septembris anno primo,[413] taxa vel fructus.

### Dunelmensis

De canonicatu et prebenda seu portione ecclesie collegiate de Deryngthon' (Darlington) (fol. 112^v)[388] Dunelmensis diocesis, de qua, vacante per obitum quondam Willelmi Kildesby extra Romanam curiam defuncti, etiam si tanto tempore vacaverit quod eius collatio est[421] ad sedem apostolicam legitime devoluta, fuit provisum Ade de Toryagthon', presbytero Eboracensis diocesis, per Urbanum xi° kalendas Septembris anno primo,[413] taxa vel fructus.

### Eliensis

De parochiali ecclesia de Harweden' (Haddenham) Eliensis diocesis, in qua subrogatus fuit Walterus de Walethon', magister in artibus, in omni iure quod competebat quondam Henrico de Harwedon, super qua dum vivebat in Romana curia litigabat, et dimittet parochialem ecclesiam de Wygherosham (Wittersham) Cantuariensis diocesis et unum beneficium de infrascriptis, videlicet prebendam Cicestrensem vel canonicatum sub expectatione prebende ecclesie Sancti Johannis Beverlacensis ⟨Eboracensis⟩ diocesis per Urbanum x° kalendas Septembris anno primo,[419] taxa vel fructus.

### Eboracensis[422]

De parochiali ecclesia de Colston', Ktkelston' nuncupata (Car-Colston), unita et incorporata dudum per archiepiscopum Eboracensem monasterio et conventui de Reddesford' communiter Werkersop' nuncupato[423] (Worksop) ordinis Sancti Augustini[424] Eboracensis diocesis, que unio et incorporatio fuerunt confirmate

vel provisum de novo per Urbanum vii° ydus Octobris anno primo,[425] taxa vel fructus.

### Herffordensis

De canonicatu et prebenda[426] de Motthon magna (Moreton Magna) in ecclesia Herffordensi,[427] de qua vacante per consecrationem Symonis de Subur' electi Londoniensis fuit provisum Johanni Gardewik, clerico Norwicensis diocesis bacallario in legibus, per Urbanum xiiii kalendas Novembris anno primo,[428] taxa vel fructus.

### Eboracensis

De parochiali ecclesia de Henynglomgh' (Hemingborough) Eboracensis diocesis, unita et incorporata per archiepiscopum Eboracensem priori et capitulo Dunelmensibus, que unio et incorporatio fuerunt confirmate vel provisum de novo per Urbanum xi kalendas Novembris anno primo,[429] taxa vel fructus.

Completum est hic de anno primo.

Anno secundo

### Norwicensis

De parochiali ecclesia de Sabur' (Sudbury) Norwicensis diocesis, de qua, vacante ex eo quod Henricus de Campedon cancellariam[430] ecclesie Londoniensis est pacifice assequtus, fuit provisum Thome de Bokthon', bacallario in legibus, per Urbanum x° kalendas Decembris anno secundo,[431] taxa vel fructus.

### Lincolniensis

De parochiali ecclesia de Edburby (Adderbury) Lincolniensis diocesis, de qua, vacatura ut supra, (fol. 113)[432] videlicet per consecrationem Thome electi Cicestrensis, fuit provisum motu proprio Domino Johanni titulo Sancti Marci presbytero cardinali vi° kalendas Decembris per Urbanum anno ii°,[433] taxa vel fructus.

### Herffordensis

De canonicatu et prebenda ecclesie Herffordensis vocata de Northon' minore (Moreton Minor), taxata x li., vacatura per consecrationem Thome electi Cicentrensis, fuit provisum Willelmo Bell', scolari in legibus, per Urbanum vi° kalendas Decembris anno secundo,[433] pro resta vi li. Et de eadem[434] sub eadem data fuit provisum Nicholao de Chadosden', que provisio fuit

---

[419] 23 August 1363.
[420] In the margin: *eadem est ecclesia*.
[421] Followed by *q* deleted by a line.
[422] *Herffordensis*, MS.
[423] *nuncupati*, MS.
[424] Follows *Benedicti* deleted by a line.
[425] 9 October 1363.
[426] Over *parochiali ecclesia* deleted by a line.
[427] *Lichfeldensi*, MS.
[428] 19 October 1363.
[429] 22 October 1363.
[430] *cancellarius*, MS.
[431] 22 November 1363.
[432] The heading *Anno secundo* is repeated at the top of the page.
[433] 26 November 1363.
[434] *eodem*, MS.

data inter inutiles quia non habuit effectum, quia Guillelmus Well' eam tenet et iam partem solvit, ut patet in recepta aliorum computorum.

## Exoniensis

De parochiali ecclesia de Newenton' Sancti Cirici (Newton, St. Cyres) Exoniensis diocesis, que post liberam resignationem Johannis Lynham, ultimi rectoris eiusdem, in manibus episcopi Exoniensis factam, tanto tempore vacavit quod eius collatio est ad sedem apostolicam legitime devoluta, licet per Willelmum de Malthon', qui se gerit pro vicario eiusdem, ipsam detineat indebite occupatam, fuit provisum Johanni Deyns, presbytero Lyncolniensis diocesis, per Urbanum iiii^to kalendas Decembris anno secundo,[434a] taxa vel fructus.

## Cantuariensis

De parochiali ecclesia Biscopeburn' (Bishopsbourne) Cantuariensis diocesis, de qua, vacante eo quod quidam Willelmus Tyngull', ipsam nuper obtinens, aliud beneficium incompassibile in ecclesia Wellensi est, ut dicitur, auctoritate apostolica pacifice assequtus, fuit provisum Johanni de Digg', presbytero Cantuariensis diocesis, per Urbanum nonas Decembris anno secundo,[435] taxa vel fructus.

## Dunelmensis

De parochiali ecclesia de Whiteburn' (Whitburn) Dunelmensis diocesis, taxata xl li., de qua, vacatura cum Johannes de Appelby decanatum Londoniensem fuerit pacifice assequtus, fuit provisum Ricardo de Whuthecombe, presbytero Wygorniensis diocesis, per Urbanum xix° kalendas Januarii anno secundo,[436] debet pro resta taxe xxxiiii li. vi s. viii d.

Summa pagine xxxix li. vi s. viii d.

## (fol. 113^v)[432] Dunelmensis

De parochiali ecclesia de Wormouth Episcopi (Bishop-Wearmouth) Dunelmensis diocesis, de qua, vacante ex eo quod Willelmus Neupport eamdem ecclesiam curatam et parochialem ecclesiam de Spafford' (Spofforth) Eboracensis diocesis non unitas aut annexas sed diversas occupavit et possedit simul per duos annos et amplius contra constitutionem *Execrabilem*, fuit provisum Willelmo de Arderne, magistro in artibus Lincolniensis diocesis, et dimittet parochialem ecclesiam de Ocestterthon' (Chesterton) eiusdem diocesis, per Urbanum xi° kalendas Januarii anno secundo,[437] taxa vel fructus. Et de ista ecclesia providetur eidem xv° kalendas Decembris anno iii°,[438] et nondum habet effectum quia de ea in curia litigatur inter David de Wloth, qui eam

possidet, et impetrantem, et impetravit comitti auditori cause quod si ei constiterit quod eam sine litteris apostolicis acceptaverit, adiudicet eam dicto David Wlorth' viii° kalendas Maii anno vii°.[439]

## Lincolniensis

De parochiali ecclesia de Haghworthyngham (Hagworthingham) Lincolniensis diocesis, taxata xii li., de qua, vacante ex eo quod Johanes de Sweyseved, olim rector eiusdem ecclesie, ecclesiam parochialem de Werelynsete (Wetheringsett) Norwicensis diocesis est pacifice assequtus, fuit provisum Thome Thottfford', clerico dicte diocesis, per Urbanum pridie nonas Januarii anno secundo,[440] debet de resta dicte taxe iiii li.

## Licheffeldensis

De parochiali ecclesia de Estlimyngthon' Asseyng' (Leamington Hastings) Licheffeldensis diocesis, de qua, vacante per obitum ultimi rectoris eiusdem extra Romanam curiam defuncti, que tanto tempore vacavit quod eius collatio est ad sedem apostolicam legitime devoluta, fuit provisum Ricardo de Thiso, bacallario in decretis, et dimittet parochialem ecclesiam de Herkegh' (Hartley) Roffensis diocesis, per Urbanum iiii° ydus Januarii anno secundo,[441] taxa vel fructus.

## Menewensis

De canonicatu et prebenda ecclesie collegiate de Awerwill' (Abergwili) Menewensis diocesis que vocatur Laniewyth (Llandygwydd), de qua vacante per resignationem Philipi de Bellocampo fuit provisum Ricardo Pagher, clerico Lincolniensis diocesis, per Urbanum pridie kalendas Februarii anno secundo,[442] taxa vel fructus.

Summa pagine iiii li.

## (fol. 114)[432] Norwicensis

De parochiali ecclesia de Snynterlee (Blakeney or Glandford) Norwicensis diocesis, de qua, vacante per obitum Walteri Mayn de Tylneys, que tanto tempore vacavit quod eius collatio est ad sedem apostolicam legitime devoluta, fuit provisum Willelmo Bell', et dimittet parochialem ecclesiam de Stannford' (Stanford) Saresbiriensis diocesis ac canonicatum et prebendam Herffordenses nuper ei collatas, per Urbanum quinto nonas Martii anno secundo,[443] taxa vel fructus. De ista ecclesia sunt alie due provisiones simul ac successive supra sub data xi° kalendas Decembris anno primo,[444] et neutra earum habuit effectum, ut certificat episcopus.

---

[434a] 28 November 1363.
[435] 5 December 1363.
[436] 14 December 1363.
[437] 22 December 1363.
[438] 17 November 1364.

[439] 24 April 1369.
[440] 4 January 1364.
[441] 10 January 1364.
[442] 31 January 1364.
[443] 3 March 1364.
[444] 21 November 1362.

### Eboracensis

De parochiali ecclesia de Buttingham (Brantingham) Eboracensis diocesis, de qua, vacante ex eo quod Willelmus Stord' ipsam per annum et ultra cessante legitimo impedimento detinuit in presbyterum non promotus, fuit provisum Johanni de Toresby, legum doctori, per Urbanum xvi° kalendas Aprilis anno secundo,[445] et dimittet parochialem ecclesiam de Lichkefford' (Lilford) Lincolniensis diocesis, taxa vel fructus.

### Licheffeldensis

De parochiali ecclesia de Wayngthon' (Warrington) Licheffeldensis diocesis, taxata xiii li. vi s. viii d., de qua, vacante per mortem quondam Johannis de Stamffordham extra Romanam curiam defuncti a tanto tempore quod eius collatio est ad sedem apostolicam legitime devoluta, fuit provisum Johanni Par seniori, clerico dicte diocesis, per Urbanum nonas Aprilis anno secundo,[446] taxa vel fructus. Ista propter nimiam potentiam ducis Lancastrie non audet possessionem intrare, et sibi opponitur qui est apostata et inhabilis ad beneficium obtinendum.

### Dunelmensis

De canonicatu ecclesie de Aukaland' (Auckland) et prebenda de Bires (Byers) in eadem Dunelmensis diocesis, de qua vacante per obitum Rogeri de Blamer' in Romana curia defuncti fuit provisum Thome Colier, clerico, dicte diocesis, per Urbanum pridie nonas Aprilis anno secundo,[447] taxa vel fructus. (fol. 114ᵛ) Sed ista provisio non habuit effectum, quia ante fuit provisum alteri supra v° ydus Junii anno [448] primo,[449] et est pauperima et quasi nichil valet, licet taxetur ad xvi li.

### Eboracensis

De parochiali ecclesia de Fereby (North Ferriby) Eboracensis diocesis, de qua, vacante per obitum Roberti de Gridalugthon', ultimi rectoris eiusdem, extra Romanam curiam defuncti, que tanto tempore vacavit quod eius collatio est ad sedem apostolicam legitime devoluta secundum statuta Lateranensis consilii, fuit provisum Willelmo Waselyn, clerico Lincolniensis diocesis, per Urbanum pridie nonas Aprilis anno secundo,[447] taxa vel fructus. Sed iste non fuit gratiam prosequtus, ymo ei renuntiavit.

### Karleolensis

De parochiali ecclesia de Wyngeston' (Wigton) Karleolensis diocesis, de qua, vacante per obitum quondam Gilberti de Wyngton' extra curiam defuncti, etiam si tanto tempore vacaverit quod eius collatio sit ad sedem apostolicam legitime devoluta, fuit provisum Ricardo de

Tyrneby, presbytero dicte diocesis, qui dimittet vicariam parochialis ecclesie de Memburn' (Newburn) Dunelmensis diocesis, per Urbanum pridie ydus Maii anno ii°,[450] taxa vel fructus.

### Londoniensis

De parochiali ecclesia de Alta Reddyrg' (High Roding) diocesis Londoniensis, quam Johannes de Langeston' per annum et ultra tenuit pacifice in presbyterum non promotus, fuit eidem de novo provisum et habititatus per Urbanum xviii° kalendas Julii anno ii°,[451] taxa vel fructus.

### Conwentrensis et Lichfeldensis

De prioratu monasterii Folapp' (Shrewsbury), vacante per obitum Rogeri de Amffrasthon', quondam prioris eiusdem, in Romana [452] curia defuncti, fuit provisum Johanni Perk, monacho dicti monasterii, per Urbanum xii kalendas Julii anno secundo,[453] taxa vel fructus. Sed iste prioratus est claustralis et nichil valet quia est solum officium et non habet nisi aliquantulum maiorem portionem in mensa.

### Wellensis

De acceptatione facte vigore litterarum apostolicarum per Willelmum Tyngill, (fol. 115) in utroque iure doctorem,[453a] et collatione subsequta de archidiaconatu de Taunton' ⟨in ecclesia Wellensi, cui prebenda est annexa, vacante per obitum Rotberti Hereward'⟩[454] extra Romanam curiam defuncti, que fuerunt confirmate vel provisum de novo eidem per Urbanum vi° ydus Augusti anno secundo,[455] et dimittet ecclesiam parochialem de Biscspebourn' (Bishopsbourne) Cantuariensis diocesis ac canonicatum et prebendam de Karenton (Crantock) Exoniensis diocesis, taxa vel fructus. De isto pendet lis in curia, et incumbens habuit pro se sententiam.

### Lincolniensis

De parochiali ecclesia de Suweldeby (Shoby) Lincolniensis diocesis, de qua ex causa permutationis fuit provisum Willelmo nato Willelmi de Wadyngton' de Hanislberch per Urbanum iii° kalendas Augusti anno secundo,[456] taxa vel fructus.

### Londoniensis

De perpetua vicaria de Lyngdon' (Luton) Lincolniensis diocesis, de qua ex causa permutationis fuit provisum Roberto de Wysente per Urbanum ydus Augusti anno secundo,[457] taxa vel fructus.

---

[445] 17 March 1364.
[446] 5 April 1364.
[447] 4 April 1364.
[448] Followed by *secundo* deleted by a line.
[449] 9 June 1363.

[450] 14 May 1364.
[451] 14 June 1364.
[452] *Pomaria*, MS.
[453] 20 June 1364.
[453a] *doctori*, MS.
[454] Supplied from above, p. 288.
[455] 8 August 1364.
[456] 30 July 1364.
[457] 13 August 1364.

Ex eadem causa et eadem die fuit provisum Willelmo Haddon' de libera capella de Cholmesford (Chelmsford) Londoniensis diocesis, que etiam datur in arayratgiis.

### Herffordensis

De canonicatu et prebenda de Hundretton' (Hunderton) in ecclesia Herffordensi, vacantibus per privationem Nicholai Heth' per dominum papam factam propter pluralitatem et multitudinem beneficiorum que obtinebat, fuit provisum Nicholao de Drayton', bacallario in legibus, per Urbanum iiii° kalendas Septembris anno secundo,[458] taxa vel fructus.

### Dunelmensis

De parochiali ecclesia de Wesyngthon' (Washington) Dunelmensis diocesis, collata ex causa permutationis auctoritate ordinaria Roberto de Warcomp', fuit confirmata, non obstante defectu natalium quem patitur de soluto genitus et soluta, vel provisum de novo per Urbanum xiiii° kalendas Octobris anno ii°,[459] taxa vel fructus. Sed supra ponitur alia provisio de eadem pridie nonas Maii anno primo [460] folio [461] pro qua solvit partem, et ideo ista debet cancellari.

### (fol. 115�v)[432] Lincolniensis

De parochiali ecclesia de Slapton' Lincolniensis diocesis, de qua, vacante cum Matheus de Assetthon' canonicatum et prebendam ecclesie Eboracensis fuit pacifice assequtus, fuit provisum Ricardo de Crayton', clerico Eliensis diocesis, per Urbanum kalendas Octobris anno ii°,[462] taxa vel fructus.

### Lincolniensis

De canonicatu et prebenda ecclesie Lincolniensis, de quibus vacantibus per obitum cardinalis Petragoracensis fuit motu proprio provisum H. cardinali Ostiensi [463] per Urbanum xi° kalendas Novembris anno secundo,[464] taxa vel fructus.

### Norwicensis

De parochiali ecclesia Sancti Gregorii de Subur' Norwicensis diocesis, cuius collatio et provisio facte auctoritate ordinaria vel apostolica Thome de Bakthon', bacallario in legibus, vacante ex eo quod Henricus de Compedor' ipsam obtinens cancellariam ecclesie Londoniensis fuit pacifice assequtus, etiam si per simplicem resignationem dicti Henrici vacaverit, fuerunt confirmate vel provisum de novo per Urbanum vii° kalendas Novembris anno secundo,[465] taxa vel fructus. Supra

ponitur alia confirmatio eiusdem facta de eadem x° kalendas Decembris eodem anno [466] supra folio [461] et utraque est infra annum, et ideo ista debet esse cancellata.

### Exoniensis

De parochiali ecclesia de Essewatr' (Ashwater) Exoniensis diocesis, de qua vacante per obitum Ricardi Gryffardi extra Romanam curiam defuncti fuit provisum Willelmo de Condesworth, clerico dicte diocesis, nisi sit alteri specialiter ius quesitum, per Urbanum pridie nonas Novembris anno secundo,[467] taxa vel fructus. Supra folio [461] providetur eidem de eadem anno eodem xviii° kalendas Januarii,[468] sed ambe sunt infra annum, et pro illa solvit, et ideo ista debet cancellari.

Completum est de anno secundo; sequitur de anno tertio.

### (fol. 116) Anno Tertio.

### Dunelmensis

De parochiali ecclesia de Wermout Episcopi (Bishop-Wearmouth) Dunelmensis diocesis, de qua, vacante per lapsum temporis ⟨concessi Willelmo⟩[469] de Neupportt' de ipsa retinenda cum quadam parochiali ecclesia, fuit provisum Willelmo de Arden', magistro in artibus, et dimittet ecclesiam parochialem de Cesterton (Chesterton) Lincolniensis diocesis, per Urbanum xv° kalendas Decembris anno tertio,[470] taxa vel fructus. Supra [461] xv° kalendas Januarii anno secundo [471] est alia provisio de eadem facta eidem, et tertia est infra, videlicet xiii° kalendas Decembris anno quinto,[472] et neutra earum habet adhuc effectum, quia David Wllorth', clericus regis, litigat in curia contra ipsum impetrantem, quia sine litteris apostolicis dictam ecclesiam acceptavit, et credo quod dictus David obtinebit quia commissum fuit per Urbanum viii° kalendas Maii anno vii° [473] quod si constiterit quod dictus impetrans sine litteris apostolicis [474] eam acceptaverit sicut fecit quod eam adiudicet dicto David.

### Dunelmensis alias Dublinensis

De hospitali Sancti Johannis baptiste extra portam civitatis Dunelmensis, quod illicite detinet Willelmus Gerandi, frater dicti hospitalis, de quo fuit provisum Henrico Baudalff', fratri dicti hospitalis, per Urbanum xiiii° kalendas Decembris anno tertio,[475] taxa vel fructus. Sed episcopus certificat quod non est in sua diocesi tale

---

[458] 29 August 1364.
[459] 18 September 1364.
[460] 6 May 1363.
[461] A blank space is left in MS.
[462] 1 October 1364.
[463] Elias de S. Eredio.
[464] 22 October 1364.
[465] 26 October 1364.

[466] 22 November 1363.
[467] 4 November 1364.
[468] 15 December 1363.
[469] Supplied from above, p. 289.
[470] 17 November 1364.
[471] 18 December 1363.
[472] 19 November 1366.
[473] 24 April 1369.
[474] Followed by *a* deleted by a dot.
[475] 18 November 1364.

hospitale, et credo quod debet esse Dublinensis in Ybernia, et tunc non debet hic poni.

## Londoniensis

De parochiali ecclesia de Hakeney (Hackney) Londoniensis diocesis, de qua, vacatura cum Thomas de Paxthon', apostolice sedis capellanus, dignitatem in ecclesia Wellensi fuerit pacifice assequtus, fuit provisum Waltero de Multon', presbytero Norwicensis diocesis, per Urbanum vii° ydus Decembris anno tertio,[476] et dimittet parochialem ecclesiam de Chyvele (Cheveley) Norwicensis diocesis, taxa vel fructus.

## Bathoniensis et Wellensis

De decanatu ecclesie Wellensis, taxato c li., in quo subrogatus fuit Stephanus Pampel, legum doctor, in omni iure quod competebat Thome de Paxton', auditori palatii apostolici, qui super eo contra dictum Stephanum ad eumdem decanatum auctoritate ordinaria electum litem movit, qui quidem Thomas postmodum iuri sibi in eo [477] competenti expresse renuntiavit, per Urbanum x° kalendas Januarii anno tertio,[478] (fol. 116ᵛ)[479] et dimittet prebendam Exoniensem ac collegiatarum Sancti Thome martiris de Glasweye (Glasnay) Exoniensis diocesis et de Awergwill' (Abergwili) Menewensis diocesis ecclesiarum, debet pro resta taxe xx li.

## Saresbiriensis

De canonicatu et prebenda ecclesie Saresbiriensis quos Ricardus de Norwico, defunctus, per nonnullos annos possederat, etiam si vacent per obitum Thome de Clypston' in Romana curia defuncti, de quibus auctoritate apostolica ⟨provisio⟩ facta Henrico de Wynterton' fuit confirmata vel provisum de novo per Urbanum nonas Januarii anno tertio,[480] taxa vel fructus. Ista prebenda vocatur Bemynstr' (Beaminster), et sunt due provisiones de eadem in antiquis arayratgiis facte diversis personis, et neutra earum, ut dicitur, habuit effectum.

## Exoniensis

De canonicatu et prebenda ecclesie collegiate de Glesenay (Glasnay) Exoniensis diocesis, de qua, vacatura cum Stephanus Pampel decanatum ecclesie Wellensis fuerit pacifice assecutus, fuit provisum Thome Waderawe, clerico Eboracensis diocesis, bacallario in legibus, per Urbanum vi° ydus Februarii anno tertio,[481] taxa vel fructus.

## Lincolniensis

De parochiali ecclesia de Hawortyngham (Hagworth-

ingham) Lincolniensis diocesis, de qua, vacante per assequitionem parochialis ecclesie de Wetlingsete (Wetheringsett) Norwicensis diocesis collate Johanni de Swynesheveden, quam Thomas de Tettefford', clericus Lincolniensis diocesis, possedit diu pacifice, licet felicis recordationis Dominus Innocentius papa VIᵘˢ quondam Henrico Ramelin, clerico Cantuariensis diocesis, de dicta ecclesia sic vacante providerit, qui litteris super hoc non confectis extra Romanam curiam decessit, fuerunt eidem Thome confirmate vel provisum de novo per Urbanum xv° kalendas Martii anno tertio,[482] taxa vel fructus. Et est alia provisio facta eidem de eadem supra nonas Januarii anno ii°,[483] pro qua partem solvit.

## Cicestrensis

De custodia domus hospitalis Beate Marie Cicestrensis, de qua, vacante per privationem Johannis de Donnutton', clerici dicte diocesis, per dominum papam, fuit provisum Symoni Bate, presbytero Lincolniensis diocesis, per Urbanum nonas Martii anno tertio,[484] taxa vel fructus.

Summa pagine xx li.

## (fol. 117)[479] Exoniensis

De canonicatu et prebenda ecclesie collegiate Beati Thome de Glasmen' (Glasnay) diocesis Exoniensis, de quo vacante cum Stephanus Pampel ipsos dimiserit fuit provisum Petro Amgov dicte diocesis per Urbanum nonas Martii anno tertio,[484] et dimittet parochialem ecclesiam de Winwolay (Landewednack) dicte dyocesis, taxa vel fructus.

## Eliensis

De parochiali ecclesia de Ditton' (Fen Ditton) Eliensis diocesis, de qua, vacatura dum Nicholaus de Wbamtorpp' dignitatem, personatum vel officium in ecclesia ⟨Exoniensi⟩ fuerit pacifice assequtus, fuit provisum Thome de Hornynggisherde Norwicensis diocesis, legum doctori, per Urbanum vi° kalendas Aprilis anno tertio,[485] taxa vel fructus.

## Eliensis

De parochiali ecclesia de Stitham (Stretham) Eliensis diocesis, de qua, vacatura dum Robertus de Stratton', auditor palatii apostolici, dignitatem,[486] personatum aut officium in ecclesia Lincolniensi fuerit pacifice assequtus, fuit provisum Roberto de Fordham, presbytero Norwicensis diocesis, per Urbanum ydus Martii anno tertio,[487] taxa vel fructus.

## Karleolensis

De parochiali ecclesia de Wegeton' (Wigton) Kar-

---

[476] 7 December 1364.
[477] *eao*, MS.
[478] 23 December 1364.
[479] The heading *Anno tertio* is repeated at the top of the page.
[480] 5 January 1365.
[481] 8 February 1365.

[482] 15 February 1365.
[483] 5 January 1364.
[484] 7 March 1365.
[485] 27 March 1365.
[486] Followed by *officium* deleted by a line.
[487] 15 March 1365.

leolensis diocesis, de qua, vacante per obitum quondam Gilberti de Wegeton' extra Romanam curiam defuncti, et si tanto tempore vacavit quod eius collatio est ad sedem apostolicam legitime devoluta, fuit provisum Ricardo de Tyrneby, presbytero dicte diocesis, per Urbanum pridie kalendas Maii anno tertio,[488] et dimittet vicariam parochialis ecclesie de Memburn' (Newburn) Dunelmensis diocesis, taxa vel fructus.

### Norwicensis

De parochiali ecclesia de Parlesdem alias de Rasehesd' (Rattlesden) Norwicensis diocesis, taxata xii li., de qua, vacatura dum Rogerus de Frethon' canonicatum et prebendam de Newethon' (North Newnton) in ecclesia de Walthon' (Wilton) Saresbiriensis diocesis fuerit pacifice assequtus, fuit provisum Thome Waderote, presbytero Eboracensis diocesis, per Urbanum vi° ydus Aprilis anno tertio,[489] et dimittet canonicatum et prebendam ecclesie collegiate de Glasenay (Glasnay) per dominum papam sibi nuper collatam, debet de resta dicte taxe x li.

### Cantuariensis

De prepositura ecclesie collegiate de Wyngham (Wingham) Cantuariensis diocesis, vacante per mortem Johannis de Teverleye extra Romanam curiam defuncti, cuius collatio (fol. 117ᵛ)[490] et provisio facte auctoritate ordinaria Willelmo Redd fuerunt confirmate vel provisum de novo per Urbanum xv° kalendas Maii anno iii°,[491] taxa vel fructus.

### Leomensis

De archidiaconatu Leomensi (Killaloe), vacante ex eo quod Thomas Othormachaym beneficium incompassible una cum dicto archidiaconatu, dispensatione legitima non obtenta contra canonum statuta, tanto tempore tenuit quod eius collatio est ad sedem apostolicam legitime devoluta, fuit provisum Donato Ocreydi, et dimittet prebendas dicte ecclesie et Cassalensis, per Urbanum xi° kalendas Maii anno tertio,[492] taxa vel fructus.

### Saresbiriensis et Wellensis

De vicaria perpetua de Jatmynstr' (Yetminster) Saresbiriensis diocesis, de qua ex causa permutationis fuit provisum Johanni Turk, presbytero Wellensis diocesis, et Willelmo Roueffaunt de vicaria perpetua[493] ecclesie de Stamenton' D'w (Stanton Drew) dicte diocesis Wellensis per Urbanum ix° kalendas Maii anno tertio,[494] taxa vel fructus.

### Eboracensis

De parochiali ecclesia de Matthon' in Crowon' (Marton in Craven) Eboracensis diocesis, cuius collatio et provisio facte vigore litterarum apostolicarum felicis recordationis Clementis pape VIᵗⁱ Johanni de Newham presbytero fuerunt eidem confirmate vel provisum de novo, per Urbanum quinto kalendas Maii anno tertio,[495] taxa vel fructus.

### Saresbiriensis

De parochiali ecclesia de Staton' (Staunton) Saresbiriensis diocesis, de qua ex causa permutationis cum vicaria de Codesdon' (Cuddesdon), pro qua fuit satisfactum in rationibus meis, fuit provisum Willelmo Lenroth' Saresbiriensis diocesis per Urbanum tertio ydus Augusti anno iii°,[496] debetur pro dicta ecclesia de Stocton' taxa vel fructus.

### Eboracensis

De prioratu Sancti Johannis Ewangeliste de Pontefracto (Pontefract) Cluniacensis ordinis Eboracensis diocesis, cuius collatio et provisio facte fratri Johanni de Melcheley monacho, licet aliquando habitum suum non tamen causa apostatandi sed causa solaciandi dimiserit, fuerunt confirmate vel provisum de novo per Urbanum iiiiᵗᵒ ydus Septembris anno tertio,[497] taxa vel fructus. (fol. 118)[479] Ista provisio nundum habuit effectum, nec credo quod habebit, quia dux Lancastrie, de cuius fundatione est, induxit alium ad presentationem abbatis Cluniacensis per devolutionem, quia prior de Caritate (La Charité-sur-Loire), de cuius collatione est, non contulit, ut dicitur, infra tempus iuris.

### Londoniensis

De parochiali ecclesia de Harwe (Harrow) Londoniensis diocesis, de qua, vacante per obitum Raymundi Peregrini extra Romanam curiam defuncti, collectoris apostolici, fuit provisum Johanni de Bokyngham, et dimittet parochialem ecclesiam de Stolton' (Stockton) Saresbiriensis diocesis per Urbanum pridie ydus Septembris anno tertio,[498] taxa vel fructus. Et itero providetur eidem de eadem ecclesia iiii° ydus Augusti anno[499] iiii°.[500]

### Lincolniensis

De prebenda de Cosynghym' (Corringham) in ecclesia Lincolniensi, taxata cxxvi li. xiii s. iiii d., de qua per obitum Raymundi Peregrini fuit provisum cardinali Aquensi[501] per Urbanum quarto nonas Septembris anno tertio,[502] debet pro taxa xliiii li. iiii s. viii d.

[488] 30 April 1365.
[489] 8 April 1365.
[490] At the foot of fol. 117. *Summa pagine x li.* At the top of fol. 117ᵛ: *anno iii°.*
[491] 17 April 1365.
[492] 21 April 1365.
[493] Followed by *de* deleted by a line.
[494] 23 April 1365.
[495] 27 April 1365.
[496] 11 August 1365.
[497] 10 September 1365.
[498] 12 September 1365.
[499] Followed by *t* deleted by a dot.
[500] 10 August 1366.
[501] Peter Itherii, bishop of Dax, bishop of Albano.
[502] 2 September 1365.

Completum est de anno tertio; sequitur de anno quarto.

Summa pagine xliiii li. iiii s. viii d.

(fol. 118ᵛ) Anno Quarto

### Saresbiriensis

De canonicatu et prebenda ecclesie Saresbiriensis, prebenda vocatur Lheword' (Highworth), vacante per obitum Raymundi Peregrini, collectoris apostolici, fuit provisum Thome de Paxthon', auditori palatii apostolici, et dimittet archidiaconatum Barbkschir' (Berkshire), in dicta ecclesia, quem [503] nundum possidet, per Urbanum quinto ydus Decembris anno iiii°,[504] taxa vel fructus.

### Saresbiriensis

De archidiaconatu Barkschir' Saresbiriensis diocesis, de quo, vacaturo cum dictus Thomas de Paxthon' dictam prebendam fuerit pacifice assequtus, fuit provisum Johanni de Harowell', et dimittet archidiaconatum Wygorniensem, per Urbanum iiii° ydus Decembris anno quarto,[505] taxa vel fructus.

### Exoniensis

De canonicatu et prebenda ecclesie Sancti Karentoci (Crantock) Exoniensis diocesis de quibus, vacantibus cum Willelmus Tynchuill' canonicatum, prebendam ac dignitatem, personatum vel officium in ecclesia Wellensi fuerit pacifice assequtus, fuit provisum Thome Cride per Urbanum ydus Decembris anno quarto,[506] taxa vel fructus.

### Exoniensis, Wellensis et Menewensis

De uno beneficiorum infrascriptorum, videlicet thesaurarie et canonicatus et prebende ecclesie Exoniensis ac canonicatuum et prebendarum ecclesiarum Wellensis et Menewensis, vacaturo dum Robertus de Midelond' prebendam ecclesie Eboracensis fuerit pacifice assequtus, fuit provisum Ricardo de Tische, presbytero bacallario in decretis, et dimittet medietatem ecclesie Wlton' (Ufton), que in ecclesia Lichfeldensi prebenda dicitur, super qua litigat in palatio apostolico, vel parochialem ecclesiam de Hertelegh' (Hartley) Roffensis diocesis, per Urbanum xiiii° kalendas Januarii anno quarto,[507] taxa vel fructus.

### Saresbiriensis

De parochiali ecclesia de Stacton' (Stockton) Saresbiriensis diocesis, de qua, vacatura ex eo quod Johannes de Bokyngham, ultimus rector eiusdem, ecclesiam de Harwe (Harrow) Londoniensis diocesis fuerit pacifice assequtus, fuit provisum Johanni de Otthon' presbytero,

et dimittet parochialem ecclesiam de Hodelene (West Hoathley) Cicestrensis diocesis, per Urbanum pridie ydus Januarii anno quarto,[508] taxa vel fructus. Non habuit effectum quia in precendenti pagina providetur alteri qui eam tenet et iam solvit. Ideo cancellatur quia datur inter inutiles.

### Londoniensis

De canonicatu et prebenda ecclesie Londoniensis, de quibus, vacantibus por mortem Raymundi (fol. 119)[509] Peregrini, capellani et collectoris apostolici, extra Romanam curiam defuncti, fuit provisum Johanni Bonlegh', clerico dicte diocesis, per Urbanum iiii° nonas Januarii anno quarto,[508] taxa vel fructus.

### Dunelmensis

De perpetua vicaria parochialis ecclesie de Northam (Norham) Dunelmensis diocesis, per clericos seculares consueta ab olim gubernari, de qua, vacante per mortem quondam Willelmi Elwyk, licet quidem frater Ricardus de Sores, monachus professus monasterii Laynlose (Kinloss) Moroniensis (Moray) diocesis ordinis Cisterciensis, habitu dicti ordinis derelicto, ipsam per tres annos et amplius occupavit indebite et iniuste, fuit provisum Johanni Mores, presbytero Lichfeldensis diocesis, et dimittet magisterium Beati Bartholomei de Twedmth' (Tweedmouth), per Urbanum iiii° nonas Januarii anno quarto,[510] taxa vel fructus.

### Dunelmensis

De vicaria perpetua parochialis ecclesie de Northam Dunelmensis diocesis, per clericos seculares consueta ab olim gubernari, vacante per mortem quondam Willelmi de Eslwyk, ultimi rectoris eiusdem, fuit provisum Johanni de Lewyk, presbytero dicte diocesis, licet Ricardus de Mores, monachus monasterii de Kynglosse Moroniensis dyocesis ordinis Cisterciensis ipsam per tres annos et amplius indebite et iniuste occupavit, per Urbanum xviii° kalendas Februarii anno iiii°,[511] taxa vel fructus. In eadem pagina ponitur iterato, et ideo altera ipsarum debet esse cancellata.

### Eliensis

De parochiali ecclesia de Ellesworth' (Elsworth) Eliensis diocesis, de qua, vacatura dum Johannes de Northon' dignitatem, personatum vel officium curatum in ecclesia Licheffeldensi fuerit pacifice assequtus, necnon de canonicatu et prebenda ecclesie Licheffeldensis vacaturis dum Johannes de Waltham canonicatum et prebendam ecclesie Lincolniensis fuerit pacifice assequtus, fuit provisum Willemo de Wethandale presbytero,

---

[503] *quam*, MS.
[504] 9 December 1365.
[505] 10 December 1365.
[506] 13 December 1365.
[507] 19 December 1365.

[508] 12 January 1366.
[509] The heading *Anno Quarto* is repeated at the top of the page.
[510] 2 January 1366.
[511] 15 January 1366.

et dimittet parochialem ecclesiam de Stamfford' (Stanford) et prebendam Herffordensem et provisionem sibi factam de parochiali ecclesia de Synterlee (Blakeney or Glandford) Norwicensis diocesis, per Urbanum xi° kalendas Februarii anno quarto,[512] taxa vel fructus. Sed de ista etiam fuit provisum alteri supra iii° kalendas Maii anno primo.[513]

### Wygorniensis

De parochiali ecclesia de Clive (Bishop's Cleeve) Wygorniensis diocesis, super qua Ricardus de Dronthon' (fol. 119v)[509] clericus et Johannes de Brian dyu in palatio apostolico litigaverunt, de qua vacatura per privationem dicti Johannis fuit provisum Ricardo predicto per Urbanum xi° kalendas Februarii anno quarto,[512] taxa vel fructus.

### Saresbiriensis

De decanatu et prebenda ecclesie monasterii monialium de Wylton' (Wilton) Saresbiriensis diocesis, de quibus vacantibus[514] per amotionem Rogeri de Chersteeffed' fuit provisum Eduardo de Cherdestok, presbytero Saresbiriensis diocesis, et dimittet parochialem ecclesiam de Cutel (East Knoyle) dicte diocesis per Urbanum xi° kalendas Februarii anno quarto,[512] taxa vel fructus.

### Wygorniensis

De archidiaconatu ecclesie Wygorniensis, non taxato, et ecclesia de Clavden' (Claverdon) eidem annexa, taxata x li. vi s. viii d., de quo, vacaturo dum Johannes de Harlewell' archidiaconatum Barchirie (Berkshire) in ecclesia Saresbiriensi fuerint pacifice assequtus, fuit provisum Symoni Clementis presbytero, et dimittet parochialem ecclesiam de Pymperne (Pimperne) Saresbiriensis diocesis, per Urbanum iiii° kalendas Februarii anno quarto,[515] pro resta.

### Exoniensis

De canonicatu et prebenda ecclesie collegiate de Crediton' Exoniensis diocesis, de qua vacante per resignationem Philipi de Bellocampo fuit provisum Johanni More, clerico[516] Saresbiriensis diocesis, per Urbanum vi° ydus Februarii anno quarto,[517] taxa vel fructus. Qui solvit l s. in partem taxe, de qua nundum constat, de quibus fuit in aliis computis responsum.

### Eboracensis

De precentoria ecclesie Eboracensis, cuius collatio et provisio facte Ade de Eboraco presbytero auctoritate

ordinaria, quam possidet pacifice, fuerunt eidem confirmate vel provisum de novo per Urbanum vi° ydus Februarii anno quarto,[517] taxa vel fructus.

### Lincolniensis

De parochiali ecclesia de Peston' (Paston) Lincolniensis diocesis, de qua, dum Johannes Thome dignitatem, personatum vel officium in ecclesia Saresbiriensi fuerit pacifice assequtus, fuit provisum Guillelmo Graule, clerico Lincolniensis diocesis, per Urbanum quinto ydus Aprilis anno quarto,[518] taxa vel fructus.

### (fol. 120)[509] Eboracensis

De parochiali ecclesia de Hersdham (Heversham) Eboracensis diocesis, in qua subrogatus fuit Thomas de Cetrefford', subdiaconus Lincolniensis diocesis, in omni iure quod competebat in ea Johanni de Waltham, presbytero Lincolniensis diocesis, super qua lis pendet in palatio apostolico inter dictum Johannem de Waltham et Nicholaum de Feriby, clericum Eboracensis diocesis, qua lite pendente[519] prefatus Johannes parochialem ecclesiam de Lyngfford' (Langford) Saresbiriensis diocesis auctoritate ordinaria sibi collata fuit pacifice assequtus, et dimittet[520] canonicatum et prebendam ecclesie collegiate de Arewill' (Abergwili) Menewensis diocesis et litem quam habet super parochiali ecclesia de Hagwortyngham (Hagworthingham) Lincolniensis diocesis, per Urbanum quinto ydus Aprilis anno quarto,[518] taxa vel fructus.

### Assawensis

De canonicatu et prebenda ecclesie Assawensis in Wallia, de quibus, dudum vacantibus per obitum Ricardi de Midelthon' in curia defuncti, Dominus Innocentum papa VI[us] providit Johanni Charode, qui, possessione[521] ipsorum[522] non habita, ipsos in manibus episcopi Assawensis libere resignavit, et subsequenter de ipsis, qui tanto tempore vacaverant per resignationem huiusmodi quod eorum collatio et provisio fuerunt ad sedem apostolicam legitime devolute, idem Dominus Innocentius ⟨Johanni⟩ Guiffandum clerico per certos exequtores provideri mandavit, qui antequam provisum ei extitisset extra curiam Romanam decessit, fuit provisum Symoni Lattebury, presbytero Limericensis diocesis, per Urbanum xviii° kalendas Maii anno quarto,[523] taxa vel fructus.

### Eboracensis

De parochiali ecclesia Sancte Helene in Staynegate in Eboraco (St. Helen in Stonegate, York), de qua vacante per mortem Thome de Langescote in Romana curia defuncti fuit provisum Henrico de Hugate,

---

[512] 22 January 1366.
[513] 29 April 1363.
[514] *qua vacante*, MS.
[515] 29 January 1366.
[516] *clerico* repeated MS.
[517] 8 February 1366.

[518] 9 April 1366.
[519] Followed by *s* deleted by a line.
[520] Followed by *parochialem ecclesiam* deleted by a line.
[521] *possessionem*, MS.
[522] *ipsius*, MS.
[523] 14 April 1366.

presbytero Eboracensis diocesis, per Urbanum xviii° kalendas Maii anno quarto,[523] taxa vel fructus. Alia provisio de eadem alteri facta est supra quinto ydus Maii anno primo.[524]

### Licheffeldensis

De canonicatu et prebenda ecclesie de Mortalle (Morehall) in ecclesia collegiata de Goushale (Gnosall) Licheffeldensis diocesis, ⟨vacantibus per privationem Nicolai Heth'⟩[525] propter pluralitatem beneficiorum que obtinebat, fuit provisum Johanni Danielis, clerico Licheffeldensis diocesis, per Urbanum (fol. 120ᵛ)[509] xvi° kalendas Maii anno quarto,[526] taxa vel fructus. Sed ista provisio non habuit effectum quia impetrans non fuit prosequtus et ex causa.

### Norwicensis

De parochiali ecclesia de Multon' (Moulton) Norwicensis diocesis, in qua subrogatus fuit Hamo Deval presbyter in omni iure quod competebat Michaeli de Hautton', super qua inter dictum Hamonem et Michaelem lis pendebat in palatio apostolico, qua lite pendente Michael decessit extra curiam, per Urbanum v° nonas Maii anno iiii°,[527] taxa vel fructus.

### Lincolniensis

De parochiali ecclesia de Harwode magna (Great Horwood) Lincolniensis diocesis, de qua collatio et provisio facte auctoritate ordinaria Johanni Sbyret de Bolkyngham, etiam si fuerit devoluta vel reservata, fuerunt confirmate vel provisum de novo per Urbanum iiii° nonas Maii anno iiii°,[528] taxa vel fructus. Ista provisio non habuit effectum quia ante habitam ipsius possessionem per dimissionem istius Johannis providetur alteri iiii° ydus Augusti eodem anno,[529] et utraque provisio est infra annum et non debet nisi una annata.

### Menewensis

De canonicatu et prebenda Sancti Martini de Arwerwell' (Abergwili) Menewensis diocesis, de quo, vacantibus dum Thomas de Tettefford' parochialem ecclesiam de Hausham (Heversham) fuerit pacifice assequtus, fuit provisum Johanni Bell', clerico Eboracensis diocesis, per Urbanum vii° ydus Junii anno quarto,[530] taxa vel fructus.

### Roffensis

De parochiali ecclesia de Suthelond' (Snodland) Roffensis diocesis, in qua [531] subrogatus fuit Johannes

de Altewe in omni iure quod competebat in ea cuidam impetranti, qui quidem impetrans super ea, eidem Johanni non obstante esset auctoritate ordinaria assequtus ex causa permutationis, in palatio apostolico litem movit, et ex tunc apud sedem apostolicam decessit, per Urbanum pridie kalendas Julii anno quarto,[532] taxa vel fructus.

### Saresbiriensis

De canonicatu et prebenda in ecclesia Saresbiriensi, de quibus, vacaturis dum (fol. 121)[509] Fortanerius de Calvomonte prioratum, canonicatum et prebendam ecclesie Sancte Radegundis Pictavensis (Poitiers) fuerit pacifice assequtus, fuit provisum Johanni Strafford', clerico Saresbiriensis diocesis, et dimittet parochialem ecclesiam de Chimark (Chilmark) dicte diocesis, per Urbanum xii kalendas Augusti anno quarto,[533] taxa vel fructus.

### Exoniensis

De canonicatu et prebenda ecclesie de Credyngthon' (Crediton) Exoniensis diocesis et prebenda bursaria nuncupata, de quibus collatio et provisio facte auctoritate apostolica Rogero Payn, vacantibus, ut credebatur, quia eam obtinens aliam prebendam inibi[534] fuerat pacifice assequtus, et cuius collatio erat devoluta non obstante quod assertum fuerit ipsum studuisse in iure civili per quinque annos et non studuerit nisi per quatuor, fuerunt confirmate vel provisum de novo per Urbanum xi° kalendas Augusti anno quarto,[535] taxa vel fructus.

### Exoniensis

De canonicatu ecclesie Sancte Crucis de Credyngthon' (Crediton) Exoniensis diocesis et de prebenda Carumwilla (Kerswell) in eadem ecclesia, de quibus, vacantibus ex eo quod Johannes Peroni, se gerens pro canonico dicte ecclesie, ipsam prebendam de Carumwilla optinens, aliam certam prebendam wlgariter nuncupatam busariam auctoritate ordinaria fuit assequtus, etiam si devoluta fuerit vel etiam alio quovis modo vacet, fuit provisum Johanni Cheyney, clerico Exoniensis diocesis, per Urbanum iii° kalendas Augusti anno quarto,[532] taxa vel fructus.

### Londoniensis

De parochiali ecclesia de Arowe alias Harwe (Harrow) Londoniensis diocesis, de qua, vacante[536] et reservata per obitum Raymundi Peregrini, quem asseverat prius esse capellanum sedis apostolice et pro certo tempore Domini Innocentii dictam capellaniam resignavit, fuit de novo provisum Johanni de Bokyngham per Urbanum iiii° ydus Augusti anno iiii°,[537] taxa vel

---

[524] 11 May 1363.
[525] Supplied from above, p. 295.
[526] 16 April 1366.
[527] 3 May 1366.
[528] 4 May 1366.
[529] 10 August 1366.
[530] 7 June 1366.
[531] Followed by *sub* not deleted.

[532] 30 June 1366.
[533] 21 July 1366.
[534] *imibi*, MS.
[535] 22 July 1366.
[536] Followed by *ex eo quod*, of which *ex eo* are deleted by a line.
[537] 10 August 1366.

fructus. Supra providetur bis eidem de eadem folio [538] iii° nonas Augusti ⟨et pridie ydus⟩[539] Septembris anno tertio,[540] et omnes sunt infra annum, et non debetur nisi una annata.

### Lincolniensis et Eboracensis

De canonicatu et prebenda de Castro (Caistor) in ecclesia Lincolniensi, vacantibus vel vacaturis per primationem Henrici Inghelby, fuit provisum Johanni Cheyne, etiam si eos causa permutationis vel alio quovis modo dimiserit, et dimittet [541] (fol. 121ᵛ)[509] parochialem ecclesiam de Kyrkeby Misperton' (Kirkby Misperton) Eboracensis diocesis, per Urbanum iii° ydus Septembris anno quarto,[542] taxa vel fructus.

### Eboracensis

De canonicatu et prebenda de Howenden' (Howden) Eboracensis dyocesis, quos Jacobus de Multhon' in eadem ecclesia solebat obtinere, de quibus, vacantibus de iure quia Willelmus Dimby presbyter vigore gratie sibi facte de canonicatu sub expectatione prebende dicte ecclesie acceptavit, tacito in dicta gratia de defectu natalium quem patitur de presbytero genitus et soluta, et in ipsis est intrusus de facto, fuit provisum Guillelmo predicto per Urbanum pridie ydus Septembris anno quarto,[543] taxa vel fructus.

### Eboracensis

De canonicatu et prebenda ac decanatu ecclesie Eboracensis, de quibus vacantibus per obitum cardinalis Petragoricensis fuit provisum Domino Anglico cardinali Avinionensi [544] per Urbanum viii° kalendas Octobris anno quarto,[545] taxa vel fructus.

### Lincolniensis

De perpetua vicaria parochialis ecclesie de Luton' Lincolniensis diocesis, de qua provisio facta vigore litterarum apostolicarum Benedicto de Masyngham, presbytero Norwicensis diocesis, qui eam possidet, licet dicatur vacasse et vacare ex eo quod quondam Robertus de Wyngssynglate, cui de ipsa vacante in curia ex causa permutationis provisum fuerat, antequam eius possessionem haberet aliam parochialem ecclesiam fuit pacifice assequtus, et sic mandatum apostolicum non videtur ad plenum exequtum, fuit confirmata [546] vel provisum de

novo per Urbanum v° kalendas Octobris anno iiii°,[547] taxa vel fructus.

### Eboracensis

De canonicatu et prebenda ecclesie collegiate de Southwelle Eboracensis diocesis, de quibus, vacantibus per Henrici [548] de Engelby ac canonicatu et prebenda ecclesie Saresbiriensis per Johannis Welbon' privationes et amontiones per dominum papam factas propter multitudinem beneficiorum, fuit provisum Johanni Cheyne, Licheffeldensis diocesis, et dimittet parochialem ecclesiam de Kyrkeby Misperton (Kirkby Misperton) Eboracensis diocesis et gratiam sibi factam de canonicatu et prebenda quos idem Henricus obtinere dicitur in ecclesia Lincolniensi, per Urbanum iii° ydus Octobris anno quarto,[549] taxa vel fructus.

### (fol. 122)[509] Dunelmensis

De capellania seu magisterio hospitalis de Scehoborn' (Sherburn) Dunelmensis diocesis, de quibus vacantibus per amotionem Alani de Scheroburghtthon' fuit provisum Waltero de Wadesborch' per Urbanum xi° kalendas Novembris anno quarto,[550] taxa vel fructus.

Completum est de anno quarto; sequitur in sequenti pagina de anno quinto.

### (fol. 122ᵛ) Anno Quinto

### Eboracensis

De prebenda Sancti Johannis et canonicatu de Beverlacho, de qua vacante per privationem Johannis de Belbury fuit provisum Rogero de Frethon', legum doctori, per Urbanum pridie ydus Novembris anno quinto,[551] taxa vel fructus.

### Dunelmensis

De parochiali ecclesia de Wermouth (Bishop Wearmouth) Dunelmensis diocesis, ad quam, vacante per obitum Willelmi Neupport, David de Wllorch fuit presentatus et auctoritate ordinaria inductus, vacante per privationem dicti David factam per dominum papam, fuit provisum Thome Holoynas, clerico Eboracensis diocesis, per Urbanum iii° kalendas Decembris, anno v°,[552] taxa vel fructus. Supra sunt due provisiones de eadem, videlicet xv° kalendas Januarii anno secundo [553] et xv° kalendas Decembris anno iii°,[554] et neutra earum habuit effectum quia dictus David Wllorch, qui est clericus regis Anglie, eam possidet et de ea litigat in curia, et obtinebit quia dominus noster papa comisit

---

[538] A blank is left in MS.
[539] Supplied from p. 292.
[540] 3 August and 12 September 1365.
[541] *et dimittet* are repeated on folio 121ᵛ.
[542] 11 September 1366.
[543] 12 September 1366.
[544] Anglicus Grimoard, priest of S. Pietro in Vincoli.
[545] 24 September 1366.
[546] *fuerunt confirmate*, MS.

[547] 27 September 1366.
[548] *Henricum*, MS.
[549] 13 October 1366.
[550] 22 October 1366.
[551] 12 November 1368.
[552] 29 November 1366.
[553] 18 December 1363.
[554] 17 November 1364.

auditori cause quod si constet quod E. de Arden' eam acceptaverit sine litteris apostolicis, sicut fecit, quod provideat de ipsa dicto David Wllorch, viii° kalendas Maii anno septimo,[555] taxa vel fructus.

### Eboracensis

De prioratu Beate Marie de Lancastre (Lancaster) Eboracensis diocesis, qui consistit in ecclesia Beate Marie Lancastrie, qui taxatur lxxx li., a monasterio Sancti Martini Saginensis (Séez) ordinis Sancti Benedicti dependente, de quo, vacante per promotionem Petri abbatis dicti monasterii ad ipsum monasterium, fuit provisum Willelmo Raymbaut, monacho dicti monasterii, per Urbanum vii° kalendas Decembris anno v°,[556] pro resta x li.

### Londoniensis

De parochiali ecclesia Sancti Martini de Vinetria (St. Martin Vintry) Londoniensis diocesis, de qua, vacatura dum Nicholaus Drayton beneficium ad collationem episcopi Wygorniensis fuerit pacifice assequtus, fuit provisum Roberto Cantello Wellensis diocesis per Urbanum vi° kalendas Decembris anno quinto,[557] taxa vel fructus.

### Lincolniensis

De parochiali ecclesia de Surfflet (Surfleet) Lincolniensis diocesis, de qua vacante per amotionem Willelmi de Kywell' fuit provisum Johanni Skreth de Bolkyngham dicte diocesis, et dimittet parochialem ecclesiam de Harwod magna (Great Horwood) dicte diocesis, per Urbanum nonas Decembris anno quinto,[558] taxa vel fructus.

Summa pagine x li.

### (fol. 123)[559] Lincolniensis

De capella perpetua sive rectoria leprosarie Sancti Juliani iuxta Sanctorum Albanum (St. Julian, Hertford) Lincolniensis diocesis, de qua, vacatura dum Johannes de Balymburg' dignitatem, personatum vel officium in ecclesia Lincolniensi fuerit pacifice assequtus, fuit provisum Hugoni de Pryngton', presbytero dicte diocesis, per Urbanum ydus Decembris anno quinto,[560] taxa vel fructus.[561]

### Saresbiriensis

De archidiaconatu Baksekine (Berkshire), taxato liiii li., qui dignitas est in ecclesia Saresbiriensi, vacante per consecrationem Johannis de Harwell' electi Batho-

niensis, fuit provisum Aley de Darby, clerico Licheffeldensis diocesis, per Urbanum xix° kalendas Februarii anno quinto,[562] pro resta dicte taxe xliiii li.

### Licheffeldensis

Item de dicto decanatu curato Sancti Johannis Cestr' (Chester) Licheffeldensis diocesis, taxato xxxvi li. xiii s. iiii d., vacante ut supra, fuit provisum Johanni de Wodehaus per Urbanum vii° kalendas Januarii anno quinto,[563] debet de resta dicte taxe xiii li. vi s. viii d.

### Wellensis

De decanatu et prebenda ecclesie Wellensis, vacaturis per consecrationem electi Bathoniensis, fuit provisum Johanni de Brompton' clerico per Urbanum xvi° kalendas Januarii anno quinto,[564] taxa vel fructus.

Summa pagine lvii li. vi s. viii d.

### (fol. 123ᵛ)[559] Licheffeldensis

De canonicatu et prebenda ecclesie collegiate [565] Sancti Johannis Cestr' Licheffeldensis diocesis, vacantibus per amotionem Johannis de Wyveley, fuit provisum Thome Eltonhed, clerico dicte diocesis, per Urbanum xvi° kalendas Januarii anno quinto,[564] taxa vel fructus.

### Licheffeldensis

De canonicatu et prebenda ecclesie Licheffeldensis, de quibus, vacantibus per amotionem Hugonis de Winnodeswold', fuit provisum Thome Aleyn presbytero per Urbanum xiiii° kalendas Januarii anno quinto,[566] taxa vel fructus.

### Lincolniensis

De parochiali ecclesia de Harwold magna (Great Horwood) Lincolniensis diocesis, vacatura dum Johannes de Bokyngham parochialem ecclesiam de Stoffelt' (Surfleet) dicte diocesis fuerit pacifice assequtus, fuit provisum Johanni Skiret, et dimittet parochialem ecclesiam de Langeston' (Lillingstone), per Urbanum iii° nonas Januarii anno quinto,[567] taxa vel fructus. De ista et de alia est provisum supra iiii° nonas Maii anno quarto,[568] et infra eodem anno kalendas Augusti,[569] sit eo alia provisio propter quam dimittet istam ecclesiam nunc ei collatam solo.

### Dunelmensis

De archidiaconatu Dunelmensi (Down), de quo, vacante per consecrationem Willelmi Mierchier episcopi Conwetrensis (Connor), fuit provisum Johanni Domen-

---

[555] 24 April 1369.
[556] 25 November 1366.
[557] 26 November 1366.
[558] 5 December 1366.
[559] The heading *Anno quinto* is repeated at the top of the page.
[560] 13 December 1366.
[561] The next two items which relate to Crediton in the diocese of Exeter repeat the items given above, p. 346. They are marked *vacat* in the margin. The second is not complete.

[562] 14 January 1367.
[563] 26 December 1366.
[564] 17 December 1366.
[565] Followed by *de* deleted by dots.
[566] 19 December 1366.
[567] 3 January 1367.
[568] 4 May 1366.
[569] 1 August 1366.

gan, qui dimittet parochialem ecclesiam de Cannelyn (Camclyn?) dicte Dunelmensis (Down) diocesis, per Urbanum xv° kalendas Februarii anno quinto,[570] taxa vel fructus.

### Eboracensis

De canonicatu et prebenda ecclesie collegiate de Harwedon' (Howden) Eboracensis diocesis, de quibus,[571] vacantibus ex eo quod Henricus Swyth, non graduatus, una cum beneficiis aliis, videlicet ecclesiam parochialem [572] de Weudele (Oundle?) Lincolniensis, canonicatus et prebendas ecclesiarum Lincolniensis, Londoniensis et Menewensis alias Albenwill (Abergwili) optinens, ipsa beneficia et eorum valorem iuxta constitutionem domini pape editam non dedit, aut per privationem, seu alio quovis modo, fuit provisum Ricardo Sufflet per Urbanum xv° kalendas Februarii anno quinto,[570] taxa vel fructus. Sed nichil valet quia non fuit prosequtus ex causa certa et rationabili.

### (fol. 124)[559] Dunelmensis

De canonicatu et prebenda ecclesie collegiate Cestrie (Chester-le-Street) Dunelmensis diocesis, de quibus, vacantibus ex eo quod David de Wlhord' plura beneficia que obtinet cum eisdem et valores [573] ipsorum secundum constitutionem domini pape non tradidit, etiam si per amotionem ipsius vacent vel alio quovis modo, fuit provisum Nicholao Sufflet per Urbanum iiii° kalendas Februarii anno quinto,[574] taxa vel fructus. Sed iste non fuit gratiam prosequtus ex causa supradicta.

### Eboracensis

De canonicatu et prebenda ecclesie Ripponensis Eboracensis diocesis quos Willelmus Dalton tempore constitutionis predicte cum nonnullis beneficiis obtinens, ipsa et eorum valores secundum constitutionem predictam non tradidit, de quibus ex causa premissa, aut alio quovis modo vacent, fuit provisum Georgio Sycilie de Hewenden per Urbanum iii° kalendas Februarii anno quinto,[575] taxa vel fructus. Sed iste non fuit gratiam prosequtus ex causa predicta.

### Exoniensis

De canonicatu et prebenda ecclesie collegiate Sancti Trioci alias Karentoci (Crantock) Exoniensis diocesis, de quibus, vacantibus propter amotionem Thome Keyns propter pluralitatem beneficiorum que obtinebat, fuit provisum Philipo Loynie Lincolniensis diocesis per Urbanum iiii° kalendas Aprilis anno quinto,[576] taxa vel

fructus. Sed non habuit effectum quia ante amotionem fuerat mortuus.

### Lincolniensis

De canonicatu et prebenda ecclesie Lincolniensis de quibus, vacaturis per consecrationem Guillelmi electi Wynthoniensis, fuit mandatum provideri Domino Anglico cardinali Avinionensi [577] per Urbanum pridie ydus Julii anno quinto,[578] taxa vel fructus.

### Lincolniensis

De canonicatu et prebenda ecclesie Lincolniensis, de quibus, vacantibus per obitum Petri episcopi Albanensis cardinalis, fuit provisum motu proprio Domino Nicholao titulo Sancte Marie in Via Lata dyacono cardinali per Urbanum pridie ydus Julii anno quinto,[578] taxa vel fructus.[579]

### (fol. 124ᵛ)[559] Lincolniensis

De canonicatu et prebenda ecclesie Lincolniensis, de quibus, vacantibus per obitum Domini H. cardinalis Hostiensis,[580] fuit motu proprio provisum Guillelmo titulo Sanctorum Johannis et Pauli presbytero cardinali [581] per Urbanum pridie ydus Julii anno quinto, taxa vel fructus.[579]

### Eboracensis

De canonicatu et prebenda ecclesie Eboracensis,[582] de quibus, vacantibus per obitum H. cardinalis Ostiensis, fuit provisum Domino Matheo cardinali Viterbiensi [583] per Urbanum pridie ydus Julii anno quinto,[578] taxa vel fructus.[579]

Sequntur reste de annatis beneficiorum collatorum per Dominum Urbanum a pridie ydus Julii anno quinto [578] usque ad vii kalendas Maii anno vii° [584]

### Cicestrensis

De decanatu ecclesie Cicestrensis, vacante per obitum Nicholai de Aston' infra duas dietas a Romana curia defuncti, fuit provisum Rogero de Frethon', legum doctori, per Urbanum viii° kalendas Augusti anno quinto,[585] taxa vel fructus.

### Wellensis

De canonicatu et prebenda ecclesie Wellensis, vacantibus per obitum Nicholai de Aston' infra duas dietas a Romana curia defuncti, fuit provisum Johanni de Langeton', clerico Lincolniensis diocesis, per Urbanum vii° kalendas Augusti anno quinto,[586] taxa vel fructus.

---

[570] 18 January 1367.
[571] *qua*, MS.
[572] *ecclesia parochiali*, MS.
[573] *valore*, MS.
[574] 29 January 1367.
[575] 30 January 1367.
[576] 29 March 1367.

[577] Anglicus Grimoard, bishop of Albano.
[578] 14 July 1367.
[579] In the margin: *Cardinalis*.
[580] Elias de S. Eredio.
[581] William Sudre, bishop of Marseille.
[582] *Lincolniensis*, MS.
[583] Mark de Viterbo, priest of S. Prassede.
[584] 25 April 1369.
[585] 25 July 1367.
[586] 26 July 1367.

(fol. 125) Anno quinto

Datur potestas episcopo aut electo Wynthoniensi aut alicui episcopo regni Anglie conferendi quatuor doctoribus in theologia, decretis aut legibus, unicum beneficium ii^c vel iii^c florenorum obtinentibus, iiii^or beneficia vacatura vel vacantia per consecrationem dicti electi per Urbanum vii° kalendas Augusti anno quinto,[586] taxa vel fructus.

### Lincolniensis

De archidiaconatu Bokyngamie in ecclesia Lincolniensi, vacante per amotionem Willelmi de Keynewill' propter pluralitatem beneficiorum que obtinebat, fuit provisum Johanni Skyrech et Bokyngham, bacallario in utroque iure, per Urbanum kalendas Augusti anno quinto,[587] taxa vel fructus.

### Lincolniensis

De archidiaconatu Oxoniensi [588] in ecclesia Lincolniensi et ecclesia de Ystele (Iffley) eidem annexa, taxata xiiii li. xiii s. iiii d., vacante per obitum cardinalis Aquensis,[589] fuit provisum Thome de Satham, clerico Licheffeldensis diocesis, per Urbanum viii° ydus Augusti anno quinto,[590] de quibus recepte fuerunt in partem primorum fructuum archidiaconatus et taxe predicte ecclesie x li.; restat quod debet de resta.

### Bangorensis

De archidiaconatu Angleseie in ecclesia Bangoriensi, vacante per mortem Hobelli Aprogenew extra Romanam curiam defuncti, fuit provisum Johanni Reys, clerico Assawensis diocesis, nisi sit alteri specialiter ius quesitum, et fuit secum super etate dispensatum, et dimittet canonicatum et prebendam ecclesie Assawensis, per Urbanum iiii° nonas Augusti anno v°,[591] taxa vel fructus.

### Licheffeldensis et Eboracensis

Concessum est Waltero de Campedon' ut parochialem ecclesiam de Wycham (Wigan) Licheffeldensis diocesis canonicatum et prebendam Eboracensis ecclesie licite retinere, resignare simpliciter vel permutare, et quod in hospitalibus Sancti Nicholai de Pontefracto (Pontefract), solito per laicos gubernari, ac leprosarum Sancte Marie Magdalene de Preston' Eboracensis diocesis, que [592] obtinet, servetur constitutio consilii Vianensis (Vienne) per Urbanum vi° ydus Augusti anno v°,[593] taxa vel fructus.

### (fol. 125^v) [594] Exoniensis

Concessum fuit Willelmo de Bukbridge ut parochialem ecclesiam de Torthon' (Great Torrington) Exoniensis diocesis, canonicatum et prebendam ecclesie Licheffeldensis, canonicatum et prebendam ecclesie collegiate de Landewebremy (Llanddewi Brefi) Menewensis diocesis, canonicatum et prebendam libere capelle regis Anglie de Astyng' (Hastings) Cicestrensis diocesis licite valeat retinere, resignare et permutare, ita quod unum ex illis teneatur dimittere, per Urbanum vi° ydus Augusti anno quinto,[593] taxa vel fructus.

### Eboracensis

De parochiali ecclesia de Beeth (Leake) Eboracensis diocesis, quam Hugo de Wymondcold' per assequutionem beneficii incompassibilis tenetur dimittere, fuit provisum Symoni Lamborn' alias Lamborny', presbytero magistro in artibus, per Urbanum pridie ydus Augusti anno quinto,[595] taxa vel fructus.

### Herffordensis

De archidiaconatu Herffordie in ecclesia Herffordensi, vacante et reservato per obitum ultimi archidiaconi, fuit provisum Rogero de Sutton', presbytero Lincolniensis diocesis legum doctori, et dimittet parochialem ecclesiam de Glaugton' (Glatton) Lincolniensis diocesis, per Urbanum pridie ydus Augusti anno quinto,[595] taxa vel fructus.

### Lincolniensis

De parochiali ecclesia de Brukton' (Broughton) Lincolniensis diocesis, cuius collatio, acceptatio et provisio facte vigore litterarum apostolicarum Roberto de Wytham, etiam si reservata fuerit vel devoluta, fuerunt confirmate vel provisum de novo, et dimittet parochialem ecclesiam de Briselee (Brisley) Norwicensis diocesis, per Urbanum iii° ydus Augusti anno quinto,[596] taxa vel fructus.

### Saresbiriensis

De canonicatu et prebenda ecclesie Saresbiriensis, vacantibus per privationem Saladini de Falletis, qui cum malis societatibus in guerris tam licitis quam illicitis incedit, fuit provisum Henrico Wyntrinton', clerico Norwicensis diocesis, et dimittet alios canonicatum et prebendam quos obtinet in ecclesia Saresbiriensi predicta, per Urbanum iii° ydus Augusti anno v°,[596] taxa vel fructus.

### Lincolniensis

Motu proprio fuit provisum titulo Sancte Praxedis presbytero cardinali [597] de archidiaconatu Oxoniensi [598] cum ecclesiis de Zestile (Iffley) et Mielton (Great Milton) eidem annexis in ecclesia Lincolniensi, vacante

---

[587] 1 August 1367.
[588] *Exoniensi*, MS.
[589] Peter Itherii, bishop of Dax, bishop of Albano.
[590] 6 August 1367.
[591] 2 August 1367.
[592] *quem*, MS.
[593] 8 August 1367.
[594] The heading *anno quinto* is repeated at the top of the page.
[595] 12 August 1367.
[596] 11 august 1367.
[597] Mark de Viterbo, priest of S. Prassede.
[598] *Exoniensi*, MS.

per obitum Petri episcopi Albanensis,[599] per Urbanum x° kalendas Octobris anno quinto,[600] taxa vel fructus.[601]

Completum est de anno quinto; sequitur de anno sexto.

(fol. 126) Anno vi°

### Norwicensis

De parochiali ecclesia de Scothewe (Scottow) Norwicensis diocesis, vacante per obitum ultimi rectoris eiusdem extra Romanam curiam defuncti a tanto tempore quod eius collatio est ad sedem apostolicam legitime devoluta, fuit provisum Johanni Bankl, clerico Karleolensis diocesis, per Urbanum v° ydus Novembris anno [602] sexto,[603] taxa vel fructus.

### Eboracensis

De vicaria perpetua parochialis ecclesie de Alne Eboracensis diocesis, vacante ex eo quod Johannes de Welton ipsam tunc optinens perpetuam vicariam parochialis ecclesie de Stafforham (Stamfordham) Dunelmensis diocesis fuerat auctoritate eadem pacifice assequtus, collatio et provisio facte per capitulum ecclesie Eboracensis Willelmo Canon' presbytero fuerunt confirmate vel provisum de novo per Urbanum pridie ydus Novembris anno vi°,[604] etiam si reservata sit vel devoluta ad sedem apostolicam, taxa vel fructus.

### Dunelmensis

De canonicatu et prebenda ecclesie collegiate de Langcestr' (Lanchester) Dunelmensis diocesis, taxata vi li. xiii s. iiii d., vacantibus per obitum Johannis de Neiwyt in Romana curia defuncti, fuit provisum Johanni de Babyngle, clerico Norwicensis diocesis, per Urbanum iiii° kalendas Decembris anno sexto,[605] debet pro resta liii s. iiii d. Infra providetur alteri xix° kalendas Januarii.[606]

### Wigorniensis

Mandatur Willelmo Guycardi, auditori palatii apostolici, ut si sibi constiterit quod duo exequtores super gratia communi facta Willelmo de Homburn', presbytero Wygorniensis diocesis, concessorum videlicet unus [607] se excusavit et alter interesse noluit, sed alter, videlicet tertius, solus ad exequtionem gratie processit in quantum potuit, ipse que postmodum vicariam parochialis ecclesie de Blokelet (Blockley) Wygorniensis diocesis infra tempus debitum acceptaverit, et quod Johannes

de Redlyngthon', vigore cuiusdem permutationis facte auctoritate ordinaria se in ipsa de facto intruserit, et dictum Willelmum fore reperiat vite laudabilis et honeste conversationis, de dicta vicaria eidem provideat et intruso predicto perpetuum silentium imponat, per Urbanum pridie kalendas Decembris anno sexto,[608] taxa vel fructus.

### Eboracensis

Gratia [609] facta per dominum nostrum papam Roberto de Pontouwe, presbytero [610] (fol. 126^v) [611] Eboracensis diocesis, de parochiali ecclesia de Acathon' (Aughton) dicte diocesis, vacante per resignationem Hugonis de Bolthon' in Romana curia factam, cui Hugoni de ipsa mandatum fuerat provideri per felicis recordationis Dominum Innocentium papam VI^tum, cui quidem mandato quidam prior et conventus se opposuerunt et litem inter se moverunt, qua lite pendente idem Hugo ipsam in dicta curia resignavit ac cessit omni iuri sibi in ipsa competenti, fuit confirmata et fuit subrogatus in omni iure quod predicto Hugoni quomodolibet [612] competebat in eadem, per Urbanum pridie nonas Decembris anno v°,[613] taxa vel fructus.

### Eboracensis

De parochiali ecclesia de Mutton' (Mitton) Eboracensis diocesis, vacante per obitum Willelmi Tatham, ultimi rectoris eiusdem, etiam si tanto tempore vacaverit quod eius collatio sit ad sedem apostolicam legitime devoluta, fuit provisum Thome Sotthoron', licet abbas monasterii Cokersand' (Cockersand) ordinis Cisterciensis ipsam prefato monasterio incorporari fecerit et uniri ac eam indebite detinuerat occupatam, et dimittet parochialem ecclesiam de Monesbyey (Mundsley) Norwicensis diocesis, per Urbanum vii° ydus Decembris anno vi°,[614] taxa vel fructus.

### Lincolniensis

De archidiaconatu de Bokyngham in ecclesia Lincolniensi, vacante per privationem Willelmi Kynewell' propter multitudinem beneficiorum que obtinebat, licet de eo provisum fuisset Johanni Skyreth, qui, litteris non confectis, in Romana curia decessit, fuit provisum Johanni de Toresby, presbytero Lincolniensis diocesis, et dimittet parochialem ecclesiam de Lilleford' (Lilford) Lincolniensis diocesis et litem quam habet de parochiali ecclesia in Bratyingham (Brantingham) Eboracensis diocesis, per Urbanum pridie ydus Decembris anno vi°,[615] taxa vel fructus. De isto archidiaconatu statim providetur alteri.

---

[599] Peter Itherii, bishop of Dax.
[600] 22 September 1367.
[601] In the margin: *Cardinalis.*
[602] Followed by *quinto* deleted by a line.
[603] 9 November 1367.
[604] 12 November 1367.
[605] 28 November 1367.
[606] 14 December.
[607] *unius,* MS.

[608] 30 November 1367.
[609] Preceded by *de* deleted by dots.
[610] At the foot of fol. 126: *Summa pagine liii s. iiii d.*
[611] The heading *anno sexto* is repeated at the top of the page.
[612] Followed by *q* deleted by a line.
[613] 4 December 1366.
[614] 7 December 1367.
[615] 12 December 1367.

### Lincolniensis

De archidiaconatu de Bokyngham in ecclesia Lincolniensi, vacante per amotionem ab eo Willelmi de Kynewell', fuit provisum Henrico Prel Lincolniensis diocesis, licet antea provisum fuisset Johanni Skyreth de Bokyngham, qui, litteris apostolicis super hoc non confectis, in Romana curia decessit, et dimittet parochialem ecclesiam de Werketon' (Warkton) Lincolniensis diocesis, per Urbanum iii° ydus Decembris, anno vi°,[616] taxa vel fructus.

### (fol. 127)[611] Wellensis et Saresbiriensis

Ex causa permutationis fuit provisum Johanni de Wolton' Wellensis diocesis de parochiali ecclesia de Templecombe Wellensis diocesis et Thome Heryngh' de vicaria perpetua ecclesie de Wermynstr' (Warminster) Saresbiriensis diocesis, taxata v li., de [617] vicaria est satisfactum, per Urbanum xi° kalendas Januarii anno sexto.[618] Restat quod debetur annata de predicta parochiali ecclesia de Templecombe.

### Eboracensis

Item Willelmo de Rippon', presbytero Eboracensis diocesis, de parochiali ecclesia de Aldyngham in Forncis (Aldingham in Furness) Eboracensis diocesis et Johanni Saffer, presbytero Eboracensis diocesis, de parochiali ecclesia Sancti Martini in Mikelgate (Micklegate, York) dicte Eboracensis diocesis, per Urbanum xix° kalendas Januarii anno sexto,[619] taxa vel fructus.

### Lincolniensis

De parochiali ecclesia de Harwode magna (Great Horwood) Lincolniensis diocesis, vacante per mortem Johannis de Bokyngham [620] in Romana curia defuncti, fuit provisum Johanni de Bokyngham [621] clerico, per Urbanum xi° kalendas Januarii anno vi°,[618] taxa vel fructus. De ista ecclesia fuit provisum isti Johanni de Bokyngham iii° nonas Januarii anno quinto,[622] et sic ambe iste provisiones sunt infra annum, et ideo non debetur nisi una annata.

Mandatur Thome de Paxton' ut si sibi constiterit Rogerum de Holure vi° fl. in redditibus et iiii°r beneficia obtinere, quod eidem Rogero super parochiali ecclesia de Patryngthon' (Patrington) quam Johannes de Mecham possedit pacifice per xii annos vel circa, super qua dicto Johanni litem movit, silentium perpetuum imponat, per Urbanum ix° kalendas Januarii anno sexto,[618] taxa vel fructus.

### Norwicensis

De parochiali ecclesia de Sotowe (Scottow) Norwicensis diocesis, vacante vel vacatura per resignationem ultimi rectoris eiusdem, fuit provisum Johanni de Carlil, clerico Karleolensis diocesis bacallario in legibus et in artibus, per Urbanum iiii° kalendas Januarii anno sexto,[623] taxa vel fructus.

(fol. 127v)[611] Item collatio et provisio facte auctoritate apostolica Johanni Cheyne, clerico Exoniensis diocesis, de canonicatu ecclesie collegiate de Credyngthon' (Crediton) de prebenda de Chaskille (Kerswell) in eadem dicte diocesis, quas possidet pacifice etiam si ex eo quod habet custodire dicta prebenda libros et vestimenta dicte ecclesie sit officium thesaurarie, fuerunt confirmate vel provisum de novo per Urbanum iiii° kalendas Januarii anno sexto,[623] taxa vel fructus.

### Cicestrensis et Wellensis

Motu proprio fuit provisum Marco titulo Sancte Praxedis presbytero cardinali [624] de canonicatu et prebenda ac precentoria ecclesie Cicestrensis ac canonicatu et prebenda de thesauraria ecclesie Wellensis, vacantibus per obitum Petri cardinalis Albanensis,[625] per Urbanum pridie nonas Januarii anno vi°,[626] taxa vel fructus.[627]

### Assawensis

De canonicatu et prebenda ecclesie Assawensis, de quibus, vacantibus per mortem Johannis de Gruffunduy clerici extra Romanam curiam defuncti, licet eorum possessionem non haberet, fuit provisum Johanni Reys, clerico Assawensis diocesis, etiam si fuerint reservati, per Urbanum vii° ydus Januarii anno vi°,[628] taxa vel fructus.

### Eliensis

De parochiali ecclesia de Ellesworthe (Elsworth) Eliensis diocesis, de qua, vacatura dum Johannes de Merthon' dignitatem, personatum vel officium curatum in ecclesia Licheffeldensi fuerit pacifice assequtus, fuit provisum Johanni de Scrap per Urbanum xv° kalendas Februarii anno vi°,[629] taxa vel fructus.

### Dunelmensis

Subrogatus fuit Johannes de Hesill' in omni iure et ad omne ius quod competebat Johanni Neswit super decanatu Langcestr' (Lanchester) Dunelmensis diocesis, super quo lis nuper pendebat in Romana curia inter ipsos, qua pendente, dictus Johannes de Neswyt in Romana curia decessit, per Urbanum xv° kalendas Februarii anno vi°,[629] taxa vel fructus.

---

[616] 11 December 1367.
[617] Followed by *quibus vacantibus* deleted by a line.
[618] 22 December 1367.
[619] 14 December 1367.
[620] Followed by *clerico per Urbanum* deleted by a line.
[621] Followed by *electi* deleted by a line.
[622] 3 January 1367.

[623] 29 December 1367.
[624] Mark de Viterbo.
[625] Peter Itherii, bishop of Dax.
[626] 4 January 1368.
[627] In the margin : *Cardinalis*.
[628] 7 January 1368.
[629] 18 January 1368.
[630] 20 January 1368.

## Lincolniensis

De archidiaconatu Lincolniensis, que dignitas curata existit, de quo, vacante per consecrationem Willelmi de Wykham episcopi Wynthoniensis, fuit provisum Ricardo de Ravensee presbytero per Urbanum xiii° kalendas Februarii anno vi°,[630] taxa vel fructus.

## (fol. 128)[611] Saresbiriensis [631]

De canonicatu et prebenda ecclesie collegiate seu conventualis monialium Schaston' (Shaftesbury) Saresbiriensis diocesis, de quibus, vacantibus per consecrationem Willelmi de Wykham episcopi Wynthoniensis, ⟨fuit provisum Johanni Blebury⟩[632] per Urbanum xiii° kalendas Februarii anno vi°,[630] taxa vel fructus.

## Wynthoniensis

De canonicatu et prebenda ecclesie collegiate seu conventualis monialium de Warewell' (Wherwell) Wynthoniensis diocesis fuit provisum Willelmo de Multho per Urbanum xiii° kalendas Februarii anno vi°,[630] taxa vel fructus.

## Londoniensis

De canonicatu et prebenda ecclesie Londoniensis, de quibus, vacantibus per consecrationem Willelmi de Wykham episcopi Wynthoniensis, fuit provisum Willelmo de Dygton' per Urbanum xiii° kalendas Februarii anno sexto,[630] taxa vel fructus.

## Dunelmensis

De canonicatu et prebenda ecclesie collegiate de Aucland' (Auckland) Dunelmensis diocesis, de quibus, vacantibus per mortem Thome de Bridekyrke in Romana curia defuncti, et de quibus sic vacantibus felicis recordationis Dominus Innocentius ⟨concessit provideri⟩ prefato Willelmo nunc episcopo Wynthoniensi, qui, antequam sibi de ipsis provisum fuisset, fuit in episcopum Wynthoniensem consecratus, fuit provisum Thome de Barnolby per Urbanum xiii° kalendas Februarii anno sexto,[630] taxa vel fructus.

## Norwicensis

De archidiaconatu Suffolchie in ecclesia Norwicensi, de quo, vacante et reservato per obitum Johannis [633] de Carleton', qui veniendo ad curiam Romanam in itinere decessit, fuit provisum Johanni Aleyn per Urbanum xiii° kalendas Februarii anno vi°,[630] taxa vel fructus.

## Lincolniensis

De canonicatu et prebenda ecclesie Lincolniensis, de quibus, vacantibus et reservatis per mortem Johannis de Carleton' extra Romanam curiam veniendo ad eam

defuncti, fuit provisum Ricardo de Lynttesford' per Urbanum xiii° kalendas Februarii anno vi°,[630] taxa vel fructus.

## (fol 128ᵛ)[611] Eboracensis

De prepositura ecclesie collegiate Sancti Johannis Beverlacensis Eboracensis diocesis, de qua, vacatura dum Ricardus Ramonscher' archidiaconatum ecclesie Lincolniensis fuerit pacifice assequtus, fuit provisum Ade de Lymberg' per Urbanum xiii° kalendas Februarii anno vi°,[630] taxa vel fructus.

## Menewensis

De canonicatu et prebenda ecclesie collegiate de Landewybremy (Llanddewi Brefi) Menewensis diocesis, de quibus, vacaturis dum Johannes de Belbury canonicatum et prebendam ecclesie collegiate et conventualis monialium Scaston' (Shaftesbury) Saresbiriensis diocesis fuerit pacifice assequtus, fuit provisum Johanni de Saxton' per Urbanum xiii° kalendas Februarii anno sexto,[630] taxa vel fructus.

## Roffensis

De parochiali ecclesia de Contefford' (Otford) Roffensis diocesis, de qua, vacatura dum Aleyn archidiaconatum Suffolchie in ecclesia Norwicensi fuerit pacifice assequtus, fuit provisum Johanni de Ledecombe per Urbanum xiii° kalendas Februarii anno vi°,[630] taxa vel fructus.

## Norwicensis

De vicaria parochialis ecclesiae in Alesham (Aylsham) Norwicensis diocesis, de qua vacante vel vacatura dum Michael de Causton' beneficium ad collationem episcopi Eliensis fuerit pacifice assequtus, fuit provisum Thome Gylury de Wodehaus presbytero per Urbanum xii° kalendas Martii anno vi°,[634] taxa vel fructus.

## Londoniensis

De parochiali ecclesia de Altabotyng' (High Roding) Londoniensis diocesis, taxata xii li., de qua ex causa permutationis cum ecclesia de Nortwolde (Northwold) Norwicensis diocesis fuit provisum Bernardo de Santre per Urbanum xi° kalendas Martii anno vi°,[635] debet pro resta taxe vi li.[636]

## Norwicensis

De parochiali ecclesia de Nortwolde Norwicensis diocesis, de qua ex simili causa permutationis cum predicta ecclesia de Altabotyng' Londoniensis diocesis fuit provisum Johanni de Glatton' per Urbanum xi° kalendas Martii anno vi°,[635] que taxatur [637] (fol. 129)[611] xli li. vi s. viii d., debet pro resta dicte taxe xiii li. vi s. viii d.

---

[631] Follows *Eboracensis* deleted by a line.
[632] The name is supplied from p. 394 below.
[633] Follows *Thome* deleted by a line.

[634] 19 February 1368.
[635] 20 February 1368.
[636] Follows *taxa vel fructus* deleted by a line.
[637] At the foot of fol. 128ᵛ: *Summa pagine vi li.*

### Norwicensis

De parochiali ecclesia de Fonrham Sancti Martini (Fornham St. Martin) Norwicensis diocesis, taxata viii li., de qua collatio et provisio facte vigore litterarum apostolicarum in forma communi Willelmo Dany, presbytero dicte diocesis, super quibus pendebat lis inter Willelmum [638] Eteswell' tunc possessorem auctoritate ordinaria, qua lite pendente idem Willelmus extra curiam decessit, fuerunt confirmate vel provisum de novo et subrogatus in omni iure competenti prefato defuncto per Urbanum viii° kalendas Martii anno vi°,[639] debet pro resta dicte taxe vi li. xiii s. iiii d.

### Dunelmensis

De canonicatu et prebenda ecclesie collegiate de Cestr' in strata (Chester-le-Street) Dunelmensis diocesis, de qua, vacante per resignationem Guidonis de Postello, fuit provisum Hugoni de Harlani, clerico dicte diocesis, per Urbanum viii° kalendas Martii anno vi°,[639] taxa vel fructus.

### Lincolniensis

De vicaria perpetua de Stotffelde (Stotfold) Lincolniensis diocesis, non taxata, de qua ex causa permutationis cum vicaria perpetua de Kerdengthon' (Cardington) eiusdem diocesis, pro qua fuit satisfactum, fuit provisum Radulpho de Beresforde per Urbanum vii° kalendas Martii anno vi°,[640] de [641] qua satisfactum est in partem fructuum de xiii s. iiii d., restat quod debet.

### Assawensis

De vicaria perpetua parochialis ecclesia de Cogidva (Cegidfa) Assawensis diocesis, non taxata, de qua collatio et provisio dudum auctoritate ordinaria facte Johanni Aprewerth, quamvis ipsam per tres menses antequam vicesimumquintum etatis sue annum attigisset possederit prout possidet pacifice, fructus ex ea percipiendo, fuerunt confirmate vel provisum de novo et mandatum ipsum habilitari per Urbanum ydus Martii anno vi°,[642] pro qua est satisfactum de iii li. vi s. viii d. in partem primorum fructuum, restat quod debet.

Summa pagine xx li.

### (fol. 129ᵛ) [643] Eboracensis

De parochiali ecclesia de Akaster' (Acaster Malbis) Eboracensis diocesis, de qua, vacante per resignationem Willelmi de Hormi, ultimi rectoris eiusdem, et que tanto tempore [644] vacavit quod eius collatio et cetera, licet abbas et conventus monasterii de Neubo illam detinuerint occupatam, fuit provisum Johanni Karolde,

bacallario in utroque iure, per Urbanum ydus Aprilis anno sexto,[645] taxa vel fructus.

### Londoniensis

De parochiali ecclesia Sancti Benedicti de Graschurche (St. Benet Gracechurch, London) Londoniensis diocesis, de qua collatio et provisio facte auctoritate apostolica Johanni de Lexham, qui eam per annum et ultra possedit pacifice, etiam si fuerit reservata vel devoluta, fuerunt confirmate vel provisum de novo per Urbanum viii° kalendas Augusti anno sexto,[646] qui composuit pro mediis fructibus medio iuramento pro viii li., de quibus solute sunt vi li., restat quod debet de resta ii li.

### Bangorensis

De archidiaconatu Angligie (Anglesey) in ecclesia Bangoriensi, de quo, vacante per obitum Howelli Aproguon extra Romanam curiam defuncti, collatio et provisio facte auctoritate ordinaria Thome de Honeberghe fuerunt confirmate vel provisum de novo, etiam si sit reservato, per Urbanum viii° kalendas Maii anno sexto,[647] taxa vel fructus.

### Eboracensis

De canonicatu et prebenda ecclesie Eboracensis quos Johannes de Appelby, legum doctor, vigore expectationis per dominum papam sibi concesse acceptavit et possedit, licet Matheus de Ascechthon' ipsos acceptaverit, quamvis ipsum Johannem sequeretur in data, dicens illos sibi declari et non dicto Johanni, ex eo quod nuper dominus noster papa dicto Johanni de canonicatu sub expectatione prebende ac decanatu ecclesie Londoniensis providit, volens quod quamprimum prebendam ipsius ecclesie Londoniensis foret pacifice assequtus vigore litterarum suarum [648] expectationem quam habet in ecclesia Eboracensi dimittere teneatur; ipseque prebendam ecclesie Londoniensis sit assequtus, et licet lite pendente super ipsis inter ipsos, prefato Johanne dicente quod, cum prebendam ipsam non vigore litterarum apostolicarum sed auctoritate ordinaria ex causa permutationis assequtus, se non debere nec teneri expectationem ipsam dimittere, et sic dictam [649] (fol. 130) [643] prebendam sibi deberi; quibus domino nostro expositis, et quod dictus Matheus non graduatus obtinet in redditibus ecclesiasticis m fl. ultra et dictus doctor non obtinet ultra viii° fl., idem dominus noster prefatum Matheum privavit et cum dicto doctore, si et in quantum indiget, contulit viii° ydus Julii anno sexto,[650] taxa vel fructus.

### Londoniensis

De archidiaconatu Excessy in ecclesia Londoniensi,

---

[638] Follows eos deleted by a line.
[639] 23 February 1368.
[640] 24 February 1368.
[641] de repeated MS.
[642] 15 March 1368.
[643] The heading Anno sexto is repeated at the top of the page.
[644] tempore repeated MS.

[645] 13 April 1368.
[646] 25 July 1368.
[647] 24 April 1368.
[648] sua, MS.
[649] At the foot of fol. 129ᵛ: Summa pagine ii li.
[650] 8 July 1368.

de quo collatio et provisio facte auctoritate apostolica [651] Henrico de Wyntryton', in utroque iure bacallario, licet idem Henricus mentionem non fecisset quod idem archidiaconatus curatus existerit, fuerunt confirmate vel provisum de nova per Urbanum xiiii° kalendas Julii anno vi°,[652] taxa vel fructus.

### Dunelmensis

De canonicatu et prebenda ecclesie collegiate Cestr' in strata (Chester-le-Street) Dunelmensis diocesis, de quibus vacaturis per resignationem Guidonis de Pestello fuit provisum Waltero de Waudefforde, clerico dicte diocesis, per Urbanum vi° ydus Julii anno vi°,[653] taxa vel fructus.

### Saresbiriensis

Mandatur provideri Johanni de Tresk, presbytero Eboracensis diocesis, de beneficio ecclesiastico spectante ad collationem episcopi Saresbiriensi per Urbanum quinto kalendas Augusti anno vi°,[654] taxa vel fructus.

### Saresbiriensis et Bathoniensis

Dum Johannes de Strekt, presbyter Eboracensis diocesis, beneficium ad collationem episcopi Saresbiriensis fuerit pacifice assequtus, dimittet rectoriam de Santton' (Stanton) Bathoniensis diocesis per Urbanum v° kalendas Augusti anno sexto,[654] taxa vel fructus.

### Eboracensis

De vicaria perpetua parochialis ecclesie de Hasill' (Hessle), a prioratu de Gliseborn' (Guisborough) Eboracensis diocesis dependente, ab antiquo consueta [655] per canonicos regulares dicti prioratus gubernari, de qua, vacante per mortem Ricardi de [656] (fol. 130ᵛ)[643] Lessebury, canonici dicti ordinis, in Romana curia defuncti, fuit provisum fratri Johanni de Dordefford', canonico Karleolensis diocesis ordinis Sancti Augustini, non obstante quod inter dictum Ricardum, possessorem dicte vicarie, et quemdam Johannem Hauby citra tamen dilationem articulorum lis penderet, et dictus Johannes de Dordefford' dimittet vicariam parochialis ecclesie de Wytingham (Whittingham) Dunelmensis diocesis, per Urbanum vi° ydus Augusti anno sexto,[657] taxa vel fructus.

### Wynthoniensis

De parochiali ecclesia de Croudon' (Croydon) Wynthoniensis diocesis, de qua, vacante ex eo quod Johannes de Tuerneby eam per annum et ultra tenuit, in presbyterum non promotus dispensatione super hoc non obtenta, et cessante impedimento legitimo, etiam si eam

permutaverit post lapsum anni huius, vel si fuerit generaliter vel specialiter reservata, fuit provisum Radulpho de Pilethon', presbytero Eboracensis diocesis, per Urbanum xii kalendas Septembris anno sexto,[658] taxa vel fructus.

### Lincolniensis

De parochiali ecclesia de Werketon' (Warkton) Lincolniensis diocesis, de qua, vacante vel vacatura dum Henricus Prel archidiaconatum de Bokyngham in ecclesia Lincolniensi fuerit pacifice assequtus, fuit provisum Robert Goere, presbytero Lincolniensis diocesis, per Urbanum pridie kalendas Septembris anno sexto,[659] taxa vel fructus.

### Exoniensis

Item collatio et provisio facte auctoritate [660] et vigore litterarum apostolicarum Nicholao Iolito, presbytero Exoniensis, de parochiali ecclesia de Blakentton' (Blackawton) Exoniensis diocesis, licet in impetratione huiusmodi litterarum dixisset idem Nicholaus quod foret Exoniensis diocesis qui tamen est civitatis Exoniensis, fuerunt confirmate vel provisum de novo per Urbanum kalendas Septembris anno sexto,[661] taxa vel fructus.

### Norwicensis

Item collatio et provisio auctoritate ordinaria ex causa permutationis Henrico de Dynniston' de parochiali ecclesia de Bengeton' (Beighton) Norwicensis diocesis, etiam si vacet per illicitam detentionem cuiusdem Johannis de novo et fuerit devoluta vel reservata, fuerunt confirmate vel provisum de novo per Urbanum kalendas Septembris anno vi°,[661] taxa vel fructus.

### (fol. 131)[643] Cicestrensis

De novo fuit provisum Henrico de Onyngge, clerico Cicestrensis diocesis de parochiali ecclesia de Blacyngton' (Blatchington) Cicestrensis diocesis, quam ultra tempus debitum detinuit, fructus ex ea percipiendo, in presbyterum non promotus, et tenetur reddere fructus indebite perceptos, et fuit etiam habilitatus, per Urbanum iiii° nonas Septembris anno vi°,[662] taxa vel fructus.

### Licheffeldensis

De vicaria perpetua ecclesie curate de Yolgrave (Youlgreave) Licheffeldensis diocesis, vacante per obitum Ricardi de Hertushull Cicestrensis diocesis in Romana curia defuncti, fuit provisum Johanni de Aptrap', presbytero Lincolniensis diocesis, per Urbanum iiii° nonas Septembris anno vi°,[662] taxa vel fructus.

### Menewensis

De prioratu de Cudyngham (Cardigan) Menewensis diocesis in Wallia, a monasterio Charteseye (Chertsey)

---

[651] Follows *ordinaria* deleted by a line.
[652] 18 June 1368.
[653] 10 July 1368.
[654] 28 July 1368.
[655] *consueto*, MS.
[656] *de* repeated MS.
[657] 8 August 1368.

[658] 21 August 1368.
[659] 31 August 1368.
[660] Followed by *ordinaria* deleted by a line.
[661] 1 September 1368.
[662] 2 September 1368.

ordinis Sancti Benedicti dependente, vacante per liberam resignationem ultimi rectoris sive prioris eiusdem in manibus abbatis ipsius monasterii factam, quem [663] idem abbas sedis apostolice licentia super hoc non obtenta illicite detinet occupatum [664] fuit provisum fratri Thome Chymy de Wallia oriundo, monacho monasterii Sancti Martini de Bello (Battle) dicti ordinis Cicestrensis diocesis, per Urbanum iiii° nonas Septembris anno vi°,[662] taxa vel fructus.

### Cantuariensis

De prepositura ecclesie collegiate de Wydgham (Wingham) Cantuariensis diocesis, vacante per consecrationem Willelmi electi Cicestrensis, fuit provisum Thome de Paxthon', legum doctori, et dimittet parochialem ecclesiam de Alloney (Hackney) Londoniensis diocesis, per Urbanum iiii° ydus Octobris anno vi°,[665] taxa vel fructus.

Completus est de anno sexto; (fol. 131ᵛ) sequitur de anno septimo.

### (fol. 132) Anno Septimo

### Bangorensis

De archidiaconatu de Manonut (Merioneth) in ecclesia Bangoriensi in Wallia, qui dignitas curata existit, de quo, vacante per obitum Edmundi Hyngham in Romanam curia defuncti, fuit provisum Johanni Beys, clerico Assawensis diocesis, et dimittet canonicatum et prebendam in dicta ecclesia, per Urbanum vi° ydus Novembris anno septimo,[666] taxa vel fructus.

### Londoniensis, Wellensis et Eboracensis

Collationes et provisiones facte Johanni de Sumfford' de canonicatibus et prebendis Londoniensis, Wellensis et Sancti Johannis Beverlacensis Eboracensis diocesis ecclesiarum, non obstante defectu natalium quem patitur de soluto genitus et soluta, cum quo alias super huiusmodi defectum extitit dispensatus, licet dum idem Johannes fuit genitus mater sua fuerat cum alio matrimonialiter copulata, cuiusmodi matrimonium tamen postmodum nullum fuit declaratum, fuerunt confirmate vel provisum de novo per Urbanum vi° ydus Novembris anno vii°,[666] taxa vel fructus.

### Dunelmensis

De vicaria perpetua parochialis ecclesie de Wytyngham (Whittingham) Dunelmensis diocesis, vacatura dum Johannes de Dodefford', canonicus Karlensis (Carlisle) ordinis Sancti Augustini, vicariam perpetuam parochialis ecclesie de Hesill' (Hessle) Eboracensis diocesis fuerit pacifice assequtus, fuit provisum Thome de Peveroth, canonico dicte ecclesie Karleolensis, per Ur-

banum quinto ydus Novembris anno septimo,[667] taxa vel fructus.

### Saresbiriensis

Motu proprio fuit provisum Bernardo xii^cim Apostolorum presbytero cardinali [668] de archidiaconatu Barkschirie in ecclesia Saresbiriensi, vacante per obitum Alexandri de Walby extra Romanam curiam defuncti, per Urbanum quinto kalendas Decembris anno septimo,[669] taxa vel fructus.[670]

### Dunelmensis

Ex causa permutationis fuit provisum Willelmo de Bronneley de thesauraria et Johanni Calton' de canonicatu ecclesie Dunelmensis per Urbanum (fol. 132ᵛ)[671] pridie kalendas Decembris vel iiii° nonas Decembris anno septimo,[672] taxa vel fructus.

### Eboracensis, Saresbiriensis

De parochiali ecclesia de Edyngton' (Edington) Saresbiriensis diocesis, de qua, vacante per obitum Nicholai Buke in Romana curia defuncti, fuit provisum Henrico Had' de Houtton', presbytero Eboracensis diocesis, et dimittet cantoriam perpetuam in ecclesia parochiali de Veldweyk (Welwick?), per Urbanum iii° kalendas Decembris anno vii°,[673] taxa vel fructus.

### Cantuariensis

Item Hugoni Hattehelle clerico de parochiali ecclesia de Wygeresham (Wittersham) Cantuariensis diocesis, vacante quia Walterus de Bakethon' parochialem ecclesiam de Hardenham (Haddenham) Eliensis diocesis est pacifice assequtus, per Urbanum quinto ydus Decembris anno vii°,[674] taxa vel fructus.

### Lincolniensis

Item collatio et provisio facte auctoritate ordinaria Laurentio de Ybstek, presbytero Lincolniensis diocesis, de parochiali ecclesia de Harwell' (Barwell) dicte diocesis, etiam si fuerit reservata, fuerunt confirmate vel provisum de novo per Urbanum xi° kalendas Februarii anno vii°.[675] Solvit in partem taxe, que est xxiii li. vi s. viii d., xiii li. vi s. viii d., restat quod debet x li.

### Wellensis

Concessum est Willelmo de Wolsham ut parochialem ecclesiam quam obtinet de Bonebury et quam dimittere

---

[663] *quam*, MS.
[664] *occupatam*, MS.
[665] 12 October 1368.
[666] 8 November 1368.
[667] 9 November 1368.
[668] Bernard de Bosqueto, archbishop of Naples, priest of Ss. XII Apostoli.
[669] 27 November 1368.
[670] In the margin: *Cardinalis.*
[671] The heading *Anno septimo* is repeated at the top of the page.
[672] 30 November or 2 December 1368.
[673] 29 November 1368.
[674] 9 December 1368.
[675] 22 January 1369.

tenebatur dum canonicatum, prebendam et dignitatem et cetera ecclesie Wellensis fuerit pacifice assequtus post assequtionem huiusmodi licite valeat **retinere, dum tamen** que expectat et obtinet iiii<sup>c</sup> fl. non excedant, per Urbanum xi° kalendas Februarii anno septimo,[675] taxa vel fructus.

### Licheffeldensis

De decanatu et prebenda de Rayton' (Ryton) in ecclesia Licheffeldensi, vacaturis dum Nicholaus de Caddesdon' canonicatum et prebendam ecclesie Eboracensis fuerit pacifice assequtus, fuit provisum Willelmo de Herseleye per Urbanum x° kalendas Februarii anno septimo,[676] taxa vel fructus.

Summa pagine x li.

### (fol. 133)[671] Norwicensis

Acceptatio et provisio facte vigore litterarum apostolicarum Roberto de Norsham, presbytero Norwicensis diocesis, de ecclesia de Turston' (Thurston) taxata xx li., vacante per obitum Roberti de Torpp', **ultimi rectoris** eiusdem, licet in impetratione dicte gratie mentionem non fecisset de quadam gratia sibi facta de parochiali ecclesia de Stretham Eliensis diocesis certo modo vacatura, fuerunt confirmate vel provisum de novo per Urbanum x° kalendas Februarii anno vii°,[676] pro resta x li.

### Dunelmensis

De canonicatu et prebenda ecclesie collegiate Auclade (Auckland) Dunelmensis diocesis, vacantibus per resignationem Roberti de Stratton', auditoris palatii apostolici, fuit provisum Petro de Burthon', clerico Licheffeldensis diocesis, per Urbanum x° kalendas Februarii anno septimo,[676] taxa vel fructus.

### Licheffeldensis et Wellensis

Dum Guillelmus Gotham prebendam, dignitatem vel personatum [677] vel officium curatum ecclesie Licheffeldensis [678] vacantem vel vacaturum in eadem fuerit pacifice assequtus, dimittet parochialem ecclesiam [679] in diocesi Wellensi, per Urbanum vi° kalendas Februarii anno vii°, taxa vel fructus.

### Saresbiriensis et Norwicensis

Dum Thomas Lexham dignitatem, personatum vel officium ecclesie Saresbiriensis vacantem vel vacaturum fuerit pacifice assequtus, dimittet ecclesiam Beate Marie de Feltowell' (Feltwell, St. Mary) Norwicensis diocesis, per Urbanum vi° kalendas Februarii anno vii°,[680] taxa vel fructus.

### Herffordensis et Eboracensis

Dum Guillelmus Flayrebourth' dignitatem et cetera ecclesie Herffordensis fuerit pacifice assequtus, dimittet parochialem ecclesiam de Gerfford' (Garford) Eboracensis diocesis, vi° kalendas Februarii anno vii°,[680] taxa vel fructus.

### Cicestrensis et Norwicensis

Dum Thomas Larynggeford' dignitatem ecclesie Cicestrensis fuerit pacifice assequtus, dimittet parochialem ecclesiam de Saham Monachorum (Monk Soham) Norwicensis diocesis eisdem die et anno, **taxa vel fructus.**

Summa pagine x li.

### (fol. 133<sup>v</sup>)[671] Lincolniensis

Dum Thomas March' dignitatem in ecclesia Lincolniensi fuerit pacifice assequtus, dimittet parochialem ecclesiam de Snayllewell' (Snailwell), vi° kalendas Februarii anno vii°,[680] taxa vel fructus.

### Norwicensis

Dum Robertus Sustede Norwicensis diocesis beneficium curatum ad collationem episcopi Eliensis fuerit pacifice assequtus, dimittet parochialem ecclesiam de Burgo (Burgh) Norwicensis diocesis, vi° kalendas Februarii anno vii°,[680] taxa vel fructus.

### Licheffeldensis et Londoniensis

De decanatu curato et electivo ecclesie Licheffeldensis,[678] vacante per obitum Guillelmi de Maniton' extra Romanam curiam defuncti, fuit provisum Anthonio de Peos, et dimittet parochialem ecclesiam de Goldesburg' (Goldsborough) et gratiam sibi factam de archidiaconatu Excessey in ecclesia Londoniensi, per Urbanum iii° nonas Februarii anno septimo,[681] taxa vel fructus.

### Londoniensis

De parochiali ecclesia Beate Marie de Wolnoth (St. Mary Woolnoth) Londoniensis diocesis, vacante per mortem Roberti Patrich' in Romana curia defuncti, fuit provisum Ricardo de Tornecombe, clerico Wynthoniensis diocesis, per Urbanum viii° kalendas Martii anno vii°,[682] taxa vel fructus.

### Wygorniensis

De parochiali ecclesia de Todyngthon' (Toddington) Wygorniensis diocesis, vacante per obitum ⟨Willelmi⟩ Traci extra Romanam curiam defuncti, fuit provisum Willelmo Lenth, licet per alium detineatur occupata, et dimittet vicariam perpetuam parochialis ecclesie Omnium Sanctorum Bristoll' dicte diocesis, per Urbanum v° nonas Martii anno vii°,[683] taxa vel fructus.

[676] 23 January 1369.
[677] Followed by *in* deleted by a line.
[678] Followed by *diocesis* undeleted.
[679] Followed by *de* deleted by a line.
[680] 27 January 1369.

[681] 3 February 1369.
[682] 22 February 1369.
[683] 3 March 1369.

### Eboracensis

Electio concorditer facta de fratre Ricardo de Kerbet, canonico prioratus de Kertemell' (Cartmel) ordinis Sancti Augustini Eboracensis diocesis, taxatum ad novam taxam xvii m., valentes xi li. vi s. viii d., ad dictum prioratum, vacantem per liberam resignationem factam de eo et confirmatio facta auctoritate ordinaria subsequta, fuerunt confirmate vel provisum de novo per Urbanum nonas Martii anno vii°.[684] Solvit vi li., restat quod debet v li. vi s. viii d.

Summa pagine v li. vi s. viii d.

### (fol. 134)[671] Barchinensis

Item collatio et provisio facte auctoritate ordinaria David Santon, clerico Barchimensis (Brechin) diocesis de perpetua vicaria parochialis ecclesie de Manross (Montrose) dicte diocesis, etiam si vacet per illicitam detentionem predecessorum suorum, fuerunt confirmate vel provisum de novo per Urbanum nonas Martii anno vii°,[684] taxa vel fructus.

### Bangorensis

De decanatu et prebenda ecclesie Bangoriensis, vacantibus [685] per obitum Edmundi Sygham in Romana curia defuncti, fuit provisum Rogero de Ossewaldestre, presbytero Assawensis diocesis, et dimittet vicarium perpetuam ecclesie de Coswaldestre (Oswestry), per Urbanum vi° ydus Aprilis anno vii°,[686] taxa vel fructus.

### Lincolniensis

Motu proprio fuit provisum Bernardo cardinali Neapolitanensi [687] de canonicatu ecclesie Lincolniensis et de prebenda de Militan' (Milton Ecclesia) in eadem, taxata xl li., vacantibus per mortem Alexandri de Dalby extra Romanam curiam defuncti, per Urbanum pridie ydus Maii anno vii°,[688] taxa vel fructus.[689]

### Menewensis

De prebenda de Karon (Tregaron) in ecclesia collegiata de Landewybremy (Llanddewi Brefi) Menewensis diocesis, vacante quia Johannes de Blebury prebendam de Allerum (Iwerne?) in ecclesia monialium de Castebury (Shaftesbury) est pacifice assequtus, fuit provisum Edmundo de le, licet de illa sic vacante alias mandatum fuerit provideri Johanni de Saxton', cui de ea non est provisum nec sibi faciet provideri, per Urbanum viii kalendas Maii anno septimo,[690] taxa vel fructus.

[684] 7 March 1369.
[685] vacante, MS. Followed by ex eo quod, of which the last two words are deleted by a line.
[686] 8 April 1369.
[687] Bernard de Bosqueto, archbishop of Naples, priest of Ss. XII Apostoli.
[688] 14 May 1369.
[689] In the margin: Cardinalis.
[690] 24 April 1369.

### Dunelmensis

Mandatur Domino [690a] Petro Flandrini, auditori palatii apostolici, quod si, sola veritate facta inspecta, reperiat Thomam Clerniaus clericum pretextu cuiusdam gratie sibi per dominum nostrum papam facte de beneficio ecclesiastico ad collationem episcopi, prioris et capituli ecclesie Dunelmensis facte in parochialem ecclesiam de Wermyuth' (Bishop Wearmouth) Dunelmensis diocesis absque litteris apostolicis et exequtoriis intrusum fore, illam David de Wllorch, cui episcopus Dunelmensis de eadem auctoritate ordinaria providit, adiudicet et super ea et ipsius possessione perpetuum silentium imponat, per Urbanum viii° kalendas Maii anno septimo,[690] taxa vel fructus.

### (fol. 134ᵛ)[671] Eboracensis et Lincolniensis

De canonicatu et prebenda de Northynwebaud' (North Newbald) in ecclesia Eboracensi, vacantibus per obitum Roberti de Midelond' extra Romanam curiam defuncti, fuit provisum Roberto Witfford', presbytero utriusque iuris doctori, et dimittet canonicatum et prebendam ecclesie Lincolniensi, per Urbanum viii kalendas Maii anno septimo,[690] taxa vel fructus.

### Lincolniensis

De canonicatu et prebenda Lincolniensibus, vacaturis dum Robertus de Witfford' prebendam de Morturwekald (North Newbald) in ecclesia Eboracensis fuerit pacifice assequtus, fuit provisum Johanni Chyne Exoniensis diocesis, et dimittet litem quam habet super prebenda de Corwesill' (Kerswell) in ecclesia collegiata de Criditon' (Crediton), per Urbanum vii° kalendas Martii anno septimo,[691] taxa vel fructus.

### Cantuariensis

Concessum est Thome de Paxton', auditori palatii apostolici, quod gratia sibi facta de prepositura ecclesie collegiate de Wengham (Wingham) Cantuariensis diocesis non possit de subreptione notarii nec obstet sibi quia in impetratione illius nullam fecit mentionem quod Thomas Ykham super ea contra Willelmum Redd, tunc illius possessorem, in Romana curia litigavit, per Urbanum vii° kalendas Maii anno vii°,[692] taxa vel fructus.

### Eboracensis

Mandatur provideri Johanni de Belthon', presbytero Eboracensis diocesis, de canonicatu et prebenda vacantibus vel vacaturis in ecclesia collegiata de Southwell' per Urbanum quinto nonas Maii anno septimo,[693] taxa vel fructus.

### Lincolniensis et Eboracensis

De parochiali ecclesia de Hnygfford abbatis (Hem-

[690a] provideri, MS.
[691] 23 February 1369.
[692] 25 April 1369.
[693] 3 May 1369.

ingford Abbots) Lincolniensis diocesis, vacante vel vacatura dum Michael de Ravendale parochialem ecclesiam de Hornse (Hornsea) Eboracensis diocesis fuerit pacifice assequtus, fuit provisum Johanni de Karlil, clerico Karleolensis diocesis, per Urbanum iiii⁰ kalendas Junii anno vii⁰,[694] taxa vel fructus.

### Wygorniensis

De prioratu de Durhustr' (Deerhurst) Wygorniensis diocesis a monasterio Sancti [695] Dyonisii (St. Denis) in Francia dependente Parisiensis diocesis, vacante per (fol. 135)[671] obitum fratris Johannis de Medunta extra Romanam curiam defuncti, fuit provisum Johanni Walkelyn, monacho monasterii Sanctorum Sergii et Bachi (Saint-Serge) Andegavensis (Angers) diocesis, per Urbanum xv⁰ kalendas Julii anno septimo,[696] taxa vel fructus.

### Wygorniensis

De novo fuit provisum Willelmo Horstleye, clerico Wygorniensis diocesis, de parochiali ecclesia Sancti Johannis Glamcestr' dicte diocesis, quam fuit nunquam canonice assequtus obstante defectu natalium quem patitur de coniugato genitus et soluta, et fuit habilitatus per Urbanum, taxa vel fructus.

### Lincolniensis

Item collatio et provisio facte vigore litterarum apostolicarum in forma communi Roberto de Brigham, presbytero Eboracensis diocesis, de vicaria perpetua parochialis ecclesie de Aston' Rowhand (Aston Rowant) Lincolniensis diocesis fuerunt confirmate vel provisum de novo per Urbanum xvi⁰ kalendas Julii anno septimo,[697] taxa vel fructus.

### Eboracensis

Provisio facta per dominum nostrum papam Johanni de Linde, presbytero, de parochiali ecclesia Omnium Sanctorum super pavimentum Eboracensi (All Saints in the Pavement, York), tunc vacante, ut credebatur, per mortem Symonis Warde in Romana curia defuncti, super qua mota est lis inter eum et Robertum Hugonis de Tholeston' de Thorparch' in ea intrusum, ⟨et⟩ ipse Johannes pro se contra dictum Robertum sententiam super possessorio et petitorio obtinuit que in rem transivit iudicatam, ac deinde idem Robertus per dominum nostrum papam ad appellandum admissus ad excludendum gratiam factam dicto Johanni quia de dicta parochiali ecclesia, vacante prout supra, per felicis recordationis Dominum Innocentium provisum fuerat cuidam David Morte, de quo dictus Johannes nullam in sua gratia fecerat mentionem, qui, ut dicitur, decessit

in partibus suis, fuit confirmata vel provisum de novo per Urbanum xv⁰ kalendas Julii anno septimo,[696] taxa vel fructus.

### Saresbiriensis

De canonicatu ecclesie Saresbiriensis et prebenda de Hussebur burbache (Hurstbourne and Burbage) in dicta ecclesia, vacantibus per obitum Johannis de Abyndon', infra duas dietas a Romana curia non remotas defuncti, fuit provisum Johanni Mere, clerico Saresbiriensis diocesis, per Urbanum vii⁰ kalendas Julii anno septimo,[698] taxa vel fructus.

### (fol. 135ᵛ)[671] Menwensis

Mandatur provideri Thome Forester, presbytero [699] Londoniensis diocesis de prebenda vacante vel vacatura in ecclesia Menewensi per Urbanum viii⁰ ydus Julii anno vii⁰,[700] taxa vel fructus.

Item Roberto de Snardeby, presbytero Eboracensis ⟨diocesis⟩, de parochiali ecclesia de Eselevent' (East Lavant) super qua litigat per Urbanum viii⁰ ydus Julii anno vii⁰,[700] taxa vel fructus.

### Cantuariensis

Item Ricardo de Bannebury, presbytero Londoniensis diocesis, de beneficio ecclesiatico, vacante vel vacaturo, spectante ad collationem archiepiscopi Cantuariensis, per Urbanum viii⁰ ydus Julii anno vii⁰,[700] taxa vel fructus.

### Eboracensis

Item Ade de Alenyn, presbytero Eboracensis diocesis, de prebenda vacante vel vacatura in ecclesia collegiata Ripponensi Eboracensis diocesis per Urbanum viii⁰ ydus Julii anno septimo,[700] taxa vel fructus.

### Lincolniensis

Collatio et provisio facte auctoritate ordinaria ex causa permutationis de parochiali ecclesia de Langeporte (Lamport) Lincolniensis diocesis Johanni Enoc, licet quidam olim ipsius ecclesie rector eam per plures annos tenuisset in presbyterum non promotus, fuerunt confirmate vel provisum de novo, etiam si alio quovis modo vacet vel fuerit reservata, per Urbanum vi⁰ ydus Julii anno vii⁰,[701] taxa vel fructus.

### Saresbiriensis

Collatio, acceptatio et provisio facte vigore litterarum apostolicarum Johanni de Soreby, presbytero Eboracensis diocesis, de canonicatu et prebenda ecclesie Saresbiriensis vacantibus per obitum Johannis de Kymefford' extra Romanam curiam defuncti, etiam si fuerint reservata, fuerunt confirmate vel provisum de

---

[694] 29 May 1369.
[695] *Sancti* repeated MS.
[696] 17 June 1369.
[697] 16 June 1369.

[698] 25 June 1369.
[699] Followed by *C* deleted by a dot.
[700] 8 July 1369.
[701] 10 July 1369.

novo, si sibi ex ordine debeatur, per Urbanum quinto idus Julii anno vii°,[702] taxa vel fructus.

## Eboracensis

Acceptatio et provisio facte vigore litterarum apostolicarum Waltero de Slarlawe, archidiacono Estridingie in ecclesia Eboracensi, de prebenda de Fenton' in eadem, vacante per obitum quondam Roberti de Walkyngton' extra Romanam curiam defuncti, etiam si sit reservata, fuerunt confirmate vel provisum de novo per Urbanum xii° kalendas Augusti vel pridie nonas Augusti anno septimo,[703] taxa vel fructus.

## (fol. 136)[671] Eboracensis

Mandatur provideri Willelmo de Ragonhill' de beneficio ecclesiastico vacante vel vacaturo spectante ad collationem archiepiscopi Eboracensis per Urbanum v° kalendas Augusti anno septimo,[704] taxa vel fructus.

## Herffordensis

De canonicatu et prebenda ecclesie Herffordensis, vacantibus per obitum Philipi Ace in Romana curia defuncti, et qui dum viveret super ipsis in palatio apostolico litigabat, et pro se diffinitivam [705] ferri sententiam obtinuit, licet per quemdam Johannem Smith' detineantur occupati, fuit provisum Thome de Arundest, clerico Cicestrensis diocesis, et fuit subrogatus in omni iure et ad omne ius quod dicto Philipo in illis competebat, per Urbanum iiii° nonas Augusti anno septimo,[706] taxa vel fructus.

## Lincolniensis et Licheffeldensis

Concessum est Laurentio de Ybestok ut parochialem ecclesiam de Bokewell' (Barwell) Lincolniensis diocesis, quam dum prebendam ecclesie Licheffeldensis foret pacifice assequtus dimittere tenebatur, post assequtionem huiusmodi licite valeat retinere per Urbanum xix° kalendas Septembris anno vii°,[707] taxa vel fructus.

De prepositura ecclesie Sancti Thome de Glasenee (Glasnay), vacante per obitum Ricardi de Grumineshawe extra Romanam curiam defuncti, fuit provisum Roberto de Hoo clerico per Urbanum xvi° kalendas Septembris anno septimo,[708] taxa vel fructus.

Motu proprio fuit provisum Symoni cardinali Cantuariensi [709] de omnibus et singulis beneficiis, etiam si tria vel quatuor eorum fuerint curata seu non curata incompassibilia, non in ecclesiis cathedralibus vel extra

dignitates, canonicatus seu prebendas,[710] que Gervasius de Wilfford', extra Romanam curiam defunctus, dum vixit, dispensative tenebat, tamquam de specialiter reservatis, per Urbanum x° kalendas Septembris anno septimo,[711] taxa vel fructus.[712]

## Cantuariensis

De parochiali ecclesia de Yvvcyrche (Ivychurch) Cantuariensis diocesis, vacante per obitum Johannis (fol. 136v)[671] Messelham in Romana curia defuncti, fuit provisum Thome Forestro, presbytero Londoniensis diocesis, per Urbanum [713] anno septimo, taxa vel fructus.

## Norwicensis

Item Thome de Blakelake, clerico Exoniensis diocesis, de ecclesia Sancti Nicholai de Feltwell' Norwicensis diocesis, vacante per obitum Thome London' presbyteri in Romana curia defuncti, per Urbanum vii° ydus Septembris anno vii°,[714] taxa vel fructus.

## Lincolniensis

Motu proprio fuit provisum Simoni titulo Sancti Sixti presbytero cardinali [715] de decanatu, canonicatu et prebenda ecclesie Lincolniensis vacantibus per obitum Johannis de Strekeley extra Romanam curiam defuncti per Urbanum xvii° kalendas Octobris anno vii°,[716] taxa vel fructus.[717]

## Cicestrensis

Ex causa permutationis fuit provisum Johanni de Landa de prioratu conventuali de Boxgrava (Boxgrove) in Anglia Cicestrensis diocesis per Urbanum nonas Septembris anno septimo,[718] taxa vel fructus.

## Eboracensis et Wellensis

Motu proprio fuit provisum Francisco cardinali Sancti Petri [719] de canonicatu et prebenda [720] de Wythodo (Wistow) in ecclesia Eboracensi et de canonicatu et prebenda ac archidiaconatu Wellensibus vacantibus per obitum cardinalis Carcassonensis [721] per Urbanum, taxa vel fructus.[717]

---

[702] 11 July 1369.
[703] 21 July or 4 August 1369.
[704] 28 July 1369.
[705] *pro se* repeated, MS.
[706] 2 August 1369.
[707] 14 August 1369.
[708] 17 August 1369.
[709] Simon Langham, priest of S. Sisto.

[710] *prebende*, MS.
[711] 23 August 1369.
[712] In the margin: *Cardinalis.*
[713] A blank space is left in MS.
[714] 7 September 1369.
[715] Simon Langham, previously archbishop of Canterbury.
[716] 15 September 1369.
[717] In the margin: *Cardinalis.*
[718] 5 September 1369.
[719] Franciscus de Thebaldeschis, priest of S. Sabina. Apparently a mistake for Simon Langham: below, p. 403; Le Neve, *Fasti* (Northern Province), p. 93; *ibid.* (Bath and Wells), p. 13.
[720] Followed by *ecclesie Eboracensis* deleted by a line.
[721] Stephen Aubert, priest of S. Lorenzo in Lucina since 22 September 1368; died 29 September 1369: Eubel, i, 19.

### Lincolniensis

Simili modo fuit provisum Philipo cardinali Ihero-solimitano [722] de archidiaconatu Leycestr' in ecclesia Lincolniensi per Urbanum nonas Octobris anno vii°,[723] taxa vel fructus.[717]

### Saresbiriensis

De canonicatu et prebenda ecclesie Saresbiriensis, vacantibus per obitum Johannis de Stretele extra Romanam curiam defuncti, fuit provisum Henrico de Torp', clerico Lincolniensis diocesis, per Urbanum v° ydus Octobris anno vii°,[724] taxa vel fructus.

Completum est de anno septimo.

(fol. 137) Sequitur de anno octavo

### Eboracensis

De canonicatu et prebenda ecclesie Eboracensis vacantibus per obitum domini cardinalis Sabinensis [725] in curia defuncti fuit provisum Roberto de Stratton', capellano commensali domini pape canonico prebendato in ecclesiis Lincolniensi et Wellensi ac dignitatem in ecclesia Lincolniensi expectanti, per Urbanum xviii° kalendas Decembris anno octavo,[726] taxa vel fructus.

### Dunelmensis

De archidiaconatu Dunelmensi, quem quondam Willelmus de Vestleye dum viveret obtinebat extra Romanam curiam defunctus, ac de canonicatu et prebenda de Coryngham (Corringham) in ecclesia Lincolniensi fuit provisum Alexandro de Nevill', vacantibus per obitum bone memorie domini cardinalis Lemovicensis,[727] per Urbanum xvi° kalendas Decembris anno octavo,[728] taxa vel fructus.

### Lincolniensis

De prioratu seu monasterio Sancte Frideswide ordinis Sancti Augustini Lincolniensis diocesis, vacante per obitum quondam Nicholai de Huggerford', fuit provisum Johanni de Dodefford', canonico ecclesie Karleolensis dicti ordinis, per Urbanum xii° kalendas Decembris anno viii°,[729] taxa vel fructus.

### Licheffeldensis

De canonicatu et prebenda de Lugdon' (Longdon) in ecclesia Licheffeldensi, vacantibus [730] per obitum Walteri Dalby, fuit provisum Laurentio de Ybestolor',

clerico Lincolniensis diocesis, per Urbanum xi kalendas Decembris anno viii°,[731] taxa vel fructus.

Item Willelmo de Hunnsterton' clerico de canonicatu et prebenda in ecclesia Herffordensi, vacantibus per mortem Willelmi Bell', per Urbanum xi° kalendas Decembris anno viii°,[731] taxa vel fructus.

### Eliensis

Acceptatio et collatio auctoritate litterarum apostolicarum facte per Michaelem de (fol. 137ᵛ)[732] Causton'. sacre theologie professorem, de parochiali ecclesia de Levryngton' (Leverington) Eliensis diocesis, vacante per mortem Ricardi de Skyteby, fuerunt confirmate seu provisum de novo per Urbanum x° kalendas Decembris anno octavo,[733] taxa vel fructus.

### Exoniensis, Dunelmensis et Lincolniensis

De archidiaconatu Cornubie in ecclesia Exoniensi, vacante vel dum vacabit per assequtionem per Alexandrum de Nevill' factam vel faciendam de archidiaconatu Dunelmensi necnon canonicatus et prebende Coringham (Corringham) in ecclesia Lincolniensi fuit provisum Willelmo de Norwico, bacallario in legibus, per Urbanum x° kalendas Decembris anno octavo,[733] taxa vel fructus.

### Eboracensis et Dunelmensis

Item Ricardo Driffeldi, clerico Eboracensis diocesis, de canonicatu et prebenda ecclesie collegiate Cutberti de Derlyngthon, (Darlington) Dunelmensis diocesis, dum vacabunt per assequtionem per dictum Alexandrum factam ut supra, per Urbanum x° kalendas Decembris anno viii°,[733] taxa vel fructus.

Item Ricardo Strode, clerico Cicestrensis diocesis, de parochiali ecclesia de Stanhope, modo premisso vacatura per dimissionem dicti Willelmi, per Urbanum x° kalendas Decembris anno octavo,[733] taxa vel fructus.

### Eliensis

Motu proprio fuit provisum Johanni cardinali Belvacensi [734] de archidiaconatu Eliensi, vacante per obitum A. cardinalis Cluniacensis,[735] per Urbanum ix° kalendas Decembris anno viii°,[736] taxa vel fructus.[737]

### Eboracensis

De canonicatu et prebenda de Bolon (Bole) in ecclesia Eboracensi, vacantibus per obitum domini cardinalis Cluniacensis,[735] fuit provisum Alexandro de Nevill' per

---

[722] Philip de Cabassole, bishop of Sabina.
[723] 7 October 1369.
[724] 11 October 1369.
[725] William d'Aigrefeuille.
[726] 14 November 1369.
[727] Nicholas de Bessia, bishop elect of Limoges, deacon of S. Maria in Via Lata.
[728] 16 November 1369.
[729] 20 November 1369.
[730] vacante, MS.

[731] 21 November 1369.
[732] The heading *anno octavo* is repeated at the top of the page.
[733] 22 November 1369.
[734] John de Dormans, bishop of Beauvais, priest of Ss. Quattro Coronati.
[735] Androin de la Roche, abbot of Cluny, priest of S. Marcello.
[736] 23 November 1369.
[737] In the margin: *Cardinalis.*

Urbanum pridie nonas Decembris anno octavo,[738] taxa vel fructus.

### Eboracensis

Motu proprio fuit provisum Anglico episcopo Albanensi de prebenda Eboracensis ecclesie vacante per obitum quondam Henrici de Ingilby, quondam dicte ecclesie canonici, per Urbanum xviii° kalendas Januarii anno octavo,[739] taxa vel fructus.[737]

### (fol. 138)[732] Bangoriensis

De parochiali ecclesia de Towyn Bangoriensis diocesis, vacante ex eo quod Tirderus Apacha ipsam ecclesiam cum una alia cum archidiaconatu de Mariomyth' (Merioneth) in ecclesia Bangoriensi, qui dignitas curata existit, per annum et amplius simul pacifice tenuit, fuit provisum Jacobo de Frestorp', clerico Lincolniensis diocesis, per Urbanum xix° kalendas Januarii anno octavo,[740] taxa vel fructus.

### Dunelmensis

Subrogatus fuit Johannes de Zwethop', clericus Dunelmensis diocesis, in omni iure et ad omne ius quod competebat Johanni de Lowyk in curia defuncto [741] in et super vicaria parochialis ecclesie de Northam (Norham) dicte diocesis, super qua idem Johannes de Lowyk contra quemdam Johannem Mores in palatio apostolico litigavit, per Urbanum xiii° kalendas Januarii anno octavo,[742] taxa vel fructus.

### Lincolniensis

Collatio et provisio facte Johanni de Dodefford de prioratu canonicali Sancte Frideswide ordinis Sancti Augustini Lincolniensis diocesis, vacante per mortem Nicholai ultimi prioris eiusdem, fuerunt confirmate vel provisum de novo per Urbanum xiiii° kalendas Februarii anno octavo,[743] taxa vel fructus.

### Lincolniensis

De canonicatu et prebenda de Leyton' Bromeswoldi (Leighton Bromswold) ecclesie Lincolniensis, vacantibus per obitum Johannis Neswynham, fuit provisum Thome de Southam, licenciato in legibus, per Urbanum xii° kalendas Februarii anno viii°,[744] taxa vel fructus.

[738] 4 December 1369.
[739] 15 December 1369.
[740] 14 December 1369.
[741] *defuncti*, MS.
[742] 20 December 1369
[743] 19 January 1370.
[744] 21 January 1370.

### Licheffeldensis

Mandatur provideri Guillelmo de Passemham, clerico Licheffeldensis diocesis, de beneficio ecclesiastico cum cura vel sine cura, vacante vel vacatura, spectante ad collationem abbatis et conventus de Romehoie (Burton?) ordinis Sancti Benedicti dicte diocesis, si cum cura xl si sine cura xxx m. sterlingorum valorem annuum non excedente, per Urbanum kalendas Februarii anno viii°,[745] taxa vel fructus.

### Eboracensis

De vicaria perpetua parochialis ecclesie de Hesill' (Hessle) a prioratu de Glyseburn' (Guisborough) dependente Eboracensis diocesis, cum vacabit per assequtionem prioratus Sancti Frideswide ordinis Sancti Augustini, fuit provisum fratri Waltero Cilteham, monacho professo Worspryng' (Woodspring) dicti ordinis, per Urbanum ydus Februarii anno octavo,[746] taxa vel fructus.

### (fol. 138ᵛ)[732] Wellensis

De prepositura ecclesie Wellensis, vacante per obitum Johannis de Nonynham extra Romanam curiam defuncti, fuit provisum Nicholao de Hecho per Urbanum viii° kalendas Maii anno viii°,[747] taxa vel fructus.

Completum est de anno octavo.

Summa universalis arrayrargiorum sive restarum de annatis beneficiorum collatorum per Dominum Urbanum a iii° kalendas Maii pontificatus sui anno primo [748] usque ad octavo kalendas Maii pontificatus eiusdem anno octavo,[747] quia de ulteriori tempore non recepi, in quibus exprimatur et ponitur est ccxl li. xviii s. Approbatum.

Item multa beneficia in quibus taxa non ponitur nec exprimatur prout in libro patet.

(fol. 139) Summa universalis restarum sive arrayrargiorum omnium beneficiorum collatorum per Dominos Clementem, Innocentium et Urbanum tempore supradicto in quibus taxa exprimatur et ponitur est iiᵐ viᶜ xliii li. iiii s. x d. Approbatum.

Summa universalis arrayrargiorum sive restarum tam denariorum Beati Petri, annui census, incluso tamen pro istis duabus restis anno LXX° dumtaxat, quam de annatis quorumcumque beneficiorum ibidem collatorum usque ad viii° kalendas Maii pontificatus Domini Urbani pape quinti anno octavo [747] est iiiᵐ cxxxvii li. viii d. sterlingorum. Approbatum.

[745] 1 February 1370.
[746] 13 February 1370.
[747] 24 April 1370.
[748] 29 April 1363.

Vatican Archives, Collectorie 13 (account of John de Caroloco, locumtenens of John de Cabrespino for 1371 and of Arnald for the period from 1372 to 1374), Collectorie 12, fols. 143-267 (account for the period from 1374 to 1378).

## First Account of Arnald Garnerii
## 1371-1374

(fol. 1, i)[2] Computa collectoris Anglie reddita camere a die viii Februarii anni a nativitate domini millesimi CCCLXX secundi usque ad diem xxvii Julii anni eiusdem LXX quarti. Arnaldi Garnerii.

(fol. 1ᵛ) Hic sequitur compotus ab isto folio primo usque ad folium cxxvii Arnaldi Garnerii, licentiati in legibus, canonici Cathalaunensis (Châlons-sur-Marne), sanctissimi in Christo patris et domini domini nostri Gregorii pape undecimi ac sedis apostolici in regno Anglie viiiᵒ idus Octobris pontificatus sui anno primo,[3] currente anno a nativitate domini Mᵒ CCCLXX primo, nuntii et collectoris deputati, de omnibus et singulis per eum nomine dicte sedis receptis, liberatis, assignatis et exspensis de quibuscumque obventionibus et iuribus ad ecclesiam Romanam in dictis partibus qualitercumque exspectantibus a vicesima secunda die Februarii anno a nativitate domini millesimo CCCᵒ LXX secundo, qua die recepit Londonie libros, quarum copia sequitur vera,[4] restarum iurium camere apostolice a domino priore Lewensi, ut locumtenente Domini Johannis de Cabrespino predecessoris sui, usque ad diem xxvii Julii anno domini millesimo CCCLX quarto, qua die xxvii versus curiam Romanam redeundo a Londonie civitate recessit pro dicto compoto reddendo camere apostolice supradicte, salvo errore calculi si reperiatur, quod non credit, et salvo quod de celario hospitii necessarii pro se vel locumtenente suo computat summam consuetam solvisse usque ad terminum seu festum Beati Michaelis tunc proxime futurum, camere apostolice per dictum Arnaldum traditus die ix Novembris anno domini millesimo CCCLXX quarto cum protestationibus quibus supra. Sic est Arnaldi Garnerii manu propria.[5]

(fol. 2, ii) Sequitur liber restarum camere apostolice debitarum et Domino Arnaldo Garnerii, licentiato in legibus collectori Anglie, per dominum priorem Lewensem, ordinis Cluniacensis Cicestrensis diocesis locumtenentem Domini Johannis de Cabrespino nuper collectoris Anglie, redditarum die vicesima secunda Februarii anno a nativitate domini millesimo CCC septuagesimo secundo.

Et dictarum restarum recepte vel solutiones reperientur scripte in toto isto libro ad pedem cuiuslibet debiti manu mea propria [6] et excusationes non solventium idem et assignationes et exspense nomine camere facte idem.

Primo restabant de denariis Beati Petri de anno LXXIᵐᵒ et precedentibus annis que secuntur.

### Cantuariensis

Archidiaconus Cantuariensis debet pro annis LXXᵐᵒ et LXXIᵐᵒ, pro quolibet viii li., et sic pro dictis duobus annis xvi li. Solvit dictas sexdecim li. in duabus vicibus, ut clarius in libro recepte habetur, et sic de aliis solutionibus michi factis.[7]

### Essexia

Item archidiaconus Essexie debet pro annis LXXᵐᵒ et LXXIᵐᵒ, pro quolibet v li. x s., et sic pro dictis duobus annis xi li. Solvit.

### Surreia

Item archidiaconus Surreie debet pro annis LXIX, LXXᵐᵒ et LXXIᵐᵒ, pro quolibet v li. xiii s. iiiiᵒʳ d., et sic pro dictis tribus annis xvii li. Solvit.

### Exoniensis

Item episcopus Exoniensis debet pro annis LXXᵐᵒ et LXXIᵐᵒ, pro quolibet ix li. v s., et sic pro dictis duobus annis xviii li. x s. Solvit.

### Eliensis

Item archidiaconus Eliensis debet pro annis LXVIII, IX, LXX et LXXIᵐᵒ, pro quolibet v li., et sic pro dictis quatuor annis xx li. Solvit.
Recepta pagine iiiiˣˣ ii li. x s.

### (fol. 2ᵛ) Norwicensis

Item episcopus Norwicensis debet pro annis LXX et LXXIᵐᵒ, pro quolibet xxi li. x s., et sic pro dictis duobus annis xliii li. Solvit.

### Lincolniensis

Item episcopus Lincolniensis debet pro anno LXXIᵐᵒ xlii li. Solvit.

---

[1] The date of the appointment of his successor. See above, p. xl.
[2] The original cover of the account. At the top six words are scribbled in a contemporary hand. I can make out only four of them: *priusquam* (two words) *vi die Decembris*. In the modern hand: *1372 ad 1375*; *912*. The last is the original number of the codex in the series of Collectorie.
[3] 8 October 1371.
[4] A stain makes the reading doubtful.
[5] This hand of the collector, in which comments are written throughout, is different from the hands in which the main entries are written.

[6] Followed by *fecit iste* deleted by a line.
[7] This and similar items are added by the hand of the collector.

### Lichfeldensis

Item episcopus Lichfeldensis debet pro annis LXX$^{mo}$ et LXXI$^{mo}$, pro quolibet x li. quinque s., et sic pro dictis duobus annis xx li. x s. Solvit.

### Herefordensis

Item episcopus Herefordensis debet pro annis LXVII, VIII,[8] IX, LXX$^{mo}$ et LXXI$^{mo}$, pro quolibet vi li., et sic pro dictis quinque annis xxx li. Solvit.

### Wygorniensis

Item episcopus Wygorniensis debet pro annis LXIX$^{no}$, LXX et LXXI$^{mo}$, pro quolibet x li. v s., et sic pro dictis tribus annis xxx li. xv s. Solvit.

### Eboracensis

Item archiepiscopus Eboracensis debet pro annis LXX et LXXI$^{mo}$, pro quolibet xi li. x s., et sic pro dictis duobus annis xxiii li. Solvit.

### Colcestrie

Item archidiaconus Colcestrie debet pro annis LXIX, LXX et LXXI$^{mo}$, pro quolibet v li. x s., et sic pro dictis tribus annis xvi li. x s. Solvit.
Recepta pagine ii$^c$ v li. xv s.

### (fol. 3, iii) Saresbiriensis

Item episcopus Saresbiriensis debet pro annis LXX et LXXI$^{mo}$, pro quolibet xvii li., et sic pro dictis duobus annis xxxiiii li. Solvit.

### Londoniensis

Item archidiaconus Middensexie Londoniensis diocesis debet pro annis LXX$^{mo}$ et LXXI$^{mo}$, pro quolibet v li. x s., et sic pro dictis duobus annis xi li. Solvit.

### Bathoniensis

Item episcopus Bathoniensis et Wellensis debet pro resta anni LXIII$^{tii}$ vi li. v s. et pro annis LXVII, VIII, IX, LXX$^{mo}$ et LXXI$^{mo}$, pro quolibet xi li. v s., et sic debet pro totali resta secunda lxii li. x s. Solvit totum.

### Wyntoniensis

Item archidiaconus Wyntoniensis debet pro anno LXXI$^{mo}$ xi li. xiii s. iiii d. Solvit.

### Roffensis

Item archidiaconus Roffensis debet pro anno LXXI$^{mo}$ v li. xii s. Solvit.
Recepta pagine vi$^{xx}$ iiii$^{or}$ li. xv s. iiii d.

(fol. 3$^v$) Arayrahgia annui census anni LXXI et precedentium

### Cantuariensis

Abbas de Faveresham debet pro annis LXX et LXXI$^{mo}$, pro quolibet xiii s. iiii d., et sic dictis duobus annis xxvi s. viii d. Solvit.

### Roffensis

Item prior de Tunebrugg' debet pro anno LXXI$^{mo}$ xiii s. iiii d. Solvit.

### Exoniensis

Item prior de Bodmyn pro anno LXXI$^{mo}$ ii s. Solvit.

### Lincolniensis

Item abbas Sancti Albani debet pro anno LXXI$^{mo}$ xiii s. iiii d. Solvit.

### Saresbiriensis

Item abbas de Malmesbury debet pro anno LXXI$^{mo}$ xiii s. iiii d. Solvit.

### Londoniensis

Item abbatissa Sancte Clare Londonie debet pro annis LXVIII, IX$^{no}$, LXX$^{mo}$ et LXXI$^{mo}$, pro quolibet vi d., et sic pro dictis quatuor annis ii s. Solvit.

### Eliensis

Item prior de Anglesey debet pro anno LXXI$^{mo}$ ii s. Solvit.

### Karleolensis

Item prior Karleolensis debet pro annis [9] LXII, III, IIII, V, VI, VII, VIII, IX, LXX et LXXI, pro quolibet xiii s. iiii d., et sic pro dictis decem annis vi li. xiii s. iiii d. Solvit.
Summa restarum et etiam recepte x li. vi s.

(fol. 4; iiii) Summa supradictorum arayrahgiorum usque hic et totum recepte iiii$^c$ xxiii li. vi s. iiii$^{or}$ d.[10] Denarii beati Petri et census.
De suprascriptis [11] denariis Petri et censu nichil dat in restis quia totum dat in recepta.

(fol. 4$^v$) Sequntur reste arrarragiorum primorum fructuum per dominum priorem Lewensem tradite ut supra folio primo

### De Cantuariensi diocesi

Primo de ecclesia de Stokebury (Stockbury) que fuit appropriata priori et conventui [12] de Ledes (Leeds) per Clementem viii idus Augusti anno xi,[13] que taxatur xxvii li. vi s. viii d., dimissa in arrarragiis pro resta vii li. vi s. viii d. Allegatur quod in dicta resta nichil

---

[8] *VII*, MS.
[9] *anno*, MS.
[10] In the margin: *vera est.*
[11] Followed by *nichil dat* deleted by a line.
[12] *conventus*, MS.
[13] 6 August 1352.

attinuit prioratui, quia erat pencio annua debita per ecclesiam dicto prioratui; tamen composuerunt ad quinque li. solvendas citra purificationem anni LXXIIII a nativitate computando, et ex post die vii Februarii anno a nativitate LXXIIII^to solvit in plenam solutionem centum solidos, v li.[14]

Capella libera de Bokinefeld' (Bockingfold), de qua per obitum Willelmi de Bradeley fuit provisum David Wygham per Innocentium iii idus Augusti anno x,[15] fuit dimissa in solidis fructibus, fructibus. Est in mandatis pluribus ad denuntiandum, sed certificat archiepiscopus quod non potest sequestrari quia in mala [16] dicione est; ideo excommunicatus et cetera.[17]

## Londoniensis

De ecclesia seu capella de Stanford (Stanford le Hope), de qua per obitum Edmundi de Grimmesby fuit provisum Johanni de Torkesseye per Innocentium viii idus Octobris anno secundo,[18] pro taxa xxvi li. xiii s. iiii d. Prohibitum per breve regium quia de patronatu regio, et Guilhermus de Wimdemaham, surgicus regius, possidet titulo regio.[19]

De ecclesia de Herlawe (Harlow) Londoniensis diocesis, de qua per assecutionem archidiaconatus Tottonie fuit provisum Magistro Ricardo Anglici per Innocentium viii idus Maii anno viii,[20] pro taxa xiii li. vi s. viii d. Non habuit effectum, ut in restis domini prioris folio tertio, et sic est ex post probatum, ideo relaxatus usque quod apareat de effectu dicte gratie vel alias per cameram fuerit ordinatum.[19]

De prebenda Sancti Pancratii in ecclesia Sancti Pauli Londonie fuit provisum ex causa premutationis Radulpho de Daventr' v nonas Martii anno predicto,[21] pro taxa xlii s. vi d.[22] Solvit viginti duos s. vi d. die xx Februarii anno LXXII, xxii s. vi.[23]

## Cicestrensis

Archidiaconatus Lewensis, non taxatus, qui fuit confirmatus Willelmo Lughtheburgh' per Clementem ii^do idus Augusti anno xi,[24] in solidis fructibus.[25] Solvit die xx Februarii anno a nativitate LXXII pro medietate veri valoris, salvo iure super procurationibus et iurisdictione, de quibus non est in Anglia, ut dicitur, solvere consuetum, quatuor li. sterlingorum, iiii^or li.[23]

Recepta pagine x li. ii s. vi d.; resta pecunie xx s.; restant fructus unius beneficii et procurationes alterius; et duo sunt beneficia inutilia; et xlvi s. viii d. sunt etiam inutiles.[26]

(fol. 5, v) Item de eodem fuit provisum Thome Bronwen' vii idus Septembris anno vi^to,[27] eo quod Willelmus predictus fuit assecutus thesaurariam dicte ecclesie, dimisso [28] in aliis solidis fructibus, fructibus. Non habuit effectum ut in restis domini prioris folio iii habetur.[29]

De archidiaconatu Cicestrensi, non taxato, permutatio facta cum decanatu ecclesie collegiate Cestrie super stratam (Chester-le-Street) Dunolmensis diocesis fuit Johanni de Skulthorp' confirmata [30] per Innocentium v^to kalendas Januarii anno vi^to,[31] fructus iiii^or li. vi s. viii d. Pro medietate veri valoris debentur quatuor li. vi s. viii d., nec reperitur quod valeat plus, et habet terminum Beati Michaelis quia pauperimus, et solvit die iiii Februarii anno a nativitate et cetera LXXIIII^to, salvo iure pluris, dictas iiii^or li. vi s. viii d.[23]

De prebenda de Ippethorn' (Upthorn) in ecclesia Cicestrensi, de qua per obitum David fuit provisum Philipo Courtenay per Innocentium x kalendas Julii anno nono,[32] pro taxa vi li. xiii s. iiii d. Non habuit effectum quia rex contulit iure suo, ut in restis folio iii.[33]

De prebenda et precentoria ecclesie Cicestrensis, taxatis liii li. vi s. viii d., de quibus per obitum cardinalis de Gordonio [34] fuit provisum cardinali Aquensi [35] per Innocentium vi^to kalendas Octobris anno nono,[36] que non fuit dimissa in primis et antiquis arraragiis quia camerarius domini pape scripserat ultima die Januarii anno LXII^do [37] quod supersederetur a petitione, dicte taxe debet de resta xxxi li. xiii s. iiii d.[38] Prohibitum per breve regium quia possessor est regius, et licet obsit in rem scripta, noluit revocare breve; quare dormit et cetera.

De decanatu ecclesie Cicestrensis ac canonicatu et prebenda sibi annexis, vacantibus per consecrationem Willemi episcopi Cicestrensis, fuit provisum Nicholao de Aston', magistro in sacra pagina, xi kalendas Decembris anno primo,[39] pro resta xxviii li. vi s. viii d. Solvit

---

[14] In the margin: *solvit.*
[15] 11 August 1362.
[16] Perhaps a mistake for *alia.*
[17] In the margin: *debet.*
[18] 8 October 1354.
[19] In the margin: *inutilis est.*
[20] 8 May 1360.
[21] 3 March 1360. The year probably should be 1363: above p. *325.*
[22] In the margin: *non est in libro alio abreveto* deleted by lines.
[23] In the margin: *solvit.*
[24] 12 August 1352.
[25] In the margin: *debet de procurationibus.*

[26] *inutilia,* MS.
[27] 7 September 1358.
[28] *dimissa,* MS.
[29] In the margin: *inutilis sit.*
[30] *confirmatus,* MS.
[31] 28 December 1358.
[32] 22 June 1361.
[33] In the margin: *inutilis.*
[34] William Farinier of Gourdon, priest of Ss. Marcellino e Pietro.
[35] Peter Itherii, bishop of Dax, priest of Ss. Quattro Coronati.
[36] 26 September 1361.
[37] Follows *LXXII* deleted by a line.
[38] In the margin: *debet* in the hand of the collector; *Cardinalis Aquensis, et agatur contra exsecutionem ut dicit possessor qui est regius* in the hand of the scribe.
[39] 21 November 1362.

in duabus vicibus, sexdecim li. xiii s. iiii⁰ʳ d., ut in libro recepte clarius habetur.[23] Item solvit xiiii die Julii anno LXXIIII^to per manus executorum domini Wygorniensis quondam undecim li. xiii s. iiii d., xi li. xiii s. iiii d.[23]

De prebenda de Middelton' (Middleton) in ecclesia Cicestrensi, dimissa inter quatuor obligatos pro diversis beneficiis ratione provisionis facte de eadem Henrico de Walton', debentur iii li. vi s. viii d.[40] Solvit xl s. die i Junii anno LXXIII, xl s.[23]

### Wyntoniensis

De hospitali Sancte Crucis, non taxato, confirmato Johanni de Edyngdon' per Clementem xviii kalendas Junii anno octavo,[41] dimisso in vii li. iii s. vi d. Solvit dictam summam.[23]

Recepta pagine xli li. xvi s. x d.; restant in pecunia xxxiii [42] li.; inutiles sunt due provisiones, scilicet prima pagine [43] et tertia.

(fol. 5ᵛ) De prebenda de Middelton' (Middleton) in ecclesia monialium Warwell' (Wherwell), de qua fuit provisum Johanni Bankatre per Innocentium vᵗᵒ kalendas Januarii anno primo,[44] pro resta xv li. Solvit dictam summam.[23]

De prioratu de Appulborthorp' (Appuldurcombe) confirmato Johanni de Osanna per Clementem v kalendas Martii anno viii°,[45] dimissa in xxx li. xvii s. ad quas taxatur, pro resta xxv li. xvii s. Est in mandato denuntiandum et sequestrandum et cetera, non obstante prohibitione per breve facta quod nichil exigeretur quia in manu regia.[46]

### Saresbiriensis

De ecclesia de Kyvelegh' (Keevil), de qua fuit provisum Magistro Thome de Trompesawe, taxata xxvi li. xiii s. iiii d., debet pro resta dimissa vi li. xiii s. iiii d. Solvit dictam summam ut in libro recepte habetur.[23]

De prebenda de Wermynstr' (Warminster) in ecclesia Saresbiriensi, de qua per obitum Johannis de Blebury fuit provisum Thome de Straguhull' per Clementem pro taxa v li. Certificat episcopus quod non habuit effectum et est probatum et processus est in archivis quare et cetera ut supra.[47]

De prebenda de Stretton' (Stratton) in ecclesia Saresbiriensi, de qua ex causa permutationis fuit provisum Johanni Thurstayn per Innocentium idus Martii anno iii^tio,[48] pro taxa xiii li. vi s. viii d. Non habuit effectum ut in restis prioris folio iiii.[47]

De prebenda de Bedmynstr' (Bedminster) in ecclesia

Saresbiriensi, de qua per resignationem Willelmi Hale fuit provisum Thome de Clipston' per Innocentium idus Decembris anno viᵗᵒ,[49] pro taxa xiii li. vi s. viii d. Non habuit effectum ut in restis folio iiii habetur.[47]

Item de prebenda Saresbiriensi acceptatio facta per Johannem Ufford' Norwicensis diocesis fuit eidem confirmata per Innocentium vii^mo kalendas Julii anno vii^mo,[50] fructus. Non habuit effectum ut in restis prioris folio iiii.[47]

De prebenda de Calne et thesauraria in dicta ecclesia, de quibus fuit provisum cardinali Nemausenensi [51] per Innocentium iii^tio kalendas Octobris anno nono,[52] pro taxa iiii^xx vi li. xiii s. iiii d.[53]

De ecclesia Sancti Petri de Wartham (Warham), de qua per resignationem Thome de Berneby fuit provisum Henrico de Worth' per Innocentium vᵗᵒ idus Octobris anno nono,[54] pro taxa iiii li. vi s. viii d. Non habuit effectum ut in restis prioris folio iiii.[47]

Recepta pagine xxi li. xiii s. iiii d.; resta pagine in pecunia cxii li. xiiii s. iiii d.; inutiles sunt provisiones v.[55]

(fol. 6, vi) De prebenda de Bedeford' (Woodford), taxata xvi li. xiii s. iiii d., et archidiaconatu Dorcestrie in dicta ecclesia, taxato lxii li., de quibus fuit provisum domino cardinali de Canilhaco episcopo Ponestrino per Innocentium iiii^to idus Martii anno ix^no,[56] pro taxa lxxviii li. xiii s. iiii d.[57] Nec Raymundus Pelegrini voluit rendere, licet monitus ante dictam mortem dicti cardinalis, ut procurator ipsius cardinalis.

De prebenda de Prestone (Preston) in ecclesia Saresbiriensi, de qua fuit provisum Thome de Setton' per Innocentium xi kalendas Novembris anno viᵗᵒ,[58] pro taxa xvi li. xiii s. iiii d. Non habuit effectum ut in restis domini prioris habetur folio iiii.[47]

De prebenda in ecclesia Saresbiriensi, videlicet Horton, vacante per obitum Willelmi de Farlee, collatio facta Nicholao de Luda, thesaurario domini regis, fuit confirmata etiam si alio quovismodo vacet vel sit reservata valeat, ac si vacasset solummodo per mortem dicti Willelmi. Solvit ii die Julii anno LXXII sexdecim li.[59] xvi li. Debet residuum, siqui sit, quia tunc non erat certum de taxa nec de residuo.[60]

De ecclesia de Dountton' (Downton) collatio et provisio eiusdem facte Thome de Edyngdon' fuerunt auc-

---

[40] In the margin: *debet residuum.*
[41] 15 May 1350.
[42] Follows *iiii* deleted by a line.
[43] Follows *folii* deleted by a line.
[44] 28 December 1353.
[45] 25 February 1350.
[46] In the margin: *debet.*
[47] In the margin: *inutilis.*
[48] 15 March 1355.

[49] 13 December 1358.
[50] 25 June 1359.
[51] John de Blanzac, bishop of Nimes, priest of S. Marco.
[52] 29 September 1361.
[53] In the margin: *Cardinalis est Nemausenensis et videat camera quia hic nichil potest haberi.*
[54] 11 October 1361.
[55] In the margin: *est vera recepta.*
[56] 12 March 1361.
[57] In the margin: *Cardinalis de Canilhaco.*
[58] 22 October 1358.
[59] Followed by *et debet residuum* deleted by a line.
[60] In the margin: *solvit. A(rnaldus), cum dicit(?) dsbet residuum siqui sit.*

toritate apostolica confirmate vel provisum de novo xvii kalendas Maii,[61] pro taxa lxvi li. xiii s. iiii d. Renuntiavit gratie et fuit relaxatus per cameram, et copia est in archivis, et forte non potuit renuntiare in preiudicio camere.[47]

De prebenda de Bisshopeston' (Bishopstone) in ecclesia Saresbiriensi, taxata xx li., de qua per obitum Petri Raymundi de Tappistagno fuit provisum Raymundo Pelegrini per Clementem kalendas Februarii anno viii°,[62] pro taxa ut supra xx li. Non habuit effectum ut in restis prioris folio iiii, et verum est quia adhuc uniebat ut est probatum.[47]

### Exoniensis

De ecclesia de Basch, de qua ex eo quod Henricus de Monte dictam ecclesiam [63] pluribus annis tenuit in presbytero non promotus fuit provisum Crenezerio de Lauff' per Innocentium vito kalendas Julii anno nono.[64] Non est talis in diocesi, ut dicitur in restis prioris folio iiii.[47]

De archidiaconatu Cornubie in ecclesia Exoniensi, non taxato, de quo per obitum Thome David fuit provisum Alexandro Nevyll' per Innocentium x kalendas Septembris anno ix,[65] fructus. Prohibitum per breve ne fiat exsecutio contra possessorem titulo regio, scilicet Thomam de Oragrave, subthesaurarium in squaquario,[66] et debetur per possessorem vel Dominum Alexandrum de Novilla licet ipse asserat contrarium.[67]

De prebenda in ecclesia Sancti Karentoci (Crantock) fuit subrogatus in omni iure quod competebat David Maynard' Johannes Trusseley, magister in artibus, per Innocentium nonas Maii anno vito,[68] pro taxa. Est probatum quod non habuit effectum dicta subrogatio et probationes sunt in archivis.[47]

De archidiaconatu Tottonie in ecclesia Exoniensi, de quo fuit provisum Ricardo de Desbunton' per Innocentium vto kalendas Novembris anno quinto.[69] Non habuit effectum ut in restis prioris folio v, et ex post idem probatum est.

Recepta pagine xvi li.; restant fructus in toto de duobus beneficiis et de una in parte; iii; inutiles provisiones sunt v; restant in pecunia lxxviii li. xiii s. iiii d.

### (fol. 6ᵛ) Wygorniensis

De ecclesia de Estlegh' (Astley), taxata xi li. vi s. viii d., de qua per obitum Henrici Stowe fuit provisum Henrico Askeby et etiam subrogatus in omni iure quod dicto Henrico competebat, qui, super hoc litigans in curia, decessit tempore Domini Clementis, pro resta viii li. Dicitur in restis prioris folio v quod non habuit effectum, sed quia est de resta, videatur melius.[67]

De hospitali Sancti Wlstani (St. Wulstan, Worcester) Wygorniensis diocesis, non taxato, de quo per resignationem Petri Francisci fuit provisum Johanni de Hareswell', canonico Sancti Martini Londonie, per Innocentium v kalendas Julii anno vto,[70] fructus. Nichil habet, ideo supersessum ut in restis prioris folio v.[47]

### Bathoniensis et Wellensis

De prepositura Wellensi, de qua per obitum Andree de Ufford' fuit provisum Ade de Hilton' per Innocentium tertio nonas Februarii anno vii°,[71] pro taxa xl li. Infra est alia provisio, et cansellarius Londonie possidet titulo regio, et habuit breve, et non potest haberi.[67]

De prebenda de Holcumbe (Holcombe) in ecclesia Wellensi, de qua, vacante aut cum vacabit per assecutionem canonicatus et prebende Thome [72] de Burton', fuit provisum Waltero Moryn per Innocentium xix kalendas Septembris anno viii°,[73] xxvi li. xiii s. iiii d. Non habuit effectum ut in restis domini prioris folio v.[47]

De prepositura Wellensi, de qua per obitum Ade de Hilton' fuit provisum Willelmo de Wykham per Innocentium nonas Januarii anno xmo,[74] xl li. Supra est alia provisio, et cansellarius Londonie possidet titulo regio, et habuit breve.[67]

### Herefordensis

De prebenda de Morton' (Moreton Magna) in ecclesia Herefordensi, taxata xx li., de qua per obitum Thome de Stauntton' fuit provisum Simoni de Sudbur' per Clementem iiiito nonas Julii anno viii°,[75] pro resta xiii s. iiii d. Prohibitum per breve ut in restis prioris folio v. Et [76] dominus Londoniensis debet, sed nondum voluit solvere, licet pluries requisitus.[67]

De eadem prebenda de Morton', de qua per promotionem [77] Simonis Thebaud in episcopum Londoniensem fuit provisum Thome Thebaud per Innocentium iiito idus Decembris anno xi,[78] pro resta xx li. Prohibitum per breve regis ut in restis prioris folio v.[67]

De decanatu Herefordensi, de quo per resignationem Thome Trilleke fuit provisum Willelmo de Bermyngham per Urbanum viimo kalendas Februarii anno primo,[79] pro resta xl s. i d. Solvit dictam summam ut in libro recepte.[80]

---

[61] 15 April (1363: *Cal. Pop. Reg. Petitions*, i, 412).
[62] 1 February 1350.
[63] Followed by *una cum* undeleted.
[64] 26 June 1361.
[65] 23 August 1361.
[66] Perhaps for *scaccario*.
[67] In the margin: *debet*.
[68] 7 May 1358.
[69] 28 October 1357. *Cf.* Le Neve, *Fasti* (Exeter), pp. 17-18.

[70] 27 June 1357.
[71] 3 February 1359.
[72] *Thoma*, MS.
[73] 14 August 1360.
[74] 5 January 1362.
[75] 4 July 1349.
[76] *Ett*, MS.
[77] *mortem*, MS.
[78] 11 December 1361. It should be *anno ix*, above, p. 328.
[79] 26 January 1363.
[80] Followed by an unfinished sentence deleted by a line so heavy as to make it in part illegible. In the margin: *solvit*.

Recepta pagine xl s. i d.; inutiles provisiones sunt due, ii[e]; restant pro quinque cviii li. xiii s. iiii d.

### (fol. 7, vii)  Norwicensis

De prioratu de Castellacre (Castle Acre), de quo ex causa permutationis fuit provisum Willelmo Warenn' per Clementem anno primo,[81] pro taxa iiii[c] iiii[xx] li. xix s. vii d. Est de patronatu laicali ut in restis folio v, et nichil potest haberi.[82]

De ecclesia de Hulmo (Holme), taxata xl li., de qua per resignationem Willelmi de Egerton' fuit provisum Thome Michiel per Clementem, pro resta x li. Prohibitum per breve regium, ideo vinctio relaxatur quousque aliud fuerit ordinatum per illum ad quem pertinet, et cetera.

De ecclesia de Derham (East Dereham), de qua per obitum Alani de Hothom fuit provisum Simoni Thebaud, nunc episcopo Londoniensi, per Clementem iii kalendas Aprilis anno decimo,[83] pro resta xl li. xvi s. viii d. Possessor est relaxatus per cameram, sed quia agatur contra dominum Londoniensem qui non vult solvere adhuc, quia dicit quod sequestrum fuit positum et levatum per Dominum Raymundum Pelegrini.[67]

De eadem per promotionem dicti Simonis Thebaud' in episcopum Londoniensem fuit provisum Bartholomeo Sidey iurisperito per Innocentum vii kalendas Decembris anno ix[o],[84] cx m. Non habuit effectum quia rex contulit ut in restis domini prioris folio v.[85]

De decanatu de Humuliard (Humbleyard), non taxato, de quo per resignationem Walteri Baltton' fuit provisum Simoni de Surbur' per Innocentum iiii[tio] kalendas Julii anno v[to],[86] fructus. Est in mandato ad denuntiandum et sequestrandum.[87]

De decanatu rurali de Fordham, vacante per obitum Johannis Hepp', fuit provisum Waltero Palmer' per Innocentium vi nonas Maii anno x,[88] fructus. Est in mandato ad denuntiandum et sequestrandum.[87]

De ecclesia de Hulmo (Holme), de qua per obitum Thome Michiel fuit provisum Roberto de Grimmeston' xviii kalendas Januarii anno primo,[88a] pro taxa xl li.[67]

Item de eadem per obitum eiusdem Thome fuit provisum Johanni Bach' eodem die. Prohibitum per breve quia possessor est regius, et non potest haberi, ipso sic possidente vivente. Et ambo fuerunt infra eumdem annum, quare una inutilis est et cetera, sed nondum potest exigi.[89]

De ecclesia de Multon' (Moulton), de qua per obitum Edmundi de Wytewell' fuit provisum Hugoni de Deval, presbytero Lichfeldensis diocesis, ii idus Martii anno predicto,[90] pro taxa xl m. Ista provisio non habuit effectum, sed alia que est infra folio xx eidem persone facta, et litigatur in curia.[85]

### Eliensis

De prioratu de Swavesey, de quo fuit provisum Stephano Bertrandi per Clementem, pro resta iiii[or] li. Prohibitum est per breve quia [91] in manu regia et de patronatu laicali, et breve est in archivis.[92]

Recepta pagine nichil; inutiles provisiones sunt iii; resta pecunie v[c] lxxv li. xvi s. iii d.; et restant fructus duarum.

(fol. 7[v]) De perpetua vicaria parochialis ecclesie de Imprington' (Impington), vacante per liberam resignationem Johannis Notlee, ultimi predicti vicari perpetue vicarie, factam in manibus Johannis Tursteyn, canonici Wellensis vicarii in spiritualibus episcopi Eliensis, fuit provisum per cardinalem Petragoricensem Johanni filio Ricardi de Chelford',[93] xii kalendas Decembris pontificatus Innocentii anno v[to],[94] pro resta xliii s. iiii d. Solvit dictam summam.[95]

De archidiaconatu Eliensi ratione provisionis facte de eodem [96] cardinali Cluniacensi [97] pro taxa xxvi li. xiii s. iiii d. Debent esse xlvi li. vi s. viii d., quia tantum taxatur, sed non habuit effectum ut in restis prioris folio vi. quia titulo regio habuit, non isto.[85]

### Lincolniensis

De prebenda de Bedeford' maiori (Bedford Maior) in ecclesia Lincolniensi, que fuit Willelmo de Wyntleseye, nunc episcopo Roffensi, confirmata per Clementem viii idus Maii anno vii vel viii,[98] pro taxa viii li. Solvit dictam summam.[95]

De prebenda de Walton' Rivaus (Welton Rivall) in ecclesia Lincolniensi, de qua ex causa permutationis cum Johanne Atton' fuit provisum Radulpho de Daventr' per Innocentium vii kalendas Maii anno v[to],[99] pro taxa xxxiii li. vi s. viii d. Est in mandato ad sequestrandum et denuntiandum, et est frater unius militis communitatis Stamford', et habet terminum Beati Michaelis, et nititur probare quod nunquam habuit effectum, et litigat coram me.[100]

De ecclesia de Trefford' (Greatford), que fuit unita

---

[81] 19 May 1342 to 18 May 1343.
[82] Followed by the unfinished and undeleted sentence *videat communiter ante d'*.
[83] 30 March 1352.
[84] 25 November 1361.
[85] In the margin: *inutilis*.
[86] 29 June 1357.
[87] In the margin: *debet fructus*.
[88] 2 May 1362.
[88a] 15 December 1362.
[89] In the margin: *ista est inutilis vel alia*.

[90] 14 March 1363.
[91] Followed by *possessor est regius* deleted by a line.
[92] In the margin: *debet*.
[93] *Schelford'*, Collectorie 13, fol. 163[v].
[94] 20 November 1357.
[95] In the margin: *solvit*.
[96] *eadem*, MS.
[97] Androin de la Roche, abbot of Cluny, priest of S. Marcello.
[98] 8 May 1349 or 1350 (*Cal. Pap. Reg. Petitions* i, 196).
[99] 25 April 1357. *Cf.* Le Neve, *Fasti* (Lincoln), p. 126.
[100] Extension doubtful. In the margin: *debet*.

monasterio Beate Marie Wyntoniensis per Clementem iii idus Julii anno xi,[101] pro taxa xiiii li. xiii s. iiii d. Non est in diocesis ut in restis folio vi, sed est iam in iiii[to] mandato.[92]

De prebenda Sancte Crucis (Spaldwick) in ecclesia Lincolniensi, taxata x li., de qua fuit provisum Johanni de Selby, pro resta ii li. x s. Possessor est regius et negat provisionem, ut in restis folio vi.[92]

De prebenda de South Scarle in ecclesia Lincolniensi, de qua per resignationem Willelmi de Kirkeby fuit provisum Johanni de Appulby per Innocentium iii[tio] idus Julii anno vi[to],[102] pro taxa xl li. Non habuit effectum ut est clare probatum.[85]

De ecclesia de Cosyngton' (Cossington), que Johanni de Melburn' fuit confirmata per Innocentium vii kalendas Julii anno vii,[103] pro taxa vi li. xiii s. iiii d.[92] Non est in diocesi ut in restis folio vi. Solvit post in partem fructuum die v Maii anno LXXIIII[to] quadraginta solidos, xl s.[104]

De prebenda de Nassyngton' (Nassington) in ecclesia Lincolniensi, taxata c li., que fuit confirmata Lodewico de Carleton' per Innocentium iii kalendas Februarii anno nono,[105] pro taxa c li. Cardinalis Ierolosomitanus[106] possidet, nec reperiuntur exsecutores Ludovici adhuc, sed videatur plus.

Recepta pagine xii li. iii s. iiii d.; inutiles sunt due ii[e]; resta pecunie pro v beneficiis clv li. iii s. iiii d.

(fol. 8, viii) Item de eadem prebenda ratione provisionis facte cardinali Carcassonensi[107] pro resta liii li. ii s. Nichil reperitur hic, quare videat camera in curia contra exsecutores.[108]

De ecclesia de Stangrunde (Standground), de eo quod ex causa permutationis fuit provisum cum ecclesia de Ripton' (Abbots Ripton) Johanni de Ditton' per Innocentium vii kalendas Octobris anno nono,[109] pro taxa xx li. Non habuit effectum ut in restis prioris folio vi.[85]

De ecclesia de Ripton' Abbatis, de qua ex causa permutationis fuit provisum Thome de Clipston' per Innocentium vii kalendas Octobris anno nono,[109] pro taxa xxiii li. vi s. viii d. Non habuit effectum ut in dictis restis folio vi.[85]

De ecclesia de parva Kynewell' (Little Kimble), de qua per assecutionem ecclesie de Cosyngton' (Garsington) per Stephanum de Gesington' fuit provisum Johanni Rocelli per Innocentium vi[to] idus Martii anno vi,[110] pro taxa iiii li. xiii s. iiii d. Non est talis in diocesi ut in restis prioris folio vi; videatur melius.

De prebenda Lincolniensi de qua per obitum Jacobi Borelay fuit provisum domino episcopo Tusculano per Innocentium xv kalendas Septembris anno vi[to].[111] Cardinalis est, et obiit, et nichil hic reperitur de suo, sed agat camera contra exsecutores.[112]

De ecclesia de Hoghton' (Houghton Regis) presentatio et institutio facte Hugoni Spalking' fuerunt eidem auctoritate apostolica confirmate vel provisum de novo per Innocentium xviii kalendas Decembris anno viii,[113] xii li. Ante providetur eidem eodem anno et ibi solvit, ut in restis prioris folio vii dicitur.[85]

De ecclesia Beate Marie Hereford (Hertford), de qua ex causa permutationis cum Johanne Dich' fuit provisum Henrico Midi per Innocentium v kalendas Aprilis anno viii°.[114] Non habuit effectum ut in restis prioris folio vii.[85]

De prebenda de Langestow (Stowe Longa) in ecclesia Lincolniensi, de qua fuit provisum Reginaldo de Tyminis per Innocentium xi kalendas Julii anno x°,[115] pro resta xix li. xvi s. viii d. Possessor est regius, et lis pendet in curia inter possessorem et unum cardinalem qui habuit post obitum Rainaudi, quare dormit pro nunc.

De prebenda in ecclesia collegiata Beate Marie iuxta castrum Leycestrie (St. Mary the Less in Castle, Leicester) intitulata, de qua fuit ex causa permutationis provisum Henrico Lymbergh' v nonas Maii anno primo.[116] Non sunt fructus ut in restis folio vii°, sed videatur melius.[117]

Recepta pagine nichil; provisiones inutiles sunt v[e]; resta pecunie lxxvii li. xvi s.; et fructus unius.

(fol. 8[v]) De magistratu de Burton' Sancti Lazari (Burton Lazars), collatio facta per Dominum Philipum patriarcham Jerosolimitanam auctoritate ordinaria Galfrido de Caddesdon', militi dicti hospitalis, fuit[118] eidem auctoritate apostolica confirmata et nichilominus subrogatus dictus Galfridus in omni iure quod competebat Roberto Haliday v nonas Martii dicto anno.[119] Non habuit effectum, nec tunc vacavit, et probationes sunt in archivis, et habetur in restis prioris folio vii.[120]

De prebenda Lincolniensi vocata Sancte Crucis (Spaldwick), vacante per obitum Willelmi de Spaldewell' fuit provisum Johanni de Kirkeby, regis Anglie clerico, xiii kalendas Maii dicto anno.[121] Non habuit effectum ut in restis folio vii, quia titulo regio possidetur.[120]

---

[101] 13 July 1352.
[102] 13 July 1358.
[103] 25 June 1359.
[104] In the margin *solvit* and *attende*.
[105] 30 January 1361.
[106] Philip Cabassole, patriarch of Jerusalem, bishop of Sabina.
[107] Stephen Aubert, deacon of S. Maria in Aquiro.
[108] In the margin: *Cardinalis Carcassonensis*.
[109] 25 September 1361.
[110] 10 March 1358.

[111] 18 August 1358.
[112] In the margin: *oscure loqueris*(?).
[113] 14 November 1360.
[114] 28 March 1360.
[115] 21 June 1362.
[116] 3 May 1363.
[117] In the margin: *inutilis est*.
[118] *fuerunt*, MS.
[119] 3 March 1363.
[120] In the margin: *inutilis*.
[121] 19 April 1363.

## Conventrensis et Lichfeldensis

De archidiaconatu Conventrensi, non taxato, de quo fuit provisum Humifrido de Hasting'. Solvit pro medietate veri valoris xvi Octobris anno lxxii quinque li., v li., salvo iure pluris super procurationibus et iurisdictione,[122] si fuerit per cameram ordinatum, quia non est consuetum ut dicitur.[123]

De eodem archidiaconatu et prebenda de Langedone (Longdon) in ecclesia Lichfeldensi, taxata xx li., de quibus post obitum Humifridi de H. fuit provisum Willelmo de Salowe per Clementem iii[tio] nonas Septembris anno vii[mo],[124] pro quibus Walterus Dalby dicitur compossuise cum camera, pro resta xiii li. vi s. viii d. Ista prebenda possidetur per alium quia non est annexa archidiaconatui, et resta est de prebenda sola, et sunt alie due provisiones infra folio xxxi et xxxvi, et ibi vide in xxxi folio.

De prebenda Lichfeldensi [125] de qua per obitum Willelmi Appeltre fuit provisum Thome Attehull' per Clementem xi kalendas Julii anno viii[o],[126] pro taxa xxx s. Solvit dictam summam xxx s. xii die Junii anno LXXII.[123]

De prebenda in ecclesia collegiata Sancti Sedde Salopie (St. Chad, Shrewsbury), de qua per obitum Willelmi Appeltre fuit provisum Roberto de Sulgrave per Clementem iii[tio] idus Decembris anno viii[o],[127] non taxata. Solvit pro medietate veri valoris die iii Junii anno LXXII decem solidos, salvo iure pluris si reperiatur de maiori valentia, x s.[123]

De prebenda de Berwyk' (Berkswick) in ecclesia Lichfeldensi, taxata xx li., de qua per obitum Guidonis de Waresio fuit provisum Willelmo Cammile per Innocentium viii[o] kalendas Maii anno primo,[128] xx li. Non habuit effectum, ut in restis domini prioris folio vii habetur.[120]

Recepta pagine vii li.; provisiones inutiles sunt iii; resta pecunie xiii li. vi s. viii d.; et procurationes unius archidiaconatus.

(fol. 9, ix) De cappellania Sancti Michaelis in castro de Cliderouwe (Clitheroe), non taxata, fuit per devolutionem provisum Johanni de Burton' per Innocentium iiii kalendas Junii anno vi[to],[129] fructus. Appropriata est ut in restis prioris folio vii; ideo non habuit effectum.[120]

De ecclesia de Codyngton' (Coddington), de qua per assecutionem ecclesie de Wynton' (Burton-in-Winhale) per Johannem Chernaux fuit provisum Waltero Linge per Innocentium iii[tio] nonas Junii anno vi[to] [130] pro taxa

vi li. xiii s. iiii d. Certificat episcopus quod non fuit talis possessor, et est tertium mandatum.[131]

De prioratu de Kirkeby (Monks Kirby), taxato iiii[xx] i li. x s. viii d., de quo per assecutionem prioratus de Veteri Belismo (Vieux Belesme) Sagiensis (Séez) diocesis per Oliverum de Desertis fuit provisum Willelmo de Grauleriis per Innocentium xiii kalendas Martii anno vii[mo],[132] pro resta xli li. xiii s. viii d. Est in manu regia, et est excommunicatus et rei gravatus non obstante excusatione et cetera. Solvit die xxvii Aprilis anno LXXIIII in partem dicte reste v li.[123]

Hic deficit una provisio secundum librum restarum camere unius ecclesie, sed non debet esse et causa redditur in restis domini prioris, et ibi vide.

De prebenda de Tervyn (Tarvin) in ecclesia Lichfeldensi, de qua per obitum Willelmi Driffeld' fuit provisum Nicholao Heeth' per Innocentium iii[tio] idus Augusti anno ix,[133] pro resta xxiiii li. ix s. vi d. Solvit quindecim li. die xxviii Junii anno LXXII, xv li.[123] Item solvit novem li. ix s. vi d. xxii die Desembris et sic totum xxiiii li. ix s. vi d.[123]

De prebenda in ecclesia collegiata de Penkrigg' (Penkridge), de qua per obitum Thome Michiel fuit provisum Thome de Eltenheed per Innocentium vii idus Aprilis anno x,[134] fructus. Episcopus est prohibitus per breve, et non audet exsequtare mandata, ideo dormit.[131]

De cantaria ecclesie Lichfeldensis, quam Thomas de Badeby debuit dimittere per assecutionem canonicatus et prebende ecclesie Lincolniensis, provisum. Non habuit effectum, ut dicitur in restis folio viii.[120]

De prebenda in ecclesia Lichfeldensi, de qua, per obitum Thome Driffeld' in curia defuncti, fuit provisum Alexandro de Dalby iiii[to] nonas Januarii anno primo per Urbanum.[135] Vocatur Tervin (Tarvin). Et non habuit effectum ut in restis folio viii.[120]

De prebenda de Gnousall' (Gnosall) in ecclesia Lichfeldensi, de qua collatio et provisio facte auctoritate ordinaria Hugoni de Carles fuerunt eidem auctoritate apostolica confirmate vel provisum de novo v nonas Martii anno predicto.[136] Non habuit effectum ut in restis folio viii.[120]

Recepta pagine xxix li. ix s. vi d.; provisiones inutiles sunt iiii[or]; resta pecunie xliii li. vii s.; et unius beneficii fructus.

## (fol. 9[v]) Assavensis

De ecclesia de Dymbergh' (Denbigh), de qua vacante de iure, ut asseritur, fuit provisum Willelmo Sinderlond' per Clementem idus Novembris anno ix,[137] pro resta xliii s. iiii d. Non est ecclesia set capella annexa ecclesie de Lavbbarchel (Llanfarchell, or Whitchurch by Den-

---

[122] *iuridictione*, MS.
[123] In the margin: *solvit.*
[124] 3 September 1348.
[125] Prebend of Darnford: Collectorie 13, fol. 164.
[126] 21 June 1349.
[127] 11 December 1349.
[128] 24 April 1353.
[129] 29 May 1358.
[130] 3 June 1358.

[131] In the margin: *debet.*
[132] 17 February 1359.
[133] 11 August 1361.
[134] 7 April 1362.
[135] 2 January 1363.
[136] 3 March 1363.
[137] 13 November 1350.

bigh), que taxatur iiii⁰ʳ li. x s., de quibus est satisfactum, ut dicitur in restis prioris folio viii.[138]

De ecclesia de Landrineaw (Llandrinio), taxata vii li., que fuit confirmata Griffino de Carleton'[139] per Innocentium iiiᵗⁱᵒ nonas Maii anno ix,[140] vii li. Solvit dictas septem li. in duabus vicibus.[123]

De ecclesia de Dymbegh' (Denbigh), de qua per obitum Willelmi Synderlond' fuit provisum ⟨Willelmo⟩ Hardeni nono kalendas Maii anno ix⁰,[141] xv li. vi s. viii d. Non habuit effectum, ut certificat episcopus; sic in restis prioris folio viii.[120]

De ecclesia de Dymbegh', de qua per obitum dicti Willelmi fuit provisum Hugoni Craster per Innocentium iiiiᵗᵒ kalendas Maii anno nono.[142] Non habuit effectum ut in restis prioris folio viii.[120]

De ecclesia de Kilkeyn (Kilken) et capella eidem annexa, de qua per obitum ultimi rectoris eiusdem fuit provisum Waltero Frestorp' per Innocentium xi kalendas Julii anno ixⁿᵒ,[143] pro taxa vii li. Non habuit effectum, ut est probatum, et atestationes sunt in archivis.[120]

### Menevensis

De ecclesia de Tanhanglarath' (Llanfihangel ar Arth), non taxata, de qua per obitum Ricardi Aprovanses fuit provisum Ludovico Cauntton' per Clementem. Non habuit effectum, ut in restis prioris habetur, et idem in computis Domini Hugonis Pelegrini ut ibi dicitur.[120]

De ecclesia de Weston' (Wiston), non ⟨taxata⟩, de qua per obitum Rogeri dicti Johannis fuit provisum Willelmo de Newehawe per Innocentium xix kalendas Junii anno iiiiᵗᵒ,[144] fructus. Non est talis in diocesi ut in restis folio viii.[120]

De ecclesia de Langedomore (Llangoedmore), taxata vi li., de qua Willelmo de Abcorg' per cardinalem Petragoricensem fuit provisum, pro resta iii li. vi s. viii d. Dicitur in restis prioris quod Dominus Hugo Pelegrini habuit, folio viii, et ostendit quitantiam, ideo assignavi hic de recepta procurationum suarum dictas iii li. vi s. viii d.[145]

De prebenda in ecclesia Menevensis de qua per obitum Thome David fuit provisum David Wygham per Innocentium xi kalendas Julii anno nono.[143] Non habuit effectum ut in restis folio ix.[120]

De prebenda in ecclesia Menevensis de qua per obitum Griffini de Cauntton' fuit provisum Willelmo de Esendon' per Innocentium iiᵈᵒ Decembris anno quinto.[146]

Non habuit effectum ut in restis prioris Lewensis folio ix.[120]

Recepta pagine x li. vi s. viii d.; alie vii provisiones [147] sunt inutiles.

(fol. 10, x) De prebenda seu portione in ecclesia Sancti Martini de Abberwill' (Abergwili), de qua per obitum Willelmi de Deybrand' fuit provisum Waltero de Fenton' per Innocentium iiiiᵗᵒ nonas Julii anno xᵐᵒ.[148] Non habuit effectum, ut in dictis restis prioris folio ix habetur.[120]

### Eboracensis

De prebenda in ecclesia Eboracensi de qua per consecrationem electi Tervinensis fuit provisum Frederico Saloman. Certificat archiepiscopus quod non fuerunt tales in ecclesia sua, et idem dicitur in restis folio ix.[120]

De prebenda de Strensall' in ecclesia Eboracensi, de qua per consecrationem Michaelis episcopi Londoniensis fuit provisum cardinali Petragoricensi per Innocentium iiᵈᵒ ⟨idus⟩ Octobris anno secundo,[149] pro taxa liii li. vi s. viii d. Cardinalis est Petragoricensis, et solvant exsecutores quia hic nichil reperitur de suo adhuc.

De vicaria de Gilling', in qua Johannes Parker fuit subrogatus in omni iure quod competebat Garlaco de Clave per Innocentium ix ⁿᵒ kalendas Maii anno nono,[150] pro taxa x li. Ista provisio et sequens fuerunt infra annum, et de sequenti est solutum priori, ut infra habetur et in suis restis folio ix.[151]

Item de eadem fuit provisum Johanni Beck' per Innocentium ixⁿᵒ kalendas Septembris anno viiᵐᵒ,[152] pro qua solvit, et videtur esse infra annum, x li. De ista provisione est solutum priori Lewensi ut in restis suis folio ix, et dicitur quod fuerit infra eundem annum, et videatur quod hic non loquitur de anno eodem ut supra.

De prebenda de Wistow in ecclesia Eboracensi, taxata c li., et archidiaconatu eiusdem ecclesie, taxato secundum estimationem ut inferius patet, de quibus per obitum cardinalis Ponestrini fuit provisum cardinali Carcassonensi,[153] pro restis prebende xxi li. xvi s. viii d. Agat camera contra exsecutores quia hic nichil de suo reperitur.[154]

Archidiaconatus Eboracensis consistit in ecclesia de Mekesburgh (Mexborough) et procurationibus, sinodalibus et denariis Beati Petri, que valent ut patet per registrum taxarum lxvii li., inde satisfactum de xxviii li. Quid restat nescio quia procurationes non solvuntur in primis fructibus, nec scio ad quam ascendit, sed in restis camere est pro v li. x s. Dicitur quod cardinalis Ierolozomitanus [155] tenuit, et dicitur quod obiit, et nichil

---

[138] In the margin: *inutilis hic.*
[139] *Charleton'*, Collectorie 13, fol. 164.
[140] Follows *v* deleted by a line. 5 May 1361.
[141] 23 April 1361.
[142] 28 April 1361.
[143] 21 June 1361.
[144] 14 May 1356.
[145] In the margin: *solvit* and the following deleted by lines: *Dominus Hugo Pelegrini respondeat, et si non rendatur, restituat summa que habuit ut hic.*
[146] 2 December 1357. Idus, kalendas or nonas is probably omitted.

[147] *provisionest*, MS.
[148] 4 July 1362.
[149] 14 October 1354.
[150] 23 April 1361.
[151] In the margin: *inutilis* and *attende* and *factam est.*
[152] 24 August 1359.
[153] Stephen Aubert, deacon of S. Maria in Aquiro.
[154] In the margin: *Cardinalis Carcassonensis obiit.*
[155] Philip Cabassole, patriarch of Jerusalem, bishop of Sabina.

reperitur hic, quare agatur camera contra executores quia ego non possum.[156]

De prebenda de Driffeld' in dicta ecclesia, de qua per obitum Willelmi de Sancto Martiale fuit provisum cardinali de Sancto Martiale,[157] pro taxa c li. Cardinalis de Sancto Martiale, et nondum voluit solvere, licet pluries et cetera.[156]

Recepta pagine nichil; inutiles videntur provisiones iiii[or]; resta pecunie ix[xx] li. xiii s. iiii d.

(fol. 10[v]) De prebenda de Northwell' (Norwell) in ecclesia Suthwellensi, in qua omni iure [158] quod competebat Johanni de Dountton' fuit subrogatus Thomas Mount de Wykham per Innocentium vi kalendas Augusti anno v[to],[159] pro taxa xxxvi li. xiii s. iiii d. Solvit xi die Octobris anno LXXII decem et octo li. vi s. viii d. et die xix Octobris decem octo li. vi s. viii d., et sic totum xxxvi li. xiii s. iiii d.[160]

De capella sive cantaria de Wentbrigg', de qua per obitum Thome Attemore fuit provisum Roberto Attewyk' per Innocentium xi kalendas Decembris anno vii[mo].[161] Non est talis in diocesi ut in restis prioris folio ix, sed post est repertum quod vocatur Feribrig' (Ferrybridge), et pro medietate veri valoris salvo iure pluris si reperiatur solvit tres li. viii s. iiii[or] d. xxii die Aprilis anno LXIII, iii li. viii s. iiii[or] d.[162]

De archidiaconatu de Estriding' in eadem ecclesia cum ecclesia de Mapelton' (Mappleton), non taxata, eidem annexa, vacante eo quod Willelmus Walcote qui ipsum optinebat aliam ecclesiam extitit pacifice assecutus, fuit provisum Waltero Skirlawe per Innocentium ii[do] kalendas Decembris anno vii[o].[163] Composuit medio iuramento et salvo iure pluris pro ecclesia de Mapalton' annexa pro medietate veri valoris xvi li. xiii s. iiii d. Solvit in duabus vicibus dictas sexdecim li. xiii s. iiii w.[162]

De archidiaconatu vero dicit quod nullus habet redditus nisi procurationes et correctiones de quibus non debetur annata determinat camera. Si debet vel non, quia dicitur quod non est consuetum solvere de talibus et de hoc est prorogatus usque ad nativitatem domini.[164]

De custodia vel sacristia capelle Beate Marie et Sanctorum Angelorum Eboraci provisio et collatio facte auctoritate ordinaria Johanni de Waltham fuerunt eidem auctoritate apostolica confirmate vel provisum de novo per Innocentium ix kalendas Januarii anno ix[no],[165] pro taxa iiii[xx] viii li. viii s. viii d. Habuit Dominus Hugo Pelegrini quinquaginta m. viii s., et ad plus non taxatur, et possessor ostendit quitantiam in prima figura, cuius

copia est in archivis. Dicit tamen dictus Dominus Hugo quod fuerunt due provisiones et de alia ipse recepit, non de ista.[166]

De capella Beati Petri de Wolvey, de qua ex causa permutationis cum Henrico Midy fuit provisum Johanni Dich' per Innocentium v kalendas Aprilis anno viii[o].[167] Certificat episcopus quod non est in diocesi, et idem dicitur in restis folio x.[168]

### Dunolmensis

De hospitali de Cretham (Gretham), non taxato, de quo per obitum Johannis de Stokton' fuit provisum Thome Johannis de Braidbrok' [169] per Clementem ii[do] idus Octobris anno ix,[170] debetur medietas exceptis tribus li. vi s. viii d. de quibus Dominus Hugo computat in resta sua. Dicitur in restis prioris folio x quod Dominus Hugo Pelegrini computat in recepta sua, sed, hoc non obstante, solvit pro quadam taxa nova ex post reperta, salvo iure pluris super antiqua, die xxviii Augusti et viii die Octobris octo li. iiii[or] s. vi d., viii li. iiii[or] s. vi d.[162]

Recepta pagine lxiiii li. xix s. iiii [171] d.; provisiones inutiles sunt una; resta pecunie videtur incerta, supra scripta nulla.

(fol. 11, xi) De prebenda in ecclesia collegiata Langcestr' (Lanchester), de qua ex causa permutationis cum Henrico de Exton' fuit provisum Galfrido de Cornetio per Innocentium xv kalendas Decembris,[172] fructus. Certificat episcopus quod non habuit effectum.[168]

De prebenda de Lumley (Lamesley) in ecclesia collegiata Cestrie super stratam (Chester-le-Street), de qua per electionem electi Norwicensis fuit provisum Willemo de Lugtheburgh' per Innocentium vi idus Februarii anno ii[do],[173] pro taxa xx li. Prohibitum per breve regium ad instantiam Domini G' Standeford', possessoris eiusdem titulo regio.[164]

De decanatu ecclesie collegiate Cestrie super stratam permutatio facta auctoritate ordinaria cum Johanne Skultorp' pro archidiaconatu Cestrie per Adam de Houton' fuit eidem confirmata per Innocentium kalendas Junii vi[to] anno,[174] qui decanatus taxatur ad xxxiii li. vi s. viii d., debet de resta xvi li. xiii s. iiii d. Litigatur in curia et fructus sunt sub sequestro auditoris et etiam camere, sed, hoc non obstante, solvit die xxvi Augusti in partem reste tresdecim li. vi s. viii d. anno

---

[156] In the margin: *cardinalis.*
[157] Hugo de Sancto Martiali, deacon of S. Maria in Portico.
[158] *iure* repeated MS.
[159] 27 July 1357.
[160] In the margin: *solvit* repeated.
[161] 21 November 1359.
[162] In the margin: *solvit.*
[163] 30 November 1359.
[164] In the margin: *debet.*
[165] 24 December 1361.

[166] In the margin: *Dominus Hugo Pelegrini medeat, et si ostendat in assignatis camere per eum solvisse, videatur si est de ista provisione quam dedit vel alia, quam non reperio in restis dedisse et ordinent* (extension doubtful) *domini.*
[167] 28 March 1360.
[168] In the margin: *inutilis.*
[169] *Bridebork',* Collectorie 13, fol. 164.
[170] 14 October 1350.
[171] Om. MS.
[172] 17 November 1353.
[173] 8 February 1354.
[174] 1 June 1358.

LXXIII xiii li. vi s. viii d., et post solvit plus in vesperis nativitatis domini tres li. vi s. viii d.[175]

De vicaria de Newton in Glondale (Kirknewton), de qua per obitum Roberti de Jarmy fuit provisum Roberto Hepp' per Innocentium nonas Septembris anno viii°,[176] pro taxa xx li. Non habuit effectum ut in restis prioris folio x.[168]

De prebenda in ecclesia de Norton', de qua per obitum Thome Drax fuit provisum Bernardo de Linario alias Luthonie Avinionie per Innocentium viii kalendas Maii anno ix^no.[177] Non habuit effectum ut in restis folio x habetur, sed videatur melius de ista.[168]

De prebenda ecclesie collegiate de Aukland' (Auckland), de qua per obitum Thome de Bridkirk' fuit provisum Willelmo Wykham per Innocentium ii^do idus Augusti anno nono.[178] Non habuit effectum ut in restis prioris folio x.[168]

De ecclesia de Santhop' (Stanhope), de qua per obitum Thome de Bridkirk' fuit provisum Willelmo de Norwico per Innocentium vii kalendas Septembris anno ix,[179] pro taxa xl s.

De eadem ecclesia collatio facta auctoritate ordinaria Ricardo de Wylington' per obitum prefati Thome fuit eidem confirmata per Innocentium iiii^to ⟨kalendas⟩ Januarii anno nono,[180] pro taxa xl s.

Item in eadem collatione predicta dicto Ricardo facta fuit confirmata per Innocentium iiii^to idus Maii anno decimo,[181] xl s.

Prohibitum de istis tribus per breve regium ut in restis folio x.

Recepta pagine xvi li. xiii s. iiii^or d.; provisiones inutiles videntur iiii^or; et in resta pecunie sunt xxvi li.

(fol. 11^v) De prebenda ecclesie collegiate de Aukland' (Auckland), de qua per obitum Thome fuit provisum Roberto de Stratton' per Innocentium xvi kalendas Septembris anno.[182] Non habuit effectum, ut habetur in restis folio xi.[183]

De capella libera de Ismouth' (Jesmond) collatio facta auctoritate ordinaria Thome Penreth' fuit eidem confirmata per Innocentum ix idus Januarii anno ix°.[184] Prohibitum per breve ne fiat exsecutio contra possessorem titulo regio, ut in restis folio xi; ideo dormit quousque aliud fuerit ordinatum et cetera.[164]

De eadem, vacante per obitum Henrici Bieufamt, fuit provisum Matheo de Bolton' per Innocentium xiii kalendas Februarii anno x^mo.[185] Prohibitum ut supra.

De hospitali pauperum Sancti Egidii de Kypitr' (Kepier), de quo per obitum Petri de Thoresbery fuit provisum Johanni Appulby per Innocentium viii kalendas Maii anno viii°.[186] Prohibitum per breve quia possessor est regius, ut in restis etiam habetur.

De ecclesia de Routhebury (Rothbury), taxata lxvi li. xiii s. iiii d., presentatio, institutio et inductio facte auctoritate ordinaria Johanni Maresscall' fuerunt eidem confirmate auctoritate apostolica vel de novo provisum per Urbanum v nonas Martii anno primo,[187] pro resta xxxvi li. xiii s. iiii d. Prohibitum per breve quia est debitor regius, et contra hoc est etiam excommunicatus et agravatus, et solvit die vi Junii anno LXXIIII^to dictas xxxvi li. xiii s. iiii d.[188]

Hic debet esse una alia provisio que est de prebenda in ecclesia de Norton', sed non videtur ut in ipsis restis habetur, quare fuit omissa in restis prioris.

## Karleolensis

De ecclesia de Crostwayt (Crosthwaite), in qua in omni iure competenti Johanni de Selario fuit subrogatus Johannes Henrici per Innocentium ii idus Januarii anno quinto,[189] pro taxa xxx li. xiii s. iiii d. Appropriata est abbati de Fontibus (Fountains), ideo non habuit effectum, sic est in restis folio xi.[190]

De vicaria de Brampton', de qua ex causa permutationis cum vicaria de Schaldeford' (Shalford) Wyntoniensis diocesis fuit provisum Johanni Amill' per Innocentium xi kalendas Septembris anno v^to,[191] pro taxa viii li. Non habuit effectum ut in restis folio xi.[190]

De vicaria de Crostwayt provisio facta Willelmo de Esyngdon' fuit eidem confirmata per Innocentium ii^do kalendas Julii anno viii°,[192] xx li. Prohibitum per breve regium ut in restis folio xi.

De ecclesia de Kirklond (Kirkland), vacante ex eo quod Johannes Kirkeby ipsam cum ecclesia de Wissehopp' (Ousby) per mensem et amplius pacifice detinuit et sine dispensatione, fuit provisum Johanni de Kirkeby per Innocentium viii kalendas Novembris anno viii°,[193] pro taxa xl li. Non habuit effectum ut in restis folio xi, et ex post est plenum probatum, et probationes sunt in archivis.[190]

Recepta pagine xxxvi li. xiii s. iiii d.; inutiles provisiones sunt iiii^or; resta pecunie xx li., et de tribus beneficiis si possunt haberi fructus.

---

[175] In the margin: *solvit* repeated.
[176] 5 September 1360.
[177] 24 April 1361.
[178] 12 August 1361.
[179] 26 August 1361.
[180] 29 December 1361.
[181] 12 May 1362.
[182] 17 August.
[183] In the margin: *inutilis videtur.*
[184] 24 December 1361. See above, p. 157.
[185] 20 January 1362.

[186] 24 April 1360.
[187] 3 March 1363.
[188] In the margin: *Dominus prior habuerat xxx li., et taxatur ii° m., et sic debet plus. Si dicatur quod secundum novam taxam est ad c m., non est ita in libro camere, quare hic presumitur favor et cetera* and *et videtur nunc* and *solvit.*
[189] 12 January 1357.
[190] In the margin: *inutilis.*
[191] 22 August 1357.
[192] 30 June 1360.
[193] 25 October 1360.

(fol. 12, xii) De quatuor obligatis sequitur resta.

### Lichfeldensis, Saresbiriensis, Londoniensis, Herefordensis

De ecclesia de Hedeneth' (Hodnet) Lichfeldensis diocesis et prebenda de Farendon' (Faringdon) in ecclesia Saresbiriensi, de Mora (Moorfields, St. Giles Cripplegate) in ecclesia Londoniensi, de Hondreton' (Hunderton) in ecclesia Herefordensi et de Ledebury (Ledbury) in diocesi Herefordensi, de quibus fuit provisum Nicholao Heth', et composuit cum camera in curia pro primis fructibus dictorum beneficiorum pro viii$^e$ l fl. ponderis camere, de quibus fuit dimissum michi pro resta in v$^e$ v fl., debet adhuc ccv fl. dymidium ii d. Solvit die xxvi Aprilis anno LXXIII in xv li. sterlingorum c fl., scilicet in xv li.[194]

Beneficia collata in Anglia per dominos cardinales

### Saresbiriensis

De prioratu seu officio nuncupato de Noion' de Mercato Novo (Neufmarché), de quo fuit provisum Nicholao Domini per cardinalem Petragoricensem, debentur fructus. Non habuit effectum, ut in restis prioris habetur folio xii.[190]

### Lincolniensis

De ecclesia de Longhous, de qua fuit provisum Waltero Bernak' per cardinalem Petragoricensem. Certificat episcopus quod talis ecclesia non est in diocesi, ut in restis folio xii.[190]

De ecclesia Sancti Clementis de Wylouiby (Willoughby) fuit provisum per cardinalem Petragoricensem Hugoni Kypas, pro taxa xxiii li. vi s. viii d. Certificat episcopus ut supra, ut in restis folio xii videatur bene.[190]

### Exoniensis

De cantaria perpetua Sancte Anne sita in ecclesia Omnium Sanctorum Exonie fuit provisum per cardinalem Urgellensem Alexandro Sporeman. Certificat episcopus quod non est in diocesi ut in restis folio xii.[190]

### Lichfeldensis

De ecclesia de Adesby, de qua per cardinalem Petragoricensem fuit provisum Johanni Daston', pro taxa viii li. Non est in diocesi ut in restis folio xii.[190]

### Lincolniensis [195]

De ecclesia de Dumeshull' (Burnhill), de qua per dominum Petragoricensem fuit provisum Hugoni de Pamberton'. Est de patronatu laycali, et non permititur a laico quod tales solvant.[190]

### Lincolniensis

De vicaria de Dorset magna (Great Dassett), de qua per dominum Petragoricensem fuit provisum Willelmo de Westbury, non taxata, fructus. Lis pendet in curia, et est de patronatu laycali.[190]

### Bangorensis

De ecclesia de Danbrugham (Llangian) fuit provisum per dominum Petragoricensem David nato Johannis. Est excommunicatus et sequestratus in primo, secundo, tertio et iiii$^o$ mandatis.[196]

### Lincolniensis

De ecclesia de Couseby (Cowesby), de qua per dominum Urgellensem fuit provisum Henrico de Helproby.[196] Dicitur in restis domini prioris quod fuit supercessum per Dominum Johannem de Cabrespino folio xii.[190]

Recepta pagine xv li.; provisiones inutiles sunt viii; resta pecunie cv fl. dimidius ii d. pro xv li. xv s. ii d.; et fructus beneficii unius.

(fol. 12$^v$) Summa universalis recepte de tempore Dominorum Clementis et Innocentii est ducentas octuaginta tres li. decem et octo s. quinque d., cclxxxiii li. xviii s. v d.[197]

Et restant in pecunia de male solventibus ab antiquo circa xiiii$^e$ xli li. ix s. ix d.

Et restant de male solventibus non taxatis fructus beneficiorum xiii.

Et de inutilibus provisionibus dimituntur fructus beneficiorum lxi.

(fol. 13, xiii) Anno i Urbani

De tempore Urbani anno primo reste

### Eliensis

De parochiali ecclesia de Elesworth' (Elsworth), vacante cum Johannes Merthen' dignitatem, personatum vel officium curatum in ecclesia Lichfeldensi fuit pacifice assecutus, fuit provisum Thome de Eltesle, clerico diocesis Eliensis bacallario in utroque iure, iii kalendas Maii.[198] Non habuit effectum quia adhuc vivit nec habuit dignitatem, ut est probatum.[199]

### Norwicensis

Item collatio et provisio facte fratri Stephano Iudicis de prepositura monasterii Sancte Marie Nottomen' ordinis Sancti Benedicti, vacante per promotionem abbatis dicti monasterii, fuerunt confirmate vel provisum de novo. Dicitur quod non est talis in Anglia, sed videatur adhuc fortius.

---

[194] In the margin: *solvit.*
[195] A mistake for Lichefeldensis.
[196] In the margin: *debet.*
[197] This item follows the following which is deleted by lines: *Summa universalis recepte de tempore Dominorum Clementis et Innocentii est ducentas octaginta quatuor li. decem et septimo d., cclxxxiiii li. xviii s. v d., ii$^e$ lxxxiii li. xviii s. v d.*
[198] 29 April 1363.
[199] In the margin: *inutilis.*

## Norwicensis

Item ordinatio facta per bone memorie Dominum Ottonum, tunc in partibus Anglie sedis apostolice legatum de una perpetua vicaria in parochiali ecclesia de Borton' (Morton) dicte diocesis fuit confirmata vel provisum de novo. Dicitur quod non habuit effectum, sed est mandatum in iii° et iiii°° et v.

## Lincolniensis

Item Johanni Ditton', clerico Lichfeldensis diocesis, de canonicatu et prebenda quos Willelmus de Askeby, sedis apostolice capellanus,[200] in ecclesia Lincolniensi optinebat, vacantibus per resignationem ipsius in manibus ordinarii aut per assecutionem alterius prebende in dicta ecclesia. Vocatur Leddford maior (Bedford Maior), et est monitus et sequestratus.

## Eboracensis

Item Petro Newbald', bacallario in legibus, de canonicatu et prebenda ecclesie collegiate de Ripon' et prebenda de Multon' (Monkton) in eadem ecclesia, vacantibus per obitum Johannis de Wyndewik'. Prohibitum per breve, ut in restis prioris habetur. Infra est alia que habuit effectum; ista non.[199]

## Herefordensis

Item Johanni Brokenhull', presbytero Herefordensis diocesis, de vicaria perpetua parochialis ecclesie de Burton' (Burrington) dicte diocesis, vacante per resignationem Ade de Alilitia in manibus ordinaria. Est in mandatis tribus, et excommunicatus et sequestratus, tamen expost certificavit episcopus quod non est talis in sua diocesi.

## Lichfeldensis

De canonicatu ecclesie Lichfeldensis et prebenda de Prees in ipsa ecclesia, vacantibus per resignationem Petri alias Johannis de Ayleston' fuit provisum Roberto de Stratton', legum doctori auditori palatii apostolici, xvii kalendas Julii.[201] Non habuit effectum, ut clare aparet in restis prioris Lewensis; ideo dormit quousque appareat de effectu.[199]

Sunt in pagina provisiones inutiles iii; et alia beneficia pro fructibus sunt in restis iiii°°.

## (fol. 13ᵛ) Eliensis

Collatio et provisio facte auctoritate ordinaria iure devoluto de prioratu seu administratione prioratus de Swavesey Eliensis diocesis, a monasterio Sancti Sergii et Bachi Andegavensis (Angers) dependentis, ordinis Sancti Benedicti, per unum religiosum dicti monasterii soliti gubernari, fratri Johanni Walkyn, monacho monasterii Westmonasterii Londondie, fuerunt confirmate vel

provisum de novo xvi kalendas Junii,[202] pro taxa temporalitatis xlviii li. xx d. Prohibitum per breve quia in manu regia; ideo dormit quousque aliud fuerit ordinatum; et quia de patronatu laycali et cetera.[196]

## Cicestrensis

Unita fuit et annexa parochialis ecclesia de Lanncynstr' (Lancing) Cicestrensis diocesis mense et usui ministri et fratrum hospitalis Sancte Trinitatis de Madindem (Muttinden) Cantuariensis, servata portione pro vicaria dicte ecclesie, v kalendas Junii.[203] Non habuit effectum ut certificat episcopus.[204]

## Landavensis

De archidiaconatu ecclesie Landavensis, vacante per resignationem Thome de Eltesle Eliensis diocesis, in utroque iure bacallario, fuit eidem Thome provisum kalendas Julii.[205] Certificat episcopus quod non habuit effectum quia dominus princeps dedit, sede vacante, et possessor est de familia Domini Guidonis de Brian et cetera.[199]

## Dunolmensis

De canonicatu et prebenda sive portione de Bires (Byers) in ecclesia collegiata de Aukesland' (Auckland) Dunolmensis diocesis, vacantibus per mortem Rogeri Blamer in Romana curia defuncti, fuit provisum Rogero de Slateburn', presbytero Eboracensis diocesis, vᵗᵒ idus Junii.[206] Certificat episcopus quod nichil valet, ut in restis folio xiii.[199]

## Eboracensis

Item Rogero de Urlam, presbytero Eboracensis diocesis, de beneficio ecclesiastico, videlicet in ecclesia parochiali Sancte Helene in Staingate (Stonegate, York) Eboracensis diocesis, vacante per mortem Johannis de Beyere vᵗᵒ idus Junii.[206] Non habuit effectum ut in restis folio xiii, et est etiam probatum.[199]

## Cicestrensis

De parochiali ecclesia de Westichenor (West Ichenor) Cicestrensis diocesis, vacante per mortem Rogeri de Lyndon', ultimi rectoris eiusdem, que [207] tanto tempore vacavit quod eius collatio est ad sedem apostolicam legitime devoluta, fuit provisum Roberto Amyas de Bremerbroghton', presbytero Lincolniensis diocesis, v idus Julii.[208] Nondum habuit effectum ut in restis folio xiii.[199]

---

[200] *capellano*, MS.
[201] 15 June 1363.

[202] 17 May 1363.
[203] 28 May 1363.
[204] In the margin: *inutilis videtur*.
[205] 1 July 1363.
[206] 9 June 1363.
[207] *qui*, MS.
[208] 11 July 1363.

### Eboracensis

De perpetua vicaria parochialis ecclesie de Skipton' Incraven' (Skipton in Craven) diocesis dicte, vacante per mortem Willelmi de Draghton', ultimi vicarii eiusdem, a tanto [209] tempore quod eius collatio est ad sedem apostolicam legitime devoluta, fuit provisum Thome filio Johannis filii Matilde Acraliato de Schirburn' in Elneto Eboracensis diocesis. Nondum habuit effectum ut in restis dicti prioris folio xiii.[199]

Resta pagine xlviii li. xx d.; inutiles provisiones sunt vi.

### (fol. 14, xiiii) Saresbiriensis [210]

Item Willelmo Person, presbytero Saresbiriensis diocesis, de parochiali ecclesia de Swyndon' (Swindon) dicte Saresbiriensis diocesis, que per assecutionem vel dimissionem Nicholai Haman, ultimi rectoris eiusdem, tanto tempore vacavit quod eius collatio est ad sedem apostolicam legitime devoluta. Non habuit effectum ut in restis prioris folio xiiii.[199]

### Dunolmensis

Item Waltero Jakes, presbytero Dunolmensis diocesis, de vicaria ecclesie parochialis de Norham dicte diocesis, vacante per mortem Willelmi de Edwyk', ultimi vicarii eiusdem, extra Romanam curiam defuncti, quam Ricardus Kine, monachus et apostata [211] ordinis Cisterciensis per ii annos et amplius occupavit pacifice et indebite. Non habuit effectum quia obiit ante adeptam possessionem, ut in dictis restis habetur folio xiiii⁰.[199]

### Eboracensis [212]

Item Johanni de Baldeston', clerico Eboracensis diocesis, de parochiali ecclesia de Mysen (Misson) dicte diocesis, vacante per resignationem sive dimissionem Johannis de Scalthorp' a tanto tempore quod eius collatio est ad sedem apostolicam legitime devoluta. Appropriata est prioratui de Madterseya (Mattersey), ideo non habuit effectum ut in restis folio xiiii.[199]

Item Willelmo de Wyncornwik', presbytero Eboracensis diocesis, de parochiali ecclesia de Manfeld' (Manfield) dicte diocesis, vacante per resignationem vel per obitum quondam Willelmi de Sturtwell', ultimi rectoris eiusdem, a tanto tempore vacavit quod eius collatio est ad sedem apostolicam legitime devoluta. Appropriata est abbati Sancte Agate (Easby) ut in restis folio xiiii.[199]

Roberto de Wadenham, clerico Lincolniensis diocesis, de parochiali ecclesia de Kayngham (Keyingham) Eboracensis diocesis, vacante per resignationem Wil-

lelmi de Brokeslesby in manibus ordinarii a tanto tempore quod eius collatio est ad sedem apostolicam legitime devoluta. Appropriata est abbati de Melsa (Meaux) ut in restis folio xiiii.[199]

De parochiali ecclesia de Elkesley Eboracensis diocesis, vacante per mortem Johannis Cambrok' a tanto tempore quod eius collatio est ad sedem apostolicam legitime devoluta, fuit provisum Roberto de Overe, clerico Eliensis diocesis. Appropriata est abbati de Welbek' (Welbeck) ut in restis folio xiiii.[199]

### Lichfeldensis

De parochiali ecclesia de Badile (Baddiley) Lichfeldensis diocesis, vacante per resignationem Willelmi Hinkele, ultimi rectoris eiusdem, in manibus ordinarii a tanto tempore quod eius collatio est ad sedem apostolicam legitime devoluta, fuit provisum Rogero de Wedemorton, presbytero Norwicensis, iii[tio] nonas Julii.[213] Non habuit effectum ut certificat episcopus, et est etiam probatum; ideo relaxatus quousque apareat de effectu, vel alias per cameram fuerit ordinatum.[199]

### Eboracensis

Item Roberto de Sathowe, presbytero Eboracensis diocesis, de ecclesia de Aghton' (Aughton), videlicet secundum communem estimationem xl li. sterlingorum. Appropriata est prioratu de Aghton' (Ellerton) ut in restis folio xiiii.[199]

Inutiles provisiones omnes istius pagine esse videntur, scilicet viii.

### (fol. 14ᵛ) Eboracensis [212]

Item Johanni Urlam presbytero de parochiali ecclesia de Usegate (All Saints Pavement in Ousegate) in civitate Eboracensi, que taxatur ad quindecim m. per annum, xv m. Non habuit effectum, ut dicitur in restis prioris folio xiiii.[199]

Item Ade de Thornton', presbytero Eboracensis, de canonicatu et prebenda in ecclesia de Rippon' et prebenda de Munkton' (Monkton) in eadem ecclesia, quorum fructus xlvi li. xiii s. iiii d. secundum taxationem non excedunt, iii[tio] nonas Julii,[213] pro taxa antiqua xlvi li. xiii s. iiii d.[196] Prohibitum per breve ut in restis folio xiiii, et supra in alio loco; debet tamen de ista provisione nisi ista provisio et alia facta cuidam Guillelmo Lond' sit ex eadem vacatione, et tunc esse debeat residuum, quia ille solvit novam taxam xx m. domino priori Lewensi et ostendit quitantiam suam; nunc est obligatus de summa marcarum restantium et cetera. Et solvit xv die Aprilis anno LXXIIII in partem dicte taxe in x m., vi li. xiii s. iiii d.[214]

Item Johanni de Otrington', presbytero Eboracensis diocesis, de parochiali ecclesia de Cato (Cotham) in dicta diocesi, vacante per resignationem Radulphi de

---

[209] *tanta*, MS.

[210] The heading *Anno i Urbani* is repeated at the top of the page.

[211] *apostota*, MS.

[212] This heading is repeated before each of the next three items.

[213] 5 July 1363.

[214] In the margin: *solvit* repeated.

Warewell' a tanto tempore quod eius collatio est ad sedem apostolicam legitime devoluta. Appropriata est prioratui de Forgarton (Thurgarton) ut in restis folio xiiii.[199]

De parochiali ecclesia de Quixlay (Whixley) Eboracensis diocesis, que per obitum Nicholai Sesay a tanto tempore vacavit quod eius collatio est ad sedem apostolicam legitime devoluta, fuit provisum Johanni de Torkesey, bacallario in legibus, vii idus Julii.[215] Non habuit effectum ut in restis folio xiiii.[199]

## Landavensis

Ex causa permutationis fuit provisum Martino de Pirtton'[216] de parochiali ecclesia de Kiltingan (St. Mary Hill) Landavensis diocesis cum prebenda ecclesie collegiate de Glanesey[217] (Glasnay) Exoniensis diocesis.[218] De prebenda est solutum, ut dicitur in libro camere folio xlvi, et quia ecclesia non taxatur, solvit pro medietate veri valoris in duabus vicibus quinque li. xiii s. iiii d., v li. xiii s. iiii d.[219]

## Londoniensis

Item Ade Thebaud' de libera capella de Chelmesford (Chelmsford) Londoniensis diocesis. Non habuit effectum ut infra sequitur in proxima provisione.[199]

## Norwicensis

Et Thome Thebaud, filio Roberti Thebaud de Gupwico, de decanatu rurali Linn' (Lynn) diocesis Norwicensis pro taxa v m. Nondum habuit effectum, ideo relaxatus quousque apareat et cetera.[199]

## Norwicensis

De decanatu rurali de Bodenhall' (Redenhall) Norwicensis diocesis, vacante per liberam resignationem Willelmi Tamworth', clerici Londoniensis, fuit provisum Thome de Draxton' Lincolniensis diocesis. Est sequestratus et excommunicatus.[220]

## Eboracensis

De parochiali ecclesia de Hornesee (Hornsea) Eboracensis diocesis, vacante apud sedem apostolicam per obitum Raymundi de Fargis quondam cardinalis, fuit provisum Nicholao Lavayus iii[tio] idus Augusti.[221] Non habuit effectum, ut certificat episcopus, titulo regio impediente, et probationes sunt in archivis.[222]

Recepta pagine xii li. vi s. viii d.;[223] resta pecunie

xl m. que valent xxvi li. xiii s. iiii d.; et restant fructus unius provisionis i; inutiles sunt v.

## (fol. 15; xv) Eboracensis

Motu proprio fuit provisum domini cardinali G. Seseraugustanensi[224] de canonicatu ecclesie Eboracensis et de prebenda de Masham in eadem ecclesia, vacantibus per obitum cardinalis Magalonensis,[225] xvii kalendas Septembris.[226] Cardinalis Sezaraugustanensis debet, et hic nichil adhuc potuit reperire, quare agat camera contra executores, quia Johannes de Estoc, qui tunc ut firmarius possidebat, dicit quod solvit totum de tempore suo, sed videatur melius per executores eiusdem cardinalis.[220]

## Bangorensis

De parochiali ecclesia Sanctorum Cirici et Julite Lanquile (Llanerfyl?) Bangorensis diocesis, vacante per obitum ultimi rectoris eiusdem extra curiam defuncti, et que tanto tempore vacavit quod eius collatio est secundum statuta Lateranensis consilii ad sedem apostolicam legitime devoluta, fuit provisum Reginaldo de Swynnesmore, presbytero dicte diocesis. Appropriata est abbati de Strata (Strata Florida) ut in restis prioris folio xv.

## Eboracensis

De vicaria perpetua parochialis ecclesie de Cokham (Kirkham) Eboracensis diocesis, vacante per resignationem Willelmi de Slateburn facta in manibus ordinarii, ⟨que⟩ tanto tempore vacavit quod eius collatio est ad sedem apostolicam legitime devoluta, vel alio quovismodo vacet, fuit provisum Simoni de Tunebrugg', presbytero Roffensis diocesis, et dimittet parochialem ecclesiam de Excete Cicestrensis diocesis. Non habuit effectum ut in restis folio xv.[222]

## Eboracensis

De perpetua vicaria parochialis ecclesie de Gilling' Eboracensis diocesis, vacante ex eo quod Garlacus de Clave, clericus Spirensis (Speyer) diocesis, eam detinuit occupatam in presbyterum non promotus infra tempus debitum, vel alio quovismodo, fuit provisum Thome filio Johannis Bristone, clerico Norwicensis diocesis. Non habuit effectum ut in restis folio xv.[222]

## Saresbiriensis

Item Roberto de Felby, clerico Eboracensis diocesis, de parochiali ecclesia Sancte Marie de Wyntebourne Stikelan (Winterborne Stickland) Saresbiriensis diocesis, vacante per mortem Thome Henrici de Chestre in Romana curia defuncti. Non habuit effectum ut in restis folio xv.[222]

---

[215] 9 July 1363.
[216] *Newton'*, Collectorie 13, fol. 165[v].
[217] Follows *Gleseney* deleted by a line.
[218] *vii idus Julii*, Collectorie 13, fol. 165[v].
[219] In the margin: *solvit*
[220] In the margin: *debet*.
[221] 11 August 1363.
[222] In the margin: *inutilis*.
[223] In the margin: *vera*.

[224] William d'Aigrefeuille, priest of S. Maria in Trastevere.
[225] Audoin Aubert, bishop of Maguelone, bishop of Ostia.
[226] 16 August 1363.

### Eboracensis

Provisum fuit Johanni Ulram, presbytero Eboracensis diocesis, de parochiali ecclesia curata Omnium Sanctorum in Usegate (All Saints Pavement in Ousegate, York), vacante in curia per mortem Simonis Warde. Non habuit effectum ut in restis predictis folio xv.[222]

### Assavensis

Item Lewelmo de Bretonia, canonico Menevensi, de parochiali ecclesia Sancti Ewdelani (Dolwyddelan) Assavensis diocesis, vacante per liberam resignationem sive dimissionem factam per Theodericum natum Johannis Oweyn, ultimum rectorem [227] eiusdem, xi kalendas Septembris,[228] pro taxa v li. Solvit dictas quinque li. penultima die Novembris anno LXXIII, v li.[219]

Recepta pagine quinque li., v li.;[229] resta pagine fructus beneficii unius; inutiles [230] provisiones sunt vi.

### (fol. 15ᵛ) Saresbiriensis

Confirmata fuit auctoritate apostolica unio facta auctoritate ordinaria de consensu capituli de parochiali ecclesia de Harewell' (Harwell) Saresbiriensis diocesis, que de patronatu Edwardi, primogeniti regis Anglie, Wallie principis, existebat, et ipsius principis infra castrum suum de Wallingford' dicte diocesis, iii kalendas Septembris,[231] pro taxa xl m. Solvit die v [232] Octobris anno LXXIII in viginti m. xiii li. vi s. viii d., et habet terminum Pasche de resta xiii li. vi s. viii d. Item solvit plus die xxi Martii in plenam solutionem taxe xiii li. **vi s. viii d.**[233]

### Norwicensis

Item Willelmo Malteby, presbytero Eboracensis diocesis, de parochiali ecclesia de Synterley (Blakeney or Glandford) Norwicensis diocesis, vacante per mortem ultimi rectoris eiusdem, que tanto tempore vacavit quod eius collatio est ad sedem apostolicam legitime devoluta.[234]

Item Andree de Borewell', presbytero Norwicensis diocesis, de parochiali ecclesia de Sniterleye dicte diocesis, vacante per mortem Willelmi Mayner de Silney extra Romanam curiam defuncti, que tanto tempore vacavit quod eius collatio est ad sedem apostolicam legitime devoluta, vel alio quovismodo, et dimittet ecclesiam parochialem de Rishull' (Rishangles) dicte diocesis.

Non habuerunt iste provisiones,[235] ut etiam habetur in restis prioris folio xv.

### Norwicensis

Item Thome Draper, presbytero Londoniensis diocesis, de parochiali ecclesia de Frenge (Frenze) Norwicensis, vacante per liberam resignationem Willelmi de Colney in manibus ordinarii factam, in tanto tempore vacavit quod eius collatio est ad sedem apostolicam legitime devoluta, xi kalendas Septembris.[236] Appropriata est prioratui Norvicensi ut in restis folio xv, et sic non habuit effectum.[222]

### Dunolmensis

Item Ade de Thornton,' presbytero Eboracensis diocesis, de canonicatu et prebenda seu portione ecclesie collegiate de Derlington' (Darlington) Dunolmensis diocesis, vacantibus per obitum Willelmi de Kyldesby extra Romanam curiam defuncti, si tanto tempore vacaverit quod eius collatio est ad sedem apostolicam legitime devoluta. Nondum habuit effectum, ut certificat episcopus.[222]

### Eliensis

Subrogatus fuit Walterus Bakton', magister in artibus, in omni iure quod competebat quondam Henrici Harewedene in ecclesia parochiali de Hadenham (Haddenham) dicte Eliensis diocesis, super qua dum viveret in Romana curia litigabat, et dimittet parochialem ecclesiam de Wygeresham (Wittersham) Cantuariensis diocesis et unum beneficium de infrascriptis, videlicet prebendam Cicestrensem vel canonicatum sub expectatione prebende dicte ecclesie Sancti Johannis de Beverlaco Eboracensis diocesis, xi kalendas Octobris,[237] pro taxa iiiiˣˣ li. Dominus Henricus Penhal, qui est cansellarius scaquarii regis, possidet, et fecit quod solverunt executores defuncti in tribus vicibus sexaginta li., lx li. Item solverunt die xxi Januarii viginti li., xx li.[238]

Recepta pagine cvi li. xiii s. iiii d.;[239] inutiles provisiones sunt iii.

### (fol. 16, xvi) Anno secundo Urbani

### Eboracensis

Unio et incorporatio dudum facte [240] per archiepiscopum Eboracensem de parochiali ecclesia Colston' communiter Karkeston' nuncupata (Car-Colston) conventui et monasterio de Radeford' [241] (Worksop) ordinis Sancti Augustini Eboracensis, fuerunt confirmate vel provisum de novo viii idus Octobris,[242] pro taxa xvii li.

---

[227] *ultimi rectoris*, MS.
[228] *22 August 1363.*
[229] In the margin: *vera.*
[230] Followed by *sunt* deleted by a line.
[231] *30 August 1363.*
[232] *die* repeated MS.
[233] In the margin: *solvit* repeated.
[234] In the margin bracketed against this item and the next: *inutiles.*

[235] Namely, this and the preceding provision.
[236] *22 August 1363.*
[237] *21 September 1363.*
[238] In the margin: *solvit* repeated.
[239] In the margin: *vera.*
[240] *facta*, MS.
[241] *Werkesopp*, Collectorie 13, fol. 165ᵛ.
[242] *8 October 1363.* This and the next two items belong in the first year.

vi s. viii d. Solvit in duabus vicibus duodecim li. Item solvit die xxviii Aprilis in plenam solutionem taxe v li. vi s. viii d., et sic totum.[238]

## Herefordensis

De canonicatu et prebenda de Morton' (Moreton Magna) in ecclesia Herefordensi, vacantibus per consecrationem Simonis de Sudbur' electi Londoniensis, fuit provisum Johanni Godewik', clerico Norwicensis baccallario in legibus, xiiii kalendas Novembris.[243] Est prohibitum, et supra in alio loco quia dicitur quod non habuit effectum quia possessor est regius, sed videatur bene, et est in mandato.[244]

## Eboracensis

Unio et incorporatio facte per archiepiscopum Eboracensem de parochiali ecclesia de Hemyngburgh (Hemingborough) Eboracensis diocesis priori et capitulo Dunolmensibus, fuerunt auctoritate apostolica confirmate vel provisum de novo, xi kalendas Novembris.[245] Nondum habuit effectum quia ad huc vivit primus possessor, videlicet Dominus Alanus de Sutlington', sed videatur cum habuerit effectum.[222]

Completum est de anno primo.

## Norwicensis

De parochiali ecclesia de Sudbur' Norwicensis diocesis, vacante ex eo quod Henricus de Campedene cancellariam ecclesie Londoniensis est pacifice assecutus, fuit provisum Thome de Bakton', baccallario in legibus, x kalendas Decembris.[246] Ante providetur eidem et ibi solvit, ut dicitur in restis prioris folio xvi, et ista provisio et alia que est in folio sequenti non debentur ut videtur, quia eidem persone facte et ex eadem vacatione; reformando totiens gratiam fuerunt facte.[222]

## Lincolniensis

Motu proprio fuit provisum Domino Johanni, titulo Sancti Marchi presbytero cardinali, de parochiali ecclesia de Edburgbury (Adderbury) Lincolniensis diocesis vi[to] kalendas Decembris.[247] Cardinalis est, et nichil hic de suo reperitur.[244]

## Herefordensis

De canonicatu et prebenda ecclesie Herefordensis, vacantibus per consecrationem Thome electi Cicestrensis, fuit provisum Nicholao de Caddesden', legum doctori, et dimittet prebendam Lichfeldensem, vii kalendas Decembris.[248] Ista provisio debet cancellari quia fuit infra annum cum sequenti, de qua debetur et cetera, ut in restis folio xvi habetur.[222]

## Herfrodensis

Item de eadem prebenda, que vocatur de Mortan minor (Moreton Minor), fuit provisum Willelmo Bello, scolari in legibus, vi kalendas Decembris.[247] Taxatur decem li. Debet pro resta vi li., ut continetur in restis domini prioris, vi li. Est in mandato ad denuntiandum et sequestrandum. Solvit xiii die Aprilis anno LXXIIII[to] in partem dicte reste quinque li., v li. Folio ix in breveto.[249]

Recepta pagine xxii li. vi s. viii d.;[250] restant provisiones iii; inutiles sunt ii; restant in pecunia xx s.

## (fol. 16[v]) Exoniensis [251]

De parochiali ecclesia de Newaton' Sancti Cirici (Newton, St. Cyres) Exoniensis diocesis, que, post liberam resignationem Johannis de Linham, ultimi rectoris eiusdem, in manibus domini episcopi Exoniensis factam, tanto tempore vacavit quod eius collatio est ad sedem apostolicam legitime devoluta, licet per Willelmum de Malton', qui se gerit pro vicario eiusdem, ipsam detinet indebite occupatam, fuit provisum Johanni Deyns, clerico Lincolniensis diocesis, iiii[to] kalendas Decembris.[252] Appropriata est prioratui de Plumton' (Plympton), ut in restis folio xvi etiam habetur.[222]

## Cantuariensis

De parochiali ecclesia de Bisschopesburn' (Bishopsbourne) Cantuariensis diocesis, vacante eo quod Willelmus Tyngull' ipsam nuper obtinens, aliud beneficium incompatibile in ecclesia Wellensi est, ut dicitur, auctoritate apostolica assecutus pacifice, fuit provisum Johanni Digg', presbytero Cantuariensis diocesis, nonas Decembris.[253] Ista provisio non habuit effectum quia ille possessor non habuit beneficium incompatibile, sed post dictus Johannes habuit eam titulo permutationis facte cum alio, ut est clare probatum.[222]

## Dunolmensis

De parochiali ecclesia de Wytebern (Whitburn) Dunolmensis diocesis, vacatura cum Johannes de Appulby decanatum Londoniensis fuit pacifice assecutus, fuit provisum Ricardo de Wynchcombe, presbytero Wygorniensis diocesis, xix kalendas Januarii,[254] debet de resta

---

[243] 19 October 1363.

[244] In the margin: *debet*.

[245] 22 October 1363.

[246] 22 November 1363.

[247] 26 November 1363.

[248] 25 November 1363.

[249] In the margin: *solvit*. The brevetum is a summary by the collector of the receipts and payments recorded more fully in the present account. It occupies folios 158[v] to 187[v]. The reference should be to fol. x (169). The entry in the brevetum is briefer than the above entry and adds nothing to it.

[250] In the margin: *vera*.

[251] Preceded by the following item deleted by lines: *Herefordensis. De canonicatu et prebenda ecclesie Herefordensis, vacantibus prout supra, fuit provisum Willelmo Bello, scolari in legibus, vi kalendas Decembris. Taxatur x li. Debet de resta vi li.* In the margin: *Supra est; ideo hic cancellata.*

[252] 28 November 1363.

[253] 5 December 1363.

[254] 14 December 1363.

xxiii li. vi s. viii d. Solvit in tribus vicibus dictas viginti tres li. vi s. viii d.[249]

### Dunolmensis

De ecclesia de Wermouth (Bishop-Wearmouth) Dunolmensis diocesis, vacante eo quod Willelmus Newport eandem ecclesiam curatam et ecclesiam curatam de Spafford' (Spofforth) Eboracensis diocesis, non unitas aut annexas sed diversas, occupavit et possedit simul per duos annos et ultra contra constitutionem *Execrabilem*, fuit provisum Willelmo Ardern, magistro in artibus Lincolniensis diocesis, et dimittet parochialem ecclesiam de Chestriton (Chesterton) eiusdem diocesis, xv kalendas Januarii.[255] Ista provisio non habuit effectum, ut habetur in restis folio xvi, et nunc possidet dominus cardinalis Carcassonensis.[256]

### Lichfeldensis

De parochiali ecclesia de Estlymelyngton' alias Lymelyngton' Hasting' (Leamington Hastings) Lichfeldensis diocesis, vacante per obitum ultimi rectoris eiusdem extra Romanam curiam defuncti, que tanto tempore vacavit quod eius collatio est ad sedem apostolicam legitime devoluta, fuit provisum Ricardo Tyscho, baccallario in decretibus, et dimittet parochialem ecclesiam de Herlegh' (Hartley) Roffensis diocesis iiii idus Januarii.[257] Non habuit effectum ut in restis folio xvi.[258]

### Menevensis

De canonicatu et prebenda ecclesie collegiate de Aburwill' (Abergwili) Menevensis diocesis, vacantibus per resignationem Philipi de Bellocampo, fuit provisum Ricardo Poger, clerico Lincolniensis diocesis, ii[do] kalendas Februarii.[259] Certificat episcopus quod non habuit effectum.[260]

Recepta pagine viginti tres li. vi s. viii d., xxiii li. vi s. viii d.; inutiles provisiones sunt vi.

### (fol. 17, xvii) Norwicensis [261]

De parochiali ecclesia de Synterlee (Blakeney or Glandford) Norwicensis diocesis, vacante per obitum Walteri Maynor de Tylneye, que tanto tempore vacavit quod eius collatio ad sedem apostolicam legitime devoluta, fuit provisum Willelmo Bello, et dimittet parochialem ecclesiam de Stanford' Saresbiriensis diocesis ac canonicatum et prebendam Herefordenses nuper sibi

collatas v kalendas Martii.[262] Ante bis providetur alteri, et nulla habuit effectum ut in restis folio xvi.[258]

### Eboracensis

De parochiali ecclesia de Brantigham (Brantingham) Eboracensis diocesis, vacante eo quod Willelmus Strode ipsam per annum et ultra cessante legitimo impedimento vel dispensatione non obtenta in presbyterum non promotus, fuit provisum Johanni de Toresby, legum doctori, et dimittet parochialem ecclesiam de Lileford' (Lilford) Lincolniensis diocesis xvi kalendas Aprilis.[263] Non habuit effectum ut in restis prioris folio xvii.[258]

### Lichfeldensis

De parochiali ecclesia de Derington' (Warrington) Lichfeldensis diocesis, vacante per mortem quondam Johannis de Stanfordham extra curiam defuncti, a tanto tempore vacavit quod eius collatio est ad sedem apostolicam legitime devoluta, fuit provisum Johanni Par seniori, clerico [264] dicte diocesis, nonas Aprilis.[265] Non habuit effectum quia de patronatu domini ducis Lencastrie, nec tunc etiam vacavit, ut est probatum.[258]

### Dunolmensis

De canonicatu ecclesie de Aukland (Auckland) et prebenda de Bires (Byers) in eadem ecclesia Dunolmensis diocesis, vacantibus per obitum Rogeri de Blamer in Romana curia defuncti, fuit provisum Thome Kokyn dicte diocesis, ii[do] nonas Aprilis,[266] taxata ad xvi li. Pauperima est, nec est aliquis possessor, nec sunt fructus adhuc quia vacat ibi agricultura et cetera.[267]

### Eboracensis

Item Willelmo Wasselyn, clerico Lincolniensis diocesis, de parochiali ecclesia de Feriby (North Ferriby) Eboracensis diocesis, vacante per mortem Roberti de Bidelington', ultimi rectoris eiusdem extra curiam defuncti, que tanto tempore vacavit quod eius collatio secundum statuta Lateranensis consilii est ad sedem apostolicam legitime devoluta, ii[do] nonas Aprilis.[266] Non habuit effectum quia est appropriata prioratui de Ferbi (North Ferriby) ut in restis folio xvii.[258]

### Londoniensis

De novo fuit provisum Johanni de Langedone de parochiali ecclesia de Alta Roting' (High Roding) Londoniensis diocesis, quam per annum et ultra pacifice tenuit in presbyterum non promotus, et fuit habilitatus, xviii kalendas Junii,[268] pro taxa xii li.[269] Est in mandato

---

[255] 18 December 1363.

[256] Stephen Aubert, bishop of Carcassonne, deacon of S. Maria in Aquiro. In the margin: *inutilis*.

[257] 10 January 1364.

[258] In the margin: *inutilis*.

[259] 31 January 1364.

[260] Followed by *sed videatur melius* deleted by a line. In the margin: *inutilis*.

[261] The heading *Anno ii Urbani* is repeated at the top of the page.

[262] 26 February 1364.

[263] 17 March 1364.

[264] *clerico seniori*, MS.

[265] 5 April 1364.

[266] 4 April 1364.

[267] In the margin: *debet*.

[268] 15 May 1364.

[269] *xii li.* repeated MS.

⟨ad⟩ sequestrandum et excommunicandum, et est infra alia provisio folio xxvi[267]

## Lichfeldensis

De prioratu monasterii Salopie (Shrewsbury), vacante per obitum Humifridi Rogeri de Omfraston', quondam prioris eiusdem in Romana curia defuncti, fuit provisum Johanni Parle, monacho dicti monasterii, xii kalendas Julii.[270] Prioratus claustralis est et nichil habet certum, ut etiam habetur in restis folio xvii.[271]

## Wellensis

Acceptatio facta vigore litterarum apostolicarum per Willelmum Tyngull', in utroque iure doctorem, et collatio subsecuta de archidiaconatu Tauntton' in ecclesia Wellensi, cui prebenda est annexa, vacante per obitum Roberti Hereward' extra curiam defuncti, fuerunt confirmate vel provisum de novo, et dimittet parochialem ecclesiam de Bisshopesbourn' (Bishopsbourne) Cantuariensis diocesis, ac canonicatum et prebendam ecclesie Sancti Karentoci (Crantock) Exoniensis diocesis, vi idus Augusti.[272] Non habuit effectum quia Thomas Arundelle tenet titulo regio, ut est probatum; ideo fuit relaxatus quousque apareat de effectu vel alias per cameram fuerit ordinatum; et dictus Willelmus non est prosecutus suam gratiam predictam adhuc et cetera; set videatur nunc.[267]

Resta pecunie xxviii li.; inutiles provisiones sunt v; restant fructus provisionum ii.

## (fol. 17ᵛ) Lincolniensis

Ex causa permutationis fuit provisum Willelmo nato Willelmi de Wadyngton' de Haneworth' de parochiali ecclesia de Syweleby (Shoby) dicte diocesis iii kalendas Augusti.[273] Est in mandato sub sequestro et excommunicatione.

## Lincolniensis

Ex causa permutationis fuit provisum Johanni Messing' de perpetua vicaria de Luigdon' (Luton) Lincolniensis diocesis viii idus Augusti.[274] Est in iii mandato.

## Londoniensis

Et Willelmo Haddon' de libera capella de Chelmesford' (Chelmsford) Londoniensis diocesis viii idus Augusti.[274] Dicitur quod nil valet, et semper mandatum.

## Herefordensis

De canonicatu et prebenda de Hondreton' (Hunderton) in ecclesia Herefordensi, vacantibus per privationem Nicholai Heeth' per dominum papam propter pluralitatem et multitudinem beneficiorum que optinebat, fuit provisum Nicholao de Wratton', baccallario in legibus, iiii kalendas Septembris.[275] Non habuit effectum, et est ita clare probatum, et probationes sunt in archivis.[271]

## Dunolmensis

Collatio facta ex causa permutationis Roberto de Waromp' de parochiali ecclesia de Wessyngton' (Washington) Dunolmensis diocesis auctoritate ordinaria, non obstante defectu natalium quem patitur de soluto genitus et soluta, fuit confirmata vel provisum de novo. Non habuit effectum, ut in restis prioris Lewensis dicitur folio xvii.[271]

## Lincolniensis

De parochiali ecclesia de Slapton' Lincolniensis diocesis, vacante cum Matheus de Assheton' canonicatum et prebendam ecclesie Eboracensis fuit pacifice assecutus, fuit provisum Ricardo Croxton', clerico Eliensis diocesis, kalendas Octobris anno secundo.[276] Dormit quia ad huc vivit dictus Matheus et possidet dictam ecclesiam, quare fuit relaxatus usque quo apareat de effectu gratie vel alias per cameram fuerit ordinatum.

## Lincolniensis

Motu proprio fuit provisum Domino H. cardinali Ostiensi [277] de canonicatu et prebenda in ecclesia Lincolniensi, vacantibus per obitum cardinalis Petragoricensis, xi kalendas Novembris,[278] pro taxa clxviii m. Cardinalis Hostiensis est, et fuit scriptum per cameram quod se sive ab exsecutoribus et cetera.[279]

## Norwicensis

Collatio et provisio facte auctoritate ordinaria Thome de Bakton', baccallario in legibus, de parochiali ecclesia Sancti Gregorii de Sudbur', tunc vacante ex eo quod Henricus de Campeden' ipsam obtinens [280] cancellariam ecclesie Londoniensis fuit pacifice assecutus, etiam si per simplicem resignationem dicti Henrici vacaverit, fuerunt confirmate vel provisum de novo, vii kalendas Novembris.[281] Ante bis providetur eidem, ut in restis prioris dicitur folio xvii, et de prima solvit ut ibi dicitur. Cave tamen qualiter viditur, quia nondum aliud scire potui.[271]

## Exoniensis

De parochiali ecclesia de Essewat' (Ashwater) Exoniensis diocesis, vacante per obitum Ricardi Griffardi extra Romanam curiam defuncti, fuit provisum ⟨Willelmo de⟩ Coddeworth, clerico dicte diocesis, nisi sit

[270] 20 June 1364.
[271] In the margin: *inutilis*.
[272] 8 August 1364.
[273] 30 July 1364.
[274] 6 August 1364.

[275] 29 August 1364.
[276] 1 October 1364.
[277] Elias de S. Eredio.
[278] 22 October 1364.
[279] In the margin: *debet; cardinalis Hostiensis*.
[280] *metuens*, MS.
[281] 26 October 1364.

alteri specialiter ius quesitum, iii$^{tio}$ nonas Novembris.[282] Ante providetur eidem infra eundem annum, et pro alia ibi solvit, ut dicitur in restis prioris folio xlii, et sic ista debet cansellari.[283]

Resta pecunie clxviii m., valent cxii li.; in recepta pagine nichil; inutiles provisiones sunt iiii; restant fructus de provisionibus v.

(fol. 18, xviii) Completum est de anno secundo.

### iii$^{us}$ annus Urbani
### Dunolmensis

De parochiali ecclesia de Wermouth' (Bishop-Wearmouth) Dunolmensis diocesis, vacante per lapsum temporis concessi Willelmo de Neuport de ipsa retinendi cum quadam parochiali ecclesia, fuit provisum Willelmo de Ardern, magistro in artibus, et dimittet parochialem ecclesiam de Chestirton' (Chesterton) Lincolniensis diocesis, xv kalendas Decembris.[284] Supra providetur eidem et infra alteri, et nulla habuit effectum, ut dicitur in restis, sed videatur bene, quia supra folio dicitur quod nunc possidet dominus cardinalis Carcassonensis.[285]

### Dunolmensis

De hospitali Sancte Johannis Baptiste extra portas civitatis Dunolmensis in Ybernia, quod illicite tenet Willelmus Gerardi, frater dicti hospitalis, fuit provisum Henrico Radulphi, fratri dicti hospitalis, xv kalendas Decembris,[284] Non est talis in regno Anglie, et sic etiam dicitur in restis.[283]

### Londoniensis

De parochiali ecclesia de Hakeney (Hackney) Londoniensis ⟨diocesis⟩, vacante cum Johannes Thomas de Paxton', sedis apostolice capellanus, dignitatem in ecclesia Wellensi fuit pacifice assecutus, fuit provisum Waltero de Multon', presbytero Norwicensis diocesis, et dimittet parochialem ecclesiam de Chivele (Cheveley) diocesis Norwicensis, vii idus Decembris.[286] Dicitur in restis prioris quod non habuit effectum.[283]

### Saresbiriensis

Provisio facta auctoritate apostolica Henrico de Wynterton', baccallario in legibus, de canonicatu et prebenda Saresbiriensibus, quos Ricardus de Norwico defunctus per nonnullos annos pacifice possedit, etiam si vacent per obitum Thome de Clypston' extra curiam defuncti, fuit [287] confirmata vel provisum de novo. Non habuit effectum, ut est clare probatum; ideo dormit ad huc.[283]

### Exoniensis

De canonicatu et prebenda ecclesie collegiate de Glaseney (Glasnay) Exoniensis diocesis, vacantibus cum Stephanus Pempel dignitatem ecclesie Wellensis fuit pacifice assecutus, fuit provisum Thome Woderove, presbytero Eboracensi baccallario in decretibus, vi idus Februarii.[288] Non taxatur. Solvit die xxi Junii pro medietate veri valoris Dominus Richardus Bokelli possessor eiusdem, salvo iure pluris super maiorem valentiam, viginti s., xx s.[289]

### Lincolniensis

Collatio et provisio facte auctoritate apostolica Thome de Tetteford', clerico Lincolniensis diocesis, de parochiali ecclesia de Hagwortyngham (Hagworthingham) Lincolniensis diocesis, vacante per assecutionem ecclesie parochialis de Wetyngs (Wetheringsett) Norwicensis diocesis collate Johanni Swinnesheved, quam dictus Thomas diu possedit pacifice, licet felicis recordationis Dominus Innocentius papa vi$^{us}$ quidam Herewico Romelyn clerico Cantuariensis diocesis, dictam ecclesiam sic vacantem providit, qui, litteris super hoc non confectis, extra Romanam curiam decessit, fuerunt confirmate vel provisum de novo. Ante providetur eidem et ibi solvit, ut dicitur in restis domini prioris folio xviii.[283]

### Cicestrensis

De custodia hospitalis domus Beate Marie Cicestrensis, vacante per privationem Johannis de Dountton', clerici dicte diocesis, per dominum papam factam, fuit provisum Simoni Bate, presbytero Lincolniensis diocesis, nonas Martii.[290] Non habuit effectum ista privatio, et est clare probatum quia non fuit executa.[283]

Recepta pagine viginti s., xx s.; inutiles provisiones sunt vi.

### (fol. 18$^v$) Exoniensis

De canonicatu et prebenda ecclesie collegiate Beati Thome Glaseney (Glasnay) Exoniensis diocesis, vacantibus cum Stephanus Pempel ipsos dimisit, fuit provisum Petro Tricrugov, presbytero dicte diocesis, et dimittet parochialem ecclesiam Sancti Wynwilay (Landewednack) dicte diocesis. Ista non habuit effectum quia alia est supra folio precedenti que habuit effectum, et ibi solvit, et est eadem vacatio et eidem persone facta collatio ut ibi.[283]

### Eliensis

De parochiali ecclesia de Ditton' (Fen Ditton) Eliensis diocesis, vacante dum Robertus de Vaghtorp' dignitatem, personatum vel officium in ecclesia Exoniensi fuit pacifice assecutus, fuit provisum Thome de Hornyngesheed Norwicensis diocesis, legum doctori. Non habuit effectum, ut est clare probatum, et probationes sunt in archivis, quare fuit relaxatus quousque

---

[282] 3 November 1364.
[283] In the margin: *inutilis.*
[284] 17 November 1364.
[285] Stephen Aubert, deacon of S. Maria in Aquiro. In the margin: *inutilis.*
[286] 7 December 1364.
[287] *fuerunt*, MS.

---

[288] 8 February 1365.
[289] In the margin: *solvit.*
[290] 7 March 1365.

apareat de effectu gratie vel alias per cameram fuerit ordinatum ut in forma.²⁸³

### Eliensis

De parochiali ecclesia de Stretham Eliensis, vacante dum Robertus de Stratton', auditor palatii apostolici, dignitatem, personatum vel officium in ecclesia Lincolniensi fuit pacifice assecutus, fuit provisum Roberto de Fordham, presbytero Norwicensis diocesis, idus Maii.²⁹¹ Nondum habuit effectum, nec auditor habet nec habuit aliquid in ipsa ecclesia, ut est clare probatum; ideo dormit et cetera.²⁸³

### Karleolensis

De parochiali ecclesia de Wiggoton' ²⁹² (Wigton) Karleolensis diocesis, vacante per obitum quondam Gilberti de Wygeton' extra Romanam curiam defuncti, si tanto tempore vacavit quod eius collatio sit ad sedem apostolicam legitime devoluta, fuit provisum Ricardo de Tirneby, presbytero dicte diocesis, et dimittet vicariam parochialis ecclesie de Newburn' diocesis Dunolmensis, ii^do idus Maii anno ii^do.²⁹³ Appropriata est prioratui de Alcoletam (Holmcultram), ut in restis prioris folio xviii.²⁸³

### Cantuariensis

Collatio et provisio facte auctoritate ordinaria Willelmo Reed' de prepositura ecclesie collegiate de Wyngham (Wingham) Cantuariensis diocesis, vacante per mortem Johannis Teverleye extra curiam defuncti, fuerunt confirmate vel provisum de novo, xv kalendas Maii,²⁹⁴ pro taxa lx m. Solvit episcopus Cicestrensis qui nunc est die xvii Julii anno domini et cetera LXXIII post monitiones et multiplicitatem requisitionum sibi factas in lx m., xl li., protestato quod si citra Pasca haberet declarationem camere quod non teneatur, quod camera sibi restituat.²⁹⁵

### Laoniensis

De archidiaconatu Laoniensi (Killaloe), vacante ex eo quod Thomas Otormachayn beneficium incompatibile una cum dicto archidiaconatu, dispensatione legitima non obtenta, contra canonum statuta tenuit tanto tempore quod eius collatio est ad sedem apostolicam legitime devoluta, fuit provisum Donato Ocenn', et dimittet prebendas dicte ecclesie et Cansellensis (Cashel), xi kalendas Maii.²⁹⁶ Non est in regno Anglie.²⁹⁷

### Saresbiriensis

Ex causa permutationis fuit provisum Johanni Turk', presbytero Wellensis diocesis, de vicaria perpetua de Jatmynstr' (Yetminster) Saresbiriensis diocesis, non taxata. Solvit die xii Maii anno LXXIII pro medietate veri valoris in quatuor m., liii s. iiii s.²⁹⁵

### Wellensis

Et Willelmo Bouefannit de vicaria perpetua de Stanntton' Drewe (Stanton Drew) diocesis Wellensis ix kalendas Maii,²⁹⁸ non taxata. Solvit pro medietate veri valoris xiii Maii anno LXXIII in quatuor m. ex compositione liii s. iiii d.²⁹⁵ Dicitur tamen in restis prioris folio xviii quod predicte provisiones non habuerunt effectum, sed post hoc non obstante solverunt ut prefertur.²⁹⁹

Recepta pagine quadraginta quinque li. vi s. viii d., xlv li. vi s. viii d.; ³⁰⁰ inutiles provisiones sunt in pagina ista vi.

### (fol. 19, xix) Eboracensis ³⁰¹

Collatio et provisio facte auctoritate litterarum apostolicarum per felicis recordationis Domini Clementis pape vi^ti Johanni de Newham presbytero de parochiali ecclesia de Merton' Cravene (Marton in Craven) Eboracensis diocesis fuerunt confirmate vel provisum de novo v kalendas Maii.³⁰² Certificat archiepiscopus ³⁰³ quod non habuit effectum.²⁹⁷

### Wygorniensis

Et Willelmo de Henereth' de parochiali ecclesia de Staunton' ³⁰⁴ iiii^tio idus Augusti,³⁰⁵ pro taxa iiii li. vi s. viii d. Est in mandato, et alias in forma.

### Lincolniensis

De prebenda ecclesie collegiate Lincolniensis, vacante per obitum Raymundi Pelegrini, collectoris apostolici extra curiam defuncti, fuit provisum episcopo Albanensi cardinali,³⁰⁶ nonas Septembris.³⁰⁷ Cardinalis Albanensis est, et nichil de suo hic reperitur.

### Eboracensis

Collatio et provisio facte fratri Johanni Mateleye, monacho de prioratu Sancti Johannis Ewangeliste de

---

²⁹¹ 15 May 1365.
²⁹² Over *Stretham* deleted by a line.
²⁹³ 14 May 1364.
²⁹⁴ 17 April 1365.
²⁹⁵ In the margin: *solvit*.
²⁹⁶ 21 April 1365.
²⁹⁷ In the margin: *inutilis*.

²⁹⁸ 23 April 1365.
²⁹⁹ In the margin: *exploratum est ex post*.
³⁰⁰ In the margin: *vera*.
³⁰¹ The heading *iii anno Urbani* is repeated at the top of the page.
³⁰² 27 April 1365.
³⁰³ Over *episcopus* not deleted.
³⁰⁴ The church in question is Staunton in Gloucestershire whose tax was iv li. vi s. viii d. (The identification of this church with Stockton in Wilts. on pages 292 and 343 is erroneous.)
³⁰⁵ 11 August 1365.
³⁰⁶ Peter Itherii, bishop of Dax.
³⁰⁷ 5 September 1365.

Pontefracto (Pontefract) Cluniacensis ordinis Eboracensis diocesis, licet aliquando habitum suum, non tamen
causa apostatandi,[308] dimiserit, fuerunt confirmate vel
provisum de novo, iiii[to] idus Septembris.[309] Non habuit
effectum quia obiit ante adeptam possessionem ut in
restis folio xix, quare dormit usque aliud sit ordinatum
per cameram.[297]

### Londoniensis

De parochiali ecclesia de Harwe (Harrow) Londoniensis diocesis, vacante per obitum Raymundi Pelegrini
extra curiam defuncti, fuit provisum Johanni Bokingham, et dimittet parochialem ecclesiam in Stokton'
(Stockton) Saresbiriensis diocesis, pridie idus Septembris.[310] Ipsemet Johannes possidet titulo regio, omissa
via reservationis predicte, quia sede Cantuariensi tunc
vacante rex vendicat sibi ius conferendi, quare dormit,
sed videat camera quid agendum, quia non vult
solvere.[297]

Completum est de anno tertio.

### Saresbiriensis

De canonicatu et prebenda ecclesie Saresbiriensis,
vacantibus per obitum Raymundi Pelegrini, collectoris
apostolici, fuit provisum Thome Paxton', auditori palatii,
et dimittet archidiaconatum Barkschir' in dicta ecclesia
quem nondum possedit, v[to] idus Decembris.[311] Obiit in
curia Romana, et ibi dominus cardinalis Cantuariensis [312] de mandato apostolico distribuit bona sua, nec
potest bene agi contra possessorem, quia dominus cardinalis de Agrefolio [313] possidet.

### Saresbiriensis

De archidiaconatu de Barkschir' fuit provisum Johanni Harewell', et dimittet archidiaconatum Wygorniensem, iiii[to] idus Decembris,[314] pro taxa liiii li.[315] Est
nunc episcopus Bathoniensis, et licet pluries requisitus,
non solvit ad huc, et dominus de Agrefolio [313] est nunc
possessor, quia.[316] Solvit xii die Julii anno LXXIIII
quatuordecim li., xiiii li. Est in breveto folio ix.[317]

In recepta pagine xiiii li.; [318] resta pecunie in secunda
et ultima provisionibus xliiii li. vi s. viii d.; et sunt tres
provisiones inutiles iii; et restant fructus duarum provisionum ii.

[308] an opostata with a general sign of abbreviation over each
word, MS.
[309] 10 September 1365.
[310] 12 September 1365.
[311] 9 December 1365.
[312] Simon Langham, priest of S. Sisto.
[313] William d'Aigrefeuille (the younger), priest of S. Stefano
al Monte Celio.
[314] 10 December 1365.
[315] In the margin: debet.
[316] Followed by two words which have been erased.
[317] In the margin: solvit.
[318] Follows nichil deleted. In the margin: Vera.

### (fol. 19[v]) Exoniensis

De canonicatu et prebenda ecclesie Sancti Karentoci
(Crantock) Exoniensis diocesis, vacantibus cum Johannes Tyngull' canonicatum et prebendam ac dignitatem, personatum vel officium in ecclesia Wellensi fuerit
pacifice assecutus, fuit provisum Willelmo alias Thome
⟨Cride⟩ pridie idus Decembris.[319] Non habuit effectum;
immo fuit provisum per mortem dicti Willelmi alteri
infra folio lxvii in libro recepte.[320]

### Exoniensis, Wellensis, Menevensis

De uno beneficiorum infrascriptorum, videlicet thesaurarie, canonicatus et prebende ecclesie Exoniensis ac
canonicatuum et prebendarum Wellensium et Mene-
vensium, vacaturo dum Robertus Middelond' prebendam
ecclesie Eboracensis fuerit [321] pacifice assecutus, fuit
provisum Ricardo Tischo, bacallario in decretis, et
dimittet medietatem ecclesie de Wilston' (Ufton), que
in ecclesia Lichfeldensi prebenda dicitur, super qua in
palatio litigat, vel parochialem de Herlegh' (Hartley)
Roffensis diocesis, iiii[to] kalendas Januarii.[322] Prohibitum est per breve regium de thesauraria et prebenda
Exoniensibus ut in restis xix folio; de prebendis Wellensi et Menevensi certificant episcopi quod non habuit
effectum dicta provisio, tamen in processu sunt moniti,
et se defendunt adhuc in camera.[315]

### Saresbiriensis

De parochiali ecclesia de Stokton' (Stockton) Saresbiriensis diocesis, vacante ex eo quod Johannes de
Bukingham, ultimus rector eiusdem ecclesie, de Harewe
(Harrow) Londoniensis diocesis est pacifice assecutus,
fuit provisum Johanni de Horton' presbytero, et dimittet
parochialem ecclesiam de Hadeleye (West Hoathley)
Cicestrensis diocesis, pridie kalendas Januarii.[323] Ante
providetur eidem et ibi solvit, ut dicitur in restis domini
prioris folio xix.[320]

### Londoniensis

De canonicatu et prebenda ecclesie Londoniensis,
vacantibus per obitum Raymundi Pelegrini, capellani et
collectoris apostolici, extra curiam defuncti, fuit provisum Johanni Bonligh', clerico dicte diocesis, iiii[to]
nonas Januarii,[324] pro taxa iii li. vi s. viii d. Vocatur
Strebun in Codigton' (Caddington Major), et solvit
dictas tres libras sex s. viii d., iii li. vi s. viii d.[317]

### Dunolmensis

De perpetua vicaria parochialis ecclesie de Norham
Dunolmensis diocesis, per clericos seculares consueta ab

[319] 12 December 1365.
[320] In the margin: inutilis.
[321] fuit, MS.
[322] 29 December 1365.
[323] 31 December 1365.
[324] 2 January 1366.

olim gubernari, vacante per mortem quondam Willelmi Estlegh' Elwik', licet quidam frater Ricardus de Sotes, monachus professus monasterii de Kenlosse (Kinloss)[325] Moracensis (Moray) diocesis ordinis Cisterciensis, habitu dicti[326] ordinis derelicto,[327] ipsam per tres annos occupavit indebite et iniuste, fuit provisum Johanni Mares, presbytero Lichfeldensis diocesis, et dimittet magistratum domus leprosarum Sancti Bertholomei de Owedemuth (Tweedmouth), iiii^to nonas Januarii,[324] pro taxa xiii li. vi s. viii d. Infra statim est alia provisio de qua debetur, et[328] ibi vide, quia illa habuit effectum ista non, sed videatur, quia de una istarum debetur, ut videtur.[329]

## Dunolmensis

De vicaria perpetua parochialis ecclesie de Norham Dunolmensis diocesis, per clericos seculares consueta gubernari, vacante per mortem quondam Willelmi de Elwyk ultimi vicarii eiusdem, fuit provisum Johanni Lowyke, presbytero dicte diocesis, licet Ricardus de Sores, monachus monasterii de Kinloss' Moracensis diocesis ordinis Cisterciensis, ipsam per tres annos et amplius indebite et iniuste occupavit, xviii kalendas Februarii,[330] taxata xiii li. vi s. viii d. Debet plus de alia provisione infra folio xlv vel circa, et est in mandato sequestrari et exequi.[329]

Recepta pagine iii li. vi s. viii d.; iniutiles sunt due provisiones ii; et de tribus debentur fructus iii; resta pecunie xxvi li. xiii s. iiii d.

## (fol. 20, xx)[331] Eliensis, Lichfeldensis

De parochiali ecclesia de Ellesworth' (Elsworth) Eliensis diocesis, vacatura dum Johannes de Merton' dignitatem, personatum vel officium curatum in ecclesia Lichfeldensi fuerit[332] pacifice assecutus, necnon de canonicatu et prebenda ecclesie Lichfeldensis vacaturis,[333] dum Johannes de Waltham canonicatum et prebendam Lincolniensis fuerit pacifice assecutus, fuit provisum Willelmo de Weterisdale presbytero, et dimittet parochialem ecclesiam de Stanford et prebendam Herefordensem et provisionem sibi factam de parochiali ecclesia de Sniterleye (Blakeney or Glandford) Norwicensis diocesis, xi kalendas Februarii.[334] Non habuit effectum quia dictus Johannes adhuc possidet ecclesiam, nec de prebenda etiam habuit effectum quia infra confirmata alteri folio lxx vel circa.[320]

## Wygorniensis

De parochiali ecclesia de Wleve episcopi (Bishop's Cleeve) Wygorniensis, super qua Ricardus Dratton' clericus et Johannes de Grian diu in palatio apostolico litigavit, vacante per privationem dicti Johannis, fuit provisum Ricardo predicto. Ante providetur eidem et ibi solvit, ut dicitur in restis prioris folio xx. Et dictus Johannes de Brian, super quo domini gratiam denegant,[335] possidet nunc titulo regio, quo titulo impediente, ipsa gratia non habuit effectum.[336]

## Saresbiriensis

De canonicatu et prebenda ecclesie monialium de Wilton' Saresbiriensis diocesis, vacantibus per amotionem Rogeri de Chestrifeld', fuit provisum Edwardo de Cherdestok', presbytero Saresbiriensis diocesis, et dimittet parochialem ecclesiam de ⟨Cutel⟩ (East Knoyle) Saresbiriensis diocesis, xi kalendas Februarii.[337] Non habuit effectum, ut certificat episcopus, et habetur in restis prioris folio xx.[336]

## Wygorniensis

De archidiaconatu ecclesie Wygorniensis, vacante dum Johannes de Harewell' archidiaconatum Barkschir' in ecclesia Saresbiriensi fuit pacifice assecutus, fuit provisum Simoni Clement' presbytero, et dimittet parochialem ecclesiam de Pomperne (Pimperne) Saresbiriensis diocesis, iii kalendas Februarii.[338] Isti archidiaconatui est annexa ecclesia de Claverden' (Claverdon), que taxata ad x li. vi s. viii d. Solvit in partem fructuum archidiaconatus pro taxa ecclesie xv li. xiii s. iiii d.; debet residuum. Sic scribitur in restis prioris folio xxi quod habet terminum Omnium Sanctorum anno LXXII^do, et atenta taxam ecclesie et quod residuum, videlicet synodaticum, non excedit vii li., quorum medietas deberetur camere. Et atenta quod procurationes recipiantur in esculentia et quod non habet aliud. Fuit relaxatus[339] salvo iure super procurationibus si fuerit ordinatum quod solvantur.[340]

## Exoniensis

De canonicatu et prebenda[341] ecclesie collegiate Criditon' (Crediton) Exoniensis diocesis, vacantibus per resignationem Philipi de Bello Campo, fuit provisum Johanni More, clerico Saresbiriensis diocesis, vi idus Februarii;[342] debet taxam extra l s. Taxatur ad lx s. et sic restant decem solidi quos solvit die vii mensis Maii anno LXXIII, x s.[343]

---

[325] Followed by *licet quidam frater Ricardus* deleted by a line.
[326] *dicit*, MS.
[327] *derelictu*, MS.
[328] Followed by *de alia infra* deleted by a line.
[329] In the margin: *debet*.
[330] 15 January 1366.
[331] At the top of the folio appears the caption: *iiii anni Urbani*.
[332] *fuit*, MS.
[333] *vacantibus*, MS.
[334] 22 January 1366.

[335] The extension of the two preceding words is doubtful.
[336] In the margin: *inutilis*.
[337] 22 January 1366.
[338] 30 January 1366.
[339] Followed by *quousque apareat* deleted by a line.
[340] In the margin: *videtur inutilis*.
[341] Prebend of Wodelond (Woodland): Collectorie 13, fol. 166.
[342] 8 February 1366.
[343] In the margin: *solvit*.

### Eboracensis

Collatio et provisio facte Ade de Eboraco presbytero auctoritate ordinaria de precentoria ecclesie Eboracensis quam possidet pacifice fuerit confirmate vel provisum de novo, vi kalendas Martii.[344] Non habuit effectum quia perdidit per sententiam contra se latam [345] in curia Romana, ut in restis folio xx.[336]

### Lincolniensis

De parochiali ecclesia de Paston' Lincolniensis diocesis, vacante dum Johannes Stevene dignitatem, personatum vel officium ecclesie Saresbiriensis fuit pacifice assecutus, fuit provisum Willelmo Cranle Lincolniensis diocesis, quinto kalendas Aprilis.[346] Non habuit effectum et atestationes sunt in archivis.[336]

Recepta pagine x s.; et sex alie provisiones sunt inutiles vi.

### (fol. 20ᵛ) Eboracensis

Subrogatus fuit Thomas Thetford', subdiaconus diocesis Lincolniensis, in omni iure et ad omne ius quod competebat Johanni de Waltham, presbytero Lincolniensis diocesis, in et super parochiali ecclesia de Heveresham (Heversham) Eboracensis diocesis, super qua lis pendet in palatio apostolico inter Dominum Johannem de Waltham et Nicholaum de Feriby, clericum [347] Eboracensem, qua lite pendente, prefatus Johannes parochialem ecclesiam de Lyngford' (Langford) Saresbiriensis diocesis, auctoritate ordinaria sibi collatam, fuit pacifice assecutus, et dimittet canonicatum et prebendam ecclesie collegiate de Abbrewill' (Abergwili) Menevensis diocesis ac litem quam habet super parochiali ecclesia de Hagworthingham Lincolniensis diocesis, quinto idus Aprilis.[348] Non habuit effectum ut est probatum, et habetur in restis prioris folio xx.[349]

### Assavensis

De canonicatu et prebenda ecclesie Assavensis in Wallia, de quibus, dudum vacantibus per obitum Ricardi de Middelton in curia defuncti, Dominus Innocentius papa VI providit Johanni Carold', qui, possessione ipsius non habita, ipsos in manibus episcopi Menevensis libere resignavit, et subsequenter de hiis, qui tanto tempore vacaverunt per resignationem huius quod collatio eorum est ad sedem apostolicam legitime devoluta, idem Dominus Innocentius Johanni Guisonden' clerico per certos executores provideri mandavit, et postquam sibi provisum extitit extra curiam decessit, fuit provisum Simoni Larthebury, presbytero Lincolniensis diocesis, xviii kalendas Martii.[350] Non habuit effectum ista pro-

visio, sed alia que est infra folio xxxv, de qua etiam in curia litigatur.[351]

### Eboracensis

De parochiali ecclesia Sancte Elene in Stayngate (St. Helen in Stonegate, York) Eboracensis diocesis, vacante per mortem Thome de Langescote in Romana curia defuncti, fuit provisum Henrico de ⟨Hugate⟩, presbytero Eboracensis diocesis. Non habuit effectum; immo possessor qui nunc est possidebat prius per vi annos, sed videatur cum habuerit effectum.[351]

### Lichfeldensis

De canonicatu et prebenda de Northall' (Morehall) in ecclesia collegiata de Gnousall' (Gnosall) Lichfeldensis diocesis, vacantibus per privationem Nicholai Heeth' propter pluralitatem quam optinebat, fuit provisum Johanni Daniel, clerico Lichfeldensis diocesis, xvi kalendas Maii.[352] Nondum habuit effectum, ut folio xx in restis habetur.[351]

### Norwicensis

Subrogatus fuit Hamo de Deval presbyter [353] in omni iure et ad omne ius quod competebat Michaeli de Hapton' in parochiali ecclesia de Multon' (Moulton) Norwicensis diocesis; inter dictum Hamonem et Michaelem lis pendet in palatio apostolico, qua lite pendente dictus Michaelis extra curiam decessit, v nonas Maii,[354] pro taxa xl m. Alia est provisio supra folio [355] que non habuit effectum, sed hic solvit die xiii Octobris anno LXXIII in decem marchis in partem taxe vi li. xiii s. iiii d.[356] Item solvit xx die Aprilis in aliis x marchis, vi li. xiii s. iiii d.[356]

### Lincolniensis

Collatio et provisio facte auctoritate ordinaria Johanni Skir' de parochiali ecclesia de Harwode (Great Horwood) Lincolniensis diocesis, etiam si fuerit devoluta vel reservata fuerunt confirmate vel provisum de novo, iiiiᵗᵒ nonas Martii.[357] Est infra alia provisio folio [358] et dicitur quod non habuerunt effectum, sed sit sub sequestro et possessor excommunicatur.

Recepta pagine xiii li. vi s. viii d.; [359] resta pagine xx m. que valent xiii li. vi s. viii d.; et sunt iiiiᵒʳ provisiones inutiles iiii.

---

[344] 24 February 1366.
[345] Reading doubtful.
[346] 28 March 1366.
[347] *clerico*, MS.
[348] 9 April 1366.
[349] In the margin: *inutilis est*.
[350] 12 February 1366. In the margin: *inutilis*.

[351] In the margin: *inutilis*.
[352] 16 April 1366.
[353] *presbytero*, MS.
[354] 3 May 1366.
[355] Blank in MS.
[356] In the margin: *solvit*.
[357] 4 March 1366.
[358] Blank in MS.
[359] In the margin: *vera*.

## (fol. 21, xxi) Menevensis [360]

De canonicatu et prebenda ecclesie Sancti Mauricii de Abrewili (Abergwili), vacantibus dum Thomas Thetford' parochialem ecclesiam de Heveresham (Heversham) fuit pacifice assecutus, fuit provisum Johanni Kerk', clerico Eboracensis diocesis. Dicitur quod non habuit effectum, ut in restis folio xxi.[351]

Infrascripta beneficia que fuerunt collata per sanctissimum in Christo patrem et dominum Urbanum papam V vii idus Junii anno iiii[to] [361] usque ad principium quinque annorum debent tradi domino priori Lewensi, quia ipse nondum habuit, et fuerunt eidem per me tradita xv die Februarii anno LXVII, licet tamen habuisset quedam alia beneficia de anno v[to], videlicet usque pridie idus Julii anno v[to].[362]

### Roffensis

Subrogatus fuit Johannes de Aschawe in omni iure quod competebat cuidam ⟨in⟩ parochiali ecclesia [363] de Soutlond' (Snodland) Roffensis diocesis, super qua, cum ipsam fuisset auctoritate ordinaria ex causa permutationis assecutus, dictus impetrans in palatio apostolico eidem Johanni litem movit et extunc apud sedem apostolicam decessit, pridie kalendas Julii.[364] Dicitur in restis domini prioris folio xxi quod ante providetur eidem et ibi solvit, et copia quitantie, quam tertius possessor exibuit, est in archivis, et ambe provisiones sunt facte eidem persone et ex eadem vacatione, quare et cetera.[365]

### Exoniensis

Collatio et provisio facte [366] auctoritate apostolica Rogero Payn de canonicatu et prebenda ecclesie de Criditon' (Crediton) Exoniensis diocesis et prebenda Bursaria nuncupata in ecclesia predicta, vacantibus, ut credebatur, pro eo qui ipsum optinens aliam prebendam inibi fuerat pacifice assecutus, cuius collatio erat devoluta non obstante quod assertum fuit ipsum studuisse in iure civili per v annos et non studuerat nisi per quatuor, xi kalendas Augusti.[367] Ante providetur eidem et ibi solvit, ut in restis prioris dicitur folio xxi.[365]

### Exoniensis

De canonicatu et prebenda Sancte Crucis Criditon' Exoniensis diocesis et prebenda de Karswell' (Kerswell) in eadem ecclesia, vacantibus ex eo quod Johannes Ponay se gerens pro canonico dicte ecclesie, ipsam prebendam de Karswell optinens, aliam certam prebendam wlgariter nuncupatam Bursariam in dicta ecclesia auctoritate ordinaria fuit pacifice assecutus, etiam si devoluta fuerit vel alio quovismodo vacet, fuit provisum Johanni Cheyney, clerico Exoniensi, per Urbanum iii[tio] kalendas Augusti.[368] Dicitur quod taxatur 1 s. Solvit dominus prior Lewensis pro ea die ix Julii anno LXXIII quinquaginta s., 1 s., et non plus taxatur, ut dicitur.[369]

### Londoniensis

De novo fuit provisum Johanni de Bukingham de parochiali ecclesia de Harewe (Harrow) Londoniensis diocesis, vacante et reservata per obitum Raymundi Pelegrini, quem prius asserat esse capellanum sedis apostolice et pro certo tempore Domini Innocentii pape sexti dictam capellaniam resignavit, per Urbanum v[to] idus Augusti.[370] Thesaurarius est domini Wintoniensis episcopi, et possidet titulo regio, et supra est alia provisio eidem facta folio,[371] et non vult solvere, sed videat camera si debet, quia postquam ipsemet impetravit, licet alio titulo possideat, videtur quod teneatur solvere, quia non potuit gratie in preiudicium camere renuntiare nec prosecutionem dimittere, maxime sine suspicione fraudis cum ipsemet possideat et cetera.

Recepta pagine 1 s.; et tres provisiones sunt inutiles iii; et de una ultima debentur fructus i.

## (fol. 21[v]) Lincolniensis

De canonicatu et prebenda de Chastre (Caistor) in ecclesia Lincolniensi, vacantibus vel vacaturis per privationem Henrici Ingelby, fuit provisum Johanni Cheyne, etiam si eos ex causa permutationis vel alio quovismodo dimiserit, et ⟨dimittet⟩ parochialem ecclesiam de Kirkeby Misperton' (Kirkby Misperton) Eboracensis diocesis, tertio idus Septembris.[372] Non habuit effectum dicta privatio, ut in restis prioris folio xxi, ideo relaxatus usque quo apareat de effectu vel alias per cameram fuerit ordinatum.[365]

### Eboracensis

De canonicatu et prebenda ecclesie collegiate de Hewden' (Howden) Eboracensis diocesis, quos Jacobus de Multon' in dicta ecclesia solebat optinere, vacantibus de iure eo quod Willelmus Dumby presbyter, vigore gratie sibi facte de canonicatu sub expectatione prebende dicte ecclesie acceptavit, tacito in dicta gratia defectu natalium quem patitur de presbytero genitus et soluta, et in ipsis est intrusus de facto, fuit provisum Willelmo predicto, pridie idus Septembris.[373] Dicitur in restis prioris quod

---

[360] The heading *Anno iiii Urbani* appears at the top of the page.

[361] 7 June 1366.

[362] 14 July 1367. In the left margin: *Titulus est.* In the right: *Sic erat scriptum in restis in archivis redditis per dominum priorem.*

[363] *parochialem ecclesiam*, MS.

[364] 30 June 1366.

[365] In the margin: *inutilis.*

[366] *facta*, MS.

[367] 22 July 1366.

[368] 30 July 1366.

[369] In the margin: *solvit.*

[370] 9 August 1366.

[371] Blank in MS.

[372] 11 September 1366.

[373] 12 September 1366.

ista provisio non est vera, et ita scripsit dominus Flandrini cum erat locumtenens domini camerarii; sic in restis prioris in effectu folio xxi.[365]

## Eboracensis

Motu proprio fuit provisum Domino Anglico cardinali [374] de canonicatu et prebenda ac decanatu ecclesie Eboracensis, vacantibus per obitum cardinalis Petragoricensis, viii kalendas Octobris.[375] Cardinalis est Avinionensis, et nichil solvit [376] in vitam, nec aliter est consuetum, ut dicitur.[377]

## Lincolniensis

Provisio facta vigore litterarum apostolicarum Benedicto de Massingham, presbytero diocesis Norwicensis, de perpetua vicaria parochialis ecclesie de Luthon' (Luton) Lincolniensis diocesis, taxata xvi li., quam possidet, licet dicatur vacasse et vacare eo quod quondam Robertus de Whyryngsete, cuidem ⟨de⟩ ipsa vacante in curia ex causa permutationis fuit provisum, antequam eius possessionem habuit alteram parochialem ecclesiam fuit pacifice assecutus, et sic apostolicum mandatum non videtur ad plenum executum, fuit [378] confirmata vel provisum de novo, v kalendas Octobris,[379] debet de resta iiii[or] li. Solvit dictas quatuor li., ut in libro recepte habetur, michi Arnaldo Garnerii.[380]

## Eboracensis, Sarisbiriensis

De canonicatu et prebenda ecclesie collegiate de Southwell' Eboracensis diocesis, vacantibus per Henrici de Ingelby ac canonicatu et prebenda Sarisbiriensibus per Johannis [381] de Wellentton' privationes et amotiones per dominum papam factas propter multitudinem beneficiorum, fuit provisum Johanni Cheyne, clerico Lichfeldensis diocesis, et dimittet parochialem ecclesiam de Kirkeby Mysperton' (Kirkby Misperton) et gratiam sibi factam de canonicatu et prebenda quos idem Henricus optinere [382] dicitur in ecclesia Lichfeldensi, iii idus Octobris.[383] Quoad prebendam de Sotoel non habuit effectum, ut in restis prioris folio xxi.[384]

## Sarisbiriensis

De canonicatu et prebenda ecclesie Sarisbiriensis, de qua per privationem Johannis de Welleontton' propter multitudinem beneficiorum fuit provisum Johanni

Cheyne, ut supra patet, iii idus Octobris.[383] Certificat episcopus in iii mandato quod dicta provisio [385] nunquam habuit effectum.[384]

## Dunelmensis

De capella sive magisterio hospitalis de Sagteburn' (Sherburn) Dunolmensis diocesis, vacante per amotionem Alani de Sareboughton', fuit provisum Willelmo de Wauthesworth', iii kalendas Novembris.[386] Non habuit effectum, ut habetur in restis folio xxii.[384]

Recepta pagine iiii[or] li.; inutiles provisiones sunt v; et restant fructus unius i.

(fol. 22; xxii) Anno v Urbani; completum est de anno quarto.

## Eboracensis

De canonicatu et prebenda Sancti Johannis de Beverlaco, vacantibus per privationem Johannis de Blebury, fuit provisum Rogero de Freton', legum doctori, pridie idus Novembris.[387] Non habuit effectum dicta provisio, ut est clare probatum, et ideo dormit quousque apareat de effectu.[384]

## Dunolmensis

De parochiali ecclesia de Wermouth' (Bishop-Wearmouth) Dunolmensis diocesis ad quam, vacantem per obitum Willelmi Newport, David de Wollore fuit presentatus et auctoritate ordinaria institutus, vacante per privationem dicti David factam per dominum papam, fuit provisum Thome Chervaux, clerico Eboracensis diocesis, xiii kalendas Decembris.[388] Dicta privatio non habuit effectum, nec provisio, sed post habuit dictam ecclesiam a domino nostro papa et ab ordinario etiam dominus cardinalis Cantuariensis et post permutavit eam; videatur quod agendum.[384]

## Eboracensis

De prioratu Beate Marie Lancastre (Lancaster) Eboracensis diocesis, a monasterio Sancti Martini Sagiensis (Séez) ordinis Sancti Benedicti dependente, vacante per promotionem Petri abbatis dicti monasterii, et dimittet officium ad ipsum monasterium, fuit provisum Willelmo Raymbaut, monacho dicti monasterii, et dimittet officium ballive dicti monasterii, consistit in ecclesia Beate Marie Lancastre, que taxatur iiii[xx] li., debet de resta pro dicta ecclesia x li.[389] Solvit dictas decem libras die xviii Octobris anno LXXII.[390] Videatur si debet plus pro aliqua temporalitate vel alia.

## Londoniensis

De parochiali ecclesia Sancti Martini in Venetria (St. Martin Vintry) Londonie, vacante dum Nicholaus

---

[374] Anglicus Grimoard, priest of S. Pietro in Vincoli.
[375] 24 September 1366.
[376] *solvunt*, MS.
[377] *dicunt*, MS. In the margin: *debet*.
[378] *fuerunt*, MS.
[379] 27 September 1366.
[380] In the margin: *solvit*.
[381] *Johannem*, MS.
[382] *pomer'*, MS.
[383] 13 October 1366.
[384] In the margin: *inutilis*.

[385] Over *provisio* is written *privatio* without sign of deletion.
[386] 30 October 1366.
[387] 12 November 1366.
[388] 19 November 1366.
[389] In the margin: *debet solvere aliquid*.
[390] In the margin: *solvit*.

Dratton' beneficium ad collationem episcopi Wygorniensis fuit pacifice assecutus, fuit provisum Roberto Canncelo, presbytero Wellensis diocesis, vi kalendas Decembris.[391] Non habuit effectum, ut in restis folio xxii.[384]

### Lincolniensis

De parochiali ecclesia de Surflet (Surfleet) Lincolniensis diocesis, vacante per mortem Willelmi Hinewell', fuit provisum Johanni Skiret de Bukingham dicte diocesis, et dimittet parochialem ecclesiam de Horwode magna (Great Horwood), nonas Decembris.[392] Nondum habuit effectum, folio xxii in restis prioris habetur.[380]

### Lincolniensis

De perpetua capella sive rectoria leprosarie Sancti Juliani iuxta Sanctum Albanum (St. Julian, Hertford) Lincolniensis diocesis, vacante dum Johannes de Herlingburgh' dignitatem, personatum vel officium ecclesie Lincolniensis fuit pacifice assecutus, fuit provisum Hugoni de Prington', presbytero dicte diocesis. Est sequestratus et monitus in iii mandato, et est de iurisdictione abbatis Sancti Albani, ut certificat episcopus, licet dicatur quod nondum habuit effectum.[393]

### Sarisbiriensis

De archidiaconatu de Barkschir', que dignitas est in ecclesia Sarisbiriensi, vacante per consecrationem Johannis Harewell' electi Bathoniensi, fuit provisum Alexandro de Walby, clerico Lichfeldensis, xix kalendas Februarii,[394] taxato liiii li., debet de resta xliiii li. Cardinalis de Agrefolio [395] possidet, et non reperiuntur bona Alexandri et cetera, et episcopus non vult solvere, licet pluries requisitus.[393]

### Lichfeldensis

De decanatu Sancti Johannis Cestr' (Chester) fuit provisum Johanni Wodhous clerico, vii kalendas Januarii,[396] taxato xxvi li. xiii s. iiii d., debet de resta x li. Est monitus et sequestratus in iii mandato.[393]

Recepta pagine x li.; inutiles provisiones sunt iiiior; resta pecunie liiii li.; et restant fructus unius provisionis i.

### (fol. 22v) Wellensis

De canonicatu et prebenda ecclesie Wellensis, vacaturis per consecrationem electi Bathoniensis, fuit provisum Johanni de Broutton' clerico, xvi kalendas Januarii.[397] Est tertio mandato, et episcopus certificat quod non habuit effectum quia rex contulit.[384]

### Lichfeldensis

De canonicatu et prebenda ecclesie collegiate Sancti Johannis Cestr' vacantibus per amotionem Johannis Wyvelay, fuit provisum Thome de Eltonheed, clerico dicte diocesis, xvi kalendas Januarii.[397] Episcopus certificat quod non habuit effectum amotio, nec fuit ibi umquam talis possessor.[384]

De canonicatu et prebenda Lichfeldensis vacantibus per amotionem Hugonis de Wymudeswold fuit provisum Thome Alayn presbytero, xiiii kalendas Januarii.[398] Non habuit effectum dicta amotio, ut est probatum.[384]

### Lincolniensis

De parochiali ecclesia de Harwode magna (Great Horwood) Lincolniensis diocesis, vacante dum Johannes de Bukingham parochialem ecclesiam de Surflet (Surfleet) dicte diocesis fuit pacifice assecutus, fuit provisum Johanni Skiret, et dimittet parochialem ecclesiam de Lilingston' (Lillingstone), iiitio nonas Januarii.[399] Alia provisio est supra folio xix et alia infra folio xxiiiito, et est mandatum iiium.[393]

### Dunensis

De archidiaconatu Dunensi (Down), vacante per consecrationem Willelmi Mort' episcopi Conventrensis (Connor), fuit provisum Johanni Donnexan, qui dimittet parochialem ecclesiam de Camelyn (Camclyn?) dicte diocesis Dunensis, x kalendas Februarii.[400] Non est in Anglia, sed dicitur quod est in Ybernia.[401]

### Eboracensis

De canonicatu et prebenda ecclesie collegiate de Howden' Eboracensis diocesis, vacantibus ex eo quod Henricus Sueth', non graduatus, ipsos cum beneficiis aliis, videlicet parochiali ecclesia de Undile (Oundle) Lincolniensis canonicatibus et prebendis ecclesiarum Lincolniensis, Londoniensis et Menevensis alias Abbrewill' (Abergwili) optinens, ipsa beneficia et eorum valores iuxta constitutionem domini pape editam non dedit, aut per privationem seu alio quovismodo, fuit provisum Ricardo Driffeld'. Nondum habuit effectum dicta privatio.[401]

### Dunolmensis

Item Nicholao Driffeld' de canonicatu et prebenda ecclesie collegiate Cestr' (Chester-le-Street) Dunolmensis diocesis, vacantibus ex eo quod David de Wallore plura beneficia que optinet cum eisdem et valores ipsorum et secundum constitutionem domini pape non tradidit, etiam si per amotionem ipsius vacent, aut alio quovismodo. Non habuit effectum ut in restis prioris folio xxiii.[401]

---

[391] 26 November 1366.
[392] 5 December 1366.
[393] In the margin: *debet*.
[394] 14 January 1367.
[395] William d'Aigrefeuille, priest of S. Stefano al Monte Celio.
[396] *Februarii Januarii* with neither deleted, MS. 26 December 1366.
[397] 17 December 1366.
[398] 19 December 1366.
[399] 3 January 1367.
[400] 23 January 1367.
[401] In the margin: *inutilis*.

### Eboracensis

Item Georgio Sicilio de Howden' de canonicatu et prebenda ecclesie collegiate de Rippon' Eboracensis diocesis, quos Willelmus Walton' tempore constitutionis predicte cum nonnullis aliis beneficiis optinens, ipsa et eorum valores constitutionem predictam non tradidit, si ex eo aut alio quovismodo vacent, iii$^{tio}$ kalendas Februarii.[402] Non habuit effectum dicta vacatio seu privatio.[401]

Titulus. Beneficia collata et confirmata in Anglia per dominum nostrum dominum Urbanum papam v$^{tum}$ a iii$^{tio}$ kalendas Aprilis citra pontificatus sui anno v$^{to}$.[403]

### Exoniensis

De canonicatu et prebenda ecclesie Sancti Karentoci (Crantock) Exoniensis, vacantibus per amotionem Thome Kenys propter pluralitatem beneficiorum que optinebat, fuit provisum Philipo de Homeye Lincolniensis diocesis, iiii$^{to}$ kalendas Aprilis.[404] Certificat episcopus quod non habuit effectum.[401]

Restant fructus unius provisionis i; inutiles sunt viii.

### (fol. 23, xxiii)[405] Lincolniensis

Motu proprio fuit provisum Nicholao Sancte Marie in Via Lata diacono cardinali de canonicatu et prebenda Lincolniensibus vacantibus per obitum episcopi Albanensis, iii$^{tio}$ idus Julii.[406]

### Lincolniensis

Motu proprio mandatur provideri Domini Anglico cardinali Avinionensi [407] de canonicatu et prebenda Lincolniensibus vacantibus per consecrationem Willelmi de Wykham, pridie idus Julii,[408] electi Wyntoniensis.[409]

### Lincolniensis

Motu proprio fuit provisum Guillelmo titulo Sanctorum Johannis et Pauli presbytero cardinali de canonicatu et prebenda ecclesie Lincolniensis, vacantibus per obitum Domini H. cardinalis Ostiensis.[410]

### Eboracensis

Motu proprio fuit provisum Matheo cardinali Viterbiensi [411] de canonicatu et prebenda Eboracensibus vacantibus per obitum cardinalis Ostiensis, pridie ⟨idus⟩ Julii.[412]

Titulus. Sequntur beneficia collata et confirmata in Anglia per Dominum Urbanum papam v$^{tum}$ pontificatus sui anno v$^{to}$ a vii kalendas Augusti [413] citra.

### Cicestrensis

De decanatu ecclesie Cicestrensi, taxato liii li. vi s. viii d., vacante per obitum Nicholai de Aston' infra duas dietas a Romana curia defuncti, fuit provisum Rogero de Freton', legum doctori, debet de resta vi li. xiii s. iiii d. Solvit vi die Junii dictas sex li. xiii s. iiii d., sed est in alio loco obligatus.[414]

### Bathoniensis et Wellensis

De canonicatu et prebenda ecclesie Wellensis, vacantibus per obitum Nicholai de Aston' in Romana curia defuncti vel prope duas dietas, fuit provisum Johanni de Blankete, clerico Lincolniensis diocesis, vii kalendas Augusti.[413] Non habuit effectum quia rex contulit, ut in restis prioris habetur folio xxiii.[415]

### Wyntoniensis

Datur potestas electo Wyntoniensi ac alicui episcopo Anglie ad conferendum iiii$^{or}$ doctoribus in theologia vel in decretis iiii$^{or}$ beneficia vacanta vel vacatura per consecrationem dicti electi. Videatur de hoc quia episcopus dicit quod nullum dedit, et fuit pluries mandatum.[415]

### Lincolniensis

De archidiaconatu de Bokyngham in ecclesia Lincolniensi, vacante per amotionem Willelmi Kinewell' propter pluralitatem beneficiorum que optinebat, fuit provisum Johanni Skiret de Bukingham, baccallario in utroque iure, et dimittet parochialem ecclesiam de Harwode magna (Great Horwood), kalendas Augusti.[416] Non habuit effectum, ut dicitur in restis.[415]

### Lincolniensis

De archidiaconatu Oxoniensi in ecclesia Lincolniensi, vacante per obitum cardinalis Aquensis,[417] fuit provisum Thome de Southam, clerico Lichfeldensis diocesis, viii idus Augusti.[418] Ecclesia de Isteley (Iffley) est annexa sibi, et taxatur ad xiiii li. xiii s. iiii d., sed archidiaconatus non taxatur. Solvit xx li. et debet residuum medietatis valoris archidiaconatus. Sic est scriptum in restis in arreragiis dimissis, quia dictus archidiaconatus

---

[402] 30 January 1367.
[403] 30 March 1367.
[404] 29 March 1367.
[405] The heading *annus v$^{us}$ Urbani* appears at the top of the page.
[406] 13 July 1367. In the margin: *Cardinalis est et cetera in Via Lata.*
[407] Anglicus Grimoard, bishop of Albano.
[408] 14 July 1367.
[409] In the margin: *Cardinalis est Avinionensis.*
[410] Elias de S. Eredio. In the margin: *Cardinalis est Sanctorum Johannis et Pauli.*
[411] Mark de Viterbo, priest of S. Prassede.

[412] 14 July 1367. In the margin: *Cardinalis Viterbiensis.*
[413] 26 July 1367.
[414] In the margin: *solvit.*
[415] In the margin: *inutilis.*
[416] 1 August 1367.
[417] Peter Itherii, bishop of Dax, bishop of Albano.
[418] 6 August 1367.

non valet ultra xl li., satis solvit pro medietate in valore, salvo iure super procurationibus si debeantur. Set solvit pro ecclesia in duabus vicibus undecim li. sex s. viii d., xi li. vi s. viii d.[414]

Recepta pagine xviii li.;[419] inutiles provisiones sunt iii; et restant fructus provisionum iiii.

### (fol. 23ᵛ) Bangorensis

De archidiaconatu Angleseye in ecclesia Bangorensi, vacante per mortem Howeli Magranew extra Romanam curiam defuncti, fuit provisum Johanni Reys, clerico Assavensis diocesis, nisi sit alteri specialiter ius quesitum super etate dispensationis,[420] et dimittet ecclesiam et prebendam ecclesie Assavensis, nonas Augusti.[421] Non habuit effectum ut in restis folio xxiii.[415]

### Lichfeldensis, Eboracensis

Concessum est Waltero de Compeden' ut parochialem ecclesiam de Wygan (Wigan) Lichfeldensis diocesis et canonicatum et prebendam ecclesie Eboracensis licite retinenti resignare simul vel permutare, et quod in hospitali ⟨Sancti⟩ Nicholai de Pontefracto, solito per laycos gubernari, ac leprosos Sancte Marie Magdalene de Preston' Eboracensis diocesis, quos optinebat, servetur constitutio, vi kalendas Augusti.[422] Prohibitum de ecclesia quia de patronatu laicali, et possessor prebende est de familia comitis Marchie, et dicit quod nunquam impetravit per se nec per alium dictam confirmationem seu dispensationem, et ita iurat, sed videatur quod agendum quia et cetera.[423]

Exoniensis, Lichfeldensis, Menevensis, Cicestrensis

Item concessum ⟨fuit⟩ Willelmo de Bokbrugg' ut parochialem ecclesiam de Torton' (Great Torrington) Exoniensis diocesis et canonicatum et prebendam ecclesie collegiate de Landewibrevy (Llanddewi Brefi) Menevensis diocesis et canonicatum ⟨et⟩ prebendam ecclesie Lichfeldensis et canonicatum et ⟨prebendam⟩ capelle regis Anglie de Hasting' (Hastings) Cicestrensis diocesis valeat licite retinere, resignare et permutare ita quod unum ex illis teneatur dimittere, vi idus Augusti.[424] Prohibitum est per breve regis de ecclesie et est in suplicatione. Et de prebenda Lichfeldensi certificat episcopus quod non habuit prebendam in ecclesia sua. De Cicestrensi et Menevensi est in mandatis monitus et excommunicatus. Et est thesaurarius domini ducis Lencastrie et cetera.[423]

### Eboracensis

De parochiali ecclesia de Leck' (Leake) Eboracensis diocesis, quam Hugo de Wymodeswold per assecutionem

beneficii incompatibilis teneatur dimittere, fuit provisum Simoni Lamburn', presbytero magistro in artibus, idus Augusti.[425] Non habuit effectum dicta gratia quia dictus Hugo ad huc possidet, ut est bene probatum.[415]

### Herefordensis

De archidiaconatu de Herefordia[426] Herefordensis ⟨diocesis⟩, vacante et reservato per obitum ultimi archidiaconi, fuit provisum Rogero de Sutton', presbytero Lincolniensis diocesis, legum doctori, et dimittet parochialem ecclesiam de Blatton' (Glatton) Lincolniensis diocesis, ii idus Augusti.[427] Non habuit effectum, ut in restis folio xxiiii.[415]

### Lincolniensis

Acceptatio, collatio et provisio vigore litterarum apostolicarum facte Roberto de Wortham de parochiali ecclesia de Bruikton' (Broughton) Lincolniensis diocesis, etiam si reservata fuerit vel devoluta, fuerunt confirmate vel provisum de novo, et dimittet parochialem ecclesiam de Brisile (Brisley) Norwicensis, iiiᵗⁱᵒ idus Augusti.[428] Non habuit effectum ista provisio, ut est clare probatum, tamen possessor qui nunc est habuit, ut dicitur, confirmationem, et est monitus et cetera.[429]

### Sarisbiriensis

De canonicatu et prebenda Sarisbiriensibus, vacantibus per privationem Saladini de Falle, qui cum malignis societatibus in guarra[430] tam licite quam illicite incedit, fuit provisum Henrico Wyntirton', clerico Norwicensis diocesis, et dimittet alios canonicatum et prebendam quos optinet in ecclesia Sarisbiriensi, iiiᵗⁱᵒ idus Augusti.[428] Non habuit effectum, ut dicitur in restis prioris folio xxiiii.[429]

### Lincolniensis

Motu proprio fuit provisum titulo Sancte Praxedis presbytero cardinali[431] de archidiaconatu Exoniensi (Oxford) cum ecclesiis de Zastile (Iffley) et Mileton' (Great Milton) eidem annexis in ecclesia Lincolniensi, vacante per obitum Petri cardinalis Albanensis,[432] v kalendas Octobris.[433] Non habuit effectum, ut dicitur in restis prioris folio xxiiii.[434]

Restant fructus duarum provisionum ii; et sunt vi inutiles vi.

(fol. 24; xxiiii) Completum est de anno quinto; anno vi Urbani. Sequntur beneficia collata et confirmata in

---

[419] In the margin: *vera.*
[420] Compare above, p. 350.
[421] 5 August 1367.
[422] 27 July 1367.
[423] In the margin: *debet.*
[424] 8 August 1367.

[425] 13 August 1367
[426] *Leek'*, MS.
[427] 12 August 1367.
[428] 11 August 1367.
[429] In the margin: *inutilis.*
[430] *guarre*, MS.
[431] Mark de Viterbo, priest of S. Prassede.
[432] Peter Itherii, bishop of Dax.
[433] 27 September 1367.
[434] In the margin: *inutilis; cardinalis est.*

Anglia per Dominum Urbanum papam quintum pontificatus sui anno sexto.

### Norwicensis

De parochiali ecclesia de Sachowe (Scottow) Norwicensis diocesis, vacante per obitum ultimi rectoris eiusdem extra Romanam curiam defuncti, tanto tempore quod eius collatio est ad sedem apostolicam legitime devoluta, fuit provisum Johanni de Karlil, clerico Karleolensis diocesis, quinto idus Novembris.[435] Appropriata est abbati de Hulm' (Hulme), ut in restis etiam habetur folio xxiiii.[429]

### Eboracensis

Collatio et provisio facte per capitulum Eboracense Willelmo, canonico, presbytero, de vicaria perpetua parochialis ecclesie de Alne Eboracensis diocesis, vacante pro eo quod Johannes de Welton', quousque tunc possidens, perpetuam vicariam de Stanfordham (Stamfordham) Dunolmensis diocesis, fuit auctoritate ordinaria pacifice assecutus, fuerunt confirmate vel provisum de novo, et si reservata fuerit vel devoluta ad sedem apostolicam, ii[do] idus Novembris.[436] Ante providetur eidem et ibi solvit, ut dicitur in restis prioris folio xxiiii.[429]

### Dunolmensis

De canonicatu et prebenda [437] ecclesie collegiate de Langcestr' (Lanchester), taxata vi li. xiii s. iiii d., Dunolmensis diocesis, vacantibus per mortem ⟨Johannis⟩ de Nesbit' in Romana curia defuncti, fuit provisum Johanni de Babingle, clerico Norwicensis diocesis, iii kalendas Decembris,[438] pro resta liii s. iiii d. Solvit in duabus vicibus dictam summam liii s. iiii d.[439]

### Wygorniensis

Mandatur domino [440] Guillelmo Gurchard, auditori palatii apostolici, ut ⟨si⟩ sibi constitit [441] quod duo executores super gratia communi facta Willelmo de Honnburn', presbytero Wigorniensis diocesis, concessorum videlicet si unus se excusavit et alius interesse noluit,[442] sed alter tertius solus ad executionem dicte gratie processit in quantum potuit, ipsamque postmodum vicariam parochialis ecclesie de Blokele (Blockley) Wygorniensis diocesis infra tempus debitum acceptaverat, et quod Johannes de Ridelyngton', vigore cuiusdem permutationis facte auctoritate ordinaria se in ipsa de facto intrusit, et dictum Willelmum fore reperiat

vite laudabilis et honeste conversationis, de dicta eidem provideat et intruso predicto silentium perpetuum imponat, ii[do] kalendas Decembris.[443] Non taxatur, sed solvit pro medietate veri valoris ad certificationem episcopi octo li. xviii d., quia certificat episcopus quod verus valor, nullis deductis expensis, est xxiiii m., viii li. xviii d. sterlingorum.[444]

### Eboracensis

Gratia facta per dominum nostrum papam Roberto de Pethowe, presbytero Eboracensis diocesis, de parochiali ecclesia de Achton' (Aughton) dicte diocesis, vacante per resignationem Hugonis de Bolthon' in Romana curia factam, cui Hugoni de ipsa mandatum fuerat per felicis recordationis Dominum Innocentium papam VI[tum], cui quodam mandato quidam prior et conventus se opposuerunt et litem inter se moverunt, qua lite pendente idem Hugo in dicta curia resignavit ac cessit omne ius [445] sibi in ipsa competentem,[446] fuit confirmata et fuit subrogatus in omni iure quod competebat prefato Hugoni quomodolibet in eadem, pridie nonas Decembris.[447] Appropriata est priori de Lortan (Ellerton) ut in restis prioris folio xxiiii.[429]

Recepta pagine x li. xiiii s. x d.; [448] inutiles sunt tres provisiones iii.

### (fol. 24[v]) Eboracensis

De parochiali ecclesia de Mitton' Eboracensis diocesis, vacante per obitum Willelmi de Tratham, ultimi rectoris eiusdem, et si tanto tempore vacaverit quod eius collatio est ad sedem apostolicam legitime devoluta, fuit provisum Thome [449] Sothoren', licet abbas et conventus monasterii Kokersand (Cockersand) ordinis Cisterciensis ipsam prefato monasterio [450] incorporari fecerunt et uniri ac eam indebite detineant occupatam, et dimittet parochialem ecclesiam de Mondesby (Mundsley) Norwicensis diocesis, vii idus Decembris.[451] Appropriata est dicto abbati ut in restis prioris folio xxv.[429]

### Lincolniensis

De archidiaconatu de Bokyngham in ecclesia Lincolniensi, vacante per privationem Willelmi Kinewell' propter multitudinem beneficiorum que optinebat, licet de ipso provisum fuisset Johanni Skir', qui, litteris non confectis, in Romana curia decessit, fuit provisum Johanni Toresby, presbytero Lincolniensis diocesis, et dimittet parochialem ecclesiam de Lilleford (Lilford) Lincolniensis ⟨et litem⟩ quam habet super parochiali

---

[435] 9 November 1367.
[436] 12 November 1367.
[437] Prebend of Langele (Langley): Collectorie 13, fol. 166[v].
[438] 29 November 1367.
[439] The sum is repeated in MS. In the margin: *solvit*.
[440] *provideri*, MS.
[441] *consistitit*, MS.
[442] *voluit*, MS.

[443] 30 November 1367.
[444] *sterlis*, MS. In the margin: *solvit*.
[445] *omni iure*, MS.
[446] *competenti*, MS.
[447] 4 December 1367.
[448] In the margin: *vera*.
[449] Followed by *Sothen'* deleted by a line.
[450] *prefatum monasterium*, MS.
[451] 7 December 1367.

ecclesia de Brantyngham (Brantingham) Eboracensis diocesis, pridie idus Decembris.[452] Nondum habuit effectum, ut habetur in restis folio xxv.[429]

## Lincolniensis

De archidiaconatu de Bokyngham in ecclesia Lincolniensi, vacante per amotionem Willelmi de Kynewell', fuit provisum Henrico Piel, licet antea provisum fuisset Johanni Skir', et dimittet parochialem ⟨ecclesiam⟩ de Werketon' (Warkton) Lincolniensis diocesis, iii[tio] idus Decembris.[453] Lis pendet in curia, et dicitur quod possessor est ordinarius.[454]

## Wellensis

Ex causa permutationis fuit provisum Johanni de Walton' Wellensis diocesis de parochiali ecclesia de Templecumbe (Templecombe), taxata xiiii m., debet de resta v li. xiii s. iiii d. Solvit in duabus vicibus quinquaginta tres s. iiii d., liii s. iiii d.[455]

## Lincolniensis

De parochiali ecclesia de Horwode magna (Great Horwood) Lincolniensis, vacante per obitum Johannis de Bokyngham in Romana curia defuncti, fuit provisum Johanni de Bokyngham. Est in mandato sequestratus et excommunicatus, et supra sunt due alie provisiones folio xx, xxii.[454]

## Eboracensis

Mandatur Domino Thome de Paxton' ut si sibi constitit Rogerum de Holm' vi[c] fl. in redditibus et iiii[or] beneficia optinere, quod eidem Rogero super parochiali ecclesia de Patrington' quam Johannes de Mecham possidet pacifice per duos annos vel circiter, super qua dicte Johanni litem movit, silentium perpetuum imponat, xi kalendas Januarii.[456] Lis pendet in curia, et dictus Johannes est obligatus ad solvendum et iuratus, lite sopita et cetera cum ordinario cum quo litigat.[454]

## Norwicensis

De parochiali ecclesia de Sochowe (Scottow) Norwicensis diocesis, vacante per mortem vel resignationem ultimi rectoris eiusdem, fuit provisum Johanni de Karlil, clerico Karleolensis bacallario, iii[tio] kalendas Januarii.[457] Ante videtur quod est appropriata[458] abbati de Ulmo (Hulme) in restis folio xxv.[459]

## Exoniensis

Item collatio et provisio facte auctoritate apostolica Johanni Cheyne, clerico Exoniensis diocesis, de canonicatu ecclesie collegiate Criditon' (Crediton) et prebenda de Kerswell' in eadem dicto diocesis, quos possidet pacifice etiam si vacet ex eo quod habet custodire dictam prebendam libros et vestimenta dicte ecclesie sic officium thesaurarie vel annexam officio thesaurarie, fuerunt confirmate vel provisum de novo, iiii kalendas Januarii.[460] Supra est alia provisio facta eidem persone folio xx, et ibi solvit ut in restis folio xxi.[459]

Recepta pagine liii s. iiii d.; inutiles provisiones sunt iiii; et de tribus[461] provisionibus debentur fructus iii; resta pecunie iii li.

## (fol. 25, xxv)[462] Cicestrensis, Wellensis

Motu proprio fuit provisum titulo Sancte Praxedis presbytero cardinali[463] de canonicatu et prebenda ac precentoria ecclesie Cicestrensis ac canonicatu et prebenda ac thesauraria ecclesie Wellensis, vacantibus per obitum Petri cardinalis Albanensis,[464] ii[do] nonas Januarii.[465] Prohibitum per breve quia rex contulit precentoriam et prebendam Cicestrenses; Wellenses possidet dominus cardinalis Carcassonensis[466] prebendam et thesaurariam.[467]

Titulus est. Beneficia collata et confirmata in Anglia per Dominum Urbanum papam V[tum] pontificatus sui anno vi[to] a vii idus Januarii[468] citra.

## Assavensis

De canonicatu et prebenda ecclesie Assavensis, vacantibus per obitum Johannis Griffundi extra Romanam curiam defuncti, licet ipse possessionem non haberet, fuit provisum Johanni Reys, clerico Assavensis diocesis, etiam si apud apostolicam fuerint reservati, et dimittet alios canonicatum et prebendam quos optinet in dicta ecclesia, vii idus Januarii. Litigat in curia cum uno ordinario ut est probatum, quare dormit pro nunc, et finita lite solvet si obtineat.[454]

## Eliensis

De parochiali ecclesia de Ellesworth (Elsworth) Eliensis diocesis, vacatura dum Johannes de Merten' dignitatem, personatum vel officium curatum in ecclesia Lichfeldensis fuit pacifice assecutus, fuit provisum Johanni de Scamp', et dimittet parochialem ecclesiam de

---

[452] 12 December 1367.
[453] 11 December 1367.
[454] In the margin: debet.
[455] In the margin: solvit.
[456] 22 December 1367.
[457] 30 December 1367.
[458] Followed by priori deleted by a line
[459] In the margin: inutilis.

[460] 29 December 1367.
[461] Over duabus deleted by a line.
[462] The heading anno vi Urbani is repeated at the top of the page.
[463] Mark de Viterbo.
[464] Peter Itherii, bishop of Dax.
[465] 4 January 1368.
[466] Stephen Aubert, deacon of S. Maria in Aquiro.
[467] In the margin: debet; cardinalis Carcassonensis.
[468] 7 January 1368.

Swattefeld' (Swafield) Norwicensis diocesis, xv kalendas Februarii.[469] Nondum habuit effectum; immo dictus Johannes ad huc possidet dictam ecclesiam, ut est probatum, et idem est in restis folio xxv.[459]

### Dunolmensis

Subrogatus fuit Johannes de Hesill' in omni iure et ad omne ius quod competebat Johanni de Nesbit' super decanatu Langcestr' (Lanchester) Dunolmensis diocesis, super quo lis pendet in Romana curia inter ipsos, qua lite pendente dictus Johannes de Nesbit' in curia decessit, xv kalendas Februarii.[469] Lis pendet in curia, et est in mandato ad sequestrandum, non obstante sequestro auditoris camere ibidem diu est aposito.[470]

### Lincolniensis

De archidiaconatu Lincolniensi, que dignitas curata [471] existit, vacante per consecrationem Willelmi de Wykham episcopi Wyntoniensis, fuit provisum Ricardo de Ravenesser' presbytero, qui dimittet preposituram Sancti Johannis Beverlacensis. Taxatur ad xx li. sicut exibuit, et, salvo iure super procurationibus si debeantur, solvit viginti sex li. xiii s. iiii d.[472]

### Sarisbiriensis

Item Johanni Blebury de canonicatu et prebenda ecclesie collegiate seu conventualis monialium Scaston' (Shaftesbury) Sarisbiriensis prout supra, et dimittet canonicatum et prebendam ecclesie collegiate Landowy brevy (Llanddewi Brefi) Menevensis, pro taxa xxx m. Possessor est gardaraulerius domine principisse, qui solvit die xxviii Septembris anno LXXIII decem li., et habet terminum de resta.[472]

### Wyntoniensis

Item Willelmo de Musho [473] de canonicatu et prebenda in ecclesia conventuali monialium de Warewell' (Wherwell) Wyntoniensis diocesis, vacantibus ut supra, xiii kalendas Februarii,[474] pro taxa xl li. Solvit in duabus vicibus viginti sex li. xiii s. iiii d.[472] Item solvit die xvi Januarii alias xiii li. vi s. viii d.[472]

Recepta pagine lxxvi li. xiii s. iiii d.; [475] inutilis est una provisio iª; restant fructus de tribus provisionibus iii; resta pecunie x li.

### (fol. 25ᵛ) Londoniensis

Item Willelmo de Dighton' de canonicatu et prebenda ecclesie Londoniensis, vacantibus prout supra, vocata

Totenhale (Tottenhall, St. Pancras, London), et taxata ad x li. xiii s. iiii d. Solvit dictas decem li. xiii s. iiii d. in duabus vicibus.[476]

### Dunolmensis

Item Thome de Barneby de canonicatu et prebenda ecclesie collegiate Auclandie (Auckland) Dunolmensis diocesis, vacantibus per obitum Thome Bridkirke in Romana curia defuncti, et de quibus sic vacantibus felicis recordationis Dominus Innocentius papa VIᵗᵘˢ prefato Willelmo nunc episcopo Wyntoniensi concessit provideri, qui [477] antequam sibi provideretur de ipsis, in episcopum [478] Wyntoniensem consecratus, xiii kalendas Februarii.[479] Non habuit effectum ut in restis folio xxvi, et unus ordinarius possidet et per plures annos possedit.[480]

### Norwicensis

Item Johanni Alayn de archidiaconatu Southfolchie [481] in ecclesia Norwicensi, vacante et reservato per obitum Johannis Kadleton', qui [477] veniendo ad curiam Romanam extra ipsam decessit, et dimittet canonicatum et prebendam ecclesie Sancti Georgii in [482] castro de Wyndesore (Windsor), xiii kalendas Februarii,[479] non taxatur. Solvit die xii Maii anno LXXIII pro medietate veri valoris tres marcas, salvo iure pluris super procurationibus et super maiore valentia, xl s.[476]

### Lincolniensis

Item Ricardo de Landeford' [483] de canonicatu et prebenda [484] Lincolniensibus, vacantibus et reservatis per mortem Johannis de Karleton' extra Romanam curiam defuncti veniendo ad eam, xiii kalendas Februarii,[479] pro taxa l s. Solvit die xiii Aprilis anno LXXIII dictos quinquaginta s.[476]

### Eboracensis

De prepositura ecclesie Sancti Johannis Beverlacensis Eboracensis diocesis, vacante dum Ricardus Ravenesher' archidiaconatum ecclesie Lincolniensis fuit pacifice assecutus, fuit provisum Ade Limbergh', qui dimittet canonicatum et prebendam lx s. in ecclesia Lincolniensi, xiii kalendas Februarii,[479] pro taxa temporalitatis xl li. Solvit die secunda Aprilis anno LXXII pro temporalitate dictas quadraginta libras, et de residuo est infra cum exploratis folio,[485] xl li.[476]

---

[469] 18 January 1368.
[470] In the margin: *debet.*
[471] *tant'*, MS.
[472] Sum repeated MS. In the margin: *solvit.*
[473] *Mulso*, Collectorie 13, fol. 166ᵛ.
[474] 20 January 1368.
[475] In the margin: *vera.*
[476] In the margin: *solvit.*
[477] *que*, MS.
[478] *episcopus*, MS.
[479] 20 January 1368.
[480] In the margin: *inutilis.*
[481] *Southfolcfolchie*, MS.
[482] Followed by *ecclesia* deleted by a line.
[483] *Lyncheford*, Collectorie 13, fol. 166ᵛ.
[484] Prebend of All Saints Thorngate, Lincoln: Collectorie 13, fol. 166ᵛ.
[485] Blank in MS.

## Menevensis

Item Johanni de Saxton' de canonicatu et prebenda in ecclesia Lamdiwybremy (Llanddewi Brefi) Menevensis diocesis, vacante dum Johannes de Blebury ⟨canonicatum et prebendam⟩ ecclesie collegiate et conventualis monialium Schaston' (Shaftesbury) Sarisbiriensis diocesis fuit pacifice assecutus, dimittet prebendam Lichfeldensem, xiii kalendas Februarii.[479] Certificat episcopus quod non habuit effectum in secundo et tertio mandatis.[480]

## Norwicensis

De vicaria perpetua parochialis ecclesie de Halesham (Aylsham) Norwicensis diocesis, vacante vel vacatura dum Michael de Causton' beneficium ad collationem episcopi Eliensis fuit pacifice assecutus, fuit provisum Thome Guilay de Wodehaus presbytero, xii kalendas Martii,[486] pro taxa xxviii m. Solvit in tribus vicibus dictas viginti octo marcas, que valent xviii li. xiii s. iiii d.[476]

## Roffensis

Item Johanni de Ledecombe de parochiali ecclesia de Otteford' (Otford) Roffensis diocesis, vacante vel vacatura dum Johannes Alani archidiaconatum Suffolchie [487] in ecclesia Norwicensi fuit pacifice assecutus, xiii kalendas Februarii.[479] Prohibitum per breve quia dictus Johannes possidet titulo regio, sede Cantuariensi vacante, et quia non debet venire contra factum proprium ipse met qui inpetravit, videant domini in camere quod agendum.[488]

Recepta pagine lxxiii li. xvi s. viii d.; [489] inutiles sunt due provisiones ii; restant fructus ultime provisionis i[us].

## (fol. 26, xxvi)[490] Londoniensis

Ex causa permutationis fuit provisum Bernardo de Sautre, presbytero diocesis Lincolniensis, de parochiali ecclesia de Alto Rotyng' (High Roding), taxata xii li., Londoniensis diocesis, debet de resta iii li.[488] Alia est provisio supra folio xvii, et est in mandato monitus, sequestratus et eccommunicatus.[488]

## Norwicensis

Item Johanni de Glatton' de parochiali ecclesia de Northwold' Norwicensis diocesis, que taxatur ad xxvii li. vi s. viii d., debet de resta iiii[or] li. Solvit dictas iiii[or] li. die xiii Junii anno LXXIII.[476]

## Norwicensis

Collatio et provisio facte vigore litterarum apostoli-

carum in forma communi Willelmo Dany, presbytero Norwicensis diocesis, de parochiali ecclesia de Fornham Sancti Martini dicte diocesis, super qua lis pendebat inter Willelmum Creswell', tunc possessorem auctoritate ordinaria, qua lite pendente idem Willelmus extra curiam decessit, fuerunt confirmate vel provisum de novo, et fuit subrogatus in omni iure competenti prefato defuncto, xi kalendas Martii,[491] taxata viii li., debet de resta vi li. xiii s. iiii d., et est monitus et sequestratus.[488] Solvit die v Novembris anno LXXIII tres li. vi s. viii d.[492]

## Dunolmensis

De canonicatu et prebenda ecclesie collegiate Cestr' in strata (Chester-le-Street) Dunolmensis diocesis, vacantibus per resignationem Guidonis de Pestello, fuit provisum Hugoni de Arlani, clerico Dunolmensis diocesis, et dimittet litem decanatus ipsius et gratiam sibi factam de parochiali ecclesia de Horncastr' (Horncastle) Lincolniensis diocesis, viii kalendas Martii.[493] Alia est provisio infra de eadem, que non habuit effectum, sicut nec ista, sed alia est supra que habuit effectum, sed de omnibus est prohibitum per breve quia possessor est titulo regio intrusus.[488]

## Lincolniensis

De vicaria de Stotteford' (Stotford) ratione provisionis facte Radulpho de Bereford', non taxata, sed composuit pro quinque marcis, debet de resta ii m. Solvit dictas duas marcas ultima die Aprilis anno LXXII, videlicet xxvi s. viii d.[494]

## Eboracensis

De parochiali ecclesia de Acastr' Malvis (Acaster Malbis) Eboracensis diocesis, vacante per resignationem Willelmi de Harmi, ultimi rectoris eiusdem, et tanto tempore vacavit quod eius collatio est ad sedem apostolicam legitime devoluta, licet abbas et conventus monasterii de Newbo illam detineant occupatam, fuit provisum Johanni Karold', bacallario in utroque iure, et dimittet parochialem ecclesiam de Launchbord (?) et capellam de Albo Fonte (Whitwell), idus Aprilis.[495] Appropriata est dicto abbati et non habuit effectum, ut in restis folio xxvii.[496]

## Bangorensis

Collatio et provisio auctoritate ordinaria facte Thome de Honerbergh' de archidiaconatu Anglesie (Anglesey) in ecclesia Bangorensi, vacante per obitum ap Gronon extra Romanam curiam defuncti, si fuerit reservato,

---

[486] 19 February 1368.
[487] *Southwell'*, MS.
[488] In the margin: *debet*.
[489] In the margin: *vera*.
[490] The heading *Anno vi Urbani* is repeated at the top of the page.

[491] 20 February 1368.
[492] Sum repeated MS. In the margin: *solvit*.
[493] 23 February 1368.
[494] In the margin: *solvit*.
[495] 13 April 1368.
[496] In the margin: *inutilis*.

fuerunt confirmate vel provisum de novo, viii kalendas Maii,[497] taxato xxvi li. xiii s. iiii d., debet de resta iiii[or] li. Solvit dictas quatuor li. die secunda Maii anno LXXIII.[494]

### Londoniensis

Collatio et provisio facte auctoritate apostolica Johanni de Lexham de parochiali ecclesia Sancti Benedicti de Grascherch' civitatis Londonie (St. Benet Gracechurch, London), quam per annum et ultra possedit pacifice, si reservata fuerit, fuerunt confirmate vel provisum de novo, viii kalendas Junii,[498] non taxata sed composuit pro viii li., debet de resta xl s. Solvit dictos quadraginta solidos.[492]

Recepta pagine xiiii li. xiii s. iiii d.; [499] inutilis provisio est i[a]; resta pecunie vi li. vi s. viii d.; et fructus duarum provisionum ii.

### (fol. 26[v]) Eboracensis

De canonicatu et prebenda Eboracensibus quos Johannes de Appulby, legum doctor, vigore expectationis per dominum papam sibi concesse [500] acceptavit et possidet, licet Matheus de Assheton' ipsos acceptavit, quamvis ipsum Johannem subsequeretur in data, dicens ipsos sibi deberi et non dicto Johanni ex eo quod nuper Johanni dominus noster papa de canonicatu sub expectatione prebende ac de decanatu Londonie providit, volens quod, quamprimam prebendam ipsius Londoniensis ecclesie fuerit pacifice assecutus vigore litterarum apostolicarum, expectationem quam habet in ecclesia Eboracensi dimittet; ipseque prebendam ipsius Londoniensis ecclesie sit assecutus, et lite super hoc pendente inter ipsos prefatos, Johanne dicente quod, cum prebendam ipsam non vigore litterarum apostolicarum sed auctoritate ordinaria causa permutationis fuit assecutus, se non, tame nfuit expectatio, habuisse dicentem,[501] et sic dictam prebendam sibi deberi; quibus domino pape expositis, et quia dictus Matheus non graduatus optinet in redditibus ecclesiasticis mille florenos et ultra et dictus doctor non optinet ultra viii[c] fl., idem dominus papa prefatum Matheum dictam prebendam privavit et eam dicto doctori, et sic in quantum indiget, contulit, xv kalendas Julii.[502] Dicitur in restis prioris infra folio xxvii quod non habuit effectum, sed infra est alia provisio de eadem folio xxix que habuit effectum, et ibi solvit.[496]

### Londoniensis

Collatio et provisio facte auctoritate apostolica Henrico Wyntirton', in utroque iure bacallario, de archidiaconatu Essexie in ecclesia Londondiensi, licet tunc

idem Henricus mentionem non fecisset quod dictus archidiaconatus curatus existerit, fuerunt confirmate vel provisum de novo, xiii kalendas Julii.[503] Alia est provisio infra eundem annum ut in restis prioris folio xxvii.[504]

### Dunolmensis

De canonicatu et prebenda ecclesie collegiate Cestr' in strata (Chester-le-Street) Dunolmensis diocesis, vacantibus per resignationem Guidonis de Pestello, fuit provisum Waltero de Waudeford', clerico dicte diocesis, et dimittet gratiam sibi factam de hospitali de Schirburn' (Sherburn) eiusdem diocesis, vi idus Julii,[505] pro taxa xx li. Prohibitum per breve regis ut in restis prioris folio xxvii, et sunt alie due provisiones supra, et prima debetur non obstante breve predicto, ut supra folio xxiiii[or].[506]

Titulus est. Beneficia collata et confirmata in Anglia per dominum nostrum Dominum Urbanum papam V[tum] anno vi[to] kalendas Augusti pontificatus sui anno vi[to].[507]

### Sarisbiriensis

Dum Johannes de Tresk', presbyter [508] Eboracensis diocesis, beneficium ad collationem episcopi Sarisbiriensis fuit pacifice assecutus, dimittet rectoriam de Stampton' (Stanton) Bathoniensis diocesis, v kalendas Augusti.[509] De hoc nihil in effectu.[510]

### Eboracensis

De vicaria perpetua parochialis ecclesia de Hesill' (Hessle) a prioratu de Gisburn' (Guisborough) Eboracensis diocesis dependente, ab antiqua consuetudine per canonicos regulares dicti prioratus gubernari, vacante per mortem Ricardi de Lesbury, canonici dicti ordinis, in Romana curia defuncti, fuit provisum Johanni de Wodeford, canonico Karleolensi ordinis Sancti Augustini, non obstante quod [511] inter dictum possessorem dicte vicarie et quemdam Johannem Kulry citra tamen dilationem lis pendet, et dictus Johannes de Dordeford' dimittet vicariam parochialis ecclesie de Withingham (Whittingham) Dunolmensis diocesis, vi idus Augusti.[512] Prorogatus est ad biennium per litteras domini camerarii, que sunt in archivis, de data xxiii die Martii anno LXXII.[513]

Inutiles sunt due et expectatio iii; restant fructus de duabus provisionibus ii.

---

[497] 24 April 1368.
[498] 25 May 1368.
[499] In the margin: *vera.*
[500] *concessam,* MS.
[501] Perhaps a mistake for *dimittere.* See above, p. 354.
[502] 17 June 1368.

[503] 19 June 1368.
[504] In the margin: *videatur si debet.*
[505] 10 July 1368.
[506] In the margin: *inutilis ista.*
[507] 27 July 1368.
[508] *presbytero,* MS.
[509] 28 July 1368.
[510] In the margin: *expectatio est inutilis.*
[511] *pro,* MS.
[512] 8 August 1368.
[513] In the margin: *debet.*

### (fol. 27; xxvii)[514]
#### Wyntoniensis

De parochiali ecclesia de Croidon' (Croydon) Wyntoniensis diocesis, vacante ex eo quod Johannes Quemby eam per annum et ultra tenuit in presbyterum non promotus dispensatione super hoc non obtento, et cessante impedimenta legitimo, etiam si eam permutavit post lapsum anni[515] huius, vel si specialiter vel generaliter reservatur, fuit Radulpho Pylaton' provisum, presbytero Exoniensis diocesis. Lis pendet in curia Romana; ideo nondum habuit effectum ut in restis folio xxviii, sed videatur, sopita lite.[513]

#### Lincolniensis

De parochiali ecclesia de Werketon' (Warkton) Lincolniensis diocesis, vacante vel vacatura dum Henricus Pryel archidiaconatum de Bokingham in ecclesia Lincolniensi fuit pacifice assecutus, fuit provisum Roberto Garre, presbytero Lincolniensis diocesis, pridie kalendas Decembris.[516] Nondum habuit effectum, sed videatur quando habebit, tunc solvat, vero.[513]

#### Exoniensis

Item collatio et provisio facte vigore litterarum apostolicarum Nicholao Thobro, presbytero Exoniensis, de parochiali ecclesia de Blakautton' (Blackawton) Exoniensis diocesis, licet impetratorem harum[517] litterarum dixisse idem Nicholaum[518] fore Exoniensis diocesis qui tamen est civitatis Exoniensis. Est in mandato, sed nondum reperitur quod sit talis in diocesi, et iam mandetur de beneficio quod ibi optinuit dictus Nicholaus.[513]

#### Norwicensis

Item collatio et provisio auctoritate ordinaria ex causa permutationis facte Henrico de Dunston' de parochiali ecclesia de Beghton' (Beighton) Norwicensis diocesis, et etiam si vacet per illicitam detentionem cuiusdam Johannis de Je et si fuerit devoluta vel reservata, fuerunt confirmate vel provisum de novo, kalendas Septembris.[519] Nondum habuit effectum ut est probatum, et hoc lite finita, quare fuit relaxatus et cetera.[520]

#### Cicestrensis

Item de novo fuit provisum Henrico de Onnyng', clerico Cicestrensis diocesis, de parochiali ecclesia de Blachyngton' (Blatchington) Cicestrensis diocesis, quam ultra tempus debitum detinuit, fructus ex ea percipiendo,

in presbyterum non promotus, et fuit etiam habilitatus, taxata xx m., debet de resta x m. Solvit dictas decem marcas que valent vi li. xiii s. iiii d.[521]

#### Lichfeldensis

De vicaria perpetua ecclesie curate de Jolegrave (Youlgreave) Lichfeldensis diocesis, vacante per obitum Ricardi de Horteshull' in Romana curia defuncti, fuit provisum Johanni de Apthorp', presbytero Lichfeldensis diocesis, et est in decanatu de Pecio, et non taxata. Set solvit pro medietate veri valoris, salvo iure pluris si reperitur in futurum decem marcas que valent vi li. xiii s. iiii d.[521]

#### Menevensis

De prioratu de Cinhingham (Cardigan) Menevensis diocesis in Wallia, a monasterio Cherteseye ordinis Sancti Benedicti, vacante per liberam resignationem ultimi prioris eiusdem in manibus abbatis ipsius monasterii, quem idem abbas apostolice sedis licentia non super hoc optenta illicite detinet occupatum,[522] fuit provisum fratri Thome Cymy de Wallia oriundo, monacho monasterii Sancti Martini de Geldo (Battle) dicti ordinis Cisterciensis, nonas Septembris.[523] Certificat episcopus quod non habuit effectum dicta vacatio nec provisio quia non vacavit et cetera.[520]

Recepta pagine xiii li. vi s. viii d.;[524] inutiles provisiones sunt ii; et restant trium[526] provisionum iii.

### (fol. 27ᵛ) Cantuariensis

De prepositura ecclesie collegiate de Wyngham (Wingham) diocesis Cantuariensis, vacante per consecrationem Willelmi electi Cicestrensis, fuit provisum Thome de Paxton', legum doctori, et dimittet parochialem ecclesiam de Hakeney (Hackney) Londoniensis diocesis, iiiᵗⁱᵒ idus Octobris.[527] Nunquam habuit effectum dicta gratia; immo obiit in curia ante adeptam possessionem.[520]

Completum est de anno sexto

Titulus est. Beneficia collata et confirmata in Anglia per dominum nostrum Dominum Urbanum papam vᵗᵘᵐ pontificatus sui anno septimo

#### Bangorensis

Et primo de archidiaconatu de Marinient (Merioneth) in ecclesia Bangorensi in Wallia, que dignitas curata existit, vacante per obitum Edmundi Hyngham in Romana curia defuncti, fuit provisum Johanni Rey, clerico Assavensis[528] diocesis, et dimittet canonicatum et pre-

---

[514] The heading *Anno vi Urbani* is repeated at the top of the page.

[515] *annum*, MS.

[516] 31 August 1368. *Decembris* is an error for *Septembris*.

[517] *huius*, MS.

[518] *Nicholaus*, MS.

[519] 1 September 1368.

[520] In the margin: *inutilis*.

[521] In the margin: *solvit*.

[522] *occupatam*, MS.

[523] 5 September 1368.

[524] In the margin: *vera*.

[525] This footnote was eliminated.

[526] Over *duarum* deleted by a line.

[527] 13 October 1368.

[528] *Aspinensis*, MS.

bendam in dicta ecclesia, vi[to] idus Novembris.[529] Est monitus, excommunicatus et sequestratus in mandatis.[530]

## Londoniensis, Wellensis, Eboracensis

Collationes et provisiones facte Johanni de Sannford' de canonicatibus et prebendis Londoniensi et Wellensi et Sancti Johannis Beverlacensis Eboracensis diocesis ecclesiarum,[531] non obstante defectu natalium que patitur de soluto genitus et soluta, cum quo alias super huius defectu existit dispensatus, licet dum idem Johannes fuit genitus mater sua fuerat cum alio copulata matrimonialiter, cuiusmodi matrimonium tamen postmodum nullum fuit declaratum, fuerunt confirmate vel provisum de novo, vi idus Novembris; [529] debet pro toto secundum librum taxe xliii li. xiii s. iiii d. Solvit die xvi Aprilis anno LXXIII dictas quadraginta tres libras xiii s. iiii d.[532]

## Dunolmensis

De perpetua vicaria parochialis ecclesie de Wyntrigham [533] (Whittingham) Dunolmensis diocesis, vacatura dum Johannes de Doedeford', canonicus Karleolensis ordinis Sancti Augustini, vicariam perpetuam parochialis ecclesie de Hesill' (Hessle) Eboracensis diocesis fuerit pacifice assecutus, fuit provisum Thome de Penreth, canonico dicte ecclesie Karleolensis, v idus Novembris,[534] pro taxa x li. Solvit die xxiiii Octobris anno LXXII dictas decem libras.[535]

## Sarisbiriensis

Motu proprio fuit provisum Bernardo titulo xii Apostolorum presbytero cardinali [536] de archidiaconatu de Barkschir' in ecclesia Sarisbiriensi, vacante per obitum Alexandri de Dalby extra Romanam curiam defuncti, v kalendas Decembris.[537] Solvit die x Martii anno domini et cetera LXXII Magister Rohgerius Kirnalorg' in partem solutionis primorum fructuum dicti archidiaconatus viginti quinque libras sterlingorum quas receperat de arayrahgiis dicto domino cardinali et eius exsecutori debitis, xxv li.[538]

## Dublinensis

Ex causa permutationis fuit provisum Willelmo de Bromley de thesauraria et Johanni Salton' de canonicatu ecclesie Dublinensis pridie kalendas Decembris vel iii[tio] nonas Decembris.[539] Non est talis in Anglia.[540]

Recepta pagine lxxviii li. xiii s. iiii d.; [541] inutiles provisiones sunt due ii; restant fructus ii.

## (fol. 28, xxviii)[542] Sarisbiriensis

De parochiali ecclesia de Hedyngton' (Edington) Sarisbiriensis diocesis, vacante per obitum Nicholai Dribe in Romana curia defuncti, fuit provisum Hode de Hunton', presbytero Eboracensis diocesis, et dimittet perpetuam vicariam in parochiali ecclesia de Vedbek' (Welwick?). Non habuit effectum ut in restis folio xxix.[540]

## Cantuariensis

Item Hugoni de Attehell' de parochiali ecclesia de Wygeresham (Wittersham) Cantuariensis, vacante quia Walterus de Bolton' parochialem ecclesiam de Hadenham (Haddenham) Eliensis diocesis est pacifice assecutus, quinto idus Decembris.[543] Prohibitum per breve bis, et copia est in archivis, et habetur folio xxix in restis prioris, sed debetur non obstante titulo regio quo se defendit possessor, et iterum est prohibitum de novo.[544]

## Wellensis, Eliensis

Concessum est Willelmi Walsham ut parochialem ecclesiam de Routeburi (Bunbury) quam optinet et quam dimittere tenebatur dum canonicatum et prebendam et dignitatem ecclesie Wellensis fuit pacifice assecutus, post assecutionem huius valeat retinere, dum tamen que exspectat et optinet quadringentos florenos non excedant. Expectatio est et non habuit effectum quia non scitum est ecclesia illa, sed videatur melius si possit reperire.[540]

## Lichfeldensis

De canonicatu et prebenda de Rayton' (Ryton) in ecclesia Lichfeldensi, vacantibus dum Nicholaus de Chaddesden' canonicatum et prebendam ecclesie Eboracensis fuit pacifice assecutus, fuit provisum Willelmo de Horsley, x kalendas Februarii.[545] Non habuit effectum ut in restis priaris folia xxix.[540]

## Dunolmensis

De canonicatu et prebenda ecclesie collegiate Aucland' (Auckland) diocesis Dunolmensis, vacantibus per resignationem Roberti de Stratton', auditoris palatii apostolici, fuit provisum Petro de Burton', clerico Lichfeldensis diocesis, x kalendas Februarii.[545] Non habuit effectum ut in restis folio xxix.[540]

---

[529] 8 November 1368.

[530] In the margin: *debet*.

[531] Prebends of Maplebury in Willesden, London, Ashill, Wells and the altar of St. Andrew in Beverley: Collectorie 13, fol. 167.

[532] In the margin: *solvit*.

[533] Wythingham, Collectorie 13, fol. 167[v].

[534] 9 November 1368.

[535] Sum repeated MS. In the margin: *solvit*.

[536] Bernard de Bosqueto, archbishop of Naples.

[537] 27 November 1368. In the margin: *Cardinalis de Agresolio* (William d'Aigrefeuille, priest of S. Stefano) *tenet*.

[538] In the margin: *solvit; debet*.

[539] 30 November or 3 December 1368.

[540] In the margin: *inutilis*.

[541] In the margin: *vera*.

[542] The heading *Anno vii Urbani* is repeated at the top of the page.

[543] 9 December 1368.

[544] In the margin: *debet*.

[545] 23 January 1369.

### Lichfeldensis

Dum Willelmus Gotham prebendam, dignitatem, personatum vel officium ecclesie Lichfeldensis fuit pacifice assecutus, dimittet quandum ecclesiam parochialem in diocesi Wellensi.[546]

### Sarisbiriensis

Dum Thomas de Lexham dignitatem, personatum vel officium ecclesie Sarisbiriensis fuit pacifice assecutus, dimittet parochialem ecclesiam Beate Marie de Feltwell' Norwicensis diocesis.

### Herefordensis

Dum Willelmus Flaynburgh dignitatem ecclesie Herefordensis fuit pacifice assecutus, dimittet parochialem ecclesiam de Gorford' (Garford) Eboracensis diocesis.

### Cicestrensis

Dum Thomas Hornyford' dignitatem ecclesie Cicestrensis fuerit pacifice assecutus, dimittet parochialem ecclesiam de Saham Monachorum (Monk Soham) Norwicensis diocesis.

### Lincolniensis

Dum Thomas March' dignitatem in ecclesia Lincolniensi fuit pacifice assecutus, dimittet parochialem ecclesiam de Snaillwell' (Snailwell).

### Eliensis

Dum Robertus Fau de Custode Norwicensis diocesis beneficium curatum ad collationem episcopi Eliensis fuerit assecutus, dimittet parochialem ecclesiam de Burg' (Burgh), v kalendas Februarii.[547]

Restant fructus unius provisionis i; et sunt ix provisiones inutiles ix.

### (fol. 28ᵛ) Lichfeldensis

De decanatu curato et electivo ecclesie Lichfeldensis, vacante per obitum Willemi de Mantton' extra Romanam curiam defuncti, fuit provisum Antonio de Ros, et dimittet parochialem ecclesiam de Goldesburgh (Goldsborough) et gratiam sibi factam de archidiaconatu Essexie in ecclesia Londoniensi, iiiᵗⁱᵒ kalendas Februarii.[548] Cardinalis Sabinensis[549] possidet, nec reperitur aliquid de dicto Antonio ad huc.[544]

### Wygorniensis

De ecclesia parochiali de Todyngton' (Toddington) Wygorniensis diocesis, vacante per obitum Willelmi Tracy fuit provisum Willelmo Lenthe, licet per alium detineatur occupata, et dimittet vicariam perpetuam parochialis ecclesie Omnium Sanctorum Bristoll' dicte diocesis, vᵗᵒ nonas Martii.[550] Est in mandatis exsecutus, monitus et excommunicatus et sub sequestro iiiiᵒʳ vicibus et cetera. Alia est provisio infra folio xcix et nulla habuit effectum, et probationes sunt in archivis ex post recepte.[540]

### Eboracensis

Electio concordata facta de fratre Ricardo[551] de Kellech', canonico prioratus de Kertmell' (Cartmel) ordinis Sancti Augustini Eboracensis diocesis, ad dictum prioratum, vacantem per resignationem liberam factam de eo, et confirmatio auctoritate ordinaria subsecuta, fuerunt confirmate vel provisum de novo, nonas Martii,[552] taxato xi li. vi s. viii d. iuxta novam taxam, debet de resta v li. vi s. viii d. Solvit dictas quinque libras vi s. viii d., salvo iure pluris super antiqua taxa.[553]

### Brechinensis

Item collatio et provisio facte David Sanntton', clerico Brecinensis (Brechin) diocesis de perpetua vicaria parochialis ecclesie de Montess' (Montrose) dicte diocesis, et si vacet per illicitam detentionem predecessorum suorum, fuerunt confirmate vel provisum de novo, nonas Martii.[552] Non est in regni Anglie talis diocesis, ut in restis folio xxix.[554]

### Bangorensis

De canonicatu et prebenda ecclesie Bangoriensis, vacantibus per mortem Edmundi Kingham in Romana curia defuncti, fuit provisum Rogero Oskvoldestro, presbytero Assavensis diocesis, et dimittet perpetuam vicariam ecclesie Oskevoldestr' (Oswestry), vi idus Aprilis.[555] Est in mandatis monitus et excommunicatus et sub sequestro.[556]

### Lincolniensis

Motu proprio fuit provisum Bernardo cardinali Neapolitanensi[557] de canonicatu ecclesie Lincolniensis et de prebenda de Multon' (Milton Ecclesia) in eadem, vacantibus per mortem Alexandri de Dalby extra Romanam curiam defuncti, pridie idus Martii.[558] Solvit Magister Rohgerius Kirnalorge die x Martii anno LXXII in partem solutionis taxe primorum fructuum tresdecim li. ix s. v d., quos receperat de arairahgiis dicto domino debitis, xiii li. ix s. v d.[553]

---

[546] Against this and the next five items in bracketed in the left margin: *inutiles*; in the right margin: *Expectationes sunt que non habuerunt effectum quod sciatur et cetera, de tempore Urbani.*

[547] 28 January 1369.

[548] 30 January 1369.

[549] William d'Aigrefeuille.

[550] 3 March 1369.

[551] *Ricardi*, MS.

[552] 7 March 1369.

[553] Sum repeated MS. In the margin: *solvit.*

[554] In the margin: *inutilis.*

[555] 8 April 1369.

[556] In the margin: *debet.*

[557] Bernard de Bosqueto, priest of Ss. XII Apostoli.

[558] 14 March 1369. In the margin: *Cardinalis Neapolitanensis est.*

## Menevensis

De prebenda de Caron (Tregaron) in ecclesia Landewybrevy (Llanddewi Brefi) Menevensis diocesis, vacante quia Johannes de Blebury prebendam de Abbe' (Iwerne?) in ecclesia monialium de Schaftebury (Shaftesbury) est pacifice assecutus, fuit provisum Edmundo Dak', licet de ipsa sic vacante ad mandatum fuit provisum Johanni de Saxton', cui de ea non est provisum nec faciet provideri, viii kalendas Maii.[559] Dicitur quod non habuit effectum, sed est in mandato ad sequestrandum et cetera, et habet nunc terminum nativitatis anno LXXIII, quia in aliis libris erat error in nomine quia dicebatur Caros et talis non reperiebatur.[556]

Recepta pagine xviii li. xvi s. i d.;[560] inutiles provisiones sunt ii; et restant fructus duarum provisionum ii.

### (fol. 29, xxix)[561] Dunolmensis

Mandatur Domino [562] Petro Flandini, auditori palatii apostolici, quod si sola veritate inspecta reperiret Thomam Clernaux clericum pretextu cuiusdam gratie sibi per dominum papam de beneficio ecclesiastico ad collationem episcopi et prioris Dunolmensis facte in parochiali ecclesia de Wermouth (Bishop-Wearmouth) Dunolmensis diocesis absque litteris apostolicis et executoriis intrusum fore, illam David de Wollore, cui episcopus Dunolmensis auctoritate ordinaria providit de eadem, adiudicet et super ea et eius possessione dicto Thome silentium perpetuum imponat, viii kalendas Maii,[559] pro taxa c li.[563] Ista provisio debetur quia dictus David obiit possessor, sed nihil reperitur ad huc de sua, et alia est infra folio xxxvi que debetur per dominum cardinalem Cantuariensem.[564]

### Eboracensis

De canonicatu et prebenda de Northmewebald' (North Newbald) in ecclesia Eboracensi, vacantibus per obitum Roberti de Middelond' extra Romanam curiam defuncti,[565] fuit provisum Roberto Wykeford', presbytero utriusque iuris doctori, et dimittet canonicatum et prebendam ecclesie Lincolniensis, viii kalendas Maii,[559] pro taxa liii li. vi s. viii d., debet de resta xl li. Solvit xxii die Januarii anno LXXIII viginta li.;[566] debet restam.[553]

## Lincolniensis

De canonicatu et prebenda Lincolniensibus, vacantibus dum Robertus de Wykeford' prebendam de Northnewebald' in ecclesia Eboracensi fuit pacifice assecutus, fuit provisum Johanni Cheyne Exoniensi diocesis, et dimittet litem quam habet super prebenda de Karswell' (Kerswell) in ecclesia collegiata de Criditon' (Crediton), viii kalendas Maii.[559] Est in mandatis ad sequestrandum et denuntiandum, et est ab et de familia domini comitis Arundell', et fuit thesaurarius Lemovicensis (Limoges).[556]

### Cantuariensis

Concessum est Thome Paxton', auditori palatii apostolici, quod gratia sibi facta de prepositura ecclesie collegiate de Wyngham (Wingham) Cantuariensis diocesis non possit de surreptione notarii nec obstet sibi quia in impetratione illius nullam fecit mentionem quod Thomas Ykham super ea contra Willelum Roose, tunc illius possessorem, in Romana curia litigavit, viii kalendas Maii.[559] Non habuit effectum ut est notorium, sed precedens supra folio xviii, et secretarius principis possidet, scilicet Fordham.[567]

### Eboracensis

Mandatur provideri Johanni de Balton', presbytero Exoniensis diocesis, de canonicatu et prebenda vacantibus vel vacaturis in ecclesia collegiata Southwell', v nonas Maii.[568] Expectatio est et nondum habuit effectum.[567]

### Lincolniensis

De parochiali ecclesia de Henygford' abbatis (Hemingford Abbots) Lincolniensis diocesis, vacante vel vacatura dum Michael de Ravenesdale presbyter ecclesiam de Hornesse (Hornsea) Eboracensis diocesis fuit pacifice assecutus, fuit provisum Johanni de Carlil, clerico Karleolensis diocesis, iiii[to] kalendas Junii,[569] pro taxa xxv m. que valent xvi li. xiii s. iiii d. Non habuit effectum ut in restis prioris est probatum folio xxx.[567]

Recepta pagine xx li.; inutiles provisiones sunt iii; restant in pecunia cxx li.; et fructus duarum provisionum ii.

### (fol. 29v) Wygorniensis

De prioratu de Durhurst (Deerhurst) Wygorniensis diocesis a monasterio Sancti Dyonisii in Francia Parisiensis [570] diocesis dependente, vacante per obitum fratris Johannis de Medinka extra Romanam curiam defuncti, fuit provisum Johanni Wallcelyn, monacho monasterii Sancti Sengii et Basii (Saint-Serge) Andegavensis (Angers) diocesis. Non habuit effectum, ut habetur in restis prioris folio xxx.[567]

---

[559] 24 April 1369.
[560] In the margin: *vera*.
[561] The heading *Anno vii Urbani* is repeated at the top of the page.
[562] Over *provideri* deleted by a line.
[563] Follows *c li.* deleted by a line.
[564] In the margin: *Cardinalis Cantuariensis tenet nunc et post permutavit, ut dicitur. Debet.*
[565] Followed by *et dimittet canonicatum et prebendam ecclesie Lincolniensis viii* deleted by a line.
[566] Sum repeated MS.

[567] In the margin: *inutilis*.
[568] 3 May 1369.
[569] 29 May 1369.
[570] *imparie*, MS.

## Wygorniensis

De novo fuit provisum Willelmo Horsleye, clerico Wygorniensis diocesis, de parochiali ecclesia Sancti Johannis Gloucestr' dicte diocesis, quam fuit nunquam canonice assecutus obstante defectu natalium quem patitur de coniugato genitus et soluta, fuit habilitatus, pro taxa vi li. xiii s. iiii d. Solvit in duabus vicibus dictas sex li. xiii s. iiii d.[571]

## Lincolniensis

Item collatio et provisio facte vigore litterarum apostolicarum in forma communi Roberto de Rukham,[572] presbytero Eboracensis diocesis, de vicaria perpetua parochialis ecclesie de Astonnewand (Aston Rowant) Lincolniensis diocesis, fuerunt confirmate vel provisum de novo, xvi kalendas Julii,[573] pro taxa vi m. et dym. Solvit die xii Octobris dictas vi m. et dym. que valent iiii\*\*or\*\* li. vi s. viii d.[571]

## Eboracensis

Provisio facta per dominum nostrum papam Johanni de Lounde de parochiali ecclesia Omnium Sanctorum super pavimentum (All Saints in the Pavement, York), tunc vacante, ut credebatur, per mortem Simonis Warde in Romana curia defuncti, super qua mota lite inter eum et Robertum Hugonis de Tholeston' de Thorpark' in ea intrusum [574] ⟨et⟩ ipse Johannes per se et contra dictum Dominum Robertum sententiam super possessorio et petitore diffinitivam optinuit, que in rem transivit iudicatam, ac deinde idem Robertus per dominum nostrum papam Innocentium ad appellandum admissus ad excludendum gratiam factam Domini Johanni quia ⟨de⟩ dicta parochiali [575] ecclesia, vacante prout supra, per felicis recordationis Dominum Innocentium provisum fuit cuidam David Morte, de quo dictus Johannes in sua gratia nullam fecit mentionem, qui, ut dicitur, decessit in partibus, fuit confirmata vel provisum de novo, dum tamen alteri parochiali ecclesie non sit preiudicate, xv kalendas Julii.[576] Valet communibus annis, ut patet certificatorium Magistri G. Fletham, xx m., nullis deductis exspensis, inde debentur x m. Solvit pro medietate veri valoris in duabus vicibus sex li. xiii s. iiii d.[577]

## Sarisbiriensis

De decanatu ecclesie Sarisbiriensis et prebenda de Husseburn' et Burbach' (Hurstbourne and Burbage) in dicta ecclesia, vacantibus per obitum Johannis de Abyndon' infra duas dietas a Romana curia defuncti,

fuit provisum Johanni More, clerico Sarisbiriensis diocesis, vii kalendas Julii.[578] Non habuit effectum quia per titulum regium fuit exclusus.[567]

## Menevensis

Mandatur provideri Thome Forester, presbytero Londoniensi, de prebenda vacante vel vacatura in ecclesia Menevensi, viii idus Julii.[579] Expectatio est et nondum habuit effectum quod sciatur.

Recepta pagine xvii li. xiii s. iiii d.;[580] inutiles provisiones sunt iii.

## (fol. 30, xxx)[581] Cicestrensis

Item Roberto Smerdeby, presbytero Eboracensis diocesis, de parochiali ecclesia de Estlecent (East Lavant), super qua litigat, viii idus Julii.[579] Certificat archiepiscopus Cantuariensis, de cuius jurisdictione est, quod non habuit effectum, titulo regio inpedimente.[582]

## Cantuariensis

Item Ricardo Bannebury, presbytero Londoniensis diocesis, de beneficio ecclesiastico, vacante vel vacaturo, spectante ad collationem archiepiscopi Cantuariensis. Expectatio que nondum habuit effectum quod possit aparere.[582]

## Eboracensis

Item Ade de Akenn, presbytero Eboracensis diocesis, de prebenda vacante vel vacatura in ecclesia collegiata de Rippon'. Expectatio est et nondum habuit effectum quod sciatur.[582]

## Lincolniensis

Collatio et provisio facte auctoritate ordinaria ex causa permutationis de parochiali ecclesia de Langeport (Lamport) Lincolniensis diocesis Johanni Onnok',[583] licet quidam olim ipsius ecclesie rector eam per plures annos tenuisset [584] in presbyterum non promotus, fuerunt confirmate vel provisum de novo, etiam si alio quovismodo ⟨vacet⟩ vel fuerit reservata, vi idus Julii,[585] taxata xxiii li. vi s. viii d., debet de resta xviii li. xiii s. iiii d. Solvit dictas decem et octo li. xiii s. iiii d.[586]

## Sarisbiriensis

Collatio, acceptatio et provisio facte vigore litterarum apostolicarum Johanni de Fereby, presbytero Eboracensis diocesis, de canonicatu et prebenda Sarisbirien-

---

[571] In the margin: *solvit.*
[572] *Brigham,* Collectorie 13, fol. 167ᵛ.
[573] 16 June 1369.
[574] *intrusio,* MS.
[575] *parochialis,* MS.
[576] 17 June 1369.
[577] Sum repeated MS. In the margin: *solvit.*

[578] 25 June 1369.
[579] 8 July 1369.
[580] In the margin: *vera.*
[581] The heading *Anno vii Urbani* is repeated at the top of the page.
[582] In the margin: *inutilis.*
[583] *Enoc,* Collectorie 13, fol. 167ᵛ.
[584] *tenuisse,* MS.
[585] 10 July 1369.
[586] In the margin: *solvit.*

sibus, videlicet Combe armam (Combe and Harnham), vacantibus per obitum Johannis de Kimefford extra Romanam curiam defuncti, etiam si fuerit reservata, fuerunt confirmate vel provisum de novo, si sibi ex ordine debeatur, v idus Julii,[587] xx m., debet de resta x m. Solvit dictas decem m. in vi li. xiii s. iiii d.[586]

### Eboracensis

Acceptatio et provisio facte vigore litterarum apostolicarum Waltero de Skirlawe, archidiacono Estriding' in ecclesia [588] Eboracensi, de prebenda de Feriton' (Fenton) in eadem, ⟨vacante⟩ per obitum quondam Roberti de Wallyngton' extra Romanam curiam defuncti, ⟨fuerunt confirmate vel⟩ fuit provisum de novo, xii kalendas Augusti vel pridie nonas Augusti.[589] Supra providetur sibi de archidiaconatu folio x, et ibi solvit salvo iure pluris solum de ecclesia annexa. Est relaxatus per litteras domini camerarii de ista provisione tamque de nulla quia negative concessa, et littere sunt in archivis.[582]

### Eboracensis

Mandatur provideri Willelmo de Ragenhull' de beneficio ecclesiastico vacante vel vacatura spectante ad collationem archiepiscopi Eboracensis, v kalendas Augusti.[590] Expectatio est et nondum habuit effectum quod sciatur.[582]

### Herefordensis

De canonicatu et prebenda ecclesie Herefordensis, vacantibus per obitum Philipi Ace in Romana curia defuncti, et qui dum viveret super ipsis in palatio apostolico litigabat et pro se diffinitivam sententiam optinuit, licet per quemdam Johannem Smyth' detineantur occupatas, fuit provisum Thome de Arundel', clerico Cicestrensis diocesis, et fuit subrogatus in omni iure et ad omne ius quod competebat dicto Philipo in illis, iiii[to] nonas Augusti,[591] pro taxa xi li. v s. iiii d. Filius est domini comitis Arundelle, et est in mandatis et cetera, et habet terminum Michaelis. Solvit xix die Aprilis anno LXXIIII[to] dictas undecim libras quinque s. iiii d.[592] Est in brevetis folio x.[586]

Recepta pagine xxxvi li. xii s.; [593] inutiles provisiones sunt iiii.

### (fol. 30ᵛ) Lincolniensis

Concessum est Laurentio de Ikestok' ut parochialem ecclesiam de Barewell' (Barwell) Lincolniensis diocesis, quam dum prebendas ecclesie Lichfeldensis foret pacifice assecutus dimittere tenebatur, post assecutionem huius licite valeat retinere, xix kalendas Septembris.[594] Alia

fuit sibi facta provisio infra eundem annum, et ibi solvit, et dictus prior Lewensis includit in recepta sua.[582]

### Exoniensis

De prepositura Sancti Thome Glaseney (Glasnay), vacante per obitum Roberti de Grinnesal' extra Romanam curiam defuncti, fuit provisum Roberto Hoo clerico, xvi kalendas Septembris.[595] Prohibitum per breve regium, quod non habuit effectum, titulo regio inpediente, et cetera.[582]

### Lincolniensis

Motu proprio fuit provisum Simoni cardinali Cantuariensi de omnibus et singulis beneficiis, etiam si tria vel quatuor illorum fuerint curata incompassibilia non in ecclesiis cathedralibus vel extra dignitates, canonicatus seu prebendas que Gervasius de Wykford, extra Romanam curiam defunctus, dum vixit dispensative tenebat, tamquam de specialiter reservatis, x kalendas Septembris.[596]

### Cantuariensis

De parochiali ecclesia de Yvechirche (Ivychurch) Cantuariensis diocesis, vacante per obitum Johannis Masselyn in Romana curia defuncti, fuit provisum Thome Forester, presbytero Londoniensis diocesis, taxata xxxv li. vi s. viii d., debet de resta xxviii li. xiii s. iiii d. Solvit dictas viginta octo li. xiii s. iiii d. in duabus vicibus.[586]

### Norwicensis

Item Thome Blakelak', clerico Exoniensis diocesis, de ecclesia Sancti Nicholai de Foltwell' (Feltwell) Norwicensis diocesis, vacante per obitum Thome Lond' presbyteri [597] in Romana curia defuncti, pro taxa xxvi m. Solvit pro dictis xxvi m. xvii li. vi s. viii d.[586]

### Lincolniensis

Motu proprio fuit provisum Domino Simoni titulo Sancti Syxti presbytero cardinali [598] de decanatu et prebenda ecclesie Lincolniensis, vacantibus per obitum Johannis Sterley extra Romanam curiam defuncti, xvii kalendas Octobris.[599]

### Cicestrensis

Ex causa permutationis fuit provisum Johanni de Landa de prioratu conventuali de Boxgrave in Anglia Cicestrensis diocesis nonas Septembris,[600] debet primos fructus extra x li. quos solvit, debet de resta iiii[xx] i li.

---

[587] 11 July 1369.
[588] *elclesia*, MS.
[589] 21 July or 4 August 1369.
[590] 28 July 1369.
[591] 2 August 1369.
[592] The sum repeated MS.
[593] In the margin: *vera*.
[594] 14 August 1369.

[595] 17 August 1369.
[596] 23 August 1369. In the margin: *Cardinalis Cantuariensis. Debet.*
[597] *presbytero*, MS.
[598] Simon Langham, previously archbishop of Canterbury.
[599] 15 September 1369. In the margin: *Cardinalis Cantuariensis; debet.*
[600] 5 September 1369.

iii s. i d. Solvit dictam summan in v vicibus ut in libro recepte.[601]

### Eboracensis

Motu proprio fuit provisum Francisco cardinali Sancti Petri [602] de canonicatu et prebenda ecclesie Eboracensis, vacantibus per obitum cardinalis M. Viterbiensis,[603] xvii kalendas Octobris.[604]

### Eboracensis, Wellensis

Motu proprio fuit provisum Simoni cardinali Cantuariensi de canonicatu et prebenda de Wistowe (Wistow) in ecclesia Eboracensi et de canonicatu et prebenda et archidiaconatu Wellensibus, vacantibus per obitum cardinalis Carcassonensis.[605]

### Lincolniensis

Simili modo fuit provisum Philipo cardinali Ierosolomitano [606] de archidiaconatu Leycestr' in ecclesia Lincolniensi, v nonas Octobris.[607] Cardinalis Ierolozomitanus qui obiit, et nichil hic reperitur, et fructus dicti archidiaconatus sunt sequestrati per dominum Lincolniensem anno LXXII post festum Omnium Sanctorum, sed non traditur nisi de mandato executoris.[608]

Recepta pagine vi[xx] vii li. iii s. i d.; [609] inutiles provisiones sunt ii[e]; et restant fructus iiii[or] provisionum iiii.

(fol. 31, xxxi) Anno viii Urbani

### Sarisbiriensis

De canonicatu et prebenda Sarisbiriensibus, vacantibus per obitum Johannis Stretlee extra Romanam curiam defuncti, fuit provisum Henrico Torp' Lincolniensis diocesis, v[to] idus Octobris.[610] Est in tertio mandato, et dicitur quod nondum habuit effectum.[608]

Completum est de anno septimo

### Eboracensis

Et primo de canonicatu et prebenda ecclesie Eboracensis, vacantibus per obitum domini cardinalis Sabinensis [611] in curia defuncti, fuit provisum Roberto de Stratton', capellano commensali pape, canonico prebendarum in ecclesia Lincolniensi et Wellensi ac dignitate ecclesie Lincolniensis expectante, xviii kalendas Decem-

bris,[612] taxata ad novam taxam cxx m., debet de resta lx m. Solvit die [613] secunda Aprilis predictas lx m., xl li.[614]

### Dunolmensis, Lincolniensis

De archidiaconatu Dunolmensi, quem quondam Willelmus de Westley dum viveret optinebat extra Romanam curiam defunctus, ac de canonicatu et prebenda de Corryngham (Corringham) in ecclesia Lincolniensi, vacantibus per obitum bone memorie domini cardinalis Lemovicensis,[615] fuit provisum Alexandro de Nevyll', xvi kalendas Decembris,[616] debet pro taxa dicte prebende cxc m.[617] Archidiaconatus non reperitur taxatus, sed ecclesia annexa bene, ac tamen solvit in tribus vicibus [618] in partem taxe dicte prebende quinquaginta li. xiii s. et iiii d.[619] Item solvit ultima die Januarii anno LXXIIII[to] vi li. viii s. iiii d.[601]

### Lincolniensis

De prioratu seu monasterio Sancte Frideswyde ordinis Sancti Augustini Lincolniensis diocesis, vacante per obitum quondam Nicholai de Hougford', fuit provisum Johanni de Doderford, canonico ecclesie Karleolensis dicte ordinis, xii kalendas Decembris.[620] Non habuit effectum.[621]

### Lichfeldensis

De canonicatu et prebenda de Langedon' (Longdon) in ecclesia Lichfeldensi, vacantibus per obitum Walteri Dalby, fuit provisum Laurentio de Ikestok' Lincolniensis diocesis, pro taxa xx li. Est in mandatis; infra est alia provisio de eadem folio xxxvi, et habet terminum Pasche iam elapsum ad habendum declaratorium camere si tenetur vel non certificare ex causis, et alia provisio est supra folio viii.[608]

### Herefordensis

Item Willelmo de Humbleton' clerico de canonicatu et prebenda in ecclesia Herefordensi, vacantibus per mortem Willelmi Belle, xi kalendas Decembris.[622] Est in mandatis tribus.[608]

### Eliensis

Acceptatio, collatio et provisio auctoritate litterarum apostolicarum facte per Michaelem de Causton', theologie professorem, de parochiali ecclesia de Leverington' Eliensis diocesis, vacante per mortem Ricardi Skyteby,

[601] In the margin: *solvit.*
[602] Franciscus Thebaldeschis, priest of S. Sabina.
[603] Mark de Viterbo, priest of S. Prassede.
[604] 15 September 1369. In the margin: *debet; Cardinalis Sancti Petri.*
[605] Stephen Aubert, priest of S. Lorenzo in Lucina. In the margin: *Cardinalis Cantuariensis; debet.*
[606] Philip de Cabassole, bishop of Sabina.
[607] 3 October 1369.
[608] In the margin: *debet.*
[609] In the margin: *vera.*
[610] 3 October 1369.
[611] William d'Aigrefeuille.

[612] 14 November 1369.
[613] *die* repeated MS.
[614] In the margin: *debet de antiqua; solvit.*
[615] Nicholas de Bessia, bishop elect of Limoges, deacon of S. Maria in Via Lata.
[616] 16 November 1369.
[617] In the margin: *debet partem.*
[618] Followed by *pro taxa* deleted by a line.
[619] Sum repeated MS. In the margin: *solvit.*
[620] 20 November 1369.
[621] In the margin: *inutilis.*
[622] 21 November 1369.

fuerunt confirmate seu provisum de novo, x kalendas Decembris.[623] Est in madatis et cetera, tamen non habuit effectum ut in restis folio xxxii.[621]

Recepta pagine iiii[xx] xvii li. vi s. viii d.; inutiles provisiones sunt due ii; restant fructus pro tribus provisionibus iii; et in partem unius restant in pecunia lxxxix li. vi s. viii d.

### (fol. 31[v]) Exoniensis

De archidiaconatu Cornubie in ecclesia Exoniensi, vacante vel dum vacabit per assecutionem per Alexandrum de Nevyll' factam vel faciendam de archidiaconatu Dunolmensi necnon canonicatu et prebenda de Corringham in ecclesia Lincolniensi, fuit provisum Willelmo de Norwico, bacallario in legibus. Prohibitum per breve, ut supra in antiquis folio.[624] Et ista etiam provisio non habuit effectum quia tunc rex dedit suo iure.[621]

### Dunolmensis

Item Nicholao Driffeld', clerico Eboracensis diocesis, de canonicatu et prebenda ecclesie collegiate Sancti Cuthberti in Derlington' (Darlington) Dunolmensis diocesis dum vacabit per assecutionem per dictum Alexandrum ut supra. Dicitur quod litigatur cum uno regio et ita est, sed finita lite pro apostolico solvat.[625]

Item Ricardo Strode Cicestrensis diocesis de parochiali ecclesia de Stanhopp' (Stanhope) modo premisso vacante per dimissionem dicti Willelmi, x kalendas Decembris.[623] Prohibitum per breve regium ut in restis folio xxxii de ecclesia predicta.[625]

### Eliensis

Motu proprio fuit provisum Johanni cardinali Belvacensi [626] de archidiaconatu Eliensi, vacante per obitum A. cardinalis Cluniacensis [627] xi kalendas Decembris,[628] pro taxa xli li. vi s. viii d.[629] Solvit die nona Januarii anno nativitatis LXXIII viginti li.[630] Solvit die i Septembris anno LXXIII viginti i li. vi s. viii d.[631]

### Eboracensis

De canonicatu et prebenda de Bolon (Bole) in eccelsia Eboracensi, vacantibus per obitum domini cardinalis Cluniacensis, fuit provisum Alexandro de Nevyll', ii[do] nonas Decembris,[632] pro taxa xvi li. Solvit dictas xvi li. die vii Julii anno LXXII.[633]

### Eboracensis

Motu proprio fuit provisum Anglico episcopo Albanensi de prebenda ecclesie Eboracensis vacante per obitum quondam Henrici de Ingelby, quondam dicte ecclesie canonico, xviii kalendas Januarii.[634] Non habuit effectum quia dictus Henricus vivit.[635]

### Bangorensis

De parochiali ecclesia de Thowyn (Towyn) Bangorensis diocesis, vacante ex eo quod Thinedus Apicha ipsam ecclesiam una cum archidiaconatu de Marinith (Merioneth) in ecclesia Bangorensi, que dignitas curata existit, per annum et amplius simul pacifice tenuit, fuit provisum Jacobo de Frestorp', clerico Lincolniensis diocesis, xix kalendas Januarii.[636] Non habuit effectum quia de patronatu domini principis et dormit.[621]

### Dunolmensis

Subrogatus fuit Johannes de Swothorp', clericus Dunolmensis, in omni iure et ad omne ius quod competebat Johanni de Lowyk' in curia defuncto [637] super vicaria parochialis ecclesie de Northam (Norham) dicte diocesis, super qua idem Johannes de Lowyle contra quemdam Johannem Mores in palatio litigavit, xiii kalendas Januarii,[638] pro taxa xiii li. vi s. viii d. Solvit in duabus vicibus iiii[or] li. xiii s. iiii d.[633]

Recepta pagine lxii li.; [639] resta pecunie viii li. xiii s. iiii d.; inutiles provisiones sunt iii; restant fructus ii.

### (fol. 32, xxxii) [640] Lincolniensis

Collatio et provisio facte Johanni de Dedeford de prioratu conventuali Sancte Frideswyd' ordinis Sancti Augustini Lincolniensis diocesis, vacante per mortem Nicholai ultimi prioris eiusdem, fuerunt confirmate seu provisum de novo xiii kalendas Februarii.[641] Lis pendet in curia, ut in restis folio xxxiii, cum ordinario, ut dicitur.[625]

### Lincolniensis

De canonicatu et prebenda Leyton' Bromeswold' (Leighton Bromswold) ecclesie Lincolniensis, vacantibus per obitum Johannis de Newenham, fuit provisum Thome de Southam, licentiato in legibus, xii kalendas Februarii,[642] pro taxa xlvi li. xiii s. iiii d. Solvit in iiii[or] vicibus viginti sex li. xiii s. iiii d.[643]

---

[623] 22 November 1369.

[624] Blank in MS.

[625] In the margin: *debet*.

[626] John de Dormans, bishop of Beauvais, priest of Ss. Quattro Coronati.

[627] Androin de la Roche, abbot of Cluny, priest of S. Marcello.

[628] 21 November 1369.

[629] In the margin: *Cardinalis Belvacensis*.

[630] Sum repeated MS.

[631] Sum repeated MS. In the margin: *solvit*.

[632] 4 December 1369.

[633] In the margin: *solvit*.

[634] 15 December 1369.

[635] In the margin: *inutilis; Cardinalis Albanensis*.

[636] 14 December 1369.

[637] *defuncti*, MS.

[638] 20 December 1369.

[639] Follows *xl li. xiii s. iiii d.* deleted by a line. In the margin: *vera*.

[640] The heading *Anno viii Urbani* is repeated at the top of the page.

[641] 20 January 1370.

[642] 21 January 1370.

[643] Sum repeated MS. In the margin: *solvit*.

## Lichfeldensis

Mandatur provideri Willelmo de Passenham, clerico Lichfeldensis diocesis, de beneficio ecclesiastico cum cura vel sine cura, vacante vel vacaturo spectante ad collationem abbatis et conventus de Bromey (Burton?) ordinis Sancti Benedicte dicte diocesis, si cum cura xl m., si sine cura xxx m., sterlingorum valentiam annuam non excedat, kalendas Februarii.[644] Expectatio est, et nondum habuit effectum quod sciatur.[645]

## Eboracensis

De vicaria ʟerpetua parochialis ecclesie de Hesill' (Hessle), a prioratu de Gyseburn' (Guisborough) dependente Eboracensis diocesis, cum vacabit per assecutionem prioratus Sancte Frideswyde ordinis Sancti Augustini, fuit provisum fratri Waltero de Colkenham, monacho professo [646] Worspanng' (Woodspring) dicte ordinis, idus Februarii.[647] Nondum habuit effectum.[645]

## Wellensis

De prepositura ecclesie Wellensis, vacante per obitum Johannis de Newenham extra Romanam curiam defuncti, fuit provisum Nicholao Heeth', vii kalendas Martii.[648] Non habuit effectum ad huc quia cansellarius Londonie tenet titulo regio.[645]

Hic finis arayraggiorum in arayraggiis traditorum per cameram

## Cicestrensis

De canonicatu et prebenda Cicestrensis vacantibus per obitum Johannis de Strokes extra Romanam curiam defuncti fuit provisum Johanni Scepdam, presbytero Norwicensis diocesis, v kalendas Martii.[649] Non habuit effectum quia alius possidet titulo regio ut in restis folio xxiii.[645]

## Wellensis

De canonicatu et prebenda de Middelton' (Milverton) et archidiaconatu Taunton' in ecclesia Wellensi simul annexis, vacantibus per obitum Ricardi Herward' extra Romanam curiam defuncti, fuit provisum Willelmo de Tyngull', utriusque iuris doctori, et dimittet canonicatum et prebendam Sancti Karentoci (Crantock) Exoniensis diocesis et parochialem ecclesiam de Bisshopeston' (Bishopsbourne) Cantuariensis diocesis, vᵗᵃˢ nonas Martii.[650] Non habuit effectum quia filius domini comitis Arundell' possidet titulo regio, et sic est clare probatum, et probationes sunt in archivis.[645]

Recepta pagine xxvi li. xiii s. iiii d.; inutiles provisiones sunt v; restant in pecunia xx li.; et fructus unius provisionis i.

## (fol. 32ᵛ) Wellensis, Sarisbiriensis

Motu proprio fuit provisum Simoni titulo Sancti Syxti presbytero cardinali de thesauraria ecclesie Wellensis, cum per munus consecrationis electo [651] Exoniensi impendendum vacabit, et de canonicatu et prebenda de Grangham (Grantham) ecclesie Sarisbiriensis, vacantibus per mortem Ricardi de Swynarton', et dimittet archidiaconatum et prebendam ecclesie Opoliensis (Oppeln) Viaceslavensis (Breslau) diocesis, nonas Martii.[652]

## Londoniensis

De parochiali ecclesia Sancti Martini in Vinetria civitatis Londonie (St. Martin Vintry), vacante vel dum vacabit per assecutionem alterius beneficii vacantis vel vacaturi ad collationem episcopi Wygorniensis faciendum per Michaelem Dratton', fuit provisum Rogero presbytero Wellensis diocesis, iii idus Martii.[653] Nunquam habuit effectum ut clare reperitur.[645]

## Norwicensis

Collatio et provisio auctoritate ordinaria facte Thome de Wuton', clerico Eboracensis diocesis, de decanatu rurali sine cura Norwicensis diocesis, et si fuerit reservata, fuerunt confirmate seu provisum de novo, iii idus Martii.[653] Est in mandatis excommunicatus et sequestratus, et dicitur quod vocatur Wastlisham (Walsingham).[654]

## Wygorniensis

Provisio et collatio auctoritate ordinaria facte Willelmo de Thuford',[655] iurisperito diocesis Norwicensis, in archidiaconatu Gloucestr' in ecclesia Wygorniensi, et si propter reservationes vel devolutiones sit sedi apostolico reservato, fuerunt confirmate seu provisum de novo, iiiᵗⁱᵒ idus Martii.[656] Solvit die xii Junii anno et cetera LXXIII in partem fructuum decem li.[657]

## Cicestrensis

De archidiaconatu Cicestrensi, vacante per mortem Henrici Folvyle, ultimi archidiaconi eiusdem extra Romanam curiam defuncti, fuit provisum Willelmo Wardri,[658] et dimittet vicariam parochialis ecclesie de Bodham (Bodiam) Cicestrensis diocesis, iiiᵗⁱᵒ idus Martii.[659] Solvit pro medietate veri valoris, salvo iure super procurationibus, iiiiᵒʳ li. vi s. viii d.[660]

## Londoniensis

De canonicatu et prebenda de Nesden' (Neasden in

---

[644] 1 February 1370.
[645] In the margin: *inutilis*.
[646] *professus*, MS.
[647] 13 February 137.
[648] 23 February 1370.
[649] 25 February 1370.
[650] 3 March 1370.

[651] *electi*, MS.
[652] 7 March 1370. In the margin: *Cardinalis Cantuariensis*.
[653] 13 March 1370.
[654] In the margin: *debet*.
[655] *Twyford*, Collectorie 13, fol. 168ᵛ.
[656] 13 March 1370. In the margin: *debet partem*.
[657] The sum repeated MS. In the margin: *solvit*.
[658] *Wardren*, Collectorie 13, fol. 168ᵛ.
[659] 13 March 1370. In the margin: *debet de parte*.
[660] In the margin: *solvit*.

Willesden) in ecclesia Londoniensi, vacantibus per munus consecrationis electo Exoniensi impendendum, vel alio et cetera, fuit provisum Simoni de Steynton' presbytero, xii kalendas Aprilis,[661] taxata iii li. ii s. Solvit dictam taxam trium li. duorum s.[660]

## Lincolniensis

De canonicatu et prebenda de Stotfeld' (Stotfold) in ecclesia Lincolniensi, vacantibus per obitum quondam Raymundi de Sancto Claro extra Romanam curiam defuncti, fuit provisum Petro Burton', clerico Lincolniensis diocesis, iii kalendas Aprilis.[662] Est in tribus mandatis sequestratus et denuntiatus.[654]

Recepta pagine xvii li. viii s. viii d.;[663] inutilis est iª provisio iª; restant fructus quinque provisionum v.

## (fol. 33, xxxiii)[664] Sarisbiriensis

Acceptatio et provisio facte vigore litterarum apostolicarum Ricardo Habet, presbytero Sarisbiriensis diocesis, de parochiali ecclesia de Donyngton' (Dinton), vacante per obitum Willelmi Peykerk' extra Romanam curiam defuncti, etiam si fuerit reservata, fuerunt confirmate seu provisum de novo, vii kalendas Aprilis,[665] pro taxa xvi li. xiii s. iiii d. Solvit dictas xvi li. xiii s. iiii d.[660]

## Eliensis

De parochiali ecclesia de Leveryngton' (Leverington) Eliensis diocesis, vacante per obitum Ricardi de Sateby extra Romana curiam defuncti, fuit provisum Johanni Barnet, presbytero Londoniensis diocesis, iiiiᵗᵒ nonas Aprilis,[666] pro taxa iiiiˣˣ v li. Solvit in vi vicibus septuaginta li.,[667] ut in libro recepte habetur.[660] Item solvit die prima Martii anno LXXIIIIᵗᵒ in plenam solutionem dicte taxe xv li.[660]

## Landavensis

De canonicatu et prebenda ecclesie Landavensis, vacantibus per munus consecrationis Henrico electo[668] ad ecclesiam Norwicensem impendendum, fuit provisum Ricardo de Croxton' Eliensis diocesis, pridie nonas Aprilis.[669] Solvit in partem fructuum die xviii Novembris anno LXXIII xxxiii s. iiii d.[660]

## Londoniensis

Ex causa permutationis fuit provisum Reginaldo Spalding', presbytero Lincolniensis, de parochiali ecclesia Sancti Benedicti de Greschirche Londonie (St. Benet

Gracechurch), quam Johannes de Lexham tunc optinebat, et dicto Johanni de parochiali ecclesia de Calesio (St. Mary, Calais) Morinensis (Thérouanne) diocesis, quam dictus Reginaldus optinebat, iiiᵗⁱᵒ nonas Aprilis.[670] Taxatur seu extimatur xii m. que valent viii li. Solvit dictas octo li. in tribus vicibus.[660]

## Herefordensis

De canonicatu et prebenda de Ewyngton' ecclesie (Ewithington) Herefordensis diocesis, vacantibus per munus consecrationis electi Exoniensis, fuit provisum Nicholao Longe, clerico Dunolmensis diocesis, nonas Aprilis,[671] pro taxa x li. Solvit dictas decem li. in tribus vicibus.[660]

## Wellensis

Item Roberto Tonelye Wygorniensis diocesis de canonicatu et prebenda ecclesie Wellensis, cum premisso modo vacabit, fuit provisum dicto Roberto, nonas Aprilis.[671] Est in mandatis tribus.[672]

## Bangorensis

Provisio auctoritate litterarum apostolicarum facte Jacobo de Frestorp' diocesis Lincolniensis de parochiali ecclesia de Towyn Bangorensis diocesis, vacante certo modo et etiam si fuerit reservata, fuit[673] confirmata seu provisum de novo, iiiᵗⁱᵒ nonas Aprilis.[670] Non habuit effectum quia infra est annum cum alia que est supra folio xxxi, quia de patronatu domini principis, ideo dormit.[674]

Recepta pagine cxxi li. vi s. viii d.;[675] inutilis est una provisio iª; restant fructus unius provisionis et partis alterius ii.

## (fol. 33ᵛ) Cantuariensis

De prepositura ecclesie collegiate de Wyngham (Wingham) Cantuariensis diocesis, que alias fuit signata Thome de Paxton', auditori palatii apostolici, cum vacaret per consecrationem Willelmi Reed, tunc electi Cicestrensis, fuit provisum de novo dicto Thome de Paxton', non obstante quod Thomas de Ikham eam detineat occupatam et cetera, vi idus Aprilis.[676] Non habuit effectum ut in restis folio xxxiiii.[674]

## Norwicensis

De parochiali ecclesia de Derham (Dereham), vacante dum Johannes Barnet possessionem parochialis ecclesie de Leveryngton (Leverington) fuit pacifice assecutus, fuit provisum Laurentio de Ikestok', vi idus Aprilis.[676]

---

[661] 21 March 1370.
[662] 30 March 1370.
[663] In the margin: *vera*.
[664] The heading *Anno viii Urbani* is repeated at the top of the page.
[665] 26 March 1370.
[666] 2 April 1370.
[667] Sum repeated MS.
[668] *Henrici electi*, MS.
[669] 4 April 1370.

[670] 3 April 1370.
[671] 5 April 1370.
[672] In the margin: *debet*.
[673] *fuerunt*, MS.
[674] In the margin: *inutilis*.
[675] In the margin: *vera*.
[676] 8 April 1370.

Non habuit effectum ut in restis folio xxxv, quia obiit ante adeptam possessionem.[674]

## Sarisbiriensis

De canonicatu et prebenda [677] ecclesie Sarisbiriensis, vacantibus per munus consecrationis impensum episcopo Norwicensi, fuit provisum Johanni Godwyk', legum doctori, iii<sup>tio</sup> kalendas Maii.[678] Dicitur quod taxatur ad xl m. Solvit die iii de Septembre anno LXXIII decem li. in partem taxe, x li.[679]

## Lincolniensis

Mandatur provideri Johanni de Stratton', bacallario in legibus, de canonicatu, prebenda, dignitate et cetera vacantibus vel vacaturis in ecclesia Lincolniensi, kalendas Maii.[680] Expectatio est et ad huc non habuit effectum.[674]

## Eboracensis

Item Johanni Fordham de canonicatu et prebenda vacantibus vel vacaturis in ecclesia [681] collegiata Sancti Johannis Beverlacensi Eboracensis diocesis, kalendas Maii. Expectatio est et ad huc non habuit effectum.[674]

## Eboracensis

Item Johanni Wodhous de canonicatu et prebenda vacantibus vel vacaturis in ecclesia collegiata de Southwell' Eboracensis diocesis, kalendas Maii.[680] Expectatio est et ad huc non habuit effectum.[674]

## Eliensis

Acceptatio, collatio et provisio facte vigore litterarum apostolicarum Michaeli de Causton', doctori in theologia, de parochiali ecclesia de Leveryngton' (Leverington) Eliensis diocesis, etiam si fuerit reservata, fuerunt confirmate seu provisum de novo, pridie kalendas Maii.[682] Non habuit effectum ut in restis prioris folio xxxv.[674]

## Eboracensis

De canonicatu et prebenda ecclesie Eboracensis, vacantibus per munus consecrationis Willelmo Courtenay electo Herefordensi ⟨impendendum⟩, fuit provisum Rogero de Freton', legum doctori, kalendas Maii.[680] Alias habuit provisionem infra eundem annum, et ibi solvit, ut in restis dicitur folio xxxv.[674]

## Lincolniensis

Dum Walterus de Aldeby, decretorum doctor, beneficium cum cura spectans ad collationem episcopi

Eliensis fuit pacifice assecutus, dimittet parochialem ecclesiam de Halewell' (Holywell) Lincolniensis diocesis, et canonicatum et prebendam de Bathelwyk' (Bathwick) in ecclesia conventuali monialium Warwell' (Wherwell) Wyntoniensis diocesis, kalendas Maii.[680] Hic non aparet de aliqua provisione, ideo inutilis ut in restis folio xxxv.[674]

Recepta pagine x li.; inutiles provisiones sunt viii; resta pecunie xvi li. xiii s. iiii d.

## (fol. 34, xxxiiii) [683] Eboracensis

De prebenda in ecclesia Eboracensi vacante per munus consecrationis impensum Willelmo electo Herefordensi fuit provisum Thome de Arundell', kalendas Maii.[680] Non habuit effectum quia per alium possidetur prius et etiam adhuc.[674]

## Dunolmensis

Collatio auctoritate litterarum apostolicarum facta Hugoni de Arlam, clerico Dunolmensis diocesis, de decanatu ecclesie collegiate Cestr' in strata (Chester-le-Street) Dunolmensis diocesis, et si fuerit reservato, fuit confirmata seu provisum de novo, vi nonas Martii,[684] pro taxa l m.[685] Est in mandatis. Solvit in vigilia nativitatis domini tresdecim li. sex s. octo d.[686] Item solvit die xxv Julii alias xiii li. vi s. viii d.[679]

## Exoniensis

Collatio auctoritate ordinaria facta Johanni Cheyne de prebenda Exoniensi vacante per assecutionem decanatus ecclesie Wellensis factam per Stephanum Pempel, et si fuerit reservata, fuit confirmata seu provisum de novo.[685] Solvit die xxi Martii in partem taxe, salvo iure pluris, xl s.[679]

## Eboracensis

De canonicatu et prebenda ecclesie collegiate de Southwell' Eboracensis diocesis, vacantibus per obitum Johannis Kendale extra curiam defuncti, fuit provisum Roberto Pedes, et dimittet parochialem ecclesiam de Rippehull' (Ripple?) Wygorniensis, iiii<sup>to</sup> nonas Maii.[687] Est in tertio mandato prebenda que fuit dicti Johannis. Certificat archiepiscopus in iii mandatis quod nunquam habuit effectum.[688]

## Eboracensis

De canonicatu et prebenda ecclesie Eboracensis, vacantibus per munus consecrationis Willelmo electo Herfordensi impensum, fuit provisum Rogero de Freton', legum doctori, v nonas Maii,[689] pro taxa xl li. Dicitur

---

[677] Prebend of Bitton: collectorie 13, fol. 168ᵛ.
[678] 29 April 1370.
[679] In the margin: *solvit*.
[680] 1 May 1370.
[681] Followed by *Lincolniensi kalendas Maii* deleted by a line.
[682] 30 April 1370.

[683] The heading *Anno viii Urbani* is repeated at the top of the page.
[684] 2 March 1370.
[685] In the margin: *debet partem*.
[686] Sum repeated MS. In the margin: *solvit*.
[687] 4 May 1370.
[688] In the margin: *inutilis*.
[689] 3 May 1370.

in restis prioris folio xxxv quod alias fuit in restis posita et ibi solvit, et fuit etiam alia provisio supra que etiam non habuit effectum, ut ibi folio xxxiii[tio].[688]

## Oscecensis

De parochiali ecclesia de Ocensaes (?) Oscecensis (Huesca?) diocesis, certo modo tunc vacante, fuit provisum Henrico de Spalt', presbytero dicte diocesis, pridie nonas Maii.[690] Non est in regno Anglie.[688]

## Sarisbiriensis

De prebenda de Cilhyngham (Gillingham) in ecclesia monialium de Schestebury (Shaftesbury), vacante per obitum Ricardi Neweton' extra curiam defuncti, fuit provisum Thome de Arundell', clerico Cicestrensis diocesis, v nonas Maii,[689] pro taxa xxx li. Solvit dictas xxx li. die prima Junii anno LXXII.[691]

## Menevensis

Mandatur provideri Johanni de Roos, clerico Landavensis diocesis, de beneficio ecclesiastico cum cura vel sine cura, vacante vel vacaturo, spectante ad collationem episcopi, decani et capituli ecclesie Menevensis, vii idus Maii.[692] Expectatio est que non habuit effectum quod sciatur ad huc.[688]

## Lincolniensis

Mandatur episcopo Lincolniensi et priori de Berkhened' (Birkenhead) ordinis Sancti Benedicti ut se informent de quibusdam delictis per Johannem de Seynebur', rectorem parochialis ecclesie Beate Marie super Montem Cestr' (Chester) dicte diocesis, et secundum informationem conferre possint dictam ecclesiam auctoritate apostolica Johanni de Altekore, clerico dicte diocesis, vii idus Maii.[692] Expectatio est que nondum habuit effectum, attamen est in secundo et tertio mandatis ad sequestrandum.[688]

Recepta pagine lviii li. xiii s. iiii d. ;[693] inutiles provisiones sunt vi, vi ; resta pecunie vi li. xiii s. iiii d. ; et fructus unius provisionis i[us].

## (fol. 34[v]) Eboracensis

Mandatur provideri Edmundo Strete, clerico Lincolniensi de beneficio ecclesiastico cum cura vel sine cura vacante vel vacaturo in ecclesia Sancti Johannis Beverlaci Eboracensis diocesis, vii idus Maii.[692] Expectatio est que nondum habuit effectum quod sciatur.[688]

## Wellensis

De canonicatu et prebenda ecclesie Wellensis, vacantibus per liberam resignationem factam in manibus Domini B. episcopi Condomiensis (Condom), fuit pro-

visum Johanni Gaylard, presbytero Wellensis diocesis, vi idus Maii.[694] Est denuntiatus et sequestratus in mandatis tribus, et est infra alia provisio folio lxii.[695]

## Sarisbiriensis

Mandatur provideri Johanni Jakesleye, clerico Londoniensis, de beneficio ecclesiastico cum cura vel sine cura spectante ad collationem episcopi, decani et capituli singulorumque canonicorum ecclesie Sarisbiriensis, idus Maii.[696] Expectatio est que nondum habuit effectum quod sciatur.[688]

## Exoniensis

Acceptatio et provisio facte per Henricum Wytefeld' presbyterum [697] de archidiaconatu Barnestapll' curato in ecclesia Exoniensi, et si fuerit reservato, fuerunt confirmate seu provisum de novo, xvi kalendas Junii.[698] Non taxatur. Solvit pro medietate veri valoris in tribus vicibus tresdecim li. vi s. viii d.,[699] salvo iure super procurationibus si debeantur.[691]

## Sarisbiriensis

Item Willelmo Hegohie de Bury, canonico Sarisbiriensi, de prebenda de Remesbury (Ramsbury) ecclesie eiusdem, non obstantibus quibuscumque etiam, fuerunt confirmate seu provisum de novo, kalendas Junii.[700] Est in mandatis ad denuntiandum, sed litigat cum domino Convenarum cardinali,[701] et est in mandatis, et est allegatum per possessorem quod duas habuit sententias contra eum.[695]

## Lincolniensis

Acceptatio et provisio facte vigore litterarum apostolicarum Willelmo Kirkestede, presbytero Norwicensis diocesis, de parochiali ecclesia de Bernak' (Barnack) Lincolniensis diocesis, et si et cetera, fuerunt confirmate seu provisum de novo, iii idus Junii,[702] pro taxa xxxiiii. m. que valent xxii li. xiii s. iiii d. Solvit in duabus vicibus xviii li.[703] Item solvit plus xxix die Martii iiii[or] li. xiii s. iiii d.[691]

## Lincolniensis

Collatio ex causa permutationis facta auctoritate ordinaria Ricardo Bidik' de parochiali ecclesia de Brinkton' (Brington) Lincolniensis diocesis, etiam si fuerit reservata, fuit [704] confirmata seu provisum de novo, iii idus Junii.[702] Alia est provisio eidem facta

---

[690] 6 May 1370.
[691] In the margin: *solvit*.
[692] 9 May 1370. If John is found guilty of homicide, he is to vacate St. Mary super Montem, Chester, Lichfield diocese: Vat. Arch., Reg. Avin. 171 fol. 277[v].
[693] Follows xxxii li. deleted by a line. In the margin: *vera*.

[694] 10 May 1370.
[695] In the margin: *debet*.
[696] 15 May 1370.
[697] *presbytero*, MS.
[698] 17 May 1370.
[699] Sum repeated MS.
[700] 1 June 1370. (William Heytesbury: Vat. Arch., Reg. Avin. 171 fol. 413.)
[701] Bertrand, priest of S. Marcello.
[702] 11 June 1370.
[703] Sum repeated MS. In the margin: *solvit*.
[704] *fuerunt*, MS.

infra eundem annum folio lxi, et ibi solvit partem quia de ista non debetur, et ambe sunt infra annum quia propter mortem Domini Urbani non potuit facere bullam et cetera.[688]

## Eboracensis

Item collatio et provisio auctoritate ordinaria facte Johanni de Leghton', presbytero Lincolniensis diocesis, de vicaria de Massham (Masham) Eboracensis diocesis, vacante per obitum quondam Alani de Otryngham extra curiam defuncti, non obstante reservatione etiam, fureunt confirmate seu provisum de novo, iii[tio] idus Junii,[702] pro taxa antiqua xxx li. et pro nova xl s. Solvit dictos quadraginta s., salvo iure super antiqua taxa, xl s.[691]

## Menevensis

De canonicatu et prebenda seu portione in ecclesia Abberwill' (Abergwili) Menevensis diocesis, vacantibus per assecutionem archidiaconatus Comorn' (Carmarthen) factam per Adam de Naas, fuit provisum Johanni Aspull' Bangorensis diocesis, xviii kalendas Julii.[705] Litigat, sed est in mandatis ad denuntiandum, et est prorogatus intro nativitatem domini anno LXXIII, et non solvit, et videatur plus.[695]

Recepta pagine xxxviii li.; [706] inutiles provisiones sunt iii; et fructus restant saltim in partes de iii.

## (fol. 35, xxxv) Anno viii Urbani

Acceptatio et collatio auctoritate apostolica facte Nicholao Buffel de parochiali ecclesia de Bluntesham (Bluntisham), vacante per mortem quondam Ricardi de Salop', ultimi rectoris eiusdem, et si et cetera, fuerunt confirmate seu provisum de novo, x kalendas Julii.[707] Non possit reperiri ad huc ubi est quia hic non nominatur diocesis, set querat quia in restis nec in libro camere est nominata.[695]

## Lichfeldensis

Motu proprio fuit provisum Francisco titulo Sancte Sabine presbytero cardinali de canonicatu et prebenda ecclesie Lichfeldensis vacantibus per obitum Antonii de Roos in Romana curia defuncti, xiii kalendas Decembris.[708]

## Menevensis

Mandatur provideri Rogero Hore, Herefordensis diocesis presbytero bacallario in legibus, de canonicatu sub expectatione prebende ecclesie Menevensis, ix kalendas Novembris.[709] Expectatio que nondum habuit effectum quod sciatur.[710]

## Lichfeldensis

Item Nicholao Suthbury, presbytero Lichfeldensis diocesis, de canonicatu sub expectatione prebende ecclesie Lichfeldensis, ix kalendas Novembris.[709] Expectatio est que nondum habuit effectum.[710]

Completum est de anno octavo et ultimo Domini Urbani, cuius anima quiescat in pace, amen.

Inutiles provisiones pagine sunt iii; restant in pagina fructus duarum provisionum ii.

Hic adde ix[xx] ii li. x s. ii d. que sunt infra folio xxxvii ad summam infrascriptam, et vide signum H—H [711] infra.

Summa recepte restarum de tempore Domini Urbani, cum summa proxime scripta et addita, milie trecentas octuaginta sex li. viii s. et duos d. sterlingorum, xiii[c] lxxxvi li. viii s. ii d.[712]

Resta pecunie dicti temporis Urbani [713] vi[c] xxxiiii li. xv s. sterlingorum.

Restant provisionum fructus de lxxv.

Et sunt de inutilibus provisionibus clxxvi.

(fol. 36, xxxvi) [714] Gregorii anno i[o]
Primus annus Domini Gregorii undecimi
Sequitur beneficia collata per Dominum Gregorium papam XI[mum] pontificatus sui anno primo in [715] Anglia tradita in restis domini prioris Lewensis [716]

## Cantuariensis

Motu proprio fuit provisum Guillelmo titulo Sancti Clementis presbytero cardinali de archidiaconatu ecclesie Cantuariensis vacante et quia dominus noster papa optinere solebat, xvii kalendas Februarii.[717]

## Sarisbiriensis

Motu proprio fuit provisum Guillelmo cardinali de Agrifolio [718] de canonicatu et prebenda ecclesie Sarisbiriensis vacantibus per mortem Thome de Paxton' in Romana curia defuncti, xvi kalendas Februarii.[719]

## Dunolmensis

Motu proprio fuit provisum seu subrogatus fuit Simoni cardinali Cantuariensi in omne iure et ad omne ius quod habuit David de Wollore in ecclesia de Wermouth' (Bishop-Wearmouth) Dunolmensis diocesis dum vixit, qui extra curiam decessit, vii kalendas Februarii,[720]

---

[705] 14 June 1370.
[706] Followed by *viii s.* deleted by a line. In the margin: *vera.*
[707] 22 June 1370.
[708] 19 November 1369. In the margin: *debet; Cardinalis Sabina Francisci nomine.*
[709] 24 October 1370.
[710] In the margin: *inutilis.*

[711] The sign is repeated in the margin. See below, n. 734.
[712] In the margin: *vera.*
[713] Repeated in MS. in the form *de dicto tempore Domini Urbani.*
[714] Folio 35[v] is blank.
[715] Followed by *collectoria* deleted by a line.
[716] In the margin: O ꝙ O *Quere signum infra folio lii. et ibi quia est de tempore Gregorii. Gregorius.* See below, n. 819.
[717] 16 January 1371. In the margin: *Cardinalis Guillelmus.*
[718] William d'Aigrefeuille, priest of S. Stefano al Monte Celio.
[719] 17 January 1371. In the margin: *Cardinalis de Agrifolio.*
[720] 26 January 1371.

debet pro taxa antiqua c li. Cardinalis Cantuariensis expost permutavit, ut dicitur, eam, et non solvit, licet teneatur. Alia est supra folio xxix que debetur etiam.[721]

### Lincolniensis

De parochiali ecclesia de Barewell' (Barwell) Lincolniensis diocesis, vacante per obitum Laurentii de Ikestok' in Romana curia defuncti, fuit provisum Philipo Kelsy Exoniensis diocesis, iiii[tio] kalendas Februarii,[722] pro taxa xxxv m. que valent xxiii li. vi s. viii d. Solvit dictam summam in tribus vicibus.[723]

### Londoniensis

De parochiali ecclesia de Hakeney (Hackney) Londoniensis diocesis, vacante per obitum Thome de Paxton' in curia defuncti, fuit provisum Ricardo de Traxton', clerico Eliensis diocesis, iii kalendas Februarii.[722] Nondum habuit effectum quia alius possidet titulo regio.[724]

### Lincolniensis

De canonicatu et prebenda de Cropride (Cropredy) in ecclesia Lincolniensi, vacantibus per obitum dicti Thome de Paxton', fuit provisum Willelmo de Gernos, presbytero Wyntoniensis diocesis, iii kalendas Februarii,[722] taxata cum capella ad c m. que valent in libris lxvi li. xiii s. iiii d. Nondum habuit effectum quia per alium titulo regio possidetur, ut in restis prioris folio xxxvii.[725]

Recepta pagine xxiii li. vi s. viii d.; [726] inutiles provisiones sunt ii[e]; restant fructus de tribus beneficiis iii; resta pecunie clxvi li. xiii s. iiii d.

### (fol. 36[v]) Lichfeldensis

De canonicatu et prebenda de Langedon (Longdon) in ecclesia Lichfeldensi, vacantibus per obitum Laurentii de Ikestok' in curia defuncti, fuit provisum Johanni Undurhull', bacallario in legibus, iiii[tio] kalendas Februarii; [722] dicitur quod taxatur xx li. Sunt alie due provisiones supra foliis viii et xxxi, et est sequestratus, habet terminum, et est in mandatis.[721]

### Exoniensis

De vicaria curata parochialis ecclesie de Brampton' (Braunton) Exoniensis diocesis, cum vacabit per assecutionem parochialis ecclesie de Barewell' (Barwell) Lincolniensis diocesis faciendam per Johannem de Kelsy, fuit provisum Deodato Clave de Wyk' presbytero, v[to] idus Februarii,[727] non taxatur. Non taxatur, sed solvit

in partem medietatis veri valoris viii die Februarii anno LXXII tres li. vi s. viii d.; [728] debet restam.[723]

### Dunolmensis

De decanatu ecclesie collegiate Sancti Andree Auclandie (Auckland) Dunolmensis diocesis, vacante per liberam resignationem Johannis de Kyngeston' extra curiam factam, fuit provisum Thome Clernaux, clerico Eboracensis diocesis, xiiii kalendas Martii.[729] Non habuit effectum ut in restis prioris folio xxxviii.[724]

### Cantuariensis

Subrogatus fuit Johannes de Fordham, clerico Norwicensis diocesis, in omni iure et ad omne ius quod competebat Thome de Paxton' dum agebat in humanis in et super prepositura ecclesie collegiate de Wyngham (Wingham) Cantuariensis diocesis, et in lite, si sit aliqua, in palatio apostolico, xiii kalendas Martii,[730] pro taxa lx m. Secretarius est domini principis, et solvit in duabus vicibus, videlicet die xvii Junii v li. et die xx Octobris alias quinque anno LXXIII, summa x li.[728]

### Assavensis

De canonicatu et prebenda ecclesie Assavensis vacantibus per munus consecrationis impensum Ludovico electo ad ecclesiam Herefordensem, fuit provisum Howelo ap David, presbytero Assavensis diocesis, v[to] idus Martii.[731] Est sub sequestro episcopi. Est sub sequestro in mandatis et est etiam sequestratum.[721]

### Cicestrensis

De canonicatu et prebenda ecclesie Cicestrensis vocata Sallesum (Selsey), vacantibus per obitum Walteri Bakton' extra curiam defuncti, fuit provisum Willelmo Palvere, presbytero Lincolniensis diocesis, v[to] idus Martii.[731] Filius domini comitis Arundelle possidet titulo regio, ideo nondum habuit effectum, sed speretur si habebit. Sic etiam in restis folio xxxviii habetur.[721]

### Lincolniensis

De parochiali ecclesia de Hundil (Hundleby) Lincolniensis diocesis, vacante per obitum dicti Walteri, fuit provisum Willelmo de Norwico, bacallario in legibus, quinto idus Martii.[731] Dicta provisio nondum habuit effectum, quia Dominus Ricardus Denatton' possidet titulo regio, quare fuit mandatum episcopo ad relaxandum; sita est quousque apareat de effectu vel alias per cameram fuerit ordinatum ut in forma consueta.[724]

Recepta pagine xiii li. vi s. viii d.; [732] resta pecunie

---

[721] In the margin: *debet.*
[722] 30 January 1371.
[723] In the margin: *solvit.*
[724] In the margin: *inutilis.*
[725] In the margin: *debet*; *inutilis.*
[726] In the margin: *vera.*
[727] 9 February 1371.

[728] Sum repeated MS.
[729] 16 February 1371.
[730] 17 February 1371.
[731] 11 March 1371.
[732] Follows *Recepta pagine iii li. vi s. viii d.* deleted by a line. In the margin: *vera.*

xlv m. que valent 1 li.;[733] inutiles provisiones sunt due ii; restant fructus de tribus provisionibus iii; summa reste pecunie istius folii ii° xvi li. xiii s. iiii d.

## (folio 37, xxxvii) Gregorii anno i

Et tradidit michi, Arnaldo Garnerii collectori predicto, dictus dominus prior Lewensis de pecuniis camere apostolice per ipsum receptis usque ad diem xxii Februarii anno a nativitate domini millesimo CCCLXXII[do] centum et sexaginta septem li. quatuordecim s. et duos d. sterlingorum.[734]

Item restituit dictus dominus prior viginti libras michi, Arnaldo Garnerii nunc collectori, de summa lxiii li. iiii[or] s. viii d. per ipsum recepta de procurationibus primi anni nuntiatoris mee pro iiii[or] mensibus quibus ipse rexit officium collectoris nomine dicti Domini Johannis de Cabrespino in mea absentia, videlicet ab viii die Octobris anno domini et cetera LXXI[mo], qua die fuit michi commissum officium, usque ad viii diem Februarii tunc proxime sequentem, qua die primo veni Londonie, licet pro rata temporis sibi non pertinerent nisi lviii li. viii d., cum omnes procurationes non ascendant ultra centum lxxiiii li. ii s. pro anno ad bursam collectoris. Et retenet de dicta summa xx librarum sic restituta quinque libras iiii[or] solidos michi pro futuro tempore debita. Allocavi pro ipso Domino Johanne eidem camere apostolice restam, videlicet xiiii li. sexdecim s. in partem solutionis xxxix li. xiii s. iiii d. quas debet camere apostolice. Idem Dominus Johannes pro supplemento de contento in restis, ut habetur infra folio xli et xlii, ubi de hoc etiam fit mentio specialis xiiii li. xvi s.[735]

Et sic de dictis iiii[or] mensibus ego, Arnaldus predictus, nichil de dictis procurationibus recepi, licet non modicum vacavit[736] officio in curia et itinere toto dicto tempore, etiam cum magnis periculis et exspensis, et plus per duos menses ante dictum tempus.

Hic finis restarum traditarum et pecunie solute michi per dominum priorem Lewensem, et alia infrascripta sunt missa de curia vel explorata expost, quorum omnium supra et infrascriptorum reperi erat[737] recepta, si qua sit, manu mei, Arnaldi Garnerii, scripta.[738]

De aliis contentis in quinque foliis sequentibus nichil ad me nisi pro memoriali ad excusationem dicti domini prioris Lewensis et ad optinendam quitantiam pro ipso.

Summa recepte pagine ix[xx] ii li. x s. ii d.; de hoc in libro recepte[739] dimisso locumtenento.

Ista summa adde supra folio xxxv quia sic est computata in breveto et ibi in signum H—H.

---

[733] It should be *xxx li.*

[734] Sum repeated MS. In the margin: H--H *supra folio xxxv continua hec. Solvit.* See above, n. 711.

[735] Sum repeated MS. In the margin: *solvit.*

[736] *vacaveri,* MS. See below, p. 476.

[737] Followed by *si qua fuit* deleted by a line.

[738] In the margin: *finis restarum.*

[739] Followed by *folio* deleted by a line.

(fol. 37[v]) Videantur contenta in tribus foliis cum duabus sequentibus.

Et dent quitantiam domino priori de receptis et redditis ut ibi continetur quia pluries me requisivit, sed non habeo potestatem quitandi nisi de receptis, et non omnia recepti ut ibi aparet.

(fol. 38, xxxviii) Pro memoriali compotorum domini prioris Lewensis sunt hic v folia sequentia

Sequentes pecuniarum summe que recepte fuerunt pro camera apostolica per Johannem de Cariloco priorem Lewensem venerabilis viri Domini Johannis de Cabrespino, doctoris decretorum, canonici[740] Narbonensis, apostolice sedis et camere in Anglia nuntii et collectoris, commissarium et subcollectorem, a festo Omnium Sanctorum anno a nativitate domini millesimo CCCLXX[mo] usque ad vicesimum secundum diem mensis Februarii anno domini ab eadem nativitate millesimo CCC[mo] LXX secundo

Denarii Beati Petri

### Essexia

De archidiaconatu Essexie pro anno sexagesimo nono v li. x s.

### Lincolniensis

De episcopatu Lincolniensi in plena solutione anni LXVIII iiii[or] li.

Item de eodem episcopatu pro annis LXIX et LXX[mo], pro quolibet xlii li., et sic pro dictis duobus annis iiii[xx] iiii[or] li.

### Roffensis

De archidiaconatu Roffensi pro annis LXV, VI, VII, VIII, IX et LXX, pro quolibet v li. xii s., et sic in toto pro dictis sex annis xxxiii li. xii s.

### Sarisbiriensis

De episcopatu Sarisbiriensi de annis LXVIII et LXIX, pro quolibet xvii li., et sic pro dictis duobus annis xxxiiii li.

### Wyntoniensis

De archidiaconatu Wyntoniensi pro annis LXVII, VIII, IX et LXX, pro quolibet xi li. xiii s. iiii d., et sic pro dictis quatuor annis xlvi li. xiii s. iiii d.

### Norwicensis

De episcopatu Norwicensi pro anno LXIX xxi li. x s.

### Cicestrensis

De episcopatu Cicestrensi de anno LXX et LXXI[mo] pro quolibet viii li., et sic pro ambobus xvi li.

### Cantuariensis

De archidiaconatu Cantuariensi pro anno LXIX viii li.

---

[740] *canonico,* MS.

### Colcestr'

De archidiaconatu Colcestrie pro anno LXVIII v li. x s.

### Eliensis

De archidiaconatu Eliensi de anno LXVI, VII, pro quolibet v li., et sic pro ambobus x li.

Summa denariorum Beati Petri dicte recepte ii° lxviii li. xv s. iiii d., quarum viii li. sunt de anno LXXI^{mo} recepte de episcopo Cicestrensi

(fol. 38^v) Annui census

### Sarisbiriensis

De abbate de Malmesbury pro anno LXX xiii s. iiii d.

### Cantuariensis

De abbate de Faveresham pro annis LXVII, VIII, IX, pro quolibet xiii s. iiii d., et sic pro dictis tribus annis xl s.

### Eliensis

De priore de Angleseye pro anno LXX^{mo} ii s.

### Wyntoniensis

De abbate de Certeseye pro annis LXVII, VIII, IX, LXX et LXXI^{mo}, pro quolibet viii s., et sic pro dictis quinque annis xl s.

### Roffensis

De priore de Tunebrugg' pro anno domini millesimo CCCLXX xiii s. iiii d.

### Eboracensis

De custode de Scardeburgh' pro anno LXXI xv d.

### Norwicensis

De abbate Sancti Edmundi de Bury pro anno LXXI^{mo} xiii s. iiii d.

### Lincolniensis

De priore de Cauchombe pro anno LXXI^{mo} xv d.
Summa annui census istius recepte vi li. iiii s. iiii d.

### Primi fructus

### Cantuariensis

De ecclesia de Yvechyrche (Ivychurch), taxata xxxv li. vi s. viii d., ratione provisionis facte de eadem Thome Forester per Urbanum, decimo kalendas Septembris anno vii,[741] in partem taxe vi li. xiii s. iiii d.

### Londoniensis

De ecclesia de Langedon' (Langdon Hills), non taxata, sed compositum est pro xl s., ratione pro-

visionis facte de eadem Willelmo de Swafeld' per felicis recordationis Urbanum, iii^{tio} nonas Januarii anno primo,[742] pro resta fructuum xxvi s. viii d.

De ecclesia de Alta Rothyng' (High Roding), taxata xii li., ratione provisionis facte de eadem Bernardo de Santon' per felicis recordationis Urbanum, xi kalendas Martii anno v^{to},[743] in partem reste lx s.

De ecclesia Beate Marie Wolnoth' Londonie (St. Mary Woolnoth) ratione provisionis facte de eadem Ricardo de Thornecumbe per felicis recordationis Urbanum, viii° kalendas Martii anno vii,[744] non taxata, sed composuit et solvit pro medietate veri valoris iiii^{or} li.

### (fol. 39, xxxix) Cicestrensis

De prioratu conventuali de Boxgrave (Boxgrove) ratione provisionis facte de eodem ex causa permutationis Johanni de Lande per felicis recordationis Urbanum, nonas Septembris anno vii,[745] in partem primorum fructuum x li.

De decanatu Cicestrensi, taxato liii li. vi s. viii d., ratione provisionis facte de eodem Nicholao de Aston' per Urbanum, kalendas Septembris anno primo,[746] in partem reste xx li.

Item de eodem decanatu ratione provisionis facte de eodem Rogero de Freton' per Urbanum, anno v^{to},[747] in partem taxe xlvi li. xiii s. iiii d.

De ecclesia de Blachington' (Blatchington), taxata xx m., per manus Domini Willelmi de Hagham, rectoris ecclesie de Samerford' Mautravers (Somerford) Sarisbiriensis diocesis, ratione provisionis facte de eadem Henrico Onyngg' per felicis recordationis Dominum Urbanum, ix kalendas Septembris anno vii,[748] in partem taxe x m.

### Sarisbiriensis

De prebenda de Durneford' (Durnford), taxata xvi li. xiii s. iiii d., ratione provisionis facte de eadem Johanni Ottford' per Urbanum, xii kalendas Augusti anno iiii^{to},[749] pro resta taxe viii li. vi s. viii d.

De prebenda de Combe et Arnham (Combe and Harnham), taxata xx m., ratione provisionis facte de eadem Johanni de Feryby per felicis recordationis Dominum Urbanum papam v^{tum}, v idus Julii anno vii,[750] in partem taxe x m.

### Bathoniensis et Wellensis

De ecclesia de Templecumbe (Templecombe), taxata ix [751] li. vi s. viii d. ratione provisionis facte de eadem

---

[741] 23 August 1369.

[742] 3 January 1363.
[743] 19 February 1367.
[744] 22 February 1369.
[745] 5 September 1369.
[746] 1 September 1363.
[747] 6 November 1366 to 5 November 1367.
[748] 24 August 1369.
[749] 21 July 1366.
[750] 11 July 1369.
[751] Follows v deleted by a line.

ex causa permutationis Johanni de Walton' per felicis recordationis Dominum Urbanum, xix kalendas Januarii anno vi,[752] in partem taxe v m. dym.

De decanatu Wellensi, taxato c li., ratione subrogationis facte de eodem Stephano Pempel' per felicis recordationis Urbanum, x kalendas Januarii anno iii[tio],[753] in plenam solutionem taxe xx li.

## Norwicensis

De ecclesia de Chevyngton' (Chevington), taxata xvi li. xiii s. iiii d., ratione confirmationis facte de eadem Hugoni Impel per Innocentium, vii kalendas Februarii anno x,[754] pro resta vi li. xiii s. iiii d.

De ecclesia de Ratlesden' (Rattlesden), taxata xx li., ratione provisionis facte de eadem Thome Woderone per Urbanum, vi idus Aprilis anno iii,[755] in partem restorem x li.

(fol. 39[v]) De ecclesia de Chyteston' (Chediston), taxata xx li., ratione confirmationis seu provisionis facte de eadem Roberto de Fordham per Urbanum, x kalendas Februarii anno vii[mo],[756] pro resta x li.

De ecclesia de Northwold', taxata xxvii li. vi s. viii d., ratione provisionis facte de eadem Johanni de Glatton' per Urbanum, xi kalendas Martii anno vi[to],[757] in partem reste ix li. vi s. viii d.

## Lincolniensis

De ecclesia de Hagworthyngham (Hagworthingham), taxata xii li., ratione provisionis facte de eadem Thome de Tetteford' per Urbanum, ii nonas Januarii anno secundo,[758] pro resta iiii[or] li.

De prebenda de Carleton' cum Thurleby (Carlton cum Thurlby), taxata xxvi li. xiii s. iiii d., ratione provisionis facte de eadem Edwardo de Cherdestoke per Innocentium, kalendas Martii anno vi,[759] pro resta vi li. xiii s. iiii d.

De ecclesia de Barewell' (Barwell), taxata xxiii li. vi s. viii d., ratione provisionis facte de eadem Laurentio de Ikestok' per Urbanum, xi kalendas Februarii anno vii,[760] in plenam solutionem taxe x li.

De vicaria de Luton', taxata xxiiii[or] m., ratione provisionis seu confirmationis de novo facte de eadem Benedicto de Massyngham per Urbanum, v kalendas Octobris anno iiii[to],[761] in partem taxe xii li.

De vicaria de Stotfold' ratione provisionis facte de

eadem Radulpho de Bereford' per Urbanum, vii idus Martii anno vi,[762] in partem reste ii m.

De ecclesia de Langeport (Lamport), taxata xxiii li. vi s. viii d., ratione provisionis seu confirmationis de novo facte Johanni de Cnol' per Urbanum, vi idus Julii anno vii,[763] in partem taxe vii m.

## Lichfeldensis

De decanatu Sancti Johannis Cestr', taxato xxvi li. xiii s. iiii d., ratione provisionis facte de eodem Johanni de Wodehouse per Urbanum, vii kalendas Januarii anno v[to],[764] in partem reste v m.

## Assavensis

De vicaria de Cogitva (Cegidfa or Guilsfield), que cum ecclesia de Cogitva taxatur ad xxv m., quarum quartem partem percipit vicarius et rector tres partes, ratione confirmationis seu provisionis de novo facte de eadem Johanni de Appulorthorp' per Urbanum, idus Martii anno vi,[765] pro resta dicte quarte partis que sunt iiii li. iii s. iiii d., xvi s. viii d.

## (fol. 40, xl) Bangorensis

De archidiaconatu de Anglesey, taxato xl m., ratione provisionis facte de eadem Thome de Haverbergh' per Urbanum, viii kalendas Martii anno vi[to],[766] in partem taxe xxii li. xiii s. iiii d.

## Eboracensis

De vicaria de Kildewyke (Kildwick) per manus Domini Johannis de Stronsall', ratione provisionis facte de eadem ex causa permutationis Willelmo Glayve de Pdyngton' per Urbanum, vii idus Julii anno primo,[767] pro nova taxa iii li. vi s. viii d.

De prebenda de Massham (Masham), taxata ad novam taxam iiii[xx] li. ratione provisionis facte de eadem Roberto de Stratton' per Urbanum, xviii kalendas Decembris anno viii,[768] in partem dicte taxe xl li., reservata cum potestate exigendi antiquam taxam si de iure debeatur.

De prebenda de Ampleford' (Ampleforth) ratione provisionis facte de eadem Rogero de Freton' per Urbanum, v[to] idus Maii anno viii,[770] pro taxa xl li.

De prebenda de Northnewebald' (North Newbald), taxata liii li. vi s. viii d., ratione provisionis facte de eadem Roberto de Wykeford' per Urbanum, viii kalendas Maii anno vii,[771] in partem taxe xiii li. vi s. viii d.

---

[752] 14 December 1367.
[753] 23 December 1364.
[754] 26 January 1362.
[755] 8 April 1365.
[756] 23 January 1369.
[757] 20 February 1368.
[758] 4 January 1364.
[759] 1 March 1358.
[760] 22 January 1369.
[761] 27 September 1366.

[762] 9 March 1368.
[763] 10 July 1369.
[764] 26 December 1366.
[765] 15 March 1368.
[766] 23 February 1368.
[767] 9 July 1363.
[768] 14 November 1369.
[769] There is no footnote for this number.
[770] 11 May 1370.
[771] 24 April 1369.

De prebenda de Bole in ecclesia Eboracensi ratione provisionis facte de eadem cardinali Cluniacensi,[772] pro taxa xvi li.

### Dunolmensis

De ecclesia de Routhebury (Rothbury), taxata lxvi li. xiii s. iiii d., ratione confirmationis seu provisionis de novo facte de eadem Johanni Marchal per Urbanum, v[to] nonas Martii anno primo,[773] in partem reste taxe xx li.

De vicaria de Pydyngton' (Pittington) ratione provisionis facte de eadem Willelmo Baty per Urbanum iiii[or] nonas Maii anno viii,[774] pro taxa vi li. xiii s. iiii d.

De ecclesia de Whiteberne (Whitburn) taxata xl li. ratione provisionis facte de eadem Ricardo de Wynchecombe per Urbanum, xix kalendas Januarii anno secundo,[775] in partem reste x li.

De beneficiis que bone memorie dominus cardinalis Carcassonensis [776] in Anglia optinebat in partem solutionis, videlicet cclxxviii li. vi. s. i d. sterlingorum recepit in partem annatorum eorundem beneficiorum camere debitorum ratione provisionum de ipsis eidem domino cardinali factorum, de qua summa responsum est in rationibus Domini Johannis de Cabrespino de ccxix li. xiii s. viiii d., lviii li.

(fol. 40[v]) Summa totalis omnium supra pro dicta camere receptorum in dicto festo Omnium Sanctorum anno domini millesimo CCCLXX usque ad vicesimum secundum diem mensis Februarii anno domini millesimo CCCLXX[mo] secundo a nativitate computando vii[c] xx li. xvi s. vi d.[777]

Sequntur assignationes et exspense dicte recepte

De quibus in quadam assignatione facta die xix mensis Decembris anno domini millesimo CCC septuaginta Petro Jacobi Marchi de societate Albertorum Antiquorum de mandato Domini Johannis de Cabrespino de centum lxxiiii li. xv s. vii d. sterlingorum cedent in deductionem dictorum receptorum pro camera cxiiii li. xvii s. vii d.[778]

Quia recepte fuerunt circa dictum festum Omnium Sanctorum, residuum vero, videlicet lix li. xviii s., quia recepte fuerunt ante idem festum Omnium Sanctorum rationibus Domini Johannis de Cabrespino redditis debebantur.

Item de mandato venerabilis patris, Domini Gaucelmi, episcopi Magalanensis (Maguelone), nuper ⟨thesaurarii⟩ felicis recordationis domini nostri pape Urbani quinti, assignate fuerunt Hugoni de Bononia, servienti

armorum domini nostri pape nuper in negotiis apostolicis ad partes [779] Anglie destinato, pro exspensis per ipsum factis ratione predictorum negotiorum xvi li.

Item eidem Hugoni pro xl fl. sibi pro redditu suo ad curiam per eundem dominum thesaurarium ordinato vi li. iii s. iiii d.

Item die quinto mensis Julii anno domini millesimo CCCLXXI[mo] assignate fuerunt ad mandatum Domini Johannis de Cabrespino Petro Jacobi de societate Antiquorum Albertorum cc li.

Item tertio die Novembris eodem anno LXXI[mo] assignate fuerunt ad mandatum dominorum de camera Johanni Credy sociorum de Guardis de Florentia clxxxxii li. xiii s.

Item die xviii Februarii anno a nativitate domini LXXII[do] liberantur venerabili viro, Arnaldo Garnerii, novo collectori, centum sexaginta septem li. quatuordecim s. duos d. sterlingorum.[780] Sic est in breveto reddito camere folio x.

(fol. 41, xli) Sequntur exspense

Item in diversis vicibus exspense facte pro mandatis camere et aliis litteris clausis per diversas partes Anglie et Wallie citra predictum festum Omnium Sanctorum deferendum iiii li. viii s. iiii d.

Item in exspensis appositis circa compota prioris facta, videlicet de recepta pro apostolica camera a dicto festo Omnium Sanctorum anno LXX[mo] usque ad vicesimum octavum diem mensis Martii anno a nativitate domini millesimo CCCLXI[mo], dicto Domino Johanni Cabrespino nuper ad curiam Romanam per Magistrum Johannem de Strensall' ad ipsa compota in curia reddenda specialiter deputatum transmissa, licet dicto Domino Johanne de Cabrespino eadem computa recipere non vacasset, c s.

Item ultra premissa in pergameno, papiro, cera, incausto et aliis pro officio emptis per idem tempus liii [781] s. iiii d.

Item pro hospitio collectoris a festo Omnium Sanctorum predicto per unum annum et tres menses et amplius viii li. vi s. viii d.

Item pro exspensis domini prioris subcollectoris et suorum in mora sua Londonie pro compotis faciendis et reddendis lx s.

Summa assignationum et expensarum dicti domini prioris Lewensis vii[c] xx li. xvi s. v d., quarum sunt pro expensis per eum factis ratione officii in dictis xv mensibus xxiii li. viii s. iiii d. Et tantundem est in sua recepta supra pagina proxima in principio.

Petit quitantiam de predictis per dominum nostrum seu cameram sibi dari quia tantum tradidit, assignavit vel expendit sicut recepit, et sic nichil debet.

(fol. 41[v]) Sequntur illa que deficiunt in restis datis et traditis michi, Arnaldo Garnerii, per cameram, de

---

[772] Androin de la Roche, priest of S. Marcello.
[773] 3 March 1363.
[774] 4 May 1370.
[775] 14 December 1363.
[776] Stephen Aubert, bishop of Carcassonne, priest of S. Lorenzo in Lucina 22 September 1368 to 29 September 1369.
[777] In the margin: *Summa recepte domini prioris, locumtenentis Domini Cabrespini.*
[778] In the margin: *assignationes et expense ipsius prioris.*

[779] Follows *parf* deleted by a line.
[780] Sum repeated in the margin.
[781] Follows *lx* deleted by a line.

quibus nichil respondetur in restis nec in recepta domini prioris Lewensis, Domini Johannis de Cabrespino locumtenentis.

### Lichfeldensis

De ecclesia de Elerkelwe (Child's Ercall), que fuit, ut in dictis restis habetur, confirmata Stephano de Eyntheton' per Innocentium vii kalendas Julii anno vii$^{mo}$,[782] pro resta taxe vi li. xiii s. iiii d.

De hoc patet folio restarum camere xxxvii. Alia dicitur quod fuit provisio infra annum ix kalendas Octobris anno viii,[783] de qua fuit satisfactum domino priori, et sic ista provisio tamquam nulla [784] debuit cancellari, et apparet quia Johannes de Cabrespino quitavit dominum priorem de dicta recepta, ut asseritur pro parte dicti prioris, sed videatur.[785]

### Sarisbiriensis

Item de prebenda de Durenford' (Durnford) in ecclesia Sarisbiriensi, taxata xvi li. xiii s. iiii d., ratione provisionis facte de eadem Johanni de Stratteford' per Urbanum, xii kalendas Augusti anno iiii$^{to}$.[786] Camera vero petit plus ultra, scilicet viii li. vi s. viii d. datas in ultimo compoto prioris, ut asseritur, in recepta alias viii li. vi s. viii d.

De hoc patet folio liiii restarum camere, et dicitur quod dictus Johannes de Cabrespino habuit et auditur a solutione billeta de solutione, ut asseritur pro parte domini prioris, et sic dictus Johannes tenetur, sed videatur cum eo.[787]

### Lincolniensis

Item de archidiaconatu Oxonie, vacante per obitum cardinalis Aquensis,[788] ratione provisionis facte Thome Southam per Urbanum viii idus Augusti anno v$^{to}$,[789] x [790] li. Folio restarum camere lix.

Quia prior dicit in arreragiis suis folio restarum suarum xxiii quod recepit xx li. et dat residuum in resta, et in restis camere dicitur quod non sunt recepte nisi x li., ideo oportet quod prior inveniat alias x li.

Dominus vero Johannes de Cabrespino habuit a dicto priore alias x li. ut in quitantia sua habetur, ideo respondeat Dominus Cabrespino si dominum priorem quitavit de dictis x li., sed videatur per dominos in camera.[791]

### (fol. 42, xlii) Eboracensis

Item de ecclesiis de Aldyngham in Fourneys (Aldingham), taxa nova x li., et Sancti Martini in Mykelgath Eboraci (St. Martin in Micklegate, York), taxata ad vii m., Eboraci, ratione provisionis facte ex causa permutationis xix kalendas Januarii anno vi$^{to}$ per Urbanum,[792] folio restarum camere lxi, duas taxas que ascendunt ut supra quatuordecim li. tresdecim s. iiii d.[793]

De utraque vero taxa est solutum Domino Johanni de Cabrespino et dominus prior habeat quitantiam, quare respondeat Dominus Johannes qui dimisit in restis suis.[794]

Summa de supplendis per Dominum Johannem de Cabrespino ut supra habetur xxxix li. xiii s. iiii$^{or}$ d. sterlingorum.

De supradicta summa recepi ego, Arnaldus Garnerii, unam partem, scilicet xiiii li. xvi s., de quibus habetur supra folio xxxvii, et ibi videatur quia ibi datur in recepta camere si sibi debeatur; alias quod dicto Domino Johanni per ipsam cameram reddatur cum et si se iustificaverit de premissis in toto vel in parte, quia hoc quod est hic et in iiii$^{or}$ foliis precedentibus est solum pro memoriali. Nam ipsa recepta cum dicto supplemento in isto et in aliis dictis foliis contento cum restis michi traditis, cuius copia vera est supra a folio secundo istius libri usque ad folium xxxvii inclusive, continetur, totum quidquid in restis michi traditis per cameram etiam continetur, prout fuit summarie Londonie exploratum anno supradicto LXXII inter me, Arnaldum Garnerii, et dominum locumtenentem Domini Johannis de Cabrespino, ad finem relationis si opus fuerit faciende

Restant quod debet, salvis excusatis suis, xxiiii li. xvii s. iiii d., de quibus non cavetur in summa reste supra folio xxxv° quia forte excusabit totum vel partem, et videatur.

Datur pro memoriali ista pagina et precedens.

Verte folium et in sequenti et sequenti invenies [795] excusationes pro predictis traditis per Dominum Johannem de Cabrespino.

### (fol. 43) [796] Iste sunt excusationes et responsiones Johannis de Cabrespino ad obiecta et impugnata in duobus foliis precedentibus per collectorem Anglie

Sequntur responssiones et excusationes Johannis de Cabrespino, olim in Anglia sedis appostolice collectoris, ad impugnata et obiecta per venerabilem virum, Dominum Arnaldum Garnerii, in illis partibus nunc collectorem, qui dicit deficere in restis datis et traditis eidem Domino Arnaldo per dominum priorem Lewensem, locumtenentem dicti Domini Johannis, licet dentur in restis camere per eundem Johannem de Cabrespino

---

[782] 25 June 1359.
[783] 23 September 1360.
[784] *nnulla* MS. without sign of abbreviation.
[785] In the margin: *ponatur in areiyahgiis quia debetur cum de ipsa ecclesia fuerunt due provisiones.*
[786] 21 July 1366.
[787] In the margin: *Dominus Johannes de Cabrespino negat dedisse quitantiam et nichil recepisse, quare ponatur in restis.*
[788] Peter Itherii, bishop of Dax, bishop of Albano.
[789] 6 August 1367.
[790] Follows *d* apparently deleted by a line.
[791] In the margin: *Dicte x libre debebantur per Dominum Johannem, sed solutum est per collectorem, ut patet supra in folio xxxvii.*

[792] 14 December 1367.
[793] Sum repeated in the margin.
[794] In the margin: *Ista provisio videtur inutilis quia sub eadem data fuit bis eidem persone provisum et de una est satisfactum.*
[795] Extension doubtful.
[796] Folio 42$^v$ is blank.

collectorem, prout ipse Dominus Arnaldus Garnerii dat in suo libro specifice declaratum.

### Lichfeldensis

Ad primum quod oponitur seu impugnatur de ecclesia de Herkelawe parva (Child's Ercall), non taxata, que Stephano de Enthython' fuit confirmata per Innocentium vii kalendas Junii pontificatus sui anno vii°,[797] pro qua petuntur, et datur in arayratgiis dicti collectoris in vi li. xiii s. iiii d.

Respondetur quod de ista ecclesia fuerunt eidem Stephano facte due confirmationes per eundem Dominum Innocentium sub diversis datis, sive una provisio de ipsa per cardinalem Urgellensem, in illis partibus tunc legatum, et una confirmatio per ipsum Dominum Innocentium, quarum una fuit sub data de qua supra et alia sub data ix kalendas Octobris anno eiusdem Domini Innocentii viii°,[798] et ambe confirmationes vel provisiones fuerunt date in restis seu arayratgiis per Dominum Hugonem Pelegrini eidem Domino Johanni de Cabrespino, de quarum una, videlicet de posteriori in data, est ipsi camere satisfactum, ut patet per computa dicti Johannis de Cabrespino et dicti domini prioris Lewensis, pro alia non data est per eundem Johannem de Cabrespino in arayratgiis, et bene, quia non sunt infra annum si bene videatur, nisi forte diceretur quod de dictis duabus confirmationibus, sive una provisione appostolica at alia confirmatione, cum sint de eodem beneficio et eidem persone non debetur nisi una annata que soluta est, super quo determinet camera, quia dictus collector, scilicet Johannes de Cabrespino, de hiis non videtur teneri.

### (fol. 43ᵛ) Sarisbiriensis; impugnatio

Item de prebenda de Durnefford' (Durnford) in ecclesia Sarisbiriensi, taxata xvi li. xiii s. iiii d., ratione provisionis facte de eadem Johanni de Strafforde per Urbanum xii kalendas Augusti anno quarto,[799] pro qua petuntur adhuc per cameram, et data est per dictum Johannem de Cabrespino camere in arayratgiis, ut patet per libros camere, viii li. vi s. iiii d.

Respondetur quod dominus prior Lewensis computat se recepisse ratione dicte provisionis et in partem dicte taxe anno LXX° viii li. vi s. viii d., et de illis est quitatus dictus prior Lewensis per dictum Johannem de Cabrespino, et ille viii libre vi s. et viii d. sunt camere asignate, et de premissis constat per dicta computa, libros et quitantiam. Et pro aliis viii li. vi s. viii d. debet esse et est in arayratgiis, et non pro maiori vel minori summa, nisi forte dictus prior Lewensis dictam restam recepisset postquam dictus Johannes de Cabrespino cum camere appostolica anno LXX° computavit, nec est verum, salva reverentia cuiuscumque

dicentis, quod dictus Johannes de Cabrespino aliquid ratione dicte provisionis receperit ultra dictas viii li. vi s. viii d. sibi asignatas per dictum dominum priorem Lewensem, quia, ut patet per computa dicti domini prioris tempore supradicto tradita et quitantiam inde sequtam, dicte viii li. vi s. et viii d. recepte fuerunt tunc in partem dicte taxe; ergo datur intelligi quod dictus Johannes de Cabrespino alias viii li. vi s. et viii d., de quibus dicitur pretendi bilheta dicti Johanni de Cabrespino, non receperat ante quia tunc solutio facta priori non fuisset facta in partem taxe, ymo in complementum taxe, nec post recepit quia extunc ibi non fuit, et bene creditur quod super hiis bilheta aliqua vera non aparebit, licet cepius[800] in illis partibus falcificentur,[801] super quo advertat diligenter idem dictus collector. Ex premissis concluditur quod dicta resta per Johannem de Cabrespino camere appostolice bene data fuit.

### Lincolniensis; iam impugnatio

Item de archidiaconatu Oxonie, vacante per obitum cardinalis Aquensis,[802] ratione provisionis facte de eo Thome de Wycham per Urbanum viii ydus Augusti anno quinto,[803] de quo dantur camere appostolice in recepta solum x li., et pro aliis x li. in arayratgiis.

(fol. 44) Respondetur quod verum est quod dictus prior in tertio computo suo computat se ratione dicte provisionis x li. recepisse et ille sunt asignate camere, et in computis ipsius Johannis de Cabrespino posite. Postea vero idem dominus prior notificavit quod receperat alias x li., quas dictus Johannes de Cabrespino in libris camere non posuit quia iam dicti libri erant scripti summati et corecti ac camere traditi, et ideo propter illas x li. noluit dictos libros iterato scribi facere, nec in eis summas radere et cancellare, maxime propter occupationes quas tunc temporis habebat de quodam fratre suo qui in eius hospitio ad mortem infirmabatur et finaliter mortuus fuit, set dictum priorem Lewensem de tota summa quitavit, sperans dictas x li. in sequentibus computis suis camere reddendis suplere pro istis x li. Recepte sunt nomine camere de pecuniis ipsius Johannis de Cabrespino, ut ipse met dat in suis computis xiiii li. xvi s., et sic restant restituende per cameram dicto Johanni de Cabrespino iiii li. xvi s. sterlingorum.

### Eboracensis; iam impugnatio

Item de ecclesiis de Aldyngham in Forneys (Aldingham), taxa nova x li., et Sancti Martini in Milgate Eboraci (St. Martin in Micklegate, York) taxata vii m. que valent iiii li. xiii[804] s. iiii d., ratione provisionis

---

[797] 26 May 1359.
[798] 23 September 1360.
[799] 21 July 1366.

[800] Presumably for *sepius.*
[801] Presumably for *falsificentur.*
[802] Peter Itherii, bishop of Dax, bishop of Albano.
[803] 6 August 1367.
[804] Follows *vi* deleted by a line.

facte ex causa permutationis per Urbanum xix kalendas Januarii anno vi°,[805] de quibus satisfactum est camere, et tamen datur in arayratgiis per ipsum Johannem de Cabrespino, ut patet per libros camere et cetera.

Respondetur quod verum est quod dicte provisiones date fuerunt per ipsum Johannem de Cabrespino camere appostolice in recepta sub data xix kalendas Januarii pontificatus Domini Urbani anno quinto, et similiter date fuerunt in arayratgiis sub eadem data sub anno tamen vi°, quia ita recepit a camera, tamen quicquid sit, quia eedem sunt perssone, ecclesie et date, licet pontificatus mutetur, non videtur quod debeatur nisi una annata, quod declaret camera ut ei placebit dicto computanti sufficit quod det in recepta vel arayratgiis que recepit, nec est obligatus ad iustificandum omnia sibi missa, set iustificet que misit, et forte fuit vitium in scribendo et in cancellando. Non est magna difficultas.

(fol. 44ᵛ) Ex premissis igitur videtur satis clare patere quod dictus Johannes de Cabrespino ratione dictarum impugnationum et pro ipsis in aliqua non teneatur, nisi dumtaxat in illis et pro illis x li. que recepte fuerunt de dicto archidiaconatu Oxonie, de quibus tenetur dicto priori vel camere respondere pro quibus dictus Dominus Arnaldus Garnerii recepit prout dat in computis suis xiiii li. xvi s., et sic restant restituende dicto Johanni we Cabrespino iiii li. xvi s. sterlingorum.

(fol. 47ᵛ)[806] De anno LXII et sequenti

Sequntur nomina illorum qui tenentur solvere denarios Beati Petri singulis annis domino nostro pape in Anglia. Et primo de anno domini millesimo CCC[807] septuagesimo secundo, quia supra in restis est de aliis annis computatum, ut per decursum ipsarum restarum potit reperiri folio ii° et iii°

Dominus episcopus Cicestrensis viii li. sterlingorum. Solvit de anno LXXII, et post etiam solvit de anno LXXIII, ideo habet litteram a et b, et sic pro ipsis annis solvit xvi li.[808]

Episcopus Sarisbiriensis xvii li. Solvit pro anno LXX secundo.[809]

Episcopus Bathoniensis et Wellensis xi li. v s. Solvit pro anno LXX secundo vii li. et post iiii li. v s. et postea in partem solutionis anni LXXIII sex li. quinque s., xvii li. x s.[809]

Episcopus Exoniensis ix li. v s. Solvit pro anno LXX secundo et LXX tertio xviii li. x s.[810]

Episcopus Norwicensis xxi li. x s. Solvit de anno LXX secundo et LXXIIItio xliii li.[810]

Episcopus Lincolniensis xlii li. Solvit de anno LXX secundo et LXXIIItio iiiixx iiii li.[810]

Episcopus Lichfeldensis x li. v s. Solvit de anno LXX secundo et LXXIII xx li. x s.[810]

Episcopus Herefordensis vi li. Solvit de anno LXX secundo.[809]

Episcopus Wygorniensis x li. v s. Solvit de anno LXX secundo et LXXIIItio xx li. x s.[811]

(fol. 48, xlvi) Dominus archiepiscopus Eboracensis[812] xi li. x s. Solvit de anno LXX secundo et LXXIII xxiii li.[810]

Archidiaconus Cantuariensis viii li. Solvit pro annis LXX secundo et LXXIIItio xvi li.[810]

Archidiaconus Roffensis v li. xii s. Solvit in duabus vicibus de anno LXX secundo.[809]

Archidiaconus Colcestrie v li. x s. Solvit de anno LXX secundo.[809]

Archidiaconus Essexie v li. x s. Solvit de anno LXX secundo et LXXIIItio xi li.[810]

Archidiaconus Middensexie v li. x s. Solvit de anno LXXII dictas quinque li. x s. et pro anno LXXIII, xi li.[810]

Archidiaconus Wyntoniensis xi li. xiii s. iiii d. Solvit de anno LXX secundo.[809]

Archidiaconus Surreie v li. xiii s. iiii d. Solvit de anno LXX secundo.[809]

Archidiaconus Eliensis v li. Solvit de anno LXX secundo.[809]

Summa dictorum denariorum ascendit quolibet anno centum nonaginta novem li. viii s. viii d.

Summa recepte istius pagine et precedentis iii° xxxvii li. viii s. viii d. Restant pro dictis duobus annis lxi li. viii s. viii d.

(fol. 48ᵛ) De anno LXXII et sequenti

Sequntur nomina illorum qui tenentur solvere annuum censum quolibet anno in Anglia domino nostro pape, et primo de anno domini et cetera septuagesimo secundo, in festo seu termino Beati Michaelis.

## Lincolniensis

Abbas Sancti Albani Lincolniensis diocesis debet solvere xiii s. iiii d. Solvit de dicto anno LXX secundo, ideo habet litteram a, et solvit de anno LXXIII, pro toto xxvi s. viii d.[810]

## Cantuariensis

Abbas de Faveresham xiii s. iiii d. Solvit de dicto anno LXX secundo et LXXIIItio xxvi s. viii d.[810]

## Wyntoniensis

Abbas de Certesey viii s. Solvit de dicto anno LXX secundo.[809]

---

[805] 14 December 1367.
[806] Folios 45 recto to 47 recto inclusive are blank.
[807] Followed by *L* deleted by a line.
[808] In the margin: *b, a.*
[809] In the margin: *a.*
[810] In the margin: *b, a.*

---

[811] In the margin: *b, a.* At the foot of the page: *Recepta pagine est infra proxima pagina* deleted by a line.
[812] On this page the name of the diocese is given also in the margin opposite each item.

### Norwicensis

Abbas Sancti Edmundi de Bury xiii s. iiii d. Solvit de anno LXX secundo et de anno LXX tertio xxvi s. viii d.[810]

### Sarisbiriensis

Abbas de Malmesbury xiii s. iiii d. Solvit de anno LXX secundo et tertio xxvi s. viii d.[810]

### Roffensis

Prior de Tunebrugg' xiii s. iiii d. Solvit de anno LXX secundo et LXX tertio xxvi s. viii d.[810]

### Exoniensis

Prior de Bodmyn ii s. Solvit pro anno LXXII et LXX tertio iiii s.[810]

### Eliensis

Prior de Anglesey ii s. Solvit de anno LXX secundo et LXX tertio iiii s.[810]

### (fol. 49, xlvii) Karleolensis

Prior Karleolensis xiii s. iiii d. Solvit de anno LXX secundo et LXXIII xxvi s. viii d.[810]

### Lincolniensis

Prior de Chaucombe xv d. Solvit de anno LXX secundo et LXXIII ii s. vi d.[810]

### Londoniensis

Abbatissa Sancte Clare Londonie vi d. Debet pro ii annis, videlicet LXXII et LXIII, xii d.

### Eboracensis

Custos de Scamdebrigg' xv d. Solvit de anno LXX secundo et tertio ii s. vi d.[810]

Summa dicti census annui iiiior li. xv s.[813] sterlingorum.

Recepta pagine et precendentis dicti census assendit ix li. xii d. Et restant in dictis paginis de dicto censu viiii s. vi d.[814]

Terminus est ad solvendum de censu quolibet anno in festo Beati Michaelis.

Et de denariis Beati Petri idem est terminus ad solvendum prelatis et archidiaconis et aliis qui habunt levare, sed ipsi communiter non rendent camere nec collectori ante terminum Pasce. Et sic habunt ad levandum a dicto festo Beati Michaelis usque ad dictum festum Pasce vel nuntiationis Beate Marie Virginis, et tunc solvere consueverunt.

Summa denariorum Beati Petri et census quolibet anno debita est iic iiiior li. iii s. viii d. Pro memoriali.[815]

(fol. 49v) Soma universalis recepte istius folii et duorum precedentium, denariorum Beati Petri et census dictorum duorum annorum, trecentas xlvi li. ix s. viiii d.[816]

Soma reste dictorum denariorum et census dictorum duorum precedentium annorum de contentis in isto folio et duobus precedentibus lxi li. xvii s. viii d.

Et sic tantum est in resta seu recepta dictorum duorum annorum quantum debetur pro dictis duobus annis.

(fol. 54, lii)[817] Primus quaternus in curiam traditus

Sequntur beneficia collata et confirmata per sanctissimum in Christo patrem et dominum nostrum, Dominum Gregorium papam undecimum, pontificatus sui anno primo, in regno Anglie, a xi kalendas Februarii[818] citra. Sunt tamen aliqua alia tradita per dominum priorem Lewensem supra folio xxxvi et sequenti, quare signum[819] supra folio xxxvi et hic continua

### Sarisbiriensis

Et primo mandatur provideri Petro Johannis, licentiato in utroque iure, de canonicatu sub exspectatione prebende ecclesie Sarisbiriensis, viii idus Februarii.[820]

### Lincolniensis

Item Nicholao de Drayton', clerico Lincolniensis diocesis, de canonicatu sub exspectatione prebende ecclesie Lincolniensis, xiii kalendas Martii.[821]

### Assavensis

Item Holwellais apDavid, presbytero Assavensis diocesis, de beneficio et cetera ad collationem et cetera episcopi Assavensis, xi kalendas Martii.[822]

### Eboracensis

Item Willelmo de Gunnthorp' de canonicatu sub exspectatione prebende ecclesie Suthwell' in Anglia, xiii kalendas Martii.[821]

### Lincolniensis

Item Rogero de Borton' de canonicatu et prebenda ecclesie Lincolniensis, xiii kalendas Martii.[823]

### Lichfeldensis

Item Willelmo de Pakyngton' Lichfeldensis diocesis de canonicatu sub exspectatione prebende ecclesie Lichfeldensis.

---

[813] Sum repeated MS.

[814] The item is repeated at the foot of the page and deleted by lines with the following comment: *supra est melius in eadem pagina.*

[815] In the margin: *Hoc est his pro memoriali totum que est*

*signatum.* The signature is opposite this item and the two preceding.

[816] Sum repeated MS. In the margin: *vera.*

[817] Folios 50 recto to 53 verso inclusive are blank.

[818] 22 January 1371.

[819] O ⊹ O is the sign given in the margin; see above, n. 716.

[820] 6 February 1371.

[821] 17 February 1371.

[822] 19 February 1371.

[823] This date, 17 February 1371, is bracketed against this and the next three items.

Wygorniensis

Item Henrico de Friston', clerico Eboracensis diocesis, de beneficio et cetera ad collationem episcopi Wygorniensis.

Sarisbiriensis

Item Willelmo Loring', licentiato in legibus clerico Lincolniensis diocesis, de canonicatu sub exspectatione prebende ecclesie Sarisbiriensis.

Quere primam receptam supra in folio xxxvi in prima pagina et secunda. Restant in ista pagina expectationes que nondum habuerunt effectum viii.

(fol. 54ᵛ) Londoniensis

Item Johanni Walde,[824] presbytero Wyntoniensis diocesis, de beneficio cum cura vel sine cura ad collationem episcopi, decani et capituli ecclesie Londoniensis, pro taxa ecclesie Sancti Botulphi ⟨iuxta Billingesgate⟩ ad quam est expeditus, vii m. Solvit in duabus vicibus pro dictis vii m. iiii li. xiii s. iiii d.[825]

Lichfeldensis

Item Petro de Burton', clerico Lichfeldensis diocesis, de canonicatu sub exspectatione prebende ecclesie Lichfeldensis, xiii kalendas Martii.[821]

Eboracensis

Mandatur provideri Radulpho de Ergam, legum doctori, de canonicatu sub exspectatione prebende, dignitatis, et cetera ecclesie Eboracensis, xiiii kalendas Martii.[826]

Eboracensis

Item Willelmo de Margeld' de canonicatu sub exspectatione prebende ecclesie Eboracensis.

Lincolniensis

Item Matheo de Assheton' de canonicatu sub exspectatione prebende ecclesie Lincolniensis.

Londoniensis

Item Waltere Power de canonicatu sub exspectatione prebende ecclesie Sancti Pauli Londonie.

Eboracensis

Item Thome Bulxbith' de canonicatu sub exspectatione prebende ecclesie collegiate Sancti Johannis Evangeliste de Beverlaco.

Dunolmensis

Item Johanni de Stubbes de beneficio et cetera ad collationem episcopi, prioris et conventus Dunolmensis.

Eboracensis

Item Johanni Seggenay ad collationem archiepiscopi Eboracensis.

Eboracensis

Item Johanni Braghton' de canonicatu sub exspectatione prebende ecclesie Sancti Johannis Ewangeliste de Hoveden' (Howden).

Recepta pagine iiii li. xiii s. iiii d.[827] Restant in ista pagina ad huc exspectationes sine effectu ix.

(fol. 55, liii) Wyntoniensis

Item Willelmo Derwent de beneficio et cetera ad collationem et cetera episcopi Wyntoniensis, xiiii kalendat Martii.[828]

Londoniensis

Item Rogero de Golborn' ad collationem episcopi Londoniensis.

Sarisbiriensis

Item Johanni de Yerdeburgh' de canonicatu sub exspectatione prebende [829] ecclesie Sarisbiriensis.

Sarisbiriensis

Item Johanni filio Martini de beneficio et cetera ad collationem episcopi Sarisbyriensis.

Bathoniensis

Item Willelmo de Tufelden' presbytero de canonicatu sub exspectatione prebende ecclesie Bathoniensis.

Wellensis

Mandatur provideri Willelmo de Pulhley de canonicatu sub exspectatione prebende ecclesie Wellensis.

Lichfeldensis

Item Johanni Cheyne presbytero de canonicatu sub exspectatione ⟨prebende⟩ ecclesie Lichfeldensis.

Wygorniensis

Item Helie de Vretwessill' presbytero de canonicatu sub exspectatione prebende ecclesie Wygorniensis.
Restant expectationes viii.

(fol. 55ᵛ) Wygorniensis

Item Petro de beneficio ecclesiastico cum cura vel sine cura ad collationem episcopi Wygorniensis, xiiii kalendas Martii.[830]

---

[824] *Wolde de Scaldewell'*, Collectorie 13, fol. 173.
[825] In the margin: *solvit*.
[826] The date, 16 February 1371, is bracketed against this and the next seven items.
[827] In the margin: *vera*.
[828] The date, 16 February 1371, is bracketed against this and the next seven items.
[829] *prebende* om. MS., but *sub exspectatione* is repeated.
[830] The date, 16 February 1371, is bracketed against this and the next six items.

### Lincolniensis

Item Johanni Clayden' presbytero ad collationem abbatis et conventus monasterii de Ramesey ordinis Sancti Benedicti.

### Eboracensis

Item Thome de Herdewyk presbytero de canonicatu sub exspectatione prebende ecclesie collegiate Sanctorum Petri et Pauli de Ripponia.

### Bathoniensis

Item Johanni Simond' presbytero ad collationem episcopi, prioris et conventus Bathoniensis ordinis Sancti Benedicti.

### Eboracensis

Item Johanni de Vretheton' presbytero ad collationem abbatis et conventus Sancte Marie iuxta Eboracum.

### Lichfeldensis

Item Johanni Hartfeld' de canonicatu sub exspectatione prebende ecclesie collegiate Omnium Sanctorum de Derby.

### Eboracensis

Item Johanni Ricardo Daudson presbytero ad collationem et cetera abbatis et conventus Selby ordinis Sancti Benedicti.
Restant expectationes vii.

### (fol. 56, liiii) Lichfeldensis

Item Johanni de Ipre presbytero ad collationem et cetera episcopi, conventus et Lichfeldensis, xiiii kalendas Martii.[831]

### Eboracensis

Item Wilelmo de Wastham de canonicatu sub exspectatione dignitatis et cetera ecclesie Eboracensis, xiii kalendas Martii.[832]

### Lichfeldensis

Mandatur provideri Johanni de Fordham, clerico Norwicensis diocesis, de canonicatu sub exspectatione prebende ecclesie Lichfeldensis

### Herefordensis

Item Thome de Lynthon', presbytero Norwicensis diocesis, de canonicatu sub exspectatione prebende ecclesie Herefordensis.

### Lincolniensis

Item Ricardo de Stratton', bacallario Lincolniensis, de canonicatu sub exspectatione prebende ecclesie Lincolniensis.

### Menevensis

Item Johanni Rose, bacallario in legibus, de canonicatu et prebenda ac dignitate in ecclesia Menevensi, x kalendas Martii.[833]

### Herefordensis

Item Thome de Chaundos, presbytero Herefordensis diocesis, de canonicatu sub exspectatione prebende ecclesie Herefordensis, v kalendas Martii.[834]
Restant exspectationes vii.

### (fol. 56ᵛ) Eboracensis

Item Johanni Tonwyk', clerico Lincolniensis diocesis, de canonicatu sub exspectatione prebende ecclesie collegiate Southwell', v kalendas Martii.[834]

### Lincolniensis

Item Thome de Sancto Botulpho, presbytero Lincolniensis diocesis, de beneficio ad collationem abbatis et conventus monasterii de Burgo Sancti Petri dicte diocesis, kalendas Martii.[835]

### Londoniensis

Item Ade Daveport Londonie, bacallario in legibus, de canonicatu sub exspectatione prebende ecclesie Londoniensis.

### Sarisbiriensis

Item Simoni Bate de canonicatu sub exspectatione prebende ecclesie monialium monasterii de Wilton' Sarisbiriensis diocesis.

### Lichfeldensis

Item Johanni de Lodelowell' de canonicatu sub exspectatione prebende ecclesie Lichfeldensis, nonas Martii.[836]

### Lincolniensis, Wyntoniensis

Item Johanni Blak', presbytero Herefordensis diocesis, de canonicatu sub exspectatione ecclesie Lincolniensis necnon de beneficio et cetera ad collationem episcopi Wyntoniensis, v idus Martii.[837]

### Eboracensis

Mandatur provideri Ade de Atum, presbytero Eboracensis, de beneficio et cetera ad collationem archiepiscopi, decani et capituli ecclesie Eboracensis, v idus Martii.[837]

### Sarisbiriensis

Item Johanni de Drayton canonicatu sub ex-

---

[831] 16 February 1371.
[832] The date, 17 February 1371, is bracketed against this and the next three items.

[833] 20 February 1371.
[834] 25 February 1371.
[835] 1 March 1371.
[836] 7 March 1371.
[837] 11 March 1371.

spectatione prebende ecclesie Sarisbiriensis, iiii idus Martii.[838]

Restant expectationes viii.

### (fol. 57, lv) Sarisbiriensis

Item Willelmo de Gimthorp' de canonicatu sub exspectatione prebende ecclesie Sarisbiriensis, v idus Martii.[839]

### Herefordensis

Item Johanni Blake, presbytero Lichfeldensis diocesis, de canonicatu sub exspectatione prebende ecclesie Herefordensis.

### Eboracensis

Item Johanni de Humbleton' de canonicatu sub exspectatione prebende ecclesie Beverlacensis Eboracensis diocesis.

### Lincolniensis

Item Eudonio de la Souche de canonicatu sub exspectatione prebende ecclesie Lincolniensis.

### Cantuariensis

Concessum est Willelmo archiepiscopo Cantuariensi ut possit conferre auctoritate apostolica ad suam collationem spectantia sex personis ydoneis et cetera, v idus Martii.[840] Certificat archiepiscopus in iii mandatis quod nunquam fuit usus, nec bullas fecit fieri, nec beneficia dedit, et cetera.

### Sarisbiriensis

Mandatur provideri Johanni Blannchard, legum doctori, de canonicatu sub exspectatione prebende, dignitatis et cetera ecclesie Sarisbiriensis.

### Exoniensis

Item Johanni Shillyngford', presbytero Exoniensis diocesis, de canonicatu sub exspectatione prebende, dignitatis, et cetera ecclesie Exoniensis.

Restant exspectationes vii.

### (fol. 57ᵛ) Cicestrensis

Item Johanni Lideford', licentiato in legibus, de canonicatu sub exspectatione prebende, dignitatis, et cetera ecclesie Cicestrensis, v idus Martii.[841]

### Lincolniensis

Item Rogero de Sutton' de canonicatu sub exspectatione prebende ecclesie Lincolniensis.

### Norwicensis

Mandatur provideri Thome de Hornynggescerthe, legum doctori, de aliqua dignitate ecclesiastica cum cura vel sine cura spectante ad collationem episcopi, prioris et capituli ecclesie Norwicensis.

### Lichfeldensis

De canonicatu et prebenda ecclesie Lichfeldensis vacantibus per obitum Raynaldi de Sancto Claro fuit provisum Andree de Buwell', presbytero Norwicensis diocesis, ii idus Martii.[842] Certificat episcopus quod talis non fuit in ecclesia ad huc.[843]

### Lichfeldensis

Mandatur provideri Willelmo de Southam de canonicatu sub exspectatione prebende ecclesie Sancti Johannis Cestrie Lichfeldensis diocesis, v idus Martii.[844]

### Wyntoniensis

Item Willelmo Everk' alias dicto Parson, presbytero Sarisbiriensis diocesis, de beneficio et cetera ad collationem abbatis et conventus monasterii de Lida (Hyde) in Anglia.

### Lincolniensis

Item Thome de Boghes, presbytero Eboracensis diocesis, de beneficio et cetera ad collationem et cetera episcopi, prioris et capituli ecclesie Dunolmensis, xv kalendas Martii.[845]

Restat una provisio iª; et exspectationes vi.

### (fol. 58, lvi) Dunolmensis

Item Hugoni de Arlam de canonicatu sub exspectatione prebende ecclesie Dunolmensis, xv kalendas Februarii.[846]

### Eboracensis

Item Waltero de Waudeford', magistro in artibus, de beneficio et cetera ad collationem archiepiscopo Eboracensis.

Item Willelmo Reed, clerico Allerdensis (Killala) diocesis de canonicatu sub exspectatione prebende ecclesie Allerdensis.[847]

Item Andree Wynfray presbytero de canonicatu sub exspectatione prebende Alberdonensis (Aberdeen).[847]

### Lincolniensis

De parochiali Sancti Johannis de Craneford' (Cranford) Lincolniensis diocesis, vacante per assecutionem parochialis ecclesie de Cestr' (Castor) dicte diocesis factam per Robertum Anstorp', fuit provisum Johanni Sunethon,[848] presbytero dicte diocesis, xiiii kalendas

---

[838] 12 March 1371.

[839] The date, 11 March 1371, is bracketed also against the next three items.

[840] 11 March 1371. The date is bracketed against this and the next two items.

[841] The date is bracketed against this and the next two items.

[842] 14 March 1371.

[843] In the margin: *provisio de vacanti.*

[844] The date, 11 March 1371, is bracketed against this and the next item.

[845] 15 February 1371.

[846] 18 January 1371. The date is bracketed against this and the next three items

[847] In the margin: *non est talis in Anglia*

[848] *Swethon*, Collectorie 13, fol. 173.

Aprilis.[849] Solvit die xiii Novembris anno LXXIII quadraginta sex s. viii d.[850] Item solvit die iii Julii anno LXXIIII in tribus marchis cum dymidia xlvi s. viii d.[851]

### Lincolniensis

Mandatur provideri Johanni de Schopedin', presbytero Norwicensis diocesis, de canonicatu sub exspectatione prebende ecclesie Lincolniensis, idus Junii.[852]

### Sarisbiriensis

Motu proprio fuit provisum Guillelmo titulo Sancti Stephani in Celiomonte presbytero cardinali, de canonicatu et prebenda de Cheremynstrebert (Charminster) in ecclesia Sarisbiriensi, vacantibus per mortem Guydonis de Pestello, regestratori litterarum apostolicarum in curia defuncti. Cardinalis de Agrifolio nec habuit ad huc effectum, sed videatur cum habebit, quia per thesaurarium domus regis possidetur titulo regio.[853]

Recepta pagine iiii li. xiii s. iiii d.,[854] inutiles sunt tres[855] provisiones iii; restant expectationes v.

### (fol. 58ᵛ) Sarisbiriensis

Motu proprio fuit provisum Bertrando titulo Sancte Prisce presbytero cardinali de canonicatu et prebenda quos in ecclesia Sarisbiriensi idem Guillelmus optinebat dum vacabit et cetera, iiii idus Junii.[856] Cardinalis de Agrifolio tenet eam adhunc, quia precedens provisio non habuit effectum.

### Eboracensis

Motu proprio fuit provisum Johanni cardinali Belvacensi[857] de canonicatu sub exspectatione prebende ecclesie Eboracensis, iii idus Julii.[858] Expectatio et videatur cum habuerit effectum.

### Eboracensis

Item Thome de Arundell' de canonicatu sub exspectatione prebende, dignitatis et cetera ecclesie Eboracensis.

### Cantuariensis

Item Hugoni de Ardene de beneficio et cetera ad collationem archiepiscopi Cantuariensis, ii nonas Junii.[859]

### Lincolniensis

Ex causa permutationis fuit provisum Johanni Valsch'

de parochiali ecclesia de Herssyngton' (Horsington) Lincolniensis diocesis et Nicholao Penne presbytero de parochiali ecclesia de Stepehaston' (Steeple Aston) dicte diocesis, idus Junii.[860] Non habuit effectum dicta permutatio quia ecclesia de Horssyngton' est de patronatu laicali et cetera, quia patronus non wlt per potentiam nisi suus interveniat concessus.[861]

### Dunolmensis

Mandatur provideri Willelmo de Osmundeston', presbytero Lichfeldensis diocesis, de beneficio et cetera ad collationem episcopi Dunolmensis, xvii kalendas Junii.[862]

### Eboracensis

Item Johanni de Humbleton' de canonicatu sub exspectatione prebende, dignitatis et cetera ecclesie Eboracensis, xiiii kalendas Junii.[863]

### Bangorensis

De canonicatu et prebenda ecclesie Bangorensis vacantibus per munus consecrationis impensus Howelo aptud ad ecclesiam Bangorensem fuit provisum Johanni Trefnant, presbytero diocesis Assavensis, xii kalendas Junii.[864] Est in mandatis ad denuntiandum et cetera, et non habuit effectum quia dominus princeps dedit Thome de Lenton', sede vacante.[865]

Hic finis primi caterni michi Arnaldo traditi in curia cum hic primo veni. Et sic est in libro recepte dimisso locumtenenti folio li scriptum

Reste sunt infra in sequenti pagina.

### (fol. 59, lvii) Secundus caternus[866]

Restant supra in precedenti pagina pro tribus provisionibus factis de vacantibus fructus iii; restant etiam quinque expectationes ad huc sine effectu v.

Summa recepte primi quaterni predicti de tempore dicti Domini Gregorii ultra denarios Beati Petri et censum xlvi li.[867] Inutiles provisiones sunt vii; restant fructus x provisionum x; restant in pecunia de taxatis ultra dictos fructus iiᶜ xvi li. xiii s. iiii d.; restant de dicto quaterno primo lxxᵗᵃ expectationes que nondum habuerunt effectum quod sciatur, lxx.

### (fol. 59ᵛ) Secundus caternus missus de curia de mense Octobris anno LXXII

### Sarisbiriensis

Mandatur provideri Lamberto de Trinkingham Lincolniensis diocesis de dignitate, personatu vel officio

---

[849] 19 March 1371. In the margin: *provisio de vacanti*
[850] Sum repeated MS. In the margin: *solvit*.
[851] In the margin: *solvit*.
[852] 13 June 1371.
[853] In the margin: *inutilis*.
[854] In the margin: *vera*.
[855] Over *duas* deleted by a line.
[856] 10 June 1371.
[857] John de Dormans, bishop of Beauvais, priest of Ss. Quattro Coronati.
[858] 13 July 1371.
[859] 4 June 1371.

[860] 13 June 1371.
[861] In the margin: *Provisio de vacanti et est duplex*.
[862] 16 May 1371.
[863] 19 May 1371.
[864] 21 May 1371.
[865] In the margin: *provisio*.
[866] A mistake; the second sheaf begins on the next page.
[867] In the margin: *vera*.

curato vel non curato ac canonicatu et prebenda eclesie Sarisbiriensis, xi kalendas Aprilis.[868]

## Lincolniensis

Dum Robertus de Somerton', presbyter Lincolniensis diocesis, assecutus fuerit gratiam ad collationem abbatis et conventus monasterii de Ramessey Lincolniensis diocesis, dimittet parochialem ecclesiam de Buckenll' (Bucknell) dicte diocesis, xi kalendas Aprilis.[868]

## Wygorniensis

Mandatur provideri Johanni de Upton' super Sabrinam, clerico Wygorniensis diocesis, de beneficio ecclesiastico et cetera ad collationem et cetera episcopi Wygorniensis, vii kalendas Aprilis.[869]

## Wyntoniensis

Item Ricardo Hexton', clerico Sarisbiriensis diocesis, de beneficio ecclesiastico et cetera ad collationem et cetera episcopi Wyntoniensis.

## Eliensis

Item Hugoni Pirinton', presbytero Lincolniensis diocesis, de beneficio et cetera ad collationem et cetera episcopi Eliensis.

## Wygorniensis

Item Ricardo Newenent, clerico Wigorniensis diocesis de beneficio ecclesiastico ad collationem et cetera episcopi Wygorniensis.

## Cantuariensis

Item Roberto de Bradegate, clerico Cantuariensis diocesis, de beneficio ecclesiastico cum cura vel sine cura spectante ad collationem et cetera archiepiscopi et capituli ecclesie Cantuariensis. Dicitur quod est expeditus de novo, et moneatur quod ecclesia quam tenet, et sic iam factum est in v mandato.[870]

Restant fructus unius i[us]; et sex expectationes vi.

## (fol. 60, lviii) Eboracensis

Mandatur provideri Roberto de Sterington', presbytero Eboracensis diocesis, de beneficio ecclesiastico et cetera ad collationem et cetera abbatis et conventus monasterii Sancte Marie Eboracensis extra Muros, vii kalendas Aprilis.[871]

## Londoniensis

Item Ricardo Helyn de Colyngham, presbytero Eboracensis diocesis, de beneficio ecclesiastico et cetera ad collationem et cetera coniunctim vel divisim decani et capituli ecclesie Londoniensis.

## Lincolniensis

Item Radulpho Botners, clerico Wyntoniensis diocesis, de beneficio ecclesiatico et cetera ad collationem et cetera abbatis et conventus monasterii de Burgo (Peterborough) Licolniensis diocesis.

## Lichfeldensis

Item Johanni Stebbing', presbytero Londoniensis diocesis, de canonicatu sub exspectatione prebende ecclesie Lichfeldensis.

## Eboracensis

Item Nicholao de Chaddesden' de canonicatu sub exspectatione prebende, dignitatis, et cetera ecclesie Eboracensis.

## Eliensis

Item Roberto Braybrok' de beneficio ecclesiastico et cetera ad collationem et cetera episcopi Eliensis. Est expeditus, ut dicitur, ad ecclesiam de Hynton' (Cherry Hinton) dicte diocesis, taxata ad xxx li., et est in mandatis et habet terminos.

## Lincolniensis

Item Reginaldo Braybrok' presbytero de beneficio ecclesiastico et cetera ad collationem et cetera abbatis et conventus monasterii de Ramesey Lincolniensis diocesis.

## Eboracensis

Item Willelmo Forester de canonicatu sub exspectatione prebende ecclesie Suthwell'.

Resta pecunie xxx li.; restant expectationes ad huc sine effectu viii.

## (fol. 60[v]) Sarisbiriensis

Mandatur provideri Ricardo Haxton' clerico de canonicatu sub exspectatione prebende, dignitatis, et cetera ecclesie Sarisbiriensis, vii kalendas Aprilis.[872]

## Lichfeldensis

Item Willelmo Chaddesle, clerico Wygorniensis diocesis, de canonicatu sub exspectatione prebende ecclesie Lichfeldensis.

## Londoniensis

Conceditur Simoni episcopo Londoniensi ut possit conferre duas prebendas in ecclesia Londoniensis et unam dignitatem in eadem et alia tria spectantia ad collationem suam in diocesi predicta. Dicitur quod nondum fecit, sed videatur melius.

---

[868] 22 March 1371.
[869] The date, 26 March 1371, is bracketed against this and the next four items.
[870] In the margin: *expeditus est.*
[871] The date, 26 March 1371, is bracketed against this item and the next seven.

[872] The date, 26 March 1371, is bracketed against this and the next eight items.

### Herefordensis

Mandatur provideri Nicholao de Herforde, presbytero Herefordensis diocesis, de canonicatu sub exspectatione prebende, dignitatis, et cetera ecclesie Herefordensis.

### Eboracensis

Item Willemo Blithe de canonicatu sub exspectatione prebende ecclesie Eboracensis.

### Exoniensis

Item Waltero [873] de Clompton' clerico de canonicatu sub exspectatione prebende ecclesie Exoniensis. Expeditus est ad prebendam Exoniensem, et est in mandato et certificatio.[874]

### Herefordensis

Item Johanni Bridwode clerico de canonicatu sub exspectatione prebende ecclesie Herefordensis.

### Eboracensis

Item Waltero Amyas de canonicatu sub exspectatione prebende ecclesie Suthwell' Eboracensis diocesis.

### Eboracensis

Item Johanni Abraham de canonicatu sub exspectatione prebende ecclesie Ripponensis Eboracensis diocesis.

Restant fructus unius expediti i^us; exspectationes sunt viii.

### (fol. 61, lix) Eboracensis

Mandatur provideri Johanni de Kepston', presbytero Cicestrensis diocesis, de canonicatu sub exspectatione prebende ecclesie Beverlacensis Eboracensis diocesis, vi kalendas Aprilis.[875]

### Eboracensis

Item Thome Sekandon' Lichfeldensis diocesis de canonicatu sub exspectatione prebende ecclesie Ripponensis.

### Eboracensis

Item Johanni de Shirfeld' clerico de canonicatu sub exspectatione prebende ecclesie Houden' Eboracensis diocesis.

### Menevensis

Item Johanni Prat de canonicatu sub exspectatione prebende ecclesie Abbrewill' (Abergwili) Menevensis diocesis, vii kalendas Aprilis.[876]

### Eboracensis

Item Thome Marie, clerico Norwicensis diocesis, de canonicatu sub exspectatione prebende ecclesie Houden Eboracensis diocesis.

### Eboracensis

Item Hugoni Attehull', clerico Lincolniensis diocesis, de canonicatu sub exspectatione prebende ecclesie Beverlacensi Eboracensis diocesis.

### Norwicensis

**Item Ricardo filio Nicholai [877] de Ligate de beneficio** ecclesiastico et cetera ad collationem et cetera abbatis Sancti Edmundi de Bury Norwicensis diocesis.

Restant expectationes vii.

### (fol. 61ᵛ) Norwicensis

Subrogatus Michael de Causton', presbyter Norwicensis diocesis, in omni iure et ad omne ius quod competebat Laurentio de Ikestok' in et super parochiali ecclesia de Esterham [878] (East Dereham) Norwicensis diocesis, iii kalendas Aprilis,[879] pro taxa lxxiii li. vi s. viii d.[880] Solvit in duabus vicibus, ut in libro recepte continetur, Laurentio dymisso, viginti sex li. xiii s. iiii d.[881]

### Lichfeldensis

Mandatur provideri Thome de Melburnia presbytero de canonicatu sub exspectatione prebende, dignitatis, et cetera ecclesie Lichfeldensis, v idus Aprilis.[882]

### Lincolniensis

Subrogatus fuit Thomas Page Norwicensis diocesis in omni iure et ad omne ius quod competebat Thome de Merston', nuper extra curiam defuncto,[883] et in parochiali ecclesia de Kalesby (Calceby?) Lincolniensis diocesis, super qua diu in curia litigaverunt, vii kalendas Aprilis.[884] Est in mandato ad exsequendum.[880]

### Lichfeldensis

De canonicatu et prebenda ecclesie de Derbeye (All Saints, Derby) Lichfeldensis diocesis, vacantibus per assecutionem de Leveryngton' (Leverington) factam per Johannem Barnet, fuit provisum Willelmo de Southam, presbytero dicte diocesis, vi kalendas Aprilis.[885] Est in mandato.[886]

---

[873] Over *Willelmo* deleted by a line.
[874] In the margin: *expeditus est.*
[875] The date, 27 March 1371, is bracketed against this and the next two items.
[876] The date, 26 March 1371, is bracketed against this and the next three items.

[877] *Michi* with a line for an abbreviation, MS.
[878] *Esterderham*, Collectorie 13, fol. 173.
[879] 30 March 1371.
[880] In the margin: *de vacanti.*
[881] Sum repeated MS. In the margin: *solvit.*
[882] 9 April 1371.
[883] *defuncti*, MS.
[884] 26 March 1371.
[885] 27 March 1371.
[886] In the margin: *de vacanti.*

### Herefordensis

Item Roberto de Wenntebrigg', presbytero Eboracensis diocesis, de canonicatu sub exspectatione prebende ecclesie Herefordensis, vi<sup>to</sup> kalendas Aprilis.[885]

### Norwicensis

De perpetua vicaria parochialis ecclesie de Aylisham (Aylsham) Norwicensis diocesis, vacante per assecutionem parochialis ecclesie Diram (East Dereham) dicte diocesis factam per Michaelem de Causton', fuit provisum Hugoni de Perington', presbytero Lincolniensis diocesis, v kalendas Aprilis.[887] Alia provisio est supra folio xxv facta eidem persone infra eundem annum, et ibi solvit partem, et sic ista non habuit effectum.[888]

Recepta pagine xxvi li. xiii s. iiii d.;[889] inutilis est provisio ultima i<sup>a</sup>; resta pecunie xlvi li. xiii s. iiii d.; restant fructus duarum provisionum ii; et expectationes ii.

### (fol. 62, lx) Sarisbiriensis

Mandatur provideri Thome de Southam de canonicatu sub exspectatione prebende ecclesie Sarisbiriensis, iii idus Januarii.[890] Dicitur quod est expeditus de novo, et est mandatum in uno mandato ad satisfaciendum et cetera.[891]

### Lichfeldensis

Item Roberto de Conelie, presbytero Wygorniensis diocesis, de canonicatu sub exspectatione prebende ecclesie Lichfeldensis.

### Menevensis

Item Rogero de Weston' de beneficio ecclesiastico et cetera ad collationem episcopi Menevensis.

### Lichfeldensis

Mandatur provideri Willelmo Seyncler, clerico Wellensis diocesis, de beneficio ad collationem et cetera episcopi Lichfeldensis.

### Lincolniensis

Item Henrico Piel de canonicatu sub exspectatione prebende, dignitatis, et cetera ecclesie Lincolniensis.

### Lincolniensis

Item Thome de Braden', clerico Londoniensis diocesis, de canonicatu sub exspectatione prebende, dignitatis, personatus vel officii ecclesie Lincolniensis.

### Eboracensis

Item Waltero de Waudeford' de canonicatu sub exspectatione prebende ecclesie Ripponensis Eboracensis diocesis.

Restant fructus unius expediti i<sup>us</sup>; et vi expectationes vi.

### (fol. 62<sup>v</sup>) Eboracensis

Item Hugoni de Arlam, clerico Dunolmensis diocesis, de canonicatu sub exspectatione prebende de Houweden Eboracensis diocesis, iii<sup>tio</sup> idus Januarii.[892]

### Eliensis

Item Roberto de Eltesle, presbytero Eliensis diocesis, de beneficio ecclesiastico et cetera ad collationem episcopi Eliensis.

### Eboracensis

Item Radulpho de Strington', presbytero Eboracensis, de canonicatu sub exspectatione prebende ecclesie Southwellensis dicte diocesis.

### Dunolmensis

Item Thome de Sakeld' de canonicatu sub exspectatione prebende Auklandie Dunolmensis diocesis.

### Wellensis

Item Petro de Burton', clerico Lichfeldensis diocesis, de canonicatu sub exspectatione prebende ecclesie Wellensis.

### Eboracensis

Mandatur provideri Waltero de Westale, clerico Norwicensis diocesis, de canonicatu sub exspectatione prebende ecclesie Suthwellensis dicte diocesis.

### Lincolniensis

Item Waltero de Aldesby, presbytero Norwicensis, de canonicatu sub exspectatione prebende, dignitatis, personatus vel officii ecclesie Lincolniensis, ii idus Januarii.[893]

Restant expectationes vii.

### (fol. 63, lxi) Tertius quaternus

### Wyntoniensis

Item Ricardo Lee, presbytero Lichfeldensis et Conventrensis diocesis de beneficio ecclesiastico et cetera ad collationem et cetera episcopi Wyntoniensis, kalendas Maii.[894]

### Eboracensis

Item Nicholao Penne, presbytero Lincolniensis dio-

[887] 28 March 1371.
[888] In the margin: *inutilis*.
[889] In the margin: *vera*.
[890] This date, 11 January 1371, is bracketed against this and the next six items.
[891] In the margin: *expeditus est ibi*.

[892] The date, 11 January 1371, is bracketed against this and the next five items.
[893] 12 January 1371.
[894] The date, 1 May 1371, is bracketed against this and the next four items.

cesis, de beneficio ecclesiastico et cetera ad collationem et cetera archiepiscopi, decani et capituli ecclesie Eboracensis.

### Eboracensis

Item Lamberto de Trinkingham, presbytero Lincolniensis diocesis, de canonicatu sub exspectatione prebende ecclesie collegiate Soutwell' Eboracensis diocesis.

### Lincolniensis

Item Roberto dicto Normen, presbytero Lincolniensis diocesis, de beneficio ecclesiastico ad collationem et cetera prioris et conventus de Burgo Sancti Petri diocesis Lincolniensis ordinis Sancti Benedicti.

### Eboracensis

Item Simoni de Leiston', presbytero Norwicensis diocesis, de beneficio et cetera ad collationem et cetera archiepiscopi, decani et capituli singuloroum quam canonicorum ecclesie Eboracensis.

### Lincolniensis

De parochiali ecclesia de Bringeton' (Brington) Lincolniensis diocesis, vacante per resignationem causa permutationis de ipsa facte[895] per David de Wellore, fuit provisum Ricardo de Bidik', presbytero Dunolmensis diocesis, xiiii kalendas Maii, pro taxa xxx li.[896] Solvit in quatuor vicibus, ut in libro recepte continetur, viginti li. xiii s. iiii d.[897] Item solvit die octava Aprilis anno LXXIIII[to] in plenam solutionem eius taxe novem li. sex s. viii d.[897]

Recepta pagine xxx li.;[898] restant expectationes v.

### (fol. 63ᵛ) Norwicensis

De parochiali ecclesia de Trington' (Terrington) Norwicensis diocesis, vacante per simplicem resignationem in manibus domini cardinalis Nemausensis[899] per Thomam Loring', fuit provisum Thome de Hintesey, clerico Cantuariensis diocesis, xviii kalendas Maii.[900] Dicitur quod nondum habuit effectum, et est probatum, et probationes sunt in archivis.[901]

### Lincolniensis

Mandatur provideri Thome de Chandos Lincolniensis diocesis de canonicatu sive dignitate cum prebenda ecclesie Lincolniensis, xvii kalendas Maii.[902]

### Lincolniensis

Item Roberto de Stratton' de personatu aut officio et cetera in ecclesia Lincolniensi, iii[tio] idus Januarii.[903]

### Lincolniensis

Item Roberto de Grendon' de canonicatu sub exspectatione prebende, dignitatis, personatus vel officii aut administratione ecclesie Lincolniensis, x kalendas Julii.[904]

### Herefordensis [905]

Item Willelmo Ives, clerico Lincolniensis diocesis, de canonicatu sub exspectatione prebende ecclesie Herefordensis.

### Wygorniensis

Item Johanni Undurhull', clerico Wygorniensis diocesis, de beneficio et cetera ad collationem episcopi Wygorniensis, xv kalendas Julii.[906]

### Wyntoniensis

Item Nicholao Undurhull' clerico de beneficio ecclesiastico ad collationem et cetera episcopi Wyntoniensis.
Inutilis est una provisio iᵃ; et restant vi expectationes vi.

### (fol. 64, lxii) Wygorniensis

Dum Robertus Undurhull' clericus canonicatum, prebendam, dignitatem, personatum vel officium cum cura vel sine cura in ecclesia Wellensi fuit pacifice assecutus, dimittet liberam capellam quam optinet in ecclesia Wygorniensi, v nonas Julii.[907]

### Herefordensis

Mandatur provideri Philipo Undurhull' clerico de canonicatu sub exspectatione prebende ecclesie Herefordensis.

### Lichfeldensis

Item Willelmo Undurhull' de canonicatu sub exspectatione prebende ecclesie Lichfeldensis.[908]

### Wellensis

Item de prebenda de Cumbe vel Cuttibe (Combe) in ecclesia Wellensi, vacante per mortem Johannis Saylardi, ultimi prebendarii eiusdem, fuit provisum.[909] Est alia provisio supra folio xxxiiii[to] et est in iiii[to] mandatis ad exequendum.[910]

---

[895] *facta*, MS.
[896] 18 April 1371. In the margin: *provisio de vacanti.*
[897] Sum repeated MS. In the margin: *solvit.*
[898] In the margin: *vera.*
[899] John de Blanzac, bishop of Nimes, priest of S. Marco.
[900] 14 April 1371.
[901] In the margin: *de vacanti; inutilis.*
[902] 15 April 1371.
[903] 11 January 1371.
[904] The date, 22 June 1371, is bracketed against this item and the next.
[905] *Sarisbiriensis*, MS.
[906] The date, 17 June 1371, is bracketed against this item and the next.
[907] The date, 3 July 1371, is bracketed against this and the next three items.
[908] Follows *Herefordensis* deleted by a line.
[909] At fol. 34ᵛ John Gaylard is given as the recipient of the provision. (Above, p. 408.)
[910] In the margin: *de vacanti.*

### Lincolniensis

De vicaria perpetua parochialis ecclesie de Astonhaut (Aston Rowant) Lincolniensis diocesis, vacante in curia per liberam resignationem Roberti de Brigham factam, fuit provisum Henrico de Brigham, presbytero Eboracensis diocesis, pro taxa iiii$^{or}$ li. vi s. viii d.[910] Solvit die xiiii Maii anno LXIII dictas iiii li. pro taxa iiii$^{or}$ li. vi s. viii d.[911]

### Wyntoniensis

De beneficio ecclesiastico cum cura vel sine cura, vacante vel vacatura communiter vel divisim ad collationem et cetera episcopi, prioris et capituli ecclesie Wyntoniensis mandatur provideri Guillelmo de Passenham, clerico Lichfeldensis diocesis.

Recepta pagine iiii li. vi s. viii d.;[912] restant fructus unius provisionis i; et quatuor expectationum iiii.

### (fol. 64$^v$) Dunolmensis, Eboracensis

Motu proprio fuit provisum Petro Sancti Eustacii diacono cardinali de parochiali ecclesia de Hoghton' (Houghton-le-Spring) Dunolmensis diocesis et de canonicatu et prebenda ecclesie Eboracensis vacantibus per obitum Willelmi de Dalton', xix kalendas Septembris.[913] Prohibitum de ecclesia per breve regis; de prebenda est in mandato, sed quia cardinalis est non sit alias exsecutum.[914]

### Cantuariensis

Mandatur provideri Roberto de Bradegare, clerico Cantuariensis diocesis, de beneficio ecclesiastico et cetera ad collationem et cetera archiepiscopi Cantuariensis, v kalendas Februarii.[915]

### Wygorniensis

Item Thome de Berford', clerico Norwicensis diocesis, de beneficio ecclesiastico et cetera ad collationem abbatis et conventus monasterii Gloucestrie Wygorniensis diocesis, v kalendas Februarii.[915]

### Eboracensis

Item Ricardo Grimesby, clerico Eboracensis diocesis, de canonicatu sub exspectatione prebende ecclesie Eboracensis, iiii$^{to}$ idus Julii.[916]

### Eboracensis

Item Henrico de Hedlam, clerico Dunolmensis diocesis, de beneficio ecclesiastico ad collationem et cetera abbatis, prioris et conventus monasterii Beate Marie extra muros Eboraci, v kalendas Julii.[917]

### Bathoniensis et Wellensis

Item Thome Salte', presbytero Bathoniensis et Wellensis diocesis, de beneficio ecclesiastico ad collationem et cetera abbatis monasterii de Glastenbury dicte diocesis, xvii kalendas Augusti.[918]

Restant fructus unius provisionis i$^{us}$; et v expectationes v.

### (fol. 65, lxiii) Dunolmensis

Item Johanni de Toresby, presbytero Lincolniensis diocesis, de beneficio ecclesiastico ad collationem et cetera episcopi, prioris et capituli Dunolmensis, xiii kalendas Augusti.[919]

### Eboracensis

Item Johanni de Wendelingburch, presbytero Lincolniensis diocesis, de canonicatu sub exspectatione prebende ecclesie collegiate Southwell' Eboracensis diocesis, x kalendas Februarii.[920]

### Eboracensis

Item Johanni de Strenssall', presbytero Eboracensis diocesis, de canonicatu sub exspectatione prebende ecclesie collegiate Suthwell' dicte diocesis.

### Exoniensis

Mandatur provideri' Johanni Burgeys de Stokeneylond', clerico Norwicensis diocesis, de beneficio ecclesiastico et cetera ad collationem episcopi Exoniensis. Expeditus est ad prebendam in ecclesia Crediton',[921] et licet litigetur in curia hactenus, tamen solvit in partem fructuum die xii Maii pro eo cuius intererit quadraginta s.[922] Item solvit die xix Julii anno LXXIIII$^{to}$ in partem fructuum xxx s.[923]

### Londoniensis

Item Johanni Wolde de Scaldewell', presbytero Lincolniensis diocesis, de beneficio ecclesiastico et cetera ad collationem et cetera decani et capituli singulorum quam canonicorum ecclesie Londoniensis.

### Eboracensis

Item Waltero de Skirlawe, bacallario in iure canonico, de canonicatu sub exspectatione prebende ecclesie collegiate Beati Johannis Beverlaci Eboracensis diocesis, v kalendas Februarii.[924]

---

[911] In the margin: *solvit.*
[912] In the margin: *vera.*
[913] 14 August 1371.
[914] In the margin: *Provisio de vacanti; Cardinalis Flandrini.*
[915] 28 January 1371.
[916] 4 July 1371. Date repeated MS.

[917] 27 June 1371.
[918] 16 July 1371.
[919] 20 July 1371.
[920] The date, 23 January 1371, is bracketed against this item and the next three.
[921] Prebend of Hentstill and Sandford: Collectorie 13, fol. 173.
[922] Sum repeated MS. In the margin: *solvit.*
[923] In the margin: *solvit.*
[924] 28 January 1371.

Recepta pagine lxx [925] s.; [926] et expectationes v restant v; et restat pars fructuum unius provisionis i[us].

### (fol. 65[v]) Lincolniensis

Item Nicholao de Dratton', bacallario in legibus, de canonicatu sub exspectatione prebende ecclesie Lincolniensis, v kalendas Februarii.[927]

### Sarisbiriensis

Item Waltero Assh' Norwicensis diocesis de canonicatu sub exspectatione prebende ecclesie Sarisbiriensis.

### Lichfeldensis

Subrogatus fuit Johannes de Mancestr', rector parochialis ecclesie de Norworthyn (Northenden) Lichfeldensis diocesis, in omni iure et ad omne ius quod Johanni de Par et Johanni de Borton' in et super capella Clidehawe (Clitheroe) sine cura Lichfeldensis diocesis competebat seu competere poterat, xiii kalendas Augusti.[928] Certificat episcopus quod est ab antiquo appropriata abbati [929] de Villa (Whalley) et quod nunquam dicta gratia habuit effectum, ideo relaxatus quousque et cetera.[930]

### Wyntoniensis

Mandatur provideri Ricardo Lee, presbytero diocesis Lichfeldensis, de beneficio ecclesiastico ad collationem et cetera episcopi Wyntoniensis, xv kalendas Augusti.[931]

### Lincolniensis

Mandatur provideri Alano de Stokers de canonicatu sub exspectatione dignitatis et cetera ecclesie Lincolniensis.

### Lincolniensis

Item Johanni de Carlton' de dignitate, personatu vel officio in ecclesia Lincolniensi.

Una est provisio inutilis i[a]; et restant v expectationes v.

### (fol. 66, lxiiii) Eboracensis

Item Johanni Curmoncestr' de canonicatu sub exspectatione prebende, dignitatis ecclesie Eboracentis, x kalendas Augusti.[932]

### Lichfeldensis

Item Reginaldo de Hulton', clerico Lichfeldensis dio-

cesis, de canonicatu sub exspectatione prebende Lichfeldensis.

### Lichfeldensis

Item Thome de Horton' presbytero de canonicatu sub exspectatione prebende ecclesie Sancti Johanni Cestrie.

### Eboracensis

Item Edwardo de Soutword' de canonicatu sub exspectatione prebende ecclesie Sancti Johannis Beverlacensis.

### Eboracensis

Item Willelmo de Norton' de canonicatu sub exspectatione prebende ecclesie Soutwellensis.

### Sarisbiriensis

Item Roberto Gloucestre de canonicatu sub exspectatione prebende ecclesie Sarisbiriensis.

### Cicestrensis

Item Hugoni Bokynhull' de beneficio ecclesiastico et cetera ad collationem et cetera prioris et conventus prioratus de Lewys (Lewes) ordinis Cluniacensis Cicestrensis diocesis.

Restant expectationes vii.

### (fol. 66[v]) Sarisbiriensis

Item Willelmo Hecghtrebury, presbytero Sarisbiriensis diocesis, de dignitate, personatu vel officio et cetera in ecclesia Sarisibiriensi, v kalendas Februarii.[933]

### Exoniensis

Mandatur provideri Henrico Whitefeld', presbytero Exoniensis diocesis, de canonicatu sub exspectatione prebende ecclesie Exoniensis.

### Lincolniensis

Item Thome Stowe, clerico Wygorniensis diocesis, de canonicatu sub exspectatione prebende, dignitatis, et cetera ecclesie Lincolniensis.

### Wygorniensis

Item Thome Hulma', clerico Wygorniensis diocesis, de beneficio ecclesiastico et cetera ad collationem episcopi Wygorniensis.

### Eboracensis

Item Johanni Caldewell', clerico Lincolniensis diocesis, de canonicatu sub exspectatione prebende [934] ecclesie collegiate de Southwell' Eboracensis diocesis.

---

[925] Follows *xxx* deleted by a line.

[926] In the margin: *vera*.

[927] The date, 28 January 1371, is bracketed against this item and the next.

[928] 20 July 1371.

[929] Follows *episcopo* deleted by a line.

[930] In the margin: *provisio de vacanti; inutius*.

[931] The date, 18 July 1371, is bracketed against this item and the next two.

[932] The date, 23 July 1371, is bracketed against this item and the next six.

---

[933] The date, 28 January 1371, is bracketed against this and the next six items.

[934] Followed by *de* deleted by a line.

Lincolniensis [935]

Item Hugoni West, presbytero Wygorniensis diocesis, de beneficio ecclesiastico et cetera ad collationem abbatis et conventus monasterii de Salop' (Shrewsbury) ordinis Sancti Benedicti Lincolniensis [935] diocesis.

Item Willelmo Feriby, clerico Eboracensis diocesis, de beneficio ecclesiastico et cetera ad collationem abbatis et conventus monasterii Beate Marie iuxta Eboracum ordinis Sancti Benedicti Eboracensis diocesis.

Restant vii expectationes vii.

#### (fol. 67, lxv) Eboracensis

Item Thome alias Johanni Scoliessle, clerico Eboracensis diocesis, de beneficio et cetera ad collationem et cetera archiepiscopi Eboracensis, v kalendas Februarii.[936]

#### Sarisbiriensis

Mandatur provideri Roberto de Walsingham, clerico Norwicensis diocesis, de beneficio ecclesiastico ad collationem abbatisse et conventus monasterii Beate Marie de Wilton' ordinis Sancti Benedicti Sarisbiriensis diocesis.

#### Lincolniensis

Item Thome de Kirketon' de Lyndeseye, clerico Lincolniensis diocesis, de beneficio ecclesiastico et cetera ad collationem et cetera decani et capituli ecclesie Lincolniensis.

#### Londoniensis

Item Johanni Paxton', clerico Lincolniensis diocesis, de beneficio ecclesiastico et cetera ad collationem et cetera prioris et conventus Westmonasterii iuxta Londoniam ordinis Sancti Benedicti Londonensis diocesis.

#### Sarisbiriensis seu Wyntoniensis

Item Thome Swyndon' alias Styne, clerico Sarisbiriensis diocesis, de beneficio ecclesiastico et cetera ad collationem episcopi Wyntoniensis, pro taxa xxiiii m. Expeditus est ad ecclesiam de Portesland' (Portland) Sarisbiriensis diocesis, et solvit in duabus vicibus eadem die xii Desembris anno LXXIII in quinque marcis lxvi s. viii d.[937]

#### Wellensis

Item Roberto Rigge, clerico Exoniensis diocesis, de beneficio ecclesiastico ad collationem et cetera abbatis et conventus monasterii de Glaston' ordinis Sancti Benedicti Wellensis diocesis.

#### Sarisbiriensis

Item Willelmo Frank', clerico Sarisbiriensis diocesis, de beneficio ecclesiastico ad collationem decani et capitulo ecclesie Sarisibiriensis.

Recepta pagine lxvi s. viii d.; [938] resta pecunie xix m. que valent xii li. xiii s. iiii d.; et restant vi expectationes vi.

#### (fol. 67ᵛ) Norwicensis

Item Johanni Lenne, clerico Norwicensis diocesis, ad collationem episcopi Norwicensis, v kalendas Februarii.[939]

#### Cantuariensis

Mandatur provideri Roberto Branlay, clerico Eboracensis diocesis, de canonicatu sub exspectatione prebende ecclesie collegiate de Malling' Cantuariensis diocesis.

#### Menevensis

Item Roberto Undurhull', clerico Wygorniensis diocesis, de canonicatu sub exspectatione prebende ecclesie collegiate de Abergvyly Menevensis diocesis.

#### Wygorniensis

Item Johanni de Middeford', clerico Londoniensis, de canonicatu sub exspectatione prebende, personatus, et cetera in ecclesia de Westbury Wygorniensis diocesis.

#### Cicestrensis

Item Johanni Tank', clerico Cicestrensis diocesis, de canonicatu sub exspectatione prebende ecclesie Cicestrensis.

#### Dunolmensis

Item Petro Voyte de Eland, clerico Dunolmensis diocesis, de beneficio ecclesiastico ad collationem et cetera prioris et capituli ecclesie Dunolmensis.

#### Bangorensis

Item Johanni Wyk', clerico Wygorniensis diocesis, de canonicatu sub exspectatione prebende, dignitatis, et cetera ecclesie Bangorensis.

Restant vii expectationes vii.

#### (fol. 68, lxvi) Londoniensis

Item Johanni Mandor, clerico Lincolniensis diocesis, de canonicatu sub exspectatione prebende, dignitatis et cetera ecclesie Sancti Pauli Londonie, v kalendas Februarii.[940] Expeditus est ad prebendam de Chswybr' (Chiswick), que taxatur ad ix m., et est in mandato et est obligatus et cetera.

#### Wellensis

Item Johanni de Langeton' de canonicatu sub exspectatione prebende, dignitatis, et cetera ecclesie Wellensis.

---

[935] Presumably a mistake for Lichfeldensis.
[936] The date, 28 January 1371, is bracketed against this and the next six items.
[937] In the margin: *solvit.*

[938] In the margin: *vera.*
[939] The date, 28 January 1371, is bracketed against this and the next six items.
[940] The date, 28 January 1371, is bracketed against this item and the next six.

### Eboracensis

Mandatur provideri Henrico Godebarn', clerico Eboracensis diocesis, de canonicatu sub exspectatione prebende ac personatus ecclesie collegiate Ripponensis dicte diocesis.

### Eboracensis

Item Johanni de Clifford, clerico Eboracensis diocesis, de canonicatu sub exspectatione prebende ecclesie Eboracensis.

### Landavensis

Item Ade Toneworth, presbytero Wygorniensis diocesis, de canonicatu sub exspectatione dignitatis et cetera ecclesie Landavensis.

### Eboracensis

Item Johanni Landreyn, presbytero Exoniensis diocesis, de canonicatu sub exspectatione prebende ecclesie Eboracensis.

### Exoniensis

Item Willelmo Trevelle, presbytero Exoniensis diocesis, de dignitate et cetera ecclesie Exoniensis.

Resta pecunie vi li.; et restant vi expectationes vi.

### (fol. 68ᵛ) Assavensis

Item Rogero Aswardby de canonicatu sub exspectatione prebende, dignitatis ecclesie Assavensis, v kalendas Februarii.[941]

### Eboracensis

Item Willelmo Durant de canonicatu sub exspectatione prebende, dignitatis ecclesie Eboracensis.

### Herefordensis

Item Johanni Middelton', presbytero Lincolniensis diocesis, de canonicatu sub exspectatione prebende, dignitatis, et cetera ecclesie Herefordensis.

### Exoniensis

Item Simoni Laborn'[942] presbytero de canonicatu sub exspectatione prebende, dignitatis, et cetera ecclesie Exoniensis. Expeditus est ad precentoriam Exoniensem, de qua litigat cum uno titulo regio impediente, et, lite sopita, est iuratus ad solvendum pro prebenda; vero solvit die ix Maii anno LXXIIII in partem fructuum quadraginta solidos.[943] Est ad finem breveti.

### Sarisbiriensis

Mandatur provideri Henrico Westbrok', clerico Sarisbiriensis diocesis, de canonicatu sub exspectatione prebende, dignitatis et cetera ecclesie Sarisbiriensis.

### Exoniensis

Item Johanni Schillingford, presbytero Exoniensis diocesis, de dignitate, personatu ecclesie Exoniensis.

### Sarisbiriensis

Item Roberto Sustede, presbytero Norwicensis diocesis, de canonicatu sub exspectatione prebende ecclesie Sarisbiriensis. Dicitur quod expeditus est et est mandatus in v.

Recepta pagine xl s.;[944] restant vi expectationes vi.

### (fol. 69, lxvii) Cicestrensis

Item Willelmo Wynndham de canonicatu sub exspectatione prebende, dignitatis et cetera ecclesie Cicestrensis, v kalendas Februarii.[945]

### Lichfeldensis

Item Johanni Durk' presbytero de dignitate et cetera ecclesie Lichfeldensis.

### Lincolniensis

Item Johanni Wiclif presbytero de canonicatu sub exspectatione prebende ecclesie Lincolniensis.

### Lincolniensis

Item Ricardo de Toneworth' presbytero de canonicatu sub exspectatione prebende ecclesie Lincolniensis.

### Menevensis

Item Willelmo Wykton' presbytero de canonicatu sub exspectatione prebende ecclesie collegiate Ackerguili (Abergwili) Menevensis diocesis.

### Cantuariensis

Item Willelmo Barton, presbytero de beneficio ecclesiastico et cetera ad collationem et cetera archiepiscopi Cantuariensis.

### Londoniensis

Mandatur provideri Willelmo Blankpain, presbytero Londoniensis diocesis, de beneficio ecclesiastico ad collationem episcopi, decani et capituli ecclesie Londoniensis.

Restant septem expectationes vii.

### (fol. 69ᵛ) Dunolmensis

Item Willelmo Daventr' presbytero de canonicatu sub exspectatione prebende, dignitatis ecclesie collegiate de Houden' (Howden) diocesis Dunolmensis v kalendas Februarii.[945]

---

[941] The date, 28 January 1371, is bracketed against this item and the next six.
[942] *Lamboren*, Collectorie 13, fol. 174ᵛ.
[943] Sum repeated MS. In the margin: *solvit*.

[944] In the margin: *vera*.
[945] The date, 28 January 1371, is bracketed against this and the next six items.

## Wyntoniensis

Item Nicholao Bedingge presbytero de canonicatu sub exspectatione prebende ecclesie collegiate de Wharewell' (Wherwell) ordinis Sancti Benedicti Wyntoniensis diocesis.

## Sarisbiriensis

Item Johanni Joskyn Roffensis diocesis de beneficio ecclesiastico ad collationem et cetera abbatis et conventus monasterii de Klendon' (Abingdon?) ordinis Sancti Benedicti Sarisbiriensis diocesis.

## Sarisbiriensis

Item Johanni Totteford de canonicatu sub exspectatione prebende ecclesie conventualis de Scaf de bury (Shaftesbury) Sarisbiriensis diocesis.

## Eboracensis

Item Ricardo de Sutton' de canonicatu sub exspectatione prebende ecclesie collegiate de Ripponia Eboracensis diocesis.

## Exoniensis

Item Roberto Clift presbytero de canonicatu sub exspectatione prebende ecclesie collegiate Beate Marie de Otrey (Ottery) Exoniensis diocesis.

## Menevensis

Item Henrico Borage de beneficio ecclesiastico et cetera ad collationem et cetera episcopi Menevensis.
Restant vii expectationes vii.

## (fol. 70, lxviii) Lincolniensis

Mandatur provideri Willelmo Ardene, presbytero diocesis Lincolniensis, de canonicatu sub exspectatione prebende, dignitatis, et cetera ecclesie Lincolniensis, v kalendas Februarii.[945]

## Herefordensis

Item Thome Furneys, presbytero Eboracensis diocesis, de beneficio ecclesiastico et cetera ad collationem episcopi, decani et capituli ecclesie Herefordensis.

## Eboracensis

Item Petro Castel alias dicto Galun, clerico Dunolmensis diocesis, de canonicatu sub exspectatione prebende ecclesie collegiate de Beverlaco Eboracensis diocesis.

## Herefordensis

Item Waltero Rennsbury, presbytero Sarisbiriensis diocesis, de canonicatu sub exspectatione prebende ecclesie Herefordensis.

## Londoniensis

Item Johanni Manndor, clerico Lincolniensis diocesis, de canonicatu sub exspectatione prebende ecclesie Londoniensis.

## Menevensis

Item Willelmo Polgrun presbytero de canonicatu sub exspectatione prebende ecclesie Menevensis.

## Lincolniensis

Item Johanni Colyntr', clerico Lincolniensis diocesis, de beneficio ecclesiastico et cetera ad collationem et cetera abbatis et conventus monasterii de Burgo Sancti Petri ordinis Sancti Benedicti Lincolniensis diocesis.
Restant septem expectationes vii.

## (fol. 70ᵛ) Wellensis

Item Johanni Langeton, clerico Lincolniensis diocesis, de canonicatu sub exspectatione prebende, dignitatis, et cetera ecclesia Wellensis, v kalendas Februarii.[945]

## Lichfeldensis

Mandatur provideri Johanni Prestwold', presbytero Lincolniensis diocesis, de beneficio ecclesiastico ad collationem abbatis et conventus monasterii Sancte Werbegie Cestr' ordinis Sancti Benedicti Lichfeldensis diocesis.

## Dublinensis

Item Willelmo Chambre, clerico Lincolniensis diocesis, de canonicatu sub exspectatione prebende ecclesie Dublinensis. Non est in Anglia.

## Lichfeldensis

Item Johanni Blexham, presbytero Lincolniensis diocesis, de canonicatu sub exspectatione prebende ecclesie Sancti Johannis Cestr' Lichfeldensis diocesis.

## Eliensis

Item Roberto Aylesham, presbytero Norwicensis diocesis, de beneficio ecclesiastico et cetera ad collationem et cetera episcopi Eliensis.

## Eboracensis

Item Willelmo Kexby, clerico Eboracensis diocesis, de beneficio ecclesiastico et cetera ad collationem et cetera ad collationem et cetera prepositi Beverlaci Eboracensis diocesis.

## Wyntoniensis

Item Johanni Hugate Eboracensis diocesis de beneficio ecclesiastico et cetera ad collationem et cetera prioris et conventus prioratus de Morton' (Merton) ordinis Sancti Augustini Wyntoniensis diocesis.
Restant vii expectationes vii.

## (fol. 71, lxlx) Londoniensis

Item Johanni Schirborn', presbytero Eboracensis diocesis, de beneficio ecclesiastico et cetera ad collationem prioris et fratrum ordinis Sancti Johannis Jerosolomitani in Anglia, v kalendas Februarii.[945]

### Lichfeldensis

Item Johanni Beneyt alias dicto Cester' de beneficio ecclesiastico et cetera ad collationem episcopi et capituli ecclesie Lichfeldensis.

### Sarisbiriensis

Mandatur provideri Ricardo Voneger, clerico Sarisbiriensis diocesis, de beneficio ecclesiastico ad collationem abbatisse et conventus monasterii de Schastebury ordinis Sancti Benedicti Sarisbiriensis diocesis.

### Karleolensis

Item Thome Karlil, presbytero Karleolensis diocesis, de beneficio ecclesiastico et cetera ad collationem episcopi, prioris et capituli ecclesie Karleolensis.

### Wyntoniensis

Item J(?) Thome Arllegham, clerico Lincolniensis diocesis, de beneficio ecclesiastico et cetera ad collationem abbatisse et conventus monialium monasterii Sancte Marie Wyntonie ordinis Sancti Benedicti Wyntoniensis diocesis.

### Cantuariensis

Item Johanni Bangrant, clerico Cantuariensis diocesis, de canonicatu sub exspectatione prebende, dignitatis, et cetera ecclesie collegiate de Wyngham dicte diocesis.

### Dunolmensis

Item Waltero Vavosova de canonicatu sub exspectatione prebende ecclesie collegiate Cestr' super stratam (Chester-le-Street) Dunolmensis diocesis.
Restant vii expectationes vii.

### (fol. 71ᵛ) Norwicensis

Item Batholomeo Dunstede, clerico Norwicensis diocesis, de beneficio ecclesiastico ad collationem abbatis et conventus monasterii Sancti Edmundi de Bury ordinis Sancti Benedicti Norwicensis diocesis, v kalendas Februarii.[946]

### Sarisbiriensis

Item Willelmo de Elynton' de canonicatu sub exspectatione prebende ecclesie Sarisbiriensis, ii nonas August.[947]

### Dunolmensis

Mandatur provideri Rogero Gisburgh', presbytero Eboracensis diocesis, de canonicatu sub exspectatione prebende ecclesie collegiate de Langhestr' (Lanchester) Dunolmensis diocesis, v kalendas Februarii.[948]

### Wyntoniensis

Item Thome Kelli diocesis Exoniensis de beneficio ecclesiastico ad collationem et cetera abbatis et conventus monasterii Sancte Marie de Hyde ordinis Sancti Benedicti Wyntoniensis diocesis.

### Dunolmensis

Item Johanni Brid, clerico Eboracensis diocesis, de canonicatu sub exspectatione prebende, dignitatis, et cetera ecclesie collegiate de Aukland Dunolmensis diocesis.

### Eboracensis

Item Johanni Jerk', clerico Eboracensis diocesis, de canonicatu sub exspectatione prebende ecclesie collegiate Sancti Sepulcri Eboracensis diocesis.

### Dublinensis

Item David Breccan de canonicatu sub exspectatione prebende, dignitatis ecclesie Dublinensis. Non est in Anglia.
Restant vii expectationes vii.

### (fol. 72, lxx) Eboracensis

Item Thome Trwrwih, clerico Eboracensis diocesis, de canonicatu sub exspectatione prebende, personatus, et cetera ecclesie [949] de Beverlaco Eboracensis diocesis, v kalendas Februarii.[950]

### Wellensis

Item Johanni Aston', presbytero Wygorniensis diocesis, de beneficio ecclesiastico et cetera ad collationem et cetera episcopi Wellensis.

### Menevensis

Item Thome [951] Cary, clerico Exoniensis diocesis, de beneficio ecclesiastico et cetera ad collationem episcopi Menevensis.

### Cicestrensis

Mandatur provideri Willelmo Middelworth', presbytero Exoniensis diocesis, de beneficio ecclesiastico et cetera ad collationem et cetera episcopi, decani et capituli ecclesie Cicestrensis.

### Lincolniensis

Item Henrico Hedlan, presbytero Dunolmensis diocesis, de beneficio ecclesiastico et cetera ad collationem et cetera prioris et conventus prioratus de Splding' (Spalding) ordinis Sancti Benedicti Lincolniensis diocesis.

---

[946] 28 January 1371.
[947] 4 August 1371.
[948] The date, 28 January 1371, is bracketed against this item and the next four.

[949] Followed by *Wellensis* deleted by a line.
[950] The date, 28 January 1371, is bracketed against this item and the next six.
[951] Follows *Johanni Aston' presbytero* deleted by a line.

Lincolniensis [952]

Item Nicholao Herford, presbytero Herefordensis diocesis, de beneficio ecclesiastico et cetera ad collationem abbatis et conventus monasterii de Salopia (Shrewsbury) ordinis Sancti Benedicti Lincolniensis [952] diocesis.

Cantuariensis

Item Johanni Grene Herefordensis diocesis de beneficio ecclesiastico et cetera ad collationem et cetera prioris et capituli ecclesie Cantuariensis ordinis Sancti Benedicti.
Restant vii expectationes vii.

(fol. 72ᵛ) Wygorniensis

Item Johanni Tretrevisa, presbytero Exoniensis diocesis, de beneficio ecclesiastico ad collationem et cetera abbatis et conventus monasterii Sancti Augustini Bristollie Wygorniensis, v kalendas Februarii.[945]

Dunolmensis

Item Waltero Brinde, clerico Eboracensis diocesis, de canonicatu sub exspectatione prebende ecclesie collegiate de Derlington (Darlington) Dunolmensis diocesis.

Wygorniensis

Item Willelmo de Wyntirton', clerico Norwicensis diocesis, de beneficio ecclesiastico et cetera ad collationem et cetera episcopi Wygorniensis.

Londoniensis

Mandatur provideri Henrico de Wyntirton' presbytero de canonicatu sub exspectatione prebende ecclesie Londoniensis.

Londoniensis

Item Johanni de Donnewich, presbytero Norwicensis diocesis, de canonicatu sub exspectatione prebende, dignitatis et cetera Londoniensis.

Menevensis

Item Radulpho de Langele, presbytero Norwicensis diocesis, de personatu et cetera ecclesie Menevensis.

Lichfeldensis

Item Willelmo Goteham, presbytero Eboracensis diocesis, de canonicatu sub exspectatione prebende, dignitatis, et cetera ecclesie Lichfeldensis.
Restant vii expectationes vii.

(fol. 73, lxxi) Sarisbiriensis

Item Ade de Lakinghith', presbytero Norwicensis diocesis, de canonicatu sub exspectatione prebende, ac dignitatis et cetera ecclesie Sarisbiriensis, v kalendas Februarii.[945]

[952] Presumably a mistake for Lichfeldensis.

Lincolniensis

Item Thome de Bakton', subdiacono Norwicensis diocesis, de canonicatu sub exspectatione prebende, digtatis et cetera ecclesie Lincolniensis.

Eboracensis

Item Willelmo Flaynburgh', clerico Eboracensis diocesis, de beneficio ecclesiastico ad collationem et cetera abbatis et conventus monasterii Beate Marie Eboraci ordinis Sancti Benedicti.

Wellensis

Item Thome de Dyngham, presbytero Eboracensis diocesis, de canonicatu sub exspectatione prebende, dignitatis, et cetera ecclesie Wellensis.

Eboracensis

Mandatur provideri Johanni de Ufford, filio quondam nobilis viri Domini Roberti de Ufford comitis Suffolchie, presbytero Norwicensis diocesis, de canonicatu sub exspectatione prebende, dignitatis, et cetera ecclesie Eboracensis.

Sarisbiriensis

Item Thome de Vormynhale, presbytero Lincolniensis diocesis, de canonicatu sub exspectatione prebende ecclesie Sarisbiriensis.

Cicestrensis

Item Ade de Voykemer, presbytero Norwicensis diocesis, de canonicatu sub exspectatione prebende ecclesie Cicestrensis.
Restant septem expectationes vii.

(fol. 73ᵛ) Eliensis

Item Johanni Kynne, presbytero Norwicensis diocesis, de beneficio ecclesiastico ad collationem episcopi Eliensis, v kalendas Februarii.[945]

Lincolniensis

Item Johanni de Smith, presbytero Lincolniensis diocesis, de beneficio ecclesiastico et cetera ad collationem abbatis et conventus monasterii de Burgo Sancti Petri ordinis Sancti Benedicti Lincolniensis diocesis.

Lincolniensis

Item Thome de Novo Mercato, clerico Norwicensis diocesis, de beneficio ecclesiastico et cetera ad collationem abbatis et conventus monasterii de Croyland (Crowland) ordinis Sancti Benedicti Lincolniensis diocesis.

Eboracensis

Item Willemo Cheophill', presbytero Eboracensis diocesis, de beneficio ecclesiastico et cetera ad collationem et cetera archiepiscopi Eboracensis.

### Cantuariensis

Mandatur provideri Roberto de Multon', presbytero Lincolniensis diocesis, de beneficio ecclesiastico ad collationem prioris et capituli ecclesie Cantuariensis.

### Wyntoniensis

Item Willelmo Welles, presbytero Wyntonieisis diocesis, de beneficio ecclesiastico et cetera ad collationem et cetera episcopi et capituli Wyntoniensis.

### Wellensis

Item Rogero de Pilberch, presbytero Norwicensis diocesis, de beneficio ecclesiastico et cetera ad collationem et cetera abbatis et conventus de Glaston' Wellensis diocesis.

Restant vii expectationes vii.

### (fol 74, lxxii) Londoniensis

Item Johanni Appulby, presbytero Lincolniensis diocesis, de beneficio ecclesiastico ad collationem et cetera prioris et fratrum hospitalis Sancti Johannis Jerosolomitani in Anglia, v kalendas Februarii.[945]

### Cicestrensis

Item Johanni Botoner, clerico Londoniensis diocesis, de canonicatu sub exspectatione prebende ecclesie collegiate Southmalling' Cicestrensis diocesis.

### Lincolniensis

Item Willelmo de Irby, presbytero Lincolniensis diocesis, de beneficio ecclesiastico et cetera ad collationem prioris et conventus de Kyme ordinis Sancti Augustini Lincolniensis diocesis.

### Cantuariensis

Item Roberto de Cousted, presbytero Norwicensis diocesis, de beneficio ecclesiastico ad collationem archiepiscopi Cantuariensis.

### Lichfeldensis

Item Nicholao de Botekesham, presbytero Eliensis diocesis, de canonicatu sub exspectatione prebende ecclesie Lichfeldensis.

### Eliensis

Mandatur provideri Willelmo de Voramby, presbytero Lincolniensis diocesis, de beneficio ecclesiastico et cetera ad collationem prioris et capituli ecclesie Eliensis.

### Londoniensis

Item Willelmo de Neuton', presbytero Eliensis diocesis, de canonicatu sub exspectatione prebende ecclesie Londoniensis.

Restant vii expectationes vii.

### (fol. 74ᵛ) Lincolniensis

Item Ricardo de Pulham, clerico Norwicensis diocesis, de beneficio ecclesiastico ad collationem abbatis et conventus monasterii de Ramsey ordinis Sancti Benedicti Lincolniensis diocesis, v Kalendas Februarii.[945]

### Dunolmensis

Item Nicholao Duris de Torgumby, presbytero Lincolniensis diocesis, de beneficio ecclesiastico ad collationem episcopi, prioris et capituli singularum quam personarum ecclesie Dunolmensis.[953]

### Menevensis

Item Johanni Attrestret, presbytero Cantuariensis diocesis, de canonicatu sub exspectatione prebende ecclesie collegiate de Abwerwyli (Abergwili) Menevensis diocesis.

### Norwicensis

Item Johanni de Carleton', presbytero Norwicensis diocesis, de beneficio ecclesiastico ad collationem et cetera abbatis et conventus monasterii Sancti Benedicti de Hulmo (St. Benet Holm) ordinis Sancti Benedicti diocesis Norwicensis.

### Norwicensis

Item Thome de Ely, presbytero Eliensis diocesis, de beneficio ecclesiastico ad collationem prioris et conventus de Castelacr' ordinis Sancti Benedicti Norwicensis diocesis.

### Londoniensis

Mandatur provideri Radulpho de Hichim, presbytero Lincolniensis diocesis, de beneficio ecclesiastico ad collationem prioris et conventus Westmonasterii ordinis Sancti Benedicti Londoniensis diocesis.

### Norwicensis

Mandatur provideri Johanni Tymon, presbytero Londoniensis diocesis, de beneficio ecclesiastico ad collationem episcopi, prioris et capituli ecclesie Norwicensis.

Restant vii expectationes vii.

### (fol. 75, lxxiii) Eboracensis

Item Michaeli de Causton' Norwicensis diocesis de canonicatu sub exspectatione prebende ecclesie collegiate de Houden' Eboracensis diocesis, v kalendas Februarii.[945]

### Norwicensis

Item Galdewino de Hadele, clerico Norwicensis diocesis, de canonicatu sub exspectatione prebende et beneficio ecclesiastico ad collationem abbatis et conventus Sancti Edmundi de Bury ordinis Sancti Benedicti Norwicensis diocesis.

[953] Follows *Lincolniensis* deleted by a line.

### Eboracensis

Item Johanni Bernet Norwicensis diocesis de canonicatu sub exspectatione prebende ecclesie collegiate Suthwell' Eboracensis diocesis.

### Lincolniensis

Item Willelmo de Aketon' Norwicensis diocesis de beneficio ecclesiastico ad collationem abbatis et conventus Leycestr' Lincolniensis diocesis.

### Eboracensis

Item Willelmo de Preshale Norwicensis diocesis de canonicatu sub exspectatione prebende ecclesie collegiate Sancti Johanni de Beverlaco Eboracensis diocesis.

### Wygorniensis

Mandatur provideri Johanni de Pulham Eliensis diocesis de beneficio ecclesiastico et cetera ad collationem episcopi Wygorniensis.

### Norwicensis

Item Henrico de Toniston', clerico Norwicensis diocesis, de beneficio ecclesiastico et cetera ad collationem et cetera episcopi Norwicensis.
Restant vii expectationes vii.

### (fol. 75ᵛ) Lincolniensis

Item Alano Tilney, clerico Norwicensis diocesis, de beneficio ecclesiastico et cetera ad collationem prioris et conventus de Spalding' ordinis Sancti Benedicti Lincolniensis diocesis, v kalendas Februarii.[954]

### Lichfeldensis

Item Waltero de Herbing' presbytero ad collationem et cetera decani et capituli ecclesie Lichfeldensis.

### Eboracensis

Item Thome de Formulawe de canonicatu sub exspectatione prebende ecclesie Eboracensis, x kalendas Augusti.[955]

### Sarisbiriensis

Item Willelmo de Trissero de canonicatu sub exspectatione prebende ecclesie Sarisbiriensis.

### Lincolniensis

Item Ricardo Hunt clerico de canonicatu sub exspectatione prebende ecclesie Lincolniensis.

### Lichfeldensis

Item Ade de Fentocher de canonicatu sub exspectatione prebende ecclesie Lichfeldensis.

### Herefordensis

Mandatur provideri Rogero de Stamford' de canonicatu sub exspectatione prebende ecclesie Herefordensis. Restant vii expectationes vii.

### (fol 76, lxxiiii) Eboracensis

Item Ade de Aton' de canonicatu sub exspectatione prebende ecclesie Sutwell' Eboracensis diocesis, x kalendas Augusti.[956]

### Eboracensis

Item Thome Veysey de canonicatu sub exspectatione prebende ecclesie Ripponensis Eboracensis diocesis.

### Lichfeldensis

Item Johanni Ludesey, clerico Cicestrensis diocesis, de canonicatu sub exspectatione prebende ecclesie collegiate Sancti Johannis Cestr' diocesis Lichfeldensis.

### Eliensis

Item Roberto de Walsam, presbytero Norwicensis diocesis, de beneficio[957] ecclesiastico ad collationem episcopi Eliensis.

### Dunolmensis

Item Alano Owithered, presbytero Dunolmensis diocesis, de canonicatu sub exspectatione prebende ecclesie collegiate de Auklandie dicte Dunolmensis diocesis.

### Dunolmensis

Item de canonicatu et prebenda ecclesie collegiate de Derlington' (Darlington) diocesis Dunolmensis, vacantibus per obitum quondam Willelmi de Kaldesby extra curiam defuncti, fuit provisum Johanni de Resham, clerico Dunolmensis diocesis, pro taxa xvi li. xiii s. iiii d.[958] Solvit die viii Maii anno LXXIII octo li. vi s. viii d.[959] Item solvit die vi Julii LXXIIII alias viii li. vi s. viii d.[960]

### Eboracensis

De parochiali ecclesia de Werkington' (Workington) Eboracensis diocesis, vacante per obitum ultimi rectoris fuit provisum Nicholao de Birland presbytero.[961] Non habuit effectum, ut est clare probatus quia ad huc vivit ille qui tunc possidebat.[962]
Recepta pagine xvi li. xiii s. iiii d.;[963] restant v expectationes v.

---

[954] The date, 28 January 1371, is bracketed against this item and the next.
[955] The date, 23 July 1371, is bracketed against this item and the next four.

[956] The date, 23 July 1371, is bracketed against this item and the next six.
[957] Follows *canonicatu sub exspectatione prebende* deleted by a line.
[958] Sum repeated MS. In the margin: *provisio de vacanti.*
[959] Sum repeated MS. In the margin: *solvit.*
[960] In the margin: *solvit.*
[961] In the margin: *provisio de vacanti.*
[962] In the margin: *inutilis est.*
[963] In the margin: *vera.*

### (fol. 76ᵛ) Eboracensis

Mandatur provideri Radulpho de Ergham de canonicatu sub exspectatione prebende, dignitatis, et cetera ecclesie Eboracensis, x kalendas Augusti.[964]

### Sarisbiriensis

Item Johanni Savage Cantuariensis diocesis de canonicatu sub exspectatione prebende, dignitatis, et cetera ecclesie Sarisbiriensis.

### Lichfeldensis

Item Roberto Prees, presbytero Lichfeldensis diocesis, de canonicatu sub exspectatione prebende ecclesie Lichfeldensis.

### Wygorniensis

Item Thome de Kersinton' Lincolniensis diocesis de beneficio ecclesiastico ad collationem et cetera episcopi Wygorniensis.

### Menevensis

Item Petro de Upton' Lichfeldensis diocesis de beneficio ecclesiastico et cetera episcopi Menevensis.

### Exoniensis

Item Johanni Podidisden', presbytero Exoniensis diocesis, de canonicatu sub exspectatione prebende ecclesie Exoniensis.

### Wellensis

Item Johanni de Odington' de canonicatu sub exspectatione prebende ecclesie Wellensis.
Restant vii expectationes vii.

### (fol. 77, lxxv) Eliensis

Item Philipo de Monte Gomer Herefordensis diocesis de beneficio ecclesiastico ad collationem episcopi Eliensis, x kalendas Augusti.[965]

### Landavensis

Item Johanni Conye Landavensis diocesis de canonicatu sub exspectatione prebende ecclesie Landavensis.

### Herefordensis

Item Johanni Merler Wygorniensis diocesis de beneficio ecclesiastico et cetera ad collationem episcopi Herefordensis.

### Eboracensis

Mandatur provideri Ricardo Boter Eboracensis diocesis de canonicatu sub exspectatione prebende, dignitatis, et cetera ecclesie Eboracensis.

### Sarisbiriensis

Item Willelmo de Karlel, presbytero Karleolensis diocesis, de canonicatu sub exspectatione prebende ecclesie Sarisbiriensis.

### Lincolniensis

Item Egidio de Caldecote, presbytero Lincolniensis diocesis, de canonicatu sub exspectatione prebende, dignitatis, et cetera ecclesie Lincolniensis.

### Eboracensis

Item Johanni Vynter, presbytero Lincolniensis diocesis, de canonicatu sub exspectatione prebende ecclesie Sancti Johannis Beverlaci Eboracensis diocesis, v kalendas Augusti.[966]
Restant vii expectatione vii.

### (fol. 77ᵛ) Eboracensis

De canonicatu et prebende et cantaria Eboracensis ecclesie, vacantibus in curia per obitum Dominici Valusci, camere apostolice subcollectoris, extra curiam defuncti, fuit provisum Fernando Gundisalvo Ulixbonensis (Lisbon), nonas Augusti.[967] Certificat archiepiscopus in tertio mandato quod dicta gratia non habuit effectum nec unquam fuerint tales in ecclesia.[968]

### Wellensis

Mandatur provideri Johanni Lovecok', clerico Exoniensis diocesis, de beneficio ecclesiatico ad collationem decani et capituli ecclesie Wellensis.

### Exoniensis

De decanatu et prebenda ecclesie collegiate Sancti Tarentoci (Crantock) Exoniensis diocesis, vacantibus per obitum Guillelmi Tyngillo alias Tynghehull' extra curiam defuncti, fuit provisum Edwardo Elier, clerico Exoniensis diocesis.[969] Taxatur, ut dicitur, ad liii s. iiii d., quos solvit die xxiii Februarii anno LXXIII, scilicet quadraginta tres s. iiii d.[970] Videatur si debet plus.

### Wyntoniensis

Mandatur provideri Nicholao Lange, clerico Dublinensis diocesis, de beneficio ecclesiastico et cetera ad collationem episcopi Wyntoniensis.

### Herefordensis

De parochiali ecclesia de Tirnoston' (Turnaston) Herefordensis diocesis, vacante per obitum David Appelewolm alias dicti Dormet', fuit provisum David

---

[964] The date, 23 July 1371, is bracketed against this and the next six items.

[965] The date, 23 July 1371, is bracketed against this and the next five items.

[966] 28 July 1371.

[967] The date, 5 August 1371, is bracketed against this and the next three items.

[968] In the margin: *provisio de vacanti; inutilis.*

[969] In the margin: *provisio de vacanti.*

[970] Sum repeated MS. In the margin: *solvit.*

Penne, acolito Menevensis diocesis, vi idus Decembris.[971]
Nondum habuit effectum quia de patronatu laicali, nec
dictus David umquam impedivit possessorem.[972]

De perpetua vicaria parochialis ecclesie de Bayling-
ham (Ballingham?) diocesis,[973] vacante per assecutionem
vicarie ecclesie parochialis de Elmendon' (Embleton)
factam per Ricardum, fuit provisum Thome de Irland
presbytero, xvi kalendas Januarii.[974] Non scribitur
diocesis nec possit scire ubi est.[975]

### Lichfeldensis

Mandatur provideri Johanni de Ecclesia, diacono
diocesis Herefordensis, de beneficio ecclesiastico ad
collationem abbatis et conventus monasterii de Salopia
(Shrewsbury) Lichfeldensis diocesis.

Recepta pagine liii s. iiii d.;[976] inutiles sunt due provisiones ii; restant fructus duarum provisionum ii; et
due expectationes ii.

### (fol. 78, lxxvi) Sarisbiriensis

Item Thome de Kington' clerico diocesis de canonicatu sub exspectatione prebende ecclesie Sarisbiriensis,
iii nonas Januarii.[977]

### Menevensis

Mandatur provideri Waltero de Hibton', clerico Lincolniensis diocesis, de canonicatu sub exspectatione
⟨prebende⟩ ecclesie collegiate de Abirwilly (Abergwili)
Menevensis diocesis, v kalendas Februarii.[978]

### Londoniensis

Item Roberto Braunche, clerico Norwicensis diocesis,
de beneficio ecclesiastico ad collationem episcopi Londoniensis.

### Wygorniensis

Item Thome de Bereforde, clerico Norwicensis diocesis, de beneficio ecclesiastico et cetera ad collationem
et cetera abbatis et conventus monasterii Gloucestr'
Wygorniensis diocesis.

### Londoniensis

Item Willelmo Govye, clerico Eliensis diocesis, de
beneficio ecclesiastico ad collationem et cetera fratrum
hospitalis Sancti Johannis Jerosolomitani in Anglia.

[971] 8 December 1371.
[972] In the margin: *provisio de vacanti.*
[973] In the margin: *provisio de vacanti, sed non scribitur diocesis; queratur tamen.*
[974] The date, 17 December 1371, is bracketed against this and
the next item.
[975] In the margin: *inutilis.*
[976] In the margin: *vera.*
[977] 3 January 1372.
[978] The date, 28 January 1371, is bracketed against this item
and the next four.

### Wygorniensis

Item Petro Godare de Tirryngton', presbytero Norwicensis diocesis, de beneficio ecclesiastico ad collationem abbatis et conventus de Evesham Wygorniensis.

Restant vi expectationes vi.

### (fol. 78ᵛ) Wellensis

Item Johanni de Welburen', clerico Lincolniensis
diocesis, de canonicatu sub exspectatione prebende ecclesie Wellensis, v kalendas Februarii.[979]

### Cicestrensis

Item Thome de Colham, clerico Sarisbiriensis diocesis,
de canonicatu sub exspectatione prebende ecclesie
Cicestrensis.

### Lichfeldensis

Mandatur provideri Waltero de Tranebonin', clerico
Herefordensis diocesis, de beneficio ecclesiastico et
cetera ad collationem et cetera episcopi Conventrensis
et Lichfeldensis.

### Eboracensis

Item Thome de Tyntesey, clerico Cantuariensis diocesis, de beneficio ecclesiastico ad collationem decani et
capituli ecclesie Eboracensis.

### Norwicensis

Item Simoni Dounk', clerico Norwicensis diocesis, de
beneficio ecclesiastico et cetera ad collationem et cetera
episcopi Norwicensis.

### Cicestrensis

Item Edmundo de Aldeforde, presbytero Norwicensis
diocesis, de beneficio ecclesiastico ad collationem prioris
et conventus de Lewes Cicestrensis diocesis.

### Lincolniensis

Item Waltero Friday, clerico Lincolniensis diocesis,
de beneficio ecclesiastico ad collationem episcopi Lincolniensis.

Restant vii expectationes vii.

### (fol. 79, lxxvii) Lincolniensis

Item Thome de Litton', clerico Lincolniensis diocesis,
de beneficio ecclesiastico ad collationem abbatis et conventus Sancti Albani Lincolniensis diocesis, v kalendas
Februarii.[979]

### Menevensis

Item Roberto Tinsed, clerico Norwicensis diocesis,
de canonicatu sub exspectatione prebende ecclesie collegiate de Landewibrevy (Llanddewi Brefi) Menevensis
diocesis.

[979] The date, 28 January 1371, is bracketed against this item
and the next six.

### Sarisbiriensis

Mandatur provideri Willelmo Radewynter, clerico Londoniensis diocesis, de canonicatu sub exspectatione prebende ecclesie conventualis monialium de Sastebury (Shaftesbury) Sarisbiriensis diocesis.

### Dunolmensis

Item Petro de Chestirton', clerico Eliensis diocesis, de canonicatu sub exspectatione prebende ecclesie collegiate de Aukland Dunolmensis diocesis.

### Lincolniensis

Item Ade alias Johanni Atteyngham, clerico Norwicensis diocesis, de beneficio ecclesiastico et cetera ad collationem abbatis conventus monasterii Sancti Albani Lincolniensis.

### Wygorniensis

Item Willelmo West, clerico Eliensis diocesis, de beneficio ecclesiastico et cetera ad collationem abbatis et conventus Gloucestr' Wygorniensis diocesis.

### Exoniensis

Item Willelmo Alisandre de Hichen, clerico Lincolniensis diocesis, de beneficio ecclesiastico et cetera ad collationem et cetera episcopi Exoniensis.
Restant vii expectationes vii.

### (fol. 79ᵛ) Lichfeldensis

Item Ricardo Moris, clerico Londoniensis diocesis, de beneficio ecclesiastico ad collationem episcopi Conventrensis et Lichfeldensis, v kalendas Februarii.[979]

### Wygorniensis

Item Johanni de Northelingham, clerico Norwicensis diocesis, de canonicatu sub exspectatione prebende ecclesie collegiate de Westbury.

### Sarisbiriensis

Mandatur provideri Johannis Sproxton', clerico Eboracensis diocesis, de beneficio ecclesiastico ad collationem episcopi Sarisbiriensis.

### Herefordensis

Item Willelmo Okham, clerico Lincolniensis diocesis, de beneficio ecclesiastico et cetera ad collationem episcopi Herefordensis.

### Norwicensis

Item Willelmo de Somersham, clerico Norwicensis diocesis, de beneficio ecclesiastico ad collationem episcopi Norwicensis.

### Norwicensis

Item Waltero de Tirrington', clerico Norwicensis diocesis, de beneficio ecclesiastico ad collationem episcopi Norwicensis.

### Eliensis

Item Willelmo de Fiswyk', clerico Eboracensis diocesis, de beneficio ecclesiastico ad collationem abbatis et conventus monasterii de Thorney Eliensis diocesis.
Restant vii expectationes vii.

### (fol. 80, lxxviii) Dunolmensis

De canonicatu et prebenda ecclesie Norton, Dunolmensis diocesis, vacantibus per obitum Thome Drax Lincolniensis diocesis, fuit provisum Ade Lok' de Lini, clerico Norwicensis diocesis, pridie idus Octobris.[980] Certificat episcopus in iii mandato quod nondum habuit effectum.[981]

### Norwicensis

De parochiali ecclesia de Risby Norwicensis diocesis, vacante per obitum quondam Alexandri Todyngton' extra Romanam curiam defuncti, fuit provisum Johanni Lulingtone de Turneye, presbytero Lincolniensis diobesis. Est in mandato.[982]

### Eboracensis

Mandatur provideri Johanni de Wodhous de canonicatu sub exspectatione prebende ecclesie Eboracensis, xviii kalendas Januarii.[983]

### Exoniensis

Item Henrico Amye Exoniensis diocesis de canonicatu sub exspectatione prebende ecclesie Exoniensis.

### Eboracensis

Item Willelmo Clerk', clerico Lincolniensis diocesis, de canonicatu sub exspectatione prebende ecclesie collegiate de Southwell' diocesis Eboracensis.

### Lincolniensis

Item Thome Chaundos, presbytero Lincolniensis diocesis, de canonicatu sub exspectatione prebende ecclesie Lincolniensis, xvii kalendas Maii.[984]

### Cicestrensis

Item Willelmo Donyngton' Eboracensis diocesis de beneficio ecclesiastico ad collationem episcopi Cicestrensis, xii kalendas Decembris.[985]
Restant fructus unius provisionis iᵘˢ; et una est inutilis 1; et quinque sunt expectationes v.

---

[980] The date, 14 October 1371, is bracketed against this item and the next.
[981] In the margin: *provisio de vacanti; inutilis.*
[982] In the margin: *provisio de vacanti.*
[983] The date, 15 December 1371, is bracketed against this item and the next two.
[984] 15 April 1371.
[985] 20 November 1371.

## (fol. 80ᵛ) Londoniensis

Item Rogero de Linton', presbytero Lincolniensis diocesis, de canonicatu sub exspectatione prebende ecclesie Londoniensis, xii kalendas Decembris.⁹⁸⁶

## Lincolniensis

Item Johanni Drafford' presbytero de dignitate et cetera vacantibus vel vacaturis in ecclesie Lincolniensis.

## Eboracensis

Mandatur provideri Johanni Ricardi Kalling', clerico Londoniensis diocesis, de canonicatu sub exspectatione prebende ecclesie collegiate Suthwell' Eboracensis diocesis, viii Kalendas Decembris.⁹⁸⁷

## Wygorniensis

De parochiali ecclesia de Marteleya (Martley) Wygorniensis diocesis, vacante per liberam resignationem Willelmi Hull' extra curiam defuncti, fuit provisum Waltero Donel, clerico Eliensis diocesis. Nondum habuit effectum quia Walterus de Brugge diocesis Wygorniensis possidet eam, et possedit iam per vi annos et ultra, quare fuit relaxatus quousque apareat de effectu vel alias per cameram fuerit ordinatum.⁹⁸⁸

## Dunolmensis

De vicaria parochialis ecclesie de Emelden' (Embleton) Dunolmensis diocesis, vacante per assecutionem alterius beneficii factam per Thomam Famwell', fuit provisum Ricardo de Irland, presbytero dicte diocesis, iii kalendas Decembris.⁹⁸⁹ Non taxatur, et quia verus valor non excedit xx li., ut patet per certificatorium episcopi, solvit in partem fructuum quinque li.,⁹⁹⁰ et die xxvii Aprilis in plenam solutionem alias solvit quinque li.⁹⁹⁰

## Eboracensis

Mandatur provideri Ricardo Killingworth', clerico Londoniensis diocesis, de canonicatu sub exspectatione prebende ecclesie collegiate Sutwell' Eboracensis diocesis.

## Herefordensis

Item Roberto de Prees, presbytero Lichfeldensis diocesis, de canonicatu sub exspectatione prebende in ecclesia parochiali de Ledbury Herefordensis diocesis, pridie idus Decembris.⁹⁹¹

Recepta pagine x li.; ⁹⁹² resta pecunie x li.; restant v expectationes v; una est inutilis provisio iᵃ.

## (fol. 81, lxxix) Eliensis

Collatio, provisio et inductio auctoritate ordinaria facte, Stephano Rote ⁹⁹³ presbytero de parochiali ecclesia de Ditton' (Fen Ditton) Eliensis diocesis fuerunt confirmate seu provisum de novo, pro taxa xxvi li. xiii s. iiiiᵒʳ d.⁹⁹⁴ Solvit die prima Novembris in partem taxe tresdecim li. vi s. viii d.⁹⁹⁵ Item solvit die vii Januarii sequentis in xx m. xiii li. vi s. viii d.⁹⁹⁶

## Wellensis

De capella Sancte Anne in Bosco Bathoniensis et Wellensis diocesis, vacante per mortem Walteri Bovet ultimi rectoris eiusdem, fuit provisum Johanni Lange, clerico diocesis Dublinensis, nonas Augusti.⁹⁹⁷ Non habuit effectum quia est unita abbassie bex Evesham, ut est probatum.⁹⁹⁸

## Eboracensis

Mandatur provideri Johanni de Mancestr', presbytero diocesis Lichfeldensis, de canonicatu sub exspectatione prebende ecclesie Eboracensis, v idus Augusti.⁹⁹⁹

## Lichfeldensis

Item Rogero dicto Dros', presbytero Lichfeldensis, de canonicatu sub exspectatione prebende ecclesie Lichfeldensis.

## Lincolniensis

Item Thome Lawart, filio Bonie nobilis viri Rogeri Lawart, clerico Lincolniensis diocesis, licentiato in artibus, de canonicatu sub exspectatione prebende, dignitatis et cetera ecclesie Lincolniensis, vi idus Augusti.¹

## Wygorniensis

Item Johanni de Prestwold', presbytero Lincolniensis diocesis, magistro in artibus, de beneficio ecclesiastico ad collationem episcopi Wygorniensis usque ad summam xxxv si cum cura, si sine cura xxv marcarum sterlingorum.

## Eboracensis

Item Ade Pikering', presbytero Eboracensis diocesis, de canonicatu sub exspectatione prebende, dignitatis, et cetera ecclesie Eboracensis, iii idus Augusti.²

Recepta pagine xxvi li. xiii s. iiii d.; ³ una provisio est inutilis i; et restant v expectationes v.

---

⁹⁸⁶ The date, 20 November 1371, is bracketed against this item and the next.

⁹⁸⁷ The date, 24 November 1371, is bracketed against this item and the next.

⁹⁸⁸ In the margin: *provisio de vacanti.*

⁹⁸⁹ The date, 29 November 1371, is bracketed against this item and the next. In the margin: *provisio de vacanti.*

⁹⁹⁰ Sum repeated MS. In the margin: *solvit.*

⁹⁹¹ 12 December 1371.

⁹⁹² In the margin: *vera.*

---

⁹⁹³ *Atterote*, Collectorie 13, fol. 173ᵛ.

⁹⁹⁴ In the margin: *provisio de vacanti.*

⁹⁹⁵ Follows *quinque li. v li.* deleted by a line. Sum repeated MS. In the margin: *solvit.*

⁹⁹⁶ In the margin: *solvit.*

⁹⁹⁷ 5 August 1371.

⁹⁹⁸ In the margin: *provisio de vacanti; inutilis.*

⁹⁹⁹ The date, 9 August 1371, is bracketed against this item and the next.

¹ The date, 8 August 1371, is bracketed against this item and the next.

² 11 August 1371.

³ In the margin: *vera.*

## (fol. 81ᵛ) Eboracensis

Acceptatio et provisio facte auctoritate apostolica Waltero de Waudeford' de canonicatu et prebenda ecclesie collegiate Ripponensis Eboracensis diocesis fuerunt, vocata de Thorp', confirmate seu provisum de novo, xvii kalendas Septembris.[4] Taxatur ad xl m. et plus, ut dicitur.[5] Solvit die xviii Octobris anno LXXIII in x m. vi li. xiii s. iiii d.[6] Item solvit plus alia vice decem li.[7]

### Lincolniensis

Mandatur provideri Henrico Piel, licentiato in legibus, de canonicatu sub exspectatione prebende, dignitatis, et cetera ecclesie Lincolniensis, v kalendas Maii.[8] Supra est iterato.

### Sarisbiriensis

Motu proprio fuit provisum Guillelmo titulo Sancti Stephani in Celiomonte de archidiaconatu Barschire (Berkshire) in ecclesia Sarisbiriensi, vacante in curia per mortem cardinalis Neopolitanensis,[9] iii kalendas Maii.[10] Solvit Magister Rohgerius Karnab' nomine dicti domini cardinalis die xi Martii in partem taxe tresdecem li. novem s. iiii d.[11] Et solvit plus in partem taxe die xx Maii decem et octo li. xviii s. vi d.[11] Solvit totum xxxii li. vii s. x d.[12]

Provisio auctoritate ordinaria facta Antonio de Neuton' preposite ecclesie Sancte Marie de Karitate Unt'tarum sine cura monasterii Sancte Marie de Neriton' (Nardo) ordinis Sancti Benedicti fuit confirmata seu provisum de novo.[13]

Item provisio auctoritate ordinaria facta Matheo de Noriton' sacristre dicti monasterii quod possidet fuit confirmata seu provisum de novo.

### Exoniensis

Mandatur provideri Waltero de Lewenant, presbytero Exoniensis diocesis, de canonicatu sub exspectatione prebende, dignitatis, et cetera ecclesie Exoniensis.

### Dunolmensis

Item Radulpho de Strington', presbytero Eboracensis

diocesis, de beneficio ecclesiastico ad collationem prioris et capituli ecclesie Dunolmensis.

Recepta pagine xlix li. xiiii d.;[14] restant iiii expectationes iiii; resta pecunie x li.[15]

## (fol. 82, lxxx) Wyntoniensis

Mandatur provideri Willelmo de Everle Sarisbiriensis diocesis de canonicatu sub exspectatione prebende[16] ecclesie monialium de Warwell' (Wherwell) ordinis Sancti Benedicti Wyntoniensis diocesis, iii kalendas Maii.[17]

### Norwicensis, Lincolniensis

Provisio facta Rogero Fabri de prioratu de Creting' (Creeting) et Eyveedon' (Everdon)[18] ordinis Sancti Benedicti Norwicensis diocesis et Lincolniensis fuit confirmata seu provisum de novo, v nonas Maii.[19] Videatur si est in Norvicensi[20] vel Lincolniensi[21] diocesi, quia laqueatur de ambobus, et non habuit effectum ut patet per certificatorium episcopi Lincolniensis.[22]

### Lincolniensis

Motu proprio fuit provisum Raymundo episcopo Penne[23] de canonicatu et prebende vacantibus in ecclesia Lincolniensi per obitum quondam Raynaudi de Teanis' in curia defuncti, iiᵈᵒ nonas Maii.[24] Cardinalis Penn' est, et non habuit effectum ad huc, et cardinalis obiit iam.

### Lincolniensis

Mandatur provideri Johanni de Botford,' presbytero diocesis Eboracensis, de beneficio ecclesiastico ad collationem abbatis et conventus monasterii de Ramesey ordinis Sancti Benedicti Lincolniensis diocesis, vᵗᵒ nonas Maii.[19]

### Eboracensis

Item Andree Bard', diacono Florentino, de canonicatu sub exspectatione prebende, dignitatis, et cetera ecclesie Eboracensis, iiiiᵒ nonas Maii.[25]

### Eboracensis

Item Willelmo Cambre, presbytero Wellensis diocesis, de canonicatu sub exspectatione prebende ecclesie Sutwell' Eboracensis diocesis, xvii kalendas Junii.[26]

---

[4] 16 August 1371.
[5] In the margin: *provisio de vacanti*.
[6] In the margin: *solvit*.
[7] Sum repeated MS. In the margin: *solvit*.
[8] 27 April 1371.
[9] Bernard de Bosqueto, archbishop of Naples, priest of Ss. XII Apostoli.
[10] The date, 29 April 1371, is bracketed against this item and the next four. In the margin: *provisio de vacanti*; *Cardinalis de Agrifolio*.
[11] In the margin: *solvit*.
[12] In the margin: *Voluit tamen quitantiam dicte summe de data xxv die Martii, quia aliter non possit computare, ut dixit et cetera*.
[13] In the margin, bracketed against this item and the next: *non dicit diocesis, nec sciatur*.

[14] In the margin: *vera*.
[15] Originally *xvi li. xiii s. iiii d.* The *vi* has been partially rubbed out and the *xiii s. iiii d.* deleted by a line
[16] *prebende* repeated MS.
[17] 29 April 1371.
[18] Both dependent upon Bernay.
[19] 3 May 1371.
[20] The *Nor* of *Norvicensi* is deleted by a line.
[21] Over *vel Lincolniensi* is written *in Lincolniensi est*.
[22] In the margin: *provisio de vacanti*.
[23] Raymond de Canillac, bishop of Palestrina.
[24] 6 May 1371.
[25] 4 May 1371.
[26] 16 May 1371.

### Sarisbiriensis

Item Johanni Sailard', presbytero Wellensis diocesis, de beneficio ecclesiastico ad collationem episcopi, decani et capituli singulorum quam canonicorum ecclesie Sarisbiriensis, ii^do idus Junii.[27]

Restant fructus ii provisionum ii; et quinque expectationes v.

### (fol. 82^v) Sarisbiriensis

Mandatur provideri de canonicatu et prebenda de Husseburn' de Burbach' (Hurstbourne and Burbage) in ecclesia Sarisbiriensi, vacantibus per obitum quondam Salatini de Fallet' extra curiam defuncti, fuit provisum Willelmo de Osmundeston', presbytero Lichfeldensis diocesis, nonas Junii.[28] Nondum habuit effectum, quia medicus regis suo titulo regio possidet, et est alia provisio supra folio [29] que etiam non habuit effectum.[30]

### Cicestrensis

De canonicatu et prebenda ecclesie collegiate de Southmalling' nuncupate Cicestrensis diocesis, vacantibus per obitum Domini Johannis de Etyngham extra Romanam curiam defuncti, fuit provisum Johanni Strensall', presbytero Eboracensis diocesis, ii idus Junii.[27] Nondum habuit effectum quia titulo regio possidetur, ideo inutilis, et per conversim aïie due provisiones facte aliis de ecclesia sua inferiore libro folio lxxxii.[30]

### Wellensis

Mandatur provideri Willelmo Cambre de canonicatu sub exspectatione prebende ecclesie Wellensis, iii idus Junii.[31]

### Eliensis

Item Edmundo Strete, bacallario in legibus, de beneficio ecclesiastico ad collationem et cetera episcopi Eliensis, ii idus Junii.[32]

### Exoniensis

Item Willelmo Cadworth', presbytero Exoniensis diocesis, de canonicatu sub exspectatione prebende ecclesie Exoniensis.

### Lincolniensis

De dignitate, personatu vel officio cum cura vel sine cura, vacante vel vacatura in ecclesia Lincolniensi mandatur provideri Ricardo de Stratton'.

### Exoniensis

Item de dignitate et personatu ecclesie Exoniensis

vacantibus vel vacaturis Johanni Cheyne, clerico Exoniensis diocesis.

Inutiles provisiones sunt ii; et restant v expectationes v.

### (fol. 83, lxxxi) Sarisbiriensis

Mandatur provideri Johanni Saylard', presbytero Wellensis diocesis, de beneficio ecclesiastico et cetera ad collationem episcopi, decani et capituli singulorum quam canonicorum ecclesie Sarisbiriensis, ii^do idus Junii.[33]

### Wygorniensis

Item Johanni Comp alias dicto Drax, presbytero Eboracensis diocesis, de beneficio ecclesiastico ad collationem abbatis et conventus monasterii de Cucestr' (Cirencester) ordinis Sancti Augustini Wygorniensis diocesis.

### Eboracensis

Collatio et provisio auctoritate ordinaria facte Nicholao de Feriby, in iure civili bacallario, de parochiali ecclesia de Heversham Eboracensis diocesis, vacante per liberam resignationem Thome de Tetteford' factam coram certis iudicibus, fuerunt confirmate et cetera, pro taxa c m., scilicet lxvi li. xiii s. iiii d.[30] Solvit in duabus vicibus viginti li.[34] Item solvit xvi die Aprilis anno LXXIIII in viginti m. xiii li. vi s. viii d.[35]

### Bathoniensis

Mandatur provideri Briano Boterwell' Wyncerstr' diocesis de canonicatu sub exspectatione prebende ecclesie Bathoniensis et Wellensis.

### Eboracensis

Item Rogero Burton' de canonicatu sub exspectatione prebende ecclesie collegiate Rippon' Eboracensis diocesis.

### Sarisbiriensis

Item Edwardo de Cherdestok', presbytero Sarisbiriensis diocesis, de canonicatu sub exspectatione prebende, dignitatis ecclesie Sarisbiriensis.

Recepta pecunie xxxiii li. vi s. viii d.;[36] restant expectationes v; restant in pecunia xxxiii li. vi s. viii d.

### (fol. 83^v) Londoniensis

Item Johanni de Stene presbytero de canonicatu sub exspectatione prebende ecclesie Londoniensis, ii idus Junii.[37]

### Lincolniensis

Mandatur provideri Johanni de Carleton', presbytero

---

[27] 12 June 1371.
[28] 5 June 1371.
[29] Blank in MS.
[30] In the margin: *provisio de vacanti*.
[31] 11 June 1371.
[32] The date, 12 June 1371, is bracketed against this and the next three items.

[33] The date, 12 June 1371, is bracketed against this item and the next five.
[34] Sum repeated MS. In the margin: *solvit*.
[35] In the margin: *solvit*.
[36] In the margin: *vera*.
[37] The date, 12 June 1371, is bracketed against this item and the next six.

thesaurario principis Aquitanie, de canonicatu sub exspectatione prebende ecclesie Lincolniensis.

### Cicestrensis

Item Hugoni Bokenhull' de canonicatu sub exspectatione prebende ecclesie Cicestrensis.

### Wellensis

Item Ricardo Bedford', bacallario in decretis, de canonicatu sub exspectatione prebende ecclesie Wellensis.

### Sarisbiriensis

De parochiali ecclesia de Wely (Wylye) Sarisbiriensis diocesis, vacante per mortem Willelmi Rath' extra curiam defuncti, fuit provisum Rogero Dawe Exoniensis diocesis. Est in iiii mandatis.[30]

### Lichfeldensis

Item Thome de Streton', presbytero Lincolniensis diocesis, bacallario in legibus ac in iure, canonico, scolari, de canonicatu sub exspectatione prebende ecclesie Lichfeldensis.

### Lincolniensis

Item Willelmo Borstall', presbytero Lincolniensis diocesis, de canonicatu sub exspectatione prebende ecclesie Lincolniensis.[38]

Restant fructus unius provisionis i; et exspectationes vi sine effectu vi.

### (fol. 84; lxxxii) Eboracensis

Item Nicholao de Feriby Eboracensis diocesis, bacallario in legibus, de canonicatu sub exspectatione prebende ecclesie Eboracensis, ii idus Junii.[39]

### Lincolniensis

Item Willelmo de Cravle, presbytero Lincolniensis diocesis, de canonicatu sub exspectatione prebende ecclesie Lincolniensis. Expeditus est ad prebendam lx s. in ecclesia Lincolniensi, et solvit triginta s. xxvii die Octobris anno LXXIII.[34] Item solvit die xxix Martii anno a nativitate LXXIIIIto alios triginta s., salvo iure pluris super maiori valentia taxe vel residui, et sic etiam quitantia manu Domini Arnaldi scripta.[34] Summa lx s.

### Eboracensis

Item Ade de Herayngton' Lincolniensis diocesis de canonicatu sub exspectatione prebende ecclesie Eboracensis.

### Dunolmensis

Mandatur provideri Henrico de Feserstonehalgh',

clerico Eboracensis diocesis, de beneficio ecclesiastico ad collationem prioris et conventus Dunolmensis usque ad summam xl m. sterlingorum.

### Dunolmensis

Item Johanni Tifford', clerico Eboracensis diocesis, de beneficio ecclesiastico ad collationem episcopi, prioris et capituli ecclesie Dunolmensis.

### Norwicensis

Item Waltero de Clee, presbytero Lincolniensis diocesis, de beneficio ecclesiastico ad collationem et cetera episcopi Norwicensis, xvi kalendas Julii.[40]

### Lincolniensis

Item Thome de Wynton', clerico Dunolmensis diocesis, de beneficio ecclesiastico ad collationem abbatis et conventus monasterii de Ramesey Lincolniensis. Recepta pagine lx s.;[36] restant vi expectationes vi.

### (fol. 84v) Cantuariensis

Item Thome de Byngham, presbytero Eboracensis diocesis, de beneficio ecclesiastico ad collationem et cetera archiepiscopi Cantuariensis, xvii kalendas Julii.[41]

### Lichfeldensis

Item Thome de Lichfeldia clerico de canonicatu sub exspectatione prebende ecclesie Lichfeldensis.

### Lincolniensis

De parochiali ecclesia de Mixebury (Mixbury) Lincolniensis diocesis, vacante vel dum vacabit per dimissionem Domini Johannis de Strensall' per assecutionem alterius beneficii vel faciendam per dictum Johannem, fuit provisum Godbain', clerico Eboracensis, xv kalendas Julii.[42] Non habuit effectum titulo regio inpediente, sed videatur si habebit. Alia est etiam provisio infrascripta folio [43] que etiam non habuit effectum quia dictus Johannes nunquam habuit beneficium incompatibile.[44]

### Lincolniensis, Exoniensis

Motu proprio fuit provisum Petro Sancte Marie in Via Lata diacono cardinali de archidiaconatu Oxoniensi in eadem ecclesia Lincolniensi, vacante per obitum Philipi de Bellocampo in curia defuncti, ac de canonicatu sub exspectatione prebende ecclesie Exoniensis, viii kalendas Julii.[45]

---

[38] Followed by *Expeditus est ad prebendam lx s. in dicta ecclesia. Solvit die xxvii Octobris triginta s.* deleted by a line and with the note: *infra est in secunda, ideo hic cancellatus.*

[39] The date, 12 June 1371, is bracketed against this item and the next four.

[40] The date, 16 June 1371, is bracketed against this item and the next.

[41] The date, 15 June 1371, is bracketed against this item and the next.

[42] 17 June 1371.

[43] Blank in MS.

[44] In the margin: *provisio; inutilis.*

[45] 24 June 1371. In the margin: *Cardinalis de Vernhio et litigat* (Peter de Vergne, deacon of S. Maria in Via Lata, and archdeacon of Exeter).

## Cantuariensis

Mandatur provideri Johanni Conventrensis et Lichfeldensis diocesis de beneficio et cetera ad collationem
archiepiscopi Cantuarensis, x kalendas Julii.[46]

## Lincolniensis

De perpetua vicaria parochialis ecclesie de Astenhaut
(Aston Rowant) Lincolniensis diocesis, vacante per
liberam resignationem in Romana curia factam per
Robertum de Brigham, fuit provisum Henrico de Brigham, presbytero Eboracensis diocesis, vii kalendas
Julii.[47] Supra est alia provisio infra eundem annum
folio,[48] et ibi solvit, ideo ista inutilis.[48]

Restant fructus unius provisionis i; et iii expectationes.

## (fol. 85, lxxxiii) Lincolniensis

De parochiali ecclesia de Myxebury (Mixbury)
Lincolniensis diocesis dum vacabit per assecutionem
decanatus de Soutmalling' Cantuariensis diocesis factam
per Johannem Strensall', fuit provisum Johanni Aspull',
clerico Bangorensis diocesis, x kalendas Julii.[46] Nondum habuit effectum, titulo regio inpediente, dicta provisio facta Johanni quia dictam ecclesiam adhuc possidet
titulo regio impediente.[48]

## Sarisbiriensis

Mandatur provideri Nicholao Russel de canonicatu
sub exspectatione prebende ecclesie collegiate monasterii
Beate Marie monialium de Wilton Sarisbiriensis diocesis, x kalendas Julii.[46]

## Sarisbiriensis

De canonicatu et prebenda[49] ecclesie Sarisbiriensis,
vacantibus per obitum Martini Manlith extra curiam
defuncti, fuit provisum Guillelmo de Osmundeston', et
dimittet canonicatum et prebendam Lemovicenses
(Limoges) et Daratenses (Le Dorat) et capellam Beate
Marie de Tallifer (La Chapelle-Taillefert) Lemovicensis
diocesis, pro taxa xxiiii m.[50] Solvit die xiii Octobris
anno LXXIII in partem fructuum decem m. que valent
vi li. xiii s. iiii d.[51]

## Lincolniensis

Mandatur provideri Thome de Buterley de beneficio
ecclesiastico ad collationem abbatis et conventus monasterii de Brame (Bruerne?) Lincolniensis diocesis, xi
kalendas Septembris.[52]

## Cicestrensis

Item Johanni Newport, clerico Landavensis diocesis,
de canonicatu sub exspectatione prebende ecclesie Cicestrensis, xii kalendas Septembris.[53]

## Norwicensis

Unio dudum facta per felicis recordationis Johannem
XXII de parochiali ecclesia de Weseleton' (Westleton)
Norwicensis diocesis ad abbatiam monasterii de Sibiton"
(Sibton) ordinis Cisterciensis dicte diocesis, quam ecclesiam de practica dictus abbas et conventus dicti monasterii possidet pacifice, fuit confirmata seu provisum de
novo, ix kalendas Septembris,[54] pro taxa xlii m., pro
quibus solvit die xi Octobris anno LXXIII xxviii li.[51]

Recepta pagine xxxiiii li. xiii s. iiii d.;[55] inutilis
provisio est i; restant iii expectationes iii; resta pecunie
ix li. vi s. viii d.

## (fol. 85ᵛ) Exoniensis

Mandatur provideri Radulpho Pylaton', presbytero,
Exoniensis diocesis, de canonicatu sub exspectatione
prebende ecclesie Exoniensis, vi kalendas Septembris.[56]

## Eboracensis

Subrogatus fuit Adam de Karleolo presbytero Karleolensis diocesis, in omni iure et ad omne ius quod
competebat quondam Thome de Sotheron' in Romana
curia defuncto[57] in et super parochiali ecclesia de Mitton' (Mitton) diocesis Eboracensis, iii kalendas Septembris.[58] Non habuit effectum quia appropriata est
abbati de Kokersind' (Cockersand) Eboracensis diocesis.[59]

## Sarisbiriensis

Collatio et provisio auctoritate apostolica facte
Roberto Bastard' de parochiali ecclesia de Wyli (Wylye)
Sarisbiriensis diocesis fuerunt confirmate et cetera, ii
kalendas Decembris.[60] Est in mandato.[61]

## Eboracensis

Collatio et provisio auctoritate apostolica facte[62]
Nicholao de Burton' de canonicatu et prebenda ecclesie
collegiate de Rippon' Eboracensis diocesis, et si et cetera,
fuerunt confirmate et cetera, iiᵈᵒ idus Septembris.[63]
Gardaraulerius domini regis possidet titulo regio, et

---

[46] 22 June 1371.
[47] 25 June 1371.
[48] In the margin: *provisio de vacanti*; *inutilis*.
[49] Prebend of Chardstock, Collectorie 13, fol. 174.
[50] In the margin: *provisio de vacanti*.
[51] In the margin: *solvit*.
[52] 22 August 1371.

[53] 21 August 1371.
[54] 24 August 1371. In the margin: *provisio est.*
[55] In the margin: *vera.*
[56] 27 August 1371.
[57] *defuncti*, MS.
[58] 30 August 1371.
[59] In the margin: *provisio de vacanti*; *inutilis.*
[60] 30 November 1371.
[61] In the margin: *provisio de vacanti*; *debet.*
[62] *facta*, MS.
[63] The date, 12 September 1371, is bracketed against this item
and the next three.

non vult solvere licet obligatio sit in rem, et dicta gratia non habuit effectum quia obiit ante adeptam possessionem.[64]

### Eboracensis

Acceptatio, collatio et provisio auctoritate apostolica facte Johanni Toresby de canonicatu et prebenda [65] ecclesie Eboracensis, si fuerint reservate, fuerunt confirmate et cetera; taxatur ad xv m.[66] Solvit pro dictis xv m. decem li.[67]

### Herefordensis

Item collatio et provisio auctoritate ordinaria facte Henrico perpetuo vicario de Ledbury Herefordensis diocesis de dicta vicaria fuerunt confirmate et cetera, pro taxa xii m.[66] Solvit dictas xii m. in viii li.[51]

### Londoniensis

De parochiali ecclesia Sancti Michaelis in Cornhill' Londoniensis diocesis, vacante per obitum Ricardi de Midford' extra Romanam curiam defuncti, fuit provisum Ricardo Lee, presbytero Lichfeldensis diocesis. Est in mandato.[61]

Recepta pagine xviii li.; [55] restant fructus ii provisionum ii; et sunt ii inutiles ii; et una expectatio i.

### (fol. 86, lxxxiiii) Cantuariensis

Mandatur provideri Galfrido Stobbe de Weshaddon', presbytero Lincolniensis diocesis, de beneficio ecclesiastico ad collationem prioris et capituli Sancte Trinitatis Cantuariensis diocesis, ii nonas Septembris.[68]

### Roffensis

Item Johanni Burbach', presbytero Cantuariensis diocesis, de beneficio ecclesiastico ad collationem episcopi, prioris et capituli singulorum quam canonicorum ecclesie Roffensis, xvii kalendas Octobris.[69]

### Londoniensis

Item Thome Hoveleye Norwicensis ad collationem abbatis et conventus monasterii de Westmonasterio Londoniensis diocesis.

### Londoniensis

Mandatur provideri Johanni Peet de Pontlee, clerico Londoniensis diocesis, de beneficio ecclesiastico et cetera ad collationem prioris et fratrum hospitalis Sancti Johannis Jherosolomitani in Anglia, x kalendas Octobris.[70]

### Londoniensis

Item Thome de Wynkelegh', presbytero Exoniensis diocesis, de beneficio ecclesiastico ad collationem prioris et fratrum et cetera ut supra.

### Menevensis

Collatio et provisio auctoritate ordinaria facte Johanni David, presbytero de prebenda de Carow [71] (Tregarow) in ecclesia Landewibrevi (Llanddewi Brefi) Menevensis diocesis, certo modo vacante, fuerunt confirmate seu provisum de novo, pro taxa nomem m., pro quibus solvit die xii Maii anno LXXIII vi li.[72]

### Eboracensis

Motu proprio fuit provisum Roberto, olim episcopo Cameracensi (Cambrai), presbytero cardinali [73] in Eboracensis ecclesiis de beneficiis et cetera [74] usque ad summam iiii^m fl., vi idus Septembris.[75]

Recepta pagine vi li.; [76] restant fructus ii provisionum ii; et v expectationes v.

### (fol. 86^v) Cantuariensis

Item simili motu Johanni titulo Sancti Marcelli presbytero cardinali in Cantuariensi usque ad summam predictam, vi idus Septembris.[77] Obiit, ideo non habuit effectum.[78]

### Lincolniensis

Mandatur provideri Thome de Byntham diocesis Eboracensis de canonicatu sub exspectatione prebende ecclesie Lincolniensis, pridie kalendas Octobris.[79]

### Menevensis

De canonicatu et prebenda ecclesie Menevensis, vacantibus per obitum Ricardi Garlandi extra curiam defuncti, fuit provisum Hugoni Attehall', clerico Lincolniensis diocesis, vii idus Octobris.[80] Certificat episcopus quod non habuit effectum ad huc.[81]

### Sarisbiriensis

Mandatur provideri Ricardi Brondons, clerico diocesis Sarisbiriensis, de canonicatu sub exspectatione ecclesie monasterii monialium de Wilton' dicte Sarisbiriensis diocesis, v idus Octobris.[82]

---

[64] In the margin: *provisio de vacanti*; *prohibitum*; *inutilis*.
[65] Prebend of Grindale, Collectorie 13, fol. 174.
[66] In the margin: *provisio de vacanti*.
[67] Sum repeated MS. In the margin: *solvit*.
[68] 4 September 1371.
[69] The date, 15 September 1371, is bracketed against this item and the next.
[70] The date, 22 September 1371, is bracketed against this item and the next two.
[71] *Caron*, Collectorie 13, fol. 174.
[72] In the margin: *provisio de vacanti*; *solvit*.
[73] Robert of Geneva, priest of Ss. XII Apostoli.
[74] In the margin: *Cardinalis est sub expectatione*.
[75] 8 September 1371.
[76] In the margin: *vera*.
[77] 8 September 1371.
[78] In the margin: *inutilis*.
[79] 30 September 1371.
[80] 9 October 1371.
[81] In the margin: *provisio de vacanti*; *inutilis*.
[82] The date, 11 October 1371, is bracketed against this item and the next.

### Sarisbiriensis

Mandatur provideri Willelmo de Gateworth', presbytero Lincolniensis diocesis, de beneficio ecclesiastico ad collationem episcopi, decani et capituli singulorum quam canonicorum ecclesie Sarisbiriensis.

### Norwicensis

De parochiali ecclesia de Saxhan parva (Little Saxham) Norwicensis diocesis, vacante per mortem Gerardi de Mota extra curiam defuncti, fuit provisum Johanni de Bokelond' minori, presbytero Londoniensis diocesis, pridie idus Octobris.[83]

### Londoniensis

Mandatur provideri Johanni[84] de Sancto Johanne, presbytero diocesis Cicestrensis, de canonicatu sub exspectatione prebende et cetera ecclesie Londoniensis, xvi kalendas Novembris.[85]

Restant expectationes iiii; et fructus unius i.

### (fol. 87, lxxxv) Norwicensis

Item Alexandro de Partenay, clerico Lincolniensis diocesis, de beneficio ecclesiastico ad collationem abbatis monasterii Sancti Edmundi de Bury ordinis Sancti Benedicti Norwicensis diocesis, xvi kalendas Novembris.[86]

### Norwicensis

Mandatur provideri Roberto Cartere, presbytero diocesis Norwicensis, de beneficio ecclesiastico ad collationem prioris et conventus prioratus de Botele (Butley) dicte diocesis ordinis Sancti Augustini.

### Norwicensis

Item Johanni Stannford', clerico Lincolniensis diocesis, de beneficio ecclesiastico et cetera ad collationem et cetera prioris et conventus prioratus de Botele diocesis Norwicensis ordinis Sancti Augustini.

### Londoniensis

Item mandatur provideri Thome de Springfeld', presbytero Londoniensis diocesis, de beneficio ecclesiastico ad collationem et cetera episcopi Londoniensis.

### Exoniensis

Item Thome de Cernebury, presbytero Exoniensis diocesis, de beneficio ecclesiastico ad collationem et cetera episcopi Exoniensis.

### Dunolmensis

Item Willelmo de Arderen, presbytero Lincolniensis

diocesis, de beneficio ecclesiastico ad collationem prioris et capituli ecclesie Dunolmensis, xiiii kalendas Novembris.[87]

### Cicestrensis

Collatio et provisio auctoritate ordinaria facte Ricardo Tangmer, presbytero Cicestrensis diocesis, de canonicatu et prebenda de Colloworth' (Colworth) in ecclesia Cicestrensi, quos diu tenuit pacifice, fuerunt confirmate seu provisum de novo, pro taxa xl m., xviii kalendas Novembris.[88] Pro taxa xl m. solvit in duabus vicibus viginti sex li. xiii s. iiii d.[89]

Recepta pagine xxvi li. xiii s. iiii d.;[90] restant expectationes vi.

### (fol. 87ᵛ) Lichfeldensis

Collatio et provisio auctoritate ordinaria facte Willelmo de Newton', presbytero diocesis Lincolniensis, de canonicatu et prebenda ecclesie Lichfeldensis, vacantibus per assecutionem canonicatus et prebende Lincolniensium factam per Johannem de Wltham, fuerunt confirmate seu provisum de novo, xiii kalendas Novembris.[91] Pro taxa vii m. quas solvit die ii Octobris anno LXXIII in iiiiᵒʳ li. xiii s. iiiiᵒʳ d.[92]

### Lichfeldensis

Collatio et provisio auctoritate apostolica facte Johanni Laas clerico de canonicatu et prebenda ecclesie collegiate Sancti Johannis Cestr' Lichfeldensis diocesis, vacantibus per obitum Ade de Warton', fuerunt confirmate seu provisum de novo. Est in v mandato.[93]

### Dunolmensis

Acceptatio et provisio auctoritate litterarum apostolicarum facte Johanni Redehond', presbytero Dunolmensis diocesis, de canonicatu et prebenda in ecclesia collegiata Cestr' in strato (Chester-le-Street) dicte Dunolmensis diocesis, vacantibus per obitum Domini David de Wallore extra curiam defuncti, fuerunt confirmate seu provisum de novo. Alia provisio est infra, et nulla habuit effectum, ut certificat episcopus in tertio certificatorio.[94]

### Eboracensis

Item Johanni de Prestwold', presbytero Lincolniensis diocesis, de canonicatu sub exspectatione prebende et cetera dignitatis et cetera ecclesie collegiate de Sutwell' Eboracensis diocesis.

---

[83] 14 October 1371. In the margin: *provisio de vacanti.*
[84] *Johanne,* MS.
[85] 17 October 1371.
[86] The date, 17 October 1371, is bracketed against this item and the next four.

[87] 19 October 1371.
[88] 15 October 1371. In the margin: *provisio de vacanti.*
[89] Sum repeated MS. In the margin: *solvit.*
[90] In the margin: *vera.*
[91] The date, 20 October 1371, is bracketed against this and the next five items. In the margin: *provisio de vacanti.*
[92] In the margin: *solvit.*
[93] In the margin: *provisio de vacanti.*
[94] In the margin: *provisio de vacanti; inutilis.*

### Lichfeldensis

Item Willelmo de Pakyngton', presbytero Lincolniensis diocesis, de canonicatu sub exspectatione prebende, dignitatis, et cetera ecclesie Lichfeldensis.

### Londoniensis

Item Johanni de Carleton, de canonicatu sub exspectatione prebende ecclesie Londoniensis.

Recepta pagine iiii li. xiii s. iiii d.; [90] restant fructus unius i; et iii expectationes iii.

### (fol. 88, lxxxvi) Eboracensis

Mandatur provideri Rogero de Burton', rectori parochialis ecclesie de Stokes, de canonicatu sub exspectatione prebende, dignitatis, et cetera ecclesie Eboracensis, xiii kalendas Novembris.[95]

### Menevensis

Item Johanni Stene Cantuariensis diocesis de canonicatu sub exspectatione prebende, dignitatis, et cetera ecclesie Menevensis.

### Cicestrensis

Item Willelmo Scelton', presbytero Lincolniensis diocesis, de canonicatu sub exspectatione dignitatis et cetera ecclesie Cicestrensis.

### Cicestrensis

Item Edwardo de Southworth', presbytero Lincolniensis diocesis, de canonicatu sub exspectatione prebende ecclesie Cicestrensis.

### Lichfeldensis

Item Thome Kyngisbury, presbytero Lichfeldensis diocesis, de canonicatu sub exspectatione prebende, dignitatis, et cetera ecclesie Lichfeldensis.

### Wellensis

Item Ricardo de Bedforde, presbytero Lincolniensis diocesis, de beneficio ecclesiastico ad collationem abbatis et conventus monasterii Glaston' ordinis Sancti Benedicti diocesis Wellensis.

### Lincolniensis

Item Willelmo de Eylesham, clerico Norwicensis diocesis, de beneficio ecclesiastico et cetera ad collationem abbatis et conventus de Ramesey ordinis Sancti Benedicti Lincolniensis diocesis.

Restant expectationes vii.

### (fol. 88ᵛ) Lincolniensis

Mandatur provideri Johanni de Cliderouwe, clerico Dunolmensis diocesis, de beneficio ecclesiastico ad collationem abbatis et conventus monasterii de Burgo Sancti Petri ordinis Sancti Benedicti Lincolniensis, xiii kalendas Novembris.[95]

### Eboracensis

Item Willelmo de Craweley, presbytero Lincolniensis diocesis, de beneficio ecclesiastico ad collationem abbatis et conventus monasterii Beate Marie extra muros Eboraci ordinis Sancti Benedicti.

### Sarisbiriensis

Item Thome de Gotne, clerico Lincolniensis diocesis, de beneficio ecclesiastico ad collationem abbatisse et conventus monasterii monialium de Wilton ordinis Sancti Augustini Sarisbiriensis diocesis.

### Eboracensis

Item Johanni Brid, clerico Eboracensis diocesis, de parochiali ecclesia de Egermond' (Egremont) dicte diocesis, cum vacabit per assecutionem alterius beneficii incompatibilis, videlicet de Mixebury (Mixbury), factam per Henricum Godbarn'. Nondum habuit effectum quia non vacavit.[94]

### Wyntoniensis

Item Thome de Bernby, presbytero Lincolniensis diocesis, de canonicatu sub exspectatione prebende monasterii monialium de Warewell' (Wherwell) ordinis Sancti Benedicti Wyntoniensis diocesis.

### Dunolmensis

Item Willelmo de Donnebrugg' Eboracensis diocesis de canonicatu sub exspectatione prebende ecclesie collegiate de Derlington' (Darlington) Dunolmensis diocesis.

### Dunolmensis

Mandatur provideri Johanni de Misterton', clerico Eboracensis diocesis, de canonicatu sub exspectatione prebende ecclesie collegiate de Derlington' Dunolmensis diocesis.

Restant vi expectationes vi; et una provisio est inutilis i.

### (fol. 89, lxxxvii) Dunolmensis

Item Waltero Dissy, clerico Eboracensis, de canonicatu sub exspectatione prebende ecclesie collegiate de Aukland' Dunolmensis diocesis, xiii kalendas Novembris.[95]

### Eboracensis

Item Thome Orgam, clerico Londoniensis diocesis, de canonicatu sub exspectatione prebende ecclesie Beati Johannis Beverlacensis Eboracensis diocesis.

### Eboracensis

Item Ricardo Orgam, clerico Londoniensis diocesis, de canonicatu sub exspectatione prebende ecclesie collegiate de Hewendon' (Howden) Eboracensis diocesis.

---

[95] The date, 20 October 1371, is bracketed against this item and the next six.

## Eboracensis

Item Willelmo Orgam, clerico Londoniensis diocesis, de canonicatu sub exspectatione prebende collegiate de Rippon, Eboracensis diocesis.

## Lichfeldensis

Item Thome Danne, clerico Lichfeldensis diocesis, de canonicatu sub exspectatione prebende ecclesie collegiate Sancti Johannis Cestr' dicte Lichfeldensis diocesis.

## Lincolniensis

Item Hugoni de Edenham, presbytero Lincolniensis diocesis, de beneficio ecclesiastico et cetera ad collationem et cetera abbatis et conventus monasterii de Croyland' (Crowland) ordinis Sancti Benedicti dicte diocesis.

## Dunolmensis

Mandatur provideri Petro de Eland, clerico Dunolmensis diocesis de beneficio ecclesiastico et cetera ad collationem et cetera prioris et conventus ecclesie Dunolmensis ordinis Sancti Benedicti.
Restant vii expectationes vii.

## (fol. 89ᵛ) Sarisbiriensis

Ex causa permutationis fuit provisum Willelmo Cherbeton' [96] de perpetua vicaria parochialis ecclesie de Northenhamne [97] (Netheravon) Sarisbiriensis diocesis et Thome Edwardi de parochiali ecclesia de Williford' (Wilsford) dicte diocesis, xiii kalendas Novembris. [98] Solverunt quilibet ipsorum equaliter quinquaginta s. pro medietate veri valoris, salvo iure pluris super maiori valentia, in summa v li. [99]

## Londoniensis

Mandatur provideri Johanni Barnet presbytero de canonicatu sub exspectatione prebende ecclesie Londoniensis, iii kalendas Novembris. [100]

## Sarisbiriensis

Item Willelmo Silvestri de canonicatu sub exspectatione prebende ecclesie collegiate monialium de Wilton' ordinis Sancti Benedicti.

## Exoniensis

Item Roberto Brok' de canonicatu sub exspectatione prebende ecclesie Exoniensis.

## Exoniensis

Item Willelmo Smith' presbytero de beneficio ecclesiastico ad collationem episcopi Exoniensis.

## Sarisbiriensis

Item Rogero Dawe, clerico Exoniensis diocesis, de beneficio ecclesiastico ad collationem decani et capituli singulorum quam canonicorum ecclesie Sarisbiriensis.

## Herefordensis

Item Johanni Prophete Herefordensis diocesis de canonicatu sub exspectatione prebende ecclesie Herefordensis.
Recepta pagine v li.; restant exspectationes vi, vi.

## (fol. 90, lxxxviii) Lichfeldensis

Mandatur provideri Rogero Daneport, presbytero Lichfeldensis diocesis, de beneficio ecclesiastico ad collationem abbatis et conventus Cestr' ordinis Sancti Benedicti Lichfeldensis diocesis, iii kalendas Novembris. [101]

## Lincolniensis

Item Thome Danecotes de canonicatu sub exspectatione ecclesie Lincolniensis.

## Sarisbiriensis

Item Edmundo de Senclow de canonicatu sub exspectatione prebende ecclesie Sarisbiriensis.

## Sarisbiriensis

Item Roberti Nube de canonicatu sub exspectatione prebende ecclesie Sarisbiriensis.

## Cicestrensis

Item Johanni Baker de canonicatu sub exspectatione prebende ecclesie Cicestrensis.

## Exoniensis

Item Radulpho Trigusion, presbytero Exoniensis diocesis, de canonicatu sub exspectatione prebende, dignitatis ecclesie Exoniensis, pridie nonas Novembris. [102]

## Londoniensis

Item Roberto Wygele Lichfeldensis diocesis de canonicatu sub exspectatione prebende ecclesie Londoniensis.

## Cicestrensis

Item Michaeli de Causton', presbytero Norwicensis diocesis, de canonicatu sub exspectatione prebende, dignitatis et cetera ecclesie Cicestrensis, nonas Novembris. [103]
Restant viii expectationes viii que nondum habuerunt effectum.

---

[96] *Cherlton'*, Collectorie 13, fol. 174.
[97] *Netherhavene, ibid.*, fol. 174.
[98] 20 October 1371. In the margin: *provisio de vacanti.*
[99] In the margin: *solvit.*
[100] The date, 30 October 1371, is bracketed against this item and the next five.

[101] The date, 30 October 1371, is bracketed against this item and the next four.
[102] The date, 4 November 1371, is bracketed against this item and the next.
[103] 5 November 1371.

### (fol. 90ᵛ) Eliensis

Item Waltero de Aldeby, presbytero Norwicensis diocesis, de beneficio ecclesiastico et cetera ad collationem episcopi Eliensis, nonas Novembris.[104]

### Eliensis

Item Johanni Newport, clerico Leodiensis (Liège) diocesis, de beneficio ecclesiastico ad collationem episcopi Eliensis.

### Londoniensis

Mandatur provideri Johanni de Domrewich', presbytero Norwicensis diocesis, de canonicatu sub exspectatione prebende, dignitatis et cetera ecclesie Londoniensis, v kalendas Februarii.[105]

### Menevensis

Item Radulpho de Langele, presbytero Norwicensis diocesis, de canonicatu sub exspectatione prebende ecclesie Menevensis de dignitate eiusdem ecclesie.

### Eboracensis

Item Thome de Sutton,' presbytero Lincolniensis diocesis, de canonicatu sub exspectatione prebende ecclesie collegiate de Southwell' Eboracensis diocesis.

### Eboracensis

Item Willelmo de Gotham, presbytero Eboracensis diocesis, de canonicatu sub exspectatione prebende, dignitatis et cetera ecclesie Eboracensis.

### Sarisbiriensis

Item Ade de Lakynghith', presbytero Norwicensis diocesis, de canonicatu sub exspectatione prebende, dignitatis et cetera ecclesie Sarisbiriensis.
Restant vii expectationes vii.

### (fol. 91, lxxxix) Lincolniensis

Item Johanni de Merton', presbytero Norwicensis diocesis, de canonicatu sub exspectatione prebende ecclesie Lincolniensis, v kalendas Februarii.[106]

### Sarisbiriensis

Item Johanni de Wormenhale, presbytero Lincolniensis diocesis, de canonicatu sub exspectatione prebende ecclesie conventualis de Chastebury (Shaftesbury) Sarisbiriensis diocesis.

### Lincolniensis

Item Thome de Bakton', subdiacono Norwicensis

diocesis, de canonicatu sub exspectatione prebende, dignitatis, et cetera ecclesie Lincolniensis.

### Lincolniensis

Mandatur provideri Rogero de Sutton', presbytero Lincolniensis diocesis, de canonicatu sub exspectatione prebende ecclesie Lincolniensis.

### Norwicensis

Item Thome de Hornyngeserth', presbytero Norwicensis diocesis, de beneficio ecclesiastico et cetera ad collationem abbatis et conventus monasterii Sancti Edmundi de Bury Norwicensis diocesis.

### Eboracensis

Item Willelmo de Flaynburgh', clerico Eboracensis diocesis, de beneficio ecclesiastico et cetera ad collationem abbatis et conventus monasterii Sancte Marie Eboracensis.

### Cicestrensis

Item Wincomer, presbytero Norwicensis diocesis, de canonicatu sub exspectatione prebende ecclesie Cicestrensis.
Restant vii expectationes que nondum habuerunt effectum, vii.

### (fol. 91ᵛ) Sarisbiriensis

Item Thome de Wormenhale, presbytero Lincolniensis diocesis, de canonicatu sub exspectatione prebende ecclesie Sarisbiriensis, v kalendas Februarii.[106]

### Eboracensis

Item Johanni de Ufford', presbytero Norwicensis diocesis, de canonicatu sub exspectatione prebende ecclesie Eboracensis.

### Eliensis

Item Johanni Kyme Norwicensis diocesis de beneficio et cetera ad collationem episcopi Eliensis.

### Lincolniensis

Item Johanni de Burgh', presbytero Lincolniensis diocesis, de beneficio ecclesiastico ad collationem et cetera abbatis et conventus de Burgo dicte diocesis.

### Lincolniensis

Mandatur provideri Thome de Novo Mercato, clerico Norwicensis diocesis, de beneficio ecclesiastico ad collationem et cetera abbatis et conventus monasterii de Croylond' Lincolniensis diocesis.

### Eboracensis

Item Willelmo Cheophill', presbytero [107] Eboracensis diocesis, de beneficio ecclesiastico ad collationem archiepiscopi Eboracensis.

---

[104] The date, 5 November 1371, is bracketed against this item and the next.

[105] The date, 28 January 1371, is bracketed against this item and the next four.

[106] The date, 28 January 1371, is bracketed against this item and the next six.

[107] *presbytero* repeated MS.

Cantuariensis

Item Roberto de Multon', presbytero Lincolniensis diocesis, de beneficio ecclesiastico ad collationem prioris et capituli ecclesie Cantuariensis.

Restant vii expectationes vii.

(fol. 92, xc) Wyntoniensis

Item Willelmo Well', presbytero Wyntoniensis diocesis, de beneficio ecclesiastico ad collationem et cetera prioris et capituli ecclesie Wyntoniensis, v kalendas Februarii.[106]

Norwicensis

Item Rogero de Pilbergch', presbytero Norwicensis diocesis, de beneficio ecclesiastico et cetera abbatis et conventus Sancti Edmundi de Bury dicte diocesis.

Londoniensis

Item Johanni de Appelby, presbytero Lincolniensis diocesis, de beneficio ecclesiastico ad collationem prioris et fratrum hospitalis Sancti Johannis Jerosolomitani in Anglia.

Cicestrensis

Item Johanni Botoner, clerico Londoniensis diocesis, de canonicatu sub exspectatione prebende ecclesie collegiate de Southmalling' Cicestrensis diocesis.

Lincolniensis

Mandatur provideri Willelmo de Irby, presbytero Lincolniensis diocesis, de beneficio ecclesiastico ad collationem prioris et conventus de Kime (Kyme) dicte diocesis.

Non dicitur diocesis

Item Roberto de Tunsted, presbytero Norwicensis diocesis, de beneficio ecclesiastico et cetera ad collationem.

Eliensis

Item Willelmo de Wramby, presbytero Lincolniensis diocesis, de beneficio ecclesiastico ad collationem episcopi Eliensis.

Restant vii expectationes vii.

(fol. 92ᵛ) Sarisbiriensis

Item Matheo de Botokesham, Eliensis diocesis presbytero, de canonicatu sub exspectatione prebende ecclesie Sarisbiriensis, v kalendas Februarii.[106]

Lincolniensis

Item Ricardo de Pulham, clerico Norwicensis diocesis, de beneficio ecclesiastico et cetera ad collationem abbatis et conventus monasterii de Ramesey Lincolniensis diocesis.

Lincolniensis

Item Rogero de Sutton', presbytero Lincolniensis

diocesis, de canonicatu sub exspectatione prebende Lincolniensis.

Dunolmensis

Item Nicholao Denys de Torgamby, presbytero Lincolniensis diocesis, de beneficio ecclesiastico ad collationem prioris et capituli singularum quam personarum ecclesie Dunolmensis.

Cicestrensis

Mandatur provideri Johanni Attestrete, presbytero Cantuariensis diocesis, de canonicatu sub exspectatione prebende ecclesie collegiate de Southmalling' Cicestrensis diocesis.

Norwicensis

Item Johanni de Cambeton', presbytero Norwicensis diocesis, de beneficio ecclesiastico et cetera ad collationem prioris et conventus monasterii Sancti Benedicti de Hulmo diocesis Norwicensis.

Norwicensis

Item Thome de Elk, presbytero Eliensis diocesis, de oeneficio ecclesiastico ad collationem prioris et conventus prioratus de Castelacr' Norwicensis diocesis.

Restant vii expectationes vii.

(fol. 93, xci) Londoniensis

Item Radulpho de Hychim, presbytero Lincolniensis diocesis, de beneficio ecclesiastico et cetera ad collationem prioris et conventus Westmonasterii Londoniensis diocesis, v kalendas Februarii.[106]

Norwicensis

Item Johanni Tinney, presbytero Londoniensis diocesis, de beneficio ecclesiastico et cetera prioris et capituli ecclesie Norwicensis.

Eboracensis

Item Michaeli de Causton', clerico Norwicensis diocesis, de canonicatu sub exspectatione prebende ecclesie collegiate de Hoveden' Eboracensis diocesis.

Norwicensis

Item Waldewino de Hadele, clerico Norwicensis diocesis, de beneficio ecclesiastico ad collationem abbatis et conventus monasterii Sancti Edmundi de Bury dicte diocesis.

Eboracensis

Mandatur provideri Johanni Barnet, presbytero Norwicensis diocesis, de canonicatu sub exspectatione prebende ⟨ecclesie⟩ collegiate Southwell' Eboracensis diocesis.

Norwicensis

Item Willelmo de Aketon', clerico Norwicensis diocesis, de beneficio ecclesiastico ad collationem prioris et conventus de Stok' (Stoke by Clare) Norwicensis diocesis.

### Eboracensis

Item Johanni de Pulham, presbytero Eliensis diocesis, de beneficio ecclesiastico et cetera ad collationem abbatis et conventus monasterii Beate Marie extra muros Eboracensis.

Restant vii expectationes vii.

### (fol. 93ᵛ) Norwicensis

Item Henrico de Couston', clerico Norwicensis diocesis, de beneficio ecclesiastico et cetera ad collationem et cetera episcopi Norwicensis, v kalendas Februarii.[106]

### Londoniensis

Item Willelmo de Pyeshale, clerico Norwicensis diocesis, de beneficio ecclesiastico ad collationem et cetera decani et capituli singulorum quam canonicorum ecclesie Londoniensis.

### Lincolniensis

Item Alano de Tilney Norwicensis diocesis de beneficio ecclesiastico et cetera ad collationem prioris et conventus de Spalding' Lincolniensis diocesis.

### Wygorniensis

Item Waltero de Toling', presbytero Norwicensis diocesis, de beneficio ecclesiastico et cetera ad collationem episcopi Wygorniensis.

### Eliensis

Mandatur provideri Johanni de Wodenhill', presbytero Lincolniensis diocesis, de beneficio ecclesiastico ad collationem et cetera episcopi Eliensis.

### Lincolniensis

Item Waltero de Felstede, presbytero Londoniensis diocesis, de beneficio ecclesiastico et cetera ad collationem abbatis et conventus monasterii de Ramesey Lincolniensis diocesis.

### Eboracensis

Item Ricardo de Ros, clerico Eboracensis diocesis, de canonicatu sub exspectatione prebende ecclesie Eboracensis.

Restant vii expectationes vii.

### (fol. 94, xcii) Lincolniensis

Item Petro de Gildesburgh', clerico Lincolniensis diocesis, de canonicatu sub exspectatione prebende ecclesie Lincolniensis, Vellensis.[108]

---

[108] *Vellensis* is bracketed against this item and the next six. Presumably it is an error for *v kalendas Februarii.*

### Lichfeldensis

Item Johanni Lingedon', presbytero Conventrensis et Lichfeldensis diocesis, de canonicatu sub exspectatione prebende ecclesie Lichfeldensis.

### Lincolniensis

Item Simoni de Multon', clerico Lincolniensis diocesis, de beneficio ecclesiastico et cetera ad collationem decani et capituli singulorum quam canonicorum ecclesie Lincolniensis.

### Eboracensis

Item Ricardo de Scrop, clerico Eboracensis diocesis, de canonicatu sub exspectatione prebende ecclesie Eboracensis.

### Eboracensis

Mandatur provideri Thome de Eltesse Juniori, presbytero Lincolniensis ⟨diocesis⟩, de canonicatu sub exspectatione prebende ecclesie collegiate Beverlacensis Eboracensis diocesis.

### Lincolniensis

Item Willelmo Rossel de Luda, presbytero Lincolniensis diocesis, de canonicatu sub exspectatione prebende ecclesie Lincolniensis.

### Vellensis

Item Johanni de Wysebech', presbytero Eliensis diocesis, de canonicatu sub exspectatione prebende ecclesie Wellensis.

Restant vii expectationes vii.

### (fol. 94ᵛ) Eboracensis

Item Johanni de Stelburg, presbytero Londoniensis diocesis, de canonicatu sub exspectatione prebende ecclesie collegiate de Southwell' Eboracensis diocesis, v kalendas Februarii.[106]

### Roffensis

Item Thome Eyne de Clive, presbytero Roffensis diocesis, de beneficio ecclesiastico ad collationem et cetera episcopi, prioris et capituli ecclesie Roffensis.

### Eliensis

Item Johanni de Pecton', presbytero Lincolniensis diocesis, de beneficio ecclesiastico et cetera ad collationem episcopi Eliensis.

### Lichfeldensis

Item Willelmo Gronne de Hengham, presbytero Norwicensis diocesis, de canonicatu sub exspectatione prebende ecclesie Lichfeldensis.

### Lichfeldensis

Item Johanni de Redham, presbytero Norwicensis

diocesis, de canonicatu sub exspectatione prebende ecclesie Lichfeldensis.

### Eliensis

Mandatur provideri Willelmo de Torp' in Gleb', presbytero Eboracensis diocesis, de beneficio ecclesiastico ad collationem episcopi Eliensis.

### Wygorniensis

Item Waltero de Eston', presbytero Norwicensis diocesis, de beneficio ecclesiastico et cetera ad collationem et cetera episcopi Wygorniensis.

Restant vii expectationes vii.

### (fol. 95, xciii) Lichfeldensis

Item Ade de Mottrum, presbytero Conventrensis et Lichfeldensis diocesis, de beneficio ecclesiastico ad collationem abbatis et conventus monasterii Sancte Werburge dicte diocesis, v kalendas Februarii.[106]

### Londoniensis

Item Thome de Aston', presbytero Conventrensis et Lichfeldensis diocesis, de canonicatu sub exspectatione prebende ecclesie Londoniensis.

### Eboracensis

Item Stephano de Houghton', presbytero Norwicensis diocesis, de beneficio ecclesiastico ad collationem episcopi Eboracensis.

### Eboracensis

Item Johanni Clerenaux, presbytero Eboracensis diocesis, de canonicatu sub exspectatione prebende ecclesie collegiate de Hovedon' dicte Eboracensis diocesis.

### Londoniensis

Item Thome de Westlee, presbytero Norwicensis diocesis, de canonicatu sub exspectatione prebende ecclesie Londoniensis.

### Wygorniensis

Mandatur provideri Edmundo de Caldecote, presbytero Lincolniensis diocesis, de canonicatu sub exspectatione prebende ecclesie collegiate de Westbury Wygorniensis.

### Dunolmensis

Item Willelmo Coliule, presbytero Eboracensis diocesis, de beneficio ecclesiastico ad collationem episcopi, prioris et capituli ecclesie Dunolmensis.

Restant vii expectationes vii.

### (fol. 95ᵛ) Dunolmensis

Item Roberto de Turkilby, presbytero Eboracensis diocesis, de beneficio ecclesiastico ad collationem epis-

copi, prioris et capituli ecclesie Dunolmensis, v kalendas Februarii.[106]

### Eboracensis

Item Johanni Tevorham, clerico Eliensis diocesis, de beneficio ecclesiastico ad collationem et cetera archiepiscopi et capituli ecclesie Eboracensis.

### Londoniensis

Item Thome de Eltessle seniori, presbytero diocesis Lincolniensis, de canonicatu sub exspectatione prebende ecclesie Londoniensis.

### Londoniensis

Item Willelmo [109] de Codenham, presbytero Norwicensis diocesis, de canonicatu sub exspectatione prebende ecclesie Londoniensis.

### Eboracensis

Item Thome de Langeton', presbytero Lincolniensis diocesis, de canonicatu sub exspectatione prebende ecclesie collegiate Suthwell' Eboracensis diocesis.

### Wyntoniensis

Item Roberto Yne, presbytero Londoniensis diocesis, de beneficio ecclesiastico et cetera ad collationem episcopi Wyntoniensis.

### Cicestrensis

Mandatur provideri de Eltessle, presbytero Lincolniensis diocesis, de canonicatu sub exspectatione prebende ecclesie Cicestrensis.

Restant vii expectationes vii.

### (foi. 96, xciiii) Cicestrensis

Item Johanni de Sumerton', clerico Norwicensis diocesis, de canonicatu sub exspectatione prebende ecclesie Cicestrensis, v kalendas Februarii.[106]

### Eboracensis

Item Johanni de Rudby, clerico Eboracensis diocesis, de canonicatu sub exspectatione prebende ecclesie collegiate Rippon' Eboracensis diocesis.

### Londoniensis

Item Thome de Gloucestr', clerico Lincolniensis diocesis, de beneficio ecclesiastico ad collationem et cetera prioris et fratrum hospitali Sancti Johannis Jerosolomitani in Anglia.

### Lincolniensis

Item Radulpho Gerners, clerico Wyntoniensis diocesis, de beneficio ecclesiastico ad collationem et cetera abbatis et conventus de Burgo Sancti Petri Lincolniensis diocesis.

---

[109] Over *Johanni* deleted by a line.

### Herefordensis

Item Johanni de Brandenfery Norwicensis diocesis de canonicatu sub exspectatione prebende ecclesie Herefordensis.

### Cicestrensis

Item Ricardo Drax, clerico Eliensis diocesis, de canonicatu sub exspectatione prebende ecclesie Cicestrenis.

### Lincolniensis

Item Roberto de Westron', clerico Norwicensis diocesis, ad collationem abbatis et conventus monasterii de Burgo Sancti Petri Lincolniensis diocesis.
Restant vii expectationes vii.

### (fol. 96ᵛ) Eboracensis

Mandatur provideri Simoni de Neylond', presbytero Norwicensis diocesis, de canonicatu sub exspectatione prebende ecclesie collegiate Southwell' Eboracensis, v kalendas Februarii.[106]

### Eboracensis

Item Thome de Wyton', clerico Dunolmensis diocesis, de canonicatu sub exspectatione prebende ecclesie collegiate Rippon' Eboracensis diocesis.

### Wyntoniensis

Item Johanni de Felbrugg', clerico Norwicensis diocesis, de canonicatu sub exspectatione ⟨prebende⟩ ecclesie conventualis monialium de Warwell' (Wherwell)[110] diocesis Wyntoniensis.

### Sarisbiriensis

Item Thome de Grey, clerico Norwicensis diocesis, de canonicatu sub exspectatione prebende ecclesie Sarisbiriensis.

### Sarisbiriensis

Item Henrico Gowet, clerico Karleolensis diocesis, de canonicatu sub exspectatione prebende ecclesie conventualis monialium de Wilton' Sarisbiriensis diocesis.

### Cantuariensis

Item Johanni de Broun de Hadelegh, clerico Norwicensis diocesis, de beneficio ecclesiastico ad collationem archiepiscopi Cantuariensis.

### Norwicensis

Item Thome de Hetershet, clerico Norwicensis diocesis, de beneficio ecclesiastico et cetera ad collationem abbatis et conventus monasterii de Welling' (Wendling) dicte diocesis.
Restant vii expectationes vii.

---

[110] Followed by *Wygorniensis* undeleted.

### (fol. 97, xcv) Wellensis

Mandatur provideri Henrico de Brandon', clerico Norwicensis diocesis, de canonicatu sub exspectatione prebende ecclesie Wellensis, v kalendas Februarii.[111]

### Lincolniensis

Item Simoni Sall', clerico Norwicensis diocesis, de beneficio ecclesiastico ad collationem abbatis et conventus monasterii de Croyland Lincolniensis diocesis.

### Eboracensis

Item Hugoni de Lymbergh' Lincolniensis diocesis de beneficio ecclesiastico ad collationem archiepiscopi Eboracensis.

### Cantuariensis

Item Thome de Feckwell', clerico Norwicensis diocesis, de beneficio ecclesiastico ad collationem archiepiscopi, prioris et capituli ecclesie Cantuariensis.

### Londoniensis

Item Roberto Ravendale, clerico Lincolniensis diocesis, de beneficio ecclesiastico ad collationem prioris et fratrum hospitalis Sancti Johannis Jerosolomitani in Anglia.

### Dunolmensis

Item Radulpho Stel, clerico Eboracensis diocesis, de beneficio ecclesiastico ad collationem prioris et capituli ecclesie Dunolmensis.

### Londoniensis

Item Radulpho Cok', clerico Lincolniensis diocesis, de beneficio ecclesiastico et cetera ad collationem prioris et fratrum Sancti Johannis Jerosolomitani in Anglia.

### Eliensis

Item Edmundo de Keylham, clerico Eliensis diocesis, ad collationem episcopi, prioris et capituli ecclesie Eliensis.
Restant viii expectationes viii.

(fol. 97ᵛ) Hic finis secundi caterni michi, Arnaldo Garnerii, missi in Anglia; quere tertium quaternum infra folio xcix.
Summa recepte secundi quaterni iiiᶜ vi li. iiii s. i d.[112]
Summa reste secundi quaterni in pecunia de beneficiis iam taxatis clii li.
Summa reste fructuum viginti unius provisionum in toto vel parte de beneficiis nondum taxatis xxi.
Et restant xiiii provisiones inutiles xiiii.
Et restant expectationes que nondum habuerunt effectum iiiiᶜ lxiiii.[113]

---

[111] The date, 28 January 1371, is bracketed against this item and the next seven.
[112] In the margin: *vera*.
[113] In the margin: *Amice Carissime. Mittimus vobis beneficia*

(fol. 98$^v$)[114] Quere signum [115] infra folio xcix ad finem de exploratis, et ibi continua et adde que sequitur in summis exploratorum.

Summa totius recepte de exploratis infra folio xcix et sequenti ad finem est infra ad signum,[115] ideo non est hic, sed [116] alie que secuntur.

Summa reste pecunie de exploratis predictis ccvii li. xi s.

Summa reste primorum fructuum beneficiorum nondum taxatorum xxix.[117]

Et est una inutilis provisio in explorata predicta i$^a$.

(fol. 99, xcvii) Explorata tempore mei, Arnaldi Garnerii.[118]

### Eboracensis

Collatio et provisio facte auctoritate apostolica Johanni de Hayton', presbytero Wyntoniensis diocesis, de perpetua vicaria parochialis ecclesie de Elmerton' (Northallerton) Eboracensis diocesis fuerunt sibi confirmate seu provisum de novo per Gregorium penultima die Decembris anno primo [119] ex relatione dicti Johannis de Hayton' facta die xxvii Novembris anno domini et cetera LXXII$^{do}$ pro taxa xx li. Die xxix mensis Novembris anno domini et cetera LXXII$^{do}$ iuravit dictus Johannes ad sancta dei ewangelia solvere dictam taxam xx li. in festo Sancti Petri ad vincula proximo x li. et in eodem festo anno extunc revoluto alias x li. pro resta, et sine ulteriori dilatione, et ad hoc obligavit se et dictam vicariam et omnia bona sua et beneficia camere apostolice, et fuit monitus per dominum sub pena excommunicationis de consensu suo et cetera. Solvit die xix Julii anno LXIII in xiiii m. novem li. sex s. viii d.[120]

### Exoniensis

Item dominus episcopus quondam, videlicet Dominus Johannes de Grandissono, legavit ecclesie Romane in testamento suo unam cappam de velveto nigro broudatam et paratam aurifrigiis [121] nobilibus ac etiam aurifrisia ampla et magna pro alia capa bene pulchra et bona ac unum librum sermonum optimum Beati Bernardi, que omnia tradidit Londonie Magister Nicholaus

Braybrok', executor dicti testamenti, canonicus que ecclesie Exoniensis, dominis vicecomiti Turensi, domini nostri pape germano, et episcopo Carpentoratensi (Carpentras) portandum et reddendum domino nostro predicto Gregorio XI, Londonie una die de mense Julii anno domini et cetera LXXII$^{do}$.[122]

### Exoniensis

Dominus episcopus qui nunc est Exoniensis misit camere per Albertos pecuniam pro servitia debita ultima die Aprilis anno LXXIII ultra duo milia v$^c$ fl.[123] in duabus vicibus.[122]

### Lichfeldensis

Provisum fuit Willelmo de Hexham [124] de ecclesia de Eccleston' Lichfeldensis diocesis per Gregorium v idus Martii anno primo,[125] qui composuit cum camera pro fructibus ante provisionem seu confirmationem receptis pro viginti marcis, pro quibus solvit xiii li. vi s. viii d. die nona Aprilis anno domini et cetera LXXII$^{do}$ et cetera, xiii li. vi s. viii d. Solvit die ix Aprilis ut supra anno LXXIII dictam summam.[126] Et debet pro taxa ratione dicte provisionis duodecim li. quas solvit die v Aprilis anno LXXIII, xii li.[126]

Recepta pagine xxxiiii li. xiii s. iiii d.;[127] restant in pecunia x li. xiii s. iiii d.

### (fol. 99$^v$) Lichfeldensis

Significatum et denuntiatum fuit domino collectori apostolico in Anglia per Leonem de Perton' diocesis [128] quod Dominus Willelmus de Kirkeby, rector ecclesie de Worwelld' (Wirswall?) Lichfeldensis diocesis quondam legavit in testamento suo, motus conscientia et in emendam domino nostro pape seu Romane ecclesie, quadringentas libras sterlingorum, et fecit executores suos Dominos Simonem de Malestang', rectorem ecclesie de Tueffeld' (Enville) dicte Lichfeldensis diocesis, et Thomam Newbury, prebendarium capelle regis de Totenhale (Tettenhall) eiusdem diocesis Lichfeldensis.[129]

Et dicti executores, facta dicta denuntiatione, fuerunt citati et moniti, qui comparentes se defenderunt et litigaverunt in camera coram dicto domino collectore, et processus est usque ad nunc habitus in archivis.

Et die ix Februarii anno et cetera LXXII, quia exhibito per eos dicto testamento in prima figura et dimissa copia, et recepto eorum iuramento non reperitur adhuc aliquid relinquerit, et ideo dormit propter defectum probationum.

---

*collata et exspectationes concessas per dominum nostrum papam in collectoria Anglie pontificatus sui anno primo, super quibus diligentiam apponatis statum patrie et negotiorum camere, dum commode poteritis, significans bene, et diu valeatis. Scriptum Avinionia die secunda Julii anno LXX$^{mo}$ secundo.*

[114] Folio 98 recto is blank.

[115] The sign given in the margin is ✝∞✝ : see below, n. 181.

[116] *se*, MS.

[117] In the margin: *infra est allocatum ad signum.*

[118] The caption in the Brevetus is *Sequitur recepta de exploratus legatis et aliis de quibus per cameram nondum fuerat scriptum nec in restis aliquid dimissum*: Collectorie 13, fol. 175$^v$.

[119] 30 December 1371.

[120] Sum repeated MS. In the margin: *solvit.*

[121] Followed by *nigris* deleted by a line.

[122] In the margin: *pro memoriali.*

[123] *ix* is written over *flor.* in MS.

[124] *Lexham*, Collectorie 13, fol. 175$^v$.

[125] 11 March 1371.

[126] In the margin: *solvit.*

[127] In the margin: *vera.*

[128] The name of the diocesis is not given

[129] In the margin, bracketed against this and the next three paragraphs: *nichil de hoc in effectu ad huc.*

Dicitur quod fuit facta dicta denuntiatio ex malitia denuntiatorum ex tunc non comparentium.

Recepta pagine nichil et resta.

(fol. 100, xcviii) Item pro legato seu relicto elimosine domini nostri pape per Dominum Robertum de Scalis militem, solvit die nona Februarii anno et cetera LXXII<sup>do</sup> Dominus Johannes Marler, executor dicti militis, in quadraginta marchis viginti sex li. xiii s. iiii d.[130]

Item recepti pro ecclesia que vocatur Welumk' (Welwick) appropriata prepositure Sancti Johannis Beverlacensis Eboracensis diocesis de explorata post restitutionem restarum xxvi li. xiii s. iiii d.[130]

### Lincolniensis

Willelmus Coleman' diocesis Lincolniensis in redemptione Terre Sancte solvit die iiii<sup>ta</sup> Maii anno et cetera LXXIII<sup>tio</sup> pro excusatione voti Romani et expensarum in eundo faciendo de consilio penitentiarii cardinalis quatuor m. que valent liii s. iiii d.[126]

Et sunt alia explorata supra folio x de viii li. iiii s. et d. de hospitali de Cretham (Gretham), de quibus ibi computatur in recepta, et supra folio xviii in fine sunt liii s. de quibus etiam ibi computatur, ideo nichil hic nisi pro memoriali de dicta summa, videlicet.[131]

Recepta pagine liii li.[127] et resta nichil.

### (fol. 100ᵛ) Cantuariensis

Dominus Johannes de Stenes optinet prebendam de Poding' (Pedding) in ecclesia collegiata de Wyngham (Wingham) Cantuariensis diocesis. Est sequestratus et excommunicatus.

### Cantuariensis

Magister Ricardus de Wexbrigg' optinet vicariam de Faversham Cantuariensis diocesis causa permutationis facte coram cardinali Cantuariensi pro taxa xx li.[132] Est sequestratus in iii° mandato et excommunicatus. Solvit die ix Aprilis anno LXXIIII in partem fructuum quinque li.[130] Est in breveto folio xviii.

### Cantuariensis

Dominus Johannes de Langham optinet ecclesiam Beate Marie Magdalene Cantuarie ex causa permutationis facte coram cardinali Cantuariensi pro taxa viii m.[132] Solvit in duabus vicibus quinquaginta tres s. iiii<sup>or</sup> d.[130]

### Cantuariensis

Dominus Ricardus Michiel optinet vicariam de Bacild' (Bapchild) Cantuariensis diocesis ex causa permuta-

tionis coram dicto domino cardinali pro taxa vi li. xiii s. iiii d.[132] Est obligatus et habet terminos et condempnatus.

### Cantuariensis

De vicaria de Eleham (Elham) ratione collationis facte per cardinalem Cantuariensem Johanni Foliot ex causa permutationis cum vicaria de Ramesey[133] (Romsey) Wyntoniensis diocesis fructus. Solvit in duabus vicibus pro vicaria de Ramsey pro medietate veri valoris sex li.[130] Item solvit plus in plenam solutionem medietatis veri valoris die vii Aprilis anno LXXIIII triginta s.[130]

### Roffensis

Ex causa permutationis fuit provisum Johanni Osbarn de ecclesia Sancte Margarete extra Roffam facte cum ecclesia supradicta Sancte Marie Magdalene Cantuarie per cardinalem Cantuariensem, non taxata. Solvit in duabus vicibus pro medietate veri valoris sexaginta quatuor s. pro medietate veri valoris.[130]

### Londoniensis

De ecclesia de Abchirch' Londonie (St. Mary Abchurch) ex causa permutationis coram domino cardinali pro taxa iiii<sup>or</sup> m.[132] Monitus est et excommunicatus, et valet plus, et petitur residuum taxe. Et valet bene xx m., quarum debet x m., de quibus solvit ix die Februarii et xi die Aprilis anno LXXIIII<sup>to</sup> in illis duabus vicibus in sex m. iiii<sup>or</sup> li.[126]

Recepta pagine xxii li. vii s. iiii d.;[127] resta pecunie xxiiii li. vi s. viii d.; et ultra restant fructus de tribus provisionibus iii.

### (fol. 101, xcix) Londoniensis

De prebenda de Rogemere (Rugmere, St. Pancras) in ecclesia Londoniensi ratione provisionis facte Johanni Wyliot fructus.[134] Est in mandato.

### Wyntoniensis

Pro ecclesia de Auton'[135] (Houghton Drayton) Wyntoniensis diocesis debentur fructus,[136] ratione provisionis facte de eadem per exspectationem Johannis Godmerston.[137] Solvit die vi Desembris anno LXXIII decem li. in partem fructuum x li.[138]

### Sarisbiriensis

Dominus Bertrandus Convenarum (Comminges)[139] est expeditus ad prebendam de Remysbury (Ramsbury)

---

[130] Sum repeated MS. In the margin: *solvit*.
[131] The sum has been rubbed. Apparently it is *ix li. xvii s. iii d.* In the margin: *pro memoriali hic summe exporatorum*.
[132] In the margin: *debet*.
[133] In the margin: *debet de ista*.
[134] In the margin: *debitantes; debet*.
[135] *Hoghton'*, Collectorie 13, fol. 176.
[136] In the margin: *debitantes*.
[137] The explanation is given in the Brevetus: Collectorie 13, fol. 176.
[138] In the margin: *solvit*.
[139] Bertrand, priest of S. Marcello.

in ecclesia Sarisbiriensi pretextu sue exspectationis debet taxam.[140] Litigatur.

### Exoniensis

Item dictus Dominus Bertrandus [139] est expeditus pretextu sue exspectationis supradicte ad unam prebendam Exoniensem fructus.[141] Nichil recepit morte preventus, ut dicitur, sed videbitur.

### Norwicensis

De vicaria de Honyng' (Honing), non taxata, fuit provisum per cardinalem Cantuariensem Ricardo Greyne, fructus. Solvit in duabus vicibus pro medietate veri valoris sexaginta quatuor s. et vi d.[142]

### Norwicensis

De ecclesia de Therne (Thurne) ratione provisionis facte Henrico de Myldehale per dominum cardinalem Cantuariensem fructus. Solvit die secunda Junii anno LXXIII viginti s.[130]

### Eliensis

De vicaria de Harleston' (Harston) fuit provisum per dominum cardinalem Cantuariensem Domino Guillelmo Tele, presbytero Eliensis diocesis, fructus. Solvit in partem fructuum die ix Maii viginti sex s. viii d.[130] Item solvit die xvii Aprilis anno LXXIIII[to] in partem fructuum xl s.[143] Item solvit xv die Julii in plenam solutionem taxe xx s.[143]

Recepta pagine xviii li. xi s. ii d.;[144] debentur in toto seu parte fructus de tribus provisionibus iii.

### (fol. 101[v]) Lincolniensis

De vicaria de Henyngford' Grey (Hemingford Grey) Lincolniensis diocesis ratione provisionis facte Johanni Templere per dominum cardinalem Cantuariensem fructus. Solvit die xii Maii anno LXIII pro medietate veri valoris quadraginta s.[130]

### Lincolniensis

De ecclesia de Sutton' in marisco (Sutton le Marsh) acceptata per Guillelmum Brien pro taxa xviii li., ut dicitur, fructus. Cadit in forma pauperum, ut asserit, et sic inutilis.[145]

### Exoniensis

De ecclesia de Sele monachorum (Zeal Monachorum)

Exoniensis diocesis collata per dominum cardinalem pro taxa iiii[or] li. vi s. viii d. Solvit dictam taxam.[143]

### Exoniensis

De ecclesia de Thorneburgh' (Thornbury) diocesis Exoniensis ex collatione domini cardinalis debentur medietatem fructuum, cum non taxatur. Solvit pro medietate veri valoris quinquaginta s. die prima Octobris 1 s.[143]

### Dunolmensis

Solvit rector Werkworth' (Warkworth) seu vicarius Dunolmensis diocesis pro quibusdam sibi in curia impositis quindecim li.[143] Et plus die viii Maii anno LXXIIII[to] solvit ex eadem causa viginti duas li. sterlingorum.[146]

### Norwicensis

Collata fuit ecclesia de Palling', non taxata, per cardinalem Cantuariensem Domino Roberto de Homerford', non taxata. Solvit die xxv Octobris anno LXXIII in v m. iii li. vi s. viii d.[143]

### Cicestrensis

Ex causa permutationis facte per cardinalem Petragoricensem fuit provisum Roberto de Attewyk' de vicaria de Bolmey (Bolney) taxata v li. Solvit die ii Octobris anno LXXIII quinquaginta s.[146] Item solvit die xviii Martii in plenam solutionem taxe l s., c s.[143]

### Cicestrensis

Et Thome Chay de ecclesia de Newyk' (Newick) taxata iiii[or] li. vi s. viii d. Solvit die secunda Octobris quadraginta tres s. iiii d.[146] Item solvit die xxv Februarii anno LXIIII[to] xliii s. iiii d.[143] Summa iiii[or] li. vi s. viii d.

### Cicestrensis

Ex causa permutationis fuit provisum per cardinalem Cantuariensem Johanni de Nonstede [147] de ecclesia de Slyndeford' [148] (Slindon) Cicestrensis diocesis, taxata vi li. xiii s. iiii d. Solvit tres li. vi s. viii d. xii Octobris anno LXXIII iii ll. vi s. vii d.[143] Item solvit die x Aprilis in plenam solutionem taxe, cuius valor non excedit xx s., ut iuravit, in quinque m. iii li. vi s. viii d.[143]

### Wyntoniensis

Et Johanni Foliot de vicaria de Romesey (Romsey) Wyntoniensis diocesis, non taxata, cum precedenti ecclesia permutata.[149] Post eodem anno permutavit iterum dictus Johannes Foliot dictam vicarium de Romesey cum vicaria de Eleham (Elham) Cantuariensis diocesis coram dicto cardinali et ibi solvit possessor qui nunc

---

[140] In the left margin: *Cardinalis Convenarum*; *inutilis*. In the right margin, bracketed against this item and the next: *non habuit effectum de prima*.
[141] In the margin: *Cardinalis Convenarum*.
[142] The sum is repeated as *lxiiii s. d.* In the margin: *solvit*.
[143] In the margin: *solvit*.
[144] In the margin: *vera*.
[145] In the margin: *inutilis*.

[146] Sum repeated MS. In the margin: *solvit*.
[147] *Monstedede*, Collectorie 13, fol. 176[v].
[148] *Slindefeld*, Collectorie 13, fol. 176[v].
[149] In the margin: *debet*.

est vicarius de Romesey supra folio precedenti.[150] et ibi videtur quia debet pro vicaria de Eleham ut ibi, et etiam pro vicaria de Romesey.

Recepta pagine lxv li. xiii s. iiii d.; [144] inutilis est iᵃ provisio iᵃ; et debetur de ultima.

### (fol. 102, xcix [151]) Eboracensis [152]

Ex causa permutationis fuit provisum per cardinalem Cantuariensem Domino Henrico Rundy de parochiali ecclesia de Feston' (Fewston) pro taxa antiqua xx m. Solvit xix die Octobris tres li. vi s. viii d.[146] Item solvit plus die xvii Martii in partem fructuum iii li. vi s. viii d.[143]

### Eboracensis

Et Domino Thome Herbert' de vicaria ecclesie de Topclif' (Topcliffe) pro taxa antiqua xx m. Solvit die xxvi Octobris anno LXXIII in quinque marchis iii li. vi s. viii d.[143] Item plus solvit die xxvii Maii anno LXXIIIIᵗᵒ iii li. vi s. viii d.[143]

### Sarisbiriensis

Provisum fuit per cardinalem Cantuariensem Roberto de Wuhtchirch' [153] de ecclesia de Folgheleston' (Fugglestone) per resignationem Johannis de Wilton', nuper rectoris eiusdem, pro taxa xx m. Solvit die xx Octobris anno LXXIII pro dictis xx marchis xiii li. vi s. viii d.[143]

### Lincolniensis

Provisum fuit per cardinalem Cantuariensem domino de Croulton', presbytero Lincolniensis diocesis, de vicaria de Burcestr' (Bicester) eiusdem diocesis, non taxata, et asseruit per iuramentum suum dictus Johannes quod verus valor dicte vicarie non excedit vii li. xiii s. iiii d., et sic debentur camere pro medietate iii li. xv s. iiii d.[154] Solvit quadraginta s. die xx Octobris anno LXXIII xl s.[143] Item solvit die xii Martii anno LXXIIIIᵗᵒ in plenam solutionem medietatis veri valoris xxxv s. ii d.[143]

### Lichfeldensis

Provisum fuit per cardinalem Cantuariensem Johanni de Eccleshale de prioratu de Rompton' (Ranton) Lichfeldensis diocesis, taxato l li. xvi d. Est obligatus et condempnatus, et habet terminum, et post solvit die xxv Novembris anno LXXIII duodecim li. x s. iiii d.[146] Item solvit xix die Junii anno LXXIIIIᵗᵒ duodecim li. x s. iiii d.[146]

### Roffensis

Ex causa permutationis fuit provisum per cardinalem Cantuariensem Domino Willelmo Daulour [155] de vicaria de Westfarle (West Farleigh) Roffensis diocesis pro medietate [156] veri valoris xxvi s. vii d. Habet terminum et est obligatus, et solvit viginti sex s. vii d. in duabus vicibus xix nona die Januarii,[146] xxvi s. vii d.

### Cicestrensis

De vicaria de Loseham (Bosham) collata per cardinalem pro taxa vi m. dym.

Et de vicaria de Hertinng' (Harting) collata per cardinalem fructus.

Recepta pagine lvi li. xv s. ix d.; [157] resta [158] pecunie x li.[159] xiii s.[160]

### (fol. 102ᵛ, xcix) Norwicensis

Collata fuit Willelmo Malot vicaria de Pesenhale (Peasenhall) per cardinalem Cantuariensem, non taxata in libro camere, sed in libro episcopi taxatur ad v m., ut asserit dictus Willelmus. Solvit die xxvii Octobris anno LXXII viginti s.[161] Item solvit die vi Jullii anno predicto xlvi s. viii d.[162]

### Lincolniensis

Collata fuit ecclesia Sancte Ebbe Oxonie Domino Johanni [163] Erle per cardinalem Cantuariensem. Solvit die xiiii Januarii anno LXIII primo triginta tres s. iiii d.[161] Et plus eadem die in alia solutione pro medietate veri valoris pro toto usque ad xl s.[161]

### Eliensis

Provisum fuit Roberto de Braybrok', bacallario in legibus, de ecclesia de Hynton' (Cherry Hinton) Eliensis diocesis pro exspectatione ad collationem episcopi Eliensis. Est obligatus et habet terminos, et solvit die xxv Martii anno LXXIIIIᵗᵒ decem li. in partem fructuum.[161] Et hic est quia non reperitur inter exspectationes.

### Lichfeldensis

Provisum fuit Rogero de Royton' [164] per cardinalem Cantuariensem de ecclesia de Donyngton' (Donington) Lichfeldensis diocesis. Possessor est obligatus et habet terminum, et solvit die xx Martii anno a nativitate LXXIIII in partem fructuum liii s. iiii d.[162]

---

[150] Follows *lxxxix* deleted by a line.

[151] In place of *c* deleted by a line.

[152] The following heading is deleted by lines: *Adhuc explorata. Sequntur beneficia vacantia et vacatura collata et confirmata per sanctissimum in Christo patrem et dominum nostrum, Dominum Gregorium, divina providentia papam undecimum, pontificatus sui anno secundo, in regnis Anglie et Hybernie.* In the margin: *infra est ultra.*

[153] *Witchirch*, Collectorie 13, fol. 176ᵛ.

[154] Sum repeated MS.

[155] *Dambour*, Collectorie 13, fol. 176ᵛ.

[156] Followed by *valoris* deleted by a line.

[157] In the margin: *vera.*

[158] Followed by *pagine* deleted by a line.

[159] Over *xxxviii li.* deleted by a line.

[160] Followed by an illegible number of pence deleted by a line.

[161] Sum repeated MS. In the margin: *solvit.*

[162] In the margin: *solvit.*

[163] *Johanne*, MS.

[164] Name supplied from Brevetus: Collectorie 13, fol. 177.

## Cicestrensis

Ex causa permutationis fuit provisum per cardinalem Cantuariensem Johanni Forester de vicaria de Kokesfeld' (Cuckfield) taxata vi li. xiii s. iiii d. Solvit in duabus vicibus sexaginta sex s. viii d.[161]

## Norwicensis

Provisum fuit, ut dicitur, per cardinalem Thome Frastorp' ex causa permutationis de ecclesia de Taterse (Tattersett) Norwicensis diocesis pro taxa xx m.

## Norwicensis

De ecclesia Sancti Andree de Tatersete (Tattersett, St. Andrew) fuit provisum per cardinalem Cantuariensem pro taxa xi m. dym., preter portionem prioris de Castellacre in eadem ecclesia xx s.

## Norwicensis

De vicaria de Pesenhale (Peasenhall) fuit provisum per cardinalem Cantuariensem fructus.

## Norwicensis

De ecclesia de Calton' (Colton) fuit provisum per cardinalem fructus.

## Norwicensis

De vicaria de Felmyngham (Felmingham) fuit provisum per cardinalem fructus.
Recepta pagine xxi li. vi s. viii d.;[157] restant fructus vii provisionum vii; resta pecunie xxv li. vi s. viii d. et pars duarum provisionum ii.

## (fol. 103, xcix) Wigorniensis

Ex causa permutationis facte per Johannem de Attheleston'[165] coram cardinali Cantuariensi fuit provisum de ecclesia Sancte Trinitatis Brisstoll' pro taxa quinque li.[166] Solvit dictas quinque li. die xxi Desembris anno LXXIII.[162]

## Sarisbiriensis

Et de ecclesia de Witeton' (Witherstone) ex causa dicte permutationis Henrico de Cotek' fructus.

## Eliensis

Vicaria de Tadlowe (Tadlow) fuit collata per dominum cardinalem Cantuariensem Nicolao Buroy,[167] que non taxatur, sed composuit pro medietate veri valoris ad quadraginta duos s. iiii d.[166] Solvit viginti unum s. ii d. die xxiiii Desembris anno LXXIII.[161]

## Roffensis

Ex causa permutationis fuit provisum per cardinalem Cantuariensem W. dicto Stok'[168] de vicaria de Kingeston' (Kingston) Roffensis diocesis, non taxata. Solvit in partem fructuum die xiii Januarii viginti s.[161] Item plus xxi Junii anno LXXIIII[to] solvit xx s.,[162] xl s.

## Norwicensis

Et Domino Nicolao de Arselle[169] de vicaria de Kumston' (Kempston?) Norwicensis diocesis fructus.

## Londoniensis, Lincolniensis

Ex causa permutationis debentur fructus ecclesie de Lkaton' (Latton) Londoniensis diocesis facte coram cardinali Cantuariensi[170] cum ecclesia de Wexham Lincolniensis diocesis.

## Eboracensis

De subdecanatu accepto in ecclesia Eboracensi per Thomam[171] Blandon fructus. Solvit xxviii die Junii in xx m. xiii li. vi s. viii d.[162]

## Eboracensis

De prebenda de Northwel (Norwell) alias vocata Palasal acceptata per Radulphum de Tertenton' in ecclesia de Suthwel fructus. Non possidetur per eum, sed per Dominum Gunfort, olim thesaurariun Calesii (Calais), auctoritate apostolica, et est obligatus et habet terminum, sed litigat, et si recipiat fructus solvere tenetur, et sic est obligatus.

## Eboracensis

De prebenda de Rapton (Rampton) acceptata per Walterum de Westhal in ecclesia de Suthowell' fructus.
Recepta pagine xxi li. vii s. x d.;[172] resta pecunie xxi s. ii d.; restant fructus v provisionum v.

## (fol. 103v) Dunolmensis

Expeditus est Laurentius Graa pro exspectatione in ecclesia Cestr' super stratam (Chester-le-Street) Dunolmensis diocesis per obitum Magistri Johannis de Borton pro taxa xx li. Solvit die xii Maii anno LXXIIII in partem fructuum in quinque marchis iii li. vi s. viii d.[162]

## Sarisbiriensis

De prebenda de Slape ratione provisionis facte Ricardo Hoxton' per obitum Rogeri White pro taxa xx m.

---

[165] The name is supplied from the Brevetus: Collectorie 13, fol. 177.
[166] Sum repeated MS.
[167] *Burray*, Collectorie 13, fol. 177.

[168] *Willelmo Attesok'*, Collectorie 13, fol. 177.
[169] *Busele* is written over *Arselle*, but the latter is not deleted.
[170] The entry is deleted by a line to this point.
[171] *Johannem*, Collectorie 13, fol. 177v.
[172] In the margin: *vera*.

### Wygorniensis

De ecclesia Beati Martini collata per cardinalem Cantuariensem Roberto James fructus pro taxa xxviii m.

### Wigorniensis

De ecclesia de Hambury iuxta Wich' (Hanbury) collata per cardinalem Johanni Sallewarre fructus pro taxa xxii m. Solvit die xx Aprilis anno LXXIIII in partem fructuum in quinque marchis iii li. vi s. viii d.[173]

### Wygorniensis

De vicaria de Berkelee (Berkeley) acceptata per Johannem Tremsa per exspectationem in forma speciali fructus. Possidetur per alium in forma pauperum, et quia Johannes est exclusus non habuit effectum adhuc.

### Lincolniensis

De ecclesia de Yvengho (Ivinghoe) ratione confirmationis facte Willelmo de Paking' per Gregorium iiii° nonas Novembris anno tertio [174] fructus. Constat de hoc per bullam missam a camera reddendam petenti cum petetur.

### Exoniensis

De vicaria de Brodhurbury (Broadhembury) ex collatione facta per cardinalem Johanni Cork' fructus. Est in v^to certificatorio sub sequestro.

### Sarisbiriensis

De archidiaconatu Dorcestr' in ecclesia Sarisbiriensi acceptato per cardinalem Gilbensem [175] fructus. Est in v certificatorio sub sequestro.

### Eboracensis

De prepositura Sancti Johannis Beverlacensis Eboracensis diocesis ratione confirmationis facte de eadem Magistro Johanni de Thoresby pro taxa temporalitatis et ecclesie de Welwyk' (Welwick) eidem annexe, de qua non est scriptum de curia, pro taxa c m. Solvit die xxii Aprilis dictas centum m. in sexaginta sex li. xiii s. iiii d.,[176] quia sic erat obligatus in curia ut dixit.

### Lincolniensis

Provisum fuit per exspectationem Domino Matheo de Assheton' de prebenda de Clifton' in ecclesia Lincolniensi pro taxa xxx m., ut patet in decanatu de Nowerck' (Newark) Eboracensis diocesis ubi est, et solvit die xxii Aprilis anno LXXIIII in partem dicte taxe in decem m. vi li. xiii s. iiii d.[173]

### Eboracensis

De novo fuit provisum Henrico Godbarn', presbytero Eboracensis licentiato in legibus, de ecclesia de Hornise (Hornsea) eiusdem per obitum Roberti de Caldewell' per Gregorium ix kalendas Januarii anno iii^tio,[177] pro taxa l m., salvo iure pluris super residuo, si plus valet, et debet taxam vel residuum et quod componat de fructibus perceptis ante confirmationem, et bulla confirmationis est hic missa per dominum camerarium reddenda petenti cum se obligavit, et habuit eam die xxvi Junii anno LXXIIII, et composuit de fructibus perceptis toto suo tempore precedenti cum iuramento suo et procuratoris, et informatio est in archivis, ad xxxvii s. v d., et quartam, et habet terminum nativitatis et cetera.

### Lincolniensis

Dominus Johannes de Templer possidet auctoritate apostolica vicariam de Hemingford' (Hemingford Grey). Est in v certificatorio episcopi sic mandatum et est ibi monitus.

### Lincolniensis

Dominus Johannes de Scaldewell' possidet auctoritate apostolica ecclesiam de Caldecote iuxta Baldok' (Caldecote near Baldock). Est in v certificatorio episcopi sic mandatum et est ibi monitus.

### Dunolmensis

De prebenda in ecclesia collegiata Norton' ratione confirmationis facte de eadem Domino Thome de Ayndyor,[178] qui fuit diu est obligatus in curia ut hic asseruit, pro taxa, que plus valet quam residuum, ut iuravit, vi li. Solvit die xvi Martii anno LXXIIII dictas sex li.[179]

### Lincolniensis

Dominus cardinalis Sancti Martialis [180] ex provisione sibi facta de prebenda de Thame in ecclesia Lincolniensi fructus. Arendatur ii^c xl m.

### Lincolniensis

Dominus Raymundus Pelegrini ex provisione sibi facta de prebenda que fuit domini cardinalis Sancti Martialis, vacante ex causa dicte provisionis, in ecclesia Lincolniensi fructus. Valet, ut dicitur, centum m.

Recepta pagine iiii^xx vi li:;[172] resta pecunie ciiii li. ix s. ii d.; restant fructus viii provisionum viii.

Summa recepte exploratorum usque ad diem xxvii Julii anno LXX^mo IIII^to, qua die exivi de Londonia, iii^c lxxxii li. xv s. vi d. Quere summas alias restantes

---

[173] In the margin: *solvit*.
[174] 2 November 1373.
[175] Robert of Geneva, bishop of Cambrai, priest of Ss. XII Apostoli.
[176] Sum repeated MS. In the margin: *solvit*.

[177] 24 December 1373.
[178] *Johanni de Grayndrop*, Collectorie 13, fol. 177^v.
[179] Sum repeated MS. In the margin: *solvit*.
[180] Hugo de Sancto Martiali, deacon of Santa Maria in Portico.

de predictis exploratis supra folio xcvi ad signum ╫∞╫.[181]

(fol. 104, xcix) iii[us] quaternus [182]

Sequntur beneficia vacantia et vacatura collata et confirmata per sanctissimum in Christo patrem et dominum nostrum, Dominum Gregorium, divina providentia papam undecimum, pontificatus sui anno secundo in regnis Anglie et Hybernie

Primo fuit provisum motu proprio Roberto duodecim apostolorum presbytero cardinali de canonicatu et prebenda de Forgonderienus (Forgandenny) in ecclesia Donkeldensi (Dunkeld), vacantibus per obitum Johannis Rede, vi idus Januarii.[183]

### Eystetensis

Dispensatum fuit cum Conrado Claffhener, rectori [184] parochialis ecclesie in Rasch' Eystetensis (Eichstätt) diocessis, qui decanatum ecclesie Eystetensis fuit auctoritate ordinaria assecutus, quod ipsos decanatum et parochialem ecclesiam licite possit retinere, pridie idus Januarii.[185] Non est in Anglia.

### Lincolniensis

Motu proprio fuit provisum Johanni titulo Sancti Marcelli presbytero cardinali de canonicatu et prebenda ecclesie Lincolniensis ac archidiaconatu Northamptonie in dicta ecclesia vacantibus per obitum Willelmi de Askeby, x kalendas Februarii.[186]

### Wygorniensis

De parochiali ecclesia de Todyngton' (Toddington) Wygorniensis diocesis, vacante per obitum ultimi rectoris eiusdem, fuit provisum David Neuton' alias de Kilgore, presbytero Landavensis, iii idus Januarii.[187] Est in mandato, nondum tamen habuit effectum, ut est probatum, ideo relaxatus in forma et cetera. Et iuravit Robbertus Undirhull', nunc possessor, die vii Aprilis anno LXXIIII infra xv dies certificare si et cum habuerit effectum. Et alia est provisio supra folio xxviii.

### Assavensis

Philippo Dilosk', presbytero Herefordensis diocesis, de vicaria parochialis ecclesie de Pola (Welshpool) Assavensis diocesis, vacante per obitum Griffini Marchalt, iii idus Januarii.[188] Non habuit effectum quia

gratia subreptitia, et copia declarationis est in archivis. Restant fructus duarum provisionum ii; et sunt tres inutiles.

### (fol. 104[v]) Lincolniensis

Mandatur provideri Edmundo Strete de canonicatu sub exspectatione prebende ecclesie Lincolniensis, et dimittet parochialem ecclesiam de Marlawe (Great Marlow) Lincolniensis diocesis, xviii kalendas Februarii.[189]

### Eboracensis

Item Ade de Hertyngdon', presbytero Lichfeldensis diocesis, de canonicatu sub exspectatione prebende ecclesie Eboracensis, etiam ad ea que archiepiscopus habet conferre in diocesi et civitate Eboracensibus, et dimittet canonicatus et prebendas de Northerheve (Netheravon) in ecclesia Sarisbiriensi et in ecclesia Exoniensi.

### Lichfeldensis

Item Thome Orgrave, presbytero Eboracensis diocesis, de canonicatu sub exspectatione prebende ecclesie Lichfeldensis.

### Sarisbiriensis

Item Thome de Bukyngham de canonicatu sub exspectatione prebende ecclesie Sarisbiriensis.

### Lichfeldensis

Ricardo de Geytington' de canonicatu sub exspectatione prebende ecclesie Licheffeldensis.

### Menevensis

Nicholao de Horton' de canonicatu sub exspectatione prebende ecclesie Menevensis.

### Sarisbiriensis

Thome de Monte Acuto de canonicatu sub exspectatione prebende ecclesie Sarisbiriensis.

Restant vii expectationes que nondum habuerunt effectum vii.

### (fol. 105, c) Cicestrensis

Motu proprio fuit provisum cardinali Tutellensi (Tulle)[190] de canonicatu et prebenda ecclesie Cicestrensis vacantibus per obitum quondam Johannis de Donutton' extra curiam defuncti, x kalendas Februarii.[191] Non habuit effectum ista provisio quia, morte preventus, non habuit possessionem. Et infra est alia provisio folio cv facta infra eundem annum alteri cardinali folio cvi, et Magister Johannes de Wendelingburch possidet auctoritate apostolica, et litigat cum titulo regio, et videatur cum habuerit et cetera.

---

[181] In the margin: *supra* ╫∞╫; *cf.* n. 115 above.
[182] Repeated in the margin.
[183] 8 January 1372. In the margin: *provisio de vacanti; inutilis; non est in Anglia.*
[184] *rectorem*, MS.
[185] 12 January 1372. In the margin: *provisio; inutilis.*
[186] 23 January 1372. In the margin: *provisio de vacanti; cardinalis est.*
[187] 11 January 1372. In the margin: *provisio de vacanti; debet.*
[188] 11 January 1372. In the margin: *provisio de vacanti; inutilis.*

[189] The date, 15 January 1372, is bracketed against this item and the next six.
[190] John Fabri, bishop of Toul, priest of Sancto Marcello.
[191] 23 January 1372. In the margin: *provisio de vacante.*

### Eboracensis

Johanni de Appulby de canonicatu sub exspectatione prebende cum dignitate, personatu vel officio in ecclesia Eboracensi, et dimittet [192] ecclesie Londoniensis, ix kalendas Februarii.[193]

### Lichfeldensis

Mandatur provideri Johanni de Fordham de canonicatu sub exspectatione prebende ecclesie Lichfeldensis, xvi kalendas Martii.[194]

### Lincolniensis

Mandatur provideri Willelmo Hunte de canonicatu sub exspectatione prebende ecclesie Lincolniensis.

### Lincolniensis

Item Roberto Mellefle, presbytero Lincolniensis diocesis, de beneficio ecclesiastico cum cura et cetera ad collationem abbatis et conventus monasterii de Croyland ordinis Sancti Benedicti Lincolniensis diocesis.

### Lichfeldensis

Item Thome More de beneficio ecclesiastico et cetera ad collationem episcopi Lichfeldensis.

### Eboracensis

Item Waltero Amyas de canonicatu sub exspectatione prebende ecclesie Suthwellensis Eboracensis.

### Londoniensis

Item Johanni de Eston', clerico Norwicensis diocesis, de beneficio ecclesiastico ad collationem prioris et fratrum hospitalis Sancti Johannis Jerosolomitani in Anglia.

Inutilis est prima provisio i; et restant vii expectationes que nondum habuerunt effectum vii.

### (fol. 105ᵛ) Lincolniensis

Thome Tythomersch de beneficio ecclesiastico ad collationem episcopi Lincolniensis, xvi kalendas Martii.[194]

### Eboracensis

Johanni Frannceys de Barewe de canonicatu sub exspectatione prebende ecclesie Eboracensis.

### Menevensis

Mandatur provideri Johanni Reys de canonicatu sub exspectatione prebende ecclesie de Akerginque (Abergwili) Menovensis diocesis, et dimittet archidiaconatum et canonicatum et prebendam ecclesie Bangorensis.

### Bangorensis

De parochiali ecclesia de Wandisvan (Llangwyfan?) Bangorensis diocesis, vacante per munus consecrationis impensum, fuit provisum David ap Hova dicte Bangorensis diocesis. Est in v mandatis.[195]

### Assavensis

Matheo Minot presbytero mandatur provideri de canonicatu sub exspectatione prebende ecclesie Assavensis.

### Assavensis

Item Amono ap Sifilo, clerico Bangorensis diocesis, mandatur provideri de beneficio ecclesiastico ad collationem episcopi Assavensis, et dimittet parochialem ecclesiam de Landrisant (Llantrisant) dicte diocesis.

### Menevensis

Mandatur provideri Howelo Kyffini, presbytero [196] Assavensis diocesis, de canonicatu sub exspectatione prebende, dignitatis, et cetera ecclesie Menevensis, iiii kalendas Martii.[197]

### Menevensis

De perpetua vicaria de Nannael [198] (Nantmel) Menevensis diocesis, vacante per non promotionem Henrici de Almania, fuit provisum Willelmo de Racadir, presbytero dicte diocesis.[195] Solvit tres li. sex s. viii d. in partem fructuum.[199]

### Lincolniensis

Mandatur provideri Johanni Huelleot, clerico Eliensis diocesis, de beneficio ecclesiastico et cetera ad collationem abbatis et conventus Sancti Albani ordinis Sancti Benedicti Lincolniensis diocesis.

Recepta pagine iii li. vi s. viii d. et restat pars; [200] restant vii expectationes vii; et fructus unius provisionis i.

### (fol. 106, ci) Lincolniensis

Johanni de Shepeyx de canonicatu sub exspectatione prebende ecclesie Lincolniensis, pridie kalendas Martii.[201]

### Lincolniensis

Mandatur provideri Willelmo de Wasseham, clerico Lincolniensis diocesis, de canonicatu sub exspectatione prebende ecclesie Lincolniensis.

### Lichfeldensis

Mandatur provideri Thome Attesate de Wisshauwe,

---

[192] *canonicatum et prebendam* are probably omitted after *dimittet.*

[193] 24 January 1372.

[194] The date 15 February 1372, is bracketed against this item and the next five.

[195] In the margin: *provisio de vacanti.*

[196] *presbytero* repeated MS.

[197] The date, 27 February 1372, is bracketed against this item and the next two.

[198] *Nannoal*, Collectorie 13, fol. 174.

[199] Sum repeated MS. In the margin: *solvit.*

[200] In the margin: *exprimatur que pars.*

[201] The date, 29 February 1372, is bracketed against this item and the next.

presbytero Lichfeldensis diocesis, de canonicatu sub exspectatione prebende ecclesie Lichfeldensis, iiii kalendas Martii.[197]

Willelmo de Walton' Lincolniensis diocesis de beneficio ecclesiastico ad collationem prioris et conventus de Landa (Launde).[202]

### Lichfeldensis

De parochiali ecclesia de Leveryngton' [203] Hasting' (Leamington Hastings) diocesis Lichfeldensis, vacante per obitum ultimi rectoris eiusdem, fuit provisum Ricardo Anbyn de Nayleston'.[195] Debet pro taxa sex li. xiii s. iiii d., de quibus solvit die xxv Octobris anno LXXIII duas li.[199] Item solvit die xxv Martii anno a nativitate LXXIIII[to] in vii m. iiii[or] li. xiii s. iiii d.[204]

### Sarisbiriensis

Acceptatio et provisio facte Rogero de Freton', legum doctori, de canonicatu et prebenda ecclesie Sarisbiriensis vacantibus per obitum Johannis Donton' fuerunt confirmate seu provisum de novo, pridie kalendas Martii.[205] Est in mandato quinto, et solvit xiiii die Julii anno LXXIIII[to] per manus executoris domini Wigorniensis iii li. xiii s. iiii d.[204]

### Londoniensis

Mandatur provideri Johanni Godewik', presbytero Norwicensis, de canonicatu sub exspectatione prebende ecclesie Londoniensis, et dimittet parochialem ecclesiam de Croydon Wyntoniensis diocesis, dum et cetera.

### Saresbiriensis

Roberto de Wortham, presbytero Norwicensis diocesis, de canonicatu sub exspectatione prebende ecclesie Sarisbiriensis, et dimittet parochialem ecclesiam in Brisele (Brisley) Norwicensis diocesis, dum et cetera, pridie kalendas Martii.[206]

Recepta pagine x li. vi s. viii d.; restant vi expectationes vi.

### (fol. 106ᵛ) Cicestrensis

Willelmo de Kirkestede, presbytero Norwicensis diocesis, de canonicatu sub exspectatione prebende ecclesie Cicestrensis, pridie kalendas Martii.[207]

### Cantuariensis

Johanni Broun de Hadlegh', presbytero Norwicensis

diocesis, de beneficio ecclesiastico ad collationem archiepiscopi Cantuariensis.

### Eliensis

Waltero de Eston', presbytero Norwicensis diocesis, de beneficio ecclesiastico ad collationem abbatis et conventus monasterii de Thorney Eliensis diocesis, et dimittet medietatem parochialis ecclesie de Seggebrok' (Sedgebrook) Lincolniensis diocesis.

### Dunolmensis

Mandatur provideri Rogero de Barneburgh', presbytero Eboracensis diocesis, de beneficio ecclesiastico ad collationem episcopi, prioris et capituli ecclesie Dunolmensis.

### Sarisbiriensis

Mandatur provideri Johanni Rolee clerico de canonicatu sub exspectatione prebende ecclesie Sarisbiriensis.

### Lichfeldensis

Mandatur provideri Alfrido Foliambe de canonicatu sub exspectatione prebende, dignitatis et cetera in ecclesia Lichfeldensi.

### Sarisbiriensis

Item Willelmo Lugoton' de canonicatu sub exspectatione prebende ecclesie Sarisbiriensis.

### Exoniensis

Item Johanni Rathawe Norwicensis diocesis de canonicatu sub exspectatione prebende ecclesie Exoniensis.

Restant viii expectationes viii.

### (fol. 107, cii) Herefordensis

Item Nicolao de Lich' de canonicatu sub exspectatione prebende ecclesie Herefordensis, pridie kalendas Martii.[208]

### Menevensis

Item Ludovico filio David de Sancto Melano presbytero de canonicatu sub exspectatione prebende ecclesie Menevensis.

### Dublinensis

Item Radulpho de Leython' Blusard Lincolniensis diocesis de beneficio ecclesiastico ad collationem episcopi Dublinensis.[209]

### Conventrensis

Item Willelmo Clek', clerico Lincolniensis diocesis, de beneficio ecclesiastico ad collationem episcopi, prioris et conventus monasterii Conventrensis.

---

[202] In the margin: *quere diocesim quia hic non est.*
[203] *Lymington,* Collectorie 13, fol. 174.
[204] In the margin: *solvit.*
[205] The date, 29 February 1372, is bracketed against this item and the next. In the margin: *provisio de vacanti.*
[206] 29 February 1372.
[207] The date, 29 February 1372, is bracketed against this item and the next seven.

[208] The date, 29 February 1372, is bracketed against this item and the next six.
[209] In the margin: *non est in Anglia.*

### Sarisbirensis

Item Johanni de Wendelinburgh' de canonicatu sub exspectatione prebende ecclesie Saresbiriensis.

### Exoniensis

Item Johanni Cheny de beneficio ecclesiastico ad collationem episcopi Exoniensis.

### Lincolniensis

Guidoni de Rouclif, presbytero Eboracensis diocesis, de canonicatu sub exspectatione prebende [210] ecclesie Lincolniensis.

Inutilis est una provisio i[a]; et restant vi expectationes vi.

### (fol. 107[v]) Eboracensis

De canonicatu et prebenda ecclesie Rippon' Eboracensis, vacantibus per obitum David de Wollore, fuit provisum Hugoni de Arlam, clerico Dunolmensis diocesis, iiii[to] nonas Martii.[211] Possidet per guadaraulerum domini regis titulo regio, et sic non habuit effectum adhuc, et alia est provisio supra.[212]

### Eboracensis

Mandatur provideri Johanni Fraunceys de Barowe presbytero de canonicatu sub exspectatione prebende ecclesie Eboracensis.

### Norwicensis

De parochiali ecclesia de Glamefford' (Glandford) Norwicensis diocesis, vacante per mortem Radulphi de Nothingham, fuit provisum Hugoni Attenhall' clerico, et dimittet canonicatum et prebendam ecclesie Menevensis. Est in mandato.[213]

### Wyntoniensis

Thome de Colingborn', presbytero Sarisbiriensis diocesis, de canonicatu sub exspectatione prebende in ecclesia monialium de Warwell' (Wherwell) ordinis Sancti Augustini Wyntoniensis diocesis.

### Dunolmensis

Mandatur provideri Johanni Lombardi, clerico Eboracensis diocesis, de beneficio ecclesiastico ad collationem episcopi, prioris et capituli ecclesie Dunolmensis,[214] v idus Martii.[215]

### Lincolniensis

Johanni Bernet presbytero mandatur provideri de canonicatu sub exspectatione prebende, dignitatis et cetera ecclesie Lincolniensis, iiii idus Martii.[216]

### Eboracensis

Willelmo Swenslete, presbytero Eboracensis diocesis, de beneficio ecclesiastico ad collationem archiepescopi Eboracensis.

Restant fructus unius provisionis i; et v [217] expectationes que nondum habuerunt effectum v.

### (fol. 108, ciii) Lichfeldensis

Hugoni de Prees Lichfeldensis diocesis de canonicatu sub exspectatione prebende ecclesie Lichfeldensis, iiii idus Martii.[218]

### Norwicensis

Stephano de Cressyngham, presbytero Norwicensis diocesis, de canonicatu sub exspectatione prebende ecclesie Norwicensis.

### Lincolniensis

Johanni Masselyn diocesis Lincolniensis [219] de beneficio ecclesiastico ad collationem abbatis et conventus monasterii de Ramesey.

### Lincolniensis

Mandatur provideri Nicholao Heth', presbytero Lichfeldensis diocesis, de canonicatu sub exspectatione prebende, dignitatis, et cetera ecclesie Lincolniensis, xi kalendas Aprilis.[220]

### Dublinensis

De archidiaconatu de Glanlagh' (Glendalough) in ecclesia Dublinensi, vacante per obitum Thome de Tamfeld', fuit provisum Simoni de Glauntfordbrigg' presbytero, viii kalendas Aprilis.[221]

### Exoniensis

Mandatur provideri Johanni Free, clerico Exoniensis diocesis, de beneficio ecclesiastico ad collationem decani et capituli ecclesie Exoniensis, xvi kalendas Maii.[222]

### Saresbiriensis

Mandatur provideri Roberto de Washam de canonicatu sub exspectatione prebende in ecclesia monialium

---

[210] *prebende* repeated MS.
[211] The date, 4 March 1372, is bracketed against this item and the next three.
[212] In the margin: *provisio de vacanti; inutilis.*
[213] In the margin: *provisio de vacanti.*
[214] Over *Dublinensis* deleted by a line.
[215] 11 March 1372.

[216] The date, 12 March 1372, is bracketed against this item and the next.
[217] Followed by *provisiones que* deleted by a line.
[218] The date, 12 March 1372, is bracketed against this item and the next two.
[219] Follows *Lichfeldensis* deleted by a line.
[220] 22 March 1372.
[221] 25 March 1372. In the margin: *provisio de vacanti.*
[222] 16 April 1372.

de Schastebury (Shaftesbury) diocesis Saresbiriensis, idus Aprilis.[223]

Restant fructus unius provisionis i; et vi expectationes vi.

### (fol. 108ᵛ) Roffensis [224]

Mandatur provideri Willelmo Loring' de parochiali ecclesia de Orpyngton' (Orpington), vacante per mortem Nicholai Regestrator' Saresbiriensis diocesis, idus Aprilis.[225] Non habuit effectum quia infra confirmatur alteri folio cix.[226]

### Cicestrensis

Item Thome de Galtorp' de canonicatu sub exspectatione prebende ecclesie Cicestrensis.

Item Hugoni de Bokenhull' de parochiali ecclesia de Waynflet (Wainfleet) vacante per obitum Willelmi de Arely.[227]

### Norwicensis

Edwardo de Southworth' de parochiali ecclesia de Ronham (Runham) Norwicensis diocesis, vacante per obitum Ade de Subdebmy. Est in v mandatis.[226]

### Herfrodensis

Johanni de Upton' super Sabrinam, clerico Wygorniensis diocesis, de canonicatu et prebenda ecclesie Herefordensis de Putesdon' (Putson) in eadem ecclesia vacantibus per obitum Egidii de Staunford', xiiii kalendas Maii.[228] Est in mandatis v.[226]

### Landavensis

Ade Wylim, presbytero Landavensis diocesis, mandatur provideri de parochiali ecclesia de Merefeld' (Marshfield) dicte diocesis, vacante per mortem Johannis Beuchamp, ultimi eiusdem ecclesie rectoris. Non habuit effectum quia appropriata est abbati Sancti Augustini.[226]

### Cassellensis

Roberto Joman clerico mandatur provideri de canonicatu et prebenda in Killabrach' (Kilbraugh) ecclesie Cassellensis (Cashel) vacante per promotionem Thome ad episcopatum Laoniensem (Killaloe), xi kalendas Maii.[229]

Inutiles provisiones sunt iii; et restant fructus trium [230] provisionum iii; et una expectatio i.

### (fol. 109, ciiii) Eboracensis

Hugoni de Feriby, presbytero Eboracensis diocesis, mandatur provideri de beneficio ecclesiastico ad collationem abbatis et conventus monasterii Beate Marie ordinis Sancti Benedicti Eboraci, ix kalendas Maii.[231]

### Bangorensis

Howelo Kyffin mandatur provideri de canonicatu sub exspectatione prebende ecclesie Bangorensis, vii kalendas Maii.[232]

### Menevensis

Johanni Trefnant, presbytero Assavensis diocesis, de beneficio ecclesiastico ad collationem episcopi Menevensis.

### Cantuariensis

Johanni Solverum de Banham, presbytero Norwicensis diocesis, de beneficio ecclesiastico ad collationem archiepiscopi, prioris et capituli ecclesie Cantuariensis.

### Norwicensis

Mandatur provideri Willelmo Wadeboys, presbytero Norwicensis diocesis, de beneficio ecclesiastico ad collationem episcopi, prioris et capituli ecclesie Norwicensis.

### Exoniensis

Johanni Faye, clerico Exoniensis diocesis, de beneficio ecclesiastico ad collationem decani et capituli ecclesie Exoniensis.

### Exoniensis

Laurentio Gonnerie, presbytero Exoniensis diocesis, de beneficio ecclesiastico ad collationem episcopi Exoniensis, vi kalendas Maii.[233]

### Londoniensis

Rogero Page de beneficio ecclesiastico ad collationem prioris et fratrum hospitalis Sancti Johannis Jerosolomitani in regno Anglie.

Restant expectationes viii.

### (fol. 109ᵛ) Exoniensis

Fratri Guillelmo de Lahare,[234] priori prioratus de Tywardrayth (Tywardreath) conceditur quod collatio et provisio sibi auctoritate ordinaria facte de dicto

[223] 13 April 1372.
[224] Follows *Saresbiriensis* deleted by a line; followed by *Cantuariensis diocesis* undeleted.
[225] The date, 13 April 1372, is bracketed against this item and the next three.
[226] In the margin: *provisio de vacanti.*
[227] In the margin: *provisio de vacanti*; *quere diocesim quia nomen non datur.*
[228] The date, 18 April 1372, is bracketed against this and the next item.
[229] 21 April 1372. In the margin: *provisio de vacanti*; *non est in Anglia.*

[230] Over *duarum* deleted by a line.
[231] 23 April 1372.
[232] The date, 25 April 1372, is bracketed against this item and the next four.
[233] The date, 26 April 1372, is bracketed against this item and the next.
[234] *de la Haye*, Collectorie 213, fol. 174ᵛ.

prioratu, vacante per mortem Willelmi Bonges, valeant et plenam optineant roboris firmitatem, vi kalendas Maii.[235] Pro taxa, ut dicitur, quadraginta li. Et solvit in duabus vicibus in partem fructuum die xxvi Octobris xi li. xiii s. iiii d.[236] Item solvit plus xvii die Junii anno LXXIIII in x marchis vi li. xiii s. iiii d.[236]

### Lincolniensis

Thome de Mapilton' de canonicatu sub exspectatione prebende ecclesie Lincolniensis, iiii[to] kalendas Maii.[237]

### Eboracensis

Item Thome Neweton' de canonicatu sub exspectatione prebende ecclesie Suthwellensis Eboracensis diocesis.

### Saresbiriensis

Item Edmundo Sentlow de dignitate, personatu vel officio in ecclesia Saresbiriensi.

### Wellensis

Item Thome Salter de canonicatu sub exspectatione prebende cum dignitate ecclesie Wellensis.

### Londoniensis

Willelmo de Chiselden' de canonicatu sub exspectatione prebende ecclesie Londoniensis.

### Eboracensis

Johanni Seggenaux de canonicatu sub exspectatione prebende ecclesie Eboracensis.

### Eboracensis

Thome de Bulwich' de canonicatu sub exspectatione prebende ecclesie Sancti Johannis de Beverlaco Eboracensis diocesis.

Recepta pagine xviii li. vi s. viii d.; restant in pecunia xxi li. xiii s. iiii d.; et vi expectationes vi.

### (fol. 110, cv [238]) Lincolniensis

Johanni Wicherewyk presbytero mandatur provideri de canonicatu sub exspectatione prebende ecclesie Lincolniensis, iiii kalendas Maii.[239]

### Lincolniensis

Motu proprio fuit provisum Petro [240] titulo Sancte Praxedis presbytero cardinali de archidiaconatu de Northamton' ac canonicatu et prebenda de Wellton' rial (Welton Rivall) in ecclesia Lincolniensi, vacantibus per mortem Willelmi de Askeby, iii nonas Maii.[241] Cardinalis est, et est alia provisio supra folio [242] eodem anno facta.[243]

### Saresbiriensis [244]

Edwardo de Cherdestok' presbytero de canonicatu et prebenda de Chalk' in ecclesia monialium de Wilton', pro taxa lxiii m., ac de canonicatu et prebenda de Yweren' (Iwerne) in ecclesia monasterii de Schaston' (Shaftesbury), pro taxa xxx m., Saresbiriensis diocesis, vacantibus per mortem Johannis Blebury, pro taxa omnium xciii m.,[245] xiii kalendas Junii.[246] Gardaraularius domine principise est, et habet terminos, sed litigat, ut dicitur. Solvit die xvi Aprilis anno LXXIIII in partem fructuum dicte prebende prime, scilicet de Chalk' in ecclesia monialium de Wilton', xxii ii.[247]

### Cicestrensis

Motu proprio fuit provisum Petro [248] titulo Sancte Prasede presbytero cardinali de canonicatu et prebenda de Fermingg' (Ferring) nuncupata in ecclesia Cicestrensi, vacantibus per obitum Johannis de Donntton', vii kalendas Junii.[249] Cardinalis est, et gratia non habuit effectum quia per Dominum Johannem Set', domini prioris Lewensis attornatum, appropriata possidetur.[243]

### Saresbiriensis

Simili motu fuit provisum Bertrandi cardinali Convenarum [250] de canonicatu et prebenda de Blebury (Blewberry) in ecclesia Saresbiriensi, vacantibus per obitum Johannis Blebury, viii kalendas Junii.[251] Cardinalis est, et nondum habuit effectum quia titulo regio possidetur.[243]

### Wygorniensis

Collatio et provisio auctoritate apostolica facte Willelmo Trifford' presbytero de parochiali ecclesia de Chivo episcopi (Bishop's Cleeve) Wygorniensis, vacante per obitum Ricardi de Drayton, fuerunt confirmate, viii kalendas Junii.[251] Non habuit effectum quia frater Domini Guidi de Brian possidet titulo regio.[243]

### Wygorniensis

Collatio et provisio auctoritate ordinaria facte Ricardo Hunte de Rougham de archidiaconatu Gloucestr' in ecclesia Wygorniensi, quem Willelmus Trifford' dimisit, fuerunt confirmate seu provisum de novo, v kalendas

---

[235] 26 April 1372. In the margin: *provisio de vacanti*; *quere diocesim*. The last two words are deleted by a line.
[236] In the margin: *solvit*.
[237] The date, 28 April 1372, is bracketed against this item and the next six.
[238] All except the bottoms of the figures are cut away.
[239] 28 April 1372.
[240] *B*, MS.

[241] 5 May 1372.
[242] A blank space is left in the MS.
[243] In the margin: *provisio de vacanti*.
[244] Repeated MS.
[245] Follows the same sum deleted by a line.
[246] 20 May 1372.
[247] In the margin: *provisio de vacanti*; *solvit*.
[248] *B*, MS.
[249] 26 May 1372.
[250] Priest of S. Marcello
[251] 25 May 1372.

Junii.[252] Non habuit effectum, ut certificat episcopus in iiii[to] mandato.[243]

Recepta pagine xxii li.; inutiles sunt iiii provisiones iiii; una restat exspectatio i; restant in pecunia xl li.

### (fol. 110[v]) Lincolniensis

Collatio et provisio auctoritate apostolica facte Gilberto Fawne alias de Stombeth'[253] de perpetua vicaria parochialis ecclesie de Spalding' Lincolniensis diocesis fuerunt confirmate, iii kalendas Junii.[254] Taxatur xxx m., ut dicitur. Solvit die xvii Julii anno LXXIII in triginta m. xx li.[247]

### Exoniensis

Thome Cari mandatur provideri de canonicatu sub exspectatione prebende ecclesie Exoniensis cum dignitate in eadem ecclesia, pridie kalendas Junii.[255]

### Eboracensis

Thome de Melborn' mandatur provideri de canonicatu et prebenda ecclesie Eboracensis, vacantibus per mortem Magistri Willelmi Dalton', iii[tio] nonas Junii.[256] Est in mandato.[243]

### Lichfeldensis

Johanni Terel, presbytero Lichfeldensis diocesis, de beneficio ecclesiastico ad collationem episcopi, decani et capituli ecclesie Lichfeldensis.

### Lincolniensis

Magistro Gaufrido Fabri mandatur provideri de canonicatu et prebenda Lincolniensibus vacantibus per obitum Magistri Johannis Beauchamp, et dimittet unum de beneficiis suis. Est in mandato.[257]

### Dunolmensis

Thome de Middelton' de beneficio ecclesiastico ad collationem episcopi Dunolmensis.

### Cantuariensis

Willelmo Truk', presbytero Londoniensis diocesis, de beneficio ecclesiastico ad collationem et cetera archiepiscopi, prioris et capituli Sancte Trinitatis diocesis Cantuariensis, pridie nonas Junii.[258]

Recepta pagine xx li; restant fructus duarum provisionum[259] ii; et restant iiii expectationes iiii.

### (fol. 111, cvi) Eboracensis

Ricardo Middelton', clerico Eboracensis diocesis,

mandatur provideri de canonicatu sub exspectatione prebende in ecclesia de Soutwell' Eboracensis diocesis, pridie nonas Junii.[260]

### Eboracensis

Waltero de Hatton' de canonicatu sub exspectatione prebende ecclesie Beverlacensis Eboracensis diocesis.

### Eboracensis

Eidem Waltero mandatur provideri de canonicatu sub exspectatione prebende ecclesie Rippon' Eboracensis diocesis.

### Saresbiriensis

Waltero Breche, clerico Saresbiriensis, de ecclesia parochiali[261] de Crisumalford (Christian Malford), vacante per dimissionem Willelmi Darby, ultimi rectoris professi in monasterio Beate Marie de Oseney diocesis Lincolniensis, iiii[to] nonas Junii.[262] Nondum habuit effectum, ideo relaxatus possessor quousque apareat de effectu seu alias per camera fuerit ordinatum.[257]

### Eboracensis

Laurentio qui clerico de canonicatu et prebenda ecclesie Eboracensis vacantibus per obitum Simonis de Brisslay. Non habuit effectum, ut certificat archiepiscopus in iiii[to] certificatorio quia possessor fuit ibi per x annos.[257]

### Lincolniensis

Willelmo de Haterington', clerico Lincolniensis diocesis, de vicaria ecclesie parochialis de Thorton' (Thornton) Lincolniensis, vacante per liberam resignationem factam per Johannem Wynter. Est in mandato.[257]

### Karleolensis

Willelmo de Feriby, clerico Eboracensis diocesis, de parochiali ecclesia de Werkington' (Workington) Karleolensis diocesis, vacante per obitum ultimi rectoris et per devolutionem. Non habuit effectum, ut certificat episcopus, sed videatur melius.[257]

Restant fructus duarum provisionum ii; et restant iii expectationes; et sunt ii provisiones inutiles ii.

### (fol. 111[v]) Wygorniensis

Johanni de Cherleton', presbytero Wygorniensis diocesis, mandatur provideri de parochiali ecclesia Sancte Trinitatis Bristollie dicte diocesis, vacante per obitum Johannis ultimi ipsius ecclesie rectoris, iiii[to] nonas Junii.[262] Non habuit effectum adhuc quia infra est alia provisio, et videatur melius.[257]

---

[252] 28 May 1372.
[253] *Fawne de Sancto Botulpho*, Collectorie 13, fol. 174[v].
[254] 30 May 1372.
[255] 31 May 1372.
[256] The date, 3 June 1372, is bracketed against this item and the next two.
[257] In the margin: *provisio de vacanti*.
[258] 4 June 1372.
[259] Over *unius expectationis* deleted by a line.

[260] The date, 4 June 1372, is bracketed against this item and the next two.
[261] *parochiali* repeated MS.
[262] The date, 2 June 1372, is bracketed against this item and the next three.

### Dunolmensis

Ricardo Bello de Beverlaco Eboracensis diocesis mandatur provideri de canonicatu et prebenda ecclesie Cestr' in strata (Chester-le-Street) Dunolmensis diocesis, vacantibus per mortem David de Wollore et per devolutionem. Non habuit effectum adhuc, ut est clare probatus, sed videatur cum habebit, et alia provisio facta alteri est supra, et nulla habuit effectum, quod non speratur.[257]

### Lincolniensis

Johanni Nampor, clerico Londoniensis diocesis, de Bedford' minori in ecclesia Lincolniensi, vacante per obitum Willelmi de Askeby, sedis apostolice familiaris. Est in mandato, et non habuit effectum quia auditor domini principis iam possedit x annos.[257]

### Dunolmensis

Johanni Lombar', clerico Eboracensis diocesis, de canonicatu et prebenda ecclesie collegiate de Aukland' Dunolmensis diocesis, vacantibus per obitum David de Wollore. Est in mandatis.[257]

### Wellensis

Ricardo Spicer, clerico Wygorniensis diocesis, mandatur provideri de beneficio ecclesiastico cum cura vel sine cura ad collationem episcopi Wellensis, vi idus Junii.[263]

### Eboracensis

Johanni de Ledes presbytero mandatur provideri de beneficio ecclesiastico ad collationem et cetera archiepiscopi Eboracensis, iiii[to] idus Junii.[264]

### Dunolmensis

Rogero de Berneburgh' presbytero de beneficio ecclesiastico ad collationem prioris conventus sive capituli ecclesie Dunolmensis, et dimittet unum de beneficiis suis.

Restant fructus unius provisionis i; et sunt iii inutiles iii; restant iiii expectationes iiii.

### (fol. 112, cvii) Eboracensis

Item Burnet Eboracensis diocesis de beneficio ecclesiastico ad collationem episcopi, decani et capituli ecclesis Eboracensis, quarto idus Junii.[265]

### Eboracensis

Johanni Ancotes de canonicatu sub exspectatione prebende ecclesie apostolorum Petri et Pauli de Rippon' Eboracensis diocesis.

### Lincolniensis

Humfrido de Aldeburgh' mandatur provideri de canonicatu sub exspectatione prebende ecclesie Lincolniensis cum dignitate et cetera.

### Eboracensis

Thome de Wodhale de canonicatu sub exspectatione prebende ecclesie de Houdon'.

### Eboracensis

Helie de Sutton' de canonicatu sub exspectatione prebende ecclesie Beate Marie Sutwellensis Eboracensis diocesis.

### Norwicensis

Willelmo Linand, presbytero Lincolniensis diocesis, de beneficio ecclesiastico ad collationem abbatis et conventus monasterii Sancti Petri de Burgo diocesis.

### Exoniensis

Johanni Mattecote Exoniensis diocesis de beneficio ecclesiastico ad collationem episcopi Exoniensis.

Willelmo de Burton' Lincolniensis diocesis de beneficio ecclesiastico ad collationem prioris et conventus de Letton' (Latton) diocesis.[266]

### Cicestrensis

Thome de Hanbyns presbytero ad collationem prioris et conventus de Lewes diocesis Cicestrensis.

Restant ix expectationes ix.

### (fol. 112[v]) Norwicensis

Thome Gudlak' presbytero Norwicensis diocesis de beneficio ecclesiastico ad collationem episcopi Norwicensis, iiii idus Junii.[267]

### Eboracensis

Thome Amcotes de canonicatu sub exspectatione prebende in ecclesia Sancti Johannis de Beverlaco Eboracensis diocesis.

### Dunolmensis

Henrico Spicer ad collationem episcopi Dunolmensis.

### Norwicensis

Henrico Ayeburgh', clerico Norwicensis diocesis, de beneficio ecclesiastico ad collationem episcopi Norwicensis.

### Dunolmensis

Johanni de Fordham mandatur provideri de beneficio ecclesiastico cum cura vel sine cura ad collationem

---

[263] 8 June 1372.
[264] The date, 10 June 1372, is bracketed against this item and the next.
[265] The date, 10 June 1372, is bracketed against this item and the next eight.

[266] In the margin: *quere diocesim quia hic non est.*
[267] The date, 10 June 1372, is bracketed against this item and the next three.

episcopi, prioris et capituli ecclesie Dunolmensis, xiii kalendas Julii.[268]

### Wyntoniensis

Simoni Fareweyre, clerico Exoniensis, de beneficio ecclesiastico cum cura vel sine cura ad collationem episcopi, prioris et capituli ecclesie Wyntoniensis, xiiii kalendas Julii.[269]

### Eboracensis

Johanni de Norton' mandatur provideri de canonicatu sub exspectatione prebende et dignitatis spectantium ad collationem episcopi in ecclesia Eboracensi et cetera, xiii kalendas Julii.[268]

### Wyntoniensis

Ricardo de Filangley diocesis Lichfeldensis de beneficio ecclesiastico ad collationem episcopi, prioris et capituli ecclesie Wyntoniensis, xvi kalendas Julii.[270]
Restant viii expectationes viii.

### (fol. 113, cviii) Dunolmensis

Thome de Norton' Eboracensis diocesis de beneficio ecclesiastico cum cura vel sine cura ad collationem episcopi, prioris et capituli ecclesie Dunolmensis, xvi kalendas Julii.[270]

### Saresbiriensis

Willelmo de Burghbr' presbytero de canonicatu sub exspectatione prebende ecclesie Saresbiriensis, iiiito nonas Julii.[271]

### Eboracensis

Willelmo de Murifeld' de canonicatu sub exspectatione prebende ecclesie Eboracensis.

### Londoniensis

Rogero de Galborne de canonicatu sub exspectatione prebende ecclesie Londoniensis.

### Eboracensis

Engelberto Belle de perpetua vicaria seu altaria Sancte Katherine sita in ecclesia Sancti Martini Eboracensis diocesis, vacante per mortem Cesarii Nese, v nonas Julii.[272] Est iterato in vto mandato quia in iiiito dicitur quod non est talis.[273]

### Londoniensis

Johanni Bierle, presbytero Eboracensis diocesis, de parochiali ecclesia seu vicaria Sancti Stephani in Colemannestret et Sancti Olavi in veteri iudaismo Londonie (St. Stephen, Coleman St. and St. Olave Upwell)

canonice unitis, vacantibus per liberam resignationem ultimi rectoris, v nonas Julii. Dicitur quod est appropriata priori de Buxelee (Butley) diocesis Norwicensis, et est scriptum episcopo.[273]

### Wyntoniensis

Ricardo Spicer, clerico Wygorniensis, de beneficio ecclesiastico ad collationem episcopi Wyntoniensis, v nonas Julii.[271]

### Maguntinensis

Theodorico dicto Walscham, clerico Maguntinensis (Mainz) diocesis, de ecclesia parochiali in Elen (Ellen) dicte diocesis, vacante ex eo quod Johannes de Elen eam tenuit per annum et ultra ad sacerdotum non promotus, v nonas Julii.[274]
Restant fructus ii provisionum ii; et una est inutilis i; est restant v expectationes v.

### (fol. 113v) Eliensis

Johanni de Misterton', clerico Eboracensis diocesis, de beneficio ecclesiastico ad collationem episcopi, prioris et conventus ecclesie Eliensis, iii idus Julii.[275]

### Wyntoniensis

Roberto Samford' mandatur provideri de aliquo beneficio ecclesiastico prioris et capituli ecclesie Montisfonte (Mottisfont) diocesis Wyntoniensis, nono kalendas Augusti.[276]

### Eliensis

Johanni de Mistertan' clerico de beneficio ecclesiastico cum cura vel sine cura ad collationem episcopi Eliensis.

### Lincolniensis

Johanni de Bannesbury, presbytero Lincolniensis diocesis, de parochiali ecclesia de Waynflet (Wainfleet) dicte diocesis, vacante per obitum Willelmi de Askeby, ultimi rectoris. Nondum habuit effectum, ut est probatus, titulo regio impediente.[273]

### Wellensis

Johanni Godeneston', clerico Wellensis diocesis, de canonicatu et prebenda de Cutibe (Combe) in ecclesia Wellensi, vacantibus per assecutionem et possessionem Willelmi Derby in ecclesia monasterii Osney. Est in v mandato.[273]

### Cicestrensis

Gilberto Fawne alias de Sancto Botulpho mandatur provideri de canonicatu sub exspectatione prebende ecclesie Cicestrensis, pridie nonas Augusti.[277]

---

[268] 19 June 1372.
[269] 18 June 1372.
[270] 16 June 1372.
[271] The date, 4 July 1372, is bracketed against this item and the next two.
[272] 3 July 1372.
[273] In the margin: *provisio de vacanti.*

[274] In the margin: *non est in Anglia.*
[275] 13 July 1372.
[276] The date, 24 July 1372, is bracketed against this item and the next three.
[277] The date, 4 August 1372, is bracketed against this item and the next.

### Norwicensis

Thome de Durem, clerico Dunolmensis diocesis, de beneficio ecclesiastico cum cura vel sine cura ad collationem prioris et conventus de Buttelee (Butley) ordinis Sancti Augustini Norwicensis diocesis.

Restant fructus unius provisionis i; et iᵃ inutilis i; et v expectationes v.

### (fol. 114, cix) Lichfeldensis

Willelmo de Swinford', presbytero Lincolniensis diocesis, de beneficio ecclesiastico cum cura vel sine cura ad collationem prioris et conventus prioratus de Killingworth' (Kenilworth) Lichfeldensis diocesis, pridie nonas Augusti.[278]

### Saresbiriensis

Roberto de Lideford', clerico Exoniensis, de parochiali ecclesia de Laking' (Locking) Saresbiriensis diocesis, vacante per assecutionem alterius beneficii, dignitatis et cetera in ecclesia Cicestrensi factam vel faciendam per Johannem de Lideford', viii idus Augusti.[279] Nondum habuit effectum, sed videatur cum habebit, et adhuc est obligatus et iuratus quod veniret infra mensem et cetera.[273]

### Menevensis

Ricardo Tauntton', clerico Menevensis diocesis,[280] de canonicatu sub exspectatione prebende, dignitatis, personatus vel officii in ecclesia Menevensi in Wallia, v idus Augusti.[281]

### Saresbiriensis

Ricardo de Croxton' mandatur provideri de canonicatu sub exspectatione prebende ecclesie Saresbiriensis, xvi kalendas Septembris.[282]

### Cantuariensis

Johanni de Bakinglee Norwicensis diocesis de beneficio ecclesiastico cum cura vel sine cura ad collationem archiepiscopi, prioris et capituli Cantuariensis, xv kalendas Septembris.[283]

### Cicestrensis

Ade Ertham presbytero mandatur provideri de canonicatu sub exspectatione prebende ecclesie Cicestrensis, xvi kalendas Septembris.[284]

### Herefordensis

Jacobo de Venne presbytero de canonicatu sub exspectatione prebende ecclesie Herefordensis.

Restant fructus unius provisionis i; et sex exspectationes vi.

### (fol. 114ᵛ) Saresbiriensis

Thome Dalby, presbytero Lincolniensis diocesis, de canonicatu sub exspectatione prebende ecclesis Saresbiriensis, xvi kalendas Septembris.[282]

### Eboracensis

Johanni de Wythornwyk' presbytero de canonicatu sub exspectatione prebende ecclesie collegiate Beverlacensis, xv kalendas Septembris.[283]

### Lincolniensis

Johanni de Godmeston', clerico Wellensis diocesis, de parochiali ecclesia de Askeby (Ashby) Lincolniensis diocesis, vacante dum Johannes de Bannebury possessionem parochialis ecclesie Beate Marie in Waynfleth' (St. Mary, Wainfleet) dicte Lincolniensis diocesis fuerit pacifice assecutus, xvi kalendas Septembris.[282] Nondum habuit effectum, et est socius domini Lincolniensis.[285]

### Lincolniensis

Thome Kendale mandatur provideri de canonicatu sub exspectatione prebende in ecclesia Lincolniensi cum dignitate et cetera, xv kalendas Septembris.[286]

### Londoniensis

Willelmo Klevele Londoniensis diocesis de beneficio ecclesiastico cum cura vel sine cura ad collationem episcopi, decani et capituli ecclesie Londoniensis.

### Cantuariensis et Roffensis

Johanni Wodehull' presbytero conceditur quod collatio et provisio sibi facte de parochiali ecclesia in Eripington'[287] (Orpington) diocesis Cantuariensis, vacante ⟨per mortem⟩ Nicholai dicti Regestrator' valeant et fuerunt confirmate, pro taxa lx m., xiiii kalendas Septembris.[288] Solvit die xxi Novembris anno LXXIII, non obstante breve regio revocato, in viginti m. xiii li. vi s. viii d.[289]

### Cantuariensis

Nicholao de Chadden' conceditur quod collatio et provisio sibi facte de parochiali ecclesia de Chevug' (Charing?) Cantuariensis diocesis, vacante causa permutationis in manibus ordinarii facte,[290] valeant et

---

[278] 4 August 1372.
[279] 6 August 1372.
[280] *Menevensis diocesis* repeated MS.
[281] 9 August 1372.
[282] 17 August 1372.
[283] 18 August 1372.
[284] The date, 17 August 1372, is bracketed against this item and the next.

[285] In the margin: *provisio de vacanti.*
[286] The date, 18 August 1372, is bracketed against this item and the next.
[287] *Orpington',* Collectorie 13, fol. 174ᵛ.
[288] The date, 19 August 1372, is bracketed against this item and the next.
[289] In the margin: *provisio de vacanti; solvit.*
[290] *factam,* MS.

fuerunt confirmate. Decanus est de Arcubus, et dicit quod numquam petiit confirmationem, et ita asserit dominus Cantuariensis, et quod cum scivit displicavit sibi, quare et cetera.[285]

Recepta pagine xiii li. vi s. viii d.; resta pecunie xx li. xiii s. iiii d.; restant fructus provisionum ii; et iiii expectationes iiii.

### (fol. 115, cx) Saresbiriensis

Henrico Fetherenstonhalgh' de canonicatu sub exspectatione prebende ecclesie Saresbiriensis, xiii kalendas Septembris.[291]

### Dunolmensis

Simoni de Kerton', clerico Karleolensis diocesis, mandatur provideri de beneficio ecclesiastico cum cura vel sine cura ad collationem episcopi, prioris et capituli ecclesie Dunolmensis, v[to] kalendas Septembris.[292]

### Lincolniensis

Willelmo de Harshamme mandatur provideri de canonicatu sub exspectatione prebende ecclesie Lincolniensis.

### Cantuariensis

Johanni Ahe Wygorniensis diocesis de beneficio ecclesiastico ad collationem prioris et conventus ecclesie Cantuariensis.

### Norwicensis

Andree Hokere, presbytero Norwicensis diocesis, de beneficio ecclesiastico ad collationem episcopi Norwicensis.

### Cantuariensis

Alano Blak', clerico Norwicensis diocesis, de beneficio ecclesiastico ad collationem archiepiscopi Cantuariensis.

### Wyntoniensis

Johanni Wendlongburgh, clerico Londoniensis diocesis, de beneficio ecclesiastico ad collationem episcopi, prioris et capituli ecclesie Wyntoniensis.

### Menevensis

Ricardo Tauntton', clerico Menevensis diocesis, in Wallia, de canonicatu sub exspectatione prebende ecclesie Memenovensis cum dignitate.
Restant viii expectationes viii.

### (fol. 115[v]) Patricii

Ade de Naas, diacono Daracensis (Kildare) diocesis

de canonicatu sub exspectatione prebende ecclesie Sancti Patricii, v kalendas Septembris.[293]

### Aladensis

Roberto Baret, clerico Aladensis (Killala) diocesis, de vicaria curata parochialis ecclesie Sancte Trinitatis de Crismolina (Crossmolina) dicte diocesis, vacante per munus consecrationis Thome episcopi Elsmensis (Emly). Non est in Anglia.[285]

### Cantuariensis

Johanni Wrigthe de Tymworth', presbytero Norwicensis diocesis, de beneficio ecclesiastico ⟨cum⟩ cura vel sine cura ad collationem archiepiscopi, prioris et capituli Cantuariensis, iii[tio] nonas Septembris.[294]

### Lincolniensis

Willelmo Campion' de Histon', clerico Eliensis diocesis, de beneficio ecclesiastico cum cura vel sine cura ad collationem episcopi, decani et capituli ecclesie Lincolniensis.

### Wyntoniensis

Johanni Rethesunte, clerico Wyntoniensis diocesis, de beneficio ecclesiastico ad collationem episcopi Wyntoniensis.

### Cantuariensis

Johanni Stok', presbytero Wyntoniensis diocesis, de beneficio ecclesiastico cum cura vel sine cura ad collationem prioris et capituli ecclesie Cantuariensis.

### Wellensis

Willelmo Hankere, presbytero Menevensis diocesis, de beneficio ecclesiastico ad collationem abbatis et conventus monasterii Glaston' Wellensis diocesis.
Inutiles sunt i[a] provisio et i[a] expectatio ii; restant v expectationes v.

### (fol. 116; cxi) Saresbiriensis

Henrico Sunyngwell', presbytero Saresbiriensis diocesis, de canonicatu sub exspectatione prebende in ecclesia monialium Schaston' (Shaftesbury) dicte diocesis, iii° nonas Septembris.[295]

### Wellensis

Wellemo de Borgonony, clerico Landavensis diocesis, de beneficio ecclesiastico ad collationem abbatis et conventus monasterii Glaston' Wellensis diocesis, iiii idus Septembris.[296]

---

[291] 20 August 1372.
[292] The date, 28 August 1372, is bracketed against this item and the next six.
[293] The date, 28 August 1372, is bracketed against this item and the next. In the margin: *non est in Anglia*.

[294] The date, 3 September 1372, is bracketed against this item and the next four.
[295] 3 September 1372.
[296] The date, 10 September 1372, is bracketed against this item and the next three.

### Sodorensis

Mandatur ⟨provideri⟩ Johanni Judicis, clerico Sodorensis (Sodor) diocesis de parochiali ecclesia Sancte Columbe de Hey (Howmore) dicte diocesis, vacante per mortem Dominici Kenuti, ultimi rectoris. Non est in Anglia.[285]

### Sodorensis

Gilberto de Ille, presbytero Sodorensis diocesis, de beneficio ecclesiastico cum cura vel sine cura ad collationem episcopi Sodorensis. Non est in Anglia.

### Turinensis

Fratri Arnaldo de Podio de beneficio ecclesiastico cum cura vel sine cura ad collationem preceptoris domus Sancti Anthonii de Remersio (Saint-Antoine-du-Rocher?) diocesis Turinensis (Tours?). Non est in Anglia.

### Lincolniensis

Ricardo Juouet de beneficio ecclesiastico cum cura vel sine cura ad collationem abbatis et conventus Leycestr' diocesis Lincolniensis, iii nonas Septembris.[297]

### Lincolniensis

Thome de Schirford', presbytero Norwicensis diocesis, de canonicatu sub exspectatione prebende cum dignitate in ecclesia Lincolniensi.

### Cicestrensis

Johanni Langristh', clerico Cicestrensis diocesis, de canonicatu sub exspectatione prebende ecclesie Cicestrensis.

Inutiles sunt iii provisiones iii; et restant v expectationes v.

### (fol. 116ᵛ) Cantuariensis

Willelmo Menesse de canonicatu sub exspectatione prebende in ecclesia collegiata de Wyngham (Wingham) in ecclesia Cantuariensi, iiiᵗᵒ nonas Septembris.[298]

### Wellensis

Johanni Mortomer de beneficio ecclesiastico cum cura vel sine cura ad collationem episcopi, decani et capituli Wellensis.

### Wyntoniensis

Phillo Conredo de beneficio ecclesiastico cum cura vel sine cura ad collationem abbatis et conventus monasterii de Hyde Wyntoniensis.

### Exoniensis

Willelmo Tongham mandatur provideri de beneficio ecclesiastico cum cura vel sine cura ad collationem decani et capituli ecclesie Exoniensis.

### Sarisbirensis

Reginaldo Attetonne, clerico Wygorniensis diocesis, de parochiali ecclesia de Fovente (Fovant) Sarisbiriensis diocesis, vacante ex eo quod Thomas Bemby in ordine ordinis Cartusiensis intravit de facto cum habitu, pro taxa xx m. Habet terminum et est obligatus cum iuramento, et solvit die prima Aprilis anno LXXIIII in decem m. sex li. tresdecim s. et quatuor d.[299]

### Norwicensis

Thome Drayton' Norwicensis diocesis de beneficio ecclesiastico cum cura vel sine cura ad collationem episcopi Norwicensis.

### Wellensis

Henrico Derby de beneficio ecclesiastico cum cura vel sine cura ad collationem abbatis et conventus monasterii de Keynesham (Keynsham) diocesis Wellensis.

Recepta pagine vi li. xiii s. iiii d.; resta pecunie vi li. xiii s. iiii d.; et vi expectationes vi.

### (fol. 117, cxii) Norwicensis

Johanni Bartot, clerico Londoniensis diocesis, de beneficio ecclesiastico cum cura vel sine cura ad collationem et cetera abbatis et conventus monasterii Beate Marie de Langele (Langley) ordinis Premonstratensis Norwicensis diocesis, iiiᵗⁱᵒ nonas Septembris.[300]

### Bathoniensis

Johanni Baleben, clerico Bathoniensis diocesis, de beneficio ecclesiastico cum cura vel sine cura ad collationem episcopi, prioris et capituli Bathoniensis, iiiiᵗᵒ idus Septembris.[301]

### Norwicensis

Parochialis ecclesia de Ronham (Rendham) Norwicensis diocesis, vacans per mortem Ade de Sudbur', Hugoni episcopo Cluanensi (Clonmacnois) usque ad apostolice sedis beneplacitum fuit data in comendam. Alia est provisio, supra folio,[302] facta alteri, et ista nichil valet.[303]

### Bangorensis

Johanni Cheyne de medietate parochialis ecclesie curate de Landyan (Llandinam?) Bangorensis diocesis dum vacabit per assecutionem parochialis ecclesie de Orpington' faciendam per Willelmum Loring'. Est in v mandato.[303]

---

[297] The date, 3 September 1372, is bracketed against this item and the next two.

[298] The date, 3 September 1372, is bracketed against this item and the next six.

[299] Sum repeated MS. In the margin: *provisio de vacanti; solvit.*

[300] 3 September 1372.

[301] The date, 10 September 1372, is bracketed against this item and the next five.

[302] A blank space is left in MS.

[303] In the margin: *provisio de vacanti.*

## Lichfeldensis

Johanni Plumme clerico de parochiali ecclesia de Audeley (Audley) Lichfeldensis diocesis, vacante per mortem Domini Ricardi de Cowper ultimi rectoris. Litigatur quia non habuit effectum adhuc propter unionem factam diu est cuidam alteri, ut pretendit.[303]

## Eboracensis

Radulpho de Fetryngton', presbytero Eboracensis diocesis, de beneficio ecclesiastico ad collationem abbatis et conventus monasterii Beate Marie extra muros Eboraci.

## Lincolniensis

Thome Yslep de canonicatu sub exspectatione prebende ecclesie Lincolniensis.

Inutiles sunt ii provisiones ii; et sunt iiii expectationes iiii; restant unius provisionis fructus i.

## (fol. 117ᵛ) Menevensis

Simoni Johannis de canonicatu sub exspectatione prebende ecclesie Menevensis, iiiiᵗᵒ idus Septembris.[304]

## Eboracensis

Roberto Lithirim de beneficio ecclesiastico cum cura vel sine cura ad collationem archiepiscopi Eboracensis.

## Wellensis

Simoni Fareweye Exoniensis diocesis de canonicatu sub exspectatione prebende ecclesie Wellensis.

## Lincolniensis

Eudoni de Anderby, presbytero Lincolniensis diocesis, de beneficio ecclesiastico ad collationem prioris et conventus prioratus de Spalding' dicte diocesis.

## Wellensis

Rogero Payn de canonicatu sub exspectatione prebende in ecclesia Wellensis cum dignitate.

## Cantuariensis

Roberto Attehalle de beneficio ecclesiastico cum cura vel sine cura ad collationem archiepiscopi, prioris et capituli ecclesie Cantuariensis.

## Cantuariensis

Johanni Delot Lincolniensis diocesis de beneficio ecclesiastico cum cura vel sine cura ad collationem episcopi, prioris et capituli Cantuariensis, vii kalendas Octobris.[305]

## Exoniensis

Gilberto Fawne alias de Sancto Botulpho de beneficio ecclesiastico cum cura vel sine cura ad collationem episcopi Exoniensis, xviii kalendas Octobris.[306]

Restant viii expectationes viii.

## (fol. 118, cxiii) Cantuarensis

Philippo de Let, clerico Lichfeldensis diocesis, de beneficio ecclesiastico cum cura vel sine cura ad collationem archiepiscopi, prioris et capituli ecclesie Cantuariensis, viii kalendas Octobris.[307]

## Lincolniensis

Thome de Lee, clerico Lichfeldensis diocesis, de beneficio ecclesiastico ad collationem abbatis et conventus monasterii de Ramsen (Ramsey) diocesis Lincolniensis.

## Cantuariensis

Hugoni Attehall' de beneficio ecclesiastico cum cura vel sine cura ad collationem archiepiscopi Cantuariensis.

## Sarisbirensis

Johanni de Northwod' presbytero de canonicatu sub exspectatione prebende in ecclesia monialium Schaston' (Shaftesbury) diocesis Sarisbiriensis.

## Londoniensis

Johanni Milis presbytero de canonicatu sub exspectatione prebende ecclesie Londoniensis.

## Eboracensis

Johanni Uppingham de canonicatu sub exspectatione prebende in ecclesie Suthwellensis.

## Exoniensis

Laurentio Gonnerie de canonicatu sub exspectatione prebende ecclesie Exoniensis cum dignitate.

Restant vii expectationes vii.

## (fol. 118ᵛ) Sarisbiriensis

Roberto de Lamborn' de canonicatu sub exspectatione prebende ecclesie Sarisbiriensis, vii kalendas Octobris.[308]

## Cicestrensis

Johanni Mori de canonicatu sub exspectatione prebende ecclesie Cicestrensis.

---

[304] The date, 10 September 1372, is bracketed against this item and the next five.
[305] 25 September 1372.

[306] 14 September 1372.
[307] The date, 24 September 1372, is bracketed against this item and the next six.
[308] The date, 25 September 1372, is bracketed against this item and the next six.

### Wellensis

Johanni Okerk' clerico de canonicatu sub exspectatione prebende ecclesie Wellensis.

### Londoniensis

Philippo Olneye de beneficio ecclesiastico ad collationem episcopi Londoniensis.

### Wyntoniensis

Johanni Attenhall de beneficio ecclesiastico cum cura vel sine cura ad collationem episcopi Wyntoniensis.

### Norwicensis

Hugoni Baudon' de beneficio ecclesiastico ad collationem abbatis et conventus monasterii Sancti Edmundi de Bury.

### Lichfeldensis

Johanni Scamper presbytero de canonicatu sub exspectatione prebende ecclesie Lichefeldensis.
Restant vii expectationes vii.

(fol. 119, cxiiii) Edmundo clerico Domini Thome Terel de canonicatu sub exspectatione prebende ecclesie collegiate de Houden' (Howden), vii kalendas Octobris.[309]

### Wyntoniensis

Johanni Ambenyle, presbytero Sarisbiriensis diocesis, de canonicatu sub exspectatione prebende in ecclesia monasterii monialium Sancte Marie Wyntonie, x kalendas Octobris.[310]

### Assavensis

Ricardo Tauntton', clerico Assavensis diocesis, de canonicatu sub exspectatione prebende in ecclesia Assavensi.

### Exoniensis

Laurentio Gonneris de canonicatu sub exspectatione prebende cum dignitate in ecclesia Exoniensi.

### Menevensis

Item Blag' presbytero de beneficio ecclesiastico ad collationem episcopi Menevensis.

### Menevensis

Johanni Dyer de Dinas de beneficio ecclesiastico ad collationem episcopi Menevensis.

### Wellensis

Johanni de Upton' de canonicatu sub exspectatione prebende ecclesie Wellensis.
Restant vii expectationes vii.

---

[309] 25 September 1372. In the margin: *quere diocesim.*
[310] The date 22 September 1372, is bracketed against this item and the next five.

### (fol. 119ᵛ) Sarisbiriensis

Johanni Godmanston' de canonicatu sub exspectatione prebende ecclesie Sarisbiriensis, x kalendas Octobris.[311]

### Sarisbiriensis

Waltero Pese, presbytero Sarisbiriensis diocesis, de parochiali ecclesia de Cnoel (Knoyle) dicte diocesis dum vacabit per assecutionem pacificam canonicatuum et prebendarum monasteriorum monialium de Wilton' et Schaftesbury ordinis Sancti Benedicti faciendam per Edwardum de Cherdestok' dicte diocesis, pro taxa xxx m. Gardaraularius domine principisse possidet ad huc dictam ecclesiam, quare gratia non habuit effectum, quia ipse non habet pacifice prebendas. Solvit die viii Junii anno LXXIIII vi li. xiii s. iiii d.[312]

### Cantuariensis

Willelmo Chaddessle, clerico Wygorniensis diocesis, de beneficio ecclesiastico ad collationem archiepiscopi, prioris et capituli ecclesie Cantuariensis.

### Cantuariensis

Johanni Digg', presbytero Cantuariensis diocesis, de canonicatu sub exspectatione prebende in ecclesie collegiata de Wyngham (Wingham) Cantuariensis diocesis, vᵗᵒ kalendas Octobris.[313]

### Londoniensis

Roberto Bradegare de canonicatu sub exspectatione prebende ecclesie Londoniensis.

### Cicestrensis

Henrico Sunningwell' de beneficio ecclesiastico cum cura vel sine cura ad collationem abbatis et conventus monasterii de Bello diocesis Cicestrensis.

### Wellensis

Johanni Mulleward', clerico Wellensis diocesis, de canonicatu sub exspectatione prebende[314] ecclesie Wellensis.
Recepta pagine vi li. xiii s. iiii d.; resta pecunie xiii li. vi s. viii d.; restant vi expectationes vi.

### (fol. 120, cxv) Wellensis

Thome Westwere, presbytero Wellensis diocesis, de beneficio ecclesiastico cum cura vel sine cura ad collationem abbatis et conventus monasterii Glaston' diocesis Wellensis, v kalendas Octobris.[315]

---

[311] The date, 22 September 1372, is bracketed against this item and the next two.
[312] In the margin: *provisio de vacanti; solvit.*
[313] The date, 27 September 1372, is bracketed against this item and the next three.
[314] *prebende* repeated MS.
[315] The date, 27 September 1372, is bracketed against this item and the next.

## Wyntoniensis

Thome Brandon de beneficio ecclesiastico ad collationem episcopi, prioris et capituli ecclesie Wyntoniensis.

## Eboracensis

Motu proprio fuit provisum Petro titulo Sancte Praxedis presbytero cardinali de archidiaconatu ac canonicatu et prebenda ecclesie Eboracensis, vacantibus per obitum bone memorie Philipi cardinalis Sabinensis, vi nonas Octobris.[316] Cardinalis est.

## Spirensis

Conrado de Duderstat de canonicatu et prebenda ecclesia Sancti Germani extra muros Spirensis (Speyer), vacantibus per obitum quondam Johannis de Ruportisburg, kalendas Octobris.[317] Non est in Anglia sed in Alamania.[318]

## Lincolniensis

Motu proprio fuit provisum Jacobi Sancti Georgii ad Velum aureum diacono cardinali de archidiaconatu Leycestr' in ecclesia Lincolniensi, vacante per obitum bone memorie Domini Philipi Sabinensis episcopi cardinalis, vi nonas Octobris.[319] Portavit litteras camere, quas sunt in archivis, quod habet usque ad iii annos prorogationem de data vii die Maii anno LXXII.[318]

## Menevensis

Johanni ap Corgone, presbytero Menevensis diocesis, de beneficio ecclesiastico cum cura vel sine cura ad collationem episcopi Menevensis, iii nonas Octobris.[320]

## Lincolniensis

Motu proprio fuit provisum Bertrando titulo Sancte Prisce presbytero Cardinali de canonicatu et prebenda Nassington' in ecclesia Lincolniensis, vacantibus [321] per obitum Philipi episcopi Sabinensis cardinalis, vi nonas Octobris.[322]

Restant fructus iii provisionum iii; iª est inutilis i; restant iii expectationes iii.

## (fol. 120ᵛ) Landavensis

Collatio et provisio auctoritate ordinaria facte Thome de Brandeston', presbytero Lincolniensis diocesis, de precentoria ecclesie Landavensis, vacante per obitum quondam Philipi Onyas, fuerunt confirmate seu provisum de novo, x kalendas Novembris.[323] Solvit die ultima Novembris anno LXXIII in partem fructuum viginti sex s. viii d.[324]

## Norwicensis

Simoni de Liston' de canonicatu sub exspectatione prebende ecclesie Norwicensis, viii kalendas Novembris.[325]

## Exoniensis

Motu proprio fuit provisum Bertrand titulo Sancti Marcelli presbytero cardinali de canonicatu et prebenda ecclesie Exoniensis et de precentoria eiusdem ecclesie, vacantibus per mortem ultimi precentoris, pridie nonas Novembris.[326] Cardinalis est Convenarum (Comminges), et ista gratia nondum habuit effectum quia unus expectans litigat cum uno regio, et cetera.[318]

## Cicestrensis

Roberto Attagrene mandatur provideri de canonicatu sub exspectatione prebende ecclesie Cicestrensis, pridie idus Novembris.[327]

## Lincolniensis

Johanni Lideford', presbytero Exoniensis diocesis, de canonicatu et prebenda ecclesie Lincolniensis vacantibus per obitum Johannis Sweyneseyd'. Non habuit effectum quia alius possidet titulo regio.[318]

## Dunolmensis

Motu proprio fuit provisum Roberto basilice xii apostolorum presbytero cardinali de parochiali ecclesia de Wermouth' episcopi (Bishop Wearmouth) Dunolmensis diocesis, vacante per obitum Thome Neuby, xv kalendas Decembris.[328] Cardinalis est.[318]

## Lincolniensis

Mandatur et comittitur archiepiscopo Cantuariensi quod parochialem ecclesiam de Bidnham (Biddenham) Lincolniensis diocesis monasterio et abbatisse et conventui monasterii de Wateberbe (Waterbeach) sub certis formis unire et incorporare possit, xvii kalendas Decembris.[329] Nondum habuit effectum dicta unio prout est clare probatum, quia ille, qui iam possidet, possidet xxii annos et cetera.[330]

Recepta pagine xxvi s. viii d.; restant fructus duarum [331] provisionum ii; et restant ii expectationes ii; et sunt ii provisiones inutiles ii.

---

[316] 2 October 1372. In the margin: *provisio de vacanti*.
[317] 1 October 1372.
[318] In the margin: *provisio de vacanti*.
[319] 2 October 1372.
[320] 5 October 1372.
[321] *vacantibus* repeated MS.
[322] 2 October 1372. In the margin: *provisio de vacanti*; *Cardinalis est Sancte Prisce*.

[323] 23 October 1372.
[324] Sum repeated MS. In the margin: *provisio de vacanti*; *solvit*.
[325] 25 October 1372.
[326] 4 November 1372.
[327] The date, 12 November 1372, is bracketed against this item and the next
[328] 17 November 1372.
[329] Followed by *et valeat* deleted by a line. 15 November 1372.
[330] In the margin: *provisio de*.
[331] Over *unius* deleted by a line.

### (fol. 121, cxvi) Londoniensis

Johanni Haukewod' Londoniensis diocesis de canonicatu sub exspectatione prebende ecclesie Londoniensis, xii kalendas Decembris.[332]

### Dunolmensis, Lincolniensis, Eliensis

Simoni titulo Sancti Sixti presbytero cardinali conceditur quod permutatio facta de parochiali ecclesia de Wermouth' episcopi (Bishop-Wearmouth) Dunolmensis diocesis cum Thoma de Newby pro canonicatu et prebenda Lincolniensibus ac ecclesia parochiali de Somersham (?) diocesis Eliensis in manibus ordinarii valeat et plenam optineat roboris firmitatem, nonas Decembris.[333] Cardinalis Cantuariensis est, et nil solvit, sicut nec alii.[318]

### Exoniensis

Deodato Clave de beneficio ecclesiastico cum cura vel sine cura ad collationem prioris et conventus prioratus de Pleynton' (Plympton) Exoniensis diocesis, xvi kalendas Januarii.[334]

### Roffensis

Eoyn Omghill' Corkegensis diocesis de beneficio ecclesiastico ad collationem episcopi Roffensis.

### Laoniensis

Demicio Otitruygh, clerico Laoniensis (Killaloc) diocesis, de canonicatu sub exspectatione prebende ecclesie Laoniensis. Non est in Anglia.

### Roffensis

Johanni de Lanwaran de Archenefeld', clerico Herefordensis diocesis, de beneficio ecclesiastico ad collationem episcopi, prioris et capituli ecclesie Roffensis.

### Cantuariensis

Hugoni de Bukinhull' de beneficio ecclesiastico ad collationem archiepiscopi, prioris et capituli Cantuariensis, xiiii kalendas Januarii.

Restant fructus unius provisionis i; iª expectatio est inutilis iª; et iiii expectationes restant iiii.

### (fol. 121ᵛ) Wyntoniensis

Johanni Grisp Eliensis diocesis de beneficio ecclesiastico ad collationem episcopi, prioris et capituli Wyntoniensis, xiiii kalendas Januarii.[335]

### Eboracensis

Willelmo de Ardern', presbytero Lincolniensis diocesis, de canonicatu et prebenda de Norwell' in ecclesia de Sutwell' diocesis Eboracensis, vacantibus per obitum Johannis de Norwell', iii nonas Januarii.[336] Per breve regium fuit data copia in cancellaria die xx Junii anno LXXIII, sed ad quem finem nescitur; est tamen in mandato.[337]

### Sarisbiriensis

Presentatio et institutio auctoritate ordinaria facte Sampsoni Trigal de prioratu de Leder (Loders) diocesis Sarisbiriensis, vacante per liberam resignationem factam per Robertum Doree, fuerunt confirmate seu provisum de novo, iii idus Januarii.[338] Est in iiii mandato ad sequestrandum et monendum et cetera.[337]

### Lincolniensis

Ricardo Bullok' de Irtlingburgh' Lincolniensis diocesis mandatur provideri de perpetua vicaria curata parochialis ecclesie Sancti Jacobi de Grimisby (Great Grimsby) dicte diocesis, vacante per mortem Johannis de Ouneby, vi idus Aprilis anno secundo,[339] pro taxa xiiii m.[337] Solvit die iii Octobris anno LXXIII in vii m. iiiiᵒʳ li. xiii s. iiii d.[340] Item solvit xii die Aprilis anno LXXIIII in plenam solutionem taxe, quia iuravit quod vix ascendit ipsam taxam et ita habetur in quitantia, iiiiᵒʳ li. xiii s. iiii d.[340]

Contenta in isto folio et xvii precedentibus fuerunt Londonie tradita dicto collectori et de camera missa die x Maii anno LXXIII domini et cetera. Et expost de provisionibus nichil de camera pro primis fructibus fuit missum, et est annus et v menses.

Recepta pagine ix li. vi s. viii d.; restant fructus ii provisionum ii; et restat i expectatio i.

Summa recepte ipsius tertii quaterni cxi li. vi s. viii d.

Summa reste istius quaterni in pecunia de taxatis beneficiis cviii li. vi s. viii d.

Summa reste fructuum de nondum taxatis provisionibus xxviii beneficiarum.

Restant etiam inutiles provisiones xxix.

Restant expectationes que non habuerunt effectum clxxxix.

### (fol. 122, cxvii) Conclusio compotorum recepte et restarum

Summa recepte primorum fructuum de tempore Domini Gregorii ultra denarios Beati Petri et census et exporata quadringentas sexaginta tres li. undecim s. duos d., iiiiᶜ lxiii li. xi s. ii d. sterlingorum.[341]

Summa universalis totius recepte a secundo folio usque ad folium cxvii inclusive facte per me, Arnaldum Garnerii, a die viii Februarii anno a nativitate domini

---

[332] 20 November 1372.
[333] 5 December 1372.
[334] The date, 17 December 1372, is bracketed against this item and the next three.
[335] 19 December 1372.

[336] 3 January 1373.
[337] In the margin: *provisio de vacanti*.
[338] 10 January 1372.
[339] 8 April 1372.
[340] In the margin: *solvit*.
[341] In the margin: *supra est per folia merius* (reading of the last word doubtful).

millesimo CCCLXX secundo, qua die prima fui Londonie, usque ad diem xxvii Julii anno sequenti LXX quarto, qua die exivi de Londonia eundo versus curiam pro computando, asscendit ad tria milia ducentas et octuaginta et sex li. novem s. et ix d., iii^m ii^e lxxxvi li. ix s. iii d.[342]

Valent, singulo floreno ponderis camere pro tribus solidis sterlingorum computando monete Anglicane, viginti unum milia nongentas novem fl. camere ii s. ix d. sterlingorum, xxi^m ix^e ix fl. ii s. ix d. sterlingorum.[343]

Vertatur folium et reperietur alias summas restarum pecunie et fructuum et cetera ad signum ‖–‖–‖ infra.

Secuntur infra assignationes et expense in duobus foliis immediate sequentibus que sunt concimiles seu quasi recepte suprascripte in quantitate.

(fol. 122^v) Conclusio compotorum recepte et restarum

Continua supra ab alia parte folii ad signum post receptam universalem totius libri istius que subsecutur.[344]

Summa reste universalis beneficiorum taxatorum ad pecuniam totius istius libri tam restarum omnium quam trium quaternorum sibi supradicto medio tempore solum missorum a camera quam etiam exploratorum assendit in pecunia usque ad dictam diem xxvii Julii anno domini et cetera LXX quarto, qua die dictus collector ressesit de Anglia, dimisso ibi locumtenenti, ii^m vii^e lxix li. sterlingorum iii s. v d., cum resta domini[345] Cabrespini supra folio xli.[346]

Valent decem et octo milia[347] quadringentos quinque fl. et dimidium vii d. sterlingorum, floreno auri pro iii s. computando, xviii^m iiii^e v fl. dym. vii d. sterlingorum.

Summa universalis reste primorum fructuum beneficiorum collatorum et nondum in pecunia taxatorum assendit ad fructus beneficiorum viii^xx xvii, cum uno restanti supra folio xli de tempore domini Cabrespini.

Summa universalis expectationum que nondum habuerunt effectum est vii^e xxiii.

Somma universalis inutilium provisionum restantium ad huc et male solventium totius istius libri ii^e lxxxviii.

Dictas vero summas omnes[348] dat camere dictus collector, salvo erore calculi et iure alieno.

(fol. 123, cxviii) Assignata camere

Memorandum quod anno a nativitate domini millesimo CCCLXX quarto, die quinta Februarii, scrutatis regestris domini collectoris Anglie, fuit repertum quod dictus collector in hoc biennio cum dymidio proxime

precedente assignaverat camere apostolice per Albertos et alios infrascriptas pecuniarum summas.

Primo tradidit Londonie Petro Marchi, socio et factori ipsorum Albertorum, nomine ipsius camere et de mandato apostolico, die duodecima Maii anno a nativitate Christi Millesimo CCCLXX secundo in centum quinquaginta li. sterlingorum mille fl. ponderis camere, cl li.

Item simili modo et forma tradidit eidem Petro Londonie die xvi mensis Augusti immediate sequenti in quadriginta quinque li. sterlingorum iii^e fl., xlv li.

Item decimaseptima die Octobris tunc sequenti in centum triginta quinque li. sterlingorum ix^e fl., cxxxv li.

Item die vii Novembris eodem anno in centum quinquaginta li. sterlingorum mille fl., cl li.

Item plus die xxvi mensis Februarii anno a nativitate domini et cetera LXXIII^tio in trescentis li. sterlingorum duo milia fl., iii^e li.

Item plus die vicesimaseptima Aprilis tunc immediate sequenti in sexaginta li. sterlingorum iiii^e fl., lx li.

Item plus die iiii^ta Maii in centum nonagintaquinque li. sterlingorum dicte monete ponderis camere mille trescentos fl., cxcv li.

Item plus die duodecima Maii statim sequenti in quadraginta quinque li. sterlingorum ccc fl., xlv li.

Item die xxv eiusdem mensis Maii in centum quinquaginta li. sterlingorum mille fl., cl li.

Item tradidit plus eidem Petro die prima Julii proxime sequentis in centum li. sterlingorum et die xix ipsius mensis in aliis centum libris et decimaquinta die Septembris in aliis centum li. duo milia fl., iii^e li.

Item simili modo et forma tradidit dicto Petro die xiiii Octobris eodem anno LXXIII^tio in centum quinquaginta li. sterlingorum mille fl., cl li.

Item plus die duodecima Novembris subsequenti in ducentis et decem li. sterlingorum mille quadringentos fl., ii^e x li.

(fol. 123^v) Item plus decimaquarta die Decembris eodem anno in centum et decem li. sterlingorum vii^e xxxiii fl. xii d. sterlingorum cx li.

Item simili modo et forma tradidit dictus collector dicto Petro die xvii Januarii anno a nativitate Christi millesimo CCCLXX quarto in septuaginta li. sterlingorum, et die tertia Februarii immediate sequenti in quindecim li. sterlingorum, octuaginta quinque li. que valent fl. ponderis camere v^e lxvi fl. li. s. sterlingorum, lxxxv li.

Postquam vero die xxvi Julii fuit simili modo repertum quod dictus nuntius tradidit dicto Petro Marchi de pecuniis dicte camere die ix Martii precedenti anno a nativitate et cetera LXX quarto in septuaginta quinque li. sterlingorum quingentos fl. ponderis camere lxxv li.

Item fuit repertum quod dictus nuntius tradiderat dicto Petro Marci, socio et procuratori Albertorum Antiquorum de Florentia, modo et forma consimili de pecu-

---

[342] In the margin: *Summa recepte totius libri.*

[343] Sum repeated MS. In the margin bracketed against this entry and the preceding: *Aprobo.*

[344] In the margin is the sign ‖–‖–‖.

[345] *domini* repeated MS.

[346] In the margin bracketed against this item and the next four: *Conclusio universalis restarum et recepte.*

[347] Follows *xv mel' fl. camere* deleted by a line.

[348] *omnis*, MS.

niis dicte camere apostolice die Jovis post quasimodo, que fuit dies xiii Aprilis, anno domini millesimo CCCLXX quarto in nonaginta li. sterlingorum sexcentos fl. ponderis camere, xc li.

Item plus die prima Maii anno supradicto tradiderat dicto Petro Marchi de pecuniis dicte camere sub modis et formis suprascriptis in ducentis et decem li. sterlingorum xiiiiᶜ fl., iiᶜ x li.

Item tradidit dictus collector plus eidem Petro Marchi nomine qua supra die decima quarta Junii anno domini millesimo CCCLXX quarto in lxxv li. sterlingorum quingentos fl. ponderis camere, lxxv li.

Item tradiderat dicto Petro Marchi modo consimili die xxi Julii anno predicto LXX quarto in centum quadraginta unam li. et decem solidos sterlingorum ixᶜ xliii fl. et tertium, cxli li. x s.

Item tradiderat dicto Petro Marchi modo consimili die xxv Julii anno domini et cetera LXX quarto tresdecim li. septem s. que valent fl. camere iiiiˣˣ ix fl., xiii li. vii s.

Summa de assignatis Albertis usque hic duo milia sexcentas octuaginta novem li. decem et septem s. sterlingorum, iiᵐ viᶜ lxxxix li. xvii s.

(fol. 124, cxix) Item fuit repertum tempora supradicta die quod dictus nuntius assignaverat die xi Martii anno a nativitate Christi et cetera LXX tertio eidem camere per Johannem Credy socium [349] Strociorum in trescentis fl. camere xlv li. sterlingorum.

Item tradidit prius pro solvendo exspensis domini vicecomitis et suorum anno LXX secundo, cum fuit missus ad Angliam per dominum nostrum papam super tractatu pacis in iiᵐ viiiᶜ fl. iiiiᶜ xx li.

Item solvit die xx Julii anno domini millesimo CCCLXX quarto pro quator aurifrisiis de mandato apostolico emptis in iiᶜ fl.[350] xxx li.

Item solvit dicta die pro duodecim pannis lecti emptis de mandato domini vicecomitis Turenn', qui sibi scripsit quod faceret sibi in compoto allocari, qui costarent viginti sex nobiles et quartum, qui valent lviii fl. et tertium, viii li. xv s.

Et solvit pro portu de Anglia usque Brug' et de Brug' usque ad Avinioniam pro medietate unius fardelli, que medietatis plus propter maiorem valentiam pertinebat predictis rebus, in xiiii fl. camere xlii s.

Summa pagine vᶜ v li. xvii s.

(fol. 124ᵛ) Item fuit repertum per decursum dicti regestri die xxvi Julii quod dictus nuntius solvit pro expensis portus litterarum officii per totum regnum quinque vicibus in dictis duobus annis cum dymidio, quarum fuit ultimus terminus ad quindenam Pasche et Beati Johannis Baptiste anno LXX quarti, xi li. xviii s. dym.

Item solvit pro papiro et incausto librorum et scrip-

turarum dictorum duorum annorum cum dymidio, viginti s. computando, ut est consuetum, pro singulo anno, pro toto valent quinquaginta s., 1 s.

Item solvit pro celario hospitii conducti Londonie dicto tempore duorum annorum cum dymidio et plus usque ad terminum Beati Michaelis anni predicti LXX quarti, ubi fuerunt duo anni et ix menses, pro singulis annis, ut est consuetum, decem m. computando, licet sibi quindecim m. costiterit hospitium et iam costet singulis annis viginti septem m. cum dymidia, que valent xviii li. vi s. viii d. sterlingorum.

Item supplicat sibi allocari pro exspensis iiiiᵒʳ mensium, videlicet a principio mensis Octobris anni LXXI, qua fuit sibi commissum officium, usque ad principium subsequentis mensis Februarii anno a nativitate domini et cetera LXXIIᵈᵒ, factis per eum in curia et extra, litteras officii et plures alias prosequendo, et versus Angliam medio tempore eundo, et in Calesio (Calais) per vi septimanas et ultra stando licentio passagii sperando, cum equitaturis et sua familia, quo tempore toto iiiiᵒʳ mensium vacavit officio et nichil de stipendiis percepit, quinquaginta octo li. sterlingorum, ad quas et plus asscendunt stipendia dictorum iiii mensium, quia sub spe recipiendi ipsa stipendia dictas exspensas et multo maiores subiit et nichil ipso tempore percepit, lviii li. sterlingorum.

Summa pagine xc li. xv s. ii d.

Summa universalis omnium assignatorum et exspensarum factarum ratione dicti officii a die viii Februarii anno a nativitate domini millesimo CCCLXX secundo, qua die primo fui Londonia, usque ad diem xxvii Julii anno sequenti LXXIIII, qua die exivi Londoniam eundo versus curiam pro computando, tria milia ducentas octuaginta et sex li. novem s. duos d. sterlingorum, iiiᵐ iiᶜ lxxxvi li. ix s. iii d.[351]

Valent, singulo floreno ponderis camere pro tribus solidis sterlingorum computando, viginti unum milia nongentos et novem fl. et duos s. ii d. sterlingorum, xxiᵐ ixᶜ fl. ii s. iii d.[352]

(fol. 125, cxx) Et quia recepta,[353] de qua habetur expresse supra folio cxvii, est concimilis dictis assignationibus, traditionibus et expensis, nichil restat debens camere appostolice dictus collector de receptis per eum ratione dicti officii dicto tempore sui regiminis que excedat ultra ii d. sterlingorum, ii d.

Ex post tamen, quod supra computat ab Anglie ressesisse, subcollector ibi dimissus, misit per cambium factum cum Albertis plures pecunias de quibus nulla sit mentio supra in dicta recepta nec in assignatis, sed ipse qui recepit et misit in suis compotis assignabit.

---

[349] socio, MS.
[350] florenis repeated MS.

[351] In the margin bracketed against this item and the next: *summa universalis.*
[352] In the margin: *Aprobo.*
[353] Followed by *est consimilis* deleted by a line.

(fol. 125ᵛ) Restarum summe in pecunia

Ultra dictam receptam restabant in pecunia dicta die xxvii Julii anno domini et cetera LXX quarto, de beneficiis per decursum libri nigri,[354] in pecuniam taxatam duo milia septingente sexaginta li. sexdecim s. et novem d., iiᵐ viiᶜ lx li. xvi s. ix d. sterlingorum.

Que valent, floreno camere pro tribus solidis computando, decem et octo milia quadringentos quinque fl. et dymidium septem denarios sterlingorum, xviiiᵐ iiiiᶜ v fl. et dym. vii d. sterlingorum.

Et restabant fructus beneficiorum nondum taxatorum centum septuaginta sex beneficiorum, viiiˣˣ xvi.

Et restabant de inutilibus provisionibus etiam ab antiquo ut in pluribus ducente octuaginta octo, iiᶜ lxxxviii.

Et restabant exspectationes que nondum haberunt effectum septingente [355] et viginti tres, viiᶜ xxiii.

Hec omnia dat salvo errore calculi et iure alieno in dictis restis.

Sic est in libro nigro reddito camere folio cxvii [356] in summa posita et per decursum ipsius libri repertum.

De dictis vero restis in pecunia erant de tempore Dominorum Clementis et Innocentii mille quadringente et quadraginta una li. x s. ix d., xiiiiᶜ xli ⟨li.⟩ x s. ix d.

Et de tempore Domini Urbani viᶜ xxxiiii li. xv s. sterlingorum.

Et de tempore Domini Gregorii de primo quaterno iiᶜ xvi li. xiii s. iiii d.

Et de secundo quaterno de dicto tempore Domini Gregorii clii li.

Et de tertio quaterno de dicto tempore Domini Gregorii cviii li. vi s. viii d.

Et de exploratis ccvii li. xi s.

Alias restas quere infra folio cxxvii ad signum H—CD

(fol. 126, cxxi) Excusationes parvitatis recepte.

Cause vero tam parve recepte dicte collectorie Anglie sicut est supra sunt septem capitula que sequntur.

i. Primo quia archidiaconi nichil solvunt ibi pro primis fructibus camere debitis de procurationibus, nec de iurisdictione, nec est consuetum, ut asserunt. Et tamen emolumenta ipsorum archidiaconatuum quasi ex toto saltim pro maiori parte in talibus consistunt.

ii. Item procuratores dominorum cardinalium nichil volunt solvere in vita eorum, nec post mortem aliquid reperitur nisi vix, et tamen habent quamplura meliora beneficia ibi et utiliora, et multi iam defuncti actenus habuerunt, qui adhuc pro magnis quantitatibus in restis camere retinentur et nichil illuc reperitur.

iii. Item quia revocatio unionum sive appropriationum per Dominum Urbanum factarum [357] a certo tempore citra et usque et etiam renovatio constitutionis

*Execrabilis* super pluralitate beneficiorum non habuit [358] locum in Anglia, collationes ea occasione quamplures expost facte non habuerunt effectum aliquod, sed dommiunt in regestris et nichil exigi potest.

iiii. Item possessores titulo regio nichil volunt solvere de eo ad quod beneficia erant obligata per prius rationem provisionum factarum predecessoribus eorumdem, licet obligationes sunt in rem seu saltim in rem scripte, inminentes quod collatio regia saltim pro tempore suo debet esse integra et cum pleno effectu.

(fol. 126ᵛ) v. Item possessores titulo regio [359] qui habuerunt collationes vel confirmationes ante vel post ⟨a sede apostolica⟩ [360] nichil volunt communiter solvere, allegantes quod non fuerunt usi illa gratia sed sola regia, licet per ipsos steterit non per sedem ipsam que fecerat in auctorizando quod in ipsa erat.

vi. Item possessores prioratuum et aliorum beneficiorum qui sunt de patronatu laycali nichil volunt solvere, licet confirmationem vel dispensationem super pluralitate vel aliqua inhabilitate alia beneficiorum ab ipsa sede optinuerint, et tamen in hoc ius presentandi patronis in aliquo non leditur nec aufertur.

vii. Item quia ibi nulle recipiuntur exspolie; ymo quia in aliquibus partibus regni sunt beneficia taxata de novo propter sterelitatem patrie vel propter guarras volunt solvere novam parvam taxam, non antiquam que maior est, asserentes quod nunquam fuerat usitatum in regno solvere nisi novam taxam vel antiquam ubi non est nova, et nunquam residuum ultra taxam fuit exactum, ut dicitur.

Et quia sunt in restis camere multa talia beneficia etiam ab antiquo restantia, videant domini quid agendum, quia magna exponitur querela cum aliquid novum a quoque in illis partibus attemptatur propter diuturnam que pretenditur taciturnitatem.

Ex causis vero predictis et aliis ipse collector tradidit bis in consilio regio x capitula infrascripta domino principe tunc inibi presidente.

(fol. 127, cxxii) Tradita bis in consilio regio pro iure camere domino principe tunc presidente.

Regie celsitudini in ipsius parliamento consilio seu cancellario supplicatur per apostolice sedis nuntium et collectorem iurium camere eiusdem in Anglia ut brevia regia in preiudicium camere nuper concessa possessoribus beneficiorum infrascriptorum dignetur revocare necnon et alia quecumque impedimenta auffere, tollens quominus camera predicta ab ipsis beneficiis et possessoribus eorundem et alias ius suum libere consequatur.

i. Primo archidiaconatus Cornubie in ecclesia Exoniensi tenetur dicte camere ad medietatem veri valoris ex collatione apostolica facta predecessori nunc auctori-

---

[354] Namely, the present book of accounts.
[355] *sextingente*, MS.
[356] Above, p. 475.
[357] *facta*, MS.

[358] *habuerunt*, MS.
[359] *regia*, MS.
[360] Supplied from fol. 183ᵛ.

tate regia possidentis, qui quidem predecessor ipsum archidiaconatum diu possedit, et fructus eiusdem auctoritate apostolica per plures annos recepit quousque per aliud beneficium incompatibile ipsum dimisit, et sic ipse archidiaconatus transit ad possesorem qui nunc est cum honore suo, attento quod ipsum debitum camere est reale seu in rem scriptum, propter quod dictus nuntius sequitur possessorem tanquam illum qui solvere tenetur de iure.

ii. Item ecclesia de Hulmo (Holme) Norwicensis diocesis tenetur dicte camere in certa summa pecunie pro provisionibus per sedem apostolicam actenus factis Thome Michiel et Roberto de Grymiston', et quia possessor auctoritate regia possidet, solvere recusat, licet obligatio sit in rem scripta que obstat possessori predicto ut in precedenti causa habetur.

iii. Item prebenda et precentoria ecclesie Cicestrensis tenentur dicte camere in certa summa pecunie pro quadam resta provisionis facta predecessori possessoris qui nunc est, qui quidem possessor solvere recusat eo solo quia auctoritate regia possidet, licet actio sit in rem ut in precedentibus casibus.

iiii. Item de prebenda de Lumley (Lamesley) in ecclesia collegiata Cestr' super stratam (Chester-le-Street) Dunolmensis diocesis ex quadam provisione facta per sedem apostolicam diu est Willelmo de Lughteburgh' debentur camere apostolice certe pecunie quas possessor qui nunc est titulo regio solvere recusat, licet obligatio sit in rem scripta ut supra in precedentibus.

v. Item de ecclesia de Torinton' (Torrington) Exoniensis diocesis et de ecclesia de Wyngham (Wigan) Lichfeldensis diocesis debetur certa pecunia ex dispensationibus factis per sedem apostolicam predecessoribus possessorum qui nunc sunt super pluralitate beneficiorum, in qua non poterat dispensare nec auctorizare patronus laycus, nec debebat, et cum dicta dispensatio nullum aufferat in iure suo presentandi preiudicium patrono layco, non debet impedire cameram quo minus ius suum ab ipso consequatur possessore, alias ipse patronus laycus dampnificaret dictam cameram absque comode suo quod esset incidere in legem fusiam.

(fol. 127ᵛ) vi. Item de prioratu de Swavesey diocesis Eliensis debetur taxa et plus ex confirmatione facta per sedem apostolicam predecessaribus possessoris qui nunc est, qui, ex eo quod de patronatu laycali est, solvere recusat quod debetur, licet ipsius proprie confirmatio nullum asserat preiudicium layco patrono in iure suo presentandi quod habet in eo.

vii. De prioratu de Lancastr' Eboracensis diocesis debentur dicte camere ex quadam obligatione facta in curia ducenti floreni, et est prohibitum per breve quod collector non compellat priorem ad solvendum, imminendo in ipso breve quod curia christianitatis in regno Anglie non habeat cognitionem nisi de testamentis vel

matrimoniis, de quibus nichil umquam collector predictus iudicialiter se intromisit sed solum de debitis camere exigendis.

viii. Item de beneficiis existentibus in manibus domini regis, sicut de prioratu de Kirkeby (Monks Kirby) et de prioratu de Swavesey et de aliis pluribus extraordinariis, et de beneficiis Domini Hugonis Pelegrini camere apostolice in magnis pecuniarum summis obligatis nichil propter ipsam occupationem regiam potest exigi per ipsum nuntium nec haberi, licet dicta manus regia debitum aes alienum non debeat de iure impedire, quia sic ipsa camera pro alieno gravaretur delicto, quod absit a tanto consilio sicut regia potestas hic habet, nam pena debet tenere actorem suum et ad alium non debet extendi de iure.

ix. Item simili modo supplicatur per dictum nuntium ut illa clausula in melius reformetur que in periculum animarum brevibus regiis prohibitoriis sibi directis de novo apponitur, videlicet *mandamus tibi districtius iniungentes quatinus sequestrum per te appositum et alias censuras tuas relaxes* et cetera, quia secundum canonicas sanctiones potestas temporalis in talibus cohercere non debet spiritualem, nam absolutio per potentiam obtenta magis ligat infelicem animam quam dissolvat.

x. Item simili modo et forma supplicatur per dictum nuntium ut sibi detur licentiam mittendi pecunias camere predicte ad curiam et ad partes externas saltim per cambium cum voluerit et sibi visum fuerit expedire, non obstantibus quibuscumque impedimentis et prohibitionibus aliis super hoc et aliis precedentibus sibi in preiudicium dicte camere factis.

Cetera suppleat dilectio iustitie celsitudinis supradicte.

(fol. 128, cxxiii) Copia litterarum directarum per collectorem Anglie ad singulos prelatos regni pro primis fructibus exspectantium obtinendis.

Reverendissimo patri et domino [361] mi recommandatione premissa.

Ex officio michi in regno Anglie per sedem appostolicam commiso significo vobis quod dominus noster papa Gregorius undecimus nuper reservavit ex certis et iustis causis ad instar nonnullorum predecessorum suorum, xv kalendas Martii anno primo,[362] ad triennium primos fructus beneficiorum per eum etiam sub exspectatione, preterquam in forma pauperum, collatorum, cum fuerint [363] ab ipsis exspectantibus acceptata. Unde cum in vestra diocesi de acceptatione ipsorum exspectantium ratione nove institutionis vel cure animarum seu ex alia fama viciniori notitiam habere debeatis satis magnam, placeat vobis me certificare quot a dicto tempore citra in vestra civitate vel diocesi sunt vigore dicte gratie apostolice beneficia, preterquam in dicta forma pauperum, usque nunc a quoque eadem auctori-

---

[361] *domine*, MS.
[362] 15 February 1371.
[363] *fuint*, MS.

tate acceptata, et alias procedere iuxta formam mandati mei super hoc et aliis officium tangentibus confecti, taliter si placet vos habentes ut nuntio apud sedem ipsam ex hoc sit vestra paternitas commendanda, que diu valeat et votive.

Datum Londonie anno a nativitate domini et cetera LXXIII^tio die viii^a Januarii.

Vester Arnaldus Garnerii, licentiatus in legibus, sedis apostolice nuntius et collector Anglie.

Et quia res nova, nondum omnes prelati beneficia certificare curaverunt, sed credo quod facient.

(fol. 130^v) [364] Repertorium contentorum in toto ipso libro

i. In isto libro nigro, qui continet centum quinquaginta tria folia, licet omnia non sunt scripta, tradito camere apostolice per Dominum Arnaldum Garnerii, collectorem Anglie, pro debitis et restis ac etiam pro compotis totius recepte per eum facte in Anglia in duobus primis annis cum dymidio vel circa, quibus iam ibi fuit nuntius apostolice sedis pro iuribus camere apostolice principaliter exigendis, sunt que secuntur.

ii. Primo fuit a principio libri, videlicet a secundo folio, usque ad folium tricesimum septimum inclusive copie restarum debitarum camere sibi traditarum per dominum priorem Lewensem locumtenentem predecessoris [365] sui in officio supradicto, una cum tota ab ipsis et aliis debitoribus camere apostolice per eum recepta.

iii. Item sunt a tricesimo octava folio ipsius libri usque ad folium xlii inclusive compota recepte, assignationis et expense sibi tradita Londonie per dominum priorem Lewensem supradictum, et ibi posita pro memoriali, una cum illis defectibus tunc repertis secundum restas dicte camere per prius redditas per dictum predecessorem, de quibus petit quitantiam prefatus dominus prior per dominum nostrum et cameram sibi dari.

iiii. Item sunt folio xlv et duobus sequentibus nomina illorum qui tenetur solvere singulis annis denarios Beati Petri et census cum solutionibus in parte factis de annis LXX secundo et tertio.

(fol. 131, cxxvi) v. Item sunt copie trium quaternorum de debitis camere Domino Arnaldo predicto traditorum vel missorum per cameram dicto tempore, una cum aliis pluribus per eum exploratis debitis et repertis, de quibus nulla fiebat mentio in dictis restis nec in dictis caternis, et hoc a folio quinquagesimo secundo usque ad folium centesimum decimum septimum inclusive.

vi. Item sunt in isto eodem libro folio centesimo decimo octavo et sequenti inclusive omnes assignationes pecuniarum camere per dictum nuntium nomine ipsius

camere de dicta recepta facte sociis Albertorum et aliis et etiam exspense ex causa dicti officii per eum facte.

vii. Item sunt folio centesimo vicesimo primo et duobus sequentibis inclusive excusationes parvitatis recepte officii et querele in scriptis tradite consilio regio super reparatione in preiudicium camere attemptatorum per consilium memoratum et copie litterarum directarum prelatis super executionem priorum fructuum ab impetrantibus preterquam et cetera.

viii. Et ultra dictum librum tradidit etiam dictus collector brevetum ubi erant triginta folia continens specialiter totam receptam et assignationes et exspensas et plura alia, de quibus supra sit mentio generalis.

Et plus etiam tradidit unum alium magis parvum brevetum de summis et restis solum, faciente mentione ubi erat sutum instrumentum obligationis subcollectoris facte camere appostolice et grosatum in forma publica redditum cum eodem [366] breveto, et infra in sequenti pagina habetur mentio de ipso.

(fol. 131^v) Obligatio subcollectoris Anglie.

Est tamen sciendum et memorandum quod dictus collector, cum exivit de Londonia pro veniendo ad curiam Romanam ut supra, dimisit ibi in Londonia in suo consueto hospitio locumtenentem suum, Magistrum Laurencium de Nigris, bacallarium in legibus civem que Romanum, cum plena potestate, et dimisit sibi consimilia compota sicut reddit camere et etiam litteras officii apostolicas et regestrum taxe beneficiorum Anglie et plura alia concernentia officium, prout continetur in instrumento publico recepto per Laurencium de Bueren' diocesis Traiectensis (Utrecht), auctoritate apostolica notarium publicum. In quo etiam instrumento dictus Magister Laurencius se obligavit cum iuramento camere apostolice de fideliter ipsum officium exercendo et compota et reliquos reddendo et fideiussores dedit, videlicet Angelum de Nigris, fratrem suum, et Petrum Marchi, socium et factorem Albertorum, prout de predictis omnibus et pluribus aliis constat et constare potest per dictum publicum instrumentum camere si voluit tradendum per collectorem sepedictum, sicut post tradidit [367] cum secundo parvo breveto loco copiature. Arnaldus Garnerii.[368]

(fol. 132, cxxvii) H—CD quere signum supra folio cxx

Restant fructus de tempore Dominorum Clementis et Innocentii de beneficiis non taxatis in toto vel in parte xiii.

Item de tempore Domini Urbani lxxv.
Item de primo quaterno Gregorii x.
Item de secundo quaterno xxi.
Item de tertio quaterno xxviii.
Item de exploratis xxix.

---

[364] Folios 128 verso to 130 recto inclusive are blank.
[365] *ppessoris*, MS.
[366] *eadem*, MS. The paragraph "Et plus . . . de ipso" is in a different hand.
[367] *tradididit*, MS.
[368] In the margin: *Obligatio subcollectoris Anglie.*

Summa omnium primorum fructuum suprascriptorum viii$^{xx}$ xvi.

Restant inutiles de tempore Dominorum Clementis et Innocentii lxi.

De tempore Domini Urbani clxxvi.

De primo quaterno Domini Gregorii vii.

De secundo quaterno xiiii.

De tertio quaterno xxix.

De exploratis i.

Summa omnium inutilium ii$^c$ lxxxviii.

Restant exspectationes primi quaterni lxx.

Exspectationes secundi quaterni iiii$^c$ lxiiii.

Exspectationes tertii quaterni clxxxix.

Summa omnium espectationum vii$^c$ xxiii.

(fol. 155, cl)[369] ++∞++ Quere infra ubi continua ad signum folio clii.

*A list of assignments made to the camera follows. It reproduces with no significant variation, except that it is in the first person singular—ego, Arnaldus Garnerii, tradidi—the last seven items on folio 123$^v$ and the last three items on folio 124.[370] The whole page is deleted by lines.*

(fol. 156, cli)[371] Secuntur assignationes facte camere appostolice de recepta istius libri.

*The entries on this folio, the verso and folio 157 repeat other entries of assignments on folios 123 to 124.[372] They are cancelled by lines. They are in the third person. The only significant variations are the following.*

*The payment of £300 to Peter Marchi, which is dated 26 February 1373 on folio 123,[373] is dated 26 February 1373 secundum computationem Anglicanam on folio 156$^v$.*

*In the entry concerning the payment of £45 to John Credy (fol. 124)[374] it is noted on folio 156 that John debet reddere in curia de die in die.*

*In the entry recording the payment of £420 to the viscount of Turenne (fol. 124)[375] it is noted on folio 156 that he was a relative of the pope and that he was sent to England several times with several others for treating of peace between the kings.*

(fol. 157$^v$) Secuntur espense facte ratione officii que sunt consuete deducere de recepta

*The items which follow duplicate those on folio 124$^v$.[376] They are cancelled by lines. The only significant difference is the statement in the entry concerning payment of £11 18 s. vi d. to couriers that they were*

*sent* cum mandatis camere ad prelatos pro exsequendo, ut est moris.

(fol. 158$^v$, cliii)[377] Hic est cum isto iii$^{um}$ caternum de tria missa, et sunt iii breveti de recepta et assignato sive summe, et repertorium debitorum est cum libro tradito per cameram et predecessorem [378]

(fol. 161, ii)[379] Recepta denariorum Beati Petri de arreragiis traditis Domino Arnaldo Garnerii, collectori Anglie, per dominum priorem Lewensem, locumtenentem Domini Johannis de Cabrespino nuper collectoris Anglie, die vicesima secunda Februarii anno a nativitate domini millesimo CCC septuagesimo secundo, et recepta aliorum sequentium annorum est infra folio xi

*The entries which follow on the recto and the verso duplicate with some unimportant changes of phraseology the entries on folios 2 to 3 recto inclusive.[380] The comments in the hand of the collector are lacking.*

(fol. 162, iii) *The entries on this folio duplicate in the same manner those on folios 3$^v$ and 4.[381]*

(fol. 163, iiii)[382] Sequntur recepta primorum fructuum dictarum restarum de tempore Dominorum Clementis et Innocentii

*The entries which follow on folios 163 to 164$^v$ give in abbreviated form and without the comments of the collector those items on folios 4$^v$ to 11$^v$ [383] which record the receipt of any payments.*

(fols. 165$^v$-169$^v$, vi-x)[384] *The entries on these folios extract in the same manner the provisions and confirmations made by Urban V from which receipts are recorded on folios 13 to 37$^v$.[385]*

(fol. 171, 171$^v$, xii)[386] *Here are recorded the items of receipt from Peter's pence found on folios 47$^v$ and 48.[387]*

(fol. 172, 172$^v$, xiii) *The receipts from the census given on folios 48 to 49$^v$ [388] are repeated in a similar manner.*

(fols. 173-174$^v$, xiiii, xv) *The items of receipt from*

---

[369] Folios 132 verso to 154 verso inclusive are blank.
[370] Above, pp. 475-476.
[371] Folio 155 verso is blank.
[372] Above, pp. 475-476.
[373] Above, p. 475.
[374] Above, p. 476.
[375] Above, p. 476.
[376] Above, p. 476.

[377] Folio 158 recto is blank.
[378] This entry is in such a loose, cursive hand that mistakes may have been made in the extension of some words. The page is the cover of the larger brevetus mentioned above several times. It contains a summary of receipts, assignments, expenses and some other material given at greater length in the preceding report. The bits of significant additional information contained in the brevetus are noted above.
[379] Folios 159 recto to 160 verso are blank.
[380] Above, pp. 363-364.
[381] Above, p. 364.
[382] Folio 162 verso is blank.
[383] Above, pp. 364-373.
[384] Folio 165 is blank.
[385] Above, pp. 374-411.
[386] Folio 170 recto and verso is blank.
[387] Above, p. 417.
[388] Above, pp. 417-418.

*provisions and confirmations made by Gregory XI recorded on folios 54 to 97ᵛ, 104 to 121ᵛ* [389] *are repeated here in summary form.*

(fols. 175ᵛ-177ᵛ, xvi-xviii) [390] *The receipts from the explorata found on folios 98ᵛ to 103ᵛ* [391] *are repeated.*

(fol. 178, xviiii) *The total sum of the receipts is given as it appears on fol. 122.* [392]

(fol. 179-181, xx-xxii) [393] *The assignments and expenses are repeated from folios 123 to 125.* [394]

(fol. 182 recto and verso, xxiii) [395] *The sums of the arrears are set forth as on folios 125ᵛ, 132.* [396]

(fol. 183 recto and verso, xxiiii) *The excuses for the small amount of receipts are repeated as they appear on folio 126 recto and verso.* [397]

(fol. 184 rector and verso, xxv) *The copy of the collector's petition to the king's council on folio 127 recto and verso* [398] *is duplicated.*

(fol. 185) *The copy of the executory letter sent by the collector to the prelates given on folio 128* [399] *is reproduced.*

(fol. 187 [400]) Pro camera apostolica de gratia. [401]

De quibus assignavit camere per manus Johannis Marchi, factoris Albertorum, in diversis vicibus iiᵐ vᶜ xlvi li. xv s. [402]

Item assignavit eidem camere diversis vicibus per manus Augustini de Benetonius, factoris sociorum de Guineriis de Luca iiiᵐ iiᶜ l li.

Item tradidit de mandato camere Domino Johanni de Tornaburi militi pro parte summe viiᵐ fl. eidem debitorum pro servitio guerre Italie lxxi li. sterlingorum. [403]

[389] Above, pp. 418-452, 459-454.
[390] Folio 175 recto is blank.
[391] Above. pp. 453-459.
[392] Above, pp. 474-475.
[393] Folio 178 verso is blank.
[394] Above, pp. 475-476.
[395] Folio 181 verso is blank.
[396] Above, pp. 477, 478-480.
[397] Above, p. 477.
[398] Above, pp. 477-478.
[399] Above, pp. 478-479.
[400] Folios 185ᵛ to 186ᵛ are blank.
[401] Apparently this is mere idle scribbling and not a caption. There is also a *Pro* and a *P* with a line through it. The folio is a continuation of an account the preceding part of which is not in this codex. The material does not relate to the account submitted by Arnaldus Garnerii in 1374. It appears to be a summary of the assignments and expenses in the account rendered in 1377: below, pp. 532-538.
[402] In the margin bracketed against this item and the next: *infra cameram.*
[403] In the margin: *extra cameram.*

Item assignavit tribus mercatoribus de mandato camere iiᵐ vᶜ lxv li. xviii s. vi d. [404]

Summa assignatorum infra cameram viiiᵐ iiiᶜ lxii li. xiii s. vi d.

Item assignavit domino archiepiscopo Rothomagensi (Rouen) de mandato camere viiiᶜ lxxxviii li. vi s. viii d.

Item assignavit Domino Rogero de Belloforti, germano Domini Gregorii m iiᶜ lxxii li. xii s. viii d.

Item assignavit pro tribus orfrisiis per ipsum emptis pro Domino Gregorio pape xlv li. xiii s. iiii d.

Item pro quibusdam expensis factis per ipsum collectorem lxx li. v s. iiii d.

Summa omnium predictorum xᵐ viiᶜ x li. xi s. vi d.

(fol. 187ᵛ) [405] Summa assignatorum de primis fructibus iiᵐ viᶜ xiii li. xv s. iii d.

Summa assignatorum de subsidio viiiᵐ xxvi li. x s. xi d.

Summa universalis omnium assignatorum tam de primis fructibus quam de subsidio xᵐ viᶜ xl li. vi s. ii d.

Summa quarundam expensarum per ipsum factarum lxx li. v s. iiii d.

Summa summarum omnium assignatorum et expensarum xᵐ viiᶜ x li. xi s. vi d. Valent, quolibet florenus pro tribus solidis computato, lxxiᵐ iiiiᶜ iiii fl. cum dimidio.

(fol. 188, i) Parvus brevetus collectoris Anglie.

(fol. 189, ii) [406] Reddit Arnaldus Garnerii, sedis apostolice nuntius et collector Anglie, de receptis per eum in dicto regno a die octava mensis Februarii anno a nativitate domini millesimo CCCLXXIIᵈᵒ usque ad diem vicesimam septimam mensis Julii anno domini et cetera LXX quarto que sequntur.

Primo reddit de restis denariorum Beati Petri sibi dimissis per dominum priorem Lewensem, tunc locumtenentem Domini Johannis de Cabrespino, de anno LXX primo et precedentium annorum totum recepisse quod erat in dictis restis, videlicet ccccxiii li. iiii d. Et reddit de restis annui census sibi etiam per eundem priorem dimissis de anno domini et cetera LXX primo et precedentibus annis totum etiam quod erat in dictis restis recepisse, videlicet decem li. sex s. Et sic reddit pro predictis restis in universo iiiiᶜ xxiii li. vi s. iiii d. [407]

Item reddit etiam recepisse de primis fructibus contentis in restis sibi consimiliter dimissis de tempore antiquo Dominorum Clementis et Innocentii usque ad tempus Domini Urbani iiᶜ lxxxiii li. xviii s. v d. sterlingorum. [407]

[404] In the margin: *infra camera.*
[405] At the top of the page deleted by a line: *viiᶜ lxx li. xvii s. iiii d. ob.*; at the bottom *xiii li. xv s. iii d.*; in the margin: *Supplicat S. V. devotus vir, Johannes Bosquern, clericus Constantiensis diocesis de quodam beneficio ecclesiastico cum cura vel sine cura spectante ad collationem et cetera.*
[406] Folio 188 verso is blank.
[407] In the margin: *Aprobo.*

(fol. 189ᵛ) Item reddit recepisse de primis fructibus contentis in restis etiam sibi dimissis de tempore dicti Domini Urbani usque ad Dominum Gregorium papam undecimum camere apostolice pertinentibus, cum traditis per dominum priorem Lewensem nomine suo et etiam nomine Domini Cabrespini, sicut in libro recepte et alio maiori breveto redditis camere clarius continetur, mille trescentas et octuaginta sex li. octo s. ii d., xiiiᶜ lxxxvi li. viii s. ii d.[407]

Item reddit recepisse pro denariis Beati Petri de annis domini millesimo CCCLXX secundo et tertio iiiᶜ xxxvii li. viii s. viii d. Et etiam reddit recepisse de annuo censu pro annis domini predictis LXX secundo et tertio ix li. xii d. Et sic pro predictis denariis et censu reddit recepisse trescentas quadraginta sex li. novem s. et octo d., iiiᶜ xlvi li. ix s. viii d.[407]

Restant de dictis denariis Beati Petri et censu pro dictis duobus annis lxi li. xvii s. viii d.

Item redidit recepisse de eisdem primis fructibus sibi dimissis in restis de tempore dicti domini nostri Gregorii et de fructibus debitis aliis etiam sibi missis de curia in tribus vicibus sine pluri, iam fuit annus in mense Maii proxime lapsi, inclusis in hoc tribus quaternis tam de exspectationibus quam de aliis, de quibus in dictis restis et quaternis cavebatur, quadrigentas sexaginta tres li. xi s. ii d., iiiiᶜ lxiii li. xi s. ii d.[407]

(fol. 190, iii) Item reddit recepisse de incertis debitis camere exploratis et per eum perquisitis[408] de quibus nullum a camera habebat speciale mandatum in dictis restis nec tribus quaternis sine pluri sibi missis, tam ratione legatorum in redemptionem Terre Sancte relictorum quam pro primis fractibus aliquorum beneficiorum per dominum cardinalem Cantuariensem in Anglia auctoritate apostolica collatorum et ex aliis causis legitimis, prout per decursum libri nigri eidem camere una cum alio maiori breveto reddito specifice et distincte plenius continetur, trescentas octaginta duas li. quindecim s. vi d. sterlingorum, iiiᶜ lxxxii li. xv s. vi d. sterlingorum.[407]

Summa universalis recepte supradicto tempore facte tria milia ducentas octuaginta sex li. novem s. tres d., iiiᵐ iiᶜ lxxxvi li. ix s. iii d.[407]

Que valent, singulo floreno pro tribus solidis sterlingorum computando, viginti unum milia nongentos novem fl. duos s. tres d. sterlingorum, xxiᵐ ixᶜ ix fl. ii s. iii d. sterlingorum.[407]

(fol. 190ᵛ) Totum vero residuum quod aeparietur in libro nigro compotorum non solutum dat in restis, salvis excusationibus plurimorum que, cum sint evidentes, frustra tempora debita occupant membranas et diu occupaverunt. Quare tollantur et deleantur de libro ipso nigro reddito camere, si dominus in ipsa camera videatur faciendum, et residuum quod clare debetur solum detur in restis pro futuro tempore exigendis.

Hic debuerunt poni reste.

(fol. 192, v)[409] Assignationes et exspense

Et de dicta summa sic, ut premittitur, recepta, dictus nuntius, de mandato apostolico assignavit camere apostolice per cambium factum Londonie cum Albertis in diversis vicibus, sicut continetur specifice in dicto libro nigro compotorum eidem camere reddito folio ci et sequenti, in toto supradicto tempore duo milia sexcentas octuaginta novem li. decem et septem s. sterlingorum, iiᵐ viᶜ iiiixx ix li. xvii s. sterlingorum.[407]

Item assignavit eidem camere etiam per cambium factum Londonie cum Johanne Credy, socio Stroziorum curiam Romanam sequentium, prout etiam in dicto libro et folio continetur, quadraginta quinque li., xlv li.[407]

Item solvit nomine camere apostolice pro exspensis per dominum vicecomitem Turrenn' factis in regno Anglie tempore quo ibi fuit cum pluribus aliis pro tractatu pacis missus, quas dominus noster ratas habuit cum bulla et acceptas, quadringentas viginti li., ccccxx li.[407]

De predictis omnibus assignatio fecit fidem per instrumenta publica.

(fol. 192ᵛ) Item solvit pro iiiiᵒʳ aurifrisiis domini nostri pape xxxᵗᵃ li. sterlingorum. Et pro duodecim pannis lecti domini vicecomitis, de suo mandato emptis, viii li. xv s. Et pro portu predictorum usque hic xlii s. Et sic solvit pro omnibus predictis quadraginta li. decem et septem s. sterlingorum, xl li. xvii s. sterlingorum.[407]

De summa que tradita fuit pro domino de Turenna ipse collector concordavit cum camera appostolica.

Item solvit nomine camere apostolico dicto tempore duorum annorum cum dymidio pro exspensis portus litterarum in quinque vicibus per regnum Anglie ad prelatos et alios missarum xi li. xviii s. vi d. Et pro celario hospitii dicto tempore et usque ad festum Beati Michaelis Septembris proxime lapsi pro maiori summa conducti, ubi fuerunt duo anni et ix menses, viginti septem marcas cum dymidia, que valent xviii li. vi s. viii d. sterlingorum. Et pro cera, papiro et incausto dicto tempore duorum annorum cum dymidio pro officio emptis l s., sicut de predictis est alias a predecessoribus computare consuetum. Et sic in summa pro predictis solvit triginta duas li. xv s. ii d., xxxii li. xv s. ii d.[407]

Loquerium hospitii fuit sibi de gratia speciali remissum.

(fol. 193, vi) Item expendit in quatuor mensibus quibus vacavit officio cum magnis exspensis in curia et in via et nichil de stipendiis percepit, sicut clarius in libro nigro compotorum et alio maiori breveto redditis camere latius continetur, ultra quinquaginta octo li. sterlingorum, ad quas et plus asscendunt stipendia dictorum iiiiᵒʳ mensium, quinquaginta octo li., lviii li.[407]

De ista summa pecunie fuit ordinatum per cameram

---

[408] *perquisitus*, MS.

[409] Folio 191 is blank on the recto and verso.

appostolicam quod ipsa camera solvet tertiam partem, dominus Arnaldus collector hodiernus, qui presentia compota redidit, aliam tertiam partem, Dominus Johannes de Cabrespino, predecessor suus, aliam tertiam, et sic fuit factum per concilium.

Summa universalis assignatorum et exspensarum supradictarum tria milia ducentas octuaginta sex li. novem s. duos d., que valent, singulo floreno pro tribus solidis computando, xxiᵐ ixᶜ ix fl. ponderis camere ii s. ii d. sterlingorum.⁴⁰⁷

Est advertendum quod de summa solvenda ut supra scriptum est Dominus Arnaldus collector hodiernus statim de parte sua satisfecit, et sibi fuit comissum quod in Anglia ipse exigeret partem tertiam quam dictus Johannes de Cabrespino solvere debet in bonis que inveniet in Anglia dicti Domini Johannis.

Et sic quasi tantum asscendunt assignationes et exspense quantum faciat recepta supradicta.

(fol. 193ᵛ) Cum isto vero breveto reddit camere plus dictus collector unum instrumentum grossatum custodiendum cum suis compotis continens obligationem subcollectoris sui dimissi in Anglia, videlicet Magistri Laurentii de Nigris, bacallarii in legibus, civis Romani, patrie Anglicane ratione dicte sue remote nationis minime suspecti.

Et omnia suprascripta tam recepte quam exspensarum et assignationum seu solutionum dat hic et in aliis duobus libris compotorum redditis camere, errore calculi et iure alieno spectante sibi salvis.

Restarum summe
Ultra dictam receptam restabant in pecunia dicta die xxvii Julii anno domini et cetera LXX quarto de beneficiis per decursum libri nigri in pecunia taxata duo milia septuagenta et sexaginta novem li. sexdecim s. novem d., iiᵐ viiᶜ lxix li. iii s. v d.⁴¹⁰

Valent, floreno camere pro tribus solidis computando, xviiiᵐ iiiiᶜ v fl. et dym. vii d. sterlingorum.

(fol. 194, vii) Restabant etiam fructus beneficiorum nondum taxatorum viiiˣˣ xvi beneficia.

Et restabant de inutilibus provisionibus etiam ab antiquo debitis ut in pluribus iiᶜ lxxxviii.

Restabant exspectationes que nondum habuerunt effectum viiiᶜ xxiii.

Hec omnia dat salvo errore calculi et iure alieno.

Sic est in libro nigro reddito camere folio cxvii in summa posita. Et per decursum ipsius libri reperitur.

Et instrumentum grosatum obligationis subcollectoris in Anglia dimissi est hic aretro loco copiature sutum, ut habetur supra in precedenti folio.

Dat etiam collector supradictus cum isto breveto in folio papiri ad partem dubia tangentia cameram, super quibus est deliberandum secrete, de quibus etiam habetur in dicto libro nigro reddito camere folio cxxi.

(fol. 196)⁴¹¹ Sequntur capitula seu dubia tradita per Dominum Arnaldum Garnerii collectorem Anglie super quibus dubitabat dominis de camera, quibus fuit singulariter per dictos dominos responsum ut sequitur in fine cuiuslibet capituli.

Prima causa est quia archidiaconi nichil volunt solvere ibi pro primis fructibus camere debitis de procurationibus nec de iurisdictione, nec est consuetum, ut asserunt, et tamen emolumenta ipsorum archidiacanatuum quasi ex toto saltim pro maiori parte in talibus consistunt.

De istis non est consuetum vacantem habere cum eorum emolumenta consistant in iurisdictione et procurationibus; quando in fructibus et in aliis consistunt, exigat collector iura pertinentia camere.⁴¹²

Item procuratores dominorum cardinalium nichil volunt solvere in vita eorum, nec post mortem aliquid reperitur nisi vix, et tamen habent quamplura meliora beneficia ibi et utiliora, et multi iam defuncti hactenus habuerunt, qui adhuc pro magnis quantitatibus in restis camere retinentur, et nichil illuc reperitur.

Executionem faciatis in predictis pro iuribus camere, cum sine culpa esse non potest quia tantum tardastis.

(fol. 196ᵛ) Item quia revocatio unionum sive appropriationum per Dominum Urbanum facta a tanto tempore citra et usque et renovatio constitutionis *execrabilis* super pluralitate beneficiorum non habuerunt locum in Anglia, et nec collationes ea occasione quamplures expost facte habuerunt effectum aliquod, sed dormiunt in regestris, et nichil exigi potest.

In illis omnibus camera habet ius qualitercumque provisum fuit per sedem apostolicam, et diligentiam habeatis meliorem quam in preterito habuistis in exigenda iura camere.

Item possessores titulo regio nichil volunt solvere de eo ad quod beneficia erant obligata per prius ratione provisionum factarum predecessoribus eorumdem, licet obligationes sunt in rem seu saltim in rem scripte, inmimentes quod collatio regia saltim pro tempore suo debet esse integra et cum pleno effectu.

Compellatis dictos possessores ad solvendum ea in quibus invenietis eorum beneficia que tenent camere apostolice obligata, et fuit male factum quia tantum tardastis, tamen dulciori et familiari modo quo poteritis procedatis.

(fol. 197) Item possessores titulo regio qui habuerunt collationes vel confirmationes ante vel post a sede apostolica nichil volunt solvere communiter, allegantes quod non fuerunt usi illa gratia sed sola regia, licet per ipsos steterit non per sedem ipsam que fecerat in auctorizando quod in ipsa erat.

---

⁴¹⁰ Over *xvi s. ix d.* deleted by a line.

⁴¹¹ Folios 194 verso and 195 recto and verso are blank.

⁴¹² In the margin: *responsum.* This notation appears in the margin opposite each answer.

Idem servetis in isto ut in precedenti utiliori et commodioso modo quo poteritis, cum ius sit acquisitum camere postquam papa et cetera.

Item possessores prioratuum et aliorum beneficiorum qui sunt de patronatu laycali nichil volunt solvere, licet confirmationem vel dispensationem super pluralitate vel aliqua inhabilitate alia beneficiorum ab ipsa sede obtinuerint, et tamen in hoc ius presentandi patronis in aliquo non leditur nec aufertur.

Compellatis predictos possessores dictorum beneficiorum ad solvendum ea in quibus tenentur camere apostolice quia alias non essetis sine culpa cum de preterito non potestis vos excusare.

(fol. 197ᵛ) Item quia ibi nulle recipiuntur exspolie, ymmo quia in aliquibus partibus regni sunt beneficia taxata de novo propter sterelitatem patrie vel propter guarras volunt solvere novam parvam taxam, non antiquam que maior est, asserentes quod nunquam fuerat usitatum in regno solvere nisi novam taxam vel antiquam ubi non est nova, et nunquam residuum ultra taxam fuerat exactum.

De exspoliis non est curandum postquam non est consuetum. De taxa recipiatis ulteriorem pro camera prout discretioni vestre videbitur, et diligentiam bonam adhibeatis, et in aliis omnibus supradictis, ut de fidelitate et diligentia consuetis valeatis commendari.

Et quia sunt in restis camere multa talia beneficia etiam ab antiquo restantia, videant domini quid agendum, quia magna exponitur querela cum aliquod novum a quoque in illis partibus attemptatur propter diuturnam que pretenditur taciturnitatem.

In isto provideat vestra prudentia collectoris quia quantumcumque sint inutilia de presenti in [413] futuro utilia possent evenire.

(fol. 198) Si de litteris indigetis pro predictis tam a domino nostro quam a domino camerario, vobis concedentur utiliori modo quo habere volueretis, forma iuris servata.

## Second Account of Arnald Garnerii
## 1374-1378.

(Collectorie 12, fol. 143)[1] Pro camera apostolica de Anglia.[2] Liber compotorum collectoris Anglie redditus camere apostolice in restis redditis eidem camere per eundem collectorem a die vicesima septima Julii anno domini millesimo CCCᵐᵒ septuagesimo IIIIᵗᵒ usque ad sextam diem Martii anno ab incarnatione domini millesimo septuagesimo septimo.

(fol. 145ᵛ)[3] Reste camere

Sequntur reste et debita Anglie camere apostolice pertinentia, salvo erore calculi, et inutilium provisionum restantia ad exigendum et levandum sexta die Martii anno ab incarnatione domini millesimo CCCᵐᵒ LXX septimo, qua die sexta Martii Dominus Arnaldus Garnerii, licentiatus in legibus ac sedis apostolice nuntius, de dicta patria, gravi et longa infirmitate detentus, recessit versus curiam Romanam et Avinionam, dimisso ibi in Anglia uno subcollectore pro exigendo dicta debita et restas sicut melius posset, videlicet Magistro Laurentio de Nigris, civi Romano ac bacallario in legibus, canonico que Lincolniensi, prout alias eum ibidem diu est dimiserat quinque annis vel circa tunc etiam proxime lapsis; et de dicta locumtenentia constat per publicum instrumentum que fuit tunc in archivis dicte camere cum primis redditis compotis retentum et in ipsa camera apostolica dimissum ad futuram rei memoriam et pro interesse ipsius collectoris et camere apostolice supradicte.[4]

### (fol. 146, iii) Reste debite camere apostolice
### Cantuariensis diocesis

Sequntur reste debite camere apostolice in Anglia die sexta mensis Martii anno ab incarnatione domini millesimo CCCᵐᵒ LXX septimo, qua die Dominus Arnaldus Garnerii, nuntius et collector sedis apostolice in Anglia, recessit de Londonia in Anglia versus curiam Romanam pro computando, et copiam restarum dimisit locumtenento suo pro exigendo, videlicet venerabili viro, Magistro Laurentio de Nigrie, civi Romano et canonico Lincolniensi.

Resta subcidi

Primo restabant ad solvendum die sexta Martii anno ab incarnatione domini millesimo CCCᵐᵒ LXX septimo[5] de summa novem milium librarum per clerum Anglie ratione subsidii promissa ixᶜ lxxiii li. ix s. sterlingorum, que valent, singulo floreno pro tribus solidis sterlingorum computando, sex milia iiiiᶜ xc fl. et xii d. Hoc est ixᶜ lxxiii li. ix s. sterlingorum vel circa, salvo semper in omnibus erore calculi, ixᶜ lxxiii li. ix s. sterlingorum.

Item restabant in diocesi Cantuariensi de parochiali ecclesia de Wyngesham (Wingham) collata per Urbanum anno septimo quinto idus Decembris[6] Hugoni Attehalle fructus pro taxa quadraginta li. folio xxiiii, xl li.

Prohibitum fuit per regem bis, quia rex contulit iure suo possessori qui nunc est, sed debentur fructus cum erit extra manus illius qui possidet titulo regio. Et vocatur dictus possessor Bartholomeus de Borne, sed per legem patrie, quia rex contulit, non possunt exigi fructus vivente illo titulo regio possidente.

---

[413] Follows *de* deleted by a line.
[1] The original cover of the codex.
[2] Repeated at the bottom of the page.

[3] Folios 143 verso to 145 recto are blank.
[4] In the margin: *vera*.
[5] Over *octavo* deleted by a line.
[6] 9 December 1368.

Resta pagine m¹ xiii li. ix s. sterlingorum.[7]

(fol. 146ᵛ) De prepositura de Wingham collata Domino Johanni de Fordham per Gregorium XI anno primo decimo tertio kalendas Martii[8] fructus, folio xxxiii.

Restavit debens adhuc in antiquis restis dictus Johannes Fordham xxx li. Dominus Willelmus de Windesore est nunc possessor, cui Dominus Johannes dimisit bene ad sufficientiam pro solvendo, ut asseruit, et est monitus et sequestratus et denuntiatus dictus Willelmus pro triginta li., et solvit post in triginta m. xx li., et habet terminum Beati Michaelis anni LXXVII pro decem li., de quibus solvit die xxiii Octobris eodem anno quinque li., et sic restant alie quinque li., v li.

De prebenda seu vicaria de Pedding' in ecclesia collegiata de Wingham collata Domino Johanni de Stenes fructus, folio liii.

Certificat episcopus quod obiit dictus Johannes et quod nunquam possedit, et fructus sunt communes et non pertinent prebende, nisi quando canonicus residet, quod non est in facto, et ideo non possunt sequestrari, sed est monitus bis. Debet tamen cum residebit tantum quantum perciperet, si personaliter resideret, exceptis distributionibus panis et vini, quia sic cavetur in littera reservationum primorum fructuum qui sunt sequestrati, et monitus est possessor in ultimo mandato anni LXXVII, et estimantur dicti fructus ad decem li., sed videatur bene quantum revera debetur, x li.

Resta pagine xv li.[7]

(fol. 147, iiii)[9] De ecclesia de Terling' (Charing) confirmata Magistro Nicholao de Scaddesden' xiiii kalendas Setempbris per Gregorium anno secundo[10] fructus, folio xlvi.

Taxa reperitur ad quinquaginta tres li. sex. s. octo d. sterlingorum. Et est decanus de arcubus, et dicit quod nunquam fuit accepta de suo consensu, nec curavit facere litteras. Ymmo dominus Cantuariensis archiepiscopus qui tunc erat ipsam confirmationem impetravit ipso nescio,[11] ut ipsemet archiepiscopus dum vivebat asseruit, et sepe michi, Arnaldo collectori, dixit. Quare videant domini de camera quid agendum, liii li. vi s. viii d.

De vicaria de Balachild' (Bapchild) quam possedit Rogerus Marchal ex causa provisionis facte coram domino cardinali Cantuariensi fructus pro taxa decem m. ⟨que⟩ valent vi li. xiii s. iiii d., folio liii.

Johannes Curtons nunc possidet istam ex causa alterius premutationis facte cum dicto Rogero coram domino cardinali Cantuariensi, et habet terminos nativitatis domini anni et cetera LXXVI et sequentis per

equales portiones, et est iuratus, condempnatus et obligatus pro vi li. xiii s. iiii d. Et videatur si debentur duplices fructus quia forte infra eundem annum fuit totum factum. Et dictus Johannes est denuntiatus in ultimo mandato anni LXXVII, vi li. xiii s. iiii d.

Dominus cardinalis de Ursinis[12] est etiam expectans ad collationem dicti domini archiepiscopi Cantuariensis et aliorum prelatorum de sua provincia, cuius pretextu plura ibi optinet beneficia, et mandetur plus ad certificandum de beneficiis acceptatis et de vero valore ipsorum cuiuslibet, et habetur de hiis in libro folio.[13] Tamen iste habuit mandatum domini camerarii ad supersedendum quia concordavit cum camera de omnibus.[14] (fol. 147ᵛ) beneficiis. Sed non forte de post acceptatis, quarum sciatur bene de omnibus beneficiis suis et aliorum dominorum cardinalium qui habunt in Anglia, et scribantur in locis et diocesibus propriis. Videatur.[15]

De vicaria de Eleham (Elham) diocesis Cantuariensis ex causa permutationis facte coram domino cardinali Cantuariensi debet Johannes Foliot, qui eam vicariam cum alio permutavit, fructus pro taxa quindecim m. ⟨que⟩ valent x li., folio liiii.[16]

Solvit in tribus vicibus novem m. que valent sex li. Et est in istis restis pro quatuor li., et habet terminum Pasche anni et cetera LXXVII de dicta resta, videlicet iiiiᵒʳ li. Solvit post die quarta Aprilis anno LXXVIIᵒ quinquaginta tres s. quatuor d., et sic remansit in istis pro viginti sex s. octo d., et habet terminum Petri ad vincula, xxvi s. viii d.

De archidiaconatu Cantuariensi ex causa provisionis facte Ademaro de Rupe idus Martii anno tertio Domini Gregorii[17] fructus, folio cxiiii. Habuit effectum et debet pro medietate veri valoris centum quinquaginta li.

Est nepos domini nostri, et dominus de Latamer est arendator, et est obligatus domino Rothomagensi procuratori suo, et nulli alii volunt solvere, et est mandatum et cetera, et fructus sequestrati, et monitus est possessor in dicto ultimo mandato, cl li.

Resta pagine cli li. vi s. viii d.[18]

(fol. 148, v)[19] De ecclesia quam possidet Magister Willelmus Berton, auctoritate apostolica fructus, folio cxl.

Non est talis persona beneficiatus in diocesi aut iurisdictione Cantuariensi, ut certificat archiepiscopus anno LXXVII. Queratur melius.

De ecclesia de Hese (Hayes) ex causa acceptationis

---

[7] In the margin: *vera*.
[8] 17 February 1371.
[9] The heading *Cantuariensis diocesis* is repeated at the top of the page.
[10] 19 August 1372.
[11] *niscio*, MS.

[12] James Orsini, deacon of S. Giorgio in Velabro.
[13] The number is not given.
[14] In the margin: *Cardinalis de Ursinis*. At the foot of the page: *Resta pagine lx li. Vera*.
[15] *Videatur* repeated in the margin.
[16] Followed by *solvit* deleted by a line.
[17] 15 March 1373.
[18] In the margin: *vera*.
[19] The heading *Cantuariensis diocesis* is repeated at the top of the page.

auctoritate apostolica facte per Willelmum Menesse fructus pro taxa triginta quinque m. ⟨que⟩ valent viginti tres li. sex s. octo d., folio cxl.

Habet terminos Omnium Sanctorum anno LXXVI et sequenti anno revoluto,[20] et est obligatus, iuratus et condempnatus, et primus terminus est elapsus nichilo soluto, et sic est excommunicatus, et denuncietur, et sic fuit missum in ultimo, et archiepiscopus certificavit quod non habuit effectum quia alius possidet titulo ordinario. Videatur melius, xxiii li. vi s. viii d.

De ecclesia de Smerden' (Smarden) acceptata auctoritate apostolica per Johannem Bon'rig' fructus pro taxa triginta m. ⟨que⟩ valent xx li., folio cxl, xx li.

Monitus est possessor et sequestrati sunt fructus in dicto ultimo mandato.

De ecclesia de Dale (Deal) ex causa acceptationis auctoritate apostolica facte per possessorem eiusdem pro taxa triginta m. ⟨que⟩ valent xx li., folio cxl, xx li.

Sequestrati sunt fructus et monitus est possessor in ultimo mandato.

De ecclesia de Norton' ex causa acceptationis auctoritate apostolica facte per Johannem Burbache fructus pro taxa viginti octo m. ⟨que⟩ valent xviii li. xiii s. iiii d., folio cxl, xviii li. xiii s. iiii d.

Sequestrati sunt fructus et monitus est possessor in ultimo mandato anni LXXVII.

Resta pagine lxxxii li.[18]

(fol. 148v) Summa reste subsidii impositi in Anglia tam in provinciis Cantuariensi quam Eboracensi ixc lxxiii li. ix s. sterlingorum.[18]

Summa restarum vacantium beneficiorum civitatis et diocesis Cantuariensis iiic xlviii li. vi s. viii d.[18]

Item restat unum beneficium non taxatum.

(fol. 149, vi) Reste diocesis Roffensis

De ecclesia de Otteford' (Otford) provisum fuit Johanni de la Combe cum vacaret per assecutionem rectoris eiusdem de archidiaconatu Soulthfolchie in ecclesia Norwicensi xiii kalendas Februarii per Urbanum anno vito [21] fructus, folio xxiii.

Non reperitur taxa sed valet centum li., et sic debet pro medietate veri valoris l li.[22] Et est prohibitum quia idem Johannes qui possidet dicit quod habet titulo regio, sede Roffensi vacante, et forte rex contulit sibi; pretextu dicte gratie alias non facturus quia negat, nec vult solvere aliqua via. Sed prosequatur melius, l li. sterlingorum.

De archidiaconatu Roffensi ex causa confirmationis seu provisionis facte Rogero de Denford' v kalendas Maii per Gregorium anno secundo [23] fructus, folio xciiii.

Alia est provisio inutilis tamen facta eidem persone et eodem anno folio cii. Et non taxatur, sed valet

l li. salvo iure pluris, et sic debet pro medietate veri valoris viginti quinque li., xxv li.[22]

Et debet etiam pro denariis Beati Petri de tribus annis, ut infra in loco proprio habetur, et ideo ibi vide. Recepit terminos qui transierunt, et sic est denuntiandus, et vide in obligatione, et fuit post denuntiatus et aggravatus anno LXXVII, etiam pro denariis Beati Petri predictis.

Reste diocesis Roffensis, resta pagine lxxv li., et i beneficium nondum taxatum.[18]

(fol. 150)[24] Reste camere diocesis Londoniensis

De parochiali ecclesia de Alta Roting' (High Roding) ex causa nove provisionis facte Johanni de Langesdon' xviii kalendas Junii per Urbanum anno secundo [25] fructus pro taxa decem et octo m. ⟨que⟩ valent xii li., folio xv.

Dominus Thomas Jordani possidet ad presentationem domini comitis Arunldell', et solvit in novem m. vi li., et habet terminum Omnium Sanctorum anno et cetera LXXVII de residuo, videlicet de aliis vi li., pro quibus est datum in istis restis, vi li.

De libera cappella de Chelmesford' (Chelmsford) ex causa provisionis facte Willelmo Haddon' viii idus Augusti per Urbanum anno secundo [26] fructus, folio xvi.

Non reperitur taxa,[27] et fructus sunt sequestrati, et monitus est possessor in secundo mandato. Videatur bene. Valet ut dicitur xv li.

De parochiali ecclesia de Harwe (Harrow) ex causa provisionis facte Johanni de Bokingham ii idus Septembris per Urbanum anno iii [28] fructus pro taxa sexaginta m. que valent quadraginta li.,[29] xl li.

Et infra est alia provisio eidem facta folio xix, sed possidet titulo regio, omisso appostolico, et non vult solvere. Videatur bene.

De parochiali ecclesia de Hakeneye (Hackney) collata Ricardo Croxton' iii kalendas Februarii per Gregorium anno primo [30] fructus pro taxa quinquaginta m. ⟨que⟩ valent xxxiii li. vi s. viii d.,[22] folio xxxii.

Nondum habuit effectum quia alius possidet titulo regio.

Resta pagine xciiii li. vi s. viii d.[18]

(fol. 150v)[31] De ecclesia de Laton' alias Acton' (Latton) ex causa permutationis facte coram cardinali Cantuariensi fructus pro taxa viginti m. ⟨que⟩ valent xiii li. vi s. viii d.[22]

Fructus sunt sequestrati et monitus est possessor in secundo mandato.

---

[20] anno revoluto repeated MS.
[21] 20 January 1368.
[22] Sum repeated MS.
[23] 27 April 1372.

[24] Folio 149 verso is blank.
[25] 15 May 1364.
[26] 6 August 1364.
[27] taxas, MS.
[28] 12 September 1365.
[29] Followed by folio xvii deleted by a line.
[30] 30 January 1371.
[31] The heading Diocesis Londoniensis appears at the top of the page.

De ecclesia de Southanynfeld' (South Hanningfield) ex causa provisionis facte Thome de Brandeston' per Gregorium xix kalendas Septembris anno iii [32] fructus pro taxa octo m. ⟨que⟩ valent v li. vi s. viii d., folio cxvi.[22]

Dominus Johannes Wik possidet auctoritate apostolica, et habet terminos Omnium Sanctorum anni et cetera LXXVI et sequenti anno revoluto, et est iuratus, obligatus et condempnatus, sed post fuit prorogatus de primo termino usque ad festum Sancti Hilarii proxime sequentem.

De ecclesia de Tollesburi (Tollesbury) ex causa unionis facte de eadem mense abbatisse de Berkingh' (Barking) per Gregorium ii idus Decembris anno iii [33] fructus pro taxa triginta m. ⟨que⟩ valent xx li., folio cxxii.[22]

Nondum habuit effectum quia Nicholaus Harper possidet auctoritate ordinaria ut vicarius, et infra xl dies postquam erunt certificati, de dicta gratia habunt certificare et concordare et cetera, et ille possidet ad presentationem dicte abbatisse ut vicarius suus et cetera.

Resta pagine xxxviii li. xiii s. iiii d.[18]

(fol. 151) [34] De prebenda de Oxegate (Oxgate in Willesden) ex causa acceptationis auctoritate apostolica facte per Johannem Donnewich' et Thomam de Aston' fructus pro taxa trium m. octo s. ⟨que⟩ valent xlviii s., folio cxl.[22]

Litigant in curia, ut certificat episcopus, et fructus sunt sequestrati, et monitus est possessor in secundo mandato, quia ambo sunt apostolici.

De prebenda de Caditon' maior (Caddington Major) ex causa acceptationis auctoritate apostolica facte per Adam Davenport fructus, folio cxl. Taxatur lxvi s. viii d., sed habet terminum nativitatis domini anni et cetera LXXVII de toto, scilicet lxvi s. viii d.

De ecclesia de Redyngdon' (Rettendon) ex causa acceptationis auctoritate apostolica facte per Johannem Kynne fructus pro taxa sexdecim m. que valent x li. xiii s. iiii d., folio cxl.[22]

Sequestrati sunt fructus et monitus est dictus Johannes in secundo mandato.

De perpetua cantaria altaris Sancti Michaelis in ecclesia Sancti Dunstani in occidente Londonie (St. Dunstan in the West, London) ex causa provisionis facte per cardinalem Cantuariensem Roberto Wicoli fructus pro taxa duodecim m. que valent octo li., viii li., ut in folio cxxxviii.[22]

Fructus sunt sequestrati et monitus est possessor in secundo mandato.

Resta pagine xxiiii li. viii s.[18]

(fol. 151ᵛ) [34] De ecclesia Sancti Gregorii seu vicaria

ecclesie Sancti Pauli Londonie (St. Gregory by St. Paul's, London) ex causa acceptationis facte auctoritate apostolica de gratia speciali per Thomam de Southam fructus, folio cxlv.

Non taxatur sed valet communiter, ut dicitur, xx m., de quibus debet decem m. pro medietate veri valoris, que valent vi li. xiii s. iiii d. Sed iuravit dictus Thomas die xxv Octobris anni LXXVII quod non valet ultra decem m. ad firmam, et ipse solvit in partem fructuum in tribus m. quadraginta s., xl s., et restat ad huc debens quatuor li. xiii s. iiii d.[22]

De thesauraria ecclesie Londoniensis ex causa provisionis sive acceptationis apostolica auctoritate facte per Johannem Maunder fructus pro medietate veri valoris lx li., ut dicitur, sed videatur melius.[22]

Possidet auctoritate ordinaria et titulo regio et cetera. Resta pagine lxiiii li. xiii s. iiii d.

Summa restarum vacantium beneficiorum civitatis et diocesis Londoniensis iiᶜ xxii li. xvi d.[18]

## (fol. 152, ix) Diocesis Cicestrensis

De prebenda et precentoria ecclesie Ciscotrensis, taxa quinquaginta tribus li. sex s. octo d., debentur de resta per cardinalem Aquensem [35] triginta una li. tresdecim s. quatuor d. ratione provisionis sibi facte per Innocentium vi kalendas Octobris anno ix,[36] in libro rubeo folio iii, xxxi li. xiii s. iiii d.

Prohibitum quia possessor est regius qui nunc est, sed videatur cum dimitteret, vel agatur contra executorem cardinalis, quia possidente illo regio non potest fieri executio contra eum.[37]

De prebenda de Fering' (Ferring) que fuit Johannis de Donnton' ratione acceptationis facte auctoritate apostolica de eadem per Johannem Wynlingburgh fructus pro taxa quadraginta quinque m. ⟨que⟩ valent xxx li., folio xlii, xxx li.

Fructus sunt sequestrati et ipse Johannes est monitus bis, et post prorogatus usque ad purificationem anni et cetera LXXVI, et litigat cum uno regio, et tunc lis debet esse sopita ut promisit, quia nimis durat.

Etiam fuit provisum de eadem viiᵒ kalendas Junii per Dominum Gregorium XI anno secundo [38] Domino Bertrando [39] titulo Sancte Prisce, sed dicta provisio [40] non habuit effectum, sed precedens. Et videatur melius.

De vicaria de Herting' (Harting) ex causa permutationis sive provisionis facte per cardinalem Cantuariensem possessori vocato Johanni fructus pro taxa octo m. que valent v li. sex s. octo d., v li. vi s. viii d.

Fructus sunt sequestrati et ipse est excommunicatus in secundo mandato.

---

[32] 14 August 1373.
[33] 12 December 1373.
[34] The heading *Diocesis Londoniensis* is repeated at the top of the page.
[35] Peter Itherii, bishop of Dax, biship of Albano.
[36] 26 September 1361.
[37] In the margin: *Cardinalis Aquensis*.
[38] 26 May 1372.
[39] *R*, MS.
[40] *promosio*, MS.

Resta pagine lxvii li.[41]

(fol. 152[v])[42] De canonicatu et prebenda ecclesie Cicestrensis vocata Waltham ex causa confirmationis facte Edmundo Strete, canonico etiam Lincolniensi et rectori ecclesie de Merlowe (Marlow) dicte diocesis Lincolniensis, per Gregorium anno iii xiiii kalendas Novembris [43] fructus pro taxa prebende Cicestrensis decem li., x li.

Est monitus bis pro prebenda Cicestrensi, ut certificat episcopus, et debet plus in diocesi Lincolniensi cum sit expeditus per expectationem ad unam prebendam in ecclesia Lincolniensi, et tunc debet de omnibus ex causa dispensationis et non alias, sed videatur bene de toto.

De prebenda in libera cappela regis de Hastings ex causa provisionis facte de eadem per dominum cardinalem Cantuariensem Willelmo Bukbrug' fructus,[44] sed ignoratur valor.

Prohibitum est per regem quia tangit coronam et cetera, ut certificat episcopus, sed debet, et queratur melius quia male certificat episcopus. Queratur verus valor.

De prebenda de Westring' (West Wittering) in ecclesia Cicestrensi ratione acceptationis facte per Willelmum de Wymundham, quam modo possidet Michael de Causton', qui optinuit in curia contra predictum Willelmum ad iuramentum Michaelis de Caston', nepotis dicti possessoris, et sic non debentur nisi uniter, fructus pro taxa quadraginta li., xl li., folio, folio et cetera.[45]

(fol. 153, x)[42] Est monitus et fructus sunt sequestrati in secundo mandato, et post obligatus et condempnatus, et habet terminum Beati Michaelis et sequentem equales portiones. Solvit die xxx Octobris anni LXXVII in decem m. sex li. tresdecim s. quatuor d. Item solvit die xxv Januarii dicti anni in viginti m. xiii li. vi s. viii d. Et sic restant ad huc viginti li. sterlingorum, xx li. sterlingorum.[46]

De prebenda de Ippeton' (Ipthorne) in ecclesia Cicestrensi ex causa acceptationis auctoritate apostolica facte per Robertum Sutton' fructus pro taxa decem m. ⟨que⟩ valent vi li. xiii s. iiii d.[47] folio, folio et cetera.

Fructus sunt sequestrati et monitus est possessor.

De prebenda de Torneye (Thorney) ex causa provisionis facte possessori fructus pro taxa decem li., x li.

De novo repertum et exploratum; queratur.

De ecclesia de Rustington' ex causa provisionis facte Thome Bundi fructus pro taxa viginti li., xx li. Prior de Arundell' dicte diocesis possidet istam ex causa appropriationis sibi facte per ordinarium, inter quem

et dictum Thomam lis pendet in curia, et ideo est relaxatus usque ad nativitatem domini anno LXXVIII°.

Resta pagine lvi li. xiii s. iiii d.[41]

(fol. 153[v]) Summa restarum vacantium beneficiorum civitatis et diocesis Cicestrensis cxxxiii li. xiii s. iiii d. Item restat i beneficium non taxatum.[41]

(fol. 154, xi) Diocesis Wintoniensis reste

De prioratu de Appuldecombe (Appuldurcombe) ex causa confirmationis facte Johanni de Osanna per Clementem v kalendas Martii pro resta taxe triginta li. decem et septem s. Debuit in aliis restis viginti quinque li. decem et septem s., folio [48] ut in libro et cetera.

Solvit in quinque vicibus de dicta resta quindecim li., et sic est in istis restis pro decem li. decem et septem s., x li. xvii s. Et habet terminos Pasche et Michaelis ad solvendum in quolibet termino l s. quousque sit totum solutum, et prioratus est valde pauper, ut dicitur, et solvit die xvi Aprilis anno et cetera LXXVII quinquaginta s., l s., et sic est in restis istis pro viii li. vii s.

De ecclesia de Wosington' (Wonston) acceptata auctoritate apostolica per Johannem Lideford' fructus pro taxa quadraginta li., xl li.,[47] folio ut in libro.

Sequestrati sunt fructus et monitus est Willelmus Durant, clericus ducis Lancastrie nunc possessor, in secundo mandato. Habetur.

De ecclesia de Trefford' (Greatford)[49] unita monasterio Beate Marie Winton' per Clementem iii idus Julii anno xi° [50] fructus pro taxa quatuordecim li. tresdecim s. quatuor d., xiiii li. ⟨xiii s.⟩ iiii d., folio ut in libro.[47]

Certificat episcopus quod non est ibi, sed videatur melius quia non est in Lincolniensi, ut est etiam certificatum per episcopum Lincolniensem. Et queratur ubi est quia hic debet esse ubi reperitur taxa.

Resta pagine lxiiii li. iiii d.[41]

(fol. 154[v])[51] De ecclesia de Godalmyng' (Godalming) ex causa acceptationis facte auctoritate apostolica per Jacobum cardinalem de Ursinis fructus pro taxa quinquaginta quinque m. que valent xxxvi li. xiii s. iiii d.,[47] folio cxli.

Certificat episcopus quod valet, ut credit, xxxvi li. xiiii s. iiii d.[52]

De ecclesia de Hoghton' (Houghton) ex causa provisionis facte Willelmo Passenham per Dominum Gregorium XI fructus pro taxa triginta m. ⟨que⟩ valent xx li., folio cxlii.

Dictus Willelmus obiit infra eundem annum in curia, per cuius obitum optinuit auctoritate apostolica ibidem quidem Ricardus nomine, qui eam pro nunc possidet,

---

[41] In the margin: *vera*.

[42] The heading *Diocesis Cicestrensis* is repeated at the top of the page.

[43] 19 October 1373.

[44] Followed by *folio* deleted by a line.

[45] At the foot of the page: *Resta pagine x li. et i beneficium nondum taxatum*. In the margin: *vera*.

[46] In the margin: *xx li. sterlis*.

[47] Sum repeated MS.

[48] Blank in MS.

[49] Identified by *Cal. Papal Regs. Petitions*, i, 230.

[50] 13 July 1352.

[51] The heading *Wintoniensis* appears at the top of the page.

[52] In the margin: *Cardinalis Jacobus de Ursinis*.

et videatur si debentur duplices fructus et per quem et quos. Dominus vero Thomas, nunc rector [53] ecclesie Sancti Gregorii Londonie fuit procurator dicti deffuncti, et recepit fructus, et ideo respondeat pro eo quia fructus sunt sequestrati in secundo pro dictis viginti li.[47]

De ecclesia Lambhith (Lambeth) ex causa acceptationis auctoritate apostolica facte per Hugonem nunc possessorem fructus pro taxa quadraginta quinque m. ⟨que⟩ valent xxx li., folio ut in libro et cetera.

Solvit in partem taxe quinque li., et habet terminos de residuo Pasche anni LXXVIII et Michaelis tunc proxime sequentis pro resta, videlicet pro xxv li.[47]

Resta pagine lxxxi li. xiii s. iiii d.[54]

Summa restarum vacantium beneficiorum civitatis et diocesis Wintoniensis cxliiii li. xiii s. viii d.[41]

### (fol. 155, xii) Diocesis Sarisbiriensis

De prebenda de Colne (Calne) et thesauraria in ecclesia Sarisbiriensi ex causa provisionis facte cardinali Nemausensi [55] per Innocentium anno ix iii kalendas Octobris [56] debentur pro taxa octuaginta sex li. tresdecim s. quatuor d., folio et cetera.

Cardinalis est et non vult solvere, sicut nec alii.[57]

De prebenda de Bedford (Woodford), taxata sexdecim li. tresdecim s. quatuor d., et archidiaconatu Dorcestrie in eadem ecclesia, taxato [58] sexaginta duabus li., ex causa provisionis facte cardinali de Canilhano [59] per Innocentium iiii idus Martii anno ix [60] debet septuaginta octo li. tresdecim s. quatuor d., lxxviii li. xiii s. iiii d.,[47] folio, folio et cetera.

Dominus camerarius scripsit quod concordaverunt cum camera, et Raymundus Pelegrini fuerat per me monitus, ipso cardinali mortuo.

De ecclesia de Dounton' (Downton) ex causa confirmationis facte Thome de Edingdon' per Innocentium xvii kalendas Martii debentur pro taxa sexaginta sex li. tresdecim s. iiiior d., lxvi li. xiii s. iiii d.,[47] folio et cetera.

Est monitus et fructus sequestrati, sed dicitur quod fuit relaxatus alias diu est per dominum priorem Lewensem de mandato domini camerarii, sed doceat de mandato dicte camere quod nondum facere potuit. Dicit tamen quod nunquam fuit optenta ipsa confirmatio de suo consensu, quod est possibile quia patronus suus, tunc episcopus Wintoniensis, qui ipsam regebat, optinuit pro eo ipsam confirmationem et cetera. Et fructus sunt etiam sequestrati et monitus est dictus Thomas, ut certificat episcopus in ultimo mandato anni et cetera LXXVII.

Resta pagine iic xxxii li.[41]

(fol. 155v) De prebenda Sarisbiriensi ex causa provisionis facte Thome de Paston' per Urbanum anno iii quinto idus Septembris [61] fructus, folio ut in libro, pro taxa, ut dicitur, sed videatur bene, xl li.

Dominus cardinalis de Agrifolio [62] possidet et tenetur ut possessor quia alter obiit in curia et non habuit alium heredem, quia dominus cardinalis Cantuariensis distribuit bona sua de mandato apostolico ut est notorium, et ideo nichil potuit haberi ad huc.[63]

De archidiaconatu de Barkchire in ecclesia Sarisbirensi, qui taxatur quinquaginta quatuor li., ex causa provisionis facte per Urbanum anno quinto [64] Alexandro de Newila debentur de resta antiqua quadriginta quatuor li., xliiii li.,[65] folio et cetera.

Infra folio xxiiii est alia provisio facta alteri. Cardinalis de Agrifolio est nunc possessor et tenetur ut possessor ipsius quia.[66] de alio non potest aliquid haberi propter suam potentiam. Videatur.[63]

De prebenda de Illerminestre (Ilminster) in ecclesia collegiata monialium de Schaston' (Shaftesbury) diocesis Sarisbiriensis, taxata triginta m., ex causa provisionis facte Johanni Bleburi per Urbanum anno vi [67] pro antiqua resta taxe debentur [68] decem li., x li.,[65] folio.

Garderaulerius domine principisse possedit [69] diu et fuit monitus et fructus sunt sequestrati, et iam obiit excommunicatus, et servetur sequestrum et agatur contra possessorem modernum, cum obligatio sit in rem scripta et sic sequitur beneficium, et debet plus infra folio sequenti. Willelmus Bukbrug' est nunc possessor et fructus sunt sequestrati in ultimo mandato, ut certificat episcopus.

Resta pagine xciiii li.[41]

(fol. 156, xiii) [70] De archidiaconatu Barkschire ex causa provisionis facte Bernardo [71] titulo xii apostolorum alias cardinalis de Napol [72] per Urbanum anno vii v kalendas Decembris [73] fructus exceptis viginti quinque li. diu est solutis, videlicet x die Martii anno et cetera LXXII, et taxatur liiii li. et forte plus; videatur bene.

Cardinalis de Agrifolio possidet et tenetur ut possessor respondere, obligatio est in rem scripta, et sic restant de ista provisione viginti novem li., xxix li.[74]

De prebenda ecclesie Sarisbiriensis que fuit Johannis Stretle ex causa provisionis facte Henrico Torp per

---

[53] *recto*, MS.

[54] Sum repeated at the bottom of the page. In the margin: *vera*.

[55] John de Blanzac, bishop of Nimes, priest of S. Marco.

[56] 29 September 1361.

[57] In the margin: *Cardinalis Nemausensis*.

[58] *taxata*, MS.

[59] Raymond de Canillac, bishop of Palestrina.

[60] 12 March 1361.

[61] 9 September 1365.

[62] William d'Aigrefeuille, priest of S. Stefano al Monte Celio.

[63] In the margin: *Cardinalis de Agrifolio*.

[64] 1367.

[65] Sum repeated MS.

[66] Followed by *nil* deleted by a line.

[67] 1368.

[68] *debet*, MS.

[69] *possedet*, MS.

[70] The heading *Sarisbiriensis* appears at the top of the page.

[71] *R*, MS.

[72] Bernard de Bosqueto, archbishop of Naples.

[73] 27 November 1368.

[74] In the margin: *Cardinalis de Agrifolio, sed debet plus, et hic debet pro facto possessoris sui*.

Urbanum anno viii° v idus Octobris [75] fructus, folio et cetera.

Certificat episcopus quod ignoratur quis ibi fuit in ultimo certificatorio et alio, et ideo nescitur que sit ista, sed queratur plus. Ista est prebenda de Rammesburi (Ramsbury), et fructus sunt sequestrati et monitus est in loco Hugo Wymundeswold' possessor, ut certificat episcopus in ultimo mandato anni LXXVII; est taxata xxxiii li. vi s. viii d.[65]

De prebenda de Grantham in ecclesia Sarisbiriensi ex causa provisionis facte Simoni Sancti Sixti per Urbanum anno viii nonas Martii [76] fructus, folio et cetera.

Dominus camerarius mandavit anno LXXVI ante festum Beati Johannis Baptiste ad supersedendum quia concordaverat cum camera, et videatur si solvit in camera taxam xliii li. vi s. viii d.[77]

De prebenda de Rammesburi in ecclesia Sarisbiriensi ex causa provisionis [78] (fol. 156ᵛ)[79] facte Willelmo de Heghtisburi per Urbanum xvi kalendas Junii anno viii [80] fructus et cetera.

Et licet diu litigaverit, possidet nunc Hugo Wymundeswold, frater Magistri Ricardi, qui cum ipso litigavit usque ad mortem, et dictus Hugo expoliavit dominum cardinalem Convenarum [81] et alium qui acceptaverat dictam prebendam post mortem dicti Willelmi, et licet per expectationem optinuerit, non vult solvere primos fructus quia de tempore Urbani et cetera, et ita iuravit et cetera, quare dormit pro taxa 1 m. ⟨que⟩ valent xxxiii li. vi ⟨s⟩. viii d.[65]

De prebenda de Gwoth (Highworth) in ecclesia Sarisbiriensi ex causa provisionis facte cardinali de Agrifolio xvi kalendas Februarii per Gregorium anno primo,[82] que fuit Thome de Paxton', fructus debentur.[83] Datur ad firmam pro octuaginta li., et sic debet pro medietate veri valoris quadraginta li. Est tamen mandatur per dominum camerarium ad supersedendum quia concordavit cum camera, et pro medietate veri valoris debet xl li.[65] Vide supra plus pro predessesore et cetera.[84]

De archidiaconatu de Barkchire ex causa provisionis facte de eodem cardinali de Agrifolio per Gregorium anno primo iii kalendas Augusti,[85] vacante per obitum

cardinalis Neapolitanensis,[86] est in restis antiquis datis camera pro solidis fructibus, exceptis triginta duabus li. septem s. decem d. solutis pro eo per Rogerum Barnabone' ante primum compotum per collectorem reditum camere, folio et libro,[87] (fol. 157, xiiii)[80] Et taxatur cum ecclesia de Morton' (Moreton) sibi annexa ad quinquaginta quatuor li. Et habet prebendam ibidem de Heyworth' (Highworth) que taxatur centum li.

Debet de resta pro predictis prebenda et archidiaconatu cxxi li. xii s. ii d., et est mandatum ad supersedendum ut supra de aliis suis beneficiis per dominum camerarium, et videatur de toto quia debetur plus forte.[84]

De prebenda de Cherdestok' (Chardstock) in ecclesia Sarisbiriensi ex causa provisionis facte Willelmo de Osmundeston' per Gregorium anno primo xi kalendas Setempbris [88] pro taxa sexdecim li. ultra sex li. tresdecim s. quatuor d. diu est solute. Remansit in restis aliis post primum compotum pro novem li. sex s. octo d., ix li. vi s. viii d.,[89] folio ut in libro rubeo et in libro antiquo nigro folio lxxiiii. Magister Johannes Cheyne possidet nunc istam, ut certificat episcopus in ultimo.

De prebenda de Chalk, taxata sexaginta tribus m., in ecclesia de Wilton', et de prebenda de Iwermynistre (Iwerne Minster), taxata triginta m., in monasterio de Schaston' (Shaftesbury) diocesis Sarisbiriensis ex causa provisionis facte Edwardo de Cherdestok per Gregorium xiii kalendas Junii anno ii [90] fructus, folio et cetera.

Est datus in restis aliis antiquis pro dicta taxa ultra tunc solutas viginti duas li. pro quadraginta li., et debet plus supra folio [91] decem li. alia de causa, et est garderaularius domine principisse, et [92] (fol. 157ᵛ)[80] est monitus, et fructus sunt sub sequestro, et denuntiatur sepius, et iam de novo obiit et procedatur quod denuntietur semper vel quod servetur sequestrum quia beneficia sunt obligata, quia obligatio est realis seu in rem scripta. Et nunc possidet Johannes Freton' prebendam de Chalk auctoritate ordinaria et Willelmus Bukbrug' possidet illam de Iwermynistre auctoritate apostolica, ut infra, et sic in istis restis pro 1 li.[89]

De ecclesia de Cristmalford' (Christian Malford) ex causa provisionis facte Willelmo Broche iiii nonas Junii per Gregorium anno secundo [93] fructus pro taxa xl li.,[89] folio et cetera.

Possidet per Thomam Alston' titulo ordinario, et sic dicta gratia nondum habuit effectum, et ideo dormit pro nunc, sed procurator suus iuravit revelare cum habuit

---

[75] 11 October 1370.

[76] 7 March 1370.

[77] Sum repeated MS. In the margin: *Cardinalis Sancti Sixti qui erat cardinalis Anglie.*

[78] At the bottom of the page: *Resta pagine cv li. xiii s. iiii d.* In the margin: *vera.*

[79] The heading *Sarisbiriensis* is repeated at the top of the page.

[80] 17 May 1370.

[81] Bertrand Cosnaco, bishop of Comminges, priest of S. Marcello.

[82] 17 January 1371.

[83] Followed by *folio* deleted by a line.

[84] In the margin: *Cardinalis de Agrifolio.*

[85] 30 July 1371.

[86] Bernard de Bosqueto, archbishop of Naples, priest of Ss. XII Apostoli.

[87] At the foot of the page: *Resta pagine lxxiii li. vi s. viii d.* In the margin: *vera est.*

[88] 22 August 1371.

[89] Sum repeated MS.

[90] 20 May 1372.

[91] Blank in MS.

[92] At the foot of the page: *Resta pagine cxxx li. xviii s. x d.* In the margin: *vera.*

[93] 2 June 1372.

effectum, et videatur tunc et videatur cum habebit effectum.

De prioratu de Ledes (Loders) ex causa confirmationis facte Sampsoni Trigal iiii idus Januarii per Gregorium anno secundo [94] fructus, folio et cetera. Taxa non reperitur sed exigatur medietas veri valoris, que est, ut dicitur, xx li.[89]

Est in manu regis, ut certificat episcopus, et dictus Sampson [95] recessit a regno et post rediit, et iam possidet ut dicitur, quare excequatur plus. Certificat etiam in ultimo mandato anni LXXVII quod est ad huc in manu regis. Videatur verus valor.

Resta pagine cx li.[96]

(fol. 158, xv) [80] Cardinalis Gibanensis [97] habet in ecclesia Sarisbiriensi archidiaconatum Dorcestrie, folio et cetera. Taxatur ad centum m. cum ecclesia de Guisshi (St. Michaels, Gussage) sibi annexa, que ecclesia taxatur ad decem m. Habet etiam prebendam de Wodeford' (Woodford) ibidem, que taxatur ad viginti li. Et datur ad firmam dictus archidiaconatus pro ducentis undecim m. que valent cxl li. xiiii s. iiii d., et sic debet pro taxa archidiaconatus cum annexa et prebenda octuaginta sex li. tresdecim s. quatuor d., lxxxvi li. xiii s. iiii d.

Et est alia magna vera provisio facta de eodem archidiaconatu dicto cardinali Gibanensi per Dominum Gregorium folio et cetera. Et ibi vide et melius hic.[98]

De prebenda in ecclesia Sarisbiriensi ex causa provisionis facte Jacobo cardinali ad Velum Aurenensem [99] per Gregorium iiii nonas Aprilis fructus, folio et cetera. Taxatur, ut dicitur, l li.[89] Videatur bene de ipsa taxa.

Et habet decanatum in eadem ecclesia qui taxatur centum li., folio et cetera. Sed est mandatum per dominum camerarium ad supersedendum quia concordavit cum camere de toto. De hoc habetur supra folio [100] et ibi vide melius, et sic hoc non est hic nisi pro memoriale.[101]

De prebenda in ecclesia monialium de Schasteburi (Shaftesbury) diocesis Sarisbiriensis que fuit Thome nunc episcopi Eliensis ex causa provisionis facte cardinali [102] Sancte Praxedis [103] per Gregorium idus Augusti anno tertio [104] fructus.[105]

Fiat executio nisi concordaverat cum camera. Dicitur quod taxatur ad xl li.[89] Videatur.

Resta pagine clxxvi li. xiii s. iiii d.[96]

(fol. 158ᵛ) [80] De prebenda de Blebury (Blewbury) in ecclesia Sarisbiriensi ex causa provisionis facte de eadem Magistro David Cabreley per Gregorium iii kalendas Augusti fructus pro taxa sexaginta m. ⟨que⟩ valent xl li.,[89] folio et cetera.

Nondum habuit effectum quia per alium possidet, videlicet per Willelmum de Salisburi, qui, ut dicitur, habuit confirmationem apostolicam et cetera, et iuravit die ii Julii anni et cetera LXXVI solvere medietatem in natali domini proximo et interim facere diligentiam suam ut sciat de dicta confirmatione veritatem. Et est frater Domine Halicie et habent breve regium die xxiii Aprilis anni et cetera LXXVII, non obstante iuramento predicto et cetera. Et post die vicesima septima Aprilis dicti anni fuit prorogatus in eodem statu ad requestum Domini Johannis de Freton' usque ad festum proximum Beati Michaelis.

De prepositura ecclesie Sancti Edmundi Sarisbiriensis diocesis ex causa provisionis facte Phillipo Brian per Gregorium vi idus Novembris fructus pro taxa decem m. ⟨que⟩ valent vi li. xiii s. iiii d.,[89] folio et cetera.

Nondum habuit effectum quia rex contulit Willelmo David, sede Sarisbiriensi vacante, ut certificat episcopus, et videatur melius.[106]

Resta pagine xlvi li. xiii s. iiii d.[96]

(fol. 159, xvi) [80] De parochiali ecclesia Sancti Petri de Esturmenistria (Sturminster Marshall) Sarisibiriensis diocesis ex causa provisionis facte nuper per sedem apostolicam Domino Ludovico Vigorosii, priori [107] prioratus monasterii Sancti Egidii prope pontem modomariam (St. Giles of Pont-Audemer), cui est annexa et dependens, fructus, folio et cetera.

Ista provisio non habuit effectum, ut certificat episcopus misero et male, quare mandetur iterum, quia tangit dictum priorem, camerarium domini cardinalis Mimatensis (Mende),[108] in cuius favorem et cetera. Sequestrati sunt fructus et monitus est possessor in loco, ut certificat in ultimo. Dicitur quod taxatur ad lx li.,[89] sed videatur, quia est in manu regis.

De prebenda Sarisbiriensi ex causa dispensationis facte Willelmo Bukbrug' super retentionem ipsius cum certis aliis beneficiis vi idus Augusti per Urbanum anno v [109] fructus, folio et cetera. Videatur bene.

Non est hic, ut certificat episcopus Sarisbiriensis, sed mandetur ad citandum dictum Willelmum qui est ibi expectans. Videatur bene.

De prebenda de Funtemel (Fontmell) ex causa provisionis facte Johanni Norwode auctoritate apostolica fructus, folio et cetera.

Sequestrati sunt fructus et monitus est Johannes Norwodo in ultimo, et taxatur xxiii li. vi s. viii d.[110]

---

[94] 10 January 1372.
[95] *Sampsoni*, MS.
[96] In the margin: *vera*.
[97] Robert of Geneva, bishop of Cambrai, priest of Ss. XII Apostoli.
[98] In the margin: *Cardinalis Gibanensis; modo est effectus papa Clemens VII*.
[99] James Orsini, deacon of S. Giorgio in Velabro.

[100] Blank in MS.
[101] In the margin: *Cardinalis ad Velum Aut', cardinalis de Ursinis*.
[102] *per cardinalem*, MS.
[103] Peter Gomez, priest of S. Prassade.
[104] 13 August 1373.
[105] Followed by *folio* deleted by a line.
[106] *videatur melius* repeated and deleted with a line, MS.
[107] *prior*, MS.
[108] William de Chanaco, priest of S. Vitale.
[109] 8 August 1367.
[110] Sum repeated MS.

De prebenda australi de Grantham ex causa subrogationis [111] (fol. 159[v])[80] facte in iure Roberti de Suthstede
Domino Willelmo Guithorp per voluntariam relationem
suam per Dominum Gregorium fructus pro taxa sexaginta quinque m. que valent xliii li. vi s. viii d., folio
et cetera.

Solvit dictus Dominus Willelmus die xxiii Julii anno
et cetera LXXVII° in viginti quinque m. xvi li. xiii s.
iiii d. Et sic restant quadraginte m. que valent viginti sex
li. xiii s. iiii d.[110] Et quia petiit hic sibi allocari xl m. per
eum indebite, ut dicit, solutas pro prebenda de Northwell' (Norwell) alias Pahisal' in ecclesia collegiata de
Suthwell' Eboracensis diocesis, ut infra et in libro folio
xcviii, quam optinet Radulphus Setrington' per litigium
in curia Romana ad huc pendens, fuit supersessum
quousque videatur an fuerunt due vacationes vel una
sola, et an duplices fructus vel uniter debeantur.

De prebenda de Ywernemynistre (Iwerne Minster)
in ecclesia collegiata monialium de Schaston' (Shaftesbury) Sarisbiriensis diocesis ex causa provisionis facte
Willelmo Bukbrug' per expectationem fructus pro taxa
viginti li.[110]

De prebenda de Cherdestok (Chardstock) ex causa
provisionis facte Johanni Cheyne fructus pro taxa xvi
li.[110]

De vicaria de Bray ex causa provisionis facte Johanni
Drax fructus pro taxa octo li.[110]

Resta pagine lxx li. xiii s. iiii d.[112]

(fol. 160, xvii) Summa restarum vacantium beneficiorum civitatis et diocesis Saresbiriensis mcxxiii li.
v s. vi d. Item restat i beneficium non taxatum.[112]

### (fol. 160[v]) Diocesis Exoniensis

De archidiaconatu Cornubie in ecclesia Exoniensi ex
causa provisionis facte Alexandro de Newill' per Innocentium x kalendas Novembris anno ix [113] fructus, folio.

Archiepiscopus est Eboracensis, et non vult solvere
quia semper litigavit cum uno regio, sed possedit x
annis et usque ad suam promotionem, et dicit quod
agatur contra possidentem, et tamen ipse est bene solvendo quia archiepiscopus est nunc Eboracensis. Et
archidiaconatus non taxatur, ut dicitur, sed valet ad
firmam pro anno iii[c] li., de quibus debet medietatem
veri valoris circa cl li.[114]

De prebenda ecclesia collegiata de Glasenay (Glasnay) diocesis Exoniensis ex causa provisionis facte
Thome Lodoron' vi idus Februarii per Urbanum anno
iii [115] ultra viginti s. diu est solutos; fuit dimissus etiam
in restis aliis redditis pro residuo.

Fructus sunt sequestrati et monitus est in primo

mandato Ricardus Loklelly possessor, et agatur contra
eum ad residuum, si quod sit, quia non reperitur
taxata, sed expost obiit dictus R., ut certificat episcopus
in ultimo mandato anni LXXVII, et videatur bene
quantum restat.

De prebenda ecclesie collegiate Sancte Crucis de
Crediton' Exoniensis diocesis vocata Carswelle (Kerswell) ex causa provisionis facte Johanni Cheyney per
Urbanum iii kalendas Augusti anno iiii [116] fructus pro
taxa septuaginta s., lxx s.

Ultra quinquaginta s. diu est pro eo solutos per
dominum priorem Lewensem in partem fructuum, est
dimissus in primis restis redditis pro residuo.[117] Et sic
debet de resta xx[ti] s.[110] Et Thomas Cari possessor est
monitus in primo mandato et aliis, sed tamen nichil fuit
factum in ultimo mandato per episcopum.

Resta pagine cli li. sterlingorum.[118]

(fol. 161, xviii) [119] De ecclesia de Torton', sic vocatur
in libro taxe magaa,[120] ex causa dispensationis facte
Willelmo Bukbrug' vi idus Augusti per Urbanum anno
v [121] fructus pro taxa xx[ti] li.,[122] folio et cetera.

Non habebit supradictam ecclesiam, sed queratur de
ista vel alia cum qua fuit dispensatum tunc, quia est
prohibitum per breve de dicta ecclesia quia nunquam,
ut dicitur, eam habuit, sed videatur melius quia vocatur
forte aliter, et videatur quia nichil fuit factum in ultimo
mandato episcopo misso.

De ecclesia de Bukington' (Bickington) seu beneficio
quod optinet Nicholaus Tobro presbyter ex causa provisionis sibi facte per Urbanum anno vi [123] fructus pro
taxa vi li. iiii s.[124]

Est monitus et fructus sunt sequestrati in secundo
mandato et denuntiatus in ultimo.

De prebenda Exoniensi que taxatur quatuor [125] li.
ex causa provisionis facte Johanni Cheyne iii nonas
Maii anno viii Urbani.[126]

Ultra quadraginta s. diu est solutos est in restis pro
residuo, videlicet pro xl s.,[110] folio.[127]

Asserit quod habet titulo regio et non isto. Prorogatus est usque ad Pascha anni LXXVII quia non vult
solvere durante titulo regio. Sequestrati sunt fructus et
monitus est dictus Johannes in ultimo.

De vicaria ecclesie de Brampton' (Braunton) ex
causa provisionis facte [128] (fol. 161[v])[119] Deodato Clave

---

[111] At the bottom of the page: *Resta pagine lxxxiii li. vi s.
viii d.* In the margin: *vera.*
[112] In the margin: *vera.*
[113] 23 October 1361.
[114] Follows *cxl li.* deleted by a line.
[115] 8 February 1365.

[116] 30 July 1366.
[117] Followed by *folio* deleted by a line.
[118] *sterlis,* MS. In the margin: *vera.*
[119] The heading *Exoniensis* appears at the top of the page.
[120] Possibly a mistake for *magno.*
[121] 8 August 1367.
[122] Repeated twice in MS.
[123] 6 November 1367 to 5 November 1368.
[124] Followed by *folio* deleted by a line. Sum repeated MS.
[125] *quatur,* MS.
[126] 5 May 1370.
[127] Blank in MS.
[128] At the foot of the page: *Resta pagine xxviii li. iiii s.* In
the margin: *vera.*

de Wik v idus Februarii per Gregorium anno primo,[129] que non taxatur. Ultra tres li. sex s. octo d. solutos in partem fructuum.

Walterus Delevenant est obligatus pro eo et ut principalis, et est datus in aliis primis restis et in istis pro residuo diu est. Hoc est pro tribus li. sex s. octo d.,[130] folio xxxiii.

Possidetur nunc, mortuo Deodato, per Johannem Godmeston', et fructus sunt sequestrati in primo mandato. Et dictus Johannes debet etiam plus, ex causa provisionis sibi facte in curia post mortem dicti Deodati, alios fructus, videlicet decem m. ad minus que valent pro toto vi li. xiii s. iiii d. Sed videatur de valore quia non taxatur ad minus nisi ad vi li. xiii s. iiii d. Et sic debentur xv m. que valent decem li. Et post solvit die iii Februarii anno et cetera LXXVII in quinque m. lxvi s. viii d. Restant vi li. xiii s. iiii d.[110]

De preceptoria et prebenda in ecclesia Exoniensi acceptata auctoritate apostolica per Symonem Lambourn' presbyterum fructus ultra quadraginta s. diu est solutos ratione prebende, folio et cetera.

Videatur quantum plus debetur quia nondum potest sciri. Precentoria possidetur per alium titulo regio, et ideo est prohibitum de precentoria sed non de prebenda, et scribatur contra possessorem prebende qui fuit in ipsa ecclesia loco dicti Symonis et cetera. Fructus sunt sequestrati in secundo mandato, et Johannes Poddeston' tunc incumbens fuit monitus, sed litigabat, et lite finita fuit iuratus concordare et cetera.[131] Exploratus fuit sic.

Resta pagine x li. et i beneficium nondum taxatum.[112]

(fol. 162, xix)[119] De archidiaconatu Exoniensi et prebenda de Aylesbury in ecclesia Lincolniensi ex causa provisionis facte domino cardinali de Vernhio[132] per Gregorium viii kalendas Julii anno primo[133] fructus, folio et cetera.

Et datur ad firmam annuam archidiaconatus octuaginta m. et non taxatur, sed prebenda taxatur ad sexaginta m., et sic debet in istis restis dictus cardinalis qui nichil solvit centum m. que valent lxvi li. xiii s. iiii d.[134]

De precentoria ecclesie Exoniensis ex causa provisionis facte cardinali xii apostolorum[135] per Gregorium anno iii v idus Februarii[136] fructus, folio et cetera.

Sed nondum habuit effectum, titulo regio impediente, sed videatur cum habuit effectum. Que taxatur, ut dicitur, xl li.

De vicaria de Tunstall' (Townstall) ex causa provisionis facte Johanni Bonefamit iii idus Aprilis per

Gregorium anno iiii[137] pro taxa, ut dicitur, septem m., folio et cetera. Valent iiii li. xiii s. iiii d.

Fructus sunt sequestrati et monitus est dictus Johannes in secundo, et post fuit prorogatus usque ad festum Sancti Hillarii anni LXXVI, et lapso termino denuntietur, sed dicitur quod obiit, et fructus sunt sequestrati in ultimo.

De prebenda in ecclesia Exoniensi ex causa provisionis facte Magistro David Calverley per obitum cardinalis Convenari[138] per Gregorium iii nonas Maii anno quarto[139] fructus pro taxa iiii li. salvo iure pluris, folio et cetera, iiii li.

Certificat episcopus quod non est talis ibi, sed dicitur quod immo est, et videatur bene. Certificat etiam episcopus in ultimo mandato quod fructus sunt sequestrati, sed tamen nescitur[140] prebenda nec nomen possessoris.

Resta pagine cxv li. vi s. viii d.[141]

(fol. 162ᵛ)[119] De prebenda in ecclesia Exoniensi que fuit Symonis Delaborun' ex causa acceptationis auctoritate apostolica facte per Johannem de Poddesdon' fructus pro taxa quatuor li., iiii li.

Litigat cum uno ordinario, scilicet Magistro Thoma de Walkington', et iuravit quod quacumque fraude cessante et cetera infra mensem veniret et concordaret postquam optinuerit contra dictum Thomam tacite vel expresse. Et debet plus de tempore dicti Symonis, et vocetur et videatur bene totum. Fructus sunt sequestrati et monitus est Johannes Attewell', procurator dicti Johannis, ut certificat in ultimo, et videatur bene quod duplices fructus debentur, et sic debentur viii li.[142]

De ecclesia Sancti Georgii Exoniensis ex causa provisionis facte per cardinalem Cantuariensem Waltero Reghlond' ii nonas Octobris fructus, folia et cetera.

Quavis litigaverit diu, nunc possidet, et non taxatur sed[143] valet, ut dicitur, pro toto xl s. Et sic solvit die x Novembris anni et cetera LXXVI pro medietate veri valoris xx s., salvo iure pluris, si plus valet. Et videatur quia pro residuo datur hic in restis. Fructus sunt sequestrati et monitus est dictus R. in ultimo, et videatur de dicto residuo, si quod sit.

De prebenda Exoniensi quam acceptavit Radulphus Piliton' auctoritate apostolica fructus, folio et cetera.

Est in curia cum domino cardinali de Vernhio, et quia absens nichil percipit et ideo nichil solvit adhuc. Fructus sunt sequestrati et monitus est Robertus Brok possessor in ultimo mandato anni LXXVII pro taxa quatuor li., iiii li.

Resta pagine xii li. et i beneficium nondum taxatum.[141]

[129] 9 February 1371.
[130] Sum repeated twice, MS.
[131] Followed by *infra est cum* deleted by a line.
[132] Peter de Vergne, deacon of S. Maria in Via Lata.
[133] 24 June 1371.
[134] Sum repeated MS. In the margin: *Cardinalis de Vernhio*.
[135] Robert of Geneva.
[136] 9 February 1373.

[137] 11 April 1374.
[138] Bertrand Cosnaco, bishop of Comminges, priest of S. Marcello.
[139] 5 May 1374.
[140] *nescit*, MS.
[141] In the margin: *vera*.
[142] Sum repeated MS.
[143] *nec*, MS.

(fol. 163, xx) Summa restarum vacantium beneficiorum [144] civitatis et diocesis Exoniensis iii⁰ xvi li. x s.
viii d. Item restant beneficia non taxata ii.[141]

### (fol. 163ᵛ) Diocesis Wigorniensis

De ecclesia de Estlegh' (Astley) ex causa provisionis
facte Henrico Haskebi per Innocentium est in restis
antiquis pro octo li.[145]

Certificat episcopus pluries quod nunquam habuit
effectum quia semper in curia litigavit et ibi obiit.
Videatur quis fuit auctoritate apostolica subrogatus.
Dictus H. non occupavit istam ecclesiam, xl annis
elapsis, sed quidam Ricardus Vi— occupat eam auctoritate ordinaria, qui est monitus et fructus sunt sequestrati, ut certificat episcopus in ultimo mandato anni
LXXVII.

De ecclesia de Staunton' ex causa provisionis facte
Willelmo de Henereth' iii idus Augusti per Urbanum
anno viii [146] fructus pro taxa quatuor li. sex s. octo d.,
folio et cetera, iiii⁰ʳ li. vi s. viii d.

Dictus Willemus resignavit istam pro meliori ecclesia
quam post tempus habuit, et nunc possidetur ista ecclesia auctoritate apostolica per Johannem Banneburi alias
Fissher. Et sic debentur duplices fructus. Iste Johannes
solvit diu est dictam taxam pro seipso, sed debet pro
alia provisione precedente, et sic habet quittantiam. Et
datur in istis restis pro illa taxa predessessoris sui. Hoc
est iiii li. vi s. viii d. vel residuo. Fructus sunt sequestrati et monitus est [147] dictus Johannes in ultimo mandato predicto.

De ecclesia de Clive (Bishop's Cleeve) ex causa
confirmationis facte Willelmo Tuford' viii kalendas Junii
per Gregorium anno primo [148] per obitum Ricardi de
Drayton' fructus pro taxa xl li.,[142] folio et cetera.

Et frater Domini Guidonis de Bran possidet titulo
ordinario, et non habuit effectum dicta gratia, et videatur bene quia debet, ut dicitur, xl li.

Resta pagine lii li. vi s. viii d.[141]

(fol. 164, xxi)[149] De ecclesia de Estington' (East-
ington) ex causa provisionis facte Johanni Rauf' xi
kalendas Junii per Gregorium anno iiii [150] fructus pro
taxa sexdecim m. que valent x li. xiii s. iiii d., folio et
cetera.

Fructus sunt sequestrati et est monitus in primo et
ultimo quidam Henricus possessor, x li. xiii s. iiii d.

De ecclesia de Bech' Sancti Martini (Eastleach
Martin) ex causa provisionis facta Ricardo Quenet
presbytero per Gregorium vi kalendas Decembris anno

iiii [151] pro taxa, ut dicitur, xviii m. ⟨que⟩ valent xii li.,
folio et cetera.

Non est talis Ricardus ibi, sed Robertus Jones
occupat dictam ecclesiam auctoritate apostolica, qui est
monitus et fructus sunt sequestrati in ultimo, xii li.

De prebenda de Aust ecclesie collegiate de Westburi
(Westbury) diocesis Wigorniensis ex causa confirmationis facte Johanni Wichif' per Gregorium anno v [152]
fructus, folio et cetera.[153]

Dicitur quod nunquam habuit confirmationem a
Domino Gregorio. Immo possidebat eam ante suam
promotionem de tempore Domini Urbani. Et taxatur,
ut dicitur, sex li. tresdecim s. iiii⁰ʳ d., vi li. xiii s. iiii d.

Resta pagine xxix li. v s. viii d.[141]

(fol. 164ᵛ) Summa restarum vacantium beneficiorum
civitatis et diocesis Wigorniensis lxxxi li. xiiii s. iiii d.[141]

### (fol. 165, xxii) Diocesis Bathoniensis et Wellensis

De prepositura in ecclesia Wellensi ex causa provisionis facte Ade de Hilton' per Innocentium iii nonas
Februarii anno vii [154] fructus pro taxa xl li.,[142] folio
et cetera.

Rogerus Helm, cancellarius in ecclesia Londoniensi,
possidet titulo regio, et est prohibitum, quo titulo
durante non possunt haberi fructus, licet ipsum beneficium sit obligatum, et tamen fuit monitus ⟨et⟩ excommunicatus ante dictum breve regium contra collectorem
optentum.

Et de eadem prepositura ex causa provisionis facte
Willelmo Wikham, nunc episcopo Wintoniensi, per
Innocentium nonas Januarii anno x [155] fructus pro taxa
xl li.[142] folio.[156]

Episcopus Wintoniensis est, et non vult solvere
aliqua via, sed citetur et vocetur iterum et cetera.

De archidiaconatu de Taunton' in ecclesia Wellensi
cum prebenda sibi annexa ex causa provisionis facte
Willelmo Tyngullun per Urbanum vi idus Augusti anno
secundo [157] fructus, folio et cetera.

Dicitur quod non habuit effectum, et est inter alias
inutiles reddita, et dominus cardinalis de Agrifolio est
nunc possessor, sed videatur melius de dicto Willelmo
si unquam possedit, quia valet bene, ut dicitur, c li.

De prebenda et archidiaconatu Wellensibus ex causa
provisionis facte cardinali Cantuariensi v nonas Octobris
per Urbanum anno vii [158] fructus, folio et cetera. Et
debet plus de thesauraria et alia prebenda Wellensibus
ex causa provisionis facte dicto cardinali Cantuariensi
ii idus Januarii per Urbanum anno vi [159] fructus, folio

---

[144] Followed by *in* deleted by a line.
[145] Sum repeated twice MS.
[146] 11 August 1370.
[147] *et*, MS.
[148] 25 May 1371.
[149] The heading *Wigorniensis* is repeated at the top of the page.
[150] 22 May 1374.

[151] 26 November 1374.
[152] 1375.
[153] In the margin: *non reperitur taxa.*
[154] 3 February 1359.
[155] 5 January 1362.
[156] Blank in MS.
[157] 8 August 1364.
[158] 3 October 1369.
[159] 12 January 1368.

et cetera, que taxatur quinquaginta m. que valent xxxiii li. vi s. viii d.[142]

Cardinalis fuit Cantuariensis, et videatur si solvit camere cum qua concordavit Avinionie ante suum obitum, et fuit scriptum ad supersedendum [160] per dominum Cantuariensem.[161]

Resta pagine ccxiii li. vi s. viii d.[141]

(fol. 165ᵛ)[162] De prebenda Wellensis ecclesie Roberti Thonneley ex causa provisionis sibi facte per Urbanum nonas Aprilis anno viii [163] fructus, folio et cetera.

Sequestrati sunt fructus et monitus est dictus Robertus [164] et denuntiatus, et iam obiit, ut certificat episcopus in secundo, sed videatur melius, et sic est denuntiatus in ultimo mandato anni LXXVII pro taxa, ut dicitur, et videatur bene, viginti li., xx li.

De prebenda ecclesie Wellensis Johannis Gaylardi ex causa provisionis sibi facte per Urbanum vi idus Maii anno viii [165] fructus, folio et cetera.

Fructus sunt sequestrati et monitus et denuntiatus est dictus Johannes, qui est mortuus, ut certificat episcopus in secundo. Videatur melius. Et sic est denuntiatus in ultimo, pro taxa, ut dicitur. Et videatur bene. xx li.

De archidiaconatu de Thaunton' et prebenda ecclesie Wellensis ex causa provisionis facte Gregorio cardinali Sancti Stephani in Celio Monte per Gregorium idus Augusti anno iii [166] fructus debentur, folio et cetera.

Cardinalis est de Agrifolio, et datur ad firmam centum tresdecim li. sex s. quatuor d., et sic debet pro medietate veri valoris lvi li. xiii s. iiii d.,[142] et fuit scriptum de camera quod de omnibus suis beneficiis concordavit cum camera, et sciatur in camera si solvit vel non.[167]

De vicaria ecclesie de Merston' (Marston Bigot) ex causa provisionis facte Henrico Bayly per cardinalem Cantuariensem xviii kalendas Februarii fructus pro taxa sex m. cum dimidia que valent iiii li. vi s. viii d., folio et cetera.[168]

(fol. 166, xxiii)[162] Fructus sunt sequestrati et monitus est dictus Henricus in secundo mandato, quare denuntiatus excommunicatus, et sic denuntiatus est in ultimo.

De perpetua vicaria in ecclesia Wellensi collata Philippo Gille per cardinalem Cantuariensem Londonie kalendas Julii fructus, folio et cetera.

Non est talis ibi, ut certificat bis episcopus, sed videatur melius quia forte erratur in nomine vel in

cognomine. Fructus sunt sequestrati in ultimo, et taxatur, ut dicitur, xx li.

De vicaria stalli prebende de Asthull' (Ashill) in ecclesia Wellensi ex causa provisionis facte Ricardo de Trendik per cardinalem Cantuariensem Londonie xviii kalendas Decembris fructus, folio et cetera, pro taxa, ut dicitur, x li.

Fructus sunt sequestrati et monitus est dictus Ricardus et denuntiatus in secundo, ut certificat episcopus, et denuntietur excommunicatus sicut est pro contumacia. Et sic est denuntiatus in ultimo. Videatur bene de ipsa taxa.

De subdecanatu et prebenda de Witlakington' (White Lackington) in ecclesia Wellensi ex causa acceptationis auctoritate apostolica facte per Thomam Byngham fructus pro taxa subdecanatus triginta m., ⟨que⟩ valent xx li., et pro taxa prebende decem et octo m., ⟨que⟩ valent xii li. Et sic valent in toto folio xxxii li.

Est de novo exploratum, quare mandatur et exequatur et fructus sunt sequestrati in ultimo.

Resta pagine lxii li.[169]

(fol. 166ᵛ)[162] De prebenda de Asthul ex causa acceptationis auctoritate apostolica facte per Willelmum Chambre fructus pro taxa viginti m., ⟨que⟩ valent xiii li. vi s. viii d., folio et cetera.

Est noviter exploratum, et mandetur et cetera. Fructus sunt sequestrati in ultimo mandato.

De prebenda de Comba (Combe) ex causa acceptationis auctoritate apostolica facte per Johannem de Longeton' fructus pro taxa octo m., ⟨que⟩ valent v li. vi s. viii d., folio et cetera.

Fructus sunt sequestrati.

De prebenda de Comba ex causa acceptationis auctoritate apostolica facte per Willelmum Welbourn' fructus pro taxa octo m., ⟨que⟩ valent [170] v li. vi s. viii d., folio et cetera.

Est noviter exploratum, et mandetur. Fructus sunt sequestrati in ultimo.

De prebenda de Comba ex causa acceptationis auctoritate apostolica facte per Johannem Mulward fructus pro taxa octo m., ⟨que⟩ valent v li. vi s. viii d.[171]

Est noviter esploratum et cetera, et sunt circa x prebende in ecclesia Wellensi vocate Comb. Fructus sunt sequestrati in ultimo mandato anni LXXVII.

De prebenda de Comba in ecclesia Wellensi ex causa provisionis facte auctoritate apostolica Johanni Brampton' in curia fructus pro taxa octo m., ⟨que⟩ valent v li. vi s. viii d., folio et cetera.

De novo exploratur. Solvit die xvi Februarii anno et cetera LXXVII in iiiiᵒʳ m. liii s. iiii d., et sic est in istis restis pro aliis iiiiᵒʳ m., videlicet pro liii s. iiii d.,[171] folio et cetera.

Resta pagne xxxii li.[169]

---

[160] *supersedum*, MS.
[161] In the margin: *Cardinalis Cantuariensis.*
[162] The heading *Bathoniensis et Wellensis* appears at the top of the page.
[163] 5 April 1370.
[164] *Ricardus*, MS.
[165] 10 May 1370.
[166] 13 August 1373.
[167] In the margin: *Cardinalis de Agrifolio.*
[168] At the foot of the page: *Resta pagine ci li.* In the margin: *vera.*

[169] in the margin: *vera.*
[170] Followed by *folio* deleted by a line.
[171] Sum repeated MS.

(fol. 167, xxiiii) Summa restarum vacantium bene-ficiorum civitatis et diocesis Bathoniensis et Wellensis iiii<sup>c</sup> viii li. vi s. viii d.[171]

### (fol. 167<sup>v</sup>) Diocesis Herfordensis

De prebenda de Morton' (Moreton Magna) in ecclesia Herfordensi ex causa provisionis facte Symoni de Sud-buri per Clementem iiii nonas Julii anno viii [172] est in restis antiquis pro tresdecim s. quatuor d. folio et cetera, xiii s. iiii d.

Archiepiscopus est Cantuariensis, et nunquam vult solvere, et debet etiam plus infra folio.[173]

De prebenda de Morton' ex causa provisionis facte Thome Thebaud' per Innocentium iii idus Decembris anno xi [174] pro taxa viginti li., folio et cetera, xx li.

Prohibitum quia possessor est regius, et est alia provisio infra folio et cetera, de qua est prohibitum ex eadem causa, et dormit quia durante titulo regio non potest excequi, sed post bene, cum obligatio sit in rem scripta, quare videatur bene cum erit locus de aliis xx li.[171]

De vicaria ecclesie de Bitton' alias Bicton' (Bicton) ex causa provisionis facte Johanni Brokenhull' pres-bytero per Urbanum anno primo [175] fructus. Est in decanatu Leomyncestrie (Leominster) que vocatur Bicton'. Et taxatur centum s., folio et cetera, v li.

Fuit mandatum sepe et nichil factum usque nunc ultimo, ubi certificat episcopus quod non est talis, quare videatur melius quia ille episcopus non certificavit semper bene, sed tamen certificat etiam in ultimo man-dato anni LXXVII quod non est talis vicaria in diocesi ista, sed videatur melius.

De prebenda de Hewithingon' in ecclesia Herfordensi, que, ut dicitur,[176] (fol. 168, xxv)[177] fuit Willelmi Belle, ex causa provisionis facte Willelmo Humbleton' per Urbanum xi kalendas Decembris anno viii [178] fructus debentur, folio et cetera, pro taxa, ut dicitur, et videatur, x li.

Fuit sepe mandatum et nichil factum ad huc deffectu episcopi, sed fuit in ultimo certificatum quod non fuit talis prebenda nec prebendarius et cetera.

De prebenda de Poteston' minori (Putson Minor) et cancellaria Herfordensi ex causa confirmationis facte seu provisionis Nicholao de Herford' per Gregorium viii kalendas Martii anno quinto.[179] Cancellaria taxatur viginti li., xx li. Dicta cancellaria habet ecclesiam annexam que plus valet. Videatur bene quia solvit pro

dicta cancellaria in duabus vicibus decem li. Et sic restant decem li. et plus, ut infra sequitur, et videatur.

Habet terminos Beati Michaelis anni LXXVI et Pasche nunc elapsos, sed est prorogatus usque ad festum Beati Hillarii anni et cetera LXXVI. Et dicitur quod litigat de prebenda cum Thoma Chandos, quia est datus in istis restis pro solidis fructibus exceptis dictis x li. in dicto folio solutis, et in recepta compotatur. Et dictus Thomas nunc possidet et optinuit dictam prebendam contra prefatum Nicholaum et cetera, qui Nicholaus est denuntiatus in ultimo, x li.

De prebenda Herfordensi Johannis Boton' ex causa provisionis sibi facte per Gregorium xi kalendas Junii anno iiii,[180] vacante per obitum Ade Esogonii, fructus, folio et cetera.

Fuit sepe mandatum et nichil fuit factum, quare mandetur plus quia communiter male certificant offi-ciales illius episcopi iam translati, et videatur bene cum isto qui nunc est ibi episcopus. Non est talis preben-darius [181] nec prebenda, ut fuit certificatum in ultimo. Dicitur quod valet x li., sed videatur bene, x li.

Resta pagine xxx li.[182]

(fol. 168<sup>v</sup>)[183] De prebenda de Gorewell' (Gorwall) et cancellaria ecclesie Herfordensis ex causa provisionis facte R. titulo Sancte Pisce presbytero cardinali [184] per Gregorium ix kalendas Octobris anno ii [185] fructus, folio et cetera.

Cardinalis est, et videatur bene quia dicitur quod non habuit effectum, sed cancellaria taxatur xx li.[186]

De prebenda de Posteston' minori (Putson Minor) in ecclesia Herfordensi, que fuit Egidii Samford', ex causa provisionis facte Johanni de Upton' xiiii kalendas Maii per Gregorium anno secundo [187] fructus pro taxa, ut dicitur, xl m. ⟨que⟩ valent xxiii li. vi s. viii d., folio et cetera.

Fuit sepe mandatum et nichil factum, et videatur melius, et infra debet plus ut videtur in sequenti pro-visione. Thomas Chandos possidet auctoritate apos-tolica, et fructus sunt sequestrati in ultimo.

De prebenda de Poteston' in ecclesia Herfordensi ex causa acceptationis auctoritate apostolica facte per Thomam Chandos fructus, folio et cetera.

Fuit mandatum et nondum certificatum. Et dicitur quod litigat de ista cum Nicholao Herfordensi, et dictus Thomas possidet contra dictum Nicholaum, et fructus sequestrati in ultimo pro taxa, ut dicitur, xx li.,[188] sed videatur bene, xx li.

---

[172] 4 July 1349.
[173] Blank in MS.
[174] 11 December 1362(?).
[175] 6 November 1362 to 5 November 1363.
[176] At the foot of the page: *Resta pagine xlv li. xiii s. iiii d.* In the margin: *vera.*
[177] The heading *Diocesis Herfordensis* is repeated at the top of the page.
[178] 21 November 1369.
[179] 22 February 1375.

[180] 22 May 1374.
[181] *prebendarius* repeated MS.
[182] In the margin: *vera.*
[183] The heading *Herfordensis* appears at the top of the page.
[184] Bertrand of S. Prisca.
[185] 23 September 1372.
[186] Sum repeated MS. In the margin: *Cardinalis est Glan-datensis* (Glandèves).
[187] 18 April 1372.
[188] Sum repeated MS.

De prebenda de Coblington' (Cublington or Medley), quam, ut dicitur, acceptavit auctoritate apostolica Johannes Midelton', fructus.

Fuit mandatum et nondum certificatum, et non bene exploratum. Dictus Johannes possidet, et fructus sunt sequestrati in ultimo. Nec alii tres predicti adhuc habunt prebendam. Valet xx li. ad taxam, ut dicitur. Sed videatur melius, xx li.

Resta pagine lxxxiii li. vi s. viii d.[182]

(fol. 169, xxvi)[183] De prebenda de Gorewell' (Gorwall) ex causa provisionis facte R. cardinali titulo Sancte Pisce fructus, folio et cetera, qui, ut dicitur, acceptavit etiam cancellariam Herfordensem per procuratores, qui sunt episcopus Londoniensis, Rogerius Oteri et Johannes Stok, et videatur quid debetur, quia noviter exploratum. Supra est in principio istius folii. Dicitur pro taxa xx li. Sed videatur melius.

De prebenda de Hompton' (Hampton Bishop), vacante per obitum Thome Hakeluit, ex causa acceptationis auctoritate apostolica facte per Johannem Budwodo fructus pro taxa xxvii s. viii d. ob., folio et cetera.

Solvit die xi Martii anni et cetera LXXV in partem fructuum viginti septem s. octo d. ob. Et valet, ut dicitur, viginti li., et sic debet pro medietate veri valoris decem li. minus dictos xxvii s. viii d. et ob. solutos. Et videatur bene quia hic dimittitur in istis restis, si ita est de dicto valore, pro viii li. xii s. iii d. ob. Nichil fuit factum in ultimo mandato, viii li. xii s. iii d. et obolum.

Resta pagine xxviii li. xii s. iii d. et obolum.[182]

(fol. 169v) Summa restarum vacantium beneficiorum civitatis et diocesis Herfordensis clxxxvii li. xii s. iii d. ob.[182]

### (fol. 170, xxvii) Diocesis Norwicensis

De prioratu de Castelano (Castle Acre) diocesis Norwicensis ex causa provisionis facte Willelmo Waron' per Clementem anno primo[189] fructus pro taxa iiiiᶜ iiiixx li. xix s. vii d. sterlingorum.

Instrumentum obligationis est in archivis, et videatur bene adhuc si poterit aliquid haberi, quia de patronatu laicali et, ut dicitur, comitis Arundelle, et nichil potest haberi nec unquam potuit, et sic dormit ad huc. Et videatur melius quia licet sit de patronatu prioris Leuensis, non tamen est de patronatu comitis predicti, quia non omnia que habet prior Leuensis sunt de patronatu dicti comitis Arundellensis. Est prorogatus usque ad festum Beati Michaelis Setempbris anni LXXVII ad requestam domini comitis predicti, et fructus sunt sequestrati in ultimo mandato anni LXXVII.

De ecclesia de Hulmo taxata quadriginta li. ex causa provisionis facte Thome Michiel per Clementem debentur de resta antiqua decem li., x li.[190]

Prohibitum est per breve, et queratur nomen possessoris qui nunc est, et sy non sit titulo regio possessor, exigatur dicta resta ab ipso possessore.

De ecclesia de Derham (East Dereham), que taxatur centum decem m., ex causa provisionis facte Symoni Thebaud nunc archiepiscopo Cantuariensi per Clementem iii kalendas Aprilis anno ix[191] pro resta, folio et cetera. Debet plus supra in precedenti diocesi Herfondensi pro alia provisione, folio et cetera, xl li. xvii s. viii d.

Et non vult solvere, licet plures fuerit requisitus, et allegat quod Dominus Raymundus Pelegrini tempore suo recepit fructus, sed non probat.

Resta pagine vᶜ xxxi li. xvii s. iii d.[182]

(fol. 170v)[192] De decanatu et prebenda de Humiliard' (Humbleyard) ex causa provisionis facte Symoni de Sudburi per Innocentium iii kalendas Julii anno v[193] fructus, folio et cetera.

Fructus decanatus sunt sequestrati et monitus est possessor in primo mandato, sed certificat de prebenda episcopus in ultimo quod non est talis in diocesi sua. Dicitur quod taxatur ad xx li., sed videatur bene, xx li.

De decantatu rurali et prebenda de Fordeham (Fordham) ex causa provisionis facte Waltero Palmer per Innocentium vi nonas Maii anno x[194] fructus, folio et cetera.

Fructus decanatus sunt sequestrati et monitus est Willelmus de Bagton' possessor in primo mandato, sed non certificat de prebenda et ideo denuntietur pro decanatu et sequestretur prebenda. Est denuntiatus in ultimo mandato, sed non est talis prebenda, ut certificat episcopus. Taxa non reperitur, sed dicitur quod valet pro medietate veri valoris viginti li., sed videatur bene, xx li.

De ecclesia de Hulmo (Holme) ex causa provisionis facte Roberto de Grimmeston' xviii kalendas Januarii per Innocentium anno primo[195] fructus pro taxa quadraginta li., xl li.

Est ibidem alia provisio de eadem ecclesia, sed infra eundem annum, quare non debetur nisi de una. Est tamen prohibitum per breve de utraque diu est, quia possessor est titulo regio et ideo dormit, sed videatur cum ille regius desinet possidere.

Resta pagine lxxx li.[182]

(fol. 171, xxviii)[196] De prepositura monasterii Sancte Marie ordinis Sancti Benedicti ex causa confirmationis facte fratri Stephano Jemdic' Stephani per Urbanum anno primo[197] fructus, folio et cetera.

Non est in Anglia, ut certificat episcopus. Ideo

---

[189] 19 May 1342 to 18 May 1343.
[190] Sum repeated MS.

[191] 30 March 1351.
[192] The heading *Norwicensis* appears at the top of the page.
[193] 29 June 1357.
[194] 2 May 1362.
[195] 15 December 1353.
[196] The heading *Norwicensis* is repeated at the top of the page.
[197] 6 November 1362 to 5 November 1363.

inutilis potest dici, sed videatur melius, quia etiam non reperitur taxa.

De vicaria ecclesie de Berton' (Barton) ex causa confirmationis facte de ordinatione ipsius vicarie per Urbanum anno primo fructus pro taxa decem li., x li.,[190] folio.[198]

Robertus Bran est nunc possessor, et fructus sunt sequestrati, et monitus est dictus R. in primo mandato, et denuntiatus et sequestrati in ultimo.

De decanatu rurali de Redenhalle ex causa provisionis facte Thome de Drayton' per Urbanum anno primo fructus pro taxa, ut dicitur, ii m. ⟨que⟩ valent xxvi s. viii s.[190]

Dicitur quod non habuit effectum, sed videatur melius, et sic in secundo mandato, ubi certificat episcopus quod non constat de tali Thoma qui est aut fuerit ibi possessor.

Archidiaconatus Southfolchie est in restis pro fructibus procurationum et iurisdictionis in libro antiquo nigro folio xxxv et in rubeo.

Fructus sunt sequestrati et monitus est possessor in primo mandato, et denuntiatus in ultimo. Dicitur quod valet l li. pro medietate veri valoris, sed videatur bene, l li.

Resta pagine lxi li. vi s. viii d.; i beneficium nondum taxatum.[182]

(fol. 171ᵛ)[196] De decanatu et prebenda rurali de Waxtonesham (Waxham) ex causa provisionis facte Thome de Witon' per Urbanum iii idus Martii anno vii[199] fructus pro taxa sexaginta duarum m. que valent xli li. vi s. viii d.[190]

Non est in diocesi, ut certificat episcopus, sed queratur melius de beneficio dicti Thome quia forte vocatur aliter ut supra, et dictus Thomas possidet illum decanatum auctoritate ordinaria, ut certificat episcopus in ultimo.

De ecclesia de Estderham (East Dereham) ex causa provisionis facte Michaeli de Causton' per Gregorium iii kalendas Aprilis anno primo[200] fructus pro taxa septuaginta trium li. vi s. octo d.

Fuit in istis restis pro triginta tribus li. sex s. octo d., folio et cetera. Fructus sunt sequestrati et monitus est possessor in primo mandato et cetera, et solvit die iiii Maii anno et cetera LXXVII in viginti quinque m. xvi li. xiii s. iiii[201] d., et sic remansit in istis restis pro aliis xvi li. xiii s. iiii d. Et post solvit plus die xvii Setembpris viii li. vi s. viii d. Et sic restat debens tantumdem, scilicet viii li. vi s. viii d.,[190] et est obligatus et condempnatus, et habet terminum Beati Michaelis anni predicti et sequentis.

De prioratu de Cretyng' (Creeting St. Olave) Norwicensis et Ewerdon' (Everdon) Lincolniensis diocesum ex causa provisionis seu confirmationis facte Rogero

Fabri per Gregorium v nonas Maii fructus, folio et cetera. Non taxatur nec valet ultra viginti duas li. Et sic debet pro medietate veri valoris undecim li.[202] (fol. 172, xxix)[199] Habet terminos Pasche anni et cetera LXXV, et sic est prorogatus per equales portiones in quatuor annis, ut in libro et cetera. Et solvit diu est pro primo termino quinquaginta quinque s., et sic est in istis restis traditus pro resta, videlicet pro viii li. v s.

De ecclesia de Saxam parva (Little Saxham) ex causa provisionis facte Johanni Bokelond Juniori ii idus Octobris per Gregorium anno secundo[203] fructus pro taxa decem et sex m. que valent decem li., folio et cetera.

Valet dicta ecclesia quadraginta m., ut dicitur, et solvit in recepta in mense Novembris anni LXXVI in una m. xiii s. iiii d. Et fructus sunt sequestrati in primo mandato et cetera, et sic est in istis restis datus pro resta medietatis veri valoris in decem et novem m. que valent xii li. xiii s. iiii d.[190] Et dictus Johannes est denuntiatus in ultimo et sequestrati.

De vicaria de Kempston' ex causa permutationis facte coram cardinali Cantuariensi Nicholao de Brisele fructus pro taxa sex m. vel residuum. Valent dicte vi m., hoc est, iiii li.[190]

Fructus sunt sequestrati in primo et cetera, et denuntiatus est Willelmus possessor in ultimo.

De vicaria de Kingesdon' ex causa permutationis facte Willelmo atte Stok' coram domino cardinali Cantuariensi ultra quadraginta s. diu est solutos fructus.

Non est in diocesi, ut certificat episcopus, quod non debet sic esse quia partem solvit, et queratur bene tamen. Non certificavit in ultimo et cetera. Videatur quantum restat.

Resta pagine xxiiii li. xviii s. iiii d. et i beneficium nondum taxatum.[182]

(fol. 172ᵛ)[199] De ecclesia de Thune (Thurne) ex causa provisionis facte Henrico de Mildehole per cardinalem Cantuariensem ultra viginti s. diu est solutos fuit datus in premissis restis pro residuo. Videatur resta.

Sequestrati sunt fructus in primo et cetera, et monitus est possessor et denuntiatus in ultimo. Videatur resta.

De ecclesia Sancti Andree de Taterset (Tattersett, St. Andrew) ex causa provisionis facte per cardinalem Cantuariensem Thome de Frastorp fructus pro taxa undecim m. cum dimidia que valent vii li. xiii s. iiii d.

Habet terminos Pasche et nativitatis domini anni et cetera LXXVI, iam elapsos,[204] et ideo sequestrati sunt fructus et denuntiatus est Willelmus Seli in ultimo.

De ecclesia Beate Marie de Westwalton' (West Walton) ex causa provisionis facte Willelmo Joksale per Gregorium vi idus Januarii anno iii[205] fructus, folio et cetera.

---

[198] Blank in MS.
[199] 13 March 1369.
[200] 30 March 1371.
[201] iii, MS.

---

[202] At the foot of the page: *Resta pagine xlix li. xiii s. iiii d.* In the margin: *vera*.
[203] 14 October 1372.
[204] *elapsis*, MS.
[205] 8 January 1373.

Fructus sunt sequestrati in primo mandato et monitus ·est dictus Willelmus in ultimo. Dicitur quod valet pro medietate veri valoris x li.

De altera portione ecclesie de Walpol (Walpole) ex causa provisionis facte de eadem Reginaldo de Walpol iii idus Januarii per Gregorium anno v$^{to}$ [206] fructus, folio et cetera. Dicitur quod valet pro medietate veri valoris x li.

Fructus sunt sequestrati in primo et cetera, et monitus est dictus R. in ultimo.

Resta pagine xxvii li. xiii s. iiii d. et i beneficium nondum taxatum.[207]

(fol. 173, xxx)[199] De ecclesia de Hopton' ex causa provisionis facte Willelmo Barton' per Gregorium anno v$^{to}$ fructus pro taxa viginti m. ⟨que⟩ valent xiii li. vi s. viii d., folio et cetera.

Noviter est exploratum et mandetur. Et fructus sunt sequestrati et monitus est dictus Willelmus in ultimo.

De ecclesia de Topcroft ex causa provisionis facte Johanni Lamport per Gregorium pro taxa sexdecim m. ⟨que⟩ valent x li. xiii s. iiii d.,[208] folio et cetera.

Fuit mandatum in secundo, sed nondum certificatum, sed sequestrati sunt fructus et monitus est dictus Johannes in ultimo.

De ecclesia de Soutreye (Southery) ex causa provisionis facte Ricardo de Ligate auctoritate apostolica fructus pro taxa decem et novem m. ⟨que⟩ valent xii li. xiii s. iiii d., folio et cetera.

Habet terminum cum iuramento Omnium Sanctorum et Pasche anni LXXVII ad concordandum [209] vel et cetera. Et fuit monitus in scriptis die xiii Februarii ut infra xv dies solveret, et solvit die ultima Februarii anni LXXVI in quatuor m. liii s. iiii d. Et sic est in istis restis pro x li., de quibus solvit post die v Novembris anni LXXVII quinquaginta s., et sic restant hic viii li.[208]

De vicaria de Middenhalle (Mildenhall) ex causa acceptationis auctoritate apostolica facte per Symonem Domynk, que taxatur ad trigenta m. ⟨que⟩ valent xx li., folio et cetera.

Fuit mandatum in secundo, et dum certificavit episcopus, et solvit die xxiii Maii anni et cetera LXXVII decem li., et sic est in istis restis pro aliis decem li.[208]

Resta pagine xxxxii li.[210]

(fol. 173$^v$)[199] De ecclesia de Letton' ex causa provisionis facte Willelmo rectoris eiusdem fructus pro taxa, ut dicitur, x li.

Sequestrati sunt fructus et monitus est dictus Willelmus.

De ecclesia de Ratlesden' (Rattlesden) ex causa provisionis facte auctoritate apostolica Roberto Aylesham fructus pro taxa triginta m. ⟨que⟩ valent xx li., folio et cetera.

Habet terminos Beati Michaelis anni et cetera LXXVII et sequentis anno revoluto, et solvit post die xxvi Setempbris in xv m. decem li., et sic restant x li.[208]

De ecclesia de Elvedone (Elveden) ex causa provisionis facte auctoritate apostolica Edmundo [211] de Warham fructus pro taxa viginti m. ⟨que⟩ valent xiii li. vi s. viii d., folio et cetera.

Fuit mandatum in secundo, sed nondum certificatum, sed sequestrati sunt fructus et monitus est dictus Edmundus in ultimo.

De vicaria de Trunton' (Terrington) ex causa acceptationis auctoritate apostolica facte per Walterum Eston' fructus pro taxa quadraginta m. ⟨que⟩ valent xxvi li. xiii s. iiii d. Et vicaria valet centum m.[212]

Est de novo exploratum, et mandetur. Et solvit die penultima Setempbris in viginti m. xiii li. vi s. viii d., et restant alie xiii li. vi s. viii d.[208]

De ecclesia de Boxford' ex causa acceptationis facte per Rogerum [213] (fol. 174, xxxi)[199] Pilbarogh' auctoritate apostolica fructus pro taxa viginti m. ⟨que⟩ valent xiii li. vi s. viii d.

Et fructus sunt sequestrati et monitus est dictus R. in ultimo.

De ecclesia de Castre (Caistor) ex causa provisionis facte per expectationem cuidam Thome de Leverington fructus pro taxa xix m. ⟨que⟩ valent xii li. xiii s. iiii d.,[208] folio et cetera.

Fructus sunt sequestrati et monitus est dictus Thomas in ultimo.

De ecclesia de Bliburgh' (Blythburgh) ex causa provisionis facte per expectationem possessori.

Fructus sunt sequestrati,[214] et monitus est possessor et cetera. Et valet, ut dicitur, pro medietate veri valoris decem li., x li.

Resta pagine xxxvi li.[207]

Summa restarum vacantium beneficiorum civitatis et diocesis Norwicensis ix$^c$ li. ii s. iii d. Item restant beneficia non taxata iii.[207]

(fol. 174$^v$) Diocesis Eliensis

De prioratu de Swavesey ex causa provisionis facte Stephano Bertrandi per Clementem est in restis antiquis pro quatuor li., iiii li., folio ut in libro.

Prohibitum per breve quia de patronatu laycaly, et debet plus infra folio [215] totam unam taxam, scilicet quadraginta octo li. viginti d., xlviii li. xx d. Sed est in manu regia quia Domina Alicia habitat ibi, sed debet

---

[206] 11 January 1375.
[207] In the margin: *vera*.
[208] Sum repeated MS.
[209] *concordendum*, MS.
[210] Followed by *vi s. viii d.* deleted by a line. In the margin: *vera*.

[211] The abbreviation can also be extended *Edwardo*.
[212] Followed by *folio* deleted by a line.
[213] At the foot of the page: *Resta pagine xlvi li. xiii s. iiii d.* In the margin: *vera*.
[214] *secrestati*, MS.
[215] Blank in MS.

totum, et prosequatur cum recesserit illa domina ab ipso prioratu. Fructus sunt sequestrati, et monitus est possessor in ultimo mandato anni LXXVII.

De vicaria de Todlowe (Tadlow) ex causa provisionis facte per cardinalem Cantuariensem Nicholao Buray ultra viginti unum s. duos d. diu est solutos debet de resta antiqua residuum, et quia reperitur taxa ad tresdecim li. sex s. octo d. debet xii li. v s. vi d., folio et cetera.

Sequestrati sunt fructus, et monitus possessor et denuntiatus in secundo et etiam in ultimo.

De archidiaconatu ecclesie Eliensis ex causa provisionis facte Jacobo cardinali Sancti Georgii ad velum aureum x kalendas Decembris per Gregorium anno iii [216] fructus, folio et cetera.

Non reperitur taxa, sed valet communibus annis ii$^c$ li., et sic debet pro medietate veri valoris c li.[217]

De ecclesia de Catenham (Cottenham) ex causa acceptationis auctoritate apostolica facte per Ricardum Strete fructus pro taxa xl. li., ut dicitur.[218]

(fol. 175, xxxii) [219] Sequestrati sunt fructus, et monitus est possessor in secundo et denuntiatus, et nunc est possessor Robertus Garlethorp auctoritate apostolica per resignationem dicti Roberti in curia factam, qui quidem Robertus solvit in duabus vicibus viginti li., et sic est in istis restis pro aliis viginti li., xx li.

De ecclesia de Tid (Tydd) ex causa acceptationis facte auctoritate apostolica per Nicholaum Drayton' fructus pro taxa quadraginta duarum li, ut dicitur, xlii li.,[208] folio.[215]

Habet terminos Beati Michaelis anni LXXVII et sequentis per equales portiones, et est obligatus, iuratus et condempnatus ut in forma, et est familiaris domini regis.

De ecclesia de Dredrayton' (Dry Drayton) ex causa acceptationis auctoritate apostolica facte per Thomam de Nous Marchato fructus pro taxa triginta m. ⟨que⟩ valent viginti li., xx li.

Habet terminos Omnium Sanctorum anni et cetera LXXVI et sequentium [220] per equales portiones. Et est obligatus, iuratus et condempnatus, et primus terminus est elapsus nichil soluto. Et dicitur quod perdidit illam ecclesiam quia non fuit infra annum promotus ad sacros ordines. Fructus sunt sequestrati, et monitus est possessor in ultimo, et videatur.

De ecclesia de Weuelngham (Willingham) ex causa provisionis facte Rogero [221] (fol. 175$^v$) [219] de Weston' auctoritate apostolica fructus pro taxa quadraginta m. ⟨que⟩ valent xxvi li. xiii s. iiii d., ut in folio et cetera,

ultra viginti novem m. cum dimidia per manus Johannis Sperhauk', procuratoris dicti rectoris, solutas. Restant hic ad huc decem m. cum dimidia [222] ⟨que⟩ valent vii li.

Et fructus sunt sequestrati, et monitus est possessor in ultimo.

De ecclesia de Weston' (Weston Colville) ex causa acceptationis auctoritate apostolica facte per Edmundum Alderfordi fructus pro taxa xxv m. ⟨que⟩ valent xvi li. xiii s. iiii d.,[208] folio.[215]

Fructus sunt sequestrati, et monitus est possessor in ultimo mandato anni LXXVII.

Resta pagine xxiii li. xiii s. iiii d.[223]

Summa restarum vacantium beneficiorum civitatis et diocesis Eliensis ii$^c$ lxx li. vi d.[223]

## (fol. 176$^v$) [224] Diocesis Lincolniensis

De prebenda de Walton' Rivaus (Welton Rivall) in ecclesia Lincolniensi ex causa provisionis facte Radulpho Daventre per Innocentium septimo kalendas Maii anno v$^{to}$.[225] Fuit datus in restis aliis primis pro taxa triginta trium li. sex s. octo d. Solvit ex post iii li. vi s. viii d., et sic [226] debentur ad huc xxx li.[227]

Et fructus sunt sequestrati, et monitus est Edmundus Staford', possessor titulo regio, et habet terminum quindene Beati Michaelis anni et cetera LXXVII de solvendo vel quod interim fuerit prosequtus contra Dominum Radulphum taliter quod solverit dictam restam medio tempore.

De ecclesia de Cosington' (Cossington) ex causa provisionis seu confirmationis facte Johanni de Melburn' alias Chaworth' per Innocentium viii° kalendas Julii anno vii,[228] que taxatur ad decem li. Fuit datus in restis antiquis pro resta dicte taxe, videlicet pro viii li.

Solvit post in tribus vicibus quinque li. sex s. octo d. Et sic debet hic restam, scilicet liii s. iiii d. Et fuit denuntiatus in secundo pro liii s. iiii$^{or}$ d.[227]

De prebenda de Nassington' ex causa confirmationis facte Ludovico de Carleton' per Innocentium iii kalendas Februarii anno ix.[229] pro taxa centum li., c li., folio.[215]

Obiit dictus L. et cardinalis Jerolosomitanus [230] est nunc possessor, ut dicitur, et respondeat ipse possessor quia non reperiuntur bona nec executores. Et fructus sunt sequestrati, et moniti sunt Robertus Nassyngton' et Johannes filius eiusdem et Robertus Child de Jarwelle, possessores fructuum, in ipso mandato, quare denuntietur excommunicati pro dictis c li.[231]

---

[216] 22 November 1373.
[217] In the margin: *Cardinalis Sancti Georgii de Ursinis.*
[218] Followed by *folio* deleted by a line. At the foot of the page: *Resta pagine clxiiii li. vii s. ii d.* In the margin: *vera.*
[219] The heading *Eliensis* appears at the top of the page.
[220] *sequentibus*, MS.
[221] At the foot of the page: *Resta pagine lxxxii li.* In the margin: *vera.*

[222] *dimidio*, MS.
[223] In the margin: *vera.*
[224] Folio 176 recto is blank.
[225] 25 April 1357.
[226] *et sic* repeated MS.
[227] Sum repeated MS.
[228] 24 June 1359.
[229] 30 January 1361.
[230] Philip Cabassole, patriarch of Jerusalem, bishop of Sabina.
[231] Sum repeated MS. In the margin: *Cardinalis Jerolosomitanus.* At the foot of the page: *Resta pagine cxxxii li. xiii s. iiii d.* In the margin: *vera.*

(fol. *177*, xxxiiii)[232] Item de eadem vacatione ratione provisionis facte cardinali Carcasonensi[233] pro resta antiqua dicte taxe debentur ad huc liii li. ii s.[227]

De ecclesia de Kinewelle (Little Kimble) ex causa provisionis facte Johanni Roucelli per Innocentium vi idus Martii anno vi[234] fructus pro taxa quatuor li. tresdecim s. quatuor d., iiii[or] li. xiii s. iiii d., folio et cetera.

Fructus sunt sequestrati, et monitus est procurator in primo mandato.

De prebenda Lincolniensi Jacoby Borelay ex causa provisionis facte cardinali episcopo Tusculanensi per Innocentium xv kalendas Setempbris anno vi[235] fructus, folio et cetera.

Cardinalis fuit et obiit nec habuit effectum, ut fuit certificatum, sed videatur melius.[236]

De prebenda de Langestowe (Stowe Longa) ex causa provisionis facte Raynaldo de Timinis per Innocentium xi kalendas Julii anno xi[237] pro resta xix li. xvi s. viii d., folio.[215]

Dominus Raymundus Pelegrini recepit illo anno, ut dicitur, fructus, et non vult solvere, et litigabat dictus Raynaldus in curia cum uno regio et obiit. Compellatur dictus Raymundus Pelegrini, nisi camera et cetera, quia forte non tenetur, licet esset procurator dicti Raynaldi.

Est prohibitum quia possessor est regius, scilicet Willelmus Tyrington', clericus residens cum privato sigillo.

De prebenda in ecclesia collegiata Beate Marie iuxta Castrum Leycestrie (St. Mary the Less in Castle, Leicester) ex causa provisionis facte Henrico Lombergh' per Innocentium v nonas Maii anno primo[238] fructus.

Fructus sunt sequestrati bis, et non certificat de monitione, quare scribatur plus, quia dicitur quod taxatur ad decem li., x li.

Resta pagine lxxxvii li. xii s. et i beneficium nondum taxatum.[223]

(fol. *177*[v])[239] De ecclesia seu prebenda de Edburgbury (Adderbury) ex causa provisionis facte Domino Hugoni cardinali Sancti Martialis per Urbanum v kalendas Decembris anno ii[240] fructus pro taxa quadraginta quinque m. que valent xxx li.[241]

Monitus est procurator suus, et ista ecclesia non reperitur taxata nec alias, sed ecclesia de Edlesburi taxatur quadraginta quinque m. ⟨que⟩ valent xxx li.[242]

De ecclesia de Sywelebi (Shoby) ex causa provisionis facte Willelmo Wadington' de Hanneworth' iii kalendas Augusti per Urbanum anno secundo[243] fructus.[244]

Certificat episcopus quod non est talis ecclesia in diocesi, quare mandetur pro beneficio dicti Willelmi et queratur ubi est ecclesia, quia in ista diocesi non reperitur taxa. Videatur bene.

De vicaria de Lingdon' (Kirtlington) ex causa provisionis facte Johanni Messing' per Urbanum viii idus Augusti fructus pro taxa iiii li. vi s. viii d., folio et cetera.

Certificat episcopus quod nil valet nec habet possessorem, sed mandetur plus.

De prebenda de Couringham (Corringham) ecclesie Lincolniensis, que fuit Domini Raymundi Pelegrini quondam collectoris apostolici, ex causa provisionis facte[245] episcopo Albanensi tunc cardinali Petragoricensi nonas Setempbris per Urbanum anno iii[246] fructus debentur pro taxa cxxvi li. xiii s. iiii d.

Nichil factum est quia obiit dictus cardinalis, nec constat capitulo de dicta provisione, ut certificat episcopus. Et vocatur Corringham, et taxatur cxxvi li. xiii s. iiii d.[247]

Resta pagine clxi li. et i beneficium nondum taxatum.[248]

(fol. *178*, xxxv)[239] De ecclesia de Risburgh' (Princes Risborough) ex causa provisionis facte Willelmo Nugin auctoritate apostolica fructus.

Nondum est mandatum quia de novo exploratum. Dicitur quod taxata ad decem li., x li.

De parochiali ecclesia de Slapton' provisa Ricero de Croxton' per Urbanum anno ii kalendas Octobris[249] fructus pro taxa duodecim li., xii li.

Nondum habuit effectum, sed videatur sy habebit quia debuit eam habere cum Matheus de Assheton' prebendam Eboracensem fuerit pacifice assecutus, et videatur bene ad huc cum erit asecutus.

De prebenda de Coringham ecclesie Lincolniensis, que fuit cardinalis Petragoricensis,[250] ex causa provisionis facte cardinali Ostiensi[251] per Urbanum xi kalendas Novembris anno primo[252] fructus debentur pro taxa cxxvi li. xiii s. iiii d.

Fuit supersessum per mandatum camere, sed dicitur quod non habuit effectum, et videatur in camera si solvit an non.[253]

---

[232] The heading *Diocesis Lincolniensis* is repeated at the top of the page.
[233] Stephen Aubert, deacon of S. Maria in Aquiro.
[234] 10 March 1358.
[235] 18 August 1358.
[236] In the margin: *Cardinalis Tusculanensis.*
[237] 21 June 1362.
[238] 3 May 1353.
[239] The heading *Lincolniensis* appears at the top of the page.
[240] 27 November 1363.
[241] In the margin: *Cardinalis Sancti Martialis.*
[242] In the margin: *queratur hic quid hoc est.*

[243] 30 July 1364.
[244] Followed by *folio* deleted by a line.
[245] Followed by *per* undeleted MS.
[246] 5 September 1365.
[247] In the margin: *Cardinalis Petragoricensis. Infra est alia provisio.*
[248] In the margin: *vera.*
[249] 1 October 1364.
[250] Elias Talleyrand, bishop of Albano.
[251] William Sudre.
[252] 22 October 1363.
[253] In the margin: *Cardinalis Ostiensis, videlicet cardinalis de ordine predicatorum qui fuit episcopus Massiliensis.*

De perpetua capella sive rectoria leprosorie Sancti Juliani iuxta Sanctum Albanum ex causa provisionis facte Hugoni de Prington' iiii idus Decembris per Urbanum anno quinto [254] fructus.

Fructus sunt sequestrati, et monitus est possessor et denuntiatus in secundo pro taxa c s.

De prebenda Lincolniensi vocata Sutton' (Sutton-le-Marsh) ex causa provisionis facte Anglico cardinali Avinionensi per Urbanum ii idus Julii anno quinto [255] fructus pro taxa ducentarum sexaginta m. ⟨que⟩ valent clxxiii li. vi s. viii d.[256]

(fol. 178ᵛ) [257] Et datur ad firmam cum capellis de Bokingham et aliis quas habet cxciii li. vi s. viii d. Et debet plus dictus cardinalis infra in diocesi Eboracensi, et ibi videatur.

De prebenda Lincolniensi ex causa provisionis facte Nicholao titulo Sancte Marie in Via Lata per Urbanum iii idus Julii anno v [258] fructus, folio et cetera.[259]

Certificat episcopus quod non apparet de effectu dicte gratie ad huc, sed videatur melius, videatur.[260]

De prebenda Lincolniensi ex causa provisionis facte Willelmo titulo Sanctorum Johannis et Pauli per Urbanum anno quinto fructus.

Taxa nescitur quia prebenda non nominatur, sed videatur.[261]

De prebenda de Multon' (Milton Ecclesia) in ecclesia Lincolniensi ex causa provisionis facte Bertrando cardinali Neapolitanensi [262] ii idus Martii per Urbanum anno vii [263] ultra tresdecim li. novem s. quinque d. diu est solutos per Rogerum Barnebone' est datus in antiquis restis pro residuo, videlicet pro triginta novem li. decem et septem s. tribus d. ⟨que⟩ valent xxxix li. xvii s. iii d.[264]

Dominus cardinalis Cantuariensis debet primos fructus omnium beneficiorum que fuerunt Gervasii Wikford ex causa provisionis sibi facte per Urbanum x kalendas Setempbris anno vii,[265] folio.[266]

(fol. 179, xxxvi) [257] Et dicitur quod nullum habuit ex ista gratia, et sic certificavit expost episcopus in ultimo mandato, sed videatur bene. Tamen dominus Cantuariensis mandavit quod concordavit cum camera de omnibus in vita sua, et videatur bene in camera que beneficia habebat. Videatur.

De prebenda de Brampton' et decanatu Lincolniensi que fuerunt [267] Johannis Utreley ex causa provisionis facte domino cardinali Cantuariensi xvii kalendas Octobris per Urbanum anno vii [268] fructus.

Dicta prebenda taxatur ad quinquaginta tres m. et decanatus cum annexa datur ad firmam pro quingentis m., et sic debet pro medietate veri valoris dicti decanatus et pro taxa dicte prebende trescentas tres m. ⟨que⟩ valent iiᶜ ii li. De quibus solvit Dominus Willelmus Palmer, procurator suus, pro istis et aliis suis beneficiis in partem fructuum centum triginta tres li. sex s. octo d., cxxxiii li. vi s. viii d. ante mandatum camere, et sic restant hic sexaginta octo li. tresdecim s. quatuor d., lxviii li. xiii s. iiii d.[269]

De ecclesia de Werketon' (Warkton) collata Willelmo Brian per Dominum Gregorium anno vi [270] fructus pro taxa decem et septem m. cum dimidia ⟨que⟩ valent xi li. vi s. viii d.

Nondum est mandatum quia de novo exploratum.

Resta pagine lxxx li. et i beneficium nondum taxatum.[271]

(fol. 179ᵛ) [257] De archidiaconatu Leycestrie in ecclesia Lincolniensi ex causa provisionis facte cardinali Jerolosomitano [272] per Urbanum anno vii [273] fructus.

Obiit, et taxa non reperitur, sed valet communibus annis cl li., et dicitur quod non habuit effectum, sed videatur melius quia debet lxxv li.[274]

De prebenda de Corringham in ecclesia Lincolniensi et portione Beate Marie de Stowe (Stow in Lindsey) sibi annexa ex causa provisionis facte Alexandro de Newill' per Urbanum anno viii, que taxatur centum octuaginta decem m. ⟨que⟩ valent viˣˣ vi li. xiii s. iiii d.

Est in restis antiquis pro sexaginta novem li. sex s. octo d., lxix li. vi s. viii d.[275] Et debet ibidem pro archidiaconatu Dunolmensis et cetera, et Willelmus Gunpthorp firmarius est monitus, et dictus Alexander est archiepiscopus nunc Eboracensis et non vult solvere, licet pluries requisitus. Et dictus archidiaconatus extimatur, ut dicitur, pro medietate veri valoris ad centum li., sed videatur bene, c li.

De prioratu seu monasterio Sancte Frideswide ordinis Sancti Augustini ex causa provisionis facte Johanni Dodeford' canonico xii kalendas Decembris per Urbanum anno viii [276] fructus.

---

[254] 10 December 1366.

[255] 14 July 1367.

[256] In the margin: *Cardinalis Albanensis Avinionensis.* At the foot of the page: *Resta pagine iiiᶜ xxvii li.* In the margin: *vera.*

[257] The heading *Lincolniensis* is repeated at the top of the page.

[258] 13 July 1367.

[259] Followed by *fructus, folio et cetera* deleted by a line.

[260] In the margin: *Cardinalis Sancte Marie in Via Lata.*

[261] In the margin: *Cardinalis Guillelmus.*

[262] Bernard de Bosqueto, priest of Ss. XII Apostoli.

[263] 14 March 1369.

[264] Followed by *folio* deleted by a line. In the margin: *Cardinalis Neapolitanensis.*

[265] 23 August 1369.

[266] In the margin: *Cardinalis Cantuariensis.* At the foot of the page: *Resta pagine xxxix li. xvii s. iii d. et ii beneficia nondum taxata.* In the margin: *vera.*

[267] *fuit*, MS.

[268] 15 September 1369.

[269] In the margin: *Cardinalis Cantuariensis.*

[270] 5 January 1376 to 4 January 1377.

[271] In the margin: *vera.*

[272] Philip Cabassole, patriarch of Jerusalem, bishop of Sabina.

[273] 6 November 1368 to 5 November 1369.

[274] In the margin: *Cardinalis Jerolosomitanus.*

[275] Sum repeated MS.

[276] 20 November 1369.

Non taxatur, sed valet cum annexis communibus annis ultra sexcentos li. Et sic debet pro medietate veri valoris trecentos li., iii$^c$ li.

Prohibitum per breve quia, omisso titulo apostolico, habuit titulo regio, et tamen litigavit diu in [277] curia et plures sententias habuit et cetera, et revera solvere debet, et rendetur quia verum titulum habuit apostolicum, et cetera.

Resta pagine v$^c$ xliiii li. vi s. viii d.[271]

(fol. 180, xxxvii)[257] De prebenda de Stotford' (Stotfold) in ecclesia Lincolniensi ex causa provisionis facte Petro Burton' iii kalendas Aprilis per Urbanum anno iiii [278] fructus pro taxa xii li.[275]

Certificat episcopus quod non habuit effectum, sed videatur melius, et sic est in mandato ultimo.

De ecclesia de Bluntesham (Bluntisham) ex causa provisionis facte Nicholao Ruffel x kalendas Julii per Urbanum anno viii [279] pro taxa viginti m. ⟨que⟩ valent xiii li. vi s. viii d.[275]

De ecclesia de Kalesby (Calceby) ex causa subrogationis facte Thome Page vii kalendas Aprilis per Gregorium anno primo [280] fructus pro taxa novem m. novem s. quatuor d. ⟨que⟩ valent vi li. ix s. iiii d.[281]

Certificat episcopus quod non habuit effectum, sed est mandatum plus, et videatur plus.

De ecclesia de Hougton' (Houghton) cum capella de Wicton' (Wyton) acceptata auctoritate apostolica per Philippum Apethorp fructus pro taxa quinquaginta m. que valent xxxiii li. vi s. viii d.[275]

Nondum est mandatum quia de nova exploratur.

De prebenda Aylesburi (Aylesbury) in ecclesia Lincolniensi ex causa provisionis facte domino cardinali de Vernhio [282] per Gregorium anno primo viii kalendas Julii [283] pro taxa quadraginta li.[275]

Et debet plus supra de archidiaconatu et prebenda ecclesie Exoniensis et ibi vide. Radulphus Piliton', procurator dicti cardinalis, est monitus et Helias et Johannes Shepman firmarii.[284]

Resta pagine cv li. ii s. viii d.[271]

(fol. 180$^v$)[257] De prebenda Sexaginta Solidorum in ecclesia Lincolniensi ex causa provisionis facte Willelmo de Combe per expectationem per Gregorium anno primo [285] ultra sexaginta s. diu est solutos fuit dimissus in restis antiquis pro residuo.

Videatur sy debeat plus quia non reperitur ad plus taxata, et noluit respondere de residuo, quare videatur melius de vero valore. Videatur residuum.

De archidiaconatu Northamptonie et prebenda de Walton' Rival (Welton Rivall) in ecclesia Lincolniensi fuerunt due provisiones facte per Gregorium anno secundo [286] cardinali Sancti Marcelli [287] et nulla habuit, ut dicitur, effectum. Archidiaconatus non taxatur, sed prebenda, ut dicitur, taxatur ad viginti duas m. que valent quatuor decim li. xiii s. iiii$^{or}$ d. Et dictus archidiaconatus valet iii$^c$ li. et sic debet pro medietate cl li.

Et videatur bene de toto.[288]

De ecclesia Beate Marie de Waynfleit (Wainfleet) ex causa provisionis facte Johanni Banneburi fructus pro taxa viginti m. cum dimidia ⟨que⟩ valent xiii li. xiii s. iiii d.[275]

Non habuit effectum quia per alium, ut dicitur, titulo regio possidetur. Et videatur melius quia monitus est incumbens, scilicet Edmundus de Staford in primo, et cetera.

De prebenda ecclesie Lincolniensis que fuit Johannis de Bentham ex causa provisionis facte Magistro Galfrido Fabri possessori fructus.

Dicitur quod non habuit effectum, nec constat de illa prebenda ut certificat episcopus, sed videatur melius, licet fuerit in tertio et quarto mandato. Videatur bene.

Resta pagine clxiii li. xiii s. iiii d. et duo beneficia nondum taxata.[271]

(fol. 181, xxxviii)[257] De ecclesia de Waynflet (Wainfleet) Omnium Sanctorum ex causa provisionis facte Hugoni Bohenhulln' idus Aprilis anno ii Gregorii [289] fructus pro taxa viginti unus m. ⟨que⟩ valent xiiii li., folio et cetera.

Fuit mandatum sed nondum certificatum.

De archidiaconatu Leycestrie in ecclesia Lincolniensi ex causa provisionis facte Jacobo cardinali Sancti Georgii [290] vi nonas Octobris anno secundo Gregorii [291] fructus.

Cardinalis de Ursinis est, et concordavit cum camera ut scripsit sepe dominus camerarius. Dictus archidiaconatus datur ad firmam ducentarum viginti quinque m., de quibus debet, cum nondum reperiatur taxatus, centum duodecim m. et dimidiam que valent lxxv li.[292]

De prebenda de Nassington' in ecclesia Lincolniensi ex causa provisionis facte Domino R. cardinali Sancte Prisce [293] sexto nonas Octobris per Gregorium anno secundo [291] fructus pro taxa, ut dicitur, centum li., c. li.[294]

De ecclesia de Bidnham (Biddenham) ex causa unionis facte de eadem abbathie et conventui monas-

---

[277] *in* repeated MS.
[278] 30 March 1366.
[279] 22 June 1370.
[280] 26 March 1371.
[281] Followed by *folio* deleted by a line, MS.
[282] Peter de Vergne, deacon of S. Maria in Via Lata.
[283] 24 June 1371.
[284] In the margin: *Cardinalis de Vernhio.*
[285] 1371.

[286] 1372.
[287] Bertrand Cosnaco, bishop of Comminges, priest of S. Marcello.
[288] In the margin: *Cardinalis Sancti Marcelli.*
[289] 13 April 1372.
[290] James Orsini, deacon of S. Giorgio in Velabro.
[291] 2 October 1372.
[292] In the margin: *Cardinalis de Ursinis.*
[293] Bertrand Latgier.
[294] In the margin: *Cardinalis Sancte Prisce.*

terii de Wateberk (Waterbeach) xvii kalendas Novembris per Gregorium anno secundo [295] fructus pro taxa, ut dicitur, quadraginta li., folio et cetera, xl li.

Nondum habuit effectum ut asseruit die x Septempbris anni LXXVI possessor qui ibi est et fuit xxiii annis, sed videatur post mortem suam vel quando dimittet, quia tunc debebuntur fructus.

Resta pagine iiᶜ xxix li.[271]

(fol. 181ᵛ) [257] De prebenda Lincolniensi que fuit Thome de Newby ex causa permutationis facte cum cardinali Cantuariensi [296] fructus pro taxa, ut dicitur, xl li.[297]

Et debet ibidem plus de duabus ecclesiis Eliensis et Dunolmensis diocesium ratione confirmationis de toto facte per Gregorium anno secundo [298] et cetera. Monitus est procurator Stephanus Neumam, receptor fructuum, et ut contumax excommunicatur.

De prebenda de Thame ex causa provisionis facte cardinali Sancti Martialis [299] per Gregorium anno iiii [300] fructus pro taxa centum sexaginta octo m., valent cxii li., folio et cetera. Et datur ad firmam pro ducentis quadraginta m., valent clxiii li. vi s. viii d. et sic debet supradictam taxam cxii li.[301]

Et certificat episcopus quod Johannes Hayward' firmarius de Thame est monitus et cetera, et denuncietur. Et post solvit Dominus Egidius secunda die Martii anni LXXVII pro eo in partem fructuum seu taxe viginti octo li. Et sic restant hic iiiiˣˣ iiiiᵒʳ li.[302]

Scripsit michi dominus thesaurarius die ultima Martii anno et cetera LXXVII quod solvit dictus cardinalis viiiᶜ lxxi fl. currentes ii s. viii d.

De ecclesia seu vicaria de Irrengho (Ivinghoe) ex causa confirmationis facte Willelmo de Pakington' per Gregorium iiii nonas Novembris anno iii [303] fructus pro taxa lv m., valent xxxvi li. xiii s. iiii d., folio et cetera.

Bulla est hic missa per cameram, et fructus sunt sequestrati, et monitus est possessor in primo et cetera.

Resta pagine clx li. xiii s. iiii d.[304]

(fol. 182, xxxix) [305] De prebenda de Castre (Caistor) in ecclesia Lincolniensi ex causa provisionis facte per expectationem Johanni Wiclif' per Gregorium anno v [306] fructus pro taxa sexaginta octo m. que valent xlv li. folio et cetera.

Fructus sunt sequestrati, et monitus est dictus Jo-

hannes in secundo, et quarta die Maii anno et cetera LXXVII solvit pro eo Robertus Wiclef tresdecim li. sex s. octo d. Et sic remansit in ista resta pro xxxii li. Sed post fuit prorogatus ad octavas Sancti Hillarii, quia fuit expoliatus per Philippum Thornburi possessorem. Restat xxxii li.[302]

De prebenda quam habet dominus cardinalis Gibanensis [307] in ecclesia Lincolniensi, que fuit domini cardinalis Penestrini,[308] ex causa provisionis sibi facte per Gregorium idus Julii anno iii [309] fructus.[310]

Debet plus de archidiaconatu Dorcestrie in ecclesia Sarum, sed concordavit cum camera, et videatur si solvit videlicet totum, ut dicitur, iiᶜ li.[302]

De ecclesia de Navemby (Navenby) ex causa provisionis facte Roberto de Longton' per Gregorium anno iii [311] fructus pro taxa triginta septem li., xxxvii li.

Solvit in dicto libro et folio in decem m. vi li. xiii s. iiii d. Et est in ista resta pro residuo videlicet pro xxx li. vi s. viii d. Fructus sunt sequestrati in primo mandato, et post conbusti. Et est prorogatus usque ad Pascha et festum Beati Michaelis anni LXXVI. Et post solvit die iiii Julii anni et cetera LXXVII in septem m. iiii li. xiii [312] s. iiii d. Et sic est nunc in ista resta pro xxv li. xiii s. iiii d.[313]

Resta pagine iiᶜ lvii li. xiii s. iiii d.[304]

(fol. 182ᵛ) [305] De ecclesia de Ingoldesbi (Ingoldsby) ex causa permutationis facte de eadem per possessorem coram cardinalem Cantuariensem [314] fructus pro taxa triginta [315] novem m. et dimidia, valent xxvi li. vi s. viii d. folio et cetera.

Fuit mandatum sed nondum certificatum.

De prebenda de Tyrington' (Corringham) in ecclesia Lincolniensi ex causa provisionis facte Guillelmo cardinali in Celiomonte [316] xii kalendas Maii per Gregorium anno iiii [317] fructus pro taxa viginti m., valent xiii li. vi s. viii d.[318]

Datur ad firmam pro centum li., et sic debet pro residuo taxe quod plus valet quam taxa quinquaginta li., l li.

De prebenda de Welleton' Bekhall' (Welton Beckhall) ex causa provisionis facte per expectationem Laurentio de Nigris [319] fructus pro taxa quindecim m. que valent decem li., x li.

Fructus sunt sequestrati, et Guillelmus Squier est

---

[295] 16 October 1372.
[296] Simon Langham, priest of S. Sisto.
[297] In the margin: *Cardinalis Cantuariensis.*
[298] 1372.
[299] Hugo de St. Martial, deacon of S. Maria in Portico.
[300] 1374.
[301] Followed by *que valent* deleted by a line. In the margin: *Cardinalis Sancti Martialis.*
[302] Sum repeated in the margin.
[303] 2 November 1373.
[304] In the margin. *vera.*
[305] The heading *Lincolniensis* is repeated at the top of the page.
[306] 1375.

[307] Robert of Geneva, priest of Ss. XII Apostoli.
[308] Simon Langham(?), bishop of Palestrina.
[309] 15 July 1373.
[310] In the margin: *Cardinalis Gybanensis.*
[311] 1373.
[312] *xiiii,* MS.
[313] In the margin a sign is followed by this statement: *hoc signum quere infra folio sequenti et hic continuatur* followed by the sign again. The sum is repeated in the margin.
[314] Simon Langham, priest of S. Sisto.
[315] *triginta* repeated MS.
[316] William d'Aigrefeuille, priest of S. Stefano al Monte Celio.
[317] 20 April 1374.
[318] In the margin: *Cardinalis in Celiomonte.*
[319] *de Nigris* repeated in the margin.

monitus in secundo, et Thomas Deystere, alias Sotham et cetera, procurator suus, recepit terminos Omnium Sanctorum proximorum et Pasche sequentis anni LXXVII cum iuramento, et primus terminus est elapsus. Videatur obiter et denuncietur.

De ecclesia de Hemynford' Abbatis (Hemingford Abbots), vacante per mortem Johannis Karbell' in curia defuncti, ex causa provisionis facte Thome de Fenton' fructus pro taxa viginti quinque m., valent xvi li. xiii s. iiii d.[302]

Walterus Fellestede expectans spoliavit dictam Thomam et possidet dictam ecclesiam per tres annos et habuit confirmationem, sed litigat cum dicto Thoma. Et valet bene xl li. Et videatur bene de residuo et quis istorum duororum tenetur.[320]

Resta pagine cii li. x s.[304]

(fol. 183, xl)[305] De ecclesia de Merlowe (Great Marlow) et prebenda Lincolniensi ex causa dispensationis facte Edmundo Strete de retinendo eandem ecclesiam cum prebenda Cicestrensi vocata Waltham per Gregorium xiiii kalendas Novembris anno iii[321] fructus pro taxa ecclesie de Merlowe magna quinquaginta m., valent xxxiii li. vi s. viii d. ut in folio et cetera.[322]

Taxa prebende Lincolniensis non reperitur quia non nominatur, et videatur bene de ecclesia si sit illa. Habet dictas ecclesiam et prebendam Cicestrensem titulo ordinario et habet nichil[323] aliud usque quo sit expeditus per expectationem ad prebendam in ecclesia Lincolniensi, et tunc debet de omnibus causa dispensationis et cetera. Et juravit dictus Edmundus die xii Maii certificare in mense cum acceptaverit prebendam in ecclesia Lincolniensi. Videatur.

De capellania de Babbeworth' (Babworth) ex causa provisionis facte Johanni Dodeford' per Gregorium iiii kalendas Decembris fructus.[324]

Est alia provisio de eadem facta Johanni Lynkeley, et fructus sunt sequestrati et monitus est possessor et denunciatus in secundo. Tamen nulla habuit effectum quia de patronatu laycali, ut dicitur. Videatur bene.

De ecclesia de Haliwelle (Holywell) ex causa provisionis facte Johanni Monig' per Gregorium pro taxa viginti m., valent xiii li. vi s. viii d.

Johannes Sparhanby est procurator dicti rectoris, et habet terminos cum iuramento Omnium Sanctorum et Purificationis anni LXXVI. Et solvit pro primo termino in decem m. vi li. xiii s. iiii d., et sic est in istis restis pro vi li. xiii s. quatuor d.[302]

Resta pagine xxxvii li. et i beneficium nondum taxatum.[304]

(fol. 183v)[305] De ecclesia de Boston' ex causa provisionis facte Domino Johanni Strensall' per expectationem per Gregorium xi kalendas Decembris anno iii[325] fructus pro taxa septuaginta septem m., valent li li. vi s. viii d. folio et cetera.

Dabatur ad firmam tempore antiquo pro centum li., et videatur residuum si plus valet quam dicta taxa. Et debet plus pro una prebenda in diocesi Eboracensi[326] optenta consimili modo per expectationem, et ibidem vide quia habet terminos de ambobus prime diei Maii anni LXXVII et sequentis anno revoluto, quia usque nunc litigavit cum uno in curia regia vocato Candal de familia domini de Newill', ideo tantum fuit prorogatus. Solvit in partem fructuum die ultima Aprilis anni et cetera LXXVII pro ecclesia viginti quinque li. tresdecim s. quatuor d., et est in istis restis pro residuo, videlicet pro viginti sex li., xxvi li vel circa.

De ecclesia de Mixeburi (Mixbury) que fuit Johannis Strensall' ex causa provisionis facte Johanni Haspul per Gregorium fructus pro taxa sexdecim m., valent x li. xiii s. iiiior d.[327]

Est in isto mandato et in ultimo.

De ecclesia de Spalton' (Slapton?)[328] ex causa provisionis facte David Mort, cum vacabit per executionem dignitatis[329] in ecclesia Lincolniensi Mathei Hassherton', iii kalendas Januarii per Gregorium anno iii[330] fructus.[331]

Nondum habuit effectum, ut est probatum. Set forte habebit, et videatur quia est iuratus possessor dictus Matheus certificare[332] infra quindecim dies postquam habebit effectum. Videatur.

Resta pagine xxxvi li. xiii s. iiii d. et unum beneficium nondum taxatum.[333]

(fol. 185, xlii)[334] De vicaria de Missendene parva alias Wissenden' (Little Missenden) ex causa provisionis facte Willelmo Belami per cardinalem Cantuariensem Londonie iii kalendas Junii fructus pro taxa quinquaginta m., valent viginti[334a] tres li. vi s. viii d., xxxiii li. vi s. viii d.

Fuit mandatum sed nondum certificatum.

De archidiaconatu Northamptonie in ecclesia Lincolniensi, non taxato, ex causa provisionis facte Henrico

---

[320] In the margin a hand with a finger pointing to a capital *E*.
[321] 19 October 1373.
[322] In the margin the sum is given as *xxx li. vi s. viii d.* In the left margin the sign given at folio 182 is repeated and followed by this statement: *hoc signum quere folio sequenti supra qui hic continuatur etiam cum pagina sequenti.*
[323] Followed by *de quo* deleted by a line.
[324] Followed by *folio* deleted by a line. In the margin: *taxa non reperitur.*

[325] 26 November 1373.
[326] In the margin: *Strinsala* (Strensall).
[327] Followed by *folio* deleted by a line. Sum repeated in the margin.
[328] Matthew de Assheton held Slapton in 1366: *Cal. Pap. Regs. Petitions*, i, 523.
[329] *dixnitatis*, MS.
[330] 30 December 1373.
[331] Followed by *folio* deleted by a line.
[332] *sertificare*, MS.
[333] In the margin: *vera*.
[334] The heading *Lincolniensis* appears at the top of the page. Folio 184 (xli) is blank except the heading *Lincolniensis* and the letter *E* at the top of each page.
[334a] MS. reads '*viginti*.'

Piel per Gregorium iiii idus Octobris anno iiii [335] fructus, folio et cetera ut in libro.

Valet de recepta, ut dicitur, quia non taxatur, iii[c] li., et sic debet pro medietate veri valoris cl li. Habet terminos Pasche anni LXXVI et sequentis cum iuramento et obligatione propria, et est condempnatus et monitus ut in forma, et primus terminus est elapsus, quia die prima Augusti anni et cetera LXXV fuit obligatus. Et debet etiam in eisdem terminis pro prebenda sua de Cropna (Cropredy?) in ecclesia Lincolniensi fructus pro taxa centum m., valent lxvi li. xiii s. iiii d., folio et cetera. Sed dicit quod litigat de prebenda, et verum est, sed si ambo sint apostolici compellantur ad solvendum. Solvit de dicta prebenda dictus Dominus H. Piel die x Novembris anni LXXVII in quadraginta m. xxvi li. xiii s. iiii d. Restant hic clxxxx li.[336]

De vicaria de Bergham (Barholm) ex causa provisionis facte per cardinalem Cantuariensem Thome Andreu Londonie vi idus Octobris fructus pro taxa sexdecim m., valent x li. xiii s. iiii d., folio et cetera.

Fuit mandatum in secundum sed nondum certificatum. Resta pagine ii[c] xxxiiii li.[333]

(fol. 185[v]) [337] De vicaria de Overton' (Everton) ex causa provisionis facte Johanni Smyth' de Overton' per cardinalem Cantuariensem vi kalendas Setempbris fructus pro taxa decem et septem m. que valent xi li. vi s. viii d., folio et cetera.

Fuit mandatum in secundo sed nondum certificatum, quia de novo repertum.

De vicaria ecclesie de Bikkelisworth' (Biggleswade) ex causa provisionis facte per cardinalem Cantuariensem Radulpho Stevene v kalendas Maii fructus pro taxa triginta duarum m., valent xxi li. vi s. viii d., folio.

Fuit mandatum in secundo, sed nondum certificatum.

De prebenda Lincolniensi et de ecclesia de Somersham Lincolniensis diocesis ex causa confirmationis facte Symoni cardinali Cantuariensi cum permutavit ecclesiam suam de Wermouth' (Bishop Wearmouth) diocesis Dunolmensis cum dictis prebenda et ecclesia cum Thoma de Newby per Gregorium anno secundo [338] fructus.[339]

Cardinalis obiit et etiam Thomas et unus alius cardinalis possidet nunc ecclesiam Thome, qui eam abstulit post mortem suam archiepiscopo Dublinensi, qui eam habuit titulo ordinario per mortem dicti Thome. Et videatur bene quia ecclesia dicti Thome [340] pro dictis fructibus obligata, et etiam prebenda Lincolniensis et ecclesia alia que est in diocesi Lincolniensi, et videantur

taxe de toto. Et debentur pro taxa dicte ecclesie de Somersham quinquaginta m., valent xxxiii li. vi s. viii d.[341]

De ecclesia de Stondon' (Upper Stondon) ex causa provisionis facte Johanni de Housbi per cardinalem Cantuariensem fructus.

Fuit mandatum in secundo, sed nondum certificatum. Videatur de taxa quia nondum reperitur.

Resta pagine lxvi li. sterlingorum et i beneficium nondum taxatum.[333]

(fol. 186, xliii) [337] De prebenda de Southcarle (South Scarle) in ecclesia Lincolniensi ex causa provisionis facte per expectationem Magistro Thome de Bakton' fructus pro taxa quadraginta li., folio et cetera.[341]

Fructus sunt sequestrati et monitus est dictus Thomas in secundo.

De prebenda de Lafford' ex causa provisionis facte per expectationem Thome de la Ware fructus pro taxa quadraginta octo m., valent xxxii li., folio et cetera.

Est obligatus per procuratorem ut in forma et iuratus et condempnatus, et habet terminos quindene Pasche anni LXXVII et Beati Michaelis et sequentis in eisdem terminis ad requestam domine principisse. Solvit xxviii Julii anni et cetera LXVII in xii m. octo li., viii li. De dicta resta solvit etiam die iiii Novembris anni LXXVII alias octo li. Et restant hic sexdecim li., xvi li.[342]

De archidiaconatu Exoniensi (Oxford) cum duabus ecclesiis annexis ex causa provisionis Thome de Southam facte debentur de procurationibus et de iurisdictione folio et cetera.

Videatur bene quia de residuo solvit et sunt sequestrati in secundo mandato. Et dictus Thomas fuit auditor cardinalis Cantuariensis. Videatur bene.

De ecclesia de Lekenore (Lewknor) ex causa provisionis facte Johanni Josekin per expectationem fructus pro taxa viginti li., xx li., folio.

Dictus Johannes obiit et Dominus Henricus Bakier, vicarius dicte ecclesie et ut executor testamenti [343] (fol. 186[v]) [337] dicti Johannis iam diu est defuncti, solvit in duobus vicibus in decem m. vi li. xiii s. iiii d. Et habet terminos de residuo Beati Johannis Baptiste et Michaelis anni LXXVII per equales portiones, et est iuratus, obligatus et condempnatus et cetera. Solvit post die xvi Junii anno predicto in quinque m. iii li. vi s. viii d., et post solvit die xv Octobris anno et cetera LXXVII in quinque m. lxvi s. viii d., et sic restant hic vi li. xiii s. iiii d.

De prebenda Sancti Martini in ecclesia Lincolniensi ex causa provisionis facte Ricardo de Streton' fructus

---

[335] 12 October 1374.

[336] Sum repeated in margin. In the left margin: *Dominus H. Piel.*

[337] The heading *Lincolniensis* is repeated at the top of the page.

[338] 1372.

[339] In the margin: *Cardinalis Cantuariensis.*

[340] Followed by *est pro dictis fructibus* deleted by a line.

[341] Sum repeated in the margin.

[342] Sum repeated MS.

[343] At the bottom of the page: *Resta pagine lvi li. et* (followed by *ii b* deleted by a line) *i beneficium nondum taxatum.* In the margin: *vera.*

pro taxa decem m., valent vi li. xiii s. iiii d., folio et cetera.

Sequestrati sunt fructus et monitus est dictus Ricardus et denuntiatus in secundo.

De prebenda Sancte Marie de Stowe (Stow in Lindsey) in ecclesia Lincolniensi ex causa provisionis facte Thome Chandos fructus pro taxa viginti li., folio et cetera.

Litigat cum Magistro Thoma de Bakton' qui est apostolicus, et tamen este Thomas Chandos possidet, et fructus sunt sequestrati per auditorem curie ad requestam dicti Bakton'. Et dictus Thomas Chandos habet terminos Beati Johannis Baptiste et Michaelis anni et cetera LXXVII per equales portiones, et est obligatus, iuratus et condempnatus, et quia non obstante lite solvit xiiii die Junii anno predicto quinque li., restat debens in dicto termino xv li. Solvit post die xxiii Octobris quinque li., et sic restant decem li., x li.

De ecclesia de Boresworth' (Husbands Bosworth) ex causa provisionis facte per expectationem Ricardo [344] (fol. 187, xliiii) [337] Eveneth' fructus pro taxa viginti octo m. cum dimidia, valent decem et novem li.

Habet terminos Omnium Sanctorum anni LXXVII et Pasche tunc sequentis per equales portiones, et est obligatus et condempnatus et cetera. Dictus Ricardus non possidet quia Rogerus Pannton' ipsum expoliavit, et optinuit duas sententias in curia, quare est mandatum contra dictum Rogerum et cetera xix li.

De ecclesia de Kirkeby Baylond' (Kirkby St. Peter or Kirkby Laythorpe) ex causa provisionis facte per expectationem Willelmo Colvile fructus, folio et cetera.

Fuit mandatum in secundo, sed nondum certificatum pro taxa, ut dicitur, x li. Videatur bene, x li.

De prebenda Lincolniensi ex causa dispensationis facte Willelmo de Bukbrugg' super retentionem ipsius cum certis aliis beneficiis per Urbanum idus Augusti anno v [345] fructus debentur, folio et cetera.

Non est ibi ut certificat episcopus Lincolniensis in secundo mandato. Videatur si est in diocesi Sarisbiriensi, ubi, ut dicitur, habet prebendam auctoritate apostolica. Videatur.

De prioratu de Burwell' ex causa confirmationis seu provisionis de novo facte Petro de Monte Ardito monacho per Gregorium XI fructus, folio et cetera.

Non reperitur taxatus, sed datur ad firmam pro viginti duabus m., et sic debet pro medietate [346] veri valoris undecim m. que valent septem li. sex s. octo d. Et videatur [347] melius. vii li. vi s. viii d.

Resta pagine xxxvi li. vi s. viii d. et unum beneficium nondum taxatum. [333]

(fol. 187v) [337] De ecclesia de Waldegrave (Walgrave), vacante in curia Romana, ex causa provisionis facte per

dominum Gregorium XI Magistro Radulpho Piloton' fructus, folio cxlvi, pro taxa viginti m., valent xiii li. vi s. viii d.

De prebenda de Castre (Caistor) ex causa provisionis auctoritate apostolica facte Philippo Thorneburi fructus pro taxa sexaginta octo m., valent quadraginta quinque li. sex s. octo d., xlv li. vi s. viii d.

De subdecanatu ecclesie Lincolniensis ex causa provisionis per permutationem nuper facte Magistro Johanni Carlton' in curia Romana fructus pro taxa sexaginta m., valent xl li., folio et cetera.

Habet terminos Beati Michaelis anni LXXVIII et sequentis, et est obligatus et cetera.

De ecclesia de Stikeneye (Stickney) ex causa dicte permutationis in curia facte Domino Thome de Luswik fructus, folio et cetera, pro taxa xviii li. xiii s. iiii d. [341]

Habet terminos Beati Michaelis anni LXXVIII et sequentis, et est obligatus et cetera.

De decanatu Lincolniensi noviter acceptato videatur taxa, quia dicitur quod valet pro medietate veri valoris cum annexis vic li. et plus sterlingorum, [348] sed videatur bene. ve li.

Resta pagine vic xvii li. vi s. viii d. [333]

(fol. 188, xlv) Summa [349] universalis omnium restarum vacantium beneficiorum civitatis et diocesis Lincolniensis iiim iiiic lxxxxvii li. xv s. iii d.; xii beneficia non taxata. [333]

(fol. 188v) Diocesis Coventrensis et Lichfeldensis

Pro resta prebende de Langedon' (Longdon) in ecclesia Lichfeldensi, taxa viginti li., ex causa provisionis facte Willelmo de Salowe per Clementem iii nonas Septembris anno vii [350] debentur de resta antiqua tresdecim li. sex s. octo d., xiii li. vi s. viii d.

Infra est alia provisio folio et cetera, et pro illa provisione ibi incepit solvere, et fructus sunt sequestrati, et Willemus Underhul nunc possessor est monitus et denuntiatus in secundo et etiam in ultimo mandato anni LXXVII, et infra vide.

De prioratu de Kerkeby (Monks Kirby) ex causa provisionis facte Guillelmo de Gralerio per Innocentium xiii kalendas Martii anno vii [351] fuit datus in restis domini prioris Lewensis pro quadraginta una li. decem s. octo d., de quibus solvit supra in recepta in duabus vicibus sexdecim li. x s., folio et cetera ut in libro. Et restat ad huc hic debens de dicta resta viginti li. octo d., xx li. viii d. [341] Et pro predictis et procurationibus trium annorum est dictus prior excommunicatus et denuntiatus, et fructus sequestrati et cetera, ut certificat episcopus in ultimo.

De prebenda in ecclesia collegiata de Penkeng' (Penkridge) ex causa provisionis facte diu est Thome de Eltonhed' auctoritate apostolica fructus folio et cetera.

---

[344] At the foot of the page: *Resta pagine xxiii li. vi s. viii d.* In the margin: *vera.*
[345] 13 August 1367.
[346] *medieta*, MS.
[347] Followed by *bene* deleted by a line.

[348] *sterlis*, MS.
[349] Followed by *summarum* deleted by a line.
[350] 3 September 1348.
[351] 17 February 1359.

Dicit episcopus quod est prohibitus per breve et non audet exequi, sed debet, et est in mandato quinto, et mandetur ad huc plus, quia male certificat episcopus quia non dicit nec misit mandatum ipsum camere quare est prohibitus. Videatur bene hoc.

Resta pagine xxxiii li. vii s. iiii d. et unum beneficium nondum taxatum.[333]

(fol. 189, xlvi)[352] De ecclesia de Wigan Lichfeldensis diocesis ex causa dispensationis facte Waltero de Campeden', thesaurario ducis Lancastrie, quod possit eam retinere cum certis aliis beneficiis vi kalendas Augusti per Urbanum anno v [353] fructus pro taxa quinquaginta m., valent xxxiii li. vi s. viii d., folio.

Obiit et habuerat prohibitorium a rege quia de patronatu laicaly, et videatur melius quia debetur eo quod petiit dispensationem, et beneficium est obligatum, et fuerat cancellarius ducis Lancastrie, et nunquam voluit solvere. Fructus tamen sunt sequestrati et monitus est possessor in loco, scilicet Jacobus de Langedon', ut certificat episcopus in ultimo.

De prebenda Lichfeldensi ex causa dispensationis facte Willelmo de Bukbrug', qui nunc est thesaurarius ducis Lancastrie, super retentionem ipsius cum certis aliis beneficiis per Urbanum vi idus Augusti anno v [354] fructus, folio et cetera.

Et licet prohibitum de certis aliis beneficiis non tamen de ista prebenda, sed non vult solvere, et certificat episcopus quod nunquam ibi habuit prebendam,[355] sed dicitur quod habet in Lincolniensi vel Sarisbiriensi. In quibus fuit mandatum in secundo et certificatum quod non fuit ibi de utraque, sed sciatur ad huc plus cum ipso Willelmo. Videatur.

De decanatu curato et electivo ecclesie Lichfeldensis ex causa provisionis facte Anthonio de Ros per Urbanum iii nonas Februarii anno vii [356] fructus, folio et cetera.

Cardinalis Sancte Sabine [357] tenet a diu et alter obiit. Et valet centum m., et sic debentur pro medietate veri valoris quinquaginta m., valent xxxiii li. vi s. octo d.[358]

Resta pagine lxvi li. xiii s. iiii d. et i beneficium nondum taxatum.[359]

(fol. 189[v])[352] De prebenda Lichfeldensi ex causa provisionis facte Francisco cardinali Sancte Sabine per Urbanum xiii kalendas Decembris anno viii [360] fructus. Taxatur, ut dicitur, viginti li., folio, xx li.[361]

Agat camera contra executores, quia hic ad huc nichil de sua reperitur, quia obiit diu est.

De prebenda de Langedon' (Longdon) in ecclesia Lichfeldensi ex causa provisionis facte Johanni Underhull' iii kalendas Februarii per Gregorium anno primo [362] fructus pro taxa viginti li.

De qua solvit tresdecim li. sex s. octo d. Et sic est in istis restis pro vi li. xiii s. iiii d.,[363] folio. Fructus sunt sequestrati, et monitus est dictus Johannes et denuntiatus in secundo et in ultimo, et supra est alia provisio facta alteri, folio et cetera.

De prebenda ecclesie Omnium Sanctorum de Derbie Lichfeldensis diocesis ex causa provisionis facte Willelmo de Southam vi kalendas Aprilis per Gregorium anno primo [364] fructus, folio et cetera.

Videatur melius si habuit effectum quia dicitur quod non habuit effectum. Sed forte est in ecclesia Sancti Johannis Cestrie ubi fuit expectans, et est nunc expeditus, ut dicitur, in dicta ecclesia Sancti Johannis Cestrie ad unam prebendam cuius fructus sunt sequestrati et ipse est monitus in secundo. Et videatur melius de alia et de ista.[365] Et sic est denuntiatus in ultimo. Dicitur quod taxatur ad decem li. Videatur bene. x li.

Resta pagine xxxvi li. xiii s. iiii d.[359]

(fol. 190, xlvii)[352] De ecclesia seu vicaria de Wenewik (Winwick) ex causa provisionis facte Willelmo Slene per Dominum Gregorium papam undecimum in forma speciali acceptata anno domini et cetera LXXV fructus pro taxa quadraginta m., valent xxvi li. xiii s. iiii d. Et dicta ecclesia seu vicaria valet iii[e] m. que valent ii[c] li., et sic debentur pro medietate veri valoris centum li, c li.

Dictus Willelmus obiit in mense Februarii anni LXXV et non habuit, ut dicitur, ius in dicta vicaria quia seculari potentia spoliavit Johannem Harewodo, nunc post ipsius Willelmi obitum dictam vicariam ocupantem, ut certificat episcopus. Et fructus sunt sequestrati, et monitus est dictus Johannes et denuntiatus in secundo.

Sed Adam Davenport, nepos Ade Fraunceys, fuit subrogatus in locum dicti Willelmi, qui adhibuit confirmationem in curia, et vocetur ipse et Magister Johannes Katerington' secrete antequam alter relaxetur, et sic post fuit vocatus, et instruxit cameram, et die xii Novembris anni LXXVII fuit dictus Johannes relaxatus quousque appareat de effectu provisionis facte defuncto vel subrogationis et cetera. Videatur bene de toto.

De prebenda de Colewich' (Colwich) ex causa provisionis facte per expectationem Johanni Chenie nunc possessori, cum quo litigat in curia Romana Richerius Tonneworth, qui dictam prebendam acceptavit,[366] fructus, folio et cetera.

Fructus sunt sequestrati, et monitus et denuntiatus

---

[352] The heading *Coventrensis et Lichfeldensis* appears at the top of the page.
[353] 27 July 1367.
[354] 8 August 1367.
[355] *prebenda*, MS.
[356] 3 February 1369.
[357] Franciscus Thebaldeschis, priest of S. Sabina.
[358] Sum repeated in the margin. In the left margin: *Cardinalis Sancte Sabine alias Sancti Petri.*
[359] In the margin: *vera.*
[360] 19 November 1369.
[361] In the margin: *Cardinalis Sancte Sabine.*

---

[362] 30 January 1371.
[363] Sum repeated in the margin.
[364] 27 March 1371.
[365] Followed by *folio* deleted by a line.
[366] Followed by *etiam* deleted by a line.

est possessor in secundo et ultimo. Et taxatur quadraginta m. que valent xx$^{ti}$ sex li, tresdecim s. quatuor d., xxvi li. xiii s. iiii d.[363]

Resta pagine cxxvi li. xiii s. iiii d.[359]

(fol. 190$^v$)[352] De prebenda Ofley (High Offley) in ecclesia Lichfeldensi ex causa provisionis facte auctoritate apostolica predecessori Johannis Turk nunc possessoris causa permutationis cum ipso predecessore facte, folio et cetera.

Videatur bene quia fuit monitus dictus Johannes in secundo, ut certificat episcopus, et nunc permutavit cum una in Sarisberiensi, pro taxa, ut dicitur, x li.

De prebenda de Bisshopeshull' (Bishopshull) ex causa acceptationis et confirmationis facte auctoritate apostolica per Robertum Conlee fructus, folio et cetera.

Sequestrati sunt fructus, et monitus est possessor et denuntiatus in secundo et in ultimo. Pro taxa, ut dicitur, x li.

De prebenda de Gaya (Gaia) minori in eadem ecclesia Lichfeldensi ex causa acceptationis auctoritate apostolica facte per Nicholaum de Bottelesham fructus pro taxa decem m., valent sex li. xiii s. iiii d., folio et cetera.

Fructus sunt sequestrati in secundo et monitus est possessor et denuntiatus, sed est prorogatus dictus Nicholaus usque ad iii septimanas post Pascha anni LXXVII. Solvit die secunda Januarii anni LXXVII in quinque m. iii li. vi s. viii d., et sic restant lxvi s. et octo d., iii li. vi s. viii d.

Pro fructibus male perceptis cappelle Sancti Thome martiris in Bermyngham per Dominum Thomam Edmund', priorem dicte capelle, sex annis cum dimidio vel circa composuit die v$^{to}$ Maii anni et cetera LXXVI in sex m., valent deductis expensis quatuor li., folio et cetera.[367]

(fol. 191, xlviii)[368] Solvit quadraginta s., xl s. Et est prorogatus de residuo usque ad festum Sancti Michaelis anni LXXVII. Et tenetur plus solvere pro primis fructibus cum apparebit de confirmatione apostolica et cetera. Solvit alios xl s. pro ipsis fructibus male perceptis die xii Novembris anni LXXVII. Et sic est in istis restis cum apparebit de confirmatione et cetera, et videatur quantum.

De ecclesia de Audeley (Audley) ex causa provisionis facte Johanni Plummer per Gregorium iiii idus Septembris anno secundo[369] fructus pro taxa viginti m., valent xiii li. vi s. viii d., folio et cetera.

Alanus Ditton' est nunc possessor et optinuit sententiam in curia, et est ibi et hic obligatus et monitus et iuratus, et laicus patronus contendit cum ipso possessore, et ista provisio facta Johanni Plummer nunquam habuit effectum, ut certificat episcopus. Sed

monitus est dictus Alanus in persona propria, sed non audet sequestrare fructus propter potentiam laicalem et cetera. Et male certificat episcopus, et ideo mandetur plus pro dicta taxa vel residuo. Sed dicitur quod Willelmus de Bassehaue possidet titulo ordinario ad presentationem patroni laicy, videlicet domini de Audelle, et sic nondum habuit effectum. Et videatur melius si intervenit aliquis collusio. Fructus sunt sequestrati in ultimo.

De prioratu de Sandewell' (Sandwell) ex causa provisionis facte Ricardo Budenham xii kalendas Februarii per Gregorium anno iiii[370] fructus.[371]

Taxatur per relationem dicti prioris ad septem m., licet ex post audiverim quod valet ultra quadraginta m., et sic pertinerit[372] (fol. 191$^v$)[373] camere, si ista est, xx$^{ti}$ m., valent tresdecim li. sex s. octo d., xiii li. vi s. viii d.,[363] vel attende ad residuum ultra taxam sy plus valet, quia duas annexas habet in diocesi Lincolniensi. Sed dictus prior litigat cum uno ordinario. Fructus sunt sequestrati et monitus est possessor in loco ut certificat in ultimo.

Resta pagine xiii li. vi s. viii d.

Summa omnium restarum vacantium beneficiorum collatorum in civitate et diocesi Conventrensi et Lichefeldensi iii$^c$ xiii li. vii s. iiii d.; iii beneficia non taxata.[359]

(fol. 192, xlix) Diocesis Assavensis

De prebenda ecclesie Assavensis ex causa provisionis facte Johanni Reys vii idus Januarii per Urbanum anno vi[374] fructus. Taxatur, ut dicitur, quinque li., v li.

Dictus Johannes obiit, et Dominus Ricardus Vincens est apostolicus et subrogatus in locum illius, et fuit spoliatus per Johannem Fordham qui possidet dictam prebendam titulo ordinario ad presentationem domini principis, et litigat cum dicto Ricero Vincens in curia, ut dicitur. Et dicitur quod nunquam recepit fructus dictus Johannes Reis. Sed videatur quid certificabit episcopus cui est mandatum et per quem fructus sunt sequestrati. Et monitus est dictus Johannes Ford in secundo. Sed non constat de dicto Johanne Reys ad huc an recepit fructus vel[375] non et an dicta provisio habuit effectum. Sed videatur bene ad huc plus. Et non certificavit episcopus in tertio certificato de isto. Videatur de taxa.

De prebenda Assavensi ex causa provisionis facte Howello ap David v idus Martii per Gregorium anno primo[376] fructus pro taxa xx s., folio et cetera.

Sequestrati sunt fructus et monitus est possessor bis et denuntiatus. Et post solvit in partem fructuum decem

---

[367] At the bottom of the page: *Resta pagine xxiii li. vi s. viii d.* In the margin: *vera*.

[368] The heading *Lichfeldensis* appears at the top of the page.

[369] 10 September 1372.

[370] 21 January 1374.

[371] Followed by *folio* deleted by a line.

[372] At the foot of the page: *Resta pagine xiii li. vi s. viii d. et i beneficium nondum taxatum.* In the margin: *vera*.

[373] The heading *Coventrensis Lichfeldensis* appears at the top of the page.

[374] 7 January 1368.

[375] Over *an* deleted by a line.

[376] 11 March 1371.

s. Habet terminum de residuo Omnium Sanctorum anni LXXVII. Videatur de vera vel residuo.

De ecclesia de Landeurvill' (Llanerfyl) ex causa provisionis facte Mauricio Apphilip, vacante ex causa dimissionis Howelli ap David, xv ⟨kalendas⟩ Octobris per Gregorium anno quarto [377] fructus pro taxa septem m. que [378] valent quatuor li. tresdecim s. iiii^or d., iiii^or li. s. iiii d.[379]

(fol. 192^v)[380] Dictus Maurus nunquam optinuit dictam ecclesiam, nec assecutus fuit gratiam, ut certificat episcopus, et etiam post asseruit idem dictus Howell'. Et videatur melius, quia fructus sunt sequestrati et monitus est possessor in secundo, et non certificat episcopus in tertio certificatorio de isto. Videatur melius.

De ecclesia de Lanwarchal (Llanfarchell or Whitchurch by Denbigh) ex causa provisionis facte per cardinalem Cantuariensem David Tegwaret, Londonie iii idus Januarii, fructus pro taxa quinquaginta s., l s., folio et cetera.

Fructus sunt sequestrati bis, sed non constat de provisore, ut certificat episcopus, et est alia provisio per cardinalem etiam facte eodem [381] anno David Bakerum.[382] Et nulla habuit effectum, ut post probatum est, titulo regio impediente. Et videatur bene.

De ecclesia de Landervel (Llandderfel) acceptata auctoritate apostolica per Tuder' Jem' fructus pro taxa septem m. cum dimidio, valent v li.

Fructus sunt sequestrati et monitus est possessor in secundo, et post recepit terminos Omnium Sanctorum anni LXXVII et Johannis Baptiste tunc sequentis, et est obligatus, iuratus et condempnatus et cetera.

De ecclesia de Dinarth' (Llandrillo-yn-Rhos) acceptata auctoritate apostolica per Lowelinum ap Howell' fructus pro taxa viginti trium m., valent quindecim li. vi s. viii d.[383]

Fructus sunt sequestrati et monitus est possessor in secundo. Et post recepit terminos Beati Michaelis anni et cetera LXXVII et Johannis Baptiste tunc sequentis, et est obigatus, iuratus, condempnatus et cetera. Et solvit in primo termino predicto vii li. xiii s. iiii d. Et sic est hic in restis istis pro vii li. xiii s. iiii d.[383]

Resta pagine xv li. iii s. iiii d.[384]

(fol. 193, 1)[380] De prebenda que fuit Gruffini ap Ith' acceptata auctoritate apostolica per Lowellinum ap Howell' fructus pro taxa xx^ti s., ut dicitur.

Fructus sunt sequestrati et monitus est possessor in secundo, et post recepit terminos ut in proxima precedenti ubi debet plus pro ecclesia sua vocata Dinarth',

ut supra in provisione ecclesie de Dinarth'. Solvit in partem fructuum die penultima Septembris anni et cetera LXXVII decem s., x s., et videatur resta decem s.,[385] si est maior vel minor et cetera. Videatur de resta.

De prebenda que fuit Roberti Voit acceptata auctoritate apostolica per Johannem Trefnant fructus pro taxa, ut dicitur, decem li., folio et cetera, x li.

Fructus sunt sequestrati et monitus est possessor in secundo, et habet terminum Omnium Sanctorum anni et cetera LXXVII.

De vicaria de Aberiw (Berriew) acceptata auctoritate apostolica per Howelinum ap David fructus pro taxa decem m. cum dimidia, valent septem li., vii li.[386]

Sequestrati sunt fructus et monitus est possessor in secundo, et post recepit terminos Omnium Sanctorum anni LXXVII et Johannis Baptiste proxime tunc sequentis.

Resta pagine xvii li. x s.[384]

(fol. 193^v) Summa omnium restarum vacantium beneficiorum civitatis et diocesis Assavensis xliii li. vi s. viii d.

### (fol. 194, li) Diocesis Menevensis

De prebenda de Mathtref'(?) in ecclesia collegiata de Abergwell' (Abergwili) Menevensis diocesis ex causa provisionis facte Howello ap Jevan v nonas Martii per Gregorium anno iiii [387] fructus, folio et cetera.

David Penne possidet istam in forma pauperum, qui post permutavit cum alio cum quo dictus Howellus litigavit in curia Cantuariensi, ipso Howello tunc possidente, sed episcopus certificat in secundo quod ipse qui habuit causa permutationis possidet ad huc. Et videatur de taxa et de toto ad huc melius, quia dicitur quod taxatur quinque li. et plus, v li.

De ecclesia de Langodomore (Llangoedmore), folio xii in libro nigro reddito camere in primo compoto, debetur magna resta. Sed dicitur quod Dominus Hugo Pelegrini habuit, et videtur bene in camera quia quittantia ostendit de taxa sibi soluta et cum ibi in illis restis est de multa [388] maiore resta. Sed forte per errorem, et ita credo quia etiam sic dicixit mihi Dominus Hugo Pelegrini. Et videatur.

De prebenda in ecclesia collegiata Landewybrevii (Llandewi Brefi) Menevensis diocesis vocata Lanverheyren ex causa provisionis facte Thome de Brandeston' vii idus Januarii per Gregorium anno iiii [389] fructus.

Infra folio est alia provisio facta Symoni Querton' vi kalendas Augusti per Urbanum anno v,[390] et fructus debentur ibi. Et episcopus certificat in secundo quod nescit prebenda nec persona dicti Thome unquam fuit ibi quod sciatur. Sed videatur.

---

[377] 17 September 1374.
[378] *qui*, MS.
[379] At the foot of the page: *Resta pagine x li. xiii s. iiii d., salvo iure pluris et minoris.* In the margin: *vera*.
[380] The heading *Assavensis* appears at the top of the page.
[381] *eadem*, MS.
[382] Followed by *folio* deleted by a line.
[383] Sum repeated MS.
[384] In the margin: *vera*.

[385] Followed by *et cetera* deleted by a line. Sum repeated MS.
[386] Followed by *folio* deleted by a line. Sum repeated MS.
[387] 3 March 1374.
[388] *multo*, MS.
[389] 7 January 1374.
[390] 27 July 1367.

De prebenda seu portione in ecclesia de Aberwill' Menevensis diocesis ex causa provisionis facte Johanni Asperulis xviii kalendas Julii per Urbanum anno viii [391] fructus.

Sequestrati sunt fructus et monitus est dictus Johannes bis et excommunicatus. Pro taxa, ut dicitur, v li.

Resta pagine x li. et ii provisiones.[384]

(fol. 194ᵛ)[392] De prebenda de Lanverheyron in ecclesia collegiata de Landewibrevii diocesis Menevensis ex causa provisionis facte Symoni de Querton' auctoritate apostolica fructus.

Non est prebenda talis in diocesi Menevensi, ut certificat episcopus in secundo. Et debet plus pro ecclesia sua in diocesi Karleolensi folio et cetera. Sed dicitur quod bullas ecclesie ipsius perdidit et cetera ut ibi reperies in diocesi Karleolensi. Taxa, ut dicitur, vi li. et videatur. vi li.

Resta pagine per se patet vi li.

Summa omnium restarum vacantium beneficiorum civitatis et diocesis Menevensis xvi li.; ii beneficia non taxata.[384]

### (fol. 195, lii) Diocesis Bangorensis

De archidiaconatu Merionneth' in ecclesia Bangorensi ex causa provisionis facte Johanni Rey idus Novembris per Urbanum anno vii [393] fructus.

Est monitus possessor et sequestrati sunt fructus, et monitus est Gervasius archidiaconus Bangorensis et officialis dicti archidiaconi, ut certificat episcopus in ultimo. Possessor qui nunc est habet docere de vero valore istius archidiaconatus et prebende sibi annexe infra Pascha anni LXXVIII. Taxatur, ut dicitur, sed videatur bene, ad quindecim li., xv li.

De prebenda Bangorensi que fuit unius Edmundi nomine ex causa provisionis facte auctoritate apostolica possessori fructus.

Ista prebenda est annexa supradicto archidiaconatui. Fuit mandatum isti novo episcopo qui iam tarde venit ad Angliam, et certificavit quod est annexa archidiaconatui supradicto in principio, sed videatur. Videatur et bene.

De medietate parochialis ecclesie de Landian ex causa provisionis facte Johanni Cheyne dum vacabit per assecutionem ecclesie de Orpington' per Willelmum Loerug' iiii idus Setempbris per Gregorium anno ii [394] fructus, folio et cetera.

Fuit in vᵗᵒ mandato et nunc in alio ubi episcopus certificavit quod non est talis ecclesia nec aliquis talis nominis beneficiatus in diocesi Bangorensi. Et videatur.

Resta pagine xv li. et ii [395] beneficia non taxata.

Summa restarum vacantium beneficiorum civitatis et diocesis Bangorensis.[384]

(fol. 195ᵛ) Summa universalis omnium restarum vacantium beneficiorum civitatis et diocesis Cantuariensis et suffraganeorum [396] suorum, qui suffraganei sunt xvi, viiiᵐ lxxxvi li. xv s. v d. ob. sterlingorum; xxviii beneficia nondum reperta taxata.[384]

### (fol. 196, liii) Diocesis Eboracensis

De prebenda de Strensall' in ecclesia Eboracensi ex causa provisionis facte cardinali Petragoriensi [397] per Innocentium vi idus Octobris anno ii [398] fructus pro taxa quinquaginta trium li. sex s. octo d., liii li. vi s. viii d.[399]

Est monitus Willelmus Snokere, perceptor fructuum possessoris [400] qui nunc est, quia obligatio est in rem.

De prebenda de Wistowe (Wistow) in ecclesia ex causa provisionis facte cardinali Carcasonensi [401] per Innocentium taxata centum li., c li[402]

Restant ab antiquo viginti una li. sexdecim s. octo d., xxi li. xvi s. viii d. Et archidiaconatus Eboracensis est etiam in eisdem antiquis restis eodem folio et cetera pro quinque li, decem s., v li. x s., xxvii li. vi s. viii d.

Sunt moniti executores testamenti Domini Willelmi de Mufeld', tunc firmarii, et debent venire infra xv dies postquam sciverint quod dictus firmarius fuerit mortuus, videlicet Helias de Sutton', Johannes de Cowik et Stephanus de Ecilishil, executores dicti Willelmi. Et iste Helias iuravit quod predicti nunquam fuerunt firmarii et cetera pro se et aliis ii, et receptores fructuum Johannes filius Thome de Calvode et Johannes de Eltonnehend'. Isti sunt in mora et, ut dicitur, excommunicati. Et videatur melius si poterit aliquid habere quia cardinalis Carcasonensis diu est obiit. Et videatur.

De prebenda de Drifeld' (Driffeld) in ecclesia Eboracensi ex causa provisionis facte Hugoni cardinali Sancti Martialis [403] per Innocentium fructus pro taxa centum li., c li.[404]

Est hic in istis restis ultra viginti quinque li. solutos nuper per manus decani Londoniensis, procuratoris sui in dicto [405] (fol. 196ᵛ)[406] pro septuaginta quinque li., lxxv li.[407] Et monitus est Willelmus Belami firmarius. Scripsit michi ultima die Martii anni LXXVII dominus thesaurarius quod ipse habuit Avinionie a domino cardi-

---

[391] 14 June 1370.
[392] The heading *Menevensis* appears at the top of the page.
[393] 13 November 1368.
[394] 10 September 1372.
[395] Followed by *provisiones* deleted by a line.
[396] *suffraganeo*, MS.
[397] Elias Talleyrand of Périgueux, bishop of Albano.
[398] 10 October 1354.
[399] In the margin: *Cardinalis Petragoricensis*.
[400] *possessorum*, MS.
[401] Stephen Aubert, priest of S. Lorenzo in Lucina after 22 September 1368.
[402] In the margin: *Cardinalis Carcasonensis*.
[403] Hugo de St. Martial, deacon of S. Maria in Portico.
[404] In the margin: *Cardinalis Sancti Martialis*.
[405] At the foot of the page: *Resta pagine lxxx li. xiii s. iiii d.* In the margin: *vera*.
[406] The heading *Eboracensis* appears at the top of the page.
[407] Sum repeated in the margin.

nali predicto viii⁰ lxxi fl. curentes ii s. viii d. et debet residuum. Sed videantur domini in camera, et vide supra in diocesi Lincolniensi pro prebenda de Thame. Videatur de ductione ipsius solutionis in camera facte.

De archidiaconatu de Estridyng' debetur de procurationibus et iurisdictione et kethedrayco.[408] Et videatur quantum quia de residuo solvit diu est, et non est in istis restis nisi predictis procurationibus et iurisdictione ex causa provisionis facte Waltero de Skirlowe per Innocentium ii kalendas Decembris anno vii.[409] Est consiliarius regius in requesto. Ideo dormit pro nunc et diu etiam in isto statu dormivit. Sed videatur quis possidet et quantum potest debere ex causis predictis. Videatur bene.

De ecclesia de Skepton' videatur si habuit effectum quia dicitur quod possessor est auctoritate apostolica folio xvii in libro nigro.

Non est talis ecclesia in diocesi Eboracensi, ut certificat archiepiscopus in ultimo mandato anni LXXVII. Videatur.

De prebenda de Massam (Masham) in ecclesia Eboracensi ex causa provisionis facte cardinali Sesare Augusti [410] per Urbanum xvii kalendas Setempbris anno primo [411] fructus pro taxa ducentum quinquaginta m., valent clxvi li. xiii s. iiii d.[412]

Dominus Johannes Stoks erat firmarius tempore mortis cardinalis [413] et nunquam voluit solvere et iam obiit. Et debetur plus pro eadem prebenda per Magistrum [414] (fol. 197, liiii) [415] Robertum Straton', qui est auditor palatii et possidet eam, et ibi vide. Sunt moniti firmarii anni LXXV, et sunt viginti firmarii, ut in certificatorio continentur. Videatur.

De prioratu Beate Marie Lancastrie ex causa provisionis facte Willelmo Raymbaut per Urbanum anno v.[416]

Est in restis antiquis pro temporalitate quam habet, quia de residuo diu est solvit ut in libro folio et cetera, sed videatur siquidem.

De decanatu et prebenda ecclesie Eboracensis ex causa provisionis facte Anglico cardinali Avinionensi [417] per Urbanum anno iii [418] fructus folio et cetera.[419]

Datur ad firmam decanatus singulis annis pro v⁰ xl m., valent iii⁰ lx li. Est sic debet pro medietate veri valoris clxxx li.[420] Et queratur valor illius prebende quam tunc etiam habuit, quia non nominatur, ideo nesci-

tur valor. Nunc vero habet aliam prebendam vocatam Decane, ut in libro folio et cetera, et ibi vide de taxa et toto.

De prebenda de Strensall' ecclesie Eboracensis que fuit Mathei cardinalis Viterbiensis [421] fructus pro taxa quinquaginta trium li. sex s. octo d.,[420] folio et cetera.[422]

Cardinalis est Viterbiensis, et videatur si solvit et si concordavit cum camera. Et est alia provisio supra facta Cardinali Petragoricensi, et est ibi monitus.

Resta pagine ii⁰ xxxiii li. vi s. viii d. et una provisio.[423]

(fol. 197ᵛ) [415] De ecclesia de Patrington' ex causa provisionis facte Johanni de Matham xi kalendas Januarii per Urbanum anno vi [424] fructus pro taxa xl li., folio et cetera.

Litigatur in curia, et est obligatus lite finita. Tamen solvit cancellarius Londonie infra folio et cetera pro alia collatione ipsi cancellario facta, et de ista etiam debetur lite finita, et ita est obligatus dictus Johannes, et videatur bene.

De prioratu de Kertmell' (Cartmel), taxato quadraginta sex li. tresdecim s. quatuor d., ex causa provisionis facte Ricardo de Kellech' per Urbanum anno vi [425] ultra undecim li, sex s. octo d. diu est solutos, debet restam taxe predicte antique folio et cetera xxxv li. vi s. viii d.

Et sic est in istis restis pro triginta quinque li. sex s. octo d. Et habet terminos quindene Pasche et Beati Michaelis anni et cetera LXXVII et sequentis per equales portiones.

De prebenda de Strensall' in ecclesia Eboracensi, taxata quinquaginta tribus li. sex s. octo d., liii li. vi s. viii d., ex causa provisionis facte cardinali Sancti Petri [426] per Urbanum anno octavo [427] fructus debentur, folio et cetera.[428]

Est supra responsum in alia provisione quia cardinalis est et iste concordavit ad tempus cum camera, ut ibi et cetera. Et videatur.

De prebenda de Wistowe (Wistow), taxata centum li., in ecclesia Eboracensi ex causa provisionis facte Symoni cardinali Cantuariensi [429] per Urbanum [430] (fol. 198, lv) [415] anno vii, v nonas Octobris,[431] fructus, folio et cetera, c li.[432]

Et debet plus ista prebenda infra ex causa provisionis facte cardinali Carcasonensi [433] de resta antiqua viginti

---

[408] Presumably a form of *cathedraco*.
[409] 30 November 1359.
[410] William d'Aigrefeuille, priest of S. Maria in Trastevere.
[411] 16 August 1363.
[412] In the margin: *Cardinalis Sesare Augusti*.
[413] A repetition of *cardinalis* is deleted by a line.
[414] At the foot of the page: *Resta pagine ii⁰ xli li. xiii s. iiii d. et ii beneficia nondum taxata.* In the margin: *vera*.
[415] The heading *Eboracensis* is repeated at the top of the page.
[416] 6 November 1366 to 5 November 1367.
[417] Anglicus Grimoard, bishop of Albano, after Sept. 17, 1367.
[418] 1364-1365.
[419] In the margin: *Cardinalis Avinionensis modo Albanensi*.
[420] Sum repeated in the margin.

[421] Mark de Viterbo, priest of S. Prassede.
[422] In the margin: *Cardinalis Viterbiensis*.
[423] In the margin: *vera*.
[424] 22 December 1367.
[425] 1367-1368.
[426] Franciscus Thebaldeschis, priest of S. Sabina.
[427] 1369-1370.
[428] In the margin: *Cardinalis Sancti Petri*.
[429] Simon Langham, bishop of Palestrina.
[430] At the foot of the page: *Resta pagine cxxviii li. xiii s. uii d.* In the margin: *vera*.
[431] 3 October 1369.
[432] In the margin: *Cardinalis Cantuariensis*.
[433] Stephen Aubert, priest of S. Lorenzo in Lucina.

unam li. sex s. octo d., xxi li. vi s. viii d.[420] et dictus cardinalis iam obiit.

De prebenda de Massam (Masham) ex causa provisionis facte per Urbanum anno vii, xviii kalendas Decembris,[434] Roberto de Straton'ultra novam [435] taxam centum viginti m. diu est solutam domino priori Lewensi. Debet quod restat pro taxa antiqua que est ducente quinquaginta m. Et sic restant ad huc centum triginta m. que valent iiii[xx] vi li. xiii s. iiii d., de quibus solvit die xxviii Aprilis anni et cetera LXXVI triginta li., xxx li. Et sic est in istis restis pro lvi li. xiii s. iiii d.[420] cum exploretur, folio et cetera. Monitus est dictus Robertus et sequestrati sunt fructus in ultimo.

Et debentur ad huc primi fructus dicte prebende de Massam ex causa provisionis facte domino cardinali Sezare Augusto per Urbanum vii kalendas Setembris anno primo [436] pro taxa antiqua clxvi li. xiii s. iiii d.,[420] folio xiiii.[437]

De prebenda Eboracensi cardinali Sancti Eustachii [438] habetur infra folio sequenti et ibi vide.[439]

De prebenda de Ripon' vocata Torp (Thorp) Eboracensis diocesis ex causa provisionis facte Waltero de Wandefford' est hic pro resta taxe quadraginta m. pro quinque li., v li., ut in folio et cetera.

Johannes de Candalle nunc possessor est monitus et fuit prorogatus, revocato iuramento, et cetera usque ad primam dominicam quadragesime anni et cetera [440] LXXVI.[441] (fol. 198[v]) [415] Solvit de dicta resta die xxviii Octobris anni LXXVII quinquaginta s. et restat debens alios [442] quinquaginta s., l s.

Cardinalis Cameracensis [443] potuit acceptare in diocesi Eboracensi et provincia usque ad quatuor milia fl. Et videatur bene si acceptavit et quot et qualia et cetera. Videatur.[444]

De perpetua vicaria seu altaria Sancte Katerine sita in ecclesia Sancti Martini Eboracensis diocesis ex causa provisiones facte Engelberto Belle v nonas Julii per Gregorium anno secundo [445] fructus, folio et cetera.

Videatur bene quia dicitur in duobus certificatoriis quod non est talis in diocesi quod videatur, et sic etiam certificavit in ultimo. Videatur.

De archidiaconatu et prebenda Eboracensibus ex causa

provisionis facte R. titulo Sancte Praxedis presbytero cardinali vi nonas Octobris per Gregorium anno secundo [446] fructus, folio et cetera.[447]

Sunt moniti iiii[or] executores Barnabonis Moreni superius nominati ubi est alia provisio, nec taxa reperitur quia prebenda non nominatur. Obiit cardinalis et nichil reperitur de suo hic, sed videatur in camera. Videatur et bene.

De vicaria de Gilling' (Gilling near Richmond) de Forset (Forcett) Eboracensis diocesis ex causa provisionis facte Thome de Hixham per sedem apostolicam fructus pro taxa centum triginta m., valent lxxxvi li. xiii s. iiii d., folio et cetera.

Est alia ecclesia eiusdem nominis que taxatur xxiiii m., et litigatur in curia cum Ricero [448] (fol. 199, lvi) [449] Upton', qui eam possidet titulo permutationis coram ordinarium facte, et ideo dormit pro nunc usque quo appareat de effectu dicte gratie ipsius Thome. Et anno et cetera LXXV de mense Octobris fuit sic relaxatus et post est monitus et sequestratus vicarius ipsius ecclesie. Et videatur de ista.

De prebenda de Norwell', vocata Palleshalle, ex causa acceptationis facte per Radulphum de Streton' fructus pro taxa quadraginta m. que valent xxvi li. xiii s. iiii d., folio et cetera.

Habet terminos dictus R. Pasche anni LXXVII, pro quo termino primo solvit xii die Maii anni LXXVI et debet pro sequenti. Et est iuratus et obligatus et in propria persona condempatus et cetera. Et sic est in istis restis pro tresdecim li. vi s. viii d., xiii li.vi s. viii d.

De prebenda de Southcave alias Cave (South Cave) in ecclesia Eboracensi ex causa provisionis facte cardinali Albanensi [450] per obitum Henrici Ingelby xvi kalendas Februarii per Gregorium anno iii [451] fructus pro taxa centum sexaginta m., valent cvi li. xiii s. iiii d., folio et cetera.[452]

Cardinalis Albanensis est, et concordavit cum camera, et dicitur quod dicta provisio nondum habuit effectum quia ad huc vivit dictus Henricus. Et videatur bene.

De archidiaconatu Eboracensi ex causa provisionis facte Symoni episcopo Penestrino viii idus Julii per Gregorium anno iiii [453] fructus, folio et cetera. Sed dicitur quod valent pro medietate veri valoris c li.

Sunt moniti, licet non personaliter, procuratores ipsius cardinalis. Et sunt alie provisiones supra, et habuit relaxamentum a camera, sed videatur si solvit quia dictus cardinalis obiit. Videatur bene de toto.

De prebenda Eboracensi vocata Garesbur (Knaresborough) ex causa provisionis facte cardinali Sancti

[434] 14 November 1368.
[435] Follows *novam* deleted by dots.
[436] 26 August 1363.
[437] In the margin: *Cardinalis Sezare Augusti.*
[438] Peter Flandrin, deacon of S. Eustachio.
[439] In the margin: *Cardinalis Sancti Eustachii.*
[440] *cetera* om. MS.
[441] At the foot of the page: *Resta pagine cccxliiii li. xiii s. iiii.* In the margin: *vera.*
[442] *alias* MS.
[443] Anglicus Grimoard was bishop of Albano. Robert of Geneva, priest of Ss. XII Apostoli, was bishop of Cambrai but he was known as Gibennensis.
[444] In the margin: *Cardinalis Cameracensis alias Albanensis.* I have found no bishop of Albanio who was bishop of Cambrai in this period.
[445] 3 July 1372.

[446] 2 October 1372.
[447] In the margin: *Cardinalis Sancte Praxedis* (Peter Gomez).
[448] At the foot of the page: *Resta pagine lxxxix li. iii s. iiii d. et ii beneficia nondum taxata.*
[449] The heading *Eboracensis* is repeated at the top of the page.
[450] Anglicus Grimoard.
[451] 17 January 1373.
[452] In the margin: *Cardinalis Albanensis.*
[453] 8 July 1374.

Eustachii [454] xix kalendas Setempbris per Gregorium anno primo [455] fructus, folio et cetera.[456]

Queratur nomen prebende et videatur taxa quia prebenda non habuit effectum. Et vocentur procuratores sui, et taxatur, ut dicitur lxx m., valent xlvi li. xiii s. iiii d.[420] Et ideo potest dici inutilis si non habuit effectum. Et videatur.

Resta pagine ii° lxvi li. xiii s. iiii d.[457]

(fol. 199ᵛ) [449] De officio seu beneficio de Bayfeld' [458] in ecclesia collegiata Sancti Johannis Beverlaci ex causa provisionis facte Waltero de Hocton' per cardinalem Cantuariensem fructus, folio et cetera.

Alia est provisio facta alteri infra folio et cetera. Et videatur bene quia fuit mandatum in secundo et nichil factum per archiepiscopum ad huc quia officialis prepositi Beverlaci nunquam exequitur mandatum. Dicitur quod valet pro medietate veri valoris quinque li. et plus, v li.

De prebenda in capella Beate Marie et Sanctorum Angelorum Eboraci ex causa provisionis facte Waltero Molin iii nonas Novembris per cardinalem Cantuariensem fructus, folio et cetera.

Et est alia provisio iterum facta folio et cetera. Et episcopus certificat in secundo mandato quod dictus Walterus nunquam habuit ibi prebendam, sed videatur melius, et sic certificat in ultimo. Videatur.

De medietate ecclesie de Trowelle (Trowell) ex causa provisionis facte Willelmo de Prestwold' per cardinalem Cantuariensem Londonie ii nonas Decembris fructus pro taxa viginti m., valent xiii li. vi s. viii d., folio et cetera.

Fructus sunt sequestrati et monitus est possessor in secundo mandato, videlicet Johannes Stowe titulo ordinario possidens.[459] Et dictus Willelmus dimissit receptis fructibus unius anni, et dictus Johannes habet terminum Pasche anni LXXVIII quod iterum prosequatur contra dictum Willelmum.

De ecclesia Sancti Martini in Milkelgate (St. Martin in Micklegate, York) ex causa provisionis facte Johanni Giffon' per cardinalem Cantuariensem idus Julii fructus pro taxa quatuor li. tresdecim s. quatuor d., iiii li. xiii s. iiii d., folio.

Dicitur quod possidetur per Robertum de la More a tribus [460] (fol. 200, lvii) [449] annis citra titulo ordinario. Et est commissum Magistro H. Fletum et cetera, et habet terminum quindene Sancti Hillarii ad certificandum et cetera. Et licet sic certificaverit tamen per

fraudem dicti Johannis et dolum dimisit dictam ecclesiam, data sibi pecunia, ut dicitur, quare tenetur et cetera. Videatur.

De prebenda in capella Beate Marie et Sanctorum Angelorum Eboraci ex causa provisionis facte Johanni de Londe per cardinalem Cantuariensem fructus, folio et cetera.

Nunquam habuit ibi prebendam dictus Johannes, ut certificavit episcopus in secundo, sed videatur melius. Et sic etiam certificavit in ultimo. Videatur.

De prebenda de Eton' (Eaton) in ecclesia collegiata de Southwelle ex causa acceptationis auctoritate apostolica facte per Johannem Strensall' fructus pro taxa decem m., valent vi li. xiii s. iiii d.

Debet etiam de ecclesia quam habet in diocesi Lincolniensi, folio et cetera, pro quibus habet terminos primi diei Maii anni LXXVII et sequentis et cetera. Et solvit die ultima Aprilis anni LXXVII in v m. lxvi s., et sic restant plus alii lxvi s.[461]

De ecclesiis de Maneffeld' (Manfield) et Soutleverton' (South Leverton) ex causa provisionis facte cardinali titulo Sancti Sexti [462] fructus, folio et cetera.[463]

Sequestrati sunt fructus in primo mandato, et moniti sunt firmarii, videlicet Nicholaus Bankewell', procurator dicti cardinalis, Petrus Proudfot et Thomas de Estwenestawe. Ecclesia de Maneffeld' taxatur xl m. et ecclesia de Soutleverton' taxatur lx m., valent lx li.

De prioratu de Novo Burgo (Newburgh) Eboracensis diocesis ex causa confirmationis facte Johanni Tresk, canonico regulari ordinis [464] (fol. 200ᵛ) [449] Sancti Augustini, per Dominum Johannem episcopum Lincolniensem, ex commissione speciali sibi super hoc, ut dicitur, facta per Dominum Innocentium quintum, fructus.

Habuit duo brevia regia quia de patronatu laycali, et fuit relaxatus in forma, ut habetur folio registri litterarum xxxiiii, videlicet possessor qui nunc est, scilicet Thomas Husthwait, prior dicti prioratus. Taxa non reperitur nec potest habere quia de patronatu laicali. Videatur.

De prebenda de Northnewold' (North Newbald) ex causa provisionis facte per Gregorium Johanni de Fordham per consecrationem archiepiscopi Dublinensis fructus pro taxa debentur octuaginta m. que valent liii li. vi s. viii d.

Dominus Henricus Snayth' possidet nunc titulo permutationis cum dicto Johanne facte coram ordinarium, et recepit terminos de una parte et Dominus Johannes Fordham de alia, videlicet Beati Michaelis anni LXXVII et sequentis per equales portiones, videlicet dictus H. pro xxviii li. et dictus Johannes Fordham pro residuo, videlicet pro xxv li. vi s. viii d. Et solvit Dominus H.

---

[454] Peter Flandrin.
[455] 14 August 1371.
[456] In the margin: *Cardinalis Sancti Eustachii.*
[457] In the margin: *vera.*
[458] Some of the prebends consisted of a share of the commuted value of the Bedern: A. F. Leach, Introduction to *Chapter Act Book of Beverley*, i, pp. xlix-liii.
[459] *possident* with sign of abbreviation over the t, MS.
[460] At the foot of the page: *Resta pagine xxiii li. et i beneficium nondum taxatum.*

[461] Sum repeated in margin.
[462] Simon Langham.
[463] In the margin: *Cardinalis Sancti Sixti qui fuit cardinalis Cantuariensis.*
[464] At the foot of the page: *Resta pagine lxix li. xix s. iiii d. et ii beneficia nondum taxata.* In the margin: *vera.*

xix die Octobris dicto anno LXXVII quatuordecim li., ut supra in recepta habetur, et sic restant hic xxxix li. vi s. viii d.

De beneficio Bereselli wlgariter nuncupato in ecclesia collegiata Sancti Johannis Beverlaci ex causa provisionis facte Ricardo Okham fructus per cardinalem Cantuariensem.

Fuit mandatum in secundo et nichil factum, sed videatur, nec etiam in ultimo ut certificavit, et hoc in deffectu officialis prepositi Beverlaci qui nunquam libenter exequitur mandatum. Videatur de taxa et quod debetur. Videatur.

De ecclesia de Kirkeby Misperton' (Kirkby Misperton) ex causa dispensationis facte Johanni Clifford' per Gregorium ix kalendas Decembris [465] (fol. 201, lviii) [449] anno iii [466] fructus pro taxa quinquaginta quinque m., valent xxxvi li. xiii s. iiii d., folio et cetera.

Debet etiam ibi pro prebenda, si sit expeditus, et de dignitate, personatu vel officio, et de beneficio permutato cum dicta ecclesia, si quod sit. Sed non pro nunc debet de ecclesia, ut dicitur, quia habet eam titulo ordinario ad presentationem patroni laici. Et de dignitate acceptata, ut dicitur, litigat, videlicet de thesauraria Eboracensi que taxatur, ut dicitur, iic li.,[461] et videatur bene quia est thesaurarius domini archiepiscopi Eboracensis et dicitur quod titulo regio etiam possidet ibi illam dignitatem. Sed litigat cum cardinali Gibanensi [467] et cetera. Et fuit tunc dispensatum, ut dicitur, cum eo quod possit retinere ecclesiam cum acceptata seu acceptanda prebenda et dignitate, dum tamen infra annum ipsam ecclesiam permutet cum aliquo beneficio compatibili et etiam non possidet dictam dignitatem cum prebenda de Wilton' sibi annexa titulo regio. Et videatur bene de toto.

De prebenda de Rampton' ex causa acceptationis facte auctoritate apostolica per Johannem Caldewell' fructus pro taxa viginti li., folio et cetera.

Habet terminos Omnium Sanctorum anni LXXVII et Pasche sequentis, et est iuratus, obligatus et condempnatus et usque tunc relaxatus. Solvit ultima die Octobris anni LXXVII decem li. et restant alie x li.[461]

De prebenda de Stilington' (Stillington) ex causa provisionis facte de eadem per Dominum Gregorium undecim Guidoni cardinali Pictavensi titulo Sancte Crusis in Ierosolomitano fructus pro taxa octuaginta m., valent liii li. vi s. viii d., folio et cetera.[468]

Et debet totum ad huc.

Resta pagine [469] iiic v li.[470]

(fol. 201v) [449] De prebenda de Bolom (Bole) in ecclesia Eboracensi ex causa provisionis et confirmationis

factarum [471] Thome Brandon' per Dominum Gregorium papam undecim fructus pro taxa viginti quatuor m., valent xvi li., folio.

De canonicatu et prebenda et archidiaconatu ecclesie Eboracensis ex causa provisionis facte domino cardinali Pictavensi per Dominum Gregorium undecim anno sexto [472] vacantibus in curia per obitum bone memorie domini cardinalis Cantuariensis fructus, folio et cetera.[473]

Et dantur ad firmam pro anno iic lx li., de quibus debet ad minus, si non taxatur, cxxx li.[461] Debet plus supra pro alia prebenda quam iam dimisit. Et videatur.

Resta pagine cxlvi li.

Summa omnium restarum vacantium beneficiorum civitatis et diocesis Eboracensis m ixc lxviii li. ii s. viii d.; x beneficia non taxata.[470]

(fol. 202v) [474] Dunolmensis diocesis

De prebenda de Lumley (Lamesley) in ecclesia collegiata Cestrie super stratam (Chester-le-Street) ex causa provisionis facte Willelmo de Lugtheburth' vi idus Februarii per Innocentium anno secundo [475] fructus pro taxa viginti li., xx li., folio et cetera.

Prohibitum per breve regium quia possessor est regius, scilicet Willelmus Standeford'. Et sunt alie provisiones infra. Et non vult solvere, sed mortuo possessore regio agatur contra beneficium quod semper remanet obligatum.

De ecclesia de Santhorp (Stanhope) ex causa provisionis facte Willelmo de Norwico per Innocentium vii kalendas Setempbris anno ix [476] fructus pro taxa quadraginta s., xl s., folio et cetera.

Prohibitum per breve. Et videatur.

De eadem ecclesia ex causa confirmationis sive provisionis facte Ricardo de Wylyngton' per Innocentium iiii idus Januarii anno ix [477] fructus pro taxa quadraginta s., xl s., eodem folio.

Prohibitum de utraque ab antiquo.

Et est alia provisio facta eidem Ricardo de eadem ecclesia eodem folio.

Et est prohibitum per breve de toto et ab antiquo, sed mortuo possessore regio, sequator beneficium quod est ex causis predictis obligatum. Et videatur.

De libera capella de Ismouth' (Jesmond) ex causa provisionis facte Thome de Penreth' per Innocentium ix idus Januarii anno ix [478] fructus, folio et cetera.

Prohibitum per breve quia possessor est regius et non potest habere. Et videatur plus.

Resta pagine xxiiii li. et ii beneficia nondum taxata.[470]

---

[465] At the foot of the page: *Resta pagine xxxix li. vi s. viii d. et ii beneficia nondum taxata.* In the margin: *vera.*
[466] 23 November 1373.
[467] Robert of Geneva, priest of Ss. XII Apostoli.
[468] In the margin: *Cardinalis Pictavensis.*
[469] Followed by *c li.* deleted by a line.
[470] In the margin: *vera.*

[471] *facte*, MS.
[472] 1376.
[473] In the margin: *Cardinalis Pictavensis.*
[474] Folio 202 recto is blank.
[475] 8 February 1354.
[476] 26 August 1361.
[477] 10 January 1361.
[478] 24 December 1361, see p. 157.

(fol. 203, lx)[479] Item de eadem ex causa provisionis facte Matheo de Bolton' per Innocentium xiii kalendas Februarii anno x [480] fructus, folio et cetera.

Prohibitum per breve quia possessor est regius et obierunt alii. Videatur.

De hospitali pauperum Sancti Egidii (Kepier) ex causa provisionis facte Johanni Appelbi per Innocentium viii kalendas Maii anno viii [481] fructus, folio et cetera.

Prohibitum quia possessor est titulo regio ibi, scilicet decanus Londonie, et dicta provisio, ut dicitur, nunquam habuit effectum, sed videatur melius. Videatur.

De prebenda de Bries (Byers Green) in ecclesia collegiata de Auklond (Auckland) diocesis Dunolmensis ex causa provisionis facte Thome Kokin ii nonas Aprilis per Urbanum anno secundo [482] fructus, folio et cetera.

Dicitur quod est pauperima, et tamen taxatur ad sexdecim li., xvi li. Mandetur plus, sed dicitur per episcopum quod nulli sunt fructus nec est possessor aliquis, quare dormit pro nunc.

De ecclesia de Wermouth (Bishop Wearmouth) fructus, folio et cetera, ex causa provisionis facte per Urbanum anno vii [483] David de Wallore pro taxa centum li., c li.

Dicitur quod non habuit effectum, et plures alie fuerunt ibi facte provisiones. Alia fuit provisio facta cardinali Cantuariensi, et alia cardinali xii Apostolorum, et alia Thome de Newbi eodem folio. Et obiit dictus David, et cardinalis Cantuariensis habuit post, et nunc Cardinalis Gibanensis habet eam, et debet pro se dictam taxam, videlicet c li. Et pro aliis quia beneficium est obligatum videatur bene de toto.

Resta pagine ii^e xvi li. salvo erore et ii beneficia nondum taxata.[470]

(fol. 203^v)[484] De prebenda ecclesie collegiate Auklond Dunolmensis diocesis ex causa provisionis facte Thome de Barnelby per Urbanum anno vi [485] fructus, folio et cetera.

Alia tamen fuit provisio que non habuit effectum infra folio. Sed iste [486] habuit nunc, ut dicitur, et est de familia domini Dunolmensis, et fructus sunt sequestrati et ipse est monitus, et dicitur quod detur pro taxa sexdecim li., xvi li.

De decanatu Langescestrie (Lanchester) ex causa subrogationis facte Johanni de Hesill' xv kalendas Februarii per Urbanum anno vi [487] fructus, folio et cetera.

Lis pendet in curia et ordinarius possidet, et est

mandatum et fructus sunt sequestrati et monitus est possessor, licet fructus sint sub sequestro auditoris palatii, quia factum ipsius non impedit ius camere. Dicitur quod debet pro taxa viginti li., sed videatur bene. xx li.

De archidiaconatu Dunolmensi et ecclesia sibi annexa ex causa provisionis facte Alexandro de Norwill' per obitum Willelmi de Westley xvi kalendas Decembris per Urbanum anno viii [488] fructus, folio et cetera.

Taxatur solum annexa centum viginti li. quas debet et medietatem veri valoris dicti archidiaconatus qui, ut dicitur, non taxatur sed valet ducente li., ii^e li. Et sic debet pro medietate veri valoris c li., salvo iure pluris et cetera. Est nunc archiepiscopus Eboracensis, et sic debet pro toto ii^e xx li.[489]

De prebenda Sancti Cutberti de Derlington' (Darlington) Dunolmensis diocesis ex causa provisionis facte Ricardo Driffeld' fructus, folio et cetera.

Litigatur in curia regia, ut dixit, diu est, et nunc possidet Willelmus de Lintton' titulo ordinario, qui est familiaris domini de Newill', et habet terminos nativitatis domini anni LXXVI et Pasche sequentis pro supplicatione domini de Newill' ad solvendum pro alio, et est obligatus, iuratus et hoc manu propria. Et debet pro taxa, ut dicitur, sed videatur bene, viginti li., xx li.

Resta pagine ii^e lxxvi li.[490]

(Fol. 204, lxi)[484] De prebenda ecclesie collegiate Cestrie super stratam, que taxatur viginti li., xx li., ex causa provisionis facte sive acceptationis per Laurentium Graa.

Et solvit in diversis vicibus tresdecim li. sex s. octo d. Restat hic debens sex li. tresdecim s. quatuor d., vi li. xiii s. iiii d., folio et cetera. Est amicus domini officialis Eboracensis et familiaris. Et habet terminos Pasche et Michaelis anni et cetera LXXVII. Solvit die vii Aprilis anno et cetera LXXVII in quinque m. iii li. vi s. viii d., et sic est in istis restis pro lxvi s. viii d.[491]

De ecclesia de Quikham (Whickham), taxa viginti li., ex causa provisionis facte Hugoni Hork xvi kalendas Junii per Gregorium anno iii [492] fructus, folio et cetera.

Fructus sunt sequestrati et monitus est possessor, et litigavit diu cum uno regio, sed die xvii Julii recepit terminos quindene beati Hillarii et sequentis per equales portiones, et est condempnatus et iuratus, et cetera, xx li.

De ecclesia de Bolum (Bolam) ex causa provisionis facte Willelmo de Berton' vii kalendas Januarii per Gregorium anno iii [493] fructus pro taxa xl li., folio et cetera.

Non habuit effectum ad huc quia est appropriata cuidam abbati, ut in libro et folio et cetera, sed videatur

---

[479] The heading *Dunolmensis* appears at the top of the page.
[480] 20 January 1362.
[481] 24 April 1360.
[482] 4 April 1364.
[483] 6 November 1368 to 5 November 1369.
[484] The heading *Dunolmensis* is repeated at the top of the page.
[485] 6 November 1367 to 5 November 1368.
[486] *ista*, MS.
[487] 18 January 1368.

[488] 16 November 1369.
[489] In the margin: *archiepiscopus Eboracensis*.
[490] In the margin: *vera*.
[491] Sum repeated in margin.
[492] 17 May 1373.
[493] 26 December 1373.

melius quia forte appropriatio non valuit propter ordinem Urbani et cetera.

Hic deficiunt due provisiones que sunt infra in sequenti pagina in principio.

De prebenda de Pilton' (Pelton) in ecclesia collegiata Cestrie in strata ex causa acceptationis auctoritate apostolica facte per Johannem de Habini fructus, folio.

Est registrator domini Eboracensis [494] (fol. 204ᵛ) [484] et habet terminum quindene Pasche ad obligandum, et concordatus et cetera. Et non reperitur taxa, sed valet viginti m. ad minus, et sic debet pro medietate veri valoris decem m., valent vi li. xiii s. iiii d.

De prebenda de Schildon' (Shildon) ex causa provisionis per expectationem facte Thome de Salkilt fructus, folio et cetera.

Sed possidetur titulo ordinario per Johannem Boring', ut dicitur, et nunc per dictum Thomam. Et videatur bene quia tarde fuit exploratum pro taxa. Debetur, ut dicitur, xvi li. Est mandatum in ultimo quia tarde exploratum.

De ecclesia de Hougton' alias Hochton' (Houghton-le-Spring) diocesis Dunolmensis, taxata iiiiˣˣ vi li. xiii s. iiii d.,[495] ex causa provisionis facte Petro Sancti Eustachii diacono cardinali xix kalendas Setempbris per Gregorium anno primo [496] fructus, folio et cetera.[497]

De archidiaconatu et prebenda [498] ecclesia Dunolmensis ex causa provisionis facte cardinali Jacobo de Ursinis [499] xviii kalendas Maii per Gregorium anno iiii [500] fructus, qui estimantur ducente li., et sic debetur hic centum li., c li. Et debet pro annexa cxx li., et sic debet pro toto iiᶜ xx li.[495]

Citati sunt Rogerus de Ripon, procurator dicti cardinalis, et Dominus Willelmus de Claxton' miles et Walterus de Hawibi', firmarii ecclesie de Hestington' (Easington) annexe archidiaconatui, sed dictus cardinalis est relaxatus per cameram et ibi debet solvere, et videtur si solvit.[501]

Resta pagine iiiᶜ xxix li. vi s. viii d.[490]

(fol. 205, lxii) Summa universalis omnium restarum vacantium beneficiorum civitatis et diocesis Dunolmensis ixᶜ viii li. xiii s. iiii d.; iiii beneficia non taxata.[490]

### (fol. 205ᵛ) Diocesis Karleolensis

De ecclesia de Ulvesbi (Ousby) ex causa provisionis facte Symoni de Querton' v kalendas Januarii per Gregorium anno quarto [502] pro taxa xi li. xix s., folio et cetera.

Litigatur in curia cum uno regio, et iuravit quod, lite sopita si optineat, infra mensem veniret concordare de primis fructibus et cetera. Idem iuravit facere de prebenda quam habet seu habere debet in ecclesia collegiata de Landewibrevii (Llandewi Brefi) diocesis Menevensis statim quando habuit possessionem pacificam. Bullas tamen perdidit, ut dicitur, et misit ad rescribendum. Et est familiaris domini de Novivilla (?) et cetera.

De vicaria de Crostwait (Crosthwaite) ex causa provisionis facte Willelmo de Hushugdon' ii idus Julii anno viii per Innocentium [503] pro taxa xx li.,[495] folio et cetera.

Prohibitum est cum breve regio in restis antiquis, sed nescitur causa quare, et videatur iterato ut sciatur causa quare.

Resta pagine xxxi li. xix s.

Summa restarum vacantium beneficiorum civitatis et diocesis Karleolensis xxxi li. xix s.[490]

Summa universalis omnium restarum vacantium beneficiorum collatorum in civitatibus et diocesibus Eboracensi, Dunolmensi et Karleolensi iiᵐ ixᶜ viii li. xv s. sterlingorum; xiiii beneficia nondum taxata reperta.[490]

(fol. 206, lxiii) Summa summarum universalis omnium restarum vacantium beneficiorum provinciarum Cantuariensis et Eboracensis et suffraganeorum ipsorum prout supra particulariter patet per civitates et dioceses xᵐ ixᶜ lxxxxv li. x s. v d. ob. sterlingorum; xlii beneficia nondum reperta taxata.[490]

Quarum xᵐ ixᶜ xcv li. x s. v d. ob. sunt de restis restantibus vacantium beneficiorum de quibus reddiderat rationem in aliis compotis proxime precedentibus m viᶜ xvii li. xvii s. xi d. ob. sterlingorum.

Item sunt tam de beneficiis que non reperiebantur in aliis computis suis proxime precendentibus ista compota taxata ad decimam que modo in istis compotis reddidit pro taxatis quam de aliis beneficiis collatis a die xxvii Julii anni LXXIIII usque ad vi diem Martii anni ab incarnatione domini M CCC LXXVII [504] in civitatibus et diocesibus et provinciis Cantuariensibus et Eboracensibus de quibus alias non computaverat ixᵐ iiiᶜ lxxviii li. xii s. vi d. sterlingorum.

### (fol. 206ᵛ) Reste denariorum Beati Petri

Sequntur reste denariorum Beati Petri de annis domini millesimo CCCᵐᵒ LXX tertio, quarto, quinto et sexto [505] usque ad sextam diem Martii anni ab incarnatione et cetera LXXVII, qua die de Anglia recessit Arnaldus Garnerii et cetera.

### Herfordensis

Et primo debet dominus episcopus Herfordensis, nunc episcopus Londoniensis, pro denariis Beati Petri annorum domini et cetera LXX tertii et quarti, pro

---

[494] At the foot of the page: *Resta pagine lxiii li. vi s. viii d.* In the margin: *vera.*

[495] Sum repeated MS.

[496] 14 August 1371.

[497] In the margin: *Cardinalis Sancti Eustachii.*

[498] *prebende*, MS.

[499] James Orsini, deacon of S. Giorgio in Velabro.

[500] 14 April 1374.

[501] In the margin: *Cardinalis de Ursinis.* **Sum repeated MS.**

[502] 28 December 1374.

[503] 14 July 1360.

[504] Followed by *de qui* deleted by a line.

[505] *et septimo* inserted above the line and deleted by a line.

quolibet anno sex li., et sic debet duodecim li., et sic restant hic xii li.[495]

### Sarisbiriensis

Dominus episcopus Sarisbiriensis debet pro anno LXX quarto pro tempore predecessoris sui dictos denarios Beati Petri, videlicet decem et septem li. Et debet pro anno LXX sexto pro se ipso decem et septem li. Somma quam debet pro dictis duobus annis xxiiii li.

### Exoniensis

Episcopus Exoniensis debet pro anno LXXVI novem li. quinque s., ix li. v s.

### Norwicensis

Episcopus Norwicensis debet de resta ultra viginti li. solutas pro anno LXX quarto triginta s. sterlingorum. Et debet pro anno LXXV viginti unam li. decem s. Et debet pro alio anno sexto xxi li. x s. Summa totalis xliiii li. x s.

### Herfordensis

Episcopus Herfordensis qui nunc est debet pro annis LXXV et sexto, pro quolibet anno sex li. Valent xii li.[495] sterlingorum. Et debet plus in principio supra.

Resta pagine cxi li. xv s.[490]

### (fol. 207, lxiiii) Roffensis

Archidiaconus Roffensis pro annis LXXIIII, quinto et sexto quinque li. duodecim s. pro quolibet anno. Valent xvi li. xvi s., de quibus solvit diu est viginti unum s. quatuor d. pro anno LXXIIII, et sic restat debens ad huc xv li. xiiii s. viii d., de quibus solvit post die xiiii Setempbris anno et cetera LXXVII iiii[or] li. x s. viii d., et hoc pro resta dicti anni LXXIIII, et sic est ad huc in istis restis pro xi li. iiii s. sterlingorum,[506] de quibus solvit post in partem dicti quinti anni quinque m. que [507] valent lxvi s. viii d. Et sic restant vii li. xvii s. iiii d.[495]

### Londoniensis

Archidiaconus Middelsexie debet pro anno LXXVI quinque li. decem s., v li. x s.

### Cantuariensis

Archidiaconus Cantuariensis debet pro anno LXXIIII de resta viii li. quia de quinto et vi annis solvit.

Resta pagine xxi li. vii s. iiii d.[490]

(fol. 207[v]) Sequntur reste census de anno ab incarnatione domini millesimo CCC[mo] septuagesimo sexto

### Wintoniensis

Abbas de Chertesey pro anno LXXVI[o] octo s.

---

[506] *sterlis*, MS.
[507] *qui*, MS.

### Karleolensis

Prior Karleolensis pro anno LXXVI[o] tresdecim s. quatuor d., xiii s. iiii d.

Resta pagine xxi s. iiii d.[490]

(fol. 208[v])[508] Sequntur nomina illorum qui tenentur solvere denarios Beati Petri quolibet anno et primo de anno ab incarnatione domini millesimo CCC[mo] LXXVII quia supra est de restis aliorum annorum precedentium.

Episcopus Cicestrensis debet quolibet anno octo li., viii li. Solvit pro anno LXXVII ut supra in recepta habetur et ibi vide.

Episcopus Sarisbiriensis debet etiam decem et septem li., xvii li.

Episcopus Batoniensis et Wellensis undecim li. quinque s., xi li. v s. Solvit pro dicto anno LXXVII ut supra in recepta habetur.

Episcopus Exoniensis novem li. quinque s., ix li. v s.

Episcopus Norwicensis viginti unam li. x s., xxi li. x s.

Episcopus Lincolniensis debet xlii li. de anno LXXVII, xlii li.

Episcopus Lichefeldensis decem li. quinque s., x li. v s.

Episcopus Herfordensis sex li., vi li.

Episcopus Wigorniensis decem li. quinque s., x li. v s.

Archiepiscopus Eboracensis undecim li. decem s., xi li. x s.

Resta pagine pro anno et cetera LXXVII cxxvii li. xv s. ultra soluta suprascripta.[490]

(fol. 209, lxvii) Archidiaconus Cantuariensis octo li., viii li.

Archidiaconus Roffensis quinque li. duodecim s., v li. xii s.

Archidiaconus Colcestrie quinque li. decem s., v li. x s.

Archidiaconus Assesie quinque li. decem s., v li. x s.

Archidiaconus Middelsexie quinque li. decem s., v li. x s.

Archidiaconus Wintoniensis undecim li. tresdecim s. iiii[or] d., xi li. xiii s. iiii d.

Archidiaconus Eliensis quinque li., v li.

Archidiaconus Surreie in ecclesia Wintoniensi quinque li. xiii[cim] s. iiii d., v li. xiii s. iiii d. Solvit pro anno LXXVII ut supra in recepta habetur.

Resta pagine pro anno LXXVII xlvi li. xv s. iiii d.[490]

### (fol. 209[v]) Resta census anno LXXVII

Sequntur nomina illorum qui tenentur solvere annuum censum quolibet anno et primo de anno ab incarnatione domini M[o] CCC[mo] LXXVII

### Lincolniensis

Dominus abbas Sancti Albani xiii s. iiii d. Solvit supra in recepta de dicto anno LXXVII.

---

[508] Folio 208 recto is blank.

Cantuariensis

Dominus abbas de Faveresham xiii s. iiii d.

Wintoniensis

Abbas de Chertesey viii s.

Norwicensis

Dominus abbas Edmundi de Bury xiii s. iiii d. Solvit de anno LXXVII ut supra in recepta habetur.

Sarisbiriensis

Abbas de Malmesbury xiii s. iiii d. Solvit de anno LXXVII ut supra in recepta.

Exoniensis

Prior de Bodmyn ii s.

Roffensis

Prior de Tornabruggi xiii s. iiii d. Solvit de anno LXXVII ut supra in recepta habetur.

Karleolensis

Prior Karleolensis xiii s. iiii d.

Eliensis

Prior de Angleseya ii s. Solvit pro anno et cetera LXXVII ut supra in recepta.

Eboracensis

Custos de Scardeburgth' xv d. Solvit de anno LXXVII supra in recepta habetur.

Lincolniensis

Prior de Chamcombe xv d. Solvit pro anno LXXVII ut habetur supra in recepta.

Londoniensis

Abbatissa[509] Sancte Clare vi d. Solvit de anno domini et cetera LXXVII ut supra in isto eodem libro habetur in recepta. Alii suprascripti sunt in istis restis. Resta pagine xxxvi s. viii d.

(fol. 210, lxvii) Lincolniensis

Magister ordinis de Sempyngham diocesis Lincolniensis debet de duobus in duobus annis in festo apostolorum Petri et Pauli, ut ipse magister dicit, de censu annuo camere apostolice unam marcam auri que communiter valet novem li. quindecim s. sterlingorum, quas solvit anno domini et cetera LXXV<sup>to</sup> die xiii Junii, ut habetur in libro recepte folio lxxxiiii. Et sic debet solvere in

---

[509] *Abbatisse*, MS.

festo Sancti Johannis anni[510] LXXVII aliam marcam que[511] valet communiter ix li. xv s., quam marcam solvit die xxii Maii anno et cetera LXXVII, salvo iure pluris et minoris valentie dicte marche. Et sic est in istis restis pro tempore futuro, non preterito, et debet solvere anno et cetera LXXIX in dicto termino pro dicta marca novem li. quindecim s.[512]

Usque hic fuit corectum cum restis aliis dimissis Londonie et hic penitus consimilibus die xxv Februarii, et iterato xx quinta die Julii anno a nativitate Christi et cetera LXXVIII fuit corectum Avinionie, et iterato etiam Avinionie de mense Octobris dicto anno LXXVIII cum ista copia.

Et corigatur melius cum reddetur liber iste vel consimilis camere propter ea que ex post, siqua sint, supervenerunt. Et semper fiat corectio salvo erore calculi.[513]

(fol. 210<sup>v</sup>) Summa universalis omnium restarum debitarum tam de denariis Beati Petri quam de aliis censibus debitis in Anglia annis LXXIII, LXXIIII, LXXV, LXXVI et LXXVII prout particulariter supra declaratur et continetur est iii<sup>c</sup> x li. x[514] s. viii d. sterlingorum.[515]

Soma restarum universalis xii<sup>m</sup> iii<sup>c</sup> xii li. vi d.[516]

(fol. 211, lxviii) Soma universalis restarum camere.

Somma universalis restarum omnium camere apostolice pertinentium ratione subsidii et primorum fructuum vel denariorum Beati Petri et annui census et alias quovismodo debitarum usque ad diem sextam Martii anno ab incarnatione domini millesimo CCC septuagesimo septimo duodecim milia ducentas et septuaginta novem li. decem[517] s. i d. ob. sterlingorum,[518] xii<sup>m</sup> ii<sup>c</sup> lxxix li. x s. i d. ob;[519] xlii beneficia nondum reperta taxata. Que valent, singulo floreno ponderis camere pro tribus solidis computando, octuaginta et duo milia et octuaginta fl. vel circa, lxxxi<sup>m</sup> viii<sup>c</sup> lxiii fl.[520] xiii d. ob. sterlingorum.

Et ultra dictam summam sunt plus supra in dictis restis plura beneficia nondum in ipso libro restarum taxata, scilicet xlii, de quibus etiam est ibi attendendum et cum diligentia sicut fieri potest explorandum.

Salvo semper erore calculi.

(fol. 211<sup>v</sup>) Ab priori de Castellario.

---

[510] Followed by *currentis* deleted by a line.

[511] *qui*, MS.

[512] In the margin: *pro memorando*.

[513] At the foot of the page: *Resta pagine ix li. xv s.* deleted by a line. In the margin: *vera*.

[514] Over *v* deleted by a dot.

[515] In the margin: *vera*. Also in the margin: *qui sunt vi li.* preceded by a word which is lost by a trimmed margin.

[516] In the margin: *xv die Novembris usque hic*. A preceding word is lost.

[517] Over *quinque* deleted by a line.

[518] *sterlis*, MS.

[519] In the margin: *vera*.

[520] Followed by a word deleted by a line so heavily that it is illegible.

Reddidit dictus collector instrumentum obligationis prioris de Castellario (Castle Acre) continentem summam reste iiii$^c$ lxxxiiii li. ix s. vii d., ut in breveto etiam continetur, et est de restis etiam antiquis que nondum potuerunt habere.[521]

(fol. 222)[522] Pro camera apostolica de Anglia.[523]

Liber compotorum collectoris Anglie, videlicet Arnaldi Garnerii, redditus camere apostolice de receptis, solutis, redditis et assignatis per eum a die vicesima septima Julii anno domini millesimo trecentesimo septuagesimo quarto usque ad sextam diem Martii anno ab incarnatione domini millesimo CCC$^{mo}$ septuagesimo septimo. Et est hic brevetus etiam.

(fol. 223)[524] Secunda copia. Recepta et asignata et reddita.

(fol. 224$^v$)[525] Compota de receptis et de redditis et asignatis.

Compota collectoris Anglie sunt hic de receptis et redditis et solutis et assignatis per eum nomine et mandato Domini Gregorii pape undecimi, seu dominorum camerarii et thesaurarii eiusdem, a die vicesima septima Julii anno ab nativitate domini millesimo CCC$^{mi}$ LXX$^{mi}$ quarti usque ad sextam diem Martii anni domini millesimi CCC$^{mi}$ LXX$^{mi}$ septimi, salvo erore calculi et provisionum inutilium et male solventium, de quibus habetur infra in alio libro restarum eidem camere apostolice per eundem collectorem modo concimili cum isto reddito folio[526] tertio et sequentibus usque ad folium lxviii.[527]

(fol. 225, iii) Recepta.

Sequitur recepta restarum primorum fructuum a die xx$^{ma}$ septima Jullii anno domini millesimo CCC$^{mo}$ septuagesimo quarto facta per Dominum Arnaldum Garnerii ut collectorem Anglie, seu per locumtenentem suum, usque ad diem sextam mensis Martii anno[528] ab incarnatione[528] domini millesimo CCC$^o$ septuagesimo vii$^o$, qua die sexta ultimo de Londonia in Anglia recessit versus curiam Romanam.

### Cantuariensis

Primo recepit pro capella libera de Bokmesfeld' (Bockingfold) diocesis Cantuariensis tunc dimissa in solidis fructibus ex causa provisionis facte David **Wingham per Innocentium anno decimo**[529] in iiii$^{or}$ m.

ix s. viii d. et ob. sexaginta tres s. et obolum, folio tertio in libro recepte habetur, lxiii s. ob.

### Londoniensis

Item recepit dictus collector de prebenda Sancti Pancratii in ecclesia Sancti Pauli Londonie, que fuit dimissa in resta dicto anno pro viginti s. sterlingorum, folio tertio, xx s. sterlingorum.

### Cicestrensis

Item de prebenda de Mildeton' (Middleton) in ecclesia Cicestrensi, que fuit dimissa in restis pro viginti sex s. viii d., folio quarto, xxvi s. viii d.

### Vintoniensis

Item decepit in diversis vicibus de prioratu de Appullercombe (Appuldurcombe), dimisso in restis pro viginti quinque li. decem et septem s., decem et septem li. decem s. sterlingorum,[530] folio quarto, xvii li. x s.

### Lincolniensis

Item recepit de prebenda de Walton' rivaux (Welton Rivall) in ecclesia Lincolniensi per manus locumtenentis in partem fructuum, folio vii$^o$, sexaginta sex s. viii d., iii li. vi s. viii d.

### Lincolniensis

Item recepit de prebenda Sancte Crucis (Spaldwick) in ecclesia Lincolniensi dimissa in restis pro quinquaginta s., folio septimo,[531] l s.

Summa pagine xxviii li. xvi s. iiii d. et ob.[532]

### (fol. 225$^v$) Lincolniensis

De ecclesia de Gosyngton' (Cossington) Lincolniensis diocesis, dimissa in restis pro octo li., folio octo, recepit in tribus vicibus quinque li. sex s. octo d. sterlingorum,[530] v li. vi s. viii d.

### Lichfeldensis

De prioratu de Kerkebi (Monks Kirby), dimisso in restis pro triginta sex li. decem s. octo d., folio ix, recepit in duabus vicibus sexdecim li. decem s., xvi li. x s.

### Eboracensis

De prebenda de Driffeld in ecclesia Eboracensi domini cardinalis Sancti Martialis[533] dimissa in restis folio x pro centum li. de taxa, recepit xxv li., viginti quinque li. sterlingorum, xxv li.

### Lichfeldensis

De ecclesia de Hedeneth' (Hodnet) Lichfeldensis

---

[521] See above, p. 497.

[522] Folios 212 to 221 verso are blank. This folio is the outside of the parchment cover of what was originally a separate codex.

[523] Heading repeated at the foot of the page.

[524] Folio 222 verso is blank.

[525] Folios 223 verso and 224 recto are blank.

[526] Followed by *quinquagesimo* deleted by a line.

[527] The next preceding report of Arnald, above, pp. 484-519.

[528] Followed by a word deleted so heavily by a line as to be illegible.

[529] 30 December 1361 to 12 September 1362.

[530] *sterlis,* MS.

[531] *septimo* repeated MS.

[532] In the margin: *vera.*

[533] Hugo de St. Martial, deacon of S. Maria in Portico.

diocesis et aliis quatuor beneficiis obligatis et in restis dimissis, folio xii, pro quindecim li. et quindecim s. solvit Nicholaus Leth' in duabus vicibus dictam restam, videlicet xv li. xv s.

### Eboracensis

De prebenda de Munkton' (Monkton) in ecclesia de Ripen' (Ripon) dimissa in restis pro xl m., folio xiiiº, solvit Adam de Torinton' in tribus vicibus dictam restam, videlicet viginti sex li. tresdecim s. iiii d., xxvi li. xiii s. iiii d.

### Londoniensis

De parochiali ecclesia de Altarothinge (High Roding) Londoniensis diocesis dimissa in restis folio xv pro duodecim li. solvit possessor eiusdem sex li. steringorum.[534]

### Herfordensis

De prebenda ecclesie Herfordensis dimissa in restis pro viginti s. folio xv solvit possessor eiusdem viginti s., xx s.

### Wigorniensis

De ecclesia de Staunton' folio xvii solvit Johannes Banneburi alias Fisher ex causa provisionis sibi facte quatuor li. sex s. viii d., iiii li. vi s. viii d. Et tamen debetur de alia provisione eodem folio in restis dimissa.
Summa pagine c li. xi s. viii d.[532]

### (fol. 226, iiii) Sarisbiriensis

De archidiaconatu de Barkschur' in ecclesia Sarisbiriensi dimisso in restis pro quadraginta li. folio xviii solvit possessor dictas quadraginta li., xl li.

### Norwicensis

De parochiali ecclesia de Multon' (Moulton) dimissa in restis folio xviii pro tresdecim li. sex s. octo d. solvit possessor dictam restam, videlicet xiii li. vi s. viii d.

### Lichfeldensis

De decanatu et prebenda in ecclesia Sancti Johannis Cestrie dimissis in restis folio xx pro decem li. solvit possessor dictam ⟨restam⟩ videlicet decem li., x li.

### Wellensis

De ecclesia de Templecumbe (Templecombe) dimissa in restis pro tribus li. folio xxi solvit possessor in duabus vicibus dictam restam, videlicet tres li., iii li.

### Lincolniensis

De ecclesia de Horwode magna (Great Horwood)

dimissa in restis pro decem li. folio xxi solvit Johannes Stret in quatuor vicibus dictam restam videlicet decem li., x li.

### Norwicensis

De ecclesia de Fornham Sancti Martini dimissa in restis pro tribus [535] li. sex s. octo d. folio xxiii solvit possessor dictos sexaginta sex s. octo d., iii li. vi s. viii d.

### Eboracensis

De decanatu et prebenda de Northnewbold' (North Newbald) dimissis in restis pro viginti li. folio xxvi solvit dictam restam, videlicet xx li.

### Eboracensis

De vicaria ecclesie de Hesill' (Hessle) dimissa in restis folio xxiii pro tresdecim li. sex s. viii d. solvit possessor xiii li. vi s. viii d.

### Lincolniensis

De prebenda de Schamelesby (Scamblesby) cum annexa de Melton' Ros (Melton Ross) dimissa in restis folio xxvi pro triginta tribus li. sex s. octo d. solvit possessor in quatuor vicibus dictam restam, scilicet xxxiii li. vi s. viii d.
Somma pagine cxlvi li. vi s. viii d.[532]

### (fol. 226ᵛ) Lincolniensis

De decanatu et prebenda in ecclesia Lincolniensi qui fuerunt cardinalis Cantuariensis dimissis in restis in solidis fructibus folio xxvi solvit procurator dicti cardinalis et pro certis aliis etiam suis beneficiis centum triginta tres li. sex s. octo d., cxxxiii li. vi s. viii d.

### Dunolmensis

De vicaria ecclesie de Norham dimissa in restis antiquis folio xxviii pro octo li. tresdecim s. quatuor d. solvit possessor in quatuor vicibus dictam restam viii li. xiii s. iiii d.

### Lincolniensis

De prebenda de Leyton Bruneswold' (Leighton Bromswold) in ecclesia Lincolniensi dimissa in restis folio xxix pro viginti li. solvit in tribus vicibus possessor dictam restam, videlicet xx li.

### Wigorniensis

De archidiaconatu Gloucestrie in ecclesia Wigorniensi dimisso in restis folio xxix pro duodecim li. tresdecim s. quatuor d. solvit possessor dictam restam, videlicet xii li. xiii s. iiii d.

### Landavensis

De canonicatu et prebenda in ecclesia Landavensi non

---

[534] Sum repeated twice.

[535] *tribus* repeated and deleted by a line, MS.

taxatis folio xxix dimissis in restis pro viginti s. solvit possessor in plenam solutionem medietatis veri valoris restam, videlicet viginti s., xx s.

### Sarisbiriensis

De canonicatu et prebenda in ecclesia Sarisbiriensi folio xxx dimissis in restis pro sexdecim li. tresdecim s. quatuor [536] d. solvit possessor in tribus vicibus dictam restam, videlicet xvi li. xiii s. iiii d.

### Dunolmensis

De decanatu ecclesie collegiate Cestrie in strata (Chester-le-Street) dimisso in restis pro sex li. tresdecim s. quatuor d. folio xxx solvit possessor dictam restam, videlicet vi li. xiii s. iiii d.

Summa pagine clxxxix li.[532]

### (fol. 227, v) Eboracensis

De vicaria ecclesie de Massam (Masham) folio xxxi dimissa in restis pro decem et octo li. solvit possessor dictam restam, videlicet xviii li.

### Lichfeldensis

De canonicatu et prebenda de Langedon' (Longdon) in ecclesia Lichefeldensi folio xxxiii dimissis in restis pro taxa viginti li. solvit posssessor in partem dicte reste tresdecim li. sex s. octo d., xiii li. vi s. viii d.

### Cantuariensis

De prepositura ecclesie collegiate de Wingham folio xxxiii dimissa in restis pro triginta li. solvit possessor de dicta resta viginti quinque li., xxv li. Restant v li.

### Assavensis

De canonicatu et prebenda ecclesie Assavensis folio xxxiii dimissis in restis pro solidis fructibus solvit in partem dicte reste decem s., x s.

### Cantuariensis

De ecclesia de Bidengdon' (Biddenden) folio xxxiiii dimissa in restis pro solidis fructibus solvit possessor in plenam solutionem taxe viginti li., xx li.

### Norwicensis

De ecclesia de Estderham (East Dereham) folio xxxv dimissa in restis pro quadraginta sex li. tresdecim s. quatuor d. solvit de dicta resta in tribus vicibus triginta octo li. sex s. octo d., xxxviii li. vi s. viii d.

### Sarisbiriensis

De prebenda de Combearulam (Combe and Harn-

---

[536] *quator*, MS.

---

ham) folio xxxv dimissa in restis pro solidis fructibus solvit in curia et hic in plenam solutionem taxe in xx[ti] m. tresdecim li. sex s. viii d., de quibus Dominus H. de Bodio habuit in curia novem li. pro lx fl. et ego collector habui Londonie iiii[or] li. vi s. viii d. sterlingorum.

### Londoniensis

De prebenda de Cheswik (Chiswick) dimissa in restis folio xxxvi pro solidis fructibus solvit possessor sex li., vi li.

Summa pagine cxxv li. x s.[532]

### (fol. 227[v]) Dunolmensis

De vicaria de Bilingham (Billingham) dimissa in restis pro solidis fructibus folo xxxvii solvit possessor in plenam solutionem taxe quinque li., v li.

### Eboracensis

De canonicatu et prebenda in ecclesia collegiata Ripon' Eboracensis diocesis folio xxxvii dimissis in restis pro decem li. solvit de dicta resta septem li. et decem s., vii li. x s.

### Norwicensis, Lincolniensis

De prioratu Creting' (Creeting St. Mary) et Eworden' (Everdon) dimissis in restis pro solidis fructibus folio xxxviii solvit in partem fructuum quinquaginta quinque s., lv s.

### Eboracensis

De ecclesia de Heversham folio xxxviii dimissa in restis pro triginta tribus li. sex s. octo d. solvit dictam restam, videlicet xxxiii li. vi s. viii d.

### Sarisbiriensis

De prebenda de Cherdestok (Chardstock) in ecclesia Sarisbiriensi folio xxxix dimissa in restis pro novem li. sex s. viii d. solvit dictam restam, scilicet ix li. vi s. viii d.

### Sarisbiriensis

De ecclesia de Wyli (Wylye) folio xxxviii solvit Rogerus Dawe pro taxa decem li., x li.

### Norwicensis

De ecclesia de Saxham folio xxxix dimissa in restis pro solidis fructibus solvit possessor in partem fructuum tresdecim s. quatuor d., xiii s. iiii d.

### Lichfeldensis

De prebenda in ecclesia collegiata Sancti Johannis Cestrie diocesis Lichfeldensis folio xxxix dimissa in restis pro solidis fructibus solvit in partem fructuum sex li. tresdecim s. iiii[or] d., vi li. xiii s. iiii d.

#### Menevensis

De vicaria de Nannaol (Llanhowell?) folio xl dimissa in restis pro tribus li. sex s. octo d. solvit dictam restam, videlicet iii li. vi s. viii d.

Summa pagine lxxviii li. xi s. viii d.[532]

#### (fol. 228, vi) Sarisbiriensis

De prebenda de Leomynstre (Beminster?) ecclesie Sarisbiriensis folio xl dimissa in restis pro novem li. tresdecim s. quatuor d. solvit dictam restam, scilicet ix li. xiii s. iiii d.

#### Exoniensis

De prioratu de Tywardrath' (Tywardreath) folio xlii dimisso in restis pro viginti una li. tresdecim s. quatuor d. solvit dictam restam, scilicet xxi li. xiii s. iiii d.

#### Lincolniensis

De prebenda de Bedeford minori folio xliiii dimissa in restis pro solidis fructibus solvit possessor in plenam solutionem fructuum quatuor li. sex s. octo d., iiii li. vi s. viii d.

#### Cantuariensis

De ecclesia de Orpington' folio xlvi dimissa in restis pro viginti sex li. tresdecim s. iiii[or] d. solvit dictam restam, scilicet xxvi li. xiii s. iiii d.

#### Sarisbiriensis

De ecclesia de Fovente (Fovant) folio xlvi dimissa in restis pro sex li. tresdecim s. quatuor d. solvit dictam restam, scilicet vi li. xiii s. iiii d.

#### Sarisbiriensis

De ecclesia de Cnoel (Knoyle) folio xlvii dimissa in restis pro tresdecim li. sex s. octo d. solvit dictam restam, videlicet xiii li. vi s. viii d.

#### Landavensis

De precentoria ecclesie Landavensis folio xlvii dimissa in restis pro quatuor li. septem s. octo solvit dictam restam quatuor li. vii s. viii d.[537]

#### Wellensis

De prebenda in Combe in ecclesia Wellensi dimissa in restis pro taxa quinque li. sex s. octo d. solvit possessor, videlicet Ricardus de Derdrabinton', dictam taxam, videlicet v li. vi s. viii d.

Summa pagine xcii li. xii d.[532]

(fol. 228ᵛ) Summa omnium receptorum per dictum collectorem de restis restantibus de vacantibus beneficiorum collatorum in civitatibus et diocesibus predictis,

de quibus alias fuerat computatum per eum, viiᶜ lxx li. xvii s. iiii d. ob. sterlingorum.

(fol. 229, vii) Recepta reste exploratorum

#### Eboracensis

De vicaria ecclesie de Alverton' folio liii dimissa in restis pro decem li. tresdecim s. quatuor d. solvit dictam restam, scilicet x li. xiii s. iiii d.

#### Cantuariensis [538]

De vicaria de Faveresham (Faversham) folio liii dimissa in restis pro quindecim li. solvit possessor in tribus vicibus dictam restam, videlicet quindecim li., xv li.

De ecclesia Sancte Marie Magdalene Cantuarie folio liii dimissa in restis pro duabus li. tresdecim s. quatuor d. solvit dictam restam in duabus vicibus, videlicet ii li. xiii s. iiii d.

De vicaria de Eleham (Elham) folio liiii dimissa in restis pro decem li. solvit in quatuor vicibus in partem fructuum octo li. tresdecim s. quatuor d., viii li. xiii s. iiii d.

#### Londoniensis

De ecclesia de Abchirche (Saint Mary Abchurch) Londonie folio liiii dimissa in restis pro duabus li. tresdecim s. quatuor d. solvit dictam restam, scilicet ii li. xiii s. iiii d.

#### Wintoniensis

De ecclesia de Hoghton' (Houghton Drayton) folio liiii dimissa in restis pro decem li. solvit possessor dictam restam, videlicet decem li., x li.

#### Lincolniensis

De ecclesia de Sutton', (Sutton le Marsh) taxata duodecim li. sex s. octo d., in marisco, folio lv dimissa in restis pro solidis fructibus solvit possessor in plenam solutionem taxe duodecim li. sex s. octo d., xii li. vi s. viii d.

#### Cicestrensis

De vicaria ecclesie de Boseham (Bosham) folio lv dimissa in restis pro solidis fructibus solvit in tribus vicibus in plenam solutionem taxe quatuor li. sex s. octo d., iiii li. vi s. viii d.

Summa pagine lxvi li. vi s. viii d.[539]

#### (fol. 229ᵛ) Eboracensis

De ecclesia de Foston' folio lv dimissa in restis pro sex li. tresdecim s. quatuor d. solvit dictam restam, videlicet vi li. xiii s. iiii d.

---

[537] Sum repeated MS.

[538] The heading is repeated before each of the next two items, MS.

[539] In the margin: *vera*.

### Eboracensis

De vicaria ecclesie de Topclif (Topcliffe) folio lvi dimissa in restis pro sex li. tresdecim s. quatuor d. solvit in duabus vicibus dictam restam vi li. xiii s. iiii d.

### Lichfeldensis

De prioratu de Rompton' (Ranton) folio lvi dimisso in restis pro viginti quinque li. octo d. solvit in duabus vicibus dictam restam, videlicet xxv li. viii d.

### Eliensis

De ecclesia de Hinton' (Cherry Hinton) folio lvi dimissa in restis pro viginti li. solvit possessor dictam restam, videlicet xx li.

### Cicestrensis

De vicaria de Cokfeld (Cuckfield) folio lvi dimissa in restis pro tribus li. sex s. octo d. solvit dictam restam, videlicet iii li. vi s. viii d.

### Norwicensis

De ecclesia de Colton', taxata decem li., folio lvii dimissa in restis pro solidis fructibus solvit possessor in duabus vicibus pro dicta taxa decem li., x li.

### Sarisbiriensis

De ecclesia de Watereton' (Water Eaton) folio lxvii dimissa in restis pro solidis fructibus solvit possessor sexaginta sex s. octo d., lxvi s. viii d.

### Lincolniensis

De ecclesia de Wexham folio lviii dimissa in restis pro solidis fructibus solvit in duabus vicibus in plenam solutionem taxe sex li. tresdecim s. iiiior d., vi li. xiii s. iiii d.

### Eboracensis

De subdecanatu Eboracensi folio lviii dimisso in restis pro quadraginta li. solvit in tribus vicibus dictam restam, videlicet xl li.

Summa pagine cxxi li. xiiii s.[539]

### (fol. 230, viii) Eboracensis

De prebenda de Norwell' alias Palishale in ecclesia collegiata de Soutwell' Eboracensis diocesis, taxata quadraginta m., folio lviii dimissa in restis pro solidis fructibus solvit possessor, scilicet Radulphus de Cetren', ex causa acceptationis auctoritate apostolica per eum facte, xii die Maii anno et cetera LXXVII in partem fructuum tresdecim li. sex s. octo d., xiii li. vi s. viii d.

### Dunolmensis

De prebenda in ecclesia collegiata Cestrie super stratam (Chester-le-Street) folio lix dimissa in restis pro sexdecim li. tresdecim s. iiiior d. solvit in quatuor vicibus de dicta resta tresdecim li. sex s. viii d., xiii li. vi s. viii d.

### Sarisbiriensis

De prebenda de Slape folio lix dimissa in restis pro solidis fructibus solvit possessor in plenam solutionem taxe tresdecim li. sex s. octo d., xiii li. vi s. viii d.

### Wigorniensis

De ecclesia de Hamburi (Hanbury) folio lix dimissa in restis pro undecim li. sex s. octo d. solvit dictam restam, videlicet xi li. vi s. viii d.

### Exoniensis

De vicaria de Brodhimburi (Broadhembury) folio lx dimissa in restis pro solidis fructibus solvit in plenam solutionem medietatis veri valoris quadraginta tres s. quatuor d., xliii s. iiii d.

### Lincolniensis

De prebenda Cliston' (Clifton) folio lx dimissa in restis pro tresdecim li. sex s. octo d. solvit in duabus vicibus dictam restam, scilicet xiii li. vi s. viii d.

### Eboracensis

De ecclesia de Hornsee (Hornsea) folio lx dimissa in restis pro triginta tribus li. sex s. octo d. solvit in duabus vicibus xxxiii li. vi s. viii d.

Et solvit etiam pro fructibus male perceptis de eadem ecclesia xxxvii s. v d.[540] Et sic solvit pro toto triginta quinque li. iiiior s. i d., xxxv li. iiii s. i d.

Summa pagine cii li. ix d.[539]

### (fol. 230v) Lincolniensis

De prebenda de Thame folio lxi dimissa in restis pro solidis fructibus solvit Dominus Egidius Sanctii, procuratoris domini cardinaliis Sancti Martialis[541] possessoris dicte prebende, in partem fructuum viginti octo li., xxviii li.

### Lincolniensis

De prebenda de Milton manerii (Milton Manor) folio lx dimissa in restis pro solidis fructibus solvit in tribus vicibus in plenam solutionem taxe quadraginta sex li. tresdecim s. iiiior d., xlvi li. xiii s. iiii d.

### Sarisbiriensis

De ecclesia de Porteslond' (Portland) folio lxi dimissa in restis pro duodecim li. tresdecim s. quatuor d. solvit in duabus vicibus xii li. xiii s. iiii d.

### Exoniensis

De prebenda de Hensthill' et Sannford' (Henstill, Sandford) in ecclesia collegiata de Crediton' Exoniensis

---

[540] Followed by *ad eadem ecclesia* deleted by a line.
[541] Hugo de St. Martial, deacon of S. Maria in Portico.

diocesis folio lxi dimissa in restis pro tribus li. solvit in plenam solutionem medietatis veri valoris iii li.

Summa pagine xc li. vi s. viii d. sterlingorum.

Summa omnium receptorum per dictum collectorem de restis restantibus de beneficiis exploratis de quibus alias computaverat est iii<sup>c</sup> lxxx li. viii s. i d. sterlingorum.

Summa universalis omnium receptorum per dictum collectorem tam de restis restantibus vacantium beneficiorum supradictorum quam de restis restantibus vacantium exploratorum de quibus beneficiis alias fuerat per ipsum computatum mcli li. v s. v d. ob. sterlingorum.[539]

(fol. 231, ix) Sequitur recepta reste denariorum Beati Petri de anno domini millesimo CCC<sup>mo</sup> septuagesimo tertio folio sexagesimo quarto.

Primo episcopus Sarisbiriensis solvit restam dictorum denariorum de anno et cetera LXX tertio, videlicet decem et septem li., xvii li.[542]

Episcopus Bathoniensis solvit[543] restam dicti anni LXXIII, videlicet quinque li., v li.

Archidiaconus Roffensis solvit restam dicti anni, videlicet quinque li. duodecim s., v li. xii s.

Archidiaconus Colcestrie solvit restam dicti anni, videlicet quinque li. decem s., v li. x s.

Archidiaconus Wintoniensis solvit restam dicti anni, videlicet undecim li. tresdecim s. quatuor d., xi li. xiii s. iiii d.

Archidiaconus Surreie solvit restam dicti anni, videlicet quinque li. tresdecim s. quatuor d., v li. xiii s. iiii d.

Archidiaconus Eliensis solvit restam dicti anni, videlicet quinque li., v li.

Sequitur recepta annui census de anno domini millesimo CCC<sup>mo</sup> LXX<sup>o</sup> secundo et tertio folio sexaginta quatuor.

### Wintoniensis

Primo solvit abbas de Chertesey restam census dicti anni et cetera LXX tertii, videlicet octo s., viii s.

### Londoniensis

Abbatissa Sancte Clare Londoniensis solvit restam census annorum et cetera LXX secundi et tertii, videlicet pro quolibet anno sex d., xii d.

Summa pagine lv li. xvii s. viii d. sterlingorum. Summa receptorum de restis denariorum Sanct Petri et censuum.[539]

(fol. 232, x)[544] Denarii Beati Petri.

Recepta denariorum Beati Petri de anno domini et cetera LXX quarto, quinto, sexto et septimo ab incarnatione domini computando.

Primo solvit episcopus Cicestrensis folio lxxx pro annis et cetera LXX quarto, quinto, sexto et septimo, pro quolibet anno octo li., valent triginta et duas li., xxxii li.[545]

Episcopus Sarisbiriensis solvit folio lxxx pro anno et cetera LXX quinto decem et septem li., xvii li.

Et debet de anno LXXIIII pro predecessore suo ut infra in restis habetur.

Episcopus Wellensis et Bathoniensis solvit folio lxxx pro annis et cetera LXX quarto, quinto, sexto et septimo, pro quolibet anno undecim li. quinque s., valent quadraginta quinque li., xlv li.

Episcopus Exoniensis solvit folio lxxx pro annis et cetera LXX quarto, quinto, pro quolibet anno novem li. quinque s., valent decem et octo li. decem s., xviii li. x s.

Episcopus Norwicensis solvit folio lxxxi pro anno LXX quarto viginti li., xx li.[546] Et debet pro resta triginta s. et de sequentibus annis totum, ut infra in restis habetur.

Episcopus Lincolniensis solvit folio lxxxi pro annis LXX quarto, quinto et sexto, pro quolibet anno quadraginta duas li., centum et viginti sex li., cxxvi li.

Episcopus Lichfeldensis solvit folio lxxxi pro anno et cetera LXX quarto decem li. quinque s. Item solvit pro annis et cetera LXX quinto et sexto viginti li. decem s. valent xxx li. xv s.

Episcopus Wigorniensis solvit folio lxxxi pro annis et cetera LXX quarto, quinto et sexto, pro quolibet anno decem li. quinque s., ascendunt triginta li. quindecim s., xxx li. xv s.

Summa pagine iii<sup>c</sup> xx li.[539]

(fol. 232<sup>v</sup>) Archiepiscopus Eboracensis solvit folio lxxxi pro anno LXX quarto, quinto et sexto triginta quatuor li. decem s., xxxiiii li. x s., videlicet undecim li. decem s. pro quolibet anno computando.[547]

Archidiaconus Cantuariensis solvit folio lxxxi pro annis et cetera LXX quinto et sexto, pro quolibet anno octo li., ascendunt xvi li. Debet de anno LXX quarto et sequentibus ut infra in restis habetur.

Archidiaconus Roffensis solvit folio lxxxi pro anno LXX quarto quinque li. duodecim s., v li. xii s. Item plus solvit sexaginta sex s. octo d. in partem anni LXX quinti, lxvi s. viii d.

Archidiaconus Colcestrie solvit folio lxxxi pro annis et cetera LXX quarto, quinto et sexto, pro quolibet anno quinque li. decem s., ascendunt sexdecim li. decem s., xvi li. x s.

Archidiaconus Essexie solvit folio lxxxi pro annis et cetera LXX quarto, quinto et sexto, pro quolibet anno quinque li. decem s., ascendunt sexdecim li. decem s., xvi li. x s.

---

[542] The name of each diocese appears in the margin opposite each item of Peter's pence.
[543] Followed by *pro*, MS.
[544] Folio 231 verso is blank.

[545] Against this and the following items of Peter's pence the name of the diocese appears in the margin.
[546] Sum repeated, MS.
[547] *computendo*, MS.

Archidiaconus Middelsexie solvit folio lxxxi pro annis et cetera LXX° quarto et quinto, pro quolibet quinque li. decem s., ascendunt undecim li., xi li.

Archidiaconus Wintoniensis solvit folio lxxxi pro annis et cetera LXX quarto, quinto et sexto, pro quolibet anno undecim li. tresdecim s. quatuor d., ascendunt triginta quinque li., xxxv li.

Archidiaconus Surrerie solvit folio lxxxii pro annis et cetera LXX quarto, quinto, sexto et septimo, pro quolibet anno quinque li. tresdecim s. iiiior d., ascendunt viginti duas li. tresdecim s. iiiior d., xxii li. xiii s. iiii d.

Summa pagine clxi li. ii s.[539]

(fol. 233, xi) Denarii Beati Petri.

Archidiaconus Eliensis solvit folio lxxxii pro annis et cetera LXX quarto, quinto et sexto, pro quolibet anno quinque li., ascendunt quindecim li., xv li.

Summa pagine xv li.[539]

Summa recepte denariorum Beati Petri de annis LXXIIII, LXXV, LXXVI et LXXVII iiiic lxxxxvi li. ii s. sterlingorum.[539]

(fol. 233v) Recepta annui census.

Sequitur recepta annui census de anno et cetera LXX quarto, quinto, sexto et septimo.

### Lincolniensis

Primo solvit abbas Sancti Albani folio lxxxii pro annuo censu de anno et cetera LXX quarto, quinto, sexto et septimo, pro quolibet anno tresdecim s. quatuor d., et sic solvit in toto quinquaginta tres s. quatuor d., liii s. iiii d.

### Cantuariensis

Abbas de Faveresham solvit folio lxxxii pro annis LXX quarto, quinto et sexto, pro quolibet anno tresdecim s. quatuor d., ascendunt duas li., ii li.

### Wintoniensis

Abbas de Chertesey solvit folio lxxxii pro anno quarto et quinto sexdecim s., xvi s.

### Norwicensis

Abbas Sancti Edmundi de Bury solvit pro anno et cetera LXX quarto, quinto, sexto et septimo, pro quolibet anno tresdecim s. quatuor d., ascendunt quinquaginta tres s. iiiior d., liii s. iiii d.

### Sarisbiriensis

Abbas de Malmesburi solvit folio lxxxii pro annis et cetera LXX quarto, quinto, sexto et septimo, pro quolibet anno tresdecim s. quatuor d., ascendunt quinquaginta tres s. quatuor d., liii s. iiii d.

### Roffensis

Prior de Tunebrugg' solvit folio lxxxiii pro annis et cetera LXX quarto, quinto et sexto, pro quolibet anno tresdecim s. quatuor d. Item solvit pro anno LXX septimo tresdecim s. iiiior d., liii s. iiii d.

Summa pagine xiii li. ix s. iiii d.[548]

### (fol. 234, xii) Exoniensis

Prior de Bodmyn solvit folio lxxxiii pro annis LXX quarto, quinto et sexto, pro quolibet anno duos s., valent vi s.

### Eliensis

Prior de Anglesey solvit[549] folio lxxxiii pro annis LXX quarto, quinto, sexto et septimo, pro quolibet anno duos s., ascendunt octo s., viii s.

### Karleolensis

Prior Karleolensis solvit folio lxxxiii pro annis LXX quarto et quinto, pro quolibet anno tresdecim s. quatuor d., valent viginti sex s. octo d., xxvi s. viii d.

### Lincolniensis

Prior de Chamcombe solvit folio lxxxiii pro annis LXX quarto, quinto, sexto et septimo, pro quolibet anno quindecim d., valent quinque s., v s.

### Londoniensis

Abbatissa Sancte Clare Londoniensis solvit folio lxxxiii pro annis LXX quarto, quinto, sexto et septimo, pro quolibet anno sex d., in totum duos s., ii s.

### Eboracensis

Custos de Sardebrugh' solvit folio lxxxiii pro annis LXX quarto, quinto et sexto, pro quolibet anno quindecim d., ascendunt tres s. novem d. Item solvit pro anno et cetera LXX septimo quindecim d., v s.

### Lincolniensis

Magister ordinis de Sempingham Lincolniensis diocesis solvit folio lxxxiii pro annis et cetera LXX quarto,[550] quinto et sexto et septimo, pro quolibet biennio novem li. quindecim s., ascendunt decem et novem li. decem s., xix li. x s. Et ista debentur camere apostolice de biennio in biennium in termino Beatorum Petri et Pauli per dictum priorem de censu annuo et cetera.

Summa pagine xxii li. ii s. viii d.[548]

(fol. 234v) Summa recepte annui census et de annis LXXIIII, LXXV, LXXVI et LXXVII xxxv li. xii s. sterlingorum.[548]

Summa universalis omnium receptorum per dominum collectorem tam de restis denariorum Beati Petri quam de restis censuum, de quibus alias fuerat computatum, quam de denariis Beati Petri et de censibus debitis annis

---

[548] In the margin: *vera*.
[549] *solvit* repeated MS.
[550] Follows *tertio* deleted by a line.

LXXIIII, LXXV, LXXVI et LXXVII est v⁰ lxxxvii li. xi s. viii d. sterlingorum.[548]

(fol. 235, xiii) Recepta vacantium.

Sequitur recepta vacantium de anno tertio Domini Gregorii XI et sequentibus ultra explorata.

### Eboracensis

De vicaria ecclesie Newerk (Newark) folio xc solvit possessor in plenam solutionem primorum fructuum ultima die Januarii anno et cetera LXXVI⁰ octo li. sex s. octo d., viii li. s. viii d.

### Cicestrensis

De ecclesia de Midalavente (Mid Lavant) folio xci solvit possessor in plenam solutionem taxa quinque li., v li.

### Eliensis

De vicaria ecclesie Sancti Johannis Baptiste in Mille strete Cantebrugie folio xci solvit possessor in plenam solutionem medietatis veri valoris tres li. sex s. octo d., iii li. vi s. viii d.

### Wintoniensis

De ecclesia de Witeley (Witley) folio xciii solvit in quatuor vicibus in plenam solutionem taxe viginti sex li. tresdecim s. iiii⁰ʳ d., xxvi li. xiii s. iiii d.

### Eboracensis

De prebenda de Northwellensi alias Palishale (Norwell) in ecclesia collegiata de Southwell' solvit Dominus Willelmus Gontorp tunc possessor in tribus vicibus in plenam solutionem taxe folio xcviii viginti sex li. tresdecim s. quatuor d.,[551] quas xxᵗⁱ sex li. xiii s. iiii d. petit sibi allocari infra in prebenda de Grantam (Grantham) in ecclesia Sarisbiriensi folio cxlvi. Et ibi vide quia est de ista prebenda ex post expoliatus per sententiam in curia.

### Cicestrensis

De prebenda de Sellesey (Selsey) in ecclesia Cicestrensi folio xcix solvit possessor in duabus vicibus in plenam solutionem taxe viginti unum li. sex s. octo d., xxi li. vi s. viii d.

Summa pagine xci li. vi s. viii d.[548]

### (fol. 235ᵛ) Sarisbiriensis

De prebenda de Axford in ecclesia Sarisbiriensi folio xcix solvit possessor in duabus vicibus in plenam solutionem taxe quinque li., v li.

### Lincolniensis

De ecclesia de Navemby (Navenby) folio cii solvit possessor in partem fructuum undecim li. sex s. octo d., xi li. vi s. viii d.

### Lincolniensis

De ecclesia de Boston' folio ciii solvit possessor in partem fructuum viginti quinque li. tresdecim s. quatuor d., xxv li. xiii s. iiii d.

### Cicestrensis

De prebenda de Huvavilla (Hove) in ecclesia Cicestrensi folio cix solvit possessor in duabus vicibus in plenam solutionem taxe triginta li., xxx li.

### Sarisbiriensis

De prebenda de Gillingham in ecclesia monialium de Schaston (Shaftesbury) Sarisbiriensis diocesis solvit possessor folio cxvii triginta li., xxx li.

### Herfordensis

De cancellaria in ecclesia Herfordensi folio cxxiiii solvit possessor in duabus vicibus in partem fructuum decem li., x li.

### Lincolniensis

De prebenda de Coprie (Cropredy) in ecclesia Lincolniensi ex causa confirmationis facte Domino Henrico Piel folio cxx in partem taxe [552] in quadraginta m. solvit die x Novembris anno LXXVII viginti sex li. tresdecim s. quatuor d., xxvi li. xiii s. iiii d.

Summa pagine cxxxviii li. xiii s. iiii d.[548]

(fol. 236, xiiii) Summa omnium receptorum per dictum collectorem de vacantibus beneficiorum collatorum annis iii, iiii, v, vi Domini Gregorii pape XI que fuerunt missa dicto collectori per cameram ii⁰ xxx li. sterlingorum.[548]

(fol. 236ᵛ) Recepta exploratorum.

Sequitur recepta exploratorum de quibus non fuerat per cameram mandatum annis LXX quarto, quinto, sexto et septimo.

### Exoniensis [553]

De ecclesia Sancti Olavi Exonie folio cxxv solvit possessor in plenam solutionem pro medietate veri valoris quadraginta sex s. octo d., xlvi s. viii d.

De ecclesie Sancti Georgii Exonie folio cxxvi solvit possessor pro medietate veri valoris viginti s., xx s.

De ecclesia Omnium Sanctorum in aurifabra Exonie folio cxxvi solvit possessor in plenam solutionem medietatis veri valoris viginti tres s. quatuor d., xxiii s. iiii d.

### Menevensis

De vicaria Beati Michaelis de Castro Walteri (Llanfihangel geneur Glyn) folio cxxvii solvit possessor in plenam solutionem taxe sexaginta sex s. octo d., lxvi s. viii d.

---

[551] Sum repeated MS.

[552] *taxatem*, MS.

[553] This heading is repeated before the next two items in the MS.

### Exoniensis

De vicaria ecclesie de Branford (Brampford Speke) folio cxxxi solvit possessor in plenam solutionem pro medietate veri valoris decem s., x s.

### Exoniensis

De vicaria ecclesie de Heckeworthi (Hockworthy) folio cxxxii solvit possessor in plenam solutionem pro medietate veri valoris quadraginta s., xl s.

### Lincolniensis

De vicaria ecclesie de Terfeld (Therfield) folio cxxxii solvit possessor in duabus vicibus in plenam solutionem pro medietate veri valoris quadraginta s., xl s.

### Menevensis

De vicaria de Lansthewell' (Llanstadwell) folio cxxviii solvit possessor in plenam solutionem taxe sex li. tresdecim s. iiiior d., vi li. xiii s. iiii d.

Summa pagine xix li.[548]

### (fol. 237, xv)[554] Sarisbiriensis

De ecclesia de Kynet (Kennet) folio cxxxii solvit possessor in plenam solutionem taxe in duabus vicibus iiiior li. sex s. octo d., iiii li. vi s. viii d.

### Wellensis

De prebenda de Holcombe in ecclesia Wellensi folio cxxxiii solvit possessor in plenam solutionem pro medietate veri valoris decem s., x s.

### Exoniensis

De ecclesia de Upton' Pyn (Upton Pyne) folio cxxxiii solvit possessor in plenam solutionem medietatis veri valoris quadraginta sex s. octo d., xlvi s. viii d.

### Wellensis

De prebenda de Wodemeremi (Wedmore?) in ecclesia Wellensi folio cxxx et quatre solvit possessor plenam solutionem taxe iiiior li.[555]

### Eboracensis

De vicaria ecclesie de Sutton' in Gaberes (Sutton on the Forest) folio cxxxiiii solvit possessor pro primis fructibus duodecim li., xii li.

### Exoniensis

De ecclesia de Bristetowe (Bridestowe) folio cxxxiiii solvit possessor in plenam solutionem taxe duodecim li., xii li.

### Sarisbiriensis

De ecclesia de Stokton' (Stockton) folio cxxxiiii solvit possessor in plenam solutionem taxe sex li. tresdecim s. quatuor d., vi li. xiii s. iiii d.

### Exoniensis

De prebenda in ecclesia Exoniensi folio cxxxiiii solvit possessor in plenam solutionem taxe pro primis fructibus iiiior li.[555]

### Londoniensis

Solvit quidem civis Londonie pro certo voto eundi ad Romam folio cxxxiiii quadraginta s. Et solverunt etiam certi alii pro expensis literarum quinque s. Et sic ascendit totum pro dictis voto et expensis quadraginta quinque s., xlv s.

Summa pagine xlviii li. xx d. sterlingorum.[548]

### (fol. 237[v]) Exoniensis

De prebenda in ecclesia Exoniensi folio cxxx solvit possessor in plenam solutionem taxe pro primis fructibus quatuor li., iiii li.

### Wintoniensis

De vicaria de Milton' folio cxxxv solvit possessor in duabus vicibus in plenam solutionem taxe sex li. tresdecim s. quatuor d., vi li. xiii s. iiii d.

### Eboracensis [556]

De ecclesia de Patington' (Patrington) folio cxxxv solvit possessor in duabus vicibus in plenam solutionem taxe quadraginta li., xl li.

Item solvit Dominus Thomas Lepton', presbyter Eboracensis diocesis, quot quodam legato per Magistrum Johannem Beron' ecclesie Romane facto folio cxxxv sexaginta s., lx s. Secundum formam in dicto folio contentam quia retinuit i nobilis pro expensis antequam alias solvere vellet.[557]

De ecclesia de Egremond (Egremont) folio cxxxv solvit possessor in plenam solutionem taxe in quatuor vicibus duodecim li., xii li.

### Lincolniensis

De prebenda de Langeford' manerii (Langford Manor) folio cxxxv solvit possessor pro compositione, primorum fructuum in duabus vicibus viginti li., xx li.

### Norwicensis

De ecclesia de Whepestede (Whepstead) folio cxxxvi solvit possessor in tribus vicibus in plenam solutionem taxe quatuordecim li. tresdecim s. quatuor d., xiiii li. xiii s. iiii d.

---

[554] The heading *Recepta exploratorum* is repeated at the top of the page.
[555] Sum repeated MS.

[556] This heading is repeated before each of the next two items.
[557] *vellent*, MS.

Eboracensis

De prebenda de Massam (Masham) in ecclesia Eboracensi folio cxxxvi solvit possessor, scilicet Dominus Robertus Stratton' procurator suus, in partem fructuum triginta li., xxx li.

Summa pagine cxxx li. vi s. viii d.[558]

(fol. 238, xvi) Lincolniensis

De prebenda Sancte Marie de Stowe (Stow in Lindsey) in ecclesia Lincolniensi folio cxxxvi solvit possessor in partem fructuum decem li., x li.

Eboracensis

De vicaria ecclesie de Chesill' (Hessle) folio cxxxvi solvit possessor in duabus vicibus in plenam solutionem taxe tresdecim li. sex s. octo d., xiii li. vi s. viii d.

Eboracensis

De prebenda de Eton' (Eaton) in ecclesia collegiata de Southwell' Eboracensis diocesis folio cxxxvi solvit possessor in partem fructuum sexaginta sex s. octo d., lxvi s. viii d.

Roffensis

De vicaria de Derteford (Dartford) folio cxxxvi solvit possessor in tribus vicibus in plenam solutionem taxe pro medietate veri valoris quinque li. tresdecim s. quatuor d., v li. xiii s. iiii d.

Cantuariensis

De ecclesia de Charte parva (Little Chart) folio cxxxvi solvit possessor in duabus vicibus in plenam solutionem taxe sexdecim li. tresdecim s. iiiior d., xvi li. xiii s. iiii d.

Lincolniensis

De archidiaconatu Bedeford et prebenda Sancte Crucis (Spaldwick) in ecclesia Lincolniensi folio cxxxvii solvit possessor in plenam solutionem taxe dicte prebende et veri valoris fructuum dicti archidiaconatus in quinque vicibus quinquaginta li., l li.

Lincolniensis

De prebenda de Castre (Caistor) in ecclesia Lincolniensi folio cxxxvii solvit in partem fructuum tresdecim li. sex s. octo d., xiii li. vi s. viii d.

Dunolmensis

De prebenda de Westureringtion' alias Eldon' in ecclesia collegiata Auklandie (Auckland) folio cxxxvii solvit possessor in tribus vicibus decem li., x li. Quia non taxa est receptum salvo iure pluris.

Summa pagine cxxii li. vi s. viii d.[558]

(fol. 238v) Norwicensis

De ecclesia de Rouham (Rougham) folio cxxxvii solvit possessor in duabus vicibus in plenam solutionem taxe triginta sex li., xxxvi li.

Norwicensis

De ecclesia de Suthorei (Southery) folio cxxxvii solvit possessor in partem fructuum in duabus vicibus quatuor li. tresdecim s. iiiior d., iiii li. xiii s. iiii d.

Exoniensis

De ecclesia de Schillingford' (Shillingford) folio cxxxviii solvit possessor in plenam solutionem pro compositione viginti sex s. octo d., xxvi s. viii d.

Exoniensis

De prebenda in ecclesia Exoniensi folio cxxxviii solvit possessor, videlicet Johannes Thodewarth', quatuor li., iiiior li.

Londoniensis

De prebenda de Rogemere (Rugmere, St. Pancras) in ecclesia Londoniensi folio cxxxviii solvit possessor in plenam solutionem taxe sexaginta s., lx s.

Norwicensis

De vicaria de Stokeneylond (Stoke by Nayland) folio cxxxviii solvit possessor in tribus vicibus in plenam solutionem taxe sexdecim li., xvi li.

Norwicensis

De vicaria de Mildenhale (Mildenhall) folio cxxxviii solvit possessor in partem fructuum decem li., x li.

Wigorniensis

De ecclesia de Bredon' folio cxxxviii solvit possessor in tribus vicibus in plenam solutionem taxe viginti sex li. tresdecim s. quatuor d., xxvi li. xiii s. iiii d.

Herfordensis

De prebenda de Hompton' (Hampton Bishop) in ecclesia Herfordensi folio cxxxix solvit possessor in partem fructuum viginti septem s. octo d. ob., xxvii s. viii d. ob.

Soma pagine ciii li. xii d. et ob.[558]

(fol. 239, xvii) Londoniensis

De ecclesia Sancti Martini Londonie iuxta Lodegate (St. Martin Ludgate) folio cxxxix solvit possessor in plenam solutionem pro medietate veri valoris quinque li., v li.

Lichfeldensis

De archidiaconatu Stafford in ecclesia Lichfeldensi folio cxxxix solvit possessor in duabus vicibus in plenam solutionem pro medietate veri valoris decem li., x li.

[558] In the margin: vera.

### Londoniensis

De ecclesia de Horsete (Orsett) folio cxxxix solvit possessor in duabus vicibus in plenam solutionem taxe sexdecim li., xvi li.

### Lichfeldensis

De fructibus capelle Sancti Thome martiris in Bernygham (Birmingham) circa sex annos cum dimidio male, ut dicitur, perceptis solvit possessor pro compositione folio cxxxix quatuor li., que sunt quasi nullius valoris, iiii$^{or}$ li. Et non aparet de confirmatione alia obtenta in curia.

### Londoniensis

De prebenda de Holburne (St. Andrew, Holborn) in ecclesia Londoniensi folio cxl solvit possessor in plenam solutionem taxe quadraginta s., xl s.

### Wintoniensis

De ecclesia de Ovinton' (Ovington) folio cxli solvit possessor in duabus vicibus in plenam solutionem taxe quinque li., v li.

### Exoniensis

De prebenda in ecclesia Exoniensi Willelmi de Dowbrug' folio cxli solvit possessor predictus pro taxa quatuor li., iiii$^{or}$ li.

### Bathoniensis

De vicaria de Evele (Avill) folio cxli solvit in plenam solutionem taxe quinque li., v li.
Soma pagine li li.[558]

### (fol. 239$^v$) Eliensis

De ecclesia de Wivelingham (Willingham) folio cxli solvit possessor in partem fructuum viginti m. Hoc est tresdecim li. sex s. octo d. Item plus solvit die decimaquarta Septembris anno et cetera LXXVII$^{mo}$ vi li. vi s. viii d. Ascendunt insimul decem et novem li. tresdecim s. quatuor d., xix li. xiii s. iiii d.

### Lincolniensis [559]

De ecclesia de Haliwelle (Holywell) folio cxlii solvit in partem fructuum sex li. tresdecim s. quatuor d., vi li. xiii s. iiii d.
De ecclesia de Lekenore (Lewknor) folio cxlii solvit possessor in quatuor vicibus in partem fructuum tresdecim li. sex s. octo d., xiii li. vi s. viii d.
De prebenda de Sleford (Sleaford or Lafford) in ecclesia Lincolniensi folio cxlii solvit possessor in partem fructuum in duabus vicibus sexdecim li., xvi li.

### Cicestrensis

De prebenda de Middelton' (Middleton) in ecclesia Cicestrensi folio cxliii solvit possessor in plenam solutionem taxe in duabus vicibus centum s., c s.

### Eliensis

De ecclesia de Herdewik' (Hardwick) folio cxliiii solvit decem li. tresdecim s. quatuor d. pro taxa tota x li. xiii s. iiii d.

### Londoniensis

De ecclesia de Reilley (Rayleigh) folio cxliiii solvit possessor in duabus vicibus in plenam solutionem taxe tresdecim li. sex s. octo d., xiii li. vi s. viii d.

### Lincolniensis

Dedit Margareta Andeley folio cxlv in redemptionem Terre Sancte viginti s., xx s.
Soma pagine lxxxv li. xiii s. iiii d.[558]

### (fol. 240, xviii) Sarisbiriensis

De prebenda Australi de Grantham in ecclesia Sarisbiriensi folio cxlvi solvit possessor scilicet pro primis fructibus sexdecim li. tresdecim s. quatuor d., xvi li. xiii s. iiii d. Et petit sibi allocari quadraginta m. supra in prebenda de Palhasal' (Norwell) in ecclesia collegiata de Stodeel (Southwell) Eboracensis diocesis in debite, ut dicit, sibi solutas folio xcviii, quia eam perdidit in curia per sententiam.

### Eliensis

De ecclesia de Cotenham (Cottenham) folio cxlvi solvit possessor in duabus vicibus, scilicet Robertus Garlethorp, in partem fructuum viginti li., xx li.

### Sarisbiriensis

De prebenda sive ecclesia de Nortlareweton' (North Newnton) in monasterio de Wilton' diocesis Sarisbiriensis ex causa provisionis facte Relberto de Walfhart' in plenam solutionem taxe capelle Omnium Sanctorum annexe [560] folio cxlvi solvit xv die Septembris anno et cetera LXXVII decem et septem li. sex s. octo d., xvii li. vi s. viii d.

### Wintoniensis

De ecclesia Sancte Marie Gidelforde (Guildford) Wintoniensis diocesis ex causa provisionis facte per cardinalem Cantuariensem Johanni de Aston' solvit folio cxxxvi de xx quarta Septembris anno et cetera LXXVII centum s., c s.

### Norwicensis

De ecclesia de Ratlesden' (Rattlesden) folio cxxxviii solvit Robertus Aylesham possessor die xx sexta Septembris anno et cetera LXX° septimo in partem fructuum decem li., x li.

---

[559] This heading is repeated before each of the next two items in the MS.

[560] *annexa*, MS.

## Assavensis

De ecclesia de Dinarth (Llandrillo-yn-Rhos) folio cxliii solvit possessor in partem fructuum die penultima Septembris anno et cetera LXX° septimo septem li. tresdecim s. quatuor d., vii li. xiii s. iiii d.

Somma pagine lxxvi li. xiii s. iiii d.[558]

## (fol. 240ᵛ) Assavensis

De prebenda Assavensi Lewellini ap Howel solvit idem Lewellinus in partem fructuum die penultima Septembris anno et cetera septuagesimo septimo decem s., x s.

## Norwicensis

De vicaria de Tyrngton' (Terrington) folio cxlii solvit possessor in partem fructuum die penultima Septembris anno et cetera septuagesimo septimo tresdecim li. sex s. octo d., xiii li. vi s. viii d.

## Norwicensis

De ecclesia de Palling' folio cxlv solvit Symon de Barton' in plenam solutionem ⟨de⟩ medietate veri valoris sexaginta sex s. octo d., lxvi s. viii d.

## Wintoniensis

De ecclesia de Lamhith' (Lambeth) solvit possessor folio cxlii in partem fructuum [561] quinque li., c s.

## Eboracensis

De prebenda de Northnewbald folio cxxxix solvit Henricus Senatham in partem fructuum ex causa provisionis facte Johanni Ford de eadem prebenda quatuordecim li., xiiii li.

## Londoniensis

De ecclesia seu vicaria Sancti Gregorii in ecclesia Sancti Pauli Londonie (St. Gregory by St. Paul's) quadraginta s., folio cxlv, xl s.

## Cicestrensis

De prebenda de Westringg' (Wittering) solvit Michael de Caston' sex li. tresdecim s. quatuor d. folio cxxxix, vi li. xiii s. iiii d. Item plus ex post in viginti m. xiii li. vi s. viii d. Ascendunt viginti li., xx li.

Somma pagine lviii li. iii s. iiii d.[558]

## (fol. 241, xix)[562] Eboracensis

De prebenda de Rapton' (Rampton) ex causa acceptationis facte auctoritate appostolica per Johannem Caldewell' solvit folio cxlii decem li., x li.

## Lichfeldensis

De prebenda de Gaya (Gaia) minori in ecclesia Lichfeldensi folio cxliiii solvit Nicolaus Botlesham in partem fructuum sexaginta sex s. octo d., lxvi s. viii d.

## Exoniensis

De vicaria ecclesie de Brampton' (Bampton) collata Johanni Godmeston' folio xxxiii solvit dictus Johannes pro provisione sibi facta in partem fructuum in quinque m. sterlingorum sexaginta sex s. octo d., lxvi s. viii d.

## Lichfeldensis

De ecclesia de Dodleston' folio cxlvi solvit Willelmus de Salopia in plenam solutionem taxe octo m. in quatuor m. quinquaginta tres s. quatuor d., liii s. iiii d. Et habuit dictus Guilhiermus de primis per prius in camera tantumden, ut dicitur, et videatur.[563]

## Wellensis

De prebenda de Combe in ecclesia Wellensi folio cxlvi solvit Johannes Brampton' ex causa provisionis sibi facte in partem fructuum in quatuor m. quinquaginta tres s. quatuor d., liii s. iiii d.

## Exoniensis

De prebenda in ecclesia Exoniensi que fuit Henrici Pik' folio xxxviii solvit Walterus Levenant pro taxa quatuor li., iiiiᵒʳ li., salvo iure pluris et cetera.

Soma pagine xxvi li.[564]

(fol. 241ᵛ) Summa omnium receptorum per dictum collectorem de vacantibus beneficiorum exploratorum que non fuerunt sibi missa per cameram viiᶜ xx li. vi s. ob. sterlingorum.[564]

Summa universalis omnium receptorum per dictum collectorem tam de vacantibus beneficiorum sibi missorum per cameram quam de vacantibus beneficiorum exploratorum que non fuerunt sibi missa per cameram et collatorum per Dominum Gregorium papam XI ab anno LXXIIII usque ad annum LXXVI ixᶜ l li. vi s. ob. sterlingorum.[564]

(fol. 242, xx) Recepta subcidii.

Sequitur recepta subsidii Domino Gregorio pape undecimo concessi per clerum Anglie in termino Omnium Sanctorum anno domini millesimo CCCᵐᵒ septuagesimo quinto, licet nondum ex toto soluti, que impositio dicti subsidii ascendit in dictis duabus provinciis ixᵐ li. sterlingorum.

## Cantuariensis

Primo solvit dominus Cantuariensis pro se et provincia sua die xxi mensis Decembris anno domini

---

[561] Followed by *in* deleted by a line.
[562] The heading *Recepta exploratorum* appears at the top of the page.

[563] This sentence was added by a different and cursive hand. I am not confident of the reading.
[564] In the margin: *vera*.

millesimo CCC<sup>mo</sup> septuagesimo quinto quingentas septuaginta sex li. tresdecim s. quatuor d., v<sup>c</sup> lxxvi li. xiii s. iiii d.

Item solvit die quarta Januarii anno a nativitate domini millesimo CCC<sup>mo</sup> LXXVI<sup>to</sup> quingentas sexaginta li., v<sup>c</sup> lx li.

Item die penultima Januarii septingentas et quinque li. viginti d., vii<sup>c</sup> v li. xx d.

Item solvit die vicesima prima Aprilis quadragentas et quinquaginta sex li. quatuor decim s. iiii<sup>or</sup> d., iiii<sup>c</sup> lvi li. xiiii s. iiii d.

Item die duodecima Maii quingentas decem et septem li., v<sup>c</sup> xvii li.

Item in crastinum Beati Johannis Baptiste quadringentas sexaginta unam [565] li., iiii<sup>c</sup> lxi li.

Item quintadecima die Julii septingentas quatuordecim li. septem s. quinque d., vii<sup>c</sup> xiiii li. vii s. v d.

Item die octava Augusti ducentas septuaginta unam li. quindecim s. quatuor d., ii<sup>c</sup> lxxi li. xv s. iiii d.

Item die decima nona Augusti sexaginta quatuor li. decem et septem s. novem d., lxiiii li. xvii s. ix d.

Soma pagine iiii<sup>m</sup> iii<sup>c</sup> xxvii li. ix s. xi d.[564]

(fol. 242<sup>v</sup>) Recepta subsidii Cantuariensis

Item die vicesima prima Augusti ducentas septuaginta nonas li. sexdecim s. octo d., ii<sup>c</sup> lxxix li. xvi s. viii d.

Item die vicesima septima Augusti trescentas [566] sexaginta octo li. tresdecim s. quatuor d., iii<sup>c</sup> lxviii li. xiii s. iiii d.

Item die septima Octobris quingentas [567] septuaginta septem li. sex s. sex d., v<sup>c</sup> lxxvii li. vi s. vi d.

Item solvit die vicesima secunda Novembris centum sexaginta septem li. duos s. quinque d., clxvii li. ii s. v d.

Item solvit die decima septima Februarii anno a nativitate domini millesimo CCC<sup>mo</sup> LXX septimo in partem dicti subsidii centum quadraginta li. sterlingorum, cxl li. sterlingorum.

Item solvit quarta die Martii in partem dicti subsidii sexaginta octo li., lxviii li. sterlingorum.

Item solvit die sexta Martii decem et octo li. duos s. ii d., xviii li. ii s. ii d.

Item solvit die decima octava Aprilis anno et cetera LXXVII<sup>o</sup> sexaginta li., lx li.

Item solvit die quarta decima Maii anno predicto dictus dominus Cantuariensis centum viginti li., cxx li.

Item solvit dominus Cantuariensis quinta decima die Julii centum viginti li., cxx li.

Soma pagine m<sup>l</sup> ix<sup>c</sup> xix li. xiii d.[564]

(fol. 243, xxi) Recepta subsidii de Eboracensi.

Dominus Eboracensis solvit in partem dicti subsidii pro se et provincia sua die decima quarta Maii anno et cetera LXX<sup>o</sup> sexto sexcentas sexaginta sex li. tresdecim s. quatuor d., vi<sup>c</sup> lxvi li. xiii s. iiii d.

Item solvit die vicesima octava Octobris quadringentas octuaginta li., iiii<sup>c</sup> lxxx li.

Item solvit Brugis per unum mercatorem de Eboraco circa medietatem mensis Decembris domino Rothomagensi quadringentas sexaginta li., iiii<sup>c</sup> lx li.

Item solvit per manus Domini Walteri Schirlowe die decima octava Februarii anno ab incarnatione domini et cetera LXX sexto in quadraginta m. viginti sex li. tresdecim s. quatuor d., xxvi li. xiii s. iiii d.

Item solvit quinta decima die Octobris anno et cetera LXXVII<sup>o</sup> per manus dicti Magistri Walteri novem li., ix li.

Item solvit dictus dominus Eboracensis in partem dicti subsidii die vicesima octava Octobris eodem anno centum trigenta septem li. tresdecim s. quatuor d. sterlingorum per manus dicti Magistri Walteri cxxxvii li. xiii s. iiii d.

Soma pagine m<sup>l</sup> vii<sup>c</sup> lxxx li.[564]

Summa universalis totius subsidii recepti in dictis duabus provinciis Cantuariensi et Eboracensi viii<sup>m</sup> xxvi li. xi s. sterlingorum.[568]

(fol. 243<sup>v</sup>) Universalis summa recepte.

Summa universalis totius recepte primorum fructuum et etiam denariorum Beati Petri et census et subcidii a folio tertio istius libri usque ad istum folium vicesimum primum inclusive decem milia septingentas et quindecim li. xiiii [569] s. et ii [570] d., x<sup>m</sup> vii<sup>c</sup> xv li. xiiii s. ii d. sterlingorum.[571]

Que valent, singulo floreno pro tribus solidis sterlinis [572] computando, sicut est pro maiori parte extimare consuetum, septuaginta unum milia et quatuor centos et xxxviii fl.[573] duos d. sterlinos,[572] lxxi<sup>m</sup> iiii<sup>c</sup> xxxviii fl. ii d. sterlinos.[574]

De supradicta recepta videatur deductio de assignatis et redditis camere per collectorem ut infra eodem libro folio xxxiii.

Erore calculi semper salvo.

(fol. 245, xxiii)[575] Secuntur assignationes facte camere

Sequntur assignationes per Dominum Arnaldum Garnerii facte camere appostolice vel aliis intra vel extra cameram, nomine et mandato ipsius domini nostri pape seu domini camerarii seu thesaurarii sui, a die vicesima septima Julii anno domini millesimo trecentesimo septuagesimo quarto usque ad diem sextam Martii anno ab incarnatione [576] et cetera LXXVII<sup>o</sup>, qua die sexta de

---

[565] *una*, MS.
[566] trescentos, MS.
[567] quingentos, MS.

[568] In the margin: *vera*. Sum repeated at the foot of the page.
[569] Over *tresdecim* deleted by a line.
[570] Over *unum* deleted by a line.
[571] In the margin: *vera*. Sum repeated in the margin and at the foot of the page.
[572] *sterlis*, MS.
[573] Followed by *tresdecim* deleted by a line.
[574] *sterlis*, MS. The sum is repeated at the foot of folio 244. In the margin: *vera*.
[575] Folio 244 recto and verso is blank except the sum noted above, n. 574 preceding.
[576] Over *a nativitate* deleted by a line.

Londonia in Anglia recessit versus Avinioniam, quia usque ad ipsam diem vicesimam septimam fuit et est per eundem Dominum Arnaldum cum ipsa camera computatum et conclusum, ut in folio tertio libri rubei habetur et folio lxvii et sequentibus qui fuit tunc positus in archivis camere apostolice Avinionie.

Primo assignavit nomine camere appostolice supradicte et de ipsius mandato Petro Marchi, socio et factori ac procuratori societatis Albertinorum Antiquorum de Florentia, per manus locumtenentis sui, Magistri Laurentii de Nigris, vicesimo quarto die Octobris dicto anno domini millesimo CCC<sup>mo</sup> LXX quarto de pecuniis dicte camere in Anglia receptis centum quinquaginta li. sterlingorum, cl li. sterlingorum.[577]

Item plus etiam assignavit in die Sancti Thome Apostoli, que fuit dies xxi mensis Decembris tunc inmediate sequentis per eundem locumtenentem alias centum quinquaginta li. sterlingorum, cl li. sterlingorum.

Item ex post modo consimili assignavit in diversis vicibus per manus ipsius locumtenentis sui usque ad diem viii Junii anni et cetera LXX quinti ducentas quindecim li. quatuor s. quinque d. sterlingorum, ii<sup>c</sup> xv li. iiii s. v d.[577]

Soma pagine v<sup>c</sup> xv li. iiii s. v d. sterlingorum.[578]

(fol. 245<sup>v</sup>) Item etiam assignavit idem Dominus Arnaldus per se ipsum eidem Petro de pecuniis camere et nomine ipsius camere xv die mensis Junii anno domini millesimo CCC<sup>mo</sup> LXX quinto in ducentis octuaginta francis quadraginta quinque li. decem s. sterlingorum, xlv li. x s. sterlingorum.

Item plus assignavit eidem Petro consimiliter die vicesima prima dicti mensis Junii triginta novem li. quinque s. septem d. sterlingorum, xxxix li. v s. vii d.

Item assignavit plus dictus dominus collector supradicto Petro Marchi socio Albertinorum nomine dicte camere appostolice secunda die Julii septuaginta quinque li. sterlingorum, lxxv li. sterlingorum.

Item assignavit etiam plus eidem Petro, nomine ⟨et⟩ ex causa quibus supra, die ante penultima dicti mensis Julii anno domini millesimo CCC<sup>mo</sup> LXX quinto quadraginta tres li. tres s. quatuor d., xliii li. iii s. iiii d.

Item assignavit plus dictus dominus collector dicto Petro Marchi de pecuniis dicte camere appostolice die xxiii Novembris anno domini millesimo CCC<sup>mo</sup> LXX quinto ducentas sex li. sterlingorum, ii<sup>c</sup> vi li. sterlingorum.

Item assignavit eadem die dicto Petro Marchi nomine quo supra undecim li. septem s. undecim d., xi li. vii s. xi d.

Item assignavit dictus dominus collector de pecuniis supradicte camere appostolice per ipsum seu ipsius nomine receptis in Anglia eidem Petro Marchi die x Aprilis anno domini et cetera LXX sexto septuaginta duas li. novem s. novem d., lxxii li. ix s. ix d.

Soma pagine iiii<sup>c</sup> xcii li. xvi s. viii d.[578]

(fol. 246, xxiiii) Et est sciendum quod de suprascriptis summis assignatis dicto Petro per me collectorem Anglie seu locumtenentem meum a vicesima septima die Julii supradicta usque ad diem sextam Maii anni et cetera LXX sexti, que summe ascendunt mille et octo li. duodecim d. sterlingorum, debuit dictus Petrus assignare camere appostolice vii<sup>c</sup> quinque li. pro quatuor milibus septuagentis fl. ponderis camere. Et retinuit in solutum residuum pro expensis per eundem Petrum solutis nomine Domini Rogeri de Belloforti et nepotis sui usque ad diem sextam Maii, scilicet iii<sup>c</sup> iii li. xiii d. sterlingorum, que valent de dicta moneta duo milia viginti fl. duodecim denarii sterlingorum, singulo floreno ponderis camere pro tribus solidis sterlingorum computando.[579]

Item Magister Laurentius de Nigris subcollector retinunit die secunda Julii anno, et cetera LXX quinto de pecuniis camere per eum receptis et Domino Rogero pro suis neccessitatibus tradidit folio lxviii cum littera manu dicti Domini Rogeri subscripta quinquaginta nobiles qui valent sexdecim li. tresdecim s. quatuor d., xvi li. xiii s. iiii d.[580]

Item solvit dictus collector, facto computato cum Petro Marchi, pro expensis quatuor mensium unius equi Domini Rogeri et alterius equi sui undecim mensium, videlicet a principio mensis Septembris anni LXX quinti usque ad xxiii diem mensis Augusti ubi fuerunt xv menses, qua die Folketus recessit versus curiam cum ipso equo, quatuor d. pro die computando pro singulo equo, septem li. decem s. sterlingorum, vii li. x s. sterlingorum.[580]

Soma pagine xxiiii<sup>or</sup> li. iii s. iiii<sup>or</sup> d. Pro Domino Rogero summa pagine iii xxvii li. iiii s. v d.[578]

(fol. 246<sup>v</sup>) Pro Domino Rogero.
Item tradidit dictus collector Petro Marchi supradicto de mandato Domini Rogerii literatorie sibi facto die xxii Julii anno et cetera LXX sexto in ducentis nobilibus auri sexaginta sex li. tresdecim s. quatuor d. sterlingorum, lxvi li. xiii s. iiii d. In quibus dictus Dominus Rogerus tenebatur dicto Petro ex amicabili mutuo sibi facto, quos quidem ducentos nobiles solvit custodibus suis in Londonia, videlicet Domino Guillelmo de Montrandre et Borgeys, pro expensis certis factis per Dominum Johannem de Rupe nepotem suum a Burdegalis usque ad primam diem Augusti tunc proxime futurum.[581]

Item consimiliter tradit dictus collector dicto Petro Marchi et de mandato dicti Domini Rogeri literatorie sibi facto die xiii mensis Augusti anno predicto LXX sexto decem et octo li. duos s. quatuor d., xviii li. ii s. iiii d.[581]

Item tradit dicto Petro pro Rogero cursore die ultima Julii misso per eum ad curiam pro factis Domini Rogeri

---

[577] In the margin: *doce.*
[578] In the margin: *vera.*

[579] In the left margin: *pro Domino Rogero.* In the other: *memorandum.*
[580] In the margin: *pro Domino Rogero.*
[581] In the margin: *Domini Rogeri.*

de Belloforte viginti s. sterlingorum.[582] Et cum rediit solvit Magistro Laurentio pro ipso Rogero quatuor francos quos sibi tradiderat pro expensis factis per duos menses in curia sperando, et sic solvit pro toto triginta tres s. quatuor d., xxxiii s. iiii d.[583]

Soma pagine lxxxvi li. ix s.[578]

(fol. 247, xxv) Pro Domino Rogero.

Item solvit dictus collector dicto Petro Marchi nomine et mandato dicti Domini Rogeri die xxviii Augusti anno et cetera LXXVI, prout continetur in uno medio folio papiri manu dicti Petri scripto continenti summam viginti quinque li. decem et novem s. decem d., in plenam solutionem dicti folii [584] sex li. decem et septem s. sex d., vi li. xvii s. vi d.[583]

Item solvit supradicto Petro Marchi nomine et mandato dicti Domini Rogeri de Belloforti et pro suis expensis die xv mensis Octobris anno domini millesimo CCC^mo LXX sexto in sexaginta nobilibus, quas habuit Dominus Montrand' pro finali solutione expensarum. Et stat instrumentum publicum. xx li. sterlingorum.[583]

Item tradidit dicto Petro de mandato Domini Rogeri literatorie sibi facto manu et signo eius subscripto die xxviii Novembris anno et cetera LXX sexto pro gonis et caligis et aliis expensis vestium ipsorum et per Folquetum etiam per prius factis decem et septem li. decem et octo d. sterlingorum, dictam literam Domini Rogeri penes se retinendo, xvii li. xviii d.[583]

Item tradidit eidem Petro Marchi dicta die xxviii Novembris anno domini predicto LXX sexto de mandato dicti Rogeri in eadem supradicta litera michi facto in quinquaginta m. sterlingorum solutis per dictum Petrum castellano et custodi suo pro expensis victus factis et faciendis per dictum Dominum Rogerum et Dominum Johannem suum [585] (fol. 247^v) [586] nepotem per dictum custodem in castello de Kelyngworth' domini ducis Lancastrie a secunda die mensis Octobris circa, qua die fuerunt primo ipsius domini ducis seu dicti castellani expensis retenti et a manibus Vasconie erecti, triginta tres li. sex s. octo d., xxxiii li. vi s. viii d.[583]

Item tradidit per manus Nicolaii de Luca, socii dicti Petri Marchi, presente Folketo, Domino Willelmo de Bukbrug', thesaurario domini ducis Lancastrie, die xx Februarii anno a nativitate et cetera LXX septimo in centum nobilibus triginta tres li. sex s. octo d., xxxiii li. vi s., viii d.[582] de mandato Domini Rogeri et pro expensis per eum factis et nepotem suum in castro domini ducis predicti et in futurum faciendis pro eisdem Dominis Rogero et Johanne.

Item solvit Nicholao de Luca, tunc administratori Domini Rogeri Belloforte, absente dicto Petro Marchi,

die xxvii Aprilis anno et cetera LXX septimo pro gonis rubeis folratis de blanqueto et pro duobus juponibus et pro speciebus et pro coralhis duobus paribus uno nigro cum expensis minorum [587] huic inde missorum et cum expensis sex li. quatuor s. sterlingorum factis Londonie per Folketum a prima die Februarii usque ad vicesimam septimam diem supradictam quindecim li. septem d., xv li. vii d. sterlingorum.

Soma pagine lxxxi li. xiii s. xi d.[578]

(fol. 248, xxvi) Pro Domino Rogero.

Item solvit supradicto Nicolao de Luca prima die Maii anno domini millesimo CCC^mo LXX septimo in centum nobilibus triginta tres li. sex s. octo d., quas ipsa die tradidit pro expensis Domini Rogeri factis et faciendis in castro de Kelingworth' Domino Willelmo Bukbrugg', nomine Johannis Dencort' capitanei dicti castri, recipienti et cum litera quittancie xxxiii li. vi s. viii d.

Die xxiii Maii que fuit dies Sabbati in vesperis Sancte Trinitatis anno et cetera LXXVII Domini Rogerus et Johannes fuerunt restituti per dominum ducem Lancastrie Londonie ante prandium Domino Archambaldo de Grili, vicecomiti de Benanias, qua die solvit Borbonetus, socius dicti vicecomitis, pro resta expensarum ipsorum Dominorum Rogeri et Johannis factarum a secunda die Octobris proxime preterita usque ad dictam xxiii diem Maii, quo tempore in gardia dicti domini ducis fuerunt, ultra trecentes nobiles per prius solutos, gardiatori ipsorum dominorum ex causa dictarum expensarum octuaginta et quinque marcas que valent centum et septuaginta nobiles qui valent quinquaginta sex li. tresdecim s. quatuor d., lvi li. xiii s. iiii d. sterlingorum.

Quas dictus Borbonetus nomine dicti vicecomitis petit sibi reddi et restitui a dictis Dominis Rogero et Johanne. Et sunt pro ii^c xxxii diebus et sic ascendit pro qualibet die una marca, videlicet ii nobiles, et plus ad totum sex nobiles, et sic ascendit totum, ut supra dicitur, videlicet iiii^c lxx nobiles de quibus petit dictus Borbonetus sibi redi, ut prefertur, dictas quinquaginta sex li. tresdecim s. iiii^or d.

Et tradidit dictus collector die ultima Maii Augustino Boneton' dictas quiquaginta sex li. tresdecim s. quatuor d. quas dictus Augustinus solvit dicto Borboneto dicta die Londonie, presente Domino Rogero et cum litera sua.

Soma pagine xc li. sterlingorum.[578]

(fol. 248^v) Pro Domino Rogero.

Item solvit pro dicto Domino Rogero pro quatuor jupponibus et caputiis duobus et quatuor paribus caligarum scarlati et quibusdem aliis dictus collector eadem die dicto Augustino sex li. duos s. duos d., vi li. ii s. ii d.[580]

Item solvit dictus collector Augustino Benoton', socio illorum de Guinegiis, die decima quinta Augusti anno

---

[582] Sum repeated MS.
[583] In the margin: *Rogeri*.
[584] *folio*, MS.
[585] At the foot of the page: *Soma pagine xliii li. xix s.* In the margin: *vera*.
[586] The heading *Pro Domino Rogero* appears at the top of the page.

[587] *minororum*, MS.

et cetera LXXVII viginti unam li. quatuor s. quatuor d. sterlingorum, per ipsum traditas, de mandato domini thesaurarii Avinionensis literatorie dicto collectori facto, Guidoni Labordonia, serventi armorum domini nostri pape, pro sexaginta septem diebus quibus fuit et esse sperabat in prosecutione financie Domini Rogeri de Belloforti duos francos pro qualibet die, hoc est iii s. et ii d. pro singulo franco computando, qui valent dictam summam, scilicet xxi li. quatuor s. iiii⁰ʳ d.[588]

Item solvit plus dicto Augustino die xxx Septembris dicto anno pro stipendiis ipsius Guidoni Bard' xlv dietis ex causa suprascripta debitis xc francos qui valent xiiii li. v s. Summa tota xxxv li. ix s. iiii d.[588]

Item solvit dictus collector de pecuniis primorum fructuum Augustino Benoton', socio illorum de Guinegiis, die xxi Augusti anno et cetera LXXVII centum li. sterlingorum in trecentis nobilibus, quas centum li. dictus Augustinus tradiderat Domino Rogero de Belloforti pro suis tunc moderatis et neccessariis expensis in Anglia faciendis, ut dicebat, et omnino habere volebat et habuit Petrus ipsa die cum litera sua, presentibus Folketo, scutifero dicti Domini Rogeri, et Domino Petro [589] (fol. 249, xxvii)[586] de Ruspis, qui ipsius nomine et mandato a dicto Augustino ipsam pecuniam receperunt Londonie in domo habitationis dicti Domini Petri de Ruspis centum li., c li. Vide etiam pecunias plures quas habuit Dominus Rogerus de subcidio ut infra folio xxix et xxx.[580]

Item tradidit dictus collector dicto Augustino xxix die Octobris anno predicto cum litera Domini Rogeri de pecuniis primorum fructuum per ipsum Augustinum solutis pro eo certis mercatoribus pannorum et telarum et aliarum rerum, ut in libro folio lxxx continetur, quadraginta tres li. quatuor decim s. decem d. pro suis, ut dixit, moderatis expensis per ipsum Dominum Rogerum receptas, xliii li. xiiii s. x d.[590]

Item tradidit dictus dominus collector Anglie Domino Guydoni de Rupe, archidiacono Turonensi, die xiiii Januarii anno ab incarnatione domini et cetera LXXVII⁰, de mandato reverendi in Christo patris domini archiepiscopi Rothomagensis auctoritate apostolica et domini thesaurarii domini nostri pape sibi facto, de pecuniis primorum fructuum camere apostolice pertinentibus centum nonaginta unam li. sex s. quinque d. sterlingorum, ultra alias summas etiam eadem die dicto Guidoni traditas de pecuniis subcidii, de quibus etiam habetur infra folio xxix et xxx. cxci li. vi s. v d.[591]

Soma pagine iii⁰ xxxv li. xv d. sterlingorum.[592]

(fol. 249ᵛ) Item tradidit dictus collector folio lxxix

Augustino Benoton' supradicto de pecuniis primorum fructuum quarta die Februarii anno et cetera LXXVII⁰ reddendo Brugiis et Rome ultra alias pecunias subcidii eadem die sibi traditas quadringentas et sexaginta li., iiii⁰ lx li. sterlingorum.[593]

Item simili modo tradidit dictus collector folio lxxix dicto Augustino de dictis pecuniis primorum fructuum die ix Junii anno predicto LXXVII⁰ ultra etiam alias pecunias subcidii eadem etiam die sibi traditas ducentas quadraginta duas li. sexdecim s. duos d. sterlingorum, ii⁰ xlii li. xvi s. ii d.[593]

Item simili modo tradidit dictus collector Londonie die xii mensis Octobris anno domini et cetera LXXVII⁰ dicto Augustino Beneton', factori illorum de Guinegiis de Luca, nomine dicte camere appostolice folio lxxix octuaginta tres li. sex s. octo d. sterlingorum de pecuniis primorum fructuum, lxxxiii li. vi s. viii d.[593]

Item tradidit supradictus dominus collector Londonie de pecuniis primorum fructuum camere apostolice pertinentibus Willelmo Hosel diocesis Lincolniensis, procuratori nomine Domini Johannis de Thornburi militis Wigorniensis diocesis, die xxvii Februarii anno ab incarnatione domini et cetera LXXVII⁰ septuaginta unam li. sterlingorum, que valent, singulo floreno pro tribus s. computando, iiii⁰ lxxiii fl. xii d. sterlingorum ponderis camere, in partem solutionis sex milium fl. eidem militi debitorum pro servitio camere apostolice in Lumbardia facto, lxxi li. sterlingorum. Et copia bulle et procurii sunt in registro.[594]

Soma pagine viii⁰ lvii li. ii s. x d.[592]

(fol. 250, xxviii) Item solvit dictus collector pro tribus orfresiis et pro uno stuch [595] corporalium ad opus domini nostri pape factis, quorum duos et lestuch sibi per Dominum Egidium de mense Martii anno et cetera LXXVII⁰ misit, et tertium est paratum et iam traditur [596] domino camerario, ut habetur in libro recepte et expensarum folio lxx, septuaginta octo marcas et dimidiam,[597] que valent cxxxvii nobiles. Hoc est xlv li. xiii s. iiii d.[598] Magister Johannes de Argentura fecit eas Londonie anno LXXVI⁰ et VII. Et habet collector quitantia de soluto.[599]

Memoradum quod Johannes Lupi, servitor camere apostolice, fuit missus ad Angliam per Dominum Gregorium XI pro negotiis Domini Rogeri et aliis, et venit Londonie de mense Decembris ante nativitatem domini anno et cetera LXXVII⁰ ubi stetit usque ad finem Martii, et recepit de subcollectore Anglie, videlicet de Magistro Laurentio de Nigris, decem li. sterlingorum de pecuniis camere apostolice de mandato domini epis-

[588] In the margin: *pro Lordonia.*
[589] At the foot of the page: *Soma pagine xli li. xi s. vi d.* In the margin: *vera.*
[590] Sum repeated MS. In the margin: *pro Domino Rogero.*
[591] In the margin: *pro Domino Rogero et pro collectore Turonensi.*
[592] In the margin: *vera.*

[593] In the margin: *de Guinegiis.*
[594] In the margin: *pro illo de Tornaburi.*
[595] *reposito,* below. p. 541.
[596] *et iam traditur* over *pro mittendo* deleted by a line.
[597] *dimiam,* MS.
[598] Sum repeated MS.
[599] In the margin: *pro domino pape orfresia.*

copi Cathaniensis (Catania), subthesaurarii [600] domini pape Rome, qui sic fieri mandaverat per suas literas. Et de dictis decem li. dictus subcollector debet in camera computare et deducere de sua recepta, quarum hic non est computatum nisi pro memoriali, quia post recessum dicti collectoris sic factum fuit.[601]

Soma pagine xlv li. xiii s. iiii d. sterlingorum ultra memoriale.

(fol. 250ᵛ) Summa omnium assignatorum per dictum collectorem de primis fructibus vacantium beneficiorum et quibusdam aliis debitis, que assignationes fuerunt facte diversis personis et etiam camere prout particulariter infra declarabit, iiᵐ viᶜ xiii li. xv s. iii d. sterlingorum.[592]

(fol. 251, xxix) Assignata camere de recepta subcidii.

Sequuntur assignationes camere apostolice seu ipsius nomine et mandato de recepta subcidii facte per collectorem Anglie usque ad diem vi Martii anni ab incarnatione domini et cetera LXXVII.

Primo habuit camera apostolica, ut in libro recepte folio lxxvi, per manus Petri Marchi in tribus vicibus usque ad diem ultimam Januarii anno et cetera LXXᵒ quinto de pecuniis subcidii, ultra alias pecunias plures primorum fructuum sibi etiam in superius assignatas, mille octingentas et quadraginta unam li. quindecim s. sterlingorum, xviiiᶜ xli li. xv s. sterlingorum.[602]

Item habuit Bartholomeus de Clanato Yporiensis (Ivrea) diocesis de mandato domini thesaurarii die vii Junii anno et cetera LXXVIᵗᵒ quadringentas et quadraginta li. decem et octo s. sex d., iiiiᶜ xl li. xviii s. vi d.[603]

Item habuit Augustinus de Massa pro illo de Interminellis die xvii Junii anno predicto mille centum viginti quinque li., xiᶜ xxv li.[604]

Item habuit Johannes Franseys de Pistorio die xxv Novembris anno predicto LXXVIᵗᵒ mille li. sterlingorum.[605]

Item habuit Brugiis dominus Rothomagensis nomine camere predicte et de mandato apostolico dicto collectori facto per manus Rogerum de Morton' mercatorem de Eboraco xv die Decembris anno predicto quadringentas sexaginta li. sterlingorum, iiiiᶜ lx li. sterlingorum. Cuius feci quitantiam de recepta.[606]

Soma pagine iiiiᵐ viiiᶜ lxvii li. xiii s. vi d. sterlingorum.[592]

### (fol. 251ᵛ) Intra Cameram

Item habuit plus dominus Rothomagensis Brugiis per manus Augustini Beneton', mercatoris de Luca et factoris illorum de Guinegiis, die xiii Decembris dicto anno quingentas li. sterlingorum, quarum quingentarum

li. septuaginta quinque li. erant pro domino Cantuariensi de servitio camere et de dicto subcidio, de quo solo subcidio hic computatur erant quadringente viginti quinque li., iiiiᶜ xxv li.[606]

Item tradidit dictus dominus collector dicto Augustino Beneton' de mandato apostolico die xxiiii Januarii anno ab incarnatione et cetera LXX sexto pro reddendo Brugiis vel Rome, facto cambio et super eo prius concordato, mille li. sterlingorum.[607]

Item consimiliter tradidit plus dicto Augustino iiii die Februarii anno predicto mille quingentas li., quarum mille quingentarum li. erant solum de subcidio predicto mille quadraginta li. sterlingorum, mxl li. sterlingorum.[608]

Item tradidit Rainaudon' de Rofinhaco de mandato domini Rothomagensis pro expensis suis in decem nobilibus de pecuniis subcidii predicti pro quo fuit missus, ut dixit, sexaginta sex s. octo d. sterlingorum, lxvi s. viii d. sterlingorum.[609]

Item consimiliter tradidit dicto Augustino die nona Junii anno et cetera LXXVIIᵒ ultra alias pecunias primorum fructuum eadem die sibi, ut supra habetur, traditas quadringentas viginti tres li. decem et septem s. duos d., iiiiᶜ xxiii li. xvii s. ii d.[610]

Soma pagine iiᵐ viiiᶜ xcii li. iii s. x d. sterlingorum.[611]

### (fol. 252, xxx) Pro Domino Rogero.

Item fuerunt assignate de dictis pecuniis subcidii quas habuit Dominus Rogerus de Bellofort' die xxx Augusti pro parte sue financie solvenda de consilio archidiaconi Turonensis per manus Augustini Benetoni centum viginti li., cxx li.[612]

Item consimiliter tradidit dictus collector die xxix Octobris anno domini et cetera LXXVII de pecuniis dicti subcidii dicto Augustino cum litera Domini Rogeri centum et tresdecim li. in partem solutionis financie sue, ut habetur folio lxxix, cxiii li. sterlingorum.

Item tradidit dictus collector Domino Guidoni de Rupe, archidiacono Turonensi, die xiiii Januarii anno ab incarnatione domini et cetera LXVII, de mandato domini archiepiscopi Rothomagensis et domini thesaurarii, de pecuniis predicti subcidii, in partem, ut dixit dictus Guido, solutionis financie Domini Rogeri de Bellofort' trigenta tres li. tresdecim s. septem s. sterlingorum, xxxiii li. xiii s. vii d. Ultra alia sibi tradita supra folio xxvii.[613]

Soma pagine cclxvi li. xiii s. vii d.[592]

### (fol. 252ᵛ) Summa omnium assignatorum per dictum

---

[600] *subthesaurario*, MS.

[601] In the margin: *Pro Johanne Lupi memorandum.*

[602] In the margin: *Albertini.*

[603] In the margin: *de Clanato.*

[604] In the margin: *de Interminellis.*

[605] In the margin: *de Pistorio.* Sum repeated MS.

[606] In the margin: *pro domino Rothomagensi.*

[607] Sum repeated MS. In the margin: *pro illis* (*illorum*, MS) *de Guinegiis.*

[608] In the margin: *pro illis de Guinegiis.*

[609] In the margin: *Raynaudi de Rofinhaco.*

[610] In the margin: *pro illis de Guineriis.*

[611] *sterlis, MS.* In the margin: *vera.*

[612] In the margin: *pro Domino Rogero.*

[613] In the margin: *Domino Guidoni de Rupe et pro Domino Rogero.* There is also in another cursive hand a much abbreviated entry which I have not been able to decipher.

collectorem diversis personis et etiam camere, prout particulariter infra declarabitur, que assignationes fuerunt facte de [614] subsidio levato, viii^m xxvi li. x s. xi d. sterlingorum.[592]

(fol. 253. xxxi) Expense facte ratione officii collectorie quatuor annis infrascriptis.

Sequntur expense ratione officii et nomine camere apostolice facte per Dominum Arnaldum Garnerii collectorem Anglie a die xxvii mensis Julii anni domini millesimi CCC^mi LXX quarti usque ad festum Beati Michaelis Septembris, et inde usque ad annum revolutum, videlicet usque ad festum Beati Michaelis anni et cetera LXX quinti, ubi fuerunt xiiii menses.

Primo solvit pro salario hospitii unius anni conducti Londonie, videlicet a die festo Beati Michaelis Septembris anni predicti LXX quarti usque ad aliud festum anni LXX quinti anno revoluto decem m., sicut est consuetum, videlicet pro anno solvere decem m., et tamen propter custodiam et periculum subcidii et guerarum oportuit conducere hospitium fortius solito et securus, que decem m. valent sex li. xiii s. iiii d., vi li. xiii s. iiii d.[615]

Item solvit pro papiro et incausto et cera totius dicti anni et registris sicut est consuetum viginti s., xx s.

Item solvit tam per manus locumtenentis sui pro portu literarum camere per dictum regnum dicto anno quam per manus suas de mense Julii anni LXX quinti pro dicto alio portu literarum ad terminum quindene Beati Michaelis anni et cetera LXX quinti cum portu quarundam aliarum literarum ad curiam missarum pro factis camere et domini nostri quadraginta duas s., xlii s.

Soma pagine sequitur infra et ibi vide.

(fol. 253^v) Item expendit dictus collector redeundo de Avinionia ad Angliam de mense Martii et Aprilis et Maii anno ab incarnatione [616] et cetera LXXV in quinquaginta diebus quibus in via et multum plus stetit, cum familia et quinque equitaturis, quorum dierum decem diebus stetit Parisius de mandato domini nostri pape cum certis literis etiam credentie ad regem, et aliis decem diebus et plus Brugiis cum aliis consimilibus literis ad tractatores pacis, etiam sperando ubique eorum responciones, pro qualibet die duos nobiles computando, centum nobiles, et pro duobus equis in ipsa via perditis quadraginta nobiles, de quibus omnibus expensis et equis perditis supplicat sibi allocare in suis presentibus compotis medietatem dicte summe, videlicet septuaginta nobiles qui [617] solum valent xxx li.[618]

Soma pagine et precedentis xxxiii li. ii s.[619]

---

[614] Followed by *primis fructibus beneficiorum et quibusdam aliis debitis* deleted by a line.

[615] The whole item is deleted by lines.

[616] *ab incarnatione* inserted above the line over *nativitate* which is not deleted.

[617] *videlicet septuaginta nobiles qui* is deleted by a line MS.

[618] Followed by *vi s. viii d.* deleted by a line.

[619] In the margin: *vera*.

(fol. 254, xxxii) Expense secundi anni ratione officii facte.

Sequntur expense sequentis anni facte per dominum collectorem ratione dicti officii collectorie in Anglia a festo Beati Michaelis anno et cetera LXXV usque ad festum predictum anni LXXVI^ti.

Item tradidit Rogero cursori literarum pro portu quinque mandatorum ad partem Wallie xvii die Decembris anno et cetera LXXV in quatuor nobilibus viginti sex s. octo d. sterlingorum, xxvi s. viii d. sterlingorum.

Item solvit pro salario hospitii conducti Londonie pro officio a termino Beati Michaelis anni et cetera LXX quinti usque ad sequens terminum Beati Michaelis anni LXX sexti, anno ipso revoluto, decem marcas, licet propter periculum custodie subcidii l milium florenorum et plus isto anno et precedenti et subsequenti collector opportuit habere cautius et securus hospitium solito, valent decem m. sex li. xiii s. iiii^or d., vi li. xiii s. iiii d.[620]

Item solvit pro literis compotorum et papiri, cera et incausto viginti s. sicut est consuetum computare, licet multum plus sibi coustet, xx s.

Item tradidit dicto Rogero cursori pro portu quarundam literarum pro iure camere ad episcopum Landavensem directarum die viii Junii anno et cetera LXX sexto pro octo diebus eundo et redeundo seu responsum sperando sex s. octo d., vi s. viii d.

Item solvit pro diversis literis missis curie et dominis camere et thesaurario pro negotiis camere diversis portitoribus earundem toto dicto anno ultra [621] vii li. xiii s. iiii d.

Soma pagine x li. vi s. viii d.[619]

(fol. 254^v) Expense tertii anni ratione officii facte.

Sequntur expense sequentis anni facte pro officio et nomine camere a festo Beati Michaelis Septembris anno domini et cetera LXX sexto, ubi quoad ista incipit annus, usque ad festum sequens Beati Michaelis Septembris anno et cetera LXX septimo.

Primo computat dictus collector pro salario hospitii conducti Londonie a dicto festo Beati Michaelis usque ad aliud subsequens festum de anno domini et cetera LXX septimo, anno ipso revoluto, decem marcas, licet propter periculum custodie et guerarum et maioris laboris [622] subdicii opportuerit conducere hospitium fortius et securus solito, videlicet sex li., vi li. xiii s. iiii d.[620]

Item solvit pro libris registris, papiro, cira, incausto viginti s., sicut est consuetum computare, licet multum plus coustent, xx s.

Item solvit pro portu literarum officii per regnum in diversis vicibus a dicto festo Beati Michaelis Septembris anni et cetera LXX sexti usque ad supradictam diem Beati Michaelis mensis Septembris predicto [623] anno et cetera LXX septimo, et pro literis regiis tribus impe-

---

[620] This item is deleted by lines in the manuscript.

[621] Followed by *viginti solidos* deleted by a line.

[622] *laboribus*, MS.

[623] *predictis*, MS.

tratis pro cambio subcidii faciendo, et pro diversis literis Avinioniam et Romam pro negotiis camere apostolice dicto anno missis quinque [624] li. et decem s., xii li. xiii s. iiii d.

Soma pagine xiii li. iii s. iiii d. sterlingorum.[619]

(fol 255, xxxiii) Expense quarti anni ratione officii facte.

Sequntur expense sequentis anni facte pro officio et nomine camere a festo Beati Michaelis Septembris anno domini et cetera LXX° septimo, ubi quo ad ista incipit annus, usque ad festum sequens Beati Michaelis Septembris anno ab incarnatione domini et cetera LXX octavi.

Primo computat dictus collector pro salario hospitii conducti Londonie a dicto festo Beati Michaelis anni et cetera LXX septimi usque ad aliud subsequens festum de anno domini et cetera LXX octavo, anno ipso revoluto, sex li. tresdecim s. iiii d., quas dicto anno coustitit et plus, vi li. xiii s. iiii d.[620]

Item solvit pro libris registris, papiro, cera et incausto viginti s., sicut est consuetum computare, licet multum plus coustent, xx s.

Item solvit pro portu literarum officii per regnum in diversis vicibus a dicto festo Beati Michaelis Septembris anni et cetera LXXVII usque ad dictum festum Beati Michaelis anni LXXVIII viginti s. sterlingorum,[625] xx s.

Item dictus collector misit domino camerario Rome per Dominum Robertum de Grantam, diocesis Lincolniensis registratorem suum, de mense Aprilis circa finem librum compotorum suorum de recepta et assignata et resta usque ad diem vi mensis Martii anno a nativitate domini et cetera LXXVIII, et licet steterit in viam eundo vel redeundo de Roma ad Angliam per sex menses, videlicet ad mensem Octobris anni predicti LXXVIII, tamen non computat pro ipso nisi, licet multum [626] plus sibi constiterit, xi li. xiii s. iiii d.

Item expendit quia carius conduxit hospitium in quo moratur propter custodiam pecuniarum subsidii quam alias conduceret v li. ii s. viii d.

Soma pagine xviii li. xvi s.[627]

(fol. 255ᵛ) Summa de assignatis intra vel extra cameram.

Summa universalis de assignatis intra vel extra cameram decem milia septingentas et decem [628] li. et undecim s. et sex [629] d. sterlis, xᵐ viiᶜ xv li. xiiii s. ii d. sterlis.

Que valent, singulo floreno pro tribus s. computando, sicut est pro maiori parte extimare consuetum, septua-

ginta unum milia quatuor centos et xxx viii fl. ii d. Hoc est lxxiᵐ iiiiᶜ xxxviii fl. ii d. sterlingorum.

Et facta deductione de recepta usque supra folio xxi de assignatis et redditis eodem libro usque ad folium xxxiii, nichil restant quod debeatur per ipsum collectorem camere apostolice quia plus receperit quam solverit, nec eque camera tenetur sibi quia plus assignaverit vel solverit quam receperit in aliquo, et sic equiparantur recepte cum expensis seu assignatis.[630] Erore calculi semper salvo.

Et est sciendum et memorandum quod iam debentur collectori culpa male solventium non sua pro stipendiis seu procurationibus suis de anno currenti millesimo CCCᵐᵒ LXXVIII° et precedentium annorum ultra mille fl., mˡ fl. et plus.[631]

De restis debitis camere usque ad sextam diem Martii anni ab incarnatione et cetera septuagesimi septimi vide infra folio secundo et tertio usque ad folium sexagesimum octavum alterius libri restarum cum isto in camera apostolica redditi.[632]

(fol. 260ᵛ, xxxix) [633] Recepta et assignata et reddita [634]

Reddiditur instrumentum obligationis prioris de Castelacro diocesis Norwicensis de iiiiᶜ lxxxiiii li. ix s. vii d., ut in breveto etiam habetur, die xxii Martii anni et cetera LXXIX. Et Dominus Geraldus Mercaderii, collector Arlatensis et auditor istorum computorum, hic cum isto papiru [635] restarum distinxit et inclusit cum ipsis restis.

(fol. 261) [636] Compotus brevis redditus camere apostolice per Dominum Arnaldum Garnerii, licentiatum in legibus sedis apostolice nuntium et collectorem in regno Anglie, de receptis per eum tam de restis restantibus de vacantibus beneficiorum collatorum per sedem apostolicam in dicto regno Anglie, de quibus beneficiis alias reddiderat dicte camere rationem, quam etiam de restis debitis in dicto regno de denariis Beati Petri et de censibus ibidem debitis, necnon de [637] receptis per eum de vacantibus beneficiorum in dicto regno collatorum per felicis recordationis Dominum Gregorium papam XI, et de denariis Beati Petri et censibus ibidem debitis a xxvii die mensis Julii anni domini MCCCLXXIIII usque ad vi diem mensis Martii anni ab incarnatione domini MCCCLXXVII, de quo tempore nunc computat, quia illa die vi Martii exivit de

---

[624] *quinque* repeated and deleted by a line, MS.
[625] *sterlis*, MS.
[626] Followed by *si* not deleted.
[627] Followed by *iiii d.* deleted by a line. In the margin: *vera*.
[628] Over *undecim* deleted by a line.
[629] Follows *septem d.* deleted by a line. The MS. contains an error in this entry.

[630] These passages deleted by lines follow: *Quinque li. duos s., sterlis v li. ii s. sterlingorum. Et ille v li. ii s. possunt esse propter marcas tribus annis primis plus solito solutas de hospitio ratione subcidii carius conducto, valent v li., propter reprobas et mali ponderis et fractas solutas pecunias et sepe decasu perditas de quibus est conciderandum et cetera.*
[631] In the margin: *debita collectori*.
[632] In the margin: *reste debite camere*.
[633] Folios 256 recto to 260 recto inclusive are blank.
[634] In the margin: *secunda copia*.
[635] Reading doubtful.
[636] This and the remaining leaves are much smaller in size.
[637] Followed by *vac* deleted by a line.

Anglia veniendo Avinioniam pro dictis suis rationibus reddendis, ac etiam computat de receptis per eum de subsidio imposito per sedem apostolicam predictam prelatis et clero Anglie anno LXXV.

Et primo apparuit restari et deberi dicte camere per finem compotorum per ipsum ultimo camere redditorum et de vacantibus beneficiorum collatorum in dicto regno Anglie usque ad dictam diem xxvii Julii anni LXXIIII usque ad quod tempus tunc computavit in camera predicta ii$^m$ vii$^c$ lxix li. iii s. v d. sterlingorum, valentes, quolibet floreno pro tribus solidis sterlingorum computando, xviii$^m$ iiii$^c$ v fl. cum dimidio vii d. sterlingorum.

Item restabat reddi ratio de vacantibus beneficiorum que tunc tempore dicti compoti per eum redditi non reperiebantur taxata per eum, que beneficia ascendebant in summa clxxvii beneficia.

(fol. 261$^v$) Item restabant de inutilibus provisionibus ab antiquo debitis ut in pluribus ii$^c$ lxxxviii beneficia.

Item restabant expectationes que nondum habuerunt effectum vii$^c$ xxiii.

Item restabant per finem dictorum compotorum ultimo per ipsum camere redditorum deberi dicte camere tam de denariis Beati Petri quam de censibus usque ad dictum annum LXXIIII lxi li. xvii s. vii d. steringorum.

De quibus quidem ii$^m$ vii$^c$ lxix li. iii s. v d. restantibus de vacantibus dictorum beneficiorum computat se recepisse in compotis modo per eum redditis a dicta xxvii Julii anni LXXIIII usque ad vi diem Martii anni ab incarnatione LXXVII mc li. v s. v d. ob.

Restant adhuc levari de dictis restis m vi$^c$ xvii li. xvii s. xi d. ob.[638]

Item computat se recepisse de dicta summa lxi li. xvii s. vii d. restantibus deberi per finem aliorum compotorum ultimo redditorum, videlicet tam de denariis Beati Petri quam de censibus, lv li. xvii s. viii d.

Restant adhuc deberi de dictis restis denariorum Beati Petri[639] et de anno LXXIII vi. li.[638]

(fol. 262) Item computat idem collector se recepisse tam de vacantibus beneficiorum collatorum per dictum Dominum Gregorium papam XI in dicto regno Anglie a dicta xxvii die Julii[640] anni LXXIIII usque ad vi diem Martii anni ab incarnatione domini LXXVII, pro quo tempore nunc computat quam de vacantibus beneficiorum que tempore alterius compoti per eum ultimo redditi non reperiebantur taxata per dictum collectorem, que modo fuerunt per ipsum reperta taxata, ix$^c$ l li. vi s. ob. sterlingorum.

Restant adhuc de dictis vacantibus dictorum beneficiorum de quibus supra proxime computat ix$^m$ iii$^c$ lxxvii li. xii s. vi d. sterlingorum.

Et sic est summa omnium restarum vacantium bene-

ficiorum que restant de beneficiis de quibus computaverat in aliis compotis proxime precedentibus quam de vacantibus beneficiorum collatorum in dicto regno Anglie annis LXXIIII, LXXV, LXXVI et LXXVII usque ad dictam vi diem mensis Martii, inclusis restis vacantium beneficiorum que tempore alterius compoti non reperiebantur taxata, x$^m$ ix$^c$ lxxxv li. x s. v d. ob. sterlingorum.

Item computat se recepisse de denariis Beati Petri debitis in regno Anglie pro dictis annis LXXIIII, LXXV, LXXVI et LXXVII usque ad dictam diem vi Martii iiii$^c$ lxxxxvi li. ii s. sterlingorum.

Restant ad solvendum de dictis denariis Beati Petri pro dicto tempore, inclusis vi li. restantibus de anno LXXIII, iii$^c$ vii li. xii s. viii d.

Item computat se recepisse de censibus debitis ecclesie Romane in dicto regno Anglie pro dictis annis LXXIIII, LXXV, LXXVI et LXXVII usque ad dictam diem vi mensis Martii anni ab incarnatione (fol. 262$^v$) domini MCCCLXXVII, incluso tam censu unius marche auri debite pro censu ecclesie Romane quolibet biennio in festo apostolorum Petri et Pauli per abbatem et fratres monasterii de Sempyngham Lincolniensis diocesis, pro qua marca recipiuntur ix li. xv s. sterlingorum, quem censum dicte marce ipse collector recepit pro annis LXXV et LXXVII, licet fuisset consuetum temporibus retroactis solvi in camera apostolica dictum censum, pro quibus omnibus computat se recepisse xxxv li. xii s.

Restant de dictis censibus pro dictis annis ii li. xviii s.

Summa omnium restarum tam de denariis Beati Petri quam de censibus de annis predictis iii$^c$ x li. x s. viii d.[641]

Advertendum tamen est quod quia dictus collector incepit recipere dictum censum biennium debitum in festo apostolorum Petri et Pauli per dictum monasterium de Sempyngham de biennio in biennio quod dictum monasterium cessavit solvere dictas marcas auri et pro uno biennio finito anno XLIX in festo predicto. Item cessavit dictum monasterium solvere dictum censum pro iiii biennis finitis annis LXIII et LXV, LXVII et LXIX, pro quibus quinque solutionibus restantibus debet adhuc dictum monasterium camere apostolice v marcas auri valent xlviii li. xv s. sterlingorum.[641]

(fol. 263) Item computat dictus collector recepisse de summa ix$^m$ li. sterlingorum impositarum pro subsidio anno LXXV in provinciis Cantuariensi et Eboracensi, videlicet a domino archiepiscopo Cantuariensi pro parte ipsum contingente dicti subsidii pro se et suffraganeis suis, que summa ipsos contingens[642] est vii$^m$ ii$^c$ li., vi$^m$ ii$^c$ xlvi li. xi s.

Restant pro dicta provincia Cantuariensi de dicto subsidio ix$^c$ liii li. ix s.

Item computat recepisse de dicto subsidio a domino

---

[638] In the margin: *resta*.
[639] Followed by *censuum* deleted by a line.
[640] Followed by *usque ad vi* deleted by a line.

[641] In the margin: *resta*.
[642] *contingente*, MS.

archiepiscopo Eboracensi pro se et suffraganeis suis pro parte ipsos contingente, que est m viii<sup>c</sup> li., m vii<sup>c</sup> lxxx li.

Restant pro dicta provincia Eboracensi de dicto subsidio xx li.

Summa totius subsidii predicti recepta per dictum collectorem a dictis duobus dominis archiepiscopis Cantuariensi et Eboracensi et eorum suffraganeis viii<sup>m</sup> xxvi li. xi s. sterlingorum.

Summa reste dicti subsidii pro dictis duabus provinciis ix<sup>c</sup> lxxiii li. ix s. sterlingorum.

Summa summarum universalis omnium receptorum per dictum Dominum Arnaldum Garnerii collectorem tam de restis restantibus de vacantibus beneficiorem collatorum in regno Anglie, de quibus reddiderat rationem camere anno LXXIIII, xxvii die Julii, quam etiam de restis denariorum Beati Petri et censibus (fol. 263<sup>v</sup>) restantibus [643] de annis LXXII et LXXIII, quam etiam de vacantibus beneficiorum collatorum in regno Anglie annis LXXIIII, LXXV, LXXVI et LXXVII usque ad diem vi Martii anni ab incarnatione domini LXXVII, inclusis receptis vacantium beneficiorum que in aliis compotis proxime redditis non reperiebantur taxata que modo reperiit taxata, quam etiam de receptis per eum de denariis Beati Petri et censibus debitis in Anglia dicte camere pro dictis annis, quam etiam de receptis per eum de subsidio imposito in Anglia per sedem apostolicam anno LXXV, x<sup>m</sup> vii<sup>c</sup> xv li. xiii s. ii d. sterlingorum.

Que valent reducte ad florenos, quolibet floreno pro tribus solidis sterlingorum computato, lxxi<sup>m</sup> iiii<sup>c</sup> xxxviii fl. ii d. sterlingorum.

Summa summarum universalis omnium restarum restantium de vacantibus beneficiorum de quibus dictus collector computaverat in camera apostolica anno LXXIIII et de aliis annis precedentibus, quam de restis restantibus tunc de denariis Beati Petri et censibus debitis ecclesie Romane in Anglia, quam de restis denariorum Beati Petri et censibus debitis annis LXXIIII, LXXV, LXXVI et LXXVII, ac de restis vacantium debitorum de beneficiis collatis in dicto regno Anglie dictis annis LXXIIII, LXXV, LXXVI et LXXVII usque ad dictam diem vi mensis Martii dicti anni LXXVII ab incarnatione computando usque ad quod tempus computat idem colector, quam etiam reste subsidii impositi in Anglia per dictum Dominum Gregorium papam XI anno LXXV circa festum Omnium Sanctorum xii<sup>m</sup> ii<sup>c</sup> lxxix li. x s. i d. ob.

Que reducte ad florenos ut supra valent lxxxi<sup>m</sup> viii<sup>c</sup> lxiii fl.[644] xiii d. ob. sterlingorum; [645] xlii beneficia que nondum reperiuntur taxata.

(fol. 264) Advertendum. In dicta vera summa restarum non includuntur xlviii li. xv s. sterlingorum debite per monasterium et fratres de Sempyngham Lincolniensis diocesis pro v bienniis quibus cessaverunt solvere censum per eos debitum, nam aliquotiens solvuntur in camera apostolica aliquotiens collectori.

(fol. 264<sup>v</sup>) Sequuntur assignationes facte per dictum collectorem.

Et primo assignavit camere apostolice xxviii die mensis Februarii anno a nativitate domini M° CCC° LXXV per manus Petri Marci, factoris et procuratoris societatis Albertorum de Florentia, ratione cuiusdam cambii per ipsum collectorem Londonie facti cum dicto Petro Marci de mense Decembris proxime tunc precedentis cl li. sterlingorum.[646]

Item eadem die et anno fuerunt habiti pro recepto [647] in dicta camera a dicto collectore ratione cuiusdam cambii per ipsum facti Londonie cum dicto Petro Marci de mense Januarii tunc proxime preteriti cl li. sterlingorum.[646]

Item die v Martii anno a nativitate domini M° CCC° LXXVI assignavit eidem camere dictus collector per manus dicti Petri Marci virtute cuiusdam cambii per ipsum facti cum dicto Petro Marci in Londonia de mense Novembris tunc proxime preteriti iiii<sup>c</sup> v li. sterlingorum.[646]

Item xxix die mensis Martii anno predicto assignavit eidem camere dictus collector per manus dictorum Albertorum ratione cuiusdam cambii per ipsum collectorem facti cum dictis Albertis in Londonia xxi die mensis Decembris tunc proxime preteriti v<sup>c</sup> lxxvi li. xiii s. iiii d., et ratione cuiusdam cambii per ipsum collectorem cum predictis Albertis facti iiii die mensis Januarii tunc proxime preteriti v<sup>c</sup> lx li., et ratione alterius cambii per ipsum collectorem cum predictis Albertis facti xxx die Januarii tunc proxime preteriti vii<sup>c</sup> v li. i s. iiii d. sterlingorum, que predicte tres summe ascendunt m viii<sup>c</sup> xli li. xv s. sterlingorum.[646]

(fol. 265) Item die vii mensis Junii anno LXXVI assignavit, de mandato camere, prout dicit, sibi facto, Bartholomeo de Clanatio Yporinensis diocesis, de qua assignatione docet per instrumentum publicum iiii<sup>c</sup> xl li. xviii s. vi d. sterlingorum.

Docuit de mandato per literas dominorum camerarii et thesaurarii eorum sigillo impendenti sigillatas et registratas in camera scriptas vii Aprilis anno LXXVI.

Item die xvii dicti mensis Junii et anni docuit per instrumentum publicum se assignasse Augustino de Massa, procuratori societatis illorum de Interminellis mcxxv li. sterlingorum.

Docuit de mandato per bullam sub dato ix kalendas Maii anno vi Domini Gregorii.[648]

Item die xiii mensis Aprilis anno LXXVII assignavit realiter dicte camere per manus Johannis Francisci de Pistorio ratione cuiusdam cambii per ipsum collectorem

---

[643] *restatibus*, MS.
[644] Followed by *cum dimidio* deleted by a line.
[645] Sum repeated MS.

[646] In the margin: *per libros*.
[647] *recepti*. MS.
[648] 23 April 1376.

facti cum dicto Johanne de mense Novembris anni LXXVI m li. sterlingorum.

Docuit per libros camere.

Item docuit per instrumenta publica se assignasse Augustino Benetoni, factori societatis de Guinegiis, videlicet iiii die Februarii anno ab incarnatione domini M° CCCLXXVII et die ix Junii et die xii Octobris ⟨eodem⟩ anno vii° lxxxvi li. ii s. x d. sterlingorum.

Item assignavit dicto Augustino de mandato camere, prout dicit, sibi facto, videlicet xxiiii die mensis Januarii anno ab incarnatione domini MCCCLXXVII et iiii die Februarii eodem anno, de quibus assignationibus docuit per instrumenta publica, ii^m iiii^c lxiii li. xvii s. ii d.

Docuit de mandato istarum duarum assignationum per bullas sub dato iiii idus Novembris anno vi Domini Gregorii.[649]

(fol. 265^v) Item die xv mensis Octobris anno LXXVI de mandato apostolico sibi facto, videlicet per bullam felice recordationis Domini Gregorii pape XI sub dato Avinionia kalendas Julii pontificatus sui anno vi [650] et per literas domini thesaurarii insertas in quodam instrumento publico, assignavit reverendo in Christo patri Domino Guillelmo archiepiscopo Rothomagensi in loco de Brugis per manus Rogerii de Morton Eboracensis, de qua assignatione docuit per literas dicti domini archiepiscopi manu sua scriptas et suo sigillo sigillatas, iiii^c lx li. sterlingorum.

Item eodem anno et xiii die mensis Decembris assignavit dicto domino archiepiscopo Brugis per manus Augustini Beneton', factoris illorum de Guinegiis, ultra lxxv li. sterlingorum quas assignavit dicto domino archiepiscopo de communi servitio debito camere per dominum archiepiscopum Cantuariensem, de quibus hic non computatur aliquo quia ipse dominus Rothomagensis debuit eas assignare dicte camere, de qua assignatione per ipsum collectorem facta docet per literas ipsius domini Rothomagensis, iiii^c xxv li. sterlingorum.

Item dixit se tradidisse de mandato dicti domini archiepiscopi Rothomagensis literatorie sibi facto Raynaudono de Rofinhaco iii li. vi s. viii d. sterlingorum.

Item dixit se assignasse de mandato domini camerarii Domino Johanni de Tornaburi militi de Anglia, seu eius procuratori, de cuius assignatione docuit per instrumentem publicum et docuit etiam de mandato dicti domini camerarii, lxxi li. sterlingorum.

(fol. 266) Item dixit se expendisse de mandato dicti

Domini Gregorii pape pro tribus orfresiis et uno reposito corporalium per ipsum emptis et missis [651] dicto domino Gregorio pape xlv li. xiii s. iiii d. sterlingorum.

Item dixit se tradidisse Domino Rogerio de Belloforti, militi germano dicti domini pape, pro expensis per ipsum Dominum Rogerium et Dominum Johannem de Rupe militem factis in Anglia, quas pecunias tradidit de mandato domini camerarii, prout docet per literas ipsius domini camerarii, et de traditione dictarum pecuniarum docet per literas dicti Domini Rogerii diversis diebus et annis factas et manu propria subscriptas, m ii^c lxxii li. xii s. viii d. sterlingorum.

Item dictus collector dixit se expendisse [652] pro quibusdam [653] expensis per ipsum factis ratione officii sui et in exequendis quibusdam literis pro dicto tempore pro quo computat, prout particulariter patet in libro rationum, lxxv li. viii s.[654] sterlingorum.

(fol. 266^v) Summa summarum universalis omnium assignationum per ipsum collectorem factarum tam infra cameram apostolicam quam etiam extra cameram de mandato sibi facto tam per dictum Dominum Gregorium papam XI quam per dominos camerarium et thesaurarium eiusdem domini nostri pape, quam expensorum per ipsum pro orfriziis ad opus dicti domini nostri pape, quam traditorum dicto Domino Rogerio de Belloforti, quam aliarum expensarum per ipsum collectorem factarum ratione sui officii, prout supra particulariter patet de omnibus predictis, x^m vii^c xv li. xiiii s. ii [655] d. sterlingorum.

Que reducte ad florenos, quolibet floreno pro tribus solidis sterlingorum computato, valent lxxi^m iiii^c xxxviii fl. ii d. sterlingorum.

Quibus x^m vii^c xv li. xiiii s. ii d. per ipsum assignatis et expensis deductis de x^m vii^c xv li. xiiii s. ii d. per ipsum receptis, apparet ipsum collectorem totum [656] assignasse vel expendisse [657] quod recepisse, ideo nichil debet camere nec camera sibi.[658]

---

[649] 10 November 1376.
[650] 1 July 1376.

[651] *missos*, MS.
[652] Followed by *pro loquerio hospitii in quo habitavit in Anglia pro iiii annis ad rationem vi li. xiii s. iiii d. pro quolibet anno et* deleted by a line.
[653] Followed by *aliis* deleted by a line.
[654] Followed by *iiii d.* deleted by a line.
[655] Over *vi* deleted by a line.
[656] Followed by *recepisse quam* deleted by a line.
[657] Followed by *et restarum debere camere in* deleted by a line.
[658] Followed by two entries deleted by lines: *v li. ii s. viii d. sterlingorum, que valent xxxiii fl. cum dimidio iiii sterlinos.*

*Petit tamen idem collector sibi assignari seu admitti in suis compotis pro loquerio sui hospitii quod asserit triennio carius conduxisse pro pecunia subsidii custodienda quam alias conduxisset x li. sterlingorum.*

# INDEX OF PERSONS

Identity of name does not necessarily signify identity of person. References to cathedral office-holders are grouped under the name of the see in the Index of Places.

Abbatesbur, John de, 94.
Abbati, Hugh, *see* Alberti, Hugh.
Abbatia, Adam de, 242, 281, 335, 375.
Abbot, Robert, 111.
Aberebury, John de, 145, 190, 230.
Aberwik, William de, 90, 102, 114, 130, 155.
Abetot, Thomas, 83.
Abirwylli, William de, 138.
Abraham, John, 424.
Abrham, Walter, 111.
Abyndon, John de, 359, 401.
Acchilii (Acciaiuoli?), society of Florence, 66.
Ace, Philip, 360, 402.
Achaliata, Thomas, 244, 282, 335, 376.
Acton, John de, 113, 135, 143, 150, 178, 188, 197, 216 273, 329, 368; *see* Hatton.
Acurcii, Henry, of Florence, 54, 64, 77.
Adany, William, 319.
Adegoris, Hugolino de, 112.
Adelvingham, William de, 48.
Ahe, John, 469.
Akae, Alan, 221.
Aketon, William de, 435, 449.
Akun, John de, 166.
Alani, Peter, 135.
Alani, William, 111.
Alayn, John, 151, 179, 198, 219.
Alberti, Antiqui, 64, 65, 66, 141, 183, 184, 203, 225, 226, 321, 322, 414, 453, 475, 476, 481, 533, 540.
Alberti, Hugh, 114, 150, 185, 212.
Alberti, Nicholas James, 225, 226.
Albi, Henry, 171.
Albo, Henry, *see* Wyth (White).
Albrogot, John, 165.
Albussato, William de, bishop of Fréjus, 165.
Alcestre, William de, 120.
Aldeburgh, Humphrey de, 466.
Aldebury, John de, 223.
Aldeby, Walter de, 407, 425, 448.
Aldeforde, Edmund de, 437, 500.
Aldyngthon, Robert de, 312.
Alenyn, Adam de, 359, 401.
Aleston, Peter alias John de, 243, 281, 335, 375.
Alexander, dean of Ross, *see* Kylwos.
Aleyn, John, 353, 394, 395.
Aleyn, Thomas, 297, 348, 389.
Allexandr', Walter, 115.
Almania, Henry de, 460.
Alsthawe, John de, 252, 295, 346; *see* Aschewade.
Alston, Thomas, 490.
Altekore, John de, 408.
Alten, Simon, 242.
Alvaro, Lupus, 109.
Alynton, Adam de, 49.
Ambenyle, John, 472.

Ambresbury, John de, 93, 104, 121.
Amcotes, Richard, 149, 178, 195, 219.
Amcotes, Thomas, 466.
Amelio, John de, 88.
Amyas, Walter, 424, 460.
Amye, Henry, 438.
Amyle, John, 158, 206, 239–240, 277, 333, 373.
Anbyn, Richard, 461.
Ancotes, John, 466.
Andeley, Margaret, 530.
Anderby, Eudo de, 471.
Andree, Thomas, 161, 177.
Andreu, Thomas, 506.
Androin, abbot of Cluny, xlvi; *see* cardinal-priest of S. Marcello.
Anglici, Richard, 169, 187, 228, 299; *see* Drax, Richard.
Angolisma, Gerald de, 104; *see* Engolisma.
Angoulême, Hugh of, xiii, xxiii, xxiv, xxviii, xlviii, 29, 32, 34.
Anneston, John, 242, 281.
Anstorp, Robert, 421.
Anthonii, William, 136, 152, 200, 220.
Anthony (Fieschi), bishop of Luni, 52.
Apacha, Tuder, 362, 404.
Apelderham, Richard, *see* Tangmere.
Apeltre, William, 100, 115, 128, 137, 152, 199, 236, 330, 370.
Apethorp, Philip, 503.
Apiorworth, John de, 320.
Appelby, John de, 118, 150, 157, 169, 197, 205, 206, 234, 239, 249, 258, 273, 277, 286, 287, 302, 315, 329, 333, 339, 354, 369, 373, 379, 396, 434, 449, 460, 516.
Appelby, William de, 253, 289, 318.
Appelewolm, David, 436.
Apphilip, Maurice, 510.
Apprelbyn (Approweyn), Theodore son of John, 242, 302.
Appulorthorp, John de, 413.
Aprewerth, John, 354.
Aprogenew, Hobell, *see* Goronwy, Hywel ap.
Apromeiis, William de, 275, 331, 371.
Aprovanseis, Richard, 101, 129, 153, 202, 237, 275, 331, 371.
Aptrap' (Apthorp), John de, 355, 397.
Aquitaine, duke of, 442; *see* Edward, Prince of Wales.
Aragon, Bertrand de, xxxiiin., 92.
Aragon, William de, 117.
Arbally, William de, 157, 205, 221.
Archenefeld, John de Lanwaran de, 474.
Archerich, Robert de, 78.
Ardene, Hugh de, 422.
Ardern, John, 240.
Ardern, William de, 250, 253, 275, 287,

289, 331, 339, 341, 371, 380, 382, 431, 445, 474.
Arderndon, John de, 161, 206, 260.
Ardi(?), Peter, 26.
Arely, William de, 463.
Argentura, John de, 535.
Arlam, Hugh de, 354, 395, 407, 421, 425, 462.
Arllegham, Thomas, 432.
Armand, bishop of Aquino (probably archbishop of Aix), xxvi.
Armeston, John de, 317.
Arselle, Nicholas de, 457; *see* Briseley.
Arundel, earl of (Richard Fitz Alan), 297, 400, 402, 405, 410, 486, 497.
Arundel, Edmund de, 85, 93, 143, 188, 216.
Arundel, Thomas, 281, 360, 402, 407, 408, 422.
Ascheburn, John de, 99, 113, 114, 118, 127, 150, 196, 219, 234, 261.
Aschewade, John de, 289, 315, 387; *see* Althawe.
Aselbech, Adam de, 116.
Askeby, Henry de, 97, 147, 193, 231, 271, 327, 367, 494.
Askeby, Robert de, 106, 110, 116, 162, 165, 175, 188, 229, 258.
Askeby, Thomas, 132.
Askeby, William de, 88, 114, 242, 281, 334, 375, 459, 464, 466, 467.
Asperulis (Haspul), John, 409, 443, 505, 511.
Assh, Walter, 428.
Assheton, Matthew de, 111, 252, 289, 341, 354, 381, 396, 419, 458, 501, 505.
Asshton, Henry de, 110.
Assier, Gerard d', xiii.
Assier, Rigaud d', xiii, xxi–xxiii, xliii–xlv, xlviii, 1.
Astacii, Philip, 321.
Asteleye, Thomas de, 35, 79, 87, 88, 94, 108, 110, 123, 145.
Aston, John de, 113, 189, 432, 530.
Aston, Matthew de, 112.
Aston, Nicholas de, 182, 187, 189, 216, 269, 326, 349, 365, 390, 412.
Aston, Richard de, 133.
Aston, Thomas de, 451, 487.
Astyng', Humphrey, *see* Hastings.
Astynges, John de, *see* Hastings.
Aswardby, Roger, 430.
Aton, Adam de, 435.
Attagrene, Robert, 473.
Attecreduk (Ralph atte Gredyk), 111.
Attegate, John, 103, 132.
Attehale, Robert, 471.
Attehall, Hugh, 424, 444, 462, 471, 484.
Attehull, Thomas de, 100, 128, 152, 199, 236, 274, 330, 370.
Attelowenill, John, 133.

Gormund, Nicholas de, 135.
Goronwy, Hywel ap, 350, 354, 391, 395; as bishop of Bangor, 422.
Gotham, William, 357, 399, 433, 448.
Gotne, Thomas de, 446.
Gouch, John, 138.
Gouf (Goch), John, 115.
Gough, John, 85, 88.
Gourney, Edmund, 86, 97, 149, 196, 233.
Govye, William, 437.
Gower, David, 248, 286.
Gowet, Henry, 452.
Graa, Lawrence, 457, 516.
Grandison, John de, bishop of Exeter, xxx, xxxi, 453.
Grantham, Robert de, xl.
Gravesend, Stephen, bishop of London, 35.
Graston, David de, 137.
Graule, William, 294, 345, 386.
Grauleriis, William de, 153, 200, 236, 262, 274, 330, 370, 507.
Grayndrop, John de, 458n.
Gregory X, pope, 32.
Gregory XI, pope, xlvi, xlvii, xlix, l.
Grenbury (Crombrygh), William de, 115, 137.
Grendon, Robert de, 426.
Grene, John, 433.
Grene, Roger, 212.
Grethull, Stephen de, 111.
Greve, John, 83.
Grey, John de, 107.
Grey, Thomas de, 452.
Greyne, Richard, 455.
Griffardi, Richard, see Giffard.
Griffi, Rayner (Azayali society), 65.
Griffin, Thomas, 194n.
Grili, Archambald de, viscount Benanias, 534.
Grimesby, Richard, 427.
Griphus, Peter, xiii.
Grisp, John, 474.
Grispini, William, 170.
Grom, John, 85.
Gronne, William (de Hengham), 450.
Groppo, Gryffin (alias Griffredi), 165.
Grose, John, 109, 110.
Gruffunduy, John de (John ap Griffith Du), 294, 345, 352, 386, 393.
Grumineshawe, Richard de, 360, 402.
Gryffin, Thomas, 98, 102, 125, 130.
Gryffyn, Adam, 155, 203, 221.
Gryffyni, John son of, 137.
Gryk, Thomas, 159, 213.
Grymesby, Edmund de, 93, 98, 110, 125, 143, 187, 194n., 228, 269, 325, 365.
Grymneston, Robert de, 196, 233, 272, 316, 328, 368, 478, 497.
Guanigre, John, 164.
Guardi of Florence, Society of, 414.
Gudlak, Thomas, 466.
Guifundum, John, see Gruffunduy (John ap Griffith Du).
Guilay (Gylury), Thomas de Wodehaus, 353, 395.
Guillelmi, Luke, son of, 240.
Guinigi Society of Lucca, 481, 534, 535, 541.
Guithorp, William, 492.
Guldesburgh, Thomas de, 88.

Gundisalvo, Fernand, 436.
Guneston, Robert de, 254, 290.
Gunfort, formerly treasurer of Calais, 457.
Gunthrop, William de, 300, 418, 421, 492, 502, 527.
Gurmunchester, John, 253, 289, 315, 428.
Gurtery, Stephen de, 98; see Bertrand, Stephen.
Guy (Egidius), 504.
Guycardi, William, 351, 392.
Gyddyng, William, see Bell, William.
Gymston, Robert de, see Grymneston.
Gynwell, John, bishop of Lincoln, 79.
Gynwell, William de, 87, 88, 114, 350, 351, 352, 390, 392, 393.

H., William, 250, 305.
Habet, Richard, 406.
Habini, John de, 517.
Habret, William, see Haket.
Hacluyt, Thomas, 79, 87, 497.
Haddon, John de, 79, 84, 88, 104, 115.
Haddon, William de, 252, 288, 341, 381, 486.
Hadele, Galdewin, 434, 449.
Hadelegh, John de Broun de, 452, 461.
Hagham, William de, 412.
Hakaill, Maurice, see Okahil.
Hake, Alan de, 204.
Haket, William, 133, 144n.
Hakton, Thomas de, 314.
Hale, William, 146, 190, 230, 270, 326, 366.
Hales, Thomas de, 6n., 7n., 61.
Haliday, Robert, 199, 235, 274, 330, 369.
Hall, William son of Robert, 133, 144, 175.
Hamnan, Nicholas, 244, 282, 335, 376.
Hamonis, William, 49, 98, 126, 196, 219, 233, 261.
Hamule, Michael, 213.
Hanbyns, Thomas de, 466.
Hankere, William, 469.
Hanneworth, John Attewode de, see Attewode.
Hanneworth, William Wadington de, see Wadyngton.
Hanneye, John, 176, 190, 191, 300.
Harden, William, 163, 201, 237.
Hardrio, John de, 166.
Hareberghe, Simon de, 84.
Harewell, John de, 109, 147, 193, 231, 271, 292, 294, 316, 327, 344, 345, 367, 385; as bishop of Bath and Wells, 297, 306, 315, 317, 348, 384, 389.
Harewodo, John, 508.
Harmi, William de, see Hormi.
Harpele, Lawrence de, 292, 317.
Harper, Nicholas, 487.
Hartfeld, John, 420.
Harweden, Henry de, 49, 87, 89, 97, 101, 130, 148, 177, 247, 285, 338, 378.
Haspul (Aspull), John, see Asperulis.
Hastings, Humphrey de, 80, 100, 104, 112, 128, 151, 152, 199, 235, 274, 330, 370.
Hastings, John, 136, 197, 219, 250, 259, 287, 305, 315.
Haterington, William de, 465.
Hattehelle, Hugh de, 356, 398.
Hatton, John de, 91, 93, 122, 127; see Acton.
Hatton, Walter de, 465.

Hauby, John, 355, 395.
Hauckynton, Vigellus de, 212.
Haukesgate, Edmund de, 101, 130.
Haukewod, John, 474.
Hauthon, Michael de, 295, 346, 386.
Hauton, Adam de, 154, 202.
Hauton, Philip de, 154, 202, 237, 301.
Haverbergh, Thomas de, 413.
Haveryng, Richard de, 53, 73.
Haward, John, 84.
Hawibi, Walter de, 517.
Haxton, Richard, 423, 457.
Haye, William de la, 463n.
Hayton, John de, 453.
Hayward, John, 504.
Hedlam, Henry de, 427, 432.
Hegham, John de, 196, 233.
Heldon, John de Skilling de, 253, 289.
Helperby, Richard (Rither) de, 155, 161, 207, 213.
Helyn, Richard, 423.
Hemesby, Richard de, 87, 91, 98, 126.
Hemmyngford, Walter de, 84.
Hemmyngton, Robert de, 15.
Hempnall, Thomas, bishop of Worcester, 39, 40.
Hemyngthon, see Hormyngton.
Henereth, William de, 292, 343, 383, 494.
Hengham, William Gronne de, 450.
Henrici (Henry), John, 103, 132, 158, 182, 206, 239, 277, 333, 373.
Henrico, Philip, 138.
Henrico, Thomas, 96, 146, 190, 217, 230, 246, 259, 284, 337, 377.
Henry- ?, 494.
Hepp, Robert, 145, 157, 205, 211, 239, 276, 332, 373.
Heraygtoft, James de, 149, 212.
Herayngton, Adam de, 442.
Herbert, Thomas, 456.
Herbing, Walter de, 435.
Herdewyk, Thomas de, 420.
Hereward, Robert, 223, 247, 252, 259, 288, 340, 381.
Herford, Nicholas de, 424, 433, 496.
Hering (Hernag), Richard, 101, 129.
Herlaston, Roger de, 109, 110.
Herneys, John, 156, 181.
Herpelby, Henry de, 241, 278, 334, 374.
Herseleye, William de, 357, 398.
Hershamme, William de, 469.
Hertelbury, William de, 121, 142, 210.
Hertushull, Richard de, 355, 397.
Hertyngdon, Adam de, 459.
Herward, Richard, 405.
Herwynton (Herwutton), William de, 110.
Heryngh, Thomas, 352.
Hesill, John de, 352, 394, 516.
Hetershet, Thomas de, 452.
Heth, Nicholas, 89, 98, 100, 107, 110, 116, 128, 140, 142, 148, 151, 152, 153, 160, 194, 200, 209, 212, 222, 236, 240, 252, 262, 274, 275, 277, 289, 295, 313, 330, 331, 333, 341, 346, 362, 370, 374, 381, 386, 405, 462, 521.
Hetton, John de, 293.
Hexham, William de, 453.
Hexton, Richard, 423, 457.
Heyneworth, Walter de, 150, 197, 219.

# INDEX OF PLACES

227, 256, 257, 268, 307, 309, 324, 364, 417, 518, 525.
prebends, 70, 419.
prior, 79, 109, 428.
Worcester (Worcs.), St. Wulstan, hospital, 147, 193, 231, 271, 327, 367.
Worcester (Worcs.), churches: St. Martin, 458; St. Swithin, 134.
Worfield (Salop.), 4.
Workington (Cumbr.), 9, 435, 465.
Worksop (Notts.), priory, 247, 285, 338, 378.
Worlington (Suff.), 18.
Worpleston (Surrey), 12.
Worsall (Yorks.), 73.
Worth (Sussex), 11.
Worthen (Salop.), 80, 137, 153, 179, 201, 218, 260.
Worthy Martyr (Hants.), 12.
Wratting, Little (Suff.), 6.
Wrawby (Lincs.), 23, 24, 80.
Wraxall (Somer.), 15.
Wraxhall, North (Wilts.), 13.
Wreningham (Norf.), 19.
Wroxeter (Salop.), 4.
Wyddial (Herts.), 84.
Wyke Regis (Dorset), 2.
Wylye (Wilts.), 13, 442, 443, 522.
Wymondham (Leics.), 7.
Wyrardisbury (Bucks.), 112.
Wyton (Hunts.), 503.

Yatesbury (Wilts.), 3.
Yattendon (Berks.), 133.
Yatton Keynell (Wilts.), 13.
Yaxley (Hunts.), church, 23, 52, 113, 115; deanery, 273.
Yealmpton (Devon), 97, 124, 147, 177.
Yearsley (Yorks.), 8.
Yeldham, Little (Essex), 11.
Yelvertoft (Northants.), 23.
Yeovil (Somer.), 34, 125, 149, 195, 233.
Yetminster (Dorset), 256, 291, 343, 383.
York (Yorks.):

archbishop, xlviii, 40, 73, 89, 109, 118, 166, 184, 248, 285, 338, 378, 379, 420, 492, 502, 516, 532.
archbishop, census, 30, 44.
archbishopric, Peter's pence, 27, 37-43, 69, 81, 82, 92, 119, 141, 172, 186, 215, 227, 256, 257, 268, 307, 309, 310, 324, 364, 417, 518, 525.
archdeacons: Cleveland, 138; East Riding, 24, 63, 163, 181, 204, 238, 276, 332, 360, 372, 402, 512; Nottingham, 55, 111, 116, 117, 251, 287, 318; Richmond, 8, 63, 89, 101, 130, 140, 154, 160, 204, 209, 221, 240, 259, 263, 269, 326; York or West Riding, 24, 156, 203, 238, 276, 309, 314, 323, 324, 331, 371, 473, 511, 513, 515.
chancellor, 90.
chapel, St. Mary and Holy Angels 138, 139, 164, 166, 204, 223, 238, 243, 245, 276, 303, 332, 372, 514.
dean, 73, 224, 264, 265n., 296, 347, 388, 512, 521.
prebends: Ampleforth, 139, 155, 156, 181; Apesthorpe, 1, 24, 49; Barnby, 89; Bole, 156, 185, 203, 238, 276, 332, 361, 404, 413, 414, 515; Bugthorpe, 9, 138; Driffield (Driffeld), 9, 80, 156, 186, 203, 238, 276, 331, 372, 511, 520; Dunnington, 90, 138, 163; Fenton, 8, 138, 167, 360, 402; Fridaythorpe, 24; Grindale, 89, 444n.; Holme Archiepiscopi, 89, 117; Husthwaite, 89, 102, 130, 154, 202, 237; Knaresborough, 9, 102, 131, 513; Laughton en le Morthen, 24, 51, 320; Masham, 90, 101, 130, 154, 156, 183, 212, 213, 246, 264, 266, 284, 337, 377, 413, 512, 513, 529; North Newbald, 358, 400, 413, 514, 521, 531; Osbaldwick, 102, 117, 118, 130, 138, 155, 180; Riccall, 50; Stillington, 90, 515; South Cave, 116, 513; South Newbald, 89; Strensall, 102, 118, 131, 155, 185, 203, 224,

225n., 226n., 238, 264, 266, 275, 331, 371, 505n., 511, 512; Weighton, 320; Wetwang, xxxi, 80, 101, 116, 130, 154, 212; Wilton, 515; Wistow, 156, 185, 203, 238, 276, 314, 331, 360, 371, 403, 511, 512.
prebends not named, 102, 116, 117, 118, 130, 155, 166, 203, 238, 252, 254, 275, 289, 290, 293, 297, 298, 317, 331, 341, 344, 349, 350, 354, 361, 362, 371, 381, 384, 390, 391, 396, 403, 404, 407, 418, 419, 420, 422, 423, 424, 427, 430, 433, 435, 436, 438, 439, 440, 442, 444, 446, 448, 450, 459, 460, 464, 465, 467, 473, 501, 505, 513, 515.
precentor, 9, 89, 90, 116, 294, 345, 386.
registrar of archbishop, 517.
subdean, 140, 160, 180, 181, 209, 222, 457, 524.
subtreasurer, 116.
treasurer, 50, 116, 117, 515.
York (Yorks.), churches:
All Saints Havergate, 8.
All Saints Pavement in Ousegate, 156, 203, 238, 245, 246, 283, 284, 295, 301, 303, 307, 336, 337, 359, 376, 378, 401.
Holy Trinity, 102, 130, 131, 155, 180.
St. Crux, 8, 89, 138.
St. Helen's in Stonegate, 243, 282, 294, 335, 345, 375, 386.
St. Martin (Coney Street), St. Katherine's Altar, 467, 513.
St. Martin in Micklegate, 244, 263, 318, 352, 415, 416, 514.
St. Michael at Ouse Bridge, 8.
St. Wilfrid, 139, 155, 180.
York (Yorks.), St. Mary, abbey (outside the walls), 55, 56, 63, 421, 423, 427, 429, 433, 446, 448, 450, 463, 471.
Youlgreave (Derby), 355, 397.
Yscifiog (Flint), 18, 137, 153, 201.

Zeal Monachorum (Devon), 455.